MAL~YA
1948-1960

EMERGENCY!!
NEVER, JUST
A FORGOTTEN
WAR

Facts and Figures Compiled by Joe P. Plant

ISBN 978-1-78222-677-2

Book design, layout and production management by Into Print
www.intoprint.net
01604 832149

Also by the author Joe P. Plant

978-1-90761-103-2   Cornwall's First Town in the Frontline:
                     Torpoint's War Diary 1939-46

978-1-78222-054-1   Up to Their Necks - the Story of a National Serviceman

978-1-78222-400-6   The Spirit Liveth On

978-1-78222-446-4   The Adventures of a Soldier's Wife

PREVIEW

The object of researching, compiling and producing this record of the events and incidents of the so called 12-year Emergency in Malaya. Was driven by my own interest of having served in that War during 1955 to 1957.

My introduction into Active Service, began within 10 hours of arriving on a troopship in Singapore. When I and many other young National Servicemen were given a .303 Lee Enfield Rifle with a magazine of 10 rounds of ammunition. Transported by lorry to Singapore Station, there to board a train enroute to Malaya. For me, 3 Coy REME LAD Ipoh Perak North Malaya. Totally unaware of what the hell was going on. With absolutely no news back home of a War in Malaya. It was a shock to one's system. Nevertheless, I soon found out that there were Regiments of British,Gurkha, Malay troops, including Squadrons of the Royal Air Force, also supported by the Federation Malay Police. All engaged in fighting the Communist Terrorist. The only news we had access too, was a rented radio in the Basha.

However, during my research discovered notes in articles and books. In the event that the British Army beat the Japanese in Malaya. Sometime in 1943, under the leadership of the Malayan Communist Party Chairman *Lai Tek*. Secret Plans were instigated. Their main objective: Once the Japanese Imperial Army had been beaten by the British Army. Then it was the time and the opportunity for them. The Communist Party of Malaya to take over and create a Communist State in Malaya. Apprently that did happen for one day only. What followed after in 1948, was a "Call to Arms" by the Malaya Communist Party then under the Leadership of *Chin Peng.* With a declaration of war against the British Governnment. The so called Emergency? Nevertheless, a war that lasted 12 long bloody years.

You may say this book, having taken many years of research to compile, is just the. 'Tip of an Iceberg.' Relating to the Actions of the Commonwealth Forces, engaged in the fight for the Freedom and Independence of Malaya. They, then the predominant Service personnel, were young National Servicemen, who died in a foreign country, fighting against a Communist led Army. Now those who have paid the ultimate sacrifice, lie forgotten in graves throughout the Peninsular of Malaya (West Malaysia).

An article in a newspaper described the fortitude of young National Servicemen serving in Malaya: -

"The young men were always careful to regret loudly their National Service, but they had a youthful enthusiasm which made light work of jungle Patrolling. To assess this, it must be remembered that according to estimates they marched 2,000 miles in three years and wore out 15,000 pairs of jungle boots."

This book is to put the records straight. And my dedication to them. All our Comrades in Arms.

THEY ARE NOT FORGOTTEN.

Joe P. Plant.

Author.

CHAPTERS

1. A FAR DISTANT LAND ....1.

2. MALAYA & WORLD WAR II...3.

3. A PERIOD OF UNREST AND PLANNING..16.

4. 1948 THE GATHERING STORM..19.

5. THE EMERGENCY ITS COST..25.

6. 1948 THE START 16TH. JUNE 1948...32.

7. 1949-...57.

8. 1950...84.

9. 1951-..115.

10. 1952-..142.

11. 1953-..168.

12. 1954-..186.

13. 1955-..202.

14 1956- ....234.

15. 1957 - 31ST AUGUST MERDEKA DAY..250.

16. 1958- ....265.

17. 1959- ....278.

18. 1960 - 31st. JULY THE END .... 288.

19. SOLVING THE MYSTERY OF THE 'MARIE CELESTE' LIBERATOR. KH326............................297.

20. MILITARY CEMETERIES MALAYA PENINSULAR ....371.

21 KNOWN COMMUNIST TERRORIST ....389.

CHAPTER 1

A FAR DISTANT LAND

Where else could you find a country shaped like a pendant jewel surrounded by sea, where gentle waves wash up the white sand beaches, laced with palm trees and thick elephant grass, only to disappear into a jungle steaming in the tropical sun. Its backbone a range of mountains running from North to South, covered in trees some nearly 200 feet high and dense jungle that the sun did not penetrate, through the high canopy of trees, with clumps of massed bamboo and areas of mangrove swamps. Truly a rain forest of natural beauty with many species of wild animal, elephants, tigers, panthers, bears, monkeys, reptiles some of the most venomous in the world, bird's insect's., ants, giant hornets, scorpions and gorgeous coloured butterflies, exotic plants that add beauty to an exciting country. Nevertheless, so full of danger to the unwary, with its swamps, snakes and other poisonous creatures lurking to strike. Its snaking rivers cutting paths through the interior jungle, which after a sudden monsoon downpour, rapidly swelled into raging torrents in its mad surge through the jungle towards the sea. Close to the equator, its climate is hot and humid all year round with constant daylight, from seven in the morning until seven in the evening, when the blackness of night descends and the searing temperature of the day, drops. almost 20 degrees. Then its jungle inhabitants, a multitude of different species of insect's and amphibian creature, begin their nightly music, with the hum of mosquitoes and the mass croaking of different species of frogs adding voice to the night air.

Its history steeped in culture from times gone by, its people originating from further North, tribes of migrating aborigines, travelled by land to seek other places to live, finally settled in its interior dense jungles, they gradually spilled out to produce the gentle rural and fishing folk of that country. A country initially colonised by the Portuguese in 1511, only to be ousted by the Dutch 130 years later and finally by the British in 1786. Who established a trading post for exporting its produce, furthermore over the space of years by various treaties, they established and occupied other regions of its land mass, albeit the same size of England without Wales. From South America, they brought rubber saplings, to Kew Gardens to propagate, then take them to Ceylon and Malaya to be planted, where the climate suited their growth, which thrived in the tropical heat, creating plantations of rubber trees. Then Tin was discovered and a mining industry sprang up, along with other produce developed later, which transformed its economy into a world market leader.

Attracted by the prospects. of work within those industries, migrating Chinese, Indians came in their droves to settle into a country known to the modern world as the Federated States of Malaya (FSOM) comprising: Perak, Selangor, Negri Sembilan, Pahang. & the: Unfederated States of Malaya (UFSOM) comprising: Johore Terengganu, Kedah, Perlis and Kelantan. All within a Peninsular of land that stretched from its borders with Siam (now Thailand) for 500 odd miles down to a narrow strip of sea, between the Island of Singapore just a mile away. The Malayan Peninsular divided two seas, on its Western shore the Bay of Bengal and the Straits of Malacca, on its Eastern shore the South China Sea. In addition, there was The Straits Settlement, comprising of the Islands of Singapore and Penang, plus two Malacca and Province Wellesley located on the West coast of the Peninsular mainland.

A brief history shows that The Portuguese settled in Malacca in 1511. In 1641 The Dutch overrun the Portuguese and took control of Malacca. In 1824 under an agreed Anglo Dutch Treaty, the British Settlement of Bencoolen on the Island of Sumatra was exchanged for the Dutch Colony of Malacca. In 1770 The East India Company arrived at the island of Penang. In 1786 George Town became its main Port for its trading, under the care of Francis Ligh. In 1832 The East India Company moved from George Town Penang to the Island of Singapore, to establish its headquarters under the control of Sir. Stanfford Rafles. In 1826 the 3 areas were united as the Straits Settlements, until 1867 when they became Crown Colonies. In 1895 the Sultans of Selangor, Perak, Negri Sembilan & Pahang, agreed with the British that the four States to become British Protectorates. (Federated States) Leaving the States of Johore, Kedah, Perlis, Kelantan & Pahang as the Unprotected States regarded as Stand Alone (Unfederated)

However, Malaya did not survive without hardship and strife. Incoming migrant countries, wanted to conquer the land, overrule the easy-going Malays and govern the land, which they had made their home. Malaya predominately of Islamic faith, became a mixture of different races, vocabularies and religions. The British colonised Malaya in 1867. Nevertheless, there are always agitators who think they know a better way of life, trusting in their own misguided belief they can turn people of different race and creed into thinking, what they themselves believe in? Is the right way for everyone else and are determined to change that? Over time immemorial. History had recorded, those factors, which have caused conflict, resulting in wars. There were two known illegal societies within the Federal States of Malaya & the Unfederated States of Malaya, which had infiltrated into Malaya. The Chinese society of. The Kuomintang Chinese Nationalist Party which had found its roots in 1919, a society not recognised by the British Government in Malaya, until 1930, and during the latter part of 1928 –1930. The Malayan Communist Party (MCP) strove to instil its doctrine amongst the Malay / Chinese. Both of these societies, apposed each other. The latter became a political thorn in the British Governments running of the country with their Communistic ideals.

During the 1930's, many members had been jailed for their activities nevertheless, both societies despised the Japanese. Having fought against them many years before during the Japanese invasion of China in 1937 until August 1945 when the Japanese finally surrendered.

CHAPTER 2

MALAYA AND WORLD WAR II

In the last century, two World Wars erupted, where practically all nations became involved. Particularly in WWII when Hitler wanted to dominate the world with his ideals, likewise the Japanese wanted to conquer the Far East with their ideals and their needs for oil and minerals available in various South East Asian countries. Shortly after the Evacuation of Dunkirk, when the French Vichy Government was on its knees and could not maintain its forces. It capitulated to the German Reich on the 22nd. June 1940. This agreement ensured that all French Colonies, would effectively come under the control of the German Reich. French Indo China became a problem to the Japanese still at war with China, and sought an agreement with the French Vichy Government to stop any arms and supplies destined for the Chinese, through the ports, the cross border with China By the end of August 1940. Japan was about to enter French Indo China, which happened on the 22 September, Japan invaded. After less than a week, took procession of many of its ports along the coast. Their intention was very obvious, as wanting to take over French Indo-China using it as a gateway into China itself. Their Action propelled the start of the war in the Pacific, with their armies carrying out sweeping thrust far into China and further within months into the Asian continent.

In June 1940, the Governor General, of Malaya. Sir. Shenton Thomas. In order to defend the Malayan Peninsular, established. The Volunteer Forces within the Federal States of Malaya and Unfederated States of Malaya & Straits Settlements. Volunteers were between the ages of 18 - 41. Basically, they were similar to the Home Guard of Great Britain.

In July 1940, after the fall of France. Winston Churchill under the guise of The Ministry of Economic Warfare, made up of four secret intelligence organizations MI6. SIS (Secret Intelligence Services) SS (Security Service) & MIDND (Military Intelligence Directorate & Naval Intelligence). In the process of forming the birth of SOE (Special Operations Executive). A certain Colin Mackenzie, a director of J.P. Coats a senior textile Company in England. Mackenzie, had lost a leg in World War I whilst serving with the Scots Guards. Was appointed the head of SOE whose principal was to train special agents in Special Training Schools (STS) in England then to infiltrate various enemy occupied countries & recruit nationals into small groups trained to carry out sabotage against the Germans. Each unit had a different numbered title. Located in Delhi India, operating under the title of Force 136, to operate against the Japanese in Burma then from Ceylon into Malaya. The first one was set up in a mansion, owned by the Stirling Family on the West coast of Scotland. Under the leadership of Bill Stirling. The purpose was to train agents to set up similar Special Training Schools within other countries. Their objectives were; generally, guerrilla warfare against the enemy, acts of sabotage, blowing up bridges, factories. One of the persons to join this clandestine Organisation was, Freddie Spencer Chapman, a serving member of the Seaforth Highlanders Territorials. He decided to transfer into that operation. There he met another person Mike Calvert, later to become known as Mad Mike Calvert, or his exploits as a leader of Chindits in Burma.

3rd. October 1940. Chapman and Calvert were chosen to go to Australia, to set up another Special Training School. They left Scotland, sailed on their voyage to Australia, via the Panama Canal. Arriving in Australia they set up their new Special Training School located on the Wilson Promontory close to the Bass Straits.

May 1941 In preparation of a possible attack by the Japanese, who since September 1940 had already occupied French Indo China. Another Special Training School was set up in Singapore called, 101 Special Training School (101 S.T.S.). Under the leadership of Col. Alan Warren. Royal Marines and Lt/Col. Jim Gavin. Royal Engineers. The school was located in an old house in Tanjong Belai, at the mouth of the Jurong River. The object of the STS was to teach selected personnel, mainly European Rubber Planters and Tin Miners or other Malays of Military or, civilian backgrounds, in small arms, explosives for use in acts of sabotage and methods of irregular warfare, to operate behind enemy lines as Special Intelligence Personnel. If, such an invasion by the Japanese occurred. These members would become. 'Stay Behind Volunteers' having been trained in the acts of sabotage, would have the means to harass the Japanese, causing as much disruption as possible. Amongst those Chinese chosen and accepted as non-Communist, were many Chinese of the Nationalist Kuomintang Society. Due to their previous hatred for the Japanese, they did not like the idea of serving under the barbaric rule of the Japanese. Many Chinese Kuomintang, living in Malaya, volunteered to join forces with the British. Obviously, they were screened before acceptance into the STS. Jim Gavin requested that Captain Freddy Spencer Chapman DSO & Bar. Be released from the Australian Training school to become his Number 2 in Singapore.

8th. September 1941. Chapman arrived in Singapore. To take up his new position and increase the progress on the section of volunteers for training, even those Chinese prisoners in various jails, were screened for selection into the Special Training School. It wasn't till December, that the establishment of 101 STS became a necessity.

On Sunday 7th. December 1941. The Imperial Japanese 25th. Army and Navy, carried out a co-ordinated attack on two fronts. The Japanese Aircraft Carriers. *Acagi, Kaja, Sorya, Hiryu, Shokaku, Zuikaku.* Sailed through the Pacific Ocean to a point, where their fighter bombers became within reach of the Islands of Guam, Wake, Midway and Hawaii. To attack the American Bases, specifically the US Naval Base at Pearl Harbour. At the same time. A second Japanese Navy fleet, sailing through the South China seas, as escorts to an Amphibious Transport fleet, carrying over 40.000 Japanese troops from Indo China. Their objective to invade the East coast of Siam and Malaya.

7th. December 1941. At 8'o'clock local time Hawaii. The Japanese bombers invaded the island of Oahu where the US Navy Fleet were based at Pearl Harbour, causing devaStations, sinking many ships and killing many Naval personnel

At 12 noon. Japanese Bombers bombed Hong Kong.

The British Navy Battleships HMS.*Prince of Wales & Repulse.* The Destroyers: *HMS Electra, Express, & Tenedos,* and HMAS *Vampire.* Having left Singapore were sailing under the code name. 'Force Z' on their way to Darwin Australia. When they were ordered to change course. Head steaming for the Gulf of Siam.

8th December 1941. During the early hours of darkness, a Japanese Amphibious Force attempted to land at Kota Bharu from 3 Japanese Navy Transport ships the *Awagisan Maru, Ayatosan Maru, and Sakuru Maru* carrying 5,200 Japanese troops These we supported by the Japanese Light Cruiser: *Sendal.* Destroyer's: *Ayanami, Isonami, Shikinami, and Uranami Minesweepers No 2 & 3, plus the Subchaser No 9.*

At 00.45. In the Gulf of Siam, about 3 miles off shore of the coast of Siam /Malaya The Japanese Amphibious Force, began their bombardment of the shore line of Kota Bharu, launching their first wave of landing craft. World War II had begun in the Far East.

The British forces of the 8th. Indian Division, the 9th. British Division supported by the 21st. Mountain Battery with 3.7 Howitzers retaliated. The RAF No 1 Squadron flying Hudson's Sunk the *Awagisan RAF* Beafighters entered into the fight but were engaged by Japanese Fighters with many losses.

During the early hours of the morning, a Squadron of Japanese bombers flew over Singapore and dropped bombs on a sleeping city.

At 6 a.m. Radio Singapore announced Great Britain was at war with Japan.

At 10.30 that day. After fierce hand to hand fighting by the British, finally with many losses to both sides, The Japanese landed in Malaya.

9th. December. 1941. Force 'Z' steaming North were to lose HMS. *Tenedos.* Being low on fuel had to return back to Singapore.

10th. December. Force 'Z' were spotted by Japanese reconnaissance planes. 84 Japanese torpedo bombers attacked and bombed both battleships the *Prince of Wales and Repulse* resulting in their sinking with great loss of life. Whilst onshore The British Forces outnumbered, taken by surprise of the speed of the Japanese forces, made a hasty withdrawal down the western side of Malaya, putting up a retreating resistance.

With this invasion by the Japanese. Increased the purpose of the 101 Special Training School. More volunteers were needed for 'Stay Behind' units. Other leading personnel to join the STS were. Captain John. Davis a Malayan Police Officer and Captain Richard Broome. Ex Malayan Civil Service. Chapman was one of the main principal architects.' at the Special Training School 101 in Singapore. However, with the Japanese Invasion. *Lai Te* the Malayan Communist Party (MCP) Secretary General, approached, Sir. Shenton-Thomas. The Governor General, to offer their Services. Sir. Shenton- Thomas well aware of their political standing and intentions rejected their offer.

12th. December. Advancing Japanese troops took the Northern town of Alor Star. The Evacuation of Penang began.

15th. December. Japanese troops secured the single line railway from Rangoon to Singapore.

18th December. The speed at which the invading Japanese forces advanced down through the Peninsula, subsequently the withdrawal of the British Forces towards Singapore Island. Acting on Lt/Gen Arthur Perceval's advice; Sir. Edward Shenton Thomas rescinded his refusal to *Lai Te's* offer of the MCP assistance & set up a meeting between a Special Group Officer. Innes Tremlett, *Lai Te's* boss (*Lai Te* was an unknown agent of the British) & Capt. Freddy Spencer Chapman, (SOE), Wong Chin Yok (Special Group Police Inspector) that took place on December 18th In a Communist Safe house in Singapore. Chapman agreed to get released from jail, those communist willing to volunteer to join the British in the pending fight against the Japanese in Malaya. The first 15 would be trained in guerrilla warfare at the 101 STS school beginning on the 22nd. December. *Lai Te* was also required to recruit all Communist Party members in towns throughout Malaya, to prepare for a guerrilla war. The training school would be in Kuala Lumpur. Following in the wake of the Japanese advance, members of the Malayan Communist Party, including farmers and local trade's peoples, seized the opportunity to retrieve any small arms and ammunition, including automatic weapons, grenades and mortar's, whether taken from dead British soldiers or Japanese or, lay abandoned in the haste of the retreating British Troops These arms were secreted into the jungle and hidden to enable the use of same, as and when in the future, the right time came to implement their plans.

19th December. Warren along with Chapman left Singapore driving up to Kuala Lumpur to set up another STS school. .in the Grounds of the Chinese Chungjing School, where 100 volunteers began their training. After training they would be sent to

Kedah or Northern Perak with gelignite, TNT & detonating wire to sabotage the railways & bridges to attempt to hinder the Japanese advance.

26th. December. Japanese troops captured the Town of Taiping their advance was swift.

30th. December. the Japanese attack was halted by, the British and 11th. Indian Infantry Division holding their defence. which they held until: -

2nd.. January. 1942, During the battle many men were lost, before the British and Indian forces withdrew back to Trolak just North of the Slim River.

On the 2nd January. 1942. On the same day, The Perak MCP State Committee including **Chin Peng**, met. As contact had been made with Chapman's Party in Tanjong Malim. Discussed how they could integrate with them?

In Singapore early in1942. Another Volunteer unit was established by Colonel Daley who had previously been responsible for counter field operations in Malaya. The Unit was called Dalforce also known as the Singapore Overseas Chinese anti-Japanese Volunteer Army. (S.P.C.A.J.V.F.) Dalforce consisted of about 2,000 Chinese civilians. only to eager to take up arms against the hated Japanese, who had driven them out of their homeland in the Sino –Jap war. They were to be trained under British officers, unfortunately, was only in existence for a couple of weeks. (In fact, prior to its formation, the authorities' in Malaya, for political reasons, vetoed this setting up of an exclusively Chinese Force).

7th. January. The battle of Slim River began. The Japanese almost walked through the British defences opening up the road to the capital Kuala Lumpur. Thus, began the initial evacuation of civilians from Malaya to Singapore who joined others fleeing before the Japanese.

9th. January. Japanese Army entered Kuala Lumpur.

10th. January. The first detachment of the Malayan Peoples Anti-Japanese Army (M.P.A.J. A).to join forces with the Force 36 was formed in Serandah.

14th. January. The Japanese Army entered Gemas South of Kuala Lumpur.

20th. January. The Second detachment of the M.P.A.J.A. were infiltrated into Gemas Johore.

30th. January. Singapore. 4,000 women, children, evacuees escaped on board the SS Wakefield, West Point, Duchess of Bedford and the Empress of Japan sailing for Batvia Dutch Eest Indies.

31st. January. Malaya was virtually under Japanese occupation. The Japanese were encamped across the causeway from Singapore Island.

5th of February. 1942. Recruits left the training camp, ill equipped and many without arms. A Company of Dalforce, fought alongside the 22nd Australian Brigade. Many without arms were pushed into the North West War Zone to fight the Japanese, many died and those left were massacred in the later. Cleansing Operation of the Japanese or, those that did escape, fled into the jungle, to eventually be formed into the origins of the Malayan Peoples Anti-Japanese Army. (M.P.A.J.A.)

8th. February. Singapore. With the evacuation of Singapore well underway. The Royal Navy had requisitioned several steamers The *Kung Wo, Tieng Kuang, and Kuala* to take evacuees away to Batavia or, other ports. The evacuation of Singapore became a similar event as that basically happened at Dunkirk, albeit an evacuation of civilians. (Read Singapore's Dunkirk. by Geoffrey Brooke.)

12th. February. The Japanese shelled & bombed Singapore.

15th February. 1942 the Japanese just walked across the Island to await the surrender by the British Army under the leadership of Lt/Gen A. E. Percival, which happened at the Singapore Railway Station. The fate of many Commonwealth soldiers, was either to be slaughtered or incaserated, including Sir. Shenton Thomas, till the end of the war in August 1945. The British surrender, came as a drastic shock, as no one realised the Japanese had the resources to wage such a war against the might of the British army in Malaya. But it did happen. .

In Kuala Lumpur. Chapman at the base camp for training members of the cladistics Force 136. Had become isolated and left behind in Malaya. He still carried on being the senior SOE Officer and co-ordinator within the Force 136 framework living in the Jungle. (He eventually left Malaya, in early February 1945 along with Broome to return to Ceylon).

Warren, had hired the *Hin Lee* a small coaster. He together with John Davis CBE. DSO. and Richard Broome had sailed to Sumatra. Made their way across Sumatra, creating an escape route through to Padang on the East coast. Returning back with the information, to Singapore, before returning again to Sumatra along the escape route they had devised.

On the 8th. March Leaving Warren behind, Davis and Broome along with 16 other SOE officers sailed to Ceylon on a junk called *Sederhana Djohannis*.arriving there 6 weeks later in mid-April. Their intention was to later return to Malaya to liaise with members of Force 136, who supplied vital intelligence reports about the Japanese activities in Malaya, with the support from the various established Guerrilla units throughout Malaya, began harassing and sabotaging the occupying Japanese communications.

In Perak after a further meeting by the MCP Committee. Enter **_Chin Peng_** who was ordered to Tanjong Talan Tin Mining area to take over as Liaison Officer, between the MCP & Capt. Spencer Chapman, also to lead a guerrilla unit in the Tanjong Malim area of Perak.

On Monday 16th. February. 1943 **_Chin Peng_** was told to meet Capt. Spencer Chapman SOE at 3 p.m. at a specific rendezvous point. He had divided his guerrilla units into 2 groups. **_Chin Peng's_** group cycled there, through many Japanese soldiers, they taking no notice of Chinese on bikes. They were after the British Soldiers. **_Chin Peng's_** group arrived two hours late. Chapman had already left with two other SOE officers. Boris Hembrey & Bill Graham, both managers of rubber plantations in Malaya, who had joined as "Stay Behinds" to fight against the Japanese. Chapman had gone on to Kuala Kabu. **_Chin Peng_** sent a courier to tell Chapman the reason they had arrived late.

The MCP were not considered by the British authorities. As likely candidates to join forces with Force 136. They were still an active Communist set-up with their ultimate aim. To work with the British against the Japanese, then at such a time in the future; to take over the running of Malaya. This is borne out by information stated in **_Chin Peng's_** book "_MY SIDE OF HISTORY_." Within the text he refers to a 9-point manifesto which set down plans for an Anti-Japanese programme to be followed by the party. A copy of this document, was given to him in March 1943, by **_Chai Ke Ming_** Senior Party Official of the MCP. The main 9 points were:

1)   The defeat of Japanese fascist and the establishments of the Malayan Republic.

2)   The formation of a national organization composed of representatives universally selected and elected from the different nationalities to govern and protect our motherland. The improvement of civilian living conditions the development of industry agricultural and commerce in order to build up Malaya as a harmonious, free and felicitous country.

3)   Freedom of speech, freedom of the press and freedom of assembly. The abolition of oppressive laws and the release of all prisoners and anti-Japanese captives.

4)   The abolition of high and unnecessary taxation and high interest Money lending.

5)   The reorganization of the Malayan Anti-Japanese Guerrillas into the National Army for the Defence of Malaya. Assistance for the guerrilla veterans and their families and the families of all those who died for the liberation of Malaya. Relief for war and disabled veterans.

6)   The development of a national culture through free education.

7)   Confiscation of all properties owned by a German, Italian and Japanese fascist, as well as confiscation of properties owned by traitors and collaborators.

8)   The establishment of commercial ties with Friendly countries.

9)   A united effort with Russia and China to support the strongholds for independence of the oppressed nations in the Far East.

In reading these nine points, it was obvious that even in the early days of the Japanese Occupation of Malaya. The MCP's intention was to create a Communist Dictatorship in Malaya, once the Japanese had been defeated.

However, it wasn't until the 30/31st December 1943, when the Malayan Communist Party, were invited to co-operate with the British against the Japanese. At a secret SOE camp at Blantan perched on the top of a Malayan mountain to the East of Tapah in Perak, a hand-written document. A TERMS OF CO-OPERATION was presented by members of the SOE Commanders of Force 136, to a selected group of members of the Malayan Communist Party (CMP) their names are as follows:

Commanders of Force 136:
Major John. L. H. Davis. - Captain Richard Broome &
Major Fredrick Spencer Chapman.

Malayan Communist Party members:
Messrs: Chang Hong (C/M) Chin Peng (Alias Chen Chin Shen). Tan Choon Lim.

Terms of Cooperation

1a   Mr. Chang Hong (C/M) is the elected representative of the Malayan Communist Party. The Anti-Japanese Force and the Anti-Japanese Union and can put into force any decisions agreed to in these meetings.

B Major. J. L. H. DAVIS., Capt. R. N. BROOME and Mr. Tan Choon Lim. Is the Military Representation (MR) of the Allied C in C Southeast Asia, and are fully empowered to cooperate with any Anti-Japanese party in Malaya.

2 CH agrees that his party will fully cooperate with the allied forces while retaking Malaya and for this purpose will follow the instruction of the Allied C in C in so far as military operation in Malaya are concerned.

B Details of Proposals and Decisions.

1   After giving a summary of the numbers and resources of the various Anti-Japanese organisations in Malaya. CH asked in what way these organisations would be expected to cooperate The MR summarised the military and fifth column activity hoped for and it was agreed that at present beyond keeping the people Anti-Japanese, the only possible Action Engaging CT's to ferment labour and carry out sabotage against Shipping, naval dockyards etc. For the next it was agreed to be a time of preparation for to use combined Action Engaging CT's.

CM also understood to emphasize in their present Propaganda the need for complete cooperation with allied Invading forces.

2   Asked what kind of help his Organisation expected, CM Replied
(a) Arms and ammunition
(b) Medical Supplies Including doctors
(c) Military training
(d) financial Assistance.

The MR stated with regard to (a) and (b) that
The Allied C in C will undertake to despatch to Malaya, by All possible means the arms and supplies needed for Effective operation. The introduction of Doctors from Outside is difficult at resent but the possibility will be Implemented.

(c) The Chinese instructors who are really in India will be Introduced as soon as communications permit. ii. Chinese students will be sent from Malaya for Training instructors and will be returned to Malaya. A Party of 6 should be prepared to proceed to India Shortly.

iii. The question of introducing European Instructors At a later date will be investigated
(d) The MR have Already asked for authority to finance. The reply is
Expected within a Month.
CH Estimates about 50-70,000 $ per Month will meet Present Requirements.

The above is subject to the Sat.isfAction Engaging CT's of members of the Headquarters of the M.C.P, AJF and AJU and is subject To agreement on the following or, similar clause to be Added.

"That cooperation shall Continue during the Period in which the army is responsible for the Maintenance of Peace and Order in Malaya."

Signatures from all parties present.

Extract from Chin Peng's book

In Malaya, the MCP with their political structure already established, had furthered their ends with the retrieval of all the weaponry, necessary to commit to a further military wing, later became known as the Malayan Peoples Anti-Japanese Army (MPAJA) made up by the Anti-Japanese Union (AJU) mainly MCP supporters and the Anti-Japanese Army (AJA) the military wing of the MCP. Also known to Force 136 as the Anti-Japanese Union and Forces. (A.J.U.F.). As time progressed many Chinese/Malays joined the MPAJA. With their intense hatred towards the Japanese and their Kempeitai (Japanese Military Police) who rounded up many senior MCP members and either incarcerate or executed them. The MPAJA in Malaya, under close supervision of the available British Officers and Senior NCO's, of Force 136, became an army within an army, and the source of the roots of the future Malayan Peoples Anti British Army. (MPABA). Nevertheless, the MPAJA became an active guerrilla force against the Japanese. They carried out acts. of sabotage and incursions, which they did with success, however the aim of the MPAJA was two fold:

a) To fight with the British against the Japanese and after the proposed later invasion and reoccupation of Malaya by the British

b) Abolish Colonialism and form a Democratic Republic of Malaya under Communist Rule.

Reference to the above is made to two published works on the activities of Force 136 and the AJUF during the interim period of 1942 –1945, F. Spencer Chapman's 'The Jungle is Neutral' Pub.1949. And **'Chin Peng'** *'My Side of History 'Pub 2003.*

The organisers of Force 136 instigated a plan to amalgamate the two separate units, the Anti-Japanese Force (AJF) and Anti-Japanese Union (AJU) into one single unit, known as the Anti-Japanese Union Force (AJUF) These were organised into various Numbered Units with code names to operate within specific areas, across the length and breadth of the Malaya Peninsular. All engaged in acts. of sabotage and disruption to the occupying Imperial Japanese Army.

In the far North operating in Kedah from the Thailand Border down to the border of Perak was AJUF 8. Code name Operation SERGEANT and FIGHTER. - In Perak AJUF 8 Code Name FUNNEL and HEBRIDES. - In Selangor AJUF 1 Code name GALVANIC. - In Negri Sembilan AJUF 2 & Western Johore. Code name HUMOUR. - In Johore AJUF 3 Code name TIDEWAY and AJUF 4 Code name CARPENTER. - In Pahang, Terengganu and Kelantan. - AJUF 6 and 7. Intelligence Communications between units was by wireless or a Courier Service where the Chinese Guerrillas could with caution, move along roadways to deliver a message to another courier and so on.

11th. May. 1943: The use of Submarines sailing from the naval base at Trincomalee in Ceylon to Malaya, with British Sino Commando Teams, began with Operation 'Gustavus I' The leader of the team was Captain John Davies. CBE. DSO., plus Chinese trained wireless operators: - Ah Piu, his bodyguard, Ah Tsing, - Ah Ying – Ah Han, Ah. Ng with their wireless/ telegraph sets, stores & folboats, left Ceylon in HMNLS 'O 24' a Dutch Submarine. Under the Command of Lt. Cmdr. W.J. de Vries enroute to Malaya.

24th. May. The Submarine resurfaced, 5 miles offshore in the area North of Pangkor Island, on the West coast of Malaya. There to transfer themselves, by folboats to their land fall at a beach near the area of Segari Perak. It was the first landing of British and Chinese soldiers since the fall of Singapore. Their objective:

(a) To obtain a Junk with a willing crew to be used for future rendezvous with Submarines

Davis, turned his trust to Ah Tsing, to secure a suitable Junk with a friendly crew. They to become the means of transport from the Submarine to the shore. Ah Tsing, made his way back to Lumutt, then across to Pulai Pangkor posing as a fish Merchant. There he made contact with a local fish Merchant, Chua Koon Eng. It took Ah Tsing three weeks before he convinced Chua. promising him his safety to him providing a suitable Junk with an equally reliable crew. It was through conversations between Ah Tsing & Chua he found out there was approximately 800 anti-Japanese Guerrillas, located in the Sitiawan area, with further Guerrilla units located and in touch throughout Perak.

(b) To set up their temporary H Q in Malaya at Bukit Segari Camp.

Subsequently, Davis could not contact HQ Ceylon with this information, due to the fact they had lost radio contact. Davis, decided he would return to Ceylon, on the next Submarine with the information.

16th June. Operation 'Gustavo's II' under the Command of Capt. Broome, Claude Fenner, together with 3 Chinese Liaison Officers: Ah Lim, – Shek Fu, - Lee Choon, a first-rate radio operator plus various stores. Sailed from Trincomalee Ceylon on board HMNLS 'O 23' under the command of Lt. Cmdr. Valkenburg en-route to the Sitiawan Islands to rendezvous wi,th the assigned Junk.

22nd. June. John Davis CBE. DSO. along with Ah Piu, were picked up from Segari beach on the requisitioned Junk. As a diversion away from their intend rendezvous with the Submarine. They set sail down the coast towards Port Swettenham, with a cargo of rice. The Junk, landed Davis & Ah Piu on an uninhabited island in the Sembilan group. There to await the return of the Junk, before proceeding back to the agreed rendezvous with the Submarine.

27th. June. The Submarine surfaced, under cover of darkness it's silhouette was seen by Davis & Piu. Soon folboats arrived at the beach. Capt. Davis Leader of 'Gustavus I'. Insisted he return back to HQ Ceylon on the Submarine. The pair were taken out to meet the waiting Broome and his party. Once on-board Davis ordered, they return back to Trincomalee with his intelligence information, together with the Japanese currency they had gathered, to be forged for future use.

6th. July. The Submarine arrived back in Trincomalee. Davis was debriefed on his latest up to date information, on the strength of the Guerrilla units in Malaya the (AJA) Anti-Japanese Army. How the Chinese trained agents of 101 STS had set up these units. Including a wider non-combatant force called the Anti-Japanese Unit (AJF) Communist led who supplied the AJA with food and Money.

24th. July. 'Operation Gustavus III.' Under the command of Major Davis, with the same team equipped with radio transmitters & other equipment left Ceylon in the Dutch Submarine. 023. With the same Dutch commander Lt. Cmdr. Valkenburg.

4th. August. The Submarine surfaced at nearly same position as the first 'Operation I' They made contact with the Junk. On board was Ah Tsing, who handed over further vital information to Claude Fenner. to take back to Ceylon. The Party transferred to the Junk and landed on the Segari beach with transmitters and other supplies. Then they joined forces with the remaining team of Davis's 'Gustavus I.' At Bukit Segari Camp. Ah Ng, in Davis's absence. had been in contact with the Guerrilla forces operating in the Sitiawan area. 4 Communist Guards had been assigned to be bodyguards to Davis's. their leader was Cheng Klang Koon. Davis, was also introduced to the Communist Acting Secretary of State. Chen Chin Seng real name Ong Boon Hua alias *Chin Peng*.

12th September. Operation 'Gustavus VI.' Capt. Broome along with Capt. E. P. W. Harrison left Trincomalee in the Dutch Submarine 024. Under the command of Lt. Cmdr. De Vries. Their intended rendezvous was South of the Sembilan Islands.

23rd. September. About to surface. De Vries spotted a Japanese convoy approaching from the South. De Vries advised that he was going to attack the convoy. Much to Broome's annoyance, a discussion took place, Broome insisted that they wait until dusk before the Submarine surfaced. Only then they take folboats and proceed with a limited amount of supplies, head for shore. Landing on the Segari beach they hid the W/T and other heavy supplies in amonst the jungle fringes before making their way to the Segari Camp.

27th. October. Operation 'Gustavus V.' A further departure by Submarine the Dutch Submarine 024 from Trincomalee. With Capt. Harrison, Claude Fenner, Lim Bo Seng (The Chinese Leader of the Chinese 136 Force) & agent Zhuan Hui Chuan. Together with more supplies & light weight W/T sets.

6th. November. The rendezvous between the Submarine & Junk occurred without incident. Lim Bo Seng was met on the Junk by *Chin Peng,* who was his escort to meet Davis. He warned of the dangers of possible capture by the Japanese, who had somehow got word of. The infiltrations of agents in the area of Pangkor. Lim Bo Seng, refused to let Harrison & Fenner off the Submarine, instead ordered them to return back with Zhuan Hui Chuan, who eventually returned to India.

Lim Bo Seng & *Chin Peng* reached the Segari beach, hid all the supplies, to be collected later. They then travelled by car, which *Chin Peng* had arranged to take them to Tapah. Then onwards to meet up with Davis, at the new camp site at Blantan.

29th November. Operation 'Gustavus VI.' On this occasion it was the first to be undertaken by a British Submarine. HMS *'Tally Ho'* commanded by Lt. Cmdr. L.W.A. Bennington. On board were Captain Harrison and Chen Teh Fu a Chinese agent.

9th. December. The Submarine surfaced, made contact with the Junk, did the exchange successfully. H.M.S *'Tally Ho'* unloading only gold coins, sterling pounds & forged Japanese yen. Plus, food supplies. Then departed back to Trincomalee

8th January.1944. Operation 'Emergency Gustavus VI.' H.M.S *'Tally Ho'* Submarine.Under the command of Lt. L. W. A. Bennington left Trincomalee. On board were Maj. Jim Hannah & Claude Fenner plus 8 Chinese agents.

19th. January. Submarine surfaced at the rendezvous position with the Junk. On board the Junk was *Chin Peng* who exchanged messages and told Fenner to return on the Submarine, as the Japanese were very active along the coast. It was in their best interest to get back to Trincomalee.

8th. February. Operation 'Remarkable I.' H.M.S *'Tally Ho'* Submarine. Under the command of Lt. Cmdr. L. W. A. Bennington. Once again Maj. Hannah & Fenner were on board, along with Chan Teh Cheok & Chen Chung Chi. failed to link up with the Junk. Due to the presence of Japanese ships & the failure to link up with the Junk. The Operation Failed.

15th. March. Operation 'Remarkable II.' H.M.S *'Tally Ho'* Submarine. Under the command of Lt. Cmdr. Bonington with Claude Fenner & Maj. Jim Hannah left. Trincomalee. But due to much Japanese shipping in the area trolled for 3 to 4 days before aborting the mission.

12th April. 1944 Operation 'Remarkable III.' A Submarine left Trincomalee with Fenner, Hannah along with. Chan Teh Cheok & Cheng Qian Koon. Once. again, the link up with the Junk was unsuccessful. Returned with all the arms ammunition, food and other supplies.

24th. April. 1944 Chen Qian Koon, did land from a Submarine at Anson. On the return journey the Submarine was attacked by Japanese air planes nevertheless, it escaped & returned to Ceylon. That was the last Submarine trip to Lumutt. That link was deemed abandoned by the HQ in India. Instead Several agents were sent to Australia from China for training.

21st September. 1944 a party of 17 OSE sailed on a Submarine ?(details unknown) The force 136 Party, under the Command of Major Martin, Major Sime with 9 British Officers (unnamed) & 7 Chinese Liaison Officers: Chen Yi Yue, Lloyd Chin Fen, Hsieh Cheng Sui, Tan Khun, Chen Chung Chi, Chan Sin Wing, Cho Tik Ming. Left the West coast of Australia.

5th. October. The Submarine surfaced on the Southern coast of Johore near Singapore. Making contact with the resistance army, the team were dispersed to six different posts in Johore.

On 23rd.January. 1945/ One other Submarine sailing, took place from Western Australia, with a British Officer. Major Sime the leader of a party. Wong Yen Dat & Leung Ming Chang along with Major Kark & three assistants of the American Intelligence Department, (unnamed).

6th.February: Submarine surfaced of the East coast of Johore, they met up with resistance parties. They were to be the last transfer of Agents by Submarine.

1st February. 1945. saw a turning point for Force 136. Radio Contact was made from Bidor in Perak, direct with HQ Ceylon giving Davies the opportunity to provide SEAC in India, with vital up-to-date information about Japanese activities in Malaya, also being able to co-ordinate between land & Aircraft. Began with the parachuting of Specialised personnel into various areas of Malaya, together with essential air drops of supplies, albeit radio silence by the aircraft was maintained, until near the intended target Drop area. The first Parachute drops. of Personnel & supplies by B24 Liberators began on: -

26th February. 1945 The 1st. B24 Liberator Bomber Flying out of Calcutta. With a team led by Major Hislop. Along with Members: Wong Sui Sang, Tsang Jan Man, Lim Hong Pei, Chan Zao Kouk, Chen Kok Ying. parachuted into thick jungle in North Kedah.

On the same day. The 2nd. B24. with a team lead by Major Harrison along with Members: Lo Ngai Soon & several British soldiers (unnambed) parachuted into Bukit Bidor.

28th April. The 3rd. B24. air drop with Major Abbott, the team leader along with Members: Har She Sun., 2 British soldiers & a Doctor (all unnamed) parachuted into Bukit Bidor.

6th.May No 4. B24. air drop with Capt. Chapman along with Members: Chiang Pak Kuan, Li Zhe and 1 British soldier (unnamed) parachuted into Pahang.

12th.May. No 5. B24. air drop with Leader Major Owen along with Members: Yuen Wai Cheong and two British soldiers (unnamed) parachuted into Bukit Bidor.

On the same day. No 6. B24. air drop with Leader Capt. Robinson along with Members: Woh Kok Shu, Lee Ki and one British soldier (unnamed) parachuted into Pahang.

30th.May. No. 7. B24. air drop with Leaders Major Broadhurst and Flight Officer Robertson along with Members: Liang Chao Zhen and Tong Shu Shen., parachuted into Selangor.

On the same day No 8. B24. air drop with Leaders Major Hunter and Captain Davies along with Members: Huang Yih Hsai and one British soldier (unnamed) parachuted into Selangor.

6th.June. No. 9. B24. air drop. 2: B24. Liberators took off from Minnariya Ceylon on a supply drop in Perak. Only 1 B24. returned. **This is covered later.

12th.June. No.10. B24. air drop with Leader Major Vsilom along with Members: Chan Phui Kong and two British soldiers (unnamed) parachuted into Perak.

18th. June. No 11. B24. air drop with Leader Major Olsen along with Members: Ho Soo Shen and two British Officers (unnamed) parachuted into Negri Sembilan.

26th.June. No.12. B24. air drop with Leader Capt. McKenzie along with Members: Hung Ling Hi, Liang She Min and two British Officers (unnamed) parachuted into North Johore.

On the same day No 13. B24. air drop with Leader Capt. Wilkinson along with Members Lee Pak Choon, Liu Sik Shand two British soldiers (unnamed) parachuted into North Johore.

On the same day No. 14. B24. air drop with Leader Major C. Miles along with Members: Diao Yi Ang and two British soldiers (unnamed) parachuted into North Johore.

2nd. July. No. 15. B24. air drop with Leader Major A. S. Olsen along with Members: Pang Har & Chan Chiok Sun. with two British officers (unnamed) parachuted into Negri Sembilan.

10th.July. No. 16. B24. air drop with Leader Major T. Walker along with Members: Seah TinToon and two British Officers (unnamed) parachuted into Selangor.

25th. July. No. 17. B24. air drop with Members: Zhang Wen Shun and several British soldiers (unnamed) parachuted into Negri Sembilan.

28th. July. No.18. B24. air drop with Members: TSun. Man Yin and several British soldiers (unnamed) parachuted into Selangor.

30th. July. No 19. B24. with Leader Major Penner along with Members: Bruce Chin Fen and two British soldiers (unnamed) parachuted into Negri Sembilan.

1st. August. No. 20. B24. air drop with Leader Major Leonard along with Members: Fu Bing and two British soldiers (unnamed) parachuted into Pahang.

1st. September. No. 21. B24. air drop with Members: Wang Shao Hua and several British soldiers (unnamed)parachuted into Negri Sembilan.

There also was possibly 10 plus other B24. Parachute drops. of British Soldiers & Chinese wireless operators into the above-mentioned States. By August 1945 The Air drops. of Parties personnel, arms and supplies, along the West coast of the Malaya States. Added towards the pending Operation 'Zipper.' Maj. Hannah just one of the British Officers. Had under his command over 800 Guerrillas, of which at the time of the British 'Zipper' Invasion, there were an estimated over 5,000 Geurrillas in the jungles.

However, there are records of two (2) B24. Liberator crashes Number 1 in Johore, known as the "Seremban Liberator. "Went missing 23 Sept 1945, possibly took off from the Cocos Islands?

And

** 6th. June: 2 known B24. Liberator Bombers.(a) **KH326 X** together with another (b) B24. "M" on the same secret mission, both bound by radio silence. Flew out of Minnariya Ceylon on the 6th. June 1945, on a supply drops. mission to members of Force 136 in North Malaya. KH326 was last seen by "M" disappearing into thick cloud just North of Penang. It was not until "M" having completed its drop, returned safely to Minnariya, that **KH326 X** well overdue. Was classified as 'Missing over Malaya.' There was a search by Force 136 Guerrilla forces, made after the failure of the pending supply drop without any results. For all intents and purposes a 'Mari Celeste.' The continuing story of the Mari Celeste KH326. Will become evident as documented during the contents of **Chapter 13.** When discovered during Operation '*Unity*' May 1955: -

(Story **to be continued in the later Chapters**).

Lai Te*.*The recognised leader of the MCP. Was aware of the forthcoming Operation 'Zipper.' In October 1944, he held a meeting in the township of Serandah North of Kuala Lumpur. Those attending were leaders of AJUF jungle units from Johore, Perak, Selangor & Pahang, amongst them was ***Liew Yao*** Central Military Committee - ***Chin Peng*** Commander of the Perak AJA - ***Liaw Wei Chung*** (Known as ***Itu***.) 5th. Regt. Perak, - ***Den Fuk Lung.*** 2nd. Regt. Negri Seremban - ***Chou Yang Pin*** Commander 1st. Regt. Selangor, - ***Chen Tien*** Commander 4th. Regt. S Johore, - ***Wang Chin*** Commander 6th. Regt. West Pahang. – ***Sun. Wen Chin*** 7TH. Regt. East Pahang.

Lai Te explained. He had agreed to assist the Allied Forces whenever Operation Zipper took place, dates unknown. This he explained was in accordance with the Terms of Co-operation signed in December 1943. He also went on to advise that by assisting the Allied Forces, to cater for future operations. Their MCP army would be split into two parts

a) An 'Open Army' to work with the British Forces &

b) The Party's 'Clandestine Army.' When the time came, this secret force would be in a position to function independently. Giving the total impression. To take the fight to the British. Upon the forthcoming landing. To change our name to the National Liberation Army & seize as much territory as possible. Including small Townships.

These plans were kept secret from Force 136.

In January / February of 1945. High ranking personnel of Force 136. Fully aware of the future plan of Operation 'Zipper' Met to discuss the role that was expected to be played by the AJUF during Operation "Zipper" The AJUF were basically an army of Malay, Chinese of significant numbers, of both Kuomintang & Malayan Communist, who had been armed to a certain degree by the British nevertheless, they did have & used arms & small ordnance, captured from the Japanese and were a source for gathering intelligence about the Japanese There certainly was a justified suspect, as to what their motives were and certainly NOT, in the political interest of the British Government. The pressing need for a solution was vital with the build up to Operation 'Zipper' Their demands were, that they should be adequately armed. It was agreed that under the control of Commissioned British officers' arms would be provided to the Malayan Resistance Movement, but with certain conditions as per the Terms of Co-operation after the re-occupation of Malaya. As it was understood, the AJUF would try to obtain the status of Malaya as an Independent Republic. The AJUF although recognised for their efforts, would receive the acclaim it deserved but, their disarmament must be ensured and they could return back to their occupation prior to joining the AJUF.

With the success of the British XIV Army pushing the Japanese back through Burma & Siam. Under the code name "Zipper," British plans had already been prepared for an invasion by land and sea, onto the Malayan Peninsular for August 1945. A pincer movement with the British Army advancing down through Malaya, whilst an amphibious sea invasion force would sail from India, to land in Southern Malaya at Morib Selangor and Port Dixon Negri Sembilan, with the final drive down to Singapore. At the same time as Operation 'Zipper 'was underway. 2 Atomic bombs were dropped 1 on Hiroshima & 1 on Nagasaki, which forced the Japanese into unconditional surrender on the 15th. August. During the Unconditional surrender of the Japanese, until it ended in capitulation. The orders of Force 136 Officers & related groups, were to ensure that Law & Order were to be upheld in all towns & villages throughout Malaya. To ensure the Japanese surrender was orderly, until the British troops arrived to take control. However, the MCP were quick to seize the opportunity. They split with Force 136 and as previously ordered for political reasons, to try and gain control of Malayan townships, including Singapore as a Communist run Island. Associations were set up throughout the land. The Association of Ex Comrades, The Anti-Japanese Alliance. Their tactics were unruly, they went on the rampage, seizing collaborators, rightly or wrongly killing, including the intimidation of the locals, forcing them into thoughts of defeating the British, and become a Communist State. Even amongst their own Leaders there were traitors. However, the British were aware of the intentions of the MCP & their military wing the MPAJA. Major. Davis CBE. DSO.Immediately set about the task of the Demobilisation of that wing. His adversary was no other than his comrade in arms & friend. ***Chin Peng,*** whom along with his trusted communist associates of the MCP Central Committee. Now the Japanese had been defeated, had set up the Malayan People's Commission. (MPC) a slight change from (MCP) with Organisation all over the country. With a directive to follow as below: -

1) The defeat of Japanese fascist and the establishments of the Malayan Republic.

   To support the Chinese, Russian & American alliance and the new international peace organisations

2) The formation of a national organisation composed of representatives. Universally selected & elected from the different nationalities to govern and protect our motherland. The improvement of civilian living conditions The development of industry agricultural and commerc, in order to build up Malaya as a harmonious, free and felicitous country.

3) To implement democracy in Malaya and establish popular will in all the state Freedom of speech, freedom of the press and freedom of assembly. The abolition of oppressive laws and the release of all prisoners and anti Japanese captives.

4) To abolish all political Organisation rules and regulations, imposed by the Japanese fascist regime.

5) The abolition of high and unnecessary taxation and high interest money lending.
6) To bring about freedom of speech publications, organisations, congregations and beliefs and to protect the legitimacy of all anti-Japanese organisations.
7) The reorganisation of the Malayan Anti-Japanese Guerrillas, into the National Army for the Defence of Malaya.
8) Assistance for the Guerrilla Veterans and their families, and the families of all those who died for the Liberation of Malaya. Relief for war and disabled veterans.
9) To abolish the old education system and replace it with democratic education through the use of the National Language.
10) The development of a national culture through free education.
11) To improve the livelihood of peoples by promoting industry and agriculture to help refugees to increase workers pay and implement the 8-hour work system.
12) Confiscation of all properties owned by a German, Italian and Japanese fascist, as well as confiscation or properties owned by traitors and collaborators.
13) To curb price fluctuations in order to maintain a stable livelihood for the people, to punish corrupt officials and all those involved in profiteering.
14) The establishment of commercial ties with Friendly countries.
15) To give preferential treatment to soldiers of the anti-Japanese war and provide compensation to families of the bereaved.
16) A united effort with Russia and China to support the strongholds for independence of the oppressed nations in the Far East.

Chin Peng, (Chinese name *Chen Ping*) One of the leaders of the Communist Party AJUF was known as a trustworthy Guerrilla by the British. Therefore, for his efforts in helping defeat the Japanese during the war,was awarded the OBE (It was rescinded in 1947). With much pomp and ceremony. Other disbandment ceremonies, took place in various state capitals of Malaya. Also, a large contingent of the AJUF travelled to England and marched in the Malayan Contingent of the Victory Parade. They were not listed as the AJUF but under the title of. "Guerrillas and Police" After the war, the existence of the Malayan Communist Party (MCP) dating back to 1928-30, was recognised by the newly formed British Administration. Their Secretary General *Lai Te* assumed command of the MCP.

The following Maps indicate the Structure of Force 136 dispersement of AJUP Regiments. 1942 -1945 together with the Similar Structure of the MPABA / MRLA Regiments.1948 -1960

THAILAND

MALAYA

FORCE 136 1942 -1945
LOCATIONS OF A.J.U.F FORCES
CODE NAMES

PERLIS

FIGHTER
SERGEANT
KEDAH   AJUF 8)

KELANTAN

HEBRIDES

FUNNEL
AJUF 5)

PERAK   BEACON

TRENGGANU

MULTIPLE

AJUF 7
(NO LIAISON)

SELANGOR   PAHANG

GALVANIC
(AJUF 1)   PONTOON
(AJUF 6)

HUMOUR
(AJUF 2)

NEGRI SEMBILAN   JOHORE

MALACCA   TIDEWAY
(AJUF 3)

O   CARPENTER
(AJUF 4)

13

PERLIS

KEDAH
8 REGT.
3 ind pln
9 pln

4 ind pln   7 ind pln

KELANTAN

1 pln   12 REGT.

MALAYA
EMERGENCY 1948 -1960
MRLA REGT. LOCATIONS

TRENGGANU
7 REGT.
12 pln

PERAK
2 pln

4 coy   3 pln
4 pln

17 pln 8 pln
12 pln   7 pln
6 pln

5 REGT. 5 pln
39 pln 37 pln

8 ind pln

36 pln

7 coy

16 pln

15 pln

8 pln

6 pln 24 coy
30 coy

PAHANG
8 pln   30 coy

7 pln

18 pln

6 REGT.

8 pln

SELANGOR   9 pln

1 REGT. 14 pln
8 batt

16 pln
28 coy   4 pln

11 pln

KUALA LUMPUR
1 pln   2 pln   3 pln   1 pln   8 ind pln
4 coy
2 REGT. 5 pln
10 ind pln,

8 ind pln

NEGRI SEMBILAN

3 plt

MALACCA

6 pln

JOHORE

12 pln   10 pln   7 pln

3 REGT. 4 coy

5 pln

3 pln

1 pln
4 REGT.
3 pln

4 pln   8 coy

9 pln

Plant.

THE ORGANISATION OF THE MALAYAN RACES LIBERATION ARMY. (MRLA)

The Organisation is divided into 2 areas
    a)   The Jungle Organisation.
    b)   The Min Yuen Movement.

The Jungle Organisation. The Malayan Peoples Anti British Army (MPABA), was renamed the Malayan Races Liberation Army (MRLA). Was the Armed Forces of the Malaya Communist Party(MCP).Organised into Regiments and Independent Platoons, was closely integrated with the Parties Organisation Policy Directives, as issued by the MCP Central Committee, usually under the title of The Military High Command.

There were 12 Regiments broken down into Platoons, that operated within the Federated States & regions within each State of Malaya. Commands were issued by each State Committees, both of Political & Military matters.

Any Independent Platoon maybe broken down into: Local Armed Work Forces (LAW). Their main objectives were for the protection of the Local Min Yuen, which consists of a Group Committee Min Yuen Workers, - Armed Section, who carry out minor acts of terrorism, sabotage & the Protection of Couriers Bodyguards.

As per the Organisation of the Regiments, as indicated on the two maps above. Their training was based upon those learnt from the British, during the days of Force 136. A Typical day in the life of a Communist Terrorist would be as follows:

4.30 a.m.	Food supply forages & messengers leave the camp after a light breakfast.
6.00 a.m.	Washing & ablutions.
6.30 a.m.	Morning Parade reciting the Red Flag Followed by a Propaganda talk.
7.00 a.m.	Cleaning weapons followed by Weapons Drill.
9.00 a.m.	Breakfast very basic Tapioca or rice, vegetables & water.
9,30. a.m.	Language lesson. everyone had to learn to read write& talk Mandarin the only language used.
12.00 noon	Lectures.
4.00 p.m.	Main Meal taken.
5.00 p.m.	General discussions for all to air their opinions.
Sundays	Day off.

This was the day in the life of a CT. Obviously, whenever Orders were given for an Ambush or act of sabotage Those chosen would leave the camp to carry out the orders Then return back to the daily routine.

This was a well Organised Army. Not a gaggle taggle band of Communist Terrorist, that the British Gurkha and Commonwealth Forces, including the Federation Police were fighting. That took 12 long bloody years to succeed and beat the Communist MRLA, to become: -The only war to defeat the uprising of Communism during the Cold War.

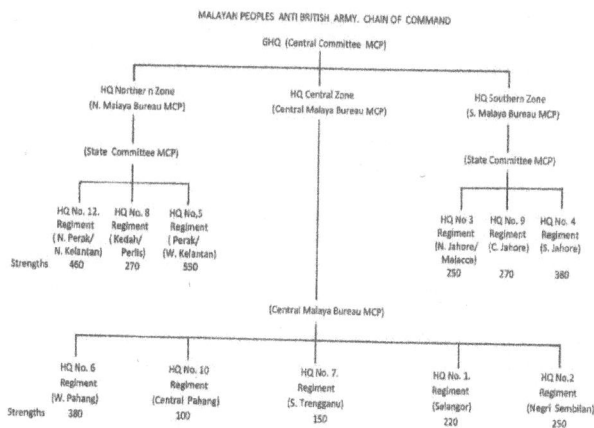

MALAYAN PEOPLES ANTI BRITISH ARMY. CHAIN OF COMMAND

GHQ (Central Committee MCP)

HQ Northern Zone (N. Malaya Bureau MCP) — HQ Central Zone (Central Malaya Bureau MCP) — HQ Southern Zone (S. Malaya Bureau MCP)

(State Committee MCP)

HQ No. 12. Regiment (N. Perak/ N. Kelantan)	HQ No. 8 Regiment (Kedah/ Perlis)	HQ No.5 Regiment (Perak/ W. Kelantan)
Strengths 460	270	590

(State Committee MCP)

HQ No 3 Regiment (N. Jahore/ Malacca)	HQ No. 9 Regiment (C. Jahore)	HQ No. 4 Regiment (S. Jahore)
250	270	380

(Central Malaya Bureau MCP)

HQ No. 6 Regiment (W. Pahang)	HQ No. 10 Regiment (Central Pahang)	HQ No. 7 Regiment (S. Trengganu)	HQ No. 1. Regiment (Selangor)	HQ No.2 Regiment (Negri Sembilan)
Strengths 380	100	150	220	250

The larger Regiments were divided into Military Sub-districts. Battalions or Companies, while the small Regiments were divided into Platoons. The Strengths shown above are approximate only and were for the period January to August 1951.

CHAPTER 3

A Period of Unrest and Planning

Following the end of the World War II with Japan, when all hostilities had ceased. The division of allied Powers with Russia in the West and China in the East, became more Political. Democracy against Communism, which could have turned into a third world war. However, it was the beginning of the Cold War. A war of politics of different ideologies that would eventually spill into unrest in many countries.

In Malaya. It was the time for rejoicing, when after 3 ½ years of ever-increasing hardship at the hands of the Japanese, during the occupation, until they surrendered on VJ day 16 August, 1945.(Victory Over Japan). There was a short delay before the British Operation 'Zipper.' Liberation forces, arrived at Penang on the 3rd. September, in Singapore the 5th. Then Kuala Lumpur on the 12th. It was during this short period of time, when the MPAJA attempted to take over the country. The Communist Guerillas emerged from the jungle, to impose terrible vengeance on traitors, real or imagined? They Killed an estimated 2,542 Chinese, Malayans, Indians and others, who they thought, collaborated with the occupying Japanese Army. The massacres stopped when the British Military Administration (BMA) Took control from September 1945 to 1st April 1946. When the Civil Government resumed their duties. One of the BMA's first jobs, was to disband the MPAJA Guerilla force, made up mainly of the Kuomintang Chinese military force and members of the MCP. Then estimated to be in excess of 7,000. On November 15th. 1945. Their disbandment, occurred. in Singapore, Penang and Seremban. Also bring to justice members of the Japanese secret Police The Kempeitai, also many Japanese Army High Ranking Officers and others, who had committed atrocities against Prisoners of War and civilians alike. Over the following months. These courts in Malaya found guilty 199 Japanese, who were executed and 126 imprisoned. Investigation were also carried out on those CT's on their action taken against civilian collaborators.

Under the British Administration, steps were taken to restore the devastated economy and bring a return to normal life. The after effects of the Japanese occupation lingered on. The Police were demoralised and alienated, what was left of their European Officers, who been interned, were recovering from their ordeal, while others joined the Civil Administration. Continuity of their Service had been disrupted. The Police required reorganising. Recruitment and training were put in hand along with the necessity of discipline. In the meantime, gangs of armed men roamed the countryside, general lawless clouded the picture. In attempt to bring unity to the prewar kaleidoscope of the Colony. The Straits Settlements with the British Protectorate, of the Federated and UnFederated Malay States. It was proposed to bring all these under the Control of the Colonial Office. Singapore was to be a Separate Crown Colony.

On December 1st. 1945 the MPAJA were formally dissolved. The hand written. "A TERMS OF CO-OPERATION" signed by the British Commanders of Force 136 and members of the MCP. On the 30/31st December 1943 Ended. They were paraded with much ceremony; each man was paid a gratuity of $ 350. All arms were to be handed in. Old Comrades Associations were formed with their own committees. Yet the purpose of the MCP was to return to the jungle, to rejoin others when the right time came?

On the 7th. January 16 Leaders of the M.P.A.J.A. were paraded in front of a large crowd at the Municipal building in Singapore to be awarded medals. The Burma Star and 1939- 1945 Star by: Supreme Allied Commander Admiral Lord Louis Mountbatten. They named as:

Chin Peng *(Chan Ping)*
Liaison Officer for Force 136 Became leader of the MPLA . Banished from Malaya after the cessation of the 'Emergency'

Liew Yau *(Lau Yew, Liu Yau)*
Chairman of the MPAJA betrayed by his bodyguard, was Killed in a Police Raid in Kedah. One Month after the beginning of the 'Emergency.'

Chan Yeung Pan
Commander of 1st. Independent Ret. MPAJA. Ulu Yang Selangor. He defected to the British at the beginning of the 'Emergency.

Lai Wei Chung *(Liao Wei Chang)'*
Commander of the 5th. Ind Regt. Simpang Pilau Perak Known as *Ito* by his call sign E-2 He was arrested at the start of the 'Emergency' and banished to China

Fook Lung *(Deng Fook Loong)*
Commander 2nd. Ind. Regt. Kuala Pulah Negri Sembilan During the 'Emergency'

Lao Wong
Commander 6th. Ind. Regt. West Pahang. During the 'Emergency'

Chen Tien
Commander 4th. Ind Regt. Johore Bahru Chairman of the Propaganda. During the 'Emergency'

Lin Chang *(Lin Tian)*
Com. 3rd.Ind. Regt. North Johore. During the 'Emergency'

Chua Seng

Com, 7th. Ind. Regt. Sungei Riau Kuantan Pahang. During the 'Emergency'

Siew Lit

Com. 8th. Ind. Regt. Kedah. During the 'Emergency'

Wu Chye Sin

Operation 'Gustavus 1.' Landed in Pulai Pangkor. May 1943 Recruited by Lim Bo Seng at Poona India Western Warfare School

Tan Sian Yau (Han Loy Boon)

Operation 'Gustavus 1.' Force 136

Che Yeop Mahidin (Mahidin bin Mohamad Sharriff)

Leader of the Pahang Cerila Wataniah. Asstn Commissioner Officer Kuala Lipis under Major I. D. Richardson established the Military Reservist of the Malay Army.

Bahai

Member of force 136 Parachuted into Malaya at Grik Peral

Abdullah bin Taaman

(not known)

Wang Siang Pu

Member of Dalforce Wore the uniform of Dalforce: Indigo Blue with a khaki cap.

13th. **January 1946**. The coffin with the remains of **Lim Bo Seng**. Were given a full Military funeral with a procession of British Troops & former Chinese Liaison Officers in attendance. Capt. Richard Broome, gave the eulogy. Lim Bo Seng was captured by the Japanese in March 1944. When the secret of Operation 'Gustavus 1' was leaked by an informer. Lim was taken to Batu Gajah Jail. Tortured by the Kempeitai. He refused giving out any information, was maltreated, subsequently died from dysentery on 29th. June 1945.

At the end of hostilities, after the surrender of the Japanese, in those far East Asian countries of Malaya, Sumatra, Java, Indo China. Countries who had been occupied by the Japanese. There was a desire to get rid of the old Colonial Administrations of the British, Dutch & French, previously Governed by them. On the other hand, The British, Dutch & French wanted to return back to Govern their old Colonies, rich in Rubber, Tin & other commodities. In Malaya the Rubber Plantations & Tin Mines, had been owned by British Companies, who had nurtured the growth over many decades, sought to regain their Plantations, which had in some ways been neglected, during the Occupation of the Japanese. Those British Planters who had been interned by the Japanese, in many cases killed. Those who had escaped before the Occupation and had joined forces with either the ISLD or SOE, Planters and Tin Miners,named as Gray, Chrystal, Hembrey, Robinson & Fenner of the Malay Police, to name a few "Stay Behind "or, had been released from interment. Were only to pleased to be able to return to their Plantations and Tin mines, which covered vast acres of the Malay Peninsula. In the case of the Tin Mines most of the machinery had been destroyed & needed to be replaced before any production could be resumed.

It was a time vacancy of employment were at their highest for the working majority.

Chin Peng was a communist through and through. He could not see Malaya or Singapore being ruled by the British Government at any price. Having wanted Malaya to become a Communist Dictatorship State, under the control of the MCP in 1945 and 46.*Chin Peng* had visited China. Upon the mysterious disappearance of *Lai Tia* on the 6th. March 1947.with all the parties' funds, leaving **Chin Peng,** then twenty-three years old. The undisputed Secretary General of the MCP.

It may be significant that Party Leaders of the MCP, did attend three important Communist Conference's in. Belgrade October 1947, the Cominform, the new International Communist Organisation. The Commonwealth Communist Parties. In Calcutta February 1948. The Conference of the Asian and Australian Communist Parties, sponsored by Russia In London 1948.... Did **Chin Peng's** World Democratic Youth and the International Union of Students trips to China and the attendance of the MCP Leaders at those three conferences. Inspire the insurrection of the pending Malaya uprising? It is perhaps necessary to believe that **Chin Peng** was given instructions to resort to violence, at any one of these conferences. (Bugle and Kukri p. 26.)

However, **Chin Peng** along with other leaders of the MCP and MPAJA. Set about planning, if necessary, by force, for the eventual overthrow of the British Rule in Malaya. The nucleus of the MPAJA had not surrendered their arms willingly. It is estimated that approx. 4,000 did not return their arms, in many cases those arms surrendered were basically useless, others in their possession, were in good condition, either supplied by the British and those taken from dead Japanese, during the raiding parties, whilst in the AJUP and MPAJA. These were put into cache of arms which lay hidden deep in various parts of the Malayan jungles. Their whereabouts known only to members of the MPAJA. Those who had become highly trained Guerrillas, in the art of the British methods of sabotage and quite capable of anything. Gradually increased the strength of its army into an unknown number.

The British were in a state of conflict with, the new state of Palestine, whilst India & Burma were seeking their Independence, from British Administration. That happened in India on the 15th. August 1947, which due to the partition caused mass killing of millions of Muslims and Hindus. Burma gained her Independence on the 4th. January 1948.

Indo China was under French Marshall Law. & the Dutch had their own problems in Sumatra & Java.

January 1947. Britain saw the beginning of more unrest in the West. In the UK. It was the worst winter experienced for many a year before. The Dockers went on strike, so did the Coal Miners, nearly bringing the country to its knees, all instigated by the Unions. Necessitating the use of the Army Personnel to carry on those working tasks. These Strikes also occurred in Singapore & Malaya. However, on a much larger scale, throughout the years of 1946/47/48 strikes, intimidation, murders & many people disappearing. (The British Government under the leadership of Prime Minister Clement Atlee, saw fit to send out to Malaya a Union delegation of 3 members of the British Trade Unions). In China the Civil War continued between the Moa Communist against the Nationalist, created masses of refugees, fleeing from mainland China, seeking refuge in other local countries, including the British Colonies of Hong Kong – Singapore & Malaya. There was no control of the numbers entering any of these Colonies including, Indo China & the Dutch East Indies. This mass unchecked entry was to cause much concern to the British in the following years of the Emergency.

11th. March 1947 John Davis CBE. DSO. (Ex Col. Force 137) Having returned to his previous occupation as Civil Servant. Sailed on the SS *Ortranto* enroute to Malaya, where he was to take over a position as an Officer In Charge of Chinese Affairs in Bentong. However, at that time, he like most people were   unaware of the future happenings in Malaya and himself the part he would play?

Throughout 1947 the legal status of the Federations of Trade Unions remained in a state of limbo. As did the Malayan Communist Party. In a top-secret meeting held in Singapore Malcom MacDonald, ommisioner Gerneral. Considered banning it. Bearing in mind this was the era of the Cold War, declared. *'Communism was the Number One Enemy.'*   The nearest Russians were in Bangkok however, their agents were at work in Malaya and Singapore.

1947. By the end of the year. In Malaya up & down the country, there had been more than 300 strikes & industrial disputes. In the State of Johore, the month of September saw one of its worst times to date.

21st.September. A gang of marauding bandits, surrounded the lonely Wessington Rubber Estate. Inside the Bungalow were the Estate Manager. Mr. & Mrs, Pratt & two friends they were entertaining. Mr Pratt, noticed flashlights outside & sensed trouble was coming. He tried to phone the Police, but the lines had been cut. Peering outside with the aid of their flashlights he was able to see and count 10 Chinese, all dressed in Japanese uniforms, each carrying rifles, which he assumed were Lee Enfield 303 rifles. The intruders were busy ransacking the Labourer's homes. Taking a long time doing it, they did not bother Mr. Pratt & his guest. Maybe dressed as Japanese, gave a false impression who they were. Nevertheless, having ransacked the Labourer's homes. Only after they had left, it was discovered they had taken hundreds of Malay dollars.

6th. October. A further incident occurred. The Manager of the Gunning Pulai Estate in South West Johore. Mr. Nicholson after a visit to Singapore. He & his wife, were travelling in their car back to the Estate. As they rounded a corner, a shot rang out puncturing a tire, out of control the car swerved & overturned. Mr. Nicholson sustained a fractured skull killing him.

Mrs Nicholson was concussed. Waking up in a daze, found a Chinese man trying to pull the rings off her fingers. In her dazed state she resisted, so he clubbed her with the butt of the stem gun he was carrying. Knocking her out. These two separate incidents against white European Planters, resulting in one death. Was just the beginning.

After the murder of Mr. Nicholson, warning signs from Planters, of the deteriorating situation, went to some extent ignored by the Governor General Sir. Edward Gent. Who had been accepted as, 'An approachable chap.' Basically he did not think the matter, although serious would & could be controlled by the Police. Unfortunately, the Police Force was unable to cope with the everyday increasing violence. In a riot in a Chinese Rubber Estate in Selangor. North Johore Police opened fire on 200 Labourers killing seven & wounding ten others.

20th. October. Wednesday, A General Strike of 24 hours was imposed by the MCP (Malayan Communist Party) caused mayhem, everything came to a standstill.

Following on. The strikes, riots, murders, still continued into 1948. Discussions were held in Kuala Lumpur & London of the then situation, which appeared totally uncontrollable.

CHAPTER 4

The Gathering Storm

At that time the British Forces based in Singapore/Malaya were

Royal Navy.
HM Ships `1948

HMS

ALACRITY – 'ALERT' – BELFAST – 'COCKADE' – NORFOLK - TERROR (Shore base) *– TRIUMPH*

Army.

1st. Battn. Kings Own Yorkshire Lt. Inf.

1st Battn. Devonshire Regt.

1st. Battn. Seaforth Highlanders

26th Field Regt. Royal Artillery.

1/6th. Gurkha Rifles

1 Battn. of the Malay Regt.

1/10th. Gurkha Rifles arrived in Penang on the 22nd. Jan 1948. Entrained to Kuala Lumpur. Then in February to Kluang

ROYAL AIR FORCE.
Squadrons on Station Krangi Singapore

Sqdn.	Location	Aircraft Type	No	Date From	Year	Date To	Year
28	Semberwang	Spitfire18	8	26th.Jan.	1948	1st. Apr.	1951
48	Changi	Dakota C4	8	26th. Jan	1948	11th. May	1949
60	Semberwang	Spitfire 18PR9	17	26th. Jan.	1948	25th. Aug.	1949
81	Tengah	Spitfire 18	17	1st. Feb.	1948	16th. Mar.	1949
	Tengah	Mosquitos PR34/34a	8	1st. Feb.	1948	16th. Mar.	1950
	Tengah	Harvard. 2B	1	16th. Mar.	1948	1st. Jun.	1948
84	Tengah	Beafighters 1	8	22nd. Mar.	1948	11th. Oct.	1948
656	Semberwang	Auster5//6/7/9	31	15th. Jul.	1947	16th. Dec.	1954
FEC	Changi	Auster 6/7	2	1st. Jul.	1948	1st. Dec.	1956

Early in 1948. Civil unrest broke out on the Rubber Estate's & Tin Mining areas of Malaya. With murders, intimidation & strikes by workers. The timing of the uprising roughly coincided with what was happening in Europe. On the 1st. April. In the divided sectors of East & West Berlin. The Soviet Communist Powers, blockaded all routes into the city. Imposing strict checks at border crossings, which caused mayhem with supplies. Subsequently this caused the Berlin Airlift to deliver supplies to its inhabitants. That lasted a year, until May 1949.

In Singapore & Malaya: -

JANUARY

Thur. 1st   Sqdn's 48. -52. -60 - 81.- 84. - 110. FEC R.A.F. Located at R.A.F. Changi---

+   Sqdn.   28   Spitfires. Located at R.A.F. Tengah---]

+   Sqdn. 209 Sunderland GR5. R.A.F. Located at R.A.F. Seletar. ---]

+   Sqdn. 656. Auster 5/6/7/9. R.A.F. Located at R.A.F. Semberwang. ---]

Fri.   9th.   850 Tin Miners' strike over wages. In the Pun Chin district 15 miles from Ipoh. 4 Tin mines were involved

Mon. 12th.   **Cfn. P. Harvey.** R.E.M.E. Died. *** *Changi Singapore ---]*

Wed. 14th.   3,500 Harbour workers ask for pay rises---]

Sat.. 17th. L/Cpl. G. Dhowa. 6th. Queen Elizabeth's Own Gurkha Rifles Killed *[No known Grave] Terandak Wall Memorial Seremba*n----]

Wed. 21st. 21 HMT EMPIRE PRIDE arrived Singapore with the 1/6th. Battn. Queen Elizabeth's Own Gurkha Rifles. ---]

Thur. 22nd. The new **Federation of Malaya Treaty** was signed. Marked The beginning of a new era for Malaya---]

Fri.   25th. **W/O.1 C.J. Lammond.** R.A.S.C. Died *** *[No known Grave] Terandak Wall Memorial Seremban.]*

Sun. 26th. R.A.F. Sqdn's. 28 & 60 Spitfires relocated from Tengah & Operational at R.A.F. Seremban

FEBRUARY

Sun. 1st   Kuala Lumpur: The new Constitution of Malaya was formerly inaugurated. Sir. Edward Gent Governor of the Malayan Union. Was sworn in at Kuala Lumpur. As first High Commissioner of the new Malayan Federation. Consisting of 9 (nine) Malay States & the British Settlements of Penang & Malacca. The Malay Rulers, the Sultans of all the nine States had on January 21st. Signed Separate treaties with Great Britain at Kuala Lumpur. Implemented the Malayan Federation. Under these Treaties, the Malay Rulers, while being confirmed all their former Powers & Privileges, undertook to promulgate for their States, and to make provision for elections. In due course both to the Central Legislative of the Federation, and to the State Council's....

+   <u>Singapore:</u> On the same day, further down the road at Klyne Street the headquarters of the MCP. A scheduled Politburo meeting headed by **Chin Peng,** was taking place. To discuss their future action, having in the Previous months, instigated many strikes & industrial disruptions. With the knowledge that the Sultans of the Malayan State's agreement to the formation of a Malay Federation. That was totally against their own intention, of Creating a Communists Dictatorship in Malaya. An intention that had been thought out and planned during the Japanese Occupation. To further the cause. The subject of armed struggle was discussed.   However, the party was in no fit state to start a military Action. Either financially or otherwise --]

+   Sqdn. 81. 5 Spitfires 8 Mosquitos R.A.F. Relocated from R.A.F. Changi to R.A.F. Tengah. ---]

+   **Spr. G.G. Crampton.** Royal Engineers Died *** *Kuala Lumpur*. ---]

Wed. 12th.   **L/Cpl W. Littlefield** R.M.P. Died Motor Veh. Acc. *Kuala Lumpur.* -----]

Thur. 26th   Calcutta The Communist Party of India held a conference in Calcutta. Mr. Laurence Sharky Secretary of the Australian Communist Party was in attendance. At the invitation of **Chin Peng,** He had already had meetings with the MCP earlier in the month. The Calcutta Congress Meeting lasted until the 6th. March. ---]

Sat. 28th.   About 1,000 workers congregated at Bedong and were confronted by the Police. Some workers reacted and one was clubbed to death. ---]

MARCH

Wed. 3rd.   <u>Malaya:</u> The dismissal of an Estate women worker, a known activist on the Bukit Sembilan Estate caused a near riot. Police arrested 66 people. 61 were put on trial and imprisoned. ---]

Mar. 7th.   7 HMT DEVONSHIRE sailed Singapore bound for Liverpool with returning Service personnel ---[

Mon. 8th.   8 MV 'SIR.DHANA' arrived in Singapore on board were the 10th. Princess Mary's Own Gurkha Rifles ---]

Sat.. 13th.   **L/Cpl. L. Tulbahadur.** 7th. Duke of Edinburgh's Own Gurkha Rifles Died. Motor Veh. Acc. Seremban *Seremban Negri Sembilan*---]

Sun. 14th.   Bandits held up the Bantu Mail train. Robbed 20 passengers. Killed a train waiter.---]

+   81 Sqdn. Harvard Relocated to R.A.F Tengah---]

Wed. 17th.   **Cpl. J. McGibbon.** 48 Sqdn. R. A. F. accidently Killed, 10 miles North of Segament. *Kuala Lumpur*---]

Thur. 18th.   Singapore: Another meeting was convened by the MCP Politburo. To discuss what further action to engage CT's to be taken. **Chin Peng** again invited Mr. Laurence Starkey to attend, who had stopped over in Singapore on his way back to Australia. During the meeting he explained to the Members what had been discussed in the Calcutta Congress Meeting. He was open for questions. One MCP Member asked. *'What they did in Australia with Strike Breakers?'* To which Starkey answered
'Kill.' Not in the cities. Only in outlying areas. The mining areas.'
A stolen Government draft document of Law. To restrict the powers of the Unions.Was read out. It was this document that triggered the call for Strike breakers to be eliminated. Copies of the Darft were further distributed to the various MCP Committees throughout the Fedreration. Albeit an open invitation to kill as indicated by Mr. Laurence Starkey. ---]

Wed. 22nd.   84 Sqdn. 8 Beaufighters R.A.F. relocated from R.A.F. Changi to R.A.F. Tengah---]

Thur. 23rd.   **AC2 .R. C. Keen.** G.W.Mech. No 2. Base Radio Dept. Paya Lebar A.C.F.E. R. A. F. M T. A *Singapore #?*---]

Mon. 27th.   **Capt. G. C. Skelley** Devonshire Regt. Died In a M. T.A *Kranji Singapore # 1/ C – 3*---]

Wed. 28th.   **Pte. L.M.C. Ward** Devonshire Regt. Died *** *Singapore # 1 / C – 4* ---]

+   **Sgt. J. McHugh** R.E.M.E. Died*** *Seremban Negri Sembila*n---]

APRIL

Fri.   2nd   2 HMT DEVONSHIRE arrived Liverpool with returning Service personnel---]

Tue.   6th.   **Capt. P.C.D. Mercer.** The Gloucester Regt. Died*** *Taiping # F / 63* Perak---]

+   **Rect. G. Birbal** 2nd. King Edwards Own Gurkha Killed in Action Engaging CT's *[No known Grave] Terendak Wall Memorial Malacca*---]

Fri.   9th.   **ASP. G.C. Swansom** MC. F. M. Police On patrol. prior to the Emergency was shot and Killed by his Chinese Guide, whilst he was leading a Platoon of Police in the dense jungle at Kati 10 miles from Kuala Kangsa Upper Perak. The Guide a known Communist was shot by the Constables.---]

Mon. 12th.   **ASP. Cadet. E. A, Freeborough** F. M. Police Killed on CT Ops. Srei Nedan Batu Pahat Johore ---]

Wed. 14th.   **ASP. R.H. Fookes.** F. M. Police + 5 PCs (**unnamed**) Killed on Ops. by Bandits at Padang Piol Jerantut Pahang *Kuala Lipis Pahang* ---]

Mon. 20th.   Whilst on a jungle operation in the Leggong region Major Bell. -Sgt. D. Price & Pte. J. Foley. K.O.Y.L.I we're trying to take shelter from a storm. When a tree fell on them. Killing **Price & Foley** severely injuring

Major Bell with a broken back. He was carried out of the jungle & transferred to a hospital _Taiping # F / 64 – 65_ Perak---]

Thur. 23rd. 23 HMT **DEVONSHIRE** sailed Liverpool bound for Singapore with replacement Service personnel---]

+ 23 HMT **ORBITA** sailed Liverpool bound for Singapore /Hong Kong with reolacement Service personnel]

Sun. 26th. On the Dublin Estate 2,000 Indian workers came out on strike, in protest against evictions. Another 1,000 Chinese came out in support. The Police opened fire on the demonstrators killing one Chinese man'---]

Tue. 28th. **Rfn. Maite Limbu**. 10th. Princess Mary's Own Gurkha Rifles Died ** _Kranji Singapore # 7 / C 10_---]

MAY

Sat. 1st. Operation '_Pepper_' & '_Haystack_' were launched against the Kuomintang Guerillas. Then operating under the name of the Malayan Overseas Chinese Self Protection Corps (OCAJA)Still causing havoc in North Perak. British & Gurkha troops were deployed in the Kinta valley in North Perak to flush them out---]

+ A one day strike was held throughout the Colony.---]

+ Kuala Lumpur The Comminist paper _Min Shang Pau_ was published---]

Sun. 2nd. Mr. R. Moon Asstn. Manager of the Sagil Estate was attacked by the Labourers with seveve injuries, was admitted to the Malacca hospital unconscious.---]

Mon. 3rd. F.M. Auxiliary Police, found 2 Japanese hand grenades in a tea kettle, in the coolie lines of the Singapore Harbour Board. They took possession and arrested 5. Suspects---].

Tue. 4th. An unsuccessful attempt to burn down the Joo Lim Saw Mill, was prevented by Labourers. Who put out the fire using chemical extinguishers.---]

Wed. 5th. Kuala Lumpur:150 Displaced. Chinese persons. Committed for deportation from George Town Penang. They would be the first of many. ---]

+ In North Johore, a secret meeting was held by the hierarchy of the MCP. **Chin Peng** the Leader of the MCP and former member of the British Force 136, who became a friend & right-hand man of Major John Davies. DSO. Had first-hand knowledge of how the British worked & trained the MCP Volunteers of Force 136. He was aware of the way they organised trained & dispersed the Guerilla forces into Regiments & smaller Units. He also knew of the various Planters who had volunteered to join Force 136, upon the surrender of the British to the Japanese in Singapore. With jungle camps still in existence, together with secret caches of arms, along with the backing of all previous Communist Guerilla Fighters, including their supporters. Those factors would form the basis of the MCP's army. If, they were to take on the British. They would take their fight to the British, but not on equal basis. Instead as per during 1943-1945. A war of Sabotage,Intimidation. Its Guerilla Forces organised into Regiments to Hit. Disengage, to fight another day. Having had several years to implement his plan. **Chin Peng's** plan of war, was to be in three phases:

1) Quick attacks on isolated Estates and Tin Mines. Police and Government buildings in small villages. Thus forcing the Governments resources back to larger Towns.

2) Occupy vacated areas. So called 'Liberated areas.'

3) Fanning out from Liberated areas to the Main Towns, attacking Railways and infrastructure before taking on the Army. With the assistance and support of the Chinese. They thought they could & would overthrow the British. It then just a case of wait until the time was right to rage war against the British Government... The meeting lasted four days, resulting in a declaration of "**Call to Arms.**" against the British Government, by the organisation, known as the Malayan Peoples Anti-British Army. (MPABA) Acting under the authority of the Malayan Communist Party.

However not one of them. Thought the British would retaliate?

Thur. 6th. England Portsmouth HMS '_MALAYA_' The battleship the Sultan's of Malaya gave to the motherland. Sailed on its last voyage from Portsmouth for the shipbreakers on the Clyde---]

+ Kuala Lumpur: A new bill was to be prepared dealing with the: Federation of Trade Unions. Whose members Are employed in similar trades. Maybe Federated ---]

Sat. 8th. Singapore: It was announced. R. A. F. Lincoln. Bomber. Will be based at Tengah air base.---]

Sun. 9th. Malaya : On the Teng Nam Estate near Seelong 3 Armed Chinese stole $ 7,000 intended as the payroll.---]

Mon. 10th. **Plt/111. J. D. Patterson**. 60 Sqdn. R. A. F. Flying Spitfire TP210 Killed in a Collision with Spitfire TP209. 6 miles North of Changi. The other Pilot survived, was picked up by a Chinese fishing boat._Singapore_---]

Tue. 11th. Singapore : Fire destroyed three quarters of the Bin Seng Rubber Factory in Bukit Timah Road Singapore. Estimated cost in excess of $ 1,700,000.---]

Wed. 12th. Approx. 18,000 bales of Rubber were destroyed by fire on the Sua Betong Rubber Estate Port Dickson---]

Thur. 13th. <u>Singapore:</u>The Singapore Labour Union threatened to. strike. If their 6 (six) demands we're not met---]
  + <u>Malaya:</u>The Malayan Railways stated they may be forced to borrow. Labourers to end the 19 day old. Strike.at Port Swettenham---]
Fri. 14th. Armed Gunmen robbed the Leong Bee Estate near Geylang Patah stole their payroll of $ 7,000.---]
  + 14 HMT DILWARA sailed Southamton bound for Singapore /Hong Kong with replacement Service personnel ---]
Sat. 15th. The Port Swettenham strike was described as.Total irregular.The mass meeting was not even Restricted to members of the Union.
Sun. 16th. F.M. CID Police. Found. 2 hand grenades of British manufacture. Believed to have been stolen from a Military base. ---]
Mon. 17th. Mr Ong Toh. The Manager of the Ghee Seng Rubber Factory was Killed by gunmen, when driving his car to the Estate---]
  + Over 1,000 picals of Rubber were destroyed in a Smoke House, owned by Harrison and Crossfield in Taiping.---]
Tue. 18th. Mr Ong Swee Leong Manager of the Ghee Seng & Co. Was found shot dead in his car. A note was found Stating: He had been Killed as a lesson to bad employers. Not Following Union Rules---]
Wed. 19th. A Bombay Merchant in Penang, who made a Complaint against. Intimidation of a Labour Union Official was found shot and wounded in his room in Penang Street. ---]
Thur. 20th. 2 Wagon loads of Rubber were destoyed by fire. In a railway siding at Port Swettenham---]
  + Mr. Tan Teck Bee. Manager for the Malayan Railways Port Swettenham. Was attacked by striking Labourers he was taken to hospital with serious injuries.---]
Fri. 21st. After arresting 7 men on an assault charge. F.M. Police Were attacked by a gang of Striking Labourers.---]
  + 21 HMT DEVONSHIRE arrived Singapore with replacement Service personnel---]
  + 21 HMT ORBITA arrived Singapore with replacement Service Personnel sailed Hong Kong 22nd. ---]
Sat. 22nd. Rfn. L. Bamprasad. 10th. Princess Mary's Own Gurkha Rifles Died*** <u>Kranji Singapore</u>---]
  + A Kongsi Tapper living in a remote part of the Sua Betong Estate, was found dead. His body was riddled with bullets----]
Sun. 23rd. The Malayan Railway Union. Demanded. 45 different Condition effecting working conditions---]
Mon. 24th. Rect. G. Dilbahadur 2nd King Edward VII's Own Gurkha Rifles Died*** <u>Batu Gajah Ipoh Perak</u>---]
  + Mr. D. L. Downie. Manager of the AmparTenang Estate was attacked by striking Labourers.---]
Tue. 25th. AC1. R.E. Hollands R.A.F. Died*** <u>Western Road</u> George Town Penang---]
  + On the same Estate Ampar Tenang. Once again Mr. D.L. Downie and his Clerk Mr. M.K. Nair. Were attacked by laborer's, with tea pruning knives, both were rushed to hospital-. ---]
  + 6 armed Chinese attacked the Laddang Geddes Estate. They Killed A Chinese Contractor & a Tapper. 2 hours Later on the same Estate, the same gang shot dead another Chinese Contractor and wounded a women---]
  + A meeting by the MCP was held in Northern Johore. To discuss an armed struggle. State by State. Setting up jungle camps. Retrieving hidden arms caches. Each State would create Two Platoons of 30 Men. Drawing on their previous knowledge of working under Force 136. Ideas and plans to set the ball rolling for The call to arms. Chin Peng intended to move up into Pahang & set up the MCP headquarters deep in the jungle. In the Interim period. He was to try & raise funds from previous MCP enterprises---]
Wed. 26th. Labourers on the Chang Swee Estate refused to leave the Estate. Intending to run it themslves. The European Manager eventualy left the Estate.---]
Thur. 27th. The Malayan Railways Union. Added 11 more request. To the 45 Conditions aready submitted---]
Fri. 28th. Sister. H. Pegram. Q. A. R. A. N. C. Died*** <u>Kuala Lumpur</u>---]
  + The Manager of the Union Estate near Batu Pahat was attacked and beaten up by his Striking Labourers.--]
  + At the Kapa Bali & Lima Blas Estate. British troops & Police Preserved order due to 79 Employees refusing to obey Court Eviction Orders.---]
  + <u>Kuala Lumpur:</u> Air Vice Marshal A. C. Sanderson. Became Air Officer Commanding Malaya---]
  + 28 HMT DEVONSHIRE sailed Singapore bound for Liverpool with returning Service personnel---]
Sat. 29th. An S.T.C. employee was attacked and stabbed over a labour dispute.---]
Sun. 30th. Cfn. D. Dawson. R.E.M.E.. Died*** <u>Tiaping? Perak</u>---]
Mon. 31st. Pte. J. R. Marritt K.O.Y.L.I. Died from Malaria <u>Tiaping # F 66</u> Perak---]
  + Striking Labourers from the Sagil Estate battled with Police in Malacca 7 Labourers including 1 woman were injured.---]
  + Soldiers of the Ceylon Royal Pioneer Corps, were due to arrive in Singapore. As Reinforcements.---]

JUNE

Tue. 1st. Operations *'Pepper'* & *'Haystack'* Against the OCAJA the Kuomintang Guerillas continued.---]
+ Police broke up a riot by Labourers on the Chang Pang Swee Rubber Estate near Jantah N. Johore 21 labouers were arrested 7 were Killed---]
+ On the Senai Estate in Johore 20 Chinese Labourers, threw blazing torches onto the roofs of the Estate Buildings estimated loss $ 30,000---]
+ Singapore: The Manger of the Joo Lim Sawmill was shot dead in a Coffee shop in Lavender road ---]
Wed. 2nd. Police offered $ 1,000 for any information for the shooting of 2 Chinese Labourers at the Factory in Kim Chan Road---]
+ Malaya: Approx 400 lbs of Rubber were destoyed by fire on the Sua Betong Estate---]
Thur. 3rd. Masked Chinese shot & Killed 2 Labourers of the Salek Tin Mine Estate near Selangor.---]
+ In a Separate incident. A sleeping Kepala (Headman) was murdered on an Oil Palm Estate.---]
+ In a further incident within the same locality. A gang of Chinese gunmen fought a gun battle with a Police Patrol---]
+ On the Chan Kang Swee Rubber Estate. Police a clashed with Labourers near Jemantah N. Johore The Laboures, armed with Spears & Changols had formed a barrier with a fallen tree across the road. During the ensuing fight. 6 men died and 30 were arrested by Police---]
+ At the 51st. m/s. in the area of Johore Bahru. A Small gang of armed & masked Chinese gunmen, Murdered the Owner of a small Estate. He was stabbed to death ---]
Fri. 4th. **Mr. E. D. Daab. MC**. Manager. of the Idris Hydraulic Mines Kampar Perak was ambushed . at the Batu Karang section of the mine & Killed by 6 Chinese gunmen. They got away with $ 2,500. Wages for the Labourers---]
+ Throughout Johore Posters were found on Estates. Stating in Chinese & Malay:
"Destroy those who rob labour by underpaying men."
" Destroy all those who work for other Races."
"Destroy all those who are running dogs of the Police." ---]
+ In Rengam, Central Johore 7 Chinese gunmen armed with Tommy guns, attacked the Consolidated East Plantation Estate.They wanted the Manager. Mr. J. Wallace, who fortunately had not returned from his normal rounds. Instead fired at Mr. Kidd the Asstn, Manager. of the Estate, who escaped before the gunmen could kill him.---]
+ Over the other side of the mountain range in Pahang. A Chinese Estate Manager, a Nationalist, was shot dead as he walked across the road in Triang. ---]
+ Singapore: The Manager and a Labourer of the Alk Hoe Rubber Factory in Kim Chuan Road.Were shot as they slept in the coolie lines ---]
+ Malaya :A Chinese Kepala was shot dead in his sleep. On the Mary Estate Batang Berjuntal by 4 gunmen.-]
+ 3 Armed Chinese gunmen burned down the Smoke House on the Siliau Estate Port Dickson. They stole $10,000 from the safe---]
+ In Ipoh Perak. 2 Malay Government officials were shot dead while on duty---]
+ Renewed. demands from the Planters. To ban the Malay Communist Party due to the then present Unlawlessnes, were issued to the Government.---]
+ Singapore An attempt to burn down Joo Lim Saw Mill, was averted by staff with chemical extinguishers.---]
Sun. 6th Guan Hong Rubber Factory in Jurong road Singapore. A Chinese worker was Killed, shot in the back by 3 Gunmen---]
+ Malaya:The Manger **Mr. Chong Chow Yam** of the Triang Esrtate Pahang was murdered by an unknown Gunman---]
Mon. 7th. Two Malay Officials **Inche Bahari** The Settlement Officer of Kuala Kangsar & **Inche Yusof** Village Headman of Ketua Kampong were Killed, shot and stabbed whilst on duty.---]
Tue. 8th. A Spitfire armed with rockets crashed upon landing. It overshot the runway at the Kuala Lumpur air strip. The Pilot escaped unhurt.---]
+ Representatives of industry demanded more stronger Powers to deal with the Present Political situation---]
Wed. 9th. The Selangor CID arrested *Yew Lit Fun.* Acting Manager. of the *Ming Shen Pau (Voice of the People)* Chinese Newspaper.Owned by the Malayan Communist Party. He was accused of publishing seditious material.---]
+ The Kedah Planters Association called on the Government to:
"FACE FACT'S. & BE POSITIVE IN ACTION ENGAGING CT'S" ---]
+ Selangor Police Officers were issued with and instructed too. Begin wearing weapons. On & off duty. ----]
+ In Rengam Johore Planters formed a "Mutual Protection Corps" Due to the many warnings they had received from Communist Sympathisers--]

+ 9 HMT ORBITA arrived Singapore with replacement Service personnel sailed bound for Liverpool with returning Service personnel 9th.---]

Thur. 10th. **Mr. John St. M. Ramsden.** Killed by Chinese gunmen near Nibong Tenang---]

+ 8 Chinese Gunmen attacked shops. and the railway Station at Niyor. 6 miles N. Johore They tied up the Station Master and 2 civilians. They escaped with more than M$ 1,000 ---]

+ 10 HMT DILWARA arrived Singapore with replacement Service personnel enroute to Hong Kong -10th.--]

Fri. 11th. Kuala Lumpur: Federation Police have been given increased special Powers to deal with the increasing Political Situation---]

+ At Rengam Johore. Chinese gunmen murdered 8 Chinese members of the local Kuomintang organization].

+ Kuala Lumpur: The Federation Government declared illegal the Communist dominated Pan-Malayan Federation of Trade Unions, including various Trade Unions in the Malay States. The High Commissioner Sir. Edward Gent declared that:
'Nearly 5,000 workers were involved in 25 strikes 16 on Rubber plantation in Malaya, all backed by the threat of intimidation and murder.—]

Sat. 12th. Mr. S.E. Thornburn. Manager of the Ulu Temis Estate Remgam. Due to the recent serious incidents in the area. Encouraged Planters in the area to band together to help the Police, ---]

+ Chinese gunmen attacked the Long Tek Hin Estate Kesang in Malacca Killing the Kuomingtang Contractor **Mr.Leong Eu Sin.** Before retreating, set alight the Smoke House.---]

+ MCP Gangs murdered 3 Local Chinese Kumingtang leaders at Rengam Johore. The Phase 1 of the MCP had really begun. ---]

+ London: In the House of Commons. The British Labour Cabinet met to discuss the Malayan situation. Questions were asked in the House of Commons. But no answers given---]

Sun. 13th. Malaya : **Recruit. Kharkabahadur Sunwar.** 7th. Duke of Edinburgh's Own Gurkha Rifles Died*** Seremban.# 11 Negri Sembilan.---]

+ 5,000 workers on various Rubber Plantation, Tin Mines and other establishment went on strike—]

+ Kuala Lumpur: In retalitation the High Commisioner, Sir. Edward Gent declared : Illegal the Communist Dominated Pan Malayan Federation of Trade Unions together with, other minor Unions in Malaya. Describing it as: 'The work of extremist elements challenging the authority of the Government.'---]

+ Kampar Perak **Chin Peng , Ah Ker & Ah Hai** (Executive members of the Malaya Commuinist Party (MCP) were visiting the Tong Fatt Tin Mine. To negotiate some funds. Having previously entered into joint Agreement of part ownership of the mine. The owner was Tong Chin, an old Friend of **Chin Peng.**---]

Mon. 14th. Kuala Lumpur. Sir. Edward Gent High Commissioner for Malaya. Called a special meeting of his Executive Council to be told:.
'Due to the current Political situation.The line of Engaging CT's to be taken. But the Malayan Communist Party were still not banned.' ---]

+ On the Sagil Estate Chinese gunmen shot and Killed a Chinese man ---]

Tue. 15th. Kuala Lumpur: Government sources stated that the recently formed. Rengam Planters Defence Force was To be Armed---]

+ A group of Malays slashed to death 4 Chinese in Lenging Perak.---]

+ London: The British Labour Cabinet. Debating about Malaya. For Political Reasons ?? Still said '**NO**' However, what was mutually agreed. The Malayan Police were given powers to banish any person connected in anyway with: 'Intimidation & Violence' in the course of any industrial dispute---]

+ The MCP reacted by shooting a Kuomintang Conductor on a Rubber Estate in Malacca---].

+ In another incident Chinese gunmen. Burnt down a Rubber smoke- house on another Estate in Malacca -]

+ Detectives detained, a senior member of the Pahang State Committee by the name of **Wang Li.** Who collaborated with the Authorities & infiltrated the Pahang organisation, providing useful information for the Authorities. Much later he was found out & shot by his so called 'Comrades.' Another Senior member also detained was **Chen Yong**. Who had collaborated with the Authorities & was paid by the British for his work with them. These two important & high ranking members of the MCP, was a big setback to their future plans.---]

CHAPTER 5
THE EMERGENCY IT'S COST

WHY IT WAS CALLED THE EMERGENCY?
AN EMERGENCY IS ONE THAT SHOULD LAST UNTIL THE IMMEDIATE PROBLEM IS SOLVED OR CONTAINED MAYBE UP TO A WEEK MAX 2/3 MONTH'S. NOT 12 BLOOD SOAKED YEARS??

During 1946 /47 /48. The Malayan Communist Party (MCP) were totally involved in causing as much disturbance, disarray, and intimidation, they could impose on the peoples of Malaya & Singapore.

Their goal was to create a dictatorship of Communism throughout Malaya. All in keeping with. Overthrowing the then British Ruling Government.

Just like other South East Asian countries. The Cold War inspired the Communist to try to take control of previous Empires of the British, Dutch. French, ruling over their countries. The MCP had planned that once their previous Government had fought and removed the Imperialist Japanese Army. The opportunity was there to take. That occurred in Malaya on June 16th.1948. What followed was a state of Emergency in one State, which rapidly spread throughout the Malayan Peninsula.

Within days the MCP 'Declared War' against the then ruling British Government. Whose response was one of caution? How could they finance it? So soon after the end of the Second World War or, would they, Declaring War against the MCP, cause the start of the third world war? In the then volatile atmosphere of the Cold War with the Western Powers at loggerheads with Russia and China. Nevertheless,taking into consideration that Malaya was the major world leader in producing rubber and tin. Vital to the outside world economy, seeing that the Plantations and Tin Mines were mainly British owned, who the MCP already knew, if their plans worked, wanted to take them over. All the Malayan owned Rubber Plantations and Tin Mines, were insured with London based Insurance Companies. Whose clauses apart from Act's. of God mentioned Acts. of War and other words as" War, Insurgents, Rebellion" or any word associated to that effect. Instead chose preferred words of "Bandits, Thugs, and Terrorist."

They choose a different line of approach Thereby the use of the connotation "Emergency " to ensure that any insurance claim, would be met by the Insurance Companies/ If, caused by any Terrorist damage under the direction of the MCP who had previously had time to plan a course of Military Action with their army of Communist Terrorists.

The Communist led Unions of England, enthusiastically supported by the British Labour Government, and against the advice of the Malaya Civil Service, The Federation Police and Employers of the Rubber and Tin Miners. Had sent out a delegation from The British Trade Union Council: John Brazier., S.S. Aubery & F.W. Dalley. To advise the working force of the Trade Unions of Malaya. As if they did not need any further advice on the MCP Policy.

The emerging Emergency became a war of "Hide and Seek" against the Guerrilla tactics of the Communist Terrorist (CT's) in the jungles of Malaya, involving various Infantry Battalions & Corps.of British Gurkha & Commonwealth Countries, including the Royal Navies & Royal Air Forces of Britain, Australia, New Zealand, & Malaya. The Royal Air Force bombing or, the Royal Navy, patrolling the surrounding seas of the Straits of Malacca and the South China Sea. When necessitated, bombardment of inshore Communist Terrorist locations as required. Plus, the Federation of Malaya Police who carried out a similar role as the Armed Forces. It was also a necessity for the reforming of the Special Air Service (SAS). Disbanded after the end of World War II. Creating units from Britain, Rhodesia & New Zealand.

The cost over the period of 12 years: Monetary Value estimated per year:

Great Britain $ 500,000.000.+ Malaya. $200,000.000.+ = $700,000,000 ++?

The loss of life of thousands of military and civilians, aeroplanes and munitions, that alone would outstretch any Insurance claims. To keep a combined Commonwealth Force engaged in an unrecognised war, declared on the British by the Malayan Communist Party. **THE ONLY WAR KNOWN TO DEFEAT THE COMMUNIST. WAS A FORGOTTEN WAR.**

But not for those conscripted National Servicemen. Some men are not born for wars. Some try to adapt. They are the ones with memories who took part throughout it ?

NB: National Service. Continued after the end of the Second World War. This was the age of Conscripting National Servicemen into the Army or, Air Force (the Royal Navy was signing on for 5 years). Every 2 weeks numerous 18 year old young Lads were called up to serve 18 months, which was then increased to 2 years with 3 years on the Reserve.

Her Majesties Troopships (HMT) engaged in ferrying various Regiments, Corps, R. A. F. (Men & Women Service Personnel plus their families too and from ports) HMT Troopships continued to be used to ship out & bring back those Service personnel who had been in Service overseas, from Gibraltar to Pusan in Korea, with stops. at Aden Columbo, Penang, Singapore, & Hong Kong (excluding India) & later to South African, Australian & New Zealand ports. Engaged in those voyages were ships listed below. However, when the Emergency in Malaya began, these voyages became more frequent due to the necessary ever changing 2-week intake & demob system of National Servicemen. This included the transportation of whole Regiment's to serve in Malaya (later Korea) who were basically made up of National Servicemen. It is estimated that during a Regiments 3-year tour of active Service, 2,000 troops would replace those returning for Demob. This would also apply to those Corps and RAF personnel; therefore, it is prudent to list those HM.Troopers as follows: -

HMT ASTURIUS – CAPTAIN COOK - DEVONSHIRE – DILWARA – DUNERA – GEORGIC - LANCASHIRE – NEW AUSTRALIA - ORBITER - OXFORDSHIRE - EMPIRE FOWEY – EMPIRE HALLADALE - EMPIRE PRIDE – EMPIRE ORWELL - EMPIRE TROOPER – EMPIRE WINDRUSH Plus a few others?

The Number of voyages outward Bound & return for the above-mentioned Troopships was: -

A single round voyage in Nautical Miles estimated for Liverpool /Singapore/ Liverpool = 16,386

No of Troopships Liverpool sailings = 9. Tot. No of voyages = 113. Tot. Nautical Mileage = 16,664,562.

A single round trip voyage in Nautical Miles estimated for Southampton /Singapore/ Southampton was 16,136

No of Troopships Southampton sailing = 10. Total No. of voyages = 236. Tot. Nautical Mileage = 38,080,960

A single round voyage in Nautical Miles estimated for Glasgow via Panama /Fremantle /Singapore /Glasgow = 16,353

No of Troopships: Glasgow sailings via Panana = 2. Total No of voyages = 10. Tot.No. Nautical miles = 327,060

During the Suez Crisis a number of Troopships sailed via Cape Town. Adding a further 3,492 avg. Nautical miles to a round trip. October 1956 to March 1957 Tot. for Liverpool & Southampton 10 sailings estimated = 34,920

Estmated overall all Troopships sailed = 55,107,502. Tot. Est. Nautical miles

29th. March 1954 : **HMT EMPIRE WINDRUSH**. On her return journey from Korea. Caught Fire. All troops & wounded onboard were saved.there were no causalities. Sunk at posn. 37N. 2.11 E. in the Mediteraenean Sea.

AIRWORK'S of London were a Company, hired by the Ministry of Defence to fly   Service personnel to and from the UK. Normally from R. A. F. Blackbushe aerodrome. Any Service Personnel flying out reported to Goodge Street Underground Station in London, which was serving as an underground transit centre. After documentation a number of Service personnel were bused to Blackbushe Aerodrome for onward flights. Normally by Hermes to Singapore via Rome, Nicosia, Bahrain, Karachi, Calcutta, Bangkok for refuelling finally Changi Singapore

A fire in May 1954 closed the Goodge Street transit centre. Transit Figures not available;

The following lists of the Three Commonwealth Armed Forces on ACTIVE SERVICE MALAYA 1948- 1960
Number of Fatalities shown in brackets [=]
Fatalities [No known Graves] THREE Services. [152] Incl. in Totals
Bodies Cremated & Repatriated THREE Services. [201] Incl. in Totals
Malayan Ordinary Ranks Two Services (Corps/RAF Regt.). Bodies Claimed by Next of KIN, [92] Incl. in Totals
Died ***Cause unknown. Unable to obtain details. Could be by Tropical Disease, Wounds, Natural Causes?
Number of Royal Navy Ships = 36 plus 1 Shore Base.
Note: Details of all Involved. Shelling from Offshore very limited information.

H.M.S.:

ALACRITY. – 'ALERT', [1] – ALBION, [1] -AMETHYST – BARWIND. [1] - BELFAST. [1] – CARDIGAN BAY. [1] - CENTAUR. [2] – CHARITY. – CHARIOT, [1] - 'CRANE'. – 'COCKADE'. [1] 'CONCORD", - CONSORT. [1] – 'COSSACK'. [1] - DEFENDER, - DRAGONFLY, - GLORY, - HART, - LLANDAFF. - LOCH QUAICH. [1] – OCEAN. - PERSEUS, - MAENAD. [1] – MAGICIENNE. [1] - MOUNTS BAY, [1] - 'NEWCASTLE' – 'NEWFOUNDLAND'. [1] - NORFOLK. [1] – SIMBANG. [3] – ST. BRIDES BAY. [1] – SUFFOLK. - TERROR. [8] – TELEMACHUS. [1] –TRIUMPH. [5] - UNICORN [1] - WARRIOR

Royal Navy Fleet Air Arm Sqdn's.

800.(Sea fires) – 827. (Fireflies) – 848 Sykorski H/C

Number of Fleet Auxiliary Ships

Gold Ganger, [1] others Not known possibly = 5

Number of Royal Marines = 3:

40. [15] - 42. [6] & 45. [12] Commandoes

Number of British Infantry Regt. = 75

Royal Artillery Field Regt.'s: -
2nd. – 4th. - 11th. (Searchlight) – 17th. - 18th. - 25th.
- 26th. 34th. - 45th. - 48th. - 95th. **[53]**
Royal Artillery (MOR's) **[10]**
4th. Queens Royal Hussars, **[20]**
1st. Inniskilling Fusiliers. **[5]**
1st Kings Own Scottish Borderers. **[3]**
1st/2nd. Kings Own Yorkshire Light Inf. **[31]**
9/12th Royal Lancers. (Prince of Wales) **[6]**
11th. Hussars. (Prince Albert's Own) **[5]**

13/18th. Royal Hussars. (Queen Mary's Own) **[9]**
15/19th. King's Royal Hussars. **[10]**.
1st. Kings Dragoon Guards. **[4]**
3rd. Royal Tank Corps. **[3]**
2nd. Coldstream Guards. **[8]**
3rd. Grenadier Guards. **[8]**
2nd. Scots Guards. **[13]**
Argyll & Sutherland Highlanders. **[3]**
Black Watch R.H.R. **[3]**
Border Regt. **[1]**

1st. Cameronians. [23]
1st. Cheshire Regt. [8]
1st. Devonshire Regt. [24]
1st/3rd. East Anglian Regt.
1st. East Yorkshire Regt. [10]
East Surrey Regt. [2]
Essex Regt. [1]
Gloucester Regt. [1]
Glider Pilot Regt.
1st. Gordon Highlanders. [18]
Green Howards. [19]
1st/2nd. King Edward VII's Own Gurkha Rifles. [97]
1st/ 2nd/ 6th. Queen Elizabeth's Own Gurkha Rifles. [92]
1st/7th. Duke of Edinburgh's Own Gurkha Rifles. [74]
1st/2nd. 10th. Princess Mary's Own Gurkha Rifles. [82]
10th. Princess Mary's Own Gurkha (Trg. Wg.) [3]
Depot Brigade of Gurkhas. [2]
Highland Light Inf. [1]
1st./2nd. King's Own Royal Regt. [1]
1st.Loyal Regt. [7]
1st. Manchester Regt. [14]
Ox' & Buck's Light Inf. [1]
1st. Queen's Royal Regt. (West Surrey) [12]

1st. Queens Own Royal West Kent's Regt. [25]
Queen's Own Cameron Highlanders. [2]
1st. Rifle Brigade.
Royal Berkshire Regt. [1]
Royal East Kent Regt. (The Buffs). [1]
1st. East Yorkshire Regt. [10]
Royal Fusiliers. [2]
Royal Northumberland Fusiliers. [1]
1st. Royal Scots Fusiliers. [8]
1st. Royal Hampshire Regt. [10]
1st. Royal Lincolnshire Regt. [10]
Royal Warwickshire Fusiliers. [1]
Royal Welsh Fusiliers. [13]
1st. West Yorkshire Regt. [5]
1st. Sherwood Foresters. [4]
1st. Seaforth Highlanders, [22]
22nd. Special Air Service Regt. [23]
1st. Somerset Lt. Inf. [22]
South Lancashire Regt. [1]
1st. South Wales Borderers.
1st. Suffolk Regt. [21]
1st. Royal Ulster Rifles. [2]
1st. West Yorkshire Regt. [5]
1st. Wiltshire Regt.
1st. Worcestershire Regt. [20]

The Number of British Corps = 23

Royal Army Service Corps Coy's
2. - 3 - 27. – 55. (Air Despatch) [99]
Royal Army Service Corps (MOR's) [18]
24. – 29. – 52. - 69 [5].
Royal Army Catering Corps. [5]
Royal Army Catering Corps (MOR's). [5]
Royal Army Chaplains Corps
Royal Army Dental Corps. [1]
Royal Army Education Corps [5]
Royal Electrical & Mechanical Engineers W/Shps.
2. – 10. -12.-13.- 14. 'LAD's' "Many". [52]
R.E.M.E. (MOR's) [18]
Royal Engineers Field Sqdn's [32]
1st.: Troop 1, -2. – 2nd. (Air Survey) 11th.
51.- 55.- 74. 84.– 305. - 410, - 554. 570.
Royal Engineers (MOR's) [16]
50 Gurkha Field Engineers [8]
Royal Army Medical Corps. [23]

R.A.M.C. (MOR's) [5]
Royal Military Police. [13]
Military Provost Staff Corps. [2]
Gurkha Military Police [2]
Royal Army Ordnance Corps, [21]
Rrmy Army Ordnance.Corps. (MOR's) [5]
Royal Army Pay Corps [4]
Royal Army Physical Training Corps. [1]
Royal Corps of Signals Units. [31]
18th. – 19th. – 24th. 28th. – 20. – 208.-230,
Royal Corps of Signals (MOR's) [16]
Malaya Sigs. Regt. Air Support Trp.
Royal Pioneer Corps. [1]
Royal Vetinary Corps.
Intelligence Corps [5}
Queen Alexandra's Royal Army Nursing Corps. [2]
Women's Royal Army Corps. [5]
General List [2]

Number of R. A. F. Squadrons = 36

Squadron No: & A/C [295 Total]
7. Lincoln.
9. Canberra.
12. Canberra.
28. Spitfire.
33. Tempest. – Hornet.
45. Hornet. -Vampire. – Venom.
48. Beverly. – Dakota .– Hastings. Valetta.
52. Dakota.– Valetta.

57. Canberra.
60. Meteor. – Spitfire.
61. Lincoln.
81. Anson. –Canberra. – Harvard. – Meteor. – Mosquito. –Pembroke. – Spitfire.
82. Canberra.
83. Lincoln.
84. Beaufighter. – Brigand.
88. Sunderland Flying Boats.

90. Valiant. – Vulcan.
97. Lincoln.
100. Lincoln.
101 Canberra.
110. Dakota. – Valletta. – Sycamore H/C.
205. Shackleton. – Sunderland Flying Boat.
209. Auster. – Dakota. – Pembroke.- Pioneer.
214. Valiant. – Vulcan.

267. Auster. –Dakota. –Harvard. –Pembroke. - Pioneer.
540. Canberra.
542. Canberra.
617. Canberra.
1311.Far East Comms. Anson. – Dakota. – Devon. –Harvard. – Hastings. – Pembroke. – Valetta. –York.

Number of R. A. F. Regiments = 5
Casualties [] included in above

Squadrons: Including MOR's
91, -92, -93, -94, - 95,- 96.

Number of African Regt's. = 6

1st. Kings African Rifles. [1]
2nd. Kings African Rifles. [2]
3rd. Kings African Rifles. [20]

1st Northern Rhodesian Regt. [5]
1st. Rhodesian Rifles. [6]
Rhodesian SAS. [3]

Number of Ceylon Corps. = 2

Royal Ceylon Pioneer Corps. [11]

Corps. of Military Police Ceylon [1]

Number of Royal Australian Navy Ships = 9

H.M.A.S: - 'ANZAC' [1] – 'ARUNTA'. – 'MELBOURNE". – 'QUADRANT'. – QUEENBOROUGH. – 'QUICKMATCH'. - 'SYDNEY". - 'TOBRUK', [1]- VAMPIRE.

Number of Royal Australian Infantry Regt's. = 4

Royal Australian Artillery [4]
100. – 101. -105. Field Batt.
1st. Royal Australian Regt. [5]

2nd. Royal Australian Regt. [14]
3rd. Royal Australian Regt. [4]

Number of Royal Australian Corps. = 9

126. Plt.Royal Australian Army Service Corps. [1]
Royal Australian Cash Office.
103.Royal Australian Army Dental Corps.
Royal Australian Electrical & Mechanical Engineers [1]
11th. Ind. Field Royal Australian Engineers

Royal Australian Medical Corps.16th. Fld. Amb. [1].
274. Field Royal Australian Military Police
368. Royal Australian Postal Unit 4 Trp.
Royal Australian Signals [2]

Number of Royal Australian Air Force. Squadrons = 6

Squadron Nos/Type A/C [11]
1
. Lincoln.
2. Canberra.

3. Sabre.
38. Dakota.

77. Sabre.
RAAF Ground Support

Number of Royal New Zealand Navy ships = 4 ships

H.M.N.Z.S.
'PUKAKI'.
'KANIERE'

'RITOITI'
'ROYALIST.'

Number of Royal New Zealand Infantry Regt's. = 5 (Including Fijian Regt.)

1st Royal New Zealand Regt. [4]
2nd. Royal New Zealand Regt. [3]
Royal New Zealand Inf. Regt. [3]

New Zealand SAS Sqdn. [2]
1st. Fijian Infantry Regt. [22]

Number of Commonwealth Royal New Zealand Air Force Squadrons = 3 [6]
Squadron No. & A/c

14. Venom,
41. Bristol Freighter. – Dakota.

75. Canberra.
Ground Base Support.

Number of Royal Malay Navy

Small Flotilla of Boats & Landing Craft.

Number of Malay Army Regt's = 7

Malayan Artillery
Royal Malay Regt's. [Incl.]

Number of Malaya Corps.

75th. Malayan Field Engineers
410th Ind. Plant Trp. Royal Engineers
Malaya Command Signals Sqdn.

1st. 2nd. 3rd. 4th. 5th. 6th. 7th. **[101]**
Federation Armoured Car Sqdn.

Number of Royal Malay Air Force = 3

Squadron No A/c

Kuala Lumpur: Chipmunk -Harvard- Tigermoth.
Penang: Chipmunk- Harvard -Tigermoth

Singapore: Chipmunk – Harvard. - Tigermoth-
Spitfire

Indian Corps. = 1

Indian Army Ordnance Corps **[1]**

Sarawak Forces = 1

Sarawak Rangers **[20]**

Federation of Malay Police Units = 5 [1026]

Fed Malaya Police
Auxiliary Force
Home Guard

Perak Aborigine Aux. Force
Malayan Aborigine Tribes

Number of Singapore Forces.

Royal Artillery 100th. – 101- 105th. Singapore Regt.s.

Medals awarded in recognition of acts of bravery

BEM. British Empire Medal (Military)	=	319	
DSO. Distinguished Service Order	=	14	
DFC. Distinguished Flying Cross	=	155 + 11 BARS	
DFM. Distinguished Flying Medal	=	39	
AFM. Air Force Medal	=	4	
MC. Military Cross	=	163 + 14 BARS	
MM. Military Medal	=	240 + 3 BARS	
GC. George Medal	=	26	
CPM .Colonial Police Medal	=	89	
KPFM Kings Police & Fire Medal	**=**	5	
AM Albert Medal	=	1	

Oher medals were awarded but not recorded within.

No purpose designed medal was minted for this WAR the only issue was the: -

GSM. 1916- 1962 GENERAL SERVICE MEDAL ARMY / R. A. F.   = 1.000,000 PLUS
GSM. 1916- 1962 GENERAL SERVICE MEDAL NAVY   =   7,800 PLUS
Mentioned in Despatches   = Too Numerous to collate

Many other different medals were awarded by the State Sultan's of Malaya. To various Military Personnel (approved by HM Queen Elizabeth II).

In September 1963. Malaya through treaties and agreements with Singapore North Borneo, Sabah, became one country Malaysia. So began the Confrontation in Borneo between Malaysia and Indonesia that lasted until 1966 Singapore decided to leave that Treaty. 1964?

The Malaysian Government awarded the **Pingat Jasa Malaysia (PJM)** to all Serving Service Personnel engaged in the Confrontation between August 1963 to August 1966 This award was also given to all Service Personnel. That were on Active service in Malaya after Malaya was awarded its Independence by the British Government. Post 31st. August 1957 to 31st August 1960. When the Emergency (War) was officially declared over.

From the 31st. August 1960 to September 1964. There was no ACT's. of war or Conflict?

Nevertheless, a New **GENERAL SERVICE MEDAL 1962** – Was Issued with Clasp/s. **MALAY PENINSULAR** & also **BORNEO**. Was awarded to all personnel serving in Malaya / Malaysia. During that period of time.

IT Does not make any sense for the 2 awards. As from August 1963 Malaya became Malaysia. ONE COUNTRY ?

However. Let us take note of the end losses of the Air Planes of the Commonwealth Air Force's. Malaya.

List of: 135 RAF / R.A.A.F ./ RNZAF / RN / Army Air Corps (AAC) Planes Crashed / Destroyed.

Austers	31 : VX114 - VX115 -VX922, VF648, VF500, VX117 VF625, VF551, VF506, VF560, VF604, VF551, VF576, VF602, VF616, VF619, VF 556, VF576, WE543, WE610, WE614, WJ408, WZ694, TJ 647, TJ602, TJ674, TJ688, TJ 321, TJ 629 + 1??. + 1 ? RSF Crash.
Beaufighter	4 : RD866, RD858, RD811, RD 859.
Brigand	9 : VS859, VS857, VS838, RH815, RH850, VS869, RH811, RH859. RH 881.
Bristol Feighter	1 : NZ5901.
Canberra	4 : WH882, WJ983, WA853, + 1 ??. (R.A.A.F.)
Dakota	7 : KN630. KN231, KN240, KN633, KN536, KJ962, KM633.
Dragonfly H/C	8 : WF 315. VF308, WT 846, WF11, WB253, WF845, XF267 VF ?.
Firefly	2 : RN No. 282 (Royal Navy) RN No ?.
Hornet	9 : WB898, WB872, WB870, PX349, WB885, WB870, PX350 PX362, PX 832.
Lincoln	1 : A73 – 40. (R.A.A.F)
Meteor	5 : A77-85, A77-643, A77-858, RR290, A77-88.
Mosquito	5 : PF624, RG254, PF623, AG524, RR290.
Pioneer	1 : XG561.
Seafire	2 : RN No.? RN. No.? (Royal Navy)
Shackleton	1 : VP254.
Spitfres	20 : TP331, TP255, TP195, VN491, TP335, TP231,TP376, TP261,TP223,TP390, TP219, TP205, TP376,TP209,TP210,TP281,TP225. TP390, VN491, SM975.
Sunderland	2 : WJ176, SZ573.
Shackleton	1 : VP254.
Sycamore H/C	3 : XE319,XF267,XL822.
Sykorski S55	2 : S55 No? S55No? (Royal Navy)
Tempest	2 : PR895, PR786.
Valetta	10 : WD164, KN161, VX521, VX491, KN861, VX525, VX540, WD160,WJ494, VX525.
Vampire	2 : WG871, WG879.
Venom	3 : WE499, WK471,WE373. (R.N.Z.R.A.F.)
Whirlwind H/C	2 : XJ413.

The Army lost many Lorries: Austin, Bedford OY's – QL's 3 Ton Vehicles, Jeeps, GMC's, Saracen APC, Daimler, Dingo's Matchless & BSA H/D's Motor Cycles Beyong repair. Plus many other Vehicles & armaments.

The Malayan Railways. Were the target for sabotage & ambush. The CT's having been taught by the British Force 136 during the fight against the Japanese, were quite able to do this on the single line railway system, operating from Singapore to Alor Star. Between June 16th. 1948 through to November 1951. There were 398 attempts by the CT's. to sabotage the railway lines resulting in 129 derailments including several fatalities.
This changed after the Communist Politburo, issued a New Policy in October 1st. 1951. Leaving the Railway to operate still under the protection of armed Guards.
Total Lives lost from 16th. June 1948 up to 31 July 1960 estimated in excess of **22,000** unconfirmed.

Casualties during the Emergency 1948 1960

Communist Terrorist

Year	Killed	Captured	Surrendered	Total per Year
1948	347	263	56	693
1949	619	337	251	1,207
1950	648	147	147	942
1951	1.079	121	201	1,401
1952	1,155	123	257	1,535
1953	959	73	372	1,404
1954	723	51	211	985
1955	420	54	249	723
1956	307	52	134	493
1957	240	32	209	481
1958	153	22	502	677
1959	21	8	86	115
1960	13	6	29	48

Totals	6,684	1,289	2,704	

There are no real figures for CT Wounded who died in the jungles either being wounded or by eradication by bombing. Est. over 3,000 ?? Overall Totals ??

Security Forces(Commonwealth Forces / Federation of Malaya Police)
Killed In Action /Died*** 16. 6.1948 - 31.8.1960)

Year	Forces Killed	Police Killed	Civilain Killed	Total per Year
1948	140	25	915	1,080
1949	210	107	834	1,151
1950	245	225	946	1,390
1951	240	307	733	1,280
1952	192	182	643	1.017
1953	151	35	445	633
1954	141	35	447	623
1955	154	49	232	435
1956	149	36	250	435
1957	59	9	132	200
1958	51	6	43	100
1959	45	8	3	56
1960	42	2	-	44
Totals	1,818 (inc. Malaya Regiments = 101)	1,026(known)	5,623 (Stats)	8,469

Figures for Civilians estimate.   A figure of over 850 Civilians reported as missing??
Above Figures do not include the Assassination of SIR. HENRY GURNEY KCMC Killed on 6th. October 1951
Security ForcesWounded

Year	Forces	Police	Civilain	Total per Year
1948	92	119	149	360
1949	77	170	200	447
1950	175	321	409	905
1951	237	454	356	1,047
1952	123	278	158	559
1953	64	53	15	132
1954	65	89	31	185
1955	43	60	24	127
1956	47	32	36	115
1957	22	11	7	40
1958	13	6	-	19
1959	1	8	-	9
1960	-	-	-	-
Totals	959 (Stats)_	1,601(Stats)	1,385(Stats)	3,945(Stats)

THE LOG of EVENTS / INCIDENTS THAT TOOK PLACE) from the 16th. June 1948 TO 31ST. August 1960 (are brief not fully detailed) as an aide memoir.
Communist Terrorist are only referred to as CT's---]
SEP (Surrendered Enemy Person.)
Unknown cause of death possibly by tropical decease is indicated by ***
NB. Authors Note: Apologies for any discrepancies, which may or, have occurred in the compilation of these sequence of events / incidents. References too many books, newspapers & documents have been researched & have found those referred too, some do not correlate to others of the same incident ---]
I did find that the Straits Times did not report all incidents on a daily basis. Therefore, for dates covered by 'Combined Operations continued throughout Malaya' There appears there was little or no information available---]

JUNE 16th. ONWARDS

Wed. 16th	16 North Perak. A predominant Tin Mining producing area. Located at the Idris Hydraulic Tin Mine Kampar. **Chin Peng** was advised by his friend Tong Chin, the Manager of the mine. That he (**Chin Peng)** would have the Money that evening. Only then **Chin Peng** would return to Johore Bahru, in readiness to move to Pahang. He totally unaware of what was about to happen approx. 40 miles North in the Kinta Valley in amongst other Rubber Estates, that straddle the town of Sungei Siput. On this specific day 2 (two) Rubber plantations. The Elphin Estate & the Phin Soon Estates. Were the scene of what was to start the Emergency. ---]
+	**At 8 'o' clock a.m.** on the Elphin Estate, the Manager. **Mr. Arthur Walker** was in his office, before returning to his bungalow for breakfast, before around about ten later, the start of a normal work schedule began for most Manager's. In the office next door, was Mr. A.H. Kumaran, his Indian Estate Clerk, (the man responsible for the morning muster roll call & collation of same, each week & Month, etc.) However, this morning was going to be different:- At 8:30 a.m. 3 (three) Chinese men rode up to his office on bikes, jumping off parked their bikes. As two slipped around the back of the office, the other one entered Mr. Walkers office. Mr. Walker's dog started barking at the intruder. As Mr. Walker pacified his dog. Next door, Mr. Kumaran overheard the commotion going on. The Chinese man spoke. 'Tabek Tuan' ('Salutation Sir.'). Arthur returned the greeting. Then 2 gun shots rang out. Mr. Kumaran hesitating, listened for a few seconds, then quickly got up & went into the next office to see **Arthur Walker** lying dead on the floor, blood and gore at the back of his head. Outside, he saw the 3 Chinese men mounting their bikes & ride away. Checking **Mr. Walker**, saw two bullet wounds in his head. Arthur died instantly. Mr. Kumaran noticed the safe was still shut with the key on the floor, possibly he upon entering had disturbed the gunmen? Nobody came to his assistance. Mr. Kumaran phoned the Police. ---]
+	**At 9'o'clock a.m.** on the Phin Soon Estate **Mr. J.M. Allison** was in his office. His Estate Conductor Mr. I.D. Christian 21 years old, (The man responsible for the supervision & distribution of the Labour force in the field) was in the outer office along with Mr. K. N. Mudaly an Indian Estate Conductor: & another Chinese Conductor, Cheah Lip Chong plus a Chinese Clerk, Tan Ah Joo. All discussing the day's work schedule. 12 Chinese gunmen surrounded the Estate office. 2 entered through the door. Ordered Christian to put his hands up. One asked Christian for his pistol. he replied. 'He did not have one'. The gunman took out a piece of string from his pocket, tied up Christian's hands behind his back. At this point Mr. Allison followed by the other three entered, they were all ordered to put their hands up. Allison was asked the same question, for his pistol, he replied. 'It was in his bungalow.' Then his hands were tied behind his back. The other gunman took the keys to the safes opened & rifled them of $ 1,000. They then marched **Allison, Christian**, Mudaly, Cheah Lip Chong & Tan Ah Joo, to the bungalow some distance away. Separating the group, leaving the three assistants outside saying: 'We are only after Europeans.' Then pushed Allison & Christian inside the bungalow. After ten minutes they came out. All were marched back to the office. Where **Allison & Christian** were each seated on chairs, before being shot dead in front of the other three. The 12 gunmen set fire to a Rubber store & drying sheds, then made good their getaway. Telephone wires hummed with the news. ---]
+	**Approx 3 miles away** on the Kumuning Estate. Mr. Boris Hembry General Manager & Mr. Reid Tweedie were discussing an outbreak of malaria. When the head office clerk Mr. Devadson interrupted and explained that

a report had come in to say **Mr. Walker** had been shot. Hembry immediately phoned the Police, who were aware of the incident & advised that Mr. Bill Powndell the Sungei Siput Officer Commanding Police District (OCPD) was on his way. Boris Hembry set out immediately in his car, upon arriving on the scene, where a Company of Gurkhas were there. Powndell informed Hembry of the other killings, on the Phin Soon Estate. Boris Hembry was. The Chairman of the Local Planters Association, therefore began to organise things. ----]

Yet two more atrocities were to take place:

+ One close by in Taiping , where a Chinese Contractor was shot dead. *(unnamed)*---]
+ In the South: On the Triang Estate. in the State of Johore . **Mr. Chung Chow Yum** the Asian Manager. Was shot dead by by 10 gunmen.who fired fifteen bullets into his body.---]
+ Notified of the atrocities. The Federation Police carried out, extensive raids on Communist Party Offices. throughout the country. They also included the Headquarters of the Singapore Communist Offices, only to find that a vast majority were empty. Their occupants having disappeared, all the leaders having gone underground. ---]
+ Kuala Lumpur: That afternoon Sir. Edward Gent. The High Commissioner of Malaya. Having been informed of the atrocities, was forced to declare. Emergency Powers, to be introduced within the States of Perak & Johore. Special Powers provided for:

   : **The Death Penalty: For unauthorized possession of arms.**
   : **The imposition of curfews.**
   : **The closing of roads, paths, & waterways.**
   : **The requisition of all means of transport.**
   : **The seizure of any article used for offensive purposes.** ---]

+ Meanwhile back at the Kampar Tin Mine. **Chin Peng,** apart from the house servants was alone & had been waiting all day to get the money. He was agitated that Tong Chin had not returned. He unaware of the atrocities that had occurred. Although, He as head of the Politburo, and his comrades. Had issued instruction to simultaneously carry out the assassinations of all White Managers of Plantations and Tin Mines. It was almost evening time when he heard the sound of trucks coming up the hill. **Chin Peng** sensed that something was not right, as they were not the sound of the mine's lorries. He decided to get out. Gathering up a few possessions, left the bungalow and hid away, there to watch the two lorries approach, stop at the bungalow. 2 European Police Inspectors, & 7 Policemen climbed out of the lorries and entered the bungalow. What for he did not know? But decided to make good his escape. ---]
+ That evening the funerals of the killed Managers were carried out. The Pall bearers led by Mr. Boris Hembry and other Planters. Boris Hembry had been a Rubber Planter in Malaya since 1930 & had risen to become the General Manager of Kumuning Estate, when the Japanese occupied Malaya. Hembry along with other Planters had escaped, made their way to Sumatra. Thus onto India to join the: Inter Services Liaison Department (ISLD) during the war with Force 136 and the Guerrilla Forces. He had come in contact with **Chin Peng** & like other members of that clandestine Group, knew it was **Chin Peng's** intention & objective to make Malaya a Communist Dictatorship servient to Communists China, which all depended on the outcome of the war? ---]
+ Kuala Lumpur: The Emergency was increased to the whole of the States of Perak & Johore. ---]
+ On the same day the organisation known as the Malayan Peoples Anti-Japanese Army' (MPAJA) issued **"A call to Arms against the British."** They having carried out many incidents of murder & intimidation of the workers on the Rubber Estates during the months of May. & early June. Moreover, although Emergency Powers had been enforced, the civil unrest had escalated. ---]
+ The Malayan CID raided the Offices of the *Min Shang Pau Publication.* Arrested 20 persons. Inside. Then closed down the Offices ---]

Thur. 17th **17 Capt. E. H. Sudbury.** BEM. Royal Engineers Died.*** *Krangi Singapore # 1 / C – 1* ---]
+ **17 P/O. S.M. S. Harford.** Royal Navy. H.M.S. *"COMMUS".* Drowned. *Kuantan Cemetery # ?* Pahang ---]
+ **17 Mr. Chong Fee Nam.** The Dublin Estate Conductor in Kedah, was shot dead whilst eating his dinner ---]
+ **17 Mr. Ooi Chng.** The Chairman of the Kuomingtang Group at Baling, was shot dead by 3 Chinese gunmen when out walking in the streets of Baling.---]
+ Singapore: The Straits Times Headlines Stated **"GOVERN OR GET OUT."**---]
+ London: In the House of Commons Sir. Antony Eden (Conservative) asked the Deputy Prime Minister Mr. Herbert Morrison (Labour) for a debate on the Political situation in Malaya.---]
+ Kuala Lumpur: In Malaya The Emergency Powers was extended to the States of Negri Sembilan. ---]
+ The MPAJA **DECLARED WAR AGAINST THE BRITISH AUTHORITIES**.---]
+ Under the Emergency Regulation. Federation of Malaya. Police (F. M. Police). Began a wide search of Malaya. On known people, suspected of being connected with the countries recent atrocities.---]

	+	Shopkeepers of Layang Layang, asked the Regam Planters Defence Force. To give them protection from looters---]
	+	Kuantan: John Davis CBE. DSO. received a teleohone call to be told. He had been made: Acting Officer Superintending Police Circle (OSPC) and ordered back to Bentong---]
Fri. 18th		Kuala Lumpur. A curfew was imposed on the area of Kampar & Sungei Siput---]
	+	*Chin Peng* making good his escape from Kampar. Was hiding in a friends house on the outskirts of Ipoh.---]
	+	The leader of the gunmen who carried out the shooting of **Mr. Walker** in Sungei Siput, was identified as a *Lui Tong Tai* ---]
	+	18 HMT DUNERA sailed Southampton bound for Singapore with replacement Service personnel---]
Sat. 19th		**19 Pte T.B. Somadasa.** Royal Pioneer Corps. Ceylon Died***_Kuala Lumpur # 237_ ---]
	+	Kuala Lumpur: Sir. Malcolm MacDonald the British High Commisioner of South East Asia. Presided over a meeting with the heads of the Civil Government :The Police and the Military.---]
	+	The Manager of the Sedenak Estate Mr. C.F.H. Pirreipont and his driver, were fired upon a few hours before a visit was due by Sir. Malcolnm MacDonald. Both received slight wounds---]
Sun. 20th		In South Kedah Mr. E. R. Rainford. Asstn. Manager of Kuala Sidim Estate Ladu Besar was fired upon by a Chinese gunman. Luckily the Gunman missed—]
Mon. 21st		**21** A Chinese Detective. **Chye Tian Kim** was shot & wounded by a Gunman at Pusang Near Batu Gajah---]
	+	**21** A Chinese Shopkeeper. **Ding Leng Kee** believed to be a member of the Kuomingtang. Was stabbed to death by 5 Chinese men at Simpang Tiga Sitiawan Perak.---]
	+	7 (seven) Important members of the Communist Party were arrested by F. M. CID Officers, under the Emergency Ordnance Regulation. Detectives raided a house in Georgetown Penang where a Member of the Politburo *Yeong Kuo* was hiding with his wife. Unfortunately, he had already left, instead they arrested his wife, who later was deported back to China with another detainee. *Liao Wei Chung* a previous Commander of the 5th. Regt. during his time with the Force 136. He too was banished to China. —]
Tue. 22nd		The Chinese Detective. **Chye Tian Kim** shot in Pusing on Monday the 21st. Died from his woumds.---]
	+	Singapore: A strong detachment of the Seaforth Highlanders. was sent to the mainland from Singapore. (Were most of these National Servicemen Infantry Lads, the first to become "The Virgin Soldiers"?)---]
	+	On that same day a communiqué from H.Q. British Land Forces Far East. Announced that it would co-operate fully with the Civil Authorities against the terrorist. It also added that that in a number of areas. Gurkha troops had relieved Malay troops & F.M. Police on static duties, enabling the latter to guard & Patrol isolated plantation---]
Wed.23rd		In a gun battle near Bameu Bahru Johore. Gurkha troops shot dead 2 CT's & wounded another. ---]
Thur. 24th		Kuala Lumpur: Essential Regulation were enacted for National Registration and Identity Cards of the entire population over the age of 12. Whilst increasing F.M. Police Powers including detentions. The recruitment of Special Constables (SC) was empowered. ---]
Fri. 25th		Singapore: The headquarters of the Malayan Communist Party, Singapore Federation of Trade Unions was closed down. Its occupants had already fled.---]
	+	42 CT's raided the town of Kuala Krau Pahang. Cutting the telephone wires, attacked the village Police Station. The CT's opened fire, the 3 Policemen inside returned fire. After half an hour of the gun fight, the CT's withdrew back into the jungle, leaving one Policeman's wife Killed (**unnamed).** Afterwards evidence of a heavy blood trails. indicated the several of the CT's had been wounded as they withdrew into the jungle. ---]
	+	Whilst down South in Johore, another gang of CT's attacked the Police Station of Sedenak. But after a fierce gun fight with the defending Police, they were driven off. 1 CT was shot dead---]
	+	Members of another CT group attacked the town of Jerantut.75 miles North East of Kuala Lumpur. After burning down the Police Station, running riot they shot several villagers & looted shops. before withdrawing back into the hills. ---]
	+	Bentong: John Davis CBE. DSO. was ordered to take over the investigation of the attacked town of Jerantut He set out with a small party of Police Volunteers to Jerantut, where at first light they found a deserted town the inhabitants had flown. They were joined by a small band of Police, who came out of hiding, and gave a brief update on the events. 20 to 30 CT's had attacked the town. Seized 3 Local Towkays (Businessmen) and took them away with the Police Sergeant. At the Police Station they found one Policeman trussed up they released him. John Davis CBE. DSO. organized a party to go and search for the missing persons. Going up into the hills, They found the camp and three corpses of the Towkays. They continued with the search and found another camp with the CT's. Engaging them Killed 3. The others ran off. The party returned to Jerantut where John Davis CBE. DSO. handed over to an incoming Platoon of the Malay Regt. Then returned to Bentong with his volunteers. ---]
	+	Discussions had been taking plaace in various centres in Malaya to form a HOME GUARD similar to the

Sat. 26th		British styled war-time units. As a possibility to combat the current situation.---]
		Singapore: Mr. Macdonald along with Gen. Sir. Neil Richie. C in C Far East Land Forces, Rear Admiral C Casion. Flag Officer Malaya, A.C. Sanderson. Air Officer Commanding Malaya. Flew to Kuala Lumpur to hold a meeting with Sir. Edward Gent.---]
	+	26 HMT DEVONSHIRE arrived Liverpool with returning Service personnel---]
Sun. 27th		Kuala Lumpur : Sir. Edward Gent was relieved of his post. Flew to Singapore enroute to Lomdon---]
Mon. 28th		London: Sir. George Maxwell. former Chief Secretay to the Fedaration of Malay called for.: *'All Malays to be armed in order to combat terrorism in Malaya.'* ----]
Tue. 29th		Bentong. About this time. John Davis CBE. DSO. was the architech and instigator of the 'Counter Insurgency Policy.' against his former ally **Chin Peng.** He was also the brains behind the formation of what became known as the 'Ferret Force.' He along with Richard Broome, Noel Alexander & Bob Thompson, all collegues in Force 136. In their own right, experts in jungle warfare. They met to disguss John's proposal of Small independent units, commanded by a number of Planters, previous members of the Inter Service Liaison Department (ISLD). They to take command of jungle patrols to seek out CT camps. These were to be joined by members of the F.M. Police from various Federal State contingents & Gurkha troops, of specially picked squad's. They estimated that they needed a force of 300 troops devided into 15: 20 man troops with a Commander and Chinese Liaison Officer. All to act independent from the others with a HQ under the command of 2 Special Officers. Supplies were to be dropped to the individual units by Dakotas of 110 Sqdn. R. A. F. All was set for a report to be drawn up and approved by the upper Authorities Approval---]
	+	29 HMT DILWARA arrived Singapore bound for Southampton---]
Wed. 30th		Heavily armed Troops & F.M. Police searched a village of Kuala Kurau searching for 40 CT's. Who had attacked the village the previous day. They engaged & fired upon the attackers for half an hour, before they withdrew, leaving many trails of blood, indicating several CT's had been wounded ---]

JULY

Thur. 1st		Operations *"Pepper"* & *"Haystack"* ended against the Kuomintang Guerrillas, then operating under the name of the Malayan Overseas Chinese Self Protection Corps (OCAJA). ---]
	+	R.A.F. Sqdn. F.E.C. "Austers" Relocated and operational at R.A.F. Changi. ---]
	+	**1 Mr. Chong Keat Ooi.** Agricultural Dept. Colonisation Officer was Killed by Chinese Gunmen in Langup Village Lower Perak---]
	+	At the 25th.m/s Pontian / Johore road, a Chinese man was battered to death by an unarmed Gang--]
	+	1 HMT DILWARA sailed Singapore with returning Service personnel ---]
Fri. 2nd		50 CT's attacked the village of Kulat 20 miles North of Johore Bahru. They Killed 3. A Chinese shopkeeper, his wife & child. (**unnamed**)They fired shots at the Police Station. ---]
	+	F.M. Police arrested 6 People: 4 men and 2 women who acted as spies for the murderous attack. ---]
	+	Police raided a house on the Riverside Estate Selangor. Arrested 2 CT's. Recovering arms & ammunition including 2 Bren guns & grenades---]
	+	In Pahang 40 miles South of Metakab. A Chinese man was Killed by 4 CT's ---]
	+	In Kedah near Jitra. F. M. Police arrested 7 CT's. One member turned out to be described of the "Highest Importance?" ---]
Sat. 3rd		In Perak at the 9th. m/s Batu Gaja /Tanjong Tualang Road. 7 CT's opened fire at the car of the hinese Manager of Phin Foon Tin Mine. Only one occupant, was wounded. ---]
	+	**3 ACI. D. Broadbent.** R.A.F. Singapore. Drowned off Fortified Island near Changi. *[No known Grave] Terendak Wall Memorial Malacca.]* ---]
Sun. 4th		**4 Pte. H.M. Karunaratne.** Royal Pioneer Corps (Ceylon) Died*** *Kranji Singapore # 239*---]
		4 London: Two planes were in a mid-air collision over Mount Vernon Hospital. A R.A.F. Command Transport plane & a Scandinavian Cloudmaster passenger plane. As they were attempting to land in bad visibility at R.A.F. Northolt London. On board the R.A.F Avro York Transport plane, flying to London to deliver a report on the Malayan Emergency was **Sir. Edward Ghent. KCMG. DSO. OBE. MC.** Governor of Singapore & Malaya. He was Killed along with all the other 37 passengers. There were no survivors of the crash. ---]
Mon. 5th		5 Malaya: **F/O. J. H. W. Moodie.** 28 Sqdn. R.A.F. Killed when his Spitfire TP261 dived into ground 4 miles North of R.A.F. Sembawang *Kranji Singapore # 3 / B - 6* ---]
	+	Kuala Lumpur: Major General. Boucher G.O.C. Malaya told the Federation Council. *'The Military were Fully Integrated with the Federation Police, furthermore as a special frontier force, mobile armoured – car units had been formed. Also, the Royal Navy & R.A.F. were operating off the East coast to prevent any seaborne reinforcements for the terrorist from landing. 2 CT radio Stations had been located deep*

		in the jungle & destroyed'---].
Tue.	6th	2 Spitfire's from 60 Sqdn. R.A.F. Tengah fired rocket propelled shells (RPS), at a CT camp deep in the jungles of Perak near Ayer Karah. It became the first air strike of the campaign. It was understood that **Chin Peng** was in that camp at the time. A follow up by a Platoon of British troops found the camp totally destroyed, however no occupants were found. Before they left, they set the Lalang alight. ---]
		N.B. *Ref: 'My Side of History'* **Chin Peng** refers to this incident. After this **Chin Peng** moved up into the Cameron Highlands. ---]
	+	F. M. CID arrested 3 of 6 Communist Agents, located in the Sungei Lui area Negri Sembilan. Who were known to have been recruiting conscripts? ---]
	+	Singapore: Mr. Malcolm Macdonald Special Commissioner for S.E. Asia announced: -
		'The Malayan Communist had been working too a deliberate plan. To stage a violent revolution. Their object to take control by armed force. Over the past eight weeks over 1,000 arrests had been made Thus throwing their plan **'Out of Gear'**--- *Action Engaging CT's taken by the Government forces, had caused them to postpone, readjust or, abandon altogether.'* He declared: *'The Federation Government would take the strongest Action Engaging CT's to supress terrorism. Trials of Terrorist would be speeded up stating. 'The expectation for a terrorist from the moment of his capture to his death - would be a matter of days.'* ---]
	+	Malaya: The Leader of the Johore Labour Union **Tan Yen** was shot dead by F.M. Police in a clash with CT's. in Johore. ---]
	+	Kuala Lumpur: At a meeting at The Malaya District HQ. John Davis CBE. DSO. proposal for the immediate formation of his Ferret Force. Was part of the agenda. This was met enthusiastically by General Boucher and given the go ahead. For Davis to organise the whole of the Ferret Force. ---]
Wed.	7th	London: In the House of Commons. Mr. Rees–Williams. Under Secretary for the Colonies announced. *'During May & June in Malaya. There had been 52 murders & attempted murders- 31 cases of arson, 31 cases of robbery, assault or, intimidation. Resulting in the arrest of 221 persons, with 7 shot dead by Police. The number of terrorists in Malaya was estimated as well over 6,000.'*----]
Thur.	8th	In the House of Commons. The Colonial Secretary Mr. Creech Jones made a statement as follows: Quote: *After paying tribute to the work of Sir. Edward Gent. Who had been Killed in the Northolt air disaster while flying to London to confer with the Government. He stated: Quote:*
		'That a:" difficult & grave "situation existed in Malaya, resulting from "an attempt by murder & violence to destroy authority & order, to reduce the economic life of the country to chaos by the murder of management of both European & Chinese therefore to impede the Malayan recovery. Support for the Malayan Government to this end. "To create some other control over Malaya." He added. 'That the most determined efforts would be to eradicate the terrorist. Promised the fullest support for the Malayan Government to this end and pointed out. That the conflict in Malaya was not unlike that now going on in China & that the same interests were involved in both, & the wilful lies regarding the Malayan situation, which have been put across from Moscow. It should be made clear, we are not faced within Malaya with the emergence of a nationalist movement, which Britain is engaged in putting down, it's not a movement of the people of Malaya, but of gangsters who are out to destroy the foundations of human society and ordinary life. Unquote. ---]
	+	Malaya: However, there was also another big problem facing the British authorities. That of the question of the Squatters. The Chinese who had fled from China to seek settlement in Malaya. These people had illegally entered the country & had spread themselves all over Malaya, specifically along the jungle fringes of the western side of the Peninsular. Since the beginning of the Emergency, they had been recognised. As a good source of information, food and recruitment, to the Communist living in the jungle. They were easy targets for the Min Yuen, the intelligence wing & supporters of the Communist. A problem which had to be resolved by detention & deportation of all Squatters. A huge task. ---].
	+	8 HMT ORBITA arrived Southampton with returning Service personnel ---]
	+	8 Mr. D W. Jennings Asstn. Manager. & Mr. J. R. Rutty Manager. of the Kuala Remam Estate Kuantan Pahang. whilst driving along the Sungei Lembing road, near Batu Sawar. Were ambushed by a number of CT's. The car ran off the road, throwing out its 4 occupants, Jennings, Rutty & 2 Dressers (Dressers were those that had basic training in medical practice) **Jennings & Rutty** and the **2 Dressers** A Malay & Indian (**unnamed**) were shot dead where they laid. Later in the day Security Forcesfound Mr. Rutty's body further along the road in a ditch,some distance from the ambush. It appeared he might have been trying to escape before being Killed? ---]
	+	A party of F. M. Police were on their way to Lankap when they ran into a number of CT's, burning down a road bridge. They opened fire on them. 1 CT was Killed identified as a High Ranking CT.---]
Fri.	9th	**9 F/Lt. R.W. Cersell.** Eng/Off. R.A.F. Sembawang Died from injuries received in a Road Traffic Accident. (RTA). On July 8th. *Kranji Singapore # 3 / B - 5* ---]

+	Gurkha troops fought a seven hour battle with a large force of CT's, at a deserted Tin Mine near Kuala Lumpur Killing four (4) CT's and capturing 19.---]
Sat. 10th	**10** At Batu Arang Selangor. The only coal mining centre in Malaya, was seized by, 100 CT's. Having cut the telephone wires isolated the town from outside calls. On the approach road in. They ambushed a Bus carrying Passengers, who were advised to sit still. Other traffic behind was also held up as they ravaged the Town. for hours, wrecking the Mining machinery plant. They began their assault around about 7 a.m. Attacking the brick-built Police Post but failed to hit any of the Police inside. The Police returning fire hit several of the CT's, who retreated, taking their wounded with them. While this was ongoing. A gang of CT's singled out several important members of the community. Killing Mr. **Peng San** Chief Mining Overseer, whilst **Marko Cheok** a leading business man, flew from a Coffee shop with his son balanced on the handle bars of his bike. They shot after him, wounding him, he fell off his bike. His son ran away. Then, the CT's moving towards his prone body they shot him in the head. They also shot a Chinese truck driver & a Chinese fitter Foreman (**both unnamed).** They entered the Kuomintang Group Office opposite the Police Station took the Clerk **Mr. Chan Kuma Yuen** outside into a side street & shot him. Half a mile outside town they held up the Railway Station. A number of CT's held up the approaching train from Rawang. Herded the passengers off & into the Station Office then robbed them of the possessions. During this period of time, the Mining machinery, compressors motors & drag lines were being damage by bullets & sledge hammers. It wasn't until 11 'o' clock. Before the Police outside being unable to make contact with Batu Arang Police Station. Realised something was wrong? Then sent a strong force of Gurkha troops, together with the Police, that forced the CT's to withdraw. During the fire fight **Pol/Insp. Katar Singh.** F. M. Police was Killed. 5 CT's were Killed & many were wounded before escaping into the jungle with their wounded. ---]
Sun. 11th	3 CT's.' were Killed by a combined Military / Police Force in the jungles of Siputeh Perak. A partially built camp near Ampang was burnt down---]
Mon. 12th	656 Sqdn Auster 5/6/7/9 Relocated at R.A.F. Semberwang ---]
Tue. 13th	The second air attack by 3 Spitfires of 60 Sqdn. took place at another CT camp high in the mountainous area of Bentong. Destroying the camp. ---]
Wed. 14th	During a raid by a Patrol of the F. M. Police on a CT jungle camp North of Kajang. A CT Commander *Liew Yao* was Killed. ---]
Thur. 15th	A further air strike by Spitfires of 60 Sqdn. Took place on a CT camp in Telok Anson Perak. The camp was surrounded by swamps & not easily accessible. A search of the area after revealed the camp had been destroyed & 10 CT's had been Killed. ---]
+	15 HMT LANCASHIRE sailed from Hong Kong with onboard the 1st. Battn. Royal Inniskilling Fusiliers as reinforcements bound for Singapore. ---]
+	R. A. F. Spitfires of 60 Sqdn. Strafed a known CT hideout in the jungle cladded hills, 35 miles N.E of Kuala Lumpur with RPS. Then strafed the area with machine gun fire. The Spitfires made 4 attacks over the area. A Dakota, flying as observer stated the area was obliterated. ---]
+	In Johore. During a raid by the F. M. Police on a house at Sungei Jel Kajang. Where CT members were hiding, amongst them was several high-ranking CT leaders, including *Lan Yan*. Un-fortunately they had been warned of the pending raid & escaped. *Lan Yan* plus two others ran off through a pineapple plantation & were followed by D/C Choo Kit who cornered *Lan Yan* who fired three shot at close range, all missing Choo Kit who shot & Killed him. Before he & others, were attacked by more CT's. For his bravery D/C. Choo Kit was awarded the Colonial Police Medal (CPM 23/11/48 LG 39464) ---]
Fri. 16th	A party of 35 F. M. Police left Kampar, on an operation into the Gunong Chanteh area of S. Perak. At a broken wooden bridge, they left a Platoon of 10 men as a "stopping Platoon" to cover any escape route. The rest pressed on. Then encountered 30 CT's in the camp, going through their morning drill. Immediately the Police opened fire, wounding several, the CT's scattered into the undergrowth taking with them their wounded. During a search of the camp, they found 1 dead CT in one of the camp huts. Meanwhile back at the broken bridge the "Stopping Platoon" engaged the retreating CT.'s killing 1 CT, they arrested the others. ---]
+	Approx. 100 CT's under the Command of *Kim Siong* attacked the Police Station at Pekan Gua Musang Pahang. The small Company of F. M. Police were surrounded & fought the CT's for nearly two hours until their ammunition ran out. The Inspector & 14 Constables surrendered & were taken away. During the fire fight one 1 F. M. Police Special Constable (SC). (**unnamed**). was Killed while another escaped. ---]
+	In response to this attack. Land Forces and RAF aerial attacks were instigated---]
+	16 HMT DUNERA arrived Singapore with replacement Service personnel---]
Sat. 17th	During a gunfight with CT's near Kajang Selangor. *Lau Yew*, the Military Commander & one of the leaders of the Malayan Peoples Anti Jananese Army. Was shot dead by. Police Superintendent Bill (Two Gun) Stafford. During the ensuing gun battle near Kapang Selangor. 10 other CT's were also shot dead, Among them was an

	Insurgent Leader (*unnamed*) During the gun fight. **L/Cpl. Dhowa Ghale.** 6th. Queen Elizabeth's Own Gurkha Rifles was Killed in Action Engaging CT's. Kajang Area [*No known Grave] Terandak Wall Memorial Malacca*-]
Sun. 18th	**18** A troop of the Malay Regiment including 10 F. M. Policemen, were ambushed at an old railway line 2 miles South of Merapoh. During the 6-hour engagement. **Major R.W. Henderson** R.A.S.C. *Kuala Lumpur # 32 / 1244* – **L /Cpl. Wan Abd Rahman bin. Wan Said** – Pte's **Ahmed. b. Gedin.-. Ahmad. Nazir. b. Lob.** Malay Regiment, were Killed in Action Engaging CT's. Gua Musang. Pahang.---]
+	**18 Recruit Dalbahadur Tamag.** 10th. Princess Mary's Own Gurkha Rifles Training Wing Died*** *Kranji Singapore # 7 / D – 2*---]
Mon. 19th	Gurkha Troops found a CT camp in the Bidor area of S. Perak during the gunfight **Capt. A. R. Pickin.** 7th. Duke of Edinburgh's Own Gurkha Rifles was Killed in Action Engaging CT's. 1 CT was Killed. *Batu Gajah # 399* Ipoh Perak. --]
+	5 Armed CT's broke into a Squatters house at Subei Toh Pahang and stole $ 60 & some jewellery in the area of Sungei Patani---]
+	Kuala Lumpur: New Regulation Powers will be introduced throughout the Federation on Malaya. ---]
+	19 HMT DEVONSHIRE Sailed Liverpool bound for Singapore with replacement Service personnel ---]
Tue. 20th	Australia: The Australian Communists dominated Seaman's Union. Declared that they would boycott vessels carrying arms & ammunition from Australia to Malaya---]
+	R. A. F. Air support was provided by Spitfires of 60. Sqdn. to a convoy of the Malay Regt. on their way to Sungei Yu in support of the Police at Gua Musang. ---]
Wed. 21st	**21 Robert Downey.** The first British child to be Killed, was shot in the head, when CT's ambushed a civilian convoy, evacuating families from the nearby Dominion Tin Mine Estate & a group of Executives from another nearby Tin-mine in the Semenyik area of Selangor ---]
Thur.22nd	Kuala Lumpur: Sir. Alexander Newboult The acting High Commissioner In response to the above attack at Gua Musang. An aerial attack was carried out by RAF Dakota's & Spitfires, supporting Ground forces on Pekan Gua Musang. Spitfires fired rockets on the area, Engaging the CT's. ---]
+	On the same day all those F. M. Police SC's, taken prisoner at Pekan Gua were released unharmed. They set the Lalang alight. The occupation of this Town lasted 5 days, before it was retaken by the British forces. ---]
+	A Squatter was Killed on the Voules Estate Tenang Segamat by 2 CT's ---]
+	Singapore. A curfew was imposed in the Straits of Johore. By the Singapore Commisioner of Police ---]
Fri. 23rd	**23 Pte. J .N. Fothergill.** 1st. Seaforth Highlanders. Killed in Action Engaging CT's. *Terandak Military Cemetery # CE / E - 1*---]
+	Kuala Lumpur: Sir. Alexander Newboult, (acting High Commissioner of the Malayan Federation) & Sir. Franklin Charles Gimson. Governor of Singapore. Announced that: '*The Malayan Communist Party & 3 affiliated organisations the:* MPAJA, *The New Democratic League & PETA Had been outlawed.*'---]
+	23 HMT LANCASHIRE arrived in Singapore with replacement Service peronnel sailed for Hong Kong 23rd.--]
+	23 HMT DUNERA sailed Singapore bound for Southamton with returning Service personnel ---]
Sat. 24th	**24 Sgt. F.T. Harris.** Cl/GD 91 Sqdn. R.A.F. Died *** *Kranji Singapore # 4 / B -3*---]
+	**24 Cadet J.A. Embery.** F. M. Police on Special Police Operation was shot by gunmen at Kememan. *Christian Cemetery Terengannu*---]
+	Army & R.A.F. carried out an Air /Ground operation to destroy a CT hideout in the jungle areas of Selangor.---]
+	In a raid by the F.M. Police 1 Chinese Gunman was shot dead, whilst 600 suspects. were captured.---]
Sun. 25th	**25 Sgt. A.F. Argyle.** Royal Fusiliers. Died *** *Kuala Lumpur. # 14 / 912*---]
+	London: Mr. Creech Jones. Speaking in the House of Commons. announced: '*3,500 Gurkha troops, had been released to take up offensive details in Malaya. The Federation of Malay Police Force would be increased by another 3,000 & 10,000 Special Constables would be recruited. 300 Palestine Police Specials, had already sailed for Malaya. To assist the Federation of Malay Police Force*'. ---]
+	Malaya. After a day and night sweep by the Police and Military Forces in the jungle area of Segamat. 21 prisoners were taken, amongst them was a well-known Communist leader of the area. During the operation. Guns, ammunition and communist documents were found. ---]
+	In another round-up by the F. M. Police and CID men, in the Teluk Mata Ikan area of Singapore. Chinese personnel who could not verify their residence were detained---]
+	6 people were murdered in the Kuala Lipis district. ----]
+	10 armed CT's entered the office of a Rubber Estate and Killed the Chinese Manager (*unnamed*) with a bayonet. The Contractor was seized. taken outside tied to a tree close to the smokehouse, which was then set

	+	alight destroying rubber. The blaze caused the death of the Contractor. (*unnamed*)---]
	+	In Perak 12 CT's attacked a lonely Police Post at Semoliang near Bidor. 1 Constable (*unnamed*) was Killed & several wounded before they drove off their attackers. ---]
Mon. 26th		In the village of Jelal North of Taiping. A group of CT's, entered the house of a Towkay a senior member of the Kuomintang *(unnamed)* and shot him dead. ---]
Tue. 27th		2 Chinese were shot dead at the village of Nanchang 13 miles away from Metakab. ---]
	+	Soldiers of the 26th Field Regt. Royal Artillery and F.M. Police Patrols, began a big sweep in the area of Semenyth 22 miles from Kuala Lumpur. Spitfires destroyed a CT headquarters. The Army rounded up the CT's killing 1. The gang were identified as the same gang that Killed **Robert Downey** the previous week. Air support was given by RAF Spitfires. During the Spitfire attack 1 CT was Killed---]
Wed. 28th		**28** CT's shot & Killed **Mr. Lee Sim** a Tapper Contractor as he got off a Bus in Sungei Siput. ---]
	+	Gurkha troops & Police Killed 2 CT's. wounded 1, arrested 2 more. During a gun battle near Bamfu Bahru 15 miles from Johore Bahru---]
	+	R.A.F Dakota's gave cover support to ground forces operating in the Gua Musang area---]
	+	Another large-scale operation was carried out in the Batu Arang area. N.W. of Kuala Lumpur. Attacking Infantry & F.M. Police. Killed 22 CT's, captured 47. Before destroying their encampment, described as a noted & troublesome centre. ---]
Thur. 29th		**29 Rect. Krishnabahadur Rai**. 10th. Princess Mary's Own Gurkha Rifles. Died from Wounds recv'd at Batu Pahat. *Kluang Johore # 3 / E - 13*---]
	+	London: It was announced in London: '*Sir. Henry Gurney former Chief Secretary to the Palastine Government will succeed Sir. Edward Gent. as High Commisioner to the Federation'.*---]
	+	The headlines in a British Newspaper stated: '**British Wipe Out Malayan Rebels'** Maybe this was referring to the retaking of Gua Musang ???? Certainly **NOT** to the MPABA ---]
Fri. 30th		**30** HMT DILWARA arrived Southampton with returning Service personnel ---]
Sat. 31st		**31 (KGO) Lt. Randhoj Gurung.** & **Rfn. Ratnabahadur Pun.** 6th. Queen Elizabeth's Own Gurkha Rifles. Killed in Action Engaging CT's *Sungei Patani # 1 – 2* .---]
	+	**31 Pte. R. Guy.** K.O.Y.L.I. Died through Cooker accident. *Western Road # 196* George Town Penang---].
	+	**31 Pte. L. Francis.** Royal Pioneer Corps (Ceylon) Died *** *Kranji Singapore # 7 / A 18*---]
	+	**31 Pte. H. Newman.** 1st. Seaforth Highlanders Died*** *Kranji Singapore # 1 / B - 6*---]
	+	In a Combined Military Police operation Several CT's were flushed out of the Limestone Cave near the San Toh Tong Cave Temple 3 miles S. of Ipoh. 4 CT's were captured---]

AUGUST

Sun. 1st		Australia: The Australian Government decided: '*If requested by the British Government Arms & ammunition would be issued & flown to Malaya by the R.A.A.F.*---]
	+	Operation '*Shawcross.'* Continued.---]
Mon. 2nd		R. A. F. Spifires made 2 attacks and destroyed many huts, that were holding about 60 CT's in camps near Pulai. They were understood to be the CT force that occupied Gua Musang in July. ---]
Tue. 3rd		**3** Gurkha Troops and F. M. Police overran a CT Stronghold 3 miles North of Pulia. Kelentan. R. A. F. Sptifires provided straffing runs. During the operation. **Rfn. Motilai Pun.** 6th. Queen's Elizabeth's Own Gurkha Rifle was Killed In Action Engaging CT's. 2 CT.s were Killed Near.Pulai Kelantan. *[No known Grave] Terandak Wall Memorial Malacca.]*---]
	+	F. M. Police Lying in ambush at Menglembu 5 miles S of Ipoh shot the President of the Miners Union known to them as the head of a CT killing gang.---]
	+	Troops of the Malay Regt. searching Squatter huts in the Baling area of Kedak found 20 people. Ordered them to stand still. 4 ran away were fired at. Killing 1 and wounding the others. All were detained. ---]
	+	R.A.F. Spitfires strafed a deep jungle area behind Ayar Kunning 10 miles S.W. of Kampar. Followed by ground forces who found. Gunpowder, arms and ammunition plus various CT propaganda items. They arrested 55 suspects. who were taken away for interrogations. ---]
Wed. 4th		**4** HMT. LANCASHIRE arrived from Hong Kong docked in Singapore. On board were the 1st. Battn. of the Inniskillings Fusiliers. Reinforcements to join other troops in the fight against the CT's. Sailed 4th. With returning Service personnel ---]
Thur. 5th		**5 Mr. J. E. Ogilvei.** General Manager. Of the Meru Tin Mines Chemor near Ipoh Perak.

		Whist driving alone was ambushed & Killed by 8 CT's. Who had been in ambush positions on the top of a double bend near a bridge, they opened fire at the car, which went on for a little way before stopping? Obviously, Mr. Ogilvei had been hit. The CT's surrounded the car & Killed **Mr. J.E. Ogilvei** with multiple shots They stole his revolver. --]
Fri.	6th	**6 Pte J. Elliott.** 1st. K. O. Y. L. I. Accidently Shot near Ipoh. _Batu Gajah # 392_ Ipoh Perak. ---]
Sat.	7th	**7 LAC. K. J. Bowen.** R.A.F. Lost at sea returning to the UK. _[No known Grave] Terandak Wall Memorial Malacca]_ ---]
	+	On the Telok Sengat Estate in Kota Tingi Johore. During a Chinese free Saturday evening film show. When 100 Tappers were watching the film. 60 CT's. attacked & demanded all the Tappers give up their I. D. cards. They Shot four children including Mr. **H. M. Rice.** the Manager. His daughter, who was witness to the murderous attack, escaped with Mrs. Rice, along with 100 workers fleeing into the jungle. The CT's set a light & burnt down every building on the Estate, before driving off with 2 lorry loads of rice. ---]
	+	In a counter operation British troops with air support from R A. F. Spitfires strafing the area, recaptured the jungle village of Pulai in Kelantan from the C.T's. Who had used it as a HQ & supply base since the 17th July? They fled before being attacked. The R.A.F. used bombs to raze it to the ground. ---]
	+	Singapore: A meeting was held by Sir. Malcolm McDonald. (Commissioner General for SE Asia) Sir. Alexander Newboult. (acting High Commissioner of the Malayan Federation) Sir. Franklin Gimson. (Governor of Singapore) Sir. Charles Clarke. (Governor of Sarawak) & Mr. James Caldor. (Officer Administering the Government of North Borneo) To discuss the situation in Malaya and the defence of British possessions in SE Asia. At the meeting of the Commissioner Generals Conference. The main point of the agenda was the situation of the Chinese Immigrants into British South-East Asia Territories. Specially at that moment in time, in Singapore & Malaya. With the MCP creating atrocities throughout the States. That there should be more rigid control over all immigration at the borders. A solution should be made and implemented. Further discussions should take place to resolve the problem---]
Sun.	8th	**8 Mr K.A.W. Burnham.** Manager of the Bukit Sindim Estate near Kulim was Killed when a CT gunman entered his bungalow and shot him in the head. His assistant Manager Mr. Rainsford saw the assailant running way fired shots after him, but he escaped. Mr. Burnham has previously been the target of the CT's, when he was shot at on July 18th, then they missed. ---]
	+	R.A.F. Spitfires attacked CT huts in the hillside area of Ampang. 6 miles East of Ipoh on the Tanjong Rambutan road. Police announced that due to dense jungle area, it would be some time before results could be followed up. ---]
	+	Kuala Lumpur: It was announced: _'Colonel W.N. Gray. former Inspector General of the Palestine Police, had been appointed Police Commissioner for the Malayan Federation.'_ ---]
Mon.	9th	Near Kuala Kabu Selangor Police and Military troops arrested 16 suspected CT's killing one. They burned down all the huts. ---]
	+	The body of the farmer who was taken prisoner by 8 CT's on Monday. Was found shot dead on a railway track with his hands tied behind his back--]
	+	A F. M. Police Patrol ran into 20 CT's near Tapah Perak. Returning fire, they Killed 2 CT's, a man and a woman. The rest escaped into the surrounding jungle. ---]
	+	9 HMT LANCASHIRE sailed Singapore for Liverpool. with returning Service personnel ---]
Tue.	10th	Singapore. An announcement stated: _'49 Dyaks (Borneo Head Hunters) had been flown to Malaya, to assist British Units tracking down CT's in the jungle. Additional numbers of Dyaks would be sent later. To form the Sarawak Rangers.'_ —]
	+	6 CT's Attacked the Senga Estate in the Rangan area of Johore and Killed 1 Rubber Tapper (**_unnamed_**)—]
	+	In another incident on the Gan Pen Estate. 20 CT's dressed in jungle green went to a Kongsi and herded the occupants into a room. Picked out 2 Chinese Tappers took them outside and shot them dead. (**_unnamed_**) ---]
	+	About the same time 3 CT's entered a house on the Consolidated Eastern Plantation Estate and shot a Rubber Tapper dead. (**_unnamed_**) ---]
Wed. 11th		In the Tanjong Tualang area of Perak. An Australian Tin Miner, **Mr. B. P. Wills** cycling along a road was shot dead by CT's. ---]
	+	30 CT's Attacked the Coronation Estate 4 miles from Kluang. Killed the School master, a Chinese Dresser & a Malay F.M. Special Constable (**_all unnamed_**) ---]
	+	A Patrol of The Ferret Force in the hours of darkness found an occupied CT. Camp, but the Sentry gave the alarm. The CT's escaped under cover of darkness, leaving all their ammunition and supplies behind ---]
	+	On the Kempas Estate Baloh. CT's burned down the Smoke House and Factory, wounding 2 Malays and 2 Chinese workers---]

	+	2 Beaufighters of 84 Sqdn R.A.F. carried out successful air strikes on CT jungle hideout camps at Batu Malatang, bordering the Kelantan / Thailand border, where it was reported 600 CT's were massing. ---]
Thur. 12th		During an attack on the Sembrock Estate by number of CT's. 'A' Platoon of 8 F. M. Police on their way to assist the defenders, were ambushed by CT 's. Coming under heavy fire, although several were wounded, they managed to break through to the Estate. For his bravery during the attack S.P. Alias B. Banking. F. M. Police was awarded the CPM 23/11/1948 LG 38464---]
	+	R. A. F. Spitfires of 60 Sqdn & 5 Beaufighters of 45 Sqdn. carried out further successful air strikes against CT jungle hideout camps in Bentong Pahang. A follow up revealed only one CT eliminated---]
Fri. 13th		Gurkha Troops engaged CT's in a remote area of Negri Sembilan. Killed 6 & wounding several others who escaped. ---]
	+	5 convicted CT's were hanged in Kuala Lumpur jail. They were the first to receive the death penalty. ---]
	+	Kuala Lumpur: Sir. Henry Gurney. sent a telegram to the Secretary of State for the Colonies: 'Advising His fears of the pending closure of the Chinese port of Swatow. on the 31st. August. ---] R.A.F. Spitfires and Beaufighters strafed & attacked a CT hideout in the area of the 37th. m/s Degong road Lower Perak. Troops following up the attack. Killed 1 CT and wounded another. Searching the area found 6 huts had been destroyed during the air attack, which were the Headquarters of the areas MPABA. They found three wounded CT's, hit during the air attack one was Identified as a known Captain of the MPABA -]
Sat. 14th		**14 Cfn. D. Hancox.** R.E.M.E. Died *** _Kranji Singapore # 1 / B -7._ ---]
	+	Following up a report that 15 civilians had been abducted or, reported missing near Kulai. A party of F. M. Police headed by S/Insp. Hisham came under heavy fire from the CT's. Returning the fire, they mortally wounded 4 CT's. S/Insp.Hisham & several Constables incurred wounds before the CT's. withdrew. ---]
	+	London: The War Office announced: 'In addition to the 4th. Queen's Hussars already in transit to Malaya and the Inniskilling Fusiliers already in Malaya. The 2nd Brigade of Guards consisting of the 2nd. Battn.'s Coldstream, Scots, & Grenadier Guards would be sent to Malaya as reinforcements.'---]
Sun. 15th		Gurkha Troops engaged a number of CT's in Negri Sembilan killing 6 and wounding others who escaped. ---]
	+	15 HMT DEVONSHIRE arrived Singapore with replacement Service personnel ---]
Mon. 16th		A Patrol of the F. M. Police searching for a missing Prospector. 20 miles North of Johore. Were ambushed by 40 CT's. Returning fire, they Killed 4 CT's. The rest fled into the jungle The Police found two big huts suitable to house 60 CT's. Also found were important CT documents & ammunition They burned down the huts. ---]
Tue. 17th		**17 Capt. M. Pickard.** R.A.S.C. Killed in Action Engaging CT's Gua Musang Perak. _Kuala Lumpur # 14 / 913._]
	+	On the Kota Estate near Rasa Negri Sembilan. Gurkhas engaged 30 to 40 CT's using Japanese machine guns. After 6 CT's had been Killed, the rest retreated. A Search found much Japanese ammunition and other items. They set alight the 20 huts where the ammunition had been stored. ---]
Wed. 18th		A Platoon of the F.M. Police engaged was ambushed by 40 CT's 20 miles North of Johore Bahru. During the fire fight 4 CT's were Killed 1 PC (**unnamed**) was Killed the Patrol leader Sen./Insp.Hisham Bin. Nawami was hit in the chest was taken to Hospital in Johore Bahru---]
	+	In another gun battle F.M. Police & Gurkha troops Killed 6 CT's on the Kota Estate near Rasa Negri Sembilan The CT's numbered at least 40 were driven off---]
Thur. 19th		**19 TO/Mech. J. J. Breen.** & **O/S. J.W. Bulmer.** Royal Navy, aboard H.M.S. 'ALACRITY' drowned whilst boarding a Motor Boat from a Sampan. _Kuala Terengganu Cemetery_ J.W.Bulmer. Lost at sea. _[No known Grave] Terandak Wall Memorial Malacca_---]
	+	**19** The crew of a R. A. F. Dakota C4 No. KJ962 110 Sqdn. **F/Lt. F. Blackburn.- F/O. D.L. Moore.- F/Lt. W.E. Lyne,|- Nav.II J. H. Ward. & Sig.1. W.G. Brown.** of 45 Sqdn R. A. F.. Whilst on a supply drop, during a second run over the Drop Zone (DZ)in the Betu Melintang area. Developed engine trouble & crashed, exploding on impact. _Kranji Singapore # 3 / D – 9 - 8 3 / C -1- 3 - 2_ ---]
	+	**19. W.O.1. A . F. Broughton.** R.E.M.E.. Died*** _Kranji Singapore # 1 / B -8._---]
	+	19. HMT DEVONSHIRE sailed Singapore enroute to Liverpool with returning Service personnel---]
Fri. 20th		**20. Sgt.Chandrabahadur. Pun**. 6th. Queen Elizabeth's Own Gurkha Rifles. Died from his wounds recv'd in an ambush. Civil Hospital Kuala Lipis _Kuala Lumpur # 24 / 2._---]
	+	5 CT's raided the house of the Supervisor **Ban Sin Kong** in the Subei Besi area of Selangor and shot dead him dead. Then looted $ 200 $ & a horde of jewellery.---]
	+	20. HMT DILWARA sailed Southampton en route to Singapore / Hong Kong. On board were The 4th. Hussars bound for Malaya.---]
	+	20. HMT DUNERA arrived Southampton with returning Service personnel---]
Sat. 21st		400 Troops & F. M. Police carried out a huge sweep in an area of Sungei Way & Sungei Bulah. Killing 7 CT.s During the Action Engaging CT's **Gnr. G. A. Vickers.** Royal Artillery. was Killed Engaging CT's

	Kuala .Lumpur # 14 / 914.---]
+	25 CT's attacked the Police Post at the Wan Lee Mine 12 miles N. of Ipoh. F.M. Police Killed 2 CT's. ---]
+	Gurkha troops Killed a well-known CT named as **Pan Yoon Yin** in the Sedenak area of Johore. ---]
+	An amphibious landing. The first of its kind in Malaya took place at several points along the Johore coast. A combined force of Gurkhas & F.M Police began a sweep of the inland. coast---]
+	On the Timor Estate. Johore. 5 F.M Police Special Constables had a gun fight with 30 CT's, wounding the CT's, they retreated. A follow up discovered blood stains at a road block, but the tracks were lost ---]
+	14 Chinese Members of the MCP were arrested by F. M. Police at Changkat Patal 10 miles S.W of Tapah ---]
+	A night Strike was carried out by Beaufighters of 54 Sqdn. On a target North of Parit Bunter Perak---]
Sun. 22nd	At dawn R. A. F. Spitfires strafed an area in the Kuantan District with rocket and machine gun fire---]
+	Later in the day Beaufighters bombed a wide area in Kedah where CT's were hiding.---]
Mon. 23rd	Gurkha troops, Royal Inniskilling Fusiliers, - Singapore & Johore State F.M. Police, together with Royal Marines from H.M.S. *SUFFOLK*. Took part in an amphibious landing. Advancing inland carried out searches of numbers of villages. Although no CT's were found, valuable information was collated. ---]
Tue. 24th	Kuala Lumpur Talks between the Thailand Government and Malayan Government regarding: *'The permission to waive Border control over British Troops & F.M Police to cross the border when persuing fleeing Communist Terrorist was agreed'---]*
+	U.S.A. The American Government announced: *'It was sending by air about US $ 50,000 of arms & ammunition for the British Authorities in Malaya. In some cases, deliveries had been made to American owned Tin and Rubber Companies. For the defence of their properties against marauding bandits.'---]*
+	24 HMT DORSETSHIRE arrived Singapore. With replacement Service personnel---]
Wed. 25th	London: Both the British and Malayan Governments realised that: *'Stern Action Engaging CT's must be taken as the armed insurrection in Malaya. Is directly associated with Communist activities throughout South East Asia'--]*
+	Kuala Lumpur: It was announced: *'200 more men of the Palestine Police Force. Will be enroute to Malaya. Increasing the number to 500. Specifically, to train Estate Guards and carry out special defence measures for Estates'---]*
+	25 HMT DORSETSHIRE sailed Singapore. Bound for Liverpool with returning Service personnel---]
Thur. 26th	26 O/S. R.W. Glen. Royal Navy H.M.S. *NORFOLK*. Died*** *Kranji Singapore # C / 10---]*
+	50 Black shirted and masked CT's. Raided the Amber Estate near Senai, 13 miles from Johore Bahru. They Killed the Estate Dresser & wounded 5 people including a 5-year-old girl (*all unnamed*). They robbed the medical supplies and set light to the Office & packing shed. A bugle was sounded before and after the attack]
Fri. 27th	Kuala Lumpur: The Federation Government have offered rewards of up to $120,000 for 12 senior men of the Malayan Communist Party named as: **Wu Tien Wang.** Chief Propagandist; **Lee Soong (alias Chuah Siew Nga); Pang Kun Yin; Fong Choon Loy; Chee Ah Kong; Teng Fook Leong** (Commander); **Chen Tien** (alias **Lau Kow.** Commander of the 7th. Regt. Johore); **Lau Mah** (Captain of the 5th Regt. Perak) Ong **Cheng Hwa; Soon Yoon Heng; Pal Tze Moke; & Wong Cheng.** ---]
Sat. 28th	28 AC2. Mohamed. Ali. Bin. Ramli. R.A.F.(MOR) Died*** *[Claimed by next of Kin] ---]*
+	Two Police squads. Killed 2 CT's. One at a Chinese Kongsi near Jempol Estate Seremban and the other in the area of Malacca ---]
+	28 In Negri Sembilan.100 C.T's attacked a village, & the nearby Tambah Tin mine. Killing the Manager. **Mr. J. Hunter.** & a F.M. Malay Constable (*unnamed*). ---]
+	In accordance with the Regulations. A CT **Tan Ah Kwang** was sentenced to death by hanging---]. 7 CT's. were captured at Chankat Chermin near Tronoh Ipoh. Police Killed 1 CT. in the raid. ---]
+	Armed CT's raided the Ulu Pedas Estate in the Seremban – Lenggeng area. Killed the Estate Syce and set light to a garage. ---]
Sun. 29th	29 Pte. A.J. Wonnacott. 1st. Devonshire Regt. Died*** *Kranji Singapore # 1 / E - 4---]*
+	Operation *"Soccer"* began. Singapore Police, Inniskilling & Gurkha troops swept the whole of the Pontian Peninsular. During the operation **C/Sgt. Karnabahadu. Limbu** 10th Princess Mary's Own Gurkha Rifles. Died in a road accident. *Kranji Singapore # 7 / D / 4* ---]
Mon.30th	London: In a broadcast to the nation, the Prime Minister Mr. Clement Attlee announced: *The Government's decision. To extend the period of National Service from, 18 Months to 2 years. Stating that the Governments full defence plans, will be laid before Parliament when it reassembled on Sept. 12th. Adding that a short bill would be introduced for the extension of the period of National Service. The White Papers dealing respectively, with the extensions of the period of National Service & with the increases in forces pay, was published (refer to Hansard 1950.) From then on due to the political state of*

	+	"**WORLD AFFAIRS**" there was little of any further debate or revision that effected the Bill. This caused wide spread concern amongst all National Servicemen who were forced into another additional 6 Months Service'.] Operation "*Shawcross*" of the Ferret Force ended. Gathering useful information on operating in the jungle also on-air drops. from the R. A. F. Sir. Grerald Harding Commander -In -Chief Land Forces. sought the assistance of Mike Calvert (Mad Mike as he was known) A former Chindit in Burma who knew all about jungle warfare. Calvert was required to carry out a survey of the position in the jungle of Squatters and how they were scattered. They being an easy source for supporting the CT's. The results of his report lead to the formation of the Malayan Scouts. Together with five points regarding the Squatters situation. That latter were integrated into & form part of The Briggs Plan. Under the guidance of Sir. Gerald Briggs. Calvert was Chosen to form the Malayan Scouts & had problems in seeking volunteers from within the Security forces. However, he began his quest to form the future Malayan Scouts Unit ---]
Tue. 31st		**31 Dvr. T. E. Brown.** R.A.S.C.. Died drowning incident. Kuala Lumpur area. *Kuala Lumpur # 32 / 1243* ---]

SEPTEMBER

Wed. 1st		At Baling Kedah near the Thailand border. A R.A.F. strike wiped out a bandit camp. ---]
	+	Troops of the Devonshire Regt. attacked & captured a CT camp in the Kluang area of Johore. The C.T's had already fled the camp back into the jungle. A search of the camp revealed a big cache of ammunition---]
	+	**Dr. Ong Cheng-Keng.** Leader of the Chinese Community in Malaya. A strong speaker against the C.T's. was found shot dead on a road near Western Road George Town Penang. ---]
Thur. 2nd		**2** CT's of the 7th. Regt. MRLA Captured at Chank Chermin on Sunday. Were identified as the 2 that Killed Australian Miner **Mr. B. P Wills.** on August 12th.---]
	+	In the Pontian District of S. Johore. During a 5-day operation "*Soccer.*" Inniskilling troops and F.M. Police discovered several camps holding large quanties of ammunition guns and clothing. All were destroyed---]
	+	In a coffee shop in Balik Paulau Penang. A Chinese F.M. Detective **Lean Hock** was shot dead by a CT---]
Fri. 3rd		**3 Gnr L. E Hanson.** Royal Artillery Died*** *Kranji Singapore # 1 / B 10* ---]
	+	A CT Camp in the jungle identified by R. A. F. air reconnaissance photos. Was found by troops of the Devonshire Regt. It was deserted. In one of the huts, ammunition was found. The Camp was destroyed.---]
	+	Kuala Lumpur: It was announced: '*Sir. Henry Gurney formerly Chief Secretary to the Government of Palestine would take up Office in the Federation on the 6th.Oct.*'---]
Sat. 4th		**4 Pte. H. M. Davies.** Sub. W. R. A. C. Died*** *Kranji Singapore # 1 / B - 11*---]
Sun. 5th		**5 Rfn. Keshabir Thapa.** 2nd. King Edward VII's Own Gurkha Rifles Killed in Action Engaging CT's. *[No known Grave] Terandak Wall Memorial Malacca* ---]
	+	**5 HMT EMPIRE TROOPER** left Southampton on board were the 2nd Brigade of Guards outward bound for Singapore for a tour of Active Service in Malaya. ---]
Mon. 6th		**6 L/Cpl's. Birdal. Rai. - Rfn. Sirinan. Limbu.** 7th. Duke of Edinburgh 's Own Gurkha Rifles. Died from wounds received in a clash with CT's in the Jalong area of Perak. *[No known Graves] Terandak wall Memorial Malacca*---]
	+	**6 Pte. M.R.D. Appuhamy.** Royal Pioneer Corps (Ceylon) Died *** *Kranji Singapore. # 7 / B - 12* ---]
	+	Kuala Lumpur: Sir. Henry Gurney was appointed High Commissioner for the Federation of Malaya. ---]
Tue. 7th		**7 C.Q.M.S. G.F. Gordon.** 1st. Royal Inniskilling Fuss. Died *** *Kranji Singapore. # 1 / B - 13*---]
	+	20 CT's attacked the Temiang Renchong Estate in the Panchor area of Batu Pahat Johore. They burnt down the Factory & Labourers huts---]
Wed. 8th		R.A.F Beaufighters carried out in two sorties a bombing raid on two camps identified as CT Training Camps. They were followed up by Spitfires, firing rocket and machine guns. During the raid after dropping a 500lb bomb on a CT Camp. As the Spitfire pulling out of the dive it stalled, span out of control & crashed into the jungle 8 mis. East of Ruab.The pilot of Spitfire TP225 of 60 Sqdn. R.A.F. **Plt.III L. Brown.** was Killed. *Kuala Lumpur # 16 / 925*---]
	+	A large party of CT's attacked the village of Yong Ping in Johore. Dividing into two section, one section attacked the Police Station, the other section entered the town, killing 2 Chinese men---]
Thur. 9th		**9 Insp. Samsudin & Sgt. Hamid.** F. M. Police were Killed in an ambush at Sintok near the Thailand Border. Other Constables were wounded and taken prisoners by the CT's---]
Fri. 10th		**10 Pte. K. K. Abraham.** Royal Pioneer Corps Ceylon Died*** *Kranji Singapore. # 7 / B - 13*---]
	+	4 Spitires attacked a Hut in the Metakab area. A follow up discovered 4 Dead CT's.
Sat. 11th		**11 Cpl. Bhagbabahadur Thapa.** 6th. Queen Elizabeth's Own Gurkha Rifle Died MRS Ipoh. *Sulva Lines # 53* Ipoh. Perak---]

Sun. 12th	**12 Mr. George Wilson**. Assistant Manager. of the Waterfall Estate near Bawang Selangor. Whilst driving his car with his son Georgie a passenger. Drove into an CT ambush, less than two miles from his Bungalow. **Mr. Wilson** opened fire, but was fatally wounded. A CT walked upto the car & ordered Georgie to run home. His mother who had heard the shots was hiding in the Rubber trees, heard him called out. *'Mummy mummy daddy's dead.'* **Mr. Wilson** was the overseer of the registration of all the Estate workers & as an example, was singled out, and shot dead.---]
+	In an area North of Johore Bahru Operation *"Mah Jon"* began to take control of the area near Poh Lee Sen. By Gurkha & Inniskilling Fusillier troops---]
+	12 HMT LANCASHIRE arrived Liverpool with returning Service personnel ---]
+	12 HMT DUNERA sailed Southampton bound for Singapore & Hong Kong On board were The 2nd part of the Guards Brigade to re-inforce the Brigade already in transit to Malaya ---]
Mon. 13th	Singapore: Police in co-operation with the Dutch authorities seized 3 ½. tons of arms from a Catalina Flying Boat of Philippine origin. It was a Cargo of arms & ammunition en-route to the C T's. Later, the seizure discovered that a large-scale gun running activity was going on into Malaya. ---]
Tue. 14th	**14 Malaya: Gnr. R. Girling.** Royal Artillery Died*** *Kranji Singapore # 1 / B – 12* ---]
+	3 Malays only armed with parangs. Beat off 3 CT's. 2 Chinese armed with a revolver & sawn-off rifle. & 1 Indian with a revolver. The Malays attacked the three, injuring the Indian and 1 Chinese who died later. The other CT escaped. The Indian was handed over to the Muar Police Johore. ---]
+	4 CT's attacked the Chong Kang Estate in the Segamat Area and shot dead 1 Malay (*unnamed*)& wounded several others---]
+	20 armed CT's attacked the Yoon HIn Mine near Tapah and set alight 3 Kongsi Houses & the Machinery House.---]
Wed. 15th	An Australian mining engineer **Mr. W.W. Archer.** working at the Rawang Tin Field. Selangor, was shot dead by a gang of C. T's. ---]
+	Near Taiping F.M. Police and Troops searching in the jungle around Bukit Palong Tinggi, for a CT camp. Engaged a Platoon of 15 CT's. During the battle they wounded several CT's, who eventually fled, carrying their wounded. In the follow up they found lying propped up against a tree a dead CT. Identified as **Chan Tsng Chuan.** A well-known communist leader from Taiping. At the camp they found a food dump, ammunition & arms. Later they arrested 4 Chinese at a Saw Mill suspected of supplying food to the CT's. ---]
Thur. 16th	**16 Mrs. Robertson.** a British civilian aged 20. Was shot & Killed by CT's in Selangor. ---]
+	4 CT's were hanged in Puku Jail Kuala Lumpur named as **Lui Chow - Wong Hing. - Khoon Kool Sang & Hiew Ah Min.**---]
+	16 HMT DILWARA arrived Singapore with the 4th. Royal Hussars on board to take up Patrol duties in Malaya]
Fri. 17th	R. A. F. Spitfires & Beaufighters carried out a concentrated attack on a CT encampment in North Selangor. Three waves of rockets and bombs destroyed the area ---]
+	A combined Military and F.M Police force. Killed 1 CT and captured 4 in the Bukit Kepong area of Muar Johore]
+	Singapore: After a 2 day wait Singapore Police seized 1 1/2. tons of arms & ammunition flown in on a Catalina Flying Boat. Run by a group of Philopene Gun Runners ---]
+	Malaya: R.A.F. Spitfires & Beaufighter in 3 waves attacked a CT encampment in deep jungle in N. Selangor with rocket and machine guns. ---]
+	Behind the Tualang Police Station 24 miles South of Ipoh. CT's Killed a Chinese man---]
Sat. 18th	Security Forcesdiscovered a Terrorist hideout containing ammunition and various other items. In the Batu Caves near Kuala Lumpur. Since September 1942. The caves had been recognised as the "Spiritual Home of the Communist Party." Due to the fate of the whole of the Communist Executive Members, who were killed by the Japanese. ---]
+	18 HMT DILWARA sailed Singapore enroute to Hong Kong---]
Sun. 19th	**19 Maj. K. M. Denning** R.A.S.C Died *** [*Ashes REP*]---]
+	The leader of the 9th. Unit MRLA *Chong Piew* was Killed by Security Forces in the area of Sungei Siput---]
+	19 HMT DEVONSHIRE arrived in Liverpool with returning Service personnel ---]
Mon. 20th	**20 AC1. J. F. Bate.** Marine Fitter of R.A.F. Seletar. Died by Accident*** *Kranji Singapore # 3 / B - 8*---]
+	At the 31 m/s Kuala Lipis / Kuantan road Pahang. A Patrol of the Malay Regt. were ambushed by CT.s
+	S/Sgt. Mohd. Nor. B. Maarof. & Sgt. Mohd. Dian.B. Kecik Malay Regt.were Killed in Action Engaging CT's]
+	John Davis CBE. DSO. No 1 of the Ferret Force set up camp in the caves, South of Ipoh ready to begin their Operational role in the jungles. 67 Recruited men of Military and Civilian backgrounds, the Malay Regt.
+	Gurkhas, plus Chinese Liaison Officer, along with a number of recruited Dyaks. Under the Command of Noel Ross the Dyak Liaison Officer.---]

Tue. 21st	A school teacher & best known Communist leader in Johore. **Tab Ah Sang** Was hanged along with 2 Other CT's (*unnamed*)---]
+	
Wed.22nd	<u>Singapore:</u> The Straits Times. Published its headlines as "***UNDISIRABLES MUST GO.***" Having constantly criticised the Government. On its lack of deporting detainees in their numbers---]
+	<u>Kuala Lumpur:</u> The civil airport of Kuala Lumpur was taken over by the ROYAL AIR FORCE Task force & basically the main centre for Air Operations in Malaya throughout the years of the Emergency. The other main aerodrome being Butterworth on the Malaya Peninsula opposite Penang ---]
Thur. 23rd	30 CT's attacked the Tan Swee Heng Estate Segamat. Burnt down the Factory and Killed the Kepala----]
Fri. 24th	R.A.F. Beaufighters in one wave, bombed a CT hideout, with bombs, rocket & cannon fire. This was followed by a second wave of Spitfires, that strafed the area. Obliterating the CT hideout on a hillside ridge. ---]
+	Gurkhas Killed 1 CT in a gun battle with 5 CT's 6 miles from Sungei Siput---]
+	<u>London</u> : In the House of Commons. The Colonial Secretary Mr. Creech Jones stated: Quote: "*That the general situation in Malaya had shown some improvement as a result of the firm measures taken, to shock the operations of the terrorists. In this "campaign of intimidation & violence "the terrorists had murdered 186 persons mainly Chinese, including 14 European; 158 terrorists had been Killed & over 200 captured; a large number of persons had been detained for "screening "; & quantities of arms had been captured.*" ---] Unquote
Sat. 25th	**25 Pte. J. B. Eglington.** Seaforth Highlanders. Died *** <u>*Taiping # K / 5*</u>.Perak---]
+	<u>Malaya</u> : 2 F. M. Police Specials trailing 3 known CT's. Killed 1 & arrested 1 other, the other escaped. 5 miles N.E. of Batu Gaja Perak. The arrested CT was known as **Siew Chong Kee** ---]
+	A small Platoon. of F.M. Police attacked a CT camp in the Utam Simpan area near Rawang. The CT's were at a better avantage than the Police. The hut was on the top of a rise with open ground In front. 4 CT's opended fire forcing the Police to throw themselves to the ground. One PC Tara Singh got up and opened fire on the CT's killing one of the CT's. His bravery ensured the other Police to fire at the CT's killing the other 3 CT's. PC Tara Singh was awarded the CPM. 23/1/48 LG 39464---]
+	Security Forces shot dead 1 CT near Pirnak Halt on the Lipid Estate Johore another CT escaped---.]
+	At the 29th. m/s Lijok road Perak. Security Forces arrested 2 Senior members of the Bukit Belong Tinggi Platoon---]
+	8 CT's attacked the Berhang River Estate Perak. Killed the Contractor (***unnamed***) using bayonets.---]
+	After a 36 hour siege. F. M. Police threw Tear Gas bombs into a cave at the 3 m/s Chemor Road near Ipoh. 3 CT's were captured 1 was **Lee Yoon Choy** Leader of the 5th. Coy 1st Unit of the MRLA ---]
Sun. 26th	**26 Pte. E.F. Anderson.** R.A.S.C. Was found Shot Dead. <u>*Kuala Lumpur # 14 / 915*</u>---]
+	<u>Kuala Lumpur:</u> Major. Gen. C. H. Boucher G.O.C. Malaya announced: '*A specially trained force had been formed known as the "Ferret Force." made up of ex-Chindit officers, including British, Gurkha, Malay Troops, including Dyaks Trackers. Their purpose was to seek out the C.T.'s in the Jungle.*'---]
Mon. 27th	In the Jungles near Metakab. A Patrol of the Ferret Force. Killed 2 CT's ---]
+	***Lim Chong*** a named CT on the wanted list, Was shot by one of his own men on the Tanah Merah Estate Port Dickson. His assailent surrendered & informed the F. M. Police of his Action .---]
+	In the Pampin- Bahau - Pertang area of Negri Sembilang. A number of CT's stopped a bus & Killed: A Bus Inspector, a Chinese Labourer & a Chinese Timber Contractor.***(all unnamed***) ---]
+	At the 43rd. m/s Kuala – Pertang road 3 CT's shot dead **Lia Ting** a Timber contractor, & 2 Labourers (***unnamed***)]---]
+	On the Ayer Puteh Estate. 15 CT's burnt down the Rubber Store.---]
+	8 CT's raided the Berhang River Estate. Seized the Chinese Labourers Contractor (***unnamed***) bayoneted him to death. Gathered all the labourerers together. Then set light to their huts---]
Tue. 28th	At Batu Gaja a Chinese School Teacher (***unnamed***) was Killed by a CT.---]
+	In an attempt to cut CT communications. Troops of the 1st. Devonshire Regt. Took to motor boats and native river craft, on the Sembrong & Legor rivers. Whilst a similar force of the Devonshires advanced through the jungles from the Kluang / Mesin road ---]
+	At the Jerentat- Choh 25 m/s. Police & Military troops Shot 2 CT's killing 1wounding the other. ---]
	In Sungei Siput. Military Troops opened fire on an armed CT. Killing him.---]
+	CT's Killed an Indian Tapper (***unnamed***) in the Sangat area.---]
+	At the 20th.m/s Bahau Dangi Road. A Military Patrol engaged 6 CT's killing 4 wounding one.Two escaped.-]
+	**28 HMT DORSETSHIRE** arrived Liverpool with returning Service personnel---]
Wed. 29th	On a road leading to the Bedford Estate Slim River area. An F.M. Police Constable shot dead a CT just as he was entering deep undergrowth.---]

	+	In the Kluang area of Johore. A Police & Military Platoon engaged 2 CT's and Killed one. The other CT threw a grenade wounding two Soldiers. The other CT escaped---]
Thur. 30th		**30 L/Cpl. Bhagbahadur Rana.** 2nd. King Edward VII's Own Gurkha Rifles Died *** _Kranji Singapore # 7 /D -5_]
	+	**30 Capt. R. Bridgett.** Royal Engineers Died *** _Kranji Singapore # 1 / A -14_ ---]
	+	In the Sungei Bulau area of Selengor Police attacked a CT camp with about 10 CT's. They threw grenades after the fleeing CT's. A follow up revealed 1 dead CT. body.---]
	+	10 CT's attacked a Mandore's house at Kampong Malak Selengor. Where the Mandore & his brother were eating. They shot dead the Mandore. His brother escaped.---]
	+	In the Kluang district of Johore. Troops and F. M. Police Killed 1 CT.---]
	+	On a small Estate near the Kampas Estate Kluang.Troops and F. M. Police Killed 1 CT ---].
	+	On the Bedford Estate, in the Kuala Kabu Kabu area. Security Forces Killed 1 CT---]
	+	Singapore/Malaya By the end of September: Figures issued stated: 'Their were 3,800 Detainees in Detention Camps The British Government regarded the Chinese Squatters, who were actively assisting the Communist Terrorist were a threat to the hinderence of the fight against the MCP. Immediate Action Engaging CT's should be taken to repatriate not banish those in detention.'---]

OCTOBER

Fri. 1st		**1 L/Cpl. N. Edland.** R.A.S.C. Died found shot dead. _Taiping # F / 70_ Perak---]
	+	In Ipoh a group of CT's threw hand grenades into the office of the Kuomintang Newspaper : Kin Kwok Daily News. Killing one reporter (**unnamed**) & wounding several others.---]
	+	1 HMT LANCASHIRE sailed Liverpool bound for Singapore & Hong Kong with replacement Service personnel ---]
Sat. 2nd		**2** Near Bidor Perak. 4 Platoon 'B' Company K.O.Y.L.I. Had been on the rifle range, under the command of Capt. D. G. Lock. (Somerset L. I.) Att/to the K.O.Y.L.I 's. Having posted two sentries & unaware of any pending danger, leaving several troops bathing in a jungle pool. When a number of C.T's opened fire upon the swimmers. The two sentries returned fire on the CT's. Killing one & wounding another. Unfortunately, the CT's fusilage Killed **Capt. D. G. Lock**.- **L/Cpl. K. Hutchinson** - **Pte.'s A. Dobson**, - **H. Woodhouse**. Wounding several others. Two of the less wounded, headed back to camp to raise the alarm. Immediately, soldiers set off to the scene of the ambush, but arrived to late. Finding the carnage & a wounded CT. Who was despatched without ceremony. Capt Lock had forty-two bullet wounds in his body. _Batu Gajah # 394 - 395 – 396 - 397_ Ipoh Perak---]
	+	On the Shenghai Estate in the Bentong area of Pahang. 3 masked Chinese men approached the Factory. When challenged by the Estate guards, they ran off.---]
	+	5 Chinese men approached the Telemog Estate in the Betong area. Where they were challenged and fired at by the Estate Guards. Without returning their fire they retreated.---]
Sun. 3rd		**3 Mr. Wata Kaya** a civilian was shot & Killed in Selengor by a Chinese gunman---]
	+	In the Metakab area. A F.M. Police together with a small Military force raided the Paya Mengkuang area & fired on 3 armed CT's, who threw grenades at the force wounding I Malay soldier. The CT's dispersed.---]
	+	2 Chinese men carrying shot guns. Fired at a Padi Planter walking along the Metakab / Meran road, wounding him in the legs ---]
	+	At the Kranmat Tin Mine 8 miles S.E of Ipoh. A gang of CT's attacked the Bungalow. The Secruity Guards opened fire on the attackers. who fled.---]
Mon. 4th		London The situation on Malaya and Demobilisation of Forces, was the subject of debates held by the Labour Cabinet. Without any conclusion.---]
	+	4 HMT EMPIRE TROOPER arrived Singapore with the Brigade of Guards ---]
Tue. 5th		Malaya : **5** During an ambush in the Lintang area. 10 Gurkha troops of the 2nd. King Edward VII's Own Gurkha Rifles were Killed: **Cpl. Bhimbahadur Thapa**.- **Rfn's . Aiman Gurung** .- **Chadrabahadur Thapa** .- **Pedambahadur. Thapa**. - **Pare. Gurung**. – **Ranbahadur. Pun**.- **Resambahadur.Gurung** – **Santabahadur Ghale**. - **Ruksing. Thapa**. - **Keshabir.Thapa**. _[No known Graves]Terandak Wall Memorial Malacca]_ ---]
	+	**5 Pte. M. R.D. Appuhamy.** R.P.C .(Ceylon) Died*** _Kranji Singapore # 7 / B 12_ ---]
	+	Singapore : Mr. Malcolm MacDonald. flew out of Singapore enroute to a meeting in London.---]
	+	5 HMT DILWARA arrived Southampton with returning Service personnel ---]
Wed. 6th		**6 Cpl. Jogbahadur Pun.** 2nd. King Edward VII's Own Gurkha Rifles. Killed in Action Engaging CT's. _[No known Grave] Terandak Wall Memorial Malacca_.---]
	+	6 HMT DILWARA sailed Singapore bound for Southampton with returning Service personnel ---]
Thur. 7th		**7 Mr. N Searson.** Asstn. Manager. Of the Rasa Estate Selangor. Died from Muliple gun shot wounds Killed by

		CT's---]
	+	In search of 2 compatriots who were kidnapped by CT's. 100 Malayan Youths of the Berisan Permuda Malayu.Formed their own search party and entered the jungle in the district area of Mantin. They found a new CT camp under construction and burnt it to the ground.---]
	+	7 At Sungei Murai village 4 miles from Bentong. 2 uniformed CT's walked into a Chinese School & in front of the children, shot the headmaster **Mr. Yim Theen Hoong**. He was a member of the Kuomingtang. Unchallenged the CT's just left the building.---]
	+	At Kampong Titi in Tanjong Tualang. 10 miles South of Batu Gaja. CT's shot dead a Pork seller. (***unnamed*** --]
	+	A number of CT's. Attacked the Budu Estate near Kuala Lipis & Killed 1 Special Constable (***unnamed)*** ---]
	+	On the Ben Heng Estate. 3 CT's attacked the Factory & Bungalow. The Estate Guards opened fire & after a short engagement the CT's withdrew.---]
Fri.	8th	2 armed CT's approached the Controller Officer of the Gemas Railway Station. When challenged by the Two Security Guards They ran off.---]
	+	600 Grenadier Guards and Officers Arrived at a camp in Sungei Besi 7 miles from Kuala Lumpur---]
	+	8 HMT DEVONSHIRE sailed Liverpool bound for Singapore with replacement Service personnel---]
Sat.	9th	**9 Pte. K K Abraham**. R.P.C. (Ceylon) Died *** *Kranji Singapore # 7 / B - 13*---]
Sun.	10th	**10 Gnr. O.K. Glynn**. Royal Artillery Died *** *Kranji Singapore # 1 / E - 11* ---]
	+	**10 Mr. A.J.F Permin**. Manager. of the Mayfield Estate Tasek Glugor Penang. Died from multiple gunshot wounds Accidental Death ---]
	+	In the jungle near Batu Sawa Pahang. A Patrol of the Malay Regt. Killed 1 CT ---]
	+	Armed Guards lined the streets of Bentong for the funeral of **Mr. Yim Theen Hoong**. Killed on the 8th. All Students from the Che Hwai school attended his funeral---]
	+	10 HMT DUNERA arrived Singapore with replacement Service personnel ---]
Mon.	11th	**11 Cpl. D. Roe**. 1st. Devonshire Regt. Died from wounds recv'd during an ambush. *Kranji Singapore # 1 / A - 15*
	+	**11 Recruit Dorje Tamang**. 10th.Princess Mary's Own Gurkha Rifles Training Wing Died*** *Kranji Singapore # 7 / D - 6*---]
	+	In jungles areas of N. Johore. After a months search, Gurkha & Royal Inniskilling Troops, captured the village of *Poh Lee Sen* the CT's HQ. Capturing munitions of various sorts, Russian flags & Communist literature. The CT's having already disappeared back into the Jungle. The village was set alight---]
	+	In two Separate attacks on the Shen Shi & Hanima Estates Johore. F. M. Police Special Constables drove off a gang of CT's ---]
	+	During an attack on the Perhentian Estate in Negri Sembilan. F.M.Police. Special Constables drove off another CT attack ---]
	+	On the Chean Estate near Kuala Kangsar. 4 CT's Burnt down the Kongsi house and Smoke House ---]
	+	11 HMT EMPIRE TROOPER sailed Singapore bound for Southampton.with returning Service personnel ---]
	+	11 HMT DUNERA sailed Singapore. bound for Calcutta. Via Penang ---]
Tue.	12th	**12 Gnr. K.H. Williams**. Royal Artillery Died *** *Kranji Singapore # 1 / B - 14* ---]
	+	F.M. CID & Police raided 3 houses 3 miles outside of Kuala Lumpur & arrested 2 important Chinese men known as CT's---]
Wed.	13th	A Chinese women. A CT Propagandist was arrested by the F.M. CID & Police in the Tenah area of Tapah ---]
	+	In the village of Kachua 2 miles S. of Kuala Kangsar. A Malay CT was Killed by F. M Police.---]
	+	A number of CT's attacked the Police Post on the Tengkin Tin Mine near Sungei Siput They were beaten off by the Special Guards.---]
	+	On the Moy Boglor Estate in Kedah.F.M.Special Police drove off an attack by a number of CT's ---]
	+	Covering an area of over 600 square mile in Johore Another large scale coordinated operation Involving troops of the Seaforth Highlanders, The Devonshire Regt., the Gurkhas, Ferret Force & F.M. Police ended with results of 27 CT's. Killed 152 detained & 12 camps destroyed. Thus gaining control of that area.---]
	+	13 R.A.F. Spitfires & Beaufighters, destroyed a CT camp in the jungles of Central Perak.---]
Thur.	14th	**14 Mr.Kenneth. G. Jenkins**. A British civilian was Killed by a lone CT. Gunman No additional details---]
	+	Auster numberTJ602 AOP5 of 656 Sqdn. R. A. A. Whilst in a forced landing. Crashed 21 miles North of Kuala Lumpur. The Pilot was unhurt ---]
	+	In the village of Pagoh near Muar. 2 CT's Killed **Mr. Heng Hock Kuan** a Hylam Bookshop keeper. & another Chinese Rice Dealer: **Mr. Sam Yet**.---]
	+	In Sampang Tiggi. 3 CT's shot and Killed **Ting See Tong** a Padi Planter ---]
	+	2 miles from the railway line at Bukit Kuan Mentakab. 6 CT's Killed a Malay worker (***unnamed)*** ---]
	+	In Langgor Kedak. A Malay carrying a shot gun. Was challenged by F.M. Police. As he raised his gun was shot

		and Killed.---]
Fri.	15th	**15 Pol/L. Shamsuudin B. Mohd. Ali.** F. M. Police. Killed on CT Ops. Kedah.---]
	+	**15 Mr. J. Moss.** DFC & Bar. Ex R.A.F. Sdn/Ldr. & Asstn. Manager. of the Jerantut Estate Pahang was shot dead by a lone CT gunman.Pahang.---]
	+	Kuala Lumpur: Emergency Regulation 17 D. were brought into force : (Aliens Immigration): Aliens who were deemed to be illegal immigrants were liable to deportation to the country of their birth or citizenship - (Travel Restriction): Perrmission required by all Persons excluding the local born landing in Malaya. ---]
	+	Operation *"Rugger"* began in Johore.---]
	+	Operation *"Kukri "* began in Perak.---]
Sat.	16th	Hidden in the jungle near Bidor Perak. A Platoon of the Coldstream Guards on their first Action Engaging CT's. Seized a CT armaments workshop---]
Sun.	17th	On information received from local Sakai's. 6 Platoon 'B' Company K.O.Y.L.I.'s . Moved into the jungle to seek out the members of the CT's, who ambushed the swimming party. On the 2nd.day, nearing twilight, they came across a Basha in the jungle. They lay in ambush positions overnight. At daybreak, the leading Scout spotted a CT guard outside the Basha. Killed him with shots from his LMG. Another CT appeared in the doorway, he too was shot with many bullets to his body, but surprisingly he escaped into the jungle. The search of the huts revealed bombs, guns, rifle butts that were used for remaking rifles. Later the area was searched & the body of the wounded guard was found dead---]
	+	Near the Pump house of the Sungei Dai Water Catchment. A Labourer of the (PWD) Public Works Department was Killed *(unnamed)* by 3 CT's who opened fire on the working party. Other Labourers escaped unharmed.---]
	+	CT's attacked the Bati Bilai Estate near Kuala Lipis Pahang and burnt down the Smoke House.---]
	+	CT's set alight a building on the Victoria Malaya Estate Negri Sembilan---]
Mon.	18th	**18 Gnr. J.A. Estell.** Royal Artillery. Killed in Action Engaging CT's *Terendak Military Cemetery # CE / E -2*---]
Tue.	19th	**19 Pte. R.F. McQuillan.** R.A.O.C. Died *** [*Ashes . REP*].---]
	+	**19 Pte. A.G. Jamis.** RPC. (Ceylon) Died*** *Singapore # 7 / C - 12.*---]
Wed.	20th	**20** On the Craigielea Estate at Muar. Johore, 30 CT's. ambushed the managers car, driven by the Asstn Manager **Mr. J. Y. Simpson.** Sat. beside him was the Manager. **Mr. S. Harper- Ball.** His normal driver was seated in the back. Who, after the killing of the 2 men, reported the incident to the Seurity Forces . The CT's ordered the two men to walk 30 yards away from the car. Then they were shot through the back of the head.-]
	+	On the Seng Heng Estate Johore. A number of CT's called out a Chinese Kepala *(unnamed)* from his house and shot him dead---]
	+	At the Kampong Ulu Sungei Long Kajang. A Police Patrol shot and Killed two Indonesian CT's and captured 2 others ---]
	+	Operation 'Radio 'began in Kedah. & Operation 'Shawcross' began in Selangor & Pahang---]
	+	Auster TJ647 AOP5 656 Sqdn. Upon landing at Seremban was damaged beyond repair---]
Thur.	21st	**21 Pte V. K. Simion.** Royal Pioneer Corps (Ceylon) Died *** *Kranji Singapore # 7 / C - 13* ---]
	+	Singapore: A further restriction was imposed on People from Singapore:. *'They will not be allowed to cross the Causeway into Malaya unless. They have their Thumb Prints visible on their I/D cards.'*--]
	+	Malaya: In the Bahua area of Negri Sembilan. 7 F.M.Police Constables were in a truck, on their way to an Estate on the main Kuala Pilah/ Bentong road. When CT's in ambush positions opened fire on them. The truck was driven off the road. The Police retunrning fire, Killed 4 CT's, wounded 3 & one escaped.---]
	+	On the Voules Estate Selengor.The President of the Labis Labour Union (*unnamed*)was shot dead by CT's---]
Fri.	22nd	In the village of Gopeng Perak, whilst waiting to have the photos taken for their I/D. Cards. 2 CT's arriving on bikes, shot and wounded 3 Malay children, a Chinese women and a Tamil man. Before riding off. The CT's threw 2 hand grenades into the crowd, which did not explode.---]
Sat.	23rd	**23 WOII. W. Golder.** Inteligence Corp.Killed whilst on CT Ops. *Western Road # 1990* George Town Penang.---]
	+	**23 Fus. J.S. Newell.** 1st. Inniskilling Fus. Died*** *Kranji Singapore # 1 / B - 15* -]
	+	Singapore: The Straits Times issued an editorial. Referring to the Chinese Secret Societies being linked with the Communist.---]
	+	23 HMT DUNERA arrived Penang ---]
Sun.	24th.	24 HMT DUNERA sailed Penang for Singapore ---]
Mon.	25th	**25 Pte. Eglington** Seaforth Highlanders Died *** *Taiping Perak # K 35*---]
	+	**25 S/Sgt. Haji. Tahir. B.Hj. Hussin.** Malay Regt. Killed in Action Engaging CT's.Pahang---]
	+	Malaya :The 2 F.M. Police Constables taken prisoners by the CT.s at Sintok. September 9th. Made their way

		back to Changloon near the Kedak / Thailand border to report their capture. Having been released by the CT's.--]
	+	**25** 6 CT's ambushed a jeep carrying the District Vetinary Inspector of Temerloh Mr. S. Kancrah, the Asstn Vetinary Officer Mr. Silimani Azariah & his son, who was driving the jeep. Shots Killed **Mr. Silimani Azariah** & wounded Mr. S. Kancrah, The CT's ordered the 2 men to walk away towards Chemor. Then set light to the jeep with **Mr. Silimani Azariah** body slumped inside.---]
	+	25 HMT DUNERA arrived Singapore ---]
Tue. 26th		**26 Pte. E.F. Anderson.** R.A.S.C.Died from wounds recv'd.during an CT ambush *Kuala Lumpur # 14 / 915.*---]
	+	**26 F/O G.C.A. Brei.** of 28 Sqdn., flying Spitfire TP376. Was Killed when he crashed on his approach to R. A. F.
	+	Semberwang. *Kranji Singapore.# 3 / A - 1*---]
	+	In the main street of Sungei Pelek 11 miles from Kuala Lumpur. An off duty Gurkha, an Estate Special Constable, together with a Malay Constable. Took on a gang of 10 CT's. The unarmed Gurkha, Killed 2 with a knife. The Malay Constable shot 2 others. The rest of the gang ran off.---]
	+	At Kuala Kangsar 2 CT's were Killed and 3 captured. They were all members of the Batu Arang killer squad. One of them was a Leader of the local MCP.---]
	+	Kuala Lumpur: Sir. Henry Gurney sent a telegram to Mr. Creech Jones. Explaining the Squatter situation: *Up to the beginning of October. There were 3,800 detainees in detention camps & the numbers would increase. What I am proposing. That it is not a case of banishment but repatriation back to their homeland.*---]
	+	In the village of Selangang 8 miles from Kuala Lumpur. 10 CT's chased a Chinese Lad down the main street, firing sten guns at him. He ran into the Police Station unhurt. During the firing 2 bystanders were wounded ---]
	+	26 HMT DILWARA sailed Soutampton bound for Singapore with replacement Service personnel --]
Wed. 27th	+	A Ferret Force Patrol going through a Squatter area of Sungei Siput. Saw 3 armed CT's run out of a hut & opened fire at them. The Ferrets Force returned fire, Killed 1 CT the other 2 escaped.---]
	+	A Sentry at the Tronoh Tin Mines. Stopped 4 CT's from entering. Killing 1. the others fled.---]
	+	CT's shot dead, **Mr. Yip Sek Yin** the Kuomintang President of the Ayer Kunning Village ---]
Thur. 28th		**28** At the 19th m/s Taiping/Selama Road Perak. In an ambush by CT's. **Pol.Insp. Mohd. Idris. B. Chek.** F. M. Police & 6 PC's (*unnamed*). were Killed ---]
		28 Operation *"Diabolo"* began in Johore.**---**]
	+	A gun battle between a Patrol of F. M. Police & 4 CT's. At Kuala Paya Buleh Kasep. The Police Killed 1
	+	captured 2. The 4th. escaped.---]
	+	Troops in an ambush near Sangil Muar Killed 1 CT. ---]
Fri. 29th.		In Lahat 5 miles S. of Ipoh. During a follow up F. M. Police Surrounded a house. When 3 CT's ran out. 1 was Killed and 2 wounded.--]
	+	A Malay Chargeman (*unnamed*) was Killed by CT's when they attacked the sub Station Pin Soon, near Batu Gaja ---]
	+	R. A. F. Beaufighters and Spitfire bombed and strafed a CT camp in the area of Sungei Penting---]
	+	29 HMT LANCASHIRE arrived Singapore with replacement Service personnel---]
Sat. 30th	+	**30 Mr. S.E. Hickman**. a Tin Miner & other Chinese miners? Of the Pahang Consolidated Tin Mines. Were Killed when C.T.'s ambushed a train.---]
		30 HMT LANCASHIRE sailed Singapore bound for Hong Kong---]
Sun. 31st	+	**31 Dvr. G. Legge.** R.A.S.C. During the Singapore riots Killed in Aid of Civil Power *Kranji Singapore # 1 / B -1---.*]
		31 B.Q.M.S. N. R. Daunt. Royal Artillery was Killed in a road ambush in the area of Johore.
	+	*Kuala Lumpur # 14 / 916.*---]
	+	Bentong. Three air strikes were made.by RAF Bombers. Destroying the camp totally. Leaving large craters.---]
	+	In the Bailing area of S. Kedah. A Patrol of the 7th. Gurkhas Killed 4 CT's ---]
	+	A Patrol of the Devonshire Regt. Killed 2 CT's in an area South of Ayer Hitan---]
	+	CT's raided the Puteh Tin Dredging Company's property and destroyed everything---]
	+	4 CT's walked into an Indian Coffee Shop. shot dead **Mr. Hong Tian Hoon.** The Manager of the Kuala Lumpur - Kluang – Port Swettenham Bus Company ---]
	+	Due to CT's attempting to blow up a bridge between Regan & Kulai. The blast damaged brickwork on the bridge, railway sleepers and lengths of rail track. The night train from Kuala Lumpur to Singapore, was delayed 8 hours. ---]
	+	A number of CT's. Opened fire at the Police Post at the 18th mile Cameron Highlands. The firing began at 7.30 p.m. & continued for two hours until reinforcements arrived'. The CT's disappeared. No casualties reported---]
	+	Kuala Lumpur.: General Boucher. Although a strong supporter of the principal of the Ferrett Force and its proven success within the months it had been on Operations. Informed John Davis CBE. DSO., the Ferrett

		Force was to be Disbanded and taken over by Army Units. Obviously to be run by Army personnel Not Civilians.---]
	+	31 **HMT DUNERA** sailed Singapore bound for Southampton with returning Service personnel ---]

NOVEMBER

Mon. 1st		A quarter of a mile away from the village of Kachau. CT's raided the Dominions Estate. They set fire to all the buildings, except the Labourers lines ---]
	+	Near the village of Kachua another group of CT's attacked the Puteh Tin Dredging Company's property and destroyed all the machinery.---]
	+	The Ferret Force on operation in the Sungei Siput area. Removed & relocated 500 Squatters along a 19 mile stretch of the Jalong road. It was a known area of CT sympathisers. ---]
Tue. 2nd		**2** In an ambush on a track running alongside the railway lines near Kuala Lipis. Pahang. Three (3) Pte.'s of the Malay Regt. were Killed & 2 were wounded: Those Killed named as **Pte's: Iajin. B. Chukut.- Aziz B. Othman. - Jamaludin. B. Abd. Chani. ---]**
	+	A F. M. Police Force went to the village of Kachau, a notorious area of CT's. In retaliation to the destruction of the Puteh Tin Dredging Company's property & Dominions Estate. They set fire to several selected buildings, leaving a few buildings intact.---]
Wed. 3rd		On the Mong Hing Tiang Estate near Manchap Malacca. 2 Javanese Laborouers **_(unnamed)_** using parangs, attempting to resist a number of armed CT's, were shot dead. The CT's then set buildings alight.---]
	+	Due to the CT's activities in the various areas in the State of Johore . 18 schools were closed. The last school to close was the Parit Jani School. The residents moved out and went elsewhere.---]
Thur. 4th		A F. M. Police convoy of 3 lorries was ambushed on the Jarantut / Kuantan Road Pahang. 3 Malay Constables **_(unnamed)_** were mortally wounded & several others wounded. The Police returned fire. The CT's fled ---]
	+	10 CT's ambushed 3 F.M. Police Special Constables carrying rations to the Police Post at Tapah. 1 of the Specials was Killed **_(unnamed)_** the other 2 escaped.---]
	+	Kuala Lumpur: The High Commisioner of Police. Mr. W.N. Gray stated: _'During the past three weeks Troops engaged in Operation 'Rugger' have destroyed several CT camp. Killed 15 CT's & possibly 6 more suspected kills & captured more.---]_
	+	**4 HMT DEVONSHIRE** arrived Singapore with more reinforcement troops. Among those were the Womens Auxillary Air Force, & the W.omens Army Corps. Who will be sent to various units as Administrators.---]
	+	**4 HMT DILWARA** arrived Southampton with returning Service personnel ---]
Fri. 5th		**5 Rfn. Chandrabahadur Gurung.** 6th. Queen Elizabeth's Own Gurkha Rifles Died from his wounds recv'd in a clash with CT's Civil Hospital Kuala Lipis. _Kranji Singapore # 7 / D - 7_---]
	+	At Broga Village in the Kajong area. Coldstream Guards on their first operation together with Gurkhas. Killed 1 CT on the Lallang Road, whilst further along the same road a Patrol of Gurkha's Killed another CT.---]
	+	F.M. Police operating in the Tai Keng area Killed I CT.---]
Sat. 6th		**6 W/O2. E. A. L. Pringle** Royal Engineers Died*** _Kranji Singapore # 1 / B - 2_ ---]
	+	**6 Pte. Mohd. Khalid. B. Ab. Chaftar.** Malay Regt. Died from his wounds recv'd. during the ambush on Tuesday the 2nd. Pahang---]
	+	A Patrol of the Seaforth Highlanders operating in the Ma-aki Forest Reserve near Bukit Kepong Killed I CT.--]
	+	A Patrol of the Iniskilling's Killed another CT near the area of Tekek Senghe---]
	+	A Patrol of the Devonshire Regt. Killed 1 CT near Cha-ah.---]
	+	A Patrol of F.M. Police Patrol near Klayan Killed 1 CT.---]
Sun. 7th		**7 Cpl. Gajrath. Mukhiya.** 6th. Queen Elizabeth's Own Gurkha rifles. Died by Accident. North of Jalong road Sungei Siput Perak. _[No known Grave] Terandak Wall Memorial Malacca_---]
	+	**7 PC Ibrahim B. Manap** F.M. Police Killed on Ops.---]
	+	**7** In the Chemor area near Ipoh Perak. In dense jungle, a large CT camp was discovered by the Ferret Force. It was capable of accommodating 100 CT's, with its own rifle range. It was the largest camp found to-date. A follow up a Platoon of Gurkhas attacked the camp . After two fellow Gurkha's had been Killed in the fire fight They fixed bayonets & charged a Platoon of CT's. They wounded many, who were carried off by the survivors. During the engagement Killed in Action Engaging CT's were: -**Cpl. Deobahadur. Thapa.** & **Rfn. Sarki. Gurung** 2nd. King Edward VII's Own Gurkha Rifles. _[No known Graves] Terandak Wall Memorial Malacca._---]
	+	In a sweep in the Muar Lenggat area of Johore. Patrols of Gurkhas & Seaforth Highlanders Killed 7 CT's ---]

		In the area of Kota Tinggi near the Nanga Estate .A Military Patrol engaged a party of CT killing 1.---]
	+	A Patrol of the Ferret Force Killed 1 CT in the Sungei Siput area.---]
	+	7 HMT DEVONSHIRE sailed Singapore bound for Calcutta via Penang ---]
Mon. 8th		**8 Mr. Norman Searson.** Manager. of the Rasa Estate, whilst motor-cycling unescorted, was shot dead in an ambush 30 miles from Kuala Lumpur. ---]
Tue. 9th		**9 Mr. B. Middleton.** Manager. of the Sungei Tekal Palm Oil Estate & a F.M. Police Lt. Went in a car to investigate a fire on the Estate, only to drive into an ambush. Returning fire.**Mr. Middleton** was Killed.---]
Wed. 10th		London: The Foreign Office informed & authorised Sir. Henry Gurney: *'It was of the utmost priority. To introduce a solution to control the problem of potential Chinese Communist Immigrants. This came about by the introduction of the Emergency Regulation 17D. Not a document for discussion, that imposed restriction on. Not only idivuduals of known Communists interest, but also innocent Chinese People. Nevertheless, the necessity of two evil. ---]*
Thur. 11th		Kuala Lumpur: However, Henry Gurney was aware of a bigger proble:. *'That of the vast numbers of Chinese Squatters living on the fringes of the jungles, who potentially could become supporters of the Min Yuen. –]*
	+	Singapore Police found an arms dump on waste ground, between Tiong Bahru Road and Alexanda Road---]
	+	11 HMT EMPIRE TROOPER arrived Southampton with returning Service Personnel---]
Fri. 12th		**12** The pilot of Spitfire TP 231 60 Sqd. R.A.F. **F/ O. P. M. Sketch.** Was Killed when pulling out of a dve bombing raid. The Spitfire crashed into trees. N.E. of Serandah. *[No known Grave]Terandak Wall Memorial Malacca---]*
	+	Later that day. A R.A.F. Dakota KN633. of 110 Sqdn. While searching for F/O. Sketch's lost Spitfire. Flying at low level in a valley, hit trees, flipped over & crashed near Rawang. Its crew on board were all Killed. **Sqdn/Ldr. D.K. Hayes. (Pilot) -Sig11.-N. Tyson. - Nav.11.-F.White.- Ft/Lt. P.G. Ballard.(Observer)** . R.A.F. **Major. R. Q. Gaitley**. King's Regt. (passenger Observer).
	+	*[No known Graves] Terandak Wall Memorial Malacca.—]*
	+	In an CT ambush in the Cameron Highlands. Cpl L.J. Whitehouse & Pte. H. Brown. R.A.S.C. were wounded & taken to the Camerons British Medical Hospital (BMH)---]
	+	Gurkhas and Members of the Ferret Force, found an arms dump in the area of Sungei Siput.---]
	+	In another area of Kampar another arms dump was found by the F. M. Police---]
	+	During a sweep by the 4th. Hussars. Patrolling the roads on the Australasia Estate. Engaged a party of CT's They shot and Killed 2 CT's wounding 4 others---]
	+	**12** 3 Malay Special Constables were Killed *(**unnamed**)*. When a sea mine blew up on the Pontian Beach Pahang---]
	+	2 CT's *(**unnamed**)* sentenced to death were hanged in Johore Bahru Prison.---]
Sat. 13th		**13 Sgt. C.J. Brading.** Royal Engineers Died***_Kuala Lumpur # 14 / 917 ---]_
	+	13 HMT DEVONSHIRE arrived Calcutta ---]
Sun. 14th		**14 Cpl. J.T. Trotter.** R.M.P. Died ***_Taiping. F / 60_ Perak ---]
	+	In the Tanjong Tualang area of Perak. Two Dredging Engineers travelling in a trolley with a dredging party. When approx. twenty (20) CT's ambushed it. Killing **Mr. R.H. Best** (Australian) & **Mr. M.S. Urquhart** (British), together with a Chinese Kepala. *(**unnambed**)* (Kepala means Headman) Several of the guards were wounded in the ambush.---]
Mon. 15th		**15 Asst/Supt. B. F. S. Cooper.** Fed. Malay Police Killed on Ops. _Seremban # ?_ Negri Sembilan ---]
	+	15 HMT DEVONSHIRE sailed Calcutta bound for Singapore via Penang ---]
Tue. 16th		The Bukit Pulai Estate was attacked twice by CT's. At 11p.m. and again at 1 a.m. On both occasions they were beaten off by the Estate Security Guards.---]
Wed. 17th		**17 Pte. H. Brown.** R.A.S.C. Died from wounds recv'd. in the ambush on the 11th.[Ashes. REP]---]
	+	**17 Capt.F. Hambrook.** MC. Seaforth Highlanders. Killed in Action Engaging CT's.Muar Johore. _Kranji Singapore # 1 / B - 3_---]
	+	Kuala Lumpur: Information released stated. During Operation '_Rugger_' in Johore. Military forces Killed 127 CT's - 152 persons were detained & 12 CT camps containing arms ammunition & food were destroyed. ---]
	+	On the Jerantut Estate Special Constables beat off an attack by many CT's ---]
Thur. 18th		Rubber trees producing latex, destroyed by CT's . The cost was estimated in the 10's of thousands of $.-]
	+	After 4 days in the Serendah jungle. 63 Guardsmen of the Scots Guards emerged from the jungle. Having not suceeded in finding the Dakota that crashed on Friday 12th.---]
	+	Near the Sungei Dai Water Catchment near Kuala Kangsar. CT's shot dead a Public Works Department (PWD)Labourer-----]
	+	CT's attacked the Batu Belai Estate near Kuala Lipis Pahang. The Estate Guards returning fire beat them off]

51

	+	On the Rubber Estate's in the area S. of Tapah. CT's used knives to slash Rubber trees. The Estate manager's estimated that over 30,000 trees had been lost to production,which would take many years before they began to produce latex---]
	+	18 HMT EMPIRE HALLADALE sailed Liverpool bound for Singapore with replacement Service personnel --]
Fri. 19th		19 Rfn. Kalibahadur. Tamang. 7th. Duke of Edinburgh's Own Gurkha Rifles. Killed in Action Engaging CT's. Negri Seremban. *Seremban # 3* Negri Sembilan. ---]
	+	CT's Shot dead 3 Fishermen fishing on a river in the area 10 miles from Danar Luat Sitiawan.---]
Sat. 20th		F. M. Police and Gurkhas screening villages of Chemor and Kathan near Sungei Siput captured 14 CT's ---]
	+	A Chinese man (**unnamed**)was shot dead by CT's at Ayar Papn Batu Gaja Ipoh. ---]
	+	The Assistant Manager and Conductor on the Sungei Ular Estate at Kulim Kedah fought off a gang of CT's--]
	+	20 HMT DEVONSHIRE arrived Penang from Calcutta sailed 20th. for Singapore---]
Sun. 21st		The Scots Guards, being aided by Air Reconaicance, found the wreckage of the Dakota Aircraft that crashed on the 12th. November. It was found in an almost inacessable jungle area.---]
	+	R. A. F. Spitfires and Beaufighters attacked a CT camp near Broga. Obsevation reports say that the straffing and bombing plastered the area.---]
	+	R. A. F. Spitfires gave air support to ground Troops in West Johore obliterating a CT Camp.---]
	+	21 HMT DEVONSHIRE arrived Singapore ---]
Mon.22nd		London Mrs.Nellie Whitehouse from Newcastle- upon -Tyne UK. Flew to be with her son Cpl. L. J. Whitehouse
	+	R.A.S.C. In the Cameron Highlands, Wounded in the ambush on the 11th. along with his freind Pte. Brown,who unfortunately died on the 17th.---]
Tue. 23rd		London: It was announced in the House of Commons: '*The Government had decided under the National Service Act. To raise the time of compulsory whole time Service. From 12 to 18 Months. To this effect the National Service (Amendment Bill) was introduced by the Minister of Labour in the House of Commons. The provisions of the bill published on November 26. (For further reading refer Hansard 1948.) The debate continued & on the same day. The third reading of the Bill was passed. The Bill was enacted on the Dec. 16th. After a unanimous second reading in the House of Lords. on December.18th.the Bill was passed---]*
	+	Malaya: Whilst on Patrol in the Kuai Area of Johore. A Sgt. Of the 6th. Gurkha Rifles charged at a CT, who fired rounds that missed him. The Sgt. Killed the CT with his bayonet. The Gurkha's captured 15 other CT's.]
	+	A gang of CT's dynamited the Railway Bridge between Labis & Bedok Johore. Immediate repair on the damaged bridge was carried out & finished. Although It was delayed by 12 hours. The night train from Singapore to Kuala Lumpur travelled slowly along it.---]
	+	3 CT's Charged with possession of arms were sentenced to death. Identified as **Lee Yoon Choy, - Wong Wee Kuen & Wong Ah Tuk.** They were smoked out of a cave in the Gonong Tunggel caves 3 miles South of Ipoh -]
	+	F. M. Police surrounded 6 huts in Layang Layang & shot dead a CT. emerging from one hut holding a pistol.--]
	+	The dead bodies of 5 CT's, were found in the jungles of Chemor near Ipoh. They were identified as those that were wounded in the bayonet Charge on the CT's, by the 2nd. King Edwards VII's Gurkha Rifles on the 7th.at Chemor—]
	+	23/11/1948 LG # 38464 p. 6137 The following awarded the Colonial Police Medal S/ISP. HISHAM B. HJ. NAWAWI. CPM FEDERATION MALAYA POLICE P/INSP. CHOO KIT. CPM FEDERATION MALAYA POLICE INSP. MOHBARAK AHMAD. CPM FEDERATION MALAYA POLICE PC. TARA SINGH. CPM FEDERATION MALAYA POLICE SC. ALIAS B. BANKING. CPM. FEDERATION MALAYA POLICE
Wed. 24th		24 Rfn. Gauraj Pun. 2Nd. King Edward VII's Own Rifles Killed in Action Engaging CT's near Ipoh. *[No known Grave] Terandak Wall Memorial Malacca]* ---]
	+	24 Sgt. G.A. Swan F. M. Police Killed on Ops.---]
	+	24 Mr. G. A. Swanson. Asstn/Manager. of the Johore Libis Palm Oil Estate was shot dead, when ten (10) C.T's attacked his house.---]
	+	24 HMT LANCASHIRE arrived Singapore from Hong Kong / sailed 24th for Liverpool with returning Service personnel---]
Thur. 25th		Kuala Lumpur: The Chief Secretary of the Malayan Federations was given the power & authority to Repatriate aliens, detained under the Emergency Regulations for assisting any Communist.---]
	+	2 CT's were Killed by F. M. Police when they ran out of a hut in the jungle near Kampong Kalong in the Kuala Kabu area. They found a load of rice in one of the huts.---]
	+	CT's attacked the Electric Sub Station at the 14th. mile in the Cameron Highlands & took the Manager Captive, taking him away.---]

Fri.	26th	**26** When 40 CT's attacked his Bungalow Mr .L Edmunds. Asstn. Manager.of the Sungei Buloh Estate & his two Sikh SC's joined him in returning fire. **Mr. L Edmunds** ran out of ammunition & was Killed. His 2 SCs were seriously wounded. His Chinese Amah escaped with his young daughter into the Labour Lines close by. The CT's ransacked the bungalow & stole provisions---]
	+	F. M. Police discovered an arms cache near the village of Batu 8 miles from Kuala Lumpur. ---]
	+	26 HMT DEVONSHIRE arrived Singapore sailed 26th.bound for Liverpool with returning Service personnel---]
	+	26 HMT DUNERA arrived Southampton with returning Service personnel---]
Sat.	27th	**27 Dvr. D.E. Saunders** R.A.S.C.. Died *** *Kranji Singapore # 11 / B - 4*.---]
	+	27 A Chinese F.M Police Detective L/Sgt. **Kok Kee Teik** while in a coffee shop in the village of Balik Pulau just outside George TownPenang, Was shot dead, when 2 CT's entered the shop. ---]
	+	27 HMT DILWARA sailed Singapore enroute to Hong Kong ---]
Sun.	28th	The night train from Kuala Lumpur was derailed, when it crashed into the already derailed Pilot train ½ a mile from Rawang Railway Station, The CT's had loosened the fish plates of the rail track.---]
Mon.	29th	**29. Rfn's . Bhuwanbahadur Limbu.- Jangbahadur. Rai.– Jangbir Rai** 7th. Duke of Edinburgh's Own Gurkha Rifles. Killed in Action Engaging CT's, between Jeniang to Loh Panggsi Sungei Patani *Sungei Patani # A /A - 4 – 3* Kedah- **---** **Rfn. Jangbir Rai** *[No known Grave] TerandakWall Memorial Malacca* ---]
Tue.	30th	The wreckage of the Pilot train, the trains Main engine & coaches were cleared & rails repaired---]

DECEMBER

Wed.	1st	**1 E/Sgt. J.A. Power.** F. M. Police.Travelling with a Platoon. of F. M. Police were ambushed at the 21st m/s Muar / Langa road Muar Johore. E/Sgt..Power died from his wounds. *[No known Grave]*---]
Thur.	2nd	A Plt. of the 6th Queen Elizabeth's Gurkhas, found a disued CT Camp in jungle North of Baling.While the search was on going. 2 CT's were seen, & fired upon, wounding both, they eacaped. A cache of arms was recovered along with other Communist items.---]
	+	At Bukit Palau Estate Johore Bahru. A Chinese Kepala *(unnamed)* was Killed by another Chinese man using a hammer.---]
	+	On the Jeta Estate Perak. Police found a tunnel leading to an underground room. Where 2 CT's were hiding. The contents were Duplicating machinery, a bicycle.and an large quantity of medical supplies.They were arrested ---]
Fri.	3rd	Singapore: Under the new Emergency Regulations. 17C. As an experiment. The first 52 detainees were repatriated to China. ---]
	+	Malaya: On the Sungei Tinggi Estate 40 miles N. of Kuala Lumpur. Two Separate attacks by 40 CT's were beaten off by the Special Constables —]
	+	R. A. F. Spitfires strafed a CT hideout in the Rengan area ---]
	+	In the Kuantan area. Security Forces destroyed a CT camp containing 1 Large and 2 smaller huts cantaining uniforms and food---]
Sat.	4th	10 CT's entered the Tankak Estate Segamat & burnt down the Rubber store.---]
	+	CT's attacked the Panjam Estate Negri Sembilan. The Special Constables returning fire. Beat them off ---]
	+	Security Forces swooped on an area of Johore Bahru and arrested 12 suspects.---]
	+	At the Kuala Krau Police Station. Police fought off several CT's in a fire fight. ---]
Sun.	5th	30 CT's attacked the Kundang Police Station 3 Miles from Ruwang They also failed to set alight the Railway Station next door. They were repelled by the 20 F. M. Policemen---]
Mon.	6th	Singapore: Under the Emergency Powers act. 52 members of the MPAJA & MCP were deported to China.---]
	+	Malaya: The body of the Malay in charge of the Electric Sub Station at the 14th. Mile.Cameron Highlands. Abducted on Thursday 25th November. His body was recovered from the river, near the Power Station in the Sungei Batang Padang---]
	+	6 HMT DILWARA sailed Southampton bound for Singapore / Hong Kong with replacement Service personnel---]
Tue.	7th	At the junction of Padu Road / Pasar Road in Kuala Lumpur. Police unearthed a cache of arms and ammunition, only 150 yards from the Padu Police Station.---]
	+	In the Kluang area of Johore F. M. Police engaged and Killed a CT.—]
	+	On the Brooklands Estate Kluang. A Group of CT's fired shots at the Managers bungalow. The Security Police returned fire, the CT's retreated.---]
	+	F.M. Police Constables in the Police Post at Yeang Hin Tapah fought off 50 armed CT's 1 CT was apparently Killed his body carried off.---]
Wed.	8th	**8 AC1 H.R. Hedges** Elect I. R.A.F. Signal Centre Singapore. Died ****Kranji Singapore # 3 / A -2*- ---]

	+	**8 /Cpl. G.H. Coomber.** Devonshire Regt. Died *** _Kranji Singapore.# 1/ B -5_ ---]
	+	Morter Bombs were used by The Scots Guards Engaging CT's. ---]
	+	A Patrol of the Inniskilling Fusilliers Killed 2 CT' in the Sedili Besar area of Johore---]
	+	The 26th Field Regt. Royal Artillery. Killed 2 CT's near Kuala Lumpur.---]
	+	Gurkha Troops Killed 4 CT's in Fire fights in North Johore.---]
Thur. 9th		Along the Silat road when a Chinese Bean cake maker got up to start work. 2 Chinese men robbed him of $150.---]
Fri. 10th		In the ealy hours of the morning.2 Chinese men waylaid a young Chinese waitress on the Greyland Road Lorong. Robbed her of $50---]
Sat. 11th		Kuala Lumpur: It was announced. _'Due to the deterioration in China. The 2/6th. Gurkha Battalion are to leave Malaya at the end of the Month & sail for Hong Kong.'_ ---]
	+	Singapore: The first batch of Armoured Cars for the Federation Police arrived ---]
Sun. 12th		Malaya : **12 E/Sgt. G. Blenkinsop.** F.M.Aux.Police.Killed in an ambush at the 17 ½ m/s.Kajang/Benji road Kajang Selangor. _Kuala Lumpur # 156_ ---]
	+	In Selangor at Batang Kali a Plt. Of the Scots Guards. Killed 28 CT's in a jungle operation' A few years later. This incident was raised in the House of Commons, the subject of some confusion of the incident ---]
Mon.13th		**13 Sgt. A. M. Jaladeen.** R.P.C. (Ceylon) Killed in Action [_No known Grave] Terandak Wall Memorial Malacca_]-]
	+	About 50 CT's entered Rawang and started shooting at the Police Station & Railway Station. Only 1 Chinese man was Killed. The CT's. were fought off by security Police.---]
		4 CT's were Killed in the Bailing area of Kedah by the Scots Guards ---]
Tue. 14th		**14 E/Sgt. R. Jones.** & **PC Hassan b. Aboo Bakar Rect. Abdullah Majid b. Jamaludin** F. M. Police Killed in a Convoy ambush on the Kuantan/Sungei Lembing Road Pahang. **Sgt. Jones** Died in Kuantan Hospital from his wounds _Kuantan_ Pahang ---]
	+	**14 Asst/Supt. B.F.S. Cooper.** F. M. Aux. Police Killed on Ops., whilst he was leading a Platoon of 15 men. Made contact with about 25 CT's. During the fire fight, he was Killed & 3 of his Platoon were wounded. Eight (8) CT's were Killed. Gemenceh Seremban Negri Sembilan ---]
	+	**14 Cadet D. Hore.** F. M. Police on Special Police Operation Killed by gunmen at Jelebu Negri Semilan---]
	+	**14 PC Hussein b. Kulop Mat Sari** F. M. Police Killed on CT Ops. Batu Gaja Perak.---]
	+	**14 Mr. Skeleson.** (Not a Planter) was shot dead by CT gunmen near Selangor No other details- --]
Wed.15th		**15 Rfn Dhanbahadur Mall.** .2nd. King Edward VII's Own Gurkha Rifles Killed in Action Engaging CT's. [_No known Grave] Terandak Wall Memorial Malacca_---]
	+	**15 Pte. T. E. Newell.** Seaforth Highlanders Died*** _Kranji Singapore # 1 / A – 13_ .---]
	+	**15 Spr. V.C. Brown.** Royal Engineers Died*** _Kuala Lumpur # 14 / 918_. ---]
	+	**15 Pte. A. Dunn.** R.A.M.C. Died *** _Batu Gajah # 402_ Ipoh Perak ---]
	+	15 HMT DUNERA arrived Singapore with replacement Service personnel---]
Thur.16th		2 miles North of Kuala Lumpur. At the Serandah Orphans Home. Two boys saw some men standing outside Mr. Mike Blake's the Superintendants house, an American from Boston Massachusetts. As they moved forward, a Chinese in unifrom pointed a gun at them & said. _'Go back to sleep or you'll get hurt.'_ The boys peeping from the dormitory window, saw Mike Blake came out of the house, stand on the top step arguing. One Chinese hit him on the head with the butt of a gun. Black stumbled, managed to crawl through the door. The CT's followed The boys heard the sound of shots, They had Killed **Mr. Mike Blake** A few moments later, the boys saw the house burst into flames.---]
	+	Kuala Lumpur: Emergency Regulation 17 D. (Aliens Ordinance): Application of Section 9 & 22A of the Alliance Ordnance of the Straits Settlements to the Malay States during the continuance of the Emergency. Was introduced ---]
	+	A Military Patrol shot & Killed 4 CT's in the Metakab area of Pahang 1 CT was a known Notorious CT---]
	+	In the Kuala Lipis area a number of CT's, burnt down the Railway Station.—]
Fri. 17th		In the Jerantut area CT's removed the fish plates from several yards of railway track.The removed fishplates were discovered & replaced before the Singapore Kuala Lumpur train arrived---]
	+	40 CT's Attacked the Prang Besar Estate near Kuala Lumpur. They were fought off. No casualties----]
	+	A Malay driver was dragged from his truck roped up, blindfolded and shot dead on the Sunkei Pangkas Estate in the Kuala Lumpur area.---]
	+	17 HMT EMPIRE HALLADALE arrived Singapore with replacement Service personnel---]
Sat. 18th		A Terengganu States Councillor **Hajir Ngar Wan Mamat** Was Killed by CT's when they attacked the Tin Mine he was a Manager at Terengganu Tin Mine---]

+	Indian Detainees complaining about being detained under the Emergency Regulations. Their case was taken up by Mr. J. A. Thivy. Indian Representative on his visit to Malaya. ---]
Sun. 19th	Bangkok : Mr. Malcolm MacDonald visited Bankok for discussions with Field Marshal Luang Pibul Songgram on joint collaboration in stopping CT's activities along the border frontier between Malaya / Thailand---]
Mon.20th	20 Pte.'s S .M. A. Davith Hamy. - W. Weerasinghe. R.P.C. (Ceylon) Died *** _Singapore # 7 / D – 12 – 13_.--]
Tue. 21st	21 Pte. Wan. Jaafar. B. Wan. Yahya. Malay Regt. Killed in Action Engaging CT's. Pahang.---]
+	21 HMT DUNERA sailed Singapore bound for Southampton with returning Service personnel---]
Wed.22nd	22 Pte. D.R. Pearson. 1st. Devonshire Regt. Died*** _Kranji Singapore # 1/ A - 12._---]
+	22 Drv. R. W. Carter R.A.S.C.died from head injuries. Transport Accident BMH _Kuala Lumpur.# 14 / 919_ ---
+	22 HMT LANCASHIRE arrived in Liverpool with returning Service personnel---]
Thur.23rd	23 Lt. (KGO) Birbahadur. Gurung. - L/Cpl. Khuile. Gurung. – Rfn's.Dhanbadur. Pun – Indrabahadur Gurung. 2nd. King Edward VII's Own Gurkha Rifles. Were Killed when their detachment was attacked in deep jungle near Tanjong Rambutan Ipoh. By a large force of C.T's, whose losses were heavy. _Sulva Lines # A 60_ - Ipoh Perak---]
+	23 Capt. C.S. Hewitt. 1st. Devonshire Regt. Died ***[_Ashes REP_]---]
+	A gunfight took place on the 36th m/s Bukit Salambau road, by a lone F.M.Detective against 4 CT's. The detective fought them off until all his ammunition had been used, then made his escape into a Tapioca plantation---]
+	2 CT gunmen **Lim Ah Ang & Chong Kah** were sentenced to 4 years hard labour for armed robbery.---]
+	Singapore: More Chinese were leaving Singapore than those arriving. This was due to the Strict Emergency Regulation imposed---]
+	4 Spitfires of 28 Sqdn. & 3 Beaufighters of 45 Sqdn, R.A.F. Carried out air strikes on Bruas Perak. This was the last air strike of 1948. In total 84 had been carried out averaging 11 per month. Significantly it was thought, the Air –Strikes had caused the CT's to disband from large groups. into smaller fighting units.---]
+	23 HMT DEVONSHIRE arrived Liverpool with returning Service personnel---]
+	23 HMT DILWARA arrived Singapore with replacement Service personnel enroute to Hong Kong sailed 23--]
Fri. 24th	Sumatra: Netherland Troops in Sumatra captured 3 CT's. They were members of the M.P.A.B.A. All three with a price on their heads. They were known as **Wong (Wang) Chin** The Leader in West Pahang.**Pa Tze Hok** Leader in Kedah & **Kan Chye Kiat** not then identified. The three were arrested in Bagan Saipiapi Indonesia. The question was. How did they get there?---]
+	24 HMT EMPIRE HALLADALE sailed Singapore bound for Liverpool with returning Service personnel---]
Sat. 25th	Malaya : 25 Pte. T. Kerr. Seaforth Highlanders Died *** _Kranji Singapore # 1 / E – 13_ ---]
+	CT's cut the Telegraph wires between Kuala Krau & Mentakab. They removed the fish plates from the railway lines. The Armoured train carrying the Telegraph repair men plus Police & Royal Artillery troops Was derailed 2 ½ miles outside Mentakab. The Driver and Firemen were slightly injured.---]
+	Penang: 370 Squatters due to be shipped from George Town Penang on the 27th. Had been delayed until the New Year.---]
Sun. 26th	50 Uniformed CT's attacked the Rampin Estate in the Bahau area of Negri Sembilan 3 Chinese Laboures were bayonetted to death. Nearly all the buildings were burnt down---]
Mon.27th	Whilst a F. M. Police Malay Special Police Corporal was walking along the Tanjong Malim Road Ipoh. He fought off an attack by 2 CT's- Killing one & wounded the other who ran off---]
+	Two CT's murdered a Coffee shop owner **(unnamed)** near Sitaiwan ---]
+	27 HMT DILWARA arrived Singapore with replacement Service personnel enroute to Hong Kong ---]
Tue. 28th	20 to 30 CT's held up a lorry on the Caledonian Estate Batu Arang. After tying up the driver they set it alight-]
+	On the Swee Lam Estate near Johore. Whilst F.M Police were searching huts. A lone CT was seen escaping, opening fire they Killed him.---]
+	On the Wallice Rubber Estate. during a CT ambush. The Mandore **Nong bin Butat** was Killed, his 2 companions were wounded. One of whom remounted the motorbike & rode off to report the incident at Jementah—]
Wed. 29th	29 Mr Vallinginham. the Estate Conductor of the Segamat Estate was found shot dead at the 10th. m/s Segamat / Labis Road---]
+	Armed CT's attacked the Bukit Nilai Estate, 22 miles from Seremban. They set alight the Conductor's house, the Factory Building & the Smoke House---]
+	Penang :The Delayed Departure of the 370 Squatters, left Penang aboard a ship bound for China ---]
+	3 Chinese men CT's were hanged in Taiping Jail. Sentenced under the Emergency Regulations Act. for processing arms---]
Thur. 30th	30 L/Cpl. G. N. F. Lawrence. Devonshire Regt. Died*** _Kranji Singapore # 1/ A - 11_ ---]

+	Kuala Lumpur: Sir. Henry Gurney sent a Telegram to Mr. Creech Jones stating:
	'Under the Emergency Regulation 17C. The first batch of 52 Detainees. Had been shipped out to Swaton China. Due to the fact they did not have Chinese Consulate passports issued by: The Chinese authorities. At the Chinese port of Swato. They were refused entry.'---]
+	Singapore : A second batch of 210 Detainees were shipped out; 53 bound for Amoy, 27 bound for Hoihow & 130 bound for Swatow.---]
+	London: Mr. Creech Jones in Whitehall presented: The Malayan Emergency Regulation 17 stated:
	'Now the Malayan Emergency Regulations had been promulgated. Whitehall had been presented with a Fait accompli----']
+	Penang: Another 291 Chinese Squatters from Perak. Were deported. sailing from Penang to China---].
+	Kuala Lumpur: In response to the refusal of the 52 deportees. Sir. Henry Gurney issued a Telegram to Mr. Creech Jones:
	'To notify the British Embassy in China. To advise the Chinese Government of its resoponsibilities. To accept its own people. We must rely on deportation to dispose of our detainees. Requirements for all detainees was unfeasible and impracticable causing more disruption to the repatriation program.---]

Fri. 31st | **31** Whilst on operational road Patrol. 4 Troop of the 4th. Hussars under the command of Lt Questier. &. 2/Lt. Sutro, along with 7 Troopers, following in the rear truck. At a 'Y' junction the point where the road divided. The convoy met with a Patrol of Gurkha's from the 2nd. King Edward VII's Own Gurkha Rifles. During an exchange of information, it was decided that the Gurkha's would take the left fork leading to Lintang & 4 Troop would Patrol the right, leading to Jalong. Both roads were narrow windy with ditches on wither side sloping up to the fringes of dense jungle, with plenty of spots ideal for any ambush. Spaced approx. 50 to 100 yards apart the convoy began their Patrol. Having cleared the 231/2. m/s, were about to navigate an 'S' bend. It was then the CT's sprang their ambush, firing first upon the rear truck, therefore stopping any means of escape, whilst concentrating fire on the 15-cwt truck with the 7 Troopers. A hail of bullets burst the trucks tyres, unable to move any further began taking hit after hit including grenades. The first truck quickly reversed past the stricken 15 cwt, to help & assist the Troopers. However, in doing so reduced the line of fire from the rear truck. All having dismounted to return fire, whilst trying to assist the other Troopers. More grenades were thrown 1 (one) went off at Lt. Questier's feet, mortally wounding him. At some point the CT's withdrew. With radios destroyed & unable to contact base. 2/Lt. Sutro took over command decided to load the dead & wounded into the truck, and make their way slowly to Jalong. At Jalong, 2/Lt. Sutro along with a driver took the rear truck back through the ambush position, to report the ambush to a Police Station. Nevertheless, the CT's had disappeared. Afterwards, a search of the area, discovered that possibly 70 CT's were involved in the ambush. Those 4th. Hussars Killed were:

Lt. M.G. Questier. - Cpl. J.E. Finch. - Trp's. B. Grayson. - S.G. Hunter. - T. Johns. – B. G. Lynch.- D. G. Mitchell. Batu Gajah # 409 / 407 / 403 /406 / 404 / 406 / 408 Ipoh Perak---]
Those wounded were : 2/Lt J.L. Sutro. - L/Cpl. H.E. Henderson. - Trp's. N. Archbold - T. Bryd. - J. Spence. - A. Clifford. – C. Carter. - J. Rowan. .- H. Smith, & C. Thompson.---]

A Black day to end 1948.

R. A. F. OPERATION "FIREDOG" END OF YEAR STATISTICS 1948

No of Sorties	No. of Strikes	1,000 Lb.Bombs	500 Lb. Bombs	350 LbCluster	20 LbBombs	R/P's	20mm	.5 mm	.303mm
70	137	/	63	-/	32	298	20,213	21,582	.

R. A. F. SUPPORT 1948

	Soties	Troops/Lift/	Casac	Pass/Lift	Supply Wt. Lbs	Leaflets drop (1,000)	B Flying Times No / hrs	Broadcsting No / hrs	Crashed
Air SupportA/C*	31	/		/	62,700	/	/	/	Spitfire 's
Auster**	N/A	/	28	/	/	/	/	/	TP225
Pioneer	/	/	/	/	/	/	/	/	TP 376
H/C Light	/	/	/	/	/	/	/	/	TP231
848 Sqdn	/	/	/	/	/	/	/	/	TP261
155 Sqdn	/	/	/	/	/	/	/	/	Dakota's
Target/MK**	/	/	/	/	/	/	/	/	KJ962
Vis/Air OBs**	/	/	/	/	/	/	/	/	KN633
Communication**	/	/	/	/	/	/	/	/	Avro York++
Leaf. Sorties*	10	/	/	/	/	/	/	/	Austers
Leaflets Drop*	/	/	/	/	/	N/A	/	/	TJ647
Leaf Sorties **	/	/	/	/	/	/	/	/	TJ 602
Leaflets Drop**	/	/	/	/	/	/	/	/	
Broad Sorties*	/	/	/	/	/	/	/	/	

Broad Hrs *	/	/	/	/	/	/	/	/
Broad Sorties**	/	/	/	/	/	/	/	/
Broad Hrs **	/	/	/	/	/	/	/	/
Photo RECCE***	542	/	/	/	/	/	./	/

* Air Support A/C Dakota -Valetta- Hastings Bristol. ** Auster. *** Photo Rec Anson,Spitfire, Mosquito, Meteor, Pembroke.++ RAF Avro York London mid air crash #

CHAPTER 7 - 1949

ROYAL AIR FORCE
OFFENSIVE AIR SUPPORT- OPERATION *'FIREDOG'*
May 1949 to December 1954

Sqdn	Location	Aircraft Type	No	Date From	Year	Date To	Year
33	Changi	Tempest F2	16	8th. Aug.	1949	17th. Mar.	1950
45	Kuala Lumpur	Beaufighter 10	8	1st. May	1949	6th. Dec.	1949
	Tengah	Brigand B1	10	6th. Dec.	1949	31st.Jan.	1952
60	Tengah	Spitfire 18	17	25th. Aug.	1949	1st. Dec.	1951
81	Tengah	Anson 19	1	31st.Oct.	1949	16th.Mar.	1950
205	Seletar	Sunderland GR4	5	15th.S.E.P..	1949	.13th. Dec.	1954
656	Changi	Auster 5/6/7/9	31	17th. Aug.	1949	17th.Aug.	1951

ROYAL NEW ZEALAND AIR FORCE
OFFENSIVE AIR SUPPORT OPERATION *'FIREDOG'*
SEPTEMBER 1949 to December 1951

Sqdn.	Location	Aircraft Type	No	Date From	Year	Date To	Year
41	Changi	Dakota C3	5	1st. S.E.P...	1949	30th. Nov.	1951

JANUARY

Sat.	1st	1 Trp. N. Archibold. 4th. Queen's Hussars died from wounds recv'd, during the previous days ambush. *Kuala Lumpur # 15 / 886* ---]
	+	Operation *'Gargoyle ' 'Octopus'* Began in the Cameron Highlands / Pahang & neighbouring states of Perak Selangor Deploying the 2nd Battn. King Edward VII's Own Gurkha Rifles against No. 5 Regt. MRLA.---]
	+	Sptfires strafed a CT camp in the Sungei Chendering area of Kampar. A follow up operation found 3 huts damaged 2 destroyed. They captured the 2nd in Command of the CT. Platoon---]
	+	Kuala Lumpur : Announced: *'Number of Detainees including dependants repatriated during 1948 = 380* ---]
Sun.	2nd	2 CT's held up a Bus at the 16th. m/s Pontian road at gunpoint. Ordered everyone off the bus. Robbed them, then told the driver to drive to Hilam Konsig where they set light to the bus.---]
Mon.	3rd	London: Mr. Creech Jones: informed Sir. Henry Gurney : *'That repatriating 2,000 detainees per month to war torn China, would cause a huge internal problem. It was impossible to continue, deportation---]*
	+	F.M. Police and Hussar Troopers Killed 1 CT during an operation at the 3rd. m/s Cheras Road near Kuala Lumpur---]
Tue.	4th	3 CT's, were Killed in the Sedenak area. One was identified as *Tan Siew* a notorious CT.---] Kuala Lumpur: Figures released show: *'From 16 June to end December 1948: 482 CT's had been Killed & 404 wounded 268 had been captured in the war against the CT's---]*
	+	HMS *CONSORT* offshore in the Straits of Malacca.. Bombarded 5 Separate CT camps in the Gulong Bongsu Forest Reserve in the Kulim area of Kedah---]
Wed.	5th	Pte. O'Reilly. The bren gunner of 'D' Coy K.O.Y.L.I. During a contact with CT's, saw a CT about to hurl a Grenade at 2/Lt. Wigg. O'Reillly, ran at the CT & with a flying leap brought him down. As they rolled down a slope, the CT released the grenade,which rolled down after them before exploding. Injuring. O'Reilly in the face and side, but still he kept hold of the CT, before 2/Lt. Wigg & O'Reillly shot the CT. For his Action Engaging CT's. Pte. O'Reilly was awarded the Distinguished Conduct Medal LG 5 /7 49 # 38657---]
	+	In Kedah Operation 'Octopus' A 5 day Operation ended in the Gunong Inas Forest Reserve. During the operation 1 CT was Killed ---]
	+	In Perak. Operation *'Kris'* continued in the area N. of Taiping. 3 CT's had been Killed & 2 Captured ---]

	+	HMS *CONSORT* sailed up the the river Lumutt & anchored opposite Lumutt to open fire on CT camps 6 miles inland to the North in the Ding Ding area of Perak. HMS *'COMMUS'* will releave HMS *CONSORT* & resume Patrolling duties in the Straits of Malacca waters---]
Thur. 6th		A Pltn. of the Inniskilling Fusiliers. Killed 2 CT's near the Pasak Estate in the Kota Tinggi district ---]
	+	1 CT was Killed when a Military Patrol discovered a CT camp capable of housing 100 CT's ---]
	+	1 CT was Killed at Tenang by a Patrol of the FM Police---]
	+	1 CT was Killed at Benting Pahang by a Patrol of the FM Police ---]
	+	At the 23 m/s Pontian to Johore road. Similar to the bus attack on the 2nd. A bus was held up by15 CT's. At gun point, they ordered the 12 passengers off. Robbed them of Money and jewellery then set the bus alight.--]
Fri. 7th		**7 Dvr. See Geok Soon.** R.A.S.C. (MOR). Died *** *Claimed by Next of Kin* ---]
	+	A number of CT' in Sampans attacked Number 221. Vehicle Stores of the R.A.O.C. Camp at Tebraun N. of Johore Bahru. They were driven off by Camp Guards 4 CT's were Killed by the Guards.---]
	+	A F.M Police Patrol Killed 1 CT in the Jerentat area of Segamat.---]
	+	Kuala Lumpur :Sir. Henry Gurney. Advised the Colonial Office London: *'That Malaya was expecting to deport 2,000 detainees per Month. In accordance with Section 2 of Emergency Regulations 17D ---]*
	+	A CT. **Lim Fong Kian** (alias **Lim Siomg**) was hanged in Pudu Jail Kuala Lumpur.---]
	+	7/01/1949 LG # 38507 p. 142 The following awarded the Colonial Police Medal L/CPL RAMILI B. HJ. IBRAHIM. CPM FEDERATION MALAYA POLICE SC. MOHAMAD B. MAT. CPM FEDERATION MALAYA POLICE SC. KRISTNA BAHAHDUR. CPM FEDERATION MALAYA POLICE
Sat. 8th		3 CT's set light to a boat on the Pahang River. It was used by Photographs taking I.D. photographs---]
	+	In a gun battle between F.M Police jungle Patrol & 30 CT's at Kampong Sawah Johore Bahru. 1 CT was Killed.---]
	+	A Scots Guards Patrol Killed 1 CT in the Benton Berguan area of Selengor.---]
Sun. 9th		**9 Spr. I. L. Gold.** Royal Engineers Died*** *Kuala Lumpur # 15 / 887*---]
	+	A Plt. of 26th. Field Artillery Royal Artillery laid an ambush in the Gumenshen area of N Tampin Negri Sembilan They captured 6 CT's---]
	+	A number of CT's Killed 2 Chinese women and 1 F. M. Special Constable (**unnamed**)---]
	+	A Plt. of Coldstream Guards Killed 1 CT during a gun battle with a Plt, of CT's. in the Ulu Langgat area---].
Mon. 10th		Singapore: Mr. Malcolm MacDonald stated: *'The new regulation 17C was drastic, but necessary for immediate Action Engaging CT's against the Squatters was imperitive.---]*
	+	Malaya : A 7 man Platoon of K.O.Y.L.I. (11 Plt. 'D' Com.) were on Patrol in a Tin Mine, near Karangan on the borders of Province Wellesley & Kedah. Came across a group of five (5) CT's below them, walking by a stream. They opened fire on them. Hearing the Platoon approach, the CT's returned fire. One (1) CT was Killed & fell into the steam to float downstream, shortly after another was Killed. The C.T's threw grenades, which fell short, however while attempting to escape over a fence, a further CT was Killed. Leaving only two, one of whom was a women, although wounded kept firing her pistol at the Platoon. Sgt. Chadwick & 4 other Private's remained in position, sending three others down to approach from the rear, they quickly Killed both. The woman was later identified as a Teacher from Penang.The bodies were searched. Medicine tablets & $4,000 in new notes were recovered.---]
	+	500 Squatters, part time CT's. Men, women & children were rounded up in the Kajang area of Selangor & sent to a detention camp for repatriation at a later date.---]
	+	Kuala Lumpur: Mr. Malcolm MacDonald sent a telegram to the Foreign Office: *'Admitting that the New Emergency Regulations 17C were drastic. Nevertheless, stern and immediate Action Engaging CT's, against the Squatters were imperative.'*---]
Tue. 11th		**E/Sgt. E. J. Aldridge.** F.M. Aux. Police while leading his Platoon on the Malay / Thailand border was Killed in Action Engaging CT's also Killed was **Cpl. Sidek.** F.M.Police. *Kranji Singapore # 18 / C – 6* ---]
	+	Kuala Lumpur: The Government & Police have Power to detain en-bloc Squatters with known association & providing help with the CT's ---]
	+	In Malacca 600 youths of all Malayan Races. Volunteered to join the British Army. After training the Recruits will be attached to British Corps units of the: Royal Engineers – Royal Signals - Royal Army Ordnance Corps. Royal Army Service Corps – Royal Army Medical Corps - Royal Electrical & Mechanical Engineers – Army Catering Corps -.Royal Military Police & Regiments of the Royal Air Force.---]
Wed. 12th		**12 Pte A. C. Kurton.** Seaforth Highlanders Died*** *Kranji Singapore # 1 / A - 10* ---]
	+	

Thur. 13th +	2 Special Constables on the Bukit Badong Estate, near Batong Barjunlai Kulang fought off 64 CT's during a fire fight lasting 45 minites, before they escaped. The CT's burnt down the store & Smoke House.---]
	12 HMT DILWARA arrived Singapore / sailed enroute to Southampton with returning Service personel 13th.--
	13 During a fire fight with a large force of CT's a Platoon of the 6th. Queen Elizabeth's Own Gurkha Rifles. The following were Killed, in the area of Sungei Patani. N. Kedah::**(QGO) Capt. Tulparsad. Pun - L/Cpl. Gaine Gurung - Rfn's . Damarsing.Thapa – Balsing Rana - Beijang.Gurung -Chhabilal Thapa - Dilbahadur. Pun - C. Girsing.Chhetri - Lalbahadur.Pun. – Tarachand Thapa – Ambersing Thapa** . _Sungei Patani # 9
Fri. 14th +	– 10 – 5 – 11-13 -16 – 8 – 14 7_ It was believed that the Commader of the CT force that killled the Gurkha Officers & men was an Ex -Japanese Officer.---]
	14 Maj. R.G. Barnes. Essex Regt. Killed in Action Engaging CT's _Taiping # E-14_ Perak---]
+	8 other people were Killed when CT's ambushed a lorry, between Lanchang Temerloh near Kuala Lumpur---]
Sat. 15th	40 CT's ambushed the Manager of the Kulai Young Estate South Johore. But his driver drove straight through the ambush. There was no casualties.---]
Sun. 16th	Gurkha Troops Killed 4 CT's and wounded 2 in the Kuala Kangsar area ---]
+	A Pahang CT Leader **Khoo Mong** was Killed by a Millitary Patrol in the Metakab area. ---]
Mon. 17th	An ammunition dump was found in Singapore holding Ammunition and guns.---]
+	**17 Maj. W. Fenton**. R. A. O. C. Died*** _Kranji Singapore # 1 / A - 9._---]
Tue. 18th	**17 Pte. J. McD. McMurdock.** Seaforth Highlanders Died*** _[Ashes REP]_---]
+	A F.M. Police Patrol Killed 5 CT's in the Karangan area of S.Kedah---]
Wed. 19th	3 F.M. Policemen were mortally wounded in an engagement with CT's a few miles from Kuala Lumpur.---]
+	**19 Gnrs. C.M. Bailey. - J. Hipwell. - F. Wallett., - W. J. Whitear.** Royal Artillery. Were Killed in a CT ambush _Kuala Lumpur # 16 / 922 - 923 – 14 / 920 – 15 / 888_---]
Thur. 20th	**19 Pte. A. Raman.** R. Pioneer. C. (Ceylon) Died.on Ops. _[No known Grave]_ Terandak Wall Memorial Malacca-]
+	After returning from a registration procedure. In Lanchang a village 20 miles from Tremerloh:- 12 Administarion Personnel were Killed.(**unnamed**) When CT's ambushed their lorry ---]
Fri. 21st	Police have offered a reward of $2,500 for information on **Hoe Lian Chye** a former leader in the MPAJA for the murder of waitress **Chew Ah Lan**. ---]
+	London: Under the Emergency Regulation 17C The Foreign Office: _'Had to continue with the programme for deporting Detainees due to the then: Position of the Chinese Nationalist against the Chinese Communist._---]
+	London: Mr. Creech Jones: Stated: _'846 mainly Chinese. Had been deported by the end of December 1948_---]
+	Malaya: Beaufighters attacked a CT camp firing Rockets at the camp located in the cliff at Gunog Rapat 3 miles S.E. of Ipoh. During a follow up by the Gurkhas, K.O.Y.L.I, & Hussars: 4 CT's were captured & 4 wounded---]
+	A CT hideout on the jungle Fringe N. of Kuala Kangsar. F. M. Police Killed 1 CT at Kampong Penagi---]
+	R. A. F. Beaufighters gave air support to ground troops Engaged in routing out CT's in the Gunang Rapat caves 3 miles S. E. of Ipoh. 4.CT's were captured. 4 Women CT's. were wounded but escaped.---]
	Two other R. A. F. air attacks, were carried out by Spitfires and Beaufighters. One on a CT target North West of Kuala Kangsar. The other was on a stretch of jungle in the Negri Sembilan Selangor border.---]
Sat. 22nd	21 HMT HALLA DALE arrived Liverpool with returning Service personnel---]
+	**22 Mr. E.D. Harding.** Manager of the Lothian Estate in the Sapang district of Negri Sembilan, whilst driving.his car to his. Bungalow, was hit by 18 bullets fired by CT's. Fotunately his only wound was a bullet in his calf. ---]
	A meeting by the Commisioner General at Bukit Serene concluded: _'The security, defence,economic & political needs required, that Chinese immigration be reduced to an_
Sun. 23rd	_absolute minimum.'_---]
+	**23** A F.M. PC. (**unnamed**) was Killed near Gurun 14 miles North of Sungei Patani---]
+	Special Police on a training excercise, came across a CT near Jemantah Village. They Killed him. He was identified as **Lee Han Boon** a former member of the MPAJA---]
+	Another. Police Patrol operating in the same area shot dead 2 CT's---]
Mon. 24th	30 CT's set fire to the buildings on the Ban Lee Estate near Sedanak ---]
+	**24 Mr. M. A. Barbour.** Died from multiple gunshot wounds. Another 2 European employees (**unnamed**) & a F.M. Policeman from the Rawang Tin Mine. Were shot dead in a CT ambush 20 miles from Kuala .Lumpur---]
+	Approx 50 CT's stopped the Collier Train near Batu Arang. 3 miles from the Colliery, Damaged the. rails, ensuring the engine & 3 wagons left the rails finishing up at the bottom of embankment. No bad casualties reported.---]

Tue. 25th	850 Squatters were evicted from the Batu Caves area & sent to a detention camp awaiting deportation---]
	A British F.M. Police Sgt. Killed a wanted CT leader *Lian Chiang* in the Bidor area of Perak---]
	On the Kelan Estate in Johore. The Manager & 16 F.M.Police Constables, engaged 20 CT's who after a 20
+	minute shoot out were driven off. ---]
Wed. 26th	3 CT's were Killed. 2 in the Segamat area near Tampah---]
	Mr. L.J. Colliers. A visiting agent while on the rounds with Mr. Wright. On the Rini Estate Skudai Johore was
+	Killed by CT's---]
Thur. 27th	26 HMT LANCASHIRE sailed Liverpool for Singapore / Hong Kong with replacement Service personnel---]
	Kuala Lumpur :It was revealed that 1,141 detained Squatters under the Emergency 17 D Regulation had been
	deported. All know to be sympathisers, had helped the CT's Only 338 had voluntarily wanted to be deported
Fri. 28th	& 216 had been repatriated. ---]
+	6 CT's were captured and 1 Killed by a Platoon of the K.O.Y.L.I. near Towar.---]
	Police discovered an arms dump hidden in a bunker in the Laonson area of Johore 1,000 of rounds of
Sat. 29th	ammunition,a number of rifles, a Japanese Machine gun and grenades.---]
+	3 Chinese Labourers (***unnamed***) were Killed by CT's on the Lim Tsion Estate.---]
+	Spitfires from 60 Sqdn. based at Changi attacked a CT camp in the Segamet area .---]
	A grenade was thrown into a vegetable shop in Rahang village 2 miles from Seremban seriously injuring 2
+	Chinese men & a 9 year old girl.---]
	CT's attacked the Ben Heng Estate in Muar. When a spotlight was directed in the direction of the firing. It
	was exstinguished by machine gun fire. Military troops were rushed to the area. Upon their arrival they
+	returned fire causing the CT's to retreat.---]
	London: In the House of Commons Mr. P. Paratin. Communist MP questioned.
	' Why the burning of the village of Kachua in Semiyeh was necessary?'
	Mr. Creech Jones atated:
	'That the 400 inhabitants of the village were known to help the Communist Terrorist''s. Therefore,under the
Sun. 30th	Ermergency Regulation. Were removed along with their possessions, before the place was burnt down.'---]
	During Operation 'Gargoyle 'Transport Aircraft of No 52 Sqdn. made supply drops, and ferried 200 Military
Mon. 31st	personnel to the area.---]
	A war time style secret amphibious landing from HMS 'COMMUS' Landed Grenadier Guards & F.M Police
	on the island of Pulau Ketan off Port Swettenham to screen the Chinese inhabtants there were no arrest
	although fired upon 2 Chinese Men escaped into the mangrove swampy area---]

FEBRUARY

Tue. 1st	Kuala Lumpur:The Emergency Travel (Restrictions) Regulation 17 C:
	Prohibiting entry into the Federation to any person unless a entry permit was first obtained. The regulations.
	Made it compulsory for all persons, excluding the local born. To have an entry permit to enter and remain in the
	Federation. The Regulation gave wide powers of mass detention before deportation of those Chinese
	Squatters supporting the Communist in Malaya---]
+	The MCP formally announced . It had renamed its Military Army Force as the :-
	"Malayan Races Liberation Army" (MRLA)
	Furthermore, claimed the War against the British was "National in Character." The single Red Star on their
	caps, would be replaced with three Red Stars. Symbolising the three Communities of Malaya. The Malays,
	The Chinese, The Indians.---]
+	The MRLA formed a No 10 Regt. from dissident Malays in Pahang---]
+	Kuala Lumpur: To counteract the formation of the MRLA No 10 Regt., of dissident Malays in Pahang. The
	formation of the Malayan Chinese Association was introduced together with 'Operation 'London' ---]
+	There was also another problem? Situated in the area of Tasek Bera on the borders of Johore and Pahang.
	The terrain of the area was rather well protected by lakes surrounded by thick jungle and swamps, where the
	CT's had set up camps & had befriended the local inhabitants. The aboriginal Semilai people, who the CT's
	were using, to grow crOps. for them. However, the task to get there. Was given to a Company of the Seaforth
	Highlanders. Under the command of Lt/Col. Douglas and F. M. Policeman. A/S W. Neil. Leaving from Bahua,
	with an estimated 2 days journey to get there.The Party accompanied by 2 Semilai guides,set out on a
	torturours journey. Even with the aid of their Semilai guides. It took three days of really tough going through the
	terrain, before they reached lake Tesa Bera. During their trek they encountered CT's. Engaging them, the
	CT's retreated back into the jungle. Upon reaching the lake, with the help of their 2 guides made friends with

	the Semilai, then set up their camp. Over the next few days. They discovered a large hidden CT camp capable of holding 150 men. It was decided, the area was definitely a staging post for the CT's. Therefore, needed to be protected by a Police Force.---]
+	Singapore: The Straits Times newspapers heading stated: **'BIG SCALE DEPORTATION URGED'**---]
Wed. 2nd	Malaya :- **Rfn. Bhimbahadur Gurung.** 2Nd. King Edward VII's's Own Gurkha Rifles. Killed in Action Engaging CT's in the area of Ipoh.
+	*[No known Grave] Terandak Wall Memorial Malacca* ---]
Thur. 3rd	2 HMT DEVONSHIRE sailed Liverpool bound for Singapore with replacement Service personnel---] Kuala Lumpur: Sir. Henry Gurney received a telegram from Mr Creech Jones stating:
Fri. 4th	*'It is impossible to continue deportation on such a large scale!'*.---]
+	4 L/Sgt. A. Ferguson. 2nd. Battn. Scots Guards. Died***Kuala Lumpur # 16 -924---]
	4/02/1949 LG. # 38530 p 629 The following awarded the Military Medal
	PTE. K. OSBOURNE MM DEVONSHIRE REGIMENT.
	L/CPL. T. CHAPMAN. MM SEAFORTH HIGHLANDERS
	PTE. E.L. THORPE MM SEAFORTH HIGHLANDERS
	SGT. D. B. RANA. MM 2nd. KING EDWARD VII'S OWN GURKHA RIFLES
	CPL. H. GURUNG. MM 2nd. KING EDWARD VII'S OWN GURKHA RIFLES
	L/CPL K. RAI. MM 7th. DUKE OF EDINBURGH'S OWN GURKHA RIFLES
	CPL. H. RAI. MM 10th. PRINCESS MARY'S OWN GURKHA RIFLES
+	SGT. O. B. ITAM MM MALAY REGIMENT.
	4/02/1949 LG.#38531 p.635 The following awarded the British Empire Medal (Military)
Sat. 5th	SGT.MOHD. ZAIN HJ. AMIN. BEM ROYAL MALAY REGIMENT.
	Auster Number TW628 AOP6 656 Sqdn. Army Air Corps Whilst landing at Muar Airstrip, overshot. Damaged
+	beyond repair. The Pilot was unhurt---]
	3 CT's Killed **Mr. Kong Yoon Hong** the Manager of a Tin Mine in the Karangan area.---]
+	9 CT's. Killed a Rubber Dealer **Mr. Trian Ho Ing** of Sungan Dua ---]
Sun. 6th	A number of CT's entered the Chong Yin Kongsi and set the engine room alight.---]
Mon. 7th	**6 Pte. K.A. Sysum.** 1st. Devonshire Regt. Drowned. In the River Pahang. [*Ashes. REP*.---] Singapore Sir. Franklin Gimson. the Govenor of Singapore stated:-
Tue. 8th	*"That they were confident that the Colony could avoid the chaos and destruction of life & propeetty, that the Communist inflicted on its inhabitants"*. ---]
	Malaya : 500 Squatters were detained during a combined raid by F.M. Police and Troops on operations. To. clear a Squatter area in Sikamat Village 5 miles from Seremban. It was a known area for the Squatters to
+	cooperate with the CT's ---]
Wed. 9th	A Patrol of Grenadier Guards. Killed a notorious killer who terrorised the Yuyow area of Sungei Besi. 2 other of his Section were captured. ---]
	A combined operation by the British & Thailand forces supported by the R.A.F. began on the Kedah /
+	Thailand borders---]
+	9 HMT DILWARA arrived Southampton with returning Service personnel---]
Thur. 10th	9 HMT EMPIRE HALLADALE sailed Liverpool bound for Singapore-with replacement Service personnel --]
Fri. 11th	**10 Lt. H. Randall.** Royal Artillery Died *** [*Ashes REP*] ---]
	11 Mr. W.A, Gutsell (JP) Lt/Col. F.M. Aux. Police A partner of the Kelross Estate Pantai Negri Sembilan. While inspecting the Estate with 2 other SC's & his driver. Drv. **P. Veerasamy.** SC's **Abdul Rahman Bin**
Sat. 12th	**Awal, Manap bin Mohd Jai** were Killed In an ambush on the Estate. *Seremban # ?* Negri Sembilan --].
	12 The crew of Beaufighter RD858 of 45 Sqdn. R.A.F. **Plt. II. M. F. J. Berry**. & **Nav.II A. I. J. Harris**. Were
+	Killed when they crashed at Butterworth. *Western Road # 1992 – 1991* George Town Penang.---]
Sun. 13th	**12 Pte. J. H. Street.** Seaforth Highlanders Died *** *Kranji Singapore # 1 / A -8* ---]
	13 The crew of Mosquito PF623. 81 Sqdn. Whilst flying, lost a propeller, then one engine fell off, before crashing at R. A. F. Tengah. **F/O. K.E.V. Price**. & **Nav. III. P. Metcalfe** were both Killed.
Mon. 14th	*Kranji Singapore # 4 / A 1 3 / A – 4 - 3* ---]
+	After 11 days the Seaforths Highlanders Patrol returned back to Bahua with their gathered information.---]
	656 Sqdn Army Air Corps (A.A.C.) Auster TJ634.AOP5. Forced landed in a paddy field 10 miles N.E of Alor
Tue. 15th	Star, It's Pilot was unhurt.---]
	Kuala Lumpur :The propagander leader of the Malayan Democratic Youth League in Kuala Lumpur
+	**Loh Liet** was shot dead at Petaling, he was carrying a revolver.---]

+ Wed. 16th	A lone F. M. Police Detective. Tet Toong. Fought with 6 CT's near the village of Sungei Chua 1 mile from Kajang. He was hit several times & taken to the local hospital ---]
+	Tapah F.M. Police Killed a CT at the 7th. m/s Cameron Highlands Road ---]
	16 Gdns. H. J. Medley. 2nd. Battn. Coldstream Guards Died***_Batu Gajah # 412_ Ipoh Perak---]
	16 Mr. F.P.W. Harrison. OBE. Manager. Of the Somme Estate Kulim Kedah was shot dead by CT's, whilst driving through road ways surrounded by jungle. Harrison a Planter before the Second World War was a former Major in Force 136 He entered Malaya 5 times by Submarine at Lumut each time the Operation
Thur. 17th Fri. 18th	was aborted through Japanese shipping. He finally parachuted into Perak on 26th. February 1945 with 1 Malay Liaison Officer & several British troops---.]
+	**Detective Tet Toong** F. M. Police Died from his wounds received on the 13th.---]
	A CT **Tan Mong Kwan** was convicted and sentenced to death with hanging in the Johore Goal.---]
Sat. 19th	Negri Sembilan F. M. Police . have offered a reward of $5,000 for information leading to the arrest of the. CT.'s. who Killed **Lt. Col Gutsel** his **Driver** & **2 Constables** on the 10th.---]
+	During the previous 3 weeks. R. A. F. Transport Squadrons made 20 seperate air drops. to troops operating in the jungle. accumalated to 47,000 lbs ---]
+ Sun. 20th	Security Guards at Kampas Estate in the Muar. Area Killed 2 CT's during a battle around the Managers Bungalow---]
	Gurkha. troops shot dead a CT sentry in the same area---]
Mon. 21st Tue. 22nd	**20 Cpl. N.J. Weyman.** Devonshire Regt. Killed in Action Engaging CT's in the Pahang jungle near Mentakab. _Kuala Lumpur. # 16 - 927_ ---]
	21 Gdmn. J. D. Brown. 2nd. Battn. Coldstream Guards Died Killed in a Transport Veh Acc._Batu Gajah # 41_---]
+	R. A. F. Spitfires strafed the jungle area near Kuantan Pahang in support of. Ground. Forces searching for CT's.---]
Wed. 23rd	In another operation 850 men women & children. Were rounded up from the Batu caves, 6 miles North of Kuala Lumpur. To be detained awaiting repatriation.---]
+	**23 Gnr. A. R. Nichols.** Royal Artillery Died *** _Kranji Singapore # 1 / A – 7_---]
+	3 wanted. CT's were Killed. One was identified as **Loh Min Sien** former president of the Malacca General Party.---]
hur. 24th	The dead body of a CT was found in the jungle near the Jabour Valley Estate. Identified as **Poo Yee** a wanted CT.---]
+	**24 Fus. P. Dunne.** Inniskilling Fusiliers Died *** _Kranji Singapore # 1 / E – 14_ ---]
Fri. 25th	24 HMT LANCASHIRE arrived Singapore with replacement Service personnel---]
+	24 HMT LANCASHIRE sailed Singapore for Hong Kong ---]
+	5 CT's shot dead **Mr. Kong Kooning.** A Tin Mine Manager of the Tong Heng Tin Mine at Karangan Kulim.---]
	CT's Killed a Rubber dealer **Mr. Tiang Ho Ing** of Simpang Dua Sittawan area.---]
Sat. 26th Sun. 27th.	Troops & FM Police whilst clearing out a Squatter area in the Batu caves 6 miles North of Kuala Lumpur 350 Squatters were taken to a detention camp---]
+	**26 Tpr. W. Lane.** 4th Hussars Died*** _Kuala Lumpur # 16 / 928_.---]
+	Gurkhas of the 1/6th engaged CT's in the Badak area of. North Kedah. Killing 1 CT and wounding 3 others--]
Mon.28th.	Gurkhas engaged a number of CT's killing 1 & wounding another near Layang Layang ---]
+	A Patrol of F.M Police Killed 1 CT & wounded another 2, near Kampong Chinah. Negri Sembilan. ---]
	28 Pte. F. M. Glass. Devonshire Regt. Killed in Action Engaging CT's. _Kuala Lumpur # 16 / 929_ ---]
	39 Dyah Trackers on operation with the Grenadier. Guards. Were presented with the cap badge of the Grenadiers. They were leaving Port Dickson for 2 weeks leave & recuperation---]

MARCH

Tue. 1st	Troops of the Devonshire Regt. With air support from R.A.F. Sqdns. attacked several suspected CT positions in the Triang region of Pahang, capturing over 100 CT's.---]
+	1 HMT DEVONSHIRE arrived Singapore- with replacement Service personnel --]
Wed. 2nd	During a Police raid the OCPD Mr. A.J.A. Blake & a Sikh F.M. PC Cpl. We're slightly wounded whilst attacking a CT. camp near Sungei Siput. The CT's withdrew. The follow up search of the camp revealed, a meal was being prepared for 70 CT's ---]
+	In the Batu Pahat area Police raided a Kongsi on the Chua Peck Seong Estate Kangsar & arrested a CT leader.on the wanted list---]
+	Police arrested 13 Chinese men, known to be assisting the CT's in Ulu Chepor & in Gopeng near Ipoh.--]
Thur. 3rd	The Village Headman **Inche Amin** of Kampong Skoti in the Jerantst area was Killed together with another

		Malay Kadir when 10 armed CT's raided the village---]
Fri.	4th	4/03/1949 LG # 38552 p.1115 The following awarded the Military Cross
		LT. J.L SUTRO. MC 4th. QUEEN'S ROYAL HUSSARS
		The following awarded the Distinguished Conduct Medal
		TRP. H.W. SMITH. DCM 4th. QUEEN'S ROYAL HUSSARS
	+	4/03/1949 LG # 38553 p.1127 The following awarded the Colonial Police Medal
		SUB/INSP. ABDUL R. B. HJ. LONG. CPM FEDERATION MALAYA POLICE
	+	A document captured from a. CT camp. Stated:
		'The Malayan Communist Party are disheartened by the way their Revolution was going'. ---]
	+	A women CT believed to be a CT leader was shot dead by Police & Gurkhas in the Jelebu area of Negri Sembilan ---]
	+	The body of a dead CT was found in the jungles of Metakab area of Pahang ---]
Sat.	5th	2 CT 's were hanged: One in Penang Goal **Soon Chen Sip** & In Johore Goal **Yong Chor** ---]
	+	5 HMT DEVONSHIRE sailed Singapore bound for Liverpool with returning Service personnel---]
Sun.	6th	**6 Lt. J. R.S. Farrar** 3rd. Battn. Grenadier Guards Died by accident. *[Ashes REP]*---]
Mon.	7th	273 Squatters were rounded up by the Security Forces in Kluang area & put into a detention camp for deportation at a later date.---]
Tue.	8th	**8 Capt. J. A. L. Smith.** R.A.S.C Killed in an ambush near Kajang Negri Sembilan *[Ashes REP]*---]
Wed.	9th	**9 Pte. D. McCreary.** Seaforth Highlanders Died*** *[Ashes REP]*---]
	+	9/03/1949 LG # 38575 p. 1603 The following awarded the Colonial Police Medal
		AUX/INSP. J. L. BODEN. CPM (Pos) FEDERATION MALAYA POLICE
		L/CPL. GHANI B. HUSSEIN.CPM FEDERATION MALAYA POLICE
	+	9 HMT DILWARA sailed Southampton bound for Singapore- with replacement Service personnel--
	+	9 HMT DUNERA sailed Southampton bound for Singapore/ Hong Kong with replacement Service personnel-]
Thur.	10th	**10 Cpl. J.W. Rayner.** Devonshire Regt. Killed in Action Engaging CT's *Kuala Lumpur # 16 -931*---]
	+	**10 LEM. J. Goggin.** Royal Navy. H.M.S. *TERROR*. Died *** *Kranji Singapore # 14 / D - 11*---]
Fri.	11th	**11 Rfn. T. Damasing Thapa.** 6th. Queen Elizabeth's Own Gurkha Rifles Killed in Action Engaging CT's Sungei Patani. *Sungei Patani # 5* Kedah ---].
	+	**11 Pte. J. C. Gardiner.** Devonshire Regt. Died from Wounds recv'd on 10th. *Kranji Singapore # 1/ A 6*--]
	+	**11 Capt. C. Taylor.** R. A. E. C. Died*** *Kuala Lumpur # 16 / 936*.---]
	+	11/03/1949 LG # 38557 p 1255 The following awarded the Military Medal
		CPL. M. THAPA .MM 2nd KING EDWARD VII'S OWN GURKHA RIFLES
	+	11/03/1949 LG # 38558 p.1265 The following awarded the Colonial Police Medal
		SC MOHD, ZAIN B. SALLEH. (Pos) FEDERATION MALAYA POLICE
	+	11 HMT EMPIRE HALLADALE arrived Singapore with replacement Service Personnel---]
Sat.	12th	12 Near Kajang Negri Sembilan, In an ambush by C.T's. Guardsmen of the 3rd. Battn. Grenadier Guards were Killed **L/Cpl. J. P. Chriscoli. MM. – Gdsmn's J.R. Hall.- V. T. Herrett.- A..E. Martin.- T. Ryan.** Killed & 1 Officer & 2 other Guardsmen wounded during the fire fight. .An uphill bayonet charge routed the C.T.'s. *Kuala Lumpur. # 16 / 937 – 932 -934 – 935 – 933*---]
	+	**12 Gnr. W.M. Maroney.** Royal Artillery Died*** *Kranji Singapore # 1 / E - 15*---]
	+	Kuala Lumpur: In a press conference Sir. Henry Gurney stated:
		'The 2nd. Brigade of Guards. Were to remain in Malaya. No truth in last Month's rumour that they would be leaving Malaya.'
		Under Emergencies Regulations 17C 3,621 Squatters had been detained living in Black Areas 781. Had been deported.---]
	+	12 HMT LANCASHIRE arrived Singapore from Hong Kong. Sailed bound for Liverpool with returning Service personnel---]
Sun.	13th	Local Planters in the Sungei Jeloh area. The area had long been a CT stronghold. Submitted a request for:
		'More Security Measures to be. Considered'---]
Mon.	14th	Singapore:In an announcement, The Commissioner General for S.E. Asia. Mr. Malcolm Macdonald stated.
		'The R.A.F. were to be reinforced with Lincoln Bombers. In addition to that, ground forces would be increased with the transfer from Hong Kong of the 26th. Gurkha Infantry Brigade.' ---]
	+	Mr. M. MacDonald, sent a telegram to Nanking:
		' Request another port of entry for deportees' ---]
Tue.	15th	**15 F/Sgt. E. Green.** Ft./MT. R. A. F Seletar Died.*** *Kranji Singapore # 3 / A -5*---]

Wed. 16th	A Chinese man, a Squatter slashed a member of a Police party in Taiping. He was shot dead by another member of the Police----]
Thur. 17th	A Gurkha Patrol . Killed 1 CT near Niyor. In the Sinklang area North Kedah ---]
+	**17 HMT EMPIRE HALLADALE** sailed Singapore bound for Liverpool with returning Service personnel---]
Fri. 18th	Royal Artillery Gunners Killed 4 CT's in the Sinklang area North Kedah---]
Sat. 19th	**19 Rfn. T. Budhiman Tamang** 7th. Duke of Edinburgh's Own Gurkha Rifles. Killed in Action Engaging CT's *Seremban # 2.* Negri Sembilan. ---]
Sun. 20th	Several CT Black Spots in Selangor. Kajang, Semenyth, Cheras, Broga, Bangi, & Denkil. Were allocated severe curfew times. Between the hours of 6 am & 6 pm. ---]
Mon. 21st	**E/Sgt. G.E.M. McBoyle.** F. M.Aux, Police Killed on Ops. Near Ipoh *Jalan Tertana # 1944* George Town Penang
+	Kuala Lumpur. It was announced : *'Lt. General Sir. Harold Briggs.Had been recalled from retirement.To co-ordinate the campaign against the CTs in Malaya. ---]*
Tue. 22nd	Under the Emergency Regulations. Consorting with CT's:- **Became A Capital Offence with a.penalty of. Death.---]**
Wed. 23rd	**23 Pte. J. Swift.** Seaforth Highlanders. Died*** *Kranji Singapore.# 1 / A - 5---*]
Thur. 24th	**24 L/Cpl. M.G. Jayasena.** Corps. Of Military Police (Ceylon) Died*** *Kranji Singapore #?* ---]
Fri. 25th	**25 E/Sgt's. W. Grant. - P. Humble.- W. Wells.** F.M.Aux.Police . Died whilst on Special Ops. with the 4th Hussars at Tasek near Ipoh. Were Killed by a member of the notorious Kepayang gang throwing a grenade. E/Sgt. Wells died in Ipoh Hospital. *Batu Gajah # 410 - 416 – 415* Ipoh Perak ---]
Sat. 26th	In Operation '*London*' in the Metakab, Jerantut & Kuala Lipis area. Police & Troops arrested 7 Chinese including 2 women. One was known to be a member of the MCP---]
+	In a raid at the 3rd. m/s Labu Road Negri Sembilan. 2 CT's were captured by Police A 3rd.CT armed with a revolver escaped. ---]
Sun. 27th	Seaforth Highlanders & F.M. Police dislodged a large force of CT's from their camp near Segamat Johore. During the gun fight. 2 CT's were Killed ---]
Mon. 28th	**28 Capt. W. G. Whitney.** Highland Light Infantry. Died*** *Seremban # RC / 371* Negri Sembilan---]
+	A Malay Regt. Patrol shot dead a CT near Kuala Medang in Kuala Lipis. A second CT fired on the Patrol but escaped.---]
Tue. 29th	Police on Patrol found a CT Camp behind the Aiken Lee Estate near Johore Bahru occupied by 6 CT's. who disappeared when the Patrol approached. 1 CT was Killed identified as *Fong Beng* the camp was destroyed. --]
+	In the Kluang area of Johore a Plt of 1/10 Gurkhas shot dead a *Saki* who was a CT messenger--]
+	Kuala Lumpur: Sir. Henry Gurney. Awarded 22 European & Malaysian officers with decorations, for their gallantry & dedication during the Emergency.---]
Wed. 30th	London: Mr. Rees Williams, the Colonial Under Secretary stated: *'There would be no more troops sent to. Malaya?? ---]*
Thur. 31st	In the Jerantut area of Pahang a Patrol of the 2nd Malay Regt. shot and Killed 2.CT's---]

APRIL

Fri. 1st	Operations: ' *Blenheim*' – Began in Pahang, Perak, Kelantan & Selangor Against No. 5 Regt.MRLA ---]
+	Operations: *Lemon, Plunder, Snow White & Triangle* Began in S.W. Pahang – Northen Negri Sembilan, Pahang & Selangor. Against No1Regt.MRLA---]
+	Operations: '*Holiday*' & '*Pussycat*'. Began in the Kedah - Perlis borders with the Thailand Police---]
+	Hong Kong. Mr. A. Grantham. Sent a telegram to the Colonial Office: *'Advising that the British Consul in Canton, Refuses to accept large numbers of Deportees.'* ---]
Sat. 2nd	Kuala Lumpur: Sir. Henry Gurney sent a telegram to Mr. Creech Jones stating.: *'In my opinion without repatriation. Britain cannot win the conflict in Malaya.'*---]
+	168 Chinese people were deported to China from Port Swettenam---].
+	A further 200 Chinese left Kuantan for Kuala Lumpur, on their first leg of their journey back to China.---]
+	**2 HMT DEVONSHIRE** arrived Liverpool- with returning Service personnel--]
Sun. 3rd	Singapore : Mr. J.K. Blackwell. Left for Hong Kong. To review the subject of deportation---]
+	3 more CT's were Killed. Gurkhas Killed 2 in the Kuantan area of Pahang & F.M.Police Killed 1 In Kedah---]
Mon. 4th	In the area of Terengganu. Police found a store of 100 bayonets & 683 rounds of 303 ammunition---]
Tue. 5th	**5 Pte J. M. Browne.** Devonshire Regt. Died*** *Kuala Lumpur. # 16 -938*---]
+	The Batu Caves Estate was attacked by 10 CT's who broke down the doors of the Factory, shot dead the F.M. Police **SC. Abdul Rahman Shar.** They escaped with his rifle & 50 rounds of ammunition---]

	+	In the coastal area of Selangor where a R. A. F. air strike had been carried out. 12 CT's. Frightened by the bombardment ran into a Police Patrol & surrendered.---]
	+	R. A. F. Spitfires & Beaufighters. Attacked a CT camp in the Kuala Langat Forest area of South Selangor. They bombed and strafed the area with rockets cannon & machine gun fire.---]
	+	Singapore: Report on Mr. J.K Blackwells recent visit to Hong Kong: *'In formulating the mass deportation of detainees from Malaya The British Consulate in Canton. Did not take into consideration receiving those deportees already in Swatow.'*---]
	+	Singapore: The Straits Times issued a editorial by Victor Purcell: Pointed out that: *The British & Rulers of the Malay States, having allowed unrestricted immigration for many years. Found themselves confronted by a situation that could only be met by the creation of Malayan Citizenship.*---]
	+	5 HMT DUNERA arrived Singapore with replacement Service personnel enroute to Hong Kong 6th.---]
Wed. 6th		2 CT's were hanged in Taiping Jail. **Teh Siew Huat & Lee Kim Yin** for possession of. Illegal arms---]
	+	3 CT's. were sentenced to hang. By the Courts in Alor Star. **Cho Seow Knoon, Kok Loy & Ng Gim Cheng.** They were captured in an previous ambush during which their leader was Killed ---]
	+	6 HMT DILWARA arrived Singapore with replacement Service personnel---]
Thur. 7th		**7 Sgmn. W.J.T. Twigg.** Royal Signals Drowned on Ops. *Kuala Lumpur # 16 / 939*---]
	+	Nanking China: Sir.. R. Stevenson: British Console: Sent a telegram to The Colonial Office London stating: *'Some deportees insisted they were Malayans'*---]
Fri. 8th		A large scale air attack by the R. A. F. on C.T. camps in the Ulu Gambak area North of Kuala Lumpur. It was the R.A.F. 100th. sortie since the Emergency began.---]
	+	A European Planter travelling with 3 Gurkha's in a jeep, came under fire from a number of CT's. The jeep caught fire. The Planter drove the jeep off the road. He & 2 Gurkhas escaped the 3rd. Gurkha reported missing. The attack happened in the Alor Gajah area of Malacca---]
	+	Beaufighters &Spitfires attacked a CT. area in the Kuala Langat area of S. Selangor ---]
	+	Singapore : Report on Mr. Davids visit to Swatow China: *'Swatow authorities refused entry to deportees for 2 reasons (a) Were not from Swatow. (b) Did not have funds to reach their home village.*---]
	+	Mr. Cheng Lock. Chairman of the Malay Chinese Association was wounded when a Chinese man threw a grenade into a meeting being held in the Chamber of Commerce building in Ipoh---]
	+	8 HMT LANCASHIRE arrived Liverpool with returning Service Personnel---]
Sat. 9th		**9 Cadet. R. H. Fookes.** Perak Aboriginal Aux. Constabulary & five **(5) Policemen (unnamed)** were Killed & three (3) wounded during an ambush by CT's on two (2) trucks near Jerantut *Kuala Lipis Cemetery* Pahang.]
	+	Kuala Lumpur: Sir. Henry Gurney sent telegram to the Colonial Office stating: *'Since most of the Detainees were being repatriated to Kwangtung Province. The Government needed to secure the right to land them at the two main ports. Swatow in the North & Hong Kong in the South.*---]
	+	Kuala Lumpur: Sir. Henry Gurney's Telegram to the Colonial Office London stating : *'Following this report and the discussions held in Hong Kong. Acknowledged the advice to seek the most practical means of acheivng the object without drawing attention.'*---]
Sun. 10th		**10 L/Cpl. Lambahadur. Gurung.** 2nd. King Edward VII's's Own Gurkha Rifles. Died by accident Bidor/Sungkai. *[No known Grave] Terandak Wall Memorial Malacca.*---]
Mon. 11th		Kuala Lumpur Sir. Henry Gurney sent a telegram to the Colonial Office in Hong Kong. who refused to provide transit assistance for Deportees advising them: *'To assist in the matter.*---]
	+	Sir. Henry Gurney sent despatch notes by Lt/Col. Gray & General Boucher: *'Communist success in China had a substantial effect on the security of Malaya'*---]
Tue. 12th		**12 Rfn. Bombahadur. Gurung.** 6th. Queen Elizabeth's Own Gurkha Rifles Drowned on CT Ops. Sungei Patani. Kedah *Sungei Patani # 22* ---]
	+	**12 L/Cpl. Guman Gurung.** 2nd. King Edward's VII's Own Gurkha Rifles Died*** *Kranji Singapore # 7 / D - 8*---
	+	**12 Asst/Sup. E.A. Freeborough.** F.M. Aux. Police was fatally wounded when leading a Patrol in the Sri Medan Squatter area of Batu Pahat area of Johore. *Kranji Singapore # 8 / D - 2*---]
	+	12 HMT DILWARA sailed Singapore bound for Southampton with returning Service personnel---]
Wed. 13th		A F. M. Police jungle squad operating in the Muar District shot dead a CT---]
Thur. 14th		Kuala Lumpur: Special Convoys were arranged to take Tourist to the Fraser Hill & Cameron Highlands to be escorted by Armoured vehicles.---]
Fri. 15th		600 Police & troops took part in an Operation. To capture or, eliminate the Kapayang gang.They cordoned off the Tanjong Rengong Estate. Using morters, the troops swept through the area. No arrest were made. The CT's made good their escape into the jungle.---]

+	**15** HMT EMPIRE HALLADALE arrived Liverpool with returning Service personnel ---]
Sat. 16th	London: In the House of Commons The Prime Minnister Mr. Atlee announced :
	'That they they had no intentions of withdrawing their support from Malaya'---]
Sun. 17th	Dehli :At the annual General meeting of the Malayan Indian Congress.
	'It was agreed to send a request to the Secretary of State for the Colonies. Requesting the
	British Government to announce a political, economic and educational programme, designed to help Malaya to
	achieve Democratic Self Government.' ---]
Mon. 18th	London: The. Sunday Times published an article stating.
	"BRITISH TROOPS WOULD BE BASED IN MALAYA FOR THE NEXT 10 YEARS
	IN A PROTECTION ROLE"---].
	19 Trp. R.D. Stares. 4th. Queen's Royal Hussars Died*** *Kuala Lumpur # 16 / 940* ---]
Tue. 19th	A Chinese schoolmaster & a Club Secretary, *(unnamed)* Both members of the Kumingtang.Were Killed
+	when CT's. attacked the village of Manchis Pahang---]
	On the same day the village of Kordua, was attacked by CT's. Two Chinese men were shot dead, both were
+	previous members of the Communist Party. Association---]
	Security Forces using flame throwers on a C.T. camp Killed 5 C.T's in an operation 4 miles N of Ipoh.---]
+	In Kuala Kangsar Perak 87 CT's known as the "Malayan Overseas Chinese Self Defence Army." surrendered
Wed. 20th	to the Police with a large quantity of arms & ammunition including Bren guns.—]
	21 Mr. E. Mackie A Tin Miner & **Pol/Lt . W. Grant** were Killed in a car accident at Batu Gajah Perak---]
Thur. 21st	**22 E/Sgt. F. J. Caffrey.** F. M. Police Killed in a Car accident near Rasa Ulu Selangor. Selangor.
Fri. 22nd	*Kuala Lumpur # 263*---]
	Singapore: The Hertogh Case: The Court ruled that Marie Hertogh. Should be returned to her biological
+	Parents the Hertogh's Aminah Mohamad filed an appeal against the decision. Therefore later the decision was
	reversed.---]
	A further 80 Chinese members of the OCAJA Gave themselves up to the Police in Perak . They had been in
+	the jungle since the beginning of the Emergecy. They stated:
	'They were not Reds & will join in with the Anti Bandit movement'---]
	23 L/Cpl. M. G. Jayasena Corps Of Military Police (Ceylon) Died*** *Kranji Singapore # ??*---]
Sat. 23rd	**23** HMT DUNERA arrived Singapore enroute to Southampton with returning Service personnel- 24th.---]
+	Five (5) C.T's including one (1) woman were shot dead by a Patrol in Bruas Perak.---]
Sun. 24th	An off duty Malay Regt. Corporal, saw a number of CT's. in a Squatter area. He raised a party of soldiers, Police
+	and Kampong guards, & went after them. In the ensuing gun fight. 8 CT's were Killed & 6 wounded: 1 of the
	dead was identified as a CT leader an ex member of the MPAJA. ---]
	Chong Hock Leng was sentenced to death for. possession of arms. He was. 1 of 3 CT's. identified who
+	boarded a bus & hit a Policeman on the head with a pistol butt. ---]
	24 HMT DUNERA sailed Singapore bound for Southampton with returning Service personnel---]
+	A women CT was captured & identified as **Chow Ah Che** Chief Subscription Collector in the Brunas area of
Mon. 25th	Perak. 4 CT's were Killed in the operation One was identified as **Wong Phool Kee** the CT leader and the girls
	sweetheart ---]
	R. A. F. Spitfires attacked a CT. hideouts in the area of East Johore Ground troops laid markers to indicate the
Tue. 26th	targets hidden by the overhead canopy ---]
	26/04/1949 LG #38593 p 2033 The following awarded the British Empire Medal (Military)
+	F/SGT. B. CLARKE. BEM ROYAL AIR FORCE
	F/SGT. SC. LEPPARD. BEM ROYAL AIR FORCE
	SGT. R.F.G. HOWARD. BEM ROYAL AIR FORCE
	SGT.J. MCWALTER. BEM ROYAL AIR FORCE
	The following awarded the Distinguished Flying Cross
	F/O. I.M. PEDDER. DFC ROYAL AIR FORCE
	Kuala Lumpur: The number of Squatters located on Rubber Estates and Tin Mines was announced as:
	'46,578. Of which 33,281 were illegally occupants.'---]
Wed. 27th	**27** HMT DEVONSHIRE sailed Liverpool bound for Singapore with replacement Service personnel---]
	A number of CT's. in the Belengu area of Temerloh Killed a compatriate. His wife still holding their baby was
+	forced to watch. They burnt his body.---]
Thur. 28th	At the 33rd. m/s Kuala Lipis to Jerantut road One F.M. Police Constable was Killed (*unnamed*)
	& two were wounded including one European Sargeant ---]
Fri. 29th	Segamet Police have offered a reward of $10,000. for the capture dead or alive for **Lim Yu Swee** alias **Lee Wei**
	30 Cadet. N.M.H. Murrin. F.M.Aux.Police. Died from Cerebal Malaria *Kuala Lumpur # 265* ---]

Sat. 30th	+ + +	An ex School teacher. Alias *Siew Yit.* The Political Officer for the N Johore Organisation in the Tenag area of Segamat. was Killed ---]

MAY

Sun. 1st		**1 Spr. W. O'Conner.** Royal Engineers Died*** *Kuala Lumpur # 16 / 941*—]
	+	Operation: *"Ramillies'- Began* in the Cameron Highlands / Pahang & neighbouring states of Perak, Selangor against No 5 Regt. MRLA ---]
	+	R.A.F. Sqdn. 45 Beaufighters Located on operations at R.A.F. Kuala Lumpur ---]
	+	Kuala Lumpur An Governent announcement stated that : *'The 13th./18th. Hussars currently serving in the Middle East along with 3 Royal Marine Commando Brigade (part in Hong Kong.) Would be transferred to Malaya.* ---]
Mon. 2nd		Two (2) CT. Leaders were shot dead in two incidents, one (1) in a Police operation in a Squatter area near Tapah Perak & the other, (2) By the F.M. Aux.Police in Segamat Johore.---]
Tue. 3rd		3/05/1949 LG # 38600 p 2167 The following awarded the Military Medal SGT. T. R. CHADWICK. MM KINGS OWN YORKSHIRE LIGHT INF. DRV. I. B. MUSA. MM ROYAL ARMY SERVICE CORPS. (MOR)
Wed. 4th		Canton: Mr. G.F. Tyrell sent telegram to Mr. Scott Foreign Office stating. *'The Consul in Canton advised the Malayan Government to resort to more realistic means, Sending Detainees to wither ports without permits was not a pernament solution given Chinase uncertain future.*---]
	+	4 HMT LANCASHIRE sailed Liverpool for Singapore/ Hong Kong with replacement Service personnel---]
Thur. 5th		5 7 Gurkha soldiers of the 2/7th. Duke of Edinburgh's Own Gurkha Rifles.. During an ambush on the Manchis/ Karak road in Pahang were wounded. Surrounded by 100 CT's who called out for them. *'To surrender'.* They refused to surrender. A young recruit. **Boy Parsuran Rai.** Stood up and fired the remaining bullets from his sten gun, before being Killed. The sound of another truck coming along the raod, had the CT's retreating. The next truck containing other menbers of the 2/7th. GurkhaTroops took command & searched the area. The wounded troops were taken to the Civil hospital. **Boy. Parsuram Rai** Depot Of the Brigade of Gurkhas. Died from wounds. *Sungei Patani # 19*---]
Fri. 6th		**6 Pte. W. G. Lawery.** Devonshire Regt. Died****Kuala Lumpur. # 16 943*---]
	+	**6 Major. H. G. G. Mills.** 4th. Royal Hussars Died*** *Kuala Lumpur # 16 / 942*---]
	+	2 Chinese Towkays. **Tan Say Hoh & Kee See Khoon,** were kidnapped by 6 CT's as they were entering the Enlee Tin Mine. 1 of the CT' s was a woman ---]
Sat. 7th		7 HMT ORBITA sailed Liverpool bound for Singapore with replacement Service personnel---]
Sun. 8th		**8 Fus. F. Whelan.** Inniskilling Fusiliers. Died****Kranji Singapore # 2 / A – 1* ---]
	+	R.A.F. made aerial attacks on two C.T. camps in the Sittawan area destroying them. These were followed up by ground forces on May. 27th, on C.T. hideouts in the jungles of S. Terengganu.---]
Mon. 9th		**9 Cfn. F. E. Biles.** R.E.M.E. Died****[Ashes REP]*---]
	+	9 HMT DILWARA arrived Southampton with returning Service personnel---]
Tue. 10th		**10 Jemadar. Kharnabahadur. Pun.** 2nd King Edward VII's Own Gurkha Rifles.Killed in Action Engaging CT's *Kranji Singapore # 7 / D 10* ---]
	+	A force of 15 CT's. attacked the United Malacca Rubber Estate. Breaking through the barbed wire fencing There was an exchange of fire and 1 F.M SC. (**unnamed**).was Killed. The CT's entered the Police Post forced their way in with bayonets. Then forced the SC's outside by bayonets. They tied the Corporal in charge to a tree then Killed hin by a bayonet, Then they burnt his body.---]
Wed. 11th		On the road to Jerantut. CT's. attacked a bus & mortally wounded the bus driver **Kungi Raman.** The CT's robbed the passengers of their possessions. They set light to the bus.---]
	+	R. A. F. Sptifires strafed a area of jungle in Sittawan. A follow up by ground troops found the camp accommodating 50 to 60. CT's was destroyed ---]
	+	No :28 Sqnd. R. A. F. left Singapore for. Hong Kong as a reserve Sqdn. In case anything should develop in China---]
	+	A Chinese F. M. Police Detective. Shot and Killed one of 4 .CT's who entered a cafe in TiTi village Negri Sembilan. The other 3 ran persued by the chasing Detective were being missed by bullets, escaped---]
	+	11 HMT EMPIRE HALLADALE sailed Liverpool bound for Singapore / Hong Kong with replacement Service personnel---]
Thur. 12th		

	+	A Kampong Guard Killed 1 of 4 CT's in the Muar area of Johore ---]
Fri.	13t	In Mentakab Pahang. A F.M. Police SP Killed 1 CT when a number of them attacked an Estate ?---]
	+	**13 Sgt. Jitu Ghale.** 2nd. King Edward VII's's Own Gurkha Rifles. Killed in Action Engaging CT's near Ipoh *[No known Grave] Terandak Wall Memorial Malacca*---]
	+	**13 Pte. M.A.W. Perera.** R. P.C. (Ceylon) Died*** *Kranji Singapore # 7 / E - 13*—]
Sat.	14th	Kuala Lumpur: Air Vice Marshal F. J. Mcllersh Became Air Office Commanding Malaya---]
Sun.	15th	After Rubber worth $7,000 were destroyed the day before, possibly by arson. A strong force of F.M. Police are guarding the Smoke Houses & Packing Shed of the Sua Petong Estate in Port Dickson. ---]
Mon.	16th	Co-ordianted Air/Ground forces & Road Patrols continued searching the jungles of Malaya ---]
Tue.	17th	Two members of the Selangor Royal Family, were involved in a vehicle crash. When a lorry laden with rice cashed into them. The Sikh lorry driver (*unnamed*) was Killed. The Members of the Royal family escaped injury---]
Wed.	18th	The Federation Police had little to report on the daily activities of the CT's. For the first time since the Emergency began, there appears to be a lull in CT activities. ---]
	+	**18 2/Lt. P. W. B. Graham-Watson.** - **L/Sgt. H. L. Lea.** 2nd. Battn. Scots Guards.Killed in Action Engaging CT's Batu Arang area.Selangor.*Kuala Lumpur # 16 -944- 945*---]
	+	**18 Rfn Kajiman. Tamang.** 10th. Princess Mary's Own Gurkha Rifles. Died*** *Kranji Singapore # 7 / D – 11*--]
Thur.	19th	**18 Cpl. E. S. Scutt.** MT Drv. R. A. F Changi Died Transport Accident *Kranji Singapore # 3 / A -6*---]
Fri.	20th	Army Auster TJ 321.AOP5 656 Sqdn. crashed in Malaya damaged beyond repair. The Pilot unhurt.---]
		Canberra Australia. The Australian Prime Minister announced: *'A Squadron of 8 R.A.A.F. Dakota crews & ground staff are to be dispatched to Malaya. To aid in the dropping*
Sat.	21st	*of supplies to ground forces.'*---]
	+	CT's attacked the Serdang Estate near Kuala Lumpur The Estate guards returned fire & beat off the CT's---]
Sun.	22nd	**21 HMT DUNERA** arrived Southampton with returning Service personnel.---]
Mon.	23rd	A Platoon of the 26th Field Regt. RA wounded 2 CT's in the jungles of Pahang---]
Tue.	24th	A CT camp of 14 huts, a parade ground & gym. Was found in the jungle by British troops? In the Bidor area of Tapah, It was destroyed ---]
		24 Rfn. Jitbahadur Rai was Killed in Action Engaging CT's 7th. Duke of Edinburgh's Own Gurkha Rifles
	+	*Kuala Lumpur # 24/ 4]*---]
	+	Two **F. M. Police Constables** (*unnamed*) were Killed during an engagement with CT's. in the Kedmask area o Terengganu---]
Wed.	25th	**24 HMT DEVONSHIRE** arrived Singapore with replacement Service personnel---]
	+	**25 Sgt. W.A.P. Raich.** 2nd. Battn. Scots Guards Klled in Action Engaging CT's Kuala Kabu Kabu Selangor. *Kuala* Lumpur # 29 – 956 ---]
Thur.	26th	**25 ACW.1 N.E. Best.** W. A. A. F. HQ ACFE R. A. F. Died*** *[Ashes REP]* ---]
		London: Mr. Scarlett. Foreign Office Memorandum stated: *'That the immigration authorities believed that individuals with residence claims in Malaya might well be*
Fri.	27th	*indoctrinated when they visit their homes.'*---]
		Kuala Lumpur: Malcolmn Macdonald. Commisioner General South East Asia . *'Believed it would be an undesirable attempt to put an end to the peripatetics habits of the overseas Chinese;*
	+	*instead he anticipated devising a system of exit / entry permits'.*---]
Sat.	28th	The R. A. F. announced: A squadron of Brigand air planes will soon arrive in Malaya---]
		28 Sgt, I.D. Lawson MBE. & **Gdsm. S. Palfrey.** Coldstream Guards. Killed in Action Engaging CT's in the
Sun.	29th	Sungkai area of N. Perak *Batu Gajah # 426* Ipoh Perak- Gdsm. Palfrey died from his wounds. *[Ashes REP]*]
		29 E/Sgt.N.H. Pullan. F. M. Police Killed on CT Ops. in the Pasir. Arus area Batu Berandam.
	+	*Kranji Singapore # 8 / D -5* --]
		Kuala Lumpur:In a farewell message by Major General Boucher. to Air Vice Marshal Sanderson. stated: *'That the valuable support the Air Force has been to the troops on the ground with the number of air strikes.*
	+	*Have gone a long way too demoralise the CT's*---]
	+	A number of CT's attacked the Manchap Police Station during the night. Throwing verey flares they fired at the Station. The Police returned fire. After 50 minutes the CT's. Withdrew. There were no casualties.---]
Mon.	30th	**29 HMT DEVONSHIRE** sailed Singapore enroute to Liverpool with returning Service personnel ---]
	+	The body of a Chinese Contractor **Liew Sow** was found on the Batu Sabelas Eatate. He had been shot with his hands tied behind his back. ---]
	+	A Patrol of the Grenadier Guards. Killed. 2 CT's in the Sungei Kathan area of Kajang Selengor---]
		London: Daily Mirror. Congratulated Mr. Hulett a civilian:
Tue.	31st	*'After stopping. 150. National Service Recruits being sent to Malaya ---]*

68

+	**31 Cpl. W. C. Byde**. Royal Signals Drowned on Ops. _Western Road # 1995_ George Town Penang ---]	
	31/05/1949 LG. # 381623 p.2681 The following awarded the Military Medal	
+	CPL. NOORDIN. MM. MALAY REGIMENT.	
	By the end of May. Inteligence reports. Regarding the whereabouts of **Chin Peng**. Had developed to his being in Ten Milestone Village, East of Mentakab. Having taken 5 months to travel through jungle to get there. ---]	

JUNE

Wed. 1st	Operation _Spitfire_ & _Sarong_. Began in the Cameron Highlands / Pahang & neighbouring states of Perak Selangor Against No 5 Regt.---
+	1 HMT LANCASHIRE arrived Singapore with replacement Service personnel ---]
+	1 HMT DILWARA sailed Southampton bound for Singapore/ Hong Kong with replacement Service personnel---]
Thur. 2nd	In the Telok Anson area of Perak. A bandit dressed in black trousers and green jacket. Ignored a challenge by The F.M. Police to halt. He was shot dead.--
+	In the same area 2 CT's. bodies were found near Pusing. Both Chinese one identified as **Ah Thye** who had $1,000 on his Head.---]
+	In Pulai 36 men 34 women & 61 children were detained. In Merapoh 90 men 64 women & 104 children were detained under the Squatters regulations ---]
+	2 HMT LANCASHIRE Men of the R. A. F. Regiment.(Malaya) All Malays. Embarked on board, they bound for Hong Kong in preparation for its. Defence ---]
Fri. 3rd	03/06/1949 LG # 38628 p. 2826 The following awarded the Colonial Police Medal
	ASS/SUPT. R. HIGGINS CPM FEDERATION MALAYA POLICE
	AUX/POL.OFF. B. M. HEMBRY CPM FEDERATION MALAYA POLICE
Sat. 4th	**4 Plt/Lt. R.A. Emuss**. 81 Sqdn. R.A.F. Died ***_Kranji Singapore # 3 / A -7_ ---]
+	No 1 Sqdn. Royal Australian Air Force Lincoln Bombers arrived in Singapore.To join in the air assault against the CT's.---]
Sun. 5th	**5 E/Sgt. C. W. H. Morgan**. & E/Sgt. Danny, along with 2 Special Constables. F. M. Police. Went to investigate a shooting of a Chinese shopkeeper, in the Sungei Senerup Estate. When 15 CT's attacked them. **Morgan** _[Ashes REP]_ & 1 F.M. Police **Special Constable _(unnamed)_** were Killed. 3 CT's were also Killed during the fire fight in the area of Segamat Johore.---]
Mon. 6th	A CT whilst attempting to throw a grenade at a F.M. Police Patrol on a Ruuber Estate, was Killed when the grenade blew up in his hand---]
Tue. 7th	Whilst they were being driven to the Eu Lee Tin Mine. 2 Tin Miners Tan Say Ho & Kee See Knoon were stopped by CT's & kidnapped them. They let the driver go who drove to Sungei Siput to report the incident-]
Wed. 8th	A F. M. Police jungle Patrol Killed 4 CT's in the Segamet District of Johore---]
Thur. 9th	London : Ministry of Defence It was announced:
	The. 1st. Battalion of the Middlesex Regt. would soon be arriving in Singapore---]
+	9 HMT DILWARA. Sailed from Greece for Singapore on board were the 1st..Battn. Suffolk Regt. ---]
+	9 HMT EMPIRE HALLADALE arrived Singapore with replacement Service personnel enroute to Hong Kong sailed 9th.---]
Fri. 10th	**10 Aux/ Insp. L. W. Litkie** F M. Aux. Police Killed on Ops. [_No known Grave_]---]
+	10 HMT ORBITA arrived Singapore with replacement Service personnel---]
Sat. 11th	**11 Capt. (QGO) Maniraj. Rai**. 7th. Duke of Edinburgh's Own Gurkha Rifles.Died*** _Kuala Lumpur # 24 / 9_ ---]
+	11/06/1949 LG #39637 p. 2884 The following awarded the Colonial Police Medal
	H/AP.INSP. L.W LITKIE CPM FEDERATION MALAYA POLICE
	PC ABDUL MAJID B. HAJIDIN. CPM FEDERATION MALAYA POLICE
Sun. 12th	**12 Pte. A. H. Ward**. Seaforth Highlanders. Died*** _Kranji Singapore # 1 / A - 4_ .---]
+	12 HMT EMPIRE TROOPER sailed Southampton bound for Singapore /Hong Kong with replacement Service personnel---]
Mon. 13th	**13 Sgt. E. Patterson**. W. R. A. C. Died*** _Kranji Singapore # 1 / A - 3_ ---].
Tue. 14th	Sixty (60) CT's attacked & burnt down the Estate Factory buildings on the Sungei Lallang Estate in Perak & destroyed Rubber stocks estimated as $12,000. ---]
Wed. 15th	Kuala Lumpur. Security chiefs announced: That the Security Forces had accounted for 2 CT's.. Each. Day.-]
+	15 HMT DUNERA sailed Southampton bound for Singapore/ Hong Kong.with replacement Service personnel]
+	15 HMT ORBITA sailed Singapore bound for Liverpool with returning Service personnel---]

Thur. 16th	**16 Rfn. Jitbahadur. Tamang**. 2nd. King Edward VII's's Own Gurkha Rifles. *[No known Grave] TerendakWall Memorial Malacca* ---]
+	**16 L/Cpl. J. Parker.** Royal Engineers Died*** *Kranji Singapore # 1 / A – 23*---]
+	London In the House of Commons. Mr. Creech Jones Stated : *'The British. Governmnet had no intentions of withdrawing from Malaya To prevent the Communist taking control'*---]
+	16 HMT LANCASHIRE arrived Singapore/ sailed for Liverpool with returning Service personnel---]
Fri. 17th.	The R.A.F. announced: *'Beaufighters of R. A. F. 45 Sqdn.are to be replaced by. Brigand Aircraft.'*---]
Sat. 18th	**18 Cpl. R. M. Vizor.** Devonshire Regt. Died*** *Kuala Lumpur # 29 – 946* .---]
+	**18 Cpl. Kabiraj Rana** . 2nd. King Edward's VII's Own Gurkha Rifles. Died***_Kranji Singapore7 / E -1_ —]
Sun. 19th	After the discovery of 2 CT camps in the Bentong area, believed abandoned. Were attacked & destroyed by R. A. F. Fighters and. Bombers.---]
Mon. 20th	Police at the Fook Hup Nam Tin Mine in Tuallang Perak fought off several night attacks by CT's, there were no casualties on the F.M. Police.---]
Tue. 21st	**21 O/S. D. Boyes** Royal Navy HMS *'LOCH QUOICH'* Died*** [*Ashes REP*] ---]
+	1 CT was Killed & a soldier (**unnamed**) Possibly Malay Regt. wounded in a clash with. CT's. in the Sungei Long Segament Squatter area near Kajang Selangor. ---]
+	21 HMT DUNERA sailed Southampton bound for Singapore/ Hong Kong.with replacement Service personnel]
Wed.22nd	Kuala Lumpur An announcement Stated: *'A. Communist plot to overthrow the Government of. Malaya and the. Singapore. Harbour Board. We're immobilised before it, could be. Put in place.'*---]
+	On the Serom Estate Segament. Insp. Hisham was wounded in the leg in a battle with CT.s which a Tamil and a Chinese women were Killed ---]
+	During a 2 hour. Battle on the Senum Estate in the Natur area,The CT's used fire crackers to ease out their. ammunitions. ---]
+	22 HMT EMPIRE WINDRUSH sailed Southampton bound for Singapore /Hong Kong with replacement Service personnel ---]
Thur. 23rd	**23 L/Smn. V. Harvey.** Royal Navy HMS *'CONSORT'* Died *** [*Ashes REP*} ---]
+	Whilst Patrolling the Kuantan to Jerentut road. An armoured car of the 4th. Hussars ran into an ambush. When all of the crew of the arumoured car were wounded. Tpr. T. F. Alden, fought a single assault on the CT's driving them off.---].
+	A Gurkha Soldier, Killed a prowler at Sungei Petani Gurkha camp---]
Fri. 24th	**24 Pte. R. Darby.** R.A.O.C.. Died*** *Kranji Singapore # 1 / A - 2* ---]
+	**24 C/El. Off. J.E. Chappell.** Royal Navy. H.M.S. *'TERROR'.* Died ***_Malacca Christian Cemetery # E 3_ ---]
Sat. . 25th	25 HMT EMPIRE HALLADALE arrived in Singapore sailed for Liverpool with returning Service personnel 25th.---]
Sun. 26th	**26 Gdsm. P.S Rowe.** Coldstream Guards Died*** *Batu Gajah # 436* Ipoh Perak---]
+	The Malay Headman of a village near Jerantat Pahang was Killed by CT's .---]
Mon. 27th	**27 Tpr. C .J. E. Hovell.** 4th Hussars Died from wounds rec'vd on the 23rd.*Kranji Singapore # 1 / A - 1*---]
+	A Patrol of the Grenadier Guards Killed 2 CT's near Kajang ---]
+	Grenadier. Guards Killed 2 of the Kajang gang a mile away from a Rubber Estate Kajang. Negrl Sembilan.-]
+	Another 3 CT's. were Killed in the same area by another Platoon of the Grenadier Guards near Bahau Negri Sembilan---]
+	27 HMT DEVONSHIRE arrived Liverpool with returning Service personnel---]
Tue. 28th	**Dato Nanning Abdullah Bin Mat Shah.** A Territorial Chief of Malacca. Was abducted by three CT's.. from his home. Nearby an ex F.M.Policeman was found shot dead.---]
Wed. 29th	Mentakab. At the new HQ of **Chin Peng**. Finally was able to hold a meeting of the Politburo. The first time they had convened, since the beginning of the Emergency. All 5 members of the Politburo. **Chin Peng Ah Dian,Yeung Kuo, Ah Tung & Sian Chung.** Discussed their agenda on the way forward.---]
Thur. 30th	Operations: *'Gargoyle Blenheim Ramillies Spitfire & Sarong'* Ended in Pahang Perak Kelantan & Selangor —]

JULY

Fri. 1st	Operations:- *'Overall'* –*'Pathfinder'* – *'Pintail'* & *'Widgeon.'* Began in Perak & Kedah to stop any CT's of Number 5 Regt. MRLA escaping North, after the previous operations ---]
+	1 HMT DILWARA arrived in Singapore. On board were 1500 troops, the 1st. Bttn. the Suffolk Regt. including

Sat.	2nd	reinforcement Women of the Queen Alexander's Nursing.C.orps & Womens.Army.Service .Corps. To take up nursing and administartuve jobs in various locations in Singapore & Malaya ---]
		Further to the Recce, done by the Seaforth Highlanders. A Police Party under the command of A/S. W. Neill. Sgt.'s Todd. - Phillips & Lowe (wireless operators) along with 50 Malays. Set out on a trip back to Lake Tasek Bera. Their objective build a runway there. Their journey took 1 day . There they relieved the rear party of the Seaforth Highlanders. They made camp and set about making an air strip and Police Post called Kampong Baapa. Over the following days helped by the Semilai. A fromidable task to clear jungle they cleared the space
Sun.	3rd	for the landing strip. 280 yds long x 40 yds wide, with roads including a habital layout for the Police Post.---]
		By this time the Min Yuen had recruited thousands of Chinese Squatters, to help supply the CT's in the jungle with food. The Squatters lived on the outskirts of the jungles. In those areas, many were employed as
Mon.	4th	Local Labourers by the Rubber Estates and Tin Mines. Nevertheless, as they were under no control & free to go about their business. They were a positive source of help to the Min Yuen and their masters the CT's--]
Tue.	5th	Tapah Police arrested two brothers. Leaders of the Reserve. Corps of Ayer Kunin Kampar an important. capture of 2 leading .CT's ---]
		5/07/1949 LG. # 38657 p. 3293. The following awarded the Distinguished Conduct Medal
		PTE. B. O'REILLY. DCM KINGS YORKSHIRE LIGHT INF.
		The following awarded the Military Medal
Wed.	6th	SGT. E.J. GULSTON. MM COLDSTREAM GUARDS
		6 The crew of Brigand RH859 of 45 Sqdn R.A.F **Fg/Off. N.B. Harben. - Nav. T.W. Smith & Sig. III C. Lloyd.** Were Killed when their plane crashed whilst on a bombing raid over Kelantan.
Thur.	7th	*[No known Graves] Terandak Wall Memorial Malacca ---]*
		A grenade was thrown into a. Chinese Circus in Kampar. Killing. 4 & injuring 43. Later Kampar Police. discovered. 4 CT's. In a. camp. They were the .CT's responbile for the grenade thrown at the circus They
Fri.	8th	were detained.---]
+		**8 Cpl. Dhanbahadur. Sunwar. 7th.** Duke of Edinburgh's Own Gurkha Rifles. Died on CT Ops. Motor Veh..Acc.
+		*Seremban # 12* Negri Sembilan.---]
+		**8. Sgt. Pharsabahadur. Rai** 10th Princess Mary's Own Gurkha Rifles. Died*** *Kranji Singapore # 7 / E – 2*]
		Capt. Asworth An officer of the Devonshire Regt. During a storm in the Lanchang area of. Pahang Was twice struck by lightning. It was the second time he had been struck, but was unhurt. When he was struck by lighning
+		he was operating a radio set, & flung. 8 yards. onto his. Commanding Officer---]
		Early one morning. A Platoon of . K.O.Y.L.I. Boarded three ton Lorries & were driven to Alor Star, the Border town between Malaya & Thailand. Where according to the Malay Police smuggling of narcotics was being carried out by CT's. There they set into ambush positions to await any further movement. Later a lone CT carrying a sub machine gun, followed by others behind, walked into the ambush 2/Lt. Thorne Killed the CT. In the chaos that followed, the CT's dropped everything, disappeared back across the Border, leaving their
Sat.	9th	narcotics behind which turned out to be worth approx. $ 500,000.---]
		9 The body of **E/Sgt. N.H. Pullen.** F.M. Police Killed on the 26th. May was discoverd & transferred to Kranji
Sun.	10th	Singapore for his burial *Kranji Singapore # 8 / D - 5*---]
		In a coffee shop 4 miles from Kuala Lumpur. 2 F.M. Police Detectives were drinking coffee, when .6 CT's entered the shop with sten guns. The Detectives Immediately opened fire, a gun battle erupted. The CT's
Mon.	11th	ran and were chase. However no casualties were reported---]
		11 Recruit. Gagansing Sunwar. 10th. Princess Mary's Own Gurkha Rifles.Training Wing Died***
Tue.	12th	*Kranji Singapore # 7 / E -3* ---]
		12 Pol/I. Katar Singh. F. M. Police & 8 Malay Police (**unnamed**) were Killed & two wounded in a clash with
+		a large force of CT's in the Rawang area Selangor.---]
Wed.	13th	**12** HMT EMPIRE TROOPER arrived Singapore with replacement Service personnel---]
		A 6 p.m. to 6 a.m. curfew was imposed on 18 towns of S.W. Pahang & N.E. Negri-Sembilan. in the area
+		covering 3,000 square miles. The curfew also extended to other areas in Selangor & Negri Sembilan---]
+		**13** HMT DUNERA arrived Singapore enroute to Hong Kong with replacement Service personnel 13th.---].
Thur.	14th	**13** HMT EMPIRE TROOPER sailed Singapore bound for Hong Kong ---]
		During the night R. A. F. Sunderlands, dropped fragmentation bombs from a great height & Havard's bombed
Fri.	15th	CT camps using parachute flares. Beaufighters and. Spitfires strafed the area---]
Sat.	16th	R. A. F. Beaufighters attacked. CT camps in North Perak.---]
+		**16 Mne. H.H. Rose.** (42 Commandos) Royal Marines accidenty shot. Ipoh Perak *[Ashes REP]* ---]
+		**16 Fus. J. J. O'Brian.** Innishkilling Fusiliers Died ****Kranji Singapore # 2 / A - 7* ---]
+		Spitfires flew several air strikes over CT camps in the area of SE Pahang---]
Sun.	17th	**16** HMT LANCASHIRE arrived Liverpool with returning Servive personnel---]

+	**17 Pte. W.G. Pearce.** Suffolk Regt. Died *** *Kuala Lumpur #29 / 949* ---]
Mon. 18th	17 HMT DILWARA arrived Singapore---]
+	R.A.F. Sqdn. 656 Relocated from R.A.F. Semberwang to R.A.F. Changi---]
Tue. 19th	18 HMT DILWARA sailed Singapore bound for Southampton with returning Service personnel---]
+	**19 Gdsn. W. Clucas.** Scots Guards. Died *** *Kuala Lumpur # 17 / 991* ---]

19 /07/1949 LG # 38668 p. 3531   The following awarded the Military Cross
JAMADAR. C. RAI. MC   BRIGADE OF GURKHAS
                                                   The following awarded the Military Medal
RFN. J. RAI. MM   BRIGADE OF GURKHA RIFLES

Wed. 20th	CPL N.B. AWANG. MM MALAY REGIMENT.
+	Two (2) Members of the "Kajang gang" were Killed & one (1) wounded, By the Scots Guards 14 miles N. of Kuala Lumpur---].
Thur. 21st	**20 HMT DEVONSHIRE** sailed Liverpool bound for Singapore with replacement Service personnel--]
+	Over 1,000. F.M. Police took part in a screening operation in Ipoh Perak. In an effort to clean up a local notorious CT. gang. Nine (9) persons were arrested in the village of Kapayang, & over 1,400 interrogated--]
	21 HMT EMPIRE WINDRUSH The advanced party of the Green Howard's arrived In Singapore aboard the Trooper. 1 Officer and 22 men of the Regiment disembarked together with various Army and R. A. F. reinforcements ---]
+	
Fri. 22nd	21 HMT ORBITA arrived Liverpool with returning Service personnel---]
Sat. 23rd.	2 CT's were Killed by Police on the Seram Estate Segamat ---]
Sun. 24th	East Kelantan began a Competition for the cleanest Kampong in the Area. It was open to all Kampongs in an effort to give pride to the inhabitants, many of whom are ex Squatters. ---]
+	It was announced by the local Authorities. '*The Curfew in the Cameron Highlands had been eased*'---]
Mon. 25th	24 HMT EMPIRE TROOPER arrived Singapore---]
+	**25 2/Lt. J.A. Forbes-Leith.** 2nd. Battn. Scots Guards Died*** *Kuala Lumpur # 30 -959*---]
+	**25 Sgt. J. Gilpin.** K. O. Y. L. I. Died of Scrub Typhus. *Taiping # E / 2.*Perak ---]
+	**25 Cad Ele/ O J. Chappel.** H.M.S '*TERROR*' Royal Navy Died*** *Military Cemetery # E.3 Malacca* ---]
	25 When travelling on the Kamaman River river to a Tin Mine. **ASP. J.A. Embury.** Perak Aboriginal Aux. Constabulary. with a **Mr. Dunne** a mining Engineer, **Mr. Amies** a Geological Surveyor. A Chinese Kepala &
Tue. 26th	**a Chinese Mining Engineer. (unnamed)**were Killed. When about 20 CT's ambushed the party.*Terengganu*]
Wed. 27th	26 Rfn. Gopilal. Gurung. 6th. Queen Elizabeth's Own Gurkha Rifles. Killed in Action Engaging CT's Sungei Patani *[No known Grave] Terendak Wall Memorial Malacca* ---]
	27 Rfn. Ranbahadur. Rana. 2nd. King Edward VII's Own Gurkha Rifles. Killed in Action Engaging CT's
+	.*Kranji Singapore # 7 / E -4*---]
+	**27 Pte. G. C. Hall.** Devonshire Regt. Died. Motor transport accident *Kuala Lumpur # 29 - 947*---].
	27 Plt.IV. A.H. Naish. 60 Sqdn. R.A.F. Killed when his Spitfire TP223 crashed 1 mile East of Seremban.
+	*Kranji Singapoe # 3 / A - 8*---]
Thur. 28th	27 HMT EMPIRE TROOPER sailed Singapore bound for Southampton with returning Service personnel---
Fri. 29th	A number of CT's broke through the wire fencing on the Sydney Estate but were driven off by F.M Police SC's security guards---]
+	**29 Pte. R.A. Mills.** Suffolk Regt. Died*** *Kuala Lumpur # 29 / 950* ---]
	29 Gdsm. J.F. Parkin. Coldstream Guards Killed in Action Engaging CT's During an ambush at a river crossing. Kuala Kras. Perak *Batu Gajah # 615* Ipoh Perak ---]
+	
+	Singapore The Hertogh Case contd: Marie Hertogh was returned to the custody of Aminah Mohamad.---]
+	29 HMT DUNERA arrived Singapore---]
Sat. 30th	29 HMT DUNERA sailed Singapore bound for Southampton with returning Service personnel---]
	30 Rfn. Lale. Pun. 2nd. King Edward VII's Own Gurkha Rifles. Died*** District Hospital Ipoh.Perak.
+	*Sulva Lines # 54* Ipoh Perak ---]
	About 20 CT's ambushed a. convoy of Holiday makers going up to the Cameron Highlands. The bus had reached the 7 m/s when the CT's. opened fire on the Hussars armoured escort, then attacked the bus. They got everyone off, took their ID cards.& poseesions. Ordered the Bus driver into the jungle then set fire to the
Sun. 31st	bus. The Hussars. rushed back to the scene. but the CT's had disappeared back into the jungle.---]
	31 Sqd.Ldr. W.J. Baser. DFC Equ.O. R A F Tengah Killed Road traffic accident
	Kranji Singapore # 3 / A - 9--]

AUGUST

Mon.	1st	2 CT's were Killed by Security Guards at Kampong Sawa in the Muar area----]
Tue.	2nd	2/08/1949 LG. # 38678 p. 3739 The following awarded the Military Medal
		SGT. B. CLUTTON MM GRENADIER GUARDS
		RFN C. SUNWAR MM BRIGADE OF GURKHAS
Wed.	3rd	A CT was Killed at Changkat Jong & 2 were arrested in the area of Kampar Perak---]
Thur.	4th	**4 Pte. R. Gee.** K.O.Y.L.I. Killed in road traffic accident assumed Taiping ???---]
	+	CT food supplier & Money collectors were arrested by FM Police in the Kuala Pilau Rea of. Negri Sembilan---]
	+	At a. house in the Kluang area of Johore. F.M. Police laid in waiting for a. CT collector. When he. appeared he was shot dead---]
	+	4 HMT EMPIRE HALLADALE arrived Liverpool with returning Serviice personnel---]
Fri.	5th	'D' Plt. of the Suffolk's found a CT camp capable of housing 20 to 30 personnel. It was deserted but large quantites of food were found. The camp was destroyed---]
Sat.	6th	Operation '*Rhubarb*' began in the Bukit Langang Forest Reserve. A Patrol of the Suffolk's Killed 1 CT identified as **Poh Seng---**]
	+	A CT was Killed by a Police Patrol in the Grik area of Kampar when they raided 6 huts. 9 men & a women were detained believed to be. CT. agents.---]
Sun.	7th	7 HMT EMPIRE WINDRUSH arrived Singapore with replacement Service personnel---]
Mon.	8th	**8 LAC. K. J. Bowen** R. A. F Died*** En-Route to UK. Lost at sea.
		[No known Grave] Terandak Wall Memorial Malacca]---]
	+	Kampong Guards in the Jerantut area of Pahang Killed CT leader **Wah Ali** boasting only a sliver bullet could kill him. He had. $10,000 on his head **Wah -Ali** & his gang. terrorised the river Kampongs between the Jerantut ferry & Kuala Krau---]
Tue.	9th	R.A.F. Sqdn 33 Located on operation R.A.F. Changi.---]
	+	Operation '*Rhubarb*' Ended---].
	+	18 Towns in the NSW area of Negri Sembilan, were placed under curfew from 6 pm to 5 30 am effective on the the 11th. till further notice.---]
	+	9/08/1949 LG. # 38685 p 3861 The following awarded the Military Medal
		CPL. H. RAI. MM BRIGADE OF GURKHA'S
Wed.	10th	10 MT EMPIRE WINDRUSH arrived Singapore with replacement Service personnel---]
	+	10 HMT LANCASHIRE sailed Liverpool enroute to Singapore/ Hong Kong- with replacement Service personnel---]
Thur.	11th	**11 Rfn. Chaman. Ale.** 1st./ 2nd. King Edward VII's Own Gurkha Rifles. Died***_Kranji Singapore # 7 /E. -5_ ---]
Fri.	12th	**12 Trp. E. Platts.** 4th. Royal Hussars Died*** _Kuala Lumpur # 29 / 951_---]
	+	CT **Chow Ah Seng** was hanged at Johore Bahru Goal he was the. 72nd. CT to be hanged---]
	+	12/08/1949 LG. # 38588 p.3907 The following awarded the Distinguished Service Order
		CAPT. E. LUCAS. DSO THE ROYAL BERKSHIRE REGIMENT.
		The following awarded the Military Medal
		SGT. A.B. IBRAHIM. MM MALAY REGIMENT.
Sat.	13th	**13 Cfn. J. Dixon.** R.E.M.E. Died*** _Military Cemetary Malacca # E / 4_ ---]
	+	**13 WOII. C.F. Roberts.** Royal Signals. Died from snake bite._Kuala Lumpur # 29 / 953_---]
Sun.	14th	In the Metakab area 7 F. M. Police (**unnamed**) were Killed in an ambush 17. Wounded with 3 Recuits missing. The we'll laid ambush took place on a high banking with on the other side, a ravine.---]
	+	F.M. Police guards in a village in the Jerantut area Killed **Wah Ali**. a CT. leader with a reward of $10,000 on his head.---]
	+	Forty (40) CT's armed with Sub.- machine guns attacked a Police Post near Kajang Selangor killing 3 Special Constables **(unnamed)** one a woman **(unnamed)** before stealing rifles & ammunition. ---]
	+	An Auster took off to fly to the new constructed air strip at Kampong Baapa and the Police Outpost. At about 10.o'clock spotted whiiffs of curllig smoke from a clearing below, which was adorned with strips of white parachute silk. He touched down but immediately took off again, circled then landed. His reason He thought he might go in nose tip up. It was just the beginng of many flights into Kampomg Baapa. ---]
Mon.	15th	Kuala Lumpur: Sir. Henry Gurney's. telegram to the Seretary of State for the Colonies:
		'*Still urging the deportation.should continue until the very last moment.*' ---]
Tue.	16th	40 CT's.. Attacked the Public Works Department (PDW) quarry, a mile outside Kajang. 4 people were Killed and 2 wounded. ---]
	+	16 HMT ORBITA sailed Liverpool bound for Singapore with replacement Service personnel---]
	+	

Wed. 17th	**16 HMT DEVONSHIRE** arrived Singapore with The 1st. Bttn Green Howard's onboard . As replacement to the Inniskilling Fusiliers, / enroute to Hong Kong 17th.---]
+	F.M Police Jungle squads. Discovered a jungle camp 11 miles N. of Kuala Lumpur. No contact was made, but there was evidence of a hurried departure ---]
Thur. 18th	**17 HMT DILWARA** arrived Southampton with returning Service personnel---]
+	**18 L/Cpl. Lalsing.Thapa.** 2nd. King Edward VII's Own Gurkha Rifles. Died***_Kranji Singapore # 7 / D_---]
+	R.A.F. Sqdn. 656 Relocaterd to R.A.F. Changi. ---]
Fri. 19th	CT's Wounded the OCPD of Kuala Kabu Selangor ---]
Sat. 20th	Air strikes by the R. A. F. carried out in the Gunog Augsi mountainous area. Limcoln bombers dropped 500 lb bombs & Sunderlands dropped 20 lb bombs.---]
+	A Patrol of the Suffolk's found a small hut raised on stilts in the swamp area of the Kuala Langat Forest containing large quantities of food. It was destroyed---]
+	A number of CT's. Shot & wounded the Officer Commanding Police District of Kuala Kabu Selangor ---]
Sun. 21st	Two Murders were reported. One a Chinese Squatter was Killed on the Labu road. Two 4 CT's knocked on the door of a Chinese man. When he opened his door, then shot him.---]
Mon.22nd	CT's took out a. Chinese labourer from his house at the Lalang Estate Jallapang road Nergri Sembilaan. Took him outside tied & gagged him then stabbed him to death---]
	A hand grenade was thrown into the house of Mr. Gim Eng Kong. Vice president of the Kulim Group of the MCA. it wounded him. His son Mr. Gim Eng Kong said:
+	_'He was not in the house at the time, when he saw 4 CT's move towards his house he also stated. 'He hoped all Chinese would join the fight for peace.'_---]
+	4 CT's were Killed in various parts of the Federation: 2 were Killed in the Kemasik area of Terengganu. The 3rd was Killed by a Patrol of the 1/10. Gurkhas in the Sungei Bronga area of Kluang & the 4th Killed by a Police. Patrol in the Ulu Jemental area near Johore also 7 were wounded during the clashes.---]
+	A Guardsman of the 2 Coldstream Guards. Helped an old lady carry her barabang during a movement of Squatters in the Cameron highlands. The incident became headlines in the Press---].
Tue. 23rd	CT's sabotaged 2 miles of the water supply pipeline at Sungei Long to Kajang. Selangor.---]
Wed. 24th	10 Plt D Comp. The Suffolk Regt. Killed three members of the CT Platoon. Assumed responsible for the sabotage of the water pipeline the previous day. Sungei Long. Kuala Lumpur.---]
+	**24 Trp's. A.J. Roberts. - P.J. Totman.** 4th. Royal Hussars Killed in ambush _Kuala Lumpur # 32 / 1217 – 1_]
+	**24 Pte. D.J.O. Spinner.** R.A.P.C.. Died***_Kranji Singapore # 1 / E - 9_---]
Thur. 25th	**24 HMT EMPIRE HALLADALE** sailed Liverpool enroute to Singapore/ Hong Kong- with replacement Service personnel---]
Fri. 26th	HQ Patrol Suffolk 's came across 10 CT's near Kampong Sungei Long & opened fire on them Killing 3 before the others retreated. It as also discovered that further along the main water pipeline 2 miles of the pipe had been sabotaged supplying water to Sungei Jeloh- Kajang.---]
+	**26 Rfn. Bhimbahadur Gharti.** 2nd. King Edward VII's's Gurkha Rifles. Died from drowning on CT Ops. _Sungei Patani. Old Gurkha Cemetery # 17_---]
+	**26 ABS P.D. Berkeley** Royal Navy H.M.S. _BELFAST_ Died *** _Western Road # 2020_ George Town Penang ---]
Sat. 27th	In Pahang. 100 CT's seized the town of Mengkarak, however their reign of terror only lasted 2 hours when a Patrol of Police attacked them. Killed 6, wounding others. The CT's withdrew---]
+	R.A.F. Sqdn. 60 Spitfires. Located on operation at R.A.F. Tengah.---]
+	Members of the **Liew Kon Kim's** CT gang raided the 'Sydney'' Estate, but were driven off by the Special Constables in charge.---]
Sun. 28th	**27 HMT DUNERA** arrived Southampton. with returning Service personnel---]
	Kuala Lumpur :The Planters & Tin Miners Associations had informed the Governement about their concerns with the Squatters living on the jungle Fringes. They being aware that they were supplying the CT's with food and Money, mainly under duress. They urged the Government to take Action Engaging CT's against the Squatters, It was necessary to cut off the supply chain to the CT's in the Jungle. Sir. Henry Gurney acknowledge their concern. In a comunique requested each of the Malay States Governing body to investigate its Squatter problem & recommend. Their Action Engaging CT's to combat it. Which as he put it.
Mon. 29th	_"Should be unifrom throughout all the Federal States."_---]
+	**29 AB. N.S. Conifray.** Royal Navy. H.M.S. _BELFAST_ Drowned at sea. _Krangi Singapore.# 14 / D -15_ ---]
Tue. 30th	Air strikes by the R. A. F. were carried out in the Gunog Augsi mountainous area by Sunderlands dropping 29 bombs & Lincoln bombers dropped 500 lb bombs.---]

Wed. 31st	+	A women CT entered a coffee shop, where a Chinese Detective was eating. She threw a hand grenade in, killing him, *(unnamed)* an elderly Chinese. Woman & a young girl were injured. by the. Grenade. The CT took flight and escaped.---]
		30/08/1949 LG # 38701 p. 4181 The following awarded the British Empire medal (Military) TRP. H. FUDGE. BEM 4th. QUEEN'S ROYAL HUSSARS TRP C.F. CAPPERDALE. BEM 4th. QUEEN'S ROYAL HUSSARS
	+	12 Plt 'D' Comp. of the Suffolk's engaged a group of CT's killing 2 and wounding 3 in the Broga area Kajang.---]
	+	Hong Kong: Letter from Sir. A. Grantham to the Secretary of State for the Colonies/: *'That the British Consulate in Swatow was ordered to close down.'---*] 31 HMT EMPIRE TROOPER arrived Southampton with returning Service personnel---]

SEPTEMBER

Thur. 1st		Operations *"Holiday"* & *Pussycat"* Began om the borders of Kedah Perlis with Thailand in conjunction with the Thailand Police.---]
	+	Operations *'Constellation & Leo'* Began in N.W. Johore & Malacca against No 3 Regt. MRLA ---]
	+	1 HMT DEVONSHIRE arrived Singapore.with replacement Service personnel ---]
Fri. 2nd		2/09/1949 LG. # 38703 p 4225 The following awarded the Distinguished Conduct Medal TPR. T. F. ALDEN DCM 4th..QUEEN'S ROYAL HUSSARS
	+	2 HMT DEVONSHIRE sailed Singapore. bound for Liverpool with returning Service personnel---]
Sat. 3rd		'D' Company Suffolk's on Patrol in the Belau area engaged 3 CT's killing 2 the other escaped & although they followed him lost his track ---]
Sun. 4th		A Hand grenade was thrown into the Coronation Park in Taiping, exploding, Killed 1 Chinese man and wounded 6 others. Police surrounded the area & arrested 83 people.---]
	+	4 HMT ORBITA arrived Singapore with replacement Service personnel.---]
Mon. 5th		5 Sdn/Ldr. J. B. Leetham. 60 Sqdn.Main Base R.A.F. Seletar. Flying Spitfire TP 335.Disappeared into cloud over the South China Sea *[No known Grave] Terandak Wall Memorial Malacca* ---]
		5 HMT ORBITA sailed Singapore enroute to Hong Kong---]
	+	Kuala Lumpur Sir. Henry Gurney. Stated:
Tue. 6th.		*'That many Communist in the jungle although wanting to give themselves up were to Fri.ghtened in case their bosess would kill them. The Emergency Act had been amended to ensure that any CT surrendering He or she would be not guilty of carrying arms without the fear of being executed.* *With the earlier formation of the Malayan Chinese Association in February along with Operation 'London' and the pressure of the Security Forces. Those dissindent Chinese who decided to go into the jungle or by dissent were placed in detention, repatriated or, re-educated resulting in the effective decline of No. 10 Regt. MRLA. The Malay Government believed. The Communist Revolt had been broken, announced* *Terms. Of Surrender for all members of the MRLA.'* ---] R.A.F. planes dropped millions of leaflets over the jungles stating information in Chinese Malay & Indian that:
	+	*If they surrendered those who had volunteered without any previous convictions and voluntarily surrendered themselves. Each case would be dealt with on its merits Thay would be pardoned.*---]
Wed. 7th		7 Flt/ Lt. J.R. Ford.*[Ashes REP]* -**Nav. G. H. W. Danton**.- **Sig. II. J.H. Armstrong**. 52 Sqn. R. A. F Killed when the Dakota KN 536. flew into trees in a valley North of Taiping Perak. *Kranji Singapore # 3 / C – 6 – 5*] 7 **Lt. T. F. Jones. DSC**. Royal Navy. H.M.S. *'TERROR'* Died***_Kranji Singapore # B / 24_---]
	+	7 **Pte. Shakudin b. Kassim**. Malay Regt. Killed in Action Engaging CT's. Kelantan.---]
	+	7 HMT LANCASHIRE arrived in Singapore with replacement Service personnel / sailed for Hong Kong.7th]
	+	8 **Mr. J. Norgemond**. a European Civilian was Killed in Action Engaging CT's fighting CT's. Died from multiple
Thur. 8th		gunshot wounds. In the Selangor area ---]
Fri. 9th		A Uniformed .CT was found shot dead on the Kuala Simpang Estate in the Kemaman area of Terengganu. Police following up a search of the area, came across a women with $ 593 in a bundle. It appeared the women was the wife of the dead CT---]
Sat. 10th		10 Five days after the announcement of surrender terms. Three – hundred (300) CT's attacked the Police & Railway Station at Kuala Krau Pahang. The CT's cut telephone wires. During the 3 hour period of attack eight (8) C.T's were Killed & four (4) Policemen *{unnamed}* Two (2) women *(unnamed)* were Killed together with two (2) European railway officials- **Mr. C.W. Price**, & **Mr. J Murgatroyd** who were dragged out of the Station & Killed. Then the CT's turned their attention on an Armoured train & derailed it. It apeared that the

	MRLA were determined to continue to wage war against the British. From then on they increased their number of attacks, murders and ambushes against the Military and Police Forces. ---]
Mon. 11th	**11 Stk/Mech.W.H. Martin**. H.M.S '*TRIUMPH*'. Killed when the port undercarriage of Firefly 282 collapsed on top of the three sailors working on it. *Hong Kong Happy Valley # 10517* ---]
+	**11 Mr. O. A. Lund**. Dredge Master Killed by CT's. Died from a fractured skull. Batu Gajah Ipoh Perak--]
Mon. 12th	**12 Rfn. Hari Thapa.** 2nd. King Edward VII's Own Gurkha Rifles Died from wounds recv'd in an ambush. *Kranji Singapore. # 7 / E. 6*---]
Tue. 13th	**13 Trp. F. Skilba**. 4th. Queen's Royal Hussars Died***_Kuala Lumpur # 32 / 1240_]
+	**13 Mne. R. Wright** (42 Commando) Royal Marines Died *** *[Ashes REP.*—]
Wed. 14th	**14 Grn. P. Chick**. Royal Artillery Died*** *Kuala Lumpur # 29 / 952*---]
Thur. 15th	**15 Capt. (KGO) Birtaman. Rai** 7th. Duke of Edinburgh's Own Gurkha Rifles. Died from Wounds recv'd Seremban *Seremban # 1* Negri Sembilan
+	2 CT's were shot dead by in the Jasin area of Malaca. 3 other camps were destroyed in the area. ---]
Fri. 16th	CT's made attacks on road traffic in two areas in Perak: On the Taiping /Alama road & in the Johore area of Segamat. Resulting in the killing of European **Mrs. M.E. Burns**. Wife of a mining official.---]
+	A force of 300 CT's. raided the Kuala Kru Estate but were beaten off by the SCs---]
+	16/09/1949 LG.# 38714 p. 4441 The following awarded the Distinguihed Flying Cross SQD/LDR. H.C.BROUGHTON AFC DFC ROYAL AIR FORCE SQDN/DR. J.H. JOHNSON DFC ROYAL AIR FORCE
+	16 HMT ORBITA arrived Singapore with replacement Service personnel enroute to Hong Kong 16th. ---]
Sat. 17th	**17 Mr. C.W.J. Brice**. British Civilian Killed by CT's. Died from multiple shotgun wounds in an area of Selangor]
Sun. 18th	HQ' Comp. of the Suffolk's whilst Patrolling the Sungei Jeloh Kajang water pipeline engaged 9. CT's Killed 3 CT's During the fire fight **Pte. J. Edwards** was Killed *Kuala Lumpur # 29 / 954* ---
+	18 HMT EMPIRE WINDRUSH arrived Southampton with returing Service personnel---]
Mon. 19th	Hong Kong: Mr. A Grantham sent telegram to Mr. Creech Jones advising:- '*Taiwan was restricting Chinese entry. Even from mainland China.'*---]
Tue. 20th	**20 Trp. G.E. Carpenter**. 13/18th. Royal Hussars Died Armoured Car Accident.*Seremban # C/ E / 51* ---]
+	20/09/1949 LG # 38718 p. 4495 The following awarded the King's Police & Fire Service Medal SGT. R. DANCY. PFSM FEDERATION MALAYA POLICE SGT C.W. MORGAN PFSM (Pos) FEDERATION MALAYA POLICE
Wed. 21st	**21 Gnr. T. Fitzgerald**. Royal Artillery Died **_Kuala Lumpur # 29 / 955_ .---]
+	Five (5) Malay Police were Killed (**unnamed**) & 6 wounded in an CT ambush in the Kroh area of Perak--]
+	21 HMT EMPIRE HALLADALE arrived Singapore. with replacement Service personnel---]
+	21 HMT DUNERA sailed Southampton bound for Singapore with replacement Service personnel.---]
Thur.22nd	In the Pentong area of Johore Bahru CT's broke into a house demanded money. Not much was offered. They captured the 8 year old girl - they murdered her father & seriously injured her mother. Then poured petrol over the daughter & set her alight, leaving the house to burn down ---]
Fri. 23rd	22 HMT LANCASHIRE arrived in Singapore enroute to Liverpool with returning Service personnel---]
+	2 BOR's of the Devonshire Regt. who robbed a shop were each given 18 months hard labour.---]
Sat. 24th	**24 Grn. T. B. Lewis** Royal Artillery Died*** *[Ashes REP]* ---]
+	A force of 50 CT's which attacked the Jerantut Estate. After tearing up railway lines on the Jerantut to Metakab railway line. Were engaged by. A Patrol of F.M. Police SC's. After a. 2 hour battle. A bugle sound The CT's retreated leaving several trails of blood ---]
Sun. 25th	**25 Gdsm. D. Moore**. 2nd. Battn. Scots Guards Died***_Kuala Lumpur # 29 -956_---]
Mon. 26th	The Suffolk Regt. Killed 4 CT's of the Kajang Gang wounding 3 One of the wounded was the notorious CT identified as *Kong Kee* he had already been wounded during a earlier clash with the Suffolk's The. Engagement happened 2 miles South of Broga.---]
+	CT *Chai Ah Chow* 2nd in Command of the Ayer Kuning Kampar Gang. Was out walking with his girlfriend. When challenged by a FM Police Patrol. *Chai Ah Chow* & his girlfriend retreated. The Police. using shotguns wounded them. *Chai Ah Chow* . Died in hospital. His wounded girlfriend was arrested---]
Tue. 27th	**27 A Plt. From 'A' Comp Suffolk's**, were ambushed. During their Action Engaging CT's. **Pte's L. Payne** & **D. Nobbs**. were Killed _Kuala Lumpur # 30 / 958 – 29 / 957_---]
+	**27 Pte. J. Philip**. R.A.O.C. Died *** *Kranji Singapore # 1 / E - 8*---]
+	A Plt. from 'D' Comp. Suffolk's. on Patrol in the Broga area. Engaged 7 CT's Killing 4 and capturing 3 others. Effectively broke up the "Kajang gang." whose leader was *Liew Kon Kim*. The notorious black bearded CT.----]

+	27 HMT EMPIRE HALLADALE sailed Singapore for Liverpool with returning Service personnel---]
Wed. 28th	150. CT's. Attacked a village in Pehang terrorising its inhabitants looting and setting fire to buildings- --]
Thur. 29th	A Patrol of the Seaforth Highlanders patrolling in the Muar area. After finding a CT camp set an ambush.
+	When the CT's returned. Opened fire fire killing one CT wounding another, before the CT's retreated, only to run into another Seaforth Patrol who Killed another CT.---]
+	A F.M. Police Patrol found the bullet ridden bodies of 2 Malays in a CT camp in the Kota Tinggi area---]
Fri. 30th	30 Bdsmn. M.S. Swann. The Suffolk Regt. Killed in Action Engaging CT's. _Kuala Lumpur # 30 / 960_ ---]
+	Operations _'Lemon.'_, _'Plunder_, _Snow White & Triangle_ Ended in S.W. Pahang,- Northern Negri-
+	Sembilan & Selangor.Against No 1 Regt. MRLA---]
+	Operation _'Pintai'_ ,_I ' Wigeon'_ , _'Pathfinder'_, _'Overall'_ Ended---]
+	30 HMT DEVONSHIRE arrived Liverpool with returning Service personnel ---]

OCTOBER

Sat. 1st	Operation _'Holiday'_ began in Kedah & Perlis. Mounted in conjunction with the Thailand Police to stop any infiltration by the Communist across borders. Thus, allowing Malay Policemen accompanied by Thailand Police, to travel across the border up to a three-mile limit in pursuit of CT's & to assist in food control. Being that the borders between the two countries were very easy to traverse. The MRLA used Thailand as rest camps and retraining places for their troops, also it was very easy for the supply of food. To get willing Thailand people to provide food and transport it freely across the unchecked borders ---]
Sun. 2nd	CT's. attacked a train between Jerantut & Mentakab. The train was stopped 4 miles South of. Gemas The CT's opened fire. 3 Police were wounded & 1 Killed including 1 Malay woman _(all unnamed)_ & several passengers wounded. The CT's ordered all off the train then drove the train towards Jerantut where they attempted to set light to the Train before ripping up the rails. ---]
Mon. 3rd	3 L/Cpl. Lalbahadur. Sunwar - Rfn's . Amberbahadur. Sunwar - Birbahadur. Limbu - Birbahadur. Rai - Chandraman Limbu - Rambahadur. Rai 7th. Duke of Edinburgh's Own. Gurkha Rifles. Killed in Action Engaging CT's at the Jelabu Pass. _Seremban # 7 - 6 – 9 – 4 - 8 – 5_ Negri Sembilan ---]
+	3 Sgt. J. R. Dowsen. 2nd. Battn. Coldstream Guards Died*** _Batu Gajah # 419_ Ipoh.Perak ---]
Tue. 4th	4 Gnr. J. Thomson. Royal Artillery Died ***_Seremban # CE / 3_ Negri Sembilan ---]
+	4 HMT ORBITA arrived Singapore ---]
Wed. 5th	5 A/B. B.R. Turner. Royal Navy. H.M.S. _'ALERT'_ Died*** _[Ashes REP]_---]
+	200 CT's attacked the Kemayan Estate in Pahang They destroyed the Managers house. Labourers quarters, a Smoke House & other buildings estimated at $200. 000---]
+	5 HMT ORBITA sailed Singapore bound for Liverpool with returning Service personnel---]
Thur. 6th	Kuala Lumpur: It was announced by the Police Commissoner that during the past three weeks 73 CT's had been Killed 29 captured & 109 CT camps destroyed---]
Fri. 7th	2 Chinese Labourers were Killed on the Langchang Estate in the Metakab area ---]
Sat. 8th	CT leader _Liew Yun Taw_ was Killed at Tromoh. 15 miles South of Ipoh. Where a F.M. Police jungle Patrol engaged 30 CT's---]
Sun. 9th	CT's shot 2 Chinese near the Hot Springs at Setapak 4 miles away from Kuala Lumpur. ---]
Mon. 10th	CT _Loh Ah Sang_ was hanged at Johore Goal. He was the 73rd. to be hanged under the Emergency Regulation.---]
Tue. 11th	During the night CT's. attacked the Police Post in the Chikus Forest Reserve in the Area of Tapah. After cutting the wire fence opened fire The Police returned heavy fire before the CT's retreated ---]
Wed. 12th	12 Gnr. R. S. C. Prett. Royal Artillery Died*** _Seremban # CE / 2_ Negri Sembilan ---]
+	12 Sto/Mec. A.F. Bouckley. Royal Navy H.M.S. _'TRIUMPH'_ Died***_Kranji Singapore 12 / C - 9_ ---]
+	CT's ambushed a bus on the Kuala Lipis/Bentis road. They Killed the driver, a Malay woman (_both unnamed_). Then set light to the bus.---]
Thur.13th.	CT's stopped a bus at the 161/2. m/s. North of Kuala Lumpur along the Betong road. They did not molest any of the passengers, instead they removed the load of sea fish, the bus was transporting.They drove the bus along a jungle path, then set light to it.---]
Fri. 14th	14/10/1949 LG.# 38735 p 4894 The following awarded the Military Cross CAPT. G.M. DARBYSHIRE MC THE SOMERSET LIGHT INF p. 4893 The following awarded the the Military Medal RFN. RAI. B. MM BRIGADE OF GURKHAS
+	14/10/1949 LG # 38736 p. 4903 The following awarded the Colonial Police Medal AGL/CPL. ABDUL GHANI B. JAMIL CPM. FEDERATION MALAYA POLICE

	L/CPL. NGAH B. SULONG. CPM. FEDERATION MALAYA POLICE
Sat. 15th	**15 Mr. R. H. B. Grant.** Assnt. Manager of the Tanah Merah Estate Port Dickson. Was found shot dead in his bungalow---]
+	A Patrol of the Seaforth's fought a gun battle in the Tangkak area of Muar. Johore no.casulties were reported.]
Sun. 16th	**16 Cpl. A. G. Mayle.** Green Howard's Died*** *Kuala Lumpur # 30 / 962*.---]
Mon. 17th	CT's stopped a. Bus on the Ruab Bentong road. Stole a box of Film cans. Due to be shown in the Theaters in Pahang. They also took 19 l. D. cards from the passengers.---]
Tue. 18th	A number of CT 's held up 5 timber lorries in the Segamat area. They sel light to all five. When a Patrol of Gurkhas arrived. There was a short gun fight, before the. CT's fled.---]
+	Gurkhas Killed a CT on in a Pineapple Plantation 6 miles from Seramban---]
+	18 HMT DUNERA arrived Singapore.with replacement Service personnel---]
Wed. 19th	**19 Cpl. Othman. b. Pandawa.- Pte's. Mohd. Taib, b.Slis.- Hussain b. Kassim.- Ibrahim b. Abd. Razak.** Malay Regt. were Killed in Action Engaging CT's & 8 wounded by C.T's in a ambush on the Jerantut /Kuala Lipis road Pahang.---]
+	Kuala Lumpur: A number of Government officers on the permanent staff were. Detained under the Emergency. Regulations ---]
+	Kuala Lumpur: It was announced: '45 CT's had been Killed last month. Captured 31 and wounded an estimated 13 who escaped.'---]
+	19 HMT DEVONSHIRE sailed Liverpool bound for Singapore/ Hong Kong with replacement Service personnel---]
Thur. 20th	**20 Rfn Harkabahadur. Rai.** 7th. Duke of Edinburgh's Own Gurkha Rifles. Killed in Action Engaging CT's at Kuala Klawang. *Seremban # 13* Negri Sembilan. ---]
Fri. 21st	**21 Lt. R.A.C McKenzie.** 2nd. Battn. Scots Guards. Killed in Action Engaging CT's. Kuala Kubu Kabu Selangor.*Kuala Lumpur # 30 -963*---]
+	21 HMT LANCASHIRE arrived Liverpool with returning Service personnel ---]
Sat. 22nd	**22 Pte. D.G. Higgins.** Green Howard's Died***Kuala Lumpur. *# 31 / 964*---]
Sun. 23rd	**23 Grn. T. B. Lewis.** Royal Artillery died in a road Accident . He was burnt to death when the driver. A Malay MOR Pte. who had only had a Military driving licence for. 1 month crashed the lorry. .*Buried???*
Mon. 24th	London: Colonial Office. Report. '*Control over the physical movement of Chinese was crutial when Malayan borders were vunerable to entry and re-entry of Chinese temporarily leaving Malaya for China*'.---]
+	24 HMT DUNERA sailed Singapore bound for Southampton.with returning Service personnel ---]
Tue. 25th	London: The Labour Government issued a statement stating that : '*The British Government recognised Chairman Moa's Peoples Republic of China. They were the first Western Power to make this move.*'---]
Wed. 26th	Kuala Lumpur:This Statement was not very helpful to the Federal Government in Malaya.. '*In their view*: '*It gave more creedence to the Malayan Chinese Communist and too the MRLA*---]
Thur. 27th	Kuala Lumpur A radio broadcast Announced*:* '*The disappearance of an Army Auster. The AAC Auster TJ674 of 656 Sqdn. Went missing on a flight from Metakab to Kuala Lumpur. Information of any interest should be. handed into the Police. The Auster was ferrying* **Brig. M. D. Erskine. DSO**. 2nd. Guards Brigade Commander. & his pilot. **Capt J. F Churcher R.A** . *Both were Killed when the Auster crashed en-route An intensive search was mounted but nothing was found. Capt.J.F. Churcher of 656 Sqdn was the first fatality of the Sqdn during Operation.*' '*FIREDOG*' *[No known Graves] Terandak Wall Memorial Malacca* ---]
+	Kuala Lumpur: Mr. Purcell Civil Service Officer Pointed out:- '*The British and Malay States. Having allowed unrestricted immigration for many years found themselves confronted by a situation tha could be met by the creation of a Malayan Citizenship.*' ---]
Fri. 28th	**28 Dvr. Ratbahadur Rai.** Gurkha Army Service Corps. Died Transport accident *Kranji Singapore # 7 / E – 7*]
+	A number of CT's took a Chinese. Labourer away from his house. Later He found dead in a ditch his hands had been tied behind his. back. A nail had been driven into his head.---]
Sat. 29th	CT's. Burnt down the engine shed at the Yin Yong Kongsi Tin Mine near Tapah---].
Sun. 30th	CT's at Layang Layang. Had a gun battle with a Chinese F.M. Detective but were driven off. ---]
Mon. 31st	R.A.F. Sqdn. 81 Anson Located at R.A.F. Tengah ---]
+	Kuala Lumpur: The flow of repatriation of detainees stopped. The number still in Malaya was estimated at
+	3,500.---]
+	Operation '*London*' ended against the Min Yuen.Oprations '*Constelation & Leo*' Ended in N.W.Johore & Malacca against No 3 Regt. MRLA

| | | . Resulting in 32 CT's Killed.- 28, wounde & 38 surrendered.---] |

NOVEMBER

Tue.	1st	Eight (8) mine workers including 2 - 10 year old boys were Killed, in an attack by a number of CT's on the Chong Hong Tin Mine in Pahang---]
Wed.	2nd	1 HMT EMPIRE HALLADALE arrived Liverpool with returning Service personnel—]
Thur.	3rd	The Armoured train was derailed between Mentakab. & Menkarak at the 65 milestone. ---]
Fri.	4th	Five (5) Plt. B Company. K.O.Y.L.I. whilst on Patrol in the jungle area of Kulim came across a small CT camp with 6 CT's. They Killed 4 & captured 2 that were women.---]
	+	4 HMT ORBITA arrived Liverpool with returning Service personnel---]
Sat.	5th	5 Sgt. Harkabahadur Thapa. 2nd. King Edward VII's Own Gurkha Rifles Died*** _Kranji Singapore # 7 / E – 8_
	+	In two Separate road ambush's. CT's On the Taiping /Selama Road Perak. They Killed **Mrs. M.E. Burne** a Tin Miners wife.---]
	+	In the Segamet area of Johore CT's Killed **Mr F. Dutton-Huttun** a planter 4 Chinese & 2 SC's (_**unnamed**_)]
Sun.	6th	**6 Mr. E.M. Farebrother.** Manager of the Voules Estate.Tenang Johore. Killed in a CT ambush.---]
	+	A F.M. Police Patrol found a CT Trophy Museum. Containing captured items of clothing of the Malay Regt. Ticket machines, various other items taken during their raids.They also found shot guns & ammunition.---]
Mon.	7th	**7 Sgt. D. Heyburn.** Royal Artillery Killed in Action Engaging CT's Rembau. Area. _Negri Sembilan # CE / 29_-]
Tue.	8th	At Tokai 5 miles from Alor Star. The Driver of a train braked, when he realised the rails had been tampered with. Too late the train was derailed.---]
Wed.	9th	9 10 Platoon 'D' Company K.O.Y.L.I. consisting of 24 men. Set off with 2/Lt.Richards & Sgt, Holmes. At about 4.45 pm, going uphill, they came under fire from about 60 CT's. At 7.30 p.m. the firing ceased. **Pte. K. W. Ward.** was the only casualty. Killed in Action Engaging CT's. His body was carried back to base camp. _Western Road # 2128._ George Town Penang. A follow up discovered eight dead CT's. 2/Lt.Rrichards was recommended for the MC & Sgt. Holmes the MM LG 7/2/50 # 38832---]
	+	**9 Mr. D.F. Hutton** Manager. of the Bruas Estate Selama Perak. And his wife **Mrs. Hutton** were shot dead whilst driving his car in the Bukit Kilian Estate by CT's. ---]
	+	In an ambush, by CT's on the Selama /Taiping Road. F.M. Police engaged the CT's Killing 7. Four (4) were Killed. Two (2) CT Chinese women & two (2) F.M. Special Constables (_**unnamed**_). ---]
Thur.	10th	British Forces began their biggest drive Against the CT's---]
Fri.	11th	Co-ordianted Air/Ground forces & Road Patrols continued searching the jungles of Malaya---]
Sat.	12th	12 During a 2 ½. hour gun battle with a large force of C.T's. **Lt. M. L. Anderson. L/Cpl. G. MacKay,** Seaforth Highlanders. Also 2 officers attached. to the Regt. **Lt. J.N.R. Hoare.** MC. Black Watch R.H.R.. _[Ashes REP]_ **Maj. W.M Campbell** Queen's Own Cameron Highlanders. Killed in Action Engaging CT's. _Kranji Singapore# 1 / E – 6 – 7 - 2 / A – 6 ---]_
	+	12 In an ambush at Jelebu Negri Sembilan. 14 F.M. Police PC's & Recruits were Killed named as:- **PC's: Ibrahim B. Manap, Othman Bin Almad.- Amin Bin Mohm Noor.- Awang bin Muda.- Abdul hid bin Jaafar. - Hussein Bin Kasman.- Ismail bim Ibrahim. Recuit's: Barharudin Bin Keling .- Abdullah Rahman b. Kelom Mohd. Jabin. - Abd. Rahman Bin Yahya.- Zainal Abindin Bin H.J. Ibrahim. - Idris Bin Kassim. - Mion Bin.NaSir.- Ahmad Bin Long.**.--]
Sun.	13th	13 'A' Plt of the Malay Regt. engaged a number of CT's who opened fire on their Patrol boats in the Gunong Musang area of Pehang. **Capt. J.M. Gibson** 1st.Battn. Queen's Royal West Kents At/t Malay Regt. & **Pte. Navi bin Jones.** Malay Regt. was Killed in Action Engaging CT's. Perhang. _Kranji Singapore #11/ A - 5_---]
Mon.	14th	A Patrol of the Seaforths Killed 4 CT's near Kampong Bahru in the Segamet area---]
Tue.	15th	**15 L/Cpl. Chetman Roka .** Gurkha Military Police. Died*** _[No known Grave] Terandak Wall Memorial Malacca]_
	+	15/11/1949 LG. # 38759 p.5407 The followimg awarded the Military Cross. JAMADAR D. GURUNG MC. DEPOT BRIGAGE OF GURKHAS SUBADAR L. RAI MC. DEPOT BRIGAGE OF GURKHAS
Wed.	16th	_Kuala Lumpur :_ Sir. Henry Gurney announced: '_Since the surrender terms announced on the 5th. September 103 CT's had surrendered. The. CT's are now, ragged, ill fed & harried by sickness. Since the beginning of the Emergency: 882 have been Killed & 549 captured._'---]
	+	16 HMT DEVONSHIRE arrived Singapore with replacement Service personnel ---]
Thur.	17th	**17 Sgt. Tecbahadur Ale.** 6th. Queen Elizabeth's Own Gurkha Rifles. Killed in Action Engaging CT's Sungei Patani. _[No known Grave]Terandak Wall Memorial Malacca_ ---]

+	17 HMT DEVONSHIRE sailed Singapore bound for Hong Kong---]
Fri. 18th	R.A.A.F. Lincoln bombers in support of ground forces made bombing raids on CT. camps in the CT. infested area of the Kelantan jungle---]
Sat. 19th	After removing a section of rail lines between Jerantut & Mentakab. 50 CT's attacked the Jenderak Estate in Pahang. After a two hour battle with the Estate Guards. With the sound of a Bugle the CT's retreated A trail of bloodstains were discovered afterward indicated several had been either wounded or Killed & had been removed ---]
+	R.A.A.F. Lincoln Bombers dropped bombs in the jungle CT infested areas of Kelantan---]
Sun. 20th	20 L/Sgt. M. Tate. 2nd, Battn. Coldstram Guards Died motor vehicle accident, near Kuala Kabu Bahru. *Kuala Lumpur # 331- 973*---]
+	20 L/Cpl. J. Ross – Wilson 9th. / 12th. Lancers Died *** *Kuala Lumpur # 19 / 1051* ---]
+	20 The crew of Sunderland NJ176 88 Sqdn. R.A.F. Seletar: Flt. Lt. D. M. Birrell.- Engr. 2A D,W, Donaldson – Cpl W.S.J. Smith. - AC2 J.E.Eaton.- AC1 W. Calthorpe. R.A.F. Kai Tak Hong Kong. Killed when swung on take off at night. *Kranji Singapore # 3 / D – 2 - 3* Donaldson & Calthorpe *[Ashes REP].* 7 other passengers on board survived.---]
Mon. 21st	21 Mne. J. Storey. 42 (Commando) Royal Marines Died By Accident *Batu Gajah # 448* Ipoh Perak ---]
+	21 PC. Koming b. Haji Mufti. F. M. Police Killed on CT Ops. ---]
+	21 Flt. Lt. D. M. Birrell. Died from his injuries rec'vd in plane crash *Kranji Singapore # 3 / D - 4* ---]
Tue. 22nd	90 of the 400 Detainees of Tanjong Briss Camp Malacca went on Hunger strike in protest to comditions---]
Wed.23rd	The bodies of 2 Malay CT's. were discovered By Police in the Metakab area---]
+	Kuala Lumpur : The Chaiman of the Planters - Association Mr. J. Mathieson stated:- *'The Government had. Failed to heed, warnings from men on the spot, which had led the country to bloodshed and bankruptcy.'*---]
Thur. 24th	24 PC Kahar. b. Sulong. F. M. Police Killed on CT Ops. ---]
Fri. 25th	Kuala Lumpur : Air Marshal F.J. Gogarty. Took over the duties of Air Officer Commanding Air Command Far East Air Force from Air Marshal Sir. Hugh P. Lloyd.---]
Sat. 26th	26 F/O. L. S. R. Smith. 45 Sqdn. R.A.F. Changi. & Nav.3 Sgt. Mr. D. A. Towner. Photographer. A passenger died when Beaufighter RD 866. lost height & crash landed in jungle 7 miles South of Duran Tipis. Another Photographer Mr.L.W. Curry very badly burnt, survived the crash. *Kuala Lumpur # 31 / 966 - 968* ---]
+	CT's. Remove a section of the rail lines between in the area of Ayer Hitam & S.E.Pahang.---]
+	26 HMT DUNERA sailed Singapore bound for Southampton with returning Service personnel ---]
Sun. 27th	27 Mr. Low Kee Yean. A Chinese Merchant, was shot dead by. 4 CT's 300 yards from his houses at Pangar Tera ---]
+	During a gun battle near Sungei Tua Estate in the Batu caves near Kuala Lumpur 1. CT. was Killed and, another wounded. ---]
Mon. 28th	A Patrol of the Suffolk Regt. was ambushed by CT's. The Patrol lesder 2/Lt. J.G. Stirling returned the attack and routed the CT's. He encouraged his Patrol to charge after the fleeing CT's until they came upon a CT camp. Engaging the CT's. wounded several. Following blood trails they eventually lost track. 2/Lt. J.G. Stirling's courage and skill was recommended for the MC. LG 7/2/50 #38832---]
Tue. 29th	The No 10 Regt. MRLA .After being harassed by the Security Forces. Within months, virtually became non existent in that area of a Kelantan / Pahang.---]
Wed. 30th	Brigadier C.I. H. Dunbar. arrived in Kuala Lumpur to take over command of the 2nd. Guards Brigade ---]
+	London : House of Commons Air Commodore Arthur Harvey stated : *'The RAF had done 24,000 hours and made 19,000 flights aganst the Communist Terrorists in Malaya.;* --]

DECEMBER

Thur. 1st	1 Pte. Yusof bin Embong. Malay Regt. Killed in acion Pahang.---]
+	Spitfire TP205 caught fire & burnt out at Butterworth airstrip ---]
+	1 HMT DEVONSHIRE arrived Singapore enroute to Liverpool with returning Service personnel 1st.---]
Fri. 2nd	2 Rfn. Khanabahadur Sunwar. 10th. Princess Mary's Own Gurkha Rifles Killed in Action Engaging CT's *Kranji Singapore # 7 / E – 9*
+	R. A. F. Beaufighters,Spitfires & Sunderlands. attacked bombed & strafed a wide area of the Sungei Jabol of Kuantan, Pahang. ---]
Sat. 3rd	3 Pte's A. Carter. - H. Kelly- J. Mills. 2nd. Battn. K.O.Y.L.I. Pte J. J. H. Godfrey. ACC. Att/ K.O.Y.L.I. - Were Killed in Action Engaging CT's at a road ambush, by forty (40) CT's on the Kroh / Klian Perak- Kedah

		Borders. When their convoy of 2 lorries were attacked. During the attack. Pte Fry. who was wounded by a grenade, lay in the road feigning dead, as his bandoliers was removed. He remained motionless, which saved his life.1 CT wounded in the ambush by the K.O.Y.L.I's died.
Sun.	4th	*Western Road # 2131 - 2396 – 2130 – 2129* George Town Penang ---]
Mon.	5th	CT attacked the Sungei Kawang Estate in the Metakab area of Pahang. Ordered everyone out and set light to all the buildings. ---]
	+	**5 L/Cpl. E. Banton.** Devonshire Regt. Died.of wounds.whilst Engaging CT's *[Ashes REP]* ---]
Tue.	6th	**5 Rfn. Hirasing Rana.- Rfn. Sun.bahadur Gurung** 6th. Queen Elizabeth's Own Gurkha Rifles. Died by accident. *[No known Graves]Terandak Wall Memorial Malacca]*. ---]
	+	In a ferocious gun battle on an Estate near Bahau, Negri Sembilan. When a force of 10 F.M. Police Patrol, consisting of six (6) Malays & four (4) Chinese, engaged a much larger force of CT's & fought to the last round. Four (4) Police were Killed (**unnamed**) & six (6) wounded. Their Malay commander **Sgt, Wahid** died from thirteen (13) bullets wounds.---]
	+	6/12/1949 LG. # 38775 p. 5769 The following awarded the Military Medal SGT.W.J. BULLEY DEVONSHIRE REGIMENT.
Wed.	7th	6 **HMT ORBITA** sailed Liverpool bound for Singapore with replacement Service personnel---]
Thur.	8th	**7 PC Ibraham. B. Manap.** F. M. Police. Killed in Action Engaging CT's in the Mersing area of Johore.---]
Fri.	9th	**8 ABS. D.J. McAdam.** Royal Navy. H.M.S. *TRIUMPH* Died *** *Kranji Singapore # 14 / D -14* ---]
Sat.	10th	9/12/1949 LG # 38778 p 5827 The following awarded the Military Medal L/CPL. W. MORGAN, MM, SCOTS GUARDS
Sun.	11th	100 CT's. laid expolsives on the train lines at the 38th. Mile, between Bahua & Kemayan. It derailed the Gemas to Metakan train, The engine 4 coaches plunged down a 15 ft embankment. Killing 2 passengers. A Malay Rail Ticket Inspector, 2 Tamil men & a Tamil boy. (**all unnamed**). A British Sgt on the train dropped onto the line, and unseen by the CT 's. walked 10 miles to report the crash.---]
Mon.	12th	A Chinese business man **Mr. Chong Lee Ing.** President of the. Kota Tinggi Group of the MCA was Killed in a CT ambush on the Kota Tinggi Mersing Road, 6 miles from Kota Tinggi. His Chinese driver named **Wong** was also Killed---]
		12 At Jelebu Police Station, Police Sgt. Jock Lovie joined the convoy of three Police trucks, containing a jungle Platoon consisting of E/Sgt. D.J. Aylott., Cadet. D. Hore. A F.M. Aux.Policeman, including fourteen (14) Malay Policemen. Jock climbed into the front seat of the second truck. The trucks were not armoured & therefore, vulnerable if involved in an ambush They left the Police Station roughly about mid morning & headed off in the direction of Seremban. When approaching a section of the winding road over the North/South mountain range. About half way up the hill, the second truck, had some minor engine trouble & was overtaken by the third truck. The three trucks were almost at the top of the hill, where the banks were at least 10 foot high above the road. It was then that all hell broke loose. The fuselage of gunfire rained down on the three trucks. Killing & wounding many of the Policemen. Jock immediately jumped from his truck & began firing towards the CT's in their ambush position. Unfortunately, a stray bullet hit his carbine taking off the foresight. Nevertheless, still continued to engage with the enemy. At this stage he was wounded in the hand, unable to fight with his carbine, instead lobbed a grenade in the direction of the CT's. The grenade hit the top of the bank & rolled back. As he went over the bank he collected five bullets in his legs slowing him down totally. The CT's had now control of the ambush position. When the firing stopped the CT's began throwing the dead & wounded bodies back onto the trucks. Before setting them ablaze. Jock could hear the CT's calling out to each other to find the remainder of the live survivors. Jock moved from his position to begin a hide & seek tactic. After about an hour of his movements, he came across another European Sergeant & a Malay. The three did not realise at the time, they were the only remaining survivors. The rest had been Killed or wounded including Jock's close Friend Sgt. 'Taffy' Aylott. The three decided their only option was to stay put. If, cornered fight it out. However the CT's left after their grissly work had been done. It was nearing twilight when the 3 decided to return back to the road to find Army & Police personnel clearing up the massacre. The three were very quickly taken to the hospital in Seremban. The names of the Dead were listed as :- **E/Sgt. D.J. Aylot. - Cadet /ASP. D. Hope.- P/C's Othman. B. Ahmd.- Amin. B. Mohd. Noor.- Awang B. Muda.- Abd. Ras. B. Jaafar.- Huss. B. Kasman.- Ismail. B. Ibrahim.- /** Recruit's: **Baharudin. B. Keling.- Abdl. B. Yahya.- Abd. Rahman. B. Kelom Mohd. Jibin.- Zainal Abidin B. HJ. Ibrahim.- Idris b. Kassain.- Mion. B. Nazir. - Ahmad. B. Long. P/C. Hussein. B. Kulop Mat. Sari. & Recr. Abdul mahmid bin Jamaludin.** F. M. Aux.Police Died K.I.A. Segamat Johore. **E/Sgt. D.J. Aylot. Cadet**
Tue.	13th	**/ASP. D. Hope.** *Seremban* ?? Negri Sembilan ---]

+	**13 Recruit Abd. Kajid. B. Jamaludin**. F. M. Aux.Police Died Motor vehicle accident 31/2. m/s Kota Tinggi/Lombong Rd Johore---]. London: House of Commons: Question on the award of the **General Service Medal** to Forces fighting in Malaya.......... **Lord John Hope** asked the Prime Minister. Mr. Atlee. *'Whether he will make a statement of the granting of a* **Gereral Service Medal** *to the forces engaged in Malaya?'* . **Mr. Atlee** : *'This Matter is at present under consideration.'* **Lord John Hope**: *'I hope the prime minister will realise that the country will be disappointed that no decision has yet been arrived at. Does not he agree, that the granting of such an award as this. Would be the best way of showing the men on the spot. That their country is not unmindful of their devotion to duty and is grateful for it?'* **Mr. Atlee** : *'I am waiting for some information from the High Commissioner on certain aspecs'.* **Sir. Ronald Ross** : *'Will the prime minister bear in mind that in the past Gereral Service Medals. Have been awarded for operations involving far less hardship and far fewer casualties. than the operation in Malaya?'* **Wing Commander Hulbert** . *'Will the right hon. gentleman give an assurance that this matter is under active consideration?'*
+	**Mr. Atlee**: *'I have already done so'?? .*---] 13/12/1949. LG # 38782 p 5906 The following in awarded the Military Cross MAJ. A.G.HEYWOOD MC. GRENADIER GUARDS 2/LT. J.B. TYSON MC ARGYLE & SUTHERLAND HIGHLANDERS
Wed. 14th	The following awarded the Military Medal RFN. GURUNG T. MM GURKHA RIFLES
+	F.M. Police Troops & R. A. F. planes are all engaged in.a massive search, after the big ambush where 100 CT's set an ambush when 3 Malay Police lorries were ambushed---] During Anti Terrorist duties **Cdt. O'Hara Murray**. MC. F. M. Police Killed on CT Ops. *Kota Bahru Kelamtan* A F.M. Police party of two PC's plus 2 Malay Regiment Pte's. Set off to an attack by CT camp, because the Orang Asli was an informer, albeit a trusted agent of the Special Group. Led them into a well planned
Thur. 15th	ambush resulting in O'Hara's death at Bertam Kelantan. Later the Orang Asli was arrested. Documents recovered named him as an important CT source of information on Security Forces movement in Kelantan--]
Fri. 16th. +	**15 2 F.M. Police PC's Hassan. B. Aboo Bakar**. & **Recruit Abd. Majid b. Jamaludin** were Killed at the 6th. m/s Seremban/ Jelebu Road Negri Sembilan ---] **16 A/C.1 W.L. Hewitt**. Cook R.A.F. Seletar Died***_Kranji Singapore # 3 / D – 5_ ---]
Sat. 17th	16 HMT DUNERA sailed Southampton. bound for Singapore/ Homg Kong with replacement Service personnel ---]
Sun. 18th	**17 Plt. III E.H. Loxton**. 60 Sqdn. R.A.F. Died while on Ops. at a C.T strike when his Spitfire TP 195. flew into the ground 11 miles S/S/West of Kuala Lumpur. *Kuala Lumpur # 31 / 969* ---]
Mon. 19th Tue. 20th	**18 SC. Rose. b. Yusof**. F. M. Police S.P. Was Killed. & 4 wounded (**_unnamed_**) . When 100 CT's attacked the Gunong Inas Rubber Estate in Perak. They were driven off by Malay Police forces. 2 C.T's Possibly more were Killed & several wounded before retreating into the jungle.---]
+	**19 Plt. I. T.E. Cantwell**. 45 Sqdn. R. A. F Died results of an accident.**_Kranji Singapore # 3 / E – 9_ ---]
Wed. 21st	**20 P/C. Koming. B. H. J. Mufti**. F. M. Police Died by Accident . 23rd m/s Muar Johore.---] 20 HMT EMPIRE HALLADALE sailed Liverpool bound for Singapore with replacement Service personnel]
Thur.22nd	**21 Bdr. G.E. Chapman., Gnrs. J.H. Gibson.- G.W. Bridgewater** [*Ashes REP]* Royal Artillery were Killed in an ambush Nr. Seremban Negri Sembilan. 5 others were wounded. *Seremban # CE / 36 RC / 384* Negri Sembilan---] Kuala Lumpur : Sir. Edward Gent announced that:
Fri. 23rd	*'All manpower will be mobilised for approximately a month. All civilian will be voluntary mobilised in an all out effort to beat the Communist Terrorist'.*----]
Sat. 24th	While pig shooting on the Karman Estate, Pahang. The Assnt Manager. Mr. J. A. Mac Donald. together with his Security Guard an SC. Fought a 15 minutes battle, against the CT's. When they fled. Mr. MacDonald gave chase, shooting at the fleeing CT's. He shot one in the head,which blew his head off.----]
Sun. 25th	**24 Rfn. Prembahadur. Limbu**. 7th. Duke of Edinburgh's Own Gurkha Rifles. Died, Fell from Truck

	on Operations.*Seremban # 16* Negri Sembilan ---]
+	**25 Rfn. J. McColl**. The Cameronians. Drowned at sea off Singapore.
	[No known Grave] Terandak Wall Memorial Malacca] ---]
Mon. 26th	**25 Pol/Insp. J. O'Neill**. F.M.Aux.Police. Died from a fractured scull, after an incident in Johore Bahru Johore *Kranji Singapore # 18 / A 10* ---]
+	**26 Pte. H. Smith**. Green Howard's Killed on operations. 1 Officer & 1 Pte.were seriously wounded, at Sungei Kundor in the Guan Musang area of Pahang. *Kuala Lumpur # 31 / 967* ---].
Tue. 27th	**26** 2 F.M. Police S.P's **(unnamed)** were Killed. in their camp near Kluang. During a. Gun battle with a a large force of CT's. At least 6 CT's. Were wounded, & upon retreating back into the jungle, taken with them,. ---]
+	**27 P/C. Kahar. B. Sulong**. F. M.Aux.Police. & E.PC. **Abu. Bakar. B. Kassim** F. M.P.olice Killed in Action
+	Engaging CT's whilst Engaging a number of CT's .in the. Yong Peng area of Johore---]
	27 F/O. K.R. Rosewell R.A.F. (Kuala Lumpur Sqdn. details unknown) Died by Accident. Hong Kong---]
+	6 CT's attacked the Bukit Seremban Estate in the Ulu Temlang area. They ordered all the Labourers out of the building before setting fire to the buildings.---]
	London: Admiralty Notice:
Wed. 28th	*'In the next two weeks HMS 'KENYA' will arrive in Singapore. She will replace. HMS 'LONDON' at present in the UK'*---]
Thur. 29th	3 CT's. held up a bus travelling from Ipoh to Kuala Kangsar. Took the I.D's cards from it's passengers and
Fri. 30th	the driver then allowed the bus to continue.---]
	During the night The telegraph lines between Bentong & Ruab & Kuala Lipis were cut.---]
	30/12/1949 LG # 38797 p. 33 The following awarded the Colonial Police Medal
	SUP/INSP. ABDULLAH B. TURFAH. CPM. FEDERATION MALAYA POLICE
	INSP. SALLEM. B. ABDUL RAHMAN. CPM. FEDERATION MALAYA POLICE
	H/INSP. D.T.LLOYD. CPM FEDERATION MALAYA POLICE
	H/NSP. G.D. TREBLE. CPM FEDERATION MALAYA POLICE
	H/INSP. N.M WARMINGTON CPM. FEDERATION MALAYA POLICE
	S/SP. BAHSHAH. B. TALIB. CPM FEDERATION MALAYA POLICE
	SUPT. F. WALLACE CPM. FEDERATION MALAYA POLICE
	DET/SUP. J.R.C. DENNY. CPM FEDERATION MALAYA POLICE
	DET. KHUA CHAN SENG. CPM FEDERATION MALAYA POLICE
	A/SUP. K.F. DAWSON. CPM FEDERATION MALAYA POLICE
	A/SUP. C.H.FENNER. MBE. CPM FEDERATION MALAYA POLICE
	A/SUP. TALIB. B. LISUT. CPM FEDERATION MALAYA POLICE
	ASUP. G.C. RIPLEY. CPM FEDERATION MALAYA POLICE
	A/SUP. R.G.SMITH. CPM FEDERATION MALAYA POLICE
	SGT. H.J. GODSAVE. CPM FEDERATION MALAYA POLICE
	SGT. PRITAH SINGH. CPM FEDERATION MALAYA POLICE
+	SGT. KHAWABAD KHAN. CPM FEDERATION MALAYA POLICE
Sat. 31st	V/SC. P.H.HOPKINS. CPM FEDERATION MALAYA POLICE
	30 HMT DEVONSHIRE arrived Liverpool with returning Service personnel---]
	Only 216 CT.s had surrendered. After the previous surrender terms had been announced in September ---]

R. A. F. OPERATION *"FIREDOG"* END OF YEAR STATISTICS 1949

No of Sorties	No. of Strikes	1,000 Lb.Bombs	500 Lb. Bombs	350 LbCluster	20 LbBombs	R/P's	20mm	.5 mm	.303mm
1,138	234	/	335	/	6,537	1,831	333,224	109,924	50,920

R. A. F. SUPPORT 1949

	Soties	Troops/Lift/	Casac	Pass/Lift	Supply Wt. Lbs	Leaflets drop (1,000)	B Flying Times No / hrs	Broadcsting No / hrs	Crashed
Air SupportA/C*	848	/	/	/	1,848.565	/	/	/	Dakota
Auster**	N/A	/	28	/	/	/	/	/	KN536
Pioneer	/	/	/	/	/	/	/	/	Sunderland
H/C Light	/	/	/	/	/	/	/	/	NJ176
848 Sqdn	/	/	/	/	/	/	/	/	Beaufighter's
155 Sqdn	/	/	/	/	/	/	/	/	RD858
Target/MK**	/	/	/	/	/	/	/	/	RD 866
Vis/Air OBs**	/	/	/	/	/	/	/	/	RD859
Communication**	/	/	/	/	/	/	/	/	Spitfires TP335
Leaf. Sorties*	14	/	/	/	/	/	/	/	TP195- TP223
Leaflets Drop*	/	/	/	/	6,404	/	/	/	Firefly RN 282

Leaf Sorties **	/	/	/	/	/	/	/	/	Mosquito's
Leaflets Drop**	/	/	/	/	/	/	/	/	PF623
Broad Sorties*	/	/	/	/	/	/	/	/	Brigand
Broad Hrs *	/	/	/	/	/	/	/	/	RH859
Broad Sorties**	/	/	/	/	/	/	/	/	Auster
Broad Hrs **	/	/	/	/	/	/	/	/	TJ 634 – TJ 674 · TJ628 · TJ321
Photo RECCE***	1136	/	/	/	/	/	/	/	

* AirSupport A/C Dakota -Valetta- Hastings Bristol *** Photo Rec Anson,,Spitfire, Mosquito, Meteor, Pembroke

CHAPTER 8 – 1950
ROYAL AIR FORCE
OFFENSIVE AIR SUPPORT OPERATION '*FIREDOG*'
March 1950 to December 1955

Sqdn	Location	Aircraft Type	No	Date From	Year	Date To.	Year
33	Tengah	Hornet 3/4	16	17th. Mar.	1950	1st. Aug.	1952
57	Tengah	Lincoln 2B(4A)	8	20th. Mar.	1950	29th.Mar.	1951
60	Tengah	Vampire FB5/9	10	1st. Dec.	1950	15th. Jan..	1951
81	Tengah	Lincoln 2B(4A)	8	20th. Mar.	1950	29th.Mar.	1951
	Seletar	Spitfire F10PR19	5	16th. Mar.	1950	15th.Oct.	1953
	Seletar	Mosquito PR34/34A	10	16th. Mar.	1950	31st. Dec.	1955
	Seletar	Anson 19	1	16th. Mar.	1950	15th.Mar.	1951
84	Tengah	Brigand	10	9th.Apr.	1950	20th.Feb.	1953
88	Seletar	Sunderland GR4	5	1st. Oct.	1950	5th. Apr.	1954
100	Tengah	Lincoln 2B(4A)	8	20th. Mar.	1950	29th. Mar..	1951
194	Changi	Dragonfly H/C 2/4	9	1st. May',	1950	2nd. Feb.	1953

MALAYAN AUXILLIARY AIR FORCE
OFFENSIVE AIR SUPPORT - OPERATION '*FIREDOG*'
March 1950 to April 1957
Kranji Singapore Squadron**

Sqdn**	Location	Aircraft Type	No	Date From	Year	Date To	Year
**	Tengah	Tiger Moth82A	4	1st. Mar.	1950	27th.Feb.	1957
		Harvard 2B	6	1st. Feb.	1951	27th. Feb.	1957
		SpitfireF24	3	1st. Jul.	1951	15th. Apr.	1953
		Chipmonk	4	Jan	1957	3rd. Apr.	1957

ROYAL AUSTRALIAN AIR FORCE
OFFENSIVE AIR SUPPORT - OPERATION '*FIREDOG*'
January 1950 to June 1958

Sqdn	Location	Aircraft Type	No	Date From	Year	Date To	Year
1	Tengah	Lincoln B30A	8	16th. Jul.	1950	31 Jun.	1958

MALAYAN AUXILLIARY AIR FORCE
OFFENSIVE AIR SUPPORT - OPERATION '*FIREDOG*'
January 1950 to April 1957
*Penang Squadron

Sqdn*	Location	Aircraft Type	No	Date From	Year	Date To	Year
*	Butterworth	Tiger Moth82A	4	1st.Mar.	1950	Mar.	1957
		Harvard 2B	4	1st. Feb.	1951	Mar.	1957
		Chipmonk	4	1st. Mar.	1957	3rd. Apr.	1957

JANUARY

Sun.	1st	Operations "*ASP.*" - "*Baxaul*"- "*Butlin*"- "*Thandiani*" Food Denial Began against No 5 Regt. MRLA.in the areas of Jerantut, Sungei Sinpang, Tremaloh. Triang. Pahang--]
Mon.	2nd	Operation -"*Thor*". In the areas of Johore against No. 1 Regt.---]
	+	During the night time. CT's blew train rail lines up for about 40 feet near Tapah Perak.The night train from Kuala Lumpur came off the rails. Mr. **G.F. Williams.** Engine Driver & 2 firemen were wounded.3 coaches were then set alight.---]
Tue.	3rd	Penang: CT's threw grenades into the Penang Power Stations Sub Stations, Fortunately did no substantial

		damage---]
Wed.	4th	The 1/6th.2/7th. & 1/10th. Gurkha Regt.'s working in co-operation with each other. Engaged about 40 CT's. Between them they Killed 3, wounding 8. The CT's first ran into the 1/2nd. Then disappeared into the jungle only to find hemselves running into the path of the 2/7th. Who contacted the 1/10th. They laid ambushes where they engaged the CT's. Killing 2 CT's. Others escaped taking their wounded with them ---]
Thur.	5th	40 R. A. F. Planes. Spitfires, Tempest, Beaufighters, Sunderland & Havards of the R. A. F. & Seafires and Fireflies of the Royal Navy's H.M.S *'TRIUMPH'*.Their target was a big concentrations of CT's in the Pedas area of Negri Sembilan---]
Fri.	6th	**6 Rfn. Bhaktabahadur. Ale.** 2nd. King Edward VII's Own Gurkha Rifles. Died *** *Kranji Singapore # 7 / E - 10*.---]
	+	**6 Sgt. Abu.Kabar.B. Ali.** F. M. Police Was Killed during a fire fight with CT's in the jungles surrounding Batu Gajah Perak---]
	+	After 6 days of chasing a gang of 200 CT's. Gurkhas of the 1/6 Gurkha Rifles, travelling through deep jungle & swamps, eventually caught up with them. Killing 9, capturing 1 and wounding at least 26 others.—]
	+	After the R.A.F. previous days air strike. The follow up by Ground troops revealed a camp for 200 had been severely damaged. They fought with a number of CT's. who escaped in the jungle---]
Sat.	7th	**7 A/P's. Abdul Aziz B. Dato Abdullah.- Baharum Bin Mat Tahar. – Mat Tahar Bin Maeker** F. M. Police Killed in Action Engaging CT's. 37m/s Kong Koi / Jelebu road Negri Sembilan ---]
	+	A CT was Killed by a Mersing F.M. Police Jungle squad, in the Endau area of Johore.---]
	+	On the Ban Hing Estate Johore. A Chinese Rubber Tapper (***unnamed***) was Killed by CT's.---]
Sun.	8th	Kuala Lumpur: Government notice : *'A total of. 6,000 persons were deported during 1949.'* ---]
	+	CT's. attacked the North bound Singapore to Kuala Lumpur mail train, North of Segamat. A woman and a British Soldier were hit by bullets. They were taken to the hospital in Segamet.---]
Mon.	9th	Singapore: (Assumed date early in January) The begining of the Marie Herttogh case. Anderline Hertogh filed a lawsuit in the Singapore Law Courts, seeking to assert their parental rights of their biological daughter Marie who at he age of 6, in 1943 during the Japanese invasion of Java, was handed over to a trusted Friend of the family named, Aiminah binte Mohamad, who moved to her home town of Kemaman Terengganu Malaya, to be brought up during the Japanese occupation as a Muslim. Her original religion was Roman Catholic. So began the saga of parental ownership which caused riots.---]
	+	9 HMT ORBITA arrived Singapore with replacement Service personnel---]
Tue.	10th	**10 Mr. Chen Choi.** A travelling Dispenser was Killed,when CT's. opened fire on his jeep. His driver was also hit. The arrival of a Troop of the 4th. Hussars stopped any further firing.---]
	+	A Gurkha scout was seriously wounded, when CT's opened fire near Tenang Kampong in the Segamet area---]
	+	In the Bahau area of. Negri Sembilan. A few seconds after a F.M. Police Patrol, traveling in a lorry along the Pahang road, towards the Kok Foh Estate. The CT's detonated a mine. blew a hole in the road. Then opened fire. The Police returned fire, throwing hand grenades into the CT's ambush positions. The search after, discovered bloodstains indicating at least 5 CT's had been wounded ---]
Wed.	11th	North of Ipoh. CT's cut the. Telegraph wires at several points, between Kantan and Sungei Siput.---]
Thur.	12th	R. A. F. Planes, attacked Bukit Champadak in the Metakab area. Strafing it with Rockets and cannon fire.-]
	+	Kuala Lumpur: In was announced in Kuala Lumpur: *'The number of CT's Killed last year was 613 & CT's captured 336* ---]
Fri.	13th	**13 F/Lt. J. A.S. Carpenter. Nav/11. G. R. Wallace. F/Off. D. A. Harker. – Nav/lll. D. A. Pointer.** 81 Sqdn. R. A. F. Died when their planes Mosquito PF624 & RG524, collided in mind-air near Seria Brunei. Buried in *Kuala Belait Cemetery Brunei*. ---]
	+	In the area of the Kuala Krau A Patrol of the 1/10th. Gurkhas Killed ***Chong Chin Nam.*** The most notorious Senior Ccommander of the 26th. Indepemdant Company of the MPABA. He had a reward of $10.000 on his head. 1 other CT was Killed.---]
Sat.	14th	A Patrol of the Suffolk's engaged two CT's wounding one who died later, the other escaped---]
Sun.	15th	**15 A/P. Abdul Raschid Bin Tagar.** F. M. Police Killed By CT's. Bukit Selembua.---]
Mon.	16th	**16 Gdsm. K. Holland.** Scots Guards was Killed during clashes with CT's. in the area of Selangor. Several CT's were Killed. *Kuala Lumpur # 31 / 970*---]
	+	**16 PC. Haron B. Idris.** F. M. Police Died from wounds recev'd in ambush on 13th.at Segamat Johore.]
	+	16 HMT ORBITA sailed Singapore bound for Liverpool with returning Service personnel---]
Tue.	17th	**17 E P/C. Sa'at Bin Mazuki.** F. M. Police Killed in ambush at 17th. m/s Kluang / Kahang rd.Johore----]
	+	A Patrol of the Coldstream Guards Killed 2 CT's in a contact North of Batu Arang.---]

	+	17/01/1950 LG # 38815 p. 302 The following awarded the Colonial Police Medal HON. AUX/POL INSP. E.C. BURNE.CPM THE FEDERATION MALAYA POLICE SGT. J. MCKENZIE. CPM THE FEDERATION MALAYA POLICE L/CPL. CHUNG AH NGOW. CPM THE FEDERATION MALAYA POLICE
Wed.	18th	**18 RSM. R.J. Read BEM.** 4th. Hussars Died. *** _Batu Gajah # 420_ Ipoh Perak---]
	+	London :Mr. Philip Noel Baker the British Secretary of State for Commonwealth Relations tated:. '_We have declared that the purpose of our presence in Malaya is to prepare the way for their. Self_ _Government.---]_
	+	The 7th. Malay Regiment MRLA had been smashed by the Security forces. They were operating along the Pahang River. 2 of their leaders, both with a. $2,000 price on their heads, had surrendered.---]
Thur.	19th	**19 Pte. C. Covell.** 1st. Battn. Seaforth Highlanders. Died*** [_Ashes REP]._ ---]
	+	**19 Sgt.I. F. Lovell** Royal Signals Died *** [_Ashes REP_]---]
	+	**19 Recruit Yaacob. B. Sulaiman.** F. M. Police Killed in an ambush Ipoh Perak.---]
	+	**19 Mrs. Burne.** was Killed during an ambush. Her husband Mr. Burne was Supt. of the Temoh section of Southern Malaya. He was driving on the Taiping /Selama Road Taiping Perak.where the ambush took place]
	+	19 HMT EMPIRE HALLADALE arrived Singapore. with replacement Service personnel---]
Fri.	20th	**20 Pilot/11. J. Janicki.** 60 Sqdn. R. A. F. Tangah. Died *** _Kuala Lumpur # 31 / 971_---]
	+	**20 SC. Leong Ah Choy.** F. M. Police Killed in Action Engaging CT's Sungei Siput Perak ---]
	+	6 CT's entered the Frazer Estate, surprised the inhabitants of a Kongsi house. Demanded food. The Security Guards hearing a commotion intervened. After a fight of 20 mins, the CT's fled. A Chinese woman was seriously hurt ---]
Sat.	21st	20 miles from Mersing. On two Seperate occasion. CT's set fire to two buses. As the Mail bus was rounding a corner. A gunshot was heard and about. 20 CT's came out of their ambush position, stopped the bus. \t gun point. Nobody was injured. They took ID cards then ordered the passengers to march away. Then they set the bus. Alight. The passengers had only gone about 200 yards. When they met the passengers. from the other ambushed bus, which had also been set alight. The CT's retreated into the jungle---]
Sun.	22nd	**22 Pilot.111. R. H. Hall.** 60 Sqdn. R. A. F. Tangah. Was Killed when his Spitfire TP219 crashed in bad weather near Kampong Solak Tampin Malacca. _Kuala Lumpur # 12 / B - 10_---]
	+	**22 Rfn. Hastabahadur Pun.** Was Killed in Action Engaging CT's. When Patrols of the 1st./ 2nd King Edward VII's Own Gurkha Rifles. Engaged & Killed 23 CT's in a gun battle near Labis Central Johore. It was later discovered that possibly 35 CT's had been Killed. _Kranji Singapore # 7 / E -11._---]
	+	The Gurkha's on Patrol found a CT camp capable of housing 100 men. Destroyed it---]
	+	22 In a road ambush by CT's at Sungei Bakap in Province Wellesley. E/**Sgt. F.R. Young.- E.PC. Abdul** **Hamid Bin. Nayar.** F. M. Police & 7 Malay Policemen were Killed. named as: PC. **Mohd. Sohar. B. Abdul** **Chani.- SC. Yeow Chew Bhik** Recruits. **Hanasi. B. Ahmad.- Johari B. Mohd.- Othman.B. H J. Omar.-** **Abdul Rahman B. Wahab.- Mohd. Sharriff B. Suleman.** _Jalan Pertana Penang # 1417_ -]
	+	CT's fired shots at a car driven by a Mr. J.F.K. Cooper. A civil engineer The attack happened at the 37th. m/s Ayer Hitam road to Johore. Luckily he escaped the bullets.---]
	+	R. A. F. planes attacked a CT camp of 9 huts, in the Rawang area NE of Batu Arang Selangor. Straffing the area destroyed it. ---]
	+	R. A. F. planes carried out another air strike at another.CT camp S.E of Kuala Lumpur in the Ulu Langat jungle near Kajang.---]
Mon.	23rd	**23 PC Ismail B. Talib.** F. M. Police Died from wounds recv'd in the ambush on the previous day.---]
	+	10 of the 23 CT's Killed by the Gurkha's, were identified. One was **Yap Pion** with a. reward o $5,000 on his. head.---]
	+	A number of CT's held up a bus travelling from Kampar to Sungei Siput. The CT's attacked it. 4 F. M. Police on the bus fought a gun battle with them, until the CT's gave up and withdrew back into the jungle. There were no casualties. ---]
	+	23 HMT DUNERA arrived Singapore with replacement Service personnel ---]
Tue.	24th	**24** A Royal Navy Seafire plane No ? from the. Aircraft carrier HMS '_TRIUMPH_' crashed at. Changi air base. The Pilot_.- Lt. W. J. Heard._ Royal Navy HMS '_TRIUMPH_' Killed._Kranji Singapore # 12 /C – 8_ ---]
	+	24 HMT DEVONSHIRE sailed Liverpool bound for Singapore/ Hong Kong with replacement Service personnel---]
Wed.	25th	5 CT's in an ambush Killed a Chinese Rubber dealer from Malim Nawar.---]
	+	A Patrol of Gurkhas Killed 1CT on the Padang Piol Estate near Jeratut Pahang.---]
	+	Under the. Emergency Regulations.The 82nd. 1 CT (_unnamed_) was hanged in Pudu Jail Kuala Lumpur ---]
	+	

Thur.	26th	A Patrol of the KOYLI Killed 3 CT's in the Kulim area of SouthKedah. One of the 3 CT's was identified as a former Captain. in the MPAJA with a reward of $ 5,000 on his head---]
Fri.	27th	26 PC. Ismail. B. Talib. F. M. Police. Killed in ambush Sungei Siput Perak---]
		27 In an road ambush on the Sungei Papan Estate Kota Tinggi area Johore. 8 Malay Special Constables & 4 Chinese Labourers were Killed & several wounded. By a strong force of C.T's. The Police are named: S/C Cpl. Ja'afar B. Abu Talis.-SC 's Embi B. Mohd. Shah.-Yusof B. Abdullah.-Sutan B. KJ. Arshad.-
	+	Abdullah B. Jaafar. –Ahmad B. Awang.- Awang B. Mamood. - Atem B. Ahmat.---]
	+	CT's fired on two trains. One in the Gurun area of Kedah between Prai and the Thailand border. The second was North of Senai in Johore. No casualties reported .---]
Sat.	28th	27 HMT EMPIRE HALLADALE sailed Singapore bound for Southampton with returning Service personnel---]
	+	28 Mr. W.M.M. MacDonald. was Killed by. CT's. Who shot him. when he was with his Contractor on their rounds of the Sabai Estate. 21 miles South of Bentong on the Manchis road.---]
Sun.	29th	In the Segamet area of Johore. 10 CT's fired shots at the Manager of the Buloh Kasap Estate. They didn't do any damage.---]
	+	Gurkha troops of the 2nd. King Edward VII Gurkha Rifles. Attacked a CT camp in the Titi area of Negri Sembilan. Engaging them Killed 3. Others escaped back into the jungle The capacity of the camp could house 350 personnel. Also found was a store for large amounts of food. The camp was destroyed.---]
Mon.	30th	A Patrol of the 2nd. King Edward VII's Gurkha Rifles Killed 3 CT's in the Kong Kol area of Jelebu.---]
		30 A/P Tai Jon. F. M. Police Killed by CT's at Pendok Batang Jesin Malacca---]
	+	4 CT's shot dead the Indian Conductor Mr. M. M. Panniker of the Kamuning Estate near Sungei Siput.---]
	+	On the Puchong road 14 miles from Kuala Lumpur. An elderly Chinese man was found dead, (unnamed) with a bullet wound in his head, his hands were tied behind his back.---]
	+	Several CT's Entered the Labourers quarters of the Sikamet Estate near Seremban. They ordered the Labourers outside. Then set light to their quarters and other buildings.--]
	+	F. M. Police and 17 Field Royal Artillery Gunners, captured a wanted women CT. in the jungle near Bahau Negri Sembilan.---]
	+	In the Batu Gajah area, The Tronoh Police Patrol laid an ambush and Killed 2 CT's. ---]
	+	Another F. M. Police Patrol, operating on the Sungei Papan Estate near Kota Tinggi Johore. Killed 2 CT's by throwing grenades into their midst.---]
	+	In the Kajang Area of Selangor CT's raided the Pak Long Tin Mine. Dragged 3 Chinese workers out and shot them dead---].
Tue.	31st	In the Muar area of Johore CT's, made a Rubber Tapper stand and watch while they stabbed his wife to death. then Killed him.(both unnamed)---]
	+	31 Gnr. J.P.Hayes. Royal Artillery Killed assumed during an engagement with CT's Seremban # RC 387 Negri Sembilan.---]
		2 F. M. Police: Abdul Ghani.- Khlid b. Rahman were Killed when CT's attacked the Rengan Water Pumping Station ---]

FEBRUARY

Wed.	1st	1 L/bdr. R. Kay. Royal Artillery Died. *** Kranji Singapore # 1 / e - 5---]
	+	1 SC Ahmad B. Hj. Ali. F. M. Police died from wounds received on the 31st. Jan. at the Rengan Water Pumping Station Johore---]
	+	An Anti- Bandit Month, was introduced during the Month of February, ending in late March employing civilians to take on the clerical tasks in the Police Stations. Therefore releasing Policemen to outside duties.This included employing more civilians in the information and propaganda office in civil departments]
	+	Mentakab Chin Peng's HQ. about this time (assumed ref: Chin Peng my side of history p.236). The Politburo learned of a breech in the party policy. Siew Lau the Malacca State Secretary, was publically annoucing and issuing documents stating : When the MCP came to power they would sieze all plantation land and redistribute it to Malay Peasants, accordingly to the Politburo: proposals. AH KOK was ordered to sort out Siew Lau's problem ----]
Thur.	2nd	2 Maj. P. M. Cook. 4th. Royal Hussars Died *** [Ashes Rep]---]
	+	2 HMT DUNERA sailed Singapore enroute to Hong Kong---]
Fri.	3rd	3 S/Major. Mohd. Noor B. Asap F. M. Police Killed on Ops. No further details ---]
Sat.	4th	R. A. F. Planes, Spitfires, Tempest, Harvards, Beaufighters & Royal Navy Fireflies including Sunderlands.

	+	carried out. 58 air strikes in the areas of Selangor & Johore ---]

<table>
<tr><td></td><td>+</td><td>carried out. 58 air strikes in the areas of Selangor & Johore ---]
CT's attacked Kampong Telekong in the Jelubu area of Negri Sembilan. The Kampong. Guards. fired on them & drove them off. A trail of blood stains, showed that several CT's had been wounded. ---]</td></tr>
</table>

+ carried out. 58 air strikes in the areas of Selangor & Johore ---]

CT's attacked Kampong Telekong in the Jelubu area of Negri Sembilan. The Kampong. Guards. fired on them & drove them off. A trail of blood stains, showed that several CT's had been wounded. ---]

Sun. 5th

+ During an air strike by Beaufighters of R.A.F. 45 Sqdn. A school was damaged and five civilians woun injured---]

A number of CT 's tried to sabotage the water main pipe, 16 miles away from Johore Bahru on the Pontiac road. Military forces heard two explosions, deployed to investigate, found. two granades had been placed under the pipe, that only dented the surface. ---]

Mon. 6th

6 A/B. C.A. CAMP. H.M.S. 'TRIUMPH' Killed during an onboard aircraft crash Firefly number ? *Kranji Singapore # 12 / c – 7*

+ Gunners of 26th. Field Artilley RA carried out firing on areas known to be used by CT's the engagement continued through to end on the 14th Feb.---]

+ The village of Simpang Tiga Perak was attacked & burnt down by CT's. Its 1,000 occupants were rendered homeless---]

Tue. 7th

7 O/Tel. A.R. Moore. H.M.S. 'TRIUMPH' Died from injurues recv'd from the day before on board air crash *Kranji Singapore # 12 / c - 6* ---]

+ CT's derailed the train on the Kemayan to Bahau rail line They removed the rails.just before the train Approached. Derailed two coaches.---]

+ Kuala Lumpur : Telegram. I.D. Higham To R.H. Scott Foreign Office :
'If the assumption is there will be appreciable banishment or repartriation to China during 1950. Then I should be inclined to thimk that the prospect's. of of ending the emergency in Malaya is small.' ---]

+ 7/2/1950 lg # 38832 p. 647   The following awarded the Military Cross
LT. P.L. RICHARDS. MC   THE SOMERSET LIGHT INF. ATT/T K.O.Y.L.I.
SABADOR. J. LIMBU MBE. MC   7TH. DUKE OF EDINBURGH'S OWN GURKHA RIFLES.
                              The following awarded the Military Medal
SGT. K. HOLMES.MM.   KINGS OWN YORKSHIRE LIGHT INF.
RFN. C. LIMBU. MM   7TH. DUKE OF EDINBURGH'S OWN GURKHA RIFLES

+ RFN. T. LIMBU. MM   7TH. DUKE OF EDINBURGH'S OWN GURKHA RIFLES
7/02/1950 lg # 38835 p. 669   The following awarded the Colonial Police Medal

Wed. 8th

AP. MOHAMAD SAID B. ALAM CPM   FEDERATION MALAYA POLICE (KAMPONG GUARD)
49 CT's. raided the Sang Lee Estate in the Ruab area of Pahang, burnt down the. rubber Storage House. the Smoke House and. Labourers lines.---].

+ A combined operation by the Bitish & Thailand forces supported by the R,A,F. began on the Kedah/ Thailand borders---]

Thur. 9th

Kuala Lumpur : Major General R.E. Urquhart: Appointed General .Officer.Commanding-. Malaya Replacing. Major General C.H. Boucher. who had been invalided home.---]

Fri. 10th

The village of Simpang Tiga. Was being. rebuilt after CT's tried to destroy it. The people are determined to. fight back. and are rebuilding the area, they still will refuse to provide food for the CT's -]

Sat. 11th

11 P/C E/Sgt. H. F. Cowan. - Ep/C Balwant Singh- A/O Kartan Singh F. M. Police .Killed on CT Ops. In ambush 20 m/s. Galong Road Sungei Siput Perak. *Batu Gajah # 421* Ipoh Perah ---]

Sun. 12th

12 Capt. G. W. R. Turrall. Intteligence Corp Killed. by CT's. *Taiping # E / 3* Perak---].

+ Bankok : Reports in the press that South Thailand's Muslems, were cooperating with Malayan Communist Terrorist were denied---]

Mon. 13th

Kuala Lumpur: John Davis CBE. DSO. DSO. In his new position of Chinese Liaison Officeer. Suggested to Gurney of forming:
'Good Chinese' into Auxilliary Police Forces Squads of 50 – 100 men' Met with credibility aand approval to proceed ---]

Tue. 14th

14 SC. Zakari B. Hj. Ahmad. F. M. Police Killed in ambush at Kota Tinggi Power Station. ---]

+ **14 Mr. H. T. Winter** was ambushed and Killed. 4 miles South of Ipoh. He and his Malay Syce, were on their way to the Dusan Bertam Estate. to pay the Labourers their wages.---]

+ 14/2/1950 lg # 38839 p.773   The following awarded the military medal
RFN. B. SUNWAR. MM   10TH. PRINCESS MARY'S OWN GURKHA RIFLES

+ 14/2/1950 lg #38884 p. 1799   The following awarded the military medal
RFN T. THAPA MM   2ND. KING EDWARD VII'S OWN GURKHA RIFLES

+ 14 HMT ORBITA arrived Liverpool with returning Service personnel---]

Wed. 15th
Thur. 16th

15 2 F. M. Police P/C's **Talib B. Kidan. Zahri B. Yob.** Killed in ambush Nankuang Pahang.—]

A Patrol of the 4th. Hussars Killed a CT leader identified as ***Ming Yuen*** on the Lipis to Kuantan road---].

	+	16 HMT DUNERA arrived /sailed Singapore enroute to Southampton with returning Service personnel---]
Fri.	17th	17 Aux.Pol/Insp. I. L. F. Campbell. CPM . F.M.Aux.P. Intelligence Officer to The 1st Battn. Green Howard's Mr. Campbell., whilst following a gang of 40 CT's. North of Bentong in an exchange of fire, he was Killed along with his Sakai Tracker. Mr.Cambell was a former member of Force 136. buried at *Kuantan Christian Cemetery # ?* Pahang ---].
	+	A Patrol from 'D'Comp. The Suffolk's located a CT camp in the Kajhua area of Kajang. They attacked it. In the ensuing fire fight 3 CT's were Killed. 2/Lt J. N.Kelly was recommended the MC. & L/Cpl. D.E.R. Wicks. The MM. LG 5/5/50 # 38903---]
Sat.	18th	Kampong Guards. Killed 2 CT's. At The 41 m/s Brunas Road Perak---]
Sun.	19th	Following the shooting of a F.M. Chinese Detective (**unnamed**). The whole of Bukit Mertajam was been placed under strict curfew.between the hours of 6 p.m to 6.am.---]
Mon.	20th	20 E.P/C's Jaafar B. Arsbad. & Md. Dap B. Lajin. F. M. Police Killed By CT's At The Bukit Kepong Police Station Muar Johore.---]
Tue.	21st	21 HMT DEVONSHIRE arrived Singapore with replacement Service personnel sailed to Hong Kong 21st
Wed.	22nd	Gunners of the 26th. Field Artilley R.A. resumed firing, on areas known to be used by CT's ---]
Thur.	23rd	23 A force of 200 CT's. under the leadership of *Mat Indra* a CT from Muar. In the early hours of the morning attacked the Police Station at Bukit Kepong Muar Johore. They attacked the Station several times, each time causing casualties. They set the married quarters alight, also the Police launch used on the river Muar. After five hours of sustained attacks, that finished about 9. o' clock. The Police Station was set alight. *Mat Indre* called this massacre a victory for the MRLA. A spotter plane flew over the burnt out Police Station & reported no sign of life in evidence. During the attack 22 F. M. Police personnel were Killed:- I/S.Jamil.B. Mohm. Shah. - Cpl. Mohm. Yassin B. Bj. A. Wahab.- L/Cpl. Jidin.B. Omar. – P/Cs Hassam B. Othman. – Abu. B. Mhm. Ali. – Hamzad. B. Ahmad. – Basiron. B Ahmad. – Awang B, Ali. - Ibrahim. B. Adom. -Abdul Kadir. -Adman. B. Jasfar. – Jaffar B. Hassam. - The Policemen are listed as: EP/C. Jaafar Bin. Arshad.- Md. Dap Bin. Lajim.- I.S.. Jamil.B. Mohd.Siha-. Moh . Besiron. B. Ahmad.- Awang B. Ali.- Ibrahim. B. Adom. Hap's Samad B. Yatim.- Mahud. B. Sa'at.- Ali Bakop Othman B. Yahya.- Redzuanb. Alias.---]
	+	In another operation 850 men women & children were rounded up from the Batu caves 6 miles North of Kuala Lumpur to be detained awaiting repatriation. ---]
Fri.	24th	24 D/Cpl. D. Chessex. F. M. Police Killed in ambush Gopeng Perak---].
	+	24/ 2/1950 LG iss. 38847 p. 961 The following awarded the Military Cross 2/LT. J.G. STARLING. MC. THE SUFFOLK REGIMENT.
Sat.	25th	Malayan. Anti Bandit. Month. Began with 350,000 volunteers being prepared if, summoned to be called up. A reward of $850.00,was announced: *'For any information leading to the capture of. any CT's alive or dead & $100 for any information leading to their capture--*]
Sun.	26th	26 Trp. W. LANE 4th. Queen's Hussars Died*** *Kuala Lumpur# 16 928.*---]
Mon.	27th	Kuala Lumpur; Major Gereral R. E. Urquhart became General Officer Commanding Malaya ---]
Tue.	28th	28 HMT EMPIRE HALLADALE arrived Southampton with replacement Service personnel.---]

MARCH

Wed.	1st	A working Party of the Trade Unions recommended: *'The immediate formation of the Malayan Trade Union Council'* ---]
Thur.	2nd	2 During an ambush at the 42 m/s, near the village of Brinchang Cameron Highlands. 6 soldiers of the R.A.S.C.**2/Lt.. W. J. Richards.** *[Ashes REP]*- **Sgt. C.R. Ritter.**- **L/Cpl. N. Hoggett.** - **Dvr. R.H. Jones.***[Ashes REP]* - **Dvr. O. B. Abdullah.**(MOR). R.A.S.C. Along with **Mr. Gates de Brazilius** New Zealander. Banker / Electrical Eng. & HonAux/Insp. & **SC. Wan Kamarudin B. Yoop Manap.** FM.P. 5 other BOR's were wounded. *Batu Gajah #423 / 424 452* Ipoh Perak. - **Dvr. O. B. Abdullah.**(MOR).*Claimed by next of Kin* ---]
	+	2/03/1950 LG # 38868 p 1423 The following awarded the British Empire Medal (Military) L/CPL. M. LEE. BEM ROYAL ENGINEERS
Fri.	3rd	3 E/Sgt. E.P. Hackett. F. M. Police. Killed on CT Ops. on the Ban Lee Estate Bentong Pahang *Kuala Lipis Cemetery* Pahang ---]
	+	3 P.E. Mackey Ex Ft./Lt. R.A.F. F. M. Police. Killed on CT Ops. . Bentong Pehang---].
	+	3 Singapore. **F.M Aux.Pol. G.de.B.B. Gates** F. M. Police was Killed by a grenade thrown by a unknown Chinese person who was shot dead.---]
Sat.	4th	

Sun.	5th	4 2 F. M. Police SC 's Othman B. Talib. & Mohd. Sujod b. Serdal Killed in Action Engaging CT's ambush on the Eldred Estate Johore. ---].
	+	5 Dvr. Cpl. F. Hand. R.A.S.C..Died from wounds recv'd on Mar. 2nd.*Batu Gajah # 614* Ipoh Perak---]
Mon.	6th	A train was derailed near Mentakab Pahang, A F.M. Policeman *(unnamed)*was Killed including several passengers were wounded, when C.T's opened fire---]
Tue.	7th	6 3 F.M. Police S C.'s Ariffin B. Awang.- Ya'Acob B. Abdul Khan. – Awang B. Mat Saman.- Killed in an ambush on the Sungei Dingin Estate Kulim Kedah---]
	+	7 Pte. J. D. Williams. R.A.M.C.. Died.*** *Kuala Lumpur # 31 / 973*---]
	+	7 8 miles from Kuala Lumpur. At an open-air Cinema in the village of Kepong Selangor. **Chan Sam Yin** the leader of a band of C.T's. Opened fire on the audience waching a Chinese.movie. Causing havoc. Killing SC. Awal Khan S/O Sab Khan F. M. Police. 17 people, including boys & girls & wounding many others.
Wed.	8th	**Chan Sam Yin**. Was a Leader in the 8th Battn. MRLA with a price of $25,000 on his head.---]
	+	The Hong Huat Sam Rubber Estate Pahang. Attacked by C.T's.Killed 2 Chinese officials.*(unnamed)* ---]
	+	8 SC Awal Khan B. S/O Sab Khan. Died from wounds rec'vd on the 6th. ---]
	+	8 SC Hashim B. Abdul Mahid F. M. Police Died from wounds received on the 4th ---]
Thur.	9th	8/3/50 LG # 38557 p. 1255 The following awarded the Military Medal.
		CPL M. THAPA. MM 2nd. KING EDWARD VII'S OWN GURKHA RIFLES
		The Deputy Comander of the 8th. Battn. MRLA. **Chan Sam Yin** Was shot dead by a village F.M. PC. When he & his men attacked the village of Kepong North Selangor. His. gang was those that had attacked a
	+	packed.canvas Cinema and opened fire on the 7th..---]
	+	9 HMT DEVONSHIRE arrived Sngapore bound for Liverpool with returning Service personnel 9th.---]
Fri.	10th	9 HMT ORBITA sailed Liverpool bound for Singapore / Hong Kong with replacement Service personnel-]
		Hong Kong: Mr. P. D. Coates Chinese Consulate Services commented :
	+	*'It was agreed at the conference the policy of severe restriction of Chinese immigrants into the Federation, Singapore, Sarawak Brunie & Borneo should be confirmed & adopted.'*---]
		Kuala Lumpur: It was announced by the Commissioner Generals Office:
	+	*'That 2000 more troops will be arriving in Malaya. To reinforce the existing Battalions, including a Squadron of Lincoln bombers '*---]
		10/03/1950 LG # 38858 p.1213 The following awarded the British Empire Medal (Military)
		F/SGT. R.G. GARTHWAITE.BEM ROYAL AIR FORCE
		F/SGT. R.F.A. HOLLOWAY. BEM ROYAL AIR FORCE
		SGT. W.F. KEABLE. BEM ROYAL AIR FORCE
		The following awarded the Distinguished Service Order
		SQDN./LDR. E.D. CREW. DSO. DFC ROYAL AIR FORCE
		The following awarded the Distinguished Flying Medal
Sat.	11th	PILOT/II A.D. CORDINER. DFM ROYAL AIR FORCE
		Along the notorious Kroh / Klian Intan road. A haven for CT ambushs.. Volunteers armed with parangs cleared 9 miles of embankments, covered in thick jungle growth. In one day only, the volunteers cleared
	+	a stretch of 6 miles. They worked under heavy guard of the Gurkha Rifles.---]
	+	Operation '*Blastoft*" began gathering information of CT activities. North East of Broda---]
	+	'B' Comp Suffolk's Killed 1 CT. wounded & captured another, in an engagement 6 miles North of Kajang--]
		Kuala Lumpur: In the wake of the Anti Bandit Month General John Harding Recommended:
Sun.	12th	*'Britain beef up its military commitmrents to Malaya. Suggesting to transferring the Commando Brigade from Hong Kong to Malaya & requesting more armoured car reinforcements.'* ---]
		12 Mr. H.M Winter. Manager. Duson Bertam Estate Perak. Killed by 3 CT's, who stopped his car whilst he
	+	was delivering Chinese New year advances for his Labourers. His Driver escaped.---]
	+	'D' Comp Suffolk's engaged & Killed 3 CT's. In the area of Broda ---]
	+	CT *Chai Ko Cha* was hanged in Taiping goal. He was the 84th CT to be hanged ---]
		Mentakab *Chin Peng's* HQ (assumed date ref: *Chin Peng* My Side of History p.236) The Politburo
Mon.	13th	Demotted *Siew Lau*---]
		13 D/PC. Gooi. Ban. Teik. & Rect. Mohd. Isa. B. Sharif. S. P/C Din Bin Endut F. M. Police were Killed in an ambush at the 39th. m/s.Bruas/Sitiwan Road Perak.---]
Tue.	14th	13 HMT EMPIRE HALLADALE sailed Liverpool enroute to Singapore /Hong Kong with replacement Service personnel---]
		2 Members of the Crown Film Unit, in Malaya to film British troops Whilst travelling in a convoy from Kuala Lumpur to Bentong. Were ambushed by CT's at a bend in the road. Opened up with Bren gun and
	+	shot guns. The camerman Mr. D Catford & Mr C. R. Stark. Plus 5 soldiers were wounded---]

Wed.	15th	Kuala Lumpur Mr. Malcomn MacDonald stated: *'That the anti- bandit operations. Had shown disirability for more air surport for the ground forces. Therfore more reinforcements including Lincoln Bombers would be sent from England. Also the 26th. Gurkha Infantry Brigade would be sent from Hong Kong'* ---] Kuala Lumpur: It was announced: *'Alsatian dogs will be used in tracking CT's in the jungle. With their handlers. Airmen of the R. A. F. Regt. They being attached to the F. M. Police Patrols. Also The 26th. Gurkha Brigade will be arriving from Hong Kong & will be centered in Kuala Lumpur.'* ---]
Thur.	16th	15 HMT DUNERA arrived Southampton with returning Service personnel---] 16 L/Cpl. C. A. Smart. R.E.M.E. Died***_Kuala Lumpur # 31/ 974_--- Australia: The MELBOURNE Herald: *'Urged the Australian Government to send immediately military forces to Malaya to help fight the communist terrorist.'* ---] Malaya: RAF 81 Sqdn. Spitfires & Mosquitoes & Anson A/C s became operational from RAF Seletar ---] Kuala Lumpur: Letter from Sir. Henry Gurney. to J.J. Parkin. Colonial Office: ... *'Authorities in the British Territories had taken every possible measures to check the movement to and from mainland China'* ....
Fri.	17th	R.A.F. 33 Sqdn. Hornet 3/4 became operational from RAF Tengah---] 17/3/1950 LG # 38866 p 1411 The following awarded the Military Cross CAPT. (KGO) D. LIMBU MC. 7th. DUKE OF EDINBURGH'S OWN GURKHA RIFLES The following awarded the Military Medal SGT. RANA. J. MM 6th.. QUEEN ELIZABETH'S OWN GURKHA RIFLES RFN. RANA. D. MM 6th.. QUEEN ELIZABETH'S OWN GURKHA RIFLES
Sat.	18th	561 Squatters were rehoused in a new village on the Seremban. Port Dickson road. They had previously been detained in detention camps---]
Sun.	19th	19 R. A. F. Planes attacked the 89th. m/s Bentong to Kuala Lumpur area. Spitfires, Brigands, Tempests & Beaufighters bombed and strafed the area infested by CT's.---]
Mon.	20th	20 Pte.N. Baldam. Green Howards Died*** _Seremban # CE / 33_ Negri Sembilan---] R.A.F. 57 Sqdn. Lincoln 2B (4A) Began Operations at R.A.F. Tengah ---]) R.A.F. 61 Sqdn. Lincoln 2B (4A) Began Operations at R.A.F. Tengah ---] }Operation 'MUSGRAVE' R.A.F. 100 Sqdn. Lincoln 2B (4A) Began Operations at R.A.F. Tengah ---] } Operation '*Blastoff*' Ended. Inteligence gathered indicated there wre at least 100 CT's active in the area Leading to a combined effort involving. The Suffolk's 1st/7th. Gurkhas. 2nd. Field Artillery , R. A. F. planes of Lincoln Bombers, & Sqrdns. of Brigands, Tempest , Sptifires & Sunderlands.
Tue.	21st	21 Rfn. Ratne. Damai. 6th. Queen Elizabeth's Own Gurkha Rifles. *[No known Grave] Terandak Wall Memorial Malacca*]---] 21 L/Cpl. R. Monteiro. Royal Signals (MOR) Died *** _Bukit Serendit Cemetery Malacca # P / 72_ ---] 21 SC Seenevasadan. F. M. Police Killed in Action Engaging CT's Badenoch Estate Kedah---] 21 E/Sgt. K.W. Davies. F. M. Police Killed on CT Ops. Ambushed on road in Badenoch Estate Sungei Patani Kedah. _Jalan Pertana # 1420_ George Town Penang ---] 21/3/50 LG # 38866 p.1411 The following awarded the Distinguished Service Order MAJ. E. GOPS.ELL. MC. DSO 6th. QUEEN ELIZABETH'S OWN GURKHA RIFLES The following awarded the Military Cross CAPT. (KGO) D. LIMBU.MC 6th. QUEEN ELIZABETH'S OWN GURKHA RIFLES LT. D.H.W. BROWN. MC GORDON HIGHLANDERS The following awarded the Distinguished Conduct Medal C/SGT. B. THAPA. DCM 6th. QUEEN ELIZABETH'S OWN GURKHA RIFLES CPL. J. NIMMO. DCM ARGYLE SUTHERLAND HIGHLANDERS The following awarded the Military Cross CAPT. D LIMBU MC 6th. QUEEN ELIZABETH'S OWN GURKHA RIFLES CAPT. (QGO) B. RAI. MC 7th. DUKE OF EDINBURGH'S OWN GURKHA RIFLES The following awarded the Military Medal PTE. H. MCPHEE.MM SEAFORTH HIGHLANDERS SGT. J. RANA MM 6th.QUEEN ELIZABETH'S OWN GURKHA RIFLES RFN. D RANA MM 6th.QUEEN ELIZABETH'S OWN GURKHA RIFLES 21/03/1950 LG # 38870 p. 1474 The following awarded King's Police & Fire Medal SC. YONG LIEW HOON. KPFM FEDERATION MALAYA POLICE

		A/SGT. ABDUL WAHID B. MOHD. SUDIN.KPFM (Pos) FEDERATION MALAYA POLICE
		The following awarded the Colonial Police Medal
Wed.	22nd	SC. UGANG B. AMIN. CPM (Pos) FEDERATION MALAYA POLICE
		SC TAN SENG. CPM. (Pos) FEDERATION MALAYA POLICE
		22 P/C. Shakarwi. B. H.J. Mohd. Daub. F. M. Police. Died from wounds recev'd in an ambush
	+	on the previous day on the Badenoch Estate Pahang---].
	+	**22 2/Lt. Hasan bin Haji Yasin. – Cpl. Salleh bin Hassan.– L/Cpl. Othman bin Abdul Samad,** --.
Thur.	23rd	**PC Sharkawi b. HJ. Mohd.Daud** .& 4 Policemen (*unnamed*) Gua Musang.---]
		'C' Company Suffolk's along with F.M. Police Patrols Killed 3 CT's in the area of the Pudu hills---]
		F.M. Police & Soldiers of the Suffolk Regt. Entered a Squatter area. During the search 2 CT's were Killed,
Fri.	24th.	5 Suffolk soldiers were slightly wounded in the engagement. The engagement took place 4 miles
	+	outside Kuala Lumpur---]
		24 Mne. D. Smith. Royal Marine 45 Commando Died *** *Kranji Singapore # 4 / E – 2*---]
		24/3/1950 LG # 38869 p.1465 The following awarded the Military Medal
		CPL. G. RAI MM 10th. PRINCESS MARY'S OWN GURKHA RIFLES
	+	L/BDR. L.S. COLLINS MM ROYAL REGIMENT ARTILLERY
		24/03/1950 LG ' 38570 p. 1474 The following awarded the Colonial Police Medal (Postumosly)
		SC . UNGANG B. AMIN. CPM FEDERATION MALAYA POLICE
		SC. TANG SONG. CPM FEDERATION MALAYA POLICE
Sat.	25th	POLI/Lt. T.W.CHARLTON was awarded the G.M. during a raid on a CT camp nr Muar Johore
		25 Sgt. M. Breese. R.A.S.C. Died from wounds recv'd in CT ambush
	+	*Western Road # 2132* George Town Penang---]
Sun.	26th	**25 PC. Lattif B. Ariffin** F. M. Police Killed on Ops. Near Ipoh ---]
		R. A. F. Sunderland SZ 573. Of 209 Sqdn. Lying offshore was being loaded up with bombs for the next
		days mission. When there was an explosion. **Flt/Lt. W. H. J. Kearney.** Nav. 209 Sqd. Was Killed & the
		R. A. F. Main Base Seletar. The bombing crew were blasted into the water. Rescue launches were
		quickly on the scene, to rescue the Airman including. **AC1. G. Gillett.** who although suffered superfial
		wounds, saw another badly injured Corporal in difficulties, although thrown a lifebelt. Gillett knowning the
		Corporal was not a swimmer, went to the aid of the drowning airman. Gave him his lifebelt. Unfortunately
		due to his own injuries and the current, was swept aay & drowned. His body was washed up two days later.
		For his courage whilst trying to save his colleague. **G. Gillett** was awarded the George Cross.*Kranji*
	+	*Singapore # 3 / D – 1 - 6*- LG 3 Oct 1950 # p.39033 ---]
	+	R. A. A.F. Lincolns made "pin point " attacks on CT camps in Central Johore---]
		26 In a road ambush in Kelantan a CT force of 250-300 strong. Killed 17 soldiers of 'A 'Plt of 'D' Comp 3rd.
		Malay Regt., They came under heavy fire, from a large force of CT's, hidden in foxholes on the opposite
		bank of the river. Those Killed were:-
		2/Lt. Hassan bin Hadj Yasin.- Cpl.Saleh bin Hassan. - L/Cpl's Mohd Ras bin Osman.- Othman bin Abdul
		Samad.- Pte's: Mohd. Yunos bin Hadj Tahar. – Pte. Ismail bin Rasol.- Ahmad bin Hadj Mohd Jan.-
		Mohd Isa bin Ahmad.- Ibrahim bin Awang.- Daud bin Ismail.- Omar bin Deris.- Mohd Yasin bin Hadji
		Ali.- Mustaffar bin Sulaiman.- Wahab bin Sidek.- Osman bin Yacob.- Mohd Sharif bin Abdul Manuf.-
		Kassim bin Mohd Amin.- Hussin bin Hadji.Yussoff. Malay Regt. & 4 F. M. Police **PC Latei. B.Arriffin.+**
	+	3 others (*unnamed*) Killed in Action Engaging CT's---]
		In the follow up after the battle it was discovered. A least 29 CT's had been Killed and many wounded, who
		may have died later. The search party also discovered 2 wounded Malay soldiers. It was the Malay
	+	Regiment biggest kill & loss.---]
		Within a week of their arrival in Singapore 8 R. A. F. Lincoln bombers. Attacked an extensive area of the.
Mon.	27th	Bahau area of Negri Sembilan known to be infested with CT's---]
Tue.	28th	**27 E/PC Dolah b. Hj. Talib.** F. M. Police Killed on Ops. No further details---]
		28 2 F. M. Police **SC 's. Kechot Osman b. Kassim - Meeroon B. Tahir** Killed in Action Engaging CT's on
	+	the Puchong Estate Johore---]
Wed.	29th	**28 HMT ASTURIAS** arrived / sailed from Singapore. with returning Service personnel ---]
		29 P/C Alias. B. Mahat. F. M. Police Died from wounds received in an ambush the previous day Bukit
Thur.	30th	Murtajam Penang---]
		30 2 F. M. Police **SC's Ujang B. Ahmad. – Maizan B. Mohamed.** Killed in Action Engaging CT's. Between
Fri.	31st	Glendak Estate & Serting Negri Sembilan---]

	+	**31 Pte's. B. Bottomley**. [_Ashes REP_]- **W. J. Daynes** - **G. S. James.**, 1st. Battn. Green Howard's including:- 2 F. M. Police **S.P/C: Dolah Bin Hj Taib AP Kee Peng Chai.** Killed in ambush. _Seremban # CE / 53 - 32_
	+	Negri Semebilan ---]
		31 E/Sgt. P.J. Murphy F. M. Police Drowned on CT Ops. Boat accidently overturned Pasir. Kemundi _Kuantan Christian Cemetery_ Pahang ---]
		1 Soldier & 1 European Estate official were wounded. When their convoy was attacked by C.T's. In Bahua Negri Sembilan.---]

APRIL

Sat.	1st	**1 L/Cpl. J. McGee.** 1st. Battn. K.O.Y.L.I.. Died ***. _Kuala Lumpur.# 17 /975_---]
	+	**1 Cpl. Salleh bin Hassam.- Pte. Yeob Ibraham bin Ngah Mat Amin.** Malay Regt. Killed in Action Engaging CT's Pahang. [_No known Graves] Terandak Wall Memorial Malacca_---]
	+	**1 P/C. Ahmad. B. Mohd. Yusuf.** F. M. Police Killed in Action Engaging CT's in Ulu Serting Kualah Pilah Negri Sembilan---]
	+	**1 SC Mamar B. Bachik.** F. M. Police. Killed in Action Engaging CT's. Batu Sables Estate Rembua Negri Sembilan---]
	+	Operation "_Jackpot_"- "_Foxhound_"- "_Autumn Double_" Began against No 2 Regt. MRLA. In Negri Sembilan-Selangor & Pahang.---]
	+	Operation "_Carp_"- "_Albermarle_"- "_Rabbit_"- "_Cleaver II._" Began against No 5 Regt. MRLA in Perak---]
Sun.	2nd	In an amusement park in Kuala Lumpur A hand grenade was thrown by an assumed CT into a crowd of people. 26 people were wounded, some seriously. It was the first attack in Kuala Lumpur, the capital, since the Eemergency began.---]
Mon.	3rd	The Anti-Bandit Month ended. Approx. 500,000 Chinese, Malays & Indians volunteered during the period doing I. D. checks, enforcing curfews imposed and special Police duties ---]
Tue.	4th	**4 Mr. A. H. Girdler.** Admin Officer for Kluang was Killed from multiple gunshot wounds & **Mr. G.B. Follett** & 4 F.M.Police **PC. Arshad. B. Siraj A/P's Abullahb/ Bor. – Wan Rasoi b. Wanln. – W. Khairrudin b. W. Mushiran.** Were Killed in an ambush at the 11th. m/s Yong Peng / Paloh Rd. Johore.---]
Wed.	5th	**5 Rfn. Dalbahadur Rana.** 2nd. King Edward VII's Own Gurkha Rifles. Killed in Action Engaging CT's Ipoh Area. [_No known Grave]Terandak Wall Memorial Malacca._---]
	+	**5 Cpl. W.J.E. Hartley.** 4th. Hussars. Killed in Action Engaging CT's. _Kuala Lumpur # 17 / 976_.---]
	+	**5 Pte Choh bin Abas.** Malay Regt. Killed in Action Engaging CT's Pahang---]
	+	_Kuala Lumpur ;_General Sir. Harold Briggs arrived in Malaya To take over the Co-ordination of all forces-]
	+	In the Jelebu area of Negri Sembilan A Gurkha Patrol Killed 7 C.T's & captured 5 ---]

	+	5/5/1950 LG # 38903 p. 2231 The following awarded the Military Cross
		2/Lt. J.N. KELLY. MC THE SUFFOLK REGIMENT.
		                                    The following awarded a BAR to his Military Cross.
		LT. R.S. CLARKE. MC & BAR THE KINGS SHROPS.HIRE LIGHT INF.
		                                    The following awarded the Military Medal
		L/CPL. D.E.R. WICKS. MM THE SUFFOLK REGIMENT.
		CPL. S. B. PAIMUN. MM MALAY REGIMENT.

Thur.	6th	**6 Mr. E.H. Dawson** an Australian official of the Straits Racing Association. Was Killed & a Chinese waiter, seriously injured. When a grenade was thrown into the Hotel Metropole in Ipoh Perak---].
	+	6 HMT DEVONSHIRE arrived Liverpool.with returning Service personnel---]
Fri.	7th	**7 L/Cpl. Abdullah bin Haji Abdul Aziz.- Deraman bin Mumat.** Malay Regt. Killed in Action Engaging CT's Pahang ---]
Sat.	8th	_Singapore: The Hertogh Case Contd._ Che Aminah binte Mohamad and Marie Hertogh arrived in Singapore from Kemaman Terengganu to meet with the Dutch Acting Consul General over the right to be returned to her biological Dutch parents. When they became separated during the Japanese invasion of the then Dutch East Indies. Their meeting was to spark off a dispute of custody to a great aftermath causing a riot---.]
Sun.	9th.	_Kuala Lumpur:_ Telegram from Malcolm MacDonald to Foreign Office: '_The Peoples Republic of China underground support for the terrorist campaign.Nake it possible for us for the time being to accept Consuls representing the Chinese Communist Government._'-----]
	+	RAF Sqdn. 84 Brigand became operational RAF Tengah ---]
	+	9 HMT ORBITA arrived Singapore with replacement Service personnel enroute to Hong Kong---]
Mon.	10th	**10 AP Liew Why Tone.** F. M. Police Killed on Ops. ---]
Tue.	11th	11/04/1950 LG # 28881 p. 1775 The following awarded the Distinguished Service Order

		LT/COL. E.P. TOWNSEND. DSO 6th. QUEEN ELIZABETH'S OWN GURKHA RIFLES
		The following awarded the Distinguished Conduct Medal
Wed.	12th	W/O. B. PUN. DCM 2th. KING EDWARD VII'S OWN GURKHA RIFLES
		Spitfire TP390 28 Sqdn. Ran out of fuel & crashed near Port Dickson. No further details.---]
	+	In the Kampar area of Perak a 24 year old Chinese women shopkeeper, was battered to death in her shop. The C.T's looted & burnt down the shop.---]
	+	Hong Kong The 2nd. Battn. Princess Mary's Own Gurkha Rifles boarded the SS ORBITA enroute to Singapore---]:
	+	12 HMT EMPIRE HALLADALE arrived Singapore with replacement Service personnel---sailed 12th Bound for Liverpool with returning Service personnel.---].
Thur.	13th	13 2/Lt. M.O.F Kimmel. Devonshire Regt. Died. of wounds received in Action Engaging CT's.
		Kuala Lumpur. # 17 - 977--]
	+	Lt. General Sir. Harold Briggs after his recent arrival in Malaya on the 5th. April .Announced:
		'He had formed a "WAR CABINET" under his chairmanship. To Co-ordinate all the resouces in Malaya in the Anti Terrorist Campaign. Those members chosen are:
		Acting Chief Seretary. Mr.M.Vel Tufol -
		The Secretary for Internal Security Mr.D,C. Watherson -
		The Commisioner for Police Mr. W.N. Gray.-
		The GOC Malaya Major General R.E. Urquuhart.-
		A.O. C. Malaya Vice Marshall F.J. Mcllersh.
Fri.	14th	Auster Number AOP V. TJ 629. 656 Sqdn. Overturned upon landing at Gua Musang.---]
Sat.	15th	15 P/C Kalid. B. Rahman. F. M. Police Died from Wounds recv'd received in CT ambush Metakab Pahang---]
	+	15 HMT ASTURIAS arrived Southamptom with returning Service personnel .---]
Sun.	16th	Singapore: The Hertogh Case: The Court ruled that Maria should be returned back to her biological parent. The Hertoghs. Which she was. However, Aminah Mohamad appealed against the decision.---]
	+	2 F. M. Police Hon In. Foo Eng Lin. - SC Mohamed Yausin B. Baba. Killed in Action Engaging CT's Sungei Kelemah Estate Negri Sembilan.---]
Mon.	17th	London : House of Commons The minister for Colonial affairs Mr. John Dugdale made a statement to the House:
		'There was no connection between the Chinese and Malayan Banditry & that the Gurkha Brigade coming form Hong Kong would meet the final military commitmets.
		His remarks raised doubts within the House of Commons and in Malaya.---]
Tue.	18th	18 Pte. R. A. James. 1st. Battn. K.O.Y.L.I. Died accidently shot.
		Western Road # 2133 George Town Penang---]
	+	18/04/1950 LG # 38888 p. 1873 The following awarded the Colonial Police Medal
		SGT. P. G. BINT. CPM (Pos) FEDERATION MALAYA POLICE
		AP. I.L.F. CAMPBELL. CPM. FEDERATION MALAYA POLICE
Wed.	19th	The Straits Times printed an article stating :
		'Unofficial Members of the Federal Legislative Council today unanimously expressed the opinion. That the manpower available in the country should be mobilised, trained and properly equipped to shoulder the responsibility of restoring peace and security Their tasks would be several :-
		1. Aid to the Civil Power
		2. Active Operations against the CT's in conjunction with and under commnd of the regular forces
		3.Consolidation and garrisoning of areas cleared of CT's
		4. Provision of Interpreters and providers of local knowledge for the Regular Forces
		5 The necessity to form a first class Inteligence Service ---]
	+	Police raided the Offices of the Malayan Communist Party HQ & arrested all the occupants. 9 in number including the man responsible for the attempted assassination of the Govenor Sir. Frank Gimson---]
Thur.	20th	20 Tpr. P.T. Ward. 4th Royal Hussars Died*** *Kuala Lumpur # 17 – 979* ---]
Fri.	21st	21 In the village of Ayer Kuning Perak. A 28 year old school teacher (unnamed)was dragged from his classroom to a tree & in front of the school children was shot dead by C. T's. ---]
Sat.	22nd	22 HMT ORBITA arrived in Singapore where the 2nd. Battn. Princess Mary's Own Gurkha Rifles disembarked. To take over the operational duties of the departing. 1st Battn. Princess Mary's Own Gurkha Rifles---]
Sun.	23rd	

Mon.	24th	23 8 F. M. Police **SC's Aziz B. Uda.- Mat B, Kassim.- Saleh B. Kulp Mat Ali. – Tan B. Abdullah.- Hamid B. Drasin.- Din B. Abdul Hamid. – Adnan B. Yahaya. A.P Laili Bin Mat Hassan.** Killed in an ambush on the Narborough Estate Sunkal Perak.---]
Tue.	25th	The Malayan Chinese Association. Protested strongly over the broadcast of the Ex Communist Terrorists **Wahi Annuar** intended to create hostile feelings towards the Chinese & create racial discrimination ---]
Wed.	26th	Canberra Australia: The Labour Party announced:

'Their rigid opposition for Australia troops to be sent to Malaya.' ---]

Singapore An attempt to assassinate the Govenor Sir. Frank Gimson as he was leaving a Stadium from seeing a boxing competion, A Chinese Man threw a hand grenade at him, although the grenage hit Sir. Frank, but failed to explode The Chinese man assumed to be a CT, escaped.---]

Thur.	27th	
	+	**27 Pte. R. Lord.** 1st. Battn. Green Howard's. Died***.*Kuala Lumpur. # 17 / 978* ---]
Fri.	28th	27 HMT ORBITA sailed Singapore bound for Liverpool with returning Service personnel---]

Kuala Lumpur: The Federation Government announced:

Sat.	29th	*'During the hours of 7 pm until 6 am the Police Circle around Segamet of main & Estate roads would*
Sun.	30th	*be enforced with the exception of the Railway trains'*---]

29 HMT EMPIRE HALLADALE sailed Singapore bound for Liverpool with returning Service personnel ---]

Kuala Lumpur. A report was issued on the problem regarding the proposed resettlement of the Squatters into new villages. The basis of the **BRIGGS PLAN.**:-

Prior to the arrival of Sir. Harold Briggs in March. Preliminary investigations had been completed, outlining the issues to be faced. On the huge problem of the resettlement of Squatters, that would take years, not a few months to complete. The Briggs Plan as it was called was: To resettle families into New Villages. Necessary in an attempt to surpress Communist Terrorism in Malaya. Beginning in the South and gradually moving up country to the North. The report outlined the Size of the problem including thirteen major areas too implement, the whole plan under the following headings:

1. STAFF ARRANGEMENTS.

The shortage of suitable Officers and trained Subordinates to undertake the laborious work in the field. Recruitment of Welfare Officers from the United Kingdom, Australia and New Zealand, for the initial resettlement and later to supervise the New Villages.

2. THE INTRODUCTION OF EMERGENCY REGULATION 17FA & 17FAA

Regulation 17F.A was made whereby any area could be declared "Controlled area." Everyone within a "controlled area "could be required to reside in a specified residential part of the area and, except within specified hours, no person could be in any part of a "controlled area" other than the permitted residential part. Regulation 17FA.A introduced on the 1st October 1951. Under this regulation owners or occupiers of land could be required to undertake the construction of buildings and other works on their land, the cost of which could be apportioned. Among various parties, including the local Government Authority.

3. USE OF EMERGENCY REGULATION 17D

Introduced in 1951 Could be used by surprise operations under the regulation to arrest and detain all persons in the areas and subsequently release and resettle those in respect of detention under the Emergency Regulation 17D.

4. SECURITY ASPECT'S OF A NEW VILLAGE.

The recruitment of full time Policemen within the villages. To protect life and property. To instil confidence Among the people and Thus to stimulate the supply of information which will eliminate Communist cells and influence. To assist and advise in the training of the Home Guard and to supervise the physical defence of the village.

5. THE DEVELOPMENT OF THE NEW VILLAGE.

Each new village to be sited, as far as possible in the light of the need for protection from Terrorist activities. The sources of livelihood of the people and other factors. The new villages mean a new way of life for those who dwell in them and after the disturbance of moving, to be more attractive than the old.

6. ECONOMIC CONSEQUENCES OF RESETTLEMENT.

The first economic consequences of resettlement were the immediate effect on the internal economy of the country, of the interruption of agricultural pursuits such as, vegetable growing, pig rearing and Rubber tapping.

7. LAND POLICY FOR NEW VILLAGES.

The policy of the State and Settlement Governments. Is to issue long term titles to appropriate cases to the inhabitants of new villages who want them.

8. AGRICULTURAL ASP.ECT'S. OF THE NEW VILLAGES.

		In each new village consideration has to be given to the type of Settler, the nature and amount of land available for crop growing and rearing of pigs and poultry.
		9. EDUCATION IN THE NEW VILLAGES.
		Education in the new villages was a special problem. The Government must take an active part in establishing primary schools. Financial aid was necessary to build schools and teacher accommodations and salaries, the supply of books and furniture and equipment. Both the English and Malay language was mandatory.
		10. MEDICAL AND HEALTH SERVICES IN THE NEW VILLAGES.
		The underlying consideration. Was that the ultimate purpose, was to absorb new villages into the general administration of the country and not to treat them as Separate sections of the population, requiring special consideration.
		11. COMMUNITY CENTRES AND ASSISTANCE FROM VOLUNTARY ORGANISATIONS.
		To be run by the Village Committee, under the guidance of the District Officers and his staff. The initial transit accommodation for newly arrived settlers, would upon the final resettlement of all the settlers, could be used as Community Centres.
		12. MALAYAN CHINESE ASSOCIATIONS CO-OPERATION.
		The support from and cooperation of these organisations in the resettlement of settlers, is a vital part in the planning of the new villages.
		13. EFFECT'S. ON THE NEW VILLAGES ON THE CAMPAIGN AGAINST THE COMMUNIST.
+		The object of resettlement. To create physical situation in which, the administration can operate effectively and the progress and welfare of the community, can be properly established and developed. It is believed that this more than anything else will help to destroy Communism in the country.
		Operations " *Butlin*"- "*Thurndiani*"-"*Bacall*"- "*Thor* " Ended---]

MAY

Mon.	1st	**1 Pte. G. B. Falconer.** 1st. Battn. Seaforth Highlanders. Died *** _Kranji Singapore # 1 / E - 3_---]
	+	**1 Rfn. Manbahadur Rai .** 10th. Princess Mary's Own Gurkha Rifles. Killed in Action Engaging CT's Temerlok Pahang Area *[No known Grave]Terandak Wall Memorial Malacca.*---]
	+	RAF Sqrn. 194 Dragonfly H/C operational from RAF Changi---]
Tue.	2nd	**2 Spr. Ahmad Bin Kassim** Royal Engineers (MOR) Died *** _Claimed by next of Kin._---]
	+	2 HMT DEVONSHIRE sailed Liverpool bound for Singapore/Hong Kong.with replacement Service personnel---]
Wed.	3rd	Kuala Lumpur: A broadcast by Sqdn/Ldr. Macfarlanes requested the need for Malay recruits to enlist for the Royal Air Force.---]
	+	Spitfire SM 975 60 Sqdn crashed on take off from Kuala Lumpur. No further information.---]
Thur.	4th	Kuala Lumpur : It was announced:
		'The 13th./18th. Hussars serving in the Middle East & the 3rd. Royal Marine Commando Brigade serving in Hong Kong will shortly.be transferred to Malaya.'---]
Fri.	5th	**5 Spr. J. Savarimutu.** Royal Engineer . Died *** _Kranji Singapore # 2 / A – 4_ --]
	+	**5 Cadet K.F. Dawson** F. M. Police Killed on CT Ops. Whilst leading a squad in a silent approach on a CT camp Batu Kulim Kedah _Jalan Petana # 2054_ Penang---]
	+	Mortar Platoon & 'C' Comp Suffolk's, together with F.M. Police jungle squad, engaged a number of CT's kiiled 5 CT's. During the engagement. Mortar Plt. Killed 4. 'C' Platoon Killed 1 & captured 4 CT's.
Sat.	6th	**6 Cpl. H. R. Simmonds.** 1st. Battn. Suffolk Regt. was Killed. _Kuala Lumpur # 17 / 990_---]
	+	**6 A.P Vaithiligam a/o Chellish** F. M. Police Killed in Action Engaging CT's 27th. m/s Tapah Rd. Perak---]
	+	Hong Kong: Telegram from the New Secretary of State for the Colonies Mr. James Griffiths. to Sir. Henry Gurney:
		'While securing the route of mass repatriation would inevitably lower the morale of the Communist Terrorist The Peoples Republic of China would have precisely the opposite consequence'.---]
Sun.	7th	Kuala Lumpur The Squatter problem Sir. Henry Gurney was requested.
		'To find an alternative within the Malaya / Boneo region'---]
Mon.	8th	**8 Sgt. J. A. Thurlby BEM.** R.A.S.C. Killed transport incident. _Kuala Lumpur # 17 / 981_---]
	+	**8 Mr. A.S. Cockram.** Manager. Hon Aux. Insp. F. M. Police. Killed by CT's on the Telemong Estate Rd. Bentong Pahang. _Kuala Lumpur ??_---]
Tue.	9th	**9 Cadet D.A. Craig** F. M. Police Killed in Action Engaging CT's Tapah Perak.---]

	+	'C' Company Suffolk's, searching the Dominion Rubber Estate. Located a camp, Engaging the CT's Killed 3 of the 4 located. 1 Surrendered. Guns & ammunition were recovered & the camp destroyed ---]
	+	Later in the afternoon 'D' Company searching the Dominion Estate to the East of Kajang. Located a CT camp and Killed 4 CT's. Guns & ammunition were recovered the camp was destroyed. ---]
Wed.	10th	**10 Jemadur. Karnabahadur Pun.** 2nd. King Edward VII's own Gurkha Rifkes Died *** _Kranji Singopore # 7 / D – 10_---]
	+	**10 P/C Saad. B. Desa.** F. M. Police Killed in ambush Kuala Nerang Pahang---].
	+	8 Plt. of 'C' Company and 12 Plt of 'D' Company. Suffolk's searching in a Tin Mine. Killed 1 CT.---]
Thur.	11th	**11 Trp. K. Guy.** 4th. Royal Hussars Died ***_Kuala Lumpur # 17 / 982_ ---]
	+	8 Platoon of C comp & 12 Platoon D comp Suffolk's searching the area of a Tin Mine Killed 1 CT---]
Fri.	12th	**12 Mr. W.A. Puddicombe.** W.A. Manager. Sepang Selnagor Killed by CT's Road ambush. No other details.]
	+	London: Mr. Strachey Secretary of State for War. Tabled 2 points on Malaya :- ' 1 To retain Territory, because it was the Colonial powers most dollar earner.' 2 To expand the Stirling expenditure to the Malayan economy.'---]
Sat.	13th	**13 Cadet P. R.J .Evans.**F.M. Aux.Police Killed on CT Ops. by a large group of Terrorist, also 6 other Police were Killed (_unnamed_) & 4 others wounded 54 m/s Simpang Neruing. Bentong / Kroh Road.Karangan Kedah. _Taiping # ?_ Perak ---]
Sun.	14th	**14** 3 F. M. Police P/C's **Adullah b. Ishak. – Aliram. S/O Din Seng. -Shariff. B. Yahaya** Killed in Ambush Padang Tasek Pahang.---]
	+	**14 PC. Amin. B. Mat.** F. M. Police Killed in Action Engaging CT's Batu Bor. Pahang.---]
Mon.	15th	**15 WOII. P. S. J. Saunderson.** R.E.M.E.. Died***_Kranji Singapore # 1 / E - 2_---]
	+	**15** 2 F. M. Police SC.'s **Mohd. Said B. Yacob. – Osman b. Mat Arof** Killed in ambush Suloh Estate Perak---]
	+	**15 PC Hassan B. Su.** F.M Police Killed on Ops. no other deatls ---]
	+	Malacca: After his demotion **Siew Lau** with his wife (also a party Member) plus 2 bodyguards, planned an escape by fishing boats to Sumatra. However, his plans was discovered, possibly by another comrade, & on the orders of **Ah Kok**, All were Detained & Sentenced to death as Military deserters. Executed CT Style ---]
Tue.	16th	**16 AP Vaithilaingham s/o Chellah.** F. M. Police Killed on Ops. no further details.---]
	+	Thailand : An Ambush on the Thailand / Malay border by 100 CT's. Surrounded a Patrol of 30 F. M. Police killing F.M. Police **ASP. P.P.J. Evans.** 4 Malay PC's, a Thailand Policeman (**all unnamed**). & wounding several others. They fought for half an hour, before the CT's withdrew. It was understood the CT's were from a CT training camp across the border in Thailand---]
	+	16/5/1950 LG # 38911 p. 2417 The following awarded the Distinguished Conduct Medal L/CPL. S. RAI. DCM 10th PRINCESS MARY'S OWN GURKHA RIFLES The following awarded.the Military Medal L/CPL D. GHALE . MM. 2nd. KING EDWARD VII'S OWN GURKHA RIFLES
Wed.	17th	**17 2/Lt. J. Bridge.** Royal Artillery Died on Ops. _[No known GraveTerandak Wall Memorial Malacca]_ ---]
	+	**17 Rect. Nandaraj Limbu.** 10th. Princess Mary's Own Gurkha Rifles Died ***_Kluang # 3 / H – 12_ Johore-]
Thur.	18th	**18 Spr. A.L. Rothnei** Royal Engineers Died***_Kranji Singapore # 1 / D – 14_ ---]
	+	**18 SC .Mohamed B. Mat Noor.** F. M. Police Killed in Action Engaging CT's. Ambushed at the 27th.m/s Tapah Road Perak---]
Fri.	19th	**19 P/C. Ismail. B. Ibraham.** F. M. Police. Died from Wounds recv'd, in an ambush on the 13th May Padang. Tesek Kedah.---]
	+	Kuala Lumpur: The Government again approached Hong Kong re: Repatriation of Detainees---]

	+	19/5/1950 LG # 38916 p. 2487 The following awarded the Distinguished Service Order
		MAJ.S.J. CAULSLY. DSO ROYAL REGIMENT ARTILLERY
		LT/COL. J.W. STEVENS. DSO DEPOT BRIGADE OF GURKHAS
		                    p. 2488 The following awarded the Military Cross
		CAPT. J. DAVIE. MC SEAFORTH HIGHLANDERS
		Lt. I. SKENE.- GIBBS. MC SEAFORTH HIGHLANDERS
		CAPT, J.N.W. MOSS. MC ROYAL REGIMENT ARTILLERY
		CAPT. (KGO) D. RAI. MC. DEPOT BRIGADE OF GURKHAS
		LT. (KGO) L. GURUNG. MC DEPOT BRIGADE OF GURKHAS
		Lt. (KGO) B. LAMA. MC 10th. PRINCESS MARY'S OWN GURKHA RIFLES
		                              The following awarded the Distinguished Conduct Medal
		W/O. D. GURUNG. DCM. DEPOT BRIGADE OF GURKHAS
		W/O. G.H.F. LEWIS. DCM ROYAL REGIMENT ARTILLERY

	MAJ. A. ORMSBY. MC & BAR	The following awarded a BAR to his Millitary Cross 10th PRINCESS MARY'S OWN GURKHA RIFLES
		The following awarded.the Military Medal
	CPL. P. BRENNAN. MM	COLDSTREAM GUARDS
	SGT C PUN. MM	GURKHA RIFLES
	CPL. P. GURUNG. MM	GURKHA RIFLES
	CPL. J. LIMBU. MM	GURKHA RIFLES
	RFN. H. LIMBU. MM	GURKHA RIFLES
	RFN. S THAPA. MM	GURKHA RIFLES
	RFN. J. SUNWAR. MM	GURKHA RIFLES

	+	19 HMT ORBITA arrived Liverpool with returning Service personnel---]
	+	19 HMT EMPIRE TROOPER arrived Singapore with replacement Service personnel---]
Sat.	20th	**20 SC. Then Choon**. F. M. Police. Killed in Action Engaging CT's Ayer Kumning. South Negri Sembilan---]
	+	20 HMT EMPIRE TROOPER sailed Singapore bound for Hong Kong---]
Sun.	21st	A Sikh caretaker (**unnamed**)was Killed. When a grenade was thrown into the offices of the China Press in Kuala Lumpur---]
Mon.	22nd	London: 7 Mothers had a meeting with the Seretary of State for war. Mr. Strachey, before he flew out to Malaya. Demanding. He did all he could to stop the War in Malaya ---]
	+	Mr. J. Strachey Secretary of State for war, was accompanied by Mr Griffiths Secreatay of State for the Colonies. Flew out from London for a visit to Singapore & Malaya ---]
Tue.	23rd	23 2 F. M. Police **SC 's Mat Eisa B. Osman**.- **Abdul Khader B. Ghani.** Killed in an ambush between the Ayah Hitam Estate & Ipoh Tin Mine. Selangor ---]
Wed.	24th	Kuala Lumpur: 6 people were injured, when 2 CT's threw hand grenades into crowds at the Lucky World Amusement Park. The 2 CT's were apprehended & arrested---]
Thur.	25th	**25 Sgmn. D.J. Plumpton**. Royal Signals Killed In Action Engaging CT's. *Kuala Lumpur # 17 / 983* ---]
	+	**Maj.(KGO)Thambir. Rai. MBE**. 7th. Duke of Edinburgh's Own Gurkha Rifles. Died***. BMH Kamunting. *Kuala Lumpur # 24 / 7* . ---]
	+	**25 Pte. D. J. Wareham.** 1st. Devonshire Regt. Died*** *Kuala Lumpur # 17 - 984* ---]
	+	**25 Sgt. Tenku Abdul Latif. Bin. Tenku Mehadi. Prince Latiff.** The adopted son of the Sultan of Negri Sembilan. Was Killed when leading a detachment of the 1st Malay Regt. in an attack on a CT camp, in the Metakab area Pahang. ---]
	+	25 HMT EMPIRE PRIDE sailed Liverpool with replacement Service personnel ---]
Fri.	26th	**26 Cfn. D. H. James.** R.E.M.E.. Died*** *Seremban # CE / 52* Negri Sembilan ---]
	+	**26 4 F. M. Police PC. Ismail b. Ibrahim. SC's Hamdan b. Elias. -Trebis b. Alias- Rect. Hamid. B. Jaafar.** Killed in Action. Engaging CT's Gunong Rapat Perak.---]
	+	26 HMT EMPIRE ORWELL sailed Southampton bound for Singapore/ Hong Kong with replacement Service personnel---]
Sat.	27th	**27 Sgt. I. D.Lawson. BEM., Gdsmn. S. Palfrey.** *[Ashes REP]* 2nd. Battn. Coldstream Guardsmen were Killed in a clash with C.T's. In the Sungkai Tapah area of Perak. 2 CT's were Killed. *Batu Gajah # 426* Ipoh Perak---]
	+	**27 Pte. B. Atkinson.** Women's Royal Army Corps Died*** *Kranji Singapore # 1 / E – 1*---]
Sun.	28th	**28 SC. Ahmed b. Ngah Mohamed.** F. M. Police Killed on Ops. no furher details ---]
	+	Hong Kong: Telegram Grantham to Griffiths: '*Hong Kong was facing its own crisis in deporting undisirables 6,000 ex Nationalist Chinese soldiers'*---]
	+	28 HMT ORBITA arrived Liverpool with returning Service personnel---]
Mon.	29th	Singapore The Death Penalty was imposed on all persons throwing grenades. Whether or not any damage was caused. Whilst a 10 year prison sentence. Was imposed on those persons, knowing about grenades thrown & not informing the Police authorities---]
	+	Singapore: Mr Stachey & Mr. Griffith arrived in Singapore to start their visit---]
	+	Hong Kong: 500 Royal Marine Commandos boarded the HMT TROOPER bound for Singapore they were the advance party of the Royal Marine Brigade---]
	+	29 HMT DEVONSHIRE arrived Singapore with replacement Service personnel ---]
Tue.	30th	**30 Rfn. Balbahadur. Pun.** 2nd. King Edward VII's Own Gurkha Rifles. Died by Drowning on Ops. Lenbui area MR.682772 *[No known Grave] Terandak Wall Memorial Malacca* ---]
	+	Malaya : Mr. Strachey & Mr. Griffiths visiting Ipoh. Were introduced to a Malay Peasant, who had been

	+	attacked on a loney road near Tapah Perak. When he was confronted by 3 CT's. He was only armed with his parang, which he swung and took off the head of 1 CT. The other 2 fled. Collecting the head & a hand grenade from the body. Took them to the Police Station. --------------
Wed.	31st	Mr. Griffiths commented: '*You are a Brave Man.*' ---]
	+	30 HMT DEVONSHIRE sailed Singapore enroute to Hong Kong ---[
	+	31 Pte. W. D. Bamblett. 1st. Battn. Green Howard's. Died ***.*Kuala Lumpur # 17 / 985*---]
	+	31 SC. Ahmad B. Hgah Mohaned. F. M. Police Killed in Action Engaging CT's. Nr. Kuala Kangsar Perak-]
		31 Det. Wong Kong Ying. F. M. Police Died from his wounds recv'd previous day. Batu Gajah Perak ---]
	+	Australia The Australian Prime Minister Mr. Menzies announced in Canberra: '*At the requaet of the UK Government. Australia would provide: Transport planes, aircrews & ground staff of the R.A.A.F.*---]
	+	Kuala Lumpur: Sir. Henry Gurney noted: The Chinese detainees , suspected of supporting the MCP had stopped in SEPTEMBER 1949. Due to the Closure of Swatow port .----]
		31 HMT EMPIRE HALLADALE arrived Liverpool with returning Service personnel--]

JUNE

Thur.	1st	1 Rfn. Patirim. Thapa. 6Th. Queen Elizabeth's Own Gurkha Rifles. Died***.*Kluang # / J – 10* Johore. ---]
	+	3 F. M. Police E/Sgt. M. Johnson & P/C's Ahmad. B. Wahab. SC. - Hilong Bin Sahat. Killed in CT ambush 6th. m/s on the Gemas / Tampin Rd. *Gutsall Road Seremban # ?* Negri Sembilan.---]
	+	"THE BRIGGS PLAN" came into operation ---].
Fri.	2nd	Kuala Lumpur :A working party of 5. Decided: '*Repatriation was still necessary*'---]
	+	2 HMT EMPIRE TROOPER. arrived Penang, with the Advance party of the Royal Marine Commandos]
Sat.	3rd	3 P/C Fais. Bux. F.M.Aux.Police Killed in an ambush in Grik Perak. 2 C.T's were Killed in the same ambush---]
	+	3 HMT EMPIRE TROOPER sailed Penang enroute to Singapore ---]
Sun.	4th	4 2 F.M. Police: SC/Sgt's. Lem Chan Poh & Chan Hong. Killed in ambush at the 74th. m/s. Lengong/Grik Road Perak---]
Mon.	5th	The night mail train from Singapore to Kuala Lumpur. Was fired upon by C.T's in Johore. 5 passengers were injured including the wife of a British Officer.---]
	+	5 HMT EMPIRE TROOPER arrived Singapore ---]
Tue.	6th	6 Pte. A. B. Bone. 1st. Battn. Devonshire Regt. Died Transport Accident *Kuala Lumpur # 17 - 096.*---]
	+	In a CT attack on a Squatter area near Segamat Johore. A Chinese youth was bayoneted to death & a Chinese women strangled.---]
Wed.	7th	7 Sgt. A. N. May. Military Provost Staff Corps. Died*** [*Ashes REP*] ---]
	+	4 CT's walked into an ambush, laid by 5 Plt. 'B' Company Suffolk's. 1 CT was Killed the others fled ---]
Thur.	8th	Kuala Lumpur: A Curfew was imposed from 6 a.m.till 7.pm. on the whole of S. Johore.----]
Fri.	9th	Operation '*Dunmow*' began in South Johore, against a large number of MRLA Engaging the Suffolk's & F.M. Police Jungle squads. Killed 1 CT'---]
	+	9 HMT EMPIRE TROOPER sailed Singapore bound for Southampton with returning Service personnel-]
Sat.	10th	10 A Platoon with 20 Troops of the 1st. Battn. K.O.Y.L.I. were in the jungle area of Ampang searching for CT's. In charge were 2 Sgt's - Hogan & Clarkson. When they came to a fork in the road. The Platoom split into 2 sections. Sgt.Hogan's section walked straight into a CT ambush, the resulting fire Killed. Pte's W. J. Boden. - J. E. Gough.- R. A. Hall. - C. M. Harrison. -. J. K. Hudson. - D. Jones., 'D' Company. *Batu Gajah # 429 - 433 - 430 – 431 - 434 - 428* Ipoh Perak. Sgt. Hogan was seriously wounded as was L/Cpl. V. Brown, who although wounded, Killed 1 of the CT's---]
	+	Operation '*Dunmow*' Ended---]
Sun.	11th	11 2/Lt. M. J. Morrice. Killed & Capt. M. G. Bax. Wounded. 2nd. Battn. Scots Guards. During an ambush by C.T's, were attacked in their jeep. 13 miles from Kuala Lumpur. Negri Sembilan. *Kuala Lumpur # 17 -987*-]
	+	11 L/Cpl. L. Sahardhoj Limbu. 5 Platoon 2nd.10th. Princess Mary's Own Gurkha Rifles. Killed in Action Engaging CT's. North East of the Fraser Estate. 3 CT's were Killed during the engagement. *Kranji Singapore # - 8 / A - 1*---]
Mon.	12th	12 Capt. M. G. Bax. 2nd. Battn. Scots Guards. Died from his wounds (see above) [*Ashes REP*]---]
	+	

		12 4 F. M. Police **AP's Lee Kai .- Yong Fook – Kassim b. Abdullah Sulaiman b. Hassan.** Killed on Ops.,---]
Tue.	13t	
		13 L/Cpl. **R. W. Price.** 1st. Battn. Devonshire Regt. Died from wounds in Action Engaging CT's.
Wed.	14th	*Kuala Lumpur # 17 – 988*]---]
		London : Telg. from Foreign Office to K.G. Younger:
		'Levels of Gurneys administration. Unanimously agreed the renewal of the repatriation of Chinese detainees
Thur.	15th	*to China, was essential. Prerequisite to the succes of Genral Briggs operational plan.'*---]
		15 HMT DEVONSHIRE arrived Singapore enroute to Liverpool via Penang with returning Service
Fri.	16th	personnel sailed 15th---]
		16 L/Cpl. **V. Brown.** 1st. Battn. K.O.Y.L.I. Died from his wounds, recv'd during the ambush on the 10th.
	+	*Batu Gajah # 435* Ipoh Perak----]
		16 Rect. **L. Maniraj Limbu .** 7th. Duke of Ediburgh's own Gurkha Rifles Died*** BMH Kinrara.
Sat.	17th	*Seremban # 19* Negri Sembilan ---]
	+	**17** Spr. **Nirmal Limbu.** Gurkha Engineers Died*** BHM *Kluang # 3 / I – 9* ---].
		17 3 F. M. Police: **Aux. P. Vaithilinhams/o Chelliah SC's Sahroni B. Sumat. – Sahat. B. Bassan**
	+	Ambushed & Killed on the Kerak / Manchia Rd. Pahang.---]
	+	**17** 2 F. M. Police. **SC. Shaoni b. Sumat. – Sahat.b.Hassan.** Killed on Ops. no further detsils---]
Sun.	18th	**10** Platoon 'D' Comp. Suffolk's engaged 3 CT's kiiled 2 wounding the other who escaped----]
	+	**18** Cpl. **Kabiraj Rana .** 2nd. King Edward VII's Own Gurkha Rifles Died *** *Kranji Singapore # 7 / E -1*---]
	+	**18** SC. **Abdullah B. Mohamad Tassim** F. M. Police Killed in Action Engaging CT's Kota Tinggi Johore ---]
		18 HMT EMPIRE PRIDE arrived Singapore on board were. The 1st. Battn. Worcester Regt.
Mon.	19th	Reinforcements to the ground troops---]
	+	**19** Pte. **G. T. James.** R.A.O.C.. Died*** *Western Road # 2134*-George Town. Penang---]
		19 3 F. M. Police. **D/Cpl. Abdul Razek B. Abu Bakar. & P/C Ahmad B. Alanh Hussein S.P/C Mohd Bin**
	+	**Rashid** Died from Wounds recv'd. Bukit Selembu Kedah ---]
		19 Mr. R. J. Wallace Manager. of the Sungei Kruit Estate Perak. Drove into a CT ambush was Killed, his
	+	3 year old son was wounded. ---]
	+	In scattered areas of the Federation Another **56 civilians** were viciously Killed by the CT's .---]
		19 HMT EMPIRE ORWELL arrived Singapore/ with replacement Service personnel sailed for Hong Kong
Tue.	20th	19th.---]
		20 Mr. V. Thambiah. Financial Asst, State Public Works Department (PWD) Ipoh. & **Mr. S. Vijaylanran**
	+	Ag.Asstn. Registrar Supreme Court Ipoh. Both Killed by a Grenade thrown into their house by CT's---]
		20/6/50 LG # 38945 p.3167 The following awarded the Distinguished Conduct Medal
		SGT. P. RAI. DCM 7th. DUKE OF EDINBURGH'S OWN GURKHA RIFLES
		The following awarded the Military Medal
	+	L/CPL. RAI. B. MM 7th. DUKE OF EDINBURGH'S OWN GURKHA RIFLES
		20 HMT EMPIRE FOWEY sailed Southampton bound for Singapore / Hong Kong with replacement Service
Wed.	21st	personnel--]
		Kuala Lumpur: The Emergency Power Was introduced:
Thur.	22nd	*'Aa a control over shops. in outlying district's.. To stop any food being supplied to CT's in the jungles---]*
		22 HMT EMPIRE WINDRUSH sailed Southampton bound for Singapore/Hong Kong with replacement
Fri.	23rd	Service personnel ---]
		23 3 F. M. Police **P/C's Jaafar B. Abdullah & Hassan B. Abdul Akas. EPC Manap b. Hj. Said.** Died in
	+	ambush Pasir. Putan Perak.---]
Sat.	24th	**23** HMT EMPIRE PRIDE sailed Singapore bound for Liverpool with returning Service personnel.---]
Sun.	25th	**24** L/AH1. **R.V. Bakar..** Royal Navy. H.M.S. *'UNICORN'* Died*** *Singapore # 12 / C - 5* ---]
	+	**25** 2 F. M. Police **SC 's Hamden B, Elias.- Trebes B, Elias** Killed on the Amaran Estate Johore---]
		25 5 F. M. Police **SC's Yacob B. Kohd Ariff .- Muhassin B. Yamen Abdul Rahim b.- Abdul.Rahman-**
	+	**Zaiton b. Hj. Ihsan. – Mansor B. Kardan.** Killed in Action Engaging CT's at the 54th. m/s Triang / Kluang
	+	Railway track.---]
		25 Mr. F.J. Blowers. British Civilian, after being attacked by CT's in .Johore. Died from fracture of skull---]
Mon.	26th	**25** L/Cpl. **Abdul Rahman B. Laudin.** F. M. Police Died from Wounds recv'd in CT Ambush Kajang Selangor.]
	+	**26** Cpl. **R.J. Siraji B. Bj. Mansor.** F. M. Police Killed in Action Engaging CT's Kemban Johore---]
Tue.	27th	'B' Compamy 2nd. 10th. Gurkha engaged CT's with no kills. 2 Gurkhas were wounded ---]
		27 Cpl. Mohd. Yunus B, Buyong. F. M. Police Died from wounds recv'd. In Ambush on 26th. June at the
	+	54th. m/s Triang / Metakab Road. Pehang---]

Wed.	28th	27 SC. Ibrahim B. Ahmad –.F. M. Police Killed in Action Engaging CT's ambushed on the Denkil Rd Selangor---]
Thur	29th	4 Platoon 'B' Comp Suffolk's engaged & Killed 2 CT's. Recovering arms & ammunition amongst them a Thompson Sub-Machine Gun.---]
Fri.	30th	F, M Police Patrol Killed 1 CT.---]
		30/06/1950 LG # 39856 p. 3366 The following awarded the Colonial Police Medal
		S/SGT. WAN YA'ACOB B. W. AHMAD. CPM. FEDERATION MALAYA POLICE

JULY

Sat.	1st	1 F. M. Police **Rect's. Kassim B, Mohd. & Othman B. Mohd. Arif.** Killed in CT Ambush at the 15th. m/s. Pontian Rd. Johore---]
	+	**1 DP/C Chong Keow.** F.M. Police Killed in Action Engaging CT's ambush. Ruab Pahang---]
Sun.	2nd	**2 S.P/C Mat Isa Bin. Mat.** F. M. Police Killed in Action Engaging CT's Terap area of Kedah.---]
	+	**2 HMT EMPIRE ORWELL** sailed Singapore bound for Southampton with returning Service personnel---]
Mon.	3rd	Gurkha Troops of the 2nd/10th. Found a camp with food ammunition, explosives and munition spare Parts. They Killed 3 CT's within the area ---]
	+	A Patrol of the Mortar Section Suffolk's. Were fired upon by CT's. At the 18th. m/s. Returning fire Killed 1 CT---]
Tue.	4th	5 Platoon 'B; Comp Suffolk's. Set in ambush positions. Engaged 4 CT's killing 2. The other 2 surendered-]
	+	**4 HMT ORBITA** arrived Singapore with replacement Service personnel---]
Wed.	5th	**5 D/PC. Chong Kong Wah.** F. M. Police Died from wounds. CT ambush Terap Kedah. ---]
Thur.	6th	**6 Rfn. Manbahadur Rai.** 7th. Duke of Edinburgh's Own Gurkha Rifles. Killed in Action Engaging CT's Kuala Lipis.*Kuala Lumpur # 27 /2.*---]
	+	**6 F/O. N. B. Harben. - NavIII. T. W. Smith.- Sig.III. C. Lloyd.** 45. Sqdn R.A.F. Died when their Brigand RH 850. Crashed into a hill near Kuala Lipis Kelantan State during a rocket attack *[No known Graves]Terandak Wall Memorial Malacca*---]
Fri.	7th	**7 Cpl. Rambahadur Gurung.** Gurkha Signal. As an escort on a train, guarding ammunition. Died by accident, *Sulva Lines Batu Gaja # 51* .Ipoh Perak---]
	+	**7 Rect. Yusof B. Abdul Rahman.** F. M. Police died from wounds received in CT Ambush on the 1st. July--]
	+	100 CT's armed with Bren guns. Attacked the Factory & Estate buildings. of the Sembrong Estate Laylang Laylang Central Johore. The assistant Managers wife. Mrs Boden and daughter were locked in the bathroom whilst the CT's looted the building. Mr. Boden and his Patrol arrived back and a fire fight ensued, The Hon Insp **J. L. Boden** CPM (Pos.) F. M Aux. Police. & Assistant Manager. Was Killed & one other SC was also Killed (**unnamed**). 3 other SC were wounded. The CT's set light to the Factory & other properties. Mr. J. L. Boden. was postumously awarded the CPM for his bravery.[*No known Grave*]---]
	+	7/7/1950 LG #38962 p.3499 The following awarded the Military Cross
		LT. K. RAI.MC 10th. PRINCESS MARY'S OWN GURKHA RIFLES
		The following awarded the Military Medal
		L/CPL D. THAPA MM . 2nd. QUEEN ELIZABEThH'S OWN GURKHA RIFLES
		CPL. D. THAPA MM 10th. PRINCESS MARY'S OWN GURKHA RIFLES
		L/CPL. M. OSMAN MM. MALAY REGIMENT
		PTE. W. B. HAMID MM . MALAY REGIMENT
Sat.	8th	**8 AP Awang Kechik b. Dosah.** F. M. Police. Killed on Ops. no further details---]
Sun.	9th	**9 2 F.M. Police Pol /Lt. J. W. Chown - E/PC Ali b. Hj. Hamid.** Killed on CT Ops. *Kranji Singapore # 8 / C – 12* ---]
Mon.	10th	**10 2/Lt.. D.S. Pyemount** 1st. Somerset Light Infantry. (Att. to K.O.Y.L.I.) Accidently shot on a Patrol *Batu Gajah #437 Ipoh Perak*---]
	+	**10 Rfn. Tikadam Rai** . 7th. Duke of Edinburgh's Own Gurkha Rifles. Died***Kranji Singapore # 8 / A - 3*---]
	+	**10 HMT EMPIRE TROOPER** arrived Southampton with returning Service personnel---]
	+	**10 HMT EMPIRE WINDRUSH** sailed Singapore bound for Southampton with returning Service personnel-]
Tue.	11th	**11 Rfn. T. Hoy.** 1st. Battn. Cameronians. Killed in Action Engaging CT's Lenga Johore. *Kranji Singapore # 2 / A – 3*]--]
Wed.	12th	**12 L /Cpl. W.H. Dowbiggin.** Royal Artillery Died *** *Kranji Singapore # 1 / D – 15*---]
	+	'B' Coy Worcestershire Regt. Although still in Jungle training at Kota Tinggi, were draftted in to serve under the 2nd./10th.Gurkha's. Involved in a large scale planned ambush, in a Rubber plantaion and to surround a

Day	Date	Event
		hut known to house CT's. They set up ambush positions ready for any later Action Engaging CT's.which occurred two days later---].
Thur.	13th	12 HMT ORBITA sailed Singapore bound for Liverpool with returning Service personnel---]
		13 Mr. R. Inder. Manager of the Dovenby Estate. Sungei Siput. Killed in an ambush at Batu Gajah Ipoh
	+	Perak. ---]
	+	13 S.P/C Sahid Bin Hj Ahmad Taib. F. M. Police Killed by accident 48th. m/s. Cameron Highlands.---]
Fri.	14th	13 HMT EMPIRE FOWEY arrived Singapore with replacement Service personnel / sailed for Hong Kong 14th. ---]
Sat.	15th	14 Pte. R.D. Vickers. R.A.S.C.. Died Transport incident. _Kuala Lumpur # 17 / 990_---]
		15 Mr. K. Lee. A European Asstn Manager on the Berading Rubber Estate Paloh, whilst on his rounds on
	+	the the next Estate – the Chamek Estate, was ambushed by CT's and Killed. Johore---]
		'B' Coy Worcestershire Regt. Lying in ambush, whilst still in training. Killed their first 2 CT's. Also they
	+	discovered the remains of a decomposed CT. The Coy then returned to Kota Tinggi to continue their Jungle training.---]
Sun.	16th	15 HMT DEVONSHIRE arrived Liverpool with returning Service personnel---]-
Mon.	17th	16 Mne. H.H. Rose. (42 Commando). Royal Marines Died Accidental gunshot wounds _[Ashes REP]_--]
Tue.	18th	R.A.A.F. No.1 Sqdn.Lincoln B30A Located on operations at R.A.F. Tengah ---]
		London : In the House of Commons after his recent visit to Malaya Mr. Stachey **contested** the view:
	+	' _**National Serviicemen were unsuitable for active Service in the campaign against the Guerrillas in Malayan**_ ---]
Wed.	19th	18 HMT EMPIRE PRIDE arrved Liverpool with returning Service personnel ---]
		19 Lt. (KGO) Rambahadur Rai. Gurkha Military Police. Died from Wounds recv'd BMH Kinrara.
Thur.	20th	_Kuala Lumpur # 26 / 1_ ---]
	+	20 E/Sgt. L. W. Wernham. Ambushed & Killed along with. **E/Sgt. K.J. Webb** & **D/Cpl Mohd. Ariff** F.M. Aux.Police. Were captured & Killed (murdered). After a gun battle between the Police & a large number
Fri.	21st	of C.T's in Taiping Perak _Christian Cemetery Tiaping_ Perak ---]
	+	21 AC1. D. G. Reeve. Cook HQ FEAF. R. A. F. Died by drowning . _Kanji Singapore # 3 / D 7_ ---]
		The Worcestershire Regt. having completed their jungle Training entrained at Singapore Station bound for
	+	Sungai Patani. Kedah.---]
		A ambush party from 'B' Plt. of the Suffolk's engaged 4 CT's on an Estate. Opening fire Killed 2, the
	+	other 2 CT's escaped. This Kill confirmed their 100th. CT Killed.---]
		21 HMT EMPIRE WINDRUSH arrived Singapore with replacemet Service personnel sailed enroute to Hong
Sat.	22nd	Kong 21st.---]
Sun.	23rd	22 Sgm. Vanisi Thamby . E. Royal Signals. (MOR) Died *** _Claimed Next of Kim_ ---]
Mon.	24th	} Combined Operations continued throughout Malaya ---]
		24 Plt.1. H. E. A. Hurn. BEM. 33 Sqdn. R. A. F. Died when his Tempest PR 786 following an engine failure
Tue.	25th.	crashed 1 mile N. of Klian Intan. _Taiping # E / 4_ Perak---]
		25/7/1950 LG # 38975 p.3812. The following awarded the Mlitary Medal
		CSM I.B.M.HAMIF MM THE MALAY REGIMENT.
Wed.	26th.	RFN K. THAPA MM 2nd. KING EDWARD VII'S OWN GURKHA RIFLES
		26 Flt/Lt. A.P. Clark 80 Sqdn R. A. F. Died by accident, when his Sptifire VN491 crashed 1 mile east of
	+	Ninepin Island _[No known Grave] Terandak Wall Memorial Malacca_ ---]
	+	26 SC . Abdul Rahim B. Abdul Rahman F. M. Police Died from Wounds recv'd during engagement with
Thur.	27th	CT's Ayer Itan Perak---]
	+	26 HMT EMPIRE ORWELL arrived Southampton with returning Service personnel---]
Fri.	28th	27 Rfn. Ranbahadur Rana. 2nd King Edward VII's Own Gurkha Rifles Died *** _Kranji Singapore 7 / E – 4_]
		The Aik Hoe Rubber Factory in Selangor was burnt down. Arson ----]
Sat.	29th	28 2 F. M. Police SC. Cpl. Zaiton B. Hj Ihsan .- SC Mansor B. Kardan Killed in CT ambush Banting Kuala Langit District Selangor.----]
Sun.	30t	4 men suspected of the arson of the Ail Hoe Rubber Factory were arrested.---]
		30 Recruit. Dhanpati. Rai 7th. Duke of Edinburgh's Own Gurkha Rifles. Died truck incident.
Mon.	31st	_Seremban # 20_ Negri Sembilan.---]
		Singapore. The Hertogh case: Maria was returned to the guardianship of Aminah Mohamad---].
		31 Flt. Lt. D. C. Marshall. - Flt Lt. R. S. Wigglesworth. - Sig.111. P. Blakey. 84 Sqdn. R.A.F. were Killed when during a dummy attack near Tapah. Their Brigand RH815 flew into a hill in the Cameron Highlands.
	+	_Batu Gajah 439 - 440 - 441_ Ipoh Perak---]
		31 Rfn. Channrabahadur. Thapa 6th. Queen Elizabeth's Own Gurkha Rifles. Died***

As described by Mr. Boris Hembry. General Manager of the Kumuning Rubber Estate in Malaya. & an Ex SOE Agent 1942-1945. In an Newspaper interview stated. (quote: Extracts from His Book 'Malayan Spymaster')

SUNDAY 16TH JULY? An article appeared in the Sunday Despatch entitled

THE (ALMOST) FORGOTTEN WAR .

'War in Korea - Banditry in Malaya?

'*At the end of 1950. The security forces – British, Gurkha, Malay Regiments, other Commonwealth and armed constabulary – numbered more than 80,000 . In addition, the RAF were flying on average more than 100 sorties a day bombing and machine gunning communist terrorist, over an area of jungle stretching 500 by 200 miles, in addition to the many operations flown, to drop supplies to the ground forces. In July 1950 Lincoln bombers dropped 41- 1,000 pounders over an area of jungle within five miles of Kumuning Estate alone.*

We have a real WAR in Malaya'

AUGUST

Tue.	1st	Operations "*Asbab*" & "*Moccasin*" began in Johore ---]
Wed.	2nd	**2 WOII. Birbahadur Rai.** 7th. Duke of Edinburgh's Own Gurkha Rifles. Whilst on a Train, was Shot & Killed on Ops. Near Ipoh *Seremban # 21* Negri Sembilan.---]
	+	**2 Pte. E. T. Summers.** R. A. M. C. Died *** *Kuala Lumpur # 17 - 992*---]
	+	**2 HMT EMPIRE TROOPER** sailed Southampton bound for Singapore / Hong Kong with replacement Service personnel---]
Thur.	3rd	**3 SC. Hussain B. Mat Lela.** F. M. Police Died from Wounds recv'd during engagement with CT's Pahang.--]
	+	**9 Plt. 'C' Company.** Suffolk's. Engaged a party of 5 CT's on the Brooklands Estate. Killed 2 with 3 escaping 1 leaving a trail of blood, who had been wounded.---]
Fri.	4th	4/08/1950 LG # 38984 p. 3997 The following awarded the Military Cross
		2/LT. J. A. McGOUGAN. MC COLDSTREAM GUARDS
		The following awarded the Military Medal
		CPL.R. G. BUTLER. MM COLDSTREAM GUARDS
	+	4/08/1950 LG # 38985 p. 4006 The following awarded the Colonial Police Medal
		PC. ABD. WAHAB B. MOHAMAD CPM FEDERATION MALAYA POLICE
		PC. ISMAIL B. BOGOK . CPM FEDERATION MALAYA POLICE.
Sat.	5th	**5 Cdt. /Spt. K. F. Dawson** F.M. Special Police. Killed on CT Ops. Kulim Kedah. *Jalan Petana # 2054* George Town Penang----]
	+	**Asstn. Supt. D. A. Craig** F. M. Police Killed on Ops. Perak *Batu Gajah # 459* Ipoh Perak---]
	+	Operation "*Rhubarb* " Began in the Jementah Forest Reserve. 8 Platoon 'C' Comp Suffolk's set out on a 2 day operation ---]
Sun. .	6th	**6 Sgt. J. A . Ashdown.** The Suffolk Regt. Killed In Action Engaging a party of Min Yuen suppliers to the CT's *Kuala Lumpur # 17 / 993*.---]
Mon.	7th	**8 Plt 'C' Comp.** Suffolk's Patrolling in the Sepong area, discovered a CT camp, suitable for between 20- 30 CT's. Including a food dump estimated last used. A fortnight before.---]
	+	**7 Plt 'C' Comp** Suffolk's found another camp, still under construction, both were destroyed. On the return journey out the Platoon engaged 5 Min Yuen. 1 CT was wounded but escaped with the others, during the brief fire fight---]
	+	**7 HMT EMPIRE WINDRUSH** arrived Singapore ---]
Tue.	8th	**8 L/Cpl.H. W. Waite.** R.A.S.C.. Killed Transport incident. *Kuala Lumpur # 17 / 994*---]
	+	Singapore : The Hertogh Case: Marie Hertogh then 13 years old. A juvenile, was married to a 22 year old teacher Mansoor Adabi. ---]
Wed.	9th	**9** 6 F. M. Police **ASP. D.A. Graig. L/Sgt's Armad B, Arshad & L/Cpl. Arrifin B, Mat. Nusu SC Mohd. Noor B. Hj. Talib.** Killed on CT Ops. when their Police Jeep was ambushed by CT's at Tapah Perak.---]
Thur.	10th	**10 Cadet D.A. Craig.** F. M. Police. Killed in Action Engaging CT's Tapah Perak---]
	+	**10 SC Ismail B. Chat.** F. M. Police Killed in Action Engaging CT's Grik Perak---]
	+	10 Platoon 'D'Company 2nd. 10th.Gurkhas engaged a number of CT's & Killed 1 CT ---]
	+	Operation "*Rhubarb*" concluded.---]

	+	10 HMT EMPIRE WINDRUSH sailed Singapore bound for Southampton via Mombasssa with returning Service personnel---]
	+	10 HMT DEVONSHIRE sailed Liverpool bound for Singapore with replacement Service personnel along with the advance party of the 1st. Battn. Gordon Highlanders ---]
Fri.	11th	11 Rfn. Charman Ale. 2nd. King Edward VII's Own Gurkha Rifles Died*** _Kranji Singapore # 7 / E – 5_ ---].
	+	11/08/1950 LG # 38990 p 4093. The following awarded the British Empire Medal (Military)
		F/SGT. R.E.S.O'NION. BEM ROYAL AIR FORCE
		F/SGT. R. PEARSON. BEM ROYAL AIR FORCE
		F/SGT. T. A. PETERS. BEM ROYAL AIR FORCE
		SGT. P. TOWNSEND. BEM ROYAL AIR FORCE
		CPL. F. TANDY. BEM ROYAL AIR FORCE
		A/C. C. MEARNS. BEM ROYAL AIR FORCE
		The following awarded the Distinguished Flying Cross
		F/LT. R. COX. DFC ROYAL AIR FORCE
		F/LT. G.W.HILL. DFC ROYAL AIR FORCE
Sat.	12th	12 Lt . J.G. Gutch. Royal Navy HMS 'TELEMACHUS ' Died *** [_Ashes REP_]---]
	+	5 Plt. 'B' Comp Suffolk's, whilst on Patrol in the Kuala Langat area. Being led by a CEP Te Chin Min found food dumps, medical supplies & printing materials. All were destroyed.---]
Sun.	13th	13 Pte. Hassan bin Ham. Malay Regt. Killed in Action Engaging CT's. Pahang.---]
	+	13 SC. Mat Dais B. Awang. F. M. Police Killed in Action. CT ambush Kendang Estate Johore---]
Mon.	14th	14 Mr. Diggens. J.A. Manager. Killed at Serdang Kedah by CT's---]
	+	14 Mrs. Nora Stutchbury. A civilian was Killed, when C.T's ambushed her car in Pahang.---]
Tue.	15th	15 (QGO) Capt. Manbahadur Rai . 10th.Princess Mary's Own Gurkha Rifles. Killed in Action Engaging CT's. _Kranji Singapore # 8 / A- 5_---]
	+	15 Sgmn. J. Cairns. Royal Signals Died*** _??? no information_---]
Wed.	16th	16 Rfn. Sukbahadur. Gurung. 6th. Queen Elizabeth's Own Gurkha Rifles. Died from Wounds recv'd N.East of Rengan. _Kluang # 3 / I – 10_ Johore --]
Thur.	17th	17 SC Abdullah B. Sangkut. F. M. Police Killed in Action Engaging CT's. Henda Estate Sungkai Perak---]
	+	Another air strike by the RAF.Was called for by the Suffolk's, in the Telok Forest Reserve---]
Fri.	18th	18 L/Cpl. Lalsing Thapa. 2nd. King Edward's Own Gurkha Rifles Died *** _Kranji Singapore 7 / D – 3_ --]
	+	18 SC Abu Bakar B. Sallah. F. M. Police Died from Wounds recv'd. Terap area Kedah---]
	+	It was about this time. Mike Calvert's Malayan Scouts 'A' Squadron were sent to Dusam Tue. Camp North of Kuala Lumpur. To begin jungle training, having already done specific sabotage training down South possible Johore. ---]
Sat.	19th	Plt. 'B' Comp Suffolk's found a camp for 20 CT's with a large food dump. It was destroyed.---]
Sun.	20th	20 Rfn, Patradhoj Rai. 7th.Duke of Edinburgh's Own Gurkha Rifles Died*** BMH Kinrara. _Seremban # 22_ Negri Sembilan---]
	+	'C' Comp Suffolk's. Patrolling in the Kuala Langat Swamp area. Found a large food dump in a small hut raised on stilts. It was destroyed.---]
	+	Plt. 'B' Comp Suffolk's. In the same area, found another camp for 40 plus CT's. With food & clothing it was destroyed.---]
	+	20 HMT EMPIRE FOWEY arrived Southampton with returning Service personnel---]
Mon.	21st	21 P/C's Hassan B. Su & Ahmad B, Puteh. F. M. Police. Killed in Action Engaging CT's Kulim Kedah---]
	+	10 Plt. 'D' Comp Killed a CT on the Soringgit Estate. Identified as Siew Moy Secretary to 2 Plt MRLA---]
	+	8 Plt 'C' Comp Suffolk's, On Patrol engaged a number of CT's. However, in the ensuing fire fight the CT's retreated back into the jungle with the Suffolk's chasing them. Lost their tracks.---]
Tue.	22nd	22 Recruit. Tulsiram. Thapa. 6th. Queen Elizabeth's Own Gurkha Rifles. Died*** MRS _Sungei Patani # 26_-]
	+	'C' Plt. Suffolk's found another camp for 40 CT's. A clothing dump & nearby yet another camp for 40-45 CT's. All were destroyed.---]
Wed.	23rd	23 P/C Omar B. Ahmad. F. M. Police. Died from wounds received on 20th. August.---]
	+	10 Plt. 'D' Comp Suffolk's whilst in ambush positions on the Sepang Estate spotted. A CT advancing. He stopped, before any Action took place. Then he retreated. He was Killed.---]
	+	9 Plt. 'D' comp Suffolk's. In ambush position near the Sepang Estate. When 5 CT's well spread out approached. The Suffolk's opened fire. Killed the last two wounding the lead CT, who escaped with the other two CT's. The two dead CT's were later identified as: La Yu Hwain Alias Huat Tah & Tong Kwee Wong alias Pak Kiang.---]

Thur.	24th	24 Rfn. Lilbahadur. Thapa. 6th. Queen Elizabeth's Own Gurkha Rifles. Killed in Action Engaging CT's Bahua area. *[No known Grave] Terandak Wall Memorial Malacca*---]
	+	24 HMT EMPIRE ORWELL sailed Southampton bound for Singapore/ Hong Kong with replacement Service personnel---]
Fri.	25th	25 Cpl. Narbahadur Thapa. 2nd. King Edward VII's Own Gurkha Rifles .Killed Mersing. *[No known Grave] Terandak Wall Memorial Malacca* ---]
	+	25 Pilot II. E. R. Taylor - Nav.III. G.C. Carpenter. 52 Sqdn.- Sig.I. T. O'Toole.DFM. 48 Sqdn. R.A. F. Maj. J. H. Proctor. 1st. Battn. The Loyal Regt. Cpl Bryant. Drv. M.Goldsmith. Drv. P.Taylor.- Drv. A. Wilson R.A.S.C.. Mr. Rentse Development Officer, P/C Mohammed bin Abd. Jalil- SC Abdullah b. Baharom & 2 Sakai guides Asip Alia Sedah- Yai Acob. When Dakota KN630.Whilst dropping marker oil bombs for an incoming raid, by 8 Lincoln bombers. Caught fire & crashed into a ravine. in the area of Kampong Jendera Ulu Kelantan. *[No known Graves] Terandak Wall Memorial Malacca*---]
		These Personnel have now been found & given a Proper Military Burials. ---]
	+	25/08/1950 LG# 39002 p.4321. The following awarded the Military Medal RFN. J. RAI. MM 10th PRINCESS MARY'S OWN GURKHA RIFLES
Sat.	26th	An Air strike was called by Security Forces. To hit a target in the Dingki area where CT's had been spotted.---]
Sun.	27th	Sir. Eddward Gent made a visit to the Resettlement area of Jelebu. Accompanied by the F. M. Police from the Chempedak Police Post. ---]
Mon.	28th	28 Pte. D. J. Frew. 1st. Battn. Seaforth Highlanders. Killed in Action Engaging CT's . *Kuala Lumpur # 17 / 995* ---]
Tue.	29th	29 Lt. K. F. McIntyre. 1st. Battn. Seaforth Highlanders. Died from wounds.recv'd previous day. *Kuala Lumpur # 17 / 996*---]
Wed.	30th	12 Plt. 'D' Company Suffolk's, together with the F.M.Police. Operating in the Kajang area engaged 3 CT's killing 2 CT's. ---]
	+	30 HMT EMPIRE TROOPER arrived Singapore with replacement Service personnel---]
Thur.	31st	31 F/O. R. J. Dench. , Flt. Lt. R. W. Richardson. Flg. Off. A. B. J. Baxter. Pilot/3. G.J. MacDonald. 38 Sqdn. R.A.A.F.. F/O. H. A. Axon. Crew members of Dakota KN 240 all of 110 Sqdn. Changi. & passengers:- Sqn Ldr. V. H. Dean. O/C 95 Sqdn R.A.F. Regt. Maj. Lowther Army. Capt. P. J. D Costerton. Royal Artillery. AC1.A.K. Caton Arm/Mech. R.A.F. LAC. Le. Bone. Arm/Asstn. R.A.F.110 dn. R.A.F. Killed when Dakota KN240 ditched into the South China sea. 80 miles NE. Kuantan *[No known Graves] Terandak Wall Memorial Malacca* ---]
	+	31 Mr.G.A.A. Denne Manager. Sabai Estate. Killed by CT's Bentong Pahang.---]
	+	31 Pol/Lt. D. J. Simmons. F.M. Police, whilst guiding a Royal Marine Commando Patrol to a CT camp, in the Batu Gajah area of Ipoh Perak. Was shot & Killed by the CT guard. *Batu Gajah # 460* Ipoh Perak ---]
	+	During the month of August. the R. A. F. & R.A.A.F. made many bombing raids in Lincoln Bombers on CT hide-outs, over a wide area of jungles in Johore, Perak, Selangor & Negri Sembilan. ---]
	+	31 HMT EMPIRE TROOPER sailed Singapore enroute to Hong Kong. On Board were 500 Gurkhas of the 67th. & 68th. Field Squadrons. Leaving Singapore for Hong Kong to replace the Argyles & Middlesex Regt.s returning from Korea ----]
	+	Operation "*Cleaver II*"- "*Mocasin*" Ended---]

SEPTEMBER

Fri.	1st	Operation "*Rose*" Began against No 8 Regt. MRLA. In Kedah.---]
	+	Operation "*Walkover*"- "*Trek*" Began against No 8 Regt. in Terengganu & Operation "*Kota*" in Kelantan---]
	+	A Chinese school teacher, (**unnamed**) was Killed by C.T's in an attack on a Perak village.---]
Sat.	2nd.	2 Lt R. Smith. Royal Navy HMS '*BARWIND*' Died*** *[Ashes REP*[----]
	+	2 E/Sgt. R.J. E. Harrison. F. M. Police Accidently shot by a Military Patrol. Kajang Selangor. *Kuala Lumpur # 271* ---]
Sun.	3rd	7 Plt 'C' Comp. Green Howards. On Patrol in the Parit Tinggi area of Johore engaged CT's. Killing 2 and fatally wounding another---]
Mon.	4th	4 PC Hussein B. Din. F. M. Police Died from Wounds recv'd in an Ambush. Batu Gajah Perak---]
	+	N E of Kuala Lumpur. The Anti-Tank Plt. Suffolk's found an explosives dump containing plastic expolsives, gun cotton, primers & slabs, 8 grenades, detonators, fuse wire & in excess of 800 rounds of ammunition ---]

Tue.	5th	5 3 F. M. Police **S/Mjr. Mohd, Noor. B. Asap.** & **P/C Salleh B. Sirona** Killed in Action Engaging CT's Bentong Pahang---]
	+	11 Plt 'D' Compny Suffolk's. Engaged 5 CT's Killing 1, the others escaped---]
	+	Auster AOP6 VX922 656 Sqdn. R.A.F. On a low run, approaching Termerloh Air strip, a wingtip made contact with the Hanger. causing the plane to crash.---]
Wed.	6th	6 **Cpl. A. G. Shennan.** 1st. Battn. Cameronians. Killed in Action Engaging CT's Johore. *[Ashes REP]*---]
	+	8 Plt. CT Company Suffolk's. Killed a CT sentry, in the Kuala Langat Forest Reserve---]
Thur.	7th	7 **Cpl. A. B. B. A. Manus.** - **LAC. Ali . B. Mohd Noor.** - **AC1. M. Y. B. Ahmad.** -**AC1. Ahmad. B. Chik.** 93 Sqdn. R.A.F. Regt. (MOR's) Died during a Mortar explosion. *Claimed by next of Kin* ---].
	+	7 **SC Cpl. S. P/C Ali bin Hj Hamid.** F. M. Police Killed in ambush on the Mersing/Endau Rd. Johore.--]
	+	7 HMT DEVONSHIRE arrived Singapore. with replacement Service personnel and the advance party of the 1st. Battn. Gordon Highlanders---]
Fri.	8th	8 **Pte. Ismail bin Jamin.** Malay Regt. Killed in Action Engaging CT's Pahang. ---]
	+	8/09/1950 LG # 39013 p. 4534 The following awarded the Colonial Police Medal CPL. SAAT B. ABD. RAHMAN CPM. FEDERATION MALAYA POLICE PC. ZAINUDUIN B. HAJI. KECHIL. CPM FEDERATION MALAYA POLICE
Sat.	9th	9 **SC/Cpl. Ahmad B. Sangkut.** F.M. Police Killed in Action Engaging CT's. 64 m/s Bentong /Ruab Rd. Pahang---]
	+	9 **Mr. J. R Dunn.** Manager. Killed in Action Engaging CT's in Bentong Pahang.---]
	+	6 Plt 'B' Comp Suffolk's. On Patrol, found dumps with clothing, guns and other equiopment.---]
	+	The 26th. Independant Company MRLA under the command of **Chin Nam** made co-ordinated attacks on the town of Kuala Kerau. Attacking the Police Station & Railway Station burning down the Railway Station Killed 2 railway engineers **(unnamed)** . Further down the line,they removed rails. Derailing an armoured truck carrying reinforcement troops ---]
Sun.	10th	10 **Pte. M. J. Greene.** 1st. Battn. Devonshire Regt. Died *** *Kuala Lumpur # 17 997*---]
	+	12 Plt Suffolk's. On Patrol in Kampong Sungei area. Killed 1 Malay CT. Identified as **Ismail Bin Sharriff** alias **Ismet** of 2 Section 2 Plt. MRLA.---]
Mon.	11th	11 2 F. M. Police **P/C Ahmad B, Esa** & **S.P/C Abdul Rahman Bin Omar**. Killed in Action Engaging CT's Kluang Johore. ---]
Tue.	12th	7 Plt 'C' Comp Suffolk's. Killed 2 CT's, wounding a 3rd. Who escaped. The 2 dead CT's were identified as **Ah Kong** a courier of the Min Yuen & **Ah Choon**,a member of 8 Section 3 Plt MRLA.---]
	+	12 HMT DEVONSHIRE sailed Singapore bound for Liverpool with returning Service personnel on board were the Regemental Band of the Suffolk Regt. ---]
Wed.	13th	13 **Mne. R. Wright.** (45 Commando). Royal Marines Died*** [Ashes REP]---]
	+	13 HMT ORBITA arrived Liverpool with returning Service personnel---]
Thur.	14th	14 **Mne's. E. J. Nevard** & **D. C. Keyes** – **H. H. Rose** (45 Commando) Royal Marines. When driving a Jeep along the Tapah / Cheneriang Road Perak. Were Killed in a C.T's ambushed. Batu Gajah # 445 - 443 Ipoh Perak Royal Marines **Keyes** & **Rose** [Ashes REP]---]
	+	The " **Malayan Scouts** " With their leader as Lt/Col. J.M Calvert. (nicknamed Mad Mike) Was formed from volunteers of the Royal Armoured Corps, Royal Artillery, & Infantry units, serving in Malaya. Having undertaken intensive training in Johore before, taking up active operations.---]
Fri.	15th	Kuala Lumpur Telegram from Griffiths to Hong Kong Office : *'Goverment request if they would accept batches of 100 / 200 repatriats on an exxperomental basis.?*---]
	+	15 HMT EMPIRE TROOPER arrived Singapore ---]
Sat.	16th	16 **S.P/C Chung Chik Yau.** F. M. Police Killed in Georgetown area Penang.---]
Sun.	17th	17 **Pte. A. Barr.** Seaforth Highlanders Died. *** *Kranji Singapore # 1/ D – 13* ---]
	+	17 3 F. M. Police **P/C Mohd Noor B. Abdullah.** **SC's Saad B. Mat.**- **Hussein B. Awang** Killed in Action Engaging CT's ---]
	+	12 Platoon 'D' Comp Suffolk's attacked a CT camp Killing 1 CT, wounding another. The Camp was built to accommodate 100 men. When firing began.Other CT's fled into the jungle. The camp was destroyed---]
	+	A Platoon of the 2nd./10th. Gurkhas came under fire during the night time, from a number of CT's throwing grenades at the CT's. The Gurkhas charged the CT's, the CT's retreated. One Gurkha was wounded----]
	+	17 HMT EMPIRE TROOPER sailed Singapore bound for Southampton with returning Service Personnel-]
	+	17 HMT EMPIRE ORWELL arrived Singapore from Hong Kong.---]
Mon.	18th	18 HMT EMPIRE WINDRUSH arrived Southampton with returning Service personnel ---]
Tue.	19th	

	+	**19 L/Cpl. Kirtidhoj Rai.** 7th. Duke of Edinburgh's Own Gurkha Rifles. Killed in Action. Engaging CT's *Seremban # 24* Negri Sembilan---]
Wed.	20th	**19 Capt. H. E. Skelton.** R. A. M. C. Died***[*Ashes REP*]---]
		20 2/Lt. G.E. Carpenter. L/Cpl. R. Hudson. [*Ashes REP*) 13/18th. Royal Hussars Killed. Armoured Car acc.
	+	*Seremban # 51* Negri Sembilan---]
Thur.	21st	Hong Kong: Telegram from Hong Kong to Gratham: *'Can see no possibility of the PRC (Peoples Republic Of China)accepting small batches*---]
Fri.	22nd	**21 Gnr. T. A. Brown.** Royal Artillery. (Att. 22nd. S. A. S). Died of grenade wounds. *Kranji Singapore # 2 / A – 2*--]
Sat.	23rd	22/9/1950 LG # 39023 p. 4748 The following awarded the Military Medal
		CPL. R. RAI.MM 7th.DUKE EDINBURGH'S OWN GURKHA RIFLES
Sun.	24th	**23 P/C Mustaffar B. Ahmad.** F. M. Police Killed in ambush. Kulai Johore.---]
		24 Sgt.W.R.N. Rowe. MC. (42 Commando) Royal Marines Killed in a battle accident.
Mon.	25th	*Batu Gaja # 445* Ipoh Perak.---]
Tue.	26th	**25 Cfn. C. R. Catchpole.** R.E.M.E Died** *Kranji Singapore*- # ?? --]
		26 SP. Wan Hussein B. W. Yussof. F. M. Police. Whilst on a raft travelling by river from Batu to Keli
	+	Kelantang. Killed by CT's ---]
Wed.	27th	Members of the 'C' and 'D' Company Suffolk's. Acting on information, made a sweep of the village of Broga East of Kajang. Successfully. Killed 4 and captured 3 CT's.---]
		27 Pte. J. Owen. Green Howard's. Killed when his truck overturned on an Estate road.Taiping Perak.
	+	*Kuala Lumpur # 17 / 998* .---]
	+	5 children were Killed & others wounded together with a number of adults. When a hand grenade was thrown into a shop in Kuala Pilan. Negri Sembilan.---]
Thur.	28th	A Patrol of the 10th Gurkhas Killed 2 CT's one was identified as **Low San** ---[
	+	**28 P/C Hamid. B. Sudin.** F. M. Police Killed in Ambush at 25th. m/s Malacca/ Seletar Rd. Malacca----]
		F. M. Police. **SC.'s Naem B. Sitam.- Mohamed.Yussof B. Sulaiman.** Killed in Action Engaging CT's
Fri.	29th	On the Eldred Estate Johore---]
		29 Sgt. R. Kabirbahadur Rai. 10th. Princess Mary's Own Gurkha Riles Killed in Action Engaging CT's in
	+	road ambush approx 78m/s between Bentong & Kuala Lumpur. *Kuala Lumpur # 27 / 13* ---]
	+	Pahang. 2 Chinese men & a boy were butchered by a number of C.T's. ---]
	+	During the month, further air strikes were carried out by the R.A.F. & R.A.A.F. over areas from Johore to the Thailand Border. Including several night attacks.---]
		29/09/1950 LG # 39030 p.4858 The following awarded the Colonial Police Medal
		SC. LAU KWEI. CPM FEDERATION MALAYA POLICE
Sat.	30th	S/SGT. LAM POH. CPM (Pos) FEDERATION MALAYA POLICE
	+	30 HMT EMPIRE ORWELL sailed Singapore bound for Southampton with returning Service personnel---]. Operation "*Rose*" against No 8 Regt. MRLA. In Kedah. Ended ---]

OCTOBER

Sun.	1st	Operations "*Jackal*"- "*Kohat*"- & "*Letter*". Began against No 4 Regt. MRLA. In Johore.---]
	+	Operation "*Autumn Double*" - Began against No 2 Regt. MRLA. In Negri Sembilan- Selangor & Pahang---]
	+	Operation "*Intiial Operation*" The first deep jungle penetration undertaken by the Malayan Scouts ---]
	+	Operation "*Hotspur*" Began against No 5 Regt. in the Tapah area of Perak---]
	+	1 HMT EMPIRE PRIDE sailed Liverpool bound for Singapore/ Hong Kong / Pusan.with replacement Service personnel---]
	+	RAF Sqdn. 88 Sunderland GR4 became operational RAF Seletar---]
Mon.	2nd	A CT disguised in normal dress, threw a grenade into a shop in Kuala Pilar. Killing 5 people & wounding 4 others. All women & children---].
Tue.	3rd	3/10/1950 LG #39033 p. 4919 The following awarded the George Medal
		A/C I.J. GILLETT. G.C (Post) ROYAL AIR FORCE
	+	3/10/1950 LG # 39033 p. 4921 The following awaded the Colonial Police Medal
		L/CPL. JAGIR SINGH. CPM FEDERATION MALAYA POLICE
Wed.	4th	**4 Mr. J. Chalmers.** Manager. of the Kinrara Estate near Kuala.Lumpur. Killed together with **PC. Dalip Singh.** F. M. Police by C.T's, who attacked the Estate. Negri Sembilan.---]
	+	4 HMT DILWARA sailed Southampton bound for Singapore with replacement Service personnel ---]
Thur.	5th	Mr Booth a Johore Planter an Asstn on the Guthrie Palm Oil Estate was ambushed & wounded by 10

		CT's. Although badly wounded, he kept driving his jeep. The lorry behind carrying workers was stopped. They were ordered to get off, then the lorry was set on fire---]
Fri.	6th	1 Plt.'A' Comp Suffolk's. Killed 1 CT. Identified as *Lee Sie Tong* a member of the Dinkit Min Yuen---].
Sat.	7th	**7 L/Cpl. C. M. Chapman**. Womens.Royal Army Corps. Died***Singapore #1 / D – 12 ---]
Sun.	8th	The Mail train from Johore to Kuala .Lumpur. Was derailed when C.T's mined the track . The train driver was Killed. *(unnamed)* 2 railway employees & 3 passengers were injured.---]
Mon.	9th	**9 Mr. J. B. Wellmott**. Asstn. Manager. of the Niyor Rubber Estate. Together with 3. **F.M. SC's: Kadir B Hj Yuus. – Ahmad B. ibraham.- Ahmid b, Sangkut.** Were ambushed & Killed by C.T's in the Kluang area of Johore.---]
	+	9 HMT EMPIRE WINDRUSH sailed Southampton bound for Singapore/ Hong Kong with replacement Service personnel ---]
Tue.	10th	9 Plt Comp Suffolk's. On Patrol in the Kuala Langat Forest Reserve, found a camp for 15-20 CT's. A CT Sentry fired on the Platoon. Who charged the camp killing the CT. Identifired as *Cheng Tuk Cho*.---]
	+	10 HMT DEVONSHIRE arrived Liverpool with returning Service personnel---]
Wed.	11th	**11 Pte. J. A. Tipler**. R. A. M. C. Att. to Cameronians. Killed in Action Engaging CT's Muar Johore.*[Ashes REP]* ---]
	+	**11 Col. E. C. Thompson**. OBE Royal Signals Died Motor Veh Acc. *Kuala Lumpur # 17 / 999*---]
	+	11 HMT EMPIRE HALLADALE sailed Liverpool enroute to Hong Kong/ Pusan/ Singapore with replacement Service personnel---]
Thur.	12th	**12 D/Cpl. Chan Ah Thiam**. F. M. Police. Died from gun wounds. Cintra Street Pahang. ---]
	+	12 HMT EMPIRE FOWEY sailed Southampton bound for Singapore / Pusan. With replacement Service personnel---]
Fri.	13th	A female Chinese Rubber Tapper on the Elvetia Estate, was held up by a lone CT & robbed of her National Registration Identity Card (NRIC)---]
	+	Operation Hammer" began in the Kuala Langat area.---]
Sat.	14th	**14 Mne. D.C. Keyes.**, *[Ashes REP]* **E.J. Nevard.** (45 Commando)) Royal Marines. Killed in ambush driving a jeep along the Tapah- Cenderiang road Perak *Batu Gaja # 443* Ipoh Perak.---]
	+	**14 AC2. J. Ross. & AC1 Y. Bin Ahmad Johd. (MOR)** .91 Sqdn. R. A. F. Regt. Tangah Kuala Lumpur. Died in Road Transport Accident. *Kuala Lumpur # 17 / 1000*.- **Y. Bin Ahmad Johd** . *[Claimed by next of Kin]*---]
	+	**14 C1. M. Y. B. Ahmad**. R.A. F. (MOR) Died*** *Claimed by next of Kin*---]
Sun.	15th	**15 SC. Barharudin B. Bima.** F.M. Police Killed in Action Engaging CT's Papan area of Batu Gajah Perak.---]
Mon.	16th	16 A strong force of CT's ambushed a lorry in the Loh Pak Long area of Ayer Kuning Perak Killing 6 F. M. Police **SC's Yacoob B. Hj Mat Asif.- Mohamed Zaib B. Yop Mat.- Salleh B. Abdul Ghani.- Suleiman B. Mat.- Yok B. Kulop Ada.-** A Telecomunications Engineer*(unnamed)* and wounding 9 others .---]
Tue.	17th	**17 8 F. M. Police: Cpl. Mohd. Yatim, B. Abdullah.- P/C's. Mohd. Noor B. Lajis. – Nordin B. Kadir. – Annuar B. Buyong. – Ismail. B. Abss -. Mohd. Shah B. Hj Abdullah. S.P/C's Mohd. B, Hussein.- Mohd Bin Salle.** All Killed in a CT ambush on the Chang Wing Estate ---]
	+	**17 Pte. A. Barr.** 1st. Battn. Seaforth Highlanders. Died***_Kranji Singapore # 1 / D – 13_ ---]
Wed.	18th	**18 EPC Itam.b. Hj, Abdullah.** F. M. Police Died from wounds recv'd previous day.---]
		18 2/Lt. C.J. Barrett. Royal Artillery. Died*** *Kranji Singapore # 1 / D - 11*---]
	+	18 HMT EMPIRE TROOPER arrived Southampton with returning Service Personnel---]
Thur.	19th	**19 2 F. M. Police. S.P/C Saad b. Mat - Hussain b. Awang.** Killed in Action Engaging CT's in the Ayer Kuning area Perak.---]
Fri.	20th	**20 6 F. M. Police. PC's Abdul Aziz B. Hussain .-Yussoff B Mat. – Kasmari B. Dimin. – Shaari B Sallah. SC. Modh. Noor b. Abdullah.** Killed in an CT ambush in Padang Kedah ---]
Sat.	21st	8 Plt Suffolk's.Operating South of the Kuala Langgat Forest. Found a large food dump .Destroyed it.---].
Sun.	22nd	CT's attacked the Railway Station at Seengor. Ordered all the staff and waiting passengers out taking chairs made them sit & watch, as they torched the Station. A nearby shop was also set on fire ---]
Mon.	23rd	**23 PC Mohd. B. Ahmad.** F. M. Police Killed on Ops. No other details---]
	+	A CT Foodstore was located by security forces in the area between Ipoh & Kuala Kangsar ---]
	+	23 HMT EMPIRE ORWELL arriuved in Southampton.with returning Service personnel---]
Tue.	24th	**24 Pte. D. C. Hicks**. 1st. Battn. K.O.Y.L.I.. Died accidently shot on Patrol. *[Ashes REP]* ---]
	+	24/10/1950 LG # 39048 p. 5292 The following awarded the Military Cross. CAPT. A. F. CAMPBELL. MC THE SUFFOLK REGIMENT.

	CAPT. J.W. LLOYD. MC	THE DURHAM LIGHT INF..
	LT. HARBORD -HAMON.D. MC.	COLDSTREAM GUARDS.
	LT. J.W.A. WRIGHT. MC.	KINGS OWN YORKSHIRE LIGHT INF.
	LT. N.T. BAGNALL. MC	THE GREEN HOWARDS
	LT. DUN GOKUL. MC	2nd. KING EDWARD VII'S OWN GURKHA RIFLES
	LT. (QGO) C. GURUNG. MC.	10th.PRINCESS MARY'S OWN GURKHA RIFLES.
		The following awarded a BAR to his Military Cross.
	MAJ. A.J.D.MacDONALD. MC & BAR	QUEEN'S OWN CAMERON HIGHLANDERS
		The following awarded the Military Medal
	SGT. H. W. BRIDGES. MM	ROYAL REGIMENT ARTILLERY
	SGT. L. WALKER. MM	COLDSTREAM GUARDS
	SGT. G. REILLY. MM	SCOTS GUARDS
	CPL. M. O'BRIEN. MM	KINGS QWN YORSHIRE LIGHT INF.
	SGT. G. CATTANACH.. MM	SEAFORTH HIGHLANDERS
+	24/10/1950 LG. Iss 39051 p. 5312	The following awarded the DISTINGUISHED FLYING CROSS
	F/Lt. K. I FOSTER. DFC	ROYAL AUSTRALIAN AIR FORCE
	CAPT. L.B. MOLYEUX-BERRY. DFC	ROYAL REGIMENT ARTILLERY 656 SDN

Wed.	25th	**25 Rfn. Narbahadur Rai.** 10th. Princess Mary's Own Gurkha Rifles. Killed in Action Engaging CT's MR 894459 _Kuala Lumpur # 27 / 14_ ---]
	+	'B' Comp Suffolk's on Patrol arrested 8 suspects. 4 male 4 female handed them over to the Police. ---]
Thur.	26th	**26 2 F.M. Police Cpl. Wan Hussin b. Wan Yusoff & P/C Mohd Desa B. Awang-** Killed by CT's at the 16th, m/s Changloon / Bintok Rd. Jitra Kedah ---]
	+	**26 3 F. M. Police SC. Lebar B. Tanir**.F. M. Police. Died from wounds during an engagement with CT's. On the Jeran Padang Estate Bahua. Negri Sembilan.---]
	+	26 HMT EMPIRE PRIDE arrived in Singapore-with replacement Service personnel---]
	+	26 HMT EMPIRE PRIDE sailed Singapore bound for Hong Kong/ Pusan---]
Fri.	27th	9 Plt. Suffolk's Operating in the Sydney Estate, were fired at, by 15- 20 CT's. In the ensuing Engagement. The CT's. retrated leaving no casualties..---]
Sat.	28th	**28 Lt. R. D. Daw. Royal Artillery** Died *** _Kranji Singapore # 1 / D -10_ ---]
Sun.	29th	**29 PC's Arshad B. Abdul Hamid.** F. M. Police Killed in Action Engaging CT's .Balik Pulau Penang.---].
Mon.	30th	12 Plt. Suffolk's On Patrol near the Kajang area. Engaged 3 CT's. Wounding 2, they escaped---]
	+	4 Plt Suffolk's operating in the Sungei Lang area contacted 3 CT's. Killing 2 identified as **Yeong Hoong** A courier for 2 Plt. MRLA **& Khe Kim Thion** a Min Yuen courier for 9 Plt. MRLA---].
	+	A Tamil Labourer on the Serenyth Estate was Killed by 2 CT's who set fire to the Smoke House and Labourers quarters. The estimated damge caused was $23,000---]
Tue.	31st	**31 Rfn. R. Rikbahadur.** 7th. Duke Of Edinburgh's Own Gurkha Rifles.Killed In Action Engaging CT's Durian Tipis _Seremban Negri Sembilan_---]
	+	**31 Mr.A. Petit C.F.** French Rubber Reseracher. & 4 F. M. Police. **SC Ibraham B Endot. Naem b. Sitam – Mohamed Yusof b.Sulaiman.** Killed in an ambush on the Johore Labis Estate Johore---]
	+	31 HMT DEVONSHIRE sailed Liverpool bound for Singapore / Hong Kong with replacement Service personnel----]
	+	31HMT EMPIRE WINDRUSH arrived Singapore with replacement Service ===]
	+	Operation _"Hotspur"_ Ended against No 5 Regt. in the Tapah area of Perak---]
	+	Operation _"Carp"_-"Albermarle"- " Rabbit"- " Cleaver II" -"Jackpot"- "Foxhound"- "Autumn Double" – "Walkover"- "Trek" "Bintang" Ended. ---]

NOVEMBER

Wed.	1st	**1 Pol/Lt. P.S. Turner.** F. M. Police on CT Ops. Died from gunshot wounds & burns. Kluang area Johore-]
	+	1 HMT EMPIRE WINDRUSH sailed Singapore enroute to Hong Kong personnel ---]
	+	1 HMT DILWARA arrived Singapore with replacement Service personnel enroute to Hong Kong 1st.----]
Thur.	2nd	**2 SC. Cpl. Biland Khan.** F.M. Police During an engagement with a number of CT's, on the Sungei Kelamah Estate Gemas. was Killed. ----]
Fri.	3rd	**3 Mne. K. Mathieson.** (40 Commando) Royal Marines. Died Motor Vehicle Accident _Taiping # E / 6_ Perak]
Sat.	4th	**4 3 F. M. Police. SC's Matahah B. Yasmin** .- **Sabtu .B. Adam- Khalid b. Hassim** were Killed. Negri Sembilan---]
	+	**4 P/C Dlip Singh.** F. M. Police. Killed in Action Engaging CT's Batu Pahat Johore-

		Kranji Singapore # 8 / D - 8 ---]
	+	4 HMT EMPIRE FOWEY arrived Singapore- with replacement Service personnel- –]
Sun.	5th	**5 Sgt. A. Lewis**. R.A.S.C. Died ***_Taiping # E / 7_ Perak---]
Mon.	6th	**6 Dvr. H. A. B. H. Z. Rahman.** R.A.S.C..(MOR) Died***_Claimed by next of Kin_ ---]
	+	**6** 3 F. M. Police **PC's Biland Khan. - Matahah b. Yassin.- Sabtu B. Adam.** Killed on Ops. ---]
	+	6 HMT EMPIRE FOWEY sailed from Singapore bound for Pusan.---]
Tue.	7th	**7 Pte. J. F. Fisher.** Green Howard's Att/t 22nd. S. A. S. Died by Accident. Gunshot wounds _Batu Gajah # 446_ Ipoh Perak.---]
	+	**7 Capt. B. W. Stedeford.** R.E.M.E.. Died*** _Batu Gajah # 447_ Ipoh Perak ---]
Wed.	8th	During a bombing raid by R. A. A. F. Lincoln Bombers on suspected CT camp. Due to adverse weather conditions the bombs were dropped short of the target. Resulting in killing 12 civilians and injuring several others.---]
Thur.	9th	On a Rubber Estate near Kulai. A Platrol of the 10th. Gurkha Rifles diiscoverd a Chinese girl Tapper tied to tree. Who had been disembowelled. A notice written in Chinese was hung around her neck . Translated " ***'Thus would perish all. Who did not pay up their subscriptions. Possibly the work of the Min Yuen?'***]
Fri.	10th	Singapore: Maria Hertogh Trial. Riots broke out in Singapore after an appeal had been heard. Police & British & Malay troops fixed bayonets to quell the rioting mob. Cars Busses were set alight 2 Eurpoean , 2 Asian , 2 Chinese were mortally wounded over 100 others were injured The mobs broke up into small groups and went on the rampaged during the night time---]
	+	10/11/1950 LG # 39064 p. 5620 The following awarded the Military Cross LT.A.N.B. MAHMOD MC MALAY REGIMENT.
Sat.	11th	**11 Mr. G.G. Duddee.** Dredgemaster of Bidor Tin Mine Perak & **D/Cpl. Chan Ah Thiam.** F. M. Police Killed by CT's.---]
Sun.	12th	**12 Mne. T.W. Barnett.** (42 Commando) Royal Marines Died *** _Batu Gajah # 616_ Ipoh Perak---]
Mon.	13th	**13 Rfn. Bakhansing Rai** 10th. Princess Mary's Own Gurkha Rifles. Killed in Action Engaging CT's Bentong _Kuala Lumpur # 27 / 15_ ---]
Tue.	14th	**14 CPM G. W. Bloomfield.** F. M. Police Killed on CT Ops. Muar Johore details of death not available---]
	+	**14** 3 F.M. Police **Pol/Lt. G.W.B. Cain. - SC Cpl. Khamis B. Yusof** . Killed on CT Ops. Muar Johore. **P/Lt. Cain.** Died from Bullet wounds shock haemorrhage. _Kranji Singapore # 8 / C - 9_---]
Wed.	15th	**15 Rfn. Subiman Sunwar.** 10th. Princess Mary's Own Gurkha Rifles. Died from his wounds recv'd in ambush BMH Kinrara ._Kuala Lumpur # 17 / 1001_ .---]
	+	**15 Mr. G.B.H. Green.** British civilian. Killed Kuala Lumpur.---]
Thur.	16th	**16 F/O. G. J. Swindells.** 33 Sqdn. R. A. F. Butterworth. Died when his Tempest PR895 overshot the runway on landing & overturned. _Western Road # 2135_ George Town Penang---]
Fri.	17th	**17** 2 PC's **Mohd. Shah b. HJ. Abdullah. – Annuar .B. Buyong.** F. M. Police Killed on Ops.---]
	+	**17** 5 F. M. Police **PC Abdul Aziz b. Hussain. - Yssof b. Mat. - Kesmari b. Dimin.- Shaari b. Salleh. SC. Dakir B. Hamid.** Killed in ambush no other details---]
	+	17 HMT EMPIRE PRIDE arrived Singapore from Pusan ---]
Sat.	18th	**18 Cpl. M. J. J. Murphy.** R. A. F. Butterworth Died *** _Western Road # 2893_ George Town Penang ---]
	+	**18 F/PC Din B. Hj. Idris.** F. M. Police Killed in Action Engaging CT's Layang Layang Johore.---]
	+	**18 SC. Chan Tong Fong.** F. M. Police Killed in Action Engaging CT's Pahang---]
	+	18 HMT DILWARA arrived Singapore bound for Southampton with returning Service personnel---]
Sun.	19th	'C ' Company 10th. Gurkhas. Engaged a large number of CT's during a fire fight. 1 CT Killed & 3 were hit. After 15 minutes the CT's withdrew. Taken their dead & wounded with them.The Gurkha's recovered 84 packs of food & clothing. Plus a small Printing press. It was estimated that the CT force was possible up to 200 strong---]
	+	19 HMT EMPIRE WINDRUSH arrived Singapore ---]
Mon.	20th	**20 Pte. Hassan bin Musang.** Malay Regt. Drowned on Ops. Pahang---].
Tue.	21st	**21 Sgt. W. C. Baddeley.** 1st. Battn. K.O.Y.L.I.. Died accidently shot._Taiping # B / 51_ Perak.--]
	+	**21 Mne. J. Storey.** (42 Commando). Royal Marines. Died by accident._Batu Gajah # 448_ Ipoh Perak---]
	+	**21 Mr. E. Legatt.** Manager. of the Coronation Estate Luang Johore. He & his driver **_(unnamed)_** were Killed in a CT ambush whilst driving through the Estate in Kluang Pahang.---]
	+	21 HMT EMPIRE PRIDE sailed Singapore bound for Liverpool with returning Service personnel---]
Wed.	22nd	**22** 2 F.M. Police **PC Sarwan b. Abu Bakar.** -**SC, Hussin b. Ahmad** . Killed in Action. Engaging CT's Coronation Estate Johore ---]
Thur.	23rd	

Fri.	24th	**23** 5 Malay Policemen were Killed in an CT ambush by C.T.'s. **P/C's NaSir. B. Salleh. - Zakaria B. Panak Rewan. E.PC's Abdul Bin Yahaya- SC's Borhan B. Mohd. Zin.- Abdul Ghani B. Lassim.** F. M. Police. On the Ladang Geddes Estate Negri Sembilan---]
	+	**24 Maj. T. R. Brook.** 1st. Battn. The Loyal Regt. Died*** *Kuala Lumpur # 17 / 1002*---]
	+	**24 L/Airman. R. V. Baker.** HMS '*UNICORN*' Died*** *Kranji Singapore # 12 / C – 5*---]
	+	**24** 2 F. M. Police **P.C's Sarwan B Abu Bakar. Kusasb, Hj, Othman** Killed at the 16th. m/s Kuantong/ Gemban Rd. Pahang.---]
Sat.	25th	**24 SC.Sgt. Khalid B. Hassim.** F. M. Police Killed in Action. Engaging CT's Kedah. ---]
	+	**25 Gnr. N. Higgs.** Royal Artillery Died *** *Seremban # CE / 28* Negri Sembilan---]
Sun.	26th	**25 PC Kusas B HJ Othman.** F. M. Police. Killed on the Ruab/Bentong Rd.---]
Mon.	27th	**26** HMT EMPIRE WINDRUSH sailed Singapore bound for Southampton with returning Service personnel
	+	**27 L/Cpl. Gamtabahadur.Thapa.** 2nd. King Edward VII's Own Gurkha Rifles Died Killed In.Action. Kota Ting aera. *[No known Grave]Terandak Wall Memorial Malacca* ---]
Tue.	28th	**27 Lt. (KGO) Shere. Thapa.** 2nd. King Edward VII's Own Gurkha Rifles. Died. Killed In Action. Engaging CT's Kamsulang Area. *[No known Grave]Terandak Wall Memorial Malacca*---]
	+	In a CT ambush. **Susan Thompson.** 2 years old English Child. In the area of Sungei Bulloh Selangor. A brutal & senseless killing of her & her Amah cook.---]
Wed.	29th	**28** HMT DEVONSHIRE arrived Singapore with replacement Service personnel enroute to Hong Kong
Thur.	30th	28nd.---]
		29 SC Dain B. Mohd. Noor. F. M. Police. Killed in Action Engaging CT's Ulu Ramis Estate Johore.---]
	+	Plt. 'D' Comp Suffolk's. Killed a CT on the Soringgit Estate, wounding 2 others who escaped. The dead CT was identified as *Yoke Fong* Secretary of 2 Plt. MRLA---]
		Operation *"Carp"- "Albermarle"- "Rabbit"- "Cleaver II"* Ended---]

DECEMBER

Fri.	1st	**1 Pte. J. D. Gregory.** 1st. Battn. K.O.Y.L.I.. Died. Accidently. Shot on Patrol. [*Ashes REP*]---]
	+	**1 Mr. J.H. Clarkson.** Manager. Killed by CT's at the Batu Caves Selangor.---]
	+	**1 SC. Adivaran a/o Yeratheran.** F. M. Police Killed In Action Engaging CT's Sungei Tun Estate Selangor]
	+	RAF Sqdn. 60 Vampires became operational RAF Tenga.---]
Sat.	2nd	**2 WOII A. Craig.** Royal Signals Died *** *Kuala Lumpur # 17 / 1003* ---]
	+	**2 ASP. A.E.B. Bulteel.** F. M. Police Killed on Ops. Ambushed by CT's on the Pokoh Sena/Nami road Alor Star Kedah *Jalan Pertana # 1420* George Town Penang ---]
Sun.	3rd	**3 Pte. Hassan Bin. Haji . Osman.** A. C. C. (MOR) Died*** *Claimed by next of Kin* ---]
Mon.	4th	**4 Drv. L. Short.** Royal Signals Killed in Action Engaging CT's. [*Ashes REP*].---]
	+	4 HMT EMPIRE HALLADALE arrived Singapore with replacement Service personnel---]
Tue.	5th	**5 Pol/Lt. W.A. Allmond.** F. M. Police. Killed in Action Engaging CT's. Bahau Estate Jerum Kuala Selangor. Selangor. Died from gunshot wounds.*Kuala Lumpur # 728* ---]
	+	5 HMT EMPIRE HALLADALE sailed Singapore bound for Liverpool with returning Service personnel---]
Wed.	6th	**6 Mr. N.F. Modder.** an Estate official on the Ampamg Tenang Estate was shot dead by an attacking force of 10 CT's in the Kajang area Selangor ---]
Thur.	7th	**7 SC Lani B. Long.** F. M. Police. Killed in Action Engaging CT's Nanyo Kluang Estate Johore---].
Fri.	8th	In the Bukit Mayang area. A Platoon from 'C' Comp Suffolk's. Killed 1 of 3 CT & wounded 2 others---]
Sat.	9th	**9 Mr. R. Judson.** Planter. Chembong Estate Rembau Negri Sembilan Died in an ambush .---]
Sun.	10th	A Plt from 'C' Comp Suffolk's. Searching the Bukit Mayang area, came across 3 CT's Killing 1 the others escaped.-----]
Mon.	11th	**11 Pte. J. Verney.** The Seaforth Highlanders Died*** *Kranji Singapore # 1 / D - 8*---]
	+	**11 Fus. W. H. Marshall**. Royal Northumberland Fusiliers. Died*** *Kranji Singapore # 2 /C -13*---]
	+	**11 Cpl. P. H. Bell.** Fit/2A. R. A. F. Seletar. Died during the Singapore Hertogh Riots. *Singapore # 3 / C - 4*---]
	+	**11 AC1.** Retro Inst Tech. **J. Y. Clark.** R. A. F. Det. Labuan. Died*** *Kranji Singapore # 4 / D -2*---]
	+	Singapore.The Hertogh Case: A court ruling decided that a Maria Hertogh a juvenile who had been raised by Muslim parents. Was to be returned to her Dutch biological Catholic parents. ---]
Tue.	12th	**12 Pte. C. Walsh.** R. A.S.C. Died*** Kuala Lipis. *Kuala Lumpur # 17 / 1004* ---]
	+	**12 SC. Mat Ross B. Saidum.** F. M. Police Killed in Action. Engaging CT's Sikamat Police Post. Negri Sembilan---]
	+	

Wed.	13th	Singapore :The previous days ruling by the court. Angered a large group of Muslims who gathered outside the court. So began the Maria Hertogh riots. ---]
	+	**13 LAC. M. O. Bartleman.** R. A. F. Died *** *[Ashes REP]*---]
	+	**13 SC. Hassan B. Che Wan.** F. M. Police Killed in Action. Engaging CT's. Bukir Pilah Estate Bahua Negri Sembilan---]
Thur.	14th	Singapore: The Hertogh Case: Marie along with her Parents. Flew out of Changi bound for Holland---]
	+	**14 W/O. H. W. Davies.** CI/GD. R.A.F.HQ. Changi Died from injuries recv'd in the Singapore Riots on the 11th. December.*[Ashes REP]*---]
		Singapore: The Hertogh Case: The 3 day riots in Singapore caused by the case ended. Resulting in the death of 18 people 7 European or of Eurarasion extract - 2 Police Officers . 9 Rioters shot by the Police
Fri.	15th	173 persons injured, 119 vehicles damaged and 2 buildings set on fire. ---]
	+	**14 HMT DEVONSHIRE** sailed Singapore enroute to Liverpool with returning Service personnel 14th.---]
		15/12/50 LG 39032 p. 6272 The following awarded the Military Medal
		CPL. K TAMANG K. MM 10th PRINCESS MARY'S OWN GURKHA RIFLES
		p. 6271 The following awarded the Colonial Police Medal
	+	INSP. TUN HAMZZAH B.TUN. CPM. FEDERATION MALAYA POLICE
Sat.	16th	PC. BARRRUDDIN B.A.M.HUSSIN.CPM FEDERATION MALAYA POLICE
		15 HMT EMPIRE PRIDE arrived Liverpool with returning Service personnel ---]
		Kuala Lumpur: It was announced in Kuala Lumpur. The War Council chaired by General Briggs was to be strengthened.:
		'The Chairman was General Briggs, Director of Operations.
		Nicole Gray Chief of Police.
		Boris Hembry, spokesman for the Malayan Planters Association
		Senior members of the Malayan Civil Service Tunku Abdul Rahman, , including representatives of the
	+	*Malay Chinese & Indian Communities'.*---]
	+	16/12/1950 LG # 407942 p?. The following awarded the Military Cross.
		2/LT. C.L. LAWRENCE. MC THE MIDDLESEX REGIMENT.
Sun.	17th	**16 HMT DILWARA** arrived Southampton with returning Service personnel---]
	+	40 CT's attacked the Galloway Estate killing 3 Labourers & set fire to newly erected buildings---]
		A follow up by the Suffolk's found 3 CT's. Assumed those in the earlier attack Killed 2 CT's 1 was
Mon.	18th	identified as *Thom Yit* ---]
		18 Rfn . Ramdhoj Limbu. 10th Princess Mary's Own Gurkha Rifles. Drowned on Ops. Sabai Area
	+	Bentong *Kuala Lumpur # 27 / 16*---]
		1 Platoon 'A' Comp Suffolk's along with 2 Platoons of the F.M. Police searching for members of the Min Yuen in the Jenderham area. Engaged 3. Opening fire Killed 1, a woman, wounded the other 2 who
Tue.	19th	escaped.---]
		19 Mr. D.A. Adamson. Asstn Manager of the Jong Landor Estate. Killed along with **Alcock** in a CT
	+	ambush in the Tapah area of Perak.---]
		Singapore: Straits Times printed an article recording the appointment to the War Council of:
		'Boris Hembry: Former Force 136 Leiutenant Colonel and experienced guerrilla fighter. Mr. Boris
		Hembry has been appointed Member to the Federal War Council in Sucession to Mr. G.D.Treble.....
		'Mr. Hembry is currently the General Manager of the Ulu Remis Estate Layang Layang Johore ,
		formerly of Sungei Siput. Where the murders of three planters started the Emergency. Mr Hembry was
		awarded the Colonial Police Medal at a ceremony in Kuala Lumpur ---]
		[**Authors Note**: Boris Hembry was in fact a not a member of Force 136 but of the Inter Service Liaison Departmemt (ISLD). A similar Clandestine Force, which worked hand in hand with Force 136 during the
	+	SOE operations in Malaya 1942-1945---]
Wed.	20th	**19 HMT EMPIRE FOWEY** arrived Southampton- with returning Service personnel ---]
	+	**20 Mr. J. M Arnold.** Manager. Kalumpang Estate near Kuala Kabu Baharu Selangor. Killed by CT's.---]
		20 5 F. M. Police **SC's. Omar B. Chilappan. – Bujang. B. Tek. – A. Bakar B. Lambak. – Yunos B.**
Thur.	21st	**Khar. – A. Wahab B. M. Yunes.** Killed in Action Engaging CT's Sisak Mines Kota Tinggi Johore---*]*
		London : Mr. Stachey & The military Staff Sent a message through to all Ranks serving in Malaya
Fri.	22nd	*'Wishing them their very best wishes for Christmas !!!*----]
		22 Mne. B. Eatough. (42 Commando) Royal Marines .Died from Wounds recv'd after being shot by CT
	+	sentry *Batu Gaja # 617* Ipoh Perak---].
		22 Rfn. J. W. Vallance. The Cameronians. Killed in Action. Engaging CT's Muer Johore.
	+	*Kranji Singapore # 1 / D - 7*---]

		22 Pol/Lt. N.R.R. Magill. F. M. Police. Killed by Terrorist during operations with Jungle squads Kuala
	+	Kabu Kabu area Selangor. *Kuala Lumpur # 292* ---]
Sat.	23rd	11 Platoon D Comp Suffolk's Patrolling along a swamp, came across a hut. As they approached an armed CT came out & was quickly shot dead. Another also in the hut was Killed---]
	+	**23 Rfn. T. Holland.** 1st. The Cameronians. Died from wounds recv'd previous day.Muar Johore *[Ashes REP]*--]
	+	**23 Gnr. A. Rawlings.** Royal Artillery Died***.*Kuala Lumpur # 17 / 1005*---]
	+	**23 Lt. Tikaram Lama.** 10th. Princess Mary's Own Gurkha Rifles. Died*** *Kranji Singapore # 1 / - 6* --]
Sun.	24th	2 F. M. Police. **P/C Omar B. Kadir. SC Abdul Maji a/o Mydin Pitchay.** Killed in Action Engaging CT's Sungei Remok Estate Selangor.---]
	+	**24 Cpl. Birbahagur Gurung.** 7th. Duke of Edinburgh's Own Gurkha Rifles. Died *** BMH Kinrara *Seremban # 26* Negri Sembilan ---]
Mon.	25th	**24 SC. Sgt. Mohd. Majid B. Hj Mokhti** F. M. Police Killed in Action Engaging CT's Ulu Kili Estate Selangor.---]
	+	**25 Drv. C.E. Whitwell.** R.A.S.C Murdered by armed robber. Ipoh. *Batu Gajah # 526* Ipoh Perak ---]
	+	**25 Rfn. Lachhimiparsad Gurung.** 6th. Queen Elizabeth's Own Gurkha Rifles.Killed in Action Engaging CT's Bahau Negri Sembilan *[No known Grave]Terandak Memorial Malacca*---]
Tue.	26th	**25 Cpl. R. Carus.** Cl. 45 Sqdn. R.A.F. Butterworth. Died from injuries received during a road traffic accident on the 23rd. December.*Western Road # 2137* George Town Penang---]
		26 PC Talip b. Mohamad. F. M. Police Killed on Ops. No further information---]
Wed..	27th	3 Chinese civilians were Killed in a Café in Ipoh When a grenade was thrown in by a CT.---]
	+	**27 Mne Sgt. S. Orr.** (40 Commando) Royal Marines Accidenty Killed. Kuala Lumpur *[Ashes REP]*---]
	+	**27 Sgt. Osman. Bin. Nasir..** A. C. C. (MOR) Died*** *Claimed by next of Kin* ---]
	+	**27 Spr. Shukor Bin Ahmad.** Royal Engineers (MOR) Died *** *Claimed by next of Kin*---]
Thur.	28th	The Asstn. Manager (*unnamed*) of the West Country Estate & his Clerk (*unnamed*) were Killed by a raiding party of 11 CT's they were heavily armed & retreated back into the Kajang Forest rReserve---]
	+	**28 Mne's. D. Parr. - L. J. Turner.** *[Ashes REP}* (45 Commando) Royal Marines. Killed in ambush. Gopeng Kampar Hills Perak. *Batu Gaja # 527 /* Ipoh Perak ---]
	+	**28 Rfn. Bhagihoj Limbu.** 7th. Duke of Edinburgh's Own Gurkha Rifles. Died*** *Kuala Lumpur # 26 /7*---]
	+	**28 Gdsmn. E. J. Duffell.** 2nd. Battn. Scots Guards. Died*** *Kuala Lumpur # 17 - 1006*---]
Fri.	29th	28 HMT EMPIRE WINDRUSH arrived Southampton with returning Service ersonnel---]
	+	**29 Pte. R. Shufflebottom.** R. A. M. C. Died*** *[Ashes REP]* ---]
	+	**29 Cadet N.H.H. Hurst.** F.M. Aux.P. Motor accident. *Seremban # ??* Negri Sembilan.---]
Sat.	30th	**29 SC Doraiseny.** F. M. Police Killed in Action. Engaging CT's. Rimba Panjong Perak---]
	+	**30 Wg/Cdr. H. E. R. Nelson.** R.A.F. Died***.*Kranji Singapore # 14 / C -14* ---]
Sun.	31st	30 2 F. M. Police **Pol/Lt. M.R. Livingstone & PC. Talip. B.Mohamed.** Killed in Action. Engaging CT's during a CT ambush, whilst in charge of a Jungle Squad, investigating a fire at a disued Tin Mine in the Grik area of Perak *Christian Cemetery* Taiping Perak ---]
	+	**31 WOII. B. Hornby.** King's Own Royal Regt. Died*** *Western Road #2894* GeorgeTown. Penang---]
	+	**31 Cfn. C. A. Legge.** R.E.M.E.. Died*** *Kranji Singapore # 1 / D - 5*--]
	+	31 8 F. M. Police Constables , including 2 Malay civilians were. Killed & 6 wounded in an attack on Police lorries by C.T's : **Sgt. A Rahman.- B. Ibrahim - Sgt. Shaari B. Yunus.- Cpl. Saidon B. HJ. A.Ramin.,- F.P.G. Alon. S/O Chuan.- Din B. Jaafar. - .Cheow Wan Chai, - A. Hamid B. Ibrahim. - Omar B. Dahaman.**---]
	+	7 C.T's were Killed during the raid.at Gurum Padang Kedah---]
		Operation "*Letter*" -"*Kohat* ""*Jackal*" – "*Rose*" Ended ---]

Dec 1950

Kuala Lumpur: Gen. Harold Briggs issueed a list of titled sections of the CMP with Monetary awards. For information on any member within those cantegories:- (Issued during. December)

Secetary General of the Central Committee. ....$30,000.
Members of the Politburo..$20,000.
State Commitee Secretaries Town Commitees Secretaries Regional Committees Secretaries. .$15,000.
Ditto + Members of Military Commands..$10,000.
District Commitee Secretaries. ....$7,000.
Ditto + Members of Companys ....$5,000.
Directing Company Members Members of Platoons.. $3.000.
Members of Group Committees Section Commanders Leaders of Min Yuen Military Work Forces

	Leaders of Protection Corps Leaders Of Special Serves Squads...$2.500. Leaders Of Part Cells..$1,500. Ordinary Part Members Combatant Members Members Of Special Service Squads Members Of Military Work Forces Members Of Protection Corps. ....$1,000. Basically Covering All The Members Of The MPBA Without Naming Them.

R. A. F. OPERATION *"FIREDOG"* END OF YEAR STATISTICS 1950

No of Sorties	No. of Strikes	1,000 Lb.Bombs	500 Lb. Bombs	350 LbCluster	20 LbBombs	R/P's	20mm	.5 mm	.303mm
4560	808	8,217	5,400	-/	10,552	19,06	970,492	564,609	77,455

R. A. F. SUPPORT 1950

	Soties	Troops/Lift/	Casac	Pass/Lift	Supply Wt. Lbs	Leaflets drop (1,000)	B Flying Times No / hrs	Broadcstin g No / hrs	Crashed
Air SupportA/C*	1412	/	/	/	1,848.565	/	/	/	Auster VX 922
Auster**	N/A	/	28	/	/	/	/	/	- TJ629
Pioneer	/	/	/	/	/	/	/	/	Dakota
H/C Light	/	/	/	/	/	/	/	/	KN630 KN240
848 Sqdn	/	/	/	/	/	/	/	/	Seafire 2RN ?
155 Sqdn	/	/	/	/	/	/	/	/	Brigand
Target/MK**	/	/	/	/	/	/	/	/	RH 815-
Vis/Air OBs**	/	/	/	/	/	/	/	/	RH850
Communication**	/	/	/	/	/	/	/	/	Spitfire
Leaf. Sorties*	14	/	/	/	/	/	/	/	TP390 SM 975
Leaflets Drop*	/	/	/	/	/	6,404	/	/	TP219 VN 491
Leaf Sorties **	/	/	/	/	/	/	/	/	Sunderland
Leaflets Drop**	/	/	/	/	/	/	/	/	SZ573
Broad Sorties*	/	/	/	/	/	/	/	/	Tempest 's
Broad Hrs *	/	/	/	/	/	/	/	/	PR 895
Broad Sorties**	/	/	/	/	/	/	/	/	PR786
Broad Hrs **	/	/	/	/	/	/	/	/	Mosquito's
Photo RECCE***	807	/	/	/	/	/	./	/	PF624

* AirSupport A/C Dakota -Valetta- Hastings Bristol
** Auster
*** Photo Rec Anson,,Spitfire, Mosquito, Meteor, Pembroke

CHAPTER 9 - 1951

ROYAL AIR FORCE
OFFENSIVE AIR SUPPORT - OPERATION 'FIREDOG'
March 1951 to July 1960

Sqdn	Location	Aircraft Type	No	Date From	Year	Date To.	Year
52	Changi	Valetta C1	10	3rd. S.E.P.	1951	1st. Oct .	1955
60	Kuala Lumpur	Vampire FB5/9	16	15th. Jan	1951	1st..May.	1957
110	Changi	Valetta C4	8	.24th. Oct.	1951	31st. Dec.	1960
656	Changi	Auster 5/6/7/9	31	1st, Aug.	1951	Jul...	1960

MALAYAN AUXILLIARY AIR FORCE
OFFENSIVE AIR SUPPORT - OPERATION 'FIREDOG'
January 1951 to April 1957
Kuala Lumpur Squadron**

Sqdn. **	Location	Aircraft Type	No	Date From	Year	Date To	Year
**	Kuala Lumpur	Tiger Moth82A	4	1st. Dec.	1951	Mar.	1957
		Harvard 2B	4	1st. Feb.	1951	Mar	1957
		Chipmonk	4	Mar	1957	3rd.Apr.	1957

JANUARY

Mon.	1st	1 2 F. M. Police **PC's Abdul Kadir B. Abdullah**.- **Arhson B. Mohd. Salleh**. were Killed during an ambush by CT's. at the Thye Hup Estate Sungei Patani. Kedah 3 others were wounded & 3 reported missing. ---]
	+	1 2 F.M. Police **SC's Osman B, Yayha**.- **Ismail B Mohd. Amin** were Killed by a number of CT's on the Grisek Estate Johore---]
	+	Operations "*Cathedral*"- "*Hustle*" & "*Kick-Off*"- "*Sabal*" Began Against No 6 Regt. MRLA. In Negri Sembilan Selangor & Pahang---]
	+	Operation "*Gallows*" followed by a series upto August "*Marker*" – "*Mermaid*" – "*Rainbow*" –"*Raven*" – "*Redskin*" –"*Rover*" –"*Rumble*" Began against No 12 Regt. MRLA in Perak. ---]
	+	Operation "*Tansing*" Began against No 3 Regt. MRLA in Pahang
	+	Singapore : A Chinese detective **_(unnamed)_** was shot dead in Singapore Chinatown by two gunmen who escaped---]
	+	1 HMT EMPIRE HALLADALE arrived Liverpool with returning Service personnel ---]
Tue.	2nd	Auster Number AOP6 VF 648 of 656 Sqdn.. R.A.F. Overturned on take-off from Bahau Air strip Negri Sembilan---]
	+	02/01/51 # 39112 p. 702 The following awarded the Military Cross MAJ. E.J.L. MOSTYN. MC SCOTS GUARDS The following awarded the Military Medal

	CPL. J. MACNAUGHT ALLAN. MM SCOTS GUARDS
Wed. 3rd	Mad Mike Calvert flew from Singapore to Rhodesia, via Cairo. To begin a selection of 100 of the 1,000 volunteers who had joined up the Southern Rhodesian Defence Force in response to Calverts request to form the Malayan Scouts. The 100 selected troops would becme the 'C' Squadron Rhodesian SAS---].
Thur. 4th	4 HMT EMPIRE TROOPER sailed Southmpton bound for Singapore with replacement Service Personnel -]
Fri. 5th	**5 Pte. S. D. Whittaker.** 1st. Battn. Worcestershire Regt. Died*** _Kranji Singapore # 1 / D - 4_---]
+	**5 PC. Idris. B. Mahadi.** F. M. Police Killed on Ops. Chemek Johore.---]
Sat. 6th	6 5 F. M. Poiice: **SC's Saman B. Taman.- Abdul Chani B. Yayha.- Yaacob B. Mat Saja.- Ibrahim B. Mohd. Noor.- Kassim B.Abdul Samat.** Were Killed in a CT ambush on the Bikam Estate Tapah Perak. ---]
Sun. 7th	7 3 F.M. Police: **SC's Ebas B, Ismail.- Ibrahim B. Noordom.- Amir B. Johari.** Killed by CT's in the area of Tapah Perak---]
Mon. 8th	**8 Pte. W. Haynes.** 1st. Battn. Worcestershire Regt. Died by accident. _Kranji Singapore # 1 / D - 3_---]
+	Acting on Police information 10 Platoon 'D' Company Suffolk's engaged CT's & Killed 1 CT, a Min Yuen---]
Tue. 9th	In the Sungei Merabua area. A small Platoon of the Suffolk's came across 2 suspicious men. Capturing them one tried to escape. After repeated warnings he was killed, the other escaped. The dead one was identified as **Soo Kow** a member of the local Min Yuen---]
Wed. 10th	**10 Mne Sgt. G. Westwood. - Mne Cpl. J.Henry. - Mne. L. O. Miller** (45 Commando) Royal Marines were Killed in a CT ambush Cameron Highlands. _Batu Gajah # 531 / 530_ Ipoh Perak. J. Henry _[Ashes REP]_---]
+	10 HMT EMPIRE PRIDE sailed Liverpool bound for Singapore-with replacement Service personnel]'
+	10 HMT EMPIRE FOWEY sailed Southampton bound for Singapore / Hong Kong with replacement Service personnel---]
Thur. 11th	11.While on a sortie near Ipoh. 2 Hornet a/c attacking a known CT target. When 1 a/c. Hornet VS838 piloted by **Sgt. Pilot G.A. Robinson - Sgt. K. Hall.-** Nav. - **Sgt. S. V. Hayler.** Sig. of 45 Sqdn R A F Suffered an explosion in its cannon bay. The plane caught fire. Sgt. Hayter baled out before the Hornet crashed into the ground. Killing the other two on impact. _[No known Graves] Terandak Wall Memorial Malacca]_---]
+	3 Plt .A. Comp & 10 Plt 'D' Comp Suffolk's found a small CT camp a fire fight ensused ! CT was Killed identified as a Min Yuen member,---]
Fri. 12th	**12 Rfn. Dirgasing. Gurung** 2nd. King Edward VII's Own Gurkha Rifles. Died*** _Kranji Singapore # 8 / A – 6]_
+	**12 Mr. W.J. Shaw.** Estate Manager. Banting Selangor was Killed by CT's. ---]
+	12 HMT DEVONSHIRE arrived Liverpool with returning Service personnel ---]
Sat. 13th	13 3 F. M. Police **SC's Mohd. Zain B. Singa.- Ismail B. Hussin.- Sn Chong.** Killed by CT's on the Samantan Estate Pahang.---]
Sun. 14th	**14 Mne. Lt. M. G. Dowling.** Royal Marines. Killed in Action Leading a Patrol in the Grik area of Perak Engaging CT's. _Taiping # B / 52_ Perak---]
Mon. 15th	**15 Mr. D.J. White** Resettlement Off. & Hon Aux/Inspt. F.M.Police. Killed in CT ambush in Pusing area of Perak _Taiping # 41_ Perak ---]
+	15 2 F. M. Police **SC's. Hassan B, Said.- Hussein B. Ahmad.** Killed by CT's in the Bentong Area.---]
+	RAF Sqdn.60 Vampire became operational RAF Changi---]
Tue. 16th	16 The body of **Sgt. S. V. Hayler** 45 Sqdn R. A. F. was found in the jungle . He had been Killed by an Aborigini poisoned tipped arrow. _Kuala Lumpur # 32 – 1239_ ---]
+	16 2 F.M. Police **SCs.Arumagam. a/o Nunian.- Adam B. Hj Omar.** Killed by CT's Batu Arang. ---]
Wed. 17th	17 **Sgt. Chandrabahadur. Ale.** 6th. Queen Elizabeth's Own Gurkha Rifles. Killed _[No known Grave]Terandak Wall Memorial Malacca_ ---]
+	**17 SC Yeop Bin Manap.**F. M. Police Killed on Ops. Telok Anson Perak---]
+	Kuala Lumpur: Air Vice Marshal R.S. Blucke. Became Air Officer Commanding Malaya ---]
Thur. 18th	A Patrol from 'D' Comp Suffolk's During a night ambush Killed 2 CT's,identified as the leader of the Kampong Jenderan Min Yuen. **Abdul Manan & his bodyguard** This killing & the fact that he was the leader in the Kampong. Under Operation ' Alka Selzer' led to the whole of the Kampong mainly Malay C.T. sympathisers being relocated in a different area ---]
Fri. 19th	**19 E/PC Wong Sin Fook** F. M. Police Killed 26th. m/s New Village Resettlement area Kulai---]
+	**19 AC2 Yunus B. Buyong** R.A.F. (MOR) Died*** _[Claimed by next of Kin]_---]
+	19/01/1951 LG # 39127 p. 364 The following awarded the Colonial Police Medal SC. TALIB.B. SIAK KAYA. CPM. FEDERATION MALAYA POLICE
Sat. 20th	**20 EPC Dahlan b. Montel** F. M. Police. Killed 32nd. m/s Muar---]
Sun. 21st	**21 Pte. D. J. Marsden.** 1st. Battn. Worcestershire Regt. Died*** _Kranji Singapore # 2 / E – 12_ ---]

+	21 HMT EMPIRE WINDRUSH sailed Southapton bound for Singapore with replacement Service personnel---]
Mon.22nd	An ambush laid by the 10th. Gurkhas, resulted in 4 CT's being Killed 2 wounded. 1 a woman & 1 captured. In an effort to escape 2 jumped into the River Karau & were swept away, assumed drowned..
+	Another section of the Gurkhas. Hearing the gunfire from the other Platoon laid a trap in anticipating the rereat of other CT's. Killed 3 more, 1 CT escaping was chased by a Gurkha rifleman who killed him in a Rubber Estate ---]
Tue. 23rd	23 SC. Ismail F. M. Police Killed on Ops. Dong Pahang.---]
Wed. 24th	CT's held up a bus at the 33rd. m/s Banting Road set it alight. A road Patrol of the 13th./ 18th. Hussars arrived the CT's retreated into the jungle fringes & were then mortored by the Hussars---]
Thur. 25th	25 Sgt. D. MacMillan. 2nd. Battn. Scots Guards. Died***_Kuala Lumpur # 18 -1008_---]
+	A Platoon of the 10th. Gurkhas met a party of 60 CT's. Killing one. Captured a 12 year old boy.---]
Fri. 26th	26 L/Cpl. J. D. Whitehead. 1st. Battn. K. O. Y. L. I. Killed in Action Engaging CT's _Western Road # 2895_ George Town Penang ---]
+	12 British soldiers & 13 civilians were wounded when a C.T threw a grenade into a dance hall in Seremban.---]
Sat. 27th	27 Pte. Hassen B. Saleh. Malay Regt. Killed in Action. Engaging CT's Pahang---]
Sun. 28th	28 Dvr. R. Baldwin. R. A. S. C. Died. Killed by bomb.outrage. _Batu Gajah # 532_ Ipoh Perak---]
Mon. 29th	29 3. F. M. Police SC's. Lee Yeong.- Ng Patt Leong.- Cheng Kam Kong Killed By CT's Ayer Kuming Perak---]
Tue. 30th	30 5 F. M. Police PC's Abdul Jalil B. Kahlu Rahman. - Yusof. B. Mohamad. - Said b. Abas & SC Sulaiman B. Abdullah.- Ahmad b. Hssein. Were Killed when 30 C.T's ambushed their Police car at the 4th. m/s Kaki Bukit/ Padang Besar Rd. Kedah. ---]

FEBRUARY

Thur. 1st	1 Sgt. Bhimbahadur Sahi. 2nd. King Edward VII's Own Gurkha Rifles. Killed in Action Engaging CT's [_No known Grave] Terandak Wall Memorial Malacca_---]
+	1 5 F.M. Policemen SC's Nazlan B. Ngah Abdul.- Sulaiman B. Abdullah.- Mohd, Yussof.B. Thamby. – Raja Malif B. Raja Mat.- Raja Aznan B. Raja Sulaiman. Killed by CT's on the Pembroke Estate Sungei Siput Perak---]
+	Operations "_Sabai_"- "_Stymei_" Began against No 6 Regt. MRLA in Selangor & Pahang.---]
+	Operations "_Mantrap_", "_Tansing_" "_Valetta_". Began against No 6 Regt. MRLA in Negri Sembilan Selengor Pahang.---]
+	Operation "_Dagger_" Began Against No 1 Regt. MRLA Labis Johore---]
Fri. 2nd	Malayan Aux Air .Force. Harvards Sqdn. became operational at RAF Kuala Lumpur ---]
+	11 Platoon 'B' Comp Suffolk's, found 3 food dumps in the Bukit Chetting area destoying all---]
+	2/02/1951 LG # 39139 p. 602 The following has been awarded the Distinguished Conduct Medal SGT. D. RAI. MM. DCM 10th. PRINCESS MARY'S OWN GURKHA RIFLES The following has been awarded the Miltary Medal CPL. D. RAI. MM 10th PRINCESS MARY'S OWN GURKHA RIFLES
+	2 HMT DEVONSHIRE sailed Liverpool bound for Singapore with replacement Service personnel---]
+	2 HMT EMPIRE FOWEY arrived Singapore with replacement Service personnel--]
Sat. 3rd	11 Platoon 'B' Comp Suffolk's Patrolling in the Kual Langat Forest Reserve came across a dead body with its hands tied behind its back. It was very decomposed & assumed abducted? A further serach revealed a second body in much the same condition---]
+	3 HMT EMPIRE TROOPER arrived Singapore with replacement Service personnel ---]
+	3 HMT EMPIRE FOWEY sailed Singapore bound for Hong Kong---]
Sun. 4th	4 Abdul Rahman bin Abdul Asis. (A Malay) the Asstn. Commander of the Singapore Special Constabulary was shot dead by a Chinese gunman in the Geyland district of Singapore.---]
+	4 HMT EMPIRE PRIDE arrived Singapore- with replacement Service personnel---]
Mon. 5th	7 Platoon 10th. Gurkhas Killed 4 CT's in the Tras road area ---]
Tue. 6th	The Penang – Kuala Lumpur Mail train, passing through South Perak. Was attacked by CT's waiting in ambush. They opened fire killing 1 Indian, a Chinese woman. (_both unnamed_) Wounding: I British soldier, 1 Malay soldier, including 2 Indians.---]
Wed. 7th	

Thur. 8th	**7 Pol/Lt. J.G. Yapp**. F. M. Police Killed on Ops. & 2 Police Constables wounded in an ambush by C.T.'s on the Jabor Valley Estate in the Kuantan.area of Pahang *Kuantan ??* Pahang.---]
+	**8 PC Man. B. Mohamed**. F. M. Police Killed on Ops. Gemas Estate Johore---]
Fri. 9th	8 HMT EMPIRE TROOPER sailed Singapore bound for Southampton with returning Service personnel --]
Sat. 10th	9 HMT EMPIRE PRIDE sailed Singapore bound for Liverpool-with returning Service personnel--]
	3 Helicopters were called out for casvac operations. 1 was in Terengannu where a Policeman was lifted with serious gunshot wounds . The 2nd. Was called out to Casvac a BOR from the jungle in South Selangor, unfortunately developed engine trouble & forced landed A 3rd Helicopter was air lifted, to lift out the BOR
Sun. 11th	to a Local Hospital---]
Mon. 12th	**11 L/Cpl. Ishak**. F. M. Police Killed on Ops. Jonkok Terengganu.---]
Tue. 13th	**12 SC Shah B. Panjang Mat Masah** F. M. Police Killed on Ops. Sungei Krudda Estate Sungei Siput Perak -]
+	**13 Rfn. L. Maitadhoj Limbu** 10th. Princess Mary's Own Gurkha Rifles. Died*** *Kranji Singapore # 8 / A 0 7*]
+	13 2 F. M. Police **SC's. Radin B. Budin. – Mohd Sa'ad Sallah**. Killed on Ops. Tanjong Malim Estate Selangor.---]
Wed. 14th	Operation *'Alka Selza'* began. 1,500 residents, the whole population of the village of Jenderam (a notorious base for C.T's) in South Selan were removed by 1,000 troops & 3 Police Companies & transferred in 50 lorries to a new camp in the Kuantan area of Pahang.---]
Thur. 15th	**14 L/Cpl. S. E. Thompsett** 1st. Battn. Suffolk Regt. Killed in Action Engaging CT's *Kuala Lumpur #18 / 1009*]
	15 Sgt. Pilot. W. Kent.- Sgt. B. A. Ellis. Nav. 45 Sqdn R.A F were Killed when their Brigand VS859 crashed near Pilau. After a cannon exploded in the Aircraft.
Fri. 16th	*Seremban # CE / 25 – 26* Negri Sembilan---]
+	**16 Pte. Anak Tulu Entap** Sarawak Rangers Killed. *[No known Grave] Terandak Wall Memorial Malacca* ---]
	16/02/1951 LG # 39150 p 857 The following awarded the Military Medal
	SGT. D. GURUNG. MM 2nd. KING EDWARD'S VII's OWN GURKHA RIFLES
Sat. 17th	RFN. B THAPA. MM 2nd. KING EDWARD'S VII's OWN GURKHA RIFLES
	17 PC. Embi. B. Hashim. F. M. Police Killed by C.T's who stopped an omnibus at the 26th. m/s Kuala Kangsar
+	Road.----]
+	17 HMT EMPIRE ORWELL sailed from Southanpton bound for Singapore/ Hong Kong with replacement Service personnel ---]
Sun. 18th	Operation *'Alka Selza'* ended---]
Mon. 19th	**18 D/Sgt. Ismail B. Hashim**. F. M. Police Killed on Ops. Sungei Dingin Estate Kulim Kedah---]
	No. 11 Platoon 10th. Gurkhas engaged a party of 10 CT's. The leading scout Rfn. D. Thapa charged them. killing 2. Threw a smoke grenade & continued charging on. Took hold of another CT & Killed him The Action Engaging CT's by the Gurkhas the remainder running. 3 Recommedations were made for the
Tue. 20th	Action Engaging CT's--- Cpl. D. Rai. DCM. Sgt. T. Limbu & Rfn.D Rai. MM
	20 L/Cpl. Hirasing. Gurung 6th. Queen Elizabeth's Own Gurkha Rifles.Died from Wounds recv'd. *Kluang #*
+	*3 / A -5 Johore---.*]
+	**20 Pte. A. G. Fee**. 1st. Battn. K.O.Y.L.I. Drowned swimming accident.*Western Road # 2896-* George Town---]
+	Patrols from 'C' Comp Suffolk's Patrolling in the Sungei Dua area Killed 4 CT's---]
	Singapore: A Special Constable was slightly hurt when he stopped 2 CT's putting up. Posters in English protesting against the Federation Governments policy of prohibiting those who evade the call-up from returning
+	to Malaya ---]
Wed. 21st	20/02/1951 LG # 387901 p. 926 The following awarded the Military Cross
	LT. J. D. A. LINN. MC KING'S OWN SCOTISH BORDERERS.ATT/ CAMERONIANS
+	**21 SC. Hamzah B. Dukin**. F. M. Police. Killed on Ops. Gambang Pahang.---]
+	*Pahang*: A combinded force of Ground & Air bombing began in the Sungei Limau Manis area where it
Thur.22nd	was believed **Liew Kon Kim** was encamped. The engagement lasted until the 23rd ---]
	22 Sgt. J. A. Rowley. Pte.'s D. C. Walker - J.C.Banner. - R. Harvey. - G. Plant. 1st. Battn. Worcestershire Regt. were Killed when a military party was ambushed by over 100 C.T's **Rowley.& Walker** *[Ashes REP]*
+	**Banner. - Harvey. - Plant.** *Kranji Singapore # 1 / C – 15 – 1 / D – 2 - 1* ---]
	A Patrol from 'B' Comp Suffolk's found a small camp still in use. Laid an ambush. Just before mid-night 2 CT's approached, both were Killed. Both Malays 1 was identified as the leader of the Kampong Jenera Min
+	Yuen.---]
Fri. 23rd	22 HMT EMPIRE WINDRUSH arrived Singapore with replacement Service personnel---]
+	**23 SC. Osman B, Alang Raja**. F. M. Police Killed on CT Ops. Sungei Siput.Perak---]
Sat. 24th	RAF Planes bombed & strafed an area of jungle where CT's were located---]
	24 D/PC. Lee. Chin Kin. F. M. Police was shot dead by a gunman in George Town Penang. ---]

119

+	**24 PC. Mohd. Nor. B. Abdul Rani.** F.M. Police Killed on the Gemas Estate Negri Sembilan---]
Sun. 25th	Searching Patrols found no results from the combined raid on the 21/22nd.--]
	25 3 F. M. Police **SC's Hassan B. Hj Hussein.- Kling B, Topa.- Bujang B. Saban.** Killed by CT's on the Kew
Mon. 26h	Estate Menchap Malacca.---]
+	**26 Pte. Zakaria B. Senek.** Malay Regt. Killed in Action Engaging CT's Kelantan---]
+	Army Auster VF 500. Hit a tree stump upon landing at Sungei Betong air strip badly damaged.---].
+	2 Civilians were Killed & 13 injured when a grenade was thrown into a cinema in Sungei Siput Perak---]
	26 HMT EMPIRE FOWEY arrived in Singapore / sailed bound for Southampton with returning Service
Tue. 27th	personnel 26th.---]
	Intelligence information was given regarding a secret meeting of the Communist State Executive Committee. To take place in a house 8 miles from 'D' Comp Suffolk's base. A trap was set surrounding the house. A party of 3 CT's were engaged. Gunshots was exchanged with no results. The house was attacked & 1 CT the only
Wed. 28th	occupant was Killed Evidence pointed to the fact a meeting had taken place, but they had already escaped -]
	28 Trp. J. E. O'Leary. Royal Artillery Att/. 22nd. SAS. Killed by a Sakai. _Kuala Lumpur # 21 / 1089_ ---]
	3 Platoon A Company Suffolk's Killed 1 CT in the Kuala Lagat Forest Reserve---]

MARCH

Thur. 1st	Operations "_Cathedral_"- "_Kick-Off_" - "_Hustle_" Began S.W Pahang Selangor Negri Sembilan-]
+	Operations "_Dagger_"- "_Prosaic_" –"_Target_". Began against 4 Regt. MRLA. In Negri Sembilan & Johore---]
+	Operations "_Rumble_"- "_Raven_" In Tapah Ipoh against No 5 Regt.
Fri. 2nd	CT's before first light. Took the ID cards from workers on the Taum Estate .. 3 Platoon 'A' Comp Suffolk' who were Patrolling the same Estate were contacted & sprang an ambush. Very soon the 5 CT's well spread out walked into it . 3 CT' were Killed. 2 escaped.---]
+	2 HMT EMPIRE TROOPER arrived Southampton with returning Service Perseonnel ---]
Sat. 3rd	3 HMT DEVONSHIRE arrived Singapore. Disembarking Royal Marines Commandos---]
+	3 HMT EMPIRE WINDRUSH sailed Singapore bound for Southampton with returning Service personnel--]
Sun. 4th	**4 Cpl. D, H. Paterson.** Argyll & Sutherland Highlanders. Died*** _Kranji Singapore # 1 / C - 14_---]
Mon. 5th	**5 Mr. D. Duclos.** Asstn. Manager. of an the Senai Estate S. Johore & 2 F. M. Police **SC's Abdul Kadie B.Awang. – Siradi. B. Mohamed.** were Killed by C.T's. _Batu Gajah_ Ipoh Perak---]
Tue. 6th	6 HMT EMPIRE PRIDE arrived Liverpool with returning Service personnel ---].
+	6 HMT EMPIRE HALLADALE sailed Liverpool bound for Singapore / Hong Kong with the 1st Battn. Gordon Highlnders bound for a tour of active servce in Malaya---]
Wed. 7th	In Separate ambushes in different areas of Perak, Sungei Rambai, where Cpl Kirkham 1st Battn. Manchester Regt., had been wounded. In an ambush with 30 C.T's Killing 2 & wounding others---]
Thur. 8th	**8 Pte. R. J. Davies.** 1st. Battn. Worcestershire Regt. Died*** _Kranji Singapore # 1 / C - 12_---]
+	**8 PC Othman B. Said.** F. M. Police Killed ¾ mile from the Police Station of Kambua South Johore.---]
+	**8 Pol/Lt. J.S.Bradley** F. M. Police Killed in Action Engaging CT's. Died through gunshot wounds in Kuala Kangsar. Perak---]
+	8 HMT DEVONSHIRE sailed Singapore bound for Liverpool with returning Service personnel---]
Fri. 9th	**9 EPC Talib b. Sudin.** F. M. Police Killed on Ops. Ruab---]
+	**9 PC. Abdhul Rahman B.K. Jesfar.** F. M. Police Killed at the Public Works Dept. Quarry Johore.---]
+	In Pahang & Johore.4 F. M. Police Special Constables (_unnamed_) were Killed by C.T's.---]
Sat. 10th	**10 Maj. R. A. S. Lisle. MC** 1st. Battn. Cameronians. Killed in Action Engaging CT's Muar Johore. _Kranji Singapore # 1 / C - 11_ ---]
Sun. 11th	**11 6 F. M. Police SC's. Mohd. B. Ali Osman.- Hussain B. Hj Karim .- Marma b.. Mohd. Tahir. – Wan Abdullah B. Rahman - Hussin B. Mohd. Salieh. – A, Rahman B. Mohd. Amin.** Killed in a CT ambush Musing Johore.---]
Mon. 12th	**12 Pte. Anak . Jugah. Jaweg.** Sarawak Rangers Killed in Action Engaging CT's _Batu Gajah # 533_ Perak--]
+	**12 EPC Abdullah b. Omar.** F. M. Police Killed in CT ambush 25th. m/s Kuantan road---]
+	12 HMT EMPIRE ORWELL arrived Singapore with replacement Service personnel / sailed for Hong Kong 12th.---]
Tue. 13th	**13 Mr. T.V. Lingham.** Supt. Of the Behrang Estate Tanjong Malim Perak Killed by CT's---].
+	**13 PC. Gurdial Singh.s/o Hiram Singh.**Killed on CT Ops. at Jalong Sungei Siput North Perak. ---]
+	A. Plt of B Company Green Howards Killed 1 CT & fatally wounded a 2nd In the swamp area of Nyer.---]
Wed. 14th	**14 PC. Mohd. B. Mohd. Arouf.** F. M. Police Killed at the 25th. m/s Kuantan Rd. Pahang---].
Thur. 15th	**15 Pte.Anak Tulu Entap.** Sarawak Rangers. Killed in Action Engaging CT's

		[No known Grave]Terandek Wall Memorial Malacca]---]
	+	**15** HMT DUNERA sailed Southampton bound for Singapore/ Hong Kong /Kure with replacement Service personnel---]
Fri. 16th		**16 Pte. J. Roxburgh.** 1st. Battn. Argyll & Sutherland Highlanders. Died***_Kuala Lumpur # 18 / 1010_---]
	+	**16 L/Cpl. R. McKee.** Black Watch. RHR. Died***_Kuala Lumpur # 18 / 1012_---]
	+	**16 Pol/Lt. J. Bradley - E/PC. Noordi. B. Hj. Ahmad** F. M. Police Killed in CT ambush 61/2. Mile Tanjon Rambutan road Tambun Perak _Batu Gajah # 466_ Ipoh Perak ---]
	+	**16** In an ambush 3 **PC's Sulaiman B. Md. Akid.- Abdul Kadir B. Buyong.- Anwar B. Sulaiman.** F. M. Police Killed in CT ambush at the 30th. m/s Asahan Rd. Malacca.---]
	+	16/03/1951 LG # 39175 p. 1442 The following awarded the Military Cross

SQDN/LDR. A.F. FURSE. MC   ROYAL AIR FORCE
F/LT. W.B. BEGY. MC   ROYAL AIR FORCE
F/LT. K.W. DALTON- GOULDING. MC   ROYAL AIR FORCE
                    The following awarded the Military Medal
F/SGT. B. COLLEEN. MM   ROYAL AIR FORCE
SGT. A EVANS. BEM   ROYAL AIR FORCE
SGT. MOHD. B. KASBAN. BEM   ROYAL AIR FORCE REGIMENT.(MOR)
L/AC. R.H. WELLER. BEM   ROYAL AIR FORCE
SGT. J.C. MOTTRAM. MM   ROYAL AIR FORCE[1]

| | + | 16/03/1951 LG #39176 p. 1429   The following awarded the British Empire Medal (Military) |

F/SGT. S.M. EAMES. BEM   ROYAL AIR FORCE
F/SGT. N.G. PEARCE. BEM   ROYAL AIR FORCE

Sat. 17th		**17 SC Cpl. Tengku Abdul Hamid.** F. M. Police Killed on Ops. Batu Ragi Buloh Kasap Johore.---]
Sun. 18th		**18 Lt. (QGO) 18 Dhanbir Thapa , Sgt. T. Durge.** 6th. Queen Elizabeth's Own Gurkha Rifles. Both Died of wounds recv'd in engagement with CT's Rengan. _Kluang # 3 / H – 9 3 / F - 14_ Johore---]
Mon. 19th		**19 Pol/ Lt. J. Stanton -Bradley.** F. M. Police. Killed by C.T's in an ambush in the Kuala Lumpur area---]
Tue. 20th		**20 Pte. Anak. Cheling. Manit.** Sarawak Rangers Killed in Action Engaging CT's
		[No known Grave]Tereandak Wall Memorial Malacca]---]
	+	**20** HMT EMPIRE FOWEY arrived Southampton with returning Service personnel---]
Wed. 21st		A Plt. Of the Green Howards came in contact with a party of CT's. Engaging them Killed 1 & badly wounded another the other CT's all making their escape into the jungle.---]
Thur.22nd		**22 AC. A. B. Ahmad. - LAC. M. Y. B. Hassam. - AC1. W. B. Warjan. - Ahmad B. Chik** R.A.F.(MOR'S) R. A. F. 94 Sqdr. R. A. F. Regt. Killed in CT ambush on the Bukit Munchong Estate _Claimed by next of Kin_
Fri. 23rd		**23 Cpl. Ahmad Bin Chik** 94 Sqdr. R. A. F. Regt. (MOR) R. A. F. Died from gunshot wounds recv'd previous day [_Claimed by next of Kin_]---]
	+	**23 Rfn. Sir.iram. Gurung** 7th. Duke of Edinburgh's Own Gurkha Rifles. Died Motor Veh. Acc. _Seremban # 29_ Negri Sembilan---]
	+	**23 PC. Engku Ahmad B. Engku Mamid.** F.M. P.olice Killed on Ops. Balik Palua Penang.---]
Sat. 24th		**24 SC. Sgt. Tengku AbduL Hamid.** F. M. Police Killed on Ops. Ruab Area Pahang---]
	+	**24 SC Jaafar \b. Kadir** F. M. Police Killed by Accident Tampin/ Gemas Rd. Negri Sembilan---]
	+	**24 SC. Darmadas.** F. M. Police Killed on Ops. Raba Estate Tronoh Perak.---]
Sun. 25th		**25 Cpl. Yaacob b. Tan** F. M. Police Killed on Ops. ??---]
Mon. 26th		R.A.F. 57 Sqdn. Lincoln 2B (4A) Completed Operations at R.A.F. Tengah ---] }
	+	R.A.F. 61 Sqdn. Lincoln 2B (4A) Completed Operations at R.A.F. Tengah ---])Operation 'Musgrave'
	+	R.A.F. 100 Sqdn. Lincoln 2B (4A) Completed Operations at R.A.F. Tengah ---] }
Tue. 27th		**27 PC. Abdul Karim B. Mohd. Yusof.** F. M. Police Killed on Ops. Waterfall Estate Rawang. ---]
Wed. 28th		**28** 3 F. M. Police **PC Shaffie B. Kamarudin. - SC. Yunos B. Malik. - Kee Peng Chai.** Killed on CT Ops. Sungei Linggui Mines Kota Tinggi ---]
Thur. 29th		**29 Rfn. Nilbahadur. Khan** 6th. Queen Elizabeth's Own Gurkha Rifles. Died from Wounds recv'd in engagement with CT's Rengam Area._Kluang # 3 / D - 11_ Johore ---]
Fri. 30th		A Rail Inspector found that the fishplates had been removed near Labis Johore. They were replaced. No delays to the trains---]
	+	

Sat. 31st	+	30 **MV TEGELBURG** arrived Singapore onboard were the first contingent of the Rhodesian Malayan Scouts to form up with Lt/Col. Calvert's Malayan Scouts (SAS)---]
		30 **HMT EMPIRE WINDRUSH** arrived Southampton with returning Service personnel ---]
	+	**31 F/Sgt. G. C. Ford.** AF/F. R. A. F. 48 Sqdn. Kuala Lumpur was Killed when struck by a loose panel from Dakota KN 231 during engine run up Kuala Lumpur. *Kuala Lumpur # 18 - 1011* ---]
		Operations *"Sabal"* -*"Mantrap"*- *"Gallows"* - *"Stymie"* Ended ---]

APRIL

Sun. 1st		**1 L/Cpl. Mohamad b. Othman.** Malay Regt. Killed in Action Engaging CT's Pulia---]
	+	**1 Pol/Lt. F.H. Jarvis** F. M. Police Died ***in Bungsar Hospital Kuala Lumpur. *Kuala Lumpur # 314*]---]
	+	Operation *"Redskin"* *"Rover"* - *"Mermaid"* Against No 5 Regt. MRLA . Ipoh Central Perak ---]
	+	Operation *"Valiant"* Against the MRLA Port Swetenham Kuala Lumpur ---]
	+	Operation *"Prosaic" "Sunset"* Malayan Scouts against the MRLA ---]
	+	R.A.F. Sqdn's. 48 - 8 Dakota C4s relocated from Changi & operational at R.A.F. Kuala Lumpur---]
Mon. 2nd		**2 Mne's. Lt. J. B. Coop. Mne. Cpl. R. T. Ryder.** (40 Commando) Royal Marines. Killed in CT ambush Kuala Kangsar. 2 CT's were Killed during the fire fight. *Taiping # E / 9 – 10* Perak---]
	+	**2 Pte Abdullah b. Zakaria.** Malay Regt. Killed in Action Engaging CT's Pahang---]
	+	**2** 3 F. M. Police. **AP. Wan Kairudin .** - **B. Hj. Wan Mushiran .,- Abdullah Bin Bor.** Killed on CT Ops.Temenggor Perak ---]
	+	Acting on information provided by the F.M. Police. A number of CT's would be collecting food from a Kongsi House, located on the Sungei Kalong Rubber Estate. The Royal West Kents laid an ambush in the hope that they could kill the CT's. They waited all day in ambush positions, until just before twilight, a movement in the scrub Alerted the ambushers. As 3 CT's approached they opened fire all three were Killed. The 3 bodies were carried out on poles for identification. It was the first kill of the Royal West Kents---]
Tue. 3rd		A' Company 10th. Gurkhas engaged a group of 10 CT's. The Gurkhas bayonet charged killing 5 & wounding 3 in the Bentong area---]
	+	3 **HMT EMPIRE ORWELL** arrived Singapore/ sailed for Southampton with returning Service personnel 3rd.]
Wed. 4th		**4 Pol/Lt. N. Wride.** F. M. Police Killed in a road ambush Kulim area Kedah. *Jalan Pertana # 1428* George Town Penang ---]
	+	A follow up from the ambush of the 2nd, by the Royal West Kents. Discovered the bodies of 2 more CT's bringing the total Killed to 5---]
	+	4 **HMT EMPIRE HALLADALE** arrived Singapore with replacement Service personnel---]
	+	4 **HMT DEVONSHIRE** arrived Liverpool with returning Service personnel---]
Thur. 5th		**5 SC. Lebos B. Ketchik** F. M. Police Killed on CT Ops. Segamat Estate Johore---]
Fri. 6th		**6 Pte. Zainalb Awang** Malay Regt. Killed in Action Engaging CT's. Perak---]
Sat. 7th		**7** 5 Malay Regt. Soldiers were Killed. **Cpl. Yunus B. Salim.- L/Cpl. Ismail b. Idris. Pte's Youhmed b. Shuhor. – Ariffin b. Mohamed- Hussein b. Awang Kecik.** During a fire fight with CT's. Negri Sembilan ---]
	+	7 **HMT EMPIRE TROOPER** sailed Southampton bound for Singapore with replacement Service Personnel--]
Sun. 8th		**8 Mne. R. J. Cherry.** (40 Commando) Royal Marines. Died ***BMH. Bukit Metajam. *Taiping # E / 11* Perak ---]
	+	**8 Rfn's Champasing Rai . Harkaman Limbu .** 7th. Duke of Edinburgh's Own Gurkha Rifles. Killed in Action Engaging CT's Ruab Pahang. *Kuala Lumpur# 27 / 18 - 17*---]
	+	11 Platoon 'D' Comp. Suffolk's were Patrolling on the Bukit Cheraka Forest Reserve North West of Kuala Lumpur. Came across a CT camp. In the ensuing battle. 2 CT's were Killed As was **Sgt. D. B. Westin**1st. Battn. Suffolk Regt.Killed in Action Engaging CT's *Kuala Lumpur # 18 / 1013* ---]
Mon. 9th		**9 F/Sgt. J. W. Bradford.** R. A. F. Died*** *[Ashes REP]*---]
	+	**9 Mne. R.H.V.Eames** (40 Commando) Royal Marines. Drowned on Ops. Kuala Lumpur *[Ashes REP]*---]
	+	**9 Rfn. L. Harkabahadur** 7th. Duke of Edinburgh's Own Gurkha Rifles Killed. *Kuala Lumpur # 25 /2* ---]
	+	**9 SC. Bahari B. Abdul Rahman** F. M. Police Killed on Ops. Sussex Estate Perak.---]
Tue. 10th		**10 Aux Insp Mr. D. Stork** F.M. Aux. Police & Manager of the Karangan Estate Kedah. Killed by CT's *Jalan Pertana # 1429* George Town Penang ---]
	+	**10 Pol/Lt. I. P Hyde.** F. M. Police On Patrol in the Badak Mati Hills Province Wellesley. For his Action was recommended for the GM. LG 24/7/1952 # 39609---]
	+	10 **HMT EMPIRE HALLADALE** sailed Singapore bound for Liverpool with returning Service personnel---]
Wed. 11th		**11 Pte. Hashim bin. Ismail.** Malay Regt. Killed in Action Engaging CT's Pahang---]

Thur. 12th	**12 A.P Liew Wye Tone.** F. M. Police Killed on CT Ops. Chemor Perak.---]
Fri. 13th	13 During a fire fight in the Kempas area. **Rfn. T. Balbahadur Tamang .** 2nd/10th. Princess Mary's Own Gurkha Rifles. Killed & 2 wounded. 1 CT was Killed & another wounded. _Kranji Singapore # 8 / A -9_]---]
	13 Pol/Lt. J.L' O. Ford. F. M. Police Drowned in a boating accident on Ops. Sungei Aur. Kuala Krau _Kranji Singapore # 18 / B -9_ ---]
+	**13** 5 F. M. Police were Killed. During an engagment with CT's: **L/Cpl. Mohd. Ali B. Baha. PC's Darus b. Mat.- Din b. Taib – Hussein b. Ngah.- Mustafah b. Din.- Yahaha B. Hamid.** In the area of Sungei Bakap.-]
+	13 HMT DUNERA arrived Singapore with replacement Service personnel enroute to Hong Kong 13th.---]
Sat. 14th	**14 EPC. Salim b. Saad** F. M. Police Killed on CT Ops. Sintok Jitra Kedah.---]
+	14/04/1951 LG # 39170 p. 1300 The following awarded the Colonial Police Medal
	CPL. J.B. OSMAN. CPM FEDERATION MALAYA POLICE
	L/CPL. G. SINGH, CPM FEDERATION MALAYA POLICE
+	14 HMT EMPIRE FOWEY sailed Southampton bound for Singapore / Hong Kong with replacement Service personnel---]
Sun. 15th	**15** 7 Malay soldiers were Killed: **Cpl. Abdul Hamid b. Hitam.- Pte's. Mohamad b. Kudus.- Ismail b. Muhamud Yusof.- Mahmud b. Mohamad. Ali b. Talib.- Don b. Daham. Abdul Hamid . Abdul Rahman.** & a British officer was wounded, when an army convoy was ambushed by C.T's in Negri Sembilan ---]
Mon. 16th	**16** 4 F. M. Police **Pol/Lt. F. P. A. Malone** F.M.Aux.Police. & **L/Cpl. Mahat B Chomik.- PC's Raban B. Said.- Saud. B. Ckek.** Killed In CT ambush at the 26th. m/s. Batu Arang Rd Rawang Selangor- _Kuala Lumpur # 394_---]
Tue. 17th	**17 SC, Mat Rashid B. Awang.** F. M. Police Killed on CT Ops. Pendok Tanjong Estate Perak---]
+	**17 Aux./Asstn.Supt. A. Brown** Auxilliary F.M Police Killed on CT Ops.---]
+	**17 EPC. Abdul Majid b. Tahir.** F. M. Police Killed CT ambush at the Lombong -Susor Rotan road Kota Tinggi]
+	**17 EPC. Mat Pimus b. Hassan** F. M. Police Killed on CT Ops. Nr. Rompin Bahau Negri Sembilan---]
+	17/04/1951 LG # 39205 p. 2185 The following awarded the Military Cross
	(KGO) B. RAI. MC 7th DUKE OF EDINBURGH'S OWN GURKHA RIFLES
		The following awarded the Military Medal
	RFN. B. RAI. MM 7th DUKE OF EDINBURGH'S OWN GURKHA RIFLES
Wed. 18th	**18** 2 F.M. Police **SC's. Ahad B. Mohamed. – Semad B. Ama..** Killed on CT Ops. New Rompin Estate Bahua.]
Thur. 19th	**19 Flt/Off. R.B. Taylor** Spitfire TP 331 Lost at Sea Hong Kong.
	[No known Grave]Terandak Wall Memorial Seremban Malacca -]
+	3 Platoon 'A' Comp Suffolk's following a trail in the Kuala Langat Forest Reserve contacted 2 Min Yuen killing both.----]
Fri. 20th	**20 Aux. Asst/Sup A. Brown** F.M. Aux.Police Killed on CT Ops. _Batu Gajah # 468_ Ipoh Perak ---]
Sat. 21st	**21 SC. Chan Chong Eng.** F. M. Police Killed on CT Ops. Segamat Johore---]
	21/04/1951. LG # 39210 p. 2317 The following awarded the George Medal
	P/LT. T.A. CHARLTON. GM FEDERATION MALAYA POLICE
	P/LT. R. GRAVER. GM. FEDERATION MALAYA POLICE
	P/LT. G.O. HARTLEY. GM. FEDERATION MALAYA POLICE
	SC/CPL. OSMAN BIN ADAM. GM. FEDERATION MALAYA POLICE
Sun. 22nd	**22 W/O. G. R. Tait.** Royal Australian Air Force. Died***._Kuala Lumpur # 18 – 1014_ ---].
+	**22** 2 F. M. Police **SC's Ali B. Mansor.- Hamzadf B. Sudin.** Killed on CT Ops. Kulai area Johore---].
+	**22 D/PC. Cpl. Lok Ah Thong** F. M. Police Killed on CT Ops. Chemor Perak---]
Mon. 23rd	**23 L/Cpl. E. Elliott.** R. M. P. Died Motor Veh. Acc. Ipoh [_Ashes REP_]---]
+	**23 Mr. E. Elliot** British civilian Killed at Batu Gajah Ipoh Perak shot by CT's---]
+	**23** 2 F.M. Police **D/PC. Cheh Soo Kiong. SPC Saad b. Hashim** Killed by gunman Penang.---]
Tue. 24th	10 Plt. The Green Howards engaged & Killed 1 CT West of Yong Peng.---]
+	11 Plt. The Green Howards in the same area contacted 2 CT's killing both of them---]
Wed. 25th	**25 Cpl. R. J. Goldsmith.** Intelligence Corps. Killed in Action Engaging CT's _Kuala Lumpur# 18 / 1015_---]
+	25 HMT EMPIRE ORWELL arrived Southampton with retrurning Service personnel---]
Thur. 26th	**26 Mr. T.A. Wight. Manager. & Mr. L. J. Collier.** A Resettlement Officer, a visiter. Were Killed in a CT ambush on the Rini Estate Estate in Sudai Johore ---]
+	12 Plt. Of the Green Howards Killed 1 CT in a swamp in the area of Yong Peng.---]
+	7 Plt. 'C' Company Green Howards Killed 2 CT's during an ambush in the Gemas Area.---]
+	A Platoon of the 2nd.10th. Princess Mary's Own Gurkha Rifles. Engaged a strong force of CT's 1 CT was Killed and several wounded who were dragged away. Rfn. L. Aitbir. Was seriously wounded. 27 packs were recovered after the engagement---]

Fri. 27th	**27 Rfn. Aitbir Limbu.** 2nd/10th. Princess Mary's Own Gurkha Rifles. Died from wounds recv'd. In the previous days engagement. *Kranji Singapore # 8 / A - 10* ---]	
+	**27 Hon. Insp A.P Foo Eng Lin** F. M. Police Killed by gunmen in Ipoh Perak.---]	
+	**27 S/C. Tan Thuran Tong.** F. M. Police Killed on CT Ops. Pek Lee Mine Sungei Siput Perak ---]	
+	**27 S/C. Soib B. Mohd. Isa.** F. M. Police Killed on CT Ops. Pusing Perak.---]	
+	27/04/19/51 LG # 39214 p. 2384	The following awarded the British Empire Medal (Military)
	S/QMS H. BARNARD. BEM	ROYAL ARMOURED CORPS
	C/SGT. A.B. LAND. BEM	ROYAL ARMY MEDICAL CORPS
	C/SGT.ISMAIL.B. ARSHAD.BEM	MALAY REGIMENT.
	W/O C.R.LAYCOCK. BEM	INTELIGENCE CORPS
	SGT. K.R. SUTCLIFFE.BEM	GREEN HOWARDS
		The following awarded the Distingished Conduct Medal
	SGT. D. SUNWAR. DCM	10th. PRINCESS MARY'S OWN GURKHA RIFLES
	SGT. R. RAI. DCM	10th. PRINCESS MARY'S OWN GURKHA RIFLES
		The following awarded the Military Cross
	2./Lt. C.F.N. CHARRINGTON.MC	THE SUFFOLK REGIMENT.
	Lt. (QGO) S. GURUNG. MC	6th. QUEEN ELIZABETH'S OWN GURKHA RIFLES.
	MAJ. P.R. RICHARDS. MC	7th. DUKE OF EDINBURGH'S OWN GURKHA RIFLES
	LT. (KGO) K. RAI.. MC	7th. DUKE OF EDINBURGH'S OWN GURKHA RIFLES
	LT. (KGO) R. RAI. MC	10th. PRINCESS MARY'S OWN GURKHA RIFLES
		The following awarded the Military Medal
	SGT. BOWDEN. MM	4th THE QUEEN'S OWN HUSSARS
	CPL. R.G.HOWELLS. MM	COLDSTREAM GUARDS
	RFN McLAUGHLAN. MM	THE CAMERONIANS
	CPL. B. GURUNG. MM	6th. QUEEN ELIZABETH'S OWN GURKHA RIFLES
	SGT. J. TAMANAGER. MM	10th. PRINCESS MARY'S OWN GURKHA RIFLES
	CPL. D. RAI. DCM MM	10th. PRINCESS MARY'S OWN GURKHA RIFLES
+	27/04/51 LG # 39215 p 2389	The following awarded the Military Cross
	Capt. D. B. HUNTER. MC	ROYAL MARINES
	LT H.B. EMSLIE. MC	ROYAL MARINES
	LT. P. GRIFFITHS. MC	ROYAL MARINES
	LT. W. B. MANSELL. MC	ROYAL MARINES
		The following awarded the Military Medal
	MNE. H.H. TYDD. MM	ROYAL MARINES
Sat. 28th	**28 S/C. Mesri B. Dinchat.** F. M. Police Killed on CT Ops. Lima Belas Estate Selangor---]	
+	**28 Mr. B.C. Desvergnes.** French Asstn. Manager Lima Belas Estate Killed along with **SC Masri B. Dinchat** F. M. Police during a CT ambush on the Estate.---]	
Sun. 29th	Auster VF 647 656 Sqdn. R.A.F. upon landing on a road near Ipoh, struck a telegraph pole crashed.---]	
Mon. 30th	Operation "*Dagger*"- "*Target*" Ended---]	

MAY

Tue.	1st	**1 Pte. J. C. Clarke**. 1st. Battn. Green Howards. Died*** _Kranji Singapore # 1/ C 11_---]
	+	**10 Plt. Green Howards** engaged 15 CT's of No. 12 Platoon MRLA killing 1 CT. Lt. Laycock Also Sgt. Winter were recommened for an award.due to their Action ---]
Wed.	2nd	**2 Rfn's Juthe. Gurung - Karnasing. Rana. - Laziprasad. Pun - Megbahadur. Gurung - Nandabahadur Thapa. Kharahabadur Pun** 2nd. King Edward VII's Own Gurkha Rifles. Killed In Action Engaging CT's. _Kranji Singapore # 8 / B – 3 -1 – 7 / A – 11 8 / B – 2 8 / A – 12 – 13_ ---]
	+	**2 Cpl. G.E. Hodds** R.E.M.E Died *** _[Ashes REP]_ ---]
	+	**2** 2 F.M. Aux. Police **Deputy/Supt. P.A. Doohan**. - **Pol/Lt. D.R.Nelder**. Investigating a train derailment were Killed by C.T's in the Batu Arang area of Selangor._Kuala Lumpur # 400 – 319_ ---]
	+	**2 SC. Attan B. Puteh**. F. M. Police Killed on CT Ops. Johore---]
	+	2 HMT DILWARA sailed Southampton bound for Singapore with replacement Service personnel---]
Thur.	3rd	**3 Capt. D. W. L. Palmer**. 1st. Battn. The Queen's West Surrey Regt. Died***[Ashes REP]---]
Fri.	4th	**4 SC. Leong Chin Chuan** F. M. Police Killed on CT Ops. Grik Perak---].
Sat.	5th	**5 Capt. P.L. Mackay.MC**.(42 Commando) Royal Marines Died from Wounds recv'd Near Pusing. _Batu Gajah # 536_ Ipoh Perak---]
Sun.	6th	**6 PC. Othman B. Abdul Hamid**. F. M. Police Killed on CT Ops. Buloh Estate Segamat Johore.---]
	+	6 HMT EMPIRE FOWEY arrived Singapore with replacement Service personnel ---]
Mon.	7th	**7 Dvr. R. C. Clarke**. R.A.S.C.. Died Transport incident. _Kranji Singapore # 1 / C – 10_ ---]
	+	**7 SC. Sudin B. Matonis**. F.M. P. Killed on CT Ops. 14th. m/s Subang Rd. Selangor.—]
	+	7 HMT EMPIRE TROOPER arrived Singapore with replacement Service personnel ---]
	+	7 HMT EMPIRE FOWEY sailed Singapore for Hong Kong ---]
Tue.	8th	**8 Drv. Adman. Bin. Ibrahim**. R.A.S.C. (MOR) Died*** _Claimed by next of Kin_ ---]
Wed.	9th	**9 Sgt. F. Weed**. The Gordon Highlands. Died***_Kranji Singapore # 1 / C –9_---]
Thur.	10th	**10 Capt. (KGO) Santabadur Gurung D.S.M.** 6th. Queen Elizabeth's Own Gurkha Rifles wounded in Action Engaging CT's died Gen. Hospital. _Seramban # 30_ Negri Sembilan---]
	+	**10 PC. Ali B. Ariffin**. F. M. Police Killed on CT Ops. Kuantan.---]
	+	**10 E/PC Kassim b. Hashim**. F. M. Police Killed Engaging CT/s near Malim Nuar---]
	+	A CT threw a grenade into the crowd whilst watching a film in the Sun Cinema in Bentong. Injuring several people---]
	+	10 Soldiers of the 10th. Gurkhas were wounded, 2 seriously in an engagement with CT's all were treated in hospital---]
Fri.	11th	**8 Platoon C Comp Suffolk's**. Patrolling in the Ulu Langat Forest Reserve, were fired up on by CT's from above Sgt Wright & 3 Suffolk's Pte's were injured in the first burst. L/Cpl Price assumed command and attacked the CT's hill position resulting in killing 3 CT's for his brave acrtion. Price was recommended for a DCM---]
	+	11 HMT EMPIRE HALLADALE arrived Liverpool with returning Service personnel ---]
	+	11 HMT DUNERA arrived Singapore enroute Southampton with returning Service personnel 11th.---]
Sat.	12th	**12 Pte.L. G. Killick**. 1st. Battn. Suffolk Regt. Died from Wounds recv'd during the previous days Action Engaging CT's. _Kuala Lumpur # 18 / 1017_---]
	+	**12 2/Lt.. W. O. Morris**. R.A.O.C.. Died***_Kuala Lumpur # 1 / C - 7_---]
	+	**12 Rfn. Jandabahadur Rai** . 7th. Duke of Edinburgh's Own Gurkha Rifles. Killed in Action Engaging CT's Selandar Area.Malacca _Seramban # 31_ Negri Sembilan---]
	+	**12 Mr. Derek Green**. British civilian Killed in his car. CT ambush Kuala Lumpur Selangor.---]
	+	**12 AC1. R. B. Harding.- ACI. L. R. Youden**. R.A.F. FEAF. Drowning accident . _Kranji Singapore # 3 / C – 7 – 8]_
	+	**12 SC. Chani B. Ludin** F. M. Police Killed on CT Ops. Kuala Kemunding Police Post Alor Gajah Malacca.—]
	+	'D' Plt. Company Green Howards Killed another CT.---]
	+	12 HMT EMPIRE TROOPER sailed Singapore bound for Southampton with returning Service personnel--]
Sun.	13th	A Platoon of the 5th. Malay Regt. engaged & Killed a CT identified as **Ah Lik** in the Kroh area---]
	+	Operation "_Tansing_" Ended ---]
Mon.	14th	2 CT's were Killed by a Platoon of the 10th. Gurkhas near Bentong. One of the CT's had a price on his head of $10,000 ---]
Tue.	15th	**15 Mr. James J. Hill**. Asstn Manager. Kinta Kellas Estate Batu Gajah Perak. Killed when single handed. He took on 15 CT's until he fell fatally wounded.---]
Wed.	16th	**16 PC. Abdul Rashid b. Mat Arof**. F. M. Police was Killed on CT Ops.---]
Thur.	17th	Kuala Lumpur : Air Vice Marshal J. L. F. Fuller-Good. Became Air Vice Marshal Commanding Malaya--]
	+	Auster VF 630 Hit Pylon on night approach at Taiping. Crashed no other information ---]
Fri.	18th	**18 Lt. J. D. R. McDonald**. R. A .O .C. Att/ Cameronians. Killed in Action Engaging CT's.

		Kranji Singapore # 1 / C - 8---]
Sat.	19th	**19 Cpl. Rukbahadur. Thapa** 2nd. King Edward VII's Own Gurkha Rifles. Died***_Kranji Singapore # 8 / A – 8_
Sun.	20th	**20 Pte. C. Walker.** 1st. Battn. K.O.Y.L.I. Killed in Action. Engaging CT'sTaiping Perak.
		Western Road # 2138 George Town Penang ---]
Mon.	21st	**21 Lt. T. Duggan.** 1st. Battn. Gordon Highlanders. Killed in Action Engaging CT's. *Kuala Lumpur #18 / 1018*--]
Tue.	22nd	**22 Pol /Lt. P. Timony** F. M. Police Killed on CT Ops. *Kranji Sinapore # 8 / D. -7* ---]
	+	**22 Rec. Abdullah B. Nathar.** F.M.Police, Killed on CT Ops. Fraser's Falls Kelantan.---]
Wed.	23rd	**23 Bdsmn. P. Parrish.** 1st. Battn. Green Howards. Died*** *Kuala Lumpur # 18 / 1019* ---]
	+	**23 3 F. M. Police Pol /Lt G.T. Mundy. & SC's Mat. B. Man. – Loh Foo Kim.** Killed while travelling with 3 trucks of a Special forces Patrol in a CT ambush 25th. m/s Ijok Rd. *Taiping # ??* Perak.---]
	+	**23 PC. Mohamad B. Talip** F. M. Police Killed on CT Ops. Dungun Terengganu---].
	+	A Patrol of the Green Howards came across a CT & Killed him.---]
Thur.	24th	**24PC. Mohamad B. Mohd, Noor.** F. M. Police Killed on CT Ops. Yong Peng Johore---]
Fri.	25th	**25 Cpl. R. R. Mitchell.** East Surrey Regt. Died***[*Ashes REP*]---]
	+	**25 Cpl. J.B. Davis** Rhodesian SAS. Died from Gunshot wounds recv'd during engagement with CT's
		Kuala Lumpur # 20 / 1085 --]
	+	25 HMT EMPIRE ORWELL sailed Southampton bound for Singapore/ Hong Kong with replacement Service personnel---]
Sat.	26th	**26 L/Cpl. Pahalman. Pun - Rfn. Padamsing Gurung** 6th Queen Elizabeth's Own Gurkha Rifles. Whilst Engaging CT's in the Bahau Area Sungei Patani. Died from wounds. *Gurkha Cem Seremban # 3* **Rfn Padamsing** *[No known Graves]Terandak Wall Memorial Malacca* ---]
	+	**26 PC Abas B. Abdul Hamid.** F.M. Police Killed on CT Ops. Muar Johore---]
	+	26 HMT EMPIRE FOWEY arrived Singapore with replacement Service personnel---]
	+	26 HMT EMPIRE FOWEY sailed Singapore bound for Southampton with returning Service personnel.--]
Sun.	27th	**27 2/Lt. W.O. Morris.** R.A.O.C Att / 1st. Battn. Worcestershire Regt. **Cpl. B. Stanton. - Pte. N. Dykes.** Worcestershire Regt. Killed during an engagement with about 50 CT's on the Ulu Paloh Rubber Estate West of Nyor Johore. *Kranji Singapore # 1 / C – 7 – 6 - Stanton [Ashes REP]* ---] Pte Awang Anak Awang was recommended a medal for his bravery. LG 20 / 11 /1951---]
Mon.	28th	**28 Rfn's. Chija Gurung. - Tekbahadur. Thapa** 2nd. King Edward VII's Own Gurkha Rifles. Killed in Action Engaging CT's *Kranji Singapore # 8 / B – 5 4*--]
	+	**28 Pte. A. Gray.** 1st. Battn. Gordon Highlanders Died***_Kuala Lumpur # 18 / 1020_---]
Tue.	29th	The Leader of the CT 's in Kuala Lumpur **Yep Heong.** was Killed.---]
Wed.	30th	**30 Cpl. Md. Yussoff B. Abdul Rahman** F.M. Police. Killed on Ops. 10th. m/s. Lipis/ Ruab Rd.---]
	+	**30 Mr. R. Eyre & Mr. F.W. Fitzpatrick** British civilians Accidental Killed. Malacca.---]
	+	30 HMT EMPIRE HALLADALE sailed Liverpool for Singapore. On board were The 1st. Battalion Manchester Regiment bound for Malaya. ---]
Thur.	31st	**31 Pol /Lt. J. T. Hugo** F. M. Police Died. fractured skull in motor accident on CT Ops.
		Jalan Pertana Cemetery #?? George Town Penang.---]
		A notorious leader of the Selangor C.T's platoon **Kong Sang.** was Killed.---]
	+	Operation "*Tansing*" Ended---]

JUNE

Fri.	1st	**1 F/Off. K. J. Fullagar. - F/Sgt. H. L. P. Gregory. – F/Sgt. C. Sharkey.** 84 Sqdn R.A.F. Killed when their Brigand VS 869 crashed approach R.A.F. Tangah. *Kranji Singapore # 3 / C – 9 - 3 / B – 1 – 3 / E - 8*---]
	+	01/06/1951 LG # 39242 p. 3013 The following awarded the Colonial Police Medal
		PC. OSMAN B. PUTIH CPM FEDERATION MALAYA POLICE
		PC. JUNID B. R. A. F.IE CPM FEDERATION MALAYA POLICE
	+	Operations "*Grasshopper*"- "*Sedge*"- "*Warbler*". Began against No 4 Regt. MRLA in Johore & Negri Sembilan]
Sat.	2nd	Operation '*Warbler*' Malayan Scouts began against the MRLA----]
Sun.	3rd	A ambush laid by a Plt 'B' Company Suffolk's. Killed 1 CT identified as a leading Min Yuen member ---]
		3 HMT DILWARA arrived Singapore with replacement Service personnel---]
	+	4 HMT DILWARA sailed Singapore bound for Southampton with returning Service personnel---]
Mon.	4th	**PC. Mohd. Noor B. Yusof.** F. M. Police. Killed on CT Ops. Johore Bahru.---]
Tue.	5th	**PC. Salleh B. Abdul Kadir.** F. M. Police. Killed on CT Ops. 33rd. m/s. Resettlement area Kulai Johore.--]
	+	5/06/1951 LG # 39252 p. 3124 The following awarded the Military Medal

	+	PTE. M.S.B. OSMAN MM MALAY REGIMENT.
Wed.	6	6 Lt. P.K. Bugden (45 Commando) Royal Marines. Died*** *Batu Gajah # 537* Ipoh Perak.—]
Thur.	7th	7 HMT DUNERA arrived Southampton with returning Service personnel ---]
Fri.	8th	9 Platoon 'C' Comp Suffolk's. Killed 1 CT near the Kuala Lumpur / Kajang Road ---]
Sat.	9th	'B' Comp Suffolk's on Patrol. Killed a CT Courier. Found a food dump with provisions along with 8 sealed drums of rice---]
Sun.	10th	10 Pol/Lt. P. Timony. F. M. Police Killed on CT Ops. Died from multiple gunshot wounds Johore Bahru---]
	+	10 PC. Mohamed Rasol B. Hj. Amin. F. M. Police Killed on CT Ops. Kuala Tenang. Labis.---]
	+	10 Rec. Ahmed B. Harun. F. M. Police Killed on CT Ops.Chegar Bongor.Gua Musang District. Kelantan. ---]
Mon.	11th	11 PC. Mat Lazin B. Ibrahim. F. M. Police Killed on CT Ops. Johore.---]
	+	11 A/P Sulaiman B. Hassan. F. M. Police Killed on CT Ops. Labis area Johore---]
	+	11 Mr.A.J. Westendorp. Asstn. Manager. Jeram Padang Estate Bahua Negri Sembilan Killed by CT's in an ambush in the Pusing area of Perak.---]
	+	A Plt 'D' Company Green Howards. Killed 1 CT in the Simpang Belok area of Malacca.Capt. Barlow was recommended for an award. Awarded the MC. LG 39507 4/4/1952---]
	+	11 HMT EMPIRE TROOPER arrived Southampton with returning Service personnel---]
Tue.	12th	12 Rfn. Chamansing. Gurung. 2nd. King Edward VII's Own Gurkha Rifles. Killed in Action Engaging CT's Ruab Pahang [*No known Grave]Terandak Wall Memorial Malacca* ---]
	+	12 Rfn. Garbajit. Rai 10th Princess Mary's Own Gurkha Rifles. Died from Wounds recv'd One REME Cfn.(a/t. 10th.) Was Killed *(unnamed)* Manchia road Bentong *Kuala Lumpur # 27 / 19*.---]
	+	12 Pte. F. Sumner. R. A. M. C. Died*** *Kranji Singapore # 18 / 1021* .---]
	+	12 PC. Kassin B. Abdullah. F. M. Police Died from wounds recv'd on 11th.---]
	+	12 3 F. M. Police PC. Bazali B. Yeop & EPC's Abdul Ghani b. Mohd. – A. Ahab nb. Ali. Killed on CT Ops. Johore---]
	+	12 2 F. M. Police A.P 's Lee Kai - Yong Fook. Killed on CT Ops. Tapah Rd. Perak---]
	+	3. Telecommunication Engineers & 3 F.M. Constables were Killed *(unnamed)* & several civilians wounded when C.T's dynamited the main railway line near Kluang Selengor---]
	+	12 HMT EMPIRE PRIDE sailed Liverpool bound for Singapore / Hong Kong with replacement Service personnel ---]
	+	12/06/1951 LG # 39267 p. 3237 The following awarded the Distinguished Service Medal CPL.. G. R. HOWE. DCM ROYAL MARINES
Wed.	13th	13 Pte. J. Thompson. 1st. Battn. Worcestershire Regt. Killed by Accident.*Batu Gajah # 538* Ipoh Perak---]
	+	13 Sgt. O.H. Ernst. Rhodesian S.A.S. Regt. Killed in Action Engaging CT's *Kuala Lumpur # 19 / 1069* ---]
	+	13 2 F. M. Police SC/Cpl. Mamat Yunos B. Abdul Malek. SC Abdul Gahni B. Mohamed. Killed on Ops. Kajang area Terengganu.---]
	+	8 Platoon 'C' Comp Suffolk's Killed a CT in the Broga area---]
	+	13 HMT EMPIRE WINDRUSH sailed Southampton bound for Singapore with replacement Service personnel---]
Thur.	14th	14 5 F. M. Police PC's .Were Killed in an ambush on CT Ops. Yahaya B.Hamid. – Darun. B.Mat.- Mustafa B. Ngah.- Mustafa B. Din. – Hussein. B. Ngah.- Din. B. Taib. Sintok Jitra Kedah ---]
	+	A Plt.of 'C' Company Green Howards Killed 1 CT. in the Jelai Gemas Forest Reserve---]
	+	In Johore Operation "*Warbler*" began Food Control---]
Fri.	15th	15 Sgt. V. Bowen. Nav. 45 Sqdn R.A.F. was Killed when Brigand VS 857 Crashed landed in Kranji Creek Singapore. The Pilot Sgt. Martin & Sig. Sgt. Weston. survived. *Kranji Singapore # 3 / B – 2* ---]
Sat.	16th	16 PC. Din b. Othman F.M. Police Killed on CT Ops. Kulim / Junjong Rd. Kedah—]
	+	16 HMT EMPIRE ORWELL arrived Singapore with replacement Service personnel /sailed for Hong Kong 16th.--]
Sun.	17th	17 Pte. Mat Nor b. Buru Malay Regt. Killed in Action Engaging CT's Pahang ---]
	+	17 Mr. D. M. Root Manager. Ludan Estate Alor Gajah. Killed. Ambushed by15 CT's Johore.---]
	+	17 SC. Baba B. Sidin F. M. Police Killed on CT Ops. Lendu Estate Malacca.---]
Mon.	18th	18 Mr. G.H. Jolly Resettlement Officer. Murdered by CT's died from Gunshot wourds. Malacca. ---]
	+	18 PC. Abduk Rashid B. Matarof. F. M. Police Killed on Ops. Perak---].
	+	18 PC. Abdul Manaf B. Samad. F.M. Police Killed in CT ambush at the 52nd. m/s Gap Rd.Pahang.---]
Tue.	19th	19 F/O. R. E. Matthews. (Navigator) R. A. F. 84 Sqdn. Was Killed when his Brigand RH 811 lost a propeller blade & the engine fell out. Aircraft abandoned near R. A. F. Tengah The Pilot survived.- *Kranji Singapore # 3 / B –3* ---]
	+	19 Rfn's Dhupdarja.Tamang - Rfn. Pahalnman. Gurung 6th. Queen Elizabeth's Own Gurkha Rifkes

		Killed in Action Engaging CT's Bahua Area---*Seremban # 34 - 33* Negri Sembilan.---]
	+	19 2 F. M. Police **SC's. Suailan B. Kasan. – Menap B. Tonkin.** Killed on CT Ops. Kuantan Area---]
Wed. 20th		20 HMT EMPIRE WINDRUSH sailed from Singapore bound for Southampton with returning Service personnel.---]
Thur. 21st		21 Pte. R. J. Hill A.C.C. Att/Worcestershire Regt.. Died***[*Ashes REP*]---]
	+	21 Pol/Lt. T. Darling. F. M. Police Wounded during an engagement with CT's in the Chiah Area of Johore. Died from gunshot woumds Gen. Hospital. Johore Bahru. *Kranji Singapore # 8 / C - 13*---]
Fri. 22nd		22 Rfn. Dhanbahadur Rai 10th Princess Mary's Own Gurkha Rifles. Died***Kranji Singapore # 8 /B - 6---]
	+	22 Rec. Abdullah B. Nathar. F. M. Police Killed on CT Ops. Fraser's Falls Kelantan---]
	+	22 HMT EMPIRE FOWEY arrived Southampton with returning Service personnel.---]
Sat. 23rd		23 SC. Mat Selidin B. Awang. F. M. Police Killed on CT Ops. Chemor Area Perak.---]
	+	23 6 F.M. Police **SC's. Osman B. Abdul Kassim, - Noman B. Salleh. – Harun B. Ibrhim. – Hadan B. Hj . Sama, -Shariff B. Daulah.** Killed in CT ambush. Kluang area Selangor.---]
Sun. 24th		24 2 F.M. Police: **SC. -Wahab B. Sulaiman. Awang. B. Ujang.** Killed on CT Ops. Bentong Pahang---]
Mon. 25th		25 Cpl. J. B. Davies. Rhodesian SAS Regt. Died from wounds recv'd Engaging CT's *Kuala Lumpur20 / 1085*]
	+	9 Platoon 'C' Comp Suffolk's Patrolling near the 9th. mile Village. Killed 1 CT.---]
Tue. 26th		26 Sgt. W. D. Hall. 1st. Battn. Cameronians. Died***Johore *Kranji Singapore # 1 / C - 5*---]
	+	26 EPC Alias B. A. Rahman F. M. Police Killed on CT Ops. Perak---]
Wed. 27th		27 D/Cpl. Foong Poon Yuen. F. M. Police Killed on CT Ops. Nibong Tebal.---]
	+	27 A Platoon of the 2nd. 10th Gurkhas acting on information. Laid a ambush at an intended CT food lift near Senai, engaged approx. 50 strong CT's. In the ensuing fire fight 4 Gurkhas were wounded including the Platoon Commander Lt.(KGO) L, Kesersing MM **Sgt. Perthilal Rai.** Died from his wounds. 4 CT's were Killed amongst then was *Lau Sui Fatt* Commander of the 5th.Platoon MRLA 4 CT's were wounded ---]
	+	27 PC. Mansoor B. Yassin F. M. Police Killed on CT Ops. Kajang Selangor---]
Thur. 28th		28 Mr. R . Goody . Manager. of the Sedgeley Estate Kajang Selangor. Killed in an CT ambush on the Dengkil road---]
	+	28 A Police Party travelling near Broda came under fire from CT's 6 F.M Police SC were Killed - **Mansor bin. Yassin – Osman Bin Abdul Kassim – Noman Bin Salleh – Harun Bin Ibraham – Handan Bin Hji. Sama –Sharrif bin Daulah .** 2 were wounded . 7 Platoon 'C' Comp Suffolk''s quickly arrived at the scene & in the follow up. Killed 1 CT.---]
	+	28 HMT. EMPIRE HALLADALE arrived Singapore disembarking were the The 1st. Battn. Manchester Regt. to begin their tour of Active Service in Malaya ---]
Fri. 29th		29 Lt.(KGO) Kesersing Limbu. MM 10th. Princess Mary's Own Gurkha Rifles. Died from his wounds recv'd. In the previous days engagement *Kranji Singapore # 8 / B -7* ---]
Sat. 30th		In Johore :Operation "*Grasshoper* "began Food Control---**]**

JULY

Sun. 1st		1 Rec. Samsudin B. Ariffin. F. M. Police Killed on Ops. Sungei Patani.---]
	+	1 2 F. M. Police **SC's. Ismail B. Mahmood .- Jaya B. Mat Tabir.** Killed on CT Ops. Kuala Krai area Kelantan]
	+	Operation "*Marker*" Began against No 5 Regt. MRLA Ipoh Central Perak.---]
Mon. 2nd		2 In N. Selangor. A detachment of the 2nd. Battn. Gurkha's was attacked by a force of 300 C.T's. The ensuing battle lasted 9 hours. During which time the C.T's sustained heavy losses. Those Killed were Gurkha Coy Comander. **Maj. T. A. Wimbush. & Rfn. Baldhoj. Rai.** 2nd. King Edward VII's Own Gurkha Rifles. Killed in Action Engaging CT's. *Kranji Singapore # 1 / C – 12 8 / B – 9* ---]
	+	1 European Tin Miner, 2 F.M. Police Special constables (all ***unnamed***) were Killed by C.T's in a ambush near Bentong Pahang.---]
	+	In another CT ambush in Province Wellesley 2 Chinese, one a young girl, were Killed by C.T's.---]
Tue. 3rd		3 HMT EMPIRE HALLADALE sailed bound for Liverpool with returning Service personnel---].
	+	3 HMT DILWARA arrived Southampton with returning Service personnel ---]
Wed. 4th		4 Hon Aux. Pol/ Insp Mr. S.S. Cook. F. M. Police Killed on CT Ops. at Manchis Pahang. Kuantan Pahang]
	+	4 2 F.M. Police **SC's. Awang B. Ujang .- Wahab B. Sulaiman.** Killed & 1 was wounded, when a number of CT's attacked the Chung King Tin Mine near Bentong Pahang ---]
	+	A Captured *Sakai* CT was Hanged in Taiping jail. ---]
	+	4 HMT DUNERA sailed Southampton bound for Singapore/ Hong Kong with replacement Service personnel.---]

Thur.	5th	**5** 2 F. M. Police **SC's Jalil. Mohamed** Killed on CT Ops. Metakab area Pahang.---]
Fri.	6th	**6 Mr. R.G.N. Cooper** Manager. Craigielen Estate Killed by CT's Panchor Muar.Kajang.---]
	+	6 HMT EMPIRE ORWELL arrived Singapore.---]
Sat.	7th	**7 Mne. J. Chadwick**.(40 Commando) Royal Marines Died Traffic accident. Lenggong Area.*Taiping # E / 13* Perak---]
	+	7 HMT EMPIRE PRIDE arrived Singapore with replacement Service personnel / sailed for Hong Kong 7th.]
Sun.	8th	**8** 2 F. M. Police Killed: **SC's Osman B. Jafarr.- Wan Boon B. Hassam** on CT Ops. Kulim Area Kedah---]
		Aux. P. Awang Kechik B. Dosah F. M. Police Killed on CT Ops. Taiping Perak.---]
	+	**8 Pol/Lt. J.W. Chown**. F.M. Aux.P. Killed on CT Ops. in Segamat Area.Johore---]
	+	**8 PC Samausin B. Hj. Omar.** F. M. Police Killed on CT Ops. Olah Limpit Kuala Langat Selangor.---]
Mon.	9th	**9 F.J. C. Ng Weng Fong.** F. M. Police Killed on CT Ops. Johore Bahru---]
	+	**9 SC. Chik B, Tabah** F. M. Police Killed on CT Ops. Bekok Johore---]
	+	9 HMT EMPIRE ORWELL sailed Singapore bound for Southampton with returning Service personnel ---]
	+	9 HMT DEVONSHIRE sailed Singapore enroute Southampton with returning Service personnel ---].
Tue.	10th	**10 2/Lt. D.S. Pyemount.** King's Yorkshire Light Inf. Accindently shot.*Batu Gajah # 437* Ipoh Perak ---]
	+	In Negri Sembilan – Johore – Malacca. Operation '*Cat* ' began Saturating the area with troops in Rubber plantations instead of Jungle.---]
	+	10 HMT EMPIRE WINDRUSH arrived Singapore ---]
Wed. 11th		**11 Mne Sgt. T.J.H. Genge.** (45 Commmdo) Royal Marines Died.*** *[Ashes REP]*.---]
Thur. 12th		10 Platoon 'D' Company 2nd. 10th. Gurkhas Killed 2 CT's One was identified as **Sua Keng** Group and District Committee Member. ---]
	+	Nairobi Kenya: In an announcement from Nairobi. Stated:-
		'*2 Infantry Battalions the 1st. Nyasaland & 3rd. Kenya Regt.'s. Would be sent to Malaya in January 1952. To strengthen forces in Malaya The Battalions would serve 18 Months in Malaya* ---]
Fri.	13th	**13 Sgt. Maitasing. Limbu** 6th. Queen Elizabeth's Own Gurkha Riflas
		[No known Grave]Terandak Wall Memorial Malacca ---]
	+	13 HMT EMPIRE FOWEY sailed Southamton enroute to Singapore / Hong Kong /Kure - with replacement Service personnel---]
Sat.	14th	**14** 3 F. M. Police : **Pol/Lt. F.J.J. Thonger. SC's Wan Endut B. Sulaiman.- Aziz B. Hashim Alias B. Yassin** Killed, also I civilian (**unnamed**) Killed & 5 Policemen wounded in a CT ambush at the 9th. m/s. Terap Rd. Kulim Kedah *Jalan Peratna # 1432* George Town Penang ---]
Sun.	15th	**15 Pte. D. Hurren** . A.C.C. Att/Camaronians Died***<u>Kranji Singapore # 2 / C -11</u>---]
	+	15/07/1951 LG.# 39228 p. 2712 The following awarded the Miltary Medal
		RFN. D.THAPA. D. MM 10th PRINCESS MARY'S OWN GURKHA RIFLES
Mon. 16th		**16 Mne.E. Lamb.** (40 Commando) Royal Marines Died from Wounds recv'd. in ambush Perak [*Ashes REP*].]
	+	In different parts of Malaya 10 people: European, Indians, Malays & Chinese were Killed in Separate ambushes. amongst those Killed was. New Zealander. **Mr. J.H. Callanan** Acting Manager. Perganang Estate.along with 3 F.M **SC's. Wan Endut Bin Sulliman. - Aziz B. Hassim. – Alias B. Embong.** in an ambush in Kota Tinggi. Others Killed in Separate incidents **(unnamed)** ---]
Tue.	17th	**17 A.P. Jamal B. Tahim.** F. M. Police Killed on CT Ops. Tapah Perak.---]
	+	**17** 2 F.M. Police **Pol/Lt. G. O Hartley (GM) SC Mohamed B. Ismail** Killed at a CT ambush on P. Kemunde Road Kuantan area Pahang. *Kuantan # ??* Pahang ---]
	+	**17** 2 F. M. Police **SC's. Mahat B. Ja'afar. – Awang B. Ali.** Killed on CT Ops. Santi Estate Pengarang Johore]
	+	**17 EPC Mohad Aris.** F. M. Police Killed CT ambush Kuantan area Pahang---]
	+	17/07/1951 LG # 39228 p.3877 The following awarded the Military Medal
		LAC. M.B. CHEROS MM R.A.F. REGIMENT.(MOR)
		ACI A.B. ISMAIL A.B. R.A.F. REGIMENT.(MOR)
	+	17/07/1951 LG # 39312 p. 4382 The following awarded the Military Medal
		CPL. N. GURUNG MM 2nd. KING EDWARD VII'S OWN GURKHA RIFLES.
		RFN. K. THAPA . MM 2nd. KING EDWARD VII'S OWN GURKHA RIFLES
Wed. 18th		**18 SAC. Ins/Mech. L. E. Burden.** R A F.Changi. Missing believed drowned.
		[No known Grave]Terandak Memorial Malacca ---]
Thur. 19th		**19 Lt. (KGO) Raj.Ranbahadur.** Gurkha Military Police Died***<u>Kuala Lumpur 26 /1</u>---]
	+	**19 Cadet. W. K. Batchelor** F. M. Police Killed on CT Ops. Dungun area of Ajil Terengganu---]
Fri.	20th	**20 Mr. E. Lamb.** British civilian Killed in CT ambush. Parit Bunta Perak.---]
	+	**20 Mr. A.D. Paterson** Manager of the Labis Bahru Estate Segamat. Killed by CT's---].
	+	**20 L/Wtr. E. Caskin.** Royal Navy H.M.S. '*TERROR*' Died *** *Kranji Singapore- # 12 / B – 26*---]

+	20/07/1951 LG. # 39290 p. 3928 The following awarded the Military Cross
	2/Lt. A.D. GAVIN MC ROYAL MARINES.
	The following awarded the Military Medal
	MNE R.G. HODGKISS MM ROYAL MARINES
+	20 HMT EMPIRE WINDRUSH sailed Singapore bound for Southmpton with returning Service personnel]
Sat. 21st	21 Pte. J. Leggat. 1st. Battn. Gordon Highlanders. Died***_Kuala Lumpur # 18 / - 1022_----]
+	21 Pol/Lt. A. E. Mothersole F. M. Police Engaging CT's. Died from gunshot wounds during contact with CT's in Ulu Yam area Selangor. _Kuala Lumpur # 339_ ---]
+	21 SC. Morad F. M. Police Died by Accident. A.M.K. Estate Jitra.---]
+	A small Platoon of the Suffolk's '8'Platoon Patrolling on the edge of a Rubber Estate spotted 4 CT's some distance away. Unfortunately they were spotted. A fire fight broke out. 2 CT's were Killed & 2 escaped into the darkness.---]
+	CT _Raja Gopal_ one of the leading CT Leaders in Selangor was Killed.---]
Sun. 22nd	22 3 F. M. Police SC.Cpl. Abu Bakar B. Ishak. - SC's Kovil Pitchay. – Yussof B. Karim. – Lon B. Wahid Killed on CT Ops. Paloh Estate Luang---].
+	22 2 F. M. Police E/Sgt. K.I. Webb . E/Sgt. L.W. Wernham Killed on CT Ops. Ambushed in the Taiping area of Perak---.]
+	22 Cpl. Abdul Manaf. b. Samad. F.M. Police Killed by CT's whilst at the Kepala Bates Rifle Range Kedah--]
Mon. 23rd	23 Rfn. Tekbahadur Gurung . 2nd. King Edward VII's Own Gurkha Rifles. Killed in CT ambush at the 56 m/s Gap Road Ruab VP722656 Pahang _[No known Grave] Terandak Wall Memorial Malacca ---]_
Tue. 24th	24 Pte. Abdul Hamid b. Mustaffa Malay Regt. Killed in Action Engaging CT's Johore---]
+	Operation 'Grasshopper' & 'Cat' ended.---]
+	After 1 Months training in Changi The Manchester Regt. Boarded a Royal Malayan Navy Tank Landing Craft named _TLC Reginald Kerr._ For their trip North to Kedah.---]
+	24/0719/51 LG #39293 p. 3995 The following awarded the Military Cross
	Lt. P.L. PHILPOX. MC THE ESSEX REGIMENT.
	The following awarded the Military Medal
	PTE. J.B. BABA . MM MALAY REGIMENT.
Wed. 25th	25 L/Cpl. Partajit Gurung . 2nd. King Edward VII's Own Gurkha Rifles. Killed Engaging CT's _[No known Grave] Terandak Wall Memorial Malacca ---]_
+	25 HMT EMPIRE TROOPER sailed Southampton for Singapore with replacement Service personnel]
Thur. 26th	26 HMT DILWARA sailed Southampton for Hong Kong/ Singapore with replacement Service personnel---]
Fri. 27th	A Plt. Of 'B' Company Green Howards. Ambushed & Killed 2 CT's, wounding a 3rd. who was thought to be _Ah Wah_ the legendary leader in the Ayer Kuning area North of where the ambush took place.---]
Sat. 28th	28 Mne Sgt. M. J. Taylor. (40 Commando) Royal Marines Died from Wounds recv'd in CT ambush at 87 m/s Grik Road.Perak._Taiping # E / 15_ ---]
Sun. 29th	The Manchester Regt. Arrived at Prai where they were to begin preperations against the CT's--]
Mon. 30th	30 F/Lt. G. L. Blewett. Med/Off. R.A.F. Seletar Died from injuries recv'd in a RTA 29th July. _Kranji Singapore # 4 / B – 5_ ---]
+	30 L/Cpl. T. Dalsing Thapa 2nd. King Edward VII's Own Gurkha Rifles. Died*** _Kranji Singapore # 8 / B -10_]
Tue. 31st	31 HMT DUNERA arrived Singapore. with replacement Service personnel ---]
+	Operation "Cathedral" "Hustle"- "Kick-Off" - "Rumble"- "Raven"- "Sedge" - "Grasshopper" 'Sun.st' Ended---]

AUGUST

Wed. 1st	1 L/Cpl. J.J. O'Neill. Royal Engineers Died*** _Kranji Singapore # 2 / A - 12_---]
+	1 Dvr. Hashim Bin. Abbas. R.A.S.C. (MOR) Died*** _Claimed by next of Kin_ - --]
+	Operations "Rebel"- "Sludge"- -"Rainbow"- "Springtide"- Began against No 5 Regt. MRLA in Central Perak Tapah, Ipoh, Cameron Highlands.---]
+	RAF Sqdn 656 Auster 5/6/7/9 became operational Changi ---]
+	1 HMT EMPIRE PRIDE arrived Singapore / sailed for Liverpool with returning Service personnel 1st.-]
+	1 HMT DEVONSHIRE sailed Liverpool bound for Singapore / Hong Kong with replacement Service personnel---]
+	1 HMT EMPIRE ORWELL arrived Southampton with returning Service personnel---]
Thur. 2nd	9 Platoon 'C' Comp Suffolk's Patrolling on the Brooklands Estate engaged & Killed 2 CT's. 1 was wounded but escaped---.]
+	2 HMT EMPIRE HALLADALE arrived Liverpool with returning Service personnel---]

Fri.	3rd	9 Plt. 'C' Company Suffolk's laying in ambush on the Brookland Estate. Just before dusk, a party of CT's entered the ambush. Opening fire 2 CT's were Killed, 1 escaped but blood trails indicated he had been wounded. Arms were retrieved.---]
	+	3 HMT EMPIRE ORWELL arrived Southampton. with returning Service personnel---]
Sat.	4th	4 F/JC. Ng Weng Fong. F. M. Police Killed on CT Ops.---]
Sun.	5th	5 Rfn. Dhanbahadur Rai 10th. Princess Mary's Own Gurkha Rifles. Killed in Action Engaging CT's *Kranji Singapore # 8 / B – 12* -]
	+	5 HMT DUNERA sailed Singapore bound for Southampton via Penang on board the troopship were the The 2nd. Battn. the King's Own Yorkshire Light Inf. Having completed their operational Duties in Malaya.---]
Mon.	6th	} Combined operations continued throughout Malaya ---]
Tue.	7th	7 L/Cpl. I. E. Fitzpatrick. 1st. Battn. Manchester Regt. Killed during a fire-fight with C.T's in the Sungei Kob area of he Bongsu Forest Reserve. During the Action Engaging CT's. Cpl. Quinn was wounded, - *Western Road # 2897*George Town Penang. The Medic. Pte. Holt. Through his bravery retrieving L/Cpl. Fitzpatrick's body under fire. Awarded the M.M (LG :2/11/1951)
	+	A Plt. Of 'C' Company Green Howards on patrol caught 2 CT's. in the area West of Gemas.Killed 1.The other escaped---]
	+	7/08/1951 LG.# 39305 p. 4227 The following awarded the Military Medal RFN. C. RAI. MM 10th PRINCESS MARY'S OWN GURKHA RIFLES
Wed.	8th	8 L/Cpl. Sancherbahadur Thapa. 7th. Duke of Edinburgh's Own Gurkha Rifles. Died*** BMH Kinrara *Kuala Lumpur # 8*---]
Thur.	9th	9 HMT DILWARA arrived Singapore sailed for Southampton with returning Service personnel 9th.---]
Fri.	10th	10 Pte. Anak. Juna Nyantau. Sarawak Rangers. Killed Engaging CT's in deep jungle. *[No known Grave]Terandak Wall Memorial Malacca*]---]
	+	10 Sgt. G. E. Howson. Pilot 33 Sqdn. R.A.F. Killed when his Hornet WB870 crashed near Kaliang *Kranji Singapore # 4 / B – 4* ---]
	+	On the Brooklands Estate. A number of cyclist were spotted with CT packs on their carriers. 8 Platoon 'C' Comp Suffolk's opened fire killing 2. The others left their bikes & fled into the gathering dusk, leaving their CT packs. Information recovered.including hand grenades.& a photo of a women CT posing with the notorious bearded *Lieu Kon Kim*---]
Sat.	11th	11 3 F. M. Police Cpl. Shahabadin.- PC's Nayan B. Omar .- Shaari B. Jafar. Killed on Ops. Batu Gajah
	+	Perak A Platoon of the 2nd/7th Gurkhas was ambushed by approx. 60 CT's in the Saroi area of Selangor. They fought a strong defending action. Engaging CT's, until reinforcements arrived. 8 CT's were Killed & a number wounded, who were carried off by the retreating CT's. No Gurkha casualties---]
Sun.	12th	12 EPC Abdul Sahid b. Yeop Darus. F.M.Aux.Police Killed by C.T's in an ambush on a Rubber Estate in the Batu Gajah Perak.---]
Mon.	13th	13 Mr. J.B. Stoker. A Manager of a plantation?. Killed by CT's.Tengkak Johore.---]
Tue.	14th	14 2 F. M. Police EPC's Moharam B. Ahmad. – Muruggth.s/o Muthur. Killed in CT ambush 6th. m/s Seremban / Jelubu road Negri Sembilan---].
Wed.	15th	15 PC. Osman B. Hanapiah.F. M. Police Killed on CT Ops. Senai Estate Johore---]
Thur.	16th	16 PC. Latif. B. Mohd. Ghani. F. M. Police Killed on CT ambush 2nd.m/s. Rawang / Kuang Rd Selangor.---]
Fri.	17th	17 L/Cpl. Kewalparsad Gurung. Rfn. Padamanbahadur Thapa .7th. Duke of Edinburgh's Own Gurkha Rifles. Killed by accident on CT Ops. Seremban. *Kuala Lumpur # 24 / 10 – 6*.---]
	+	17 Mr. B.H. Johnston Manager. Killed by CT's at Kendong Negri Sembilan. No futher details.---]
	+	17 2 F. M. Police PC's Othma B Hassam.- Mohd. B. Hitam. Killed on Ops.Ayer Kroh Malacca---]
	+	17 6 Plt. 'B' Company Green Howards ambushed a CT. Killed him. In the area N.E. of Batang Malacca---]
Sat.	18th	18 ASP. E. F. Rainford DSO. MC. F. M. Police Killed in an CT ambush on the Cheras /Sungei Besi Road Kluang Johore. *Kuala Lumpur # 430* ---]
Sun.	19th	19 Cadet. W.K Bachelor. F. M. Police Killed by a terrorist in an ambush on the Aji /Terengganu Rd. in the Dungun area Terengganu---]
Mon.	20th	20 Rfn. Dhanbahdur Limbu . 7th, Duke of Edinburgh's Own Gurkha rifles. Killed by accident on Ops. Muar Area. *Seremban # 43* Negri Sembilan---]
Tue.	21st	21 PC Mohd. Zaman B. Abd. Majib. F. M. Police Died from wounds recv'd in CT ambush at 2nd.m/s on the 16th.---]
	+	21 2 F. M. Police PC Abdulla Rahman.b. Long. Latif b. Mohd Ghani. Killed on CT Ops.---]
	+	21 SC. Ibrahim Bin Hassan. F. M. Police Killed on CT Ops. Kuantan Pahang---]
Wed.22nd		22 Pte. L. G. Hollebon. 1st. Battn. The Queen's Own Royal West Kents. Died from wounds recv'd in ambush He continued firing, while other troops quickly dropped from the lorry to engage the CT's. Holleman was the

	last to jump down and was Killed. *Kuala Lumpur # 18 / 1023*---]
	+ 22 HMT EMPIRE WINDRUSH arrived Southampton.with returning Service personnel--]
Thur. 23rd	23 Cdt . ASP. V. K. Batchelor . F.M. Aux. Police Killed on Ops. *Terengganu* ---]
	+ Plt. 'A' Company Green Howards on Patrol in a Rubber Estate in the Chabau area came across a CT. and was Killed.---]
	+ 23 HMT EMPIRE TROOPER arrived Singapore with replacemet Service personnel---]
Fri. 24th	Auster. Number AOP 6 VF625 656 Sqdn R.A.F. Whilst landing in gusty conditions, struck the ground at Johore Bahru Air strip. Was blown over. No injuries to Pilot---]
Sat. 25th	A CT leader. **Choo Ah Kong.** (scourge of Bahua) was Killed by F.M. Police ---].
Sun. 26th	On the Crescent Estate near Tampin Support Company Green Howards Killed 2 CT's---]
Mon. 27th	27 During an investigation of a burning Bungalow. A section of the 1st. Battn. Manchester Regt. Came under fire from a well organised ambush laid by 40 CT's, under the command of the local DC Secretariat **Pak Yam** who opened fire on the Platoon, from close range in dense jungle. During the fire fight **Pte. E. McGibbons**. Killed.*Western Road # 2139*- George Town Penang---]
	+ 27 HMT EMPIRE FOWEY sailed for Southampton with returning Service personnel ----]
Tue. 28th	28 **Pte. B. D. E. Taylor.** 1st. Battn. Worcestershire Regt. Died***[*Ashes REP*]---]
	+ Kuala Lumpur: It was announced that :- 'General Sir. Bob Lockhart would succeed General Sir. Harold Briggs.' ---]
Wed. 29th	**29 Pol/Lt. R. Watson MM.** F. M. Police Killed on CT Ops. Tampin area. *Seremban ??* Negri Sembilan ---]
	+ **29 SC. Abdul Aziz B. Alang Abdul** F. M. Police Killed on CT Ops. Chemor Perak---]
	+ 29 HMT DEVONSHIRE arrived Singapore with replacement Service personnl enroute to Hong Kong---]
	+ 29 HMT EMPIRE TROOPER sailed Singapore bound for Southampton with returning Service personnel---]
Thur. 30th	11 Plt. 'D' Company Green Howards. Killed 2 CT's S.E. of Selangor Malacca.---]
	+ 30 HMT EMPIRE ORWELL sailed Southampton bound for Singapore / Hong Kong with replacement Service personnel---]
	+ 30 HMT DEVONSHIRE sailed Singapore bound for Hong Kong ---]
Fri. 31st	31/07/51 LG # 39323 p. 4610 The following awarded the Military Medal L/CPL. R. PUN. MM 6th DUKE OF EDINBURGH'S OWN GURKHA RIFLES
	+ CT *Ting Fook* (The terror of Taiping. A leading member of the MCP) was Killed by Royal Marine Commandos]
	+ Operations "*Grasshopper*"- "*Sedge*"- "*Warbler*"- "*Redskin*" "*Rover*". Ended ---]

SEPTEMBER

Sat. 1st	1 **Rfn. Kharkabahdur Pun** 2nd. King Edward VII's Own Gurkha Rifles Died from Wounds recv'd in CT ambush .*[No known Grave] Terandak Wall Memorial Wall Malacca*]
	+ 1 **Trp. J. Burgess** 13/18th. Royal Hussars Died *** *Kranji Singapore # 2 / A – 11* ---]
Sun. 2nd	CT's held up and stole the Mail Truck from Kuala Kangsar to Lenggong. Air mail was also in the packets]
Mon. 3rd	3 **Mr. L.V Brown. –2** F.M.Police **Aux/ P. R. Park. Colin.** - **PAAC** - **A.P. J.L Garnham.** Killed in Action Engaging CT's Sungei Siput *Batu Gajah # 475 - 474 - 473.* Ipoh Perak---]
Tue. 4th	RAF Sqdn. 52 Valetta became operational RAF Changi ---]
	+ 4 HMT EMPIRE HALLADALE sailed Liverpool enroute to Singapore / Hong Kong with replacement Service personnel---]
	+ 4 HMT DUNERA arrived Southampton with returning Service personnel---]
Wed. 5th	Kuala Lumpur: **Chin Peng** was named as the CT Leader, directing all CT operations throughout Malaya. A reward of $ 80,000 was offered his capture alive & $ 60,000 for his dead body.---]
	+ Bentung: About this time **Chin Peng** was hiding in Bentung along with **Lee An Tung, Siao Chang & Ah Chung,** who had managed to join them from East Pahang. The three Politburo leaders discussed their previous Action Engaging the Security Forces. Their purpose of the fight, to establish a Communist led Ditatorship in Malaya. All agreed many mistakes had been made, during their military objectives. That basically had failed. Therefore wrote up a new Policy. For all too adhere too. This eventually was circulated within the MRLA on the 1st October. 1951---]
Thur. 6th	6 **Pte. D. R. I. Elsley.** 1st. Battn. The Queen's Own Royal West Kents. Killed in Action Engaging CT's. *Kuala Lumpur # 18 / 1024*---]
	+ 6 **2/Lt. J.B. Harden.** 13/18th. Royal Hussars.Killed in Action Engaging CT's. *Seremban # CE / 48* ---]
Fri. 7th	7 **Dvr. T. F. J. Hopper.** R.A.S.C. Killed in CT ambush. *Batu Gajah # 618* Ipoh Perak---]
	+ 7/09/1951 LG # 39328 p. 4714 The following awarded the Military Cross LT. F.E. JOHNSTON MC ROYAL MARINES

		The following awarded the Military Medal
		MNE. T. SPEAKE. MM ROYAL MARINES
Sat.	8th	8 Plt. ' C' Company Green Howards discovered a CT camp in the S.E. Gemas Forest. Attacked the Bashas Killed 1 CT, the rest escaped into the jungle---]
Sun.	9th	**9 Cfn. S. E. Robinson**. R.E.M.E. Died***_Kranji Singapore # 2 /C - 10_---]
	+	9 HMT DILWARA arrived Singapore bound for Southampton with returning Service personnel---]
Mon. 10th		**10 Aux/Asstn.Spt. L.V. Brown. Aux/Pol. J.J. L.Graham, Aux.Pol. D.J.White** Perak Aboriginal Aux. Constabulary. Killed in CT ambush ---]
Tue.	11th	**11 SC. Mat Rasul B. Wan Chik** F.M. Police Killed on CT Ops. 771/2. m/s Grik/ Lenggong Rd. Grik Perak---]
Wed.	12th	12 HMT EMPIRE ORWELL arrived Singapore/ with replacement Service personnel sailed for Hong Kong 12th.---]
Thur. 13th		**13 Sgt. Rambahadur Rai** . 10th. Princess Mary's Own Gurkha Rifles Killed in Action Engaging CT's [No known grave] Terandak Wall Memorial Malacca---]
Fri.	14th	**14 Cpl. Muda B. Otham**. F. M. Police Killed on CT Ops. 53rd. m/s. Pana Rd. Terengganu---]
Sat.	15th	**15 SC. Sgt. Mohamed Yassim B. Lezis.** F. M. Police Killed on CT Ops. Johore---]
Sun.	16th	3 Soldiers of the Royal West Kents, whilst on leave in Penang. Were shot by a gunman in the Pitt Streat area. Two were seriously injured. Pte Ellis & Pte Smith, Pte Hodson escaped with minor injuries all three taken to the local hospital---]
Mon. 17th		**17 CQMS. S. C. Petherbridge.** 1st. Battn. Worcestershire Regt. Died***_Kranji Singapore # 2 / F - 10_ ---]
Tue.	18th	18/09/1951 LG. 39336 p. 4884 The following awarded a Bar to Distinguised Flying Cross
		S/LDR. A.C. BLYTHE. DFC + BAR ROYAL AIR FORCE
		The following awarded the Distinguished Flying Cross
		F/LT. K. FRY. DFC ROYAL AIR FORCE
		CAPT. R.P.F. WARNER. DFC ROYAL ARTILLERY REGIMENT.
		The following awarded the Distinguished Flying Medal
		SGT. A.E. COVER. DFM ROYAL AIR FORCE
	+	18 HMT EMPIRE FOWEY arrived Southampton. with returning Service ersonnel---]
Wed. 19th		**19** F. M. Police **SC's Hussein B. Buyong. – Arshad B. Silong**. Killed on CT Ops. Semenyth Estate Kajang---]
	+	19 HMT EMPIRE PRIDE sailed Liverpool bound for Singapore / Hong Kong with replacement Service personnel---]
Thur 20th		**20 SC. Santhanan a/o Kulandai** F. M. Police Killed on CT Ops.Kapa Bahru Estate Rawang---]
Fri.	21st	**21 SC. Mohomed B. Lazis** F. M. Police Killed on CT Ops. Ainsdale Estate Labu District.---]
	+	21 2 F. M. Police **Aux/PC Mustapha B. Tacob. - SC Wan Empak B. Osman** Killed on CT Ops.Kemaman Terengganu ---]
Sat. 22nd		**22 Sgmn. P.G. Boylan.** Royal Signals. a/t 22nd. SAS. Killed accidental shooting._Kuala Lumpur # 18 / 1028_]
Sun. 23rd		**23 W/OI. T. Lee.** 2nd. Battn. Royal Welsh Fusiliers. Died***_Kranji Singapore # 2 / C - 9_---]
	+	**23 BQMS E. Taylor** Royal Artillery. Died***-_Kuala Lumpur # 18 / 1029_----]
Mon. 24th		**24 PC. Zakariah B. Mohamad** F. M. Police Killed on Ops. Lima Kongsi Sungei Bakap P. Wellesley ---]
	+	**24** 2 F. M. Police **SC's Idris B. Mohamed Darus. – Khalip B. Samsudin** Killed on Ops. Tanjong Malim ----]
	+	**24 SC. Lin B. Saad** F.M. Police Killed on CT Ops. Lima Kongsai Sungei Bakap---]
	+	**24 SC. Abdullah B. Maidin** F. M. Police Killed on CT Ops. Sungei Besi Selangor.---]
Tue. 25th		**25 Mne. P. D. Fordham** (45 Commando) Royal Marines. Died from Wounds recv'd. _Batu Gagah_ # 549 Ipoh Perak---]
Wed. 26th		**26 Mr. H. C.Travers – Drakes**. Manager. Killed in CT ambush. Kluang Johore---]
Thur. 27th		**27 SC. Ong Kok Han** F. M. Police Killed on CT Ops. Bruas/Batu Hampur Rd. Perak.---]
	+	27 HMT EMPIRE ORWELL arrived Singapore enroute to Hong Kong with replacement Service personnel---]
	+	27 HMT EMPIRE WINDRUSH arrived Southampton with returning Service personnel---]
	+	27 HMT EMPIRE TROOPER sailed Southampton bound for Singapore with replacement Service personnel]
	+	27 HMT DEVONSHIRE arrived Singapore enroute to Liverpool with returning Service personnel---]
Fri.	28th	**28Aux.Pol/Off. Mr. K.D. H. Reader.** Asstn. Manager of the Central Puloh Estate. Killed in CT ambush.---]
Sat.	29th	29 HMT DUNERA sailed Southampton bound for Singapore with replacement Service personnel---]
Sun. 30th		**30 Cpl. T. H. Henderson.** 1st. Battn.The Queen's Own Royal West Kents. Died from wounds recv'd in CT ambush _Kuala Lumpur # 18 / 1030_----]

OCTOBER

133

Mon.	1st	**1 Rfn. Kharakbahadur Pun.** 2nd. King Edward VII's Own Gurkha Rifles. Killed in Action Engaging CT's *[No known Grave] Terandak Wall Memorial Malacca]* ---]
	+	Operations *"Mahalkal"* . Began against No 8 Regt. MRLA. In Negri Sembilan, Selengor & Pahang. ---]
	+	7 Plt. Joined by 8 Plt Green Howards, when searching in a jungle area. Discovered another dead CT who had died from his wounds.---]
	+	Auster VX 115 656 Sqdn. R.A.F. whilst flying S.W. from Grik to Taiping crashed into a mountain No casualties]
	+	The night train from Singapore to Kuala Lumpur was derailed by CT's. no cashualties reported---]
	+	Bentong: Oct 1st. The changed conditions of the Politburo Comminist Policy, under the leadership of **Chin Peng** for Terrorists was issued. Were as follows:-
		I.) Stop seizing I.D. & ration Cards
		II.) Stop Burning villages and Coolie lines
		III.) Stop attacking Post Office's, reservoirs, power Stations, and other Public Services.
		IV.) Refrain from derailing civilian trains with high expolisives.
		V.) Stop throwing grenades to be exploited rather than attack.
		VI.) No new Village are to be destroyed but reasonable and acceptable conditions to protect the interest of resettled Chinese Squatters. Are to be put forward and wherever possible. Their demands are to be fulfilled by lawfull means.
		VII.).The formation of Home Guards Units to be delayed, obstructed, dismantled or. Made use of. Stubborn reaction engaging CT's. Are to be Killed or, others are to be persuded too help the party or remain neutral.
		There was further instructions to all members based on increasing the CPM 's MRLA change in method towards the populations. education on the Comminist Doctrine, infiltration on the Trade Unions in an attempt to try and gain the Populace confidence. ---]
		A copy of this document came into the hands of the Seccurity Forces. It was found on the body of a dead CT. After an engagement ---]
Tue.	2nd	**2 L/Cpl. Hassan b. Awang** Malay Regt. Killed in Action Engaging CT's Pahang---]
	+	**2** 2 F. M. Police **Pol/Lt. B.Talks. - SC Ismail B. Abdullah** Killed on CT Ops. in the Batu Padang Kertah Kemasik area of Terengganu ---]
		In the same location 7 Plt. Green Howards. Contacted a lone CT. Killed him Kertah Kemasik Terengganu --]
	+	2/10/1951 LG # 39348 p 5119 The following awarded the Military Medal
	+	L/CPL. D.H.J. JOLLY. MM ROYAL ELECTRICAL MECHANICAL ENGINEERS
Wed.	3rd	**3**. A Platoon 'D' Comp. Suffolk's were attempting to cross the river Sungei Langat. Wading through **Pte.R. Moore.** 1st. Battn. Suffolk Regt. got into difficulties & drowned. As light was failing, it was difficult to find him. His body was found the next day. Obvious the weight of his equipment plus the strength of the current was the cause of his drowning.. *Kuala Lumpur # 18 / 1031.*---]
	+	**3** HMT EMPIRE HALLADALE arrived Singapore with replacement Service personnel / sailed for Hong Kong 3rd..---]
Thur.	4th	**4 Mr. Bob Evans.** Miner. Accidently Shot by a Gurkha Road Block at Batu Gajah Perak.---]
Fri.	5th	**5 Pte. J. Jackson.** ACC. Died*** *Kuala Lumpur # 18 / 1032*---]
	+	**5 Mne. G. A. Dayes.** (40 Commando) Royal Marines. Killed in Action Engaging CT's *Taiping # E / 16* Perak.
	+	**5Pol / LtH. G. Marcon** F. M. Police Killed on CT Ops.*Kuantan # ???* Pahang--]
Sat.	6th	Kuala Lumpur : **Sir. Henry Gurney.** KCMG. High Commisioner for the Federation of Malaya was Killed by C.T's in a road ambush, whilst on their way up to Frasers Hill. With an F.M.Police escort, of a land Rover followed by Sir. Henry's Rolls Royce, A radio van, then an ammoured car with 10 Policemen. They set off from the King's House about 11 o' clock. On the way up. The radio van broke down, leaving Sir Henry Gurney's Rolls Royce and Landrover continuing up the hill. Thus leaving their escorts behind. After a short time, the armored car overtook the broken van and went after Sir. Henry Gurney's Rolls Royce. When just a mile from the Gap Rest House. They were fired upon. returning fire, they carried on to find the Rolls Royce Stationary, with a body laying too one side. Still the firing continued from the CT's, with the Police returning fire with bren guns, before the CT's stopped firing. The ambush took place at the 151/2. m/s Gap Road. Pahang /Selangor Border. --]
	+	**6 SC. Muda B. Yussof.** F. M. Police Killed on CT Ops. Pahang.---]
	+	Operation *"Pursuit"* Immediately began against the perpetrators' of **Sir. Henry Gurney's** Assassination. Known as No 6 Regt. MRLA led by **Siew Ma**.---]
	+	**6** HMT EMPIRE ORWELL arrived in Singapore / sailed for Southampton with returning Service personnel- 6th.---]
Sun.	7th	10 miles from Kulim. A Public Works Depaetment (PWD) Lorry, a Bus were ambushed by CT's.The ambush

	took place on the main road. The CT's set light to the Bus & Lorry before Securrity Forces arrived on the scene.They pursued after the CT's, caught up & engaged them.. 3 CT's were wounded but escaped leaving their packs behind---]
Mon. 8th	8 5 F. M. Police **Pol/Lt. F.C. Belshom. PC.'s Abdul Aziz. B. Mahmood. - Babjee.- SC's Ali Deman B. Mat – Mat Taha B. Othman.** Killed in Action Engaging CT's on anti terrorist duties, in an area of Endua River Mersing Johore *Kranji Singapore # 8 / C – 7* ---]
Tue. 9th	9 **Pol/Lt. H.G. Marcon.** F. M. Police Killed on CT Ops. Kuantan Pahang.---]
+	9 HMT DILWARA arrived Southampton with returning Service personnel---]
Wed. 10th	10 **Pte D. C. Coleman.** 1st. Battn. The Queen's Own Royal West Kents. Died *** *Kuala Lumpur # 18 / 1033*]
+	10 2. F. M. Police **SC's. Mohd,Tahir B. Ngah Mat Arof. – Haron B. Abdul Samad.** Killed on CT Ops.Kota Bahru Mapar District Perak. ---]
+	10 HMT EMPIRE FOWEY sailed from Southampton bound for Singapore / Hong Kong with replacement Service personnel---]
Thur. 11th	11 **SC.Cpl. Abdul Aziz B. Abdul Rahman** F. M. Police Killed on Ops. Segamat Johore.---]
+	11 **SC.Mohd. Yussof B. Omar** F. M. Police Killed on CT Ops. Juasseh Estate Kuala Pilah Negri Sembilan-]
+	10 miles from Kulim. F.M. Police engaged a number of CT's, who disappeared into the Jungle---]
Fri. 12th	In the Durian Tunggal area 2nd. Plt. 'D' Company Green Howards. Killed 1 CT.---]
Sat. 13th	13 **WOII. W. F. Garrett.** Devonshire Regt. A/t 22nd.SAS. Killed in Action Engaging CT's *Seremban # CE / 47*]
	13 3 F. M. Police **AG. L/Cpl Haron B. Suek. PC Abdullah B. Bidin. F/JC. Abdullah B. Bidin.** Killed whilst Engaging CT's on Ops. Johore.---]
Sun. 14th	14 **SC. Mohamed B, Samet** F. M. Police Killed on CT Ops. Ayer Pasir. Estate Malacca---]
+	14/10/1951 LG # 39333 p. 4822 The following awarded the Colonial Police Medal
	POL/LT. E.C KILFORD CPM FEDERATION MALAYA POLICE
	EPC. WAN MAT ALIB. WAN SUIMAN CPM FEDERATION MALAYA POLICE
	SAC. NAYAN B. HASSAN CPM FEDERATION MALAYA POLICE
	SC ISMAIL B. MAT. ESA CPM FEDERATION MALAYA POLICE
	SC KASSIM B. MOHAMMAD CPM FEDERATION MALAYA POLICE
	CPL. GULDIAL SINGH CPM FEDERATION MALAYA POLICE
+	14 HMT EMPIRE PRIDE arrived Singapore/ sailed for Hong Kong with replacement Service personnel14]
Mon. 15th	15 **SC. Mohd. Taib B. Dali** F. M. Police Killed on CT Ops. Ulu Choh Water Works Galang Patah Johore Bahru]
+	London: A delegation from Malaya representing, The Rubber Owners Association, the Malayan Chamber of Commerce the Association of British Malaya The Rubber Trade ssociation of London The Eastern Exchange Banks Association the British Association of Straits Settlements & the Incorporated Society of Planters were in London to meet Mr. Lyettleton. The Colonial Secetary & Mr Lennox Boyd. Minister of State for Colonial Affairs To discuss the situation in Malaya ---]
Tue. 16th	16 **Capt. G. Caulfield.** 1st. Battn.Gordon Highlanders. Killed in Action Engaging CT's. *Kuala Lumpur # 18 / 1034* ---]
+	16 HMT EMPIRE ORWELL arrived Singapore enroute to Southampton with returning Service personnel16th.
Wed. 17th	17 **SC Shararudin B. Jai.** F. M. Police Killed on CT Ops. Sungei Sidu Estate Kuala Langat Selangor ----]
Thur. 18th	18 **A/B. D. J. Heaton** Royal Navy HMS *'TERROR'* Died ***]*Ashes REP*]---]
+	Kuala Lumpur: It was announced in Kuala Lumpur: 'The " **Federal War Council** " was to be expanded to include Communal & Industrial Leaders,with the addition of Planters & Miners ---]
Fri. 19th	19 **Rfn. Chandrabahadur Rai .** 10th.Princess Mary's Own Gurkha Rifles. Killed In Action Engaging CT's Bentong Area *Kuala Lumpur # 27 / 1*---]
+	19/10/1951 LG # 39361 p. 5431 The following awarded the British Empire Medal (Military)
	W/O. D. ARMITAGE. BEM 4th. QUEEN'S HUSSARS
	SGT. W. H. BIRKETT. BEM ROYAL ENGINEERS
	cont. p. 5432
	C/SGT. A. CALVER. BEM SUFFOLK REGIMENT.
	W/O. K.W.LAMA. BEM 10th PRINCESS MARY'S OWN GURKHA RIFLES
	C/SGT. J. M. MATHISON. BEM THE CAMERONIANS
	SGT. P.L.POINTON. BEM SCOTS GUARDS
	The following awarded the Military Cross.
	Capt. D.C. MAHONEY. MC ROYAL MARINES
	LT. R. P. CARTER. MC ROYAL MARINES
	Lt. J . D. SHALLOW. MC ROYAL MARINES

| | Lt. A.H.V. GILLMORE MC | THE SUFFOLK REGIMENT. |
| | 2/LT. F. LAYCOCK MC | THE GREEN HOWARDS |

The following awarded the Military Medal

	CPL. J. McKNIGHT MM	THE CAMERONIANS
	SGT. N.WINTER. MM	THE GREEN HOWARDS
	RFN. A. GURUNG. MM.	2nd. KING EDWARD VII'S OWN GURKHA RIFLES.
	L/CPL. T. GURUNG, MM.	2th KING EDWARD VII'S OWN GURKHA RIFLES
	SGT. H. RANA MM	6th QUEEN ELIZABETH'S OWN GURKHA RIFLES
	L/CPL. S GURUNG MM	6th QUEEN ELIZABETH'S OWN GURKHA RIFLES
	RFN. P. TAMAG MM	7th. DUKE OF EDINBURGH'S OWN GURKHA RIFLES
	SGT. T. LIMBU. MM	10th PRINCESS MARY'S OWN GURKHA RIFLES
	RFN. C. RAI MM	10th PRINCESS MARY'S OWN GURKHA RIFLES
	PTE. R.B. HUSSIN. MM	MALAY REGIMENT

The following awarded the Colonial Police Medal

| | SC. LO SWEE KIM CPM (POS) | FEDERATION MALAYA POLICE |

Sat. 20th 20 2 F. M. Police **PC's. Abdullah B. Hassan - Nayan B. Akil.** Killed on CT Ops. Gelang Patah Rd. Johore Bahru---]

Sun. 21st 21 **Rfn. Tekbahadur Rai** . 6th. Queen's Own Gurkha Rifles. Died from Wounds recv'd Engaging CT's Hind 1035Sht 3l3 VP 142606 *Kluang # 3 / F - 19* Johore---]

+ 21 2 F. M. Police **AG. Pd L/Cpl. Sulaiman B. Mustapa – PC Md. Noor B. Abd. Karim.**. Killed on CT Ops. 5th m/s. Sungei Kob Rd. Kulim Kedah---]

Mon.22nd 22 **Capt. E. A. Deed. - Cpl. H. Sulley. - L/Cpl.R. J. Chambers. - L/Cpl. D. P. Molland . - Pte. J. Bardell. Pte. D. P. Brown. - Pte. J. Cheesman. - Pte. L. J. Hand . - Pte. G. H. Heath. - Pte. J. A. C. Knight. – Pte. M. Pelling.** 1st. Battn. The Queen's Own Royal West Kent Regt. & **Pte's. Anak Gadong Kelambu - Anak Kasaw Bulan - Anak. Engan Untang.** Sarawak Rangers. **SC's Abu Bakar b. Sulaiman - Bathurmalai a/l Pandiah** F. M. Police were Killed, on the New Caledonian Estate Batu Arang. In an area of N. Selangor including 12 troops, wounded in a gun battle with a large force of C.T's (several were Killed & wounded). *Kuala Lumpur # 19 / 1042 – 1048 – 1050 – 1040 – 1056 – 1058 – 1054 – 1046 – 1052 – 1044 – 1060 - 18 / 1039 – 1035 - 1037*---]

+ 22 **Sgmn. P. G. Boylan** Royal Signals. A/t SAS. Killed in Action Engaging CT's *Kuala Lumpur # 18 / 1028*---

Tue. 23rd 23 **SC .Bataumalai a/l Pandiah.** F. M. Police Killed on CT Ops. Kalumpang Estate Tanjon Malim.---]

+ 23 **Mr E.M.T.A. De Clercq.** The Belgium Manager of the TMR Estate. Killed by CT's at Tanjong Malim Perak.]

Wed. 24th 24 **Pte. A. G. Lepper.** 1st. Battn. The Queen's Own Royal West Kent Regt. Died from wounds recv'd. On 22nd. *Kuala Lumpur # 1 /1041*---]

+ 24 **SC Saad.** F. M. Police Died from wounds recv'd on 22nd .Kulim Kedah---]

+ RAF Sqdn. 110 Valetta C4 became operational RAF Changi ---]

Thur. 25th 25 **Pte. F. L. Lewis.** 1st. Battn. Suffolk Regt. Killed in Action Engaging CT's. 1 CT was Killed during the fire fight. *Kuala Lumpur # 10 / 1043*---]

+ Dragonfly WF308 Sqdn 194 R.A.F. Cas/Vac flight. Dived into ground near Ruab---].

Fri. 26th London: In the General Election The Labour Government were defeated. Losing to the Conservative Party Mr. Winston Churchill was elected the new Prime Minister---]

+ 26 HMT DUNERA arrived Singapore- with replacement Service personnel---]

Sat. 27th 27 **W/O Clk. F. Cain.** R.A.F. Regt. Butterworth Died from Wounds recv'd Engaging CT's. *Western Road # 2140* George Town Penang---]

+ 27 HMT LANCASHIRE arrived Liverpool with returning Service personnel---]

+ 27HMT EMPIRE WINDRUSH arrived Singapore with replacement Service personnel---]

+ 27 HMT DEVONSHIRE arrived Liverpool with returning Service personnel---]

Sun. 28th 28 **SC Hassan B. Sohor** F. M. Police Killed on CT Ops. Degong Rd Resetlement Post.---]

Mon. 29th Another Bus was ambushed near the Kampong of Terap. A Platoon of the 1st. Lancashire Regt. On their way to investigate the incident, were ambushed by a group of CT's. Returning fire Engaged them. After a short time the CT's fled.. In the follow up. Trails of blood proved some of them were wounded. Unfortunately due to nightfall the engagement was called off.---]

Tue. 30th 30 **Rfn. R. Shaw.** 1st. Battn. Cameronians. Killed by accident. Muar Johore *[Ashes REP]*---]

Wed. 31st 31 **Maj. F. C. Blucke.** R.A.O.C. Died*** *[Ashes REP]*---]

+ Kuala Lumpur: An announcement was issued stated.
A Fijian Infantry Battalion would be sent to Malaya to strengthen forces already there. Their tour of Active Service would be 2 Years.'.---]

	+	31 HMT DILWARA sailed Southampton bound for Singapore / Hong Kong with replacement Service personnel---]
	+	Operation *"Mahakal" 'Warbler' Marker'* Ended---]

NOVEMBER

Thur.	1st	**1 Sgmn H.W. Marr.** Royal Signals Died***. *Kranji Singapore # 2 / C -8*---]
	+	1 HMT DUNERA sailed Singapore bound for Southampton with returning Service personnel---]
	+	1 HMT EMPIRE FOWEY arrived Singapore with replacement Service personnel enroute to Hong Kong sailed 2nd.---]
Fri.	2nd	2/11/1951 LG #39374 p.5716 The following awarded the Nritish Empire Maedal
		PTE. E.G. TWIGDEN, B.E.M THE SUFFOLK REGT. ATT/ MALAYAN SCOUTS
		p 5718 The following awarded the BAR to his Military Cross
		LT. (KGO) D. GURUNG.MC & BAR 7th. DUKE OF EDINBURGH'S OWN GURKHA RIFLES
		The following awarded the Miltary Medal
		SGT. D. RAI. MM 7th. DUKE OF EDINBURGH'S OWN GURKHA RIFLES
		RFN.. H. RAI.MM 7th. DUKE OF EDINBURGH'S OWN GURKHA RIFLES
		PTE. R. HOLT. MM THE MANCHESTER REGIMENT.
		The following awarded the Colonial Police Medal
		SC.SHEIKH SULIMAN B. SHEIKH HAFFUU CFM. FEDERATION MALAYA POLICE
	+	2 HMT EMPIRE HALLADALE arrived Singapore/ sailed for Liverpool with returning Service personnel. ---]
Sat.	3rd	**3 Rfn. Kalbahadur Rai .** 10th. Princess Mary's Own Gurkha Rifles. Died*** *Kranji Singapore # 8 / B -12*---]
Sun.	4th	Auster AOP 6 VF 551 656 Sqdn. R.A.F. After engine failure crashed in jungle. Pilot Sgt. E. Webb & Pol/Cad.J. Underhill F. M. Police, survived the crash although were slightly injured.---]
Mon.	5th	**5 Cpl. J. Broadbent.** 1st. Battn. Manchester Regt. Killed during an ambush in the Kuala Nau area of Kulim. Sgt. Taylor, Pte Johnson were wounded. *Western Road # 2141* George Town Penang.---]
	+	**5 Pte. H. Rowberry.** 1st. Battn. Worcestershire Regt. Died*** *[Ashes REP]*---]
	+	London: It was announced that the Colonial Secretary:-
		Sir. Oliver Lyttelton, would leave London on the 26 November for a 3 weeks tour of Malaya. To report on the then current situation in Malaya ---]
Tue.	6th	A section of the 'Iban' Platoon Suffolk's attacked a hut close to a cultivation plot. 3 CT's in the hut were Killed]
Wed.	7th	**7 Rfn. G. Tejbahadur.** King Edward VII's Own Gurkha Rifles. Killed in Action Engaging CT's Ruab Pahang VP818790 *[No known Grave]* Terandak Wall Memorial Malacca---]
	+	**7 Sgt. C. Chew.** R. A. S. C. Died*** BMH Kinrara *Kuala Lumpur # 19 / 1045* ---]
Thur.	8th	**8 Cpl. Ibrahim B. Mat. - PC. Haris B. Md Nafis.** F. M. Police Killed on CT Ops. Kampah Perak.---]
	+	Auster AOP6 VX114 656 Sqdn when Taking off from Kuala Lumpur crashed---]
	+	6 Platoon B Comp Suffolk's engaged and Killed 1 CT in the Kuala Langat Forest Reserve---]
	+	8/11/1951 LG 38374 p 5718 The following awarded the Military Medal
		PTE. HOLT R. MM MANCHESTER REGIMENT.
	+	8 HMT EMPIRE ORWELL arrived Southampton- with returning Service personnel--
Fri.	9th	**9 Pol/Lt. R.L Good.** F. M. Police Killed in a bobby trap incident, trying to remove a CT flag from overhead telegraph wires. Engaging the CT's.3 Special Constables received minor injuries. In the Chendering area of Perak.---]
Sat.	10th	**10 PC Ahmad.** F. M. Police Killed in Train Derailment.Kampah Perak---]
Sun.	11th	**11 Gnr. F. R. Houghton** Royal Artillery Killed in CT Road ambush Negri Sembilan *Kuala Lumpur # 19 / 1047*---]
	+	**11 Lt. J.A. Hibbs** Royal Tamk Corps Killed in Ambush North of Guran *Taiping # E / 17* Perak ---]
	+	A European planter (*unnamed*)& 2 SC's **Jaffa B. Joharri. – Ismail B. Omar.** F. M. Police Were Killed in an ambush by C.T's in the Kluang area of Johore---]
	+	**11 Mr. G. R. Tilley.** Asstn. Manager. of the Menkibol Estate. Kluang. Killed by CT's.--
	+	Auster VX 115 656 Sqdn. R.A.F. Waiting to take off from Kuala Lumpur was struck by Auster VX117.---]
	+	11/11/1951 LG # 39406 p 6472 The following awarded the Military Medal
		SGT. MON.K MM . GREEN HOWARDS
Mon.	12th	**12 PC Omar B. Yussof.** F. M. Police Killed on Ops. Kuala Lipis. Pahang---]
Tue.	13th	**13** 7 F. M. Police **Daud B. Olong .- Lee Kim Huat. – Lee Tiam Soy. – Abdul Wahab B. Ismail. -Mohd. Yanus B. Pandak. – Abdul Hamid B, Alias.- Ahmaed B. Tahir.** The ambush was laid under the leadership of *Yong Hoi* a dreaded CT. ---]

+	**13 Mr. I.E.H. Corbett.** Director of Bidor Estate (former Chairman of the Rubber Growers Asstn. In London Who had only arrived in Malaya the week before) Was ambushed & Killed Together with **C.W. Dicks** & 9 F.M.Police SC's *(unnambed)*.---]
+	13 HMT EMPIRE WINDRUSH sailed Singapore bound for Southampton. with returning Service personnel On board were the 4th. Hussars. returning after their tour of Active Service in Malaya ---]
Wed. 14th	**14 PC. Ahmad B. Mempri.** F. M. Police Killed in CT ambush CT Ops. ---]
+	**14** 2 F.M. Policemen (*unnamed*)were Killed & 2 wounded in a raid by C.T's on a Estate in Segamat Johore].
+	**14 Pol/Lt. R.L. Good.** F.M. Aux.Police & his driver *(unnamed)* were Killed in a road ambush by C.T's in the Tapah area of Perak *Batu Gajah # 554* Ipoh Perak ---]
+	An Indian CT leader *A.S.Malan* was Killed in Selangor.---]
Thur. 15th	**15 Pte. E. A. Riches.** 1st. Battn. Suffolk Regt. Died from Wounds recv'd in engagement with CT's *Kuala Lumpur # 19 / 1049*---]
Fri. 16th	**16 Sig. J. W. M. Gibson** DFM. R.A.F. Seletar.. Flying Boat Wing Died*** *Kranji Singapore # 4 / B – 9* ---]
+	**16 Capt. G. Caulfield.** The Gordon Highlanders Killed in Action Engaging CT's. *Kuala Lumpur #18 /1034* ---]
Sat. 17th	**17 SC. Karim Bin. Dasara.** F.M. Police Killed on CT Ops. ---]
+	10 Platoon 'D' Comp Suffolk's. Engaged 5 CT's in the Ulu Langat Forest Reserve. Killed 1 the other escaped. ---]
+	17 HMT DEVONSHIRE sailed Liverpool bound for Singapore / Hong Kong via Mombassa with replacement Service personnel---]
Sun. 18th	**18 SC. Idris B.Haji. Ahmad.** F.M. Police Killed on CT Ops.---]
Mon. 19th	**19 SC. Suleiman B. Mohamed.** F. M. Police Killed on CT Ops.Jabau area Tapah. ---]
+	In Negri Sembilan 6 CT's were Killed. & in Johore. 2 CT's were Killed, by Security Force---]
+	HMT EMPIRE ORWELL sailed Southampton bound for Singapore/ Hong Kong with replacement Service personnel---]
Tue. 20th	**20 Pte. Anak Cheling Manit** Sarawak Rangers.Killed Engaging CT's *[No known Grave]Terandak Wall Memorial-Malacca*---]
+	**20 L/Cpl. J. Ross-Wilson.** 9th./12th. Royal Lancers Died***￼*Kuala Lumpur # 19 / 1051* ---]
Wed. 21st	21 HMT EMPIRE TROOPER arrived Singapore with replacement Service Personnel---]
Thur.22nd	**22 Sto.Mech. D. Burns.** Royal Navy HMS *'MAGIEICNE'* Died *** *[Ashes REP]*---]
Fri. 23rd	Three air strikes were carried out by R.A.F. Lincoln & Vampire Aircraft, on a CT camp. In the area of Naka. A follow up by ground forces, found the camp decimated. Evidence of a hasty retreat by the CT's including bloodstained clothing. ---]
Sat. 24th	**24 Rfn's. Ajirbahadur Rai. - Jalbahadur Tamar.** 7th. Duke of Edinburgh's Own Gurkha Rifles Killed by Accident. Bahua Camp.*Sembilan # 41 - 40* Negri Sembilan ---]
+	24 HMT EMPIRE TROOPER sailed Singapore bound for Southampton with returning Service Personnel--]
Sun. 25th	Two Separate engagements by the Suffolk Regt. occurred. One: 12 Platoon 'D' Comp acting on Information sprung an ambush on the jungle edge on the Kuala Lumpur Kajang Road, when 2 CT's emerged from the jungle both Kiiled. ----]
+	The second engagement occurred to 'D' Comp. Again acting on information 10 Platoon, set an ambush on the edge of a Rubber Estate near Kajang. One CT came out to meet up with another. Both were instantly Killed. ---]
+	25 HMT EMPIRE PRIDE sailed Singapore bound for Liverpool with returning Service personnel ---]
Mon. 26th	**26 Pte. L.W. Holman** The Queen's Own Royal West Kents. Killed in Action Engaging CT's. *Kuala Lumpur # 19 / 1053*---]
Tue. 27th	**27 2/Lt.. W. Grey.** 1st Battn. Cameronians. Died*** Muar Johore. *[Ashes REP]*---]
+	**27 Cpl. T. R. Mawdsley** 9th./12th. Royal Lancers. Died***￼*Kuala Lumpur # 19 / 1055*--]
+	A further Air strike carried out by the same R. A. F. strike force. Began early in the morning. After which ground forces moved in to report of the damage. Again the strike was accurate & a fourth camp was destroyed--]
+	A follow up by ground forces found no bodies. Rcovered both men & womens clothing.---]
Wed. 28th	**28 Rfn. Kirtinarayan Rai** . 7th. Duke of Edinburgh's Own Gurkha Rifles. Killed in Action Engaging CT's Kualah Pilah *Kuala Lumpur # 26 / 4*---]
+	**28 Mne. R.A. Clark** (40 Commando) Royal Marines Died from Wounds recv'd in engagement with CT's *Taiping # B / 53* Perak---]
+	28 HMT EMPIRE FOWEY arrived Singapore ----]
+	28 HMT DILWARA arrived Singapore with replacement Service personnel enroute Hong Kong 28th. ---]
Thur. 29th	Kuala Lumpur: Sir. Oliver Lyttelton. At the direction of Mr. Winston Churchill the Prime Minister. Arrived in Kuala Lumpur at the beginning of his 3 week tour. To report back on the grave situation in Malaya.---]

	+	29 HMT DUNERA arrived Southampton with returning Service personnel ---]
Fri.	30th	**30 Pte. A. Reeves.** R. A. O. C. Died*** *Kuala Lumpur # 19 / 1057* --]
	+	Kuala Lumpur: Sir.Oliver Lyttelton met with General Sir. Robert Lockhart & Lt/General Sir. Harold Briggs. With his focus on resettlement.:

'Lt General Briggs, de-emphasized the sort of fruitless "jungle bashing" on which the army had wasted valuable resources in the war's early years. Too many Brigade Commanders, newly arrived from Europe and, in the words of one officer, "nostalgic for World War II" Would send their troops thrashing through the dense vegetation, only to discover nothing but empty guerrilla camps. "You can't deal with a plague of mosquitoes by swatting each individual insect," Briggs said. "You find and disinfect their breeding grounds. Then the mosquitoes are finished---]

		A Bus was ambushed by a number of CT's in the Rawand area of Selangor they Killed the Bus Inspector
	+	**Siew Kim Seng** ---]
		CT's slashed rubber trees in the areas of Kluang, Johore Bahru & Ipoh ---]
	+	HMT EMPIRE FOWEY sailed Singapore bound for Southampton with returning Service personnel---]
	+	

DECEMBER

Sat.	1st	Sir. Oliver Lyttelton was driven from Johore Bahru. In a 7 ton armoured car, armed with a 2 inch cannon, to The Free Town New Settlement 33 miles from Johore Bahru. There he met with Planters & Leaders of the local Chinese Communities before he went onto Kuala Lumpur ---]
	+	Malayan Aux. Air Force Sqdn. Kuala Lumpur Tiger Moths became operational. RAF Kuala Lumpur ---]
	+	1 HMT EMPIRE HALLADALE arrived Liverpool with returning Service personnel---]
Sun.	2nd	**2 Cpl. H. D. Marsh.** R. A. S. C. Died Transport accident. *Kuala Lumpur # 19 /1059* ---]
Mon.	3rd	In the same area of the previous air strikes In a follow up by Troops. Another camp was found to house at least 40 CT's still in use. An ambush was set up by the Manchester Regt. to await the possible return of the CT's---]
	+	A S.E.P. led a Platoon of the 10th. Gurkhas to a basher,where 2 CT's were located. A grenade was thrown and a bren gun was fired into the basha. Investigation revealed 2 dead CT's.Both were important MRLA CT's within the district ---]
	+	Bentong Pahang: A Chinese man dressed in Black, acting supsisiously was arrested by F.M. Police He had a grenade in his pocket. His intention was to attempt o kill Sir. Oliver Lyttelton who was on his way to meet Dignitaries of Bentong.---]
	+	Kuala Lumpur: Mr. Lyttlteon met with leaders of the Malay Communities. Had talks with Sir. Rob Lockhart & attended a meeting with various. Rulers of the Federation States. The leaders of all three communities Malay, Chinese & Indian, urged Mr. Lyttleton:-
		'Immediate poitical reforms as an essential part of Malaya's struggle against militant Communist.' ---]
Tue.	4th	Kuala Lumpur: It was announced: General Sir. Rob Lockhart. Became Director of Operations Malaya ---]
	+	3 Plt 'A' Comp Suffolk's. Killed 1 CT in the area S. of Kajang. He was the last CT's to be Killed by the Suffolk's]
	+	3 CT's approached an ambush by the Wocestershire Regt. The lead CT was immediately shot dead the other two, scattered into the brush on either side.---]
Wed.	5th	**5 2 F. M. Police SC's Mohd. Amin B. Saeman – Jabbar B. Raben** Killed Engaging CT's on CT Ops.Sagil Area Tankok Muar---]
	+	Ipoh: Mr. Lyttlteon met with a delegation of Planters who voiced their opinion:
		'Of the very serious situation regarding the Rubber Plantations that had been brought to a standstill by the activities of the CT's---]
Thur.	6th	**6 Pte. B. Wilson.** 1st. Battn. Worcestershire Regt. Died*** *Kranji Singapore# 2 / D -1*---]
	+	**6 Pte. Gill.** of 9 Platoon. 'C' Company Green Howards. Killed during an ambush Lt.J. A. Davies was wounded in the chest & arm The ambush took place in the Gemas jungle. Pte.Gill's *[Ashes REP]*---]
Fri.	7th	**7 Sgt. C. Barker.** 1st. Battn. Cameronians. Died drowned on Ops. Muar Johore. *Kranji Singapore# 2 / C 15]*
	+	**7 Dvr. C. Kearney.** R. A. S. C. Died Transport incident.*Kuala Lumpur # 19 / 1061*---]
Sat.	8th	A Platoon of the Royal West Kents. Killed 3 CT's. Identified as **Ah Ngew, Siew Kool , & a woman Yap Kong Thye** ---]
Sun.	9th	Penang: Continuing on his tour. Sir. Oliver Lyttelton, flew from Ipoh to Penang, where the plane a R. A. F. Valetta, approaching the runway, when approx. 50 yds away. Its wheel hit & ploughed through mud bungs. before crashing on the runway. Careeing on down the runway, before finishing up in a field.
		Sir. Oliver Lyttelton narrowly missed being Killed, along with other passengers. Members of his

	party:- Act/Chief Sec of State Mr. D.C Watherstone, his Sec Mr J.J Paskin - Und/Sec of State fo the Colonies - Mr. H. Fraser - Insp/Gen. Colonilal Police.Col. W. Mulle -. Mr. A.K. Mackintosh - Mr. Welbore Kerr. - Mr. J. Deval F. M. Police When he got out Mr. Lytteton said.
	'This is nothing I have been in crashes before'--.]
Mon. 10th	**10 Rfn. Manparsad Limbu** . 7th. Duke of Edinburgh's Own Gurkha Rifles. Died****Kranji Singapore #8 / B 13*]
+	A Royal Marine Officer 1 Sgt , 2 R M Commandos along with 2 F.M. Police Insp & 3 F.M. PC's. Set in a moonlight ambush near Kampar Perak. Killed 4 CT's.---]
Tue. 11th	**11 Cpl. N. S. Howe** (42 Commando) Royal Marines Died*** [*Ashes REP*] ---]
+	**11 D/PC Ong Kok Lye** F. M. Police Killed on CT Ops. Bukit Tambun Rd. P. Wellesley Penang.---]
+	Singapore: Mr.Oliver Lyttelton returned to Singapore for further talks on the situation in Malaya---]
+	11/12/1951 LG # 39406 p. 6472 The following awarded the Military Medal
	SGT. G. MON.K . MM GREEN HOWARDS
Wed. 12th	**12 SC Itam B. Saad.** F. M. Police Killed on CT Ops. Kuala Kangsar Perak---]
+	12 HMT EMPIRE ORWELL arrived Sun.gapore with replacement Service personnel/ Sailed for Hong Kong 12th.---]
Thur. 13th	**13 SC Mat Nasb B Pandar Shubor.** F. M. Police Killed on CT Ops. Kuala Kangsar. Perak---]
+	13 HMT EMPIRE WINDRUSH arrived Southampton. with returning Service personnel---]
Fri. 14th	**14 Pte. D. Wilson.** 1st. Battn. Suffolk Regt. Killed in an accident, when a grenade with a faulty fuse blew up wounding Sgt. Wilce and Cpl. Baily. *Kuala Lumpur # 19 / 1062*---]
+	Another Plt No 4 of 'B' Company of the Suffolk's ambushed and Killed a CT identified as ***A.S.Maniam*** the leader of an Indian section of the MRLA ---]
+	Singapore: Mr Lyttleton held a press conference before he flew off to Hong Kong, he stated:-
	He would begin writing up his report on what he had discovered during his tour of Malaya & the prevailing situation in Malaya. There were 6 major points he would make recommendation on.
	a) *The overall directions of all forces Military Civil, against the Communist.*
	b) *Re-Organisation of the Police Force.*
	c) *The extension of education as it appeared most Malayans did not know what they were fighting for & that education could help to win the war of ideas.*
	d) *A higher measure of protection for the new settlements.*
	e) *Proper Organisation of the Home Guard.*
	f) *Recruitment of the best men for the Malayan Civil Service from both Britain & Malaya*
	g) *Yet still, there were a lot of minor issues to be tackled & resolved ----*]
+	14 HMT EMPIRE ORWELL sailed Southampton bound for Singapore / Hong Kong with replacement Service personnel---]
Sat. 15th	Singapore: G.V. Kitson Office of the Commisioner General sent Telegram to R.H. Scott Foreign Office London:
	'Suggesting consideration of sending detainees to Taiwan.'?---]
+	Kuala Lumpur: A Sub Committee was set up by the Commisioner General, with M.V. del Tufuo Malayan Chief Secretary. G.V. Kitson. for Chinese Affairs, J. M. Addis Foreign Office Hong Kong. To try and sort out the Chinese Detainees and deportation problem.---]
+	London: G.V. Kitson. Telegram to R.H. Scott Foreign office London.
	'It was doutful if they could be sent to Taiwan. The Deportees may not be willing to go there'.---]
Sun. 16th	**16 Sgt. H. G. Holloway** R. A. S. C. Died***Sak Kong *Kranji Singapore #??---*]
+	**16 Pol/Lt. R.E. Lord** Killed along with his Driver (**unnamed**) F. M. Police Killed on CT Ops. when they were attacked by CT's on a side road in the Cheendering area of Perak 3 other Special Constables were wounded *Batu Gajah # 555* Ipoh Perak ---]
+	Kuala Lumpur. The Sub Committee sought the assistance of the Foreign Office London to:-
	'Instruct the British Consul in Tamsui to approach the Formosan authorities.' ---]
+	Kuala Lumpur: **The** appointment of a **"SUPREMO"** for Malaya was agreed by the 9 Rulers of Malaya or their representatives This was their response of the 2 hour meeting, Sir. Oliver Lyttelton held with the Rulers. During his tour of Malaya & would form the cornerstone of his report---]
+	16 HMT DILWARA arrived Singapore sailed for Southampton 16th. with returning Service personnel ---]
Mon. 17th	Kuala Lumpur: Mr. Lyttleton arrived back in Kuala Lumpur from Hong Kong, to complete his report on what he had discovered during his tour of Malaya, which took a further 2 days ---]
	17 HMT EMPIRE PRIDE arrived Liverpool with returning Service personnel ---]
+	**SC Awi B. Matahah** F. M. Police Killed in CT ambush 14th. m/s Kuantan /Gambang Rd. Pahang.---]
	2 F. M. Police **PC Imbrahim B. Mat. SC's Koming B. Hj. Ariffin** Killed on CT Ops. Kulai Perak. ---]

140

+	A S.E.P. led a Platoon of the Mancheser Regt. to 2 CT camps in the jungle understood to be camps used by the MRLA the **Leng- Kaus Protection Force** operating in the area. They were destroyed.---]
Tue. 18th	18 AG. Pd.L/Cpl. **Rattan Singh** F.M. Police Died by accident. Rifle range Kuala Kabu Bahru Selangor.---]
+	CT Camps have been found by Jungle Patrols in areas of Kedah, Selangor,Pahang, Perak , Johore, Negri Sembilam, all were destroyed.---]
Wed. 19th	Military & F.M Police on Patrol near Gunog Rapat engaged & Killed 4 CT's 6 miles South of Ipoh.---]
Thur. 20th	Singapore : After further talks with Sir. Malcolm Macdonald. Mr. Oliver Lyttelton left Singapore in an Argonaut Plane enroute to London.---
+	20/12/1951 LG 39387 p. 6053 The following awarded the George Medal PTE. AWAND ANAK RAWANG GM SARAWAK RANGERS A/T WORCS The following awarded te Colonial Police Medal CPL, MAHARUDDIN. B. UDIN CPM FEDERATION MALAYA POLICE PC BAHARUDDIN B. ALANG MAT HUSSIN CPM FEDERATION MALAYA POLICE The citation for Pte. Awand Anak Rawang reads: 'During a fire fight.The Worcestershire Regt. engaged with 50 CT's. The leading scout was killed along with their section Commander. Pte.Awand Anak Rawang. Sarawak Rangers. Was hit in the leg above the knees, another Worcestershire Soldier was hit below the knee, shattering the bone. Both were lying in the open surrounded by intense fire. Awang collected his and the wounded soldier's rifle and dragged him under cover. From there returned fire on the CT's. Awang was hit once again in the shoulder & with his other hand drew a hand grenade, pulling out the pin with his teeth. Threw it at the CT's who retreated. When after 40 minutes other reinforcements arrived -]
+	20 HMT LANCASHIRE sailed Liverpool bound for Singapore/ Hong Kong with replacement Service Personnel---]
+	20 HMT EMPIRE FOWEY arrived Southampton. with returning Service personnel---]
+	20 HMT EMPIRE HALLADALE sailed Liverpool for Singapore with replacement Service personnel---]
Fri. 21st	21 Cpl. **Mustaffa b. Ahmad** Malay Regt. Killed in Action Engaging CT's Pahang---]
+	21 HMT DUNERA sailed Southampton bound for Singapore with replacement Service personnel--]
Sat. 22nd	22 PC. **Abdul Karim B.Hadi.** F. M. Police Killed on Ops. Ruab Pahang---]
Sun. 23rd	London: Mr. Oliver Lyttelton arrived back in London to report back to Mr. Winston Churchill---]
+	23 HMT EMPIRE TROOPER arrived Southampton with returning Service Personnel---]
Mon. 24th	England Chequers Mr Winston Churchill studying Mr.Oliver Lytteltons Report on Malaya. Stated:- 'There was only one good thin, he had found in Malaya, which was the New Villages Plan instigated by Lt. General Briggs. During his tour he had been heavily guarded by armed escorts. Spoken with many officials of all races & creeds, including senior officers in the Army & R AF. Who advised him of the difficulty in finding the enemy in the jungles. Ideally suited to guerrilla warfare. Since the murder of Sir. Henry Gurney. The countries Administrative Office, had been in disarray with nobody in charge. The Chief of Police did not see eye to eye. With the Chief of Intelligence. The Planters were up in arms as were other Associations. His report painted a scene of despair, written by a man of integrity with his knowledge of military matters who had himself lived in Malaya during the thirties & recommended that one **Senior Supremo** be assigned the task. To bring the then current state of disarray into a workably state of affairs. Of new plans to defeat the Communist Terrorist in Malaya. Winston Churchill agreed with the report as it stood. 3 Names were discussed Montgomery., Vye. & Slim. For the job of Supremo. Also plans to be urgently put in place--]
+	The Manchester Regt. Killed 1 CT. in the Kulim area---]
Tue. 25th	25 LAC/Stomn. **H. Wormald.** R.A.F. Butterworth Died motor vehicle accident. *Western Road # 2142* George Town Penang---]
Wed. 26th	5 CT's were Killed over the Christmas period. 3 were Killed on Christmas Day by Security Forcesin the area of Ipoh near a river bank: 2 were Killed in the Bentong area of Pahang: 1 was Killed by a Patrol of the Royal West Kents on the Caladonian Estate---]
Thur. 27th	27 SC **Snusi B. Hassan** F. M. Police Killed on CT Ops. 6th. m/s Jalan/ Lombong Kota Tinggi Johore---]
Fri. 28th	28 LAC/Clk. **R. C. F. Cooper.** R.AF. Changi. Died climbing in Penang. *Western Road # 2143* George Town Penang ----]
+	28/12/1951 LG 39420 p. 6740 The following awarded the Colonial Police Medal SC. ABDUL. MOH. B. A. SAMAT. CPM FEDERATION MALAYA POLICE
+	28 HMT ASTURIUS sailed Southampton bound for Singapore via Panama Canal /Sydney ---]
Sat. 29th	

Sun. 30th Mon. 31st	**29 Mr. W. G. Hudson.** British Civilian Killed in CT ambush Died from gunshot wounds to the heads Johore Bahru Johore.---] **30 SC Jafar B. Abdul Hamid.** F. M. Police Yong Peng River Estate Kluang Johore.----] Operations *"Mermaid"*- *"Valiant"* *"Rebel"*- *"Sludge"*- *"Springtide"*- *"Rainbow* Ended ---]

R. A. F. OPERATION *'FIREDOG'* END OF YEAR STATISTICS 1951

No of Sorties	No. of Strikes	1,000 Lb.Bombs	500 Lb. Bombs	350 LbCluster	20 LbBombs	R/P's	20mm	.5 mm	.303mm
6,498	1,001	5,081	13,845	384	34,968	19,960	528,999	643,685	703,915

R. A. F. SUPPORT 1951

	Soties	Troops/Lift/	Casac	Pass/Lift	Supply Wt. Lbs	Leaflets drop (1,000)	B Flying Times No / hrs	Broadcsting No / hrs	Crashed
Air SupportA/C*	1239	/	/	/	3,164,744	/	/	/	Auster'sVX117
Auster**	/	/	/	/	/	/	/	/	VX115 VX114
Pioneer	/	/	/	/	/	/	/	/	VF500 VP648
H/C Light	'	/	/	/	/	/	/	/	VF630- VF647
848 Sqdn	/	/	/	/	/	/	/	/	VF551 VF 625
155 Sqdn	/		/	/	/	/	/	/	Brigand's
Target/MK**	/	/	/	/	/	/	/	/	VS838-
Vis/Air OBs**	/	/	/	/	/	/	/	/	RH811
Communication**	/	/	/	/	/	/	/	/	VS857
Leaf. Sorties*	255	/	/	/	/	'	/	/	Dakota
Leaflets Drop*	/	/	/	/	/	10,066	/	/	KN231
Leaf Sorties **	/	/	/	/	/	/	/	/	Spitfire
Leaflets Drop**	/	/	/	/	/	/	/	/	TP331
Broad Sorties*	/	/	/	/	/	/	/	/	Hornet
Broad Hrs *	/	/	/	/	/	/	/	/	WB870
Broad Sorties**	/	/	/	/	/	/	/	/	Dragonfly
Broad Hrs **	/	/	/	/	/	/	/	/	VF308
Photo RECCE***	1131	/	/	/	/	/	J	/	

* AirSupport A/C Dakota -Valetta- Hastings Bristol

** Auster

*** Photo Rec Anson,,Spitfire, Mosquito, Meteor, Pembrok

CHAPTER 10 – 1952

ROYAL AIR FORCE

OFFENSIVE AIR SUPPORT - OPERATION 'FIREDOG'
January 1952 to May 1957

Sqdn	Location	Aircraft Type	No	Date From	Year	Date To.	Year
33	Butterworth	Hornet 3/4	16	1st. Aug.	1952	31st. Mar.	1953
45	Tengah	Hornet 3/4	16	31st. Jan .	1952	31st. Mar	1955
48	Changi	Valetta C4	10	1st, Apr.	1952	1st. May.	1957

JANUARY

Tue.	1st	Operation *"Broderick"* Began against No 5 Regt. MRLA Kroh Chikos Forest Reserve ---]
	+	Operation *"Noah"* *"Techchi"* Began against No 5 Regt. MRLA Triang Bentong SW Pahang ---]
	+	Operation *"Pancake"* Began against No 8 Regt. MRLA Kedah ---]
	+	1/01/1952 LG # 39433 p.136 The following awarded the Distinguished Flying Cross
		F/LT. L. TEBBUTT. DFC ROYAL AIR FORCE
		F/LT. C.B.URWIN. DFC ROYAL AIR FORCE
		The following awarded the Distinguished Service Medal
		SGT. K.J. JACKMAN. DSM THE CAMERONIANS
		The following awarded the Colonial Police Medal
		HON/INSP. R.D. WILLIAMSON. CPM FEDERATION MALAYA POLICE
		SC TALIP B. SIAK KAYA. CPM FEDERATION MALAYA POLICE
Wed.	2nd	2 Rfn. Khimbahadur Pun. 2nd. King Edward VII's Own Gurkha Rifles. Died*** *Kluang # 3 / A – 4* Johore]
	+	2 S/C. Jasmany B. Yussof F. M. Police Killed on CT Ops. Terap area Kedah/Perlis---]
Thur.	3rd	3 SC. Tor Sai Lim. F. M. Police Killed on CT Ops. At the Sin Cheong Hin SC. Post Lahat Ipoh Perak---]
	+	The A/T Plt. Support Company Green Howards engaged in a fire fight with 7 CT's at Ker Halt. Area of Bukit Keru. Attempting to cross a swamp, became under fire from 7 CT's in position on a small overlooking hill. Fortunately the Plt. took evasive Action. Engaging CT's & encircled the CT's. During the ensuing gun fight 1 CT was Killed & another wounded, as they made their escape. It was later discovered that this group were the HQ unit of 6 Plt. MRLA. Sgt. Bishorek was awarded the BEM (Military) for his leadership.-----]
Fri.	4th	4 Pte. P. A. Whitmore. 1st. Battn. The Queen's Own Royal West Kents Regt. Died Transport Veh. Acc. *Kuala Lumpur # 19 / 1063* ---]
	+	4 F/Off. T. R. Woods. 80 Sqdn R.A.F. Reported missing. When in his Hornet WB 900 went missing 90 miles East of Seletar *[No known Grave] Terandak Wall Memorial Malacca]*---]
Sat.	5th	5 Pol/Lt. J.G. Quick. F. M. Police Killed on CT Ops. Died from gunshot wounds in Batu Sawah Kuantan Pahang. *Kuala Lumpur # 367* ---]
Sun.	6th	6 SC Sgt. Yakob b. Yussof. F. M. Police Killed Engaging CT's on CT Ops. Kuan Pahang---]
Mon.	7th	7 SC Tasar B. Sastro. F. M. Police Killed in CT ambush Kepong/Rawang Rd ---]
	+	7 HMT EMPIRE ORWELL arrived Singapore enroute to / Hong Kong with replacement Service personnel]
Tue.	8th	8 SC Mohd. B. Kahar. F. M. Police Killed in CT ambush on CT Ops. Sungei Taho EstateTapah Perak---]
	+	8 HMT EMPIRE ORWELL sailed Singapore enroute to Hong Kong with replacement Service personnel]
Wed.	9th	9 8 F. M. Police Sgt. Mohd. Ali B. Sudin. - PC's Baharon B. Suraidi. – Malek B. Mohd, - SC 's Arshad B. Ibraham. –Tamg Ah Chong. – Sulaiman B. Yunas.– Chew Fui .- Razek B. Tarang Killed In ambuah by C.T's at the 31st. m/s Dagong Rd Kampar Perak.---]
	+	1 Plt. A Company Suffolk's engaged 2 CT's. Killed 1 wounding the other who escaped---]
Thur.	10th	10 Lt.'s N. Harris. – N. Marrris - T. Cooke. Asstn / Supt. G. E. Devon Pol/Lt. J.H. Thompson F. M. Police Killed during engagement with CT's on Ops. Johore *[Graves Unknown]*---]
	+	10 HMT ASTURIUS arrived Singapore from Suva on Board were the 1st. Battlion Fijian Regt. reinforcements for Malayan Command.---]
Fri.	11th	11 Sgmn. E. A. Moore Royal Signals Killed in Action Engaging CT's *Kranji Singapore # 2 /C / 14*---]
	+	11 Pte. Anak Talap Nyaru. Sarawak Rangers was Killed during a brief engagement with CT in dense jungle. the CT's broke off the engagement. *[No known GraveTerandak Wall Memorial Malacca]* ---]
	+	

		11 Hon. Insp. **P. R. Butler- Madden** F.M Aux. Police & Manager. of the Tanah Mersh Estate Killed in a CT
	+	ambush Port Dickson Negri Sembilan. _Seremban # ??_ Negri Sembilan ---]
		11/01/1952 LG # 39438 p. 262 The following awarded the Distinguished Conduct Medal
Sat.	12th	SGT/MAJ.D.M. MORGAN. DCM ROYAL MARINES
		A 4 man Patrol of the Green Howards in ambush position. Laid in waiting in the Bukit Batu area. Their
		patience was rewarded when 5 CT's appeared. Opening fire Killed 2, the other 3 escaped. For his
	+	leadership 2/Lt Harrop was later awarded the MC.(LG 24/06/1952)---]
		12 HMT EMPIRE FOWEY sailed Southampton bound for Singapore/ Hong Kong/Kure with replacement
Sun.	13th	Service personnel---]
		Kuala Lumpur: Being the results of Mr. Oliver Lyttelton's report on Malaya The resignations of 2 senior
		Police officials was announced:
		'Mr. W.N. Gray Police Commisioner for the Federation of Malaya &
Mon.	14th	_Sir. William Jenkin. Director of Inteligence'._ ---]
		14 6 F. M. Police **L/Cpl Noor Mohd. B. Tahir - PC Mohd. B. Abdul Kadir – Abdullah b. Kechil. SC's Norbi**
		B. Songah. – Idris B. Zainal – Wan Man B Wan Nek . In an ambush by CT's in the Sungei Siput area
	+	of Perak on the Hock Lian Estate. In the fierce fight 3 C.T's Killed. ----]
Tue.	15th	**14** HMT DILWARA arrived Southampton with returning Service personnel ---]
		15 LAC. G. Horsman. Nursing Attd.1 HQ FEAF R.A.F.Changi Killed motor transport accident.
	+	_Kranji Singapore # 4 / B – 8_ ---]
Wed.	16th	**15** HMT EMPIRE PRIDE sailed Liverpool bound for Singapore with replacement Service Personnel-
		London: In a press conference Mr. Oliver Lyttelton announced:
		'In succession to the late Sir. Henry Gurney. **General Sir. Gerald Templar.** _Is to become High_
		Commissioner for the Federation Of Malaya. With his expert knowledge as Director of military
		intelligence, would be a greatest value in Malaya. His expertise in dealing with delicate political
		problems. General Lockhart would continue as Deputy Director of Operations under General Sir. Gerald
		Templar. Mr Lyttelton also pointed out:
		General Sir. Gerald Templar would only be responsible for affairs in Malaya not Singapore where there
Thur.	17th	_was no threat from the Communist.'_ ---]
		On information from the Federation Police An ambush was laid by the 10th. Gurkhas in Karak's
		Chinese cemetery. It was the way Rubber Tapper workers took, when on their way to work. Rifleman
		Kanaksing Limbo, saw a line of the workers carrying latex buckets. Noticed that one was not, but saw a
		grenade was peeping out of the Tapper's shirt. He became suspiciuos. Immediately, took aim opened
		fire instantly Killed him. The Tapper a CT, was handed over to the Police for indentification. Who
		immediately stated: He was **Hoi Koi Meng,** the most wanted CT in the area, who had escaped many
Fri.	18th	ambushs laid by the 10th. Gurkhas . They had finally got their man---]
		18 A/Cpl. L. C. Ireland . (40 Commando) Royal Marine Killed during an attack on a C.T camp in S. Perak
	+	_Batu Gajah # E / 18_ Ipoh Perak ---]
		18 HMT EMPIRE WINDRUSH sailed from Southampton bound for Singapore/ Hong Kong with
Sat.	19t	replacement Service personnel ---]
		19 Mne. C. Alexander. (40 Commando) Royal Marines Died from Wounds recv'd previous day
	+	_Taiping # E / 19_ Perak.---]
	+	**19** HMT DUNERA arrived in Singapore with replacement Service Personnel ---]
Sun.	20th	**19** HMT EMPIRE HALLADALE arrived in Singapore with replacement Service personnel.---]
		20 Rfn. Bhaktabahadur Magar . 10th. Princess Mary's Own Gurkha Rifles. Died***
	+	_Kranji Singapore # 8 / C – 1_---]
	+	**20 Cfn. B. Hitchen.** R.E.M.E. Died*** _Kuala Lumpur # 19 / 1064_---]
		20 LAC. E. Jones. Eng/Mech. Far East Flying Boat Wing. R.A.F.Seletar Drowning accident.
	+	_Kranji Singapore # 4 / B – 7_---]
Mon.	21st	**20** HMT ASTURIAS sailed Singapore bound for Southampton with returning Service personnel---]
		A Patrol from the Training Wing Green Howards saw a CT crossing the Railway line The CT ran away &
		was shot dead. His body was found. The train to Tampin was stopped. The dead CT's body was loaded
		onto the train to take it to Tampin, there to be collected by the F.M. Police.---]
	+	**12** Plt 'D' Company Suffolk's. Patrolling in the Kuala Langat Forest Reserve engaged and Killed 1 CT ---]
	+	**21** HMT DEVONSHIRE arrived Singapore- with replacement Service personnel 1,500 African troops of
Tue.	22nd	the Nyasa & Kenya Infantry Battn.'s. arrived in Singapore--]
		22 Pol/Lt. A.E. Benson. F. M. Police Killed in Action Engaging CT's, while leading a Police party in Sendu
		Gopeng area. 3 CT's were also Killed. Pol/Lt.Benson was shot in the stomach by a CT sentry & died

	+	soon after. Colonel H. Montgomery Hyde. MP for Belfast, who was in Malaya & Mr. T.Q. Graffinkin CPO Perak. congratulated them for this success. *Batu Gajah # 458* Ipoh Perak.---]
		22/01/1952. LG # 39446 p. 459 The following awarded the Distinguished Flying Cross
		S/LDR. L.H. WILLIAMSON. DFC ROYAL AUSTRALIAN AIR FORCE
		p. 458 The following awarded the Distinguished Conduct Medal
		PTE J. L. PANNELL. DCM QUEEN'S OWN ROYAL WEST KENTS
		The following awarded the Military Medal
		L/CPL J.C. MARTIN. MM QUEEN'S OWN ROYAL WEST KENTS
		p. 456 The following awarded the Colonial Police Medal
Wed.	23rd	A/SUP. D.H.KENT. CPM FEDERATION MALAYA POLICE
Thur.	24th	23 HMT DUNERA sailed Singapore bound for Southampton via Penang with returning Service personnel]
	+	A composite Plt. Of the Mortar & M/C gun Comp. Green Howards came across 2 CT's. on a jungle path in the Tampin Forest Reserve. Both killed.---]
	+	12 Plt D Company Suffolk's Patrolling in the Kuala Langat Forest Reserve engaged and Killed another CT-]
Fri.	25th	Operation "*Pancake*" began. British, Gurkha & Malay troops carried out several anti C.T. raids in Sembilan, Kedah, & Pahang resulting in 12 C.T.'s Killed.---]
	+	A CT of the 5th. Independent Platoon MRLA surrendered to Police in Terap---]
		London: The Colonial Office announced:
	+	'Colonel A. Young. Commisioner of Police for the City of London would be the new Commisioner of the Federation of Malaya Police to carry out the reorganisation of The Federation Police Force.' ---]
Sat.	26th	25 HMT DEVONSHIRE sailed Singapore enroute to Hong Kong/Kure with replacement Service personnel]
	+	26 Aux.Pol/Insp. K .D.Harding F. M. Police & Manager. of the Lothian Estate Nilai. Was Killed when a landmine laid by CT's exploded. at Sepang Selangor *Seremban # ??* Negri Sembilan ---]
Sun.	27th	26 HMT EMPIRE HALLADALE sailed Singapore bound for Liverpool with replacement Service personnel]
	+	27 Capt. S. J. Huntley. Royal East Kent Regt.(The BUFFS) Died***_Kranji Singapore # 2/C -13_---]
	+	27 Pte. A. Jeeves. R.A.S.C. Killed on CT Ops. In aid of Civil Power.[*Ashes REP*]---]
Mon.	28th	A Combined Police / Military Screening of the inhabitants of Jujong, Sungei Koh & Terap resulted in the arrest of 21 persons: 15 Chinese males, 3 Chinese females & 3 Malay males---]
Tue.	29th	28 Tpr. J. F. Britnell. 9th./12th. Royal Lancers. Died***_Taiping # B / 54_ Perak.---]
	+	29 F. M. Police SC's Othman B, Abdullah – Ya'acob B, Mat Killed on Ops. Gunong Inis Selaman Perak-
		8 Plt 'C' Company Suffolk's Patrolling in the Ulu Klang Forest Reserve East of Kuala Lumpur engaged a number of CT's. During the fire fight 2 CT's were Killed. Lt. Pensotti. Pte's Johnston and Norwood were
	+	wounded ---]
Wed.	30th	29 HMT LANCASHIRE arrived in Singapore with replacement Service personnel.---]
	+	30 Tpr. J. Skillen. 13/18th. Queen's Royal Hussars Died*** _Kranji Singapore # 2 / A – 9_ ---]
Thur.	31st	30 HMT EMPIRE ORWELL arrived Singapore /enroute to Southampton with returningService personnel]
	+	31 L/Cpl. A. E. Morton-Jones. R. M. P . Died Motor. Veh. Acc. _Seremban # CE / 41_ Negri Sembilan---]
		31 2 F. M. Police Pol/Lt F.L. Bruce. SC Cpl. Ahmed B. Awang. Killed during engagement with CT's on the
	+	Wan Lee Hydraulic Mine Chemor Perak. *Batu Gajah # 557* Ipoh Perak ---]
	+	RAF Sqdn. 45 Hornet became operational RAF Tengah---]
		31 HMT LANCASHIRE sailed enroute to Hong Kong with replacement Service personnel.---]

FEBRUARY

Fri.	1st	Operations "*League*" -"*Puma –Noah*". Began against No 5 Regt. MRLA in Perak---]
	+	Operation " *Helsby*" Began against No 12 Regt. MRLA Headquarters Belum Valley N Perak 1st Para Drop many were injured jumping into high trees.---]
	+	Operation "*Pancake*". Began against No 8 Regt. In Kedah.---]
Sat.	2nd	2 Cpl. H. Holland 1st. Battn. Suffolk Regt. Died***. [*Ashes REP*]---]
	+	2 SC. Mohamd Sain B. Ahmed. F. M. Police Killed on CT Ops. Muar Johore---]
	+	2 SC. Jasmany B. Yussof. F. M. Police Killed on CT Ops. Terap Area Kedah/ Perlis---]
	+	2 Rfn. Birbahadur Rana. 10th. Princess Mary's Own Gurkha Rifles Died *** _Kranji Singapore # 8 / C -2_ -]
Sun.	3rd	3 Pte. E. Docherty. Argyll & Sutherland Highlanders. Died*** _Taiping # B / 55_ Perak---]
	+	3 Capt. J. Geddes. R.A.M.C. Att./Gordon. Higlamders Died***[*Ashes REP*]---]
	+	R. A. F. air strikes were carried out in the Relau Forest Reserve---]
Mon.	4th	4 WO/I. S. Vatabua. 1st Battn. Fijian Regt.Killed in Action Engaging CT's [*Ashes REP*]---]
	+	4 PC. Osman B. Hj. Menan. F. M. Police Died from wounds recv'd on Jan 31st. ---]

145

	+	4 HMT EMPIRE FOWEY arrived Singapore with replacement Service personnel---]
Tue.	5th	**England Sandringham : ANNOUNCED:** **'THE DEATH OF HIS MAJESTY KING GEORGE VI.'** **'HIS MAJESTY HAD DIED PEACEFULLY IN HIS SLEEP'**---]
	+	5 HMT EMPIRE FOWEY sailed Singapore enroute to / Hong Kong / Kure .---]
Wed.	6th	**6 Pte. H. C. Walker.** SP. Plt. 1st. Batn. Suffolk Regt. Killed in Action Engaging CT's it was during a combined force of 50 members of the F.M Police 2 Flights of the RAF Regt. (MOR's) and 3 Plt 'A' Comp Suffolk's in the first sweep 2 CT's were Killed. another was Killed on the second sweep of the area. *Kuala Lumpur-# 19 / 1065]*
	+	Auster AOP 6 VX925 656Sqdn. R.A.F. during a flight over Penang, force landed on a railway line? ---]
	+	A CT member of the 5th. Platoon MRLA Surrendered to a Police partrol. He admitted he had Killed a comrade in order to escape---]
	+	Another Plt:- 2 Plt 'A' Company Suffolk's Patrolling in the rubber near Jenderam engaged and Killed 1 CT. ---]
	+	6 HMT DILWARA sailed Southampton bound for Singapore with replacement Service personnel---]
Thur.	7th	**7 Cfn. F. J. Marles**. R.E.M.E.. Att/ Cameronians Died ***Kuala Lumpur # 19 / 1066---]
	+	7 SC Hussein B. Yahay F. M. Police Drowned on CT Ops. Sungei Endua Mersing Johore---]
	+	Kuala Lumpur: Lt/General Sir. Gerald Templer. flew into Kuala Lumpur to become High Commissioner of Malaya.---]
Fri.	8th	**London: Princess Elizabeth whilst on her honeymoon with Prince Phillip was pronounced** **'QUEEN ELIZABETH THE II'**---]
Sat.	9th	**9 Mr. M. Lesse** British civilian Killed by CT's---]
Sun.	10th	10 HMT EMPIRE PRIDE arrived Singapore with replacement Service personnel.---]
	+	10 HMT ASTURIAS arrived Southampton with returning Service personnel---]
Mon.	11th	**11 Mr. R.D. Harrison.** Manager. of the Voulles Estate Tenang Johore. Killed by CT's.---]
	+	11/02/1952 LG # 39467 p. 866 The following awarded the Military Cross LT. D.C TYSON MC THE WORCESTERSHIRE REGIMENT. The following awarded the Military Medal SGT. R.G. FOWLER MM THE SUFFOLK REGIMENT.
Tue.	12th	**12 Asst. Supt. R.H. Jesse.** F.M. Aux.Police & 3 Police Constables (**_unnamed_**) were Killed by C.T's in a car ambush, in the Jerum Area Kuala Selangor *Kuala Lumpur # 374* .---]
	+	12 2 F. M. Police **SC's Hashim B. Mohd. Ali.** –**Sulaiman B. Hj. Abdul Rahman** Killed on CT Ops. Merbua Estate Selangor---]
	+	Plt. 'D' Company Green Howards ambushed 3 CT's. Killed 2, hitting the 3rd. who went into the jungle never to be found, assumed died of his wounds. 1 of the CT's was identified as *Ghani* with a price on his head of $10,000.---]
	+	12 HMT DUNERA arrived Southampton with returning Service personnel---]
Wed.	13th	**13 Capt. R. D. Duff.** 1st. Battn. Gordon Highlanders. Killed by accident. *Kuala Lumpur # 20 / 1105* ---]
	+	Kuala Lumpur :Air-Vice Marshal G. H. Mills. Became Air Officer Commanding Malaya ---]
Thur.	14t	14 HMT LANCASHIRE arrived Singapore from Hong Kong / Sailed 14th. bound for Liverpool with returning Service personnel---]
Fri.	15th	**15 Pol/Lt. A.J. Brosnan.** F. M. Police Killed on Ops. on the Sapuloh Estate Paloh near Kluang Selangor *Kranji Singapore # 8 / C – 8* ---]
	+	15 HMT EMPIRE PRIDE sailed Singapore bound for Liverpool with returning Service personnel---]
Sat.	16th	**16 Spr. Zainal Bin Abd. Latif.** Royal Engineers (MOR) Died *** *Claimed by next of Kin*---]
	+	**16 SC. Samion B. Zainal** F. M. Police Killed on Ops. Kampas Estate Paloh Johore---]
	+	**16 PC. Bahron B. Wan Teh.** F. M. Police Killed on Ops. Kalumpang Village Selangor.---]
	+	16 HMT EMPIRE TROOPER sailed Southampton bound for Singapore with replacement Service personnel]
Sun.	17th	**17** An Ambush on a Rubber Estate 53 miles South of Ipoh 1 Officer & 7 Soldiers of the The Gordon Highlanders were Killed In Action Engaging CT's. **2/ Lt.. K. S. Rose.-. Pte's. J. H. Fairgrieve.- J. S. MacKenzie.- K. W. Wrght**. *Taiping # E / 21 – 22 – 24 - 26*---] **L/Cpl. Learmouth. - A. Newlands - J. Nutt. T. Wright** [*Ashes REP*]---]
	+	**17 Rfn. P. J. Foley.** Royal Ulster Rifles. Killed on Ops. [*Grave unknown*] *Terandak Wall Memorial Malacca* -]
	+	17 HMT EMPIRE WINDRUSH arrived Singapore with replacement Service personnel---]
Mon.	18th	**18 SC. Mat Sap B Mhd, Jai** F. M. Police Killed on CT Ops. Kelapa Bali Estate Tampin/Gemas Rd---],
Tue.	19th	**19** 3 F. M. Police **PC. Abdullah B. Kamad.- Kamarudin. B. Chee.- Mat.Desa B. Yeop**. Killed in CT ambush on Ops. near Kuantan. ---]
Wed.	20th	**20** 2 F. M. Police: **PC's Manan B. Fakir.- Mohd. Noor B. Mohd**. Killed in an ambush Ruab Pahang---].

Thur.21st	+	20 HMT EMPIRE WINDRUSH sailed Singapore enroute for Hong Kong ---]
		21 Sgt. R. J. Gratton. Nav. 45 Sqdn R.A.F. was Killed when Mosquito RR290 port wing broke off crashed into sea 24 miles West of Tengah the Pilot Sgt. Holden - Rushworth. bailed out survived.
	+	*Kranji Singapore # 4 / C – 1]*]
		21 HMT EMPIRE ORWELL arrived Southampton with returning Service personnel---]
Fri. 22nd		22 3 F. M. Police SC's Mohamed B. Awang – Ismail B. Limbo. – Sariman B.Keromotinoyo Killed on CT Ops. 10th. m/s Jalan Kulai Johore.---]
	+	22 HMT EMPIRE HALLADALE arrived Liverpool with returning Service personnel---]
Sat. 23rd		23 PC Hassam B. Mohd. Zain F. M. Police died from wounds recv'd on 21st.during an ambush---]
Sun. 24th		24/02/52 LG ? P The following awarded the George Medal
		SC. ABU HASSAN BIN MOHD ZAIN. GM- FEDERATION MALAYA POLICE
Mon. 25th		25 5 F. M. Police PC's Ahmad B. Johari.- Wan Selleh B. Wan Ismail.- Loo Thye Lim.- Abd. Rhman B.Che Ali.- Haron B. Ismail. Killed on Ops. Tanjong Malim Perak---].
Tue. 26th		26 SC. Yussof B. Suki F. M. Police Killed on CT Ops. Rengan Johore---]
	+	26 HMT EMPIRE FOWEY arrived Singapore with replacement Service personnel---]
	+	26 HMT EMPIRE FOWEY sailed Singapore bound for Southampton with returning Service personnel---]
Wed. 27th		27 Pol/Lt. R.H. Newson F. M. Police Killed Engaging CT's on CT Ops. Died from gunshot wounds Shock & haemorrhage Kolam Air Lane.Johore *Kranji Singapore # 18 / C -5* ---]
Thur. 28th		28 Pte. E. F. Buckley. 1st. Battn. Manchester Regt. Killed accidentally.
		Western Road # 2144 George Town Penang ---]
	+	28 Rfn. H. McGlinchie 1st. Battn. Cameronians. Died*** Awat Segamat Johore.*Kranji Singapore # 2 / A – 8*]]
	+	28 SC. Ahmad B. Ali. F. M. Police Killed on CT Ops. Kluang Area Johore---]
	+	28 SC. Yin B. Mat Isa. F. M. Police Killed CT ambush on Konsang Timah Resettlement Camp Batu Gajah Perak---]
Fri. 29th		29 SC. Said B. Sakariah. F. M. Police Killed on CT Ops. Bedak Mati Sungei Bakap Province Wellesley.---]
	+	'C' & 'D' Company Green Howards was involved in an ambush. returning from another Patrol. Pte. Johnson the driver of the scout car, finally got his Scout Car over the fallen tree. Whilst Mr.Harradine a Planter who had been given a lift in the Scout Car, returned fire with the mounted Bren gun, keeping the CT's at bay. For their courage Pte. Johnson was MID & Mr. Harradine was awarded the George Medal.---]
	+	29 Mr. D. A. Lees. a British consulting engineer. Aux.Hon/Insp. L.A. Murray- Lease. (Perak Aboriginal Auxilliary Constabulary) SC Aminudin B. Abd, Manap. F. M. Police Killed in C.T's ambush on the Heawood Estate Rubber / Tinnear Sungei Siput *Batu Gajah # 483* Ipoh Perak .---]
	+	29 SC Ahmed B. Rashim F. M. Police Killed on Ops. Sungei Bakap Provice Wellesley ---]
		Operation *"Noah" "Techchi"* Ended.---]

MARCH

Sat. 1st		1 Sgmn. Tejbahadur. Gurung Gurkha Signals Died*** Kuala Lipis area *Kuala Lumpur # 27 / 3*---]
	+	PC. Ismail B. Busu. F. M. Police Killed Motor Veh Acc. Ipoh / Kuala Kangsar Rd. Perak---]
	+	Operation 'Grease' began SAS against the MRLA ---]
Sun. 2nd		2 REM 2. R.W. Rutherford. Royal Navy. H.M.S. 'ST. BRIDES BAY.' Went Missing from recreational party In Malaya . Presumed dead. *[No known Grave Terandak Wall Memorial Malacca]*---]
Mon. 3rd		3 Mr. R.K. Mylvaganam. Asian Manager. Layang Layang Estate. Killed by CT's.---]
	+	A Plt. 'B' Company Green Howards operating in the Rubber jungle edge of the Alor Gaga area engaged 2 CT's killed one of them, seriously wounding the other, who crawled away, assumed he died of his wounds in the jungle.---]
	+	Near Rampin Negri Sembilan. A train track was dynamited & the train derailed. A number of C.T's attacked the train 7 people were Killed (*unnamed*) & 15 injured. ---]
Tue. 4th		4 Maj. V. T. Champion De Crespigny. (Bart OBE) R.A.S.C.. Died*** *Kranji Singapore # 2 / E - 26*---]
	+	4 In an CT ambush 5 PC's were Killed.PC's Haron B. Ya'acob.- Omar B. Saamah,- Daub B. Idris.- Ali B. Mohammad.- Mamat B. Husin. F. M. Police Kula Krai District ---]
	+	4 HMT DILWARA arrived Singapore with replacement Service personnel ---]
Wed. 5th		Operation *"Crossbones"* began a joint Police / Military operation supported by No. 38 Sqdn R. A. F. located at Butterworth---]
	+	*Russia* : The Kremlin announced the death of JOSEF STALIN---]
Thur. 6th		6 Rfn. W. Ure. The Cameronians Killed In Action Engaging CT's Segamat Johore *Singapore*---]

Fri.	7th	**7 Sgt. A. J. Woods.** Far East Training Wing R.A.F. Whilst training to be a Pilot when his Hornet WB910 overshot the runway at Butterworth & overturned. He was Killed. _Western Road # 2145_ George Town Penang---]
	+	AusterT7 WE543 656 Sqdn Lost height on landing approach at Kuala Lumpur crashed.---]
Sat.	8th	**8 Sgt. E. H. S. Bryant.** 9th./12th. Royal Lancers. Died***_Taiping # E / 28_ Perak---]
	+	**8 Pte. K. Hiscox.** A driver of the 1st. Battn. Manchester Regt. was Killed accidently returning from a Patrol _Western Road # 2146_ George Town Penang ---]
	+	8 3 F. M. Police **Zainal B. Ibrahim.** Pc's **Sidek B. Muda.- Kamaruddin B.A. Rahman** Killed on Ops. Batu Pahat Johore.---]
	+	H.M.S. '_AMETHYST._' Having sailed 30 miles up the Sungei Perak river. Bombarded C.T camps in dense Jungle areas infested by C.T's. Follow up Ground forces discovered 17 C.T camps destroyed---]
Sun.	9th	**9 Mr. G.C. Stevens.** Resident Manager. Idris Hydraulic TinLtd. Perak. Accidently shot by an F.M. SC.---]
	+	'A' Platoon of the 1st Manchester Regt. found a C.T camp, occupied by approx 30 C.T's. in the jungle near Sungei Rambei area. 2 C.T's Killed. During the fire fight. Cpl Kirkham was wounded. The CT camp was destroyed.---]
	+	9 HMT EMPIRE WINDRUSH arrived Singapore from Hong Kong ---]
	+	9 HMT DILWARA sailed Singapore bound for Southampton sailed bound for Southampton with returning Service personnel---]
Mon. 10th		**10 Capt. J. P. Gray.** R.A.S.C.. Died***_Kranji Singapore # 5 / C -4_ ---]
	+	Auster AOP6 VX117 656 Sqdn AAC Overturned on force landing at Selengor.---]
	+	10 HMT EMPIRE FOWEY arrived Southampton with returning Service personnel ---]
Tue.	11th	11 3 F. M. Police. **Asst/Supt. V.H. Franks.** & **PC's Karim B, Tahir.- Hassan Bassari B. Endut. Of the** Jungle Squad were Killed in a gunfight with CT's. in the Kulim area Kedah In a follow up by the F.M.Police they engaged 8 CT's Killed 1 CT. wounding 3 C.T's. **V.H. Franks.** _Jalan Pertana #?_ George Town Penang]
	+	11 2 F. M. Police **SC Jamhary B. Mat. – Hairudin B. Ysin.** Killed on CT Ops. Between Kuala Kangsar / Sauk Perak---]
	+	11 HMT EMPIRE PRIDE arrived Liverpool with returning Service personnel ---]
Wed. 12th		**12 Rfn. Budhibahadur Rai.** 7th Duke of Edinburgh's Own Gurkha Rifles. Died Motor Veh. Acc. Kuala Pilah _Kuala Lumpur. # 26 / 5_ ---]
	+	**12 Pte. K. Kipkorir.** 3rd. King's African Rifles. Died*** _Kranji Singapore # 8 / C – 3_ ---]
	+	12 HMT EMPIRE HALLADALE sailed Liverpool bound for Singapore- / Hong Kong-with replacement Service personnel---]
	+	12 HMT EMPIRE ORWELL sailed Southampton bound for Singapore with replacement Service personnel--]
	+	12 HMT EMPIRE WINDRUSH sailed Singapore bound for Southampton with returning Service personnel]
Thur. 13th		**13 S/Sgt. W.D. Gay.** 656 Sqdn. Glider Pilot Regt. Killed when his Auster AOP 6 VF576 on approach to Kuala Besar Air strip spun into the ground _Kranji Singapore # 2 / D - 5_---]
	+	**13 Capt. R. M.Brown.** R. A. M. C. Died***_Taiping # E / 28_ Perak—]
	+	13 HMT LANCASHIRE arrived Liverpool with returning Service personnel---]
Fri.	14th	A CT **Chong Ah Chem** a member of the 5th Platoon MRLA. Surrendered at Nibong Tebal Police Station. Freely given information. He was disillusioned with his Platoon Commander who had his own members named as : **Phony Liew, Chai Fook Seng, Ooi Ah Yin, Bah Kiah, Ah Chat & Woh Seong.** All Executed---]
Sat.	15th	**15 PC. Katan B. Mohd.** F. M. Police Killed in CT ambush. Jerantut /Kuantan Rd. Pahang.---]
	+	**15 PC. Tuan Yahaya.** F. M. Police Killed on CT Ops. Krai District---]
Sun.	16th	**16 Pol /Lt. L.R. Mansfield** F.M.Aux.Police Killed on CT Ops. Engaging CT's Sungei Lembing area of Kuantan Pahang _Kuantan # ??_ Pahang ---.]
	+	16 HMT EMPIRE TROOPER arrived Singapore with replacement Service personnel ---]
Mon. 17th		**17 F/Sgt. Wojeichowski.** 60 Sqdn. R.A.F. Whilst on a night navigation exercise in Vampire WG871. went missing. Lost without trace presumed dead. _[No known GraveTerandak Wall Memorial Malacca]_---]
	+	**17 Sgt. Manbahadur.** 6th.Queen Elizabeth's Own Gurkha Rifles. Died***_Kranji Singapore # 8 / C -4_ ---]
	+	17 HMT EMPIRE TROOPER sailed Singapore for Hong Kong ---]
Tue.	18th	**18 PC. Sudin B. MD. Yumon.** F. M. Police Killed In Pengarang Police Station Johore---]
Wed. 19th		**19 Bdr. Ismail Bin Md. Moor.** Royal Artillery (MOR) Died ***_(Claimed by next of Kin)_ ---]
	+	19 HMT DUNERA sailed from Soutampton bound for Singapore/ Hong Kong with replacement Service personnel ---]
Thur. 20th		**20 Sgt. G. F. W. Couzens.** 80 Sqdn R.A.F. Flying Hornet WB907 crashed into the sea 1 mile of Staheli Point Hong Kong._[No known GraveTerandak Wall Memorial Malacca]_---]
Fri.	21st	**21 L/Cpl. D. MacDonald.** Royal Signals Killed in Action Engaging CT's._Kuala Lumpur # 19 /1067_ ---]

+	**21 Pol/Lt. E.J. Miller**. F.M. Aux.Police Killed during an ambush of two lorries carrying F.M. Police by about 30 CT's,in the Tras. Raub area of Pahang. For his gallant Action Engaging CT's. Pol/Lt. Miller was recommended for a medal _Ruab # ??_ Pahang —]	
+	A CT Ambush Killed 12 Public Works Department (PWD) men including a district officer & an engineer._(all unnamed_) ---]	
+	21/03/1952 LG # 39497 p.1609 The following Wrded the British Empire Medal (Military)	
	FLT/SGT. W.M. P. MEARS. BEM ROYAL AIR FORCE	
+	21/03/1952. LG # 39497 p.1610 The following awarded the Distinguished Service Order	
	S/LDR. G.C.UNWIN. DFC DS0 THE ROYAL AIR FORCE	
	The following awarded the Distinguished Flying Cross	
	F/LT. S. MILLS DFC. ROYAL NEW ZEALAND AIR FORCE	
	MAJ. D. P. D. OLDMAN DFC ROYAL REGIMENT. OF ARTILLERY	
	p. 1611 The following awarded the Distinguished Flying Medal	
	SGT. M. R. CLARKE. DFM ROYAL AIR FORCE	
	The following awarded the Military Medal	
	F/SGT. L. C. E. HARRIS MM ROYAL .AIR FORCE. REGIMENT.	
	The following awarded the Air Force Medal	
	SGT. J.C.DOWMAN. AFM ROYAL AIR FORCE	
	The following awaded the Colonial Police Medal	
	S/CPL. JAAFAR B. OSMAN CPM FEDERATION MALAYA POLICE	
	S/CPL. NG. KOON HWA CPM FEDERATION MALAYA POLICE	
Sat. 22nd	**22 Major. H.P. Chadwick**. East Yorkshire Regt. A/T Cameron Highlanders. Killed in Action Engaging CT's in ambush [_Ashes REP_]---]	
+	HMS '_AMETHYST_' sailed from Penang on her homeward journey back to the UK---]	
Sun. 23rd	**23 Pte. S. Lesukukwa**. 3rd. King's African Rifles. Killed in Action Engaging CT's _Kuala Lumpur #21 / 1116_--]	
Mon. 24th	A Platoon of The Manchester Regt. found a Camp in the Bongsu area of Kedah which had been vacated earlier that day. They began a search. Later that day they made contact with several CT's. In the ensuing fire fight 1 CT. Killed. It was close to darkness when the CT's withdrew. Several of the Platoon were slightly wounded ---]	
Tue. 25th	**25 Pte. K. Dinnen**. Royal Army. Dental. Corps. Died*** _Kuala Lumpur # 19 / 1068_ ---]	
Wed. 26th	**25 Mr. R. Codner. MC**. Asstn.Manager. District Officer Tanjong Malim. - **Tooh Eng Kiew** PWD Eng. were Killed including 12 men **(unnamed)** & 8 wounded including Mr.W.H. Fourniss. When 40 C.T's ambusded a repair working party, on their way to repair the pipeline damaged by C.T's at Tanjong Malim Perak /Selangor border---]	
+	Pol/Lt. I.P. Hyde & SC. Samion F. M. Police Awarded the GM for their gallant Action . During road ambush near Ruab Pahang.(LG 24/7/52 39609)---]	
Thur. 27th	RAF Planes dropped bombs on the area, close to the Pipeline where it was thought the CT's responsible for the ambush were located ---]	
Fri. 28th	**28 Mr. W.H.Fourniss** Ex. Eng. of Public Works died from his wounds recv'd the previous day.---]	
Sat. 29t	_Kuala Lumpur_.After the ambush at Tanjong Malim. Possibly information given by informers to CT's Lt/Gen Templer. Stormed into Tanjong Malim. Imposed a 22 hour curfew from Tanjong Malim to Trolak 18 miles to the North. No one could leave the area. Shops, would only be open for 2 hours a day. School was closed. Bus Services suspended. All would be reduced to half ration portions. (population 5,000) due to the recent rise in C.T activities in the immediate vicinity---]	
Sun. 30th	**30 Spr. Arbat Bin Haji Sen** Royal Engineers (MOR) Died *** _Claimed by next of Kin_.---]	
+	30 2 F. M. Police **SC Abdul Hamed B. Alang – Mohamed Abas B. Hj Taib**. Killed on CT Ops. Nam Fan Police Post Menglembu Perak.---]	
Mon. 31st	**31 Tpr. L.W. Hammond**. 13th./18th. Royal Hussars. Killed in Action Engaging CT's. _Kranji Singapore # 2 / D - 4_ ---]	
+	**31 Mr. L. J. Fitzgerald**. A British Capt. in the Penang Aux.Police & his Asstn.**SC. Baharom B. Yeop Mohamed**. Were Killed by C.T's in a road ambush on the Ayer Hill Penang _Jalan Pertana # ??_ George Town Penang—]	
+	**31 SC Manickal s/o Sinsamy** F. M. Police Killed Engaging CT's on the . Gapis Estate Padang. ---]	
+	31 HMT DEVONSHIRE arrived Singapore enroute to Liverpool with returning Service personnel sailed 31st.---]	
+	Operation '_Helsby_' Ended ---]	
+		

+	Kuala Lumpur: The Number of New Villages erected by the end of March 1952 was 410. Resettleing some 170,000 Persons. John Davis CBE. DSO. was appointed New Village Liaison Officer by Maj. Gen Templar---]

APRIL

Tue.	1st	Operation *"League"*. Began against No 5 Regt. MRLA In Perak & Selangor.---]
	+	Operation *"Hive"*. Began against No 2 Regt. MRLA In Negri Sembilan---]
	+	Operation *"Question"*- *"Ginger"*. & *"Service"* Began. A public relations operation between the civilians &
	+	Kuala Lumpur A letter in Malay, Chinese & Tamil. Signed by General Templer was delivered to every household in the area under curfew by the F.M. Police. Stating: *'If you are a communist. I do not expect you to reply.* *If you are not. I want you to. On this sheet of paper, provide as much information as you can. To help my forces catch the communist terrorist in your area. Signed General Templer.* The letters were distributed in evelopes & when completed to be placed in sealed boxes before being collected & delivered to General Templer---]
	+	1 HMT EMPIRE PRIDE sailed Liverpool bound for Singapore with replacement Service personnel--]
Wed.	2nd	Support Company. Green Howards Engaged & Killed 1 CT. ---]
Thur.	3rd	3 5 F.M. Malay Policemen were Killed in an ambush by C.T.'s in the Kuala Kraa area of Kelantan.names:
Fri.	4th	**Insp. Harun B. Ya'acob -Omar B Sa'amah – Daub B.Idria -Ali B.Mohammad -Kamat B. Husin---]**

	+	4/04/52 LG 39507 p 1879	The following awarded the British Empire Medal (Military)
		SGT. V. MACGOWAN. BEM	ROYAL MARINES
		p.1880	The following awarded the British Empire Medal (Military)
		QMS. T. LEONARDS. BEM	4th QUEEN'S HUSSARS
		QMS. R. W. GARDNER. BEM	ROYAL CORPS SIGNALS
		SGT.J.D.BLENKINSON. BEM	ROYAL ENGINEERS
		C/SGT. J.G. LEDINGHAM. BEM	THE BLACK WATCH
		W/O. W. O'NEILL. BEM	ROYAL ARMY ORNANCE CORPS
		SGT. T. WINNING. BEM	ROYAL ARMY SERVICE CORPS
		CPL. R.E. WEIGHELL. BEM	ROYAL CORPS SIGNALS
			The following awarded the Military Cross
		CAPT. L.H. JOLE. MC	ROYAL MARINES
		LT. M.G.R.M. DARWELL. MC	ROYAL MARINES
		CAPT. P.K. BRYCESON MC	THE CAMERONIANS
		CAPT. J. BARLOW MC	THE GREEN HOWARDS
		LT. J.C. CAIGER MC	THE EAST SURREY REGIMENT.
		2/Lt. F.A. GODFREY MC.	THE SUFFOLK REGIMENT.
		LT. (KGO) J. SUNWAR.MC	7th. DUKE OF EDINBURGH'S OWN GURKHA RIFLES.
			The following awrded the Military Medal
		SGT. J.S. AUBERIN.MM	ROYAL MARINES
		CPL P.L. SIMPSON. MM	ROYAL MARINES
		MNE P. E. DALE P.E.MM	ROYAL MARINES
		SGT. F. F. TURNER. MM	13/18th ROYAL HUSSARS.
		PTE. J. W. APPLEBY. MM	GREEN HOWARDS
		PTE P. GILMOUR. MM	SEAFORTH HIGHLANDERS
		SGT. B. PUN MM	2nd. KING EDWARD VII'S OWN GURKHA RIFLES
		L/CPL J. CHALE MM	6nd QUEEN ELIZABETH'S OWN GURKHA RIFLES
		CPL. D. LIMBU. MM	7th. DUKE OF EDINBURGH'S OWN GURKHA RIFLES
		CPL. P. SUNWAR .MM	7th. DUKE OF EDINBURGH'S OWN GURKHA RIFLES
		CPL. L. LIMBU MM	10th PRINCESS MARY'S OWN GURKHA RIFLES
		RFN. H. RAI. MM	10th PRINCESS MARY'S OWN GURKHA RIFLES
		SGT. I.B.H.TAHIR .MM	MALAY REGIMENT
		L/CPL. M.B. TOHID M.B.MM	MALAY REGIMENT

	+	4 HMT DILWARA arrived Southampton with returning Service personnel ---]
Sat.	5th	10 Plt. 'D' Company Green Howards. Lay in ambush position for three days & were rewarded for patience when an armed CT came along the track & was instantly Killed---]
Sun.	6th	**6 Rfn. W. Ure.** 1st Battn. Cameronians. Died*** *[Ashes REP]* ---]

	+	**6 Sgmn. H.A. Ellery** Royal Signals Died *** *Kranji Singapore # 2 / D -3* ---]
	+	6 HMT EMPIRE ORWELL arrived Singapore with replacement Service Personnel---]
Mon. 7ᵗʰ		The sealed voting boxes from Tanjon Malim, were delivered to General Templar in the presence of Senior representative from Tanjon Malim they were opened and counted.---]
Tue. 8ᵗʰ		8/04/1952 LG. # 39518 p. 2114 The following awarded the Military Cross
		2/LT. G.H. W. HOWLETT. MC THE QUEEN'S ROYAL WEST KENTS
	+	8/04/1952.LG # 39511 p.1958 The following awarded the Military Medal
		CPL.H THAPA. MM 6ᵗʰ. QUEEN ELIZABETH'S OWN GURKHA RIFLES
Wed. 9ᵗʰ		The results of the secret ballot in Tanjong Malim. Led to the capture of 30 Chinese Communist, mainly shop keepers of Tanjon Malim. The curfew restrictions imposed on March. 27ᵗʰ. was eased & the reduced portion of rice rations restored---]
Thur. 10ᵗʰ		**10 Pte. S. Kipkorir.** 3ʳᵈ. King's. African Rifles. Killed in acrion. *Kuala Lumpur # 21 / 1114*---]
	+	**10 Pte W.J. Lowday** 1ˢᵗ. Battn. The Queen's Own Royal West Kent Regt. Killed in Action Engaging CT's *Kuala Lumpur # 19 / 1071* --]
	+	10 HMT EMPIRE ORWELL sailed Singapore bound for Southampton with returning Service personnel---]
	+	10 HMT EMPIRE WINDRUSH arrived Southampton with returning Service personnel---]
Fri. 11ᵗʰ		**11 L/Cpl. K. Kiptebelio.** 3ʳᵈ. King's African Rifles, died from wounds.recv'd previous day *Kuala Lumpur # 21 / 1115]* ---]
	+	11 HMT EMPIRE HALLADALE arrived Singapore with replacement Service personnel / sailed for Hong Kong / Kure 11ᵗʰ.---]
Sat. 12ᵗʰ		**12 Capt. R.B. Tarleton.** The Black Watch R.H.R. Died***Kuala Lumpur # 19 / 1070*---]
	+	12 HMT EMPIRE FOWEY sailed Southampton bound for Singapore/ Hong Kong /Kure with replacement Service personnel---]
Sun. 13ᵗʰ		**13 Mr. J. Ward.** Manager. of the Kamuning Estate Sungei Siput Perak. Killed in a CT ambush Perak.---]
Mon. 14ᵗʰ		**14 PC's Karim B Tabir.** F. M. Police Killed on Ops. Sungei Dingin Kulim Kedah---]
	+	14 HMT DUNERA arrived in Singapore with replacement Service personnel enroute to Hong Kong 15ᵗʰ.-]
Tue. 15ᵗʰ		**15 Rfn. Padamsing Thapa** 6ᵗʰ. Queen Elizabeth's Own Gurkha Rifles Died*** BMH – *Kluang # 3 // A – 3*---] Johore---]
Wed. 16ᵗʰ		**16 SC. Hassam B. Jaafar** F. M. Police Killed on CT Ops. Sungei Ulah Estate Kulim Kedah---]
	+	Support Company Green Howards Killed a CT Sentry at a CT Camp.---]
Thur. 17ᵗʰ		**17 2 F.M. Police Pol/Lt. L.C. Cawthra.** F.M.Aux.P. **SC Abdul Majid B. Abdul Karim** Killed in CT ambush 15ᵗʰ.m/s Johore Bahru / Pontian Rd. Johore *Kranji Singapore # 8 / C -10* .---]
	+	12 Plt. 'D' Company whilst on Patrol encountered 2 CT's resting. Opening fire Killed both of them.---]
	+	Support Company Green Howards Killed 1 CT.---]
Fri. 18ᵗʰ		**18 Sgt. Bije Rai.** 10ᵗʰ. Princess Mary's Own Gutrkha Rifles. Died*** *Kranji Singapore # 8 / C - 5*---]
	+	**18 12 F. M. Police PC's . Mohd. Taib B, Tahir. – Ibrahim B. Ahmed.** Killed in CT ambush Simpang Pertang Durian Tipis Negri Sembilan.---]
Sat. 19ᵗʰ		**19 4 F. M. Police PC's Salleh B. Wok. – Ahmad B. Idris – Razili B. Dollah. Tuan Yahaya.** Killed in Motor Veh. Acc. Temerloh Pahang---]
	+	2 Plt. 'A' Company Green Howards Killed 1 CT. in the Alor Gajah Area who was identified as **Ah Fook** a notoriously local leader with a $ 10,000 reward on his head.---]
Sat. 20ᵗʰ		**20 Sgt. J. McGuire.** 1ˢᵗ Battn. Cameronians. Killed in an accident Segamat Johore [*Ashes REP*]---]
Sun. 21ˢᵗ		**21 SC .Mohamed B. Yussof.** F. M. Police Killed on CT Ops. Kuala Reman Estate Kuantan Pahang ---]
Mon.22ⁿᵈ		**22 W/O G.R. Tait.** Royal Australian Air Force Died*** *Taiping # ? ?* Perak ---]
Tue. 23ʳᵈ		**23 Cpl. V.E. Visagei.** Rhodesian Special Air Service Regt. was Killed in the area of the Cameronrn Highlands. When the Platoon came with a few yards of a CT camp, the CT's opened fire. Killing **Visagei** instantly. The rest of the Platoon engaged with the CT's, who after a short period retreated. The SAS troops found a large camp with the food still hot, obviously they had desturbed the CT's midday dinner. They enjoyed the hot meal before destroying the camp. Evacuating **Visagei's** body. *Kuala Lumpur # 19 / 1072* .--]
Wed. 24ᵗʰ		**24 Cpl. J. O'Sullivan.** Eng/Fit.48 Sqdn. R.A.F. Died***.*Kuala Lumpur # 10 - 1074*---]
		10 Plt. 'D' Company Green Howards Killed another CT with a price of $ 15,000 on his head. Identified as **Yau Ming.** By this time The CT's had Killed 1,250 Chinese, 221 Malays, 184 Indians & 89 British all unarmed & defenceless---]
	+	24 HMT EMPIRE TROOPER called Singapore for Southampton with returning Service Personnel---]
Thur. 25ᵗʰ		**25 L/Cpl. Abu Mansor b. Alang Ahmad** Malay Regt. Killed in Action Engaging CT's Batu Gajah Perak---]
	+	Soldiers of the Suffolk Regt. Killed 10 C.T's in different engagements One of the C.T's Killed was **Long Pin** Commander of the 1ˢᵗ. Regt. MRLA.---]

	+	25 HMT EMPIRE PRIDE arrived Singapore with replacement Service personnel---]
Fri.	26th	26 HMT DILWARA sailed Southampton bound for Singapore/ Hong Kong with replacement Service personnel]
Sat.	27th	27 Cpl. A. W. Bucknell. Royal New Zealand Air Force Died***[*Ashes REP*]---]
	+	27 Lt. (QGO) Rasbahadur Rai . 7th. Duke of Edindurgh's Own Gurkha Rifkes. Died from Wounds recv'd in ambush *Seremban # 38* Negri Sembilan ---]
Sun.	28th	28 SC. Zainal Abindin B. Hj. Baka F. M. Police Killed on CT Ops. Naa Estate Kuantan Pahang---]
Mon.	29th	29 Sgt. A. W. Bucknell. 1st. Battn. Fijian Regt. Killed in Action Engaging CT's [*Ashes REP*]---]
	+	29 Lt. P. W. Hunt. Intelligence Corps Died*** *Taiping # E / 31* Perak---]
	+	29 HMT DEVONSHIRE arrived Liverpool with returning Service personnel ---]
Tue.	30th	London The *DAILY WORKER* Newspaper published in England. Printed an article under the headlines :- "*THESE ARE NO FAKES*" Showing a picture of a Royal Marine holding the head of a decapitated Chinese Communist Terrorist. Insinuating: *That it was the practice by British Troops. To sever the heads of dead Communist Terrorist & bring them out of the jungle for Identification purposes. This was later denied in the House of Commons. With the answer. Although it did happen, it was not the practice of The British Soldiers, but carried out by the Dyak Head hunters, who were being used as trackers, in the search for Communist Terrorist. Due to the terrible jungle terrain & tropical conditions. The dead CT bodies could not be carried out for identification porposes]*
Wed.	31st	Kuala Lumpur: Lt/Gen Templar trebled the price on *Chin Peng's* head to $250,000 alive. if dead $120,000 others. Included *Au Tien Tsin, Chen Tien, Tsin Lee. An Rung* ----]
	+	Operation "*League*" - "*Puma*" "*Helsby*" Ended ---]

MAY

Thur.	1st	Operation "*Habitual.*" Began against No 8 Regt.MRLA In Pahang & Terengganu---]
	+	1 HMT EMPIRE PRIDE sailed Singapore bound for Liverpool with returning Service personnel---]
	+	1 HMT DUNERA arrived in Singapore bound for Southampton with returning Service personnel 1st. ---]
Fri.	2nd	2 Sgt. A. Wray, - Pte's. R.W. Porter. - F. L. Crosswaite. - W. Hartley of the Green Howards. Were Killed. When the truck they were travelling in, went out of control on a steep hill & crashed into a static water tank. *Seremban # RC / 66 - CE / 63 - 65 – 64* Negri Sembilan.---]
	+	2/05/1952 LG # 39531 p. 2569 The following awarded the Military Cross Lt. D. L. S. LANGLEY MC ROYAL MARINES 2/05/1952 .LG # 39534 p.2450 The following awarded the George Medal REC CONST. TAN SIEW. GM FEDERATION MALAYA POLICE SC. WA N AMRAN B. WAN MANAF GM FEDERATION MALAYA POLICE
	+	2 HMT EMPIRE ORWELL sailed Southampton enroute to Singapore / Hong Komg with replacement Service personnel---]
Sat.	3rd	3 Pte. M. Moulana. 3rd. King's African Rifles. Killed in Action Engaging CT's *Kuala Lumpur #19 / 1073* ---]
	+	3 2/Lt. J.H. P Broughton 9th./12th. Lancers Died*** [*Ashes REP*] ---]
	+	3 F/O. B.A.D. Cochrane. - Sgt. J.B. Armstrong. - Jn/Tech. C.J.A. Cox. 84 Sqdn. R.A.F. Killed when their Brigand RH755 in a rocket attack lost a wing & crashed 40 miles S.E .of Butterworth. *Kuala Lumpur #33 – 1255 1256 – 1257* ---]
Sun.	4th	3 F. M. Police L/Cpl. Omar B. Chik. SC's Abindin B. Sumi. – Abdul Rahman B. Mohamed. Killed in a road ambush on CT Ops. 71/2. m/s. Jemaluang Road Mersing Johore ---]
	+	4 HMT EMPIRE FOWEY arrived Singapore with replacement Service personnel enroute to Hong Kong / Kure sailed 5th.---]
Mon.	5th	Search parties of Troops found the wreckage of the crashed Brigand RH755, that crashed on the 3rd. In deep jungle in an area of North Perak. The 3 dead bodies of the crew were carried out for a Military burial. The plane was destroyed---]
Tue.	6th	6/05/1952 LG. # 39535 p. 2456 The following awarded the Colonial Police Medal L/CPL. PILAS. B. SILONG. CPM FEDERATION MALAYA POLICE SC. MOHD. DIN B, OMAR CPM FEDERATION MALAYA POLICE SC. MUSA B. KHAMIS. CPM FEDERATION MALAYA POLICE SC. DAVID NAGANALAI.CPM FEDERATION MALAYA POLICE AP. ISMAIL B. HJ. TAHIR. CPM FEDERATION MALAYA POLICE
	+	6 HMT EMPIRE HALLADALE arrived in Singapore ---]
Wed.	7th	London: In the House of Commons Colonial Secretary Mr. Oliver Lyllteton. Answered a question raised by MP Mr. Awbury:

	'Whether he had any statement to make regarding the severing of heads in Malaya?' **Mr. Lyttleton** confirmed:
	'The photo shown in the Daily Worker was genuine, which happened in April 1951 (the previous year) When a jungle Patrol was ambushed by CT's. The British Officer & Corporal were Killed & two members of the Patrol badly wounded. One bandit was shot dead. After the CT's had retreated. A Tribesmen. Not a Royal Marine decaptitated the body. The head was brought out of the jungle for identification by the Police authorities---]
+	7 HMT EMPIRE HALLADALE sailed Singapore bound for Liverpool with returning Service personnel ---]
Thur. 8th.	**8 Rfn. Gangaman Rai .** 7th. Duke of Edinburgh's Own Gurkha Rifles. Died by Accident Near Sikamat Camp *Seremban # 37* Negri Semilan---]
+	**8 Maj. G. O. Herbert**. South Lancashire Regt. Died***.*Kranji Singapore # 2 / D -2*---]
Fri. 9th.	**9 WOII. A. W. Kirk.** R.E.M.E.. Died***.*Kranji Singapore # 2 / D -10*---]
+	**9 Pol/L. t. D. Wed.gewood.** F M.Police Killed on CT Ops. At Daong Kuala Terengganu. *Kota Bahru J / ??* -]
+	A leading CT in the Tampin area **Chin Ah Ming** together with his wife **Mee Chun** surrendered to the Green Howards. He was to provide valuable information on the CT' in that area.---]
Sat. 10th	**10 Cpl. S. J. Bailly.** 1st. Battn. Suffolk Regt. Killed in Action Engaging CT's *Kuala Lumpur # 19 / 1075*---]
+	**10 L/Cpl. K. Moso.** 3rd. King's African Rifles. Killed in Action Engaging CT's *Kuala Lumpur # 21/ 1113* ---]
+	**10 Major J. Black** Royal Engineers Died*** *Kranji Singapore # 2 / D – 11* ---]
Sun. 11th	**11 Trp. A. Fergus.** Royal Ulster Rifles Att/ 22nd. S. A. S. Died *** *Kranji Singapore # 2 / D -9* ---]
+	**11 Mr. W. A. Puddlecombe.** Asstn. Manager. of the Sepang Estate near Sungei Pelak was Killed in an ambush by 20 C.T's---].
Mon. 12th	**12 Gnr. Kulshak Bin Ku Ahmad** Royal Artillery (MOR) Died***.*Claimed by next of Kin*---]
+	**12** 3 F. M. Police A/P **Mr. R Berling.** F. M. Police & Aastn. Man. & FM. Aux. P.olice Insp . **SC. Yassin B. Moharam** .- **Kassim B. Awang**.. Were Killed while on anti Communist Duties on the Telok Sengat Estate Gentong Kota Tinggi area of Johore. [*Graves Unknown*]---]
Tue. 13th	**13 Cpl. Shanmugham (Kennedy)** A. S. Royal Signals (MOR) Died*** *Claimed by next of Kin*] ---]
Wed. 14th	**14** 7 Plt. 'C' Company Green Howards Killed 2 CT's in the Ayer Kuning area. One of the two dead CT's was identified as **Ah Wah**---]
Thur. 15th	A Platoon of the 5th.Malay Regt., Killed a CT identified as **Ah Lik.** In the Kroh area.--]
Fri. 16th	16/05/1952 LG 39542 p. 2653 The following awarded BAR to the Distinguished Flying Cross W/CDR. H.A. CONAGHAN. DFC+BAR ROYAL AUSTRALIAN AIR FORCE
	p. 2651 The following awarded the George Medal CPL. H.FOSTER. GM. LANCASHIRE FUSILIERS
	The following awarded the British Empire Medal (Military) PTE. G. HAMILTON. BEM. ROYAL MILITARY POLICE FUS. J.E. MYERS. BEM LANCASHIRE FUSILIERS
Sat. 17th	} Combined Operations continued throughout Malaya---]
Sun. 18th	**18 Pte. T. Kelly.** 1st Battn. Manchester Regt. Killed in Action Engaging CT's. [*Ashes REP*]---]
Mon. 19th	**19 SC Mohamed B. Ismail** F. M. Police Killed on CT Ops. Lunok Bongor Kuala Krai Kelantan.---].
Tue. 20th	**20 Rfn. Ranbahadur Gurung .** 7th. Duke of Edindurgh's Own Gurkha Rifkes. Died from Wounds recv'd Coy Camp area South Johore. *Seremban # 45* Negri Sembilan---]
+	20 HMT EMPIRE TROOPER arrived Southampton with returning Service Personnel---]
Wed. 21st	**21** In the South Gemas Forest Reserve. A Patrol of 'D' Company Green Howards on Patrol engaged 3 CT's. Killed 3. During the fire fight **Pte. Alcock** a Dog handler received fatal wounds & died later in the ambulance. *Seremban # CE / 68* Negri Sembilan---]
+	**21 Mr. A Nicholl.** Manager. Belata River Estate Kerling Selangor. & **SC Mat. B, Busoh** F. M. Police Killed by CT's. Months later, Mr.Nicholl's revolver was recovered on the body of **Ah Chee.** N.Selangor Terrorist Leader.---]
+	Acting on information from a young Chinese girl who had been approached by a CT on a Rubber Estate A Combined Patrols of 'D' & Support Companies Green Howards encircled a cave. The CT's inside opened fire, then the exchange of fire bought 4 CT' running in all directions. 2 CT's were Killed 1 CT, a man identified as **Ah He** & I Female CT **Peck Ha.** 1 CT was wounded in the exchange but escaped with the other one assumed as **Chong Ping.** For her betrayal the Chinese Girl was later Killed by **Chong Ping**---]
+	21 HMT EMPIRE ORWELL arrived Singapore enroute to Hong Kong with replacement Service personnel]
Thur.22nd	**22 PC Ahmed Shahar.** F. M. Police Killed on CT Ops. Perak.---]
+	**22 SC Ajat B. Alok.** F. M. Police Killed on CT Ops. Bukit Tinndal Phang.---]
+	**22 Mr. Lim Oo Lee.** A leading Chinese Rubber Merchant was Killed by C.T's on his Bukit Minyak Estate.---]

	+	A Patrol of the Manchester Regt. captured a Sakai CT, in possession of a shotgun identified as **Ah Sin** he was handed into the Police and later charged & sentenced to Death---]
	+	22 HMT DILWARA arrived Singapore with replacement Service personnel enroute to Hong Kong 22nd.-]
Fri. 23rd		'C' Company Patrol 10th. Gurkhas whilst on Patrol in the Sungei Lembing area. Came across a CT The leading Scout Killed the CT.. Continuing forward came under fire and charged to find themselves in a CT camp with accommodation for 15 CT's, who had already fled. Leaving packs & rations. The dead CT was identified as a high ranking CT **Manap Jepun** who had a price of $75,000 on his head. The Commander of the 10th (Malay) Communist Regt. ---]
Sat. 24th		24 2 F. M. Police **Pol/Lt. A.R. Frazer.** F.M.Aux.Police **PC. Mohamed.** Killed on Ops. Kulai Johore. *Kranji Singapore # 8 / D – 1* ---]
Sun. 25th		25 **PC. Ali B. Salleh** F. M. Police Killed Engaging CT's on CT Ops. Tekka mlne Perak---]
	+	25 HMT EMPIRE PRIDE arrived Liverpool with returning Service personnel.---].
Mon. 26th		26 **Tpr. R. Hall** 13/18th. Royal Hussars. Died by accident. *Kuala Lumpur # 20 / 1076* ---]
	+	26 HMT EMPIRE FOWEY arrived Singapore Roads Bound for Southampton with returning Service personnel 26th.---]
Tue. 27th		A support Company of the 10th. Gurkhas. Killed 2 CT's near the Jabor Valley Estate the rest fled.---]
Wed. 28th		28 HMT LANCASHIRE sailed Liverpool for Singapore with replacement Service personnel.---]
	+	28 HMT DUNERA arrived Southampton with returning Service personnel---]
Thur. 29th		The same Support group of Gurkhas caught up with the CT's engaged on the 25th. & Killed 1 CT---]
Fri. 30th		30 **L/Cpl. J. McInnes.** 9th/12th. Royal Lancers. Died ***Kuala Lumpur # 20 / 1077* ---]
	+	The same Support group of Gurkhas, having chased the CT's. Killed another 2 CT's---]
	+	30/05/1952.LG #39554 p.2951 The following awarded the Distinguished Conduct Medal
	+	CPL. P THAPA. DCM 6th QUEEN ELIZABETH'S OWN GURKHA RIFLES
		The following awarded the Military Medal
		RFN. L. GURUNG.MM 6th QUEEN ELIZABETH'S OWN GURKHA RIFLES
		RFN T. ROKA .MM 6th QUEEN ELIZABETH'S OWN GURKHA RIFLES
Sat. 31st		Operation *'League'* Ended ---]

JUNE

Sun. 1st		Operation *"Phantom"* Began A joint operation of Air & Ground forces---].
	+	1 7 F.M. Malay Policemen out of a Platoon of 14 were Killed, when they ran into an ambush of about 50 C.T's in position at the 31/2. m/s Kamrat Pulai Tin Mine Estate near Ipoh.named as- F. M. Police, **SC's Hussein B. Ahmed. – Abdullah B, Ayob.- Abu. B. Sultan Sallah. – Salleh B. Ajim. – Chen Ah Hong. – Abdul Rani B. K. Salleh. -Azri B. Baki.** –. After heavy fighting the C.T's retreated to the jungle leaving behind 2 dead CT's. ---]
Mon. 2nd		2 HMT DUNERA sailed Southampton bound for Singapore/ Hong Kong with replacement Service personnel]
Tue. 3rd		3 **Maj. A. J. D. McDonald.** 1st. Battn. Cameronians. Died***[*Ashes REP*]---]
	+	3 **Maj W. Shaw** Queen's Own Cameron Highlanders Died*** *Seremban # RC / 69* Negri Sembilan---]
	+	3 **Cfn. L. M. Gallacher.** R.E.M.E.. Died****Kuala Lumpur # 2 / 1078*---]
Wed. 4th		Auster VF602. 656 Sqdn. R.A.F. Flew into trees near Taiping. Sgt. J. Roley. Glider Pilot Regt.and passenger A/Supt. D. Lockinton F. M. Police Both escaped unharmed.---]
	+	4 HMT DEVONSHIRE sailed Liverpool bound for Singapore/ Hong Kong with replacement Service personnel-
Thur. 5th		5 HMT EMPIRE HALLADALE arrived Liverpool with returning Service personnel---]
Fri. 6th		6 **F/Lt. D. B. Stebbing.** 91 Sqdn. R.A.F. Regt. Killed during C.T .engagment *Kuala Lumpur # 20 – 1079*--]
	+	6/06/52.LG # 39565 p. 3120 The following awarded the Military Medal
		CPL. KHATRI B. MM 6th QUEEN ELIZABETH'S OWN GURKHA RIFLES
Sat. 7th		7 **Mr. M. Thomanson Manager.** of the Johore Labis Estate Johore. Killed.---]
Sun. 8th		8 HMT DILWARA arrived Singapore sailed for Southampton with returning Service personnel 8th —]
Mon. 9th		9 **Pte. J. Grady.** 1st Battn. Manchester Regt. Killed in an ambush in the Sungkei area S.Tapah. *Taiping # / 57* Perak---]
Tue. 10th		In two attacks in different parts of Malaya. In the Segamat area of Johore. C.T's Killed 4 Chinese. They tied one Chinese man to a tree then stabbed him to death. Took another 4 away & murdered them. 2 were women Whilst in the Kuantan area of Kelantan. C.T's mined a road & blew up a truck, injuring 14 people including children.---]
Wed. 11th		11 **Pol/Lt.C.E.A. Bates.** F.M. Police Motor Killed vehicle accident on the Sg. Lenbing road *Kuantan # ??* Pahang---]

	+	During raids in the Grik area of N Perak. Gurkha troops Killed 6 senior CT Commanders of the MRLA. amongst those Killed were **Lau Chan** Political Commissar & **Ah Pinh** Commander of the 12th Regt. MPLA **Chin Nam Fook** Group Secretary of the Min Yuen & most notorious of the Tampin District.---]
	+	A S.E.P. Was prepared to lead the M & M/G Plt. & Support Company Green Howards to a camp high up in the Tampin Forest reserve. Where they engaged the CT's. killing 6 namely: **Chong Ping** - **Chin Kong** - **San Moi Kow Ming** - **Wong Koi** - **Kow Foo** & **Lam Kwai**. Arms & ammunition found were handed over to the F.M. Police. **Chong Ping** was identified as the CT. who earlier had assassinated the young Chinese girl who had informed where their cave was---]
Thur. 12th		The Support Company of the 10th. Gurkhas came across a lone CT. Killed him. He was identified as a Min Yuen Courier ---]
	+	'C' Company 10th. Gurkhas on another separate Patrol Killed 1 CT---]
	+	Kuala Lumpur: Major General Sir. Hugh Stockwell. Became General Officer Commanding Malaya --]
	+	Kuala Lumpur: Air Marshal A. C. Sanderson Became Air Officer Command Far East Air Force---]
	+	12 HMT EMPIRE ORWELL arrived Singapore with replacement Service personnel---]
Fri. 13th		**13 Rfn. Lalbahadur Rai .** 10th. Princess Mary's Own Gurkha Rifles. Died South Terengganu Jungle *[Grave unknown] Terandak Memorial Malacca.*---]
	+	13/06/1952 LG.# 39571 p. 3234 The following awarded he Colonial Police Medal INSP.WONG YOK CHEE. CPM. FEDERATION MALAYA POLICE
	+	13 HMT EMPIRE ORWELL sailed Singapore enroute to Hong Kong /Pusan ---]
Sat. 14th		A Platoon of the Green Howards attacked a C.T H.Q. camp in dense jungle near Tampin Negri Sembilan & Killed 7 C.T's, capturing several others.---]
Sun. 15th		**15 SC. Jom B. Abu.** F. M. Police Killed CT road ambush CT Ops. 31/2. m/s Johore Bahru/ Ayer Hitam Road Johore---]
Mon. 16th		**16 SC Mohamed B. Yob Mat Sach** FM.P. Killed on CT Ops. Kuala Kuang New Village Chemor Perak.---]
	+	A Platoon of the Manchester Regt. Killed 1 CT---]
	+	16/06/1952 LG 39542 p. 2653 The following awarded BAR to Distinguisded Flying Cross W/CDR. H.A, CONACHAN. DFC +BAR ROYAL AUSTRALIAN AIR FORCE 16/06/1952 LG 39542 p. 2651 The following awarded the George Medal CPL. H. FOSTER. GM THE LANCASHIRE FUSILIERS The following awarded the British Empire Medal (Military) PTE. J.E. MYERS. BEM THE LANCASHIRE FUSILIERS PTE. G. H. BROWNE BEM ROYAL MILITARY POLICE
Tue. 17th		17 /06/1952 LG # 39571 p. 3234 The following awarded the Colonial Police Medal L/CPL. A.B. BIN OTHMAN CPM FEDERATION MALAYA POLICE
	+	17 HMT EMPIRE FOWEY arrived Southampton with returning Service personnel---]
Wed. 18th		18 HMT EMPIRE PRIDE sailed Liverpool bound for Singapore/ Hong Kong with replacement Service personnel---]
Thur. 19th		**19 Pte. T. Arands., Pte. W. M. Baillie., Pte. M. Harrison., Pte.R. H. Smith., Pte. T. Traynor.** 1st Battn. Manchester Regt. were Killed. During a near perfect C.T ambush led by **Pak Lam** LDCS C.T's in the Tanah Rata area of the Cameron Highlands. Including L/Cpl E. Nicholas. Ptes. T. Mc Kibbon & S. King were wounded. A Malay Policeman **Insp. Din Bin Ibrahim** F. M. Police & a civilian **(_unnamed_)** were also Killed- *Taiping # B / 58 – E / 34 – 35 -33 B / 59* Perak.... Pte. F. Mrozek for his Gallantry was awarded the M.M. (27/10/195 LG 40000) ---]
Fri. 20th		20/06/1952 LG 39678 p. 3397. The following awarded the Colonial Police Medal POL/INS. H.R MAUDSLEY..CPM FEDERATION MALAYA POLICE INSP. WANG YOH CHEE.CPM FEDERATION MALAYA POLICE SC. WONG YEE PANG. CPM FEDERATION MALAYA POLICE
Sat. 21st		**21 Mr. A Sargeant.** Manager. of the Panel Estate Kluang Pahang. Killed by CT's. in a road ambush in Johore.]
	+	3 Platoon of the 10th. Gurkhas were deployed in the area of the Cherul Gorge where 3 Separate CT cultivation plots had been photographed from the air. During their operation Killed 5 CT's & destroyed the plots.---]
Sun. 22nd		**22 L/Cpl. B. A. Bissell.** R. E. M. E. Died*** *Singapore # 2 / D – 8* ---]
		22 Mr. J.W. Barrel. Asstn Manager. of the Selaba Estate. In the Teluk Intan area of Perak was ambushed and Killed by CT's---]
Mon. 23rd		A Platoon of East African troops Killed 2 CT's in Terengganu---]
Tue. 24th		24/06/1952 LG # 39582 p. 3465 The following awarded the Military Cross
	+	2/LT. J. D. HARROP. MC THE GREEN HOWARDS
Wed. 25th		**25 Rfn. J. H. Mezzetti.** 1st. Battn. Cameronians. Killed in Action Engaging CT's. Tenang Johore *[Ashes REP]*

	+	25 HMT **LANCASHIRE** arrived Singapore- with replacement Service personnel sailed bound for Liverpool with returning Service personnel 25th.----]
Thur. 26th		Support Company 10h Gurkhas Killed another 3 CT's during an engagement South of the Cherul Gorge--]
	+	26 HMT **EMPIRE HALLADALE** sailed Liverpool bound for Singapore / Hong Kong with replacement Service personnel---]
Fri. 27th		27 Pte. **J. A. Thorn**. R.A.O.C.. Died*** _Kuala Lumpur # 20 / 1084_---]
	+	27 L/Cpl. **S. A. Smith**. R.E.M.E. Died*** _Kuala Lumpur # 20 / 1082_---]
	+	27 SAC. **C. D. Slater**. Trans/Dvr. R.A.F. Died from his injuries received in a road Traffic Accident on the 23rd. June- _Kuala Lumpur # 20 -1080_. --].
	+	27/06/52. LG # 39584 p3523 The following awarded the Military Medal
		CPL.A. BARKER.MM ROYAL MARINES
Sat. 28th		28 Sgt **Pirithlal**.Rai 10th. Princess Mary's Own Gurkha Rifles. Killed in Action Engaging CT's - _Kranji Singapore # 8 ./ B – 8_---]
	+	28 Sgt. **Rajbahadur Rai** 10th. Princess Mary's Own Gurkha Rifles. Killed in Action Engaging CT's _[No known Grave] Terandak Memorial Malacca_].---]
	+	28 A/B N. **Warburton**. Royal Navy. H.M.S. 'MAENAD'. Died *** _Kranji Singapore # 14 / D – 13_ ---]
Sun. 29th		4 Platoon 10th. Gurkhas engaged a large force of CT's & charged into them killing 4 CT's. The rest scattered & fled from the onslaught. Rfn. Budhari Rai was recommended for a medal LG 26/09/1952---]
	+	A prominent Communist Commisar in the 5 Regt.MRLA **Moo Yat Mei** surrendered to the Security forces---]
	+	29 2 F. M. Police **AP. Insp. F.H. Wilkins** . AP Yahya B.Abbas Killed on CT Ops. Chen Wing Estate Segamat _[Graves Unknown]_----]
Mon. 30th		30 A/B SC. **Bradbury- Flint**. Royal Navy.H.M.S. "COCKADE" Died car accident. _Kranji Singapore # 14 / D – 12]_---]
	+	30 Mr. **P.F Wilkins**. Hon Aux. Inspt.F.M. Police Killed in Anti Communist Duties Chan Wing Estate Kuala Terengganu---]
	+	London: The War office announced: '_Major General Sir. Hugh Stockwell would succeed Major General H.E. Urquhart as G.O.C. Malaya Effective from 1st June._' ---]
	+	In different parts of Malaya British, Gurkha, East African & Fijian troops Killed 12 C.T' in several attacks.---]
	+	30 HMT **LANCASHIRE** sailed Singapore for Liverpool with returning Service personnel---]
	+	30 HMT **EMPIRE ORWELL** arrived Southampton with returning Service personnel---]

JULY

Tue. 1st		1 2 F. M. Police **SC's Jaffar B. Abdul Ghani**. – **Mohd B. Dena Khan**. Killed on CT Ops. Anglo Johore Estate Segamat---]
	+	1 Pte. **P. J. Staples**. R.A.S.C. Died from injuries recv'd in climbing incident. _Taiping # E / 36_ Perak---]
		Operation 'Churchman' began against **Lieu Kon Kim** the Commander of the 4th. Ind. Comp. No 1 Regt. MRLA]
Wed. 2nd		HMT **DEVONSHIRE** arrived Singapore with replacement Service personnel enroute to Hong Kong 2nd.---]
Thur. 3rd		3 Major. **W. Shaw**. Queen's Own Cameron Highlanders. Died*** _Seremban #RC 69_ Negri Sembilan---]
Fri. 4th		4 3 F. M. Police **C/Sgt. Jali B. Hj. Taib**. – **SC's Sahek B. Long**. - **Ahmed B. Achid**. Killed on CT Ops. Bukit Cheading Estate Kuala Langat Selangor.---]
Sat. 5th		5/07/1952 LG# 39617 p 4204 The following awarded the Military Cross
		LT. G. THAPA. MC 6th. QUEEN ELIZABETH'S OWN GURKHA RIFLES
		CAPT. E.H. MORGAN. MC THE SUFFOLK REGIMENT.
Sun. 6th		6 Pte. **B. V. Ansell**. 1st. Battn. Suffolk Regt. Killed in Action Engaging CT's accidental battle accident . _Kuala Lumpur # 20 / 108_]---]
	+	During attacks near Kajang Selangor. A Notorious C.T leader **Liew Kon Kim** was Killed by Lt . Hands of the Suffolk Regt. His mistress **Ah Ying** was also shot dead by Lt. Hands. **Kong Fah** Commander of No. 3 Platoon was Killed by Cpl. Hollamby. The 3 bodies were poled out of the jungle through swamps and dense jungle, before being loaded onto a truck & taken to Telok Datoh Police Station. Where they were put on public display. Purely to convince the locals that **Liew Kon Kim** the bearded terrorist. Was really dead & after three years, would cease to terrorise them & the district ever again. He was also taken to Tanjon Sapat. A New Settlement to exibit him there before disposal.--]
Mon. 7th		7 3 Malay Regt. Ptes. were Killed in Action Engaging CT's during an ambush. **Pte.'s Mohamad Khalid b. Abdul Ahmed**. – **Mohd. Sharif b. Adun**. Pahang ---]
	+	One British Lt. (_unnamed_) & a civilian Mr. A. L Morgan were caught in an ambush when the car driven by Mr. Morgan a Planter on the Voules Estate, had to stop where a tree had been felled across the road. As they

		got out of the car, several CT's fired on them, wounding both men. The British Lt. As he lay in the road, feigned death as they stripped him of his uniform. Mr. Morgan was bayoneted twice, in the head and back by a C.T, but survived his wounds. When found they were taken to Kluang Hospital Johore Bahru.---]
Tue.	8th	**8 SC Sulaiman B. Ayob.** F. M. Police Killed in road ambush on CT Ops. 91/2. m/s Segamat /Labis Rd. Johore]
	+	**8 Pol/Lt. D. Wedgewood.** F.M. Aux. P. Killed on CT Ops. Sungei Krai Kelantan ---]
Wed.	9th	9 HMT EMPIRE FOWEY sailed Southampton bound for Singapore / Hong Kong with replacement Service personnel---]
	+	9 HMT DILWARA arrived Southampton with returning Service personnel---]
	+	9 HMT EMPIRE PRIDE arrived Singapore with replacement Service personnel---]
Thur.	10th	In different areas of the Federation. Hungry CT's. attacked 2 food lorries In the Labis area CT's held up a lorry loaded with fish and stole 2/3rd. of its laod. Near the uninhabited town of Tras CT's held up a lorry loaded with flour & made off with 21 sacks. It appears "**Starve The Communist** " Programme is working]
	+	Acting on a information from a S.E.P. A Patrol of 'B'Company 10th. Gurkhas re-established an ambush at the Cultivation plots in the area of the Cherul Gorge to await any potrential CT activity---]
Fri.	11th	Next day 3 CT's approached the area within the ambush. A burst from a bren gun Killed 2. As the 3rd. CT escaped. He was shot by a Gurkha acting as a backstop. The 3 CT's were identified as all senior members of the 7th. Regt. HQ . The Commissar, the Quartermaster & Sub Unit Commander ---]
Sat.	12th	**12 Pte. Ahmad b. Yusof** Malay Regt. Killed in Action Engaging CT's Pahang---]
Sun.	13th	CT's slashed, 2,000 Rubber trees, and smahed latex cups. In the Johore Bahru area.---]
	+	13 HMT EMPIRE PRIDE sailed from Singapore enroute to Hong Kong. On Board were the advance party of Airmen of 84 Sqdr. R. A. F. Regt.(Malaya) who will relieve 93 Sqdr. R. A. F. Regt. (Malaya) Due back the end of the Month of July ---]
Mon.	14th	In Perak CT's in the Slim river area sawn down 120 Rubber trees and over 1.000 half sawn through, other Rubber trees were slashed---]
	+	A Patrol of the Malay Regt. found a big CT camp, with Slit trenches surroumding the area of 11 huts, a Lecture room, a Canteen, Cookhouse estimated to cater for 60 CT's A second camp was found with a food dump. All were destroyed.---]
Tue.	15th	**15 Mr. I. Corley** Manager. Killed in Action Engaging CT's in the Layang Layang area of Johore.---]
Wed.	16th	**16 Dvr. G. Hodgson.** R.A.S.C. Died Motor Transport Acc *Kuala Lumpur # 20 / 1083*---]
Thur.	17th	17 HMT EMPIRE WINDRUSH arrived Singapore with replacement Service personnel---]
Fri.	18th	**18 SC. Weir. B. Darbar.** F. M. Police Killed on CT Ops. Kluang Johore ---]
	+	**18 Pol/Lt. R. Dixon.** FM Aux.Police Killed on CT Ops. Charging a number of CT's in ambush Kampong. Kuala Medang *Kuala Lipis # ??* Pahang---].
		18 HMT DUNERA arrived in Singapore with replacement Service personnel enroute to Hong Kong .---]
Sat.	19th	19 HMT DUNERA The remaining Airmen of 84 Sqdr. R. A. F. Regt.(Malaya) left Singapore for Hong Kong]
Sun.	20th	The Communist Party Group Committee member **Ah Chee** was Killed in an ambush laid by the Royal West Kents Held in his hand was a revolver, which was identified as the one owned by Mr. A .Nicholls who was Killed the previous month.---]
Mon.	21st	A Platoon of the 10th. Gurkhas Killed 2 CT's in the Slim river area of Perak---]
Tue.	22nd	**22 Lt. (KGO) Kalibahadur Limbu .** 2nd.10th. Princess Mary's Own Gurkha Rifles. was Killed in Action Engaging CT's during a fire fight with a number of CT's on a Rubber plantation. 3 CT's were Killed & several wounded, who were carried away. *Kranji Singapore # 8 / C - 6- .*---]
Wed.	23rd	**23 Pte. R. E. Dunn.** 1st. Battn. Worcestershire Regt. Died*** *Taiping # B / 60* Perak---]
Thur.	24th	24/07/52 LG # 39609 p. 4066. The following awarded the George Medal
		MR. R. F.C.V. HARRADINE. GM ASSTN. ESTATE /MANAGER
	+	p. 4067
		POL/LT. I.P. HYDE. GM FEDERATION MALAYA POLICE
		SC. SAMION B. ABDULLAH. GM FEDERATION MALAYA POLICE.
Fri.	25th	F.M.P. Special Branch Officers raided a house in Lahat Road Ipoh & arrested two women CT suspects. **Lee Ten Tai** alias **Lee Meng** & **Cheow Yin** . Took them away for trial.---]
	+	25 HMT EMPIRE HALLADALE arrived Singapore with replacement Service personnel ---]
Sat.	26th	**26 Flt/Lt. J. B. Jones.** Eng. R.A.F. Butterworth. Died*** *Western Road # 2147* George Town Penang---]
	+	**26 SC Hasrack B. Jemjan.** F. M. Police Killed on CT Ops. Kulai Johore.---]
	+	26 HMT EMPIRE WINDRUSH sailed Singapore bound for Southampton with returning Service personnel-]
	+	26 HMT EMPIRE HALLADALE sailed Singapore for Hong Kong/ Kure ---]
Sun.	27th	**27 SC Wan Mat B. Wan Ngah.** F. M. Police Killed on Ops. Grik Perak---]
Mon.	28th	} Combined operations continued throughout Malaya ---]

Tue. 29th		Gurkha Patrols Killed 3 CT's In the Sungei Cherul area.All members of the 7Th. Regt. HQ.---]
	+	29/07/1952 LG 39610 p. 4075 The following awarded the Colonial Police Medal
		SC. KASSIM B. MAT. CPM FEDERATION MALAYA POLICE
		SC.MOH. ARIS B.PUTCH CPM FEDERATION MALAYA POLICE
		The following awarded the King's Police & Fire Medal
		POL/LT. D.J.MILLER PFM (Pos) FEDERATION MALAYA POLICE
Wed. 30th		**30 Dvr. L. F. McAllister**. R.A.S.C.. Died. by accident. *Kuala Lumpur # 20 / 1086*---]
	+	**30 Cpl. Mohammad . Bin . Kassim**. RA.M.C. (MOR) Died***_Claimed by next of Kin_ --]
	+	30 HMT LANCASHIRE arrived Liverpool with returning Service personnel---]
	+	30 HMT DEVONSHIRE arrived Singapore enroute to Liverpool with returning Service personnel 30th.---]
	+	30 HMT EMPIRE TROOPER sailed Southampton bound for Singapore / Hong Kong with replacement Service personnel---]
	+	30 HMT EMPIRE PRIDE arrived Singapore sailed bound for Liverpool with returning Service personnel 30th.]
Thur. 31st		_Kuala Lumpur:_ The trial of the **Lee Meng** began. The charges were for three offences under the Emergency Regulation Act the second women **Cheow Yin** had committed suicide while in custody..---]
	+	31 HMT EMPIRE FOWEY arrived Singapore roads with replacement Service personnel---]

AUGUST

Fri. 1st		Operation "*Hammer*" Began against No 1 Regt. MRLA in Selangor. Seremban Kuala Lumpur ---]
	+	Operation '*Lambley*' SAS against the MRLA---]
Sat. 2nd		**2 F/Off. W. J. Visard.- Sgt. D. Mann. -Sgt. J. D. Pickrell**. 52 Sqdn. R A F. & 4 from 55 Coy RASC **Cpl. W.H. Lane. - Dvr. D. Dagg. - Dvr. F. McShane. - Dvr. A. Whitty**. Were Killed when Valletta VX540 on a supply drop crashed into the jungle. N. of Kuala Lumpur.. *[No known Graves] Terandak Wall Memorial Malacca* -]
	+	**2 Cfn. T. Wright**. R.E.M.E. Died*** *Western Road George Town Penang # 2148* ---]
	+	2 HMT EMPIRE FOWEY sailed Singapore enroute to Hong Kong / Kure with replacement Service personnel---]
Sun. 3rd		_Kuala Lumpur:_ The trial of **Lee Meng** was suspended due to the 2 Asian Assessors. Passing a not guilty verdict, which was overuled ---]
Mon. 4th		A" Plt. of 'A' Company Green Howards engaged & Killed **Chee Hong** A senior Member of the MRLA.---]
Tue. 5th		**5 SAC. M. V. Morling**. Arm/Mech. R.A.F. Tengah. Died result of a Motor transport accident on 3rd. August. *Kranji Singapore # 4 / C - 4*---]
	+	**5 Rfn. Tikaram Chhetri** 1st,10th. Princess Mary's Own Gurkha Rifles. Killed in Action Engaging CT's *Kranji Singapore # 7 / A -7* ---]
	+	5/08/1952 39617 p. 4204 The following awarded the Military Cross
		LT. G. THAPA. MC 6th QUEEN ELIZABETH'S OWN GURKHA RIFLES
		CAPT. E.H. MORGAN. MC SUFFOLK REGIMENT.
	+	5 HMT DUNERA arrived in Singapore enroute to Southampton with returning Service personnel-5th. ---]
Wed. 6th		6 Plt 'B' comp. Patrolling in the Sepong area discovered a CT camp suitable for between 20-30 CT's including a food dump. Estimated last used a fortnight before. 7 Plt 'C' Comp found another camp still under construction both were destroyed. 1 CT was Killed---]
	+	Operation "*Rhubarb* " Began in the Bakit Langat Forest Reserve The Suffolk's Killed one CT identified as **Poh Seng** Another abandoned camp was discovered and destroyed.---]
	+	6 HMT DILWARA sailed Southampton bound for Singapore with replacement Service personnel ---]
Fri. 7th		A Plt of the M & M/C G. Plt. of the Green Howards Shot & wounded a CT who surrendered. His capture led to others leading to another 5 CT's in another camp. The Patrol found the camp opening fire Killed all 5 CT's. One of the shot CT was identified as **Phang Ngen** alias **Kin Keong** District Committee member for Ayer Kuning with a price on his head of $13,000---]
Sat. 8th		**8 Rfn. Kumbasing Ale** . 7th. Duke of Edinburgh's Own Gurkha Rifles. Died*** *Kuala Lumpur # 27 / 20* --]
	+	10 Plt. 'D' Company Green Howards Killed 1 CT---]
	+	Operation "*Rhubarb*" concluded.---]
	+	08/08/1952 LG 39619 p. 4246 The following awarded the Colonial Police Medal
		HON.INSP. A.C. MACKEMZIE. CPM FEDERATION MALAYA POLICE
Sun. 9th		9 12 Plt. 'D' Company Green Howards took up ambush positions in the Sungei Sungkai Estate Egaged 3 CT's. Killed 1 the other 2 escaped.---]

Mon. 10th	**10 Cpl. Lalbahadur Pun** . 2nd. King Edward VII's Own Gurkha Rifles. Died Sungei Basi. *Kranji Singapore # 7 / A – 8* ---]
Tue. 11th	**11** 7 Plt 'C' Comp Killed 2 CT's wounding a 3rd.who escaped .The 2 dead CT's were identified as **Ah Kong** a courier of the Min Yuen & **Ah Choon** a member of 8 Section 3 Plt MRLA.---]
Wed. 12th	**12 L/Cpl. G. R. Greenwood.** R. M. P. Died****Kranji Singapore # 2 / D -7* ---]
+	**12 Capt. R.B. Tarleston.** The Black Watch. Died****Kuala Lumpur # 19 / 1070*---]
+	**12 Pol/LT. Arthur Abishagam.** F. M. Police was Killed along with 7 F. M. Police **L/Cpl. Ahmid B, Yakim. PC's. Alias B. Tamin. – Yusof B. Mohd.SC Mohd Yasin B. Mohamed.- Tan Ah Lee .- Mohamed Jani B. Pais.- Manap B. Mohamed.**in CT ambush Ayer Kuning Negri Sembilan. ---]
Thur. 13th	5 Plt. 'B' Comp Suffolk's whilst on Patrol in the Kuala Langat area. Being led by a CEP **Te Chin Min** found food dumps, medical supplies & printing materials. All were destroyed.---]
+	Kuala Lumpur : The trial of **Lee Ming** began with 2 new Assesors . I Asian the other European and a New Judge. The court ruled that she was guilty of possessing arms and was sentenced to death. **Lee Ming** was taken to Taiping jail to await her fate. However, her trial had stirred up such concern that an appeal was lodged with the Federal Court of Appeal in Kuala Lumpur. Which in turn was taken up by the Privy Council in London. As time progressed **Lee Ming**'s case was to cause an International intrigue.---]
Fri. 14th	The M/G Plt. of the Green Howards set up an ambush Engaging 3 CT's. Killed all 3---].
Sat. 15th	Another air strike was called for by the Suffolk's in the Telok Forest Reserve---]
+	A Patrol of 12 Plt 'D' Company Green Howards set an ambush on the Selabak Estate 3 CT.s approached the ambush position. 2 were Killed instantly. the 3rd. Managed to escape, followed by Mr. Nightingale The Estate Asstn. Manager. The escaping CT returned fire & shot **Mr. Nightingale** who died later from his wounds.--]
Sun. 16th	**16 L/Cpl. Abirdhoj Rai.** 2nd/10th. Princess Mary's Own Gurkha Rifles. Killed in Action Engaging CT's whilst the Platoon was engaged in an uphill encounter, with a large number of CT's who retreated. Around the slopes of the hill 6 dead CT's were found & 2 wounded. The wounded informed their captives that they were part of the 10 Platoon MRLA of 39 strength. However the search continued chasing the fleeing CT's *Kranji Singapore # 7 / A - 9*---] For their gallantry during the hour long engagement Cpl Tamang was awarded the DCM & Rfn. N.Rai was awarded Military Medal---]
+	**16 Rfn. R. Tilbahadur Rana** . 2nd. King Edward VII's Own Gurkha Rifles. Died****Kranji Singapore # 7 / B – 1*
+	**16 Dvr. G. Hodson.** R.A.S.C.. Died. Transport incident. *Kuala Lumpur # 20 / 1083*---]
Mon. 17th	**17 SAC. R. R. Nesbit.** Den/Mech. R.A.F. Changi . Killed Motor Veh. Acc. *Kranji Singapore-#4/ C / 2*--]
+	**17 Pte. M. Saulos.** 3rd. King's African Rifles Died*** *Kuala Lumpur # 20 / 1093* ---]
+	**17 Pte. B. Larman.** 1st. Battn. Suffolk Regt. Killed in Action Engaging CT's *Kuala Lumpur # 20 / 1091*---]
+	**17 Aux /Insp. A. F. Nightingale.** FM Aux Police Died from his wounds recv'd 15th. *Teluk Intan # ??* Perak ---]
+	A Plt. of the A/T Company Green Howards engaged 3 CT's.' Killing all 3.---]
Tue. 18th	Platoons of the 2nd./10th.Gurkhas following up the incident of the previous day were given formation by civilians who had seen several CT's, carrying a wounded comrade crossing the Muar/Tankar road, in the area of the 121/2 m/s. There a wounded CT was found near the m/s. But no further contact was made of the other CT's]
Wed. 19th	**19 Hon. Insp AP. G. M. Burns** F. M. Police & Manager. of the Riverveiw Estate Killed in an ambush -Together with 6 F. M. Police **SC's .Jamludin B. Mat Ali. – Kathmubu s/o Kannusamy. -Noordin B. Abdullah.- Abdullah B. Minti. -Kassam B. Osman. -Yang B. Mat Ali. – Mhd. Nor B. Hj Asip** Killed in the Telok Tualang area of Perak. *Batu Gajah # 489* Ipoh Perak ---]
Thur. 20th	**20 Rfn's. R. Sobhasing. Rana – Padambahadur Gurung** 2nd. King Edward VII's Own Gurkha Rifles.Killed in Action Engaging CT's. *Kranji Singapore # 7 / A - 10 - 11*---]
+	'C' Comp Suffolk's found a large food dump in Kuala Langat Swamp area in a small hut raised on stilts. It was destroyed.---]
+	5 Plt. 'B' Comp Suffolk'sfound a camp for 20 CT's with a large food dump. It was destroyed---]
+	6 Plt. 'B' Comp Suffolk's found another camp for 40 plus CT's plus food & clothing It was destroyed.---]
+	10 Plt. 'D' Comp Killed a CT on the Soringgit Estate identified as **Siew Moy** Secretary to 2nd. Plt. MRLA--]
+	20 HMT EMPIRE ORWELL sailed Southampton bound for Singapore /Kure /Pusan with replacement Service personnel---]
Fri. 21st	8 Plt 'C' Comp Suffolk's whilst on Patrol, engaged a number of CT's. However in the ensuing fire fight the CT's retreated back into the jungle. Being followed their tracks were lost---]
Sat. 22nd	**22 Major G.E, Harper.** Royal Engineers Died *** *Kranji Singapore # 2 / D – 6*
+	**22 F/Off. G. E. Sykes.** 60 Sqdn. R.A.F. Killed when his Vampire WL556 overshot the runway & crashed at R.A.F. Tengah. *Kranji Singapore # 4 / C – 3* ---]
+	

+	**22 Rfn. Dhojbir Limbu.** 7th. Duke of Edinburgh's Own Gurkha Rifles. Died by Accident on Ops. Paroi Camp *Seremban # 46* Negri Sembilan---]
Sun. 23rd	22 HMT EMPIRE HALLADALE arrived Singapore- --]
	'C' Plt Suffolk's, found another camp for 40 CT's a clothing dump & nearby another camp for 40-45 CT's.
+	All destroyed.---]
+	23 HMT EMPIRE HALLADALE sailed for Glasgow with returning Service personnel---]
	23 HMT EMPIRE FOWEY arrived Singapore Roads / sailed bound for Southampton with returning Service
Mon. 24th	personnel 23rd---]
	10 Plt. 'D' Comp Suffolk's whilst in ambush positions on the Sepang Estate spotted a CT coming towards
+	them. He stopped retreated before any Engaging CT's took place.---]
Tue. 25th	24 HMT EMPIRE WINDRUSH arrived Southampton with returning Service personnel ---]
	9 Plt. 'D' Comp Suffolk's in ambush position near the Sepang Estate when 5 CT's approached well spread
	out. The Suffolk's opened fire Killed the last two, wounding the lead CT who escaped with the other two
	CT's. The two dead CT's were later identified as *La Yu Hwain* alias *Huat Tah* & *Tong Kwee Wong* Alias
+	*Pak Kiang*.---]
Wed. 26th	25 HMT EMPIRE PRIDE arrived Liverpool with returning Service personnel ---]
Thur. 27th	An Air strike was called to hit a target in the Dingki area where CT's had been spotted. ---]
	Near Sepamg 5 CT's walked into an night ambush of 9 Platoon 'C' Comp. Suffolk's although the CT's were
+	well spread out 2 were Killed & a 3rd. wounded who subsequently died ---]
Fri. 28th	27 HMT EMPIRE TROOPER called SIngapore enroute to 'Hong Kong with replacement Service personnel]
	28 Off. R. Jackson. 45 Sqdn R.A.F. Killed when his Hornet WB912 stalled recovering from a diving straffing
+	run & crashed into trees 6 miles East of Seremban. Body recovered *[Ashes REP]* ---]
	11 Plt. D Comp Suffolk's Killed a CT on the Soringgit Estate wounding 2 others who escaped . The dead CT
+	was identified as *Yoke Fong* 2nd. Plt MRLA ---]
Sat. 29th	28 HMT DEVONSHIRE arrived Liverpool with returning Service personnel---]
+	**29 Mr. Mark Richford- Venfil.** European Civilian Killed by CT's Bukit Merah Selangor.---]
+	**29 Mr. M.R. Perfit.** Manager. Triang Estate Johore Killed By CT's.---]
	29/08/1952 LG # 39634 p. 4587 The following awarded the British Empire Medal
	F/SGT. P. LAIDLER. BEM ROYAL AIR FORCE
	F/SGT. R. D. REYNOLDS. BEM ROYAL AIR FORCE
	The following awarded 2nd. Bar to Distinguished Flying Cross
	S/LDR. W.G.G D. SMITH. DFC +BAR +BAR ROYAL AIR FORCE
	The following awarded the Distinguished Flying Cross
	S/LDR. A.P. NORMAN. DFC. ROYAL AIR FORCE
	F/LT. W. BANKS. DFC ROYAL AIR FORCE
	F/LT. K. W. JOHNSON. DFC ROYAL AIR FORCE
	The following awarded the Distinguished Flying Medal
+	SGT. A. LAMBERT. DFM. ROYAL AIR FORCE
	29/08/1952 LG 36190 4075 The following awarded the Colonial Police Medal
	SC. K BIN MAT {Post} FEDERATION MALAYA POLICE
	SC.M. A. BIN PUTEH (Post) FEDERATION MALAYA POLICE
Sun. 30th	A CT cap, uniform, a printing machine & CT literature. Was sent to the British Film makers currently in
Mon. 31st	production of the film entitled 'THE PLANTERS WIFE ' as advertisement material---]
	2 more CT's were Killed 1 by a F.M Police Patrol in the Huantan area of Pahang The 2nd was Killed by a
	Gurkha Patrol in the Jelebu area of Sembilan---]

SEPTEMBER

Tue.	1st	1 HMT DILWARA arrived Singapore with replacement Service personnel---]
+		Operation *'Hive' 'Demon.'* Began SAS against the MRLA ---]
Wed.	2nd	A Patrol of the F. M. Police Killed 1 CT in the area near Kuantan---]
+		Another F. M. Police Patrol Killed 1 CT in the area of Jelebu Kuala Kangsar---]
Thur.	3rd	10 CT's raided a Tin Mine in the Kampar area of Perak & batterd to death a Chinese worker (*unmamed*).--]
Fri.	4th	4 HMT DUNERA arrived Southampton with returning Service personnel ---]
Sat.	5th	Kuala Lumpur: General Sir. Gerald Templar, has won the first round against the CT's Records indicate
		that the number of kill , captured or surrendered CT's have been the highest on record since his arrival 4
		months ago---]

Sun.	6th	<u>Penang:</u> An all Island land wide operation was started to seek out CT's. Road blocks were set up and everyone was searched including all vehicles. Rumours were abound about the possibility **Chin Peng** was Hiding in Penang --]
	+	6 HMT DILWARA sailed from Singapore bound for Southampton.with returning Service personnel---[
Mon.	7th	**7 SC Abu B. Sam.** F. M. Police Killed on CT Ops. Muar Johore---]
Tue.	8th	A F. M. Police Patrol. Killed 1 CT in the Mersing area of Johore ---]
Wed.	9th	9 7 Platoon 'C' Comp. Suffolk's on Patrol in the Kuala Langat Forest Reserve located a small occupied camp for 3 persons. Charging the camp Killed 2 CT's ---]
Thur.	10th	A CT who was about to throw a hand grenade at a Patrol of the 3rd. Malay Regt. was shot dead ---]
Fri.	11th	**11 Pte. C. Denton.** 1st. Battn. The Queen's Own Royal West Kents. Killed in Action Engaging CT's. <u>*Kuala Lumpur # 20 / 1095*</u>]---]
Sat.	12th	A Fijian Patrol Killed 1 CT in the Bahau Area of Johore---]
	+	12 HMT EMPIRE ORWELL arrived Singapore with replacement Service personnel sailed enroute to Hong Kong/ Kure / Pusan ---]
Sun.	13th	The Operation in Penang continued ---]
Mon.	14th	Police checked the identity of all the visitors to the village of Ayer Itam 5 miles from Penang---]
	+	14 HMT EMPIRE FOWEY arrived Southampton with returning Service personnel ---]
Tue.	15th	In the Kuala Pilah area of Negri Sembilan A Patrol of the Fijian Regt. Engaged 3 CT' s killing 1 wounded another the 3rd. surrendered ---]
Wed.	16th	In the Triang area of Pahang a Patrol of the 3rd Kings African rifles found 2 CT's in a hut killing 1 wounded the other whilst escaping, got away ---]
Thur.	17th	**17 SAC, R. R. Nesbitt Den.** Mech R. A.F. Changi Died*** <u>*Kranji Singapore # 4 C - 2*</u> ---]
	+	17 HMT EMPIRE WINDRUSH sailed Singapore with replacement Service personnel---]
Fri.	18th	**18 Rfn. Indrabahadur Rai .** 7th. Duke of Edinburgh's Own Gurkha Rifles. Died from Wounds recv'd <u>*Kuala Lumpur # 26 / 8*</u> ---]
	+	**18 Gnr. P.M.P. Kemp.** Royal Artillery Killed in Action Engaging CT's <u>*[No known Grave]Terandak Wall Memorial Malacca*</u> ---]
Sat.	19th	**19 Sgt. K. Mambaua.** 3rd. King's African Rifles. Killed in Action Engaging CT's <u>*Kuala Lumpur # 20 / 1088*</u>---]
Sun.	20th	A dramatic fall in the incidents by the CT's has thrown Malayan Observers into speculation. The CT's might be. Regrouping ready for an onther wave of attacks. Last month figure for the first 18 days was 118 this months figure for the same period was 67---]
Mon.	21st	**21 Cpl. S. Alfred.** 3st. King's African Rifles. Killed in Action Engaging CT's <u>*Kuala Lumpur # 20 / 1090*</u> ---]
Tue.	22nd	**22 L/Cpl. A. D'Arcy.** 1st. Battn. Cameronians. Killed in Action Engaging CT's Johore. <u>*Kranji Singapore # 2 / A - 14*</u>---]
	+	22 HMT DEVONSHIRE sailed Liverpool bound for Singapore / Hong Kong with replacement Service personnel---]
Wed.	23rd	23/09/1952. LG # 39651 p.5036 The following awarded the George Medal LT W. J. WADGE GM FEDERATION MALAYA POLICE Lt W.J. ROBERTSON GM FEDERATION MALAYA POLICE L/CPL.WAN. HASSAN. b. WAN AWANG. GM FEDERATION MALAYA POLICE SC/CPL. SAMAD BIN BABA. GM FEDERATION MALAYA POLICE
	+	23 HMT EMPIRE HALLADALE arrived Glasgow with returning Service personnel & for repairs.---]
Thur.	24th	<u>Singapore</u> The Straits Times. Head lines were about the CT **Ah Koek** known as **"Shorty "** Who The Government had placed a sum of $150, 000, for information for his capture alive. As he was 4'- 9 " tall he would be worth $3,000 per inch---]
Fri.	25th	The A/T Platoon Support Company Green Howards Killed 1 CT.---]
	+	11 Platoon 'D' Comp Suffolk's acting upon information laid an ambush surrounding a building on the Saranggit Estate near Kajang 2 CT's approached the building, being well spaced appart. The sentry's opened fire, Killed 1, whilst the other escaped.---]
Sat.	26th	At 6 am a 7 hour Curfew was imposed on the residens of George Town Penang under the code name Operation *"Box 5,000"* The Police and troops screened all the ocupants 4 suspect CT's were detained, after questioning 2 were realesed. Of the other 2 one was identified as a CT the other under investigation.]
	+	26/09/1952 LG 39655 p. 5093 The following awarded the Colonial Police Medal PC. LEE SOW KUNG CPM. FEDERATION MALAYA POLICE
Sun.	27th	**27 Lt. C. F. D. Sutton.** FM Aux. Police Killed on Ops. <u>*Kuantan # ??*</u> Pahang ---]
	+	10 Platoon in a follow up to the ambush on the 26th. contacted another CT recognised as the second CT they opened fire. Killed the CT.---]

Mon. 28th	28 HMT EMPIRE TROOPER arrived Singapore from Hong Kong ---]
+	**28 Mr. R.E. Bogle** was Killed during an ambush by about 30 CT's on the Fraser Estate Kulai.---]
+	The same Plt of the Green Howards. Killed ***Yong Hoi*** a Senior Section Leader of 39 Independent Plt. MRLA---]
Tue. 29th	**29 SC. Ibraham B. Mohamed**. F. M. Police Killed on Ops. Fraser Estate Kulai---]
+	29/09/1952 LG 39636 p. 4656 The following awarded the Colonial Police Medal
	ASSTN/SUPT. W.F. STAFFORD. CPM. FEDERATION MALAYA POLICE
	SC. HASSAN.B. DERANI. CPM FEDERATION MALAYA POLICE
+	29 HMT EMPIRE TROOPER sailed Singapore bound for Southampton with returning Service personnel--]
Wed. 30th	**30. Capt. (KGO) Padamial Rai. MC.** 7th. Duke of Edinburgh's Own Gurkha Rifles. Died Kumingtang *Sungei Patani # 66* Kedah---]
+	Operation "*Hammer*" – Ended ----]

OCTOBER

Thur. 1st	Operation '*Copley*' '*Churchman*' Began SAS against the MRLA ---]
+	1 HMT DUNERA sailed Southampton bound for Singapore / Hong Kong with replacement Service personnel---]
Fri. 2nd	**2 L/Cpl. R. T. Tennant**. 1st. Battn. Cameronians. Died from Wounds recv'd, Labis Johore. *Kranji Singapore # 2 / D – 13*----]
+	A female Chinese Rubber Tapper on the Elvetia Estate was held up by a lone CT who robbed of her NRIC (I.D. CARD)---]
+	'D' Comp 10th. Princess Mary's Own Gurkha Rifles Killed 1 CT. ---]
Sst . 3rd	'C' Company 10th. Princess Mary's Own Gurkha Rifles. Killed another CT---]
+	3 HMT DILWARA arrived Southampton with returning Service personnel---]
Sun. 4th	4 HMT EMPIRE FOWEY sailed Southampton bound for Singapore / Hong Kong with replacement Service personnel---]
Mon. 5th	**5 Tpr. D. R. Cook.** 13th./18th. Royal Hussars Died *** *Seremban #CE / 73* Negri Sembilan---]
+	1 Plt. 'A' Comp Suffolk's Killed 1 CT identified as ***Lee Sie Tong*** a member of the Dinkit Min Yuen.--]
Tue. 6th	6 HMT EMPIRE ORWELL arrived Singapore sailed bound for Southampton with returning Service personnel---]
Wed. 7th	**7 Mr. R. P. Herman.** Dutch Eurasion civilian Killed by CT's. Place not known? Gunshot wounds to head.---]
+	7/10/1952 LG # 39664 p. 5276 The following awarded the Distinguished Conduct Medal
	W/O. K. A. TAMUI. DCM KINGS AFRICAN RIFLES
Thur. 8th	'A' Plt Comp Suffolks on Patrol in the Kuala Langat Forest Reserve found a camp for 200 CT. Destroyed---]
Fri. 9th.	Platoon 'C' Comp Suffolk's located a CT camp near Sepang. As they entered a CT entered at the opposite end. A burst of fire Killed the CT Sentry. The camp was built to accommodate 15 was destroyed.---]
Sat. 10th	**10 L/Cpl. Makarbahadur Rawat.** 7th. Duke of Edinburgh's Own Gurkha Rifles. Died BHM Kinrara *Kuala Lumpur # 26 / 6*---]
+	10/10/1952 LG. # 39667 p. 5329 The following awarded the Military Cross
	2/LT. J.C. DUNTON. DFC THE GREEN HOWARDS
	2/LT. L.R. HANDS. DFC THE SUFFOLK REGIMENT.
Sun. 11th	11/10/1952 LG # 39667 p. 8485 The following awarded the Distinguished Flying Cross
	LT/CDR. M. WILLIAMS DFC ROYAL NAVY
Mon. 12th	Operation "*Hammer*" begen in the Kuala Langat area.---]
Tue. 13th	**13 Rfn. Badalsing Sunwar.** 10th. Princess Mary's Own Gurkha Rifles. Died*** *Kuala Lumpur # 7 / B 2*---]
Wed. 14th	A Police jungle Patrol engaged a CT in the Pondok Tanjon Forest area near Taiping wounding him but he escaped---]
+	During a jungle contact. A CT Sentry fired on the F. M. Police Lt. who charged the camp killing the CT identifired as ***Cheng Tuck Cho.***---]
Thur. 15th	15 HMT EMPIRE WINDRUSH arrived Singapore with replacement Service personnel--]
Fri. 16th	**16 SC Wan.** F. M. Police Drowned on Ops. Jitra Kedah /Perlis---]
Sat. 17th	**17 Cpl. J. R. H. Gooch.** No. 2 R.A.F. Police Died Road traffic accident *Kranji Singapore # 4 / C – 6* .---]
Sun. 18th	18 A convoy of trucks carrying te 19th. Gurkhas back to camp was fired upon by about 60 CT's In the ensuing fight Killed 2 CT's wounding several other who retreated into the jungle---]
Mon. 19th	19 F/Lt. P. E. Poling. R.A.F. Seletar Died*** *Kranji Singapore # 4 / C -5*---]

Tue. 20th	20 HMT DEVONSHIRE arrived Singapore enroute to Hong Kong with replacement Service personnel 21st.
Wed. 21st	21 **Rfn. Indrabahadur Gurung. MM.** 6th. Queen Elizabeth's Own Gurkha Rifles. Died from Wounds recv'd
	BMH Kluang. *Kluang # 3 / A - 5* Johore---]
+	21/10/1952 LG # 39675 p5527/8 The following awarded the Brotish Empire Medal (Millitary)_

RSM. P. J.T. READING. BEM   ROYAL MARINES
C/SGT J.G. BUXTON. BEM   ROYAL MARINES
SGT K. R. HONEYSETT.BEM   ROYAL MARINES

                              The following awarded the Distinguish Service Order
LT/COL P. A. MORCOMMBE. DSO   SUFFOLK REGIMENT.
                              The following awarded the Military Cross
MAJ. J. T. STEWART. MC   WEST YORKSHIRE REGIMENT.
CAPT. (QGO) K. RAI. MC   10th. PRINCESS MARY'S OWN GURKHA RIFLES
CAPT. S. GURUNG. MC   10th PRINCESS MARY'S OWN GURKHA RIFLES
LT.J. P. GARDNER. MC   ROYAL MARINES
LT.J. J. MOORE.   MC   ROYAL MARINES
Lt. A.B. HORREX. MC   THE SUFFOLK REGIMENT.
2/Lt. L.F. HANDS. MC   THE SUFFOLK REGIMENT.
                              The following awarded the Military Medal
CPL. T.A. WANT. MM   ROYAL MARINES
CPL. C.J. MacNISH. MM   ROYAL MARINES
MNE. E.C.R. GOUGE MM   ROYAL MARINES
MNE J. JONES. MM   ROYAL MARINES
L/BDR. R.H. ABU MM   ROYAL ARTILLERY
CPL R . GRUNDY. MM   THE GREEN HOWARDS
RFN D PUN . MM   2nd. KING EDWARD VII'S OWN GURKHA RIFLES
SGT. L. GURUNG.. MM .   6th QUEEN ELIZABETH'S GURKHA RIFLES
C/SGT. D. THAPA. MM.   6th QUEEN ELIZABETH'S GURKHA RIFLES
RFN .I GURUNG. MM.   6th QUEEN ELIZABETH'S GURKHA RIFLES
CPL. L. RAI. MM   7th. DUKE OF EDINBURGH'S OWN GURKHA RIFLES
L/CPL. B. TAMANG.MM   7th. DUKE OF EDINBURGH'S OWN GURKHA RIFLES
CPL. D. RAI. MM   10th PRINCESS MARY'S OWN GURKHA RIFLES
CPL. R. RAI. MM   10th PRINCESS MARY'S OWN GURKHA RIFLES
RFN. B.. RAI. MM .   10th PRINCESS MARY'S OWN GURKHA RIFLES

	22 8 Plt Suffolk's operating South of the Kuala Langgat Forest found a large food dump---].
Thur.22nd	23 **Sgt. A. Sellwood.** 1st. Battn. Worcestershire Regt. Died by Accident *Taiping # E / 37* Perak---]
Fri. 23rd	23 HMT EMPIRE WINDRUSH sailed Singapore bound for Southampton with returning Service personnel.
+	On board were The Green Howard Regt. having completed their tour of Active Service in Malaya---]
	24. Dvr. Syad .Hamzad. Bin. Ali. R.A.S.C.. (MOR) Died***_Claimed by Next of Kin_ ---]
Sat. 24th	Auster T7 VF 616 656 Sqdn R.A.F. Hit a building at Port Dickson. Plane was damaged beyond repair.---]
+	**25 Pte. S . Willard** 3rd. King's African Rifles Killed in Action Engaging CT's *Kuala Lumpur # 20 / 1092* ---]
Sun. 25th	'B' Comp Suffolk's on Patrol arrested 8 suspects. 4 male 4 female handed them over to the F.M. Police.---]
+	**26 Rfn. Bhupalsing Gurung.** 7th. Duke of Edinburgh's Own Gurkha Rifles. Drowned on Ops. Sungei Basi
Mon. 26th	area *Kuala Lumpur # 26 / 9* .---]
	9 Plt. Suffolk's Operating in the Sydney Estate were shot at by 15- 20 CT's the ensuing engagement
+	No casualties. The CT's retreated.---]
+	26 HMT EMPIRE HALLADALE arrived Liverpool from Glasgow---]
+	26 HMT EMPIRE FOWEY arrived Singapore ----]
+	**27 L/Cpl. Ganbahadur Pun** . 6th. Queen Elizabeth's Own Gurkha Rifles Killed in Action Engaging CT's Kuala
Tue. 27th	Kangsar **Rfn. G. Kharkabahadur**. Died from Wounds recv'd BHM Kamunting.
	Sungei Patani # 71 – 70 . Kedah---]
	27 HMT EMPIRE HALLADALE sailed Liverpool bound for Singapore/Hong Kong ---]
+	27 HMT EMPIRE FOWEY sailed Singapore bound for Soutjhampton with returning Service personnel---]
+	**28 L/Cpl. Idris . Bin. Ismail** R.A.S.C.. (MOR) Died*** _Claimed by next of Kin_ ---]
Wed. 28th	**28 SC's Kamis B. Salleh.- Bujang B. Hj. Sanusi.** F. M. Police Killed on CT Ops. Pekan Jabi New Village
+	Segamat Johore.---]
+	28 HMT DUNERA arrived in Singapore with replacement Service personnel ---]
+	28 HMT DILWARA sailed from Southampton bound for Singapore with replacement Service personnel on

+	board were the 1st. Battn. Somerset Light Inf. ---]
	29 HMT EMPIRE ORWELL arrived Southampton with returning Service personnel---]
Thur. 29th	29HMT EMPIRE TROOPER arrived Southampton with returning Service personnell---]
+	29 HMT DUNERA sailed Singapore enroute to Hong Kong---]
+	12 Plt. Suffolk's on Patrol near the Kajang area engaged 3 CT's. wounding 2 they escaped---]
Fri. 30th	31 Dvr. T. G. Hoye. R.A.S.C. 3 Coy. Died Transport Acc. Kamunting..*Taiping # E / 48* Perak---]
Sat. 31st	31/10/1952 LG. 39684 p. 5739 The following awarded the Distinguidhed Flying Cross
	CAPT. T.N.W. LACY. DFC ROYAL ARTILLERY REGIMENT. 656 SDN
	LT. J.F. CAMPBELL. DFC ROYAL ARTILLERY REGIMENT. 656 SDN
	LT. D.T. YOUNG. DFC ROYAL ARTILLERY REGIMENT. 656 SDN
+	Operation *"Habitual"* -*"Hive"*- Ended---]

NOVEMBER

Sun. 1st	Operation *"Copley."* Began against 12 Regt. MRLA in Kelentan.---]
Mon. 2nd	**2 Lt/Col. G. Gelder.** Army Physical Training Corps Died***[*Ashes REP*]---]
+	2 Hon. Insp. W.J. Berry. F. M. Police Killed on Ops. Ulu Remis Estate Kluang Johore.---]
Tue. 3rd	3 12 Plt Suffolk's while on Patrol in the Kampong Sungei Killed 1 Malay CT identified as ***Ismail Bin Sharriff*** alias *Ismet* of 2 section 2 Plt. MRLA.---]
+	6 Plt. 'B' Comp Suffolk's at Sungei Didu found dumps with clothing , guns and other equipment ---]
+	4 Plt Suffolk's operating in the Sungei Lang area contacted 3 CT's killing 2 identified as ***Yeong Hoong*** A courier for 2 Plt. MRLA & ***Khe Kim Thion*** a Min Yuen courier for 9 Plt. MRLA.---]
Wed. 4th	A Tamil Labourer on the Serenyth Estate was Killed by 2 CT's who set fire to the Smoke House and Labourers quarters. The estimated damge caused was $23,000.---]
+	4/11/1952. LG #39688.p 5823 The following awarded the Distinguished Conduct Medal
	CPL. M. TAMANG. DCM 10th PRINCESS MARY'S OWN GURKHA RIFLES
	The following awarded the Military Medal
	RFN. N. RAI. MM 10th PRINCESS MARY'S OWN GURKHA RIFLES
Thur. 5th	At Temoh Perak a CT ambush wounded two F. M. Police SC's. One of the SC's led a Patrol of the Manchesters to follow a trail of blood & found a CT who when challenge raised his rifle was Killed.---]
Fri. 6th	6 Pte. D. W. Latter. 1st. Battn. The Queen's Own Royal West Kents. Killed in Action Engaging CT's *Kuala Lumpur # 20 / 1094* ---]
Sat. 7th	7 CT's ambushed a Police Patrol in the Temoh Area of Perak. 2 F. M. Police were Killed on Ops. **Pol/ Lt. J.Thompson.** 1 PC **(unnamed)** [*No known Grave*] & 2 wounded 1 CT was Killed.---]
Sun. 8th	1 Platoon 'D' Comp Suffolk's acting on information Killed 1 CT near to Kajang ---]
Mon. 9th	9 HMT EMPIRE FOWEY arrived Singapore ---]
+	9 HMT EMPIRE FOWEY sailed bound for Southampton with returning Service personnel---]
Tue. 10th	CT's Cut the telephone wires on the Sungei Chonoh Estate in the Slim River area. Perak---]
Wed. 11th	A Patrol of the RAF Regt. (All Malays) Killed a CT in the Buit Langong Forest Reserves Selangor----]
Wed. 12th	**12 Rfn. A. Weir.** 1st. Battn. Cameronians. Died from Wounds recv'd, Segamat Johore. *Kranji Singapore # 2 / D - 12*---]
+	12 HMT EMPIRE PRIDE sailed Liverpool bound for Singapore/ Hong Kong with replacement Service personnel---]
Thur. 13th	**13 Lt. R. R. G. Bald.** 1st. Battn. Cameronians. Killed in Action Engaging CT's Johore [*Ashes REP*]---]
+	**13 Fus. R.E. Villers.**The Royal Fusiliers Died*** *Kuala Lumpur # 20 / 1096*---]
+	**13 Pol/Lt. I.C.F. Whilstone.** F.M. Aux. Police Killed on Ops. *Kuala Lumpur # 432* ---]
+	**13 Sgt. F. J. Morley.** 60 Sqdn. R.A.F. Killed whilst flying Vampire WG 881 Collided with Vampire WG 882 at Kampong Sadili Bazaar 14 mile North of Kota Tinngi [*No known Grave*] *Terandak Wall Memorial Malacca*] The other pilot Sgt. W. Gosill baled out & was rescued by Gurkhas. ---]
Fri. 14th	1 Plt 'B' Comp Suffolk's engaged 2 CT's in a small camp killing 1 Identified as ***Yong Teck Cheong*** Member of the Sungei Kontan Min Yuen the other CT escaped ---].
+	14/11/1952 LG # 39695 p. 6012 The following awarded a Bar to the Military Medal
	CPL. H. GURUNG . MM + BAR 2nd KING EDWARD VII'S OWN GURKHA RIFLES
	The following awarded the Military Madel
	RFN.K, RANA MM 2nd. KING EDWARD VII'S OWN GURKHA RIFLES.

+	14 HMT DUNERA arrived Singapore ---]
Sat. 15th	6 Plt. 'B' Comp Suffolk's Killed 1 CT in the Tanjong Duables Malay Reserves. Identified as *Gansze Hoot* of 1Plt. Sungei Siput Platoon---]
+	15 HMT DUNERA sailed from Singapore enroute to Southampton. with returning Service personnel ---]
Sun. 16th	16 Rfn. G. Purnabahadur. 2nd King Edward VII's Own Gurkha Rifles. Died***_Kuala Lumpur #24/ 5_ ---]
Mon. 17th	Platoon 'B' Comp Suffolk's led by a S.E.P. located 1 CT in the Tanjong Duables area & Killed him---]
Tue. 18th	Kuala Lumpur: In a 90 min Brief Sir. Gerald Templer urged that: 'Non Malay Asians. Be permitted into the Malyaan Civil Service that would allow a stronger Malayan Nation'---]
+	18 HMT ASTURIAS sailed Southampton bound for Singapore with replacement Service personnel---]
Wed. 19th	19 SC Hassam B. Shafie F. M. Police Killed on Ops. Kroh Upper Perak---]
+	19 Pol/Lt. H.R. Hemsley. F.M. Aux. Police Killed on Ops., Batu Kurau _Taiping # ??_ Perak.---]
+	During an engagement with a number of CT's were Killed by Rfn. Krisnabahadur. Newar. 10th.Princess Mary's Own Gurkha Rifles. Unfortunately he himself was Killed by another CT. _Kranji Singapore #/ B – 4_ ---]
+	6 Plt. 'B' Comp Suffolk's engaged 3 CT's in the Kampong Tanjon Mennach area killing 1, wounding another. The dead CT was identified as *Ah Kow* .a courier.---]
+	19 HMT DEVONSHIRE arrived Singapore enroute to Liverpool with returning Service personnel 20th
+	19 HMT EMPIRE ORWELL sailed Southampton bound for Singapore/ Hong Kong / Pusan with replacement Service personnel---]
Thur. 20th	20 SC Mohamed B. Saton. F. M. Police Killed on Ops. Johore---]
+	11 Plt. 'D' Comp Suffolk's contacted 2 CT's at Sungei Merabu. Killed 1 & wounded the other escaped. The dead CT was identified as *Tek Liew* . Commander of the 2 Plt. MRLA On The Wanted List.---]
Fri. 21st	21 HMT EMPIRE WINDRUSH arrived Southampton with returning Service personnel ---]
Sat. 22nd	22 HMT LANCASHIRE sailed Liverpool bound for Singapore./ Hong Kong with replacement Service personnel---]
Sun. 23rd	23 HMT DILWARA arrived Singapore. Disembarking the 1st. Battn. Somerset Light Inf. Sailed for Southampton with returning Service personnel 23rd.---]
Mon. 24th	24 Cpl. Amberbahadur Rai. 7th. Duke of Edinburgh's Own Gurkha Rifles. Died*** _Seremban # 47_ Negri Sembilan ---]
+	12 Plt. Comp Suffolk's found a CT camp for 20-30 CT's in the process of being built.Destroyed it---]
+	24 HMT EMPIRE TROOPER sailed Southampton bound for Singapore with replacement Service personnel]
Tue. 25th	6 Plt. B Comp Suffolk's contacted 2 CT's killing 1, wounding the second who escaped. In the follow up he was discovered dying. Killed without ceremony. They also ran into another 10 CT's they charged killing 2 CT's. Unfortunately L/Cpl. F.T.C. Mallows of 5 Plt. was Killed. _Kuala Lumpur # 20 / 1097_ The dead CT's were identified as *Ong Ling & Hon Kwong*. 1 Plt. Bodyguard of *Lee Chay Tit* alias *Kong Har*. Commander of 4 Comp *Fan Yon Oof* 1 Plt. & *Wong Lo Dej*. Section leader of 1 Plt. Serandah. --]
+	25 HMT EMPIRE HALLADALE called Singapore Roads Sailed for Hong Kong 25th.---]
Wed. 26th	26 L/Cpl. J. Wealleans. Royal Engineers Died*** [_Ashes REP_]----]
+	26 5 F. M. Police SC Sgt. Tahir B. Zaini .- Cpl. Ahmad B. Jais.- SC's Zainal B. Ayen. -Jais B. Shib. - Ahmad B. Shafie. Killed on CT Ops. Kota Tinggi Johore---]
Thur. 27th	27 Rfn. G. Thompson. 1st Battn. Cameronians. Died from Wounds recv'd in ambush Labis Johore [_Ashes REP_]---]
Fri. 28th	28 Hon. Insp. A.P. R.W. Saunders. (Lt. Col) F. M. Police Killed on CT Ops. CEP. No 3 Regam Johore.---]
Sat. 29th	29 Pte. J. Rooney. RA.M.C.. Died*** [_Ashes REP_]---]
	Iban Plt Suffolk's contacted 2 CT's in the Ulu Semenyth Killing 1 CT identified as *Kam Yiam* Section leader of 2 Plt MRLA ---]
Sun. 30th	30 2/Lt. J. V. Mack. 1st. Battn. The Queen's West Surrey Regt. Died***_Kuala Lumpur # 20 / 1098_---]
+	30 HMT EMPIRE FOWEY arrived Southampton- with returning Service personnel---]
+	Operation 'Demon.' Endied ---]

DECEMBER

Mon. 1st	Operation 'Hammer' Began SAS against the MRLA ---]
+	Iban Plt Suffolk's, Patrolling in the Jeloh Forest Reserve found a CT camp occupied by 3 CT's. They opened fire killing all 3 Identified as *Siew Yin Dg* Section Commander 2 Plt. *Chey Song* & *Chin Lee Sang* 2 Plt. MRLA---]

Tue.	2nd	**2 L/Cpl. Bahadurman**. Rai. 10th. Princess Mary's Own Gurkha Rifles.Killed in action engaging CT's *Kranji Singapore # 7 / B – 6* ---]
Wed.	3rd	A Platoon of he 10th. Princess Mary's Own Gurkha Rifles.engaed a number of CT's. 1 Gurkha was seriously wounded ---]
Thur.	4th	**4 Rfn. Kharhabahadur Gurung** . 10th. Princess Mary's Own Gurkha Rifles.died from his wounds of the previous day *Sulva Lines # 61* Ipoh Perak---]
	+	Auster AOP 6 VF619 656 Sqdn R.A.F. Overturned during forced Landing near Kluang.---]
	+	In Terengganu 3 CT's walked into the Dungu Police Station and surrendered. Identified as **Tin Boo** his wife **Foo Tee** & **Foo Bac Hoo**. ---]
Fri.	5th	**5 Pte. R. J. Clare**. 1st. Battn. Somerset Light Infantry. Died by Accident (Att. to K.O.Y.L.I.) [*Ashes REP*]---]
	+	In the Kamanman area 2 CT's. Surrendered to Police Identified as **Foo Jong See & Kau Chin Boo**. They were starving & informed the Police Three of their Comades had died from starvation the previous month their names were.**Ji Chou Boo, Foo Wa Khian, & Tomh Paw**.---]
	+	In Perak another CT surrendered to Police The former Member of the Self Protection Company **Lee Kap Chin** walked into the High street Police Station in Tampin and surrendered ---]
Sat.	6th	F. M. Police Jungle Patrols killed 4 CT's in different engagements in the area of North Perak---]
	+	Iban Platoon Suffolk's engaged & killed 3 CT's who were working on a new cultivation plot---]
	+	Singapore : About this date The Straits Times made a comment as too the new leader of the CMP. She was a Chinese spy by the name of **Hsia Hsuch Hung** The New Red Boss of the MCP. Therefore being in charge of **Chin Peng**. She still being in China would soon be coming to Malaya. It was a mystery how true this was? It never did happen.---]
Sun.	7th	6 Pln. 'B' Comp Suffolk's Patrolling in the Kuala Langat Forest Reserve (North) Killed 1 CT ---]
	+	7 EMPIRE PRIDE called Singapore with replacement Service personnel / sailed for Hong Kong /Pusan 7th.]
Mon.	8th	2 Chinese men suspected CT's were charged with possession of explosives. When arrested in Johore they were in possession of 328 Detonators, 84 reels of wire , & various weights of Dynamite & Gelignite---]
Tue.	9th	**9 Cpl. F. G. Cooper**. R.A.S.C. Died Transport Acc. Kluang *Kramji Singapore # 2 / E - 1*---]
	+	9/12/52.LG # 39714 p 6496 The following awarded the Military Medal SGT. I .LIMBU .MM 7th DUKE OF EDINBURGH'S OWN GURKHA RIFLES
Wed. 10th		**10 PC. Abdul Rashid** F. M. Police Killed on CT Ops. Tohallang Chinese TinKongsi Perak.---]
	+	'B' Platoon 'C' Comp Suffolk's on Patrol in the Kuala Langat Forest Reserve (South) North of Sepang killed 1 CT.---]
	+	Kuala Lumpur:Mr. MacDonald revealed: *'The Communist were planning to change Tactics. The situation in Malaya was improving but prodicted that a change would meke it worse. Instead of violence would be changed to infiltration'.*---]
	+	A Platoon of the Suffolk's killed a leading member of the Baty Laul Selangor Committee Identified as **S. Dharmaraj**.---]
	+	A F. M. Police Patrol killed 1 of a number of 10 CT's when they engaged them in a jungle clash.---]
	+	In the Semban area of Kuala Kangsar A Platoon of the 6th. Gurkhas killed 1 CT.---]
Thur. 11th		**11 Cpl. W. Benham**. [*Ashes REP*], **Cpl. G. H. Low**. R.A.O.C. Accident *Kranji Singapore # 2 / D – 15* ---]
	+	1 CT surrendered to the Police in the Seremban area Identified as **Kok Fool Cheong**---]
	+	The Asstn.Manager Mr. Byne of the Penkalan Bukit Estate in the Pogoli area of Johore beat off 20 CT's during a fiece fire fight on the estate. 2 of the SC's were wounded The CT's before they retreated set light to an estate Lorry ---]
	+	11 HMT ASTURIAS arrived Singapore with replacement Service personnel sailed 12th. Bound for Austarilia]
Fri.	12th	In the Jelibu area. A Patrol of the 7th. Gurkhas trapped 4 CT's Killing 3, & wounding the 4th. who escaped. 2 of the CT's killed were women.---]
	+	12 HMT DEVONSHIRE arrived Liverpool with returning Service personnel ---]
	+	12 HMT EMPIRE ORWELL arrived Singapore enroute to HongKong / Pusan with replacement Service personnel---]
	+	12 HMT DUNERA arrived Southampton with returning Service personnel ---]
Sat. 13th		2 CT's were killed by a Patrol of the F. M. Police in the Kota Tinggi area ---]
Sun. 14th		1 CT was killed by a Patrol of the F. M. Police in the Jasin District of Malacca---]
	+	1 CT was killed and 30 routed by F. M. Police Patrols when they attacked a CT Camp in Baling---]
Mon. 15th		**15 Pte. J. Lewel**. 1st. Battn. Fijian Infantry Regt. Was the first Fijian soldier to be killed in action engaging CT's when his Patrol engaged 12 CT's in the Batu Pahat area in Johore [*Ashes REP*]---]
Tue.	16th	Kuala Lumpur: The Sultan of Selangor stated: *'The Emergency would be hopefully over by Next Year!!*---]

Wed. 17th	10 Platoon 'D' Comp Suffolk's engaged 5 CT's in the Ulu Langat Forest Reserve Killing 1 the rest escaped.]
+	In the Changloon area of Kedah 2 miles from the scene of an previous ambush. Security forces found a hastily made grave revealing the body of a CT wounded in the ambush.---]
Thur. 18th	**18 SC Bakar B. Abdullah** F. M. Police Killed on Ops. Nami Police Post Kuala Nerang Kedah.---]
+	18 HMT EMPIRE WINDRUSH sailed Southampton bound for Singapore / Hong Kong with replacement Service personnel---]
Fri. 19th	**19 2/Lt.. P. M. Hargest**. New Zealand Infanty Regt.Died. Killed in Road accident.[*REP New Zealand*]---]
Sat. 20th	**20 F/Lt. B. Massey**- **F/Sgt. E. C. Powell** - **LAC. D. Kay**. Armn Mech Guns. 84 Sqdn R.A.F. Were killed when their Brigand RH 823. Lost a wing & crashed 8 miles South of Kota Tinngi. *Kranji Singapore # 3 / E -7 – 8 - 9* --]
Sun. 21st	**21 Pol/Lt. R.B. Dixon. - SC Noh B. Mohd. Amin**. F. M. Police Killed on CT Ops. During an attack on Terrorist Dixon charged them & was shot dead in the Kuala Medang area of Kuala Lipis Pahang.---]
+	The Chinese Manaager of the Paku Mining *(unnamed)* Kongsi was found murdered near Bidor Perak---]
+	4 CT's were killed in clashes. 2 Killed by a Patrol of the 2nd. Gurkhas in the Kaula Kangsarg area. 1 was Killed by a new Chinese F. M. Police SC Patrol in the Menong Kaula Kangsar area. 1 was killed ny a F. M. Police Patrol in the Chemor area North of Ipoh.---]
+	21 HMT LANCASHIRE arrived Singapore with replacement Service personnel---]
Mon.22nd	**22 Mr. B.E.M Beard**. Planter. Accidently shot by a member of the Special Force in the Tanah Merah area of Negri Sembilan---]
+	22 HMT LANCASHIRE sailed Singapore bound for Hong Kong---]
Tue. 23rd	**23 Recruit. Khulie** . 2nd King Edward VII's Own Gurkha Rifles . Died B.M.H. Kamunting.Sungei Patani *Sulva Lines # 65* Ipoh Perak.---]
+	23/12/1952 LG.39726 p. 6735 The following awarded the British Empire Medal (Military) SGT. R.C. HAWKINS. BEM ROYAL AUSTRALIAN AIR FORCE The following awarded the Distinguished Flying Cross SQDN/LDR. R. CARLING. DFC ROYAL AUSTRALIAN AIR FORCE
+	23 HMT EMPIRE HALLADALE arruived Singapore Sailed bound for Liverpool with returning Service personnel----]
+	23 HMT ASTURIAS arrived / sailed Singapore bound for Southampton with returning Service personnel---]
Wed. 24th	Auster AOP 6 VF556 656 Sqdn.AAC . Crashed on take –off at Seremban.---]
Thur. 25th	**25 L/Cpl. A. D. Row. - L/Cpl. D. J. Taylor**. R.M.P.. Died Motor Veh Acc. *Kranji Singapore # 2 / E – 5 - 4* .---]
+	25 HMT EMPIRE HALLADALE sailed for Liverpool with returning Service personnel---]
Fri. 26th	**26 D.S.I. Kok Ah Lek** F. M. Police. Killed on Ops Cuming Rd Seremban---]
+	'D' Comp Suffolk's engaged 2 CT's killed 1, fatally wounded another, Found him dying from his wounds. Identified as *Ah Ngew* member of the Min Yuen. The other killed unknown.---].
+	**26 6 F. M. Police SC's Omar B Ali** .- **Mohd. Hon B. Kasman** .- **Ishak B. Chandi**,- **Abd. Hamid B. Budin**. – **Abd. Hamid B. Hj. Mohd. Pamin**.- **Aziz B. Sahom**. Killed on Ops Sungei Bekok Estate Johore---]
Sat. 27th	**27 Pte. Ismail Bin Mohd. Wall**. R.A.O.C. (MOR) Died****Claimed by next of Kin* ---]
Sun. 28th	28 HMT EMPIRE TROOPER arrived Singapore with replacement Service personnel---]
Mon. 29th	**29 Pte. G. F. Cleveland** 1st.Battn. Somerset Light Infantry. Died*** *Kuala Lumpur # 21 / 1130* ---]
Tue. 30th	A prominent CT Leader **Phien Wek** alias **Chok Song Aaatn**. Platoon leader of the 12th. Regt. operating the Kedak North Perak area. Walked into a Police Station and surrendered. In his possession he had a Governments Surrender leaflet, 1 carbine, 2 rifles a hand grenade. He stated he was totally disillusioned with the MCP.---]
Wed. 31st	**31 Pol/Lt.C.S. Tozer** F. M. Police Killed on CT Ops. Johore Straits Johore. [*Grave unknown*]---]

R. A. F. OPERATION "FIREDOG" END OF YEAR STATISTICS 1952

No of Sorties	No. of Strikes	1,000 Lb.Bombs	500 Lb. Bombs	350 LbCluster	20 LbBombs	R/P's	20mm	.5 mm	.303mm
3,699	675	2,418	10,573	678	25,301	10,490	864,792	634,313	462,749

R. A. F. SUPPORT 1952

	Soties	Troops/Lift/	Casac	Pass/Lift	Supply Wt. Lbs	Leaflets drop (1,000)	B Flying Times No / hrs	Broadcsting No / hrs	Crashed
Air SupportA/C*	988	/	/	/	3,021,645	/	/	/	Brigand's
Auster**	/	/	/	/	/	/	/	/	RH755
Pioneer	/	/	/	/	/	/	/	/	RH 823
H/C Light	144	144	/	/	/	/	/	/	Hornet's
848 Sqdn	/	/	/	/	/	/	/	/	WB907

155 Sqdn	/		/	/	/	/	/	/	WB910 WB907
Target/MK**	/	/	/	/	/	/	/	/	Vampire's
Vis/Air OBs**	/	/	/	/	/	/	/	/	WG871WG882
Communication**	/	/	/	/	/	/	/	/	WG881
Leaf. Sorties*	53	/	/	/	/		/	/	Valetta
Leaflets Drop*	/	/	/	/	/	12,419	/	/	VX540
Leaf Sorties **	/	/	/	/	/	/	/	/	Mosquito
Leaflets Drop**	/	/	/	/	/	/	/	/	RR290
Broad Sorties*	/	/	/	/	/	/	/	/	Auster
Broad Hrs *	/	/	/	/	/	/	312	/	VX925 VX117
Broad Sorties**	/	/	/	/	/	/	/	/	WE543 VF 576
Broad Hrs **	/	/	/	/	/	/	/	/	VF602 VF616
Photo RECCE***	2195	/	/	/	/	/	/	/	VF556 VF619

* AirSupport A/C Dakota -Valetta- Hastings Bristol

** Auster

*** Photo Rec Anson,,Spitfire, Mosquito, Meteor, Pembroke

ROYAL NAVY FLEET AIR ARM
OFFENSIVE AIR SUPPORT - OPERATION 'FIREDOG'
January 1953 to Dec. 1956

Sqdn	Location	Aircraft Type	No	Date From	Year	Date To	Year
848	Semberwang	Sykorski S55 H/C	10	23rd. Jan.	1953	1st. May	1953
	Kuala Lumpur		10	1st. May	1953	26. Mar.	1956
	Then Semberwang		10	26th. Mar	1956	15th. Nov.	1956

JANUARY

Thur.	1st	**1 Pol /Lt. A Grant** F. M. Police . Died***. Johore Bahru. *Kranji Singapore # 8 / D – 3 –*]
	+	Operation *"Broderick"* Began against No 5 Regt. MRLA In Perak---]
	+	Operation *'Techchi.'* Began against No 6 Regt. MRLA. In Pahang---]
	+	Operations *"Cornwall"-" Commodore⌐"* "Began against No 3 & 4 Regt.'s. MRLA. In Johore---]
	+	Operation *"Question"* -*"Service"* Relationship between the Public & Police Continued---]
	+	Operation *"Ginger"* Began Public Attitude Relations ---]
	+	Operation. *'Eagle'* SAS against the MRLA---]
	+	Kuala Lumpur: Air Vice Marshal F.R.W. Scherger became Air Officer Commading Malaya ----]
Fri.	2nd	**2 Spr. Omparsad.Gurung.** Gurkha Engineers. Died by Accident BMH *Kluang #3 / A - 2*. Johore---]
	+	10 Plt 'D' Comp Suffolk's engaged 2 CT's on the Low Tikok Estate Killed both---]
Sat.	3rd	'A' Platoon of the Manchester Regt. Killed 1 CT ---]
Sun.	4th	Hong Kong: Letter from G.E. Aldington. Colonial Office to J.M. Addis Foreign Office Ref. Chinese Deportees in Malaya :
		'Though these Chinese deporteses were of Chinese origin and born in Formosa, the British were sceptical that the Taiwanese would accept them on the basis of them decent and their nationality.'---]
Mon.	5th	5 HMT EMPIRE ORWELL arrived Singapore sailed bound for Southampton with returning Service personnel]
	+	5 HMT GEORGIC arrived Singapore with replacement Service personnel---]
Tue.	6th	6 HMT GEORGIC sailed Singapore for Hong Kong ---]
Wed.	7th	7 The Somerset Light Infantry having finished jungle training relocated to Selangor. Their main object was the elimination of Number 1 Plt. MRLA under the leadership of **Liew Siew Fook** in command of about 25 CT's --]
	+	7 HMT EMPIRE PRIDE arrived Singapore bound for liverpool with returning servi personnel--]
Thur.	8th	Formosa: Letter from E.H. Jacobs-Larson British Consulate to J.M. Addis Hong Kong Foreign Office ref:
		'Anti Communist sympathisers deserved a special consideration , because their lives would be in danger if repatriated to Comminist China.' ---]
	+	8 HMT DUNERA sailed Southampton bound for Singapore/ Hong Kong with replacement Service personnel---]
Fri.	9th	**9 Rfn. Rudrabahadur Mall.** 2nd. King Edward VII's Own Gurkha Rifles. Died****Kranji Singapore # 7 / B – 7*]
	+	**9 Lt.(QGO) Manbir Taman** . 10th. Princess Mary's Own Gurkha Rifles. Died*** *Kranji Singapore # 7 / B - 8*]]
Sat.	10th	**10 Supt. A.W. Milton** F. M. Police Died***. *Kuala Lumpur.# 445*]---]
	+	10 HMT EMPIRE FOWEY arrived Southampton with returning Service personnel---]
Sun.	11th	Kuala Lumpur: The State Government issued Strict food controls were to introduced into Selangor in an effort to wipe out the Kajang Gang to starve them out Kill and illiminte their remenants Road blocks were to be installed to restrict all foods including rice. The restriction shall last as long as necessary ---]
Mon.	12th	Kuala Lumpur: The High Commisioner Sir. Gerald Templer greeted three ophan boys he has adopted from the Sernadah Boys Homes ---]
Tue.	13th	Penang: At the Gertak Sangul village 2,000 villagers were questioned with hand out questionaires containing photos of known Communist in the area of South Penang. The questionaires were to be handed back completed placed in lock up boxes for review This was done on the High Commisioners Sir. Gerald Templers instructions ---]
	+	13 HMT ASTURIAS arrived Southampton with returning Service personnel---]

Wed. 14th	A Platoon of the Manchester Regt. Engaged 2 CT's in thick Lalang grass. The CT's retreated firing. A burst from a bren gun Killed 1. The Patrol continued persuing the 2nd. CT wounded him capturing him handed over to the Police. The CT immediately agreed to assist in tracking down others. ---]
Thur. 15th	With the recently captured S.E.P.. Idenified as *Tuan Thiam* Former President of The Miners Union in Bidor Acting as a guide. The same Manchester Patrol set out in search of other CT's & came across a CT camp 1 CT made a dash for it into the jungle In the camp, two women CT's were Killed identified as *Yoke Chin & Pitt Yuen*. The escaped CT was identified by the S.E.P. as *Yoke Kuon* A Committee Member---]
+	15 HMT EMPIRE WINDRUSH arrived Singapore with replacement Service personnel/ sailed for Hong Kong 16th.---]
Fri. 16th	**16 L/Cpl. Yusof Bin . Othman.** R. A. S. C.(MOR). Died*** *Claimed by next of Kin* ---]
+	16/01/1953. LG # 39714 p358 The following awarded the Militsry Medal SGT. B. LIMBU MM 10th. PRINCESS MARY'S OWN GURKHA RIFLES
Sat. 17th	A Platoon of the 10th. Gurkhas laid a trap for a known CT Gang operating in the Gelang Patah area of Johore who were searching for food. Waiting for 2 days. Eventually 5 CT's arrived. 3 were Killed, two escaped without any food. Several sacks of potatoes and onions were retrieved by the Gurkhas---]
Sun. 18th	**18 Pte. E. W. V. Pheasant.** 1st. Battn. Somerset Light Infantry. Died by accident.*Kuala Lumpur #20 / 1099*
+	**18 L/Cpl. Jagatbahadur Limbu .** 7th Duke of Edinburgh's Own Gurkha Rifles. Died Dura Tipis Area MR WQ197976 *Seremban # 49* Negri Sembilan---]
+	18 HMT LANCASHIRE arrived Singapore from Hong Kong / Sailed for Liverpool with returning Service personnel 18th.---]
Mon. 19th	London: Letter from J.C. Jerrom Colonial Office to E.T. Briggs Foreign Office: '*The Malayan Government was cautioned by the Colonial Office and the Foreign Office, of the implication of sending deportees with communist sympathies to Formosa . Such a case might compromise H.M. Consul's position. ---]*
Tue. 20th	20 HMT GEORGIC The Suffolk Regt. sailed Singapore bound for England. With a record of 196 CT's Killed, which for British Regiments, was to remain thoughout to the end of the Emergency.---]
Wed. 21st	21 During a flight from Ipoh to a jungle Fort in Legap Perak a S51 Army Dragonfly H/C WT 848. Casualty Evac. Sqdn R.A.F. Changi Crashed when its rotor failed.1 mile from Chemor Perak. **The pilot F/O. B. F. Walters.** Was Killed also **Major E.C.R. Barker.** BEM Beds & Herts Regt. Att/22Nd SAS, & Asstn/ **Comd. G.D. C. Toulson KPM CPM** F. M. Police. *Kuala Lumpur # 21 – 1100 - RC / A – 1 - Batu Gajah 502 Ipoh* Perak---]
+	**21 Lt. P.B.S. Cartwright.** Royal Scots Fusilliers - **2/Lt. F.M . Donnelly-Woods.** The Queen's.- **Trp. B. Duckworth.** Royal Engineers.- **Trp. B. Watson** Wiltshire Regt. All Att/ 22 SAS Drowned on Operations.. *Kuala Lumpur # 20 / 1110* ---]
+	21 HMT EMPIRE CLYDE sailed Liverpool bound for Singapore with replacement Service personnel---]
Thur.22nd	**22 Pol/ Lt. J.D..A. Abercronie** F. M. Police Killed on Ops. *Batu Gajah # 505* Ipoh Perah.---]
Fri. 23rd	Royal Navy Fleet Air Arm 849 Sqdn. Sykorski S55 H/C Began operations from Semberwang---]
+	2 CT's surrendered to a Platoon of the Somersets ---]
Sat. 24th	300 Policemen set an 8 mile cordon across the centre of the city, in search of the Limping gumamn who shot Detective **See Chong Yee** last Wednesday---]
Sun. 25th	Six masked gunmen entered a shop at Bukit Panjang village. They looted the shop, got away with $100 they are thought to be associates to the Linping gunman?---]
Mon. 26th	The Sultan of Pahang. Invited Sir. Gerald Templer to visit New Villages and Kampongs in Pahang. To raise the morale of the people, as he had also done recently in Johore ---]
+	A Plt. of the Somersets engaged 4 CT's shot and wounded 1 and captured 3. The wounded one was identified as a District Committee Member ---]
Tue. 27th	**27 Sgt. R. Beaumont.** 1st. Battn. Somerset Light Infantry. Killed 2 CT's, unfortunately in the returning fire he was Killed in Action Engaging CT's.*Kuala Lumpur #20 / 1101*---]
Wed. 28th	**28 Trp. J. A. S. Morgan.** Middlesex Regt. Att/22nd. S.A.S . Died from wounds.*Kuala Lumpur # 20 / 1103* ---]
+	28 HMT EMPIRE FOWEY sailed Southampton bound for Singapore /Hong Kong with replacement Service personnel --]
+	28 HMT EMPIRE ORWELL arrived Southampton with returning Service personnel---]
+	28 HMT EMPIRE TROOPER arrived Southampton with returning Service personnel---]
Fri. 29th	**29 Cpl. D. M. Clothier.** 1st. Battn. Somerset Light Infantry. Killed In Action Engaging CT's. *Kuala Lumpur # 20 / 1104*---]
+	Kuala Lumpur :The Secretary of state for the Coloniesappointed: Mr. J.M.A. Nicholss as the new Deputy Commissioner of Federation of Malaya Police succeeding Mr. Robinson. ---]
Sat. 30th	**30 Rfn W.S. McHale.** 1st. Battn. Cameronians. Killed In Action Engaging CT's Kluang Johore

	Kranji Singapore # 2 / A – 13 ---]
+	30/01/1953 LG #39768 p. 701 The following awarded Bar to Military Cross
	CAPT. (QGO) K. RAI. MC + BAR IOM 10th. PRINCESS MARY'S OWN GURKHA RIFLES
Sat. 31st.	**31 Pte. Samek b. Kidam** Malay Regt. Killed in Action Engaging CT's Kedah---]
+	31/01/1953 LG # 39765 p. 625 The following awarded the Colonial Police Medal
	S/SGT. MOHAMMAD TAHIR B. AHMAD CPM THE FEDERATION MALAYA POLICE
	L/SGT. MANSOR. B. ALI. CPM THE FEDERATION MALAYA POLICE
	SC. DARTO B. AHMAD. CPM THE FEDERATION MALAYA POLICE
+	31 HMT EMPIRE PRIDE arrived Liverpool with returning Service personnel---]
+	Operation. *'Churchman' Hammer* Ended ---]

FEBRUARY

Sun.	1st	Operation *'Hardcastle'* Began SAS against the MRLA ---]
	+	A Patrol of the 2nd. Malay Regt. Killed a CT in the slim River area. Perak---]
	+	1 HMT EMPIRE WINDRUSH arrived Singapore with replacement Service personnel---]
Mon.	2nd	R.A.A.F. Lincoln Bombers dropped bombs on CT hideouts near Seremban Negri Sembilan---]
	+	A Patrol of the SAS shot and wounded a CT later he died ---]
	+	2 HMT DILWARA sailed Southampton bound for Singapore / Hong Kong with replacement Service personnel]
		RAF Hornets carried out several attacks on CT Camps in the same area of Seremban ---]
Tue.	3rd	A Patrol of the Kings African Rifles Killed a CT in the area of Bentong Pahang---]
	+	3 HMT EMPIRE WINDRUSH sailed Singapore bound for Southampton with returning Service personnel---]
Wed.	4th	4 HMT ASTURIAS sailed Southampton bound for Singapore / Hong Kong with replacement Service personnel]
Thur.	5th	*Ah Chin* CT boss of the Kahang district near Kluang was Killed by the F.M. Police Tiger force who came across 4 CT's drinking coffee with Rubber tappers the other 3 CT's escaped ---]
	+	5 HMT DUNERA arrived Singapore with replacement Service personnel---]
Fri.	6th	The Kinta Public Authorities in Ipoh Perak. Issued thousands of pamphlets requesting Residents should look aftter Ipoh and keep it clean---]
	+	6 HMT DUNERA sailed from Singapore bound for Southampton via Mombassa with returning Service personnel---]
Sat.	7th	**7 Pte. A. K. Johnson.** 1st. Battn. Somerset Light Infantry. Engaged 4 CT's killing 1 wouded another during the engagement Johnson was Killed in Action Engaging CT's *Kuala Lumpur. # 20 / 1102]*---]
Sun.	8th	Kuala Lumpur: Sir. Gerald Templer and Lady Templer set off on a 3 day tour of Kelantan travelling by boat, Rail & car. They were to visit many New villages and Kampongs on a Good Will visit.---]
Mon.	9th	A. F.M. Police Platoon were ambushed on the Sungei Siput / Kras road by a group of CT's. The Platoon opened fire on the CT's who did not return fire, instead just ran away ---]
Tue.	10th	A Fijian Patrol called for an air strike on a CT camp in the Langat Forest Reserve---]
Wed.	11th	RAF Hornets based at Butterworth carried out several attacks on the designated area---]
	+	A Fijian Patrol Killed 2 CT's. in the Pulai area---]
Thur.	12th	12 13/18th Hussars carried out a continuous barrage from their armoured cars, into the hills behind the village of Bukit Metajam near Taiping. Villagers stood and watched the barrage, that lasted for 90 minutes. A
	+	follow up by ground forces in progress--]
	+	12 HMT EMPIRE ORWELL sailed Southampton bound for Singapore with replacement Service personnel--13
Fri.	13th	**13 L/Cpl. Isak Bin. Din.** REME. (MOR) Died*** *Claimed by next of Kin* ---]
	+	**13 Capt. R.D. Duff.** The Gordon Highlanders Died by accident. *Kuala Lumpur # 20/ 1105*---]
	+	**13 Spr. G.F. Brennan.** Royal Engineers Died*** *Kranji Singapore # 2 / D – 14* ---]
Sat.	14th	Kuala Lumpur: John Davis CBE. DSO.Took on the position British Adviser in Pahang ---]
	+	14 HMT GEORGIC arrived Liverpool with the returning 1st. Battn. Suffolk Regt. ---]
Sun.	15th	15 HMT EMPIRE CLYDE arrived Singapore with replacement Service personnel 800 soldiers of the Sommerset Light Infantry 70% of the Battalion were National Servicemen. After 6 weeks training at Kota Tinggi they will join the Gurkha Brigade---]
Mon.	16th	London: The fate of *Lee Ming.* Still in Taiping jail was petitioned in the Privy Council in London. *Lee Ming* was represented by Mr. Dingle Foot a most respected legal eagle. The findings were that as she was deemed a pauper her appeal could not be upheld. However, a firm of London Solicitors took up her case. Called a press conference, therefore raised the situation in the House of Commons, with a petition for the death sentence to be lifted. It was signed by 50 MP's and sent to the Sultan of Perak. This was the beginning of an inquisition. And being the time of the Cold War & Spying was carried on by the East and West alike.

	Moscow, Hungary, China and the MCP became involved. The passivity of swopping one spy for another was the thought of the day. In Hungary there was one such name of a spy called Mr. E. Sanders who had been in a Hungarian jail since 1948. Therefore, would this be the case for negotiations between Hungary and the United Kingdom. Albeit *Lee Ming* was not a spy???---]
+	Penang: The curfew in Penang will be lifted overnight. To allow voting to be carried out---]
Tue. 17th	17 HMT LANCASHIRE arrived Liverpool with returning Service personnel ---]
Wed. 18th	London : A petition for clemency is being drawn up in London for *Lee Tan Tai* alias *Lee Ming* whose application to appeal by the Privy Council against Sentence of death was refused on Tuesday---]
+	London: 60 Members of Parliament have signed a petition to the Sultan of Perak requesting a pardon for *Lee Ming* the condemned woman Terrorist. The Petition will be flown out by a Comet aircraft this evening.]
Thur. 19th	The Commander of Number 1 Plt. MRLA *Liew Siew Fook* surrendered to the Somersets. *He* decided to become a SEP. Leading the Somersets to one of the Top CT's in Selangor. *Lau Cheng* ---]
+	19 HMT EMPIRE FOWEY arrived Singapore with replacement Service personnel---]
Fri. 20th	CT's cut the telephone wires in the Kuala Krai district of Kelantan---]
+	20 HMT EMPIRE FOWEY sailed Singapore enroute to Hong Kong ---]
Sat. 21st	R.A.A.F. Sqdn 1 Lincolns bomber bombed CT hideouts in dense jungle of Johore ---]
+	21 HMT EMPIRE CLYDE sailed Singapore bound for Liverpool with returning Service personnel---}
Sun. 22nd	RAF Hornets of 45 Sqdn. attacked CT camps in the area of Yong Peng Johore ---]
Mon. 23rd	Ipoh The petition for Clemancy for the convicted Communist *Lee Ming* was delivered to the Metri Besar of Perak. It will be the subject for discussion at the next meeting---]
Tue. 24th	In the Kulim District of Kedah 1 CT was Killed identified as *Lian How* on the wanted listed ---]
Wed. 25th	**25 Pte. M. Rabonu.** 1st. Battn. Fijian Regt. Killed in Action Engaging CT's [*Ashes Rep]* ---]
+	25 HMT ASTURIAS arrived Singapore with replacement Service personnel 26---]
Thur. 26th	Kuala Lumpur: Mr.W.L. Blythe of the Legislative State Council Stated : '*The Emergency Powers. Cannot be relaxed'* ---]
+	26 HMT ASTURIAS sailed Singapore enroute to Hong Kong---]
Fri. 27th	A Patrol of the Fijian Regt. Killed the Group Committee member of the Parit Sulong Group in Johore he was identified as *Chu Kee*. A woman with him escaped capture ---]
+	27 HMT EMPIRE TROOPER sailed Southampton bound for Singapore 'Hong Kong with replacement Service personnel---]
Sat. 28th	London: Britain will not. Trade *Lee Ming* under sentence of Death in Tiaping Jail, for Mr. Edgar Saunders in a Hungarian Jail accused of spying ---]

MARCH

Sun. 1st	Operation *"Cato"* Began against No 6 Regt. MRLA in Pahang.---]
	Operation *"Matador"* - *"Sword"* Began against No 6 Regt. MRLA Ruab Mentakab Bentong SW Pahang--]
+	6 Hornets a/c of 45 Sqdn. Provided air cover for ground troops in the jungle area of Bahat.---].
+	Intelligence information claimed: *Chin Peng* was encamped somewhere in the Cameron Highlands---]
Mon. 2nd	The Somersets led by the SEP *Liew Siew Fook*. Located *Lau Cheng* and Killed him and his bodyguard, 6 CT's surrendered.---]
+	Hornets a/c of 45 Sqdn. Attacked a target where approx. 100 CT's were being hunted by the 1st. Fijian Regt.]
+	2 HMT EMPIRE WINDRUSH arrived Southampton with returning Service personnel ---]
Tue. 3rd	3 HMT DILWARA sailed Southampton bound for Singapore with replacement Service personnel---]
Wed. 4th	**4 Cpl. D. Watkins.** Eng. Fit. R.A.F. Seletar Died from injuries recv'd, Motor traffic accident. on the 3rd. . *Kranji Singapore # 4 / D – 1* ---]
Thur. 5th	Operation *"Thrush"* began. The object was Food Denial throughout Lower Perak.---]
Fri. 6th	2 Hornets a/c of 45 Sqdn, provided air cover for ground troops in the Labis area.---]
+	06/03/1953 LG. # 39793 p.1299 The following awarded the British Empire Medal (Miliary)

F/SGT. E.M. M. MILLS. BEM	ROYAL AIR FORCE
SGT. R. J. JOHNSON. BEM	ROYAL AIR FORCE
SGT. J.G. LEDSON. BEM	ROYAL AIR FORCE

p. 1300

S/TECH. H. M. SOAMES. BEM	ROYAL AIR FORCE
CPL. P.R. RICHARDS. BEM	ROYAL AIR FORCE
CPL. J. S. ELLIS . BEM	ROYAL AIR FORCE REGT.
CPL. B. b. OTHMAN. BEM	ROYAL AIR FORCE REGT. (MALAYA)

	The following awarded the Distinguished Flying Cross	
	F/LT. P. J. BARDON.DFC	ROYAL AIR FORCE
	F/LT. I.S. MACPHERSON. DFC	ROYAL AIR FORCE
	F/LT. R. D. A. SMITH. DFC	ROYAL AIR FORCE
	The following awarded the Distinguished Flying Medal	
	F/SGT. N. GROVE. DFM	ROYAL AIR FORCE
	SGT. C. A, CORNFORD. DFM	ROYAL AIR FORCE

Sat. 7th — A Patrol of the Fijian Regt. Killed 3 CT's in the Gelang Patah area of Johore---]

Sun. 8th — In the same area another Patrol of the Fijians Regt. Killed 3 CT's---]

Mon. 9th — R. A. F. Aircraft attacked the. Camp where **Chin Peng** was supposedly hiding. A follow up revealed 2 CT's. were Killed three others wounded but no evidence of **Chin Peng** ---]

Tue. 10th — A Gurkha Patrol Killed 2 wanted CT's identified as **Phun Kow & Kim Kon Sang** ---]

Wed. 11th — 6 Hornet a/c of 45 Sqdn, attacked a number of CT's attempting to climb hills to avoid the flooding lower down. In the Kulang area---]

+ — The same number of Hornet a/c of 45 Sqdn, repeated their attack in the same area.---]

Thur. 12th — 12 Cpl. M. Adjetumbaya. 1st. King's African Rifles. Killed in Action Engaging CT's. *Ampan Road Mohammedan Cemetery #?* Kuala Lumpur. Together with **Pte. U. Saimon.** 3rd King's African Rifles. *Kuala Lumpur # RC / A -2* . ---]

+ — 12 HMT LANCASHIRE sailed Liverpool for Singapore- with replacement Service personnel --]

Fri. 13th — 13 Cpl. T. Pahalman. 6th.Queen Elizabeth's Own Gurkha Rifles.Killed on Ops. *Sungei Patani # 82*---]

+ — 6 Hornet a/c of 45 Sqdn, repeated their attack on the CT's in the same area. As previous day ---]

+ — 13 HMT EMPIRE FOWEY arrived Singapore sailed bound to Southampton with returning Service personnel-13th.---]

Sat. 14th — 4 Hornet a/c of 45 Sqdn, provided air cover for troops of the 6th.Malay Regt. Landing by Helicopter in the jungle near Kuala Lipis.---]

Sun. 15th — 15 Cpl. M Sahal. 3Rd. King's African Rifles. Killed in Action *[No known Grave]Terandak Wall Memorial Malacca]*

Mon. 16th — London: In The House of Commons Mr. Earnest Daves asked the Prime Minister Mr. Churchill: *'If he can announce the decision that had been reached on the offer made by the Hungarian Government. In regard to the release of Mr. Sanders in exchange for **Lee Ming**?'* Mr. Churchill The Prime Minister of Her Majesty's Government stated: *'After earnest consideration, have decided that they cannot entertain the proposals made by the Hungarian Government. There were other points raised regarding the release of Mr. Sanders .Nevertheless the question of **Lee Ming** stood.'*---]

Tue. 17th — Hong Kong: Letter from J.M. Addis to J.F .Brewis Singapore: ref Deportees to Formosa: *'It would not be Proper to ask the Formosan authorities to accept deportees who were not born in Formosa.]* Kuala Lumpur: Under the guidance of General Templer. The Government administrations Document ER 17D Deportation policy was abolished. Ceasing the need for deportation of Chinese Squatters & their dependants that had been in place for the previous 5 years.---]

+ — 17 HMT EMPIRE HALLADALE sailed Liverpool bound for Singapore / Hong Kong with replacement Service personnel ---]

+ — 17 HMT EMPIRE CLYDE arrived Liverpool with returning Service personnel---]

Wed. 18th — 2 Hornet a/c of 45 Sqdn. Attacked a pin point target South of Kuala Lumpur with RPS and Cannon fire---]

Thur. 19th — 19 Rfn. Partap Ale. 10th. Princess Mary's Own Gurkha Rifles. Killed in Action Engaging CT's *Kranji Singapore # 7 / B -9-*]

+ — 19 HMT EMPIRE ORWELL sailed Singapore bound for Southampton with returning Service personnel---]

+ — 19 HMT ASTURIAS arrived Singapore ---]

Fri. 20th — A F.M. Police force of 150 men completed an arduous trek along the Malay /Thailand Border their task was to cut off 3 escape routes used by CT 's to cross the border into Thailand in the Belum Valley---]

+ — 20 HMT ASTURIAS sailed Singapore bound for Southampton with returning Service personnel---]

Sat. 21st — 21 Lt. P.B.S. Cartwright. R.S.F. 2/Lt. F.M. Donnelly-Woods. The Queen's., **Spr. B. Duckworth.** R.E., **Trp. B. Watson.** Wiltsshire Regt. Att/ 22nd. S.A.S. All Drowned on Ops. *Kuala Lumpur # 20 / 1110 – RC / A -3 20 / 1108 – 20 1106* ---]

Sun. 22nd — A Patrol of the Kings African Rifles, Killed a woman CT, identified as **Chow Ying Pa**. She was with another 3 CT's who fled when the Africans discovered them, the woman was at the rear of the file---]

Mon. 23rd —

Tue. 24th	A CT surrendered to the Somersets He was identified as the last member of Number 1 Plt MRLA, Thus he being the last. So! eliminating the whole of Number 1 Platoon. The Somersets then moved to Sepang. Their
+	objective there, was another high ranking CT. **Yong Kwo** ---]
+	**24 Lt. F.S. Tulk**. 22nd. SAS. Died Motor Veh. Acc. _Singapore # 2 / E – 7_.---]
	24 Cfn. Mohd. Yassin. Bin. Talib. R. E. M. E. (MOR) Died*** _Claimed by next of Kin_ ---]
Wed. 25th	2. Hornet a/c of 45 Sqdn, provided air cover for troops landing by H/C in the jungle near Kuala Lipis. Operation
+	"_Running Jack_"---]
Thur. 26th	**25 Sgt. L. C. Patten**. Womens Royal Army Corps. Died*** _Kranji Singapore # 2 / E -3_---]
	2 R.A.F. Hornets a/c provided air cover for troops landing by H/C in the jungle near Kuala Lipis---].
+	**26 Pte's. A. Campbell**. - **T.E. Cronin** The Gordon Highlanders Drowned on Patrol.
	Kuala Lumpur # 20 / 1109 - 1107.---]
	26 Pol/Lt. D.H. Chapin. F.M. Aux. Police Killed in Action Engaging CT's near Lasah. 2 CT's were Killed & 1
Fri. 27th	captured. **Chapin** died as he threw himself upon a Terrorist, whose escape would otherwise have been certain.
+	His group made contact with the party of CT's in the Lasah area Sungei Siput. _Batu Gajah # 504_ Ipoh Perak]
Sat. 28th	**27 PC. Ri B. Alang Ahmed**. F. M. Police Killed Bukit Yong Police Station. Kelantan---].
	27 Mr. R. Castle .British Civilian Killed by a CT. Selangor.---]
Sun. 29th	**28 F/O. A.J. Rosser**. Att. To 77 Sqdn R.A.A.F.. Killed when his Meteor A77-858 was lost over the jungle.
+	_[No known Grave]_ Terandak Wall Memorial Malacca.---]
Mon. 30th	**29 L/Cpl. E.J. Down**. 1st. Battn. Somerset Light Inf. Died***_Kuala Lumpur # 21 / 1112_---]
Tue. 31st	**29 HMT EMPIRE WINDRUSH** sank Mediterranean Sea. 37 N. 211 E. All Passengers Survived---]
	3 Hornet a/c of 45 Sqdn, R.A.F.provided air cover for troops landing by H/C in the Jungle near Kuala Lipis--]
+	31/03/1953 LG # 39813 p 1804/5 The following awarded the George Medal
	IBAN T. MENGGONG ANAK PENGGIT GM SARAWAK RANGERS
	31 HMT DILWARA arrived Singapore enroute to Hong Kong with replacement Service personnel 31st. ---]

APRIL

Wed.	1st	**1 Sgt. H. Bocek** Far East Training Sqdn R.A.F. Killed when his Hornet PX344. Crash landed 14 miles East of Malacca. _Singapore # 4 / D – 6_ ---]
	+	Operation "_Screw_ "Began against No 3 & 4 Regt. MRLA in Johore---]
	+	Operations "_Cornwall_"-"_Screw_" Began against No 5 Regt.MRLA Tapah Perak---]
	+	Operation '_Pageant_' Began SAS against the MRLA---]
	+	1 HMT EMPIRE TROOPER arrived Singapore with replacement Service personnel sailed for Hong Kong 1st]
	+	1 HMT DUNERA arrived Southampton returning Service personnel---]
Thur.	2nd	} Combined Operations continued throughout Malaya---]
Fri.	3rd	3 EMPIRE FOWEY arrived Southampton with returning Service personnel---]
Sat.	4th	} Combined Operations continued throughout Malaya---]
Sun.	5th	Kuala Kangsar: The Sultan Of Perak received notice from London: '_The Death Sentence on_ **Lee Ming** _should be recinded to that of a Life sentence in Prison_' ---]
Mon.	6th	} Combined Operations continued throughout Malaya---]
Tue.	7th	}
Wed.	8th	**8 Sdn/Ld. C. T. White. MBE**. Eng/Off. R.A.F.Seletar Died ***_Kranji Singapore # #4 / D – 5_ ---]
Thur.	9th	**9 F/O. R.L James** Att. to 77 Sqdn R.A.A.F. Killed when his Meteor A77- 643 was lost over the jungle
		[No known Grave] Terandak Memorial Malacca ---]
	+	**9 W/O. H. B. Brown**. R. A. A. F Died ** _Kranji Singapore- # 4 / D - 4_---]
	+	9 HMT EMPIRE ORWELL arrived Southampton with returning Service personnel---]
Fri.	10th	10 6 F.M. Police: **SC's Mohamed Rashid B. Ngah M. Noh** .-- **Mohamed Kahlid B. Manchick**. - **Ismail B. Meod**. – **Hassan B. Ahmed** .- **Manap B. Aj. Sait**. – **Ahmad Zuki B. Putah Abdullah**. F. M. Police Killed on CT Ops.Sungei Siput Area Perak.---]
	+	10 HMT LANCASHIRE arrived Singapore with replacement Service personnel---]
	+	10 HMT ASTURIAS arrived Southampton with returning Service personnel---]
Sat.	11th	} Combined Operations continued throughout Malaya---]
Sun.	12th	}
Mon.	13th	**13 Cpl. T. Pahalman Thapa** 6th. Queen Elizabeth's Own Gurkha Rifles Died Motor Veh. Acc. _Sungei Patani # 82_ Kedah ---]
Tue.	14th	**14 Rfn. Amersing Thapa**. Queen Elizabeth's Own Gurkha Rifles Died from wounds recv'd previous day Motor Veh Acc._Sungei Patani # 83_.---]

+	**14 Rfn. Tilakbahadur Chhetri.** 10th. Princess Mary'sOwn Gurkha Rifles. Killed Kamunting. ---] *Kranji Singapore # 7 / B / 10 ---]*	
+	14 HMT LANCASHIRE sailed from Singapore bound for Mombassa ---]	
+	14 HMT EMPIRE HALLADALE arrived Singapore with replacement Service personnel---]	
Wed. 15th	} Combined Operations continued throughout Malaya---]	
Thur. 16th	16 HMT EMPIRE HALLADALE sailed for Hong Kong---]	
Fri. 17th	**17** 2 F. M. Police **SC's Mohamed Tap. B. Mohamed Zin B. Mohamed.** Killed on Ops. Gemas Bahru New Village Johore---]	
Sat. 18th	Combined Operations continued throughout Malaya---]	
Sun. 19th	**19 Gp/Capt. P. C. Hilton.** Sen/Per/O. R.A.F. HQ FEAF. Died Nat. causes *Kranji Singapore # 3 / B – 9* ---]	
+	19 HMT EMPIRE TROOPER arrived Singapore from 'Hong Kong ---]	
Mon. 20th	20 HMT EMPIRE TROOPER sailed bound for Sothampton with returning Service personnel---]	
Tue. 21st	**21** 2 F. M. Police **Pol/Lt. A. B. Wilmot. Pol/Lt. A. Bernard** Killed on CT Ops. Kulim area Kedah *Jalan Pertana # ?? 1488* George Town Penang ---].	
Wed.22nd	22 HMT ASTURIAS sailed Southampton bound for Singapore / Hong Kong with replacement Service personnel---]	
Thur. 23rd	**23 2/Lt. D. W. Manning.** 1st. Battn. The Queen's Own Royal West Kent Regt. Killed in Action Engaging CT's *Kuala Lumpur # 21 / 1111*---]	
+	23/04/1953 LG. # 39833 p. 2261 The following awarded the Military Cross LT. J.M.C. THORNTON. MC 7th DUKE OF EDINBURGH'S OWN GURKHA RIFLES.	
Fri. 24th	} Combined Operations continued throughout Malaya---]	
Sat. 25th	}	
Sun. 26th	26 HMT DILWARA arrived Singapore ---]	
Mon. 27th	27 HMT DILWARA sailed Singapore bound for Southampton with returning Service personnel---]	
Tue. 28th	28/04/1953 LG # 39839 p.2605 The following awarded the British Empire Medal (Military)	
	S/SGT. J. BEALE. BEM	ROYAL CORPS SIGNALS
	S/SGT. F. W. OFFARD. BEM	ROYAL CORPS SIGNALS
	SGT. F. R. RIDER. BEM	ROYAL SUFFOLK REGIMENT.
	SGT. K. SUDELL. BEM	ROYAL NORFOLK REGIMENT.
	W/O. A. DALLEN. BEM	QUEEN'S OWN ROYAL WEST KENTS
	W/O. GODFREY son of MHANOO. BEM	KINGS AFRICAN RIFLES
Wed. 29th	**29 L/Cpl. E. J. Down** 1st. Battn. Somerset Light Infantry. Died*** *Kuala Lumpur # 21 1112*---]	
Thur. 30th	30 HMT DUNERA sailed Southampton bound for Singapore / Hong Kong with replacement Service personnel---]	
+	Operation *'Hardcastle'* Ended ---]	

MAY

Fri. 1st	Operation *"Commodore"* Began SAS in the Kemesul Forest Reserve---]	
+	1 Royal Navy Sqdn. 848 became operational RAF Kuala Lumpur ---]	
+	1/05/53 LG #39839 p2406 The following awarded a Bar to the Military Cross	
	Lt. N.T. BAGNAL. MC & BAR	THE GREEN HOWARDS
		The following awarded the Military Cross
	CAPT. (QGO) L. THAPA. MC	6th.QUEEN ELIZABETH'S OWN GURKHA RIFLES
	LT. R.B.RUSBY. MC	THE NORTH STAFFORDSHIRE REGT.
	LT. HITAM. MC	MALAY REGIMENT.
		The following awarded the Distinguished Conduct Medal
	SGT. B. LIMBU. DCM	10th PRINCESS MARY'S OWN GURKHA RIFLES
		The following awarded the Military Medal
	SGT. G. CARSON. MM.	ROYAL SCOTS.
	SGT. J. G. THOMAS. MM	13/18th ROYAL HUSSARS.
	SGT. R. EVANS. MM	THE SUFFOLK REGIMENT.
	CPL. C. HELMAN. MM	THE GREEN HOWARDS
	RFN. D. ROKA. MM	2nd. KING EDWARD VII'S OWN GURKHA RIFLES
	L/CPL K. GURUNG. MM	6th QUEEN ELIZABETH'S OWN GURKHA RIFLES
	L/CPL.K. THAPA. MM.	6th QUEEN ELIZABETH'S OWN GURKHA RIFLES
	CPL. K. GURUNG. MM	10th PRINCESS MARY'S OWN GURKHA RIFLES

SGT. B. RAI. MM	10th PRINCESS MARY'S OWN GURKHA RIFLES
WO2 G. RAI. DSM. MM	10th PRINCESS MARY'S OWN GURKHA RIFLES
SGT. M. B. ALIT. MM	MALAY REGIMENT
CPL. D.B. INGGAL. MM	MALAY REGIMENT
L/CPL ALI s/o LALE. MM	KING'S AFRICAN RIFLES
WOPC K.A. MATTO. MM	KING'S AFRICAN RIFLES

	+	Royal Navy Fleet Air Arm 849 Sqdn. Sykorski S55 H/C Tansferred to Kuala Lumpur---]
	+	1 HMT EMPIRE ORWELL sailed Southampton bound for Singapore/Hong Kong /Kure /Pusan with replacement Service personnel---]
Sat.	2nd	Singapore – The London bound Comet jet airliner flew out of Changi with 4 members of the Rubber Producer Council. Bound for a Conference in Copenhageen of the Rubber Study Group ---]
Sun.	3rd	Auster T7 WE614 656 Sqdn A.A.C. Nosed over on landing at Noble Field Selengor S/Ldr F. Tamms badly injurded. survived the crash.---]
Mon.	4th	Singapore: The Comet airliner which flew out of Changi on Saturday. Crashed in a storm 22 miles from Calcutta their were no survivors ---]
Tue.	5th	A fire in the New Village of Batu Dua Bias destroyed 5 homes.It was the 2nd. fire in 3 Months it partly destroyed the Police Station. 53 families became homeless ---]
Wed.	6th	Kuala Lumpur: Go Ahead For Federal Elections. Sir. Donald MacGillivray president of the Fereration Council announced: 'The High Commisioner and Rulers have agreed that it is time for a pratical examination of the pratical issues to be looked at.'---]
Thur.	7th	7 L/Cpl. A. J. Secrett. 1st. Battn. The East Yorkshire Regt. Died Battle Accident. Kranji Singapore # 2 / E – 6]
Fri.	8th	8 S/Mech. T.J. McTaggart H.M.S 'UNICORN' Died*** Western Road # 2898 George Town Penang---]
Sat.	9th	} Combined Operations continued throughout Malaya---]
Sun.	10th	10 Rfn. Ishorbahadur Rai . 10th. Princess Mary's Own Gurkha Rifles. Died*** Kranji Singapore # 8/ B -3-]
Mon.	11th	11 Cpl. J. G. White. R.A.F. Police Changi. Died*** Kranji Singapore # 4 / D – 3 ---]
Tue.	12th	Kuala Lumpur:The National Conference working Committee held its second meeting on the Unity of Malaya---]
	+	The Kelantan –Tenggannu Express bus whilst attemting to board the river ferry, drove into the river Terengganu. It was completely immersed, all 12 passengers swam to the river bank---]
	+	12 /05/1953 LG # 39851 p. 2649 The following awarded the Military Cross

Lt. J.A. BUTLER. MC	THE CAMERONIANS.
SC MURAD B. ALI. CPM	THE FEDERATION MALAYA POLICE
ASP. G. D. HODGSON PM	THE FERERATION MALAYA POLICE .

Wed.	13th	The Royal Navy exploded 50 tons of Japanese bombs that had been dumped in the sea since August 1945. East of Pulah Tekong Besar 1,000 people were evacuated from the area. Prior to the explosion that set for & went of at 12.30 pm.---]
Thur.	14th	14 F/Lt. D. R. Parsons. 33 Sqdn R.A.F. Killed when his Hornet WB872 dived into the ground at Kroh airstrip after leading an attack at Kroh. Perak. Western Road # 2149 George Town Penang ---]
Fri.	15th	A search was carried out to find the crashed Hornet---]
	+	15 HMT EMPIRE HALLADALE called Singapore with returning Service personnel enroute to Liverpool--]
Sat.	16th	16 Major. C.F.F. Anderson. Royal Artillery Died*** Kranji Singapore # 2 / E -9---]
	+	Dragonfly HAR4 WF311 Casvac Flight After engine failure crashed near Kuning.F/Lt. W. Pinner unhurt.---]
Sun.	17th	17 F/O G. P. Doolittle. Att./to 77 Sqdn R.A.A.F Killed whilst flying Meteor A77-85 [No know grave] Terandak Wall Memorial Malacca ---]
Mon.	18th	London: Sir. John Nichols. Governor of Singapore in transit by Comet after meetings in London ---]
Tue.	19th	} Combined Operations continued throughout Malaya---]
Wed.	20th	20 HMT EMPIRE TROOPER arrived Southampton with returning Service personnel also on board were The Malayan /Singapore Delegation arriving for the Queen's Coronation. A welcome message to the Malayan Singapore Delegation, was read out by the Senior Commision for the Police Mr. T. Gafikin on behslf of Sir. Gerald Templer.---[
Thur.	21st	21 A/B L.M. Galipeau H.M.S. 'TERROR' Died*** Kranji Singapore # ??---]
Fri.	22nd	1,000 troops of the East Yorks Regt. The Gurkhas, Field Artillery units, F. M Police & Home Guards were airlifted by Helicopters from Kluang, into the jungle to seek out & destroy The Communist Committee of South Johore---]
Sat.	23rd	23 Rfn. Balbir Gurung 2nd. King Edward VII's Own Gurkha Rilfes Killed. [No known Graves]TerandakWall Memorial Malacca---]

+	23 HMT DILWARA arrived Southampton with returning Service personnel---]
Sun. 24th	The Operation to lift 1,000 troops Took 2 days to complete.---]
+	24 HMT EMPIRE ORWELL arrived Singapore with replacement Service personnel enroute to Hong Kong--
Mon. 25th	25 Rfn. Gyanbahadur Gurung . 2nd. King Edward VII's' Own Gurkha Rifles. Drowned on Operations
	[No known Grave]Terandak Wall Memorial Malacca---]
Tue. 26th	Shots were fired at a convoy of the 12th. Lancers on the Chemor Jalpang Rosd near Ipoh.
	1 shot went through the Land Rovers glass, just missing the driver. The Lancers returned heavy fire
	throwing grenade in the direction of the shots. There were no Casualties---]
+	26/05/1953 LG # 39869 p. 3012 The following awarded the British Empire Medal (Military)
	SGT. J. NEWAR. BEM 7th. DUKE OF EDINBURGH'S GURKHA RIFLES
	W/O. N.G.E. STEVENS. BEM ROYAL ELECTRICAL MECHANICAL ENGINEERS
	SGT. M. DACRE. BEM ROYAL AIR FORCE
	S/TECH. W. W PERRYMAN. BEM ROYAL AIR FORCE
	The following awarded the Bar to the Distinguished Flying Cross
	F/LT. J.R. DOWLING. DFC + BAR ROYAL AIR FORCE
	F/LT. R. HARLING. DFC + BAR ROYAL AIR FORCE
	F/O. S. EDMON.DSON. DFC + BAR ROYAL AIR FORCE
	The following awarded the Distinguished Flying Medal
	F/SGT. AM MOSS DFM ROYAL AIR FORCE
+	26 HMT ASTURIAS arrived / sailed Singapore bound for Southampton with returning Service personnel---]
Wed. 27th	27 HMT LANCASHIRE arrived Singapore- with replacement Service personnel onboard were the 2nd..
	Battalion King's African Rifles arriving to reinforce the 1st Battlion Kings African Rifles --]
Thur. 28th	28 HMT DUNERA arrived Singapore with replacement Service personnel ---]
+	28 HMT EMPIRE CLYDE sailed Liverpool bound for Singapore / Hong Kong with replacement Service
	personnel---]
Fri. 29th	29 HMT EMPIRE HALLADALE arrived Liverpool with returning Service personnel---]
Sat. 30th	Sir. Gerald Templer For his Service in Malaya was awarded the:
	Insignia of a Knight Grand Cross of the Order of St, Michael and St. George. ---]
Sun. 31st	R.A.A.F. Lincoln Bombers of 1Sqdn during the week flew 15 sorties dopping 4.000 lb bomba on the jungles
	below The Blockbusters blasted huge craters in the canopy. A total of over 57 tons were dropped---]
+	31 HMT LANCASHIRE sailed for Liverpool with returning Service personnel---]

JUNE

Tue. 1st	1 Trp. B. Powell. Seaforth Highlanders. Tpr. A.E.Howell Att/22nd. SAS. Died from injuries received in
	Dragonfly No? Helicopter crash. Kuala Lumpur # 21 – 1138 – RC / A – 6 ---]
+	Operation 'Eclipse' Began against No. No 8 Regt. MRLA In Kedah.---]
+	Operation 'Jekyll 'began against No 2 Regt. MRLA in the Bahau area of Negri Sembilan---]
+	Operation 'Matador ' Flame" Began. SAS against the MRLA ---]
+	1 HMT DUNERA sailed Singapore bound for Southampton with returning Service personnel---]
Wed. 2nd	2 Cpl. B. Mason.Den. Admin. R.A.F. Changi Drowning accident Kranji Singapore # 4 / A – 5 ---]
Thur. 3rd	London: The Coronation of her Majesty Queen Elizabeth the II took place in West Minister Abbey---]
Fri. 4th	4 Mr. R. Chestnut Manager. & Mr. W. R. Mc Connachei Asstn.Manager. Harewood Estate Sungei Siput.
	were Killed in an ambush by 6 CT's in Perak.---]
Sat. 5th	5 HMT EMPIRE FOWEY sailed Southampton enroute to Singapore / Hong Kong with replacement Service
	personnel sailed 6th.---]
Sun. 6th	6 Rfn. Kajibahadur Rai . No 3 Platoon A Company 10th. Princess Mary's Own Gurkha Rifles. was Killed in
	Action Engaging CT's. The CT's escaped Kranji Singapore # 7 / B -3---]
Mon. 7th	An air strike was called by the Gurkha's. To try & stop the reteating CT's. The designated area was
	plastered with bombs from the R. A. F. Planes.---]
+	Acting on information given by a captured CT, who himself had Killed 3 high ranking CT's. Operation "Goliath"
	Began in search of the three graves, by the 1st Malay Regt.---]
Tue. 8th	} Combined Operations continued throughout Malaya but no contacts. made ---]
Wed. 9th	CT's cut telephone wires in the Batu Pahat area of Johore ---]
Thur. 10th	A CT surrendered to the Kota Tingi Police Informing them of the air strike without any casualties---]
Fri. 11th	Patrols of the Gurkha's went out in search of the other CT's & successfully Killed I CT'---]
Sat. 12th	

Sun. 13th	An Armoured car of the 11th. Hussars was held up on the road by a CT, with his hands raised in surrender. The Hussar's Bren gunner noticed other figures under cover in the side foliage & opened fire The CT's dispersed & got away.---] Kuala Lumpur: It was announced that the Troop lifting Operation on the 24th May, resulting in the elimination
Mon. 14th	of *Meng Soon, Chow Lup,* & a woman CT *Luan Chu Klok* senior members of the South Johore Committee & responsible for many atrocities ---]
Tue. 15th	} Combined Operations continued throughout Malaya ---]
+	**15 Sgt. T. H. Ashworth**. Royal Signals Died *** *[Ashes REP]*---] 15/06/1954 LG. # 40206 p. 3595 The following awarded the British Empire Medal (Military)
Wed. 16th	CAPT. D.R. BOYNS MD. BEM ROYAL ARMY MEDICAL CORPS
+	**16 HMT ASTURIAS** arrived Southampton with returning Service personnel---]
+	**16 HMT EMPIRE ORWELL** called Singapore enroute to Southampton with returning Service personnel---] Operation *"Goliath"* ended. With the 3 bodies being found. One of the bodies was identified as *Lau Fatt*
Tue. 17th	the 5th. top wanted CT.---] Kuala Lumpur Mr. Josiah Francis The Australian Army Minister flew back to Canberra to report back to the
+	Australian Governemnt on his meeting with Sir. Gerald Templer on the situation in Malaya ---] **17 HMT DILWARA** sailed Southampton bound for Singapore / Hong Kong via Mombassa with replacement
+	Service personel ---]
Fri. 18th	**17 HMT EMPIRE TROOPER** sailed Southampton bound for Singapore with replacement Service personnel] Kuala Lumpur: Figures issued by the Security Force show that 87 CT's were illuminated last Month with 8
+	Captured and 14 surrendered---] 18/6/54. LG # 40206 p. 3596 The following awarded the Military Medal CPL. T. THAPA. MM 6th QUEEN ELIZABETH'S OWN GURKHA RIFLES
Sat. 19th	RFN. B. GURUNG. MM 6th QUEEN ELIZABETH'S OWN GURKHA RIFLES
Sun. 20th	**19 Drv. Bickley.** R.A.S.C Killed in Transport Accident *Taiping #?* Perak---] Members of the Red Cross Girl Guides. Visited the British Military Hospital Kinrara. near Kuala Lumpur to see the treatment administered to British and Commonwealth troops some 200 patients of British Gurkha and African and 1 Sarawak Ian amongst them, are Tuberculosis patients. Kinrara has 100 such sufferers and it the
Mon. 21st	largest Hospital to treat the disease. ---]
Tue. 22nd	} Combined Operations continued throughout Malaya ---]
Wed. 23rd	**22 HMT EMPIRE CLYDE** arrived Singapore enroute Hong Kong with replacement Service personnel---]
+	**23 L/Cpl. Siray Rai .** 7th. Duke of Edinburgh's Own Gurkha Rifles Died****Kranji Singapore #7 / B - 5* ---]
Thur. 24th	**23 HMT EMPIRE CLYDE** sailed Singapore enroute Hong Kong ---]
Fri. 25th	Operation *"Matador"* began. To destroy CT cultivation plots deep in the jungle--] **25** Acting on information provided by the F.M. Police of the noise of firing, possibly an ambush on the Kulai Oil Palm Estate Johore. A Officer of the 10th. Gurkhas along with his driver of the Scout car arrived on the scene to find a burnt out landrover, the dead body of **Mr. P . A. Gregoire** lying in the middle of the road & F.M. Police SC, lying wounded by the side of the road. Further searching found the Estate Manager Pol/Inspt. W. A. Gibson, who was seriously wounded. The call for assistance went out & later a Platoon of Gurkhas arrived. The Estate Manager & the F.M. SC were taken away to the Johore Bahru hospital, 20 miles away. Without much hope of catching them, the Gurkha's gave chase after the CT's. However, unknown at the time there was a third member of the ambushed party. Mr. C. Shawcross who was found later. He explained that he had been led well away, questioned by the CT's. He answered he was staying in Singapore investigating an air crash. Only then did the CT's release him. Possibly was the reason why he was
+	released unharmed ?---] 25/06/54 LG# 40217 p. 3820 The following awarded the Military Cross CAPT. D.R.L WYMAN MC ROYAL REGIMENT ARTILLERY ATT/T MALAY REGT. CAPT. J.A. LYS MC 6th. QUEEN ELIZABETH'S OWN GURKHA RIFLES LT. (QGO) S. RAI.MC 7th. DUKE OF EDIMBURGH'S OWN GURKHA RIFLES Lt. P.S. LEIGH MC QUEEN'S OWN ROYAL WEST KENTS 2/Lt. R.A. DOUGLAS. MC. THE SOMERSET LIGHT INF. The following awarded the Mlitary Medal SGT.V.C. R. HEALEY.MM . QUEEN'S OWN ROYAL WEST KENTS RFN T. THAPA. MM 2nd. KING EDWARD VII'S OWN GURKHA RIFLES WO2 L. THAPA MM 6th QUEEN ELIZABETH'S OWN GURKHA RIFLES SGT. B. RAI MM 7th. DUKE OF EDINBURGH'S OWN GURKHA RIFLES RFN. G. SUNWAR. MM 7th.DUKE OF EDINBURGH'S OWN GURKHA RIFLES

Sat. 26th	CPL. B. B.H. BUSIN MM MALAY REGIMENT.
Sun. 27th	SGT. S. RAVOKA. MM FIJI REGIMENT.
	26 Pol/Inspt. W. A, Gibson died from his wounds received during the previous days ambush.---]
Mon. 28th	London: Sir. Oliver Lytleton advised the House of Commons:
+	*'It was estimated to be 380 CT's active on the Malaya / Thailand Border.' ---]*
Tue. 29th	**28 Cpl. Jamaludin b. Rejab** Malay Regt. Killed in Action Engaging CT's Kedah---]
	28 HMT EMPIRE FOWEY arrived Singapore with replacement Service personnel enroute to Hong Kong
Wed. 30th	29 HMT EMPIRE HALLADALE sailed Liverpool bound for Singapore/ Hong Kong with replacement Service personnel ---]
	Kuala Lumpur: A Communist issued document retrieved from a captured CT. Rvealed that Operation *'Sting'*
+	Had a devastating effect on the CT's. They were being starved. In response they issued instruction for
+	more cultivation plots to be made in remote parts iof the Jungles ---]
	30 HMT DUNERA arrived Southampton with returning Service personnel---]
	Operation *Pageant'* Ended ---]

JULY

Wed. 1st	**1 Pte. H. C. Stevenson** 1st. Battn. The Queen's Own Royal Wests Kent Regt. Died by Accident *Kuala Lumpur # 21 / 1118*---]
+	Operation "*Sword*" began against No 8 Regt. MRLA in Kedah.---]
+	Operation ' *Mustang' 'Biter'* Began SAS against the MRLA---]
Thur. 2nd	2 HMT LANCASHIRE arrived Liverpool with returning Service personnel ---]
Fri. 3rd	3/07/53 LG # 39904 p 3682 The following awarded the Military Cross
	LT. (QGO) B. LAMA. MC 10th. PRINCESS MARY'S OWN GURKHA RIFLES.
	The following awarded the Military Medal
	L/CPL. N. LIMBU. MM 10th PRINCESS MARY'S OWN GURKHA RIFLES
	WO2 H. RAI. MM 10th PRINCESS MARY'S OWN GURKHA RIFLES
	SGT. N. LAGI. MM FIJI REGT.
Sat. 4th	**4 Cfn. W. Greenwood.** R.E.M. E. Died*** *Kuala Lumpur # 21 / 1120* ---]
Sun. 5th	} Combined Operations continued throughout Malaya---]
Mon. 6th	}
Tue. 7th	7 HMT ASTURIAS sailed Southampton bound for Singapore /Hong Kong with replacement Service personnel---]
Wed. 8th	8 HMT EMPIRE CLYDE arrived Singapore enroute to Liverpool with replacement Service personnel 8th.]
Thur. 9th	**9 Cpl. Barandhoj Rai** . 10th. Princess Mary's Own Gurkha Rifles. Died*** *Kranji Singapore # 7 / C -2* ---]
+	9 HMT EMPIRE ORWELL arrived Southampton with returning Service personnel---]
Fri. 10th	**10 Sgnm. N. De Costa.** Royal Signals Died*** *Seremban # P / 1009* Negrei Sembilan---]
Sat. 11th	} Combined Operations continued throughout Malaya---]
Sun. 12th	**12 Maj. G. V. Seymour. MC.** 1st. Battn. Royal Scots Fusiliers. Died*** *Kranji Singapore # 2 / E – 8* ---]
Mon. 13th	} Combined Operations continued throughout Malaya
Tue. 14th	**14 Spr. Sidi Bin Shafi** Royal Engineers (MOR) Died*** *Claimed by next of Kin* ---]
Wed. 15th	**15 F/O. B. P. H. Lacy.** 45 Sqdn. R.A.F. Killed when his Hornet WB898 crashed dived into ground.10 miles N.W Butterworth. *Western Road # 2150* George Town Penang---]
+	15 HMT DILWARA arrived with replacement Service personnel---]
Thur. 16th	**16 Pol/Lt. A.I. M cKinven** F. M Aux.Police Killed on Ops. [*Grave unknown*]---]
Fri. 17th	**17 PC Awang B. Yacob.** F. M. Police Killed on Ops. Kuala Selangor.---]
Sat. 18th	**18 L/Cpl. Pahari. Bin. Awal.** R. E. M. E. (MOR) Died*** *Claimed by next of Kin* ---]
Sun. 19th	**19 Cpl. V. W. Isaacs.** Mov/Clk. R.A.F. Changi Died. Road Traffic Accident. *[Ashes REP]*---
+	19 HMT DILWARA sailed Singapore enroute to Hong Kong ---]
Mon. 20th	20 HMT EMPIRE HALLADALE arrived Singapore with replacemnet Service personnel ---]
+	20 HMT EMPIRE TROOPER arrived Singapore with replacement Service personnell---]
Tue. 21st	**21 Cpl. Abdul Rahman** F. M. Police Killed on Ops. Pekan Nanas Johore.---]
+	21/07/53 LG # 39920 p 4012. The following awarded the Military Cross
	CAPT. R.E.W. ATKINS MC 6th. QUEEN ELIZABETH'S OWN GURKHA RIFLES.
	The following awarded the Distinguished Conduct Medal
	L/CPL P. THAPA. DCM 6th. QUEEN ELIZABETH'S OWN GURKHA RIFLES.
	The following awarded the Albert Medal

	MR. H. E. WILLKINDSON. AM (Pos) BRITISH CIVILIAN.
+	21 HMT DUNERA sailed Southampton bound for Singapore/ Hong Kong with replacement Service personnel]
	21 HMT EMPIRE FOWEY Called Singapore enroute to Southampton with returning Service personnel 21st.]
Wed.22nd	22 Pte. G. P. Murray. 1st.Battn. Gordon Highlanders Died by accident. *Kuala Lumpur # 21 / 1119*---]
Thur. 23rd	23 Maj. C. A. L. Watt. 1st. Battn. Gordon Highlanders Died***_Kranji Singapore # 2 / E - 10_---
+	23 Cpl. C. Houlsley. 11th. Hussars Died***_Kuala Lumpur # 21 / 1121_---]
+	23 HMT EMPIRE TROOPER sailed Singapore with returning Service personnel---]
Fri. 24th	24 Pte. Akob b. Sabah Malay Regt. Killed in Action Engaging CT's Kelantan ---]
Sat. 25th	25 Rfn. Gajurman Rai 10th. Princess Mary's Own Ghuka Rifles Died *** *Sungei Patani # 90*---]
+	25 HMT EMPIRE HALLADALE sailed Singapore bound for Hong Kong---]
Sun. 26th	A CT leader *Tan Cheong See* was Killed by Security Forces in the Jemantah area of Johore---]
Mon. 27th	} Combined Operation continued throughout Malaya ---]
Tue. 28th	28 Rfn. Gorebahadur Limbu. 7th. Duke of Edinburgh's Own Gurkha rifles. Died from Wounds recv'd *Seremban # 52* Negri Sembilan ---]
Wed. 29th	29 Drum Maj. K. Garnett. 1st. Battn. The East Yorkshire Regt. Died Battle Accident *Kranji Singapore # 2 / B – 1* ---]
Thur. 30th	30 Sgt. Bahrudin b. Ariffin. 6th. Malay Rgt. & Pte. Anak. Akit. Mat. Sarawak Rangers.Att /6th. Malay Regt. was Killed in Action Engaging CT's During the gunfight 1 CT was Killed & 1 captured. 2 Malay Ptes. were wounded in the area South of Ruab *[No known Grave]Terandak Wall Memorial Malacca* ---]
Fri. 31st	Operation *"Matador"* - *"Sword"* Ended

AUGUST

Sat. 1st	Operation *"Ibex"* Began against No7 Regt. MRLA in Pahang. ---]
Sun. 2nd	In the Kluang area of Johore a British F.M. Ploice Lt. shot & Killed *Hok Hoi* a senior member of the MRLA---
Mon. 3rd	} Combined Operation continued throughout Malaya ---]
Tue. 4th	4 SC Hassam B. Saibom. F. M. Police Killed on Ops. Tapah Area Perak---]
Wed. 5th	5 5 F. M.Police SC B. Maniam. .- S. Mohamed Hanifa .- M. Mabor. – Abdul Ghani B. Abdullah. -M. Sheik Mohamed. Killed on CT Ops.Sungei Siput Area Perak.---]
+	5 AC1 Sallen . b. Jaffr. R.A.F. Regt. 94 Sqdn. (MOR) Died***[_Claimed by next of Kin_]---]
Thur. 6th	6 LAC. G. Habergham. Ins/Mech. R.A.F. Changi Died Ground accident no further details. *Kranji Singapore # 4 / D – 7*
Fri. 7th	Washinton U.S.A. The State department endorsed Britains fight against Communism. *'Warmly congratulated Sir. Gerald Templer on his leadership against the CT's. To free the world of the threat of communism'*---]
Sat. 8th	8 HMT EMPIRE ORWELL sailed Southampton bound for Singapore / Hong Kong with replacement Service personnel---]
Sun. 9th	9 Pol/Lt.J.D.A. Abercrombie. F.M. Aux.Police Killed while leading his Platoon on the Malaya /Thailand border during Operation *"Knot"* . A/Cpl. Sidek was also Killed. He was then with the 18th Federal Jungle Comp.---]
Mon. 10th	10 L/Cpl. A. M. Sims. 1st. Battn. Cameronians. Died***- *[AshesREP]* ---]
+	10 Cfn. J. T. C. Hanson. R.E.M.E. Died. Electricuted in an accident at Base Workshops. Singapore. *Kranji Singapore # 2 / E -13* —]
+	10 HMT EMPIRE CLYDE arrived Liverpool with returning Service personnel---]
Tue. 11th	A Platoon of Gurkhas Killed *Chan Pun* leader of the 6th. Regt. in an area of South Pahang His killing dealt a serious blow to the MRLA---]
Wed. 12th	}
Thur. 13th	} Combined Operations continued throughout Malaya ---]
Fri. 14th	A Home Guard Chief. shot and Killed a bandit in the main street of Kampar. It was discovered that the CT had just robbed Mr.Teh Hian Tat a leading Miner of the town of $1,000 ---]
Sat. 15th	15 Rfn. Sherbahadur Rai . 2nd /10th. Princess Mary's Own Gurkha Rifles. Killed in Action Engaging CT's *Sungei Patani # 94 Kedah]* ---]
Sun. 16th	1 CT was Killed by a Patrol of the Manchester Regt.---]
Mon. 17th	17 L/Cpl. Balbir Thapa . 10th. Princess Mary's Own Gurkha Rifles. Died*** _Kranji Singapore # 7 / C – 3_ ---]
Tue. 18th	During a pre-dawn attack on the village of Sungei Pelek. The village Sir. Gerald Templer called a 'Bad' Village 1 Month before. 10 arrest were made ---]
Wed. 19th	A Platoon of the Special Volunteer Force were relocated to the village of Sungei Pelek ---]
Thur. 20th	20 HMT EMPIRE FOWEY arrived Southampton with returning Service personnel .---]

	+	20 HMT DUNERA arrived Singapore enroute to Hong Kong with replacement Service personnel ---]
Fri.	21st	21/08/53 LG # 39943 p. 4535 The following awarded the Military Cross
		MAJ. R.S.R. CARR. MC 7th. DUKE OF EDINBURGH'S OWN GURKHA RIFLES.
Sat.	22nd	22 Pte. D. C. Sayner. 1st. Battn. West Yorkshire Regt. Killed in Action Engaging CT's. _Kuala Lumpur # 21 / 112_]---]
	+	22 HMT EMPIRE HALLADALE arrived Singapore Roads sailed for Liverpool with returning Service personnel 22nd. ---]
Sun.	23rd	} Combined Operations continued throughout Malaya ---]
Mon.	24th	24 L/Cpl. Jagatbahadur . - Rfn. L. Phulbahadur. 2nd/10th. Princess Mary's Own Gurkha Rifles. Killed in Action Engaging CT's _Sungei Patani # 95 - 96_---]
	+	24 HMT DILWARA arrived Singapore with replacement Service personnel ---]
Tue.	25th	25 HMT DILWARA sailed Singapore enroute to Hong Kong / Kure ---]
	+	25 HMT EMPIRE CLYDE sailed Liverpool bound for Singapore/ Hong Kong with replacement Service personnel---]
	+	25 HMT ASTURIUS arrived Singapore with replacement Service personnel ---]
Wed.	26th	26 HMT ASTURIAS sailed Singapore bound or Southampton with returning Service personnel ---]
	+	26 HMT EMPIRE TROOPER arrived Southampton with returning Service personnel---]
Thur.	27th	27 Rfn. D.Jite Damai 6th. Queen Elizabeth's Own Gurkha Rifles Killed [No known Grave]_Terandak Wall Memorial Malacca_---]
	+	27 HMT LANCASHIRE sailed Irom Liverpool bound for Singapore / Hong Kong-with replacement personnel---]
Fri.	28th	28 Pte. E.A. Vukica. Fiji Regt. Killed in Action Engaging CT's. [_Ashes REP_]---]
	+	2nd./10th. Gurkhas Killed 2 CT's in the Plentong area Kota Tinggi. They were identified as two Group Committee Members.---]
Sat.	29th	29 HMT EMPIRE ORWELL called Singapore with replacement Service personnel sailed 29th.---]
Sun.	30th	After a 10 day operation on the River Pinn a Platoon of the 6th. Malay Regt. returned to report no contact--]
Mon.	31st	Operation _"Ibex"_ _'Mustang'_Ended---]

SEPTEMBER

Tue.	1st	1 Rfn. Lalbahadur. Gurung. 6th.Queen's Elizabeth's Own Gurkha Rifles Died from Wounds recv'd Segamat.
	+	_Kluang # 3 / F – 10_ Johore---]
		Operation 'Boxer' Began SAS against the MRLA ---]
	+	R.A.F. 7 Sqdn. Lincoln 2B(AA) Began Operations at R.A.F. Tengah---)
	+	R.A.F. 83 Sqdn. Lincoln 2B(AA) Began Operations at R.A.F. Tengah---) Operation '_BOLD_'Tengah---]
	+	R.A.F. 148 Sqdn. Lincoln 2B(AA) Began Operations at R.A.F. Tengah---)
Wed.	2nd	A Platoon of the 6th. Malay Regt. whilst changing ambush position, were attacked by a number of CT's led by a woman CT recignised as **Ah Wong.** During the exchange of fire. No casualties were reported.---]
	+	2 HMT NEW AUSTRALIA sailed Southampton bound for Singapore / Hong Kong with replacement Service Personnel---]
Thur.	3rd	3 Pte.B. Willcox. 1st. Battn. The East Yorkshire Regt. Died from his wounds _Kranji Singapore # 2 / E - 11_---]
Fri.	4th	4 L/AM R. N. Noakes H.M.S. '_SIMBANG_' Died*** _Kranji Singapore #4 / E -1_---]
Sat.	5th	5 PC. Abdul Hadi B. Yusof F. M. Police Killed on Ops. Gua Chah Kelantan---].
Sun.	6th	6 Mr. Chan Chin Chuan. The hero of the recent shooting of a CT in Kampar, was accidently Killed---]
	+	A Plt. of the Somersets engaged 4 CT's killing the first 2. The other 2 escaped. It was later that the 2 Killed were the bodyguards of **Yong Kwo** who had escaped---]
Mon.	7th	Penang: 92 CT's were still active in Penang and Province Wellesley. 61 on Penang Island & 31 located In Province Wellesly---]
Tue.	8th	8 HMT EMPIRE FOWEY sailed Southamppton bound for Singapore/ Hong Kong with replacement Service personnel---]
Wed.	9th.	A woman CT who surrendered to the authorities in Province Wellesly in January. She surrendered after reading a leaflet stating. '_There was a new way of life._' Announced: She is soon to get married ---]
Thur.	10th	10 AC1. L. L. Kilbank. Arm/Mech 60 Sqdn R.A.F. Died by accident on duty..[_Ashes REP_]---]
Fri.	11th	London: General Sir. Charles Keightly. flrew out of London on his way to Singapore to take up the post of Commander in Chief Far East Land Force, replacing General Sir. Cameron Nicholson.---]
Sat.	12th	Penang: 2 CT's were Killed in the fishing village of Tanjong Gertak Senggat ---]
Sun.	13th	

Mon. 14th	A surrendered CT informed the F.M. Police Kampar that **Yong Hoi** who had claimed to have Killed 100 people was Killed by one of his own guards---]
Tue. 15th	Kuala Lumpur: Demands were made by the Labour Party's National Conference that: '*A British Cabinet Mission should be sent to Malaya . To be involved with future negotiations.*' ---]
+	**15 Drv, B. Waterhouse,** R.A.S.C. Killed on CT Ops.Ruab Pahang *Kuala Lumpur # RC / A - 4*---]
Wed. 16th	15/09/1954 LG # 39962 p. 4937 The following awarded the Distinguished Conduct Medal RFN. N. LIMBU. DCM 10th PRINCESS MARY'S OWN GURKHA RIFLES
+	**16 Pol/Off. B. Owen.** R.A.F. 60 Sqdn. Flying Vampire FB9 WG 879 crashed on a navigation Ops. at Labis. *Kanji Singapore # 4 / D – 8 .* ---]
+	16 HMT DUNERA arrived Singapore enroute to Southampton with returning Service personnel. Major General A.G.O'Carroll Scott. General Officer Commanding Singapore was booed & jeered at by the troops When he went on board the DUNERA. Troops were demanding ' *What about some shore leave for us*' The reason for no shore leave was that the DUNERA was only calling, and sailed after 3 ½ hours at anchorage---]
Thur. 17th	16 HMT ASTURIAS arrived Southampton with returning Service personnel---]
Fri. 18th	Penang: The Village of Tanjong Gertak Senggat was cordoned off by land and seaway whilst all the inhabitants were shown a photo of a wanted CT.---]
Sat. 19th	6 CT's were Killed by the Fijian Regt. in the Batu Pahat area. After stalking them for 9 ½ hours ---]
Sun. 20t	**19 Capt. W. Cushway.** R.E.M.E.. Died***Kranji Singapore # 2 / E – 25* ---]
+	**20 Rfn. Jasbahadur Limbu .** 10th. Princess Mary's Own Gurkha Rifles.Killed in Action Engaging CT's. *Sungei Patani # 99* ---]
+	**20 Rfn. G. Lalbahadur.** 6th. Queen Elizabeth's Own Gurkha Rifles. Killed in Action Engaging CT's *Sulva Lines # 59* Ipoh Perak-]
+	20 HMT EMPIRE CLYDE arrived Singapore with replacement Service personnel.---]
Mon. 21st	20 HMT EMPIRE ORWELL called Singapore enroute to Southampton with returning Service personnel 20th.]
Tue. 22nd	Operation "Sword" Ended ---]
+	**22 Cpl. C. Ellingworth.** East Yorkshire Regt.Died***. [*Ashes REP*] ---]
Wed. 23rd	A premature release of a stick of 6 bombs, from a Canberra. Killed 1 British officer & 7 ORs (***unnambed***)?
+	**PC. Kasbi B. Suraldi.** F. M. Police Kilied on Ops. Tanah Merah Kelantan.---]
+	23 HMT EMPIRE TROOPER sailed Southanpton bound for Singapore /Hong Kong with replacement Service personnel---]
Thur. 24th	23 HMT EMPIRE HALLADALE arrived Liverpool with returning Service personnel ---]
+	24 HMT LANCASHIRE arrived Singapore / with replacement Service personnel sailed for Hong Kong 24th.]
Fri. 25th	24 HMT NEW AUSTRALIA called Singapore with replacement Service personnel enroute to Hong Kong-]
Sat. 26th	25 HMT EMPIRE CLYDE sailed Singapore enroute to Hong Kong---]
+	**26 F/Lt. L Langley. DFM. - F/O J.A. Shillaker.** [*Ashes REP*] (Nav) **F/O.R. A. Craddock. (Nav)** . **Sgt. R. F.De Rosa** 48 Sqdn. R. A. F. **Dvr. D.A. Jones.- Dvr. J. C. Jones.- Dvr. W. Janes.- Dvr. E. H. Muller** -. 55 Coy. R.A.S.C. Were Killed when their Aircraft Valetta WD164 flying into mist crashed in high ground near Bertam. *Kranji Singapore # 12 / A – 3 - 4 - 5 - 11 / A – 6 – 7 8 – 9*---]
Sun. 27th	26 HMT DILWARA arrived Singapore enroute to Southampton with returning Service personnel 27th. ---]
+	Auster T7 WE610 AAC Flight. Badly damaged by forced landing at Noble Field Kuala Lumpur. Pilot Lt.R. Gale injured. ---]
Mon. 28th	27/09/53 LG # 39973 p.5173 The following awarded Bar to his Military Cross CAPT. (QGO) B. RAI. MC & BAR. 7TH. DUKE OF EDINBURGH;S OWN GURKHA RIFLES.
Tue. 29th	Auster AOP6 VF506 AAC Flight Overturned during forced landing at Bruas 20 miles North of Taiping. Sgt. S. Mousley injured.---]
Wed. 30th	Kuala Lumpur: Genral Sir. Gerald Templer warned: '*The village of Jarkoh near Benta. To Stop feeding the CT's or?*'---]
	30 HMT EMPIRE FOWEY called Singapore with replacemet Service personnel enroute to Hong Kong.--]

OCTOBER

Thur. 1st	Operation '*Valliant*' Began against No 5 Regt. MRLA in Pahang---] Operaion '*Galway*' Began SAS against the MRLA ---]
Fri. 2nd	**2 Pte. A. Waqamatia.** 1st. Battn. Fijian Regt. Killed in Action Engaging CT's [*Ashes REP*]--]
Sat. 3rd	3 2 F. M. Police SC's **Abdullah B. Saibon - Haron B. Ramli** Killed on Ops. Scudai area Johore---]
Sun. 4th	An ambush laid by a Platoon of the 6th. Malay Regt. On the 5th. resulted in no contact----]

Mon.	5th	**5 Mr. A.L Subramaniam.** Asstn. Manager. Segamat Elminia Estate Killed by CT's Johore ---]
	+	5 HMT NEW AUSTRALIA called Singapore enroute to Southamton with returning Service personnel---]
Tue.	6th	06/10/1953 LG # 39977 p. 5287. The following awarded the Distinguished Flying Cross
		CAPT. F. C. RUSSELL. DFC ROYAL REGIMENT ARTILLERY 656 SQDN
		CAPT. J. P. SELLERS. DFC ROYAL REGIMENT ARTILLERY 656 SQDN.
Wed.	7th	7 HMT EMPIRE CLYDE arrived in Singapore- --]
	+	7 HMT ASTURIUS sailed Southampton bound for Singapore with replacement Service personnl---]
Thur.	8th	} Combined Operation continued throughout Malaya
Fri.	9th	09/10/53 LG # 39989 p. 5421 The following awarded Military Cross.
		LT. (QGO) D. GURUNG DCM MC 6th. QUEEN ELIZABETH'S OWN GURKHA RIFLES
		The following awarded the Miltary Medal
		RFN. G. PUN MM 6th. QUEEN ELIZABETH'S OWN GURKHA RIFLES
		The following awarded Bar to his Military medal.
		RFN. B. RAI. MM & BAR 2nd. KING EDWARD VII'S OWN GURKHA RIFLES .
Sat.	10th	A Platoon of the 6th. Malay Regt. went out on Ops.,after information that 14 CT's had been seen in the area of Kuala Lipis. There was no sign of them ---]
	+	10 EMPIRE FOWEY sailed Southampton bound for Singapore / Hong Kong with replacement Service personnel---]
Sun.	11th	Kuala Lumpur: Mr.John Blacking was appointed Advisor on all Aborigines matters. Mr. Blacking served in Malaya with the Coldstream Guards during 1948 -1949 in the Cameron Highlands ---]
Mon.	12th	12 HMT EMPIRE CLYDE sailed Singapore bound for Liverpool with returning Service personnel---]
Tue.	13th	Kuala Lumpur: General Sir. Gerald Templer warned:
		'The village of Seudal Johore. Their area was the worst area in the Federation for communisum They are making the biggest mistake in their lives '–]
Wed.	14th	14 HMT EMPIRE ORWELL arrived Southampton with returning Service personnel---]
Thur.	15th	**15 SC Alang B. Kulap Pachet** F. M. Police. Killed on CT Ops. Batu Gajah area Perak---]
Fri.	16th	16 HMT DUNERA arrived Southampton with returning Service personnel---]
	+	16/10/53 LG. # 39989 p. 5557 The following awarded the Military Medal
		SGT. S. THAPA MM . 2nd KING EDWARD VII'S OWN GURKHA RIFLES
Sat.	17th	**17 Pte. Abdul Majid b. Mat Yusof** Malay Regt. Killed in Action Engaging CT's Perak---]
Sun.	18th	**18 Pte. J. B. Clarke.** 1st. Battn. West Yorkshire Regt. Died Motor transport Accident *[Ashes REP].*---]
Mon.	19th	A Gurkha Patrol Killed 1 CT in the Segament area ----]
Tue.	20th	A Patrol of the Fijian Regt. Killed 1 CT in the Pohgo area ---]
Wed.	21st	A F. M. Police Patrol Killed a woman CT in the Pontian area ---]
Thur.	22nd	**22 Sgt. P. Bamford., Pte. W. B. Green.** 1st. Battn. The East Yorkshire Regt. Killed in Action . *Kranji Singapore # 2 B – 11 – 10* ---]
	+	22 HMT EMPIRE TROOPER arrived Singapore with replacement Service personnel---]
	+	22 HMT LANCASHIRE Called Singapore/ sailed for Liverrpool with returning Service personnel .---]
Fri.	23rd	2 CT's surrendered to the Security Forces 1 of the CT's had shot and Killed his comrade ---]
	+	23 HMT EMPIRE TROOPER sailed Singapore bound for Hong Kong with replacement Service personnel]
Sat.	24th	A Section of a Platoon of the Manchester Regt. came under fire from about 50 CT's, located on a hill above them. Returning Fire were outnumbered, they withdrew back to their main base.---]
Sun.	25th	**25 Pol/ Insp. R. W. Saunders** F. M. Police Killed on Ops. *Kranji Singapore # 18 / B – 8*---]
	+	The same Patrol of the Manchester Regt.Returning back to the same location of the previous day engagement with CT's. Found 3 dead CT 's One was Identified as **Thep Min** the Bodyguard of the Joint State Committee Member---]
Mon.	26th	**26 Sgt. Yamsing Thapa** 6th. Queen Elizabeth's Own Gurkha Rifles. Died*** *Sulva Lines # 48* Ipoh Perak---]
	+	A CT surrendered to a Railway employee at Ayer Kunning. Identified himself as one of the CT engaged in the recent engagement with the Manchester Regt.---]
	+	Dragonfly HAR 4 WT 846 194 Sqdn.R.A.F. Crashed 34 miles North West of Kuala Lumpur.---]
	+	26 HMT DILWARA arrived Southampton with returning Service personnel---]
	+	26 HMT NEW AUSTRALIA arrived Southampton with returning Service personnel---]
Tue.	27th	**27 L/Cpl. Ganbahadur Pun. . Rfn. Kharkabahadur Gurung** 6th. Queen Elizabeth's Own Gurkha Rifles. Died. *Sungei Patani # 71- 70*---]
	+	27/10/53 LG # 40000 p. 5772 The following awarded the Military Cross.
		CAPT. J.H. JACOB. MC. THE DURHAM LIGHT INF.
		CAPT. (QGO) N. RAI.MC 7th. DUKE OF EDINBURGH'S OWN GURKHA RIFLES

	LT. K.S, BEALE. MC	QUEEN'S OWN ROYAL WEST KENTS
		The following awarded the Military Medal
	PTE F. MROZEK. MM	THE MANCHESTER REGIMENT.
	SGT. J. C. HANNAH. MM	THE CAMERONIANS
	SGT. K.J. WILDE. MM	QUEEN'S OWN ROYAL WEST KENTS
	CPL. D. CLARKE. MM	MIDDLESEX REGT. A/T ROYAL WEST KENTS
	RFN J. GURUNG. MM	2nd. KING EDWARD VII'S OWN GURKHA RIFLES.
	RFN. G. PUN. MM	6th QUEEN ELIZABETH'S OWN GURKHA RIFLES
	L/CPL. D. RAI. MM	7th. DUKE OF EDINBURGH'S OWN GURKHA RIFLES
	SGT. K. RAI. MM	7th. DUKE OF EDINBURGH'S OWN GURKHA RIFLES
	SGT. M.TAMANG. MM.	7th. DUKE OF EDINBURGH'S OWN GURKHA RIFLES
	CPL. K. LIMBU. MM	10th PRINCESS MARY'S OWN GURKHA RIFLES
	WOPC K MUTHAMI.MM	KING'S AFRICAN RIFLES
Wed. 28th	28 HMT ASTURIAS arrived Singapore with replacement Service personnel.---]	
Thur. 29th	29 Snr. Tech. F. Stothard. Eng /Fit. R.A.F. Kuala Lumpur Killed in accident when he was struck by H/C Dragonfly WF315. [Ashes REP]---]	
+	29 HMT ASTURIAS sailed Singapore bound for Hong Kong/ Kure ---]	
Fri. 30th	} Combined Operations continued throughout Malaya---]	
Sat. 31st	31 Rfn. Birkhabahadur Limbu . 10th. Princess Mary's Own Gurkha Rifle Died*** Kranji Singapore # 7 / C -4]	
	Operations 'Flame' 'Biter' Ended ---]	

NOVEMBER

Sun. 1st	1 S/Sgt. J. Cox R.A.S.C.. Died*** no further information---]	
+	RNZN HMNZS 'PUKAKI' began her first support role of duty in Malayan coastal waters---]	
+	1 HMT EMPIRE CLYDE arrived Liverpool with returning Service personnel---]	
Mon. 2nd	2 Mr. W.J. Berry GM. Security Officer & F.M. Aux.Police Inspector. Killed in an ambush on the Ulu Remis Estate Layang Layang area of Johore. Kranji Singapore # 18 A – 9 ---]	
Tue. 3rd	Platoons of 'A' & 'D' Companies 2nd/10th. Gurkhas ambushed 5 CT's near the Fraser Estate. All 5 CT's were Killed.---]	
Wed. 4th	4 Mr. A.J. Hawkins British Civilian Killed gunshot wounds to head Selangor.[grave unknown]---]	
Thur. 5th	} Combined Operations continued throughout Malaya---]	
Fri. 6th	}	
Sat. 7th	7 Rfn. Tekbahadur Limbu . 10th. Princess Mary's Own Gurkha Rifles. Died*** Kranji Singapore # 7 / C -6 -]	
+	7 Cfn. Loke Ming Kool. R.E.M.E. (MOR) Died*** Claimed by next of Kin ---]	
+	Dragonfly HAR4 XB 253 H/C. 194 Sqdn. R.A.F. Extensively damaged whilst landing in Jungle clearing Cameron Highlands. Pilot Sgt Manson & Brigadier Howard unhurt.--]	
+	7 HMT EMPIRE ORWELL sailed Southampton bound for Singapore / Hong Kong with replacement Service personnel---]	
Sun. 8th	8 Trp. J. A. Godrich . 9th. / 12th. Royal Lancers Died*** Kuala Lumpur # 21 / 1123 ---]	
+	8 Pte. M. Barnet. 3rd. King's African Rifles. Died***Kuala Lumpur # RC / A – 5 ---]	
Mon. 9th	9/11/53. LG # 40009. p. 5979 The following awarded the Military Medal	
	RFN. B. PUN. MM 2nd. KING EDWARD VII'S OWN GURKHA RIFLES	
Tue. 10th	10 Pte.J.J. Itumo. 3rd. King's African Rifles.Killed in Action Engaging CT's	
	[No known Grave Terandak Memorial Malacca]---]	
+	10/11/1953 LG # 40012 p. 6005 The following awarded the British Empire Medal (Military)	
	SGT. L. DALY. BEM. ROYAL AUSTRALIAN AIR FORCE	
	The following awarded the Distinguished Flying Medal	
	F.SGT. E. R. CHENEY. DFM ROYAL AUSTRALIAN AIR FORCE	
Wed. 11th	}	
Thur. 12th	} Combined Operations continued throughout Malaya---]	
Fri. 13th	}	
Sat. 14th	14 Pol/Lt. T.J. Bennet. F.M. Auxilliary Police. Killed on Ops. Taiping # ?? Perak---]	
+	14 HMT EMPIRE FOWEY called Singapore enroute to Southampton with returning Service personnel14th. -]	
Sun. 15th	} Combined Operations continued throughout Malaya---]	
Mon. 16th	16 Rfn. Purnabahadur Gurung . 2nd. King Edward VII's Own Gurkha Rifles. Died By Accident Selangor Kuala Lumpur # 24 / 5 ---]	

Tue. 17th	} Combined Operations continued throughout Malaya---]
Wed. 18th	**18 Pte. J. Sinclair.** 1st. Fijian Regt. Killed in Action Engaging CT's [*Ashes REP*]---]
Thur. 19th	Bangkok: A Japanese member of the CT's operating along the Thailand /Malaya border surrendered to the Thailand Authorities he was identified as **Yak Saki** who had been fighting in the Japanese army in Siam]
Fri. 20th	20 HMT DILWARA sailed Southampton bound for Singapore with replacement Service personnel---]
+	20 HMT ASTURIUS arrived Singapore. ---]
+	20 HMT EMPIRE TROOPER called Singapore enroute Southampton with returning Service personnel---]
Sat. 21st	Kuala Lumpur: General Sir. Gerald Templer arrived back from his trip to London:. *'With Good news regarding the future Financial aid Malaya with be afforded ---]*
+	21 HMT ASTUR1US sailed Singapore bound for Southampton with returning Service personnel---]
Sun. 22nd	**22 Pte. Mohd. Tahar b. Ahmad.** Malay Regt. Killed in Action engag ing CT's Kelantan---]
+	**22 Mr. H.D Gerhold.** British Civilian Killed Johore Bahru Johore.---]
Mon. 23rd	**23 Rfn. R. Dangadhoj Rai .** 10th. Princess Mary's Own Gurkha Rifles. Died***_Kuala Lumpur 26 / 3_---]
Tue. 24th	**24 Pte. Anak.Dugu.Empati.** Sarawak Rangers. Killed in Action. *[Grave unknown Terandak Wall Memorial Malacca]*
+	24 HMT EMPIRE CLYDE sailed Liverpool bound for Singapore / Hong Kong with replacement Service personnel---]
Wed. 25th	**25 Mr. R.W. Saunders.** Manager. CEP No 3 & **Aux. Inspt. Rengam** F.M. Police Johore Killed by CT's---].
Thur. 26th	**26 Cpl. K. Bancroft.** East Surrey Regt. Att/ 22nd.SAS. Died from Wounds recv'd. **Pte . F. W. Wilkins.** A.C.C. 22nd. SAS Died from Wounds recv'd. *[No known Graves Terandak Wall Memorial Malacca]* ---]
+	26 HMT EMPIRE FOWEY arrived Singapore with replacement Service personnel---]
Fri. 27th	**27 2/ Lt. M. W. Raingill.** 1st. Battn. Manchester Regt. & **Cpl Adrian Anak Tandang.** Sarawak Rangers were Killed during an assault on a CT camp in the Sungei Inas Forest Kedah- *[No known Graves Terandak Wall MemorialMalacca].*---]
+	27 HMT EMPIRE FOWEY sailed Singapore bound for Hong Kong---]
Sat. 28th	**28 Sgt. N. Wara.** DCM 1st. Battn. Fijian Regt. Killed in Action Engaging CT's [*Ashes REP*]---]
+	Another CT **Ah Yee** surrendered to a Rubber Tapper. He claimed he had shot another CT, while attempting to escape the other CT's body was later found & Identified as **Cheng Chee**. ---]
Sun. 29th	**29 SC Daub B. Abdullah** F. M. Police Killed on CT Ops. Besut Terengganu---]
+	CT **Siow Hong** surrendered to the Home Guard near Kuala Nerang---]
Mon. 30th	**30 Rfn. Rambahadur Rai** 10th. Princess Mary's Own Gurkha Rifles [*Ashes REP*]
+	'D' Platoon 2nd.10th. Gurkhas Killed 1 CT---]
+	30 HMT EMPIRE ORWELL arrived Singapore en route to Hong Kong with replacement Service personnel-- Operation 'Valiant' Ended ---]

DECEMBER

Tue. 1st	**1 Cpl. P. G. R. Eakin.** Inniskilling Fus. Att / 22nd. SAS. Died shooting incident. *Western Road # 211* George Town Penang ---]
Wed. 2nd	Malay Home Guards in Pahang Killed a known Malay Communist aborigine **Bah Petankan** who had been responsible of killing 30 of his own people----]
Thur. 3rd	} Combined Operations continued throughout Malaya---]
Fri. 4th	**4 Rfn. Kharkbahadur Gurung .** 10th. Princess Mary's Own Gurkha Rifles. Died from Wounds recv'd BMH Kamunting *Sulva Lines #61* Ipoh Perak---]
+	**4 L/Cpl. A. May.** R.M.P.. Died Motor Veh. Acc [*Ashes REP*] ---]
Sat. 5th	**5 L / Cpl. G. W. J. Edgar.** R.M.P.. Died from Injuries recv'd on 4th. *Seremban # 21 / 1127* Negri Sembilan---]
+	**5 Drv J.M. Ford** Royal Signals Killed in Action Engaging CT's *Kuala Lumpur # 21 / 1129* --]
Sun. 6th	} Combined Operations continued throughout Malaya---]
Mon. 7th	2 Pltn. Manchester Regt. surprised a group of 4 to 5 CT's. killing 2 The rest escaped. Food, arms & ammo were recovered.---]
Tue. 8th	}
Wed. 9th.	} Combined Operations continued throughout Malaya---]
Thur. 10th	}
Fri. 11th	}
Sat. 12th	5 armed CT's stopped 2 lorries carrying 30 Labourers on the Tanah Hitam–Kilian Intan road ordered everyone off before setting fire to the lorries then Killed 1 male & 1 female (**_unnambed_**), another male & female decided to volunteer to go with them. ---]

Sun. 13th	**13 Pol/Lt. A.E. Middleditch.** F.M.Aux.Police Killed on CT Ops. during an engagement with a mixed force of CT's & Orang Asli in Sungei Telum area Cameron Highlands.Perak *Batu Gajah # 508* Ipoh Perak ---].
+	13 HMT ASTURIAS arrived Southampton with returning Service personnel . ---]
Mon. 14th	**14 Pte. G. J. Cox.** 1st. Somerset Light Infantry. Died*** *Kranji Singapore # 2 / B - 9*---]
Tue. 15th	} Combined Operations continued throughout Malaya---]
Wed. 16th	A Patrol of the Lancashire Regt. found a dead CT who was in wounded in the previous engagement on the 7th. Identified as *Kam Yin* of 5 Ind Plt.MRLA.---]
Thur. 17th	17 HMT DILWARA arrived Singapore with replacement Service personnel ---]
Fri. 18th	**18 Lt. J.L.C. Fotheringham** 22nd. SAS Died *** Killed in Action. *Kuala Lumpur # 21 -1125* ---]
+	**18 L/Cpl. C. Morrison.** R.M.P.. Died*** *Kranji Singapore # 2 / B - 8* ---]
+	18 HMT DUNERA sailed from Southampton bound for Singapore with replacement Service personnel---]
Sat. 19th	19 HMT EMPIRE CLYDE arrived Singapore enroute to Hong Kong with replacement Service personnel 20th.]
Sun. 20th	20 HMT EMPIRE TROOPER arrived Southanpton with returning Service personnel---]
+	20 HMT EMPIRE FOWEY sailed Southampton bound for Singapore/ Hong Kong with replacement Service personnel---]
Mon. 21st	**21 Rfn. Birbahadur Limbu** . 7th.. Duke of Edinburgh's Own Gurkha Rifles. Drowned on CT Ops. *Sungei Patani # 102* Kedah---]
Tue. 22nd	22 HMT EMPIRE ORWELL arrived Singapore en route to Southampton with returning Service personnel 22nd]
+	'D' Platoon Manchester Regt. engaged & Killed a CT. name (**unknown**) but one of the bodyguards of the Commander of 5 Ind. Plt. MRLA. ---]
Wed. 23rd	23 HMT DILWARA sailed Singapore bound for Southampton with returning Service personnel---]
Thur. 24th	**24 LAC. Othman . Bin. Ahmad.** Gnr. 94 Sqdn. R.A.F. Regt. (MOR) Died***. *Claimed by next of Kin* ---]
Fri. 25th	} Combined Operations continued throughout Malaya---]
Sat. 26th	**26 Cpl K Bancraoft Trp. F.W Wilkins** 22nd. SAS Killed Engaging CT's. *Kuala Lumpur # 1124- 1126*---]
Sun. 27th	**27 Cfn. D. F. Pipe.** R.E.M.E. Died.****Kuala Lumpur # 21 / 1128* ---]
Mon. 28th	**28 Pte G.F. Cleveland** 1st. Battn. Somerset Light Inf. Died*** *Kuala Lumpur # 21 1130*--]
Tue. 29th	**29 Sgt. H.H. Hamilton** Royal Signals Died *** *Kranji Singapore # 2 / B - 7*.---]
Wed. 30th	} Combined Operations continued throughout Malaya---]
Thur. 31st	Operation*"Cornwall"*-*"Screw"* Ended ---]

R. A. F. OPERATION *"FIREDOG"* END OF YEAR STATISTICS 1953

No of Sorties	No. of Strikes	1,000 Lb.Bombs	500 Lb. Bombs	350 LbCluster	20 LbBombs	R/P's	20mm	.5 mm	.303mm
7,603	298	3,132	6,719		13,800	5,975	600,386	371,555	223,730

R. A. F. SUPPORT 1953

	Soties	Troops/Lift/	Casac	Pass/Lift	Supply Wt. Lbs	Leaflets drop (1,000)	B Flying Times No / hrs	Broadcsting No / hrs	Crashed
Air SupportA/C*	1346	/	/	/	4,561,995	/	/	/	Vampire's
Auster**	14,276 hrs	/	/	/	/	/	/	/	WG879
Pioneer	/	/	/	/	/	/	/	/	Meteor's
H/C Light	317	9,998	/	/	3,804	/	/	/	A77-88
848 Sqdn	169	/	/	/	/	/	/	/	A77-643
155 Sqdn	471	/	/	/	/	/	/	/	A77-858
Target/MK**	/	/	/	/	/	/	/	/	Hornets
Vis/Air OBs**	/	/	/	/	/	/	/	/	WB898
Communication**	/	/	/	/	/	/	/	/	WB872
Leaf. Sorties*	184	/	/	/	/	61,585	/	/	PX349
Leaflets Drop*	/	/	/	/	/	/	/	/	Valetta
Leaf Sorties **	327	/	/	/	/	/	/	/	WD164
Leaflets Drop**	/	/	/	/	/	/	/	/	Dragonfly
Broad Sorties*	327	/	/	/	/	/	/	/	WT846 WF311
Broad Hrs *	/	/	/	/	/	/	312	/	WB253WF845
Broad Sorties**	/	/	/	/	/	/	/	/	Auster's
Broad Hrs **	/	/	/	/	/	/	/	/	WE 614
Photo RECCE***	1065	/	/	/	/	/	/	/	WE610 VF506

* AirSupport A/C Dakota -Valetta- Hastings Bristol
** Auster
*** Photo Rec Anson,,Spitfire, Mosquito, Meteor, Pembroke

CHAPTER 12 -1954.
JANUARY

Fri.	1st	Operations *'Galway'*- *'Inland'* & *'Termite'* Began against No 5 Regt. MRLA In the areas of Sungei Siput, Ipoh & South Perak---]
	+	Operations *'Hawk'* & *'Apollo'* began against No 6 Regt. MRLA In the areas of Ruab, Kuala Lipis, Pahang --]
	+	Operations *'Kitchener'* & *'Ajax'* began against No 4 Regt. MRLA In the areas of Rengam & Kulai Johore---]
	+	Operation *'Sword'* Began SAS against the MRLA ---]
	+	1 HMT EMPIRE WINDRUSH sailed Southampton bound for Singapore/ Hong Kong with replacement Service personnel.---]
Sat.	2nd	**2 Dvr. P. Smith.** R. A. S. C. Died by accident. _Kuala Lumpur # 21 / 1132_ ---]
	+	A section from 'D' Company 10th. Gurkhas on a Patrol East of Kulai, ran into a herd of Elephants with babies. The Bull elephant, charged scattering the Platoon. Unfortunately, 1 Gurkha Rfn.Chandrabahadur Gurung was tossed into the air, landing in front of the Elephant, with one of its tusks pierced his chest.Gurung was casvac'ed out & taken to hospital---]
	+	2 HMT ASTURIUS sailed from Southamton bound for Singapore/ Hong Kong with replacement Service personnel---]
Sun.	3rd	3 HMT EMPIRE CLYDE arrived Singapore enroute to Liverpool with returning Service personnel 3rd.---]
Mon.	4th	A Platoon of the 'D' Company 2nd.10th. Gurkhas Killed a CT in the Kota Tinggi area. He was identified as a high ranking member of the Johore State Communist Committee .A Rfn. was seriously wounded in the engagement & Cas/Vac to hospital---]
Tue.	5th	' B' Company 10th. Gurkhas Killed 3 CT's during an engagement. One of the CT's was Identified as a prominent CT who had been in the Victory Celebration in London in 1946.---]
Wed.	6th	} Combined Operations continued throughout Malaya---]
Thur.	7th	**7 Mr. J.B. Ritson** .Manager. & Aux. Pol /Insp. Killed on CT Ops. Bahau Area. _Seremban # ??_ Negri Sembilan---]
Fri.	8th	**8 SC. Ahmed** F. M. Police Killed on CT Ops. Bahau North Sembilam.---]
Sat.	9th	'A' Company Platoon 10th Princess Mary's Own Gurkha Rifles Killed a number of CT's. ---]
Sun.	10th	1 Patoon 10th. Princess Mary's Own Gurkha Rifles acting on information. A number of CT's were in a Palm Oil Estate near Lalang Lalang. Went to investigate. A CT Semtry fired at them. The Platoon Sgt. ordered a charge & Rfn.Birbahadur Rai raced ahead of the rest firing his LMG. Killed the CT carrying on. Shot another. Going through long grass, engaged another killing him. He then Killed a 5th. CT. Awarded the DCM LG 7/05/1954---]
Mon.	11th	**11 Pte. A. Cooper.** 1st. Battn. Manchester Regt. Died accidentally Killed during a jungle training Patrol. _Western Road # 2152_ George Town Penang ---]
	+	**11 Flt/Lt. M. Short.** P/A CIC FEAF R.A.F. Died Road Traffic Accident. _Kranji Singapore # 3 / E - 3_---]
Tue.	12th	12 HMT EMPIRE FOWEY arrived Singapore/ Sailed enroute to Hong Kong 12th.---]
	+	A Platoon of the Lancashire Regt. engaged in an ambush Killed 2 women CT's. Identified as **Yoke Chin & Pitt Yuen** ---]
	+	12/01/1954 LG 40073 p. 303 The following awarded the Colonial Police Medal ASTN/SUPT. W. M. HUMBLE. CPM FEDERATION MALAYA POLICE
Wed.	13th	A Fijian Patrol Killed 5 CT's in the Rengam area of Johore ---]
Thur.	14th	14 HMT EMPIRE ORWELL arrived Sothampton with returning Service personnel---]
Fri.	15th	**15 Pte. Ismail b. Uda** Malay Regt. .Killed in Action Engaging CT's Perak---]
	+	15 HMT DUNERA arrived Singapore with replacement Service personnel---]
Sat.	16th	} Combined Operations continued through out Malaya ---]

Sun. 17th	}
Mon. 18th	**18 Lt. G. J. L. Goulding.** Royal Artillery **L/Cpl. C. W. Bond** (R.E). Att/ 22nd. S.A.S. Killed in Para Drop into the Ulu. _Taiping # EW / 40 – 39_ Perak.---]
Tue. 19th	19 HMT DILWARA arrived Southampton with returning Service personnel ---]
Wed. 20th	**20 Capt. J. R. Moffat.** Royal Artillery. att/ 22nd. S.A.S. Died from injuries after Para drop into Ulu. _Taiping #_ 41 Perak---]
+	20 HMT DUNERA sailed Singapore enroute to Hong Kong ---]
Thur. 21st	**21 Sgt. A.W Perry** Army Glider Pilot Regt. **F/Lt. J. R. Maulden** 194 Sqdn. R.A.F. Killed when his Auster
+	AOP 6 VF604 went missing on a weather Recce _Kuala Lumpur # 23 – 1211 – w23 1209_ ---]
+	21 HMT EMPIRE FOWEY arrived Singapore/ sailed bound for Southampton with returning Service personnel 22nd.---]
Fri. 22nd	**Spr. Yunus Bin Mohmud** Royal Engineers (MOR) Died *** _Claimed by next of Kin_ ---]
Sat. 23rd	A Platoon of the 6th. Malay Regt. Killed 1 CT. near Kuala Lipis---]
+	23 HMT ASTURIUS arrived Singapore with replacement Service personnel enroute to Hong Kong 23rd. --]
Sun. 24th	A Platoon of the 6th. Malay Regt. encountered a CT sentry & fired at him. He ran into the jungle, no further contact was made in the Ulu Dong area---]
Mon. 25th	**25 W/O. F. W. Wilson.** Royal Artillery Died*** [_Ashes REP_] ---]
+	A Platoon of the 6th. Malay Regt.Killed 3 CT's during an ambush. 3 miles from Kuala Lipis. The 3 were identifired as: _Lim Men Sek, Chan Ban Sek, Ah Wei & Sani Bin Mat Buscat._ All of the 12th. Regt. MRLA. _Lim Men Sek_ was known as the Terror of Lipis.---]
Tue. 26th	HMT EMPIRE HALLADALE arrived Singapore/ sailed for Liverpool with returning Service personnel 26th.---]
Wed. 27th	27 HMT EMPIRE CLYDE arrived Liverpool with returning Service personnel---]
+	27 HMT EMPIRE TROOPER sailed Southanpton for Singapore with replacement Service personnel---]
Thur. 28th	**28 Pte. Anaak Utut Ugap.** Sarawak Rangers. Killed in Action Engaging CT's _Taiping #_ Q / 1 _Perak ---]
+	**28 Pte. P. S. Brown.** 1st. Battn. West Yorkshire Regt. Killed in Action Engaging CT's. _Taiping # E / 42_ Perak]
Fri. 29th	**29 3 F. M. Police SC. Cpl.Abdul Ghani Besu.** SC's. **Abdul Razek B.Besu.** & **Asri B. Hassen.** Killed on
+	Ops. Bidor Perak.---]
Sat. 30th	**30 PC. Mohd. Amin B. Yusof.** F. M. Police Killed on Ops. Pahang ---]
Sun. 31s	A Patrol of the 6th. Malay Regt. returned from a long spell in the jungle, with no contacts. made---]

FEBRUARY

Mon. 1st	Operation ‘_Galway_’ Began against No 5 Regt. MRLA in Perak---]
Tue. 2nd	**2 Lt. /Col. A.I. Forester- Walker** MBE. 2nd. King Edward VII's Own Gurkha Rifles Died*** _Seremban # 83_ Negri Sembilan---]
+	**2 Rfn's. Kaluman Tamang. – Balbahadur. Rai** 7th. Queen Elizabeth's Own Gurkha Rifles. Killed in Action Engaging CT's _Seremban # 57 - 56_ Negri Sembilan---]
Wed. 3rd	**3 Rfn. P. Partu.** 2nd. King Edward VII's's Own Gurkha Rifles Died from Wounds. Kerling Estate Negri Sembilan. _Kuala Lumpur # 24 - 1_---]
+	**3 Plt/Off. P.M. Rathbone** 45 Sqdn. R.A.F. Butterworth. Was Killed when his Hornet WB885. Overshot when landing overturned. _Western Road # 2153_ George Town Panang---]
Thur. 4th	4 HMT EMPIRE ORWELL sailed Southampton bound for Singapore/ Hong Kong with replacement Service personnel---]
Fri. 5th	5 HMT EMPIRE WINDRUSH arrived Singapore- with replacement Service personnel--]
Sat. 6th	**6 Mr W. R. McConnachei.** Astn. Manager. of the Harewood Estate Sungei Siput Perak. Together with another Planter **Mr. R Chestnut.** were Killed in an ambush Perak---]
Sun. 7th	} Combined Operations continued throughout Malaya---]
Mon. 8th	}
Tue. 9th	9 HMT EMPIRE WINDRUSH sailed Singapore to Hong Kong./ Kure ---]
Wed. 10th	**10 Capt. J.K. Tarling.** Royal Engineers Died*** _Western Road # 2154_ George Town Penang.---]
Thur. 11th	11 HMT DEVONSHIRE sailed Liverpool bound for Singapore / Hong Kong/Kure with replacement Service personnel---]
Fri. 12th	} Combined Operations continued throughout Malaya---]
Sat. 13th	**13 Pte.W.B. Mathews.**1st. Battn. Somerset Light Inf. Died by accident. _Kuala Lumpur # RC A / 6_---]
Sun. 14th	14 HMT EMPIRE FOWEY arrived Southampton with returning Service personnel---]

Mon. 15th	**15 Pte. Abdul Hamid b. Abdul Hadi.** Royal Malay Regt. Killed in Action Engaging CT's Perak---]
Tue. 16th	16 HMT DUNERA arrived Southampton with returning Service personnel---]
+	16 HMT ASTURIUS arrived Singapore ---]
Wed. 17th	17 HMT ASTURIUS sailed Singapore bound for Southampton with returning Service personnel---]
Thur. 18th	} Combined Operations continued throughout Malaya---]
Fri. 19th	**19 Pte. J. G. Annders.** 1st. Battn. The East Yorkshire Regt. Died****Kranji Singapore # 2 / B – 13* ---]
	19/02/1954 LG # 40108 p. 1160 The following awarded the George Medal.
	SC ABDUL. HJ. B. M. ZAIN. GM FEDERATION OF MALAYA POLICE
Sat. 20th	} Combined Operations continued throughout Malaya---]
Sun. 21st	**21 F/Off S Ainsley – F/Sgt. J.M. Price** Air /Sig. 52 Sqdn.R.A.F. **F/Off. B.R. Landbeck** Nav. 204 Sqdn, R.A.F. Were Killed when their Valetta WJ 494, on approach to Changi. Lost height hit trees and crashed The Pilot F/O R.C.F. Hamilton, survived as did all the other 10 passengers, *Kranji Singapore # 3 / E – 2 – 4 / A – 1 – / E -1 -*]
+	**21 Pte. J. A. Leeworthy.** 1st. Battn. Somerset Light Inf. Died****Kuala Lumpur # 21 / 1131*---]
Mon.22nd	**22 L/Cpl. E.C. Newell** The Queen's Royal West Kent Regt. Died.*** *Kuala Lumpur # 21 / 1133*---]
Tue. 23rd	**23 F/O A. Ashton. SAC M.Gooding.** Loud Hailer operator. *[No known Grave]Terandak Wall Memorial Malacca* **F/O P. Starling Nav. – Sgt. F. McConnell Air Sig.** *Kranji Singapore # 4 / B – 2 - 3 /E- 4* All Killed when Valetta C1 WD 160 Far East Transport Wing R.A.F. While engaged on a Voice mission, hit trees on top of a ridge and crashed into the valley below near Tampin.---]
Wed. 24th	24/02/1954 LG # 40110 p. 1174 The following awarded the Colonial Police Medal SC. NADZAL B. KUANTAN CPM FEDERATION OF MALAYA POLICE
Thur. 25th	25 HMT EMPIRE HALLADALE arrived Liverpool with returning Service personnel---]
Fri. 26th	26 HMT LANCASHIRE sailed Liverpool for Singapore/ Hong Kong with replacement Service personnel]
+	26 HMT EMPIRE ORWELL arrived Singapore with replacement Service personnel---]
Sat. 27th	} Combined Operations continued throughout Malaya---]
Sun. 28th	HMT EMPIRE TROOPER arrived Singapore with replacement Service personnel---]

MARCH

Mon. 1st	Operation "*Inland*" began against No 5 Regt. MRLA In Perak.---]
+	1 HMT EMPIRE TROOPER sailed Singapore bound for Southampton with returning Service personnel---]
Tue. 2nd	4 CT's were Killed by 'A' Company 2nd.10th. Princess Mary's Own Gurkha Rifles. Pengarang Peninsular ---]
+	Dragonfly HC2 H/C WF315 194 Sqdn. Crashed at Fort Chabi Kedah.No casualties.---]
+	2 HMT EMPIRE WINDRUSH arrived Singapore from Hong Kong/Kure ---]
Wed. 3rd	3 HMT EMPIRE ORWELL sailed Singapore en route to Southampton with returning Service personnel---]
Thur. 4th	**4 Pte. Alias. Bin. Mohd. Yusof.** R. M. P. (MOR) Died*** *Claimed by next of Kin*---]
Fri. 5th	5 HMT EMPIRE WINDRUSH sailed from Singapore bound for Southampton with returning Service personnel---]
Sat. 6th	Singapore: The entire Police Force was searching for the escaped Communist Leader **Wong Fook Kwong** who escaped from the Remand Ward of the General Hospital. Wednesday night --]
Sun. 7th	London : Labour Government were defeated in a Commons vote....
	'National Service remains at 2 years' ---]
Mon. 8th	Kuala Lumpur : 6 CT's were Killed over the week-end. 'B' Plt. Of the Fijian Regt. Killed 3 CT's in a firefight in the Gelong Patah area of Johore.---]
+	In another engagement with CT's. 'A' Plt. of the Fijian Regt. Engaged and Killed 3 more CT's ---]
Tue. 9th	**9 Pol/Lt. T. A. Charlton. (GM)** F.M.Aux. Police. Killed on Ops. Sungei Buntu Penggang Johore *Kranji Singapore # 8 C – 11* ---]
+	9/03/54 LG # 40122 p.1521 The following awarded the Military Medal SGT. B. H. OTHMAN MM MALAY REGIMENT PTE. S. A. JANTI. MM SARAWAK RANGERS A/T QUEEN'S ROYAL WEST KENTS
+	9 HMT EMPIRE FOWEY sailed Southampton bound for Singapore.with replacement Service personnel--]
Wed. 10th	**10 Rfn. Pitambahadur Rai .** 10th. Princess Mary's Own Gurkha Rifles. Died*** *Kranji Singapore # 7 / C -8*]
Thur. 11th	Kuala Lumpur : Announced: *'Plans are underway for the future Develepment of 2 Malayan Civil Services'* ---]
Fri. 12th	**12 2/Lt. A.V. Palmer.** The Queen's West Surrey Regt. Died****Seremban # CE 4* Negri Sembilan---]
+	12 HMT DEVONSHIRE arrived Singapore bound for / Hong Kong with replacement Service personnel sailed 12th.---]

Sat. 13th	13 **Rfn.Jaibahadur Limbu** . 10th. Princess Mary's Own Gurkha Rifles. Died Motor Veh. Acc, Kuala Pilah _Seremban # 58_ Negri Sembilan ---]
+	13 HMT ASTURIUS arrived Southamton with returning Service personnel ---]
Sun. 14th	'A' Company 2nd./10th. Princess Mary's Own Gurkha Rifles. Killed 6 CT's in the same area as those on the 2nd.---]
Mon. 15th	Support Company 2nd. 10th. Princess Mary's Own Gurkha Rifles Gurkhas Operating in the Pengarang Peninsular Killed 3 CT's .& captured one in a well planned ambush---]
Tue. 16th	16 HMT DUNERA sailed Southampton bound for Singapore / Hong Kong with replacement Service personnel---]
Wed. 17th	London: The Cabinet are wavering about the exchange of **Lee Meng** for Mr. Edgar Sanders. Not yet ready to agree a swop deal---]
Thur. 18th	18 HMT DILWARA sailed Southampton bound for Singapore/Hong Kong with replacement Service personnel---]
Fri. 19th	Kuala Lumpur : Announcement: _'A big step forward. Leading members of the Malayan Political and Communal Parties are to meet on the 27th. to thrash out the way forward for the Federation'_ ---]
Sat. 20th	20 SVF. **Sgt. Sam Weng.** F. M. Police Killed on CT Ops.Ruab area Pahang.---]
Sun. 21st	Singapore: The Attorney General. Mr. E.J.Davis, is prepared for talks with Mr. Oliver Lytelton on the Rendell Commission for Constitutional reforms in the Colony---]
Mon.22nd	22 **Pte. C. Ziyalure.** 3rd. King's African Rifles. Killed in Action Engaging CT's _Kuala Lumpur # 32 / 1245_---]
+	22 **Rfn. Kharkabahadur** . 7th. Duke of Edinburgh's Own Gurkha Rifles Died***_Kranji Singapore- # 7 / C 7_]
Tue. 23rd	Penang: George Town was under strict curfew after two suspects escaped. In the murder trial of the killing of **Mr. David Chan**. ---]
Wed. 24th	M.F. Police. Issued the description on the 2 escaped Prisoners known as **Lee Khan Kau, alias Ah Khen, alias Lee Telk & Chan. & Ah Siew. alias Chan Kwong Siew.** ---]
Thur. 25th	25 HMT EMPIRE ORWELL arrived Southampton with returning Service personnel---]
Fri. 26th	Kuala Lumpur:The 1st Malayan Officer to be commissioned into the R.E.M.E. Wiil arrive on board HMT LANCASHIRE Lt. Idris Bin Abdul enlisted in the R.E.M.E. in 1947. Had just completed courses at the Eaton Hall Officers Training College England---]
Sat. 27th	27 **Major. A. E. Amor.** Royal Hampshire Regt. Died Motor Transport Acc. _Kuala Lumpur # 21 / 1134_---]
+	27 HMT LANCASHIRE arrived Singapore with replacement Service personnel----]
Sun. 28th	28 HMT LANCASHIRE sailed for Hong Kong with replacement Service personnel---]
+	Kuala Lumpur : The Recruitement Drive for volunteers to join the Malay Auxiliary Air Force stated: ' _'30 applicants had been selected for interviews.'_ ---]
Mon. 29th	HMT EMPIRE WINDRUSH SANK WHILST BEING TOWED. BY HMS '_SAITES_' between Algiers and Gibraltar---]
+	
Tue. 30th	Auster AOP 6 VF560 656Sqdn. ACC Hit trees in a down draft, crashed 2 miles South West of Kroh. Perak.-]
Wed. 31st	31 HMT EMPIRE FOWEY arrived Singapore with replacement Service personnel---]
+	Operation "_Sword_" came to a successful end---]

APRIL

Thur. 1st	Operation '_Hawk_' began against No 6 Regt. MRLA In Pahang---]
+	1 HMT ASTURIUS sailed Southampton bound for Singapore/ Hong Kong with replacement Service personnel. On board were the 1st. Battalion The Royal Scots Fusiliers bound for Malaya ---]
Fri. 2nd	The area of Batu Pahat was declared "White" ---]
Sat. 3rd	3 **SC Poun s/o Endin Froom.** F. M. Police Killed on Ops. Gurun Kedah.---]
Sun. 4th	Platoons of the 2nd. 10th. Princess Mary's Own Gurkha Rifles. Went to Sang Kang village where a number of CT's had been seen in an area of swamp nearby. During the search 2 CT's submerged below water level were Killed. Gunfire from within the swamp area, indicated there were other CT's in the swamp. Another search found 5 CT's hiding submerged in the water. All were Killed. One of the dead CT's was identified as **Foo Ah Kwong**. A Prominent leader in South Johore, with a price on his head of $100,000. He had been responsible for the sabotage, murders & other atrocities carried out in Johore since the beginning of the Emergency---]
Mon. 5t	5 HMT EMPIRE FOWEY sailed Singapore bound for Southampton on board were the 1st. Battn. Gordon Higlanders having completed their tour of active Service in Malaya ---]
Tue. 6th	6 **Spr. N. Collins.** Royal Engineers Died***_Kuala Lumpur # 16 / 930_ ---]

Wed. 7th	**7 Mr. Heathy.** British Civilian Died Gunshot wounds to the head. Selangor---]
Thur. 8th	Kuala Lumpur : Lieutenant -General Sir. Geoffrey Bourne. Became Officer Commnding Malaya---]
+	8 HMT DEVONSHIRE arrived Singapore ---]
+	8 HMT DEVONSHIRE sailed Singapore bound for Liverpool with returning Service personnel---]
Fri. 9th	The crack CT 3rd. Independent Platoon. Were officialy missing. The Secruirty forces admitted. They were well organised, well trained & equally heavily armed Platoon, in the area of Layang Layang; Perhaps due to food control they have moved. To where was the question? However ground forces are to remain active in the area ---]
Sat. 10th	**10 Rfn. Harkabahadur Limbu.** 7th. Duke of Edinburgh's Own Gurkha Rifles. Killed in Action Engaging CT's
+	*Kuala Lumpur # 25 – 2]* ---]
Sun. 11th	Kuala Lumpur: 'After talks on the proposed Railway Strike with the Unions demanding a further 18 demands to be considered The threat was removed until after negotiations had taken place.'---]
Fri. 12th	12 HMT DUNERA arrived Singapore with replacement Service personnel enroute to Hong Kong 12th---]
+	12 HMT LANCASHIRE arriived Singapore/ sailed for Liverpool with returning Service personnel 13th.-]
Tue. 13th	} Combined Operation continued throughout Malaya ---]
Wed. 14th	14 HMT EMPIRE ORWELL sailed Southampton bound for Singapore / Hong Kong with replacement Service personnel---]
Thur. 15th	15 HMT DILWARA arrived Singapore enroute to Hong Kong with replacement Service personnel 15th.]
Fri. 16th	**16 Pte. D. A. J. Braybrooks.** 1st. Battn.The Queen's West Surrey Regt. Died*** *Kuala Lumpur # 21 – 1135]*
Sat. 17th	**17 Rfn. Sukdeo Gurung .** 6th. Queen Elizabeth's Own Gurkha Rifles. Died from Wounds recv'd. Labis Johore *Kluang # 3 / C – 10* Johore---]
+	17 HMT EMPIRE TROOPER arrived Southanpton with returning Service personnel---]
Sun. 18th	Malacca : 2,000 protesters heard. UMNO MCA Leaders:
	'Condemn as the most Unreasonable regrettable and intolerable" The British Colonial Offices Rejection of the Reliances request to be allowed to be heard in London But the leaders are still going to London' --]
Mon. 19th	A CT was shot dead by Security Forces in Negri Sembilan.---]
Tue. 20th	Singapore: Crowds shouted Merdeka (Freedom) as a UNOMCA Delegation flew out of Kallang Airport enroute to talks in London---]
Wed. 21st	Kuala Lumpur: In an announcement:
	'The Government last month. Spent $ 120,000. On information leading to the capture or killing of known Communist Terrorist'- --]
Thur.22nd	**22 Rfn. Birkhabahadur Rana** . 2nd. King Edward VII's Own Gurkha Rifles Died from Wounds recv'd BMH Kinrara *Kuala Lumpur # 25 / 5* ---]
Fri. 23rd	**23 SC Kader B. Mahmad.** F. M. Police Killed on Ops. Nibomg Tibor Province Wellesley---]
+	23 HMT ASTURIUS arrived Singapore with replacement Service personnel---]
Sat. 24th	24 HMT EMPIRE HALLADALE sailed Liverpool for Singapore.with replacement Service personnel---]
Sun. 25th	Kuala Lumpur: The President of the Malayan Chinese Association refused to fly to London to meet Mr. Oliver Lytelton, for informal talks He stated due to ill health he would be going on the Liner CHUSAN sailing on May the 7th ---]
Mon. 26th	26 HMT EMPIRE FOWEY arrived Southampton disembarking the 1st Battn. Gordon Highlanders ---]
Tue. 27th	A Patrol of the 2nd. 10th. Gurkhas Killed 1 CT.in Central Johore---]
+	27/04/1955 LG # 40765 p. 2536 The following awarded the George Medal
	T/INSP. HASSAN, B. SHAHABUDIN. GM FEDERATION MALAYA POLICE
Wed. 28th	} Combined Operations continued throughout Malaya---]
Thur. 29th	**29 Pte. Sirat. Bin. Sujab.** R.A.S.C. (MOR) Died*** *Claimed by next of Kin* ---]
+	**29 Pte. H. Turagavakace.** 1st. Fijian Infantry Regt. Killed in Action Engaging CT's. [*Ashes REP*]---]
Fri. 30th	Seremban: 6 girls and 3 boys of the Kuala Pilah School are throught to have sailed on a boat to Communist China last Saturday. Their parents are desperate for them to return---]

MAY

Sat. 1st	Operation "Appolo"- "Hawk"- "Apollo" Began against No 6 Regt.Ruab Kuala Lipis Pahang ---]
Sun. 2nd	2 HMT DILWARA arrived Singapore sailed enroute to Southampton with returning Service personnel ---]
Mon. 3rd	**3 Fus. H. Scott.** 1st. Battn. Royal Scots Fusiliers. Died*** *Kranji Singapore # 2/ B - 6*---]
Tue. 4th	4/05/1954 LG # 40163 p. 2617 The following awarded the British Empire Medal (Military)
	SGT. J.H. SWAN. BEM ROYAL AIR FORCE
	F/SGT, G, MAY. BEM ROYAL AIR FORCE

		SGT. RH. THOMPSON. BEM	ROYAL AIR FORCE
		SGT. J WILLIAMS. BEM	ROYAL AIR FORCE

	SGT. RH. THOMPSON. BEM	ROYAL AIR FORCE
	SGT. J WILLIAMS. BEM	ROYAL AIR FORCE
	The following awarded the Distinguished Flying Cross	
	W/CDR. C. C. F. COOPER.DFC	ROYAL AIR FORCE
	F/LT. D. M. FLEMING. DFC	ROYAL AIR FORCE
	F/LT. K. KINGMOTT. DFC.	ROYAL AIR FORCE
	F/O. C. P. FLAVELL. DFC	ROYAL AIR FORCE
	The following awarded the Distinguished Flying Medal	
	SGT. R.I. CROSS. DFM	ROYAL AIR FORCE
	SGT. C. J. TURLEY. DFM	ROYAL AIR FORCE
	4/05/1954 LG # 40164 p. 2627	The following awarded the British Empire Medal (Military)
	C/A/ART. W.G. KEEN	ROYAL NAVY
	A/ART. P.J.HUNT. BEM	ROYAL NAVY
	The following awarded the Distinguished Flying Cross	
	LT/COM. J.E. BREESE. DFC	ROYAL NAVY 848 SQD.
	LT/COM. S.H. SUTHERS. DFC	ROYAL NAVY 848 SQD.
+	4 HMT ASTURIUS arrived Singapore. ---]	
Wed. 5th	5 L/Cpl. R. Jefferies. R.A. S. C. 3 Coy. Died by accident Taiping # E / 43 Perak---]	
+	5 Pol/Lt. T. A. Charlton.GM. F.M. Aux.P. & 3 SC's Chin Yon. – Teo Hock Sai. – Omar B. Kasbar . F. M. Police were Killed in Action Engaging CT's. In a one hour fire fight in the jungle, against many CT's. Charlton, died from Gunshot wounds.Penggaring Johore---]	
+	5 HMT ASTURIAS sailed Singapore bound for Southampton onboard were the 1st.Battn. Lancashire Regt.	
Thur. 6th	6 Sgt. Choten Tshering Sherpa. 6th. Queen Elizabeth's Own Gurkha Rifles. Died*** Kranji Singapore 7 / C - 9---]	
Fri. 7th	7/05/1954 LG. 40166 p. 2685	The following awarded the Disinguished Conduct Medal
	RFN. B. RAI . DCM	10Th. PRINCESS MARY'S OWN GURKHA RIFLES
	The following awarded the Military Medal	
	CPL. A.R. B. ISMAIL. MM.	MALAY REGIMENT.
+	7 HMT DUNERA arrived Singapore enroute to Southampton with returning Service personnel 7th. ---]	
+	7 HMT DEVONSHIRE arrived Liverpool with returning Service personnel---]	
+	7 HMT EMPIRE ORWELL arrived Singapore with replacement Service personnel enroute to Hong Kong –]	
Sat. 8th.	8 Cpl. G. Thompsom. R. E.M. E. Died***Kranji Singapore # 2 / B -12 ---]	
Sun. 9th	9 HMT EMPIRE FOWEY sailed Southampton bound for Singapore/ Hong Kong with replacement Service personnel ---]	
Mon. 10th	10 Lt. J. Davies. Royal Navy HMS 'CARDIGAN BAY' Died *** [Ashes REP]---]	
Tue. 11th	11 Pol/Lt. E. D Boxhall. F. M. Police Killed on Ops. Boxhall was an outstanding shot. A first rate instructor, devoting a lot of his energies, to the improvement of shooting. [Grave Unknown] ---]	
+	11 Pte. Chazali b. Hassam. Malay Regt. Killed in Action Engaging CT's Perak---]	
+	11 HMT LANCASHIRE arrived Liverpool with returning Service personnel---]	
Wed. 12th	A Platoon of Gurkha Troops? Killed a CT leader Chen Kim-Tou in the Rawang area of Selangor---]	
Thur. 13th	Singapore: Riots broke out in Singapore against the Governments announcement: 'All males aged 18 to 20 had to register by end of May. To undergo. Part-time National Service. Failure to do so would result in a fine or a period in jail.'---]	
+	500 Students opposed to the demand and more sympathetic to the Communist. Gathered outside the Government House. The Police were called to disperse the crowd, which turned into a riot. 26 people were injured and 48 students arrested.---]	
Fri. 14th	4 CT's held up a bus at the 25th m/s Pogah /Langat road Johore. Lectured the passengers, stole $30 from the driver then let the bus go---]	
Sat. 15th	Gurkhas? surrounded a Group of CT's in the jungle area of Bahau Negri Sembilan Nevertheless they escaped---]	
Sun. 16th	Combined Operations continued throughout Malaya---]	
Mon. 17th	17 Dvr. P.O. King. R. A. S. C. Drowning incident. Western Road # 2156 George Town Penang ---]	
Tue. 18th	18 Sgt. R. E. Jones. - Pte. R.W. Fisher. 1st. Battn. The Queen's West Surrey Regt. Died*** Seremban # CE – 86 – RC – 484 Negri Sembilan---]	
Wed. 19th	19 Rfn. Hastabahadur Thapa . 2nd.King Edward VII's's Own Gurkha Rifles.Killed in ambush [No known Grave] Terandak Wall Memorial Malacca]---]	
+	19 Rfn. Gubersing Limbu. 10th. Princess Mary's Own Gurkha Rifles. Died*** Kranji Singapore 7 / C -5---]	

+	19 HMT EMPIRE TROOPER sailed Southanpton bound for Singapore / Hong Kong with replacement Service personnel- --]
Thur. 20th	20 A/Comm/P L.A. Searle. F. M.Police. during a night time ambush Killed in Action Engaging CT's Selangor [Grave unknown].---]
Fri. 21st	The Royal Navy 848 Sqdn. Sikorsky Helicopters became operational. When 8: S55 H/C landed to take troops of the 2nd. 10th Princess Mary's Own Gurkhas Rifles. To a jungle clearing, to deploy and engage with CT's during Operation "Commodore"---]
Sat. 22nd	Kuala Lumpur: An Anouncement stated. 'The Malayan Civil Service is losing its attraction. For non Malay Asians. Reasons given: Outside Companies are giving higher saleries to Non Malay Asians --]
Sun. 23rd	23 HMT HALLADALE arrived in Singapore with replacement Service personnel---]
Mon. 24th	Gurkha Patrols? Killed 4 CT's in Central Malaya ---]
Tue. 25th	Fijian Patrols. Killed 3 CT's in the area of Johore---]
+	25 /05/1955 LG # 40181 p.3072 The following awarded the Colonial Police Medal SC SAKHAWAT HUSSAIN S/ORAHMALI. CPM. FEDERATION MALAYA POLICE SC. ALIMON. B. SENU. CPM. FEDERATION MALAYA POLICE
+	25 HMT ASTURIUS arrived Southampton with returning Service personnel---]
Wed. 26th	26 L/Cpl. N. Nadaku. 1st. Fijian Infantry Regt.Killed in Action Engaging CT's [Ashes REP] ---]
Thur. 27th	27 SC. Aziz B. Mat. F. M. Police Killed on CT Ops. Ipoh Perak ---]
Fri. 28th	28 Asst/Comm. Chief of Kedah Police C.M. Godwin. F. M. Police. Killed in an ambush at Kedah Peak enroute to the Rest House on Kulai Oil Palm Estate Johore. It appeared it was a well planned ambush. Jalan Pertana # 1467 George Town Penang ---]
+	28 HMT HALLADALE sailed from Singapore bound for Liverpool.---]
Sat. 29th	29 Pte. W. F. McAuley. R.E.M.E. Died*** Kranji Singapore # 2 / B - 15---]
+	29 HMT DILWARA arrived Southampton with returning Service personnel---]
+	29 HMT EMPIRE ORWELL arrived Singapore enroute to Southampton with returning Service personnel---]
Sun. 30th	Kuala Lumpur :General Templar having completed his time in Malaya, stated: 'The emergency might be contained. But certainly was not at an end. Those that understood jungle warfare Realised it could drag on interminably.' Handed over his duties to Sir. Donald MacGillivray. His successor as Director of Operations was:- Lt. General Sir. Geoffrey Bourne.---]
Mon. 31st	31 Pte.W. Hill. 1st. Battn. Royal Hampshire Regt. Died from Wounds recv'd in Ambush. Kuala Lumpur # 21 / 1136---]

JUNE

Tue. 1st	1Trp. B. Powell. Seaforth Highlanders. Tpr. A.E.Howell Att/22nd. SAS. Died from injuries received in Helicopter No ? Crash. Kuala Lumpur # 21 – 1138 – RC / A – 6 ---]
+	Operation 'Eclipse' Began against No. No 8 Regt. MRLA In Kedah.---]
+	Operation 'Jekyll 'Began against No 2 Regt. MRLA in the Bahau area of Negri Sembilan---]
+	Operation 'Termite' Began SAS against the MRLA---]
+	1 HMT LANCASHIRE sailed Liverpool for Singapore/ Hong Kong.with replacement Service personnel---]
Wed. 2nd	2 Cpl. B. Mason. Den. Admin. R.A.F. Changi Drowning accident. Kranji Singapore # 4 / A – 5 ---]
Thur. 3rd	3 Mr. R. Chestnut Manager. & Mr. W. R. Mc Connachei. Asstn.Man. Harewood Estate Sungei Siput. were Killed in an ambush by 6 CT's in Perak.---]
+	3 HMT DUNERA arrived Southampton with returning Service personnel ---]
Fri. 4th	600 to 800 Pupils at the Chinese High School at Bukit Timah. Staged a sit in. In an attempt to seek assurance. If they are still at school and they sign up for National Service. They will not be called up. ---]
Sat. 5th	5 HMT EMPIRE FOWEY arrived Singapore with replacement Service personnel---]
Sun. 6th	6 Rfn. Kajibahadur Rai . No 3 Platoon 'A' Company 10th. Princess Mary's Own Gurkha Rifles. was Killed in Action Engaging CT's. The CT's escaped Kranji Singapore # 7 / B -3---]
+	6 HMT EMPIRE FOWEY sailed Singapore enroute to / Hong Kong---]
Mon. 7th	} Combined Operations continued throughout Malaya---]
Tue. 8th	4 CT's approached 5 Indian Tappers, working on an Estate at the 29th mile Lenggong road. They lectured them bbefore taking one Kanniah alias Kanna. They tied his hands behind his back, led him away from the other 4. Then shot and Killed him---]
Wed. 9th	A CT. surrendered to the Kota Tingi Police. Informing them of an air strike, without any casualties--]

+	Patrols of the Gurkha's? went out in search of the other CT's & successfully Killed I CT--]'
Thur. 10th	} Combined Operations continued throughout Malaya---]
Fri. 11th	40 CT's ambushed a Plt. of the F.M. Police. Patrolling a Canal in the area of Kuala Kabu Kabu. They returned fire but soon ran out of ammunition. The CT's surrounded them took all their weapons before retreating. Their prize being guns. The Commander of this MRLA section, was the much wanted *Heap Theong* a very nasty character with a long record of murders---]
Sat. 12th	A follow up was put into motion with the Somersets, taking up the chase into the swamp area. The RAF were called in to assist in trying to stop the CT's moving. Lincoln bombers, dropped a series of bombs along an assumed escape route. But to no avail the CT's had gone---]
Sun. 13th	13 HMT EMPIRE CLYDE sailed Liverpool bound for Singapore / Hong Kong with replacement Service personnel---]
Mon. 14th	30 CT's ambushed a landrover driven by a F.M. Policeman. 10 miles North on Seremban killing the Policemen (*unnamed*) and wounding 3 SC's. They took their arms and ammunition before they left---]
Tue. 15th	15 Sgt. T. H. Ashworth. Royal Signals Died *** *[Ashes REP*]---]
+	15/06/1954 LG.40206 p.3595 The following awarded the British Empire Medal (Military)
	CAPT. D.R. BOYNS MD. BEM ROYAL ARMY MEDICAL CORPS
Wed.16th	} Combined Operations continued throughout Malaya ---]
Tue. 17th	17 HMT NEW AUSTRALIA sailed Suthamptom bound for 'Sydney / Singapore via Panama ---]
Fri. 18th	18/6/54. LG # 40206 p 3596 The following awarded the Military Medal
	CPL. T. THAPA. MM 6th QUEEN ELIZABETH'S OWN GURKHA RIFLES
	RFN. B. GURUNG. MM 6th QUEEN ELIZABETH'S OWN GURKHA RIFLES
+	18 HMT EMPIRE TROOPER arrived Singapore with replacement Service personnel---]
Sat. 19th	19 HMT EMPIRE TROOPER sailed Singapore for Hong Kong ---]
+	19 HMT ASTURIUS sailed Southampton bound for Singapore / Hong Kong with replacement Service personnel---]
Sun. 20th	Operation *"Matador"* Began to destroy CT cultivation plots deep in the jungle--]
Mon. 21st	21 HMT EMPIRE ORWELL arrived Southampton with replacement Service personnel---]
Tue. 22nd	22 HMT DILWARA sailed Southampton bound for Singapore / Hong Kong / Kure with replacement Service personnel ---]
Wed. 23rd	23 L/Cpl. Siray Rai . 7th. Duke of Edinburgh's Own Gurkha Rifles Died***_Kranji Singapore #7 / B - 5_ ---]
Thur. 24th	} Combined Operations continued throughout Malaya---]
Fri. 25th	An ambush laid by the Somersets resulted in killing the leading CT of a group, whilst the others escaped.--]
+	25/O6/54 LG# 40217 p3820 The following awarded the Military Cross
	CAPT. D.R.L WYMAN MC ROYAL REGIMENT ARTILLERY ATT/T MALAY REGT.
	CAPT. J.A. LYS MC 6th. QUEEN ELIZABETH'S OWN GURKHA RIFLES
	LT. (QGO) S. RAI.MC 7th. DUKE OF EDIMBURGH'S OWN GURKHA RIFLES
	Lt. P.S. LEIGH MC QUEEN'S OWN ROYAL WEST KENTS
	2/Lt. R.A. DOUGLAS. MC. THE SOMERSET LIGHT INF.
	The following awarded the Mlitary Medal
	SGT.V.C. R. HEALEY.MM . QUEEN'S OWN ROYAL WEST KENTS
	RFN T. THAPA. MM 2nd. KING EDWARD VII'S OWN GURKHA RIFLES
	WO2 L. THAPA MM 6th QUEEN ELIZABETH'S OWN GURKHA RIFLES
	SGT. B. RAI MM 7th. DUKE OF EDINBURGH'S OWN GURKHA RIFLES
	RFN. G. SUNWAR. MM 7th.DUKE OF EDINBURGH'S OWN GURKHA RIFLES
	CPL. B. B.H. BUSIN MM MALAY REGIMENT.
	SGT. S. RAVOKA. MM FIJI REGIMENT.
Sat. 26th	A similar ambush by the Somersets. Killed 1 more CT from the same Plt commanded by *Heap Theong*---]
Sun. 27th	27 HMT EMPIRE FOWEY arrived Singapore enroute to Southampton with returning Service personnel --]
Mon. 28th	28 Cpl. Jamaludin b. Rejab. Malay Regt. Killed in Action Engaging CT's. Kedah---]
+	28 HMT HALLADALE arrived Liverpool- with returning Service personnel--]
Tue. 29th	} Combined Operations continued throughout Malaya---]
Wed. 30th	}

JULY

Thur. 1st	Operation *"Termite"* Began against No. 12 Regt. MRLA in Perak---]

194

	+	1 HMT LANCASHIRE arrived Singapore with returning Service personnel sailed for Hong Kong /Kure 1st.-]
Fri.	2nd	SC.Sayono B. Mahmood. F. M. Police Killed on Ops. Telok Anson Area Perak---]
Sat. .	3rd	} Combined Operations continued throughout Malaya---]
Sun.	4th	4 Rfn. Bakhiljar Rai. 7th. Duke of Edinburgh's Own Gurkha Rifle. Killed in Action Engaging CT's. *Seremban # 60* Negri Sembilan---]
Mon.	5th	4 Cpl. L. Creighton. Royal Engineers Died*** *Kuala Lumpur # 21 / 1140* ---]
Tue.	6th	Operation *"Matador"* Ended. During the Operation. 4 CT's were Killed---]
	+	6 HMT EMPIRE TROOPER arrived Singapore fron Hong Kong---]
Wed.	7th	7 W/O. E. S. Baxter. (GRF) R.A.F. Seletar. Died***.*Kranji Singapore # 4 / A – 4* ---]
	+	7 HMT EMPIRE TROOPER sailed Singapore bound for Southanpton with returning Service personnel--]
Thur.	8th	8 Pte. B. W. G. Plympton. 1st. Battn. Somerset Light Infantry. Died***Kuala Lumpur # 21 / 1137---]
	+	8 L/Cpl. R. C. Watton. 1st. Battn. Royal Hampshire Regt. Died*** *Kuala Lumpur # 21 / 1139* ---]
	+	8 HMT DEVONSHIRE sailed Liverpool bound for Singapore / Hong Kong'Kure with replacement Service personnel---]
Fri.	9th	9 HMT EMPIRE ORWELL sailed Southampton bound for Singapore / Hong Kong/ Kure with replacement Service personnel. On board were the Advance party of the Royal Welch Fusiliers destined for Korea---]
Sat.	10th	10 Pte. M. Willie. 3rd. King's African Rifles. Died***Kuala Lumpur # 21 / 1141---]
	+	10 HMT ASTURIUS arrived Singapore enroute to Hong Kong 10th. with replacement Service personnel---]
Sun.	11th	11 Pte. P. W. P. Spurr. 1st Battn. Somerset Light Infantry. Died by accident *Kuala Lumpur #21 / 1142*----]
	+	11 Pol/ Insp, W. A, Gibson. F. M. Police Killed on CT Ops. *Kranji Singapore # 17 / A – 8* ---]
	+	11 Sgt. Singh. Bachan. R.A.O.C. Died***Kuala Lumpur # 25 / 37---]
	+	11 HMT EMPIRE CLYDE arrived Singapore with replacement Service personnel/ sailed 11 Hong Kong--
Mon.	12th	12 HMT EMPIRE CLYDE arrived Singapore enroute to Hong Kong with replacement Service personnel sailed 12th.----]
Tue.	13th	13 Capt. P. Gibbs. R.A.E.C. Died*** *Kranji Singapore # 2 / B – 14* ---]
	+	13 LAC. M. Poole. W/Mech R.Att. to No 1 (Ceylon) Radio HQ 90 Group R.A.F. Died ***. *Kranji Singapore # 4 / A – 3* -]
Wed.	14th	} Combined Operation continued throughout Malaya ---]
Thur.	15th	15 HMT EMPIRE HALLADALE sailed Liverpool bound for Singapore / Hong Kong with replacement Service personnel---]
Fri.	16th	RAF Fighters blazed away with rockets and machine gun fire at CT hideouts in the hills. The villages of isolated Pergal Jelubu 15 miles from Kuala Klawang Negri Sembilan watched the air stikes Less than 5 mins after the attack. Royal Navy Helicopters took 100 Gurkhas from the main road up into the hills to clear out the CT Camps---]
Sat.	17th	Singapore: Power workers threatened to Strike at midnight ---]
Sun.	18th	Singapore:10,000 Power workmen went on strike in Singapore demanding more pay.---]
Mon.	19th	} Combined Operations continued throughout Malaya ---]
Tue.	20th	20 Pte. S. P. King. 1st. Battn. The Queen's Royal Regt. Died***Seremban # RC -487 Negri Sembilan---]
	+	20 Rfn. G. Lalbahadur Gurung. 6th. King Edward' s Own Gurkha Rifles. Killed in Action Engaging CT's Perak.Sulva Lines # 59 Ipoh Perak.---]
	+	20 L/S C.B. Larkin. H.M.S. *'TERROR'* Died*** *Kranji Singapore # 12 / C - 14*---]
Wed.	21st	Operation *"Sword"* Began against the Kedah State Committee 8th. Regt. MRLA whose leader was **Ah Sui**--]
	+	21 HMT EMPIRE FOWEY arrived Southampton with returning Service personnel.---]
Thur.	22nd	22 SC Saris B, Samen. F. M. Police Killed on Ops. Jelabu Area Johore---]
Fri.	23rd	23/07/1954. LG. # 40236 p 4309 The following awarded the Military Medal
	+	SGT. L. SAILADA .MM FIJI INFANTRY REGT.,
Sat.	24th	24 2/Lt.. R.M. Townsend. 1st. Battn. The Queen's West Surrey Regt. Accidently shot on patrol. *Kuala Lumpur # 21 -1143*---]
Sun.	25th	A Patrol of the 2nd. 10th. Princess Mary's Own Gurkha Rifles came under heavy fire from a Number of CT's. 2 Gurkhas were wounded. One fell down a steep ridge. Rfn. Naprasad continued firing until the CT's retreated. Then Naprasad, tended to the wounded, before searching for the other rifleman down the ridge, without success. He had to give up due to fading light. He continued next morning with other reinforcements & found **Rfn. Gajuman Rai**. had died from his wounds. *Sungei Patani # 90.* For his courage & dedication Rfn. Naprasad was recommended for The DCM---]
Mon.	26th	26 HMT EMPIRE CLYDE arrived Singapore---]
Tue.	27th	27 HMT EMPIRE CLYDE sailed Singapore bound for Liverpool with returning Service personnel-

Wed. 28th	28 HMT LANCASHIRE arrived Singapore from Kure / sailed for Liverpool with returning Service personnel]
Thur. 29th	29 P/O. AS.C. Perkins.Royal Navy HMS 'TERROR' Died ***[Ashes REP]---]
Fri. 30th	} Combined Operations continued throughout Malaya ---]
Sat. 31st	}

AUGUST

Sun. 1st	RNZN HMNZS "KANIERE". began her support role of duty, whilst 'PUKAKI'. Completed her first, support role of duty in Malayan coastal waters---]
+	1 HMT NEW AUSTRALIA arrived Singapore with replacement Service personnel ---]
+	1 HMT EMPIRE ORWELL arrived Singapore enroute to / Hong Kong/Kure with replacement Service personnel---]
Mon. 2nd	2 Cpl. Tajudin. Bin. Rosch. R.A.S.C.. (MOR) Died*** Claimed by next of Kin---]
+	2 HMT ASTURIUS arrived Singapore with replacement Service Personnel---]
+	2 HMT NEW AUSTRALIA sailed Singapore bound for Southampton with returning Service Personnel---]
Tue. 3r+	3 Rfn. R. Tulparsad Rana. 6th. Queen Elizabeth's Own Gurkha Rifles. Died*** Kluang # 3 / E – 3 Johore]
+	3 HMT ASTURIUS sailed Singapore bound for Southampton with returning Service personnel--]
Wed. 4th	4 Sgt. Hamzah b. Abu Kassim. Malay Regt.Killed in Action Engaging CT's Perak---]
Thur. 5th	Operation "Ajax" Began against No 4 Regt. MRLA. In Johore---].
Fri. 6th	6 HMT DEVONSHIRE arrived Singapore with replacement Service personnel enroute to / Hong Kong sailed 6th.---]
Sat. 7th	7 HMT DUNERA sailed Southampton bound for Singapore / Hong Kong with replacement Service personnel---]
+	7 HMT EMPIRE TROOPER arrived Southanpton with returning Service personnel---]
Sun. 8th	The Group Committee Member of the Karrangan section identified as Soon Peng, Surrendered to a Patrol of the 2nd10th. Princess Mary's Own Gurkha Rifles. He gave information regarding, where a camp for CT's was located. Lleading the way for the Gurkhas to ambush the CT's---]
Mon. 9th	} Combined Operations continued throughout Malaya---]
Tue. 10th	10 HMT EMPIRE FOWEY sailed from Southampton bound for Singapore / Hong Kong/Kure with the 2nd. Battn. Royal Welch Fusiliers bound for Korea ---]
Wed. 11th	11 Pte. B. D. Smith. 1st. Battn. Royal Hampshire Regt. Killed in Action Engaging CT's Rawang. Kuala Lumpur # 21 / 1144 ---]
Thur. 12th	12 Mr. B.P. Wills Dredge Master. Tronoh Tin Mines Kampar Perak. Killed in ambush by CT's---].
Fri. 13th	13 SC Mayon B, Hihak F. M. Police Killed on CT Ops. Kota Tinggi area Johore.---]
Sat. 14th	The Patrol of 2nd. 10th. Gurkhas along with the CT. SEP Soon Peng engaged and Killed 3 CT's---]
+	14 HMT DILWARA arrived Singapore enroute to Southampton with returning Service personnel ---]
Sun. 15th	15 HMT EMPIRE HALLADALE arrived Singapore with replacement Service personnel ---].
+	15 HMT EMPIRE HALLADALE sailed Singapore enroute to Hong Kong ---].
Mon. 16th	} Combined operations continued throuout Malaya---]
Tue. 17th	17 L/Cpl. Deobahadur 6th. Queen Elizabeth's Own Gurkha Rifles. Died from Wounds recv'd Segamat Kluang # 3 / B – 3 Johore---]
+	17 Rfn. Kharkabahadur Sunwar . 10th. Princess Mary's Own Gurkha Rifles. Died*** Kranji Singapore # 7 / C -11 [Ashes REP]---]
Wed. 18th	} Combined Operations continued throughout Malaya---]
Thur. 19th	19 Mr. M.A. William a British civilian was accidently shot near Sungei Buloh---]
Fri. 20th	Singapore: CT's stole 49 Bombs from the RAF air base at Tengah Singapore. The bombs easy to conseal, hold enough high expossives to make 100 homemade land mines or 20,000 hand grenades ---]
Sat. 21st	} Combined Operations continued throughout Malaya---]
Sun. 22nd	}
Mon. 23rd	23 Spr. G.W. Sidebottom. Royal Engineers Died***Kuala Lumpur # 21 / 1145 ---]
+	23 HMT NEW AUSTRALIA arrived Southampton with returning Service Personnel---]
+	23 HMT EMPIRE ORWELL arrived Singapore enroute to Southampton with returning Service personnel23
Tue. 24th	24 HMT ASTURIUS arrived Southampton with returning Service personnel ---]
Wed. 25th	25 HMT EMPIRE CLYDE arrived Liverpool with returning Service personnel---]
Thur. 26th	Support Company 1st.10th. Princess Mary's Own Gurkha Rifles. Killed 2 CT's in the Pontian area Identified as a State Committee member & his girl friend ---]
+	26 London: The War Office issued a statement:

		' The destination of the Royal Welch Fusiliers has been changed from. Service in Korea to Active Service in Malaya' ---]
Fri.	27th	27 2/Lt. J. A. Davies. 15/19th. The Kings Royal Hussars Died Armoured Car overturned.Ruab/Grik Road._Taiping # E / 44_ Perak---]
Sat.	28th	28 L/Cpl. W. Salubeniq. 3rd. King's African Rifles. Killed in Action Engaging CT's. [No known Grave]Terandak Wall Memorial Malacca]---]
Sun.	29th	29 Rfn's Dhanman Limbu. – Ganesh Tamang . 10th. Princess Mary's Own Gurkha Rifles. Killed in Action Engaging CT's _Sungei Patani # 107 - 106_
	+	29 Rfn. Purnabahadur Rai. 10th. Princess Mary's Own Gurkha Rifles. Killed in Action Engaging CT's. _Kranji Singapore # 7 / D 9_ ---]
	+	29 HMT EMPIRE FOWEY arrived in Columbo Ceylon. To embark the Advance party of the Royal Welch Fusiliers who were to be re transported to Singapore---]
Mon.	30th	30 Pol/Lt. Harrison. A. F. M. Police Died*** _Kuantan_ Pahang.---]
Tue.	31st	30 HMT LANCASHIRE arrived Liverpool with returning Service personnel---]
	+	30 HMT EMPIRE HALLADALE arrrived Singapore---]
	+	Operation _"Galway"-"Termite"- "Inland"_ Ended---]

SEPTEMBER

Wed.	1st	1 Cpl. J. E. B. Noel. Eng/Fit. (A) R.A.F. Changi Died*** _Kranji Singapore # 4 / a – 2_ ---]
	+	Operation "Shark" Began against No 5 Regt. MRLA In Sungei Siput Perak.---]
	+	1 HMT EMPIRE HALLADALE sailed Singapore bound for Liverpool with returning Service personnel---]
Thur.	2nd	2 HMT DUNERA arrived Singapore enroute to Hong Kong with replacement Service personnel 3rd. ---]
Fri.	3rd	A high ranking CT. Number 4 in the Negri Sembilan area, was Killed. Identified as **Sallahbin Yussof**---]
	+	3 HMT DUNERA sailed Singapore enroute Hong Kong ---]
	+	3 HMT EMPIRE TROOPER sailed Southanpton bound for Singapore via African Ports/ Singapore ---]
	+	3 HMT EMPIRE FOWEY arrived Singapore disembarking the advance party of the 2nd. Battn. Royal Welch Fusiliers as replacement Service personnel ---]
Sat.	4th	4 HMT EMPIRE FOWEY sailed Singapore bound for Hong Kong---]
Sun.	5th	5 SAC. J. N. Hill. Eng/Mech. R.A.F. Seletar Drowned in boating incident. _Kranji Singapore # 3 / E – 6_ ---]
	+	5 HMT DEVONSHIRE arrived Singapore ---]
Mon.	6th	6 HMT DEVONSHIRE sailed Singapore bound for Liverpool with returning Service personnel---]
Tue.	7th	7 Sgmn. Raghudhoj Chhetri . Gurkha Signals Died by Accident on CT Ops. Nobart Camp Gurun Kedah _Sungei Patani # 108_ ---]
Wed.	8th	} Combined Operation continued throughout Malaya ---]
Thur.	9th	09/09/1954 LG # 40272 p. 5147 The following awarded the Colonial Police Medal PC.CHAN THAN SEND. CPM FEDERATION MALAYA POLICE
	+	9 HMT ASTURIUS sailed from Southampton bound for Singapore/ Hong Kong with replacement Service personnel---]
Fri.	10th	10 Whilst on take off at Kuala Lumpur.Mosquito PR 34. 81 Sqdr. R.A.F. swung and hit a Landrover killing **Drv. J. A. McCleary.**_55 Coy R.A.S.C. Kuala Lumpur # 22 / 1146_ .---]
	+	10/09/1955 LG # 40725 p. 5245 The following awarded the Military Cross MAJ.G.S. MATE. MM MC FIJI iNFANTRY BRIGADE
Sat.	11th	CT's cut 250 yards of telephone wire and felled several telegraph post in the Kluan Area of Johore ---]
Sun.	12th	A CT was shot dead whilst guarding 4 packs of clothing. By a Patrol of the Fijians in the Regam area]
Mon.	13th	13 L/Clp. G. Robertson. Royal Signals Died*** _Kuala Lumpur # 22 / 1147_ .---]
Tue.	14th	14 SC Hasan B. Klang. F. M. Police Killed on Ops. Bahau Area Negri Sembilan---]
Wed.	15th	15 HMT EMPIRE ORWELL arrived Southampton with returning Service personnel---]
Thur.	16th	16 Pte. Esa. bin. Mohd Lajim. Malay Regt. Killed in Action Engaging CT's Perak---]
Fri.	17th	Operation "Sword" Ended. 8 CT's had been eliminated. 25 Camps destroyed & 27 food dumps found in the Bongsu area---]
Sat.	18t	For the past week R.A.A.F. Lincoln Bombers have plastered the area of Mount Ophir, a CT hideout. As did the Royal Artillery Gunners. At daybreak, a Voice Plane flew over the area.Loud hailed: _A cease fire had been imposed to allow any CT's to Surrender._ Eventually 3 CT's came out and gave themselves up to the Security Forces---]
	+	18 HMT EMPIRE FOWEY arrived Singapore from Korea with the 2nd. Battn. Royal Welch Fusiliers to join up with the advance party 2nd. Battn. Located in Nee Soon Camp Singapore---]

Sun.	19th	A Patrol of the Queen's Royal Regt. ambushed 3 CT's in the area of Gemas. 1 CT was wounded all three were captured---]
Mon.	.20th	15 Home Guards were arrested in the new village of Paloh near Kluang. While the Viilage was celebrating the Sultans Birthday. CT's sneaked in and stole rifles and ammunition. The Guards did not return any fire ---]
Tue.	21st	Kuala Lumpur: **Mrs Sheilla Cuff** . The wife of a RAF Cpl. Was Killed when she accidently touched a live wire in her house Pengalang Road Her husband was on duty at the time. She leaves 2 chidren---]
Wed.	22nd	**22 Cpl. C. Ellingworth.** 1st. Battn. The East Yorkshire Regt. Died*** [*Ashes REP*]---]
+		22 HMT NEW AUSTRALIA sailed Southampton via Panama Canal bound for Sydney / Japan /Singapore]
Thur.	23rd	CT's broke through the barbed wire fence, rushed the Home Gaurds Post and surrounded it. Villagers came out and demanded they let the Guards go. There were no Casualties ---]
Fri.	24th	24 HMT LANCASHIRE arrived Singapore .with replacement Service personnel---]
Sat.	25th	**25 Pte. H. M. C. A. Duff.** 1st. Battn. The Queen's West Surrey Regt. Died***_Kuala Lumpur # 22 - 1149_---]
+		25 HMT LANCASHIRE sailed Singapore bound for Hong Kong ---]
Sun.	26th	Kampon Machap new village Johore. The village was a notorious Larder for the CT's. Had to be broken up. Its 57 families were being sent elsewere .---]
Mon.	27th	Gurkhas of the 2/7th. Killed 3 CT's in he area of Seremban details? being withheld for security reasons---]
Tue.	28th	**28 Tpr. N. Hornigold.** 11th. Royal Hussars Died ***_Kuala Lumpur- # 22 / 1150_ ---]
Wed.	29th	Combined Operations continued throughout Malaya---]
Thur.	30th	**30 Sgt. Bhagtabahadur Gurung** . 6th. Queen Elizabeth's Own Gurkha Rifles. Died*** _Sulva Lines # 58_ Ipoh Perak---]
+		30 HMT ASTURIUS arrived Singapore enroute to Hong Kong with replacement Service personnel 30th.---]
+		Operation "Hawk"- "Apollo" - "Jeklyll Ended

OCTOBER

Fri.	1st	Operation *"Hotspur"* R. A. F. Air Strike ---]
+		Operation '*Axe "Hilt'* Began SAS aaaaagainst the MRLA ---]
Sat.	2nd	**2 Pte. S. Vukaruru., Pte. A. Waqamatia.** 1st. Battn. Fijian Infantry Regt. Killed in Action Engaging CT's [*Ashes REP*]---]
–		2 HMT EMPIRE HALLADALE arrived Liverpool sailed for Glasgow ---]
+		2 HMT DUNERA arrived Singapore ---]
Sun.	3rd	**3 P/Off. Salleh. B. Hassan.** 93 Sqdn R.A.F. Regt. (MOR) Killed on Ops._Claimed by next of Kin_ ---]
+		**3 Cpl. Ahmid b. Isin** Malay Regt. Killed in Action Engaging CT's Selangor---]
+		3 HMT DUNERA sailed Singapore bound for Southampton with returning Service personnel---]
Mon.	4th	4 HMT EMPIRE ORWELL sailed Southampton bound for Singapore / Kure, Hong Kong with replacement Service personnel---]
+		4 HMT EMPIRE FOWEY arrived Singapore with replacement Service personnel---]
Tue.	5th	**5 Pte. P. J. Archer.** 1st. Battn. Royal Hampshire Regt. Died*** _Kuala Lumpur # 22 / 1151_---]
+		**5 Rfn. Gunabir Rai.** 7th. Duke of Edinburgh's Own Gurkha Rifles. Died Motor Veh Acc. _Seremban # 61_ Negri Sembilan---]
+		5 HMT DEVONSHIRE arrived Liverpool with returning Service personnel ---]
Wed.	6th	6 HMT EMPIRE FOWEY sailed Singapore bound for Southampton with returning Service personnel---]
Thur.	7th	**7 Cpl. L. Winecon.** 3rd. King's African Rifles. Killed in Action Engaging CT's _Kuala Lumpur # 24 / 11_ ---]
Fri.	8th	**8 Rfn. Debilal Thapa** 2nd. King Edward VII's Own Gurkha Rifles. Died*** _Kranji Singapore # 8 / A - 2_---]
Sat.	9th	} Combined Operations continued throughout Malaya---]
Sun.	10th	**10 Pte. D. Juvenalisi.** 3rd. King's African Rifles. Killed in Action Engaging CT's _Kuala Lumpur # 32 / 1242_ -]
+		**10 S/Sgt. W. T. F. Howle.** R.A.E.C.. Died*** [*Ashes REP*]---]
+		10 HMT DILWARA arrived Southhamton with returning Service personnel---]
Mon.	11th	**11 ? G. A Grierson.** Royal Navy HMS '*SIMBANG*' Died *** _Kranji Singapore # 12 / C – 13_---]
Tue.	12th	12 HMT EMPIRE CLYDE arrived Singapore with replacement Service personnel ---]
+		12 HMT EMPIRE FOWEY sailed Singapore bound for Singapore with replacement Service personnel--]
Wed.	13th	13 HMT EMPIRE CLYDE sailed Singapore bound for Hong Kong ---]
Thur.	14th	**14 Pte. Yaha B. Alip.** Malay Regt. Killed in Action Engaging CT's Perak---]
Fri.	15th	A Shopkeeper was detained after a shooting incident between an area Security force and CT's on the South Johol Estate Kuala Pilah District of Negri Sembilan---]

Sat. 16th	16 4 F. M. Police **SC's Ahmed B. Amzd. – Abdul Wahan B. Tamey. – Yasin B. Ahmad. – Mohd Yassin B Marimin**. Killed on CT Ops. Pontian Area Johore---]
Sun. 17th	Kuala Lumpur: Sir.. Donald MacGillivray announced: ' *'At the request of General Sir. Geofrey Bourne (Director of Operations in Malaya) To expand the War Cabinet responsible for the day to day running of the war against the Terrorist. He had invited Tunku Abdul Rahma. (President of the United Malays Nation Association. Dato Sir. Onn Bin Ja'afar (Leader of the Nagara (National) party:H.S. Lee (Malayan Chinese Association):Mr. V. N Menon (Indian Trade Union and Labour): Mr. R. B. Carey (Member for Works)-To attend.'*
Mon. 18th	}Combined Operations continued throughout Malaya---]
Tue. 19th	}

Wed. 20th	20/10/1954 LG. 40312 P. 6121 The following awarded the British Empire Medal (Military)
	SGT.D.A. HOWARD. BEM ROYAL AIR FORCE
	SGT. B. b. BAKIR. BEM ROYAL AIR FORCE (MOR)
	CPL. D.N. GIBBONS. BEM ROYAL AIR FORCE
	CPL/TECH. H.F COBB. BEM ROYAL AIR FORCE
	     The following awarded the Distinguished Flying Cross
	LT. CDR. C.J. KNIGHT. DFC ROYAL NAVY
	LT. CDR. G.D LUFF. DFC ROYAL NAVY
	CAPT. V. K. METCALFE. DFC ROYAL CORPS SIGNALS
	F/O. H. MARSHALL DFC ROYAL AIR FORCE
	F/LT. R. W. J. ANDRUSIKIEWICZ.. DFC ROYAL AIR FORCE
	F/O. R. G. J. SNELLER. DFC ROYAL AIR FORCE
	F/LT C. COX. DFC ROYAL AIR FORCE
	F/LT. V.J. HURRING.DFC ROYAL AIR FORCE
	     The following awarded the Distinguished Flying Medal
	S/SGT. J.I. FORD. DFM ROYAL CORPS SIGNALS
	CPL. A. G. GILBERT. DFM ROYAL ARMY SERVICE CORPS.
	F/SGT. C.KIRKHAM. DFM ROYAL AIR FORCE
	SGT. C. FENWICK . DFM ROYAL AIR FORCE

Thur. 21st	**21** Pol/Lt. R.I. Ollerton. F. M. Police Killed by Accident Johore [*Grave Unknown*] ---]
+	On the Fraser Estate a Patrol of 2nd.10th. Princess Mary's Own Gurkha Rifles Killed 1 CT---]
Fri. 22nd	**22** HMT LANCASHIRE arrived / sailed Singapore bound for Liverpool with returning Service personnel--]
+	**22** Maj. QM. F. J. Moon. R.A.S.C.. Died*** *Kuala Lumpur # 22 / 1152*--]
+	**22** HMT ASTURIUS arrived Singapore enroute to Southampton with returning Service personnel 23rd. ---]
Sat. 23rd	**23** Mr. T.W. Hunt. Asstn. Manager. Glendale Estate. Bahau. Killed in Ambush together with a Chinese Contractor(**unnamed**)---]
Sun. 24th	A Platoon of the 2nd. 10th. Princess Mary's Own Gurkha Rifles ambushed & Killed 3 CT's whilst they were picking up food at a food dump---]
Mon. 25th	London: The Ruler of Negri Sembilan whilst on a visit to London awarded Jonathan Serale with his fathers medal. Mr. L.A. Searle former Selangor Special Group Chief. was awarded posthurmously The **Selangor Distinguished Conduct Medal** ---]
+	A Platoon of the 6th Malay Regt. Killed 1 CT in the Metakab area ---[

Tue. 26th	26/10/54 LG # 40308 p 6053 The following awarded the British Empire Medal (Military)
	SGT. D.G. GODDARD. BEM ROYAL REGIMENT ARTILLERY
	SGT. K.J. KING. BEM THE QUEEN'S ROYAL WEST KENTS
	S/SGT. L.R. KNIGHT. BEM ROYAL MILITARY POLICE.
	W/O. M.T.B. M. AKIL. BEM MALAY REGIMENT.
	W/O. J.M PATTERSON. BEM QUEEN'S ROYAL WESTKENT REGIMENT.
	C/SGT. S. GURUNG. BEM BRIGADE OF GURKHAS
	     p. 6504 The following awarded the Miltary Cross
	MAJ. J.A. LLYOD WILLIAMS MC 2ND. KING EDWARD VII'S OWN GURKHA RIFLES.???
	LT. (QGO) N. LIMBU. 7th. DUKE OF EDINBURGH'S OWN GURKHA RIFLES.
	LT. (QGO) D. LIMBU. MC 10th. PRINCESS MARY'S OWN GURKHA RIFLES.
	Lt. R.W. NEVE. MC QUEEN'S ROYAL WEST KENTS
	LT. A.M.B. ABAS. MC. MALAY REGIMENT.
	     The following awarded the Military Medal
	CPL. S.G. MILES. MM ROYAL ARMY SERVICE CORPS (LEP)

	PTE. A.B.H. YAACUB.MM	MALAY REGIMENT.
	PTE.B.M ZAIN. MM	MALAY REGIMENT.
	CPL. E.MORRIS. MM	KINGS AFRICAN RIFLES
	CPL. J DIMURI. MM	FIJI REGIMENT.
Wed. 27th	27 HMT EMPIRE ORWELL arrived Singapore with replacement Service personnel sailed 27 bound for Southampton with returning Service personnel---]	
Thur. 28th	28 **Sgt. Bhagtabahadur.** 6th. Queen Elizabeth's Own Gurkha Rifles Killed in Action Engaging CT's Perak. # *58 Sulva* Lines Ipoh Perak---]	
+	28 HMT EMPIRE TROOPER arrived Singapore with the 1st Battn. Northern Rhodesian Riles replacement Service personnel---]	
Fri. 29th	29 HMT DUNERA arrived Southampton with returning Service personnel---]	
Sat. 30th	} Combined Operations continued throughout Malaya---]	
Sun. 31st	}	

NOVEMBER

Mon. 1st	Operation *"Inswinger* "Began against No 1 Regt. In Selangor.---]	
+	**1 Cpl. F. S. Walters.** M.T/Dvr. R.A.F. Seletar Died Vehicle accident *Kranji Singapore # 4 / A – 6* ---]	
Tue. 2nd	**2 PC Samion B. Mohamed.** F. M. Police Killed on Ops. Pokok Sena /Naka Rd. Kuala Perlis.---]	
Wed. 3rd	**3 SC Ismail B. Hassan.** F. M. Police Killed on Ops. Kuala Nerang Area Kedah---]	
Thur. 4th	4 HMT EMPIRE FOWEY arrived Singapore with replacement Service personnel.]	
Fri. 5th	5 HMT EMPIRE TROOPER sailed Singapore bound for Southanpton with returning Service personnel---]	
+	5 HMT EMPIRE CLYDE arrived Singapore with replacement Service personnel---]	
Sat. 6th	6 HMT EMPIRE CLYDE sailed Singapore bound for Liverpool with returning Service personnel---]	
+	6 HMT EMPIRE FOWEY sailed Singapore bound for Pusan---]	
Sun. 7th	} Combined Operations continued throuout Malaya ----]	
Mon. 8th	A CT surrendered to the 10th Gurkhas he was the 6th.member of the gang of 5 Killed on the 3rd.---]	
Tue. 9th	**9 Major. G.S. Davis.** Royal Artillery Died***Kranji Singapore # 2 / C 2 ---]	
+	09/11/1954 LG # 40323 p. 6366 The following awarded the Colonial Police Medal	
	POL/LT. R. GRAVER. G.M .CPM	FEDERATION MALAYA POLICE
	SC. HUSSEIN BIN. LUMUT. CPM	FEDERATION MALAYA POLICE
	SC HUSSEIN B. LUMAT. CPM	FEDERATIOM MALAYA POLICE
+	9 HMT EMPIRE HALLADALE sailed Liverpool bound for Singapore via Mauritius with replacement Service peronnel ---]	
+	9 HMT EMPIRE HALLADALE arrived Liverpool from Glasgow ---]	
Wed. 10th	10 HMT DEVONSHIRE sailed Liverpool enroute to Singapore / Hong Kong /Kure with replacement Service personnel---]	
+	The 2nd. Battn. Royal Welch Fusiliers moved to a Camp in Negri Sembilan ---]	
Thur. 11th	11 HMT ASTURIUS arrived Southampton with returning Service personnel---]	
Fri. 12th	Kuala Lumpur: Air Marshal F.J. Fressages. Became Air Officer Commanding Air Command Air Far East---]	
Sat. 13th	3 CT's were Killed by a Security Patrol in the Ruab area. 1 was a woman another women escped but was badly wounded. The CT's were identified as **Meng Chuan. alias Cheong Swee Sang.** District Member of the Choroh area. The woman **Ah Lan.** Group Secretary **& Phui Wah.**---]	
Sun. 14th	14 During a CT road ambush near Yong Peng . **Pte. M. Canavanua. Pte. L. Kasivo.- Pte. Luwei. - Pte V. Marawa. - Pte Tanicawau.** 1st Fijian Regt. Killed in CT ambush along with 6 being wounded (*Ashes REP*)]	
Mon. 15th	Hunt for 30 heavtly armed CT's in the swamp area of South West Yong Peng. Responsible for the ambush attack on the Fijians the previous day. R.A.A.F. Vampire Jets and Lincoln Bomber together with RAF Hornets plastered the area---]	
Tue. 16th	**16 L/Cpl. D. W. F. Grindley.** R.M.P.. Died***KranjiSingapore # 2 / C – 1 ---]	
+	**16 Spr. R. Broardley.** Royal Engineers Died*** *Kranji Singapore # 2 / A – 15* ---]	
+	16 HMT EMPIRE ORWELL arrived Singapore wth replacement Service personnel / sailed bound for Kure /Pusan/Hong Kong 16th.---]	
Wed. 17th	17 HMT LANCASHIRE arrived Liverpool with returning Service personnel ---]	
Thur. 18th	**18 Sgt. G. Nepia.** RNZIR. att. to Fijian Infantry Regt.) **Sgt. P Taloga. - Pte. J. Sinclair.** [*Ashes REP*] 1st Fijian Regiment Killed Shooting accident *Kranji Singapore #2 / E - 27*---]	
+	18 HMT DILWARA sailed Southampton bound for Singapore/Hong Kong with replacement Service personnel---]	

Fri. 19th	**19 Pte. S.Nagata**. 1st. Battn. Fijian Infantry Regt. Died from wounds recv'd previous days ambush [Ashes REP]---]
Sat. 20th	While driving back to his Bungalow Mr Soon Boon Leong Manager of the Nyalas Estate Jasin was ambushed at the 2nd. m/s Jasin Road. He drove through it, the bullets smashed all the windows ---]
Sun. 21st	Bangkok: 5 Secret Society Members organised by Chinese Communist were detained on the Thailand Malay Border--]
Mon.22nd	**22 Pte. A. Baleilakeba**. 1st. Battn. Fijian Infantry Regt. Killed in Action Engaging CT's [*Ashes REP*]---]
Tue. 23rd	23 HMT DUNERA sailed Southampton bound fior Singapore/ Hong Kong with replacement Service personnel ---]
+	23 HMT EMPIRE FOWEY arrived Seletar ---]
Wed. 24th	} Combined Operations continued throughout Malaya ---]
Thur. 25th	25 HMT EMPIRE FOWEY sailed Seletar enroute to Southampton with returning Service personnel 25th.
Fri. 26th	Combined Operations continued throughout Malaya---]
Sat. 27th	Acting on information Platoon of the 2nd.10th Princess Mary's Own Gurkha Rifles. Killed 3 CT 's in a hut In the serach they found a dead Chinese baby approx. 1 Month old. It was taken to the Seremban Welfare Organisation for identification. One of the dead CT's was identified as ***Ah Cheng***. Bodyguard of ***Mao Sze Chuan***. Political Commisar for the 6th. Independent Platoon MRLA---]
Sun. 28th	Wellington New Zealand: General Howard Kippenberger informed a Number of Ex New Zealand Returned Service Association Members: 'Malaya was a running Sore'---]
Mon. 29th	CT's shot Inspector Tan Kean and three children. One of them was his son. They were at Poppy day fun fair. All Four were hit in the legs it happened in Bukit Mertajm---]
Tue. 30th	
+	Operations 'Termite "Axe' Ended.---]

DECEMBER

Wed. 1st	Operation "Latimer North." "Latimer South." Began against Nos 5 & 6 Regt.'s in Perak Negri Sembila & Pahang---]
+	The 1st Battn. Somerset's were relocated to the area of Bentong – Temerloh and the Pahang River --]
+	1 HMT EMPIRE CLYDE arrived Liverpool with returning Service personnel---].
Thur. 2nd	**2 PC. V. P. Devarajan**. F. M. Police Killed on Ops. Port Shean Pahang---]
Fri. 3rd	} Combined Operations continued throughout Malaya---]
Sat. 4th	}
Sun. 5th	**5 Trp. P.J. Fitchett**. 15/19th The King's Royal Hussars. Died*** *Taiping # E / 45* Perak---]
+	5 HMT EMPIRE TROOPER arrived Southanpton with returning Service personnel---]
Mon. 6th	} Combined Operations continued throughout Malaya---]
Tue. 7th	**7 Rfn. Narsingbahadur Sunwar** . 10th. Princess Mary's Own Gurkha Rifles. Died from Wounds recv'd Kuala Pilah *Seremban # 62* Negri Sembilan --]
Wed. 8th	} Combined Operations continued throughout Malaya---]
Thur. 9th	**9 Spr. Ahmad Bin Taib**. Royal Engineers (MOR) Died*** *Claimed by next of Kin* ---]
+	9 HMT DEVONSHIRE arrived Singapore with replacement Service personnel---]
Fri. 10th	10 HMT DEVONSHIRE sailed Singapore bound for Hong Kong /Kure /Pusan---]
+	10 HMT ASTURIUS sailed Southampton bound for Singapore with replacement Service personnel---]
Sat. 11th	11 HMT NEW AUSTRALIA called Singapore enroute to Southampton with returning Serrvice personnel--
+	11 HMT EMPIRE ORWELL arrived Southampton with replacement Service personnel---]
Sun. 12th	**12 Cpl. Wan Mahmud b. Wan Hassan**. Malay Regt.Killed in Action Engaging CT's Perak---]
Mon. 13th	**13 L/Cpl. A.A.M. Webb. L/Cpl. Abu Baker Rasidi Bin K. Raman. (MOR)** Royal Engineers Died*** *Seremban # CE / 93* Negri Sembilan .Abu *Claimed by next of Kin* ---]
Tue. 14th	} Combined Operations continued throughout Malaya---]
Wed. 15th	**15 Pte's T. Tanicakua. - E. Qaasevakaatini**. Fiji Regt. Killed in Action Engaging CT's [*Ashes REP*] 6 others were seriously wounded in the ambush---]
+	15 HMT EMPIRE HALLADALE arrived Singapore with replacement Service personnel---]
Thur. 16th	16 HMT DILWARA arrived Singapore with replacement Service personnel ---]
Fri. 17th	2 Soldiers 1 Malay and 1 British (*unnamed*) were swept away in the raging torrent of waters of the river Muar. Their bodies have not been recovered and it is throught they were swept out to sea. [*No known Graves*] *Terandak Wall Memorial Malacca*---]
+	17 HMT DILWARA sailed Singapore enroute to Hong Kong---]

Sat. 18th	18 Rfn. Kharke Thapa 6th. Queen Elizabeth's Own Gurkha Rifles. Died***_Kranji Singapore #7 / A – 1_ ---]
Sun. 19th	19 HMT EMPIRE FOWEY arrived Southampton with returning Service personnel---]
Mon. 20th	20 HMT DUNERA arrived Singapore with replacement Service personnel enroute to Hong Kong 21st.---]
Tue. 21st	21 HMT DUNERA sailed Singapore personnel enroute to Hong Kong.---
Wed.22nd	22 Capt. R. Prynne. Border Regt.Att/ 2nd. 10th. Gurkhas. An Explosives Technician was Killed, when booby trap exploded _Seremban # CE - 94_ Negri Sembilan---]
+	} 22 HMT EMPIRE CLYDE sailed Liverpool bound for Singapore/ Hong Kong with replacement Service personnel---]
+	22 HMT EMPIRE HALLADALE sailed Singapore bound for Liverpool.with returning Service personnel---]
Thur. 23rd	23 Mr. R.D. Willamson. Manager. of a Southern Malay Pineapples. Pontiam Rengam Johore Pineapple Estate was shot dead in a CT ambush at Simpang Rengam Johore.---]
+	23 HMT DILWARA arrived /sailed Singapore bound for Southampton with returning Service personnel---].
Fri. 24th	} Combined Operations continued throughout Malaya---]
Sat. 25th	25 Pte. S. Esekia. Northern Rhodesia Regt. Killed in Action Engaging CT's _Kuala Lumpur # 27 / 12_ ---]
Sun. 26th	26 Sldr. J. J. Timmerman. The. Netherlands Army. Part of the UN Forces fighting in the Korean War. Timmerman was on his way back to the Netherlands, when he became ill & died from Jaundice in a Singapore Hopital _Kranji Singapore #?_ ---]
Mon. 27th	3 CT's Killed 2 Chinese /men at Ulu Choh New village Gelong ---]
Tue. 28th	4 CT's clubbed to death another Chinese man in the same area ---]
Wed. 29th	CT Osman China. District Committee member along with 8 other members. 2 of them women surrendered at Kampong Ulu Atok near Kuala Lipis Osman a wanted Terrorist with a price on his head. Stated he Thought about it for 15 Months. His comrades identified as Moh YaTinbin Mukasan. District Committee Member Moh. Katmam bin Mohamad. Section Leader Rosman bin Mugajat -. Mat jasa Bin Timin -Teh Singat - Kiah Binte Mat ---]
Thur. 30th	3 Other CT's of the same gang gave themselves up to a Padi Farmer identified as: Jamalu bin Mat., Mat Aris - & bodyguard Zukaria bin Buyan. ---]
Fri. 31st	31 Pte. D. Michaya. 2nd. King's African Rifles. Killed in Action Engaging CT's _Kranji Singapore # 2 C – 3_ ---]
+	31/12/1954 LG # 40365 p. 7389 The following awarded the British Empire Medal (Military) SGT. E.A. WEEKS. BM ROYAL AUSTRALIAN AIR FORCE The following awarded Bar to the Distinguished Flying Cross W/CDR. A.R. EMSLIE. DFC +BAR ROYAL AUSTRALIAN AIR FORCE
+	31/12/1954 LG # 40366 p. 37 The following awarded the Co;onial Police Medal
+	31 HMT NEW AUSTRALIA arrived Southsmpton with returning Service personnel---]
+	Operation "Hotspur" Ended ---]

R. A. F. OPERATION "FIREDOG" END OF YEAR STATISTICS 1954

No of Sorties	No. of Strikes	1,000 Lb.Bombs	500 Lb. Bombs	350 LbCluster	20 LbBombs	R/P's	20mm	.5 mm	.303mm
1,955	426	3,457	22,993	/	7,167	3,905	305,330	497,321	164,928

R. A. F. SUPPORT 1954

	Soties	Troops/Lift/	Casac	Pass/Lift	Supply Wt. Lbs	Leaflets drop (1,000)	B Flying Times No / hrs	Broadcsting No / hrs	Crashed
Air SupportA/C*	2071	/	/	/	6,793.142	/	/	/	Valetta's
Auster**	14,276 hrs	/	/	/	474	/	/	/	WD160
Pioneer	1172	1502	34	Incl1502	83650	/	/	/	WJ494
H/C Light	167	/	377	1,589	31,488	/	/	/	Hornet's
848 Sqdn	N/A	/	/	/	/	/	/	/	WB885
155 Sqdn	471	6.534‑	204	955	170,449	/	/	/	Auster
Target/MK**	/	/	/	/	/	/	/	/	VF604
Vis/Air OBs**	/	/	/	/	/	/	/	/	VF560
Communication**	/	/	/	/	/	/	/	/	Dragonfly
Leaf. Sorties*	240	/	/	/	/	70,700	/	/	WF315
Leaflets Drop*	/	/	/	/	/	/	/	/	VF???
Leaf Sorties **	/	/	/	/	/	388	/	/	
Leaflets Drop**	/	/	/	/	/	/	/	/	
Broad Sorties*	256	/	/	/	/	/	/	/	
Broad Hrs *	/	/	/	/	/	/	355.5	/	
Broad Sorties**	174	/	/	/	/	/	/	/	
Broad Hrs **	/	/	/	/	/	/	118.5	/	
Photo RECCE***	1065	/	/	/	/	/	/	J	

* AirSupport A/C Dakota -Valetta- Hastings Bristol
** Auster
*** Photo Rec Anson,,Spitfire, Mosquito, Meteor, Pembroke

CHAPTER 13 - 1955

ROYAL NEW ZEALAND AIR FORCE
OFFENSIVE AIR SUPPORT- OPERATION 'FIREDOG'
January 1955 to July 1960

Sqdn	Location	Aircraft Type	No	Date From	Year	Date To	Year
14	Tengah	Venom FB1	16	10th. Apr.	1955	1st, S.E.P..	1958
41	Changi	Bristol Freighter	4	1st. Jul.	1955	Jul	1960
75	Tengah	Canberra B2	8	1st. Jul .	1958	Jul	1960

JANUARY

Sat.	1st	**Spr. M. S. Scaff.** Royal Engineers Died***[_Ashes REP_ ---]
	+	Operation "*Rooster*" "*Huntsman*" "*Latimer North*" "*Latimer South*" '*ASP.*' Food denial Began against the No. 6 Regt. MRLA In Perak & Pahang.---]
	+	Operation *"Latimer North"* Began SAS Operation against the CT's---]
	+	Operation 'Cato' began against No 6 Regt. MRLA Ruab, Mentakab, Pahang
	+	Operations 'Nassau' began in Kuala Langat, S. Selangor
Sun.	2nd	5 Vampire Jets of 14 Sqdn NZ.R.A.F. took off from Tangah to carry out strikes against CT camps located in the Pulai area of Johore---]
	+	2 HMT ASTURIUS arrived Singapore with replacement Service personnel sailed enroute to Hong Kong / Kure 2nd.---]
Mon.	3rd	Kuala Lumpur: In a radio broadcast from. Lt/General Sir. Geoffrey Bourne announced:- '*The Terrorist activities had caused less hindrance to the life of the Malayan economy during 1954, than any period since the start of the Emergency. During 1954 a total of 713 CT's had been Killed or captured & 210 had surrendered. The figures were down on 1953 when 981 had been Killed or captured with 379 surrendering to the security forces. However, the necessity for the present momentum must remain.*'---]
Tue.	4th	Kuala Lumpur: A further radio announcement by a spokesman for the Federation Government:- 'Backed up Lt/General Sir. Geoffrey Bourne statement: '*Gave the number of Communist Terrorist active in the Jungles had more than halved since 1951. Figures quoted were from 8,000 down to approx. 3,500. This drop-in figure were caused by the Action of the Security forces. Engaging CT's. Killing Capturing or, by surrender. As opposed to the evidence of a new factor which the Communist had to cope with. That of death by malnutrition or wounds, which they were having to cope with living in the jungles. However, they were still aggressive in many parts of the Federation specifically in Pahang & Johore.*' ---]
	+	4 HMT EMPIRE ORWELL sailed from Southampton enroute to Singapore/ Hong Kong with replacement Service personnel.---]
Wed.	5th	**5 Sgt. S. Hylton.** CI/GD. R. A. F. Seletar Died***._Kranji Singapore. # 4 / A - 8_---]
Thur.	6th	6 HMT DEVONSHIRE sailed Singapore bound for Liverpool with returning Service personnel 6th. ---]
Fri.	7th	Combined Operation continued throuout Malaya ---]
Sat.	8th	**8 Pte. B. Msope.** Northern Rhodesian Regt. Killed in Action Engaging CT's _Kuala Lumpur r# 32 / 12 41_ --]
	+	8 HMT EMPIRE TROOPER sailed Southanpton bound for Singapore / Hong Kong via African Ports with replacement Service personnel---]
Sun.	9th	**T/Insp. Appu Veloo.** F. M. Police Killed in Action Engaging CT's Pahang ---]
	+	HMS ''*COMMUS*' Combined Operation '*Nassau* 'Shelled identified CT position in deep Jungle in the Kuala Langgat area, where the Artillery gunners were ineffective 'out of range' Began Shelling on the 9th continued until the 14th. ---]

Mon. 10th	'C' Company 10th. Princess Mary's Own Gurkha Rifles Killed 3 CT's. in the Kulai area ---]
+	HMS 'COMMUS' Operation 'Nassau' continued bombardment ---]
Tue. 11th	HMS 'COMMUS' Operation 'Nassau' continued bombardment ---]
Wed. 12th	HMS 'COMMUS' Operation 'Nassau' continued bombardment ---]
+	12 HMT DILWARA arrived Singapore sailed bound for Southampton with returning Service personnel12th.]
Thur. 13th	13 Fus. G. R. Evans. 2nd. Battn. Royal Welch Fusiliers. Died***.[Ashes REP]---]
+	HMS 'COMMUS' Operation 'Nassau' continued bombardment ---]
Fri. 14th	14 LAC. A. E. Ryan. Des/Rider Main. Base R. A. F. Seletar. Motorcycle accident Kranji Singapore # 4 / A – 7 --]
+	HMS 'COMMUS' Operation 'Nassau' ceased bombardment during which Fired 507 4.5 shells were Directed & 6 Star shells---] Kuala Lumpur : Air Vice Marshal W.H. Kyle. Became Air Officer Commanding Malaya---]
Sat. 15th	16 HMT DUNERA arrived Singapore ---]
Sun. 16th	Pol/Lt. C.A. O'Keefe F. M. Police Killed on CT Ops. during Anti Communist duties in the Benta area of
+	Pahang. Kuala Lipis # ?? Pahang ---]
	17 HMT DUNERA sailed Singapore bound for Southampton with returning Service personnel---]
Mon. 17th	18 HMT EMPIRE HALLADALE arrived Liverpool with returning Service personnel---]
Tue. 18th	PC. Jan Thiagara. F. M. Police Killed Fort Dixon Pahang---]
Wed. 19th	19 HMT EMPIRE CLYDE arrived Singapore.with replacement Service personnel ---]
Thur. 20th	PC. Mohd. B. Mahmood F. M. Police Killed on Ops. near Kluang Johore.---]
+	20 HMT EMPIRE CLYDE Sailed for Hong Kong ---]
Fri. 21st	21 EMPIRE FOWEY sailed Singapore bound for Southampton with returning Service personnel----]
Sat. 22nd	Sgt. Khalil b. Burok. Royal Malay Regt. Killed in Action Engaging CT's Kelantan ---]
+	HMS 'COMMUS' Operation 'Nassau' resumed its roll of bombardment of CT positions in deep Jungle for the next 4 days---]
Sun. 23rd	Cpl. Ibrahim .B. Hanefi. & PC. S. B. Awang. F. M. Police Killed on Ops. at Kampong. Sayak Bukit Meriam.Kuala Perlis.---]
Mon. 24th	'C' Compamy 10th. Princess Mary's Own Gurkhas Killed 1 CT in the Kulia Area---]
+	24 HMT ASTURIUS arrived Singapore sailed for Southampton with returning Service personnel 25th.---]
Tue. 25th	D/Sgt. Lee Kwang Keong. F. M. Police Killed on Ops. Seremban Negri Sembilan---]
	HMS 'COMMUS' Operation 'Nassau' ceased its 4 day bombardment targeting. Fired 415 4.5 HE shells & 24 Star shells---]
Wed. 26th	Along the Pahang River a Plt. of the Somerset's were fired upon. In the ensuing fire fight with the CT's who after a short engagement gave up and fled. Leaving behind 3 dead, Identified as *Chin Tai and Cheong*, 1 wounded identified as *Kiew*. a women. From papers found in the nearby camp, It appeared that at least 32 CT's had been there for a special meeting---]
Thur. 27th	27 HMT EMPIRE ORWELL arrived Singapore with replacement Service personnel enroute to Hng Kong / Kure 27th. ---]
Fri. 28th	HMS 'NEWCASTLE' Operation 'Nassau' began a 2 day bombardment of CT positions in deep jungle--]
Sat. 29th	HMS 'NEWCASTLE' Operation 'Nassau' Ended a 2 day bombardment of CT positions in deep jungle Fired 349 6 inch HE shell---]
Sun. 30th	HMS 'CONCORD" Operation 'Nassau' began a 2 day bombardment of CT positions in deep jungle---]
Mon. 31st	HMS 'CONCORD" Operation 'Nassau' ended the 2 day bombardment Fired 117 4.5 inch HE shells---] Operation 'Hilt' Ended ---]

FEBRUARY

Tue. 1st	Combined Operation 'Nassau' continued ---]
Wed. 2nd	London The Under-Secretary at the British Colonial office. Lord Lloyd announced:-
+	'That the Malayan Police Forces were in a position to undertake operations against terrorist bases in Southern Thailand. These would be with the full co-operation of the Thailand Authorities. If the occasion did rise. An agreement had been reached that both Malayan & Thailand Police Forces could operate across the borders for a distance of up to 10 to 20 miles. A joint intelligence centre had been set up in Sengkla Southern Thailand. British Helicopters as well as supply dropping & reconnaissance Aircraft, might operate across the frontier in support of joint Police Action Engaging CT's.' ---]
Thur. 3rd	3 Pte. A. Silverwood. 1st. Battn. West Yorkshire Regt. Died from wounds recv'd in ambush.

		Taiping #B / 63] Perak---]
Fri.	4th	**4 Cpl. M. Komaiwai.** 1st. Battn. Fijian. Infantry Regt. Killed in Action Engaging CT's [*Ashes REP*]---]
	+	4 HMT DEVONSHIRE arrived Liverpool with returning Service personnel---]
Sat.	5th	5 HMT EMPIRE CLYDE arrived Singapore / sailed bound for Liverpool with returning Service personnel-]
Sun.	6th	**6 LAC. A. S. B. Dol.** (MOR) No 95. R.A.F. Regt. Accidentally Shot on duty.[*Claimed by next of Kin*]---]
Mon.	7th	7 HMT DILWARA arrived Southampton with returning Service personnel---]
Tue.	8th	**8 Gnr. G.O. Hughes.** Royal Artillery Died***_Seremban # CE / 95_ Negri Sembilan.---]
	+	HMS 'CONCORD" Operation 'Nassau' began a 2 day bombardment of CT potitions in deep jungle---]
Wed.	9th	**9 Cpl. M. Vala.** 1st. Battn. Fijian Infantry Regt. Killed in Action Engaging CT's [*Ashes REP*]---]
Thur.	10th	HMS 'CONCORD' Operation 'Nassau' ended its 2 day bombardment of CT potitions in deep jungle Fired 88 4.5 inch HE shells---]
Fri.	11th	11 HMT EMPIRE FOWEY arrived Southampton with returning Service personnel---]
Sat.	12th	Combined Operation 'Nassau' continued. ---]
Sun.	13th	**13 L/Cpl. Anak. Jugam. Ungkok.** Sarawak Rangers. Killed Jalan Langgar Alor Star Kedah [*No known Grave] Terandak Wall Memorial Malacca* ---]
	+	13 HMT EMPIRE ORWELL arrived Singapore ---]
Mon.	14th	14 HMT EMPIRE ORWELL sailed Singapore bound for Southampton with returning Service personnel
	+	14 HMT ASTURIUS arrived Southampton with returning Service personnel---]
Tue.	15th	**15 SAC. W. H. Leppard.** Armament Mech. (G) 60 Sqdn. R. A. F. Butterworth Ground Accident. *Western Road # 2159* George Town Penang---]
Wed.	16th	Operation 'Nassau' continued ---]
Thur.	17th	Operation 'Nassau' continued ---]
Fri.	18th	'A' Company 10th. Princess Mary's Own Gurkha Rifles Killed 2 CT's in the Kulai area ---]
Sat.	19th	19 HMT EMPIRE TROOPER arrived Singapore with replacement Service personnel enroute to Hong Kong 19th. ---]
Sun.	20th	Combined Operation 'Nassau' continued ---]
Mon.	21st	**21 Cpl. W. J. Vine.** 1st. Battn. Royal Scots Fusiliers. Died*** *Western Road # 2160* George Town Penang.-]
	+	**21 Maj. R.Genge.** 1st. Battn. Fijian Infantry Regt. was Killed in an ambush in Southern Johore another
	+	Fijian officer & Soldier although both wounded survived the ambush.[*Ashes REP*]---]
Tue.	22nd	**22 Cpl. G. H. Shaw.** 1st. Battn. Somerset Light Infantry. Was Killed by a CT dressed as one of the Security Forces. In the confusion 2/Lt. Heath, was shot and wounded. *Kuala Lumpur # 22 / 1154* ---]
Wed.	23rd	23 HMT DUNERA arrived Southampton with returning Service personnel---]
Thur.	24th	After a bombing attack by the R. A. F. In the follow up 'B' Company 10th. Princess Mary's Own Gurkha Rifles. Killed 2 CT's North East of Kulai---]
Fri.	25th	}Combined Operations 'Nassau' continued ---]
Sat.	26th	}
Sun.	27th	}
Mon.	28th	**28 Fus. J. Lyon.** 1st. Battn. Royal Scots Fusiliers. Died***_Western Road # 2161_ George Town Penang ---]
	+	Operation 'Nassau' continued ---]
	+	Operation *"Latimer North "* Completed---]

MARCH

Tue.	1st	**1 L/Cpl. Birbahadur Sunwar** . 10th. Princess Mary's Own Gurkha Rifles. Killed in Action Engaging CT's *Kranji Singapore # 7 / A - 2*---]
	+	R.A.F. 7 Sqdn. Lincoln 2B(AA) Completed Operations at R.A.F. Tengah---)
	+	R.A.F. 83 Sqdn. Lincoln 2B(AA) Completed Operations at R.A.F. Tengah---) Operation 'BOLD'
	+	R.A.F. 148 Sqdn. Lincoln 2B(AA) Completed Operations at R.A.F. Tengah---)
	+	R.A.F. 9 Sqdn. Canberra B6 Began Operations at R.A.F. Butterworth.---)
	+	R.A.F. 12 Sqdn. Canberra B6 Began Operations at R.A.F. Butterworth.---)
	+	R.A.F. 101 Sqdn. Canberra B6 Began Operations at R.A.F. Butterworth.---) Operation Mileage'
	+	R.A.F. 617 Sqdn. Canberra B6 Began Operations at R.A.F. Butterworth.---)
	+	1 HMT DEVONSHIRE sailed Liverpool bound for Singapore with replacement Service personnel---]
Wed.	2nd	**2 Cpl. Krishnabahadur Limbu** . 10th. Princess Mary's Own Gurkha Rifles. Died from wounds. *Kranji Singapore # 7 / A -3* --]
	+	2 HMT EMPIRE CLYDE arrived Liverpool with returning Service personnel---]
Thur.	3rd	} .Combined Operations continued throughout Malaya---]
Fri.	4th	**4 Sgt. D. Shaw**. East Surrey Regt. Died*** *Kuala Lumpur.# 22 – 1155* ---]
	+	4 HMT EMPIRE FOWEY sailed Suthampton bound for Singapore/ Hong Kong- with replacement Service Personnel---]
Sat.	5th	A Gurkha Patrol ambushed & Killed 6 C.T's in the Seremban area of Negri Sembilan---]
Sun.	6th	**6 Cfn. C. E. Baker**. R. E. M. E. Died ***. *Kranji Singapore # 2 / C - 4*---].
Mon.	7th	**7 Cpl. Wong Ah. Nyang**. F. M. Police Killed on Ops. Jalia Pahang.---]
Tue.	8th	**8 Pte. B. J. Leedham**. 1st. Battn. Worcestershire Regt. Died*** [*Ashes REP*]---]
	+	08/03/1955 LG # 40426 p. 1408 The following awarded the Colonial Police Medal
		SC MAROF B. ABDUL RAHMAN. CPM. FEDERATION MALAYA POLICE
Wed.	9th	9 HMT ASTURIUS sailed Southampton bound for Singapore / Hong Kong with replacement Service personnel---]
Thur.	10th	10 HMT EMPIRE TROOPER arrived / sailed Singapore bound for Southanpton with returning Service personnel 10th.-----]
Fri.	11th	**11 PC.Othman B. Mohamed**. F. M. Police Killed on Ops. Johore.---]
Sat.	12th	**12 L/Cpl. G. C. Brocklesby**. 1st. Battn. The East Yorkshire Regt. Died from injuries recv'd whilst working on an Ulu Landing Zone. Strip [*Ashes REP*]---]
Sun.	13th	13 HMT EMPIRE ORWELL arrived Southampton with returning Service personnel ---]
Mon.	14th	**14 POAF(E) J.C. Scrimener**. H.M.S. *'CENTAUR'* Died*** *Kranji Singapore # 12/E/12*---]
	+	**14 Mr. K.D. Paul**. Manager. of the Penggerang Rubber Estate near Kota Tinggi (Johore) was Killed by C.T.'s]
Tue.	15th	**15 2/Lt.. B. B. Heath**. 1st. Battn. Somerset Light Infantry. Died from his wounds recv'd during the fire fight with CT's on the 22 February. *Kuala Lumpur # 22 / 1156*---]
Wed.	16th	} Combined Operations continued throughout Malaya---]
Thur.	17th	17 HMT DUNERA sailed Southampton bound forSingapore /Hong Kong with replacement Service personnel]
Fri.	18th	18 HMT DILWARA sailed Southampton bound for Singapore with replacement Service personnel---]
Sat.	19th	**19** 5 F. M. Police **S/C.'s Mat. Henson B. Jaffa., Salleh B. Mat., Tuan Abdullah. B. Tuan Muda., & Ar Lek,** Police Killed in ambush Kuala Krai area Kelentan---]
Sun.	20th	20 HMT EMPIRE CLYDE sailed Liverpool bound for Singapore /Hong Kong with replacement Service personnel ---]
Mon.	21st	**21 Spr. Mod. Nasir. Bin Din.** Royal Engineers (MOR) Died *** *Claimed by next of Kin* ---]
Tue.	22nd	**22 Pol/Lt. L. Whittingham**. F.M. Aux. Police. Due to illness after a long spell on Jungle Patrol in the Kinat Hills Ipoh caught Scrub fever and died. *Batu Gajah # 522* Ipoh Perak .---]
Wed.	23rd	**23 PC. Michael Yoong** F. M. Police Killed on Ops. Bagan Larut Taiping.---]
Thur.	24th	Operation *'Rex'* Began against the CT 9th. Independent Platoon in the Kota Tinggi & Pengerang district's. Involving combined operations of Infantry Navy & Air support ---]
Fri.	25th	Operation *'Rex'* continued ---]
Sat.	26th	**26 Sgt. C. A. M. Brown**. MTF. R.A.F. Changi Died *** *Kranji .Singapore #4 / B - 1*---]
		Combined Operation *'Rex'* Malayan Navy M/L ferried 80 Troops onto the shore at Panggerang---]
Sun.	27th	HMS *'COCKADE'* Operation 'Rex' Phase I. Bombarded inland areas until 6th. April ---]
Mon.	28th	Combined Operation *'Rex'* Malayan Navy M/L ferried 80 Troops onto the shore at Panggerang---]
Tue.	29th	29 HMT EMPIRE FOWEY arrived Singapore/ sailed enroute to Hong Kong with with replacement Service personnel 29th.---]
Wed.	30th	30 HMT DEVONSHIRE arrived Singapore ---]
Thur.	31st	**31.LACW. A.M. Golding**. Nursing Asstn. R. A. F. Changi Drowning Accident. *Kranji Singapore # 4 / A -* ---]

APRIL

Fri.	1st	Operation *"Mileage"* Began. R. A. F. Sqdns 9-12-101-617. Butterworth---]
	+	*Operation Beehive:* Began SAS against the MRLA---]
	+	1 HMT EMPIRE ORWELL sailed Southampton bound for Singapore with replacement Service personnel
Sat.	2nd	2 F/O. J. E. Bowler. 45 Sqdr. Flying Hornet F3PX832 collided with- F/O. R. G. Russell. Hornet PX350 over Butterworth. Both were Killed. *Western Road # 2163 – 2162* George Town Penang---]
Sun.	3rd	Relying on information that some 200 CT's, were active in the Bukit Besam Ambat area on the Borders of Negri Sembilan & Selangor. Operation *"Beehive"* was launched. An air attack was mounted comprising 11 Lincolns, No 1 Sqdn R.A.A.F. : 4 Canberra's & 12 Hornets bombed & strafed the area .Supported by an H/C air drop of troops into the area. They found no trace of any CT activity.---]
Mon.	4th	4 HMT DEVONSHIRE sailed Singapore bound for Liverpool with returning Service personnel ---]
	+	Combined Operation *'Rex'* Malayan Navy M/L ferried 80 Troops onto the shore at Panggerang & removed 1 dead CT---]
	+	4/04/1955. LG #40164 p. 2627 The following awarded the British Empire Medal (Military) LT. A.W LLOYD. BEM. ROYAL NAVY 848 SQD
Tue.	5th	Operation 'Rex' HMS *'COCKADE'* ceased its bombardment of inland areas having fired 652 4.5 inch HE Shells---]
Wed.	6th	6 Spr. N. Collins. Royal Engineers Died *** *Kuala Lumpur # 16 / 930*---]
	+	Combined Operation *'Rex'* Malayan Navy M/L casvacd 3 sick soldiers from the shore at Panggerang
Thur.	7th	7 Cpl. Abu Baker B. Bahu. F. M. Police Killed on Ops. Parit Keliling, Jasin Malacca.---]
Fri.	8th	Combined Operations 'Rex' continued---]
Sat.	9th	Combined Operations 'Rex' continued---]
Sun.	10th	10 HMT EMPIRE TROOPER arrived Southanpton with returning Service personnel---]
	+	10 HMT EMPIRE FOWEY arrived Singapore with replacement Service personnel ---]
	+	10 HMT EMPIRE FOWEY sailed for Southampton with returning Service Personnel---]
Mon.	11th	11 PC. Attan. F. M. Police Killed on Ops. Near Segamat Johore.---]
Tue.	12th	14 Sqdn RNZAF Venom FB1 Began Operations at R.A.F. Tengah ---]
Wed.	13t	HMS *'ALERT'* Operation *'Rex' Phase I* Began its 2 day bombardment of inland areas ending 14th Fired 180 4 inch shell---]
	+	13 HMT DUNERA arrived Singapore enroute to Hong Kong with replacement Service personnel 13th.---]
Thur.	14th	Combined Operation *'Rex' Phase I* Malayan Navy M/L withdrew 7 Troops from the shore at Panggerang]
Fri.	15th	Combined Operation *'Rex' Phase I* Malayan Navy M/L. Ferried 84 Troops to the shore of Penggarang-]
Sat.	16th	Combined Operation *'Rex' Phase I* Malayan Navy M/L 'Casvacd1 sick Soldier from the shore of Penggarang]
Sun.	17th	17 Mr. B.P. Exshaw.Civilian. Killed by CT's Fractured skull Kluang Pahang.---]
Mon.	18th	Combined Operations *'Rex' Phase I* Malayan Navy M/L Ferried troops to the shore of Penggarang---]
	+	18 HMT EMPIRE CLYDE sailed from liverpool bound for Singapore / Hong Kong with replacement Service personnel---]
Tue.	19th	19 Spr. Abdul Hamid Bin Marth. Royal Engineers (MOR) *Claimed by next of Kin* ---]
Wed.	20th	20 PC. Ahmad. B. Yasin. F. M. Police Killed on Ops. Near Seremban Negri Sembilan---]
Thur.	21st	Combined Operations *'Rex' Phase I* Malayan Navy M/L Withdrew 84 Troops from the shore of Penggarang]
	+	HMS *'PELANDOK'* Operation *'Rex' Phase II* Began its bombardment of inland areas Penggarang---]
	+	21 HMT ASTURIUS arrived Singapore enroute to Southampton with returning Service personnel 21st.---]
Fri.	22nd	Combined Operations 'Rex' continued---]
Sat.	23rd	23 Sgt. M. J. Hanlon. 1st. Battn. Somerset Light Infantry. Killed in a CT ambush on a civilian food convoy Action Engaging CT's. *Kuala Lumpur # RC A / 8* ---]
Sun.	24th	24 Cpl. J. Davidson. Royal Engineers Died*** *Kranji Singapore # 2 / C -7* ---]
Mon.	25th	25 HMT EMPIRE ORWELL arrived Singapore with replacement Service persoannel enroute to Hong Kong / Kure 25th.---]
Tue.	26th	HMS *'PELANDOK'* Operation *'Rex' Phase II'* Ended its bombardment of inland Penggarang areas having Fired 100 4.5 inch HE Shells & 60 Star shells ---]
	+	26/04 1955 LG # 40400 p. 2405 The following awarded te Military Medal CPL. J. L. P. BALLANTYNE. MM SOMERSET LIGHT INF.
Wed.	27th	Singapore: The Drivers and Conductors of the Hok Lee Bus Company came out on strike.-----]
Thur.	28th	28 L/Cpl. E. G. Martin. 1st. Battn. Somerset Light Infantry. Killed in Action Engaging CT's. *Kuala Lumpur # 22 / 1158* ---]

	+	HMS 'NEWFOUNDLAND' Operation 'Rex' *Phase II* Shelled inland areas Penggarang fired 200 6 inch Shells ---]
Fri. 29		**29 Capt. M. R. Mather.** Royal Artillery Died *** *Kuala Lumpur # 22 / 1159* ---]
	+	Singapore: The Bus Strike called by the Hok Lee Drivers and the Conductors was all due to; The new work rosters introduced to prevent any further strikes and the formation of any more Unions between the Singapore Bus Workers Union a Communist driven body Thousands of Students supported the Strikers by turning up with food and entertainment---]
	+	29 HMT DUNERA arrived Singapore ---]
	+	29 HMT DUNERA sailed Singapore bound for Southampton with returning Service personnel.—]
Sat. 30th		Kuala Lumpur: The Federation Government stated: '*Two large areas in Pahang & Trengannu were officially declared "WHITE" These two areas covering 7,300 square miles, consisting of a population of approx.125,000. inhabitants.'*---]
	+	Alor Star : During the month of April. Thailand Police forces operating in Malaya near the border. Seized one of the largest arms cache found, since the beginning of the Emergency. A surrendered CT had led them to the arms dump, where some 2,000 rounds of ammunition, 200 Japanese manufactured hand grenades, 200 detonators & 317 sticks of dynamite, were recovered. During the firefight 1 CT was Killed]
	+	Singapore :Other Unions affiliated to the Middle Rock Group Dockers, came out on strike in support of the Hok Lee Bus Drivers strikers---]

MAY

Sun. 1st		Operation *"Unity"* Began against No 12 Regt. MRLA In Perak.---]
	+	41 Squadron. New Zealand Air Force flew from their base in New Zealand to Kranji Singapore as part of New Zealands air support in the Malayan Emergency. Mr. Holland. The Prime Minisiter stated.: '*That Malaya was now the front line of New Zealands defence system, and was not going to fall under Communist influence*'---]
	+	1 HMT EMPIRE FOWEY arrived Southampton with returning Service personnel---]
Mon. 2nd		**2 A/B P.W.A. Rhodes** H.M.S. '*TERROR* ' Died*** *Kranji Singapore 12 / B -25* ---]
Tue. 3rd		HMS '*PELANDOK*' Combined Operations '*Rex*' *Phase IIIA* Began its bombardment of Penggarang areas-]
Wed. 4th		**4 S/C. Lim Tian Watt.** F. M. Police Killed on CT Ops. Ayer Kroh area Malacca ---]
Thur. 5th		Combined Operations '*Rex*' Redeployed 30 Troops Malayan Navy L/C ferrying them to the shore of Penggarang---]
Fri. 6th		HMS '*COSSACK*' Operation '*Rex*' *Phase IIIA* Began its bombardment of Penggarang areas---] HMS '*PELANDOK*' Combined Operations '*Rex*' *Phase IIIA* Completed its bombardment of the Penggarang areas. Firing 156. 4.7 inch HE shells 56. 6 inch HE shells 44. Star shells---]
Sat. 7th		Kuala Lumpur: Due to the change in the Colonial Rule to that of future Malaya Indeopence The Alliance Party proposed: '*An amnesty agreeing to meet with **Chin Peng** the Secetary General of the MCP for further discussions & too clarify the terms of Surrender. Under those conditions it was seen too impose certain restrictions upon the Security Forces*' ---]
Sun. 8th		The strike by the Hok Lee Bus Company escalated into a riot. 20 lorry loads of students joined the rioting Strikers. A mob of 2,000 attacked the Police. A Chinese Policeman was doused in petrol and set alight the riot continued through on the 11th and 12th until 3.00 am on the 13th. ---]
Mon. .9th		**9 Sgt. C. E. Slack.** 11th Royal Hussars Died *** *Kuala Lumpur # 22 / 1160*.---]
	+	HMS '*COSSACK*' Operation '*Rex*' *Phase IIIA* Began its bombardment of Penggarang areas ---]
	+	Operation '*Rex*' *Phase IIIA* Malayan Navy L/C relocated 30 Soldiers on the shore line at Penggarang---]
Tue. 10th		R.A.F. 58 Sqdn. Canberra PR7 Began Operations at R.A.F. Changi.---]
	+	R.A.F. 82 Sqdn. Canberra PR7 Began Operations at R.A.F. Changi.---]
	+	R.A.F. 540 Sqdn. Canberra PR7 Began Operations at R.A.F. Changi.---]
	+	R.A.F. 542 Sqdn. Canberra PR7 Began Operations at R.A.F. Changi.---]
Wed 11th.		HMS '*CONCORD*'' Operation '*Rex*' *Phase IIIA* Began its bombardment of Penggarang areas ---]
	+	11 HMT ASTURIUS arrived Southampton with returning Service personnel---]
Thur. 12th		**12 2/Lt.. K. A. Hensley.** Royal Warwickshire Fusiliers Died*** *Kuala Lumpur- # RC A/ `10*---]
	+	Operation '*Rex*' *Phase IIIA* Malayan Navy L/C relocated 32 Soldiers on the shore line at Penggarang---]
Fri. 13th		Singapore: The Hok Lee Bus Strike was resolved between the Government and the Unions. ---]
	+	HMS '*COSSACK*' Operation '*Rex*' *Phase IIIA* Completed its bombardment of inland Penggarang areas Firing 180 4.5 inch HE shells ---]

+ Sat. 14th	13 HMT EMPIRE ORWELL arrived Singapore enroute to Southampton with returning Service personnel-- Singapore: After the Bus strike riots.. 4 people had been Killed and 31 injured. Bus Services resumed to normal roster times. ---]
+	14 HMT DEVONSHIRE arrived Liverpool with returning Service personnel---]
Sun. 15th	**15 Cfn, J.J. Turner.** R.E.M.E Died***_Kuala Lumpur # 22 / 1161_ ---]
+	15 HMT EMPIRE CLYDE arrived Singapore with replacement Service personnel ---]
Mon. 16th	HMS 'CONCORD" Combined Operation 'Rex' Completed its bombardment of Penggarang. Firing 150 4.5 inch HE shells ---]
+	16 HMT EMPIRE CLYDE sailed Singapore enroute to Hong Kong.---]
Tue. 17th	**17 Dvr. Hassan. Bin . Osman.** R.A.S.C. (MOR) Died*** _Claimed by next of Kin_ ---]
Wed. 18th	Under the code name Operation "Canterbury" 6 Lincoln Bombers No 1 Sdn. R.A.A.F. 8 Venoms 60 Sqdn R. A. F. & * Venoms 41 Sqdn RNZAF bombed an area of Kelang Central Johore, released 14,545 kg. of bombs, into the jungle below---]
Thur. 19th	Operation 'Rex' Phase IIIA Malayan Navy L/C casvaced 1 soldier off the shore line at Penggarang---]
+	Operation 'Rex' Phase IIIA Malayan Navy L/C relocated 33 Soldiers on the shore line at Penggarang---]
Fri. 20th	Kuala Lumpur: Lieutenant General Sir. Roger Bower. Became Director of Operations & General Officer Commanding Malaya ---]
+	HMS 'NEWCASTLE' Combined Operation 'Rex' Began its bombardment of Penggarang areas---]
+	HMS 'NEWCASTLE' Operation 'Rex' Phase IIIA Completed its bombardment of Penggarang areas. Firing 265 6 inch HE shells ---]

+	20/05/1955 LG # 40482 p. 2921	The following awarded the Distinguished Flying Cross
	CAPT. C. H. C. PICKTHALL. DFC	ROYAL REGIMENT ARTILLERY
	CAPT. D.H. G WISDOM. DFC	ROYAL REGIMENT ARTILLERY
	CAPT. D. H. GOODACRE. DFC	ROYAL REGIMENT ARTILLERY
		The following awarded the Distinguished Flying Medal
	CPL. A. ABBOTT. DFM	ROYAL ARMY SERVICE CORPS.
+	20/05 1955 LG # 40483 p. 2930	The following awarded the Distinguished Flying Cross
	S/LDR. W.H. MILLS. DFC	ROYAL AIR FORCE
	F/LT. P. J. LANGLEY. DFC	ROYAL AIR FORCE
	F/O. D. DOBIE. DFC	ROYAL AIR FORCE
	F/O. F.S SOUNESS. DFC	ROYAL AIR FORCE
		The following awarded the Distinguished Flying medal
	SGT. T. WALL .DFM	ROYAL AIR FORCE.
		The following awarded the British Empire Medal (Millitary)
	S/TECH D. M. HARPER. BEM	ROYAL AIR FORCE
	CPL. P. J. BARKER. BEM	ROYAL AIR FORCE
	CPL. H. F. JURY. BEM	ROYAL AIR FORCE
	CPL/TECH C. JOHNSON. BEM	ROYAL AIR FORCE.

Sat. 21st	About this time the first of **4,000lb** bomb was dropped into the jungle in Central Johore. Operation 'Commodore' Their effect was not as great as the 1,000 lb bomb. Very few **4,000 lb** bombs were used during the Emergency. They were only used with the express permission of the High Commisioner of Malaya---]
Sun. 22nd	**22 Pte. Hassam B. Ismail** Malay Regt. Killed in Action Engaging CT's Perak---]
Mon. 23rd	} Combined Operations 'Rex' continued---]
	A Plt of the Somerset's led by a SEP in the area of Kuala Krau. Shot an Killed 2 CT's who were his comrades in arms.---]
Tue. 24th	24/05/55. LG # 40487 p. 3014 The following awarded the Military Medal PTE. J. KOBITI. MM FIJI REGIMENT.
Wed. 25th	**25 Cpl. R.R. Mitchell.** East Surrey Regt. Died*** _[Remains REP]_
+	HMS 'PELANDOK' Operation 'Rex' began its bombardment of Peggarang areas ---]
Thur. 26th	} Combined Opration 'Rex' Continued ---]
Fri. 27th	27/05/55 LG # 40492 p. 3150 The following awarded the Military Medal L/AC H.B. RAJAB. MM ROYAL AIR FORCE REGIMENT. (MOR)
+	27 HMT DEVONSHIRE sailed Liverpool bound for Singapore / Hong Kong with replacement Service personnel---]
+	27 HMT EMPIRE FOWEY sailed Southampton bound for Singapore /Hong Kong with replacement Service personnel. ---]

+	27 HMT DUNERA arrived Sothampton.with returning Service personnel---]	
Sat. 28th	HMS 'PELANDOK' Operation 'Rex' Completed its bombardment of Peggarangareas Firing 100 4.7 inch HE shells & 100 Star shells ---]	
Sun. 29th	29 Pte. A. B. Bennett. 1st. Battn. Somerset Light Infantry. Killed in an CT ambush. The Plt. returning fire at the hidden CT's, who fled leaving behind bags of rice, sufficient for at least 3 weeks rations *Kuala Lumpur-* # 22 / 1162--]	
+	29 Capt. M.R. Mather. Royal Artillery Army Air Corps Flying Auster Mk 6 WJ 408. Hit tree whilst dropping leaflets Killed near Jerantut *Kuala Lumpur* # 22 / 1159 ---]	
Mon. 30th	30 2 F. M. Police SC's. Zakaria B. Mat Piah. – Bakar B, Saad. Killed on CT Ops. Tapah area Perak---]	
+	HMS 'COMMUS' Operation 'Rex' Began its bombardment of Penggarang areas ---]	
+	30 HMT EMPIRE CLYDE arrived Singapore ---]	
+	30 HMT EMPIRE CLYDE sailed Singapore bound for Liverpool with returning Service personnel ---]	
Tue. 31st	31 Trp. D.C. Bruce. 15/19th. The King's Royal Hussars. Died*** *Taiping* # E / 47 Perak---]	
+	HMS 'COMMUS' Operation 'Rex' Completed its bombardment of inland areas of Penggarang using 120 4.5 inch HE shells---]	
+	31/05/55 LG # 40492 p. 3148	The following awarded the British Empire Medal (Military)
	A/ART. R.R. FERRIS. BEM	848 SQD. ROYAL NAVY
	CPL. L.C, BENTLEY. BEM	ROYAL HAMPSHIIRE REGT.
	QMS. R. CUNNINGHAM . BEM	ROYAL CORPS SIGNALS
	QMS. J. R. LATIMER. BEM	ROYAL CORPS SIGNALS
	SGT. R.S. CRABB. BEM	ROYAL CORPS SIGNALS
	SGT. L. KENDRICK. BEM	ROYAL CORPS SIGNALS
	SGT. M. MALETA. BEM	KING'S AFRICAN RIFLES
	C/SGT. W,Y.C.R. THICK. BEM	EAST YORKSHIRE REGIMENT.
	CPL. M. TAMANG. BEM	7th. DUKE OF EDINBURGH'S OWN GURKHA RIFLES
		The following awarded the Military Cross
	Lt. (QGO) A. LIMBU. MC	7th. DUKE OF EDINBURGH'S OWN GURKHA RIFLES
	LT. N.M. B. SUTTON. MC	MALAY REGIMENT.
	LT. K.M TAGIVETAUA. MC	FIJI REGIMENT.
		The following awarded a BAR to the Military Cross
	MAJ. R.S.R CARR MC & BAR	7th. DUKE OF EDINBURGH'S OWN GURKHA RIFLES
	LT.(QGO) S. RAI. MC & BAR.	7th. DUKE OF EDINBURGH'S OWN GURKHA RIFLES.
		The following awarded the Military Medal
	WOII R.A. PUDDY. MM	1st. BATTN. SOMERSET LIGHT INFANTRY
	L/CPL B. RAI. MM	2nd. KING EDWARD VII'S OWN GURKHA RIFLES
	RFN B. LIMBU. MM	2nd. KING EDWARD VII'S OWN GURKHA RIFLES
	SGT. B. RAI. MM	7th. DUKE OF EDINGIRGH'S OWN GURKHA RIFLES
	L/CPL L. BUDHIRAJ. MM	10th PRINCESS MARY'S OWN GURKHA RIFLES
	L/CPL. R. RAI. MM	10th PRINCESS MARY'S OWN GURKHA RIFLES
	CPL. I.B.A RAZAK . MM	MALAY REGIMENT
	SGT. J MUSA. MM	KINGS AFRICAN RIFLES
	SGT. R. NAVAKAKASAI. MM	FIJI REGIMENT.
	LAC H.B RALPH. MM	ROYAL AIR FORCE. REGIMENT.
		The following awarded the Distinguished Flying Cross
	LT/COM. B. PATTERSON DFC	848 SQDN. ROYAL NAVY
	LT. R. LEONARD. DFC	848 SQDN. ROYAL NAVY
		The following awarded the Distinguished Flying Medal
	A/C J.J. HAYALL. DFM	848 SQDN. ROYAL NAVY
		The following awarded the Royal Red Cross Medal
	MAJ. C O'NEILL. RRC	QUEEN ALEXANDRA'S ARMY NURSING CORPS

---oOo---

THE DISOVERY OF THE B24 LIBERATOR BOMBER (' MARIE CELESTE')DISAPEARED ON 6TH. JUNE 1945.

[Authors Note] The below Operational report (copied from the original, and reproduced by kind permission of the Royal Scots Fusiliers). This details the jungle conditions & period of time, faced by all British & Commonwealth Infantry Soldiers operating in jungle terrain. Operation' UNITY' was carried out in the jungles near the Malay / Thailand Borders beginning the 1st May 1955. finishing on the 2nd July 1955. (A period of 8 weeks living in extreme jungle conditions) It also gives a detailed description of an area, following a RAF air strike with Bombs. However, further on during the patrol. A most unusual nevertheless, very interesting find. Read on: -

ROYAL SCOTS FUSILIERS OPERATION REPORT

Ops. Log.   'D' Coy. Op UNITY.
Pers.   Maj. G. D. Wilmot.
             2/Lt. C. A. Robertson.
             53 OR all of "D" Coy 1 RSF
             1 Dog handler with Dog (AlSat.ian)

Maps:- 2 1/4., 2 j/1. (revealed but Not shown in this publication)
Mission to search out & eliminate any C T's in the area bounded by Northing 40 in the NORTH, Northing 30 & the MALAYA/THAILAND border in the South, the MALAYA/THAILAND border in the EAST, ' & the Easting 80 in the WEST on no account was any British soldier to cross the border into Thailand
Tues 3 May
   Reveille 0400hrs. Breakfast 0445 hrs. Enbus & move off from KROH at 0530hrs. Via BALING to helicopter LZ. At GR 662283 debussed a mile from this & walked rest of way as road potholed & tpt had difficulty in negotiating ruts. Petrol trucks carrying gas for helicopters managed to get to LZ. C.O. Public Relations Officer & his Chinese photographer accompanied forces. Arrived at LZ 0730. Three Helicopters arrived at 0815. Hills cloudy. First Lift took off at 0910 to LZ prepared by SAS Sgt. WILLIAMS & 14 OR of SAS Regiment. dropped yesterday morning. LZ. At GR 913375. C.O. saw us in & went back. All down by 1140. Split force into 2.

   Force 1   Mission
   Coy HQ.   To investigate CT camp at GR 849857.
   10 Pl
   12 Pl
   Force 2
   2/Lt. Robertson   To investigate CT camp at GR 877336.
   11 Pl.
   Force 1
Went WESTalong river S. BAHO then to SW camp at GR 880369. Slow going down stream running SW. On inconvenient spur but based at 1700 hrs. as time running short for setting up camp.
   Force 2
Left DZ at 1200hrs went S via border to stream junct GR 895353. Based up for night.
   Force 1
Downstream at river junction at GR 878364 & then WEST to river junct .GR 868366 Saw Tiger footprints the whole way along river between these river juncs.
Up river to GR864359.Lots of waterfalls. Fus. Barr delayed us at spur GR 858350 as bad cramp. Thought we may have difficulty finding water, but small stream at second valley we looked in at GR 855343. In contact with Bn HQ at KROH on wrls but heavy interference
   Force 2
Arrived at 876340 at 1400hrs. Force Patrolled S in direction of CT camp which was our target. Patrols only located natural clearings & no signs of human activity
THUR. 5 MAY
   Force 1
Carried on SOUTH up ridge all morning till reached stream at GR 854321. One man 's footprints wearing same sort of shoe going upstream. Got Alsatian on to them but soon lost. Possibly one day old. Found old CT camp to hold 30 at GR 848319 not occupied for at least 2 years. On uphill till stream petered out. Camped in pouring rain at GR 848316.

   Force 2
Force Patrolled area of reported this time from G. 859319.

FRI. 5 MAY
   Force 1
Auster gave us bearing of 50 & distance off 1300yds to CT camp. Hard going with elements of 10 Pl. prepared DZ for airdrop near Camp . Nothing found of CT camp So returned.
   Force 2
Patrolled to clearing in area of reported eamp. Auster told us that this clearing, which we had found 2 days previously was site of suspected CT camp. Clearing was a natural one.

SAT. 7 MAY

Force 1

With 10 Pl on 670 bearing up ridge to Thailandlland border at GR 863322 N.T.R. then down stream to GR 854321. C sent Sgt. Shanley & 12 Pl to investigate camp in GR 852328.

12 Pl.

Found camp & base for 6 at 1430hrs at GR852328 evac in morning. Clearing at GR854337 of tapioca. Supplied by Auster to stay out night & return tomorrow to Coy HQ via clearing reported by Auster at GR 859335.

Force 2

Cut DZ. Patrolled upstream to GR 872333. Then NW end back NE along spur.

SUN. 8 MAY

Force 1

Waited at DZ for airdrop until 1030 hrs. then Bn HQ ordered Force 1 to join 12 Pl at GR859340 & abandon 12 Pls kit. Packed up hurriedly wrapping up 12 Pls in ponchos & burying it in a hole. Went down stream in heavy rain. Up ridge GR851326 where we found large CT camp capable of holding over 60. Difficulty in getting water.
2 Austers dropped food to us at 1820. Having had no food that day cooked in the dark. All hungry & wet.

12Pl

An airstrike arranged at QY838359 on suspect CT camp, had orders from Bn HQ to follow up-strike & not to return to our kits. By1900 hrs had reached GR 857339 & got Auster drop of 2 days rations & 12 packs.

Force 2

Received airdrop. Auster reported large camp at GR 867335. Set of at 1500 hrs. in the direction. Found old camp for 100 C.T.'s in this area, 18 Months old, evacuated 9 mths ago. Tracks leading to NW & SW. Followed former track onto main spur then returned to base. Found empty food dump at GR868338. Reached base at 1930hrs. a Narrow shave.

MON. 9 MAY

Force 1

Tried unsuccessfully to contact Bn Hq on wrls, went on downstream to join12 Pl. Very steep waterfalls GR 856332,where we came across 12 PL's tracks. These went too far S so we left them When slightly up tributary by river junc at GR 853333 our med orderly fell & stick penetrated along side his anus. Looked deep & as Fus. McFADDEN in agony made him as comfortable as possible. Dog handler S/Sgt Fulcher treated him. This happened at 1200hrs. Went up right & cleared small DZ did not get through to Bn on wrls until 1600 hrs. Auster dropped med sups & instrs from M.O. Fus. McFADDEN in much less pain by nightfall.

12Pl.

Found camp for 6 at 1300hrs.at GR 846343 not used for one month cultivation 80yds x40yds not planted. Canberra tgt is 500yds NORTH. On to GR 838359 but camp not found.

Force 2

Patrolled to area of camp found yesterday. Auster confirmed that this is camp reported by him yesterday. Followed up tracks. One leading SW faded after 250yds. NW turned SW after a short distance, & at GR 864333 formed a "Y" junction with track leading N down spur. This latter track had been recently used. Patrol followed up track & found that it had been made by security forces.
Cas. evac party (HUNTER)left for LZ (1).

TUE. 10 MAY

Force 1

Most of the force received airdrop while stretcher party carried cas. across river & up ridge. The whole force proceeded up ridge to GR 863333. Cleared small DZ there.

12 PL

Proceeded to GR 846369 at scene of camp for 6 evac 4-6hrs. Track leading WEST followed for 200yds one man barefoot one wearing hockey boots.

Force 2

Patrolled to NW of base to GR870350& back due E to stream & along ridge on far side running S&SE. Started building LZ (2) at GR 882347.

WED. 11 MAY

Force 1

Rainy & low cloud. Started off down ridge. Found we were going down wrong ridge & were on one at GR 856337. Receed to EAST but decided going with stretcher too hard & returned up ridge. Received airdrop where we camped & had cut DZ last night. Slow going on up ridge- machetes party following scouts & stretcher party then stretcher party's kit. Stretcher was then dumped & carriers went back to collect their kit. Could not get EAST as thick Bamboo valley so had to go up to top which we reached at 1600hrs. Down ridge till 1615 hrs. No water. Camped at GR 863331. Fus. McFADDEN all right & not in pain. Heard 11 Pl. blowing up trees preparing LZ for cas evac.

12Pl.
Same loc.

Force 2
Continued building LZ(2)Sgt Gilmore escorted to LZ(1) received airdrop.

THUR. 12 MAY
Force 1
On downstream to water eventually. Lost our signaller Cpl. Boyd for a time & Fus. Hunter who had Septic tenia on his feet . MAJ WILMOT & signaller Fus. Mc Masters went on downstream to small clearing at GR 877350 Cleared DZ 0-joined by whole force by 1600 hrs. Got Auster fix & learnt that 11 Pl were 500yds away at bearing of 122o . Had airdrop from Auster & arranged by wrls with 11 Pl For them to send party to carry stretcher party's packs tomorrow.

12 Pl.
Same Loc.

Force 2
Continued to build LZ(2)

FRI. 13 MAY
Force 1
At 0810 hrs party from 11 Pl arrived & carried packs & led way to LZ at GR 823447 being prepared by their Pl for casvac. Sycamore Helicopter arrived in the afternoon & successfully evacuated Fus. Mc FADDEN. Remained on edge of LZ for a good wash. Message from HQ for Force 1 To return to LZ where we originally came in on 3 MAY by 1200 hrs tomorrow.

12 Pl.
Same loc.

Force 2
LZ(2) completed Casvac away.

SAT. 14 MAY
Force 1.
Went downstream to GR 887 352 then upstream to GR 908358 & along excellent wide path leading along MALAY/THAILAND border & down to LZ at GR 913375. Here we met troops sent out on 12 May by Helicopter. At 1320 Sycamore Helicopter arrived with Helicopter carrying Lt. Staheli. This did 4 trips from KROH to LZ carrying in 1 Labrador, & carrying out Cpl. Boyd, Fus Simpson due for demob, Fus Hunter Fus ROBINSON, Fus. TOPPING sick, the Alsatian & Maj. Wilmot.

12 Pl
2/3 CT tracks being followed , 2/3 days old.

Force 2
Supplied guide party to CS 59 back to LZ(1) Rest day for remainder.

SUN. 15 MAY
Force 1.
Airdrop day. Spent time in sorting out both this & immediate plan. of Action Engaging CT's with reinforcements & 10 Pl who were then at LZ . 12 Pl found track 2/3 days old crossing river to NORTH at GR 846369. Followed up.

Force 2
Received airdrop.

MON. 16 MAY
Force 1
Patrolled to 3 largest cultivations which were reported by Auster & were approx 200-300 x G of LZ. All these were considerable size approx 50 x 100 . Cultivation was stage 1v. Crops. were tapioca & concealed under this was growing a vast assortment of green vegetable. No signs of bashas were seen. Gardening implements such as hoes were discovered & also destroyed, & all the crops. uprooted & cut. It was estimated that these ladangs must have been cultivated until recently. Tracks leading out of them were followed enthusiastically by our dog but persuit had to be abandoned when they disappeared over the border. The quantity of food growing made it appear that they were the vegetable gardens of a camp some 100 strong. Returned to base & found that 12 Pl had joined us. Received orders to expect big Sunray following day.

Force 2
2 day Patrol proceeded to GS 8931 at GR 883327. Natural Clearing containing young trees here . Based up at 893320.

TUE. 17 MAY

Force 1

No Patrol today. Big Sunray arrived by Helicopter after lunch. New plan was decided upon. All the forces in the Coy to be split up into two parties. Lt. Robertson to command one, self the other. Also areas to be changed . Lt Robertson who was on the move to LZ was to operate from there. A base party was to be left at the LZ & the remainder were to move into the area to the W. Boundaries were left to be mutually agreed. Fus.Waldron was evac with foot trouble.

Force 2

Ordered to move to LZ (1) Short Patrol failed to locate camp reported by Auster at 895319.

WED. 18 MAY

Force 1.

Reinforcements were divided up according to Pls. It was decided that 10Pl should be split up into 2 parts one half to be attached to 12 Pl. the other to 11 Pl. were unable to arrive until approx 1700 hrs. & by time plans had been discussed for the future it was decided to postpone move until the following morning. Also the route was to be altered to enable more ground to be Patrolled during the move.

Force 2

Moved back to LZ

THUR. 19 MAY

Force 1

Moved off at 0730hrs From LZ & headed S to join border track. We proceeded along this to GR 90033. There was no sign of movement here so we moved due W to stream at GR 886334 & followed this N to junction with S Baho Followed along S Baho & based up for the night at GR 882358 There was no sign during the days march of any CT activity Were not even able to pick up any signs of footprints. The track running along the S Baho was however good & easy to follow & had been cut up in places suggesting that was a used route.

Force 2

Patrolled to GR 925385 Only natural clearing here. Found CT camp at 920374 Evac.2-3 weeks , 6 months old 1 Basha for 10 persons Nearby ladang 50 x 60 contained lettuce beans & cucumber. CT camp even 6 months found at 903387 Camp 1 year old overgrown ladang close at hand .

FRI. 20 MAY

Force 1

Moved at 0730 hrs & continued to travel along S Baho to stream junction at GR 846379 & there turned S along the small stream. We revisited the ladang at GR 845373. which had been visited by Sgt Shahley's section some days before. Found no signs of CT 's had returned. Then continued upstream & climbed up circular feature in M.S. 8336. Here we had a shock for we had chosen the route as being the least steep one on our final destination & found that we had to climb up a nearly vertical slope. We then moved along S ridge . GR 835350 & cut NE to ladang at GR 845356. This was to be our base for operating from in the area & from there we proposed to carry out our task of searching the ladangs in the area.

FRI. 20 MAY

Force 2

Completed food destruction in ladangs near LZ followed up track from ladang at GR 917374. Head back to LZ (1)natural clearing at GR 912378.

SAT. 21 MAY

Force 1

Airdrop day Improved cultivation to receive airdrop . However we do not appear to have been very good at this for some considerable time was later spent in collecting the packages dropped in trees & undergrowth.

Force 2

Natural clearing at GR 929385. Patrol returned to GR 924374.

SUN. 22 MAY

Force 1

Patrol moved N along stream to bombed area at GR 848368. We had been asked to investigate this as a visual air recce had reported seeing basha's at the N end of the clearing. The approach to the clearing was easy but once we hit the edge of the actual bombing we were scrambling over a mass of fallen trees & splintered timber. We searched the whole of the area thoroughly but could find no sign of any basha's there. Had there been one in the actual clearing itself I doubt if anything recognisable could have been left. The effect of the bombing was devastating extremely accurate. One bomb having landed in the centre of the ladang. The actual clearing which must have been 50 x 60 had been increased to about 300x x 200x . We split up into two parties & searched the high ground E & W of the lading without success & then returned to base camp.

3 day Patrol set out for 9140. Based up at 920397. Located 1 Stage(11) ladangs, one at GR 920408 other at GR 913402. Tracks from both led to border. Natural clearing at both ladangs had basha spaces for 4-6 men & Had been evacuated for 1 month. Ladangs about 4-6 months old.

MON. 23 MAY

Force 1

Proposed today to search other ladangs in our area. However we received message telling us to suspend everything as we were moving to a new location as an effective Patrol would have meant being away for at lest 36 hrs. It was not practical to send one out. Auster dropped us fresh instructions 1700hrs that night & we were instructed to move S. to bandit camp at GR 818303. We were to establish our base & if possible to search N within our boundaries which were W S. Baho & E. S Baho To the S. boundary was to be the border.

Force 2

Patrolled to SW of LZ

TUE. 24 MAY

Force 1

Moved off at 0800hrs we planned to get to our destination along the ridge. Firstly we were going to climb up the S. bound ridge which starts at MS84.34. We then proposed to follow this along until it hit the border ridge, which we would then follow along until we reached the camp. Our initial move brought us to far N.W. & while we thought that according to the map we should be at GR646351!! We were then directed by Auster onto the correct ridge & he stayed with us giving us checks for the remainder of the march. During the first halt we had on the march before the Auster arrived we spotted a black panther, which at first we thought to be war dog "Peter" a black Labrador. Peter at the time was sitting with S/Sgt. Fulcher. After that everyone kept doubly 'ALERT'. We arrived without further incident at the border ridge & based up at 1700hrs. The going all the way was hard & much more up & down than the map suggested . there were no tracks along the ridge . Our base camp that night was just on the source of a stream at GR843323.

Force 2

Still on 3 day Patrol.

WED. 25 MAY

Force 1

Moved off at 0715. Initial 200x took approx 1 hr. as we found we were going though thick bamboo. Once we got onto the border ridge the going was easy & the whole ridge had an excellent track along it the whole way. At 1300 hrs we reached .366 at GR 824305. Auster then gave us bearing to & location of camp we were heading for. Fortunately we found track running to camp from ridge & arrived at 1330. Our original estimate had been 1400hrs. Auster came over at 1400 hrs. to check that we were in the right place. Fortunately we were. We Patrolled the immediate area of the camp to make certain all was clear & then based up for the night.

Force 2.

Still on 3 day Patrol.

THUR. 26 MAY

Force 1

We were due to receive airdrops. today at approx 1100 hrs. Owning to engine trouble this did not come in until approx 1700hrs. Everyone was getting rather hungry & very anxious by then. Delighted to see Valletta whose Pilot apologised for delay. Spent the day searching the camp. The Police who had visited this before & however had made a very thorough job of both searching & destroying it. Nothing came to light except tattered remains of clothing & hockey boots A few strips of material, some used medical eqpt & strips of material.

Force 2

Patrolled to GR908389. Found Natural clearing.

FRI. 27 MAY

Force 1

Started today on the task of searching the four map squares. Two Patrols were sent out to 8031.8131. Nothing found except game tracks along tops. of ridges . Going in this area quite difficult. Steep hills., thick undergrowth & a large amount of bamboo near to the streams No sign of CT activity.

Force 2.

Found Natural clearing of fern at GR881390. & one of bamboo at GR 873393. Both these had been repeated as being a suspected hill paddi.

SAT. 28 MAY

Force 1.

Two Patrols out today to search ms's 8030, 8130. Patrol into area 8030 found nothing but animal trap at 815309. on the way out along ridge. Also Elephant tracks along stream in this area. Patrol l 8130 on the way S. whilst following the stream cut up through bamboo thicket & **found the remains of a crashed wartime Liberator Bomber with British markings on tail & wings. Bomber was found at GR818300.** Wreckage was scattered about over a considerable area & part of the fuselage had burnt out. Clothing , arms , ammunition, grenades, medical eqpt & personal clothing (kit) had been packed in CLE containers which remained in the bomb bays or were scattered near it. The Aircraft was presumed to have been on a supply run for Force 136. Also what we thought to be the charred remains of human bones were unearthed. This was later stated by experts not to be the case l (Lt. Staheli) still feels very sceptical & from personal clothing found later feel quite convinced that crew did not bale out. This find made by Fus. McGill who was leading scout of Sgt. Dummelow's Patrol was reported to Bn HQ we started to salvage eqpt. whilst awaiting instructions.

Force 2

Patrolled boundary from 907360 to B.P 49. No tracks other than intermittent game trail along border Patrolled GR9240.

SUN. 29 MAY.

Force 1

Salvaging of eqpt. Continued today. We were told to get out all we could without disturbing wreckage unduly. We asked for tools to dismantle 2 brownings from the rear turret which were dropped to us by Auster. By the end of the day we had recovered, approx 2,000 rounds of .5, .303,.300, .45, .9 mm ammunition , two .5 browning guns, 22 sten-guns, 1 bren gun, 18 -.38 revolvers, 1 .38 Police special revolver, 1-.45 mm pistol. Two medical kits, an assortment of army clothing, ,Also, 3 survival knives, a charred remains of BD with whistle attached, charred flying boots, & goggles a lighter, 1pr of civilian shoes, charred flying jackets, remains of Mae West & navigators protractors. All those later articles together with the position of the wreck convinced us that some at least of the crew members must have crashed with the aircraft. The amo with the exception of the .300 was in excellent condition of the stens was assembled & undoubtedly would have worked, also about 40 sten mags were Serviceable . The bren gun was in a poor shape externally though the inside of the barrel & working parts were as new. The revolvers if cleaned by an armourer l am certain would have worked. The .5 brownings seemed to be in good condition . Thay had however been adapted for electric firing & would have needed some modification for use by ground troops With the exception of about 2 pairs of gym shoes all articles of clothing were US. In the medical packs, such items as plaster, bndages etc:- were US. However bottles of iodine, insect repellant etc:- also jars of Whitfields ointment were in perfect condition & were used by Pl Medical Ord. We also salvaged in Serviceable condition two artery forceps, a pair of surgical scissors, three thermometers & a scalpel. All these were immediately appropriated by the Pl Med. Ord. Who was hovering around seizing all useful items to make up his kit? All arms & stores were evacuated to base camp. We then started to clean & assemble weapons whilst awaiting instructions as to there disposal.

Force 2

Patrolled to GR8939via GR8739. NTR. Continued crop destruction in Ladangs.

MON. 30 MAY

Force 1

Received instructions today to cut LZ so that experts could be flown in. to view wreckage. Requested drop of explosives, saws, axes etc:- took airdrop of rations & eqpt. Started cutting L.Z. Continued to search a/c but could find nothing of interest . Searched surrounding area but found nothing but scattered wreckage. Large piece of broken wing was discovered further down the valley next to large tree which had its top broken off. From this we assumed that a/c must have hit tree & thought this might be reason for crash. Searched wreckage for a/c identification number. Which we were unable to find. We were instructed that we were not to move out of M.S. we were in & the Police were Patrolling to our S. Our task was to finish the cutting of the L.Z. as quickly as possible.

Force 2

Made ready to move to L.Z. (2)

TUE. 31 MAY

Force 1

Continued with preparing L.Z. also blasting trees with plastic explosives dropped. Progress was regretfully much slower than expected.

Force 2

Move to L.Z.

ROYAL SCOTS FUSILIERS REPORT

CONTINUED FROM MAY

WED. 1 JUNE

Force 1

Still cutting L.Z. Work was going rather slowly owing to axes & saws breaking. At the end of the day L.Z. virtually completed. Target day for completion was P.M. 2nd.

Force 2
Received airdrop. Patrolling area around base.

THUR. 2 JUNE

Force 1
L.Z. completed . During the course approx 1430 hrs. shooting was heard to the S. of our location. This was two single shots followed by a burst of automatic fire 5-6 rounds . took out Patrol immediately & searched around our location but discovered nothing. It was discovered subsequently that this shooting was due to the Police who had had a contact Took our airdrop today.

Force 2.
Patrolled spur N. of base to GR 863333 also area GR8835. NTR.

FRI. 3 JUNE

FORCE 1
Helicopter with R.A.F. pers arrived in approx 0930 hrs. Took them down to examine wreckage also S/Sgt. from War Graves Commission R.A.F. removed portions of a/c for identification. War Graves Commission Sgt looked for remains but could find none

Party finally left with "spoils" at approx 1600hrs. I.O came in with helicopter & briefed us on further task. This was to Patrol & ambush along border track to our N & E within our area. All weapons were evacuated by Heli & all visitors left the same night. Sgt. Fulcher & War Dog evac. Dog handler & Dog arr.

Force 2
Patrolled to 870368 also area 8934. NTR

SAT. 4 JUNE

Force 1 This was observed as a rest day.
Force 2.
Ambushed track at GR864333 Patrolled area of food dump at GR868338 NTR

SUN. 5 JUNE

Force 1
Went out on 36hr Patrol going N along border track. Patrol left 0800hrs. Moved along border track & it was decided to follow this . Track eventually led onto S. Tebus & along tracks in parts rather vague but quite possible to follow. Footprints of one person seen along this track going N. track was followed & fresh footprints following track going S. were seen at GR815343. tracks were 12 to 14 hrs old. They were followed up & within 50x led into CT camp. this camp consisted of one basha for approx 8-10 men. Also cookhouse basha. It had recently been abandoned. The camp had obviously been very thoroughly cleaned for nothing of value remained. Basha floor had been uprooted & table overturned . This gave the appearance of C.T.'s having removed stores hidden under them. the camp appeared to have been a courier or supply carriers staging post. The depth of the footprints suggested that C.T.'s were heavily laden Unfortunately we had no food or wireless & were Thus unable to follow up. Based up for the night in Basha. Very convenient as it poured with rain.

Force 2.
Patrolled border between GR886320-878322, also between 987330-900333. Thick bamboo along border. No recent signs of C.T.'s.

MON. 6 JUNE

Force 1 Destroyed CT camp Cookhouse etc:- by fire. Returned to base camp. During absence remainder had taken airdrop for us. Also fresh instructions received that we were not to Patrol in that area but to start search for camp in caves at GR803294. Police who were operating in the same area to S. of us were ordered to be clear by 2359hrs. 6th.

Force 2
Patrolled border from GR 897329 to GR886320 NTR.

TUE. 7 JUNE.

Force 1
At 0800 hrs 36hr Patrol went out to search for cliffs & search for camp in their vicinity. Route selected was to go along border track to GR 814289 & then along ridge, which was done. A good track was discovered running along G.W. ridge which led directly over the top of the cliffs, this then turned S. & dropped to low ground by river at GR 798293. it then joined track going S. along river. This was followed for approx 1000x & Patrol then based up.

Force 2
Patrols searched area in which 68 set was lost from Auster. Unsucessful. C/S 51 left for new location.

WED. 8 JUNE

Force 1.

Patrol moved off & searched M.S. 8028, then moved back onto W. found ridge & along track to border & back to camp. Except for tracks nothing was found.

Force 2

Patrolled to CT camp at GR867336, investigated stream lines between here & base NTR.

THUR. 9 JUNE

Force 1.

0800hrs 36hr. Patrol again left for area of cliffs. Same route out was used & thorough search on M.S. 8029 made. Nothing but old cooking fire at GR809293 was found. No indication of activity in that area seen. Patrol moved down onto river at GR798296 & based up for night.

Force 2

Patrolled to GR852313 via CT camp at 867336. Followed border to 865324 found temporary 1 basha CT camp at GR859320 & GR868328. both occupied 1 week. 3-4 months old. Track from 2nd camp led down spur leading to N. faded at GR8088330. Trouble in camp include dysentery, swollen crutch & non-functioning 68 set.

FRI. 10 JUNE.

Force1.

Patrol moved off downstream to stream junction at G.R798299 & then followed track along stream to E. Although, the track was good there were no signs of its use recently. Searched area alone edge off cliffs, which run parallel to mainstream, until it reached junction, at GR806297. Where the cliff features then followed the line of the tributary strain. This stream was followed to top of Ridge. No signs of caves or activities seen. Climb up here was, very sleep. Patrol then moved along ridge onto border track back to base camp.

Force 2

Patrolled to GR9035.NTR.

SAT. 11 JUNE

Force 1.

Patrolled to area cliff features both along the top & the bottom. We made an attempt to get at the cliffs from the top of the feature but came to a sheer drop & were unable to go any further. Signs of tracks seen on the steep slope going down to cliffs, these petered out & led to nothing. Presume these were animal. No signs off any activity. Patrol returned to base.

Force 2

Patrolled to GR9034. Two troubles of the ninth in student & starvation.

SUN. 12 JUNE

Force 1

Airdrops. day. Ordinary day Patrol went out to area of stream at GR805297. Investigated stream valley. Returned to place via N. running stream at GR 812299. Elephant tracks seen following this stream otherwise nothing seen. During course, of night, light, was seen flashing act regular interval off 10 secs, on bearing of 232o from base camp. First, estimated as about 2000x. away subsequently it was decided that it must be between 7000x x 10000x a way. We thought this might have been a C. T. signal though later on rather doubted this of although no other natural reason was forthcoming. One peculiar feature in regard to light was the fact that had not an L. Z. been out. We should never have seen it. However, there was a sentry platfrom in camp, which had what appeared to be a lamp bracket fitted on it. Even if no trees, had been cut one could have stood behind the lamp bracket & seen the light. This was only place in the camp from, which it was at all possible. I still wonder if this was just pure coincidence, we never did manage to get an explanation of this.

Force 2

Airdrop.

MON. 13 JUNE

Force 1

decided to try & trace light. Moved out with Patrol at 1600hrs & based on top of cliffs at GR803294, from which one could normally get a wonderful view of all the surrounding jungle. Unfortunately, that night, heavy clouds came down & blotted out everything, also it poured with rain. The result was we spent a very wet night, & uncomfortable night, & achieved nothing.

Force 2.

Patrolled to GR897333 Then along border to GR909355.

TUE. 14 JUNE.

Force 1.

Moved off at 0700 hrs to investigate feature3075 atGR789273. Route taken was along N running stream until level with feature then due W on to feature. Area around whilst Patrolled but nothing discovered except the inevitable game tracks, along ridge is & tracks a long stream. We had been given smoke code for Auster, but unfortunately, the N.T.R code was blue smoke. Of six dropped only two were Serviceable, & one of those turned out to be a dud. The Auster, was unable to see the one we set off as he flew over. While we were in the upstream valley. He continued to circle us, but we were unable to contact him & tell him we were OK. Returned to base camp via EW Cliff feature & border ridge. Arrived at 1900hrs.

Force 2.
Patrol for the from GR882322 to GR866325. Found track running W from GR880323. Faded out after 100yards.

WED. 15 JUNE
Force 1.

0800hrs Patrol moved off to search area just Patrolled by us. They took approximately same route. Searched Hill feature N of GR3075, going there was very difficult. Thick attap, nothing was discovered. Patrol moved based up for might at GR789288.
Force 2.
Patrolled to GR864336, then W & then NE. Found sentry basha for camp for 100 well hidden in. re-entrant at GR 866337.

THUR. 16 JUNE
Force 1.

Patrol moved over ridge & onto running stream & followed this to stream junction at GR798299. Then moved along stream westward. Intention was to search all along stream valley. Resting places at GR813294 & GR818297. All indications were that at resting places At GR 818297 had been re-visited by C.T.'s during the last 4-7 days. The reason for this surmise were that cut bamboo, used as water containers looked fresh. Also cooking fires & ridge pole for one poncho type basha. Patrol searched around the camp , but found nothing else & returned to base. The same day we were told that "C" Coy were moving up from the S to join us at our location. WE were asked to take their airdrop for them the following day.

Force 2
Patrolled to 8733. Fond temporary basha 6 months old at GR873333. Occupied one week. Heffron flown out.C/S51 return.

FRI. 17 JUNE

Force 1
Took "C" Coy's airdrop. Two chutes stuck up trees & spent several hours getting them down. "C" Coy arrived at about 1600 hrs & based up about 100x away from us on another flat place of ground. Signal from I.O. told us to expect C.O. & I.O. at 0900hrs next day.

Force 2
Airdrop.

SAT. 18 JUNE

Force 1
0930hrs. C.O. & I.O. arrived in Navy Helicopter. C.O. visited all the men & spoke to them. Fus. Moran who had been suffering from toothache was evacuated & also Cpl Kirkwood who was due to go back to the depot as instructor. C.O. then briefed NCO's & Offrs of "D" & "C" Coy's. Plan was to concentrate on cliff features & search this until we found cave & were 100% certain none existed. We were told that cave was unlikely to be large entrance but might be cleft in rock leading to a cave . Similar thing had happened in IPOH. Area was to be divided between Coys. "D" Coy were to Patrol bottom of cliff & W. "C" Coy top of cliff & south. Requested toggle ropes & also asked if it was at all possible to obtain Ibans as, due to a lot of heavy rains it was very difficult to be able to say with any degree of certainty whether they had been used. I.O. then examined sentry position with lamp bracket suggested that night Auster recce might solve problem. Helicopter Brought in & took out mail. Also brought us some extra rations & fresh bread which C.O. had organised & which was more than welcome.

Force 2
Morale -boosting visit from C.O. as well as morale boosting mail.

SUN. 19 JUNE

Force 1
Went out today on joint Patrol with "C" Coy reps. Went over both our areas & agreed the boundaries. During the course of this found an excellent shortcut down them to the bottom. Found no sign of CT activity. Base party took airdrop of toggle ropes for us.

Force 2

Working on L.Z.

MON. 20 JUN

Force 1 Patrolled along all bottom of cliff –face. No sign of obvious cave entrance or fissures. Attempted to climb up likely looking places but were unable to go more than halfway up. Returned to base.

Force2

Work on L.Z. completed for mentime.

TUE. 21 JUNE

Force 1.

Patrol again searched bottom of cliffs & attempted to climb, still without success.

Force 2

Rest day.

WED. 22 JUNE

Force 1

Again Patrolled same area without success. Could not find anything at all suggestive of any activity in that area & still no sign of entrance to caves. Took airdrop today.

Force2

Airdrop.

THUR. 23 JUNE

Force 1

Still Patrolling & searching same area. Still finding nothing new.

Force 2

English, Coull, Cpl. Wilson airlifted out.

FRI. 24 JUNE.

Force 1

Patrolling cliffs . Found way up cliffs to N side at W end. Footprints of one person found. Thought this might be the way the Police contact vanished.

Looking at this route from the top it looks quite impossible but is in fact quite easy & fast to get away. Apart from this nothing found.

Force 2.

Hooker, Main airlifted. Ordered to new position.

SAT. 25 JUNE

Force 1

Patrols are still searching area of cliff features. Still unable to find wither cave or signs of enemy activity. Airdrop today.

Force 2

McRailt feverish. Had to unpack all our kit. Rebuild basha, unit for copter to take him out.

SUN. 26 JUNE

Force 1

Decided to Patrol area of resting places discovered by us & Police. There were no signs of these, having been revisited by C.T.'s, since they were last Patrolled. No sign of activity.

Force 2

McRailt evacuated.

MON. 27 JUN

Force 1

Patrol again. searched around area resting places. Unable to find any signs of activity.

Force 2

Moved towards new location. Found food dump at GR882325. Contained 8 cwts of rice, 18 tins of condensed milk & 16 tins of porridge oats. Scots element in raptures. Based up on border at GR882322.

TUE. JUNE 28

FORCE 1.

Patrol visited resting place at GR818297 found carefully & cleverly hidden food dump. This was built off ground on stilts & thatched with attap. It was located just outside resting place in patch of attap. Dump contained quantity of rice & maize armourers kit of pliers, 5, cartridge case & other tools in pouch. Immediate 24hr ambush was laid & dump left undisturbed.

Force 2

68 set was again US, 4 Patrols out locally. Food dump found at GR874324. Contained 6 cwts of rice in oil cans, 2 gallons groundnut oil, cereal, 5 newspapers (2-10th June), 2 parachutes, SF pack containing SF JG clothing in good condition & 1 green lightweight blanket. This dump had been visited within last week or 10 days. A few vague tracks in the area lead nowhere in particular. CT camp for 4-6 found at GR878235. Occupied about 1 week evacuated 6-8 weeks ago.

WED. 29 JUNE

Force 1

Continued day & night ambush on food dumps. Still no success. Receuivedinstrs to move to L.Z. at GR883347. We were to link up there with 11 Pl & be evacuated July 2nd. Requested airdrop 2 days rations on the following day & this agreed. Told airdrop would be 0900hrs.

Force 2

CT camp for 6 found at GR878327. Pieces of SF ration pack & eqpt left lying around. Camp occupied for about 1 month evacuated 3-4 weeks. No definite tracks.

THUR. 30 JUNE

Force 1

Waited until 1630hrs for airdrop. Which was delayed owing to engine trouble with Aircraft. When it arrived it consisted if 1 days fresh rations, 1 days 24hr ration packs & NAFFI goods. Fresh rations absandoned and the rest distributed as quickly as possible. Moved off at 1730hrs and based up for night at GR840320 which we reached approx 1915hrs. No water or time to build bashas. Very cold.

Force 2.

Returned to L.Z.

FRI. 1 JULY

Force 1

Moved of at 0700hrs. along border to 4152 feature. Thence due E to stream Where we had breakfast. Moved E again and re-joined border track and followed this to GR 873323. From there followed stream along to L.Z. Linked up with 11 Pl and based up. Here Fus. McIntyre cut his hand badly with a machette but luckily helicopter that was bringing in axes and explosives to clear three large trees from L.Z. arrived at that moment and we were able to get him into it and away. This was a great relief as injury looked quite serious.

Force 2
Improved L.Z.

SAT. 2 JULY

Force 1
Evac. by helicopter to-day. Met by Coy Comdr. On L.Z. N. Baling. Coy then moved to new camp at Lintang.

Force 2
Evacuated.

"OPERATION UNITY"

"COMMENTS ON OPERATION"

1. "INFORMATION"

As we were working in liaison with the Police and other Coys of the Bn, it would have been appreciated if we could have been given more info of the activities of those groups. At the beginning of the Op this was quite good but latterly outside news

2. "ORDERS"

Owing to the fact that two 'Ops.' rooms were being run in the same Bn at the time orders sometimes arrived from two different sources and on thoise occasions were contradictory. This caused some confusion.

3. R.T.

Times of opening up clash with the routines calls at Coys. This caused delay in sending messages. The code for sitrep and airdrop which was used was found to save a great deal of wireless time and was thought to be a good idea.

4. AIRDROP

(1) Auster. Smoke grenades were dropped by Auster and in the majority of cases over 50% were rendered US by free dropping.

(2) Valetta Resup For approx 4 successive airdrops. we received 24 hr A&B packs despite repeatedly asking for compo. We were never able to get compo dropped even when we did eventually get the C&D 24 hr rations. This monotony in food was very much noticed and resulted in many people buying food from NAFFI rather than eat rations & incurring sizable airdrop bills.

GEN SUMMARY

At the time of the Op the morale was very high though we were all very disappointed at our lack of success. A very morale boosting visit from the C.O. and the I.O Who fully explained the situation was greatly appreciated. Untill then we felt that the war was being run entirely off a map & our requests to search where we felt there might be C.T.'s were refused & we never knew quite why. It would be a great help if Pls could be allowed a bit more freedom of movement if this did not conflict too violently with the overall plan. Failing that, as already mentioned, it would if we could be told the overall plan more frequently, as we were in the C.Os visit. Why we were being so restricted. In regard to moves from one location to another we found we were always set a strict time limit. Often this was if not impossible, very difficult to adhere to and resulted in jungle bashing at its worst in order to arrive on time. A little more leniency in this matter in case the type of vegetation or ground should prove hard going would be a great help.

GEN SUMMARY FORCE 2.

1. Everyone was feeling the strain of being out for so long, but morale was high all along and the men deserve praise for the way they stuck it out.

2. For two successive airdrops. 2/3 of our rations were type 'A'. This is the least popular of the 4 types and after a few days of eating corned beef, chopped bacon and vegetables salad mayonnaise one feels that further consumption of these foods will turn the stomach, and in a few cases it did. The deal arrangement is a fair representation of each type in the diet.

3. As most people have difficulty in making 5 days rations last five days a poor view is taken of losing a day's food by stretching out a five day ration pack over 6 days. This should be avoided whenever possible.

[Authors Note] The outcome of the discovery of the 'Marie Celeste' B24 Liberator Bomber KH365 will be revealed After 'Chapter – 1960'.........

ooOoo

JUNE

Wed.	1st	RAN Ships 'ANZAC' – 'ARUNTA' - 'QUADRANT' & 'TOBRUK' came on Station as part of their attachment role to the BCFESR---]
	+	RNZN, 'PUKAKI' Began her second support role of duty in Malayan coastal waters---]
Thur.	2nd	Operation 'Shark' Began SAS against the MRLA---]
Fri.	3rd	**3 Mr. B.L. Sheppard.** Manager. of the Oh Sing Estate (Malacca) was Killed by C.T's in an ambush---]
	+	HMS 'CRANE' Operation 'Rex' Phase III began shelling the inland area of Penggarng---]
Sat.	4th	HMS 'MODESTE''' Operation 'Rex' Phase III Shelled the inland area of Penggarang firing 60: 4 inch HE Shells---]
Sun.	5th	HMS 'CRANE' Operation 'Rex' Phase III Completed shelling the inland area of Penggarng Firing 100: 4 inch HE shells---]
Mon.	6th	} Combined Operations 'Rex' continued ---]
Tue.	7th	} Combined Operations 'Rex' continued ---]
Wed.	8th	**8 WOII. K. Hardwick.** Royal Corp Signals. Died *** *Kranji Singapore # 2 / C/ 8* ---]
	+	**8 SC. A. Bakar. B. Rani.** F. M. Police Killed.on CT Ops. Gelang Patah area Johore---].
Thur.	9th	9 HMT EMPIRE ORWELL arrived Southampton with returnin Service personnel
Fri.	10th	**10 Maj. E. M. Salter.** MBE. MC. Royal Ulster Rifles. Died*** *Taiping # B / 64* Perak---].
		10/06/1955. LG # 40506 p375 The following awarded the Military Medal
	+	SGT. A.M.B, SIDEK. MM MALAY REGIMENT
		RFN. N. THAPA. MM 6th QUEEN ELIZABETH'S OWN GURKHA RIFLES

+	10 HMT ASTURIUS sailed Southampton bound for Singapore/ Hong Kong with replacement Service personnel---]
Sat. 11th	Kuala Lumpur: Air Vice Marshal V. E. Hancock. became Air Officer Commanding Malaya---]
Sun. 12th	}
Mon. 13th	} Combined Operations 'Rex' continued ---]
Tue. 14th	}
Wed. 15th	Canberra Australia: The Australian Prime Minister Mr. Menzies, announced:- *'The 2nd Battalion Australian Infantry Regt. Would leave for Malaya towards the end of the year & would be available for use against the Communist Terrorist if necessary'.*---]
Thur. 16th	In 1955 (Thur. assumed date)The wreckage of the Auster Plane TJ 674 was found by members of the Hampshire Regt. Near the top of the Bentong Gap. The only identification to enable it was that of **Brig.Erskine.** Was his Medal Ribbons, shoes & a shirt tab of a Officers outfitters in London. ---]
Fri. 17th	17 **C/Sgt. J. P. Pearce.** The Queen's Att/ 22nd. S.A.S. Died from wounds recv'd in Action Engaging CT's *Kuala Lumpur # 22 / 1163* ---]
+	**17 Lt. G. M. Green.** (QM)R. A. M. C. Died*** Kuala Lumpur.[*Ashes REP*]---]
Sat. 18th	Operastion 'Rex' *Phase III* Continued---]
Sun. 19th	19 HMT EMPIRE FOWEY arrived Singapore with replacement Service personnel sailed enroute to Hong Kong 19th.---]
Mon. 20th	HMS 'NEWCASTLE' Operastion 'Rex' *Phase III* Began shelling the inland area of Penggarang---]
+	20 HMT DUNERA sailed Southampton bound for Singapore / Hong Kong with replacement Service personnel---]
Tue. 21st	Operastion 'Rex' *Phase III* Continued---]
+	HMS 'NEWCASTLE' Operastion 'Rex' *Phase III* Completed shelling the inland area of Penggarang Firing 300 6 inch HE shells---]
Wed.22nd	22/06/1955. LG # 40212 p. 3689 The following awarded the 2nd. BAR to Disinguished Flying Cross W/CDR. N.T. QUINN. DFC & BAR+BAR ROYAL AUSTRALIAN AIR FORCE The following awarded the Disinguished Flying Cross F/LT. D. C. NICHOLLS. DFC ROYAL AUSTRALIAN AIR FORCE
Thur. 23rd	**23 Pte. Din. Bin . Senawi.** A. C. C. (MOR) Died****Claimed by next of Kin* ---]
+	Singapore: A communiqué from GHQ FARELF Singapore to Army HQ MELBOURNE' confirmed the proposal by the WAR Office in London:- *'The formation of the new 28th Commonwealth Infantry Brigade. Be set up. The time & details of the Group would be discussed in the proposed meeting to be held in MELBOURNE. Australia'*---]
Fri. 24th	**24 Pte. G. Bessant.** 1st. Battn. Somerset Light Infantry. Killed in Action Engaging CT's. *Kuala Lumpur # 22 / 1164*---]
+	24 HMT EMPIRE CLYDE arrived Liverpool with returning Service personnel---]
+	Kuala Lumpur: An official announcement by the Federation Government, stated:- *'A Letter had been received via the United Planters Association, which had been posted in Southern Thailand on June 7th. for transmission to the Malayan Political & Communal Association. The subject letter called for representatives of those communities to hold a round table conference at an early date, to discuss the problems of ending the War & achieving Peace & the Independence of Malaya. Written in Chinese & signed by a certain* **Ng Heng** *Representative of the Supreme Communist Headquarters of the Malayan Liberation Army. No one by that name was known to the Federation Police. However, it was believed that it was another alias for* **Chin Peng** *Secretary General of the Malayan Communist Party. The communiqué, read as a "Peace Offer." Was rejected, not only by the Federation Government but all Political & Various Community Association.'* The Government statement went on to add: *'We have seen these sudden shift in Communist policy before, & we shall not be mislead by this one. Knowing the true purpose of, the Communist offer & the motives which underwrite it. The Government reject's. it absolutely & has no intentions of negotiating with the Communist Terrorist. If the Communist genuinely wish to end the emergency. They can do this today'.*---]
Sat. 25th	The R.A.F. began a 7-day operation in which 20,000,000 leaflets were dropped throughout the Federation Explaining the rejection of the "Peace Offer" Urging the Terrorist to surrender under the Liberal terms already on offer to them.---]
Sun. 26th	26 HMT DEVONSHIRE arrived Singapore.with replacement Service personnel---]
Mon. 27th	**27 Pte. D. P. Seaton.** 1st. Battn. Kings Own Scottish Borderers Died *** [*Ashes REP*]---]
Tue. 28th	**28 Rfn. Balbahadur Thapa** . 6th. Queen Elizabeth's Own Gurkha Rifles. Killed in Action Engaging CT's East of Pantai Village. *Seremban # 65* Negri Sembilan---]

+	**28 Grn. M.H. Stansbie.** Royal Artilery Died*** _Kuala Lumpur # 22 / 1165_---]	
+	**28 Cfn. R. W. Biddle.** R. E M E. Died***[_Ashes REP_]---].	
Wed. 29ᵗ	**29** 2 F. M. Police **S/C's Zakaria B. Mat. Piah., Bakar B. Sead.** Killed on Ops. Tapah Area Perak.---]	
Thur. 30ᵗʰ	**30** HMT DILWARA sailed Southampton bound for Singapore.with replacement Service personnel---]	
+	**30** HMT DEVONSHIRE sailed Singapore bound for Liverpool with returning Service personnel---]	

JULY

Fri. 1ˢᵗ	**1** HMT ASTURIUS arrived Singapore sailed bound for Southampton with returning Service personnel 1ˢᵗ.---]	
	41 Sqdn. RNZAF relocated to Kuala Lumpur. Their Bristol Freighters to be used for supply drops.---]	
Sat. 2ⁿᵈ	Combined Operations continued throughout Malaya ---[	
Sun. 3ʳᵈ	**3 Capt. G. N. B. Hart.** 6ᵗʰ. Queen Elizabeth's Own Gurkha Rifles. Died ***_Suvla Lines# 425_ Batu Gaja Ipoh Perak.---]	
+	**3 Cpl. J. R. Grant.** Coxswain R. A. F. Seletar Drowning Accident. _Kranji Singapore # 4 / B – 6_ .---]	
+	RAN Ships: 'ANZAC' - 'QUADRANT' & 'TOBRUK'. Having completed their tour of duty were replaced by the	
+	RAN Ship 'WARRAMUNGA' to commence her tour of duty. ---]	
+	RNZN HMNZS 'KANIERE'. completed her first support role of duty in Malayan coastal waters---]	
Mon. 4ᵗʰ	**4 Cpl. L. Creighton** Royal Engineers Died *** _Kuala Lumpur # 21 / 1140_---]	
Tue. 5ᵗʰ	5/07/1955 LG # 40527 p 3861 The following awarded the Military Medal .	
	CPL. GURUNG. M. MM 6ᵗʰ QUEEN ELIZABETH'S GURKHA RIFLES	
Wed. 6ᵗʰ	Operation "Rex Phase III' began on the Penarang Peninsular to eliminate the CT's operating in that area 2ⁿᵈ. 10ᵗʰ. Gurkhas were assigned to that operation---]	
Thur. 7ᵗʰ	**7. PC. Ishak B. Din.** F. M. Police Killed on CT Ops. Perak---]	
Fri. 8ᵗʰ	**8. SC. Hasim B. Abu.** F. M. Police .Killed on CT Ops. Jerom Padang Bahau Negri Sembilan---].	
Sat. 9ᵗʰ	**9. SC. Tan B. Buyong.** F. M. Police Killed on Ops. Pahang.---]	
Sun. 10ᵗʰ	**10 W/O I A. E. White.** Royal Engineers Died *** _Kranji Singapore # 2 / E – 14_ ---]	
+	**10** HMT EMPIRE FOWEY arrived Singapore with replacement Service personnel sailed bound for Southampton with returning Service personnel-10ᵗʰ.---]	
+	HMS 'COSSACK' Combined Operations _Nassau'_ shelled CT targets deep in the Jungles of Kuala Langgat Firing 180 4.5 inch HE shells---]	
Mon. 11ᵗʰ	**11 Mr. A.K. Bhomwick.** Manager of an Estate??? Killed in ambush Malacca---]	
+	HMS 'CRANE' Operation 'Rex' Phase IIIB Shelled the inland area of Penggerang Firing 70 4 inch HE shells]	
Tue. 12ᵗʰ	**12** HMT "NEW AUSTRALIA arrived Penang on board were The 2ⁿᵈ. Battn. Royal Australian Regt. bound for Minden Barracks Penang---]	
Wed. 13ᵗʰ	**13 L/Cpl. G. Satalsing Gurung.** 6ᵗʰ. Queen Elizabeth's Own Gurkha Rifles. Killed in Action Engaging CT's,. near Batu Gelang _Seremban # 66_ Negri Sembilan---]	
Thur. 14ᵗ.	**14 Spr.'s Abdul Manaf Bin Hassan. – Mohd.. Bin Mohd. Idras.** Royal Engineers (MOR's) Died*** unknown incident _Claimed_ by next of Kin ---]	
Fri. 15ᵗʰ	HMS 'COSSACK' Operation 'Rex' Phase IIIB Began shelling the inland area of Penggrang---]	
+	HMS 'COSSACK' Operation 'Rex' Phase IIIB Completed shelling the inland area of Penggarang Firing 180 4. 5 inch shells ---]	
Sat. 16ᵗʰ	}	
Sun. 17ᵗʰ	} Combined Operations 'Rex' Phase IIIB continued ---]	
Mon. 18ᵗʰ	}	
Tue. 19ᵗʰ	**19 Gnr. D. A. Little.** Royal Artillery Died***_Taiping. # E / 48_ Perak.---]	
+	**19** HMT EMPIRE CLYDE sailed Liverpool bound for Singapore/ Hong Kong. On boaud were The 1st. Batn. Royal Lincolnshire Regt. Bound for a tour of active Service in Malaya ---]	
+	19/07/1955 ? The following awarded the Military Cross	
	CAPT. F. E. KITSON MC THE RIFLE BRIGADE	
Wed. 20ᵗʰ	**20** HMT DUNERA arrived Singapore enroute to Hong Kong with replacement Service personnel 20ᵗʰ.---]	
Thur. 21ˢᵗ	HMS 'OPPOSUM' Combined Operations 'Nassau Phase VI Began shelling CT targets deep in the jungle area of Kuala Langgat for the next 3 days---]	
Fri. 22ⁿᵈ	**22 SC. Zalani B. Pajang Ismalan.** F. M. Police Kiled on Ops.---]	
+	**22** HMT ASTURIUS arrived Singapore with replacement Service personnel---]	
+	**22** HMT EMPIRE ORWELL sailed Southampton bound for Singapore with replacement Service personnel--]	
Sat. 23ʳᵈ	**23 Pte. M. Simushi.** Northern Rhodesia Regt. Killed on CT Ops. Kuala Kangsar area Perak.	

	Kuala Lumpur # 22 / 1166 ---]
+	23 HMT ASTURIUS sailed Singapore bound for Southampton with returning Service personnel---]
Sun. 24th	HMS *'OPPOSUM'* Combined Operations 'Nassau' ended shelling CT targets deep in the jungle area of Kuala Langgat Firing 190 4 inch HE shells---]
Mon. 25th	Operation *"Rex Phase IIIB* continued
Tue. 26th	**26 W/O. W. Harvey.** CI/GD R.A.F. Changi Died ******Kranji Singapore # 4 / C – 7* ---]
+	**26 Bdsn. B. J. Pearse.** Royal Marines H.M.S. *''NEWFOUNDLAND''* Died *** *[Ashes REP]*
+	26/07/1955 LG. # 40547 p. 4307. The following awarded the British Empire Medal (Military)
	F/SGT. J. B. JARRETT. BEM ROYAL AUSTRALIAN AIR FORCE
	p.4308. The following awarded the Distinguished Flying Cross
	W/CDR. H. F. MOORE.DFC ROYAL AUSTRALIAN AIR FORCE
Wed. 27th	**27 Rfn. Tulbahadur Gurung** . 2nd, King Edward VII's Own Gurkha Rifles. Died***
	Kranji Singapore # 7 / A – 4---]
+	Kuala Lumpur: The first Election of The Federation of Malaya. resulted in an over-whelming victory for the Triple Alliance Party formed by the United Malay's National Organisation, (U.M.N.O.), the Malayan Chinese Association (M.C.A.) & the Malayan Indian Congress (M.I.C.) under the leadership of Tengku Abdul Rahman. Who won 51 of the 52 elected seats against the opposition. The Negara (National) Party. Led by Dato Sir. Onn bin Ja'afar. After the election Tengku Abdul Rahman spoke of the need to: *Initially go "dead slow" for the first few months rather the "rush into it" in their quest to gain independence. On the question of amnesty for terrorists, he stated that this would not be put into effect until, "the right time & with the advice of experts". If the Communist excepted the amnesty, the leaders would be deported & the other Guerrillas rehabilitated. An Amnesty, should cover Guerrillas (other than leaders) guilty of atrocities because "if we want peace we must forget them." If the terrorist leaders refused an amnesty, however ever able-bodied man over the age of 18 would be mobilised for part -time military Service in the Federation. ---]*
+	27 HMT NEW AUSTRALIA sailed Southampton bound for SYDNEY via Penang ---]
Thur. 28th	28 HMT DILWARA arrived Singapore. with replacement Service personnel---]
Fri. 29th	} Combined Operations *'Rex' Phase VI* continued ---]
Sat. 30th	30 HMT DEVONSHIRE arrived Liverpool with returning Service personnel---]
Sun. 31st	} Combined Operations *'Rex' Phase VI* continued ----]

AUGUST

Mon. 1st	Operation *"Rex' Phase VI"* began deploying 130 Gurkhas by Malayan Navy motor launch further up the Penggarang Peninsular same operational instructions against the CT's. & withdrew 30 troops ---]
Tue. 2nd	**2 L/Cpl. A.W. Fleming.** 1st. Battn. Royal Scots Fusilliers Died****Taiping # E / 49* Perak---]
+	2 HMT DILWARA sailed from Singapore bound Southampton. with returning Service personnel---]
Wed. 3rd	HMS *'COMMUS'* Combined Operations 'Rex' *Phase IV* Began shelling inland areas of Penggarang ---]
Thur. 4th	HMS *'COMMUS'* Combined Operations 'Rex' *Phase IV* Completed shelling inland areas of Penggarang Firing 160. 4.5 inch shells---]
+	4 HMT EMPIRE FOWEY arrived Southampton. with returning Service personnel---]
Fri. 5th	**5 PC. Ishak B. Din.** F. M. Police Killed on CT Ops. Perak.---]
Sat. 6th	**6 Pte. B. Malia.** 3rd. King's African Rifles Rifles Died*** *Kuala Lumpur # RC / A - 11* ---]
+	**6 SC. Hasim B. Abu.** F. M. Police Killed Jerom Padang Bahau Negri Sembilam ---]
Sun. 7th	**7** 2 F. M. Police **SC's. Atan. B. Panjang Ismalam. – Masman B. Sukeimei.** Killed on CT Ops.Johore.---]
Mon. 8th	**8 Rfn. Narbahadur Limbu.** 10th. Princess Mary's Own Gurkha Rifles Died*** *Kranji Singapore # 7 / A -5* -]
Tue. 9th	**9 SC Abdullah B. Ismail.** F. M. Police Killed on CT Ops. Kulim area Kedah.---]
+	'C' Company 10th . Princess Mary's Own Gurkha Rifles, engaged & Killed 1 CT in the area of Landang Gegges---]
Wed. 10th	**10 Pte. J.R. Ainsley.** 1st. Battn. Royal Hampshire Regt. Died*** *Kuala Lumpur # 22 / 1167*---]
Thur. 11th	**11 Dvr. E. Halliwell.** Royal Signals Killed in Action Engaging CT's *Kuala Lumpur # 22 / 1170* --]
+	**11 Pte. F. Salweko.** Northern Rhodesian Regt. Killed in Action Engaging CT's *Kuala Lumpur # 18 /* 1036 ---]
+	**11 Capt. M.A. Wright.** The Devonshire Regt. Died*** *Kuala Lumpur- # 22 - 1168*---]
+	**11 Rfn's. Birbahadur Gurung. - Indrabagadur Newar. - Jahasing Thapa.-** Killed in Action Engaging CT's . **Pahalsing Thapa.** (Died from Wounds recv'd). 2nd. King Edward VII's's Own Gurkha Rifles Killed in ambush. Near Sungei Basi. *Kuala Lumpur # 27 / 10 - 8 - 6 – 28 – 1* ---]
+	HMS *'COSSACK'* Bombarded an area of deep jungle where CT's were known to be hiding Firing 180 4.5 inch HE shells ---]

Fri. 12th	**12 PC. Tan B. Buyong.** F. M. Police Killed on CT Ops. Pahang ---]	
+	**12 HMT EMPIRE CLYDE** arrived Singapore with replacement Service personnel The 1st Battn. Royal Lincolnshire Regt. Destination Bentong West Pahang---]	
+	**12 HMT ASTURIUS** arrived Southampton with returning Service personnl---]	
Sat. 13th	**13 L/Cpl. R.J. Malsom.** R.A.S.C. Killed accidental bomb explosion at Seremban *Kuala Lumpur # 22 / 1169*]	
+	**13 L/Cpl. Satalsing. Gurung** 6th. Queen Elizabeth's Own Gurkha Rifles. Killed in Action near Batu Gelanggand *Seremban # 66* Negri Sembilan---]	
+	**13HMT EMPIRE CLYDE** sailed Singapore enroute Hong Kong ---]	
Sun. 14th	**14** During a night time bombing attack by a Canberra bomber the intended target North of the Landan Geddes Estate was missed, resulting in 1 British officer 4 Pte.'s *(unnamed)* 1 Gurkha Rifleman Killed **Siridhoj Rai.** *Kranji Singapore ???* 2 British Pte.'s & 1 Gurkha wounded.---]	
Mon. 15th	Operation *'Rex'* Phase VI Malayan Navy M/L redeployed 30 Soldiers further along the Penggarang Shore	
Tue. 16th	**16 L/Cpl. D.J. Catleugh** Royal Welch Fusilies Died*** *Kuala Lumpur # 22 / 1171*---]	
+	16/081955 LG # 40562 p. 4694 The following awarded the Coloniial Police Medal PC. MOKHTAR B. JAAFAR. CPM FEDERATION MALAYA POLICE	
+	16/08/1955 LG # 40563 p.4739 The following awarded the Military Medal PTE. P.P. OCALLAGHAN. MM ROYAL HAMPSHIRE REGIMENT.	
Wed. 17th	**17 HMT DUNERA** arrived Singapore enroute to Southampton sailed with returning Service personnel17th.]	
Thur. 18th	9 Platoon 'C' Company 10th. Gurkhas. Killed a CT who was identified as Min Yuen Courier **Ng Ki.** the kill was recorded as the 300th. to the 10th Princess Mary's Own Gurkha Rifles---]	
+	Operation *'Rex'* Phase VI Malayan Navy M/L withdrew 30 Troops from the shore of Penggarang ---]	
+	HMS *'NEWFOUNDLAND'* Operation *'Rex'* Phase VI Began shelling inland areas of Penggerang ---]	
Fri. 19th	**19 Pte. C. Charnock.** R.E.M.E. Died*** *Kuala Lumpur # 2 / E - 2* ---]	
+	HMS *'NEWFOUNDLAND'* Operation *'Rex'* Phase VI Completed shelling inland areas of Penggerang Firing 150 7inch shells ---]	
+	**19 HMT EMPIRE FOWEY** sailed Southampton enroute to Singapore/ Hong Kong.-with replacement Service personnel-----]	
Sat. 20th	**20 SC. Zalani B. Pajang Ismalan.** F. M. Police Killed Kuala Kangsar area Perak.---]	
Sun. 21st	**21 Lt.Col. G. Ford.(MBE)** Staff & General List. Died***Kuala Lumpur 18 / 1038 ---]	
Mon.22nd	**22 HMT EMPIRE ORWELL** arrived Singapore with replacement Service personnel enroute to Hong Kong / /Kure 22nd.---]	
Tue. 23rd	**23 SC. Mohd. Yassin B. Bashik.** F. M. Police Killed on CT Ops.Kluang Area Johore.---]	
Wed. 24th	**24 Spr.Birsuba Gurung.** Gurkha Engineers. Died Motor Veh. Acc.BMH *Kluang # 3 / B -6.*Johore---]	
+	**24 HMT DEVONSHIRE** sailed Liverpool bound for Singapore with replacement Service personnel on Board were the 1st Battn. Kings Own Scottish Borderers ???---]	
Thur. 25th	**25 L/Cpl. A.C.H. Farrance.** 1st. Battn. Somerset Light Inf. Died*** *Kuala Lumpur # 18 / 1027*---]	
+	**25 SC. Aman B. Ali.** F. M. Police Killed on CT Ops. Kepong Selangor---]	
+	**25 HMT LANCASHIRE** sailed Liverpool for Singapore with replacement Service personnel ---] [**Authors note:** This was the Troopshire Myself and 5 REME Mates sailed for a Sunshine Holiday in Singapore?? Read my Book '**UP TO THEIR NECKS'** Chapter Thirteen. Relates to our passage out to Singapore & other destinations---]	
Fri. 26th	**26 Rfn. Dhanraj Gurung.** 6th. Queen Elishabeth's Own Gurkha Rifles Died *** *Kranji Singapore # 7 / A - 6* --] + The Deputy General Secretary of the CT *Yeung Kuo.* was Killed by Security Forces---]	
Sat. 27th	**27 Rfn. Tulbahadur. Gurung.** 2nd King Edward VII's Own Gurkha Rifles. Died***Kranji Singapore # 7 / A – 4]	
Sun. 28th	**28 HMT EMPIRE CLYDE** arrived Singapore with replacement Service personnel---]	
Mon. 29th	**29 HMT EMPIRE CLYDE** sailed Singapore bound for Liverpool with returning Service personnel--]	
Tue. 30t	**30 HMT DILWARA** arrived Southampton with returning Service personnel ---]	
Wed. 31st	Operation *''Rex Phase III'* Ended with no contacts.---]	
+	Operation "Rex Phase V" Began a civilian part of the operation to search all Civilians in the Pengarang Peninsular---]	
+	Operation *'Shark'* Ended ---]	

SEPTEMBER

Thur. 1st	Kuala Lumpur: During SEPTEMBER the air offensive under the code name Operations 'Shark'; 'Latimer North & Latimer South ' Began in the areas of Sungei Siput, Perak; Temerloh, Triang & South Pahang---]

Fri.	2nd	2 3 Malay Regt. Soldiers were Killed in Action Engaging CT's during an ambush. **Cpl. Othman b. Abdullah-Pte's Dimin b. Mat - Osman b. Ngah Ahmad.** Perak---]
Sat.	3rd	3 HMT ASTURIUS sailed Southampton bound for Singapore/ Hong Kong with replacement Service personnel] Combined Operations *"Rex Phase 'V'* continued---]
Sun.	4th	Operation *"Rex Phase 'V'* Ended---]
Mon.	5th	**5 Cpl.G. J. Boreham.** 1st. Battn. The East Yorkshire Regt. Killed in .Action Engaging CT's.[*Ashes REP*]
Tue.	6th	**6 Mr. T.G. Devonshire.** British Civilian Killed. Shot in the face. Kluang Johore.---]
Wed.	7th	Kuala Lumpur: The High Commissioner Sir. Donald MacGillivray. broadcast the terms of the amnesty which were as follows: -
		'Terrorists who surrendered would be given a free pardon for crimes committed under Communist direction before, or in ignorance of the amnesty offer.
		Terrorist could surrender to whom they wished, including members of the public.
		Although there would be no general cease – fire, the Security Forces would be on the 'ALERT' to help those who accepted the offer, & local cease-fires would be arranged for this purpose.
		The Government would conduct and investigate into those who surrendered. Individuals who showed that they genuinely intended to be Loyal Citizens, & to give up Communist Activities, would be helped to gain a normal position in society & would be reunited with their families. As regards other persons restriction would be placed on their liberty, but if they wished to be sent to China? Their requests would be given consideration. Terrorist could surrender in any of the 186 designated "safe "area, which no troops would be present. (The designated areas included street checks of road, railway- lines, Rubber Estates, Tin Mines, vegetables gardens, temples etc.) There would be no Time limit to the amnesty, the termination depending on the progress made---].
Thur.	8th	Immediately after the High Commissioner's Broadcast 20,000,000 leaflets were dropped by air over suspected Communists hide-outs in the jungles. Also, millions more were handed out to all local inhabitants to ensure that news did each the C.T.'s. An embargo was placed on air offensive, until a later date. to see what the outcome of the amnesty gave. However, the response was not encouraging. By the end of November only 80 in number surrender of the estimated 3,000 plus still in the jungle.---]
Fri.	9th.	Combinded Operation *'Nassau'* ended with Land forces firing 5,835 4.5 inch Mortars, 25,248 3 inch mortars 127,000 rds of .303 being expended by 10 Separate Regiments mortar Platoons. 55,885 :25 pound shells & 1,595 5.5 inch shells fired by the Royal Artillery Field Regt.s. ---]
Sat.	10th	**10 Rfn. Aspur Gurung.** 6th. Queen Elizabeth's Own Gurkha Rifles Died in BMH Kamunting. *Sulva Lines # 57* Ipoh Perak.---]
Sun.	11th	11 HMT EMPIRE FOWEY arrived Singapore enroute to /Hong Kong with replacement Service personnel sailed 11th.---]
Mon.	12th	**12 Pte. J. H. Kirby.** 1st. Battn. Cheshire Regiment. Died***[*Ashes REP*] ---]
	+	1st. Battn. Lincolnshire Regt. arrived in Bentong and took over from the 1st Battn. Somerset Light Inf.---]
	+	12 HMT NEW AUSTRALIA arrived Penang enroute to Southampton with returning Service personnel---]
Tue.	13th	**13 PC. Suboh. B. Mohd. Yussof.** F. M. Police Killed on CT Ops. Kota Tinggi. Johore---]
Wed.	14th	} Combined Operations continued throughout Malaya---]
Thur.	15th	15 HMT DUNERA arrived Southampton with returning Service personnel---]
Fri.	16th	} Combined Operations continued throughout Malaya---]
Sat.	17th	**17 Pte. P. M. Fenelon.** Q.A.R.A.N.C. Died***. *Taiping # B/ 65* .Perak ---]
Sun.	18th	} Combined Operations continued throughout Malaya---]
Mon.	19th	**19 SQMS W.A, Curd.** Royal Signals Died ***. *Kranji Singapore # 18 /1026*---]
	+	**19 W/OPC. M. Peterson.** Northern Rhodesia Regt. Killed in Action Engaging CT's *Kuala Lumpur # 22 / 1172]*
Tue.	20th	} Combined Operations continued throughout Malaya---]
Wed.	21st	21 HMT DILWARA sailed Southampton with replacement Service personnel. On Board were the 1st. Battn. South Wales Borderers ---]
Thur.	22nd	Combined Operations continued throughout Malaya---]
Fri.	23rd	23 HMT EMPIRE CLYDE arrived Liverpool with returning Service personnel---]
	+	23 HMT DEVONSHIRE arrived Singapore with replacement Service pearsonnel---]
	+	23 HMT LANCASHIRE arrived Singapore with replacement Service personnel. Disembarking with other R.E.M.E. troops was The Author Cfn. Plant.---]
Sat.	24th	"D" Coy of the Royal Lincolnshire Regt. captured CT. Party Official. *Phui Wak* & his bodyguard in the area of West Pahang.---]
Sun.	25th	Kuala Lumpur.: It was announced :-

+	'Letters had been received by Tenku Abdul Rahman & other members of the Malayan Government stating theSecretary of the Malayan Communist party **Chin Peng** was willing to send an emissary to negotiate with the Government, on the restoration of peace in Malaya. The letters were dated 24th. SEPT & post marked Kilian Intan a few miles from the Malay Thailand Border.'---]
+	RAN Ships *'ANZAC' 'QUADRANT' & 'TOBRUK'* having completed their tour of duty were replaced by ---] RAR ship *'WARRAMUNGA'* to commence her tour of duty. RNZN *'KANIERE'*. completed her first support
Mon. 26th	role of duty in Malayan coastal waters---]
Tue. 27th	} Combined Operations continued throughout Malaya---]
Wed. 28th	}
+	28 HMT DEVONSHIRE sailed Singapore enroute to Liverpool with returning Service personnel onboard were the 1st Battn. Somerset Light Inf. Having completed their tour of Active Service in Malaya ---]
	28 HMT LANCASHIRE sailed Singapore bound for Liverpool via African Ports with returning Service
Thur. 29th	personnel---]
	29 Rfn. Dalbahadur Limbu . 7th. Duke of Edinburgh's Own Gurkha Rifles. Died ***at Segamat
+	*Kluang Gurkha Cem # 3 / E – 8* Johore---]
Fri. 30th	29 HMT EMPIRE ORWELL arrived Southampton with returning Service personnel---]
	} Combined Operations continued throughout Malaya---]

OCTOBER

Sat. 1st	**1 Dvr. J. Humpherson**. R.A.S.C.. Died***[*Ashes REP*]----]	
+	**1Brig. H.A. Skone**. CBE. DSO. HQ Kuala Lumpur Garrison Died*** *Kuala Lumpur # 22 / 1173r*---]	
+	Operation 'Subsidiary OP' (South Johore) Began SAS against the MRLA---]	
Sun. 2nd	2 HMT EMPIRE FOWEY arrived Singapore with replacement Service personnel ---]	
+	2 HMT EMPIRE FOWEY sailed Singapore bound for Southampton with returning Service personnel---]	
Mon. 3rd	} Combined Operations continued throughout Malaya---]	
Tue. 4th	4 HMT NEW AUSTRALIA arrived Southampton with returning Service personnel---]	
Wed. 5th	} Combined Operations continued throughout Malaya---]	
Thur. 6th	}	
Fri. 7th	}	
Sat. 8th	} Combined Operations continued throughout Malaya---]	
Sun. 9th	**9 Pte. N. C. Pedley**. R.A.O.C.. Died***[*Ashes REP*]---]	
Mon. 10th	'D' Company 2nd. 10th. Gurkhas .Located 3 CT's working on a cultivation plot 1 was kiiled the other 2 were wounded but escaped---]	
Tue. 11th	11/10/1955. LG. 40603 p. 5693	The following awarded the Distinguished Flying Cross
	S/LDR. B.V. KERWIN. DFC	ROYAL AIR FORCE
	S/LDR. S. J. RAWLINGS. DFC	ROYAL AIR FORCE.
	S/LDR. M.E.J. HICKMOTT. DFC.	ROYAL AIR FORCE
	F/O. C.J. CALVERT. DFC	ROYAL AIR FORCE
	F/O. P. GRAY. DFC	ROYAL AIR FORCE
	CAPT. D. W. SMITH. DFC	ROYAL REGIMENT ARTILLERY
+	11/10/1955. LG. # 40604 p. 5074	The following awarded the Distinguished Flying Cross
	F/O. J. SHERBURN. DFC.	ROYAL AIR FORCE
		The following awarded the Distinguished Flying Medal
	F/SGT. J.F.E. ERASMUS.DFM	ROYAL AIR FORCE
+	11/10/1955 LG # 40605 p. 5714	The following awarded the Distinguished Flying Cross
	LT/COM. M.W. WORTHERSPOON	ROYAL NAVY 848 SQDN
+	11 HMT DUNERA sailed Southampton bound for Singapore / Hong Kong-with replacement Service personnel]	
Wed. 12th	3 CT's Surrendered to Support Company 2nd. 10th.Princess Mary's Own Gurkha Rifles in the Ulu Timram area---]	
Thur. 13th	**13 Capt. J. M. B. Davies. Fus.J. Evans**. 2nd. Battn. Royal Welsh Fusiliers.Killed .*Kuala Lumpur # 22 / 1174 – 1176* **Pte. D. J. Durham**. R.A.P.C. Att/Royal Welsh Fusiliers *Kuala Lumpur # 22 / 1178* Killed in ambush near Seremban whilst delivering pay. After they were Killed. The CT ambush squad, poured petrol on their bodies & set them alight. ---]	
+	Support Company 2nd. 10th. . Princess Mary's Own Gurkha Rifles Killed 1 CT wounded 2 others ---]	
Fri. 14th	14/10/1955 LG #40607 p. 5773	The following awarded the Colonilal Police Medal

228

	S/SGT. SIDEK . B. NORDIN . CPM. FEDERATION MALAYA POLICE
+	'D' Company 2nd. 10th. . Princess Mary's Own Gurkha Rifles Killed 1 CT in deep jungle---]
+	A preliminary meeting took place at Kelian Intan between 2 representavies for the Government Mr.S. Wylie, Dept. Police Commissioner & Mr. Too Joon Hing Asstn. Minister for Education. & *Chin Peng* accompanied by a guide. This was the first time *Chin Peng* had been seen in 7 years & Mr. Wylie who was personally acquainted with *Chin Peng* though the war time years of 1942 – 45. After the meeting the Government representatives flew back to Kuala Lumpur. ---]
+	A Rubber Tapper was murdered by approx 10 C.T.'s in a district? in Pahang. ---]
Sat. 15th	15 HMT EMPIRE ORWELL sailed Southampton bound for Singapore /Hong Kong /Kure with replacement Service personnel ---]
Sun. 16th	16 Fus.J. Gibson. 1st. Battn. Royal Scots Fusiliers. Died*** *[Ashes REP]*---]
Mon. 17th	17 Pte. Abu Hassan b. Abdul Rahman. Malay Regt. Killed in Action Engaging CT's Kedah---]
+	A road Patrol of the 11th. Hussars operating on the Kuala Pilah / Serting road. Killed 1 CT & captured another.---]
Tue. 18th	} Combined Operations continued throughout Malaya ---]
Wed. 19th	19 HMT GEORGIC arrived at Penang Island with the 2nd. Battn. Royal Australian Regt.---]
+	Mr. C.G. Stanley the Manager. of a Rubber Plantation was seriously wounded when C.T.'s attacked the Plantation near Labis in Johore.---]
+	19 HMT DILWARA arrived Singapore with replacement Service personnel on board were the 1st. Battn. South Wales Borderers ---]
Thur. 20th	20 Cfn. Latip. Bin. Jaapar. R. E. M. E. (MOR) Died*** *Claimed by next of Kin* ---]
+	2nd/10th. Gurkha's Mortor Platoon captured a Women CT who had medical items on her person, indicating she was looking after another wounded CT.---]
Fri. 21st	21 Rfn. Jhgarbahadur Rai . 1st./10th. Princess Mary's Own Gurkha Rifles accidentally Killed in the Bahru area of Negri Sembilan *Kuala Lumpur # 27 / 9* ---]
+	21 HMT ASTURIUS sailed Southampton bound for Singapore / Hong Kong with replacement Service personnel 21 ---]
Sat. 22nd	22 Lt/Col. J. D. Cruikshank. R. A. M. C. Died*** { *Ashes REP]* ---]
Sun. 23rd	23 PC. Udin B. Salleh. F. M. Police Killed on Ops. Perak.---]
+	A wounded Women CT gave herself up to a Pln. of the 2nd./10th. . Princess Mary's Own Gurkha Rifles . She was the one who had been looked after by the woman CT captured on the 21st.---]
Mon. 24th	24 Pte. E. P. Leather. R. A. O. C. Died***. *Kranji Singapore # 2 / B – 3* ---]
+	24 HMT EMPIRE FOWEY arrived Southampton with replacement Service personnel---]
+	24 HMT DILWARA sailed Singapore bound for Southampton via Mombassa with returning Service personnel---]
Tue. 25th	25 /10/1955 LG # 40613 p 5966 The following awarded the British Empire Medal (Military)
	W/O. O BETHAM. BEM FIJI REGT.
	SGT. P. R. JERRARD. BEM ROYAL ARMY SERVICE CORPS
	S/SGT. P. R. JOHNSTON. BEM ROYAL CORPS SIGNALS
	CPL. O. R. LEVET. BEM LIFE GUARDS A/T 22nd.SAS
	SGT. J. SAUL. BEM MIDDLESEX REGIMENTT. A/T. 22nd SAS.
	The following awarded the Military Cross
	MAJ. P. HAIG. MC THE SOMERSET LIGHT INF.
	MAJ. M.A. LOWRY MC QUEEN'S ROYAL WEST SURREYS
	LT. D.G.H ANREWS MC ROYAL SCOTS FUSILIERS
	The following awarded BAR to the Military Medal
	SGT. L. LIMBU MM+BAR 10th PRINCESS MARY'S OWN GURKHA RIGLES
	The following awarded the Military Medal
	CPL. D.I. CLEMENTS MM THE SOMERSET LIGHT INF
	PTE. F.G. DAVIS MM THE SOMERSET LIGHT INF.
	RFN. D.RANA. MM 2nd. King Edward VII's Own GURKHA RIFLES
	L/CPL. B. RAI MM 7th. Duke Of Edinburgh's Own GURKHA RIFLES
	CPL. C. CAKAU. MM FIJI REGIMENT.
	L/CPL. S. JAMANI MM NORTHERN RHODESIAN REGIMENT.
Wed. 26th	} Combined Operations continued throughout Malaya---]
Thur. 27th	27 Pte. D. P. Seaton. 1st. Battn. King's Own Scottish Borderers. Died***[Ashes REP]---]
+	27 HMT DEVONSHIRE arrived Liverpool with returning Service personnel disembarking were the

	1st. Battn. Somerset Light Inf. ---]
Fri. 28th	Kuala Lumpur: The Federation Government announced:- ' 'A large area of 8,464 sq. miles of Central Pahang had been declared 'WHITE'. It also stated that the CT strength had reduced from 8,000 in 1951 to its present strength of approx 3,000 indicating that their Organisation had been largely disrupted & the decimation of No. 6 Regiment MRLA. & its supporting Min Yuen cell. This had been the direct result of intensive 'Food Denial ' operations under the code names in various areas of Pahang 'Rooster ' in the area of Kuala Lipis; 'Huntsman' in the area of Ruab; 'Latimer North"- "Latimer South" & "ASP.' in the areas of Temerloh & Triang.---]
Sat. 29th	**29 Rfn. G. Narbahadur Gurung.** 6th. Queen Elizabeth's Own Gurkha Rifles. Died in BMH Kinrara. _Seremban # 74_ Negri Sembilan---].
Sun. 30th	**30 Sgt. G. Hayes.** Sup 2. FETW 6 R. A F. Kranji Singapore Died in Road traffic accident _Kranji_ _Singapore # 12 / A – 1_ ---]
+	**30 Cpl. J. Kellet.** M/T/F R. A. F. Changi Died *** _Kranji Singapore #.3 / A – 5_ ---]
Mon. 31st	**Dvr. Ahmad Bin Sir.at** R. A. S.C (MOR) ** _Claimed by next of Kin_ ---] Operation 'Subsidiary OP'(South Johore) Ended---]

[**Authors Note**] The following is a transcript of an article which appeared in the <u>News of the World</u> in London written by one of their reporters under the title

Quote: **THE FORGOTTEN MEN**

THIS IS WORSE THAN BURMA.

By A. Noyes Thomas who is on a flying visit to British Garrisons overseas

I have just travelled by night through the jungle area of Kluang in Central Johore, where British army and Security Forcesare beginning the biggest operation of the entire seven-year Campaign in Malaya. What I have seen and learned of the conditions in which these soldiers are operating leaves no doubt that if, the 14th. Army in Burma was the forgotten army of World War II than these jungle fighters of ours, are certainly the forgotten men of 1955.

Theirs is a story of great heartedness, which is little realised in Britain. Yet it is one, which I believe, should be known to every man, women and child in the land – and be remembered always with pride. Do not forget these troops the majority of whom are National Servicemen, fighting this lonely battle cheerfully in a World supposedly at peace. While they struggle through the undergrowth, wade the swamps, pluck bloodsucking leeches from their sweating bodies, and exchange shots with Communist bandits, their brothers and Friends back home are leading ordinary peaceful lives.

Look for instance at the battle scene as I glimpsed it on my way North. It seemed even darker and more fore bidding than usual, amongst the steamy jungles of South Malaya. Heavy storm clouds hung low and still over the tree tOps. Here and there a searchlight cut suddenly and blindingly through the trees. That was the sign of a 'bad village' where, during the dusk to dawn curfew, guards keep watch to prevent anyone creeping in or out, and to make it impossible for food to be supplied to the Reds. Apart from the searchlights there was no hint of what was going on. There was no sign that five battalions of infantrymen and a squad of jungle paratroopers were plunging relentlessly through almost unbelievably difficult terrain and converging on some 800 of Malaya's toughest terrorists.

The operation is an all-out bid to break up a group which threatens, by continued and, indeed increasing terrorist activity to undo much of the good work which has been done in restoring law and order to many parts of Malaya. When the offer of an amnesty, which still holds well was made to all bandits on 09 SEPTEMBER, about 5,000,000 leaflets were dropped in the Johore area from low flying R. A. F. Aircraft. But these did not produce a single surrender. Instead the jungle toughs of Kluang replied by stepping up their reign of terror on local villages.

Any Chinese or Malayan peasant who refuses to co-operate with the bandits faces death or worse. One man suspected by bandits of being uncooperative was held up while he was cycling along a road with his wife. The bandits politely asked his wife to step aside and while she watched slit her husband's throat. Another man suspected of being a traitor to Communism was visited in his home by bandits. They seated him with his wife and numerous children around the walls of the room. Then they called into the centre of the family circle the eldest son and, while all watched, slowly strangled the boy to death. This sought of thing obviously tended to encourage terrorist elsewhere to launch new attacks. The ambush 100 miles North of Kluang last 'Thursday, in which a British Army Officer and two British soldiers were first Killed, then set on fire, was almost certainly inspired by the way in which Kluang Thur.gs were getting away with murder. But the defiant terrorist of the Southhave failed to consider that, Lieutenant General Sir. Geoffrey Bourne, the director of Operations, is now able to concentrate just as much strength as he believes he needs in any one place.

They have probably been shaken to learn that within the past few days he has been able to send by road, train and helicopter and ordinary plane the 1st Battalions of the Royal Hampshire and Northern Rhodesia Regiments and a squadron of the crack 22nd. Special Air Service Regiment, the brilliantly successful Unit of all volunteers and all Regular jungle paratroopers. Along with the 1st. Battalion of the East York's and the Queen's Royal Regiment, a Battalion of Ghurkha's and strong Police force, all of whom were already on the scene, have plunged into the jungle. No one knows how long it will be before they emerge. Aborigine porters are with them, carrying stores sufficient for many days. More supplies will be dropped by parachute.

This Malayan Jungle is worse than anything in Burma, say many soldiers who have served in both countries. And from that opinion tens of thousands of old Burma hands in Britain may be able to judge in the peace and coolness of Sunday in autumn just what thousands of young Malaya hands are up against out here in the steamy jungle tonight. The astonishing part of it is these youngsters seem actually to enjoy it.

Unquote   *(Within the above transcript It is assumed. The incident referring to the British soldiers ambushed was on Thursday Oct. 13th. as stated above) ---]*

NOVEMBER

Tue. . 1st	1 WOII G. C Yates. Royal Engineers Died*** _Kranji Singapore # 11 / A – 14_ ---]
+	Singapore The New Zealand SAS flew into Changi. As replacements to the Rhodesian SAS Squadrons who had returned to Rohdesia. In preparation to join the other 22 SAS force operationg in deep jungle areas They first task Jungle training and Parachute jumping.---]
Wed. 2nd	2 PC Khalid B. Din. F. M. Police Killed on Ops. Labis Johore.---]
Thur. 3rd	Australia Canberra: The Labour party announced:-
	'If they win the forthcoming Election on the 12th. December. Australian forces with be withdrawn from the Conflict in Malaya' ---]
Fri. 4th	4 A/B P.W.A. Rhodes Royal Navy HMS ''NEWCASTLE' Died*** _Kranji Singapore # ??_---]
+	London The Colonials Chief Minister stated:-
	'Agreement had been reach by all parties that. The way is open for an Independent United Malaya' ---]
+	A Patrol of the Fijian Regt. led by Cpl. A. Kakua MM added 2 more kills to his score 1 Killed was the Bodyguard to a CT District Committee Leader He was Identified as _Lee Swee_, the other Killed was a CT woman identified as _Hong Moi_.---]
Sat. 5th	5 Pte Mohd Sabu b. Mohd. Yusof. Royal Malay Regt. Killed in Action Engaging CT's Selangor---]
Sun. 6th	Johore Bahru 2 Rubber Tappers **Wong Yuen Kee & Low Chong.** were sentenced to 3 years & the Lstter to 4 years for supplying food to the CT's---]
Mon. 7th	A Patrol of the 10th. Gurkhas Killed a CT in the Bahau district of Negri Sembilan Identified as **Ko Fatt** a CT who had been in the jungle since 1948---]
Tue. 8th	Kuala Lumpur : The formation of the **28th. Commonwealth Independent Infantry Brigade** Group came into force in Malaya. It comprised of the following Regiments, Corps & Support units under the control of 28th Brigade HQ Butterworth Perak.....
	1st. Royal Lincolns Fusiliers- 1st. Royal Scots Fusiliers - 2nd. Royal Australian Regiment- 105 Field Battery Royal Australian Artillery.- 11 Indep. Field Sqdr. Royal Engineers – 3 Coy R.A.S.C. IPOH. The HQ Royal Australian Army Service Corps - The attached. 3 Coy R.E.M.E. LAD. - 16 Field Amb. Royal Australian Medical Corps.- 103 Australian Army Dental Corps.- 2 Inf. Wksp. R.E.M.E.Taiping – Australian Provost Group.- 257 Field Pay Cash Office- 368 Postal Unit. Designated Places: Penang, - Butterworth, Ipoh, Taiping, Sungei Besi, Kuala Lumpur. ---]
+	8 HMT DUNERA arrived Singapore with replacement Service personnel.Sailed for Hong Kong 8th.---]
+	8 HMT EMPIRE ORWELL arrived Singapore with replacement Service personnel enroute to Hong Kong / Kure. ---]
Wed. 9th	9 Rfn. Ganeshabahdur. Rai.10th.Princess Mary's Own Gurkha Rifles. Killed in Action Engaging CT's.Dang Geddes Camp. _Kuala Lumpur # 28 / 5_ ---]
+	9 PC. Meor Saidin B. Meor Ahmad. F. M. Police Killed on CT Ops. Perak---]
Thur. 10th	10 Cpl. D. Booth. Royal Corps Signals Died***_Kuala Lumpur # 22 / 175_ .---]
Fri. 11th	11 Capt. M. A. Wright. 1st. Battn. Devonshire Regt. Died***_Kuala Lumpur # 22 /1168_---]
+	11 Boy. Purnabahadur Pun. Depot the Brigade of Gurkhas Died at BMH Kamuntan _Sungei Patani # 115_ Kedah---]
+	11 Cfn. Hussein. Bin. Duras. R. E. M. E. (MOR) Died*** _Claimed by next of Kin_---]
+	11 HMT ASTURIUS arrived Singapore enroute to Southampton with returning Servie personnel 11th. ---]
Sat. 12th	

Sun. 13th	**12 Lt.J Bawden** H.M.S. '*SIMBANG*' 848 Sqdn was Killed when his Sykorski S55 helicopter crashed returning from a troop lifting Operation in the Seggamat Area of Johore *Ulu Pandan Cemetery Singapore # 2C / D1*
Mon. 14th	Australia : The UMNO passed a motion: *'To ban Australian Troops entering Malaya.' ---]*
	Kuala Lumpur: In an Interveiw Tenku Abdul Rahman stated.
Tue. 15th	*'He opposed the MCP but If, in the future they were recognised. His Party the Alliance would certainly win.'---]*
+	The new Crew of HMS "*NEWCASTLE*" landed at Changi airport, they were first Royal Navy Crew to be flown to their ship---]
Wed. 16th	In the Rengam area of Johore.Mr. J. Hall. & Mr. E. King were seriously wounded when C.T.'s attacked the Rubber Estate ---]
Thur. 17th	**16 Dvr.'s. Ismail Bin Ishak.- Ab Manap Bn Saringat.** R. A. S. C. (MOR) Killed on Ops. *Claimed by next of Kin---]*
	17 A second meeting took place in Kelian Intan between Mr. I. S.Wylie & Mr. Too. Federation Representatives & **Chen Tian**. MRLA. To further discuss the possibility of an amnesty. **Chin Peng** was not present, but replaced by his representative **Chen Tian**. The meeting did not resolve the point & was concluded with notice of a further meeting time & date set for 20th. However Ministers in several War Cabinets were sceptical about **Chin Peng's** intentions . Nevertheless Tengku Abdul Rahman said: *'**Chin Peng's** Proposal of an International Commission was nonsense & would never recognise the Malayan Communist Party. Suggested that a meeting should take place. He was 'not going to negotiate or treat with **Chin Peng** as an equal.' The meeting would not take place in Kuala Lumpur but at another venue, to be*
Fri. 18th	*agreed.'---]*
+	**18 Sgt. P. Talogo.** 1st. Battn. Fijian Infantry Regt. Killed in Action Engaging CT's [*Ashes REP*]---]
Sat. 19th	18 HMT DUNERA arrived Singapore.with replacenet Service personnel enroute to Hong Kong 18th.---]
	Baling A 2nd.meeting was resumed. In attendance was Mr. Wylie, Mr. Too & **Chen Tian**. MRLA representative. Once again it resulting in no conclusion except, that of a further meeting should be held in Kuala Lumpur, Between Tengku Abdul Rahman, Mr. Marshall Chief Minister of Singapore. **Chin Peng** MRLA Demanding the security of himself & his emissaries to be guaranteed & an International Committee be set up
+	to discuss any further. 'Peace talks' Also the Governments terms of amnesty to be 'more liberal'---]
	On the same day. Over 100 C.T. has attacked the New village of Kea Farm in the Cameron Highlands. Killing F.M. Police **PC. Omar. B. Mohd**, & seriously wounding **PC Ahmad B. Salmon**. who died the following day.
Sun. 20th	They also murdered a villager before escaping with a number of weapons & many rounds of ammunition--]. Due to the failure of the CT's to observe a potential cease fire . The restriction imposed on the Security
Mon. 21st	Forces since the 9th. SEPTEMBER were lifted. ---]
	21 HMT EMPIRE FOWEY sailed Southampton bound for Singapore/ /Hong Kong with replacement Service
+	personnel---]
Tue. 22nd	21 HMT DEVONSHIRE sailed Liverpool bound for Singapore with replacement Service personnel---]
Wed. 23rd	**22 Pte J. A. Marshall**. Royal Lincolnshire Regt. Died***. *Kuala Lumpur # 22- 1177--*]
Thur. 24th	23 HMT DUNERA arrived Singapore ---]
Fri. 25th	24 HMT DUNERA sailed Singapore bound for Southampton with returning Service personnel---]
	With the latest attack by the CT.'s on the New Village of Kea. The air offensive resumed under the previous stated code names. Canberras of 12 Sqdn. from Butterworth bombed CT camps in the Taiping
Sat. 26th	Area---]
	A CT Platoon Commander surrenderd with 7 of his Platoon. They gave themselves up in the Brapit New
Sun. 27th	Village near Bukit Mertajam.---]
	Kuala Lumpur :Tenku Abdul Rahman made a statement: *'The Alliance party meeting to take place in London in January will be. Name the day for Malaya's*
Mon. 28th	*Independence'---]*
	Acting on information that two senior members of the Johore Secretariat. **Yang Kwo**. Vice Secretary General & **Ah Ho**. State Committee Secretary were in a CT hill camp located South West of Simpang Pertang New village Negri Sembilan. Operation *"Saturation"* was mounted. Involving Air Strikes & grounds Troops from 5
Tue. 29th	British & Gurkha Battalions attempted to seal off the area---]
	29/11/1955 LG # 40644 p. 6731 The following awarded the British Empire Medal (Military) F/SGT. V. MAC. TURNBULL ROYAL AUSTRALIAN AIR FORCE. <div align="center">The following awarded the George Medal</div>
+	INSP. T.S. SAMBAN THAMBURTHI T.S. GM FEDERATION MALAYA POLICE
Wed. 30th	29 HMT EMPIRE ORWELL arrived / sailed Bound for Southampton with returning Service personnel---]

	+	Operation *"Cobble Shoe " "Lagoon"* ended.---]
		30 HMT EMPIRE CLYDE sailed from Liverpool bound for Singapore / Hong Kong with replacement Service personnel---]

DECEMBER

Thur.	1st	Kuala Lumpur: General Bourne announced:-
		'Full Scale Operation would return after the recent attack by the Communists Terrorists on the New Village in the Cameron Highlands.'---]
	+	Operation *'Saturation'* began against the Perpetrators---]
	+	1 HMT DILWARA arrived Southampton with returning Service personnel---]
Fri.	2nd	RAN Ship *'ANZAC'* returned on Station. To commence her 2nd tour of duty.---]
	+	2 HMT ASTURIUS arrived Southampton with returning Service personnel---] .
Sat.	3rd	A Patrol of the 11th. Hussars captured a CT ---]
	+	RAN Ships *'ARUNTA'* & *'WARRAMUNGA'* Having completed their tour of duty left Malayan coastal waters.--]
Sun.	4th	**4 Rfn. Mitrabahadur Rana.** 6th. Queen Elizabeth's Own Gurkha Rifles. Died***
		Seremban # 76 Negri Sembilan---]
Mon.	5th	Kuala Lumpur: Mr. A,P.H. Humphreys stated:-
		'The MCP has a Lunatic "Core" which makes it necessary for the Malayan Federation Police to maintain its vast numbers of Police'. ---]
Tue.	6th	**6 L/Cpl. D. G. Rowlands** 2nd. Battn. . Royal Welsh Fusiliers. Died***_Kuala Lumpur # 22 / 1179_.---]
Wed.	7th	**7 Pte. Anak Ujon Unggat.** Sarawak Rangers. Att/22nd. S. A. S Killed in Action Engaging CT's.
		Batu Gajah # 547 Ipoh Perak ---]
Thur.	8th	8 Province Wellesley was declared 'White' The area covers 59 square miles--]
	+	A Starving CT gave himself up to a Rubber Tapper at Sungei Seyang Regam named as **Tan Chew Gee.** Security forces are searching for 4 other CT's who had been tied up to prevent them from surrendering---]
Fri.	9th	**9 PC. Abdul Gahni.** F. M. Police Killed on Ops. Kuantan/ Maran Rd. Pahang.---]
Sat.	10th	**10 LAC. W. G. Woodward.** Eng/Mech (Turb) 60 Sqdr. R. A. F. Tanga Died***._[Ashes REP]_---]
Sun.	11th	} Combined Operations continued throughout Malaya---]
Mon.	12th	Operation *'Saturation'* ended after a period of 10 days, R.A.F. Lincolns & Canberra's had made repeated bombing raids. Dropping 752: 1,000 lb bombs into the area of Bukit Mertajam The operation resulted in no finds---]
Tue.	13th	During an ambush in the Ulu Langat Kajang Forest Reserve Selangor. The Hampshire Regt. Killed 11 C.T.'s, wounded 1 & captured another. Amongst the identified dead were **Chang Lo** Secretary of the Selangor State Committee the No 1 in Selangor. **Wahab** A District Committee member & **Sarlip** A Group Secretary. the camp was wiped out---]
	+	13/12/1955 LG # 40655 p 7059 The following awarded the British Empire Medal (Military)
		L/CPL K. R. HAW. BEM ROYAL CORPS SIGNALS
		L/CPL. R. WILSON. BEM ROYAL ARMY SERVICE CORPS.
Wed.	14th	14 HMT EMPIRE FOWEY arrived in Singapore enroute to Hong Kong with replacement Service personnel Sailed 14th.---]
Thur.	15th	**15 PC. Bahari B. Amat.** F. M. Police Killed on Ops. Penang.---]
Fri.	16th	**16 Pte. P. J. Masterman.** 1st. Battn. Royal Hampshire Regt. Died***_Kuala Lumpur. # RC A / 12_ ---]
Sat.	17th	13 Children from the Slim School Cameron Highlands. Who have been stranded at Port Swettenham by the floods. To be picked up by H.M.S.*'CONSORT'* and taken to Singapore to be reunited with their parents]
Sun.	18th	Top CT in South Malaya **Lau Lee** (alias **Lim Tong – Lau Lim**) was Killed by a Patrol of the F. M. Police Force in the area of Tangkak Johore. He was the right hand man of **Chin Peng**---]
Mon.	19th	} Combined operations continued throughout Malaya ----]
Tue.	20th	20 HMT DEVONSHIRE arrived Singapore with replacement Service personnel---]
	+	20 HMT LANCASHIRE arrived Liverpool with returning Service personnel---]
Wed.	21st	**21 Cpl. H. O.M J. R. De Rohan.** Royal Engineers Died *** _Kranji Singapore # 2 / B – 2_ ---]
	+	21 HMT DUNERA arrived Southampton with returning Service personnel---]
	+	21 HMT EMPIRE ORWELL arrived Southampton with returning Service personnel---]
Thur.	22nd	On a Rubber Estate near Pusing 'B Comp Malay Regt. surprised 3 CT's. All 3 were Killed & identified as **Kong Po, Ng Ngah, & Lap Kong,** all members of the Local Armed Work Force (AWF)---]
Fri.	23rd	Kuala Lumpur: A letter addressed to Tenku Abdul Rahman was received in Kuala Lumpur from the Communist leader **Chin Peng**. Its contents proposed & described an 8 point. " United front programme which stated:

233

	A cessation of hostilities by negotiations;
	The abolishment of the Emergency Regulation;
	Independence for all Malayan citizens of the political system;
	Guarantees for all Malaya citizens of the "democratic rights" in their
	religious & political beliefs:
	Equality of the sexes;
	Improvement of culture, education, health & welfare;

These were the proposals by the Communist that were to lead to a meeting between the Federation of Malaya and the Communist led MRLA ---]

Sat. 24th Kuala Lumpur: The election of Musa Bin Ahmad a Malayan as chairman of the Central Committee & an Indian named Balan as its vice chairman.---]

+ 24 HMT DEVONSHIRE sailed Singapore bound for Liverpool with returning Service personnel---]

Sun. 25th 25 HMT EMPIRE CLYDE arrived Singapore enroute to Hong Kong 26th.with replacement Service person-]

Mon. 26th 26 Rfn. Purnabahadur Ale. 6th. Queen Elizabeth's Own Gurkha Rifles. Died from wounds received in an ambush Cameron Highlands *Sulva Lines # 56* Ipoh Perak .---]

Tue. 27th 27 SC. Aman B. Ali. F. M. Police. Killed Kepong Selengor.---]

+ Kroh. : John Davis CBE.DSO . having known *Chin Peng* as a friend during the period of time they were both in Force 136. Was to be the escort for *Chin Peng's* Party. To ensure his parties safety throughout the forthcoming talks Also to make sure Reporters were kept well away from the Talks. He arrived in Kroh in preparation for the following day.---]

Wed. 28th Kilan Intan /Baling Road: At about 10'o'clock John Davis CBE DSO was to meet *Chin Peng*.

John's greeted *Chin Peng*. In Cantinese. *'Long time No see.'* Both were delighted to meet once again.

Much to *Chin Peng's* Surprise at this meeting with his old Senior Officer.of days gone by.

They precceeded under heavy ared escorts to the meeting at Baling.

+ Baling The prior arranged meeting of the hostilities in Malaya, took place at a venue accepted by *Chin Peng*, which was 20 miles this side of the Malay / Thailand Border in the town of Baling. Prior to the meeting a cease fire had been ordered to commence on the on the 22nd. December, covering an area of 400 square miles around Baling. The two parties taking part in the talks for the Federation Government were:

Tengku Abdul Rahman, Mr. David Marshall & Sir. Cheng Lock Tan : -

For the Communist –*Chin Peng, Abdul Rashid bin Malden & Chen Tian*.

The talks began at 2:30 Opened with Tengku Abdul Rahman emphasising that: *He & Mr. Marshall were the elected Leaders to conduct the talks.*

The Communists Leaders recognised that fact & asked:

'For recognition of the Malayan Communist Party. If, they ceased hostilities?'

This was not accepted by Tengku Abdul Rahman who insisted that:

'The Malayan Comunist Party be dissolved & that they become loyal to the Federation. & the conditions as laid down previously'---]

The Communist:

'Did not except the "loyalty" clause & declare they would rather continue the struggle.'

Thur. 29th 29 Sgt. E. E. Preddice. 11th. Royal Hussars Died *** [*Ashes REP*]---]

+ Bailing: The Talks broke down at1.o'clock. Tenku Abdul Rahman concluded: on the fact that:

'The amnesty which had been offered to the Communist in SEPTEMBER would cease on February the 8th 1956. Furthermore the war against them would be intensified adding that he had no intention of meeting the Communist leader again, unless the Communist indicate before hand their deSir.e to see me, in order to make a full & complete surrender.' Tengku Abdul Rahman stated:

'The Malaysian people were 'sick & tired' of the state of the emergency but that the Communist leaders had turned down the Governments offer to end the struggle. The war must be intensified. I will not give in & betray the Malayan People. So the Malayan Communist Party must' ---]

Fri. 30th Kilan/Intan/ Baling road. John Davis CBE DSO and *Chin Peng* with hs party parted company .Davis's job done.--]

Sat. 31st Kuala Lumpur: Tenku Abdul Rahman before his departure to London. Revealed his secret fear:

'Chin Peng will go on fighting to the last Man' ---]

R. A. F. OPERATION *"FIREDOG"* END OF YEAR STATISTICS 1955

No of Sorties	No. of Strikes	1,000 Lb.Bombs	500 Lb. Bombs	350 LbCluster	20 LbBombs	R/P's	20mm	.5 mm	.303mm
1,831	300	4,552	5,705	/	2,680	3,096	352,674	282,187	33,300

R. A. F. SUPPORT 1955

	Soties	Troops/Lift	Casac	Pass/Lift	Supply Wt. Lbs	Leaflets Drop (1,000)	B Flying Times No / hrs	Broadcsting No / hrs	Crashed
Air SupportA/C*	56	/	/	/	1,523,701	/	/	/	
Auster** Total	23,069	/	/	/	/	/	/	/	Hornet
Anson ***	Inc	///	/	/	/	/	/	/	PX832
Pioneer	N/A	830	13	110	96.807	/	/	/	PX350
H/C Light	N/A	/	/	/	/	/	/	/	Sykorski
848 Sqdn	Disbanded	/	/	/	/	/	/	/	H/C??
155 Sqdn	N/A	4.033	173	378	91,854	/	/	/	
Target/MK**	365	/	/	/	/	/	/	/	
Vis/Air **	8,284		/	/	/	/	/	/	
Communication**	6,853	/	/	/	/	/	/	/	
Leaflets Sories*	365	'/	/	/.	/	9,894	/	/	
Leaflets Drop*	388,000	/	/	/	944	/	/	/	
Leaflet Sorties **	/	/	/	/	/	/	/	/	
Leaflet Drop**	/	/	/	/	/	/	/	/	
Broad Sorties *	582	/	/	/	/	/	/	///	/
/Broad Hrs*	/	/	/	/	/	/	/	611.5	
Broad Sorties **	340	/	/	/	/	/	/	/	
Broad Hrs **	/	/	/	/	/	/	/	254	
Photo Recc***Tot	833	/	/	/	/	/	/	/	
AirOP**	18	/	/	/	/	/	/	/	

** Auster**
*** Photo RECCE Anson, Spitfire, Mosquito, Meteor

CHAPTER 14 - 1956

JANUARY

Sun. 1st	Operation 'Latimer North 'Began SAS against the MRLA ----]
+	Operation "Deuce" began with the first involvement of 2 RAR (Royal Australian Regiment) Troops to be deployed into Malaya since arriving in October. They had been located in Minden Barracks Penang undergoing training. The purpose of Operation 'Deuce' was aimed at the disruption & clearance of CT's from the State of Kedah, where 4 MRLA Armed Work Forces, operated in supplying food & supplies to the CT's. in the areas of Kulim, Sungei Ula, Anak Kulim & Sungei Bakap. 2 RAR along with the Intelligence Service, Police, Home Guard, 105 Field Battery RAA with air support from R.A.F. Butterworth, began their first Patrols finding evidence. However, no contacts.. ---]
Mon. 2nd	London: A conference was held in London chaired by the British Colonial Secretary Mr Lennox –Boyd in the presence of a Malayan delegation led by Tengku Abdul Rahman. The conference, which was to last until the 8th Februay .Was held to discuss the future constitutional developments of the Federation of Malaya. The meeting ended with: 'A proposal of full Independence for Malaya would be introduced at the earliest possible date & full Self-Government & Independence within the Commonwealth for the Federation of Malaya would be proclaimed, if possible by August 1957. Obviously, there were certain ideals, which the Federation Government would install & implement before the proposed date finance, internal defence & security, prosecution against the C.T's, whilst Britain would continue with direct responsibility of external defence relations of the Federation of Malaya']
Tue. 3rd	3 HMT EMPIRE FOWEY arrived in Singapore sailed for Southampton 8th.with returning Service personnel]
Wed. 4th	4 Cpl. J. J. Plumtree. A/F R.A.F.Changi. Accidental shooting on duty. Kranji Singapore # 12 / A – 2 ---]
+	4 Gnr. Alias Bin Othman. Royal Artillery Died *** Claimed by next of Kin.---]
Thur. 5th	2 RAR had their first break when they sighted 3 C.T's Opening fire they wounded & captured 1 Whilst two others, possibly wounded got away. The captured CT turned out to be a 20 year old Chinese volunteer who had only joined the MPLA in March 55. He was armed with a Japanese rifle & a number of rounds of ammunition---]
Fri. 6th	A 'Coy 1st Battn. Royal Lincolnshire Regt. engaged and Killed 2 CT's in the jungles of West Pahang---]
Sat. 7th	} Combined Operations continued throughout Malaya ---]
Sun. 8th	8 HMT EMPIRE FOWEY sailed for Southampton with returning Service personnel---]
Mon. 9th	9 PC.Abdul Gahni F. M. Police Killed on Ops. Kuantan/Maran Rd. Pahang.---]
Tue. 10th	10/01/1956 LG # 40680 p.205. The following awarded the Distinguished Conduct Medal
+	SGT. R. RAI. DCM 6th. QUEEN ELIZABETH'S OWN GURKHA RIFLES
Wed. 11th	Kuala Lumpur : The 'Cease Fire Over' Was announced by Tenku Abdul Rahman. 'The hunt for Chin Peng & his followers was on once again. ---]
+	In the area of the Bukit Sidum Estate lines. A F. M. Police Jungle Patrol engaged 4 CT's opened fire but they escaped. An elderly Chinese man was discovered with gunshot wounds, he was taken away as a suspect for helping the CT's---].
+	Searching for Chin Peng. Combined Operations continued along the Malay / Thailand Border. Road blocks were in place checking all travelling towards Thailand ---]
+	11 HMT EMPIRE CLYDE arrived Singapore Roads with replacement Service personnel ---]
Thur. 12th	12 L/Cpl. J. Brandon. R. M. P. Died ***Seminyth Selangor.Kuala Lumpur # 22 / 1180 ---]
+	12 2/Lt. D. W. Bolam. Royal Hampshire Regt. Killed in Action Engaging CT's & 1 soldier wounded in an operation near Kajang. Kuala Lumpur. # 23 / 1186---]
+	12 HMT EMPIRE CLYDE sailed Singapore bound for Liverpool with returning Service personnel ---]
Fri. 13th	} Combined Operations continued throughout Maya ---]
Sat. 14th	14 HMT EMPIRE ORWELL sailed Southampton bound for Singapore/ Hong Kong with replacement Service personnel---]
Sun. 15th	A Patrol of the 2nd. RAR Killed a man (unnamed) who had walked into their ambush. Identified as a local man. Although the locals had been warned of an area of potential incident. These incidents did occur. -]
Mon. 16th	'B Coy Royal Lincolnshire Regt. Engaged a number of CT's Captured 2 and wounded another who later surrendered. ---]
Tue. 17th	17 PC. Bahari B. Amat. F. M. Police Killed on Ops. Penang---]
Wed. 18th	18 HMT DUNERA sailed Southampton bound for Singapore / Hong Kong with replacement Service personnel---]
Thur. 19th	19 Pol/Lt. E.J. Hughes. F.M.Aux.P.olice Fatally wounded in a freak accident during an ambush. A bullet entered A slit hole 6"x3" in their GMC armoured car, ricocheted around inside, before striking Hughes in the

		head. Fatally wounding him. Kota Tinggi Johore *Kranji Singapore # 8 / D – 3* .---]
Fri.	20th	**21 Tpr. J. F. Myers.** 11th Royal Hussars Died*** *[Ashes REP*]---]
Sat.	21st	21 HMT ASTURIUS arrived Singapore with replacement Service personnel enroute to Hong Kong 21st--]
Sun.	22nd	Under the Code Name "*Kingly Pie*" 7 Lincoln Bombers No 1 Sqdn R.A.A.F. & 4 Canberra's from No 12 Sqdn. Carried out a bombing raid on an area near Kluang Central Johore where the notorious Commander **Goh Peng Tuan** of the 7th. Independent Platoon MRLA was encamped. Guided by ground forces 2 1.000lb bombs were dropped followed by attacks from the Canberras. The resulting finds by ground forces claimed the bodies of **Goh Peng Tuan** plus 13 other bodies found. However, it was estimated that evidence of possibly a further 8 had been disintegrated.---]
	+	Operation "*Bukit Tapeh*"The first undertaken by the New Zealand SAS in deep jungle areas of Pahang.---]
	+	22 HMT DEVONSHIRE arrived Liverpool with returning Service personnel---]
Mon.	23rd	**23 Mr. G. Roderick.** Dredgemaster Trenoh Tin Mines Kampar Perak. Killed in the Bikam Estate whilst test Boring.---]
Tue.	24th	}Combined Operations continued throughout Malaya---]
Wed.	25th	}
Thur.	26th	26 HMT DILWARA arrived Singapore roads with replacement Service personnel ---]
Fri.	27th	**27 Pte. Anak Bagi Rejap.** Sarawak Rangers. Died***.*Kuala Lumpur # 23 / 1182* ---]
Sat.	28th	28 HMT EMPIRE FOWEY arrived Southampton with returning Service personnel .---]
Sun.	29th	29 HMT ASTURIUS sailed Southampton bound for Singapore/ Hong Kong with replacement Service personnel---]
Mon.	30th	**30 Rfn. Kale Gurung.** 6th. Queen Elizabeth's Own Gurkha Rifles. Died *** Simpang Patang. *Seranban # 77* Negri Sembilan---]
Tue.	31st	**31 Sgt. K.H. Ewald.** 2nd. Battn. R.A.R. Died by accident during ambush.*Taiping # E / 51* Perak----]

FEBRUARY

Wed.	1st	**1 Mr. Richard McVeigh** Asstn. Estate Manager. was Killed along with 2 F. M. Police **SC's Abdul Rahmn B.Hasan - Othman B. Hj. Bdul Hamid.** Killed in an ambush in the Kulai area of Johore.---]
	+	1 HMT DILWARA sailedSingapore bound for Southampton with returning Service personnel ---]
Thur.	2nd	}
Fri. .	3rd	} Combined Operations continued throughout Malaya---]
Sat.	4th	}
Sun.	5th	6 HMT EMPIRE CLYDE arrived Liverpool with returning Service personnel ---]
Mon.	6th	Kuala Lumpur An announcement by **Chin Peng** received in Kuala Lumpur declared : **"THE AMNESTY WAS OVER."---]**
Tue.	7th	7 HMT EMPIRE ORWELL arrived Singapore with replacement Service personnel enroute to Hong Kong-]
Wed.	8th	Kuala Lumpur: Upon his return from London Tengku Abdul Rahman broadcast: '*His thanks to Britain for granting the future Independence of Malaya.*'---]
Thur.	9th	} Combined Operations continued throughout Malaya ---]
Fri.	10th	**10 Pte. L. W. J. Smith.** 1st. Battn. The Queen's West Surrey Regt. Died*** *Kranji Singapore # 11/ A -10*---]
Sat.	11th	11 HMT ASTURIUS arrived Singapore enroute to Southampton with returning Service personnel 11th.---]
Sun.	12th	12 7 F. M. Police **Sgt. Abu Baker B. Mat Said., Cpl. Mohd. Sharif. B. Hj. Abdulla Salam., S/C. Abdullah . S. HJ. Abd. Majid., Naam B. Abu Hassan., Abd. Samnat B. P., Abdullah. Zulkifil B. Yoop Ibrahim., Abdul Rahman b. Hassa.** Were blown up when a landmine exploded. It was understood approx 30 C.T's had set & exploded the landmine in the Langkap area of Perak. ---]
Mon.	13th	'C' Company 2nd.10th. Princess Mary's Own Gurkha Rifles Killed 4 CT's one a Woman in the area of Ulu Tinram ---]
Tue.	14th	} Combined Operations continued throughout Malaya---]
Wed.	15th	}
Thur.	16th	16 HMT DUNERA arrived Singapore.with replacement Service personnel---]
Fri.	17th	**17 LAC. J. G. J. Ellens**. Mus. R.A.F. Changi Died*** *Kranji Singapore # 12 / A – 6* ---]
	+	17 HMT EMPIRE FOWEY sailed Singapore enroute to Hong Kong ---]
	+	17 HMT DUNERA sailed Singapore enroute to Hong Kong ---]
Sat.	18th	} Combined Operations continued throughout Malaya---]
Sun.	19th	19 HMT EMPIRE FOWEY arrived Singapore sailed Bound for Sothampton with returning Service personnel]
Mon.	20th	**20 S/Ldr. S. Foster.** R.A.F. Kuala Lumpur Died***.*Kuala Lumpur # 23 - 1183*---]
	+	'C' Company 2nd.10th. Princess Mary's Own Gurkha Rifles in the same area of Ulu Tinram engaged

	4 CT's killing one a Woman identified as a member of the local Communist Group Committee---]
+	20HMT EMPIRE ORWELL arrived Singapore with ---]
Tue. 21st	**21 Cpl. T. M. Quinn.** 3 Coy R. A. S. C. Died ***. Ipoh Perak *Taiping # 66* Perak.---]
+	21 HMT EMPIRE ORWELL sailed Singapore bound for Southampton with returning Service personnel
Wed.22nd	22 HMT EMPIRE FOWEY sailed Southampton enroute to Singapore / Hong Kong with replacement Service personnel---]
Thur. 23rd	A R.A.F. air strike on a CT Camp near Kluang Johore. Killed 13 CT's. Their bodies were identified by British & Fijian Troops---]
Fri. 24th	24/02/1956. LG # 40716 p 1137 The following awarded BAR to the Miltary Cros
	MAJ. J.M. SYMES. MC + BAR ROYAL HAMPSHIRE REGIMENT.
	The following awarded the Miltary Medal
	CPL. WHEELER MM ROYAL HAMPSHIRE REGIMENT.
	CPL. H.T. SMITH. MM ROYAL HAMPSHIRE REGIMENT.
Sat. 25th	Operation "Bukit Tapeh" ended. The New Zealand 22 SAS recorded they got lost. Map reading & navigation in the jungle was a skill that had to be leant.---]
Sun. 26th	} Combined Operations continued throughout Malaya ---]
Mon. 27th	}
Tue. 28th	28 HMT EMPIRE CLYDE sailed Liverpool bound for Singapore with replacement Service personnel---]
+	28 HMT DILWARA arrived Southampton with returning Service personnel ---]
Wed. 29th	Operation *'Latimer North'* Ended---]

MARCH

Thur. 1st	} Combined Operations continued throughout Malaya---]
Fri. 2nd	**2 F/Lt. D. J. McColl. - F/O. C. R. Clisby.**(Nav). - **Sgt. D. Brodie.** - A/Sig. 48 Sqdn. R.A.F. **L/Cpl. T. H. Randle.- Dvr. H. F. Boardman.- Dvr. A. A Driver.- Dvr. A. H. G. Hickman.** R. A. S. C. 55 Coy Killed when the Valetta VW861. Supply Aircraft on a supply drop to the SAS crashed into trees and cartwheeled into the jungle in the Cameron Highlands. *Kuala Lumpur # 33 / 1249 – 1248 – 1250 - 1254 – 1251- 1252 – 1253* .---]..
+	The Crashed Aircraft was sighed by F/Sgt. Shuvalski of 194 Sqdn. R. A. F.---]
+	A Dragonfly H/C XF267 of 194 Sqdn R. A. F. took off to survey the crash site, which was quite unsuitable for a landing or parachute evac. They received a casvac call. Set a course to the pick up area. After they took off all was going well, when after 10 minutes the H/C engine stopped & it skewered downwards to crash near a river bank. Sustaining a couple of slight injuries to its occupants. They followed the river until they came across a SAS Patrol & were taken back to the casvac pick up area. To be picked by another H/C to return to Kuala Lumpur ---]
Sat. 3rd	3 HMT ASTURIUS arrived Southampton with returning Service personnel---]
Sun. 4th	**4 Sgt. C.C. Anderson.** 2nd. R.A.R. died from wounds received when a Patrol were fired upon by 6 C.T's the fire fight lasted 45 min's. Reinforcements from a second RAR Platoon ran into the fleeing CT's opening fire Killed 1 & wounded others who got away. Sgt Anderson for his Bravery was M.I.D(Pos). *Taiping # B / 67* Perak---]
Mon. 5th	Singapore: Big Hunt for 3 other men in connection with the stealing of 1,400 bombs found hidden in Jervois Road Singapore. 1 man was detained with leg injuries ---]
Tue. 6th	**6 Rfn. Purnabahadur Thapa** . 6th. Queen Elizabeth's Own Gurkha Rifles. Died*** Brinchan Cameron Highlands *Sulva Lines # 55* Ipoh Perak.---]
Wed. 7th	The 10th. Princess Mary's Own Gurkha Rifles left Singapore on board the **MS TJILUWAH** bound for Hong Kong having completed there tour of Duty in Malaya ---]
Thur. 8th	Singapore : Sir. Ivor Jennings arrived in Singapore to advise them on the road to Merdeka with 3 hurdles: *'The smallness of the Colony. The short interim period. the Rendell Constitution to Merdeka. Thought The Communist threat was not a major proplem to Merdeka'* ---]
Fri. 9t	**9 Capt. D.C. Howard.** Royal Engineers Died*** *Kranji Singapore # 11 / A / - 11*---]
Sat. 10th	A Patrol of the 2Nd. RAR engaged a lone CT who was shot in the leg, managed to escape. Tracker dogs were used in the follow up without success---]
+	HMAS *'QUEENBOROUGH'* began her first engagement in Malayan coastal waters.---]
Sun. 11th	**11 Pol/Lt. B.A. Hathaway.** F. M. Police Killed in road accident Kedah *Jalan Pertana # 2503* George Town Penang---]
Mon. 12th	**12 Rfn. Palbahadur Gurung.** 6th. Queen Elizabeth's Own Gurkha Rifles. Died from wounds Seremban Civil Hospital *Seremban # 78* Negri Sembilan.---]

Tue. 13th	**13 Cpl. Kalunsing.Lepcha** 7th. Queen Elizabeth's Own Gurkha Rifles. Killed in Action Engaging CT's. Segamat Area MR VJ627444 *[Kluang Gurkha Cemetery #3/C/ 9*---]
+	RAN HMAS *'QUADRANT'*. Began its second tour of duty in Malayan coastal waters was joined by RAN *'QUICKMATCH'* on her first engagement in Malayan coastal waters---]
+	13 HMT DUNERA arrived Singapore with replacement Service personnel l---]
Wed. 14th	**14 Pte. S. B. Duad**. R. A. M. C. (MOR) Died*** *Claimed by next of Kin* ---]
+	**14 Spr. D. Armstrong.** Royal Engineers Died*** *Kuala Lumpur # 23 / 1184*---]
+	**14 POAF(E). J.C. Scrivener.** Royal Navy. H.M.S. *'CENTAUR'.* Died***.*Kranji Singapore # 12 / C – 2* ---]
+	14 HMT EMPIRE ORWELL arrived Southampton with returning Service personnel ---]
+	14 HMT DUNERA sailed Singapore bound for Southampton with returning Service personnel---]
Thur. 15th	Security Forces Killed 2 C.T's wounding 1 In the Kuantan Kubu area of Selengor.---]
Fri. 16th	16/03/56. LG # 40732 p 1575 The following awarded the Military Medal
	SGT. G..A..R. WESTALL. MM ROYAL HAMPSHIRE REGIMENT.
+	16 HMT EMPIRE FOWEY arrived Singapore----]
Sat. 17th	'A' Coy. 1st. Battn. Royal Lincolnshire Regt. Killed 1 CT ---]
+	17 HMT EMPIRE FOWEY sailed Singapore bound for Southampton with returning Service personnel---]
Sun. 18th	'B' Coy. 1st. Battn. Royal Lincolnshire Regt. Killed **Awf Hor Par** a leading Party Member.---]
Mon. 19th	**19 MEI l. Campbell.** Royal Navy HMS *''COCKADE''* Died *** *[Ashes REP]*---]
Tue. 20th	11 CT's raided Kampong Simpang Pulai. Demanded where all the shotguns were? The women refused so they raided all the households and got away with 11 shotuns & 320 rounds of ammunition ---]
Wed. 21st	Upon returning from a jungle operation whilst dischaging rilfes a Pte. **(name& Regt. Unknown)** Was shot & seriously wounded but lived to tell the tale---]
Thur.22nd	22 HMT ASTURIUS sailed Southampton bound for Singapore / Hong Kong with replacement Service personnel---]
+	22 HMT EMPIRE FOWEY arrived Southampton with returning Service personnel ---]
Fri. 23rd	**23 Rfn. Charam Rai .** 10th. Princess Mary's Own Gurkha Rifles. Died base camp accident *[Ashes REP]*----]
+	**23** A similar incident happened when **Pte. C.A. Jay**. 2nd. Battn. R.A.R. Died in base camp accident. *Taiping # E / 52* Perak---]
+	**23 Pte. J. Decent.** 2nd. Battn. R.A.R. Died***.*Taiping #B / 68* Perak---]
+	**23 Rfn. Tikaram Gurung.** 6th. Queen Elizabeth's Own Gurkha Rifles. Died MVA Muar to Gawa Rd. *Kluang # 3 / D – 15* Johore---]
Sat. 24th	24 HMT EMPIRE CLYDE arrived Singapore sailed for Beira 24th.---]
Sun. 25th	6 Platoon 'B' Company 2nd. RAR Engaging a CT & opened fire. However he mananged to escape leaving his pack. Documents identified him as a member of No 4 AWF Tageted under Operation *'Deuce–*]
Mon. 26th	The Recovery of the Whirlwind Helicopter, forced down into a shallow mountain river near the Malaya/Thailand Border continued. RAF Engineers were stacking sandbags flown in by Pioneer aircraft. In an attempt to divert the river, before building a metal sheet platform to allow the Helicopter to take off once repaired---]
Tue. 27th	12 CT's stopped a Lorry carrying workers to the Rubber Plantation Singled out one Chinese named **Kim Seong** Told the driver to carry on. Who reported the incident. A Patrol of the Hampshire Regt. Found his body. His head had been slashed open with a parang.---]
Wed. 28th	Air strikes in support of ground forces & Road Patrols searching for CT's continued throughout Malaya---]
Thur. 29th	Kuala Lumpur: New safeguards will be in force after Merdeka. Giving the right for Britain to intervene if civil unrest does occur—]
Fri. 30th	} Combined Operatuions continued throughout Malaya---]
Sat. 31st	}

APRIL

Sun. 1st	RNZN *'KANIERE'*. Began her second support role of duty whilst RNZS *'PUKAKI'.*completed her second support role in Malayan coastal waters---]
Mon. 2nd	New Zealand Squadron 22 SAS became fully operational under Operation "*Gabe South*" from the Fort Serve Blue Valley Estate Cameron Highlands up to the borders of Thailand---]
Tue. 3rd	Air strikes in support of ground forces & Road Patrols searching for CT's continued throughout Malaya---]
Wed. 4th	**4 Flt/Sgt. R. Fraser** No 5 Sqdn. RNZAF Died.*** *[Ashes REP]*---]
Thur. 5th	**5 Pol/Lt. D. W. Needham.** F.M. Police Died from gunshout wounds recieved in Action Engaging CT's Johore]

	+	RANS *'QUADRANT'*. Completed its second engagement of duty in Malayan coastal waters.---]
Fri.	6th	**6 W/SC Mary Leong.** F. M. Police Killed on CT Ops. Kajang Selangor.---]
	+	Support Compnay 2nd.RAR were fired upon by CT sentries when they discovered a camp they opened fire & at least 12 CT's within the camp scattered escaping into the jungle---]
	+	6 HMT EMPIRE ORWELL sailed Southampton bound for Singapore /Hong Kong / Kure with replacement Service personnel---]
Sat.	7th	London: Talks began in The Commonwealth Office between a Delegation from Malaya . Under Tenku Abdul Raham & the Commonwealth Seretary About the forthcommimg Day of Malaya Independence--]
Sun.	8th	**8 LAC. D. J. Veale.** A/M (Bbs) R.A.F. Seletar Died*** *Kranji Singapore #12 / A – 7* ---]
	+	8 HMT EMPIRE FOWEY arrived Singapore with replacement Service personnel--]
Mon.	9th	**9 SC. Ahmad B. Idris.** F. M. Police Killed On CT Ops. Rompin Negri Sembilan.---]
	+	The NZ SAS. Fired their first shot when they encountered a naked CT bathing in a river .Opening fire they heard a scream, he must have been wounded. However the CT escaped. Their mission was to eliminate the CT **Ah Ming** leader of a Platoon of Chinese & aboriginals, who operated in the area of Fort Brooke The Department of Aborigines had placed a reward of $4,500 on the head of **Ah Ming** & a further $1,500 for any of his followers. ---]
	+	9 HMT EMPIRE FOWEY sailed Singapore bound for Southampton with returning Service personnel---]
Tue.	10th	Penang: A CT **Tsang Hing Luen** walked into the Ayah Itam Police Station & surrendered. He was the last CT to surrender before the end of the amnesty. He was a member of the 11th. Penang Anti British Army---]
	+	10 HMT DUNERA arrived Southampton with returning Service personnel---]
Wed.	11th	} Combined Operations continued throughout Malaya---]
Thur.	12th	}
Fri.	13th	13 HMT ASTURIUS arrived Singapore with replacement Service personnel enroute to Hong Kong 13th.-]
Sat.	14th	Fijian troops Killed 5 CT's near Tangkak Johore. Identified as members of the Indepentant State Committee: Secretary **Chiang Koon,** Group Secretary **Ong Boon Chiew,** Group Committee Member **Yap Jib Hai,** Courier **Lim Mam Wan & Wong Ah Chin.** The courier had important documents in his possession. All five CT's had been in the jungle since the beginning of the Emergency in 1948---]
Sun.	15th	} Combined Operations continued throughout Malaya---]
Mon.	16th	**16 Sgt. C. Thompson.** 15/19th. The King's Royal Hussars. Died by Accident *Taiping # E / 53* Perak---]
	+	**16 Lt. P.E. Reynolds.** 1st. Battn. R. A. R. Died*** *Krangi Singapore # 17 / B -1*---]
	+	16 6 F.M. Police SC's, were Killed in an ambush 1 1/2 miles from Langkap on the Teluk Anson / Kampar Road when the lorry carrying 12 SC's entered a CT ambush where they had laid land mines at both ends of the area, which were blown up. As the F.M. SC's debused to seek shelter in the roadside ditch, jumping down they fell upon hidden bamboo stakes. Impaled they were shot dead by the CT's The remaining SC's returned fire that turned into a gun battle before the CT's withdrew. Those Killed named as: **Sgt Abu Bakar B.Mat Said. -Cpl. Mohamad Sharrif B. Haji. Abdul Salem. SC's Hassim Abdul B. Haji Abdul Mohamad. Abdul Maji. Abdul Samatt Pandak Abdul. & Zulkiff bin Yeop Ibraham'** ---]
Tue.	17th	A large Police and troop force began a search for the CT's involved in the previous days ambush---]
Wed.	18th	**18 Cpl. Mohd, Deva.** F. M. Police Killed on Ops. Scudal Johore---]
Thur.	19th	A Patrol of the 1st Battalion the Rifle Brigade. Killed **Young Kio** Deputy Secretary-General of the MCP. & the chief responsible for the MCP's Political Offensive. In an area near Kuala Lumpur. Documents found in his possession provide comprehensive details on the MCP plans to subjugate Malaya by subversion---] .
Fri.	20th	}
Sat.	21st	} Combined Operations continued throughout Malaya---]
Sun.	22nd	}
Mon.	23rd	Kuala Lumpur A letter from **Chin Peng** was delivered to Tenku Abdul Rahman suggesting that:
Tue.	24th	*'A meeting to be set up in the little village of Naka along the Malaya Thailand border to meet his Boss* **Chen Tian** *?'* The Tenku remarked.: '*Someone is trying to be funny. I am not aware that* **Chen Tian** *was* **Chin Peng's** *Boss. No way am I going to meet him.*'---]
	+	Operation *'Hustler'* Air strike carried out by bombers of the R. A. F. R.A.A.F. RNZAF. Killed 13 CT's of the 7th. Ind. Troop led by **Goh Peng Taun** Political Commisar. 2 Camps were obliterated. Possibly more bodies maybe found---]
	+	3 C.T's including a District Committee Member were Killed in Johore.- by a F.M.Police Jungle Patrol---]
	+	R.A.A.F. Lincoln Bombers dropped 20 tons of bombs at Klang Gates Dam 8 miles from Kuala Lumpur. The explosions raatled windows in Kuala Lumpur.- The body of a CT was found in a swamp.--]
Wed.	25th	**25 PC Ong Huan Seng.** F. M. Police Killed on Ops. Petaling Jaya Selangor.---]

Thur. 26th		26 HMT EMPIRE CLYDE arrived Singapore from Beira---]
Fri. 27th		A troop of the NZ SAS found a hut near Fort Brooke set an ambush. When 2 CT's appeared they opened fire. Killed one, wounding the second,who ran off followed by a Trooper. After a short while the Trooper returned with the dead CT, straggled across his neck like a deer. ---]
		Sgt. Shahabudin. F.M. Police was awarded for his bravety. He was in charge of a party of Police SC's during the repair of Rifle Butts near Tanjong Malin. When 25 CT's fired upon them. Killing 1 SC sentry & wounding a Sgt. PC. Whilst returning fire, **Shahabudin** sent for help & continued to engage the CT's, killing and wounding several. The Sgt was hit again and Killed. The fire fight continued untill a Police Patrol arrived. Only then did the CT's disperse back into the jungle fringes---]
	+	27 HMT EMPIRE CLYDE redocked Seletar ---]
Sat. 28th		105 Field Battery RAA carried out harassing fire on an area of the jungle where known CT's were hiding--]
	+	28 HMT DEVONSHIRE sailed Liverpool bound for Singapore via Suva -with replacement Service personnel]
Sun. 29th		**29 Fus. G.C.Fieldhouse.- Fus.C. B. Taylor.** 2nd. Battn. Royal Welch Fusiliers Killed no further information. *Kuala Lumpur #23 / 1187 – 1188* ---]
	+	Under the terms of the amnesty 11 CT's surrendered. 5 were women CT's. At Kalumpang 5 miles South of Tanjon Malim. Their leader ***Hrap Thong*** was Killed a few weeks before ---]
Mon. 30th		2 CT's were Killed by F.M. Police jungle Patrols in the Selam area of Central Perak.---]
	+	1 RAR Ended their tour of Operation under the code name '*Deuce*' which continued under the control of the 1st. Battn. The Malay Regt.---]
	+	30 HMT EMPIRE ORWELL arrived Singapore with replacement Service personnel enroute to Hong/Kong
	+	Kure 30th.---]
	+	Kuala Lumpur: Tenku Abdul Rahman. Expected to announce future Plans for Malaya ---]

MAY

Tue. 1st		Operation "*Shark North*." Further restriction of food & concentration on harassment to CT Armed Work Forces in the Sungei Siput area of Taiping. 2nd Battn. RAR began operation ---]
	+	Operation "*Corner Key*" "*Gabes North*" Began SAS operation against the CT's---]
Wed. .2nd		**2 Trp. A. R. Thomas.** Royal New Zealand . S.A.S. Accidently shot was airvac'd out. Died from his wounds Sungei Perolak.*Kuala Lumpur # 23 / 1189* ---]
Thur. 3rd		} Combined Operations continued throughout Malaya---]
Fri. 4th		4 HMT ASTURIUS arrived Singapore enroute to Southampton with returning Service personnel sailed 4th. ---]
	+	4 HMT EMPIRE CLYDE redocked Singapore---]
Sat. 5th		**5 Maj. C. J. G. Mumford.** 1st. Battn. Royal Hampshire Regt. Died*** *Kuala Lumpur # 23 / 1190*---]
	+	5 HMT EMPIRE CLYDE sailed for Liverpool with replacement Service personnel---]
	+	5 HMT DILWARA sailed Southampton bound for Singapore with replacement Service personnel via Mombassa East Africa---]
Sun. 6th		} Combined Operations continued throughout Malaya---]
Mon. 7th		'D' Coy Royal Lincolnshire Regt. engaged a pnumber of CT's Killing 3 and wounding 2 others . One of those Killed was State Committee Member. ***Chi Ying***. For his Action Engaging CT's during the engagement. Lt. P. Surtees was awarded the the MC.---]
Tue. 8th		8/05/56 LG # 40772 p 2689 The following awarded the British Empire Medal (Military)

W/O. M. MAXWELL. BEM	NORTHERN RHODESIAN REGIMENT.
BQMS. E. HARDY. BEM	ROYAL REGIMENT ARTILERY
SQMS. T. JONES. BEM	ROYAL CORPS SIGNALS
C/SGT. C. LIMBU. BEM	10th. PRINCESS MARY'S OWN GURKHA RIFLES
C/SGT. G. WATSON. BEM	EAST YORKSHIRE REGIMENT.
S/SGT. J. GREAVES. BEM	ROYAL ELECTRICAL MECHANICAL ENGINEERS
CQS. R. J. BRANDRETH. BEM	ROYAL ARMY SERVICE CORPS
SGT. J.W. MCCULLOCH. BEM	ROYAL CORPS SIGNALS
SGT. B. F. STONE. BEM	ROYAL ELECTRICAL MECHANICAL ENGINEERS
SGT. J.E THORNTON. BEM	EAST YORKSHIRE REGIMENT.
p. 2690	The following awarded the Military Cross
MAJ. W.A. ROBINSON. MC.	THE EAST YORKSHIRE REGIMENT.
MAJ K.W. NIVIENS. MC	THE GREEN HOWARDS
LT. M.N.B. MULHALANDIN. MC,	MALAY REGIMENT.
LT. HASHIM. MC	MALAY REGIMENT.

		The following were awarded the Military Medal..
	SGT. M.F.E. PIKE. MM	ROYAL HAMPSHIRE REGIMENT.
	RFN. T.GURUNG. MM	2th. KING EDWARD VII'S OWN GURKHA RIFLES
	RFN. P RAI. MM	7th. DUKE OF EDINGBURGH'S OWN GURKHA RIFLES
	RFN. G RAI. MM	10th PRINCESS MARY'S OWN GURKHA RIFLES
	CPL. K RAI. MM	10th PRINCESS MARY'S OWN GURKHA RIFLES
	SGT.M.Z.B. IBRAHIM. MM	MALAY REGIMENT
	L/CPL. I.B.YAHAYA. MM	MALAY REGIMENT
	CPL. R. TIKOIYANNCA. MM	FIJI REGIMENT.
	p. 2691	The following awarded the Distinguished Flying Cross
	CAPT. R.O.I WOODBRIGE. DFC	ROYAL REGIMENT ARTILLERY
		The following awarded the Distinguished Flying Medal
	CPL. D. WADE, DFM	ROYAL ARMY SERVICE CORPS
	8/05/1956 LG. Iss.40773 p. 2701	The following awarded the British Empire Medal (Millitary)
	SGT. C. H. IRELAND. BEM	ROYAL AIR FORCE
		The following awarded the Distiguished Flying Cross
	S/LDR. J.A. PEMBERTON. DFC	ROYAL AIR FORCE
	F/O. T. A. PIDWELL. DFC	ROYAL AIR FORCE
	F/LT. G. FRANCIS. DFC	ROYAL AIR FORCE
	F.LT. G. GARFORTH. DFC	ROYAL AIR FORCE
	F/O. W. J. W. CURRY. DFC	ROYAL AIR FORCE
	F/O. T.A. POWELL. DFC	ROYAL AIR FORCE
	F/O. D. P. RIORDAN. DFC	ROYAL AIR FORCE
		The following awarded the Distinguished Flying Medal
	SGT. J.R. HUNTTINGTON. DFM	ROYAL AIR FORCE
	S/A/C. D. R. GUDGEON. DFM	ROYAL AIR FORCE
	p 2703	The following awarded the Distinguished Flying Cross
	W/CDR, C.H. SPURGEON. DFC	ROYAL AUSTRALIAN AIR FORCE
	S/LDR. T. S. FAIRBAIRN. DFC	ROYAL AUSTRALIAN AIR FORCE

+	8 HMT EMPIRE FOWEY arrived Southampton with returning Service personnel ---]	
Wed. 9th	} Combined Operations continued throughout Malaya ---]	
Thur. 10th	10 SAC. L. B. Blackmore. A/M (Bbs) R.A.F. Accidental Death due to discharge of Aircraft rocket gun Butterworth *Western Road # 2154* GeorgeTown Penang---]	
Fri. 11th	11/05/56 LG # 40775 p. 2761 The following awarded the Military Medal	
	CPL. J.J. CLARKE MM ROYAL HAMPSHIRE REGIMENT.	
Sat. 12th	12 Recuit Manbahadur Rai.10th. Princess Mary's own Gurkha Rifles. Died*** Kamunting *Sungei Patani # 119* Kedah. ---]	
Sun. 13th	}	
Mon. 14th	} Combined Operations continued throughout Malaya---]	
Tue. 15th	}	
Wed. 16th	16 L/Cpl. B. D. Swain. 1st. Battn. Royal Hampshire Regt. Killed in Action Engaging CT's. *Kuala Lumpur # 23 / 1194* ---]	
+	16 Spr. Soomana Charles. Royal Engineers (MOR) *Claimed by next of Kin* ---]	
Thur. 17th	17 Fus.. J. Owen. 2nd. Battn. Royal Welsh Fusiliers. Died*** *[Ashes REP]*---].	
+	17 L/Cpl. Purkhalal Pun. 7th. Duke of Edinburgh's Own Gurkha Rifles. Killed. *[No known Grave]Terandak Wall Memorial Malacca* ---]	
Fri. 18th	} Combined Operations continued throughout Malaya---]	
Sat. 19th	*Kuala Lumpur:* Lieutenant General Sir. Roger Bower Became General Officer Commanding Malaya ---]	
Sun. 20th	A Troop of the NZ.SAS Killed 1 CT Identified as *Kum Chin.* He was *Ah Ming's* 2 I/C ---]	
Mon. 21st	21 HMT EMPIRE ORWELL arrived Singapore ---]	
Tue. 22nd	22 Grn. J. G. Harper. Royal Artillery Died.*** *Kuala Lumpur # 23 / 1192* ---]	
+	22 HMT EMPIRE ORWELL sailed Singapore bound for Southampton with returning Service personnel	
Wed. 23rd	23 PC. Kassim B. Jasmat. F. M. Police Killed on Ops. Labis Estate Rd. Johore.---]	
+	An Army Auster flying between Ipoh & Kuala Lumpur went missing enroute A search is underway to locate it and its pilot Sgt Ken McConnell Royal Artillery- --]	
Thur. 24th	24 Sgt. J. B. Joyce R.E.M.E.. Died *** *[Ashes REP]*---].	
Fri. 25th	25 LAC. Abdullah. Bin . Haji. Ahmad. R.A.F.(MOR) 91 Fld. Sqdn. FAF Regt. Drowned,	

	No known Grave] Terandak Wall Memorial Malacca---]
Sat. 26th	**26 S/Sgt W. Boyd** R. E.M .E Died *** _Kranji Singapore 2 / B -.5_ ---]
+	26 HMT DEVONSHIRE arrived Singapore with replacement Service personnel.---]
Sun. 27th	**27 Gnr. A.R. Brooks** Royal Artillery Died ***._Kuala Lumpur # 23 / 1193_ ---]
+	**27 HMT EMPIRE FOWEY arrived Singapore--]**
Mon. 28th	28 HMT EMPIRE FOWEY sailed Singapore bound for Southampton with returning Service personnel via Cape Town ---]
+	28 HMT DEVONSHIRE sailed Singapore bound for Suva ---]
Tue. 29th	**29 Sgt. E. W. Hargreaves.** R. A.E. C. Died***._[Ashes REP]---]_
Wed. 30th	30 HMT EMPIRE CLYDE arrived Liverpool with returning Service personnel---]
Thur. 31st	Operation _"Corner Key"_ Completed---]

JUNE

Fri. 1st	} Combined Operations continued throughout Malaya---]
Sat. 2nd	**2 SC Amri B. Bakri.** F. M. Police Died Motor Veh. Acc. Yong Peng area Johore.---]
Sun. 3rd.	**3 SC's Cpl. Ahmad B. Abdul Ghani.- Pali B.Jem.** F. M. Police Killed on Ops. Nanyo Estate Kota Tinggi Johore---]
Mon. 4th	} Combined Operations continued throughout Malaya---]
Tue. 5th	5 HMT EMPIRE FOWEY sailed Southampton bound for Singapore/ Hong Kong- with replacement Service personnel---]
Wed. 6th	In the area of Poh Lee Sen. A Patrol of the 2nd. 10th. Prince Mary's Own Gurkhas Rifles.engaged 40 CT's killing 1. The rest retreated into the jungle---]
Thur. 7th	**7 Capt. L. Griffiths.** Royal Artillery Pilot - **Maj. G. Pahalmansing.** MBE.(IDSM), **Maj. D. A. Truss.** 2nd. King Edward VII's's Own Gurkha Rifles. Were Killed. When the Piltot of Auster WZ694 was making a low level left turn over the jungle near Kuala Pilah, 4 miles from Kuala Lumpur. It struck a tree crashed into the jungle & caught fire. There were no survivors.._Kuala Lumpur # 23 / 1195 - 1198_ .---]
+	7 HMT DILWARA arrived Singapore with replacement Service personnel ---]
Fri. 8th	} Combined Operations continued throughout Malaya---]
Sat. 9th	**9 L/Cpl. G. A. Hanslar.** R. A. S. C. 55 Coy Died Transport incident. _Kuala Lumpur # 23 / 1196_---]
Sun. 10th	The Selengor Labour Party condemned Australia's constant interference into Malayan affairs Calling on the Governemnet to take Action ---]
Mon. 11th	A combined Police and South Wales Borderers Patrol Killed 2 CT's. 1 a women dentified as **Ten Geok Lan** was Killed instantly the 2nd. A Tamil although wounded got away. Fortunately the follow up found him Killed him---]
Tue. 12th	6 Suspected helpers of the CT's were arrested in the village of Semenyih a notorious place for CT' helpers 30 residents have been arrested there since January this year---]
Wed. 13th	The 1st Battn. Kings Own Scottish Borderers after Beating the Retreat. Left Singapore for mainland Malaya to fight the CT's---]
Thur. 14th	14 HMT ASTURIUS sailed Southampton bound for Singapore/ Hong Kong with replacement Service personnel---]
	14 HMT EMPIRE ORWELL arrived Southampton with returning Service personnel
Fri. 15th.	**15 Plt. P. C. M. De Boer.** - M/Nav.- **Sgt. P. J. Sherlock. Sgt.G. B. Manners.** A/Sig. 48 Sqdn. R.A.F. Changi. **Capt.W.R. Franklin - Cpl. L. M. McKay. - Dvr. T. E. Bolden. - Dvr. J. Dixon. - Dvr. J. McMullin.- Dvr. J. Smith.** 55 Coy. R.A.S.C. Killed when Valetta VX521. Supply Aircraft crashed into hillside in the area of Ipoh. _Kuala Lumpur # 32 / 1232 – 1231 – 1233 - 1230 – 1234 1235 – 1236 -1237 – 1238_ ---]
+	15 HMT DILWARA sailed Singapore bound for Southampton wth returning Service personne---]
+	15 HMT CAPTAIN COOK sailed from Glasgow bound for Hong Kong/Singapore via Panama ---]
Sat. 16th	**16 Pte. Anak . Linkoi . Janggak.** Sarawak Rangers Killed on Patrol Kranji _Singapore # 19 / A – 1_ ---]
Sun. 17th	} Combined operations continued through out Malaya
Mon. 18th	5 CT's stopped at lorry at the 331/2 m/s Kluang /Mersing road and stole 5 Katis of dried fish then got away the driver and his mate stayed in the jungle overnight. Reported the theft the next morning at the Kahang Police Station---]
Tue. 19th	A Security forces took up the chase and retracing steps and a fishy smell caught up with the 5 who fired shots before reteating. Leaving the dried fish behind---]
Wed. 20th	_Kuala Lumpur_ : Tenku Abdul Rahman voiced his opinion Stating: _'There would be no Merger with Singapore after Merdeka' ---]_

Thur. 21st	**Sgt. Ken McConnell.** The Auster Pilot. 21 says after he crashed his Auster No? into the jungle on May 23rd.Found his way out of the jungle. He was taken to Taiping Hospital to recover from his ordeal--
Fri. 22nd	**22** Patrols of the 2nd. RAR carrying out reconnaissance sorties of the water pipeline from the Sungei Bemban Reservoir to Sungei Siput .Ran into a CT ambush. 1 land mine was exploded, then opened fire on the Troops. Some of the troops were blown off the ground by the force. but quickly regained firing positions. **Cpl. J .N. Allan.** Was Killed in the cross fire **& Pte. G.C. Fritz.** was wounded in the well planned ambush by a group of 25-30 C.T.'s. Although Friz kept firing, He soon died from his wounds. A reinforcement Platoon arrived on the scene & raked the C.T's from above. In the return fire **Pte. C.C. Ingra.** was Killed. 2 CT's were Killed & several wounded, who disappeared into the jungle. 1 was identified as a member of the local AWC The other a member of the 13/15th. Platoon. Lt Campbell was awarded the MC. Pte Pennant & Falk. were awarded the MM. Pte Fritz was posthumously M.I.D. *Taiping #B / 69 – 55 - 56* Perak---
Sat. 23rd	} Combined Operations continued throughout Malaya---]
Sun. 24th	**24 Trp's. G. Campbell. - R.F.D. Jones.- G. Summers. - W.J. Smith.** 15/19th The King's Royal Hussars. Died when their APC collided with a train at a level crossing. *Taiping # E / 57 – 58 - 60 -* **Smith** [*Ashes REP*] Perak]
+	**24 Trp. W. R. J. Marselle.** Parachute Regt. att. to 22nd. S.A.S. Died from Gunshot wounds *Kuala Lumpur # 23 .- 1197 ---*]
Mon. 25th	} Combined Operations continued throughout Malaya---]
Tue. 26th	}
Wed. 27th	**27 L/Cpl. J.S. Leiper.** 1st. King's Dragoon Guards Died*** [*Ashes REP*]---]
+	**27** HMT EMPIRE FOWEY arrived Singapore with replacement Service personnel---]
Thur. 28th	**28 Pte. F. W. Barratt.** R. A. M. C. Died***.*Kuala Lumpur # 23 / 1199 ---*]
Fri. 29th	29/06/56. LG # 40817 p 3789 The following awarded the Distinguished Service Order LT/CON. P. KANATABATU. DSO. FIJI REGIMENT The following awarded the Miltary Medal PTE. P KEDRATI. MM FIJI REGIMENT PTE. J RAGORE. MM FIJI REGIMENT
+	29/06/1956. LG # 40819 p 3867. The following awarded the George Medal INSP CHEW KIM CHUAN.GM FEDERATION MALAY POLICE INSP. LOH KWANG SEANG.GM FEDERATION MALAY POLICE CONST. TONG SONG LING.GM FEDERATION MALAY POLICE
Sat. 30th	**30 Rfn. Bhimbahadur Rana** 2nd. King Edward VII's Own Own Gurkha Rifles. Died***[*Ashes REP*]---]
+	**30 Rfn. Bhaijalsig Rai .** 10th. Princess Mary's Own Gurkha Rifles. Died***[*Ashes REP*]---]
+	**30** HMT EMPIRE FOWEY sailed for Hong Kong---]

JULY

Sun. 1st	**1 Cpl. H. S. Shaffle.** R.A.F.(MOR) R. A. F. Regt. Died*** [*Claimed by next of Kin*]---]
+	Operation " *Cloud*" Began SAS Operation against the CT's---]
Mon. 2nd	**2 Pol/Lt. D.W. Needham.** F.M. Aux.Police Killed on CT Ops. Johore *Kranji Singapore # 18 / B -10* ---]
Tue. 3rd	03/07/1956 LG # 40822 p. 3889 The following awarded the Colonial Police Medal D.SGT. TAI KIM HONG. CPM FEDERATION MALAYA POLICE PC. NANCHIR B. SUIN. CPM FEDERATION MALAYA POLICE
Wed. 4th	} Combined Operations continued throughout Malaya---]
Thur. 5th	**5** HMT ASTURIUS arrived Singapore with replacement Service personnel ---]
+	**5** HMT EMPIRE ORWELL sailed Southampton bound for Singapore/ Hong Kong / Kure with replacement Service personnel---]
Fri. 6th	**6 Pte. J. A. Purves.** 1st. Battn.The Queen's West Surrey Regt. Died*** *Kranji Singapore # 11/ A-12*---]
+	**Ch/Tech. C. W. Longstaff.** Arm/F. R.A.F.Seletar Died Nat. Causes *Kranji Singapore # 12 / A – 8* ---]
+	**6** HMT ASTURIUS sailed Singapore enroute to Hong Kong —]
Sat. 7th	} Combined Operations continued throughout Malaya ---]
Sun. 8th	5 C.T's were Killed by Security Forces in an engagement in Johore.---]
Mon. 9th.	**9 Srn. Cd. Eng.J. Smith.** Royal Navy. H.M.S. '*SIMBANG*' Died****Kranji Singapore # 12 / C -11*---]
Tue. 10th	10/07/1956 LG # 40825 p 4009 The following awarded the British Empire Medal (Military) SGT. H.W. BAXTER. BEM ROYAL ARMY MEDICAL CORPS A/T 22nd SAS SAP. H. B. BLYTH. BEM ROYAL AUSTRALIAN ENGINEERS. The following awarded the Military Cross

	LT. P. P. H. SURTEES. MC ROYAL HAMPSHIRE REGIMENT., The following awarded a BAR to his MC. LT. J.M. SYMES. MC & BAR SOUTHATAFFORDSHIRE REGIMENT. CAPT. R. HARKASING. MC & BAR 6th.QUEEN ELIZABETH'S OWN GURKHA RIFLES
Wed. 11th	**11 C/Sgt. A. H. Brookes.** 1st. Battn. Worcestershire Regt. Died*** [_Ashes REP_]---]
+	**11 L/Cpl. D. A. Drummond.** R. E.M .E. Died***. _Kuala Lumpur # 23 / 12_ ---]
Thur. 12th	} Combined Operations continued throughout Malaya---]
Fri. 13th	}
Sat. 14th	'C' Coy Royal Lincolnshire Regt. Wounded and captured 1 CT.---]
Sun. 15th	Surrendered CT **Tan Tak Shin** atated : '_Communist leaders lived of roast pork and keep mistresses The troops he added were forbidden the pork and the mistresses'_---]
Mon.16th.	} Combined Operations continued throughout Malaya---]
Tue. 17th	17 HMT EMPIRE CLYDE sailed Liverpool bound for Singapore / Hong Kong with replacement Service personnel---]
+	17 HMT DILWARA arrived Southampton with returning Service personnel---]
Wed. 18th	} Combined Operations continued throughout Malaya---]
Thur. 19th	**19 Pte. Wonyana.** 1st. Rhodesian African Rifles. Died*** _Kranji Singapore # 4/E/3_---]
Fri. 20th	20 HMT EMPIRE FOWEY arrived Singapore with replacement Service personnel --]
Sat. 21st	21 HMT EMPIRE FOWEY sailed Singapore bound for Southampton via Cape Town with returning Service personnel---]
Sun. 22nd	Operation "_Slimforce_" was undertaken by a Squadron of the NZ SAS . The first operational jump by parachutes into the Sungei Besi area. where it was know that a force of 20 CT's were operating The Jump ended in disaster. Jumpimg into the jungle canopy, left the chute at least 150 feet above ground level, therefore personnel had to absail down. Resulting in 2 SAS sustaining broken ankles one with a damaged back the operation had to be aborted---]
Mon. 23rd	} Combined Operations continued throughout Malaya---]
Tue. 24th	**24 F/O F. W. T. Hobson.** 45 Sqdn. R.A.F. Flying Venom, WE373 Crashed into the sea 2. ½. miles off Yen. Kedah. LAC B. Hancock Royal Australlan Air Force using his own diving equipment volunteered to recover the pilots body. After 3 attempts he was sucesfull in retrivineg the body.of **F/O F. W. T. Hobson** _Western Road # 2165_ George Town Penang---]
Wed. 25th	25 HMT DEVONSHIRE arrived Singapore with replacement Service personnel---]
+	25 HMT ASTURIUS sailed Singapore enroute to Southampton with returning Service personnel Diverted vis Cape Town due to Suez Crisis & closure of the Suez Canal. The ASTURIUS was to be the first Troopship to visit Cape Town since the end of World War II.--]
Thur. 26th	A troop of the NZSAS laid an ambush where 7 CT's had been spotted by local aborigines. Just before dusk 2 CT's emerged into sight both were hit by gunshots 1 got up & ran away 2 others were Killed. 7 packs were found therefore 4 had been Killed with 1 escapee.---]
Fri. 27th	5 C.T.'s were Killed by Security Forcesin areas of Kelantan & Perak.---]
Sat. 28th	During a Combined Operation in the District of Bahau. 'C' Coy Royal Lincolnshire Regt. Killed 2 CT's; one of which was identified as **Au Ha Ho** the Leader of the District Committee.---]
Sun. 29th	29 HMT EMPIRE ORWELL arrived Singapore with replacement Service personnel enroute to Hong Kong /Kure 29th.---]
Mon. 30th	} Combined Operations continued throughout Malaya---]
Tue. 31st	31 HMT DEVONSHIRE sailed Singapore enroute to Liverpool via Mombassa with returning Service personnel]

AUGUST

Wed. 1st	}
Thur. 2nd	} Combined Operations continued throughout Malaya---]
Fri. 3rd	}
Sat. 4th	**4 L/Cpl. N. Indrabahadur Newar.** 6th. Queen Elizabeth's Own Gurkha Rifles. Died*** Kamunting. _Sulva Lines # 52_ Ipoh Perak ---]
Sun. 5th	**5 Gnr. F.D. Cunniff.** Royal Artillery Died*** _Taiping I- 7_Perak.---]
Mon. 6th	A Platoon of 1/6th. Gurkhas ambushed a number of CT's, on a food gathering forage in the Tanah Rata area of the Cameron Highlands killing 1 the others got away---]
Tue. 7th	} Combined operation continued throughout Malaya

Wed. 8th	A reward of $2,000 as been posted as a reward for information leading to the capture of CT **Kassin bin Arahad** a former paddi planter now bodyguard to **Sin Yuen** Committee member of a Platoon in the Taiping area If **Kassim** is found dead, the reward reduces down to $1,500---]
Thur. 9th	} Combined operation continued throughout Malaya
Fri. 10th	}
Sat. 11th	**11 Cpl. L. J. Bligh**. R.E.M.E.. Died accidental death. Kamunting _Taiping # E / 61_ Perak---]
Sun. 12th	12 HMT EMPIRE CLYDE arrived Singapore with replacement Service personnel enroute to Hong Kong 12th
Mon. 13th	2 CT's surrendered to a railway worker at Klang Rawang. They were identified as **Keh Sen** and his wife **Chong Tong** ---]
Tue. 14th	Troops of 'C' Coy 2 Bttn Malay Regt. Scaled 800 ft up the sheer cliffs of Gunog Rapat limestone near Ipoh surprising 3 CT's in their camp. Killed one and captured the other 2 ---]
Wed. 15th	**15 Pte. Othaman Bin.Jafar**. Malay Regt. Killed in Action Engaging CT's Perak---]
Thur. 16th	**16 LAC. R. Brothwick**. Eng/M 194 Sqdn R.A.F. Killed in road traffic accident _Kuala Lumpur # 23 – 1201_]
Fri. 17t	} Combined Operations continued throughout Malaya---]
Sat. 18th	**18 Pte. H.M. Jephson**. 2nd. Battn. R. A.R. Died transport accident _Taiping # E / 62_ Perak---]
Sun. 19th	} Combined Operations continued throughout Malaya---]
Mon. 20th	Singapore: A Royal Nany Helicopter resucued a seriously ill Sailor from a grounded freighter off the coast of Singapore He was picked up and flown directly into the grounds of the Singapore General Hospital---]
Tue. 21st	**21 Pte. Abdullah b. Mohamed Jadi**. Malay Regt. Killed in Action Engaging CT's Perak---]
Wed.22nd	22 HMT CAPTAIN COOK arrived Singapore sailed bound for Glasgow with returning Service personnel---]
Thur. 23rd	**23 Rect. Manbahadur Sunwar**. 10th.Princess Mary's Own Gurkha Rifles Died*** _Sungei Patani # 127_ Kedah]
Fri. 24th	**24 Sgt. J. B. Joyce**. R. E.M .E. Died***. _[Ashes REP]_---]
Sat. 25t	**25 Spr. R.J. E. Watson**.Royal Engineers Died*** _Taiping # E / 63_ Perak---]
+	25 HMT EMPIRE ORWELL arrived Singapore with replacement Service personnel ---]
Sun. 26th	The deputy commander of the C.T's **Yeung Kuo** was shot dead during an engagement in SouthSelangor.---]
Mon. 27th	27 HMT EMPIRE ORWELL sailed Singapore bound for Southampton via Cape Town with returning Service personnel---]
+	27 EMPIRE FOWEY arrived Southampton with returning Service personnel---]
Tue. 28th	28 HMT EMPIRE CLYDE arrived Singapore with replacement Service personnel---]
Wed. 29th	29 HMT ASTURIUS arrived Southampton with returning Service personnel---]
+	29 HMT EMPIRE CLYDE sailed Singapore with returning Service personnel---]
Thur. 30th	30 HMT DILWARA arrived Southampton with returning Service personnel. ---]
Fri. 31s	R.A.F. 9 Sqdn. Canberra B6 Completed Operations at R.A.F. Butterworth.---]
+	R.A.F. 12 Sqdn. Canberra B6 Completed Operations at R.A.F. Butterworth.--]
+	R.A.F. 101 Sqdn. Canberra B6 Completed Operations at R.A.F. Butterworth.---]
+	R.A.F. 617 Sqdn. Canberra B6 Completed Operations at R.A.F. Butterworth.---]
+	Operation " _Cloud_" Completed---]

SEPTEMBER

Sat. 1st	Operation "_Latimer South_" Began the SAS Operation against the CT's ---]
Sun. 2nd	Combined Operations continued throughout Malaya---]
Mon. 3rd	An Aborignee CT named **Abeklum** Surrendered to the NZSAS---]
Tue. 4th	Combined Operations continued throughout Malaya---]
Wed. 5th	RAN _QUEENBOROUGH_ Completed her first engagement left Malayan coastal waters---].
Thur. 6th	**6 L/Bdr. Omar Bin Buyong**. Royal Artillery (MOR) Died ***_Claimed by next of Kin_ ---]
+	4 C.T's were Killed by Security Forces in an engagement in the jungles of Perak.---]
Fri. 7th	**7 Mr. T.G. Devonshire**. A British civilian Killed, by CT's Gunshots to head Kluang Johore.---]
Sat. 8th	'B' Coy, Royal Lincolnshire Regt. Engaged and Killed 1 CT identified as **Kwan Yuk** a leading CT Member---]
Sun. 9th	} Combined Operations continued throughout Malaya---]
Mon. 10th	**10 Spr. H.Langstaff**. Royal Engineers Died***_Kuala Lumpur # 23 / 12 02_ ---]
Tue. 11th	11/09/1056 LG.# 0874 p. 5151 The following awarded the Distinguished Flying Cross CAPT. P. T. A. MUSTERS. DFC ROYAL REGIMENT. ARTILLERY 11/09/1956 LG # 40874 p. 5151 The following awarded the Distinguished Flying Medal CAPT. P.T.A. MUSTERS. DFC ROYAL REGIMENT ARTILLERY CAPT N.P.W. RICKARD. DFC ROYAL REGIMENT ARTILLERY

+	11/09/1956 LG 30875 p.5159 The following awarded Bar to the Distinguished Flying Cross SDR/LDR.L.L. HARLAND. DFC +BAR ROYAL AIR FORCE The following awarded the Distinguished Flying Cross F/LT. T. W. SMAIL. DFC ROYAL AIR FORCE F/O. J. AULT. DFC ROYAL AIR FORCE
Wed. 12th	} Combined Operations continued throughout Malaya---]
Thur. 13th	}
Fri. 14th	**14 PC. Hussain B. Shariff.** F. M. Police Killed on Ops. Thailand / Malay Border.---]
Sat. 15th	15 HMT DEVONSHIRE arrived Liverpool with returning Service personnel---]
Sun. 16th	5 C.T's were Killed during an engagement in Negri Sembilan.---]
Mon. 17th	**17 Cpl. P. R. Coulter.** 1st. Battn. King's Own Scottish Borderers. Died***[*Ashes REP*]---]
+	17 EMPIRE FOWEY arrived Southampton with returning Service personnel----]
Tue. 18th	18/09/1956 LG # 40879 p. 5283 The following awarded the Military Medal SGT. F. C. ISSACS. MM ROYAL FUSILIERS A/T QUEEN'S OWN ROYAL WEST KENTS
Wed. 19th	} Combined Operations continued throughout Malaya---]
Thur. 20th	}
Fri. 21st	}
Sat. 22nd	} Combined Operations continued throughout Malaya---]
Sun. 23rd	}
Mon. 24th	} Combined Operations continued throughout Malaya---]
Tue. 25th	Whilst engaged clearing a Helicopter Landing Zone 'A' Company of the 2nd. 10th. Princess Mary's Own Gurkha Rifles discovered a CT camp. 1 CT guard fired at them & was Killed in the return fire. Upon a search, another dead CT was found in one of the huts, along with 6 packs in line. The corpse had been dead for approx. 4 days.---]
Wed. 26th	} Combined Operations continued throughout Malaya---]
Thur. 27th	RANS *'MELBOURNE"* & *'SYDNEY"* began their first engagement in Malayan coastal waters were joined by
Fri. 28th	*'QUADRANT'* on her third *whilst 'QUEENBOROUGH'* & *'QUICKMATCH'* *began* their second engagement, in Malayan coastal waters to commence their tour of duties as attachments to the BCFESR.---]
Sat. 29th	RANS HMAS *'TOBRUK'* & *'ANZAC'* Carried out Naval gunfire support to land forces on shore.---]
Sun. 30th	Combined Operations continued throughout Malaya---]

OCTOBER

Mon. 1st	Operations *'Cobble Shoe'* & *'Lagoon'* Began SAS against the MRLA ---]
Tue. 2nd	**2 Spr. Yaacob Bin Dollah.** Royal Engineers (MOR) Died *** [*Claimed by next of Kin*]----]
Wed. 3rd	} Combined Operations continued throughout Malaya---]
Thur. 4th	4 HMT CAPTAIN COOK arrived Glasgow with returning Service personnel---]
Fri. 5th	} Combined Operations continued throughout Malaya---]
Sat. 6th	6 HMT EMPIRE CLYDE arrived Liverpool with returning Service personnel ---]
Sun. 7th	7 HMT EMPIRE ORWELL arrived Southampton with returning Service personnel---]
Mon. 8th	**8 Mr. F.H. Sykes.** British Civilian Killed by a CT in Johore.---]
Tue. 9th	} Combined Operations continued throughout Malaya---]
Wed. 10th	}
Thur. 11th	**11 Gnr. Ahamad Bin Yaacob.** Royal Artillery (MOR) Died *** *Claimed by next of Kin* ---]
Fri. 12th	**12 PC. Saad B. Din.** F. M. Police Killed on Ops. Temerloh Pahang.---]
Sat. 13th	} Combined Operations continued throughout Malaya---]
Sun. 14th	}
Mon. 15th	} Combined Operations continued throughout Malaya---]
Tue. 16th	}
Wed. 17th	} Combined Operations continued throughout Malaya---]
Thur. 18th	Acting on information from an Aboriginee. Who informed the NZ SAS that 2 CT's had demanded food & taken 4 of his Friends as hostage. The NZ SAS went to seek out the 2 CT's. Made their way to a basha assumed where they were hiding along with their hostages . As 1 CT emerged from inside to relief himself. Shots rang out, killing him. This brought out the second CT inside the Basha he came out screaming. Another shot hit the CT, wounded him, but in the following confusion he escaped.---]
Fri. 19th	**19 D/Cpl. Wong Wee Choon.** FM.Police Killed on CT Ops. Kulai New Village Johore--]
Sat. 20th	} Combined Operations continued throughout Malaya---]

Sun. 21st	**21 Pte. A.W. Keen.** 2nd. Battn. R.A.R. Died ***. *Tiaping E / 64* Perak---]
Mon.22nd	**22 MAA. S.V. Spicer.** Royal Navy HMS *'TERROR* Died *** [*Ashes REP*]---]
Tue. 23rd	A Patrol of 2 RAR located a group of 4 CT's at a Tin Mine at Kongsi. Cpl. N. Byquar opened fire on the C.T's who got away. For his Action Engaging CT's Cpl. Byquar was M.I.D---].
Wed. 24th	**24 Mr. J.M. Wood.** Assnt Manager Amber Estate Johore Killed by CT's---].
+	The body of a CT was discovered by Rubber Tappers. Identified as one of the group of CT's previously seen on the 18th..---]
Thur. 25th	A Patrol of the Royal Lincolnshire Regt. Led by Lt. E.M.C.D. Taylor engaged a number of CT's Killing 2 identified as **Ah Chi** and **Ah Khee** 2 others were wounded also idebntified as **Ah Po** & **Mui Fong**.For their Action Engaging CT's during the fire fight. Lt Talyor was awarded the Military Cross and Iban tracker Pte. Reji Annuk Tapua MID.---]
Fri. 26th	**26 Mr. J.B.D Edwards.** Manager. Sungei Krudda Estate. Killed along with 2 F.M. Police **SC's Osman B. Mat Noor.- Yussof B. Mat Diah.** When approx 15 CT's attacked the Estate. Near Sungei Siput Perak.---]
+	Singapore: The Chinese Middle School riots in Singapore. Activated by the Communist Party were out of control---].
+	Singapore: The Pro Communist leader **Lim Chin Siong** held a workers meeting and together joined the students .---]
+	Singapore: More reinforcements were required from Battalions on Military Operation in Malaya: Operation *'Phot'* Initiated 6 Infantry Battlions, 2 Armoured Car Squadrons from Malaya to be despatched to Singapore-]
+	26/10/1956 LG # 40912 p. 6107 The following awarded the British Empire Medal (Military)
	W/O. E. R. WORSWICK. BEM ROYAL ARMY ORDNANCE CORPS
	The following awarded the BAR to Military Cross
	MAJ, A. S. HARVEY. MC BAR 6th QUEEN ELIZABETH'S OWN GURKHA RIFLES
	p. 6108 The following awarded the Military Cross.
	MAJ. LLYOD WILLIAMS. MC. 2nd. KING EDWARD VII'S OWN GURKHA RIFLES
	CAPT. D. RA.I MC 10th.PRINCESS MARY'S OWN GURKHA RILFES
	The following awarded Bar to the Military Cross
	MAJ. A,S, HARVEY. MC & BAR 6th. QUEEN ELIZABETH'S OWN GURKHA RIFLES
	The following awarded the Military Medal LG 6108/9
	CPL. I, GURUNG. MM 6th. QUEEN ELIZABETH'S OWN GURKHA RIFLES
	SGT. P. RAI. MM 7th. DUKE OF EDINBURGH'S OWN GURKHA RIFLES
	CPL. G. RAI. MM 10th. PRINCESS MARY'S OWN GURKHA RIFLES
	PTE. A.B.R. FALK. MM 2nd BATTN. ROYAL AUSTRALIAN REGIMENT
	PTE. L.A PENNANT. MM 2nd BATTN. ROYAL AUSTRALIAN REGIMENT
	p. 6109 The following are posthurmously Mentioned for Distinguished Service
	SGT. C.C. ANDERSON. 2nd BATTN. ROYAL AUSTRALIAN REGIMENT
	PTE G. C. FRI.TZ. 2nd BATTN. ROYAL AUSTRALIAN REGIMENT
Sat. 27th	RAN HMAS *'MELBOURNE'* & *'SYDNEY'*. Completed their first tour of engagement whilst *'QUADRANT'* Completed her third & final engagement. & *'TOBRUK'* Completed her first engagement In Malayan coastal waters. ---]
Sun. 28th	} Combined operations continued throughout Malaya ---]
Mon. 29th	**29 Capt. J.H. Villar.** Royal Artillery Died*** *Batu Gajah # 158* Ipoh Perak---]
Tue. 30th	RAN HMAS *'ANZAC'* completed her second tour of duty departed Malayan coastal waters---]
Wed. 31st	Combined Operations continued throughout Malaya---]

NOVEMBER

Thur. 1st	The NZSAS were removed from Fort Brooke area to take part in Operation " *Latimer South*"--]
+	1 HMT CAPTAIN COOK sailed from Glasgow bound for Wellington NZ---]
Fri. 2nd	**2 Pte. D. MacVicar.** 2nd. Battn. RAR. Died by accident. *Taiping # E / 65* Perak ---]
Sat. 3rd	Singapore: The riots in Singapore ended. Resulting in 13 deaths and more than 100 injured.---]
Sun. 4th	**4 Pte. C. E. A. Hobbs.** R.A.M.C. Died. Transport incident. [*Ashes REP*]---]
Mon. 5th	'B' Coy Royal Lincolnshire Regt. Killed 1 CT. during a Patrol in the jungle.---]
Tue. 6th	Combined Operations continued throughout Malaya---]
Wed. 7th	Kuala Lumpur: It was announced:
	'The Special Group is to be expanded and become totally Independent from The Federation Police ---]
Thur. 8th	**8 2/Lt. R.D. Ogden.** The Royal Lincolnshire Regt. and 2 Home Guards were accidently Killed when

Fri. 9th		they walked into a 'A" Coy's Lincolnshire ambush position. Battle Accident. _Kuala Lumpur # 23-12 03_---]
Sat. 10th		} Combined Operations continued throughout Malaya---]
Sun. 11th		Kuala Lumpur: Tenku Adul Rahman stated:
		'Merdeka will not end the war, in our determination to destroy the Communist Terrorrist' ---]
Mon. 12th		**12 L/Cpl. W. M. Goodwin.** 1st. Battn. Royal Scots Fusiliers. Died***[_Ashes REP_]
Tue. 13th		}
Wed. 14th		} Combined Operations continued throughout Malaya---]
Thur. 15th		}
Fri. 16th		**16 Pte. B. Ward.** R.A.O.C.. Died *** ._Kranji_ _Singapore # 2 / B – 4_ ---]
Sat. 17th		**17 LAC. R. F. Smith.** Elec/M R.A.F. Seletar Died*** ._Kranji Singapore # 12 / A - 9_ ---]
Sun. 18th		**18 Cpl. D. V. Giles.** R.E.M.E. Died accident in 12 Inf. Workshops.Ipoh. _Taiping # E / 66 Perak_—]
+		18 EMPIRE FOWEY sailed Southampton bound for Singapore with replacement Service personnel----]
Mon. 19th		19 HMT DEVONSHIRE sailed Southampton bound for Singapore with replacement Service personnel--]
Tue. 20th		The right hand man of **Chin Peng - Lau Lee** was ambushed & Killed at Tangkak Johore---]
+		20/11/56 LG #40928 p6571 The following was awarded the Military Medal
		SGT. E.J. O'SULLIVAN. MM. ROYAL WELCH FUSILIERS
Wed. 21st		} Combined Operations continued throughout Malaya---]
Thur.22nd		}
Fri. 23rd		**23 F/O J. A. N. Selth** [_Ashes REP]_.- F/O J. H. Witham._[Ashes REP]_ **Nav.-Sgt. K. L. Benton** A/Sig. _[Ashes REP]_ 48 Sqdn. RAF. **Cpl. J.E.Wellman.- Dvr. F. J. Merrett.- Dvr. E. Roberts. Dvr. P. Studd** 55Coy R.A.S.C.. Killed when Valetta VX525. Supply Aircraft making a steep turn crashed in the Cameron Highlands _Kuala Lumpur # RC / 23 -1206 23 / 1210 – 1208 – 1204_ ---]
Sat. 24th		}
Sun. 25th		} Combined Operations continued throughout Malaya---]
Mon. 26t.		}
Tue. 27th		27/11/1956 LG # 40934 p. 6707 The following awarded the Distinguished Flyng Cross
		F/LT. K. M. DEE. DFC. ROYAL AUSTRALIAN AIR FORCE
Wed. 28th		} Combined Operations continued throughout Malaya---]
Thur. 29th		In South Johore 174 Communist Sympathisers were arrested by the F. M Police. 101 are being detained under the Emergency Regulation 17C---]
Fri. 30th		30/11/1956 LG. # 40937 p. 6775 The following awarded Order British Empire Medal (Military)
		W/O. W.E. HUGHES.OBE ROYAL AUSTRALIAN SIGNALS CORPS.
		The following awarded the British Empire Medal (Military)
		PTE. K,N GRIBBLE. BEM 2st. BATTN. ROYAL AUSTR ALIAN REGIMENT,

DECEMBER

Sat. 1st		HMT DILWARA arrived Southampton.with returning Service personnel ---]
+		MV SKAUBRYN A Norwegian ship. Due to the Suez Crisis was hired by the MOD to take home returning Service personnel---]
Sun. 2nd		**2 Mr. B. R. Entwhistle** Manager. Killed by a Malayan Air Force sentry at night, on the Semenyih/Bangi track Selengor.---]
Mon. 3rd		**3 LAC. M . Murphy.** No 1 Sqdn. R.A.A.F.. Accidental Death ._Kranji Singapore # 3 / G – 5_ ---]
Tue. 4th		4 HMT DEVONSHIRE sailed Liverpool bound for Singapore with replacement Service personnel---]
Wed. 5th		**5 Rfn. Sangaparsad Thapa.** 6th. Queen Elizabeth's Own Gurkha Rifles. Died by accident. Seremban Hospital. _Seremban # 79 Negri Sembilan_.---]
Thur. 6th		**6 F/Lt. N. J. Gee. M.O.** R.A.F. Hospital Changi Died ***._Jewish Cemetery Singapore_---]
Fri. 7th		Army Bomb Disposal teams were on the scene at a Police Compound in Port Swettenham where a gardener found a war time British bomb. Believed to be left by the retreating British in 1942--]
+		7 HMT EMPIRE FOWEY arrived Singapore ---]
Sat. 8th		}Combined Coperations continued throughout Mlalaya ---]
Sun. 9th		}
Mon. 10th		10 **S/Ldr. A. S. Tie.**- F/O **W.A. Deviscovi.** - F/Off. **D.F. Nelson.** 41 Sqdn. RNZAF. Changi. _Kuala Lumpur #32 / 124 32/1226- 32 1225_ ----] **Sgt. B. R. Mathews.**- **Cpl. M. S. Walters.**- **Dvr. M. Wakefield.** 55 Coy R.A.S.C. 2 Cameramen Passengers **Low Hong Chye. – Louis Paul.** Were also Killed, when Bristol Freighter MNZ5901 Supplies airplane crashed, when it flew into a steep ridge approx 4,500 ft in the Cameron Highlands.

	An Auster spotter plane discovered the wreckage & the SAS found it.---]
	At the time it was assumed all 9 on the plane perished & were given temporary burials. Later interned at Cheras Road *Kuala Lumpur # 32 / 1224 – 1225- 1226 -1227 – 1229 – 1228*]---]
+	10 EMPIRE FOWEY sailed Singapore bound for Southampton with returning Service personnel----]
Tue.. 11th	} Combined Operations continued throughout Malaya---]
Wed. 12th	**12 Lt. J. Bowden.** Royal Navy HMS '*SIMBANG*' Died*** [*Ashes REP*]---]
Thur. 13th	The SAS and Malay Regt. found the bodies of the 9 RNZAF crew members of the crashed Bristol Freighter Last Monday. 5 bodies were found and a search for the other 4 continued ---]
+	*Cameron Highlands* R.A.A.F. Lincoln Bombers dropped bombs on a suspected CT hideout---]
Fri. 14th	The follow up by Gurkha troops involved a helicopter carrying the Gurkhas. After taking off from Tana Rata the Helicopter lost power dropping 15 feet. crashed upon landing to the East. There were no casualties But it was yet another victim of the Ghost mountain Gunong Patu Pateh---]
Sat. 15th	Home Gaurds at Aenai retuning to their Post after Patrolling the perimeter wire fence. Were fired upon by 2 CT's who fled when return fire was directed at them---]
Sun. 16th	A young Home Guard identified as **Wong Kim Pat** & his comrade **Chong Soh Mei** who deserted and joined the CT's was Killed by Gurkhas three others were captured in the Kluang District---]
Mon. 17th	A Landslide in the Cameron Highlands removed a large section of the road. British and Gurkha Troops travelling in a lorry, following a Saracen APC.16 were injured. The 15/19th. Hussars Saracen APC Slipped 200 ft down the ravine ---]
Tue. 18th	A rescue operation began involving the REME Recovery teams from 12th. Infantry Workshops. & 3 Coy LAD REME including the 15th/19th. Kings Royal Hussars. All from the Ipoh Garrison ---]
+	**18** The bodies of **Cpl. S. W. J. Wells.**- **Trp. A.G. Walker.** 15/19th. The King's Royal Hussars.were recovered from the APC Killed in the accident in the Cameron Highlands. Perak.*Taiping # E/ 67 – B/ 70* Perak---]
+	18 HMT DEVONSHIRE arrived Singapore with replacement Service personnel
Wed.19th	**19 Pte Anak Berain Dempi.** Sarawak Rangers Killed in Action Engaging CT's *Kranji Singapore # 19 / A 2* –
+	**19 PC. Mohd. Yussof B. Abd, Zain.** F. M. Police Killed on Ops. Johore.---]
Thur. 20th	*Drv. T. Lee. 55 Coy R.A.S.C.. Having survived the crash of the Bristol Freighter* Had already left the crash site before the SAS arrived. Sustained by rations off the plane, he was discovered on the 12th day by a Platoon of Malay Soldiers. Malay Infantry Regt.---]
Fri. 21st	**21 Air.Vice Marshall. F. J. St. G. Braithewaite.** CBE. R.A.F. Died***. [*Ashes REP*].-- -]
Sat. 22nd	}
Sun. 23rd	} Combined Operations continued throughout Malaya---]
Mon. 24th	}
Tue. 25th	25 HMT DEVONSHIRE sailed Singapore bound for Souhampton with returning Service personnel --]
Wed. 26th	**26 S/Sgt. W. E. M. Harris.** *Kuala Lumpur # 23 / 1205* R.E.M.E.. & **Cfn. A.B. Hassan.** (MOR) R.E.M.E [*Claimed by next of Kin*] - **Capt. Shukor bin Chik.** - **Sgt. Ibrahim bin Almad Badawi.**- **Pte. Ismail bin Yusoff.**- **Pte. Mohamad bin Khamis.**- **Pte. Ibrahin bin Abdul Kasim.** 6th Malay Infantry Regt. Were Killed in an ambush whilst on their way to recover a broken down Scout Car. In the Ayer Hitem area Pahang. 45 minutes after the ambush had occurred. An Officer of the 2/6th. Gurkhas. Major A.M. Morrison who was the first person to arrive at the ambush scene. Found S/Sgt. Harris's son. Arnold sitting beside his father's wrecked Land Rover & the dead Malay soldiers in the Austin Gantry recovery lorry. He immediately ordered his men of the 2/6th. Gurkhas & Home Guard to search the area, without finding any CT's---]
Thur. 27th	} Combined Operations continued throughout Malaya---]
Fri. 28th	**28 Rfn. Madbarsing Bura.** 6th. Queen Elizabeth's Own Gurkha Rifles. Killed in Action Engaging CT's Ipoh.*Sulva lines # 2* Ipoh Perak ---]
Sat. 29th	29 HMT DILWARA sailed Southampton. bound for Singapore/ Hong Kong.with replacement Service personnel ---]
Sun. 30th	**30 Cfn. R. Brown.** R.E.M.E. Died *** *Taiping # E / 68* Perak---]
+	30 EMPIRE FOWEY arrived Southampton with returning Service personnel----]
Mon. 31st	With the H.M Queen's approval The following awards were made to Members of the Royal Limcolnshire Regt. approval of the Negri Sembilan State Meritourious Medal to :-
+	SGT. G. L. BENCH. M.M N.S.S. ROYAL LINCOLNSHIRE REGIMENT. Negri Sembilan State Conspicious Gallantry Medal to L/CPL. C.J HENDERSON N.S S C & PTE. R.C. POWELL. G M N.S S C ROYAL LINCOLNSHIRE REGIMENT.
+	31 HMT CAPTAIN COOK arrived Singapore Roads ---]

R. A. F. OPERATION "*FIREDOG*" END OF YEAR STATISTICS 1956

No of Sorties	No. of Strikes	1,000 Lb.Bombs	500 Lb. Bombs	350 LbCluster	20 LbBombs	R/P's	20mm	.5 mm	.303mm
800	139	2,579	2,283	/	3,351	873	109,900	75,943	/

R. A. F. SUPPORT 1956

	Soties	Troops/Lift	Casac	Pass/Lift	Supply Wt. Lbs	Leaflets(1,000)	B Flying Times No / hrs	Broadcsting No / hrs	Crashed
Air SupportA/C*	56	/	/	/	1,523,701	/	/	/	Valetta's
Auster**	16,205	/	/	/	/	/	/	/	KN861
Anson ***	Inc.	/	/	/	/	/	/	/	VX521
Pioneer	N/A	830	13	110	96.807	/	/	/	VX525
H/C Light	N/A	/	/	/	/	/	/	/	Bristol
848 Sqdn	Disbanded	/	/	/	/	/	/	/	MNZ2901
155 Sqdn	N/A	4.033	173	378	91,854	/	/	/	Venom
Target/MK**	137	/	/	/	/	/	/	/	WE373
Vis/Air **	6,111	/	/	/	/	/	/	/	Dragonfly
Communication**	9536	/	/	/	/	/	/	/	XF267
Leaflets Sorties*	333	'/	/	/.	/	/	/	../	Sykorski S55
Leaflets Drop*	/	/	/	/	/	96,568	/	./	RN No?
Leaflets Sorties**	inc	/	/	/	/	/	/	/	Auster
Leaflets Drop**	/	/	/	/	/	/	/	/	WZ694
Broad Sorties*	485	/	/	/	/	/	1311.5	/	McConn?
Broad Hrs *	/	/	/	/	/	/	/	563.8	
Broad Sorties**	294	/	/	/	/	/	371.3		
Broad Hrs **	/	/	/	/	/	/	/	363.2	
Photo Rec*** Tot	974	/	/	/	/	/	/		
AirOP**	127	/	/	/	/	/	/	/	

** Auster
*** Photo Rec Anson,Spitfire, Mosquito, Meteor

CHAPTER 15 – 1957

31st AUGUST MERDEKA DAY

ROYAL AIR FORCE
OFFENSIVE AIR SUPPORT - OPERATION 'FIREDOG'
January 1957 to December 1960

Sqdn	Location	Aircraft Type	No	Date From	Year	Date To	Year
48	Changi	Hastings C1/2	8	1st. May	1957	Jul	1960
214	Changi	Valient B	2-4	31st. Oct.	1957	27th. Mar.	1959

JANUARY

Tue. 1st	Operations *'Latimer South'* began in the Bahau & Rompin area of Negri Sembilan ---]
+	Operations *'Shark North' 'Shark South'* & *'Cheiftan'* began in the Ipoh , Tapah & Cameron Highlands area
+	Operations *'Shoe" Huckster'* began in the Gemas Segamat Kuala Lipis area ---]
+	Operations *'Gabes'* began in the Perak Kelantan area --]
+	Operation *'Tartan Rock'* began in the Kluang Kualai area --]
Wed. 2nd	2 MV SKAUBRYN arrived Southampton with returning Service personnel---]
+	2 HMT CAPTAIN COOK sailed Singapore bound for Liverpool with returning Service personnel---]
Thur. . 3rd	3 EMPIRE FOWEY sailed Southampton via Cape Town for Singapore / Hong Kong with replacement Service personnel---]
Fri. 4th	4/01/1957. LG # 40968 p. 143 The following awarded the Military Cross LT E.M.C.D. TAYLOR. MC ROYAL LINCOLNSHIRE REGIMENT. The following awarded the Military Medal L.CPL A. RANA. MM 2nd KING EDWARD'S OWN GURKHA RIFLES
Sat. 5th	} Combined Operations continued throughout Malaya---]
Sun. 6th	6 Pte. A. D. Barson. 1st. Battn.Royal Lincolnshire Regt. Killed Road traffic accident. *Taiping # E – 69* Perak---]
Mon. 7th	} Combined Operations continued throughout Malaya---]
Tue. 8th	Near Pontian Security forces raided CT lairs. Arrested 12 Students Mainly Chinese ---]
Wed. 9th	A Lincoln Bomber of No 1 Sqdn R.A.A.F. No.A73 -40 Mk.3OA crashed into the sea 400 yrds off shore near Pontian 7 crew members were injured, all were brought ashore safely---]
Thur. 10th	London: A Defence Minister ? Stated: *'There would be no cuts to the forces in Malaya'* ---]
Fri. 11th	11 Sgt. W.T. McNichol-Moncur. R.E.M.E.. Died*** *Kuala Lumpur # 11 /A – 13* ---]
Sat. 12th	The wreckage of Auster VF604 lost on 21/1/1954 was found in deep jungle near Kuala Lumpur. The bodies were not found, However, the 2 Occupants have been listed as buried in Kuala Lumpur see date of crash-]
Sun. 13th	}
Mon. 14th	} Combined Operations continued throughout Malaya---]
Tue. 15th	15 HMT DUNERA sailed Southampton bound for Singapore via CapeTown with replacement Service personnel---]
Wed. 16th	16 HMT DEVONSHIRE arrived Singapore with replacement Service personnel---]
Thur. 17th	17 Sgt. H. W. Richards. R.E.M.E. Died*** *Taiping # E / 70* Perak---]
+	CT *Li Yau* surrendered to Troops of the NZ SAS Regt.---]
Fri. 18th	'D' Coy of the 1st. Battn. Royal Lincolnshire Regt. Killed *Ah. Ku.* In an ambush near Sungei Siput.---]
+	18 HMT DEVONSHIRE sailed Singapore for Hong Kong ---]
Sat. 19th	A Patrol of the NZSAS Regt. Killed *Leong Chuen* a CT courier. Important documents were found on his body. Another CT who was wounded escaped.---]
Sun. 20th	20 Maj. H. E. Bryde. 1st. Battn. 2nd. Battn. Royal Welsh Fusilliers Died*** *[Ashes REP]*---]
Mon. 21st	21 Cfn. B. Caley. R.E.M.E.. Died*** *[Ashes REP]*---]
+	Auster VF604 lost during a weather recce .The two occupant Sgt J. Perry Army Air Corps & F/lt. J. Maulden Never found *[No known Grave}* Terandak Memorial Malacca]---]
Tue. 22nd	22 HMT EMPIRE ORWELL sailed Southampton bound for Singapore via Cape Town with replacement Service personnel---]
Wed. 23rd	A Communist Party Secretary *Chau Choi* & his *mistress* was shot dead near Ipoh---]
Thur. 24th	RAN HMAS *'QUICKMATCH'* & *'QUEENBOROUGH'* Carried out Naval gunfire support to Land Forces ---]

Fri. 25th	} Combined Operations continued throughout Malaya---]
Sat. 26th	**The Author** Joe Plant after 18 Months in Ipoh. Left 3 Coy REME LAD entrained to Singapore ---]
Sun. 27th	} Combined Operations Continued throughout Malaya---]
Mon. 28th	A Game warden shot and Killed a Tiger who had previously Killed a 12 year old Girl near Bentong---
Tue. 29th	**29 QGO) Lt. Pemba Tshering Lama** 6th. Queen Elizabeth's Own Gurkha. Rifles. Died from Wounds recv'd Sikamet Camp. _Seremban # 80_ Negri Sembilan---]
+	29.**The Author** Joe Plant Flew out of Changi Airport Singapore, enplaned on a BOAC Super Constalation Flight to London Hearthrow. Due for Demob on the 3rd. February?----]
Wed. 30th	Combined Oerations continued throughout Malaya ---]
Thur. 31st	Operation _'Huckster'_ 24- Gemas Segamat Kedah ended ---]

Transcript from Straits Times Jan. 3rd. 1957.

AMBUSH BOY'S STORY.

as reported by Nelson Rutherford. (Ref Ambush 26th. December 1956)Quote

It took 15 minutes for Arnold Harris to become a man - 15 horrifying minutes in which he saw his father & seven others shot down in a terrorist ambush.

His story began at 4am on Boxing day when he & 10 other men of the 6th. Bttn. Malay Regt. Set off for Ayer Hitam to repair a broken down scout car.With Arnold in the Land Rrover were his, father S/Sgt. William Harris 38 R.E.M.E. att. to the Malay Regt. Captain Shukar bin Chik & two Malay soldiers. Behind was an Austin Gantry Recovery wagon. With six Malay soldiers aboard. They were in high spirits, Arnold was thinking of the Aircraft carrier kit his father had given him for a Christmas present. He would start to build it as soon as they got back. The time was 6.45 a.m. as they approached a bend in the road beyond it, 30 Terrorist would be waiting in ambush positions. Arnold told me "We were all laughing, Captain Shukur had just made a joke. Suddenly I heard firing I thought something had happened to the engine. Then the windscreen was shattered & Captain Shukur shouted to me to get down. He & my father had been hit by bullets. The Captain died in the next burst of fire & dad was hit.

The two soldiers sitting in the back with me grabbed their rifles out of the gun clips, hitting me on the head in the process, jumped out & were shot down. I was hit by shotgun pellets but did not feel it. I got my head down near the door , There were more shots, then I heard voices. I looked up & saw the Chinese terrorist around me. They were taking the canvas off the Land Rover. They were fully uniformed & wore peaked hats with red stars on & twigs for camouflage, all carried guns. One asked me if I or my father had a gun. I shook my head. Then a short fat man helped me out into the road & laid me on the grass verge. He was very gentle, he gave me two Asprins, I swallowed one but decided not to touch the other because thought it might be poison. Then they threw everything out of the Land Rover including a box containing two mouse deer given to me earlier, then bayoneted them. The gang went over to my father, who had been hit in the first burst & searched him. They also searched the other bodies.& took everything they could find.

MYSTERY CAR.

The reds stole two rifles, a pistol. S/Sgt. Harris's camera containing shots taking the previous day at a Christmas party, jungle boots, wallets & shirts, they also took Arnolds hat.

As they finished a P.W.D jeep with three men in it arrived from the direction of Bentong. The bandits stopped it & the man sitting next to the driver got out smiled & spoke to them . I saw him give something to one of the terrorist, I think it was a piece of white paper. Then he got back into the jeep & then drove away. The driver saw me besides the road but pretended not to notice me. A few seconds later a terrorist on the bank above shouted & began waving his hands. The whole gang ran up the bank & disappeared. I knew they had seen the recovery waggon, it had been travelling about four minutes behind us. The bandits opened fire above me with Bren guns from three different positions. A soldier leant out of the window with his gun ready he was about to shoot when a bullet caught him.

ESCAPE BID.

Then Dad called me, he was lying by the Land Rover & he told me to drive it away. I said would not leave him behind. "Never mind me" he said. I dragged him into the vehicle & was trying to start it, when the gang started firing again. I thought they were shooting at me & took cover. My father fell out, he asked me for some water & asked me to find a stream. There were no streams, then I remembered the radiator of the Land Rover. I hope it wasn't punctured.

I'M GOING'.

I filled the lid of a cardboard box with water & gave it to dad. One of the soldiers lying in the drain had come too. I tied a piece of string around his leg, it was bleeding badly.Suddenly my dad said.

" I'm going Arnold, look after the family ." He didn't say anything more .

Arnold paused for a moment. his eyes on the floor, then he murmured. I waited beside dad for a car to come along. Five minutes later a black car packed with people arrived I shouted to the driver but he would not stop. ---]Unquote.

FEBRUARY

Fri.	1st	**1 Pte. Mjikijelwa**. 1st. Rhodesian African Rifles. Died***_Kranji Singapore # 4 / E -4_ --]
		1st Battn. Royal Lincolnshire Regt. relocated to North Perak with their HQ at Taiping.---]
Sat.	2nd	2 HMT DEVONSHIRE arrived Singapore sailed for Liverpool with returning Service personnel 2nd..---]
Sun.	3rd	}
Mon.	4th	} Combined Operations continued throughout Malaya---]
Tue.	5th	}
Wed.	6th	6 EMPIRE FOWEY arrived Singapore with replacement Service persoannel---]
Thur.	7th	7 EMPIRE FOWEY sailed from Singapore for Hong Kong. ---]
	+	A Malay Terrorist CT. **Rompah** Head of the State propaganda & Press surrendered to the NZ SAS Regt.---]
Fri.	8th	**8 AC. G. A. Pickering**. R.A.F. Police Seletar Died***_[Ashes REP]_---]
Sat.	9th	} Combined Operations continued throughout Malaya---]
Sun.	10th	}
Mon.	11th	11 HMT CAPTAIN COOK arrived Liverpool with returning Service personnel---]
Thur.	12th	5 Troop NZ SAS came across 4 Indians dressed like CT's. They opened fire and Killed them only to discover they were Tamils from nearby Estates, hunting in a prohibited area.Unfortunate accident.---]
	+	12/2/1957.LG # 40999 p 975. The following awarded the George Medal
		ASST SUP. A. J. V. FLETCHER .GM FEDERATION MALAYA POLICE
		INSP. GOH CHIN HEE..GM FEDERATION MALAYA POLICE
Wed.	13th	The 2nd. Battn. Royal Welch Fusiliers took over Security duties in Singapore---]
Thur.	14th	**14 Dvr. M. Burke**. R.A.S.C.. Died Railway incident. _Kuala Lumpur # 33 / 1207_ ---]
	+	**14 Spr. Harkabahadur Gurung.** Gurkha. Engineers. Died Motor Veh. Acc. _Kuala Lumpur 26 / 11_---]
	+	14./2/57. LG # 40999 p. 975 The following awarded the George Medal
		ASP. A.J.V. FLETCHER. GM FEDERATION MALAYA POLICE
		INSP GOH CHIN HEE. GM FEDERATION MALAYA POLICE
		The following awarded the Colonial Police Medal
		D/PC. IDRIS B. ABDULLAH. CPM FEDRATION OF MALAYA POLICE
Fri.	15th	}
Sat.	16th	} Combined Operations continued throughout Malaya---]
Sun.	17th	}
Mon.	18th	}
Tue.	19th	19 EMPIRE FOWEY arrived Singapore enroute to Southampton with returning Service personnel sailed 19th.---]
Wed.	20th	**20 Spr. Othmaan Bin Saad** Royal Engineers (MOR)Died*** _Claimed by next of Kin_ ---]
Thur.	21st	London Publication of the report of the Federation of Malaya Constitutional Commission headed by Lord Reid were published in London & Kuala Lumpur on the future Independence of Malaya---]
Fri.	22nd	}
Sat.	23rd	} Combined Operations continued throughout Malaya---]
Sun.	24th	}
Mon.	25th	}
Tue.	26th	**26 Cfn. Abdul Aziz . Bin. Ahmad** R.E.M.E. (MOR) Died***_Claimed by next of Kin_---]
	+	26 HMT EMPIRE ORWELL arrived Singapore with replaceenet Service personnel---]
Wed.	27th	Combined Operations continued throughout Malaya---]
Thur.	28th	28 HMT OXFORDSHIRE sailed Liverpool bound for Singapore / Hong Kong with replacement Service personnel---]

MARCH

Fri.	1st	London: House of Commons: A new revision to the National Service Act. When Mr. Duncan Sandys, the then Defence Minister, issued a White Paper outlining the Government's future defence policy & foreshadowing sweeping changes effecting all three Services. Officially described as:
		"The biggest change in defence policy ever made in normal times." The main point in the new policy that directly effected National Servicemen was:
	+	**A progressive reduction in National Service intake with no further call -up after the end of 1960---]**
	+	1 HMT DUNERA sailed Singapore bound for Southampton via Cape Town with returning Service personnel]

Sat. 2nd	2 HMT EMPIRE ORWELL sailed Singapoe bound for Southampton via Cape Town .with returning Service personnel ---]
Sun. 3rd	A Patrol of the RAR captured an arms Factory of the CT's near Kuala Kangsar it was one of the biggest caches discoved during the Emergency---]
Mon. 4th	Kuala Lumpur: Tenku Abdul Rahman strongly criticized the demand made by 85 British Labour MPs for the withdrawal of all British Service personnel from Malaya – stating: 'It is as much the duty of the British people as the Malayans themselves to meet and crush the Communist challenge. It is accepted by all the free world that the fight against the Communists in Malaya is not Malaya's concern alone'---]
Tue. 5th	CT *Kadir* surrendered to the NZ SAS He became a valuable S.E.P. ---]
Wed. 6th	6 PC Abd. Rahman B. Abd, Wahab. F. M. Police Killed on Ops. Bentong/ Kuala Lumpur Rd. Pahang---]
Thur. 7th	}
Fri. 8th	}
Sat. 9th	} Combined Operations continued throughout Malaya --]
Sun. 10th	}
Mon. 11th	}
Tue. 12th	12/03/1957. LG # 41020 p1575 The following awarded the Military Medal CPL. GTHAPA. MM 2nd. KING EDWARD VII'S OWN GURKHA RIFLES The following awarded the British Empire Medal (Military) FUS. J. GALLAGHER. BEM ROYAL SCOTS FUSILIERS
Wed. 13th	} Combined Operations continued throughout Malaya---]
Thur. 14th	15 HMT ASTURIUS sailed Southampton bound for Singapore / Hong Kong with replacement Service
Fri. 15th	personnel---] 'A', 'B' & 'HQ' Comps of the Royal Lincolnshire Regt. Were involved in a rescue operation when a three
Sat. 16th	story Rubber Factory collapsed. Five bodies were recovered.---]
Sun. 17th	17 Cpl. J.M. O'Donnell. Royal Australian Air Force. Died by Accident *Western Road # 2166* George Town Penang---]
Mon. 18th	18 HMT DEVONSHIRE arrived Liverpool with returning Service personnel---]
Tue. 19th	} Combined Operations continued throughout Malaya---]
Wed. 20th	A Troop of the NZ SAS Killed 1 CT Identified as *Wong Kwai – (Li Hak Chi's* No 2I/c) ---]
Thur. 21st	} Combined Operations continued throughout Malaya---]
Fri. 22nd	22 Pte. E. F. Thompson. R.A.A.S.C. 127 Plt 3 Coy Died Transport incident. *Taiping I / 1* Perak---]
+	22 F/Lt. R. L. Hollands HQ R.A.F. Changi. Died ***.*[Ashes REP]*---]
+	22 EMPIRE FOWEY arrived Southampton via Cape Town with returning Service personnel ---]
+	Kuala Lumour :The Malayan Communist are making another attempt to start up Peace agreements with
Sat. 23rd	the Malayan Government. The Tenku stated: 'He was unaware of any such letter' --] } Combined Operations throughout Malaya continued---]
Sun. 24th	A Wanted CT identified as *Yua Fook* was shot dead by a F.M. Police Sgt. In the Gunong Rapat area of
Mon. 25th	the caves near Ipoh. He was I of the last 2 remaining CT's of the Gunong Rapat Cell--] London : The Last details have been agreed for the Self Government of Singapore The Documents will
Tue. 26th	be signed Next week by both British and Singapore Delegates---]
Wed. 27th	} Combined Operations continued throughout Malaya ---]
Thur. 28th	}
Fri. 29th	29 HMT DILWARA sailed Southampton bound for Singapore with replacement Service personnel via Cape Town---]
Sat. 30th	} Combined Operations continued throughout Malaya---]
Sun. 31st	}

APRIL

Mon. 1st	1 Cpl. R. G. Kiddell. R.A.M.C.. Died***[Ashes REP]---]
+	Operation 'Cobble' began in the Gemas Segamat Kluang area ---]
+	1 HMT OXFORDSHIRE arrived Singapore with replacement Service personnel enroute to Hong Kong 1st.]
Tue. 2nd	} Combined Operations Continued throughout Malaya ---]
Wed. 3rd	3 Pte. D. E. Allen. 1st. Battn. The Loyal Regt. Died*** *Kranji Singapore # 11 / A – 15* ---]
Thur. 4th	4 HMT EMPIRE ORWELL arrived Southampton with returning Service personnel---]
Fri. 5th	In the area of Gemas a 5 Man Plattoon of the 2nd. 10th. Gurkhas engaed 5 CT's killing 2 CT's. Identified as

		members of the local Min Yuen Group--]
Sat.	6th	}
Sun.	7th	} Combined Operations continued throughout Malaya---]
Mon.	8th	}
Tue.	9th	RAN HMAS 'MELBOURNE' & 'WARRAMUNGA' Began their second tour whilst 'ANZAC' & 'TOBRUK' their third attachment to the BCFESR.---]
Wed.	10th	10 Cpl. Mohamad. Bin. Yusoff. (MOR) Malay R.A.F. Regt. Kuala Lumpur. Killed in Action Engaging CT's Seremban Area.[Claimed by next of Kin]---]
	+	10 HMT DUNERA arrived Southampton with returning Service personnel ---]
Thur.	11th	11 Cpl. Mehsar Thapa . 2nd. King Edward VII's Own Gurkha Rifles. Killed in Action Engaging CT's Seremban area- Seremban # 81 Negri Sembilan ---]
	+	11 HMT EMPIRE FOWEY sailed Southampton bound for Singapore/ Hong Kong.via Cape Town with replacement Service personnel--]
	+	11 HMT OXFORDSHIRE arrived Singapore ---]
Fri.	12th	12 Sgt. A. Barrie. R.A.S.C.. Died. Transport incident. Kranji Singapore # 11 / A – 16 ---]
	+	Another Malay Terrorist CT Kadir surrendered to the NZSAS Regt. S.E.P. Li Yau had led to his whereabouts.]
Sat.	13th	} Combined Operations continued throughout Malaya---]
Sun.	14th	}
Mon.	15th	15 HMT ASTURIUS arrived Singapore with replacement Service personnel.---]
Tue.	16th	16 Cpl. R. F Martin. A/F/Fit. R.A.F. Seletar Died when the Whirlwind XJ427 Crashed at Seletar. The two other crew members survived. Kranji Singapore # 12 / A – 10 ---]
	+	16 HMT ASTURIUS sailed Singapore enroute to Hong Kong---]
Wed.	17th	17 Cfn. G. Beck. R.E.M.E.. Died***Kuala Lumpur # 23 / 1212 ---]
	+	While on Patrol on the Nam Fatt Yen Estate nearTapah. The East Kent Regt. engaged 3 CT's killing 2 and wounding the third who was captured. During the engagment Lt. Hodges followed one of the CT's and Killed him. Later he was identified as a notorious CT on the wanted list ---]
Thur.	18th	18 HMT OXFORDSHIRE sailed Singapore bound for Liverpool via Durban with returning Service personnel]
Fri.	19th	19 Troops of the NZSAS Regt. lying in ambush. Shot & Killed Wong Quai the assistant to the group leader Li Hak Chi.More important documents were also found on his body. Again S.E.P. Li Yau led to this ambush.-]
Sat.	20th	}
Sun.	21st	} Combined Operations continued throughout Malaya---]
Mon.	22nd	}
Tue.	23rd	23 J/Tech. P. Arundell. SAC. A. Ledson. [Ashes REP] R.A.F. Tengah wore both Killed when their Land Rover was hit by a Venom VE399. Kranji Singapore # 12 / B – 6 ---]
Wed.	24th	}Combined Operations continued throughout Malaya---]
Thur.	25th	}
Fri.	26th	26 A/B. W.S. Spooner. HMAS 'TOBRUK' Was Killed when struck by a Star shell casing fired by HMS 'COCKADE' during an engagement off the East coast of Malaya near Pulau Tioman. Buried at Sea [No known Grave]Terandak Wall Memorial Malacca---]
	+	26 HMT EMPIRE ORWELL sailed Southampton bound for Singapore via CapeTown with replacement Service personnel---]
	+	26/04/1957 LG # 40156 p. 2571 The following awarded the Distinguished Conduct Medal W/O. E. R. MASON. DCM ROYAL WELCH FUSILIERS
Sat.	27th	27 HMT ASTURIUS arrived Singapore enroute to Southampton with returning Service personnel---]
Sun.	28th	Combined Operation continued throughout Malaya---]
Mon.	29th	RAN HMAS 'WARRAMUNGA' Completed her second tour of duty in Malayan coastal waters.---]
Tue.	30th	} Combined Operations continued throughout Malaya ---]

MAY

Wed.	1st	Operation "Cheiftan" Began SAS operation against the CT's---]
Thur.	2nd	} Combined Operations continued throughout Malaya---]
Fri.	3rd	In an area of Negri Sembilan a CT leader Tong Fook Leong was Killed by Security Forces in an ambush-
Sat.	4th	} Combined Operations continued throughout Malaya---]
Sun.	5th	5 Capt. Sunwar. Gurung 2nd. King Edward VII's Own Own Gurkha. Rifles. Died*** [Ashes REP]---]
Mon.	6th	} Combined Operations continued throughout Malaya---]

Tue. 7th	5 Lincoln Bombers No 1 Sqdn R.A.A.F. 12 Venoms No 60 Sqdn R. A. F. & No14 Sqdn RNZAF made a co-ordinated strike on a suspected CT Camp of **Ten Fook Long** Ground forces reported the area had been devastated & impossible to carry out further investgations---]
Wed. 8th	8 HMT DILWARA arrived Singapore with replacement Service personnel---]
Thur. 9th	} Combined Operations continued throughout Malaya---]

Fri. 10th	10/05/1957 LG # 41066 p. 2787 The following awarded the George Medal
	L/Cpl. AS RAMAN B. AWANG GM. 4th. MALAY REGIMENT.
	                     For saving life from the swollen River Woh S Perak.
	                  The following awarded the Disinguished Conduct Medal
	PTE. AHMAD. B, UDIN. DCM 6th MALAY REGIMENT.

Sat. 11th	11 T/Cpl. **A. G. Buchanan**. RNZ SAS. Regt. Died on operations at Kuala Pilah. *Kuala Lumpur # 23 / 1213*]
Sun. 12th	} Combined Operations continued throughout Malaya---]
Mon. 13th	13 Cpl. **L. Kalunsing Lepcha. - Cpl. Kabir Rai** . 7th. Duke of Edinburgh's Own Gurkha. Rifles Killed in Action Engaging CT's *Kluang # 3 / C 9 3 / D – 13* ---]
Tue. 14th	14 HMT DUNERA sailed Soutampton bound for Singapore via Cape Town with replacement Service personnel ---]
+	14 HMT DILWARA sailed Singapore with replacement Service personnel bound for Penang---]
+	14 HMT EMPIRE FOWEY arrived Singapore enroute to Hong Kong with replacement Service personnel sailed 14th.---]
Wed. 15th	15/05/1957 LG # 40169 p.2869 The following awarded the British Empire Medal (Military) LAC B HANCOCK. BEM THE ROYAL AUSTRALIAN AIR FORCE
Thur. 16th	16 HMT DILWARA arrived Penang ---]
Fri. 17th	A night time strike by No 1 R.A.A.F. Lincoln Bombers dropped 70,000 lbs of bombs, on a known CT camp.---]
+	A follow up by ground forces Identifed the bodies of **Ten Fook Long & his wife** along with others not named----]
+	17 HMT DILWARA sailed Penang bound for Southampton via Cape Town.with returning Service personnel With the 1st Battn. Royal Scots Fusiliers, having completed their 3 year tour of active Service in Malays---]
Sat. 18th	18 HMT OXFORDSHIRE arrived Liverpool with returning Service personnel---]
Sun. 19th	} Combined Operations continued throughout Malaya---]
Mon. 20th	20 F/Sgt. **J. Marrey**. A/Eng. R.A.F. Seletar Died****Kranji Singapore # 14 / A – 21* ---]
+	In an ambush near Ipoh **Chin Voon** a High ranking CT on the wanted list was captured---]
Tue. 21st	} Combined Operations continued throughout Malaya---]
Wed.22nd	The Seretary of the MCP State Committee **Ah Fatt** was shot dead in an ambush by the Security Force]
Thur. 23rd	} Combined Operations continued throughout Malaya ---]

Fri. 24th	24/05/1957 LG # 41079 p 3156 The following awarded the Military Cross
	MAJ MIRYLEES. M.C THE LEICESTERSHIRE REGIMENT.
	Lt. I.H. BURROWS. MC NEW ZEALAND SPECIAL AIR SERVICE
	Maj J.B.C. PALMER. MC QUEEN'S WEST SURREY REGIMENT.
	LT. R.I HYWEL – JONES. MC THE SOUTH WALES BORDERERS
	MAJ. A.B. ISMAIL. MBE MC. MALAY REGIMENT.
	                  The following awarded BAR to Military Cross
	MAJ. J.E.G. VIVIEN. MC & BAR 2nd. KING EDWARD VII'S OWN GURKHA RIFLES.
	                  The following awarded the Military Medal.LG 3156
	SGT. G.R.TURNBULL. MM ROYAL REGIMENT ARTILLERY ATT/T SAS.
	PTE. C. NEWMAN..MM SOUTH WALES BORDERERS
	CPL. B. RAI. MM 10th PRINCESS MARY'S OWN GURKHA RIFLES
	SGT. H.B. AWANG. MM MALAY REGIMENT
	CPL. R.B.S.B ISMAIL. MM MALAY REGIMENT

Sat. 25th	} Combined Operations continued throughout Malaya ---]
Sun. 26th	26 Pte. **R. M. Harper**. 1st King's Own Scottish Borderers. Died*** *Kranji Singapore # 11/ A – 17*---]
Mon. 27th	27 HMT ASTURIUS arrived Southampton with returning Service personnel ---]
+	27 HMT EMPIRE FOWEY arrived Singapore ---]
+	27 HMT EMPIRE FOWEY sailed Singapore bound for Southampton with returning Service personnel---]
Tue. 28th	28/05/1957 LG #41079 p 3156 The following awarded the Military Cross LT.A.W. CAMPBELL. MC 2nd BATTN. ROYAL AUSTRALIAN REGIMENT. The following were awarded the Military Medal.

	CPL. D.J. HUMPHREYS. MM	ROYAL WELCH FUSILIERS
	PTE. Y. B UMAT. MM	MALAY REGIMENT
Wed. 29th	} Combined operations continued throughout Malaya ---]	
Thur. 30th	**30 L/Cpl. Tongogara.** 1st. Rhodesian African Rifles. Killed in Ambush _Kranji Singapore # 4 / E – 7_ ---]	
+	30 HMT EMPIRE ORWELL arrived Singapore.with replacement Service personnel---]	
Fri. 31st	**31 Pte. Josephe.** 1st. Rhodesian African Rifles. Died from wounds recvd on previous days ambush _Kranji Singapore # 14 / A – 25_ ---]	
+	31/05/1957 LG # 41084 p 2333 The following awarded the Military Cross	
	LT. D.G. HOOD. MC	THE SHERWOOD FORESTERS

JUNE

Sat. 1st	A four man Patrol of 'C' Coy the Royal Lincolnshire Regt. led by Capt. P. F. Walter successfully beat off a band of 30 CT's in an ambush on the Jalong Tinggi Estate near Sungei Siput. During the fire fight **Wan Tai Lui** was Killed. In recognition their Action Engaging CT's. Capt. P. F. Walter was awarded the MC Pte. Taylor & Iban Tracker. Pte Anak. Alo Empang were MID.---]	
Sun. 2nd	} Combined Operations ontinued throughout Malaya---]	
Mon. 3rd	3 HMT EMPIRE ORWELL sailed Singapore bound for Southampton via Cape Town with replacement Service personnel--]	
Tue. 4th	The 2nd. Battn. Royal Welch Fusiliers became non operational handing over Duties to the 1st. Battn. South Wales Borderes---]	
+	4 HMT ASTURIUS sailed Southampton bound for Singapore/ Hong Kong with replacement Service personnel---]	
Wed. 5th	} Combined Operations continued throughout Malaya---]	
Thur. 6th	}	
Fri. 7th	7/06/1957 LG #41096 p 3495 The following awarded the Distinguished Flying Medal	
	W/O. C.D. JENKINS. DFM	THE PARACHUTE REGIMENT.
	CPL. T. E. WESTBROOK. DFM	ROYAL ARMY SERVICE CORP
Sat. 8th	**8 Rfn. Manbahadur Gurun.** 6th. Queen Elizabeth's Own Gurkha. Rifles Died by Accident Cameron Highlands. _Sulva Lines # 50_ Ipoh Perak. ---]	
Sun. 9th	**9 Capt. D. C. Howard.** Royal Signals Died ** _Kranji Singapore # 11 / A -11_ ---]	
+	**9 Dvr. Abdul Ghanfer. Bin .Abdul . Mamid.** R.A.S.C.. (MOR) Died***_Claimed by next of Kin_]---]	
Mon. 10th	} Combined Operation continued throughout Malaya ---]	
Tue. 11th	11/06/1957 LG # 40197 p.3505 The following awarded the British Empire Medal	
	SGT. W. DODDS. MBE	ROYAL AIR FORCE.
	SGT. J.M.YOUNG.MBE	ROYAL AIR FORCE.
		The following awarded Bar the Distinguished Flying Cross
	SDN/LDR. E.W.FORWELL DFC +BAR	ROYAL AIR FORCE.
	MAS/NAV J. LANCASTER DFC +BAR	ROYAL AIR FORCE.
	F/LT. R. B. MORGAN. DFC	ROYAL AIR FORCE.
	F/LT. W.F. J. STEVENS. DFC	ROYAL AIR FORCE.
	F/LT. W. F. BURKE. DFC	ROYAL AIR FORCE
		The following awarded the Distinguished Flying Medal
	F/SGT. E. E. ROSSITTER. DFM	ROYAL AIR FORCE
+	11/06/1957 LG. 41098 p.3513 The following awarded the Distinguished Flying Cross	
	LT. K. MITCHELL. DFC	ROYAL NAVY
+	11/06/1957 LG. # 41097 p.3505 The following awarded the British Empire Medal(Military)	
	SGT.W. DODDS BEM	ROYAL AIR FORCE
	SGT. J.M. YOUNG. BEM	ROYAL AIR FORCE
		The following awarded the Bar to Distinguished Flying Cross
	SDN/LDR. E.W.FURWELL. DFC +BAR	ROYAL AIR FORCE
	MAS/NAV. J. LANCASTER DFC+BAR	ROYAL AIR FORCE
		The following awarded the Distinguished Flying Cross
	SDN/LDR. E.W.FURWELLDFC.	ROYAL AIR FORCE
	F/LT. R.B..MORGAN DFC	ROYAL AIR FORCE
	F/LT. W.F.J. STEVENS DFC	ROYAL AIR FORCE

	The following awarded the Distinguished Flying Medal
	F/SGT. E.E. ROSSITER DFM ROYAL AIR FORCE
Wed. 12th	12 HMT OXFORDSHIRE sailed Liverpool bound for Singapore/ Hong Kong via Durban with replacement Service personnel ---]
Thur. 13th	13 DSP J. Purdy. F.M.Aux.P. Killed on CT Ops. through motor accident. Johore Bahru *Kranji Singapore # 8 / D – 6* .-]
Fri. 14th	} Combined Operations continued throughout Malaya---]
Sat. 15th	Air strikes in support of ground ooperations along with Road Patrols cont, throughot Malaya ---]
Sun. 16th	16 Spr. M. H. Clark. Royal Signals Died*** *Kranji Singapore # 11 / B* – 14 ---]
Mon. 17th	} Combined Operations continued throughout Malaya---]
Tue. 18th	}
Wed. 19th	Phase II of 'Eagle Swoop' began by the 2 RAR against **Wai Shan** the local leader around the Kroh to the Thailand Border---]
Thur. 20th	20 HMT DUNERA arrived Singapore with replacement Service personnel ---]
Fri. 21st	4 R. A. F. Venoms dropped 8 : 1,000lb bombs on an area in support of Support Platoon 2 RAR who had located a CT Camp.---]
Sat. 22nd	In the follow up Pte. Clark threw a grenade at the CT sentry killing him, a fire fight ensured with approx. 30 CT's Killed 2 Australians **Pte's. T.B. Hallard., J.P. Potts** were Killed in Action Engaging CT's *Taiping K / 1 - I / 3* Perak Pte T.G. Hogg was wounded & casvac'd out Cpl Kennet was awarded the Military Medal 1 CT was Killed & 1 wounded during the fire fight.---]
+	22 Pte. Anak Kusing Letang. Sarawak Rangers Att. to 1st. Royal Lincolnshire Regt. was Killed in an ambush in the jungle. *Taiping # Q / 2* Perak---]
Sun. 23rd	23 Capt. W. H. Moore. MBE 6th. Queen Elizabeth's Own Gurkha. Rifles. Died*** *Western Road # 2177* George Town Penang---]
Mon. 24th	} Combined Oerations continued throughout Malaya---]
Tue. 25th	25/06/57. LG # 41108 p 3793 The following awarded the Military Medal
	PTE G.J. HICKS. MM SOUTH WALES BORDERERS
+	RAN HMAS *QUEENBOROUGH* & *'QUICKMATCH'* Completed their second tour of duty in Malayan coastal waters.---]
+	A Platoon of the 2nd, RAR contacted 3 CT's about a mile away from the previous days engagement In the exchanged of fire Pte Hewitt was slightly wounded but contact was lost.--]
Wed. 26th	26 F/Lt. H.W. Crocker. AHQ R.A.F. Died*** *[Ashes REP]*---]
+	26 HMT DUNERA sailed Singapore bound for Southampton via Cape Town with the 2nd. Battn. Royal Welch Fusiliers having completed their tour of active Service duties in Malaya ---]
Thur. 27th	27 HMT DILWARA arrived Southamton with returning Service personnel ---]
+	27 HMT ASTURIUS arrived Southampton with returning Service personnel ---]
+	27 HMT EMPIRE FOWEY arrived Southampton.with returning Service personnel---]
Fri. 28th	8 R. A. F. Venoms armed with 16 1,000lb bombs. Attacked the area 2 miles South of the previous day contact, in an attempt to elliminate the fleeing CT's. 2 Patoons of the 2nd. RAR following up on the air drop. Set 2 ambushs. 1 Platoon RAR ran into the second & **Pte J. J.Wilson** was accidently Killed *Taiping # I / 4* Perak---]
Sat. 29th	29 HMT CAPTAIN COOK sailed from Glasgow bound for Wellington NZ ---]
Sun. 30th	Air strikes in support of ground operations along with Road Patrols cont, throughout Malaya--]

JULY

Mon. 1st	1 Pte.J.N. Metcalfe 2nd. Battn. R.A.R. Died Transport incident. *Taiping # K / 2* Perak---]
+	Operation "Parchment" began the SAS operation against the CT's---]
Tue. 2nd	RNZN HMSNZS *ROYALIST* Began her support role of duty in Malayan coastal waters.---]
Wed. 3rd	A massive air strike was carried out by R. A. F. & R.A.A.F. Aircraft 8 Venoms each with 2 : 1,000 lb bombs & 5 Lincoln Bombers each loaded with 14: 1.000 lb. bombs on two CT camps ---]
Thur. 4th	A follow up by 2nd. RAR revealed the camp obliterated but no sign of any CT's---]
Fri. 5th	5 HMT EMPIRE ORWELL arrived Southampton with returning Service personnel---]
Sat. 6th	Another air attack by 8 Venoms attacking with Rockets on a jungle camp thought to be that of **Wai Shan** Followed by harassing fire from he Field guns of 105 Field Battery before a follow up revealed no sign of CT's ---]
Sun. 7th	Operation 'Eagle II 'ended with little or, no success---]

Mon. 8th	**8 F/O. J. T. Lincoln**. 60 Sqdn. R.A.F. Killed when his Venom WK471 Stalled Taking-off at R.A.F. Tengah. *[Ashes REP]---]*
Tue. 9th	}
Wed. 10th	} Combined Operations continued throughout Malaya---]
Thur. 11th	}
Fri. 12th	2 CT's were Killed by a Patrol of the NZSAS Regt. identified as ***Ah Kiu & Cheong Tong*** ---]
Sat. 13th	<u>Kuala Lumpur</u> : Air Marshal The Earl of Bandon Became The Officer Commanding Air Command Far East--]
+	**13 HMT OXFORDSHIRE** arrived Singapore with replacement Service personnel enroute to Hong Kong
Sun. 14th	**14 Capt. Stephen-Smith**. (DFM) Intelligence Corps. Died Motor Veh Acc.Alor Star. Kedah *[Ashes REP]* --]
Mon. 15th	**15 HMT ASTURIUS** arrived Singapore with replacement Service personnel ---]
Tue. 16th	**16 HMT ASTURIUS** sailed Singapore enroute to Hong Kong ---]
Wed. 17th	HMNZS "*ROYALIST*" sailed into Singapore to become part of the 5th Cruiser Squadron.---]
Thur. 18th	**18 HMT EMPIRE FOWEY** sailed Southampton bound for Singapore/ Hong Kong with replacement Service personnel. Via Cape Town ---]
Fri. 19th	19 **Lt. A. G. H. Dean**. 3rd. Carabiniers Att/ 22nd. S.A.S. Killed in Action Engaging CT's <u>Kuala Lumpur #23 – 1214---</u>]
+	**19 Pte. Wonyana** 1ST.Rhodesian African Rifles Died*** <u>Kranji Singapore # 4 / E – 3</u> ---]
Sat. 20th	} Combined Operations continued throughout Malaya---]
Sun. 21st	**21 SAC Arshad B. Maasin**. R.A.F. Regt. 96 Sqdn.(MOR) Died by accident [*Claimed by next of Kin*]---]
Mon.22nd	} Combined Operations continued throughout Malaya---}
Tue. 23rd	23/07/1957 LG # 41132 p. 4369 The following awarded the Distinguished Flying Cross
	SQDN /LDR. L. BRITT. DFC ROYAL AUSTRALIAN AIR FORCE
Wed. 24th	**24 Sgt. J Hunt**. R.A.O.C.Died*** <u>Kranji Singapore # 11 / B - 15</u>---]
Thur. 25th	**25 Pte Kassim Bin Ibrahim**. Royal Signals (MOR) Died*** <u>Claimed by next of Kin</u>---]
+	HMNZS "*ROYALIST*" In its first operational role bombarded the jungle area of Tanjon Lampat South East Johore, Firing 86 HE shells, where several CT's camps were known to exist ---]
Fri. 26th	RAN HMAS '*ANZAC*' Carried out Naval gun bombardment support to Land Forces.---]
Sat. 27th	**27 Pte. Hssain. Bin. Mohajir**. R.A.O.C. (MOR) Died***<u>Claimed by next of Kin</u> ---]
+	**27 Gnr. Abu Hassan Bin Haran** Royal Artillery *** <u>Claimed by next of Kin</u> ---]
Sun. 28th	**28 HMT OXFORDSHIRE** arrived / sailed Singapore bound for Liverpool with returning Service personnel]
Mon. 29t	}
Tue. 30th	} Combined Operations continued throughout Malaya---]
Wed. 31st	}

AUGUST

Thur. 1st	} Combined Operations continued throughout Malaya---]
Fri. 2nd	**2 Bdr. D.K. Sutton**. Royal Australian Artillery. Died transport incident <u>Taiping # I / 5</u> Perak---]
Sat. 3rd	} Combined Operations continued throughout Malaya---]
Sun. 4th	**4 HMT ASTURIUS** arrived / sailed Singapore enroute Southampton with returning Service personnel---]
Mon. 5th	**5 Pte. H.R. Peke**. Royal New Zealand Infantry Regt. Died*** [*Ashes REP. NZ*]---]
+	**5 Spr's J. R. Bullock. - J. J. Ryan**. Royal Engineers Died incident not known <u>Taiping # I / 6 – K / 3</u> Pera
+	<u>Kuala Lumpur</u>: The official signing to end the 88-year period of British indirect rule in Malaya also, Terminating direct British Sovereignty over the former Straits Settlements of Malacca & Penang. Was signed by Sir. Donald McGillivray. The High Commissioner & The Rulers of the Malay States.In the presence of Tenku Abdul Rahman Chief Minister of the Federation & members of the Federation Cabinet.---]
Tue. 6th	**6 HMT DUNERA** arrived Southampton with returning Service personnel disembarking were the 2nd. Battn. Royal Welch Fusiliers---]
Wed. 7th	Sycamore XJ381 On a Flight from Fort Telanok to Tanah Rata losing height crashed trying to land at the Helipad. P/Off J. McCorkle & his passenger were unhurt.---]
Thur. 8th	} Combined Operations continued throughout Malaya---]
Fri. 9th.	}
Sat. 10t	**10 Maj. G. D. Meilkejohn**. MBE Royal Signals Died*** <u>Western Road # 2167</u> George Town Penang ---]
+	**10 HMT EMPIRE FOWEY** arrived Singapore with replacement Service personnel---]
Sun. 11th	**11 HMT EMPIRE FOWEY** sailed Singapore bound for Hong Kong- --]
Mon. 12th	}

Tue. 13th Wed. 14th	} Combined Operations continued throughout Malaya---] }
Thur. 15th	An ambush by Secruity forces was laid at a known located food dump. During the nighttime the food was lited by a number of CT's led by *Li Hak Chi.* Without a shot being fired. So cunning were the CT's.---]
+	15 HMT NEW AUSTRALIA sailed Southampton bound for Sydney via Panama Canal---]
Fri. 16th	16/08/1957 LG # 41151 p. 4835 The following awarded the Military Cross LT. J.D.B. HODGES. MC ROYAL EAST KENT REGIMENT.
Sat. 17th Sun. 18th	} Combined Operations continued throughout Malaya---] }
Mon. 19th	Another ambush set up by the RNZSAS in the same locality as the night ambush on the 15th.Intercepted a party of CT's carrying food. Killing one CT identified as *Li Hak Chi* State Group Committee member. His bodyguard *Ah Sang* was mortally wounded, others escaped dropping the food. It was the food lifted on the 15th All were destroyed---]
Tue. 20th	} Combined Operations continued throughout Malaya---]
Wed. 21st	21 HMT OXFORDSHIRE arrived Liverpool- with returning Service personnel---]
Thur.22nd	22 F/Sgt. R. Pound. Pilot.- M/Nav. J. J. A. Tucker. -Sgt. B. T. Boyatt. A/Sig. 110 Sqdn. R.A.F. Capt. *Kuala Lumpur # 32 – 1221 – 1223- 1222* Killed when Valetta VX 491 Supplies plane flew into hills in Perak. The 55 Coy R.A.C.S. Dispatcher's L/Cpl. R. Travis. – Dvr's E. Roe. – A. Downes. – I. Moore. Were injured but survived. .L/cpl. Travis & Drv. Downes Set off to walk out of the jungle. After 4 days they met a Military Patrol, subsequently the other two Drivers were rescued. ---]
Fri. 23rd	23 Reel. Manbahadur Sunwar . 10th. Princess Mary's Own Gurkha. Rifles. Died by accident *Sungei Patani.#127*]
+	23/08/57 LG # 41158 p 5033 The following awarded the Military Cross CAPT. P. F. WALTER. MC THE ROYAL LINCOLNSHIRE REGIMENT. The following awarded the Military Medal L.CPL. M. TAMANG. M M. 7th. DUKE OF EDINBURGH'S OWN GURKHA RIFLES PWO. PISAY. MM RHODESIAN AFRICAN RIFLES
Sat. 24th	Information of a Food Lift in the village of Bukit Siput would take place 28/29 An ambushed was set in place]
Sun. 25th	RAN HMAS *'TOBRUK'.* Carried out Naval guns barrage in support to Land Forces.---]
Mon. 26th	During a night time engagedment 'B' Platoon 2nd. 10th. Gurkhas Killed 5 CT's in the Bukit Siput Village This single engagement began in February when information was gathered & over the Months before the ambush was laid known as the "*Chicken Coop*" ambush One CT was identified as the Leader of the 32 Platoon. The ambush practically eliminated the 32 Platoon MRLA in the Bukit Siput area ---]
Tue. 27th	27 HMT EMPIRE FOWEY arrived Singapore with replacement Service personnel.---]
Wed. 28th	28 HMT EMPIRE FOWEY sailed Singapore bound for Southampton with returning Service peraonnel--]
+	28 HMT ASTURIUS arrived Southampton with returning Service personnel---]
Thur. 29th	29 F/Lt. A. R. Walker. AHQ R.A.F. Died ***[Ashes REP]---]
+	29 HMT DUNERA sailed Southampton bound for Singapore with replacement Service personnel ---]
Fri. 30th	A Patrol of 'B' Coy Royal Lincolnshire Regt. shot dead a CT courier *San Fatt* two hours before the declaration of Independence was granted Malaya its Independence. By the British Government. Which occurred upon the stroke of Mid-night. Thus bringing to an end 170 years of British Rule in Malaya.---]
Sat. 31st	MERDEKA DAY Malaya Celebrates its Day Of independence. Kuala Lumpur: In his speech Chief Minister Tenku Abdul Rahman. 'Praised the troops who quelled the Communist rebellion & called upon the People of Malaya to rid itself of Communism. He also paid tribute to the British for being blessed with a good administration. Let the legacy left by the British not suffer in efficiency & integrity in the years to come. It also brought to a close the second phase of the fight against the MRLA that due to the intense pressure & success of Commonwealth Forces over the past 3 years & before, had reduced the numbers quite considerably causing them to loose Heart. It was also estimated that approx 1,830 CT's had basically lost heart & fled to the safety over the border Thailand there to join *Chin Peng* who had been there for some years to regroup & continue the fight---]
+	Operation *"Parchment"* Completed SAS operation against the CT's---]

SEPTEMBER

Sun. 1st	Kuala Lumpur : SEPTEMBER the 1st the number of CT's still active were estimated as 1,830 of which 550 were located near the Malay /Thailand Border with a known 450 located in Thailand The War Cabinet With the change in Administration. Phase Three of the Offensive began. The mopping up of the remnants

	of the MRLA.]
Mon. 2nd	A Patrol of 'D' Coy Royal Lincolnshire Regt. Killed **Yee You & Ang Heng** near Solak being recorded as the first CT's to be Killed after Merdeka Day.---]
Tue. 3rd	} Combined Operations continued throughout Malaya---]
Wed. 4th	}
Thur. 5t	**5 Gnr. F. D. Cuniff.** Royal Artillery. Died*** _Taiping # 1 / 7_ Perak ---]
Fri. 6th	A Platoon of the 1st. 7th. Gurkhas Killed 4 CT's ---]
Sat. 7th	}
Sun. 8th	} Combined Operations continued throughout Malaya---]
Mon. 9th	}
Tue. 10th	**10 Spr. H. Langstaff.** Royal Engineers Died*** _Kuala Lumpur # 23 / 1202_ ---]
Wed. 11th	} Combined Operations continued throughout Malaya---]
Thur. 12th	A Troop of the NZ SAS tracked 2 CT's through a tropical downpour only to lose ttheir tracks---]
Fri. 13th	2 CT's one identified as **Li Hak Chi's** wife & another CT (**unnamed**) surrendered. They had been in the 3 recent engagments by the NZ SAS, which were to be their last operations---]
Sat. 14th	**14 Cpl. Dalbahadur Rana** . 6th. Queen Elizabeth's Own Gurkha. Rifles. Died*** BMH Kamunting _.Sulva Lines # 49_ Ipoh Perak.---]
Sun. 15th	} Combined Operations continued throughout Malaya ---]
Mon. 16th	**16 Sgt. F. R. Duckett.** 1st. Battn. Royal Lincolnshire Regt. Died***_Taiping # K- 4_ Perak--]
Tue. 17th	17 HMT EMPIRE FOWEY arrived Southampton with returning Service personnel---]
+	17 HMT OXFORDSHIRE sailed Liverpool bound for Singapore / Hong Kong with replacement Service
+	personnel---]
Wed. 18th	}Combined Operations continued throughout Malaya---]
Thur. 19th	}
Fri. 20th	**20 F/Lt. E. W. Draper. Pilot.**- A/Fit's **Cpl. R. Simpson**. & **Cpl. P. A. S. Cosens**. 155 Sqdn R.A.F. Killed when Whirlwind H/C XJ413. Tail Rotor broke off .Crashed 5 miles from Slim River Padang. _Kuala Lumpur # 33 –1258 – 1260 -1259 - ---_]
Sat. 21st	}
Sun. 22nd	} Combined Operations continued throughout Malaya---]
Mon. 23rd	}
Tue. 24th	Kuala Lumpur: It was announced Kuala Lumpur & the surrounding area as declared 'WHITE'---]
Wed. 25th	Combined Operations continued throughout Malaya ---]
Thur. 26th	26 HMT DUNERA arrived Singapore with replacement Service personnel ---]
Fri. 27th	**27 Pte. Jonah.** 1st. Rhodesian African Rifles. Died*** _Kranji Singapore # 14 / A - 24_---]
Sat. 28th	}
Sun. 29th	} Combined Operations continued throughout Malaya---]
Mon. 30th	}

OCTOBER

Tue. 1st	**1 PC. Thye Nyong Yaw** F. M. Police Killed on Ops. Serdang Kuala Perlis---]
Wed. 2nd	2 HMT DUNERA sailed Singapore bound for Southampton with returing Service personnel ---]
Thur. 3rd	}
Fri. 4th	} Combined Operations continued throughout Malaya---]
Sat. 5th	}
Sun. 6th	}
Mon. 7th	CT's attacked a Military Vehicle & Killed 1 civilian & wounded 1 Soldier in the area of Johore ---]
Tue. 8th	**8 Spr. C.M. Binmore.** Royal Engineers Died ***_[Ashes REP]_---]
Wed. 9th	} Combined Operations continued throughout Malaya---]
Thur. 10th	**10 Pte. D. T. Thompson.** 1st. Battn. Lincolnshire Regt. Killed in Action Engaging CT's (with Peter his Tracker dog _[Ashes REP]_---]
+	10 HMT OXFORDSHIRE arrived Singapore enroute to Hong Kong 10 th with replacement Service personnel---]
+	10 HMT NEW AUSTRALIA arrived Singapore with The 3rd. Battn. Royal Australian Infantry Regt. aboard the then enroute by train to Penang ---]
Fri. 11th	} Combined Operations continued throughout Malaya---]
Sat. 12th	A Patrol of the 7th. Gurkhas engaged 3 CT's. L/Cpl. Limbu stood up & fired at the CT's killing 2

	the other CT turned & fled, persued by the L/Cpl, who after a chase caught the CT & brought him back to the rest of his Platoon. He was recommended for an award.LG 41287 14/01/1958---]
Sun. 13th	} Combined Operations continued throughout Malaya---]
Mon. 14th	}
Tue. 15th	15 CAPTAIN COOK sailed Glasgow bound for Singapore via Panama / Wellington NZ ---]
Wed. 16th	} Combined Operations continued throughout Malaya---]
Thur. 17th	17 HMT NEW AUSTRALIA sailed Singapore bound for Penang ---]
+	17 HMT EMPIRE FOWEY sailed Southampton bound for Singapore with replacement Service personne---]
Fri. 18th	18 HMT NEW AUSTRALIA arrived Penang---]
Sat. 19th	19 HMT NEW AUSTRALIA sailed Penang bound for Southampton via Sydney with returning Service Personnel---]
Sun. 20th	20 Rfn. J. P. Moore. Royal Berkshire Regt. Died***_Kuala Lumpur # 32 / 1216_ ---]
Mon. 21st	} Combined Operations continued throughout Malaya---]
Tue. 22nd	22/10/1957 LG # 41209 p. 6177 The following awarded the Miltary Cross
	2/LT. J.S,PEEL. MC THE RIFLE BRIGADE
	CPL. J. GURUNG. MM The following awarded the Miltary Medal
	6th. QUEEN ELIZABETH'S OWN GURKHA RIFLES
Wed. 23rd	} Combined Operations continued throughout Malaya---]
Thur. 24th	24 HMT OXFORDSHIRE arrived Singapore---]
Fri. 25th	25 Pte. D. Jack. 1st. Battn. Royal Lincolnshire Regt. Died*** (3 wks from Demob) _Taiping # K- 7_ Perak---]
+	25 HMT OXFORDSHIRE sailed Singapore bound for Liverpool with returning Service personnel---]
	Salisbury Rhodesia: Statemnent
	'There would be no Rhodesian troops left in Malaya after the return of the Rhodesian Rifles in February 1958' ---]
Sat. 26th	}
Sun. 27th	} Combined Operations continued throughout Malaya---]
Mon. 28th	}
Tue. 29th	29 HMT DUNERA arrived Southampton with returning Service personnel ---]
Wed. 30th	} Combined Operations continued throughout Malaya---]
Thur. 31st	}

NOVEMBER

Fri. 1st	Operation 'Gabes South' Began SAS against the MRLA ----]
Sat. 2nd	} Combined Operations continued throughout Malaya---]
Sun. 3rd	}
Mon. 4th	}
Tue. 5th	}
Wed. 6th	}
Thur. 7th	} Combined Operations continued throughout Malaya---]
Fri. 8t	}
Sat. 9th	}
Sun. 10th	}
Mon. 11th	}
Tue. 12th	} Combined Operations continued throughout Malaya---]
Wed. 13th	}
Thur. 14th	}
Fri. 15th	}
Sat. 16th	} Combined Operations continued throughout Malaya---]
Sun. 17th	17 W.O II P.R. Broughton Royal Pioneer Corps Died*** _Kranji Singapore # 11 / B – 16_ ---]
+	17 HMT OXFORDSHIRE arrived Liverpool with returning Service personnel---]
Mon. 18th	18 Cpl. J. W. Sinclair. R.E.M.E.. Died*** _Kranji Singapore # 11 /B 17_ ---]
+	18 A civilian Mr. C.M. Gonsalvez. Killed in Action Engaging CT's details unknown.---]
Tue. 19th	}
Wed. 20th	} Combined Operations continued throughout Malaya---]
Thur. 21st	}
Fri. 22nd	22 Mr. H.J. Wates. British Civilian Killed by CT's .Batu Bahat. Johore.---]

Sat. 23rd	}	Combined Operations continued throughout Malaya---]
Sun. 24th	}	
Mon. 25th	}	
Tue. 26th	}	Combined Operations continued throughout Malaya---]
Wed. 27th	**27**	4 Royal Artillery (MOR's) Killed in Action Engaging CT's **Bdr. Omar Bin Manap– L/Bdr. Zakaria Bin Othman - Gnr.'s Hashim Bin Saad – Salleh Bin Yunos** *Claimed by next of Kin*---]
Thur..28th	}	Combined Operations continued throughout Malaya---]
Fri. 29th	**29**/11/1957 LG. # 41242 p.7039 The following awarded the Distiguished Flying Cross	
	CAPT.J. E. NUNN. MC ROYAL REGIMENT. ARTILLERY A/T 22 SAS	
	The following awarded the Distiguished Flying Medal	
	SGT. D.H. ROSE. BEM MM ROYAL ARMY SERVICE CORPS	
Sat. 30th	Operation *'Cobble'* ended ---]	

DECEMBER

Sun. 1st		Operation *"Goblet"* – *"Hippo "* & *"Dazzle"* SAS mounted operation against the CT's---]
+		3 RAR became Operational against the Armed Work Force(AWF) in the Lintang Sungei Siput area of Perak under Operation *"Shark North".*---]
+		1 HMT NEW AUSTRALIA arrived Southampton with returning Service personnel---]
Mon. 2nd	}	Combined Operations continued throughout Malaya---]
Tue. 3rd		3/12/1957 LG.41244 ISS. p. 7059 The following awarded the Distinguished Flying Cross
		LT/CDR. R. D. E. WILSON. DFC MC ROYAL NAVY 858 SQDN.
Wed. 4th	}	Combined Operations continued throughout Malaya---]
Thur. 5th		HMS *'NEWCASTLE'* bombarded overnight the inland area of South Johore where CT's where still hiding were some CT's---]
Fri. 6th		6 /12/1957 LG # 41248 p. 7191. The following awarded the Distinguished Flying Cross
		F/LT. T. CARBIS. MC ROYAL AIR FORCE
		F/LT. D. S. LOCKHART. MC ROYAL AIR FORCE
		F/LT. S MCINTYRE. MC ROYAL AIR FORCE
		F/O. K.R. STEER. MC ROYAL AIR FORCE
		MAST/PILOT. A.F.B. WEBB. MC ROYAL AIR FORCE
		The following awarded the BAR to Distinguished Flying Cross
		SDN/LDR. S. MACREATH. AFC DFC +BAR ROYAL AIR FORCE
		The following awarded the Distinguished Flying Medal
		F/SGT. E.J. TATAM. DFM ROYAL AIR FORCE
		SGT. R. F. BROOKS. DFM ROYAL AIR FORCE
Sat. 7th		7 HMT EMPIRE FOWEY arrived Singapore with replacement Service personnel---]
Sun. 8th	}	Combined Operations continued throughout Malaya---]
Mon. 9th	**9**	Pte. R. Nelson. 1st. Battn. The Loyal Regt. Died***_Taiping # K / 8_ Perak---]
Tue. 10th		10 HMT EMPIRE FOWEY sailed for Southamton with returning Service personnel---]
Wed. 11th	**11**	PC. Hussain B. Dahari F.M. Police Killed on Ops.---]
+		11 HMT OXFORDSHIRE sailed Liverpool bound for Singapore / Hong Kong with replacement Service personnel via Cape Town ---]
Thur. 12th	}	Combined Operations continued throughout Malaya---]
Fri. 13th	**13**	F/Lt. L. G. Hall.- M/Nav. D. H. M. Brown. 45 Sqdn. R.A.F. Whilst in transit from R.A.F. Coningsby to FEAF postings. Were Killed when their Canberra WH882 collided with Canberra WJ983 at Pontian. Singapore. **Flt. Lt. H. Hartley. F/Sgt. E. E. Stevens.** Canberra WJ 983.
		Kranji Singapore # 12 / B – 10 - 8 - 9 – 7 ---]
Sat. 14th		14 HMT CAPTAIN COOK arrived Singapore on board were the 1st Battn. New Zealand Regt. ---]
Sun. 15th		A Patrol of 'B' Coy Royal Lincolnshire Regt. Killed CT *Ah Tong* near Tanjung Rambutan.---]
Mon. 16th	**16**	Cook. A. C. Cooper. HMAS. *'ANZAC'* Drowned in Singapore Harbour..Buried at sea
		[No known Grave] Terandak Wall Memorial Malacca --]
Tue. 17th	**17**	Pol/Lt. G.E.T. Southey F. M. Police Killed in Action Engaging CT's Kuala Lumpur Selangor._Malacca # 131_]
+		17/12/1957 LG. # 41257 p.7427 The following awarded the British Empire Medal (Military)
		SGT. R. REA. BEM. INTELIGENCE CORPS.
		BDR. H.A. RIDZAMN. BEM ROYAL REGIMENT ARTILLERY (MOR)

	TRP. SC. WATENE. BEM NEW ZEALAND REGT. A/T 22 SAS
	CPL. B. b. H. SAMSUDUN. BEM ROYAL ARMY SERVICE CORP (MOR)
	SGT. J. GURUNG BEM 2nd. KING EDWARD VII'S OWN GURKHA RIFLES
	The following awarded Bar to Distinguished Service Order
	L/COL. R.C.H. MIERS. DSO +BAR SOUTH WALES BORDERES
	The following awarded the Distinguished Service Order
	LT/COL. G.H. LEA. DSO LANCASHIRE REGIMENT.
	The following awarded the Military Cross
	LT. I.A CHRISTIE. MC KINGS OWN SCOTISH BORDERES
	MAJ. A.G. JONES. MC SOUTH WALES BORDERES
	CAPT. A. L.H. NAPIER. MC SOUTH WALES BORDERES
	CAPT. J.O. LAWES. MC 2nd. KING EDWARD VII'S OWN GURKHA RIFLES
	LT. M. GURUNG. MC 6th. QUEEN ELIZABETHS OWN GURKHA RIFLES.
	The following awarded the Red Cross
	MAJ. E. BALLERTY.RC QUEEN ALEXANDERS ROYAL ARMY NURSING CORPS
	The following awarded the Military Medal
	CPL. G. HARRIS. MM SOUTH WALES BORDERES
	L/CPL.K. LIMBU. MM 7th. DUKE OF EDINBURGH'S OWN GURKHA RIFLES
	CPL. J.C. TUCKER. MM ROYAL WELCH FUSILIERS
	P.W/O ALEXANDER. MM 1st. RHODESIAN AFRICAN RIFLES
	CPL. LENOU. MM 1st. RHODESIAN AFRICAN RIFLES
Wed. 18th	18 HMT CAPTAIN COOK sailed Singapore enroute to Glasgow with returning Service personnel---]
Thur. 19th	} Combined Operations continued throughout Malaya ---]
Fri. 20th +	20/12/1957 LG #41527 p 7428 The following awarded the Military Cross
	LT. I.A. CHRISTIE. MC QUEEN'S OWN SCOTTISH BORDERERS
	MAJ. A GWNNE-JONES. MC SOUTH WALES BORDERERS
	CAPT' A.L.H. NAPIER. MC SOUTH WALES BORDERERS
	CAPT. J.O. LAWES. MC 2nd. KING EDWARD VII'S OWN GURKHA RIFLES.
	LT. M. GURUNG. MC 6th. QUEEN ELIZABETH'S OWN GURKHA RIFLES.
	The following were awarded the Military Medal
	CPL. G. HARRIS. MM SOUTH WALES BORDERERS
	CPL. J.C TUCKER. MM ROYAL WELCH FUSILIERS
	L/CPL. K LIMBU. MM 7th. DUKE OF EDINBURGH'S OWN GURKHA RIFLES
	WO2 K DUKPA. MM 10th PRINCESS MARY'S OWN GURKHA RIFLES
	PWO ALEXANDER. MM RHODESIAN AFRICAN RIFLES
	CPL. LENGU. MM RHODESIAN AFRICAN RIFLES
Sat. 21st	} Combined Operations continued throughout Malaya---]
Sun. 22nd +	22 Lt. Bishnabahadur Gurung 2nd. King Edward VII's Own Gurkha. Rifles . Died*** *Sungei Patani # 6*---]
	A Patrol of 'D' Coy Royal Lincolnshire Regt. Killed CT *Tsang Tung* near Tanah Hitam one other CT was reported Killed.---]
Mon. 23rd	In the border town of Chang Looi near Alor Star. More than a 1,000 people of the Town held a march as long as half a mille in support of Anti Communist. They supporting the Surrender terms given to the CT's to become good citizens.---]
Tue. 24th	A CT of the 13/15 Platoon 5th. Regt. MRLA. *Yip Ah Chu.* Surrendered to the Royal Lincolnshire Regt.---]
Wed. 25th	25 A dead body was discovered by a F.M. Police jungle Patrol. In the jungles of Pahang . It was identifiesd as **Mr. A. C. Cooper**. A civilian Australian Killed by CT's---]
Thur. 26th	} Combined Operations continued throughout Malaya---]
Fri. 27th	}
Sat. 28th	}
Sun. 29th	} Combined Operations continued throughout Malaya---]
Mon.30th	30 Pte. K. B. Bancroft. 1st. Battn. Cheshire Regt. Died*** *Kuala Lumpur # 23 / 1215*---]
+	30 Cpl, W. Dodd. 1st. Battn. Royal Lincolnshire Regt.Died from Wounds recv'd in battle *Taiping # K - 9* Perak]
+	30 HMT EMPIRE FOWEY arrived Southampton with returning Service personnel---]
Tue. 31st	31 Cpl. Tayengwa 1st. Rhodesian African Rifles Died *** *Kranji Singapore # 4 / E - 8*---]
	Operation *"Gabes North "* Completed---]

R. A. F. OPERATION *"FIREDOG"* END OF YEAR STATISTICS 1957

No of Sorties	No. of Strikes	1,000 Lb.Bombs	500 Lb. Bombs	350 LbCluster	20 LbBombs	R/P's	20mm	.5 mm	.303mm
373	49	1,205	2,283	/	1,992	382	40,216	5.130	/

R. A. F. SUPPORT 1957

	Soties	Troops/ Lift	Casac	Pass/Lift	Supply Wt. Lbs	Leaflets(1,000)	B Flying Times No / hrs	Broadcsting No / hrs	Crashed
Air SupportA/C*	1683	/	/	/	4,818,799	87.988	/	/	Valetta
Anson***	Inc	/	/	/	/	/	/	/	VX491
Auster**	15,321	/	/	/	/	/	/	/	Canberrra 's
Pioneer	1361	4052	2659	106	923.968	/	/	/	WH882
H/C Light	10,013	2890	536	2,292	181,667	/	/	/	WJ983
848 Sqdn	Disbanded	/	/	/	/	/	/	/	Venom's
155 Sqdn	10.057	16,282	96	363	238.249	/	/	/	WK499
Target/MK**	174	/	/	/	/	/	/	/	WK471
Vis/Air **	5,772	/	/	/	/	/	/	/	Whirlwind
Communication**/***	5,975	/	/	/	/	/	/	/	XJ413
Leaflets Sorties*	322	/	/	/	/	/	/	/	XJ427
Leaflet Drops. *	/		/	/	/	87.088	485	/	Auster
LealetSorties **	320	/	/	/	/	/	/	/	VF604
Leaflets Drop**		/	/	/	/	N/A	294	/	Lincoln
Broad Sorties*	523	/	/	/	/	/	1619.9	/	R.A.A,FA73-40
Broad Hrs *	/	/	/	/	/	/	/	536.2	
Broad Sorties**	163	/	/	/	/	/	5387.5	/	
Broad Hrs **	/	/	/	/	/	/	/	1619	
Photo Rec	709	/	/	/	/	/	/	/	
AirOP**	178	/	/	/	/	/	/	/	

* AirSupport A/C Dakota -Valetta- Hastings Bristol
** Auster
*** Photo Rec Anson,Spitfire, Mosquito, Meteor, Pembroke

CHAPTER 16 - 1958

ROYAL AIR FORCE
OFFENSIVE AIR SUPPORT - OPERATION 'FIREDOG'
January 1957 to December 1960

Sqdn	Location	Aircraft Type	No	Date From	Year	Date To	Year
81	Tengah	MeteorPR10	8	.1st. Apr.	1958	Jul	1960
		PembrokeCP	4	1st. Apr.	1958	Jul	1960
90	Butterworth	VulcanB1	2-4	6th. Jun.	1958	26th. Jun	1960
110	Seletar	SunderlandGR5	4	1st. Nov.	1958	31st. May	1960
205	Changi	Shackelton MR1	8	26th.Feb.	1958	Jul.	1960
	Kuala Lumpur	ShackletonMR1	2	1st.Oct.	1958	1stNov.	1958
	Seletar	TE Pioneer CC1	9	1st.Nov.	1958	---------1st	1959
209	Seletar	Pembroke C1	5	1st. Nov.	1958	Oct.	1960
	Kuala Lumpur	Dakota C4	3	1st.Nov..	1958	26th. Jun	1959
214	Changi	Auster6/7	2	1st. Nov.	1958	1st. Oct.	1959
						18th. Mar.	

ROYAL AUSTRALIAN AIR FORCE
OFFENSIVE AIR SUPPORT - OPERATION 'FIREDOG'
January 1958 to July 1960

Sqdn	Location	Aircaft Type	No	Date From	Year	Date To	Year
2	Butterworth	Canberra B1	9	1st. Jul.	1958	Jul.	1960
3	Butterworth	Sabre 32	16	11.Nov.	1958	Jul	1960
77	Butterworth	Sabre 32	16	11th. Feb	1958	Jul .	1960

MALAYAN AUXILLIARY AIR FORCE
OFFENSIVE AIR SUPPORT - OPERATION 'FIREDOG'
January 1958 to July 1960
Kranji SingaporeSquadron

Sqdn	Location	Aircraft Type	No	Date From	Year	Date To	Year
	Seletar	Chipmonk	4	1st.Apr.	1958	Jul	1960

MALAYAN AUXILLIARY AIR FORCE
OFFENSIVE AIR SUPPORT - OPERATION 'FIREDOG'
January 1957 to July 1960

Sqdn	Location	Aircraft Type	No	Date From	Year	Date To	Year
656	Kuala Lumpur	Chipmonk	4	3rd. April	1957	Dec.	1958
	Butterworth	Chipmomk	4	""	""		
	Kranji SingaporeTengah	Chipmonk	4	""	""		
	Then Seletar			1st. April	1958	1st July	1960

JANUARY

Wed.	1st	Operation Cheiftain Continued & operation 'Ginger' In Perak & 'Bintang'in Selangor began .---]
	+	Operation "Ladder" & "Thrust" Began. SAS operation against the CT's---]
Thur.	2nd	Combined Operations continued throughout Malaya---]
Fri.	3rd	A Patrol of the Royal Lincolnshire Regt. engaged CT.s in the jungle wounding 2 . 1 later died from his wounds..A 3rd CT surrenedered. As a result of this Action Engaging CT's. Maj.G.D. Cole was awarded the Military Cross and Cpl. F. Shaftoe awarded the Military Medal
Sat.	4th	**4 Cpl. Othman B. Sulaiman.** F.M. Police Killed on Ops.---]
Sun.	5th	5 HMT OXFORDSHIRE arrived Singapore with replacement Service personnel---]
Mon.	6th	6 HMT OXFORDSHIRE sailed Singapore enroute to Hong Kong ---]

Tue. 7th	Kuala Lumpur: Maj. Gen. F.H. Brooke. succeeded Lt. Gen. Sir. James Cassels. as Director of Emergency Operations & concurrently Chief of Staff of the Federations armed forces---].
+	7/01/1958 .LG # 41279 p. 207 The following awarded the Military Medal
	RFN. B TAMANG. MM 7th. DUKE OF EDINBURGH'S OWN GURKHA RIFLES
Wed. 8th	A Patrol of 3 RAR engaged a number of CT's with success. Killing 3. 1 RAR Pte. was wounded in the elbow & hip.---]
Thur. 9th	} Combined Operations continued throughout Malaya---]
Fri. 10th	10 HMT DILWARA sailed Southampton bound for Singapore / Hong Kong with replacement Service personnel]
Sat. 11th	}
Sun. 12th	} Combined Operations continued throughout Malaya---]
Mon. 13th	}
Tue. 14th	14/01/1958 LG# 41287 p.392 The following awarded the Military Medal
	L/CPL. K. LIMBU.MM 7th. DUKE OF EDINBURGH'S OWN GURKHA RIFLES
Wed. 15th	} Combined Operations continued throughout Malaya---]
Thur. 16th	Operation "Ginger" began against No 5 MRLA in Sungei Siput & Ipoh.---]
Fri. 17th	} Combined Operations continued throughout Malaya---]
Sat. 18th	}
Sun. 19th	19 HMT OXFORDSHIRE arrived Singapore enroute to Liverpool with returning Service personnel 19th.---]
Mon. 20th	RAN HMAS 'ANZAC'.Completed her first tour of duty in Malayan coastal waters. Whilst HMAS 'WARRAMUNGA' Began her third tour of duty & HMAS 'VOYAGER". Began her first attachment to the BCFESR.]
+	Another Platoon of 3 RAR made contact with CT's wounded some who escaped. ---]
Tue. 21st	3 RAR Followed up on the previous days contact ---]
+	21 HMT EMPIRE FOWEY sailed Southampton bound for Singapore with replacement Service personnel]
Wed.22nd	3 RAR Continued the follow up but lost contact---]
Thur. 23rd	23 HMT CAPTAIN COOK arrived Glasgow with returning Service personnel---]
Fri. 24th	}
Sat. 25th	} Combined Operations continued throughout Malaya---]
Sun. 26th	}
Mon. 27th	}
Tue. 28th	28 Cpl. Chandrabahadur Gurung . 2nd. King Edward VII's Own Own Gurkha Rifles. Died***[Ashes REP]--]
Wed. 29th	RAN HMAS 'TOBRUK' Completed her third tour of duty in Malayan coastal waters---]
Thur. 30th	} Combined Operations continued throughout Malaya---]
Fri. 31st	31 Pte. A. J. Tulloch. 3rd. Battn. R.A.R. Died*** Taiping # I / 8 Perak---]
	Operation "Hippo" & "Dazzle" the SAS Operation against the CT's finished---]

FEBRUARY

Sat. 1st	} Combined Operations continued throughout Malaya---]
Sun. 2nd	}
Mon. 3rd	3 SAC. M. N. B. Awang. R.A.F. (MOR). Died***Claimed by next of Kin ---]
Tue. 4th	4/02/1958 LG. # 41301 p. 771. The following were awarded the British Empire Medal
	F/SGT. D.R. PHINN. BEM ROYAL AIR FORCE
	SGT. F.J. MULHOLLAND. BEM ROYAL AIR FORCE
	SGT.J.H. PACKER. BEM. ROYAL AIR FORCE
	The following were awarded the Distinguished Flying Cross
	F/LT. G.G. BAYLISS. DFC ROYAL NEW ZEALAND AIR FORCE
	F/LT J. DAVIDSON. DFC ROYAL AIR FORCE
	F/LT. L.J. WITTINHAYDEN.DFC ROYAL AIR FORCE
	F/LT. N. O. LEARY. DFC ROYAL AIR FORCE
	F/LT. D. TRAINER. DFC ROYAL AIR FORCE
Wed. 5th	} Combined Operations Continued throughout Malaya
Thur. 6th	}
Fri. 7th	}
Sat. 8th	} Combined Operations continued throughout Malaya---]
Sun. 9th	}
Mon. 10th	} Combined Operations continued throughout Malaya---]
Tue. 11th	11 HMT OXFORDSHIRE arrived Liverpool with returning Service personnel---]

Wed. 12th	12 HMT DILWARA arrived Singapore enroute to Hong Kong with replacement Service personnel---]
Thur. 13th	13 HMT DILWARA sailed Singapore bound for Beira---]
Fri. 14th	**14 Capt. P. J. L. Dalley.** Army Air Corps Died*** _Taiping # K / 10_ Perak.--]
+	**14 Trp. A. J. Forte** 1st. King's Dragoon Guards Died ** _Kranji Singapore # 11 / E – 20 ---]_
Sat. 15th	15 HMT EMPIRE FOWEY arrived Singapore with replacement Service personnel---]
Sun. 16th	A Patrol of the 3 RAR ambushed 2 CT's South of Sungei Siput without much results . 1 Pte was wounded i the incident---]
Mon. 17th	} Combined Operations continued throughout Malaya---]
Tue. 18th	**18 Asstn. Comd. L. G. Valpy** F. M. Police Died*** Pahang---]
Wed. 19th	19 HMT EMPIRE FOWEY sailed Singapore bound for Southampton with returning Service personnel--]
Thur. 20th	HMNZS "_ROYALIST_" Laying offshore of the South East coast of Johore fired 152 shells bombarded the inland area of Tanjong Punggai, where CT's camps were. An Auster of the Army Air Corps directed the salvos.---]
Fri. 21st	**21 Trp. T. Walsh.** Kings Dragoon Guards Died*** _Kranji Singapore # 11 / E – 21_ ---]
Sat. 22nd	} Combined Operations continued throughout Malaya---]
Sun. 23rd	**23 Pte. T. Kawha.** 1st. Royal New Zealand Regt. Att./Royal Lincolnshire Regt. Accidently Killed while cutting down a tree for a clearing area. of a Landing Zone, in the Chimor area.. Half the tree broke in half hit the ground & sprung back onto him _Taiping # K / 11_ Perak.--]
Mon. 24th	A Patrol of the Royal Licolnshire Regt. Killed **Lou Swee** A prominent member of the CT's--]
Tue. 25th	}
Wed. 26th	} Combined Operations continued throughout Malaya---]
Thur. 27th	}
Fri. 28th	**28 Cpl. D.A. Seesink.** 3rd. Battn. R.A.R. Died*** _Taiping # K / 12_ Perak---]
+	Operation " _Thrust_" – "_Ladder_ " Completed the AS operations against the known CT's---]

MARCH

Sat. 1st	Operation "_Ginger_" began SAS operations against the CT's---]
Sun. 2nd	} Combined Operations continued throughout Malaya---]
Mon. 3rd	}
Tue. 4th	4 HMT OXFORDSHIRE sailed Liverpool bound for Singapore/ Hong Kong with replacement Service personnel---]
Wed. 5th	**5 SAC Mohd. Noor B. Awang** R.A.F. 94 (LAA) Sqdn Tengah (MOR) Died *** [_Claimed by next of Kin_]---]
Thur. 6th	} Combined Operations continued throughout Malaya---]
Fri. 7th	7/04/1958 LG #.41329 p.1499　　　　The following awarded the Military Cross
	CAPT. J.D.W. JONES MC　　　　　　ROYAL MARINES
	MAJ. G.D. COLE MC　　　　　　　ROYAL LINCOLNSHIRE REGIMENT.
	The following awarded the Military Medal
	L/CPL. F. SHAFTOE MM.　　　　　ROYAL LINCOLNSHIRE REGIMENT.
Sat. 8th	The 1st Battalion Royal New Zealand Regt. Relieved the 1st Battn. Lincolnshire Regt. having completed their tour of operations in Malaya.---]
Sun. 9th	A Patrol of 3 RAR contacted 2 groups of CT's of equal numbers.During the engagement there were no casualties on wither side. The CT's just retreated---]
Mon. 10th	} Combined Operations continued throughout Malaya----]
Tue. 11th	}
Wed. 12th	**12 Sgt. C. B. Young.** R.E.M.E.. Died***_Kuala Lumpur # 32 / 1218_---]
Thur. 13th	2 Platoon NZ Regt. engaged 1 CT guarding a water hole. He avoided the shots & escaped---]
+	13 HMT EMPIRE FOWEY arrived Southampton with returning Service personnel---]
Fri. 14th	14/03/58 LG.# 41355 p1667　　　　The following awarded the Military Medal
	CPL. W.D. KENNEDY. MM　　　　　2nd BATTN. ROYAL AUSTRALIAN REGIMENT.
Sat. 15th	} Combined Operations continued throughout Malaya---]
Sun. 16th	16 HMT DILWARA arrived Singapore back from Beira ---]
Mon. 17th	17 HMT DILWARA sailed bound for Hong Kong ---]
Tue. 18th	} Combined Operations continued throughout Malaya---]
Wed. 19th	2 Platoon N Z Regt. engaged 2 CT's on a ridge above them. Engaged them, but they escaped.. A follow up found a well protected camp which was destroyed.---]
Thur. 20th	**20 L/Cpl. S. Stone.** 1st. Battn. Royal Lincolnshire Regt. Killed by a falling tree during storm.

		Kranji Singapore # 11- B-18----]
Fri.	21st	**21 WOII. H. M. Allcock**. R.A.O.C. .Died***_[Ashes REP]_---]
Sat.	22nd	**22 Sgmm. E.R. Norris**. Royal Australian Signals. Died*** _Taiping # K / 13_ Perak ---]
	+	**22 Pte. W. Hart.** 1st. Battn. Cheshire Regt. Died***_[Ashes REP]_---]
Sun.	23rd	} Combined Operations continued throughout Malaya---]
Mon.	24th	}
Tue.	25th	RAN HMAS _MELBOURBE._ Began her third tour of duty in Malayan coastal waters ---]
Wed.	26th	**26 Sgt. J. T. Bragginton.** A/F/Fit.R.A.F. Died Natural Causes. _Kuala Lumpur # 32 1220_ ---
Thur.	27th	} Combined Operations continued throughout Malaya---]
Fri.	28th	28 HMT DILWARA arrived Singapore ---]
	+	28 HMT OXFORDSHIRE arrived Singapore with replacement Service personnel enroute to Hong Kong 28th
Sat.	29th	}
Sun.	30th	} Combined Operations continued throughout Malaya---]
Mon.	31st	}

APRIL

Tue.	1st	R.A.F. 81 Sqdn. Meteor. PR10 Completed Operations R.A.F. Seletar---]
	+	1 HMT EMPIRE FOWEY sailed Southampton bound for Singapore / Hong Kong with replacement Service personnel via Cape Town l--]
Wed.	2nd	2 HMT DILWARA sailed Singapore bound for Southampton with returning Service personnel---]
Thur.	3rd	} Combined Operations continued throughout Malaya---]
Fri.	4th	}
Sat.	5th	}
Sun.	6th	} Combined Operations continued throughout Malaya---]
Mon.	7th	}
Tue.	8th	}
Wed.	9th	}
Thur.	10th.	}
Fri.	11th.	} Combined Operations continued throughout Malaya---]
Sat.	12th	12 HMT OXFORDSHIRE arrived Singapore with replacement Service personnel sailed bound for Liverpool with returning Service personnel 12th.---]
Sun.	13th	} Combined Operations continued throughout Malaya---]
Mon.	14th	}
Tue.	15th	Operation '_Tiger_' Began in the Semangar Triangle when the Royal Artillery & the R. A. F. began a bombardment of the area This was to last 3 days---]
Wed.	16th	} Combined Operations continued throughout Malaya---]
Thur.	17th	9 Platoon 3rd RAR on Patrol in the Lintang area engaged a CT fired at him but he disappeared into the jungle---]
Fri.	18th	**18 Capt. P. B. Jessop.** R.A.S.C. Died***_Batu Gajah # 427_ Ipoh Perak---]
	+	**18 M(E)1 J. Richardson.** Royal Navy. H.M.S. '_TERROR_'. Died*** _Kranji Singapore # 14 / D -19_ ---]
Sat.	19th	**19 Spr. J. Haycock** Royal Engineers Dired** _Kranji Singapore # 11 / B – 19_ ---]
	+	The follow up by ground Forces of the bombardment Operation ' _Tiger_' resulting in no contacts.---]
Sun.	20th	A Member of the 31 Independent Platoon MRLA. Identified as **Wong Chan** stopped & surrendered to a Plt. Of the 1st. Battn. Cheshire Regt. ---]
Mon.	21st	Whilst driving along in an armoured car. It was stopped by a CT. In charge of the armoured car was Major Voss NZ Regt. He got down & approached the CT who surrendered. He was identified as The Secretary General of the South Malaya Bureau **Hor Lung** .---]
Tue.	22nd	Near Lintang New Village a Platoon of 3 RAR engaged CT's during a night ambush unfortunately no casualties were reported. Perak ---]
Wed.	23rd	On the Sungei Reyla Rubber Estate in the area of Lintang another contact was made by 3 RAR against 3 CT's. Once again resulted in no casualties reported. Perak---]
Thur.	24th	A follow up by 7 Platoon RAR. 3 miles South of the previous nights ambush. Found the 3 CT's hiding in the Rubber trees. The 3 made a run for it, chased by the Platoon, who opened fire at the 3 CT's. Killing 2 the third escaped. The 2 dead CT's 1 a Malay the other a Chinese,were members of the Lintang AWF --]
Fri.	25th	25 HMT EMPIRE FOWEY arrived Singapore with replacement Service personnel---]

Sat. 26th	26 HMT EMPIRE FOWEY sailed Singapore for Hong Kong---]
Sun. 27th	3 CT's engaged a Patrol of the 3 RAR in the Sungei Plus Forest Reserve without any results.Perak --]
Mon. 28th	} Combined Operations continued throughout Malaya---]
Tue. 29th	29/04/1958 LG # 41692 p. 2763 The following awarded the British Empire Medal
	S/SGT. A. HOLTSBY. BEM ARMY CATERING CORPS
	S/SGT. F.E. THOMAS. BEM ROYAL ARMY SERVICE CORPS
	SGT. M.A..TREE. BEM ROYAL ELECTRICAL MECHANICAL ENGINEERS
	SGT. B. TURNBULL.BEM 1ST. DRAGOON GUARDS
	CPL. I .F.A . JONES. BEM WOMENS ROYAL ARMY CORPS.
	p. 2764 The following awarded the Military Cross
	LT. N. RAI. MM 10th PRINCESS MARY'S OWN GURKHA RIFLES
	p. 2764 The following awarded the Military Medal
	SGT. N.C. JAMEISON. MM NEW ZEALAND INF. REGIMENT.
Wed. 30th	30 Pte. J. Davies. 1st. Battn. Royal Lincolnshire Regt. Died by Accident *Kranji Singapore # 11-B-20*---]
+	30 HMT DILWARA arrived Southampton with returning Service personnel ---]

MAY

Thur. 1st	RNZN HMNZS *ROTOITI*. Began her first support tour of duty in Malayan coastal waters.**---]**
+	Operation *"Juno"* began the SAS Operation against known CT's Independent Platoons ---]
+	Phase II of Operation *'Tiger'* began in search of the Group Leader **Ah Cheung** of Gelang Patch the wanted CT & 9 Platoon Commander MRLA ---]
Fri. 2nd	} Combined Operations continued throughout Malaya---]
Sat. 3rd	}
Sun. 4th	} Combined Operations continued throughout Malaya---]
Mon. 5th	}
Tue. 6th	}
Wed. 7th	} Combined Operations continued throughout Malaya---]
Thur. 8th	8 F/Sgt. A. Stirk. A/Sig 52 Sqdn R.A.F. Changi. Died*** *Kranji Singapore # 12 / B – 11* ---]
+	8 J/Tech. A. V. L. Hatcher. Eng/Fit. R.A.F. HQ Changi Road traffic accident. *[Ashes REP]*.---]
+	8/05/1958 LG # 41701 p.2979 The following awarded the Military Cross
	LT. C.H. DUCKER. MC. 3rd. BATTN. ROYAL AUSTRALIAN REGIMENT.
	The following awarded the Military Medal
	L/CPL. M.P. HAMLEY. MM. 3rd. BATTN. ROYAL AUSTRALIAN REGIMENT.
+	8 HMT EMPIRE FOWEY arrived Singapore sailed bound for Southampton with returning Service personnel]
Fri. 9th.	} Combined Operations continued throughout Malaya---]
Sat. . 10th	A Patrol of the Royal Lincolnshire Regt. During an ambush near Yong Peng Killed 1 CT and wounded 7 other CT's. This engagement cumulated in the decimation of the last fighting CT Platoon in the area of Yong Peng Cpl. M. Harriman was MID This was the last Active Service enganement of the Royal Lincolnshire Regt.---]
Sun. 11th	} Combined Operations continued throughout Malaya---]
Mon. 12th	}
Tue. 13th	}
Wed. 14th	} Combined Operations continued throughout Malaya---]
Thur. 15th	}
Fri. 16th	}
Sat. 17th	} Combined Operations continued throughout Malaya---]
Sun. 18th	} Combined Operations continued throughout Malaya---]
Mon. 19th	19 Rfn. Panjabsing Rai . 10th. Princess Mary's Own Gurkha Rifles. Died*** *[Ashes REP]*---
Tue. 20th	20/05/1958 LG # 41389 p3165 The following awarded the Military Cross
	MAJ. R. JAMES MC INNISKILLINGS FUSILIERS ATT/TO MALAY REGT.
	The following awardedbar to the Military Medal
	SGT. D.B NINGGAL MM +BAR MALAY REGIMENT
	The following were awarded the Military Medal
	SGT. B.A. BAKAR MM MALAY REGIMENT
	SGT. M.N.B. HASSAN MM MALAY REGIMENT
	SGT. H.B.P SU. MM MALAY REGIMENT
Wed. 21st	} Combined Operations continued throughout Malaya---]

Thur.22nd	22 HMT DILWARA sailed Southampton bound for Singapore with replacement Service personnel ---]
Fri. 23rd	**23 Cpl. P.L. Haynes**. 3rd. Battn. R.A.R. Died*** _Taiping # I / 9_ Perak ---]
+	23/05/58 LG # 41392 p. 3238 The following awarded a Bar to Military Cross
	CAPT. F.E. KITSON MC & BAR THE RIFLE BRIGADE.
	The following awarded the Military Cross
	MAJ. F. RENNIE MC NEW ZEALAND. S A S
	The following awarded the Military Medal LG 3238
	WO2 ROSS W.H. MM GREEN HOWARDS . ATT/TO SAS
	L/CPL I. GURUNG. MM 6th QUEEN ELIZABETH'S OWN GURKHA RIFLES
	C/SGT. K. GURUNG. MM 6th QUEEN ELIZABETH'S OWN GURKHA RIFLES
Sat. 24th	**24 Capt. B. Agutter.** 2nd. Battn. K.O.Y.L.I.. Died*** _Kranji Singapore # 15 / E - 10_---]
Sun. 25th	} Combined Operations continued throughout Malaya---]
Mon. 26th	}
Tue. 27th	}
Wed. 28th	} Combined Operations continued throughout Malaya---]
Thur. 29th	A Central Member of the Pulai Armed Work Force. Identified as CT. **Man Ko** Was Killed by the 1st. New Zealand Regt.---]
Fri. 30th	During the Phase II of Opeartion _'Tiger'_ only 1 CT was eliminated---]
+	30 HMT OXFORDSHIRE sailed from Liverpool bound for Singapore / Hong Kong with replacement Service personnel---]
+	30 HMT EMPIRE FOWEY arrived Soujthampton with returning Service personnel---]
Sat. 31st	R.A.F. 205 Sqdn. Sunderland GR5 Completed Operations R.A.F. Seletar---]

JUNE

Sun. 1st	} Combined Operations continued throughout Malaya---]
Mon. 2nd	}
Tue. 3rd	4 CT's were ambushed by the 1st. NZ Regt. They Killed 1 CT identified as **Itam Bin Pandak** a member of the Asi group. While the other 3 CT's possibly wounded escaped.---]
Wed. 4th	**4 SC's Pahib. Jeva – Ahmad B. Abdul Ghani** F.M. Police Killed on Ops.--]
Thur. 5th	} Combined Operations continued throughout Malaya---]
Fri. 6th	}
Sat. 7th	} Combined Operations continued throughout Malaya---]
Sun. 8th	}
Mon. 9th	} Combined Operations continued throughout Malaya---]
Tue. 10th	**10 Pte. Anak Pasang Nyambik.** Sarawak Rangers.Killed engaging CT's _Taiping # Q / 3_ Perak---]
Wed. 11th	}
Thur. 12th	} Combined Operations continued throughout Malaya---]
Fri. 13th	}
Sat. 14th	**14 Cpl. S. J. Readioff**. 1st Battn. Cheshire Regt. Died*** _Kranji Singapore # 11 / E- 21_ ---]
Sun. 15th	} Combined Operations continued throughout Malaya---]
Mon. 16th	}
Tue. 17th	17 HMT CAPTAIN COOK sailed from Glasgow bound for Wellington NZ Via Panama ----]
Wed. 18th	} Combined Operations continued throughout Malaya---]
Thur. 19th	19 HMT DILWARA arrived Singapore with replacemet Service personnel ---]
Fri. 20th	20 HMT EMPIRE FOWEY sailed Southampton bound for Singapore via Mombasa with replacement Service personnel---]
Sat. 21st	**21 Pte. B. Coupland**. 1st. Battn. Royal Lincolnshire Regt. Died in a RTA [Ashes REP] Perak ---]
Sun. 22nd	"D" Patrol 1st.NZ Regt. Killed another Asi member identified as **Bah Payang** who had been wounded in the engagement of the 3rd. ---]
Mon. 23rd	The other 2 CT' s wounded in the engagement with the N.Z Regt. .on Monday the 3rd. Were located as they crossed a clearing. Both were Killed by shots fired by the troops They were Identified as **Kwong Ming & Anjan Bin Pandak. (Anjan Bin Pandak** was **Itam Bin Pandak** brother), who was Killed on the 3rd. ---]
+	A senior Member on the Central MCP Printing Press **Phong Kee Sang** surrendered to a Private of the 1st NZ Regt. in the Bekor area ---]
+	23 HMT OXFORDSHIRE arrived Singapore with replacement Service personnel---]
Tue. 24th	24 HMT OXFORDSHIRE sailed Singapore enroute to Hong Kong ---]

+	24 HMT DILWARA sailed Singapore bound for Southampton with returning Service personnel ---]
Wed. 25th	A wounded CT was captured by the Mortar M/Gun Platooon of the 2nd. 10th. Princess Mary's Own Gurkha Rifles.)dentified as **Ong Chin Tong** 2nd Senior CT of the Kota Tinggi Group---]
Thur. 26th	}
Fri. 27th	} Combined Operations continued throughout Malaya---]
Sat. 28th	}
Sun. 29th	29 Pte. B. J. Taxworth. 1st. Royal New Zealand Regt. Killed in an ambush in the area of the Cameron Highlands. _Taiping # K / 14_ Perak---]
Mon. 30th	In an ambush by the NZ Regt. 1 CT. was Killed. Identified as **Ah Yoong** the personal bodygaurd. to **Chan Hong** the Senior State Committee member in the Kinta Hills of Perak---]
+	R.A.A.F. 1 Sqdn.Lincoln B30A completed operations at R.A.F. Tengah.---]
+	RAN HMAS 'MELBOURNE". Completed her third tour of duty in Malayan coastal waters---]
+	RNZN HMNZS ROYALIST. Completed her first support role of duty & left Malayan coastal waters.---]
+	Operation "Juno" began by the SAS against known CT's---]

JULY

Tue. 1st	R.A.A.F. 2 Sqdn. Canberra B1 Began Operations at R.A.F. Butterworth---]
+	01/07/1958 LG.# 41433 p. 4141 The following awarded the British Empire Medal (Military)
	F/SGT. TW. MOULD. BEM ROYAL AIR FORCE
	The following awarded the Disinguished Flying Cross
	F/LT. K.J.ROBINSON. DFC ROYAL AIR FORCE
	F/LT. B. ROWBOTTOM. DFC ROYAL AIR FORCE
	F/O. G. ALEXANDER. DFC ROYAL AIR FORCE
	F/O. N.E.BURLOW. DFC ROYAL AIR FORCE
	The following awarded the Distinguished Flying Medal
	F/SGT. J.G. WARD. DFM ROYAL AIR FORCE
Wed. 2nd	} Combined Operations continued throughout Malaya---]
Thur. 3rd	A Platoon of 3 RAR found a CT camp & was fired at by the Sentry. In the return fire he was Killed. The Patrol followed after the other retreating CT's. Another Patrol hearing the gunfire, returned to find the camp deserted. The Dead CT was identified as **Lan Shui Mia** of the Lingtang / Sungei Siput AWF---]
Fri. 4th	}
Sat. 5th	} Combined Operations continued throughout Malaya---]
Sun. 6th	}
Mon. 7th	7 Jrn. Tech. N. Pithey. A/Rad/Fit R.A.F. Tengah Killed in Road traffic accident _Kranji Singapore # 12 / B -12_ ---]
Tue. 8th	8 HMT OXFORDSHIRE arrived Singapore enroute to Southampton with returning Service personnel 8th.---]
Wed. 9th	}
Thur. 10th	} Combined Operations continued throughout Malaya---]
Fri. 11th	}
Sat. 12th	12 PC. Wong Chin Thiam F.M. Police Killed on Ops.---]
Sun. 13th	} Combined Operations continued throughout Malaya---]
Mon. 14th	14 Spr. Lakhman. Tamang. Gurkha Engineers. Died BMH Kumintang _Sungei Pantani #141_ Kedah ---]
Tue. 15th	A Platoon of 3 RAR made contact with CT's who fled into the jungle ---]
Wed. 16th	} Combined Operations continued throughout Malaya---]
Thur. 17th	}
Fri. 18th	18 HMT DUNERA sailed Southampton bound for Singapore with replacement Service personnel ---]
Sat. 19th	} Combined Operations continued throughout Malaya---]
Sun. 20th	20 PC. Che Wan F.M. Police Killed on Ops. ---]
Mon. 21st	Another Platoon of 3 RAR made contact with a number of CT's who quickly dispersed in the fading light ---]
+	3 RAR Followed up on the previous days contact picked up the trail ---]
+	21 HMT EMPIRE FOWEY arrived Singapore with replacement Service personnel---]
Tue. 22nd	3 RAR Continued the follow up but lost contact---]
Wed. 23rd	} Combined Operations continued throughout Malaya---]
Thur. 24th	24 Rfn. Kalibahadur Limbu . 7th. Duke of Edinburgh's Own Gurkha Rifles. Died BHM _Kluang # 3 / M -2_---].
Fri. 25th	25 HMT EMPIRE FOWEY sailed Singapore onboard were The Royal Lincolnshire Regt. bound for Blighty having finished their tour of Active Service in Malaya ---]

+	25 HMT DILWARA arrived Southampton with returning Service personnel ---]
Sat. 26th	In a Mangling shed 2 bins filled with sweet potatoes, were found by members of 3 RAR. With Food control in operation, the sweet potatoes were possibly intended for a pick up by CT's. An ambush was laid to await developments.---]
Sun. 27th	27 Tpr. D. Readman 1st King's Dragoon Guarrds Died [Ashes REP] ---]
Mon. 28th	A leading member of the Bekok Min Yuen CT. Yeung Cheong was Killed by the 1st. NZ Regt. .---] A further contact was made by a Platoon of 3 RAR without results---]
Tue. 29th	The 3 RAR ambush laid for the sweet potatoes pick up. Sprung into Action Engaging CT's when 5 CT's entered the shed. The intial burst of fire.Killed 3 CT's, the two others escaped, one was hit.The 3 were identified as Tsaung Foo, Sui Ming & Wan Tin all Members of the 31 Independent Platoon.---]
Wed. 30th	3 RAR began a follow up the folowing morning near the ambush area. They spotted a figure dash across the road, stopped raised up its arms in surrender. It turned out to be a womam CT. Lying in the grass was another body, wounded who had been shot, possibly the night before. He was identified as Lam Poh Leader of the Jalong A.W.F. The women revealed she was his wife Fan Heung Mui. Lam Poh who surrendered was taken to hospital for treatment.---]
+	Later that day another CT surrendered another Patrol of 3 RAR He was identified as Hoi Ming--]
Thur. 31st	31HMT OXFORDSHIRE arrived Southampton with returning Service personnel---]

AUGUST

Fri. 1st	Operation's " Brooklyn" " Boulder" SAS operation began against the CT's---]
Sat. 2nd	Combined Operations continued throughout Malaya---]
Sun. 3rd	Kuala Lumpur : Tuanku Abdul Rahman Ruler of Negri Sembilan for 24 years. Was elected first Yang di Petuan Agong or, Paramount Ruler of Independent Malaya (King) for a 5 year period Having defeated the seanior Ruler of Pang Sultan Abu Bakar by 8 votes to 1. ---]
+	The surrendered CT Hoi Ming Turned S.E.P. led a Police Patrol into the jungle to meet 2 other CT's who were to surrender They were idendified as 2 Indians Ramasanay Moothi & Magalam --]
Mon. 4th	} Combined Operations continued throughout Malaya---]
Tue. 5th	5 Cpl. R. V. Jessop. R. A. M. C. Died*** Kranji Singapore # 11 / B – 22 ---]
Wed. 6th	} Combined Operations continued throughout Malaya---]
Thur. 7th	}
Fri. 8th	8 Rfn. Minbahadur. Mall 6th. Queen Elizabeth's Own Gurkha Rifles Died from Wounds recv'd in an engagement with CT's Tanah Hitam. Sulva Lines # 97 Ipoh Perak---]
Sat. 9th	9 HMT EMPIRE FOWEY arrived Aden where the Royal Lincolnshire Regt. disembarked as a reserve Battn.-]
Sun. 10th	CT. Lim Kim a courier of the Tanjong Rambutan Work Party was Killed by by the 12 Plt. D Comp. 1st. NZ Regt.---]
Mon. 11th	} Combined Operations continued throughout Malaya---]
Tue. 12th	}
Wed. 13th	}
Thur. 14th	} Combined Operations continued throughout Malaya---]
Fri. 15th	RAN HMAS QUIBERON. Began her first tour of duty attached to the BCFESC. Whilst HMAS 'VOYAGER". Completed her first tour of duty & HMAS 'WARRAMUNGA' completed her third & final tour of duty in Malayan coastal waters.---]
+	15 HMT DUNERA arrived Singapore with replacement Service personnel ---]
Sat. 16th	16 Pte. R. M. Breitmeyer. 1st. New Zealand Regt. Accidently Killed road accident. Taiping # I / 10 Perak ---]
+	2 CT's Wai Ming & his wife. Were captured by a Patrol of the 1st. NZ Regt. in the Korbu Forest Reserve N.E Kinta Hills. Information given to the Special Group, about Ah Fuk led to several ambushes over the following days. ---]
+	16 HMT CAPTAIN COOK arrived Singapore---]
Sun. 17th	} Combined Operations continued throughout Malaya ---]
Mon. 18th	18 HMT CAPTAIN COOK sailed Singapore bound for Southampton with returning Service Personnel---]
Tue. 19th	19 HMT DILWARA sailed Southampton bound for Singapore with replacement Service personnel ---]
Wed. 20th	20 HMT DUNERA sailed Singapore bound for Southampton with returning Service personnel ---]
Thur. 21st	CT. Ah Fuk was captured by the 1st NZ Regt. His capture was due to information given by Wai Ming---]
+	A Patrol of the 1st NZ Regt. Engaged 4 CT's.near Tanah Itam. Killing 3: 2 men & 1 women & capturing the 4th CT.---]
Fri. 22nd	22 In a Separate contact L/Cpl. P. Brown. 1st. RN Z Regt. Killed on operations North of Ipoh.

		Taiping # K / 16 Perak---]
	+	22 HMT EMPIRE FOWEY arrived Southampton with returning Service personnel---]
	+	22 HMT DEVONSHIRE sailed Southampton bound for Aden with replacement Service personnel---]
Sat. 23rd		} Combined Operations continued throughout Malaya---]
Sun. 24th		A 6 man Plt of D Comp 1st. NZ Regt. During a night operation near Tanah Itam Killed 3 CT's and captured another.---]
Mon. 25th		A Platoon of the 3 RAR made contact with CT's without results---]
Tue. 26th		26 HMT OXFORDSHIRE sailed Southampton bound for Singapore / Hong Kong with replacement Service personnel---]
Wed. 27th		Information was received of a Food Lift in the Penggarang area, which led to an ambush being laid by the 2nd.10th. Princess Mary's Own Gurkha Rifles . They were successful killing 2 CT's One was identified as the Group Committee Secretary **Chia Siow Hwa** a ruthless CT . Who had Killed his own brother the ex school teacher of Pungai ---]
Thur. 28th		**28 Maj. P. G. F. Sutton.** MC. 1st. Battn. Royal Welsh Fusiliers Died***_Kuala Lumpur # 33 / 1261_---]
Fri. 29th		29/08/1958 LG # 41519 p. 6093 The following awarded the Miltary Medal
		TRP J. J. LADNER ROYAL REGIMENT. ARTILLERY ATT/22 SAS
Sat. 30th		} Combined Operations continued throughout Malaya---]
Sun. 31st		Operations _"Chieftan"- " Goblet" - "Hippo" -"Dazzlle" -"Ginger "_ Completed by SAS against the CT's---]

SEPTEMBER

Mon. 1st		RNZAF 14 Sqdn Venom FB1 Completed Operations at R.A.F. Tengah —]
	+	R.A.F. 110 Sqdn. Whirwind H/C Completed Operations at R.A.F. Kuala Lumpur---]
	+	Operation _"Jumlah"_ began SAS operation against the CT's---]
Tue. 2nd		2/09/58.LG 41486 p 5401 The following awarded the Military Cross
		CAPT D. L. BRUCE MERRIE MC LOYAL REGIMENT.
		The following awarded the Military Medal
		CPL. R.H. COPEMAN MM ROYAL REGIMENT ARTILERY ATT/ TO 22nd. SAS.
Wed. 3rd		A member of the 10th. North District Asi group surrendered to the NZ Regt., named as **Chan Sau Po** ---]
Thur. 4th		**4 Dvr. Kassim. Bin. Raok.** R.A.S.C. (MOR). Died***_Claimed by next of Kin_ ---]
Fri. 5th		} Combined Operations continued throughout Malaya---]
Sat. 6th		}
Sun. 7th		**7 Pte. Mustafah bin Hamad** Malay Regt. Killed in Action Engaging CT's Perak---]
Mon. 8th		8 HMT DEVONSHIRE arrived Aden with replacemnet Service personnel to replace the Royal Lincolnshire Regt. ---]
Tue. 9th		**9 Pte. Yahaya Bin Abdul Samat** Royal Signals (MOR) Died*** _Claimed by next of Kin_---]
Wed. 10th		10 HMT DEVONSHIRE sailed Aden bound for Southampton on Board were the 1st. Battn. Lincolnshire Regt.']
Thur. 11th		Plt. D Comp 1st. NZR ambushed and Killed **Sui Lin wife of Low Ming** a member of the Ipph District Committee.---]
Fri. 12th		7 CT's of the North District Asi Group .1 Indian 4 Chinese including 2 women & 2 Aboriginnes surrendered to the NZ Regt., Perak—]
	+	12 HMT EMPIRE FOWEY sailed Southampton bound for Singapore/ Hong Kong with replacement Service personnel ---]
Sat. 13th		) Combined Operations continued throughout Malaya---]
Sun. 14th		14 HMT CAPTAIN COOK arrived Southampton with returning Service personnel---]
Mon. 15th		A Patrol of 3 RAR captured a CT who surrendered. He was identified as **Mo Yuen Sheng** of the Lingtang / Sungei Siput Group ---]
Tue. 16th		16 HMT DILWARA arrived Singapore with replacement Service personnel---]
Wed. 17th		17 HMT OXFORDSHIRE arrived Singapore with replacement Service personnel enroute to Hong Kong sailed 17th---]
Thur. 18th		18 HMT CAPTAIN COOK sailed Southampton for Glasgow---]
Fri. 19th		**19 Sgmm. K.V. Jones.** Royal Australian Signals. Died*** _Taiping # I / 14_ Perak---]
	+	19 HMT DUNERA arrived Southampton with returning Service personnel ---]
Sat. 20th		Combined Operations continued throughout Malaya---]
Sun. 21st		21 HMT DILWARA sailed Singapore bound for Southampton with returning Service personnel---]
Mon.22nd		CT's including 1 woman of the 25/26th.Section of the 31 Independent Platoon MRLA surrendered to 6 Platoon D Company NZ Regt. Their leader **Tsei Ko Yin with his wife and baby**.' Stated

	'They had become disolusioned & had enough' Perak---]
Tue. 23rd	} Combined Operations continued throughout Malaya---]
Wed. 24th	}
Thur. 25th	A CT surrender to the 2nd. 10th. Princess Mary's Own Gurkha Rifles. He was named as **Kim Soon** from 9 Platoon. A significant turn in events against 9 Platoon MRLA. There was only 29 left ---]
Fri. 26th	RAN HMAS *'QUICKMATCH'* Began her third tour of duty in Malayan coastal waters---]
Sat. 27th	Combined Oerations continued throughout Malaya ---]
Sun. 28th	**28 Sgt. R. Burness.** R.E.M.E.. Died***[Ashes REP]---]
Mon..29th	A Patrol of the 3 RAR found a deserted CT' Camp destroyed it North Perak---]
Tue. 30th	**30 L/Cpl. Damberbahadur Limbu.** 7th. Duke of Edinburgh's Own Gurkha Rifles. Died by Accident Telok Sangat Area. _Kluang # 3 / E -15_ Johore ---]
+	30/09/58 LG 41508 p. 5951 The following awarded the British Empire Medal (Military)
	W/O.C.N. BATES. BEM THE ROYAL ENGINEERS
	W/O. H.G. GIBBS. BEM THE ROYAL ENGINEERS
	W/O. T.W. JAMES. BEM ROYAL REGIMENT. ARTILLERY ATT/SAS
	C/SGT. R .PEADHAN. BEM 10th.PRINCESS MARY'S OWN GURKHA RIFLES.
	The following awarded the Distinguished Service Order
	LT/COL. A.N. L.VICKERS. DSO 2nd. KING EDWARD VII'S OWN GURKHA RIFLES
	p. 5952 The following awarded the Military Cross
	MAJ H.A.I.THOMPSON. MC ROYAL SCOTS FUSILIERS A/T 22SAS REGT.
	Lt. W.K.L. PROSSOR. MC THE CHESHIRE REGIMENT.
	Lt. P.H. SURTEES MC ROYAL LINCOLNSHIRE REGIMENT.
	The following awarded the Military Medal
	SGT. H. SANDILANDS. MM ROYAL REGIMENT ARTILLERY ATT/ TO SAS.
	CPL D.SWINDELLS.MM MIDDLESEX REGIMENTT. ATT/ TO SAS
	CPL.A. BOND. MM. ROYAL LINCOLNSHIRE REGIMENT.
	SGT. I. GURUNG. MM 2nd. KING EDWARD VII'S OWN GURKHA RIFLES.
	RFN. P. LIMBU. MM 7th. DUKE OF EDINBURGH'S OWN GURKHA RIFLES
	CPL. D. RAI. MM 7th. DUKE OF EDINBURGH'S OWN GURKHA RIFLES

OCTOBER

Wed. 1st	R.A.F. 52 Sqdn. Valetta C1 relocated fron R.A.F. changi to R.A.F. Kuala Lumpur ---]
+	R.A.F. 60 Sqdn. Venom FB1/4 Completed operations R.A.F. Tengah ---]
Thur. 2nd	2 HMT OXFORDSHIRE arrived Singapore bound for Southampton.with returning Service personnel---]
Fri. 3rd	3/10/1958 LG # 41514 p. 6581 The following awarded the Military Medal
	TRP. J. I. LADNER. MM ROYAL REGIMENT. ARTILLERY ATT/SAS
Sat. 4th	}Combined Operations continued throughout Malaya---]
Sun. 5th	5 HMT EMPIRE FOWEYarrived Singapore with replacement Service personnel sailed 5th. Hong Kong -]
Mon. 6th	} Combined Operations continued throughout Malaya---]
Tue. 7th	}
Wed. 8th	}
Thur. 9th	}
Fri. 10th	} Combined Operations continued throughout Malaya---]
Sat. 11th	} Combined Operations continued throughout Malaya---]
Sun. 12th	}
Mon. 13th	}
Tue. 14th	} Combined Operations continued throughout Malaya---]
Wed. 15th	}
Thur. 16th	}
Fri. 17th	} Combined Operations continued throughout Malaya---]
Sat. 18th	18 HMT EMPIRE FOWEY arrived Singapore sailed bound for Southampton with returning Service personnel 18th. ---]
Sun. 19th	} Combined Operations continued throughout Malaya---]
Mon. 20th	20 HMT DILWARA arrived Southampton with returning Service Personnel---]
Tue. 21st	}Combined Operations continued throughout Malaya---]
Wed.22nd	}

Thur. 23rd		5 CT members including 1 women & a small child. Surrended to the 1st. NZR They were members of the 31 Independent Platoon MRLA. One of them was identified as **Tsei Ko Yin**. The women was his wife with the child ---]
Fri. 24th		24/10/1958 LG # 41533 p. 6581 The following awarded the Distinguished Flying Cross SQDN.LDR. L.A. TUCKER. DFC ROYAL NEW ZEALAND AIR FORCE
	+	**24 HMT OXFORDSHIRE** arrived Southampton with returning Service personnel---]
Sat. 25th		}Combined Operations continued throughout Malaya---]
Sun. 26th		}
Mon. 27th		**27 HMT DEVONSHIRE** arrived Southampton with the returning 1st Battn. Lincolnshire Regt.---]
Tue. 28th		}Combined Operations continued throughout Malaya---]
Wed. 29th		**29 WOII. D.B. Keeble** R.A.P.C.. Died*** _Kranji Singapore # 11 / B – 23---]_
Thur. 30th		} Combined Operations continued throughout Malaya---]
Fri. 31st		**31 Rfn. Dharmabahadur Rai** 10th.Princess Mary's Own Gurkha Rifles Died*** _[Ashes REP]_---]
		Operation _"Brooklyn" "Jumlah"_ completed by SAS against the CT's---]

NOVEMBER

Sat. 1st		R.A.F. 205 Sqdn. Sunderland GR3 Completed Operations at R.A.F. Seletar ---]
	+	R.A.F. 205 Sqdn. Shackleton MR1 Completed Operations at R.A.F. Changi---]
	+	R.A.F. 267 Sqdn. SE Pioneer CC1.- Pembroke C1.- Auster 6/7. – Harvard 2B.- Dakota C4. Completed Operations at R.A.F. Kuala Lumpur---]
	+	R.A.F. Sqdn. 92 & 93 Royal Air Force Regt.(Malaya) Disbanded---]
Sun. 2nd		} Combined Operations continued throughout Malaya---]
Mon. 3rd		RAN HMAS 'QUICKMATCH' Completed her third tour of duties in Malayan coastal waters---]
Tue. 4th		}
Wed. 5th		} Combined Operations continued throughout Malaya---]
Thur. 6th		}
Fri. 7th		}
Sat. 8th		**8 Rfn. Minbahadur Mall** . 6th. Queen Elizabeth's Own Gurkha Rifles. Died*** _Sulva Lines # 97_ Ipoh Perak]
	+	**8 Cpl. B. L. Thorpe** A/F/Fit. 194 Sqdn. R.A.F. Killed when Sycamore H/C. XL 822 crash landed in a thicket 8 miles from Tanah Rata _Kuala Lumpur # 33 1263_ ---].
Sun. 9th		Combined Operations continued throughout Malaya---]
Mon. 10th		R.A.A.F. 3 Sqdn. Sabre 32 began Operations at R.A.F. Butterworth---]
Tue. 11th		**11 HMT EMPIRE FOWEY** arrived Southampton with returning Service personnel ---]
Wed. 12th		**12 PC. Hussain B. Dahari.** F. M. Police Killed on Ops. Penang.---]
Thur. 13th		**13 WOI. Kulbahadur Limbu** . 10th. Princess Mary's Own Gurkha Rifles. Died***_[Ashes REP]_---]
	+	**13 L/Cpl. D. Naylor. - Dvr. L. Birnie.** R.A.S C. Died. Transport incident._Taiping # 18 – 17_ Perak.---]
	+	**13 F/Lt. A. E. Pike.** MF Flight R.A.F Seletar. Killed when his Beufighter RD811 after engine failures, lost height & crashed into the sea 3 miles North of Changi..His other crew member survived _Kranji Singapore # 12 / B – 15_ ---]
	+	**13 HMT OXFORDSHIRE** sailed Southampton bound for Singapore / Hong Kong with replacement Service personnel---]
Fri. 14th		} Combined Operations continued throughout Malaya---]
Sat. 15th		A Patrol of the 3.RAR made contact with CT's without any results---]
Sun. 16th		} Combined Operations continued throughout Malaya---]
Mon. 17		}
Tue. 18th		**18 F/Lt. J. I. T. Rolfe.**_[Ashes REP]_ - **F/O B. S. Casling**. 45 Sqdn. R.A.F. Killed when Canberra WH853 engine cut after take-off & crashed in the sea 2 miles North of Tengah. The third crew member survived. _Kranji Singapore # 4 / B – 13_ ---]
	+	18/11/58 LG #41553 p 7113 The following awarded the Military Medal PTE.P. DILLON. MM ROYAL NEW ZEALAND REGIMENT.
Wed. 19th		**19 CPO(A) G.A. Lobb.** Royal Navy. H.M.S. 'MOUNTS BAY'. Killed Road Accident. _Kranji Singapore # 12 / C - 4_ ---]
Thur. 20th		In the hills NW of Lasah Platoon of 3 RAR engaged a number of CT's Killing 3 identified as: **Ah Chin,-Sui Kwai Ming & Chan Nana** Members of the Lintang North A.W.F. **Ah Chin**,was a member of the CT gang that ambushed & Killed Sir. Henry Gurney. Lt. Claude Dunker for his Action Engaging

		CT's during the engagement was recommended for an award.(LG 2/05/1959) ---]
Fri.	21st	An area of approx 3,000 square miles of the State of Perak was declared 'WHITE'---]
Sat.	22nd	} Combined Operations continued throughout Malaya---]
Sun.	23rd	}
Mon.	24th	}
Tue.	25th	} Combined Operations continued throughout Malaya---]
Wed.	26th	**26 Sgt. E. Turner.** 1st Battn. The Loyal Regt. Died***_Taiping # K / 19_ Perak---]
Thur.	27th	} Combined Operations continued throughout Malaya---]
Fri.	28th	}
Sat.	29th	Another contact was made by 3 RAR with CT's without results ---]
Sun.	30th	**30 Cpl. Mahmud Bin. Matzim.** R.A.S.C. (MOR) Died***_Claimed by next of Kin_ ---]
		Operation 'Cheiftan' Ended ---]

DECEMBER

Mon.	1st	) Combined Operations continued throughout Malaya Operation 'Bintang' 'Ginger'---]
Tue.	2nd	RAN HMAS 'QUICKMATCH' Completed its third tour of duty in Malayan coastal waters.---]
Wed.	3rd	**3 Rfn. Antabur Sunwar** 10th. Princess Mary's Own Gurkha Rifles. Died* [Ashes REP]*---]
Thur.	4th	) Combined Operations continued throughout Malaya---]
Fri.	5th	5 HMT OXFORDSHIRE arrived Singapore with replacement Service personnel---]
	+	5/12/1958 LG # 41567 p. 7407 The following awarded the Distinguished Flying Cross
		CAPT. M.G. BADGER. DFC CORPS ROYAL ENGINEERS
		CAPT. H.G. CRUTCHLEY. DFC ROYAL REGIMENT. ARTILLERY 656 SQDN
		The following awarded the Distinguished Flying Medal
		S/SGT. R.. BOWLES. DFM ARMY AIR CORPS
Sat.	6th	6 HMT OXFORDSHIRE sailed Singapore enroute to Hong Kong ---]
Sun.	7th	} Combined Operations continued throughout Malaya---]
Mon.	8th	}
Tue.	9th	**9 F/Lt. W.A.S. Bouttell. – F/Lt. S. Bowater. DFC AFC.- F/Lt. A.C. Moore - F/Off. M.A.C. Jones. Sgt P. Marshall.- F/Sgt. D.H.J.N. Dancy DFC.-M/A/Sig. J Stewart- F.Sgt. E.L Owen. Sgt. P. C. Barnley. Sgt. J. E. Sixsmith** Nos 205/209 Sqdn R.A.F. Killed whilst on a Anti piracy Patrol when Shackleton VP 254 Crashed into the South China Sea. Off Labuan. _[No known Graves] Terandak Wall Memorial Malacca_
		F/Sgt. G.H.G.N. Dancy DFC Body recovered. _Kranji Singapore # 12 / B – 14_ ---]
	+	9/12/1958 LG # 41568 p. 7508 The following awarded the British Empire Medal (Military)
		F/SGT. A.N. PATIENT. BEM ROYAL AIR FORCE
		The following awarded the Distinished Flying Cross
		F/LT. J. HUBICKA. DFC ROYAL AIR FORCE
		F/LT. J.H. LEVERSIDGE. DFC ROYAL AIR FORCE
		F/LT. C.E. SLATER.DFC ROYAL AIR FORCE
Wed.	10th	**10 Rfn. Kuluman. Rai** 10th. Princess Mary's Own Gurkha Rifles. Died*** [Ashes REP]---]
Thur.	11th	**11 Rfn. Dambarbahadur. Rai.** 7th. Duke of Edinburgh's Own Gurkha Rifles. Died*** [Ashes REP]--]
Fri.	12th	} Combined Operations continued throughout Malaya---]
Sat.	13th	}
Sun.	14th	**14 Sgt. M. Ryan.** 3rd. Battn. R.A.R. Died Transport incident. _Taiping # I / 11_ Perak ---]
Mon.	15th	By the 15th. December the end of Operation 'Tiger' & Badak." There was only 8 members of the 9 Platoon MRLA left in the Pengaran area, all others had been eliminated by the ground forces engaged in the operation in the area. Senior Members identified, as **Ah Fun** Leader of the Kota Tinggi Group & **Chia Chee Fong** Leader of the Pengarang Group---]
Tue.	16th	} Combined Operations continued throughout Malaya---]
Wed.	17th	}
Thur.	18th	} Combined Operations continued throughout Malaya---]
Fri.	19th	}
Sat.	20th	} Combined Operations continued throughout Malaya---]
Sun.	21st	21 HMT OXFORDSHIRE arrived Singapore with replacement Service personnel--]
Mon.	22nd	Combined Operations continued throughout Malaya---]
Tue.	23rd	6 CT's of 9 Platoon MRLA surrenderd to Security Forces leaving just 2 from the original 29---]
Wed.	24th	24 HMT OXFORDSHIRE sailed Singapore bound for Southampton with returning Service personnel--]

Thur. 25th	} Combined Operations continued throughout Malaya---]
Fri. 26th	}
Sat. 27th	} Combined Operations continued throughout Malaya---]
Sun. 28th	}
Mon. 29th	} Combined Operations continued throughout Malaya---]
Tue. 30th	30/12/1958. LG # 41586 p. 7949 The following awarded the Distinguished Flying Cross
	W/COM. K.V. ROBERTDON. AFC DFC ROYAL AUSTRALIAN AIR FORCE
Wed. 31st	M.A.A.F. Penang Sqdn Chipmonk Completed Operations Disbanded at R.A.F. Butterworth—]
+	M.A.A.F. Kuala Lumpur Sqdn. Completed Operations Disbanded at R.A.F. Kuala Lumpur ---]
+	The whole of the Johore State was declared 'White' 8 ½. years since the Emergency began---]
+	Operation *'Tiger'* & *'Badak'* ended ---]

R. A. F. OPERATION *"FIREDOG"* END OF YEAR STATS 1958

No of Sorties	No. of Strikes	1,000 Lb. Bombs	500 Lb. Bombs	350 Lb. Cluster	20 Lb Bombs	R/P's	20mm	.5 mm	.303mm
927	47	1963	3220	-	1452	351	111313	-	-

R.A.F. SUPPORT 1958

	Soties	Troops/Lift/	Casac	Pass/Lift	Supply Wt. Lbs	Leaflets drop (1,000)	B Flying Times No / hrs	Broadcsting No / hrs	Crashed
Air SupportA/C*	1250	/	/	/	5,018,733	/	/	/	Sycamore
Auster**	/	/	/	/	/	/	/	/	XL822
Pioneer	3211	2744	43	923	508,943	/	/	/	Canberra
H/C Light	11,843	7113	505	1873	213,927	/	/	/	WA853
848 Sqdn	Disbabded	/	/	/	/	/	/	/	Shackleton
155 Sqdn	11,846	19,655	217	841	415,283	/	/	/	VP254
Target/MK**	/	/	/	/	/	/	/	/	Beaufighter
Vis/Air OBs**	/	/	/	/	/	/	/	/	RD811
Communication**	/	/	/	/	/	/	/	/	
Leaf. Sorties*	314	/	/	/	/	/	/	/	
Leaflets Drop*	/	/	/	/	/	86,100	/	/	
Leaf Sorties **	0	/	/	/	/	/	/	/	
Leaflets Drop**	/	/	/	/	/	/	/	/	
Broad Sorties*	523	/	/	/	/	/	/	/	
Broad Hrs *	/	/	/	/	/	/	1475	395	
Broad Sorties**	163	/	/	/	/	/	/	/	
Broad Hrs **	/	/	/	/	/	/	315.5	94.6	
Photo RECCE***	725	/	/	/	/	/	./		

*   AirSupport A/C Dokota -Valetta- Hastings Bristol
** Auster
*** Photo Rec Anson,,Spitfire, Mosquito, Meteor, Pembroke

CHAPTER 17 - 1959

JANUARY

Thur.	1st	**18 Spr. J. Gibson** Royal Engineers Died*** *Kuala Lumpur # 33 / 12 65* ---]
Fri.	2nd	Combined Operations *'Brooklyn'* *'Bamboo'* & *'Selandang'* continued in Kedah Perils & Central Pahang Mopping Up continued throughout Malaya---]
Sat.	3rd	**3 F/Sgt. D. J. Waterman.** BEM A/Fit 209 Sqdn. R.A.F. Died Accident**[*Ashes REP*]---]
Sun.	4th	**4 Cpl. E. Johnson.** 1st. Battn. Sherwood Foresters. Died*** *Kranji Singapore # 11/ B - 24*---]
Mon.	5th	**5 Spr. Khumansing Bura.** Gurkha Engineers Died BMH Kumintang *Sungei Patani # 149* Kedah---]
	+	**5 Cpl. Othman B. Sulaiman** F. M. Police Killed on Ops. "*Pengerang*" Johore---]
	+	**5 Capt. C.C Treherne** R.A.S.C. Died*** [*Ashes REP*]---]
Tue.	6th	} Combined Operations continued throughout Malaya---]
Wed.	7th	}
Thur.	8th	**8 Cpl. T. W. Hodge.**(Adm) R.A.F. Tengah Died Natural Causes *Kuala Lumpur # 33 - 1262r*---]
Fri.	9th	9 HMT EMPIRE FOWEY sailed Southampton bound for Singapore/ Hong Kong with replacement Service personnel ---]
Sat. .	10th	Following the surrender of the last two CT's in the State of Johore to security Guards The whole of Johore State was declared 'WHITE' ---]
Sun.	11th	}Combined Operations Continued throughout Malaya--]
Mon.	12th	}
Tue.	13th	13 HMT OXFORDSHIRE arrived Southampton with returning Service personnel ---]
Wed.	14th	} Combined Operations continued throughout Malaya---]
Thur.	15th	}
Fri.	16th	**16 Cfn. B.A.D. Henderson.** RAEME. Died ** *Taiping # K / 20* Perak---]
Sat.	17th	Combined Operations continued throughout Malaya---]
Sun.	18th	**18 Spr. J. Gibson** Royal Engineers Died* *Kuala Lumpur # 33 / 1265*---]
Mon.	19th	**19 Cfn. R. Parker.** R.E.M.E.. Died*** [*Ashes REP*]---]
Tue.	20th	} Combined Operations continued throughout Malaya---]
Wed.	21st	}
Thur.	22nd	} Combined Operations continued throughout Malaya---]
Fri.	23rd	}
Sat.	24th	} Combined Operations continued throughout Malaya---]
Sun.	25th	**25 Gnr. R.M. Ducat.** Royal Australian Artillery. Died Transport incident. *Taiping # K / 21* Perak---]
	+	**25 Rfn. Nare. Rana** 6th. Queen Elizabeth's Own Gurkha Rifles. Died by Accident *Sungei Patani#150* ---]
Mon..	26th.	} Combined Operations continued throughout Malaya---]
Tue..	27th	**27 Pte. A. McAdam.** 2nd. Battn. The K. O. Y. L. I.. Died*** *Kranji Singapore # 2 / A - 5*---]
Wed.	28th	} Combined Operations continued throughout Malaya---]
Thur.	29th	}
Fri..	30th	The Last known CT in Negri Sembilan. Surrenderd to Security Forces---]
Sat..	31st	Following the surrender of the last CT. in the State of Negri Sembilan. It was declared 'WHITE'----]

FEBRUARY

Sun.	1st	} Combined Operations continued throughout Malaya---]
Mon.	2nd	}
Tue.	3rd	}
Wed.	4th	) Combined Operations continued throughout Malaya---]
Thur.	5th	**5 Capt. C. C. Treherne.** R.A.S.C.. Died*** [*Ashes REP*] ---]
	+	5 HMT OXFORDSHIRE sailed Southampton bound for Singapore/ Hong Kong with replacement Service personnel ---]
Fri.	6th	Kuala Lumpur: Lt. General Sir. James Cassels. The Director of Emergency Operations & Chief of Staff of the Federations armed forces was succeeded by Maj. General F.H. Brooke.----]
	+	6 HMT EMPIRE FOWEY arrived Singapore with replacement Service personnel sailed Hong Kong 6th. –]
Sat.	7th	**7 L/REM1. B.J. Harding.** ? .[*Ashes REP*]---]
Sun.	8th	**8 PO/RE W. L. Jones.** Royal Navy. H.M.S. *'TERROR'.* Died. Road Accident. *Kranji Singapore # 12 C - 3*---]
	+	Kuala Lumpur: The State of Selangor was declared "WHITE" After an ambush, when two CT's were Killed

	& one surrendered.**Siu Mah** with a reward of M$150,000 (£18,000) 0n his head & one of the highest ranking members of the MRLA. Responsible for the killing of Sir. Henry Braithwaite Gurney in Oct 1951. Was shot dead by The Loyal Regt. It was reported that **Siu Mah** hiding in a cave, had sent two of his bodyguards into Ipoh for food. Instead they surrendered & led the ambush party to the cave.---]
Mon. 9th	RAN HMAS '*QUEENBOROUGH*'. Began her third tour of duty in Malayan coastal waters.---]
Tue. 10th	Kuala Lumpur: The Prime Minister Tengku Abdul Rahman before his resignation. Announced: '*There were 859 known Communist Terrorist left in the Malayan Federation. With another 484 in the jungles astride the borders of Malaya & Thailand. Further details were announced as follows: Since the beginning of the Emergency 10,527 Communist Terrorist had been Killed, captured or, surrendered 86 Communist terrorist had been eliminated since Malaya had achieved Independence.*'---]
Wed. 11th	} Combined Operations continued throughout Malaya---]
Thur. 12th	**12 Capt. (QGO). Rane Gurung** . 6th. Queen Elizabeth's Own Gurkha Rifles. Died BMH Kinrara *Sulva Lines # 96* Ipoh Perak---]
Fri. 13th	} Combined Operations continued throughout Malaya---]
Sat. 14th	}
Sun. 15th	}
Mon. 16th	} Combined Operations continued throughout Malaya---]
Tue. 17th	}
Wed. 18th	}
Thur. 19th	} Combined Operations continued throughout Malaya---]
Fri. 20th	**20 F/Lt. H. T. Albutt.** 224 Group Sig. HQ R.A.F. Kuala Lumpur. Died***. *Kuala Lumpur # 33 - 1264* ---]
+	**20 HMT EMPIRE FOWEY** arrived Singapore sailed bound for Southampton bound with returning Service personnel 20th. ---]
Sat. 21st	**21 F/Lt. A. G. A. Mitchell.- F/Lt. T. Hillman.** 194 Sqdn R.A.F. Killed when flying Sycamore H/C XE 391. Crashed 6 miles South of Kuala Lumpur. *Kuala Lumpur # 33 – 1268 – 1266* ---]
Sun. 22nd	} Combined Operations continued throughout Malaya---]
Mon. 23rd	}
Tue. 24th	}Combined Operations continued throughout Malaya---]
Wed. 25th	}
Thur. 26th	}
Fri.. 27th	} Combined Operations continued throughout Malaya---]
Sat. 28th	**28 HMT OXFORDSHIRE** arrived Singapore with replacement Service personnel enroute to Hong Kong 28th.]

MARCH

Sun. 1st	}
Mon. 2nd	} Combined Operations continued throughout Malaya---]
Tue. 3rd	}
Wed. 4th	**4 LAC. D. J. Hall.** Royal Australian Air Force. Died*** *Western Road # 2168* George Town Penang---]
Thur. 5th	**5 Pol/Lt. C. W. Tate.**F.M. Aux Police .Killed on Ops. *[Grave Unknown]* ---]
Fri. 6th	} Combined Operations continued throughout Malaya---]
Sat. 7th	}
Sun. 8th	8/03/1959.LG 41701 p2979 The following awarded the Military Medal L/CPL. M.P. HANLEY. MM ROYAL AUSTRALIAN REGIMENT.
Mon. 9th	The Cameron Highlands. were declared" WHITE". Bringing a total figure of 4/5ths. of the Federation free of CT's with the exception of CT activity in the the Thailand Border & part of Perak.---]
Tue. 10th	} Combined Operations continued throughout Malaya---]
Wed. 11th	}
Thur. 12th	}
Fri. 13th	}
Sat. 14th	} Combined Operations continued throughout Malaya---]
Sun. 15th	**15 Sigm S. Narbahadur** Gurkha Signals Died By Accident. *Kluang # J / K – 6* Johore --]
+	**15 HMT OXFORDSHIRE** arrived /sailed Singapore enroute to Southampton with returning Service personnel 15th.---]
+	**15 HMT EMPIRE FOWEY** arrived Southampton with returning Service personnel ---]
Mon. 16t	R.A.F. 209 Sqdn. Auster 6/7 Completed Operations R.A.F. Kuala Lumpur---]
Tue. 17th	**17 2 F.M. Police Sgt. Mohd. Shah s/o Nabi Bakhsh - MM Zanal Abidin B. Talib.** Killed in CT ambush ---]

Wed. 18th	**18 PC. Murad B. Abdullah F.M. Police** died from wounds recv'd previous day ---]
Thur. 19th	}Combined Operations continued throughout Malaya---]
Fri. 20th	}
Sat. 21st	**21 LAC. J.A.R. Gudsell.** Royal New Zealand Air Force. Died*** [*Ashes REP*]---]
Sun. 22rd	}
Mon. 23rd	} Combined Operations continued throughout Malaya---]
Tue. 24th	}
Wed. 25th	RAN HMAS *'MELBOURNE'*. Began her fourth tour of duty, whilst HMAS *'VOYAGER'*. Began her second tour of duty in Malayan coastal waters.---]
Thur. 26th	} Combined Operations continued throughout Malaya---]
Fri. 27th	}
Sat. 28th	RAN HMAS *'ANZAC'*. Began her second tour of duty whilst HMAS *'TOBRUK'*. Began her third tour of duty in Malayan coastal waters.---]
Sun. 29th	}
Mon. 30st	} Combined Operations continued throughout Malaya---]
Tue. 31st	}

APRIL

Wed. 1st	**1 Pol/Lt. J. Stead** F. M. Police . Killed on Ops. *[Grave Unkown]*---]
Thur. 2nd	} Combined Operations continued throughout Malaya---]
Fri. 3rd	}
Sat. 4th	}
Sun. 5th	}
Mon. 6th	} Combined Operations continued throughout Malaya---]
Tue. 7th	**7 HMT OXFORDSHIRE** arrived Southampton with returning Service personnel---]
+	**7 HMT EMPIRE FOWEY** sailed Southampton bound for Singapore / Hong Kong with replacement Service personnel ---]
Wed. 8th	} Combined Operations continued throughout Malaya---]
Thur. 9th	All 7 Malay Regiments Awarded the title **"ROYAL MALAY REGIMENTS"---**]
Fri. 10th	} Combined Operations continued throughout Malaya---]
Sat. 11th	**11 SPO/V B. J. Barrett** Royal Navy HMS *'CHEVIOT* Died***[*Ashes REP*]--]
Sun. 12th	} Combined Operations continued throughout Malaya---]
Mon. 13th	}
Tue. 14th	}
Wed. 15th	}
Thur. 16th	} Combined Operations continued throughout Malaya---]
Fri. 17th	**17J/Tech. B. W. Hayes.** Eng/Fit R.A.F. Seletar. Died Road Traffic Accident. *Kranji* *Singapore* # 14 / A – 22
Sat. 18th	}
Sun. 19th	}Combined Operations continued throughout Malaya---]
Mon. 20th	}
Tue. 21st	Operation *'Ginger'* ended having destroyed the MCP's Organisation in the Ipoh area .Since the beginning 45 CT's had surrendered 35 Killed & 5 captured. Accordingly they had had enough some having been in the jungle since 1948.----]
Wed.22nd	} Combined Operations continued throughout Malaya---]
Thur. 23rd	}
Fri. 24th	}
Sat. 25th	}
Sun. 26th	} Combined Operations continued throughout Malaya---]
Mon. 27th	**27 S/Ldr. J. E. Scott.- F/Lt. P. de B. Daly.- F/Lt. L.W. D. Dray.** 194 Sqdn R.A.F. Killed when Sycamore H/C XF267 crashed near Kuala Lumpur. *Kuala Lumpur* # 33 – 1267 - 1269 - 1271 ---]
Tue. 28th	28/04/59 LG # 41692 p 2765. The following awarded the Military Medal SGT. N.C. JAMIESON. MM NEW ZEALAND REGT.
Wed. 29th	**29 Lt. R. H. Morley.** 1st. Battn. The Loyal Regt. Died*** *Taiping # K / 22* Perak---]
Thur. 30th	RAN HMAS *'QUEENBOROUGH'*. Completed her third tour of duty in Malayan coastal waters.---]
+	RNZN HMNZS *'ROTOITI'*. Completed her first support role of duty in Malayan coastal waters---
+	30 HMT OXFORDSHIRE sailed Soiuthampton bound for Singapore / Hong Kong with replacement

	+	Service personnel ---]
	+	**30 HMT EMPIRE FOWEY** arrived Singapore with replacement Service personnel sailed Hong Kong 5th]
	+	Operation '*Ginger*' Ended ---]

MAY

Fri.	1st	} Combined Operations continued throughout Malaya---]
Sat.	2nd	}
Sun.	3rd	**3 Gnr. S.J. Blanch**. Royal Australian Artillery Died transport incident. *Taiping # K / 23* Perak --]
Mon.	4th	} Combined Operations continued throughout Malaya---]
Tue.	5th	}
Wed.	6th	}
Thur.	7th	} Combined Operations continued throughout Malaya---]
Fri.	8th	8/05/59 LG # 41701 p.2979 The following awarded the Military Cross.
		LT. C.H. DUNKER MC. 3rd. BATTN. AUSTRALIAN REGIMENT.
		The following awarded the Military Medal
		L/CPL M.P. HANLEY MM . 3rd. BATTN. AUSTRALIAN REGIMENT.
Sat.	9th	} Combined Operations continued throughout Malaya---]
Sun.	10th	}
Mon.	11th	}
Tue.	12th	} Combined Operations continued throughout Malaya---]
Wed.	13th	**13 HMT EMPIRE FOWEY** arrived Singapore sailed bound for Southampton with returning Service personnel 13th.---]
Thur.	14th	Combined Operations continued throughout Malaya---
Fri.	15th	**15 Cfn. W. J. H. Johnston**. R.E.M.E. Died*** .*[Ashes REP]* ---]
Sat.	16th	**16 Sgt. W. C. Woods**. Arm/Fit R.A.F. Kuala Lumpur Died***.*Kuala Lumpur # 33 – 1270* ---]
Sun.	17th	} Combined Operations continued throughout Malaya---]
Mon.	18th	}
Tue.	19th	}
Wed.	20th	} Combined Operations continued throughout Malaya---]
Thur.	21st	}
Fri.	22nd	} Combined Operations continued throughout Malaya---]
Sat.	23rd	23 HMT OXFORDSHIRE arrived Singapore with replacement Service personnel enroute to Hong Kong 23rd]
		RAN HMAS '*MELBOURNE*". Completed her fourth. Tour of duty in Malayan coastal waters.---]
Sun.	24th	}
Mon.	25th	} Combined Operations continued throughout Malaya---]
Tue.	26th	}
Wed.	27th	}
Thur.	28th	**28 Tpr. R. Richardson**. 13/18th. Royal Hussars. Killed Battle accident. *Taiping # K / 24* Perak---]
Fri.	29th	**29 Sgt. W. Christie**. 1st. Battn. Seaforth Highlanders. Died***.*[Ashes REP]*---]
Sat.	30th	} Combined Operations continued throughout Malaya---]
Sun.	31st	}

JUNE

Mon.	1st	RNZN HMNZS '*PUKAKI*'.. Began her third support role of duty in Malayan coastal waters.---]
Tue.	2nd	Combined Operations continued throughout Malaya---]
Wed.	3rd	R.A.F. 155 Sqdn. Whirlwind H/C Completed Operations at R.A.F. Kuala Lumpur---]
Tur.	4th	4 HMT EMPIRE FOWEY arrived Southampton with returning Service personnel ---]
Fri.	5th	} Combined Operations continued throughout Malaya---]
Sat.	6th	)
Sun.	7th	7 HMT OXFORDSHIRE arrived Singapore enroute to Southampton with returning Service personnel 7th.--]
Mon.	8th	} Combined Operations continued throughout Malaya---]
Tue.	9th	}
Wed.	10th	}
Thur.	11th	} Combined Operations continued throughout Malaya---]
Fri.	12th	**12 A/B. J. Brennan** Royal Navy. H.M.S. "*COSSACK*" 'Died*** Buried at Sea.-

		[No known Grave Terendak Wall memorial Malacca ---]
+		**12 Dvr. J. Atkinson.** R.A.S.C.. Died*** *Kranji Singapore # 11 / C - 22* ---]
+		Kuala Lumpur: Air Vice Marshal R.A. Ramsey Rae. Became Air Officer Commanding Malaya---]
		12/06/1959 LG. 41738 p. 3897 The following awarded the Distinguished Flying Cross
		CAPT. I.E. BELL. DFC ROYAL REGIMENT. ARTILLERY 656 SQDN.
		CAPT. M.P.E. LEGG. DFC ROYAL REGIMENT. ARTILLERY 658 SQDN
		The following awarded the Distinguished Flying Cross
		SGT. B.A. HORSEY. DFM ROYAL REGIMENT. ARTILLERY 858 SQDN
Sat. 13th	}	
Sun. 14th	} Combined Operations continued throughout Malaya---]	
Mon. 15th	}	
Tue. 16th	16/06/1959 LG. # 41739 p. 3905 The following awarded the British Empire Medal	
	CPL/TECH. L.W. BOSWELL. BEM ROYAL AIR FORCE	
	The following awarded the Distinguished Flying Cross	
	F/LT. (AFC) W. H. SPENCER. AFC DFC ROYAL AIR FORCE	
	F/LT. J. W. PECKOWSKI. DFC ROYAL AIR FORCE	
	MAS/P. W.H. ATKINS. DFC ROYAL AIR FORCE	
	The following awarded the Distinguished Flying Medal	
	F/SGT. W.H. MACEACHEN. DFM ROYAL AIR FORCE	
Wed. 17th	**17 Cpl. N. Stobie.** R.E.M.E. Died*** *Singapore 1 /B -4 #* ---]	
Thur. 18th	} Combined Operations continued throughout Malaya---]	
Fri. 19th	}	
Sat. 20th	RAN HMAS 'VOYAGER''. Completed her second tour of duty in Malayan coastal waters---].	
Sat. 21st	**21 Capt. Q. M F. L. Hoyle.** R.A.S.C.. Died***_Taiping # R / 2_ Perak ---]	
+	**21 J/Tech. M. Hauxwell.** Arm/Fit. R.A.F. Tengah Killed Road traffic accident. *Kranji Singapore # 14 / A – 1*	
Mon.22nd	} Combined Operations continued throughout Malaya---]	
Tue. 23rd	}	
Wed. 24th	**24 Pte. K. Gardner.** 1st. Battn. The Loyal Regt. Died***_Taiping # K / 25_ Perak---]	
Thur. 25th	} Combined Operations continued throughout Malaya---]	
Fri. 26th	}	
Sat. 27th	}	
Sun. 28th	} Combined Operations continued throughout Malaya---]	
Mon. 29th	29 HMT OXFORDSHIRE arrived Southampton with returning Service personnel ---]	
Tue. 30th	30 HMT EMPIRE FOWEY sailed Southampton bound for Singapore /Hong Kong with replacement Service personnel ---]	

JULY

Wed. 1st	01/0/1958 LG # .41433 P. 4141 The following awarded the Distinguished Flying Cross	
	F/LT. B. ROWBOTHAM. DFC ROYAL AIR FORCE	
	F/LT. K.J. ROBINSON. DFC ROYAL AIR FORCE	
	F/O. G. ALEXANDER. DFC ROYAL AIR FORCE	
	F/O. N.R. BURLOW. DFC ROYAL AIR FORCE	
Thur. 2nd	}	
Fri. 3rd	} Combined Operations continued throughout Malaya---]	
Sat. 4th	}	
Sun. 5th	**5 SAC. A. N. Mulligan.** A/Mech. R.A.F. Changi Killed. Road Traffic accident Singapore [Ashes REP]]	
Mon. 6th	} Combined Operations continued throughout Malaya---]	
Tue. 7th	}	
Wed. 8th	}	
Thur. 9th	} Combined Operations continued throughout Malaya---]	
Fri. 10th	}	
Sat. 11th	}	
Sun. 12th	} Combined Operations continued throughout Malaya---]	
Mon. 13th	**13 PC. Wong Chin Thiam** F. M. Police Killed on Ops. 22nd. m/s Ipoh /Kampar Perak.---]	
+	**13 Pte. Sulaiman Bin. Mohd.** A. C. C. (MOR)Died ***_Claimed by next of Kin_ ---]	
Tue. 14th	**14 Lt/Col. G. F. Blyth.** Royal Engineers Died *** *Kranji Singapore # 11 / C -23*---]	

Wed. 15th	} Combined Operations continued throughout Malaya---]
Thur. 16th	}
Fri. .17th	**17SAC. I. B. Mahmood.** R.A.F. Regt. (MOR) Died*** [*Claimed by next of Kin*] ---]
Sat. 18th	Combined Operations continued throughout Malaya---]
Sun. 19th	**19 PC. Che Wan** F. M. Police Killed on Ops. Kg. Bahru Penang.---]
Mon. 20th	} Combined Operations continued throughout Malaya---]
Tue. 21st	}
Wed.22nd	**22 HMT OXFORDSHIRE** sailed Southampton bound for Singapore / Hong Kong with replacement Service personnel---]
Thur. 23rd	**23 HMT EMPIRE FOWEY** arrived Singapore with replacement Service personnel sailed Hong Kong 23rd.-]
Fri. .24th	} Combined Operations continued throughout Malaya---]
Sat. 25th	}
Sun. 26th	**26 LAC. W.P. Duffy. - A/C J.G. Lawson.** Royal Australian Air Force. Killed *** *Western Road # 2171 – 2170* George Town Penang----]
Mon. 27th	)Combined Operations continued throughout Malaya---]
Tue. 28th	28/10/1958 LG. ISS 41533 P. 6581 The following awarded the Distinguished Flying Cross S/LDR. A. F. TUCKER DFC ROYAL NEW ZEALAND AIR FORCE
Wed. 29th	)Combined Operations continued throughout Malaya---}
Thur. 30th	**30 A/B. B. Rolph** Royal Navy HMS *'TERROR'* Died*** [*Ashes REP*]---]
Fri. 31st	)Combined Operations continued throughout Malaya---]

AUGUST

Sat. 1st	} Combined Operations continued throughout Malaya---]
Sun. 2nd	}
Mon. 3rd	}
Tue. 4th	} Combined Operations continued throughout Malaya---]
Wed. 5th	**5 HMT EMPIRE FOWEY** arrived Singapore bound for Southampton with returning Service personnel ---]
Thur. 6th	} Combined Operations continued throughout Malaya---]
Fri. 7th	}
Sat. 8th	}
Sun. 9th	}
Mon. 10th	} Combined Operations continued throughout Malaya---]
Tue. 11th	}
Wed. 12th	}
Thur. 13th	} Combined Operations continued throughout Malaya---]
Fri. 14th	**14 HMT OXFORDSHIRE** arrived /sailed Singapore with the 1st./2nd. 10th. Princess Mary's Own Gurkha Rifles for Hong Kong. Having completed their long sucessful tours of operation in Malaya.---]
Sat. 15th	**15 Cpl. Mohamid Noor B, Hamid** F.M. Police Killed on Ops. ---]
Sun. 16th	} Combined Operations continued throughout Malaya---]
Mon. 17th	}
Tue. 18th	}
Wed. 19th	} Combined Operations continued throughout Malaya---]
Thur. 20th	**20 HMT OXFORDSHIRE** arrived Singapore enroute to Hong Kong with replacement Service personnel
Fri. 21st	} Combined Operations continued throughout Malaya---]
Sat. 22nd	}
Sun. 23rd	}
Mon. 24th	}
Tue. 25th	} Combined Operations continued throughout Malaya---]
Wed. 26th	The advanced party of the 2nd. Battn., New Zealand Regt. arrived in Kuala Lumpur in replacement for the 1st. Battn. NZ Regt.---]
Thur. 27th	)Combined Operations continued throughout Malaya---]
Fri. 28th	**28 HMT EMPIRE FOWEY** arrived Southampton with returning Service personnel ---]
Sat. 29th	**29 HMT OXFORDSHIRE** arrived Singapore enroute to Southampton with returning Service personnel---] going on board were the 1st. Battalion of the Loyal Regiment on their way home after their tour of duty in Malaya.---]
Sun. 30th	Combined Operations continued throughout Malaya---]

Mon. 31st	**31 Sgt. Gyanbahadur Gurung** 6th. Queen Elizabeth's Own Gurkha Rifles. Died*** *Sulva Lines # 95* Ipoh Perak---]

SEPTEMBER

Tue. 1st	} Combined Operations continued throughout Malaya---]
Wed. 2nd	}
Thur. 3rd	}
Fri. 4th	}
Sat. 5th	} Combined Operations continued throughout Malaya---]
Sun. 6th	**6 S/Lt. R.H.C. McKenzie.** Royal Navy. H.M.S.' *CENTAUR*' Died*** *Kranji Singapore # 12 / C - 2*---]
Mon. 7th	} Combined Operations continued throughout Malaya---]
Tue. 8th	}
Wed. 9th	}
Thur. 10th	}
Fri. 11th	}Combined Operations continued throughout Malaya---]
Sat. 12th	}
Sun. 13th	}
Mon. 14th	) Combined Operations continued throughout Malaya---]
Tue. 15th	}
Wed. 16th	16 HMT EMPIRE FOWEY sailed Southampton bound for Singapore / Hong Kong with replacement Service personnel ---]
Thur. 17th	}
Fri. 18th	} Combined Operations continued throughout Malaya---]
Sat. 19th	}
Sun. 20th	20 HMT OXFORDSHIRE arrived Southampton with returning Service Personnel---]
Mon. 21st	} Combined Operations continued throughout Malaya---]
Tue. 22nd	}
Wed. 23rd	**23 Sgmn. Narbahadur Suwar.** Gurkha Signals. Died *** *Kluang # 3 / K -6* Johore---]
Thur. 24th	24 HMT CAPTAIN COOK sailed Glasgow bound for Wellington NZ ---]
Fri. 25th	} Combined Operations continued throughout Malaya---]
Sat. 26th	}
Sun. 27th	}
Mon. 28th	} Combined Operations continued throughout Malaya---]
Tue. 29th	}
Wed. 30th	}
Wed. 31st	} Combined Operations continued throughout Malaya---]

OCTOBER

Thur. 1st	R.A.F. 209 Sqdn. SE Pioneer CC!.- TE Pioneer CC1 .- Pembroke C1. – Dakota C4. – R.A.F. Kuala Lumpur Completed Operations---]
Fri. 2nd	} Combined Operations continued throughout Malaya---]
Sat. 3rd	}
Sat. 4th	**4 Sgt. D. Anderson** R.A.S.C. Drowned *Kranji Singapore # 11 / C – 24* ---]
Mon. 5th	**5 Cpl. B. S. Powell** Royal Engineers Died *** *Kuala Lumpur # 33 / 1272* ---]
Tue. 6th	}Combined Operations continued throughout Malaya---]
Wed. 7th	}
Thur. 8th	8 HMT EMPIRE FOWEY arrived Singapore with replacement Service personnel sailed Hong Kong 8th.---]
Fri. 9th	} Combined Operations continued throughout Malaya---]
Sat. 10th	}
Sun. 11th	}
Mon. 12th	} Combined Operations continued throughout Malaya---]
Tue. 13th	13 HMT OXFORDSHIRE sailed Southampton bound for Singapore/ Hong Kong with replacement Service personnel---]
Wed. 14th	} Combined Operations continued throughout Malaya---]
Thur. 15th	}

Fri. 16th	} Combined Operations continued throughout Malaya---]
Sat. 17th	}
Sun. 18th	}
Mon. 19th	} Combined Operations continued throughout Malaya---]
Tue. 20th	20 HMT EMPIRE FOWEY arrived Singapore with replacement Service personnel --]
Wed. 21st	21 HMT EMPIRE FOWEY sailed Singapore bound for Southampton with returning Service personnel --]
Thur.22nd	} Combined Operations continued throughout Malaya ---]
Fri. 23rd	23 F/Lt. A. E. Johnson. Pilot- SAC. D. J. D. Motton. 209 Sqdn. R.A.F. Killed when Pioneer XG 561 Hit a pylon in the grounds of Radio Malay Ipoh. *Kualu Lumpur # 33 – 1274 - 1276* ---]
Sat. 24th	}
Sun. 25th	} Combined Operations continued throughout Malaya---]
Mon. 26th	}
Tue. 27th	27 Pte. Anak Tinggi . Kumpang. Sarawak Rangers. Killed in Action Engaging CT's*Taiping # Q / 4* Perak -]
Wed. 28th	} Combined Operations continued throughout Malaya---]
Thur. 29th	}
Fri. 30th	31 Pte. Anang. Bin. Hji. Amari. ACC. (MOR) Died*** *Claimed by next of Kin*---]
Sat. 31th	Operation *'Planters Punch'* ended---]
+	R.A.F. 58 Sqdn. Canberra PR7 completed Operations at R.A.F. Changi.---]
+	R.A.F. 82 Sqdn. Canberra PR7 completed Operations at R.A.F. Changi.---]
+	R.A.F. 540 Sqdn. Canberra PR7 completed Operations at R.A.F. Changi.---]
+	R.A.F. 542 Sqdn. Canberra PR7 completed Operations at R.A.F. Changi.---]

NOVEMBER

Sun. 1st	} Combined Operations continued throughout Malaya---]
Mon. 2nd	}
Tue. 3rd	}
Wed. 4th	} Combined Operations continued throughout Malaya---]
Thur.. 5th	5 HMT OXFORDSHIRE arrived Singapore enroute to Hong Kong with replacement Service personnel sailed 5th.---]
Fri. 6th	6 SC. M.M. Zainal Abidin B. Talib F. M. Police Killed on Ops. Location not known ---]
+	6 HMT CAPTAIN COOK sailed from New Zealand with the 2nd. Battn. New Zealand Regt. on board bound for Penang.---]
Sat. 7th	7 Cpl. G. W. A. Bawden. R.E.M.E.. Died*** *Kranji Singapore # 11/ C – 25* ---]
Sun. 8th	} Combined Operations continued throughout Malaya---]
Mon. 9th	}
Tue. 10th	}
Wed. 11th	} Combined Operations continued throughout Malaya---]
Thur. 12th	12 HMT EMPIRE FOWEY arrived Southampton with returning Service personnel ---]
Fri. 13th	} Combined Operations continued throughout Malaya---]
Sat. 14th	14 Cpl. R. E. Faulkner Ins/Fit. R.A.F. 205 Sqdn. Changi Died***. *[Ashes REP]*---]
+	14 Lt. (QGO) Chengba. Tamag 10th. Princess Mary's Own Gurkha Rifles. Died*** *[Ashes REP]*---]
Sun. 15th	15 Cpl. B. C. McAuley. R.E.M.E.. Died*** *Kranji Singapore # 11 / E -22*---]
Mon. 16th	16 L/Cpl. R. Whipp. 13/18th. Royal Hussars. Died***\u200bTaiping # K / 26 Perak.—
+	R.A.F. FEC Sqdn. Meteor T7 Completed Operartions at R.A.F. Changi---]
Tue. 17th	17 Sgt. T. J. Day. 1st. Battn. The Queen's Regt. Died*** *[Ashes REP]*.---]
Wed. 18th	18 Trp. M. J. Warner. 13/18th. Royal Hussars Died **Taiping # K / 28 Perak.--]
Thur..19th	Combined Operations continued throughout Malaya---]
Fri. 20th	20 /11/1959 LG # 41876 p. 7447 The following awarded the Air Force Medal SQD/LDR. D.C. HARVEY. DFC AFC ROYAL AIR FORCE
+	20 HMT OXFORDSHIRE arrived Singapore with replacement Service Personnel enroute to Southampton with returning Service personnel 20th. ---]
Sat. 21st	}Combined Operations continued throughout Malaya---]
Sun. 22nd	22 Pte. B. Walker. 1st. Battn. Cheshire Regiment. Died*** *Kranji Singapore # 11 / D - 4*--]
Mon. 23rd	}Combined Operations continued throughout Malaya ---]
Tue. 24th	24 HMT CAPTAIN COOK arrived Penang .---]
Wed. 25th	}Combined Operations continued throughout Malaya---]

Thur. 26th	26 HMT CAPTAIN COOK sailed Penang bound for Singapore with the 1st. Battn. New Zealand Regt. on board ---]
Fri. 27th	27 HMT CAPTAIN COOK arrived Singapore sailed bound for Wellington NZ with retrurning Service personnel] RAN HMAS 'ANZAC'. Completed her second tour of duty. ---]
Sat. 28th	HMAS 'QUICKMATCH' & 'TOBRUK' Completed their third tour of duty & HMAS VENDETTA Began her first
Sun. 29th	tour of duty with the BCFESR.---]
Mon. 30th	}Combined Operations continued throughout Malaya---]

DECEMBER

Tue. 1st	1/12/59 LG 41884 # p. 7667 The following awarded the British Empire Medal S/SGT. C. ATKINS. BEM THE CHESHIRE REGIMENT. S/SGT. C.E. ETHERINGTON.BEM ARMY CATERING CORPS S/SGT. R. LEE. BEM ROYAL ARMY SERVICE CORPS S/SGT. D. SKELTON.BEM ROYAL ARMY SERVICE CORPS SGT. L.F. LARSSON.BEM ROYAL AUSTRALIAN INF. REGIMENT. S/SGT. H. JAMES.BEM NEW ZEALAND INF REGIMENT.
Wed. 2nd	2 HMT EMPIRE FOWEY sailed Southampton bound for Singapore / Hong Kong with replacement Service personnel --]
Thur. 3rd	} Combined Operations continued throughout Malaya---]
Fri. 4th	}
Sat. 5th	}
Sun. 6th	} Combined Operations continued throughout Malaya---]
Mon. 7th	R.A.F. 209 Sqdn. Pembroke C1 Competed Operations R.A.F. Seletar--]

Tue. 8th	8/12/1959 LG. # 41887 p.7773 The following awarded the British Empire Medal (Military)
	F/SGT. K.E.B. DALLY BEM ROYAL AIR FORCE
	     The following awarded the Distinguished Flying Cross
	F/LT. D. GEDDES. DFC ROYAL AIR FORCE
	F/LT. P.K. WOODRIDGE. DFC ROYAL AIR FORCE
	F/O. J.A. BOARDMAN. DFC. ROYAL AIR FORCE
	     The following awarded the Distinguished Flying Medal
	SGT. P.J. CUNNINGHAM. DFM ROYAL AIR FORCE

Wed. 9th	9/12/1958 LG # 41567 p. 7497 The following awarded the Distinguished Flying Cross CAPT. M.G.BADGER. DFC ROYAL ENGINEERS A/T ARMY AIR CORPS 656 SDN. CAPT H. G. CRUTCHLEY. DFC ROYAL REGIMENT. ARTILLERY 656 SDN. The following awarded the Distinguished Flying Medal SGT. R.W. BOWLES. DFM ARMY AIR CORPS 656 SDN.
Thur. 10th	} Combined Operations continued throughout Malaya---]
Fri. 11th	}
Sat. 12th	} Combined Operations continued throughout Malaya---
Sun. 13th	13 Dvr. B. F. Davidson. R.A.S.C.. Died Transport Incident. *Kuala Lumpur # 33 /1273* ---]+
Mon. 14th	14 HMT OXFORDSHIRE arrived Southampton with returning Service Personnel--]
Tue. 15th	} Combined Operations continued throughout Malaya---]
Wed. 16th	}
Thur. 17th	} Combined Operations continued throughout Malaya---]
Fri. 18th	}
Sat. 19th	} Combined Operations continued throughout Malaya---]
Sun. 20th	}
Mon. 21st	} Combined Operations continued throughout Malaya---]
Tue. 22nd	}
Wed. 23rd	23 HMT EMPIRE FOWEY arrived Singapore with replacement Service personnel ---]
Thur. 24th	24 HMT EMPIRE FOWEY sailed Singapore bound for Hong Kong---]
Fri. 25th	}Combined Operations continued throughout Malaya---]
Sat. 26th	}
Sun. 27th	27 AC. J. Mcguire. Arm/Mech. R.A.F. Tengah Died*** *Kranji Singapore # 14 / A – 21* ---]
Mon. 28th	Combined Operations continued throughout Malaya---]
Tue. 29th	29 Cpl. Abdul 29 Majid. Bin . Mohamed. R.A.O.C.. MOR) Died****Claimed by next of Kin* ---]

Wed. 30th	30/12/1959 LG. ISS.? P. ?	The following awarded the Distinguished Flying Cross
	W/CDR. K. V. ROBERTSON DFC	ROYAL AUSTRALIAN AIR FORCE.
Thur. 31st	Combined Operations continued throughout Malaya---]	

R. A. F. OPERATION "*FIREDOG*" END OF YEAR STATISTICS 1959

No of Sorties	No. of Strikes	1,000 Lb.Bombs	500 Lb. Bombs	350 LbCluster	20 LbBombs	R/P's	20mm	.5 mm	.303 mm
137	2	/	/	/	/	/	/	/	/

R. A. F. SUPPORT 1959

	Soties	Troops/Lift/	Casac	Pass/Lift	Supply Wt. Lbs	Leaflets drop (1,000)	B Flying Times No / hrs	Broadcsting No / hrs	Crashed
Air SupportA/C*	69	/	/	/	4,566,209	/		/	
Auster**	/		/	/	/	/	/	/	Sycamore XE391
Pioneer	N/A	1357	41	427	227,646	/	/	/	XF267
H/C Light	N/A	/	/	/	/	/	/	/	Pioneer
848 Sqdn	Disbabded	/	/	/	/	/	/	/	XG561
155 Sqdn	N/A	2397	136	329	76,186	/	/	/	
Target/MK**	/	/	/	/	/	/	/	/	
Vis/Air OBs**	/	/	/	/	/	/	/	/	
Communication**	/	/	/	/	/	/	/	/	
Leaf. Sorties*	N/A	/	/	/	/	9.899	/	/	
Leaflets Drop*	/	/	/	/	/	/	/	/	
Leaf Sorties **	/	/	/	/	/	/	/	/	
Leaflets Drop**	/	/	/	/	/	/	/	/	
Broad Sorties*	/	/	/	/	/	/	/	/	
Broad Hrs *	/	/	/	/	/	/	/	/	
Broad Sorties**	/	/	/	/	/	/	/	/	
Broad Hrs **	/	/	/	/	/	/	/	/	
Photo RECCE***	/	/	/	/	/	/	./	/	

* AirSupport A/C Dakota -Valetta- Hastings Bristol

** Auster

*** Photo Rec Anson,,Spitfire, Mosquito, Meteor, Pembroke ---

ROYAL AIR FORCE
OFFENSIVE AIR SUPPORT - OPERATION 'FIREDOG'
January 1959 to December 1960

Sqdn	Location	Aircraft Type	No	Date From	Year	Date To	Year
48	Changi	Beverley C1	4	1st. Jun.	1959	Jul	1960
52	Kuala Lumpur	Valetta C1	10	1st. Oct.	1959	Jul	1960
60	Tengah	Meteor NF14	12	1st. Oct.	1959	Jul	1960
110	Kuala Lumpur	WhirlwindH.CH4	5	3rd.Jan.	1959	Jul.	1960
	Butterworth	SycamoreH/CH4	13	13th. Jan.	1959	Jul.	1960
209	Kuala Lumpur	Pembroke C1	4	1st. Oct.	1959	15th. Dec	1959

ROYAL AIR FORCE
OFFENSIVE AIR SUPPORT - OPERATION 'FIREDOG'
January 1960 to July 1960

Sqdn	Location	Aircraft Type	No	Date From	Year	Date To	Year
81	Tengah	Canberra PR7	3	13th.Jan	1960	Jul .	1960

JANUARY

Fri.	1st	} Combined Operations continued throughout Malaya---]
Sat.	2nd	}
Sun.	3rd	}
Mon.	4th	} Combined Operations continued throughout Malaya---]
Tue.	5th	5 HMT EMPIRE FOWEY arrived/ sailed Singapore bound for Southampton with returning Service personnel]
Wed.	6th	6 HMT OXFORDSHIRE sailed Southampton bound for Singapore / Hong Kong with replacement Service Personnel---]
Thur.	7th	} Combined Operations continued throughout Malaya---]
Fri.	8th	8 HMT CAPTAIN COOK arrived Singapore enroute to Glasgow with returning Service personnel---]
Sat.	9th	} Combined Operations continued throughout Malaya---]
Sun.	10th	}
Mon.	11th	}
Tue.	12th	} Combined Operations continued throughout Malaya---]
Wed.	13th	}
Thur.	14th	}
Fri.	15th	} Combined Operations continued throughout Malaya---]
Sat.	16th	16 Rfn. Bhartaman Rai . 7th. Duke of Edinburgh's Own Gurkha Rifles. Killed in Action Engaging CT's *Sungei Patani # A / A -1* Pahang ---]
Sun.	17th	]
Mon.	18th	} Combined Operations continued throughout Malaya---]
Tue.	19th	}
Wed.	20th	20 Cpl. S. L. I. Douglas. (Stat Clk) R.A.F. Seletar. Attacked & Killed.[*Ashes REP]*---]
+		20 Sgt. W. J. Mc Cammont. 1st. Battn. The Cameronians. att. Army Air Corps. Died in air accident *Kuala Lumpur # 33 / 1277* ---]
+		20 Pte. J. Finnerty. 1st. Battn. Cheshire Regt. Died***_Kranji Singapore # 11 / E - 23_---]
Thur.	21st	} Combined Operations continued throughout Malaya---]
Fri.	22nd	}
Sat.	23rd	}
Sun.	24th	}
Mon.	25th	}
Tue.	26th	} Combined Operations continued throughout Malaya---]
Wed.	27th	27 HMT EMPIRE FOWEY arrived Southampton with returning Service personnel ---]
Thur.	28th	} Combined Operations continued throughout Malaya---]

Fri.	29th	29 HMT OXFORDSHIRE arrived Singapore with replacement Service personnel enroute to Hong Kong 29th.]
Sat.	30th	} Combined Operations continued throughout Malaya---]
Sun.	31st	}

FEBRUARY

Mon.	1st	} Combined Operations continued throughout Malaya---]
Tue.	2nd	}
Wed.	3rd	}
Thur.	4th	} Combined Operations continued throughout Malaya---]
Fri.	5th	**5 Cpl. P. R. Peach.** Royal Signals Drowning accident .*Kuala Lumpur # 33 / 1275* ---]
Sat.	6th	} Combined Operations continued throughout Malaya---]
Sun.	7th	}
Mon.	8th	}
Tue.	9th	} Combined Operations continued throughout Malaya---]
Wed.	10th	10 HMT CAPTAIN COOK arrived Glasgow with returning Service personnel---]
Thur.	11th	} Combined Operations continued throughout Malaya---]
Fri.	12th	}
Sat.	13th	13 HMT OXFORDSHIRE arrived/ sailed Singapore enroute to Southamton with returning Service personnel-13th.--]
Sun.	14th	**14 Rfn. Parsad Gurung.** 6th. Queen Elizabeth's Own Gurkha Rifles Killed in Action Engaging CT's *Sulva Lines # 94* Ipoh Perak [
Mon.	15th	**15 Sgmn. S. Narbahader.** Gurgkha Signals Died***_Kluang #3/K/6_ Johore---]
	+	**15 Sgt. Narbahadur Chhetri.** Gurkha Signals Died BMH Kinrara _Seremban # 82_ Negri Sembilan---]
Tue.	16th	} Combined Operations continued throughout Malaya---]
Wed.	17th	}
Thur.	18th	}Combined Operations continued throughout Malaya---]
Fri.	19th	}
Sat.	20th	}
Sun.	21st	} Combined Operations continued throughout Malaya---]
Mon.	22nd	}
Tue.	23rd	}
Wed.	24th	}
Thur.	25th	} Combined Operations continued throughout Malaya---]
Fri.	26th	**26 Maj. D. M. A. Wedderburn.** 3rd. Battn. Grenadier Guards Died*** _Kranji Singapore.# 11- D- 5_---]
Sat.	27th	9 CT's Surrendered to the 2nd. Battn. N.Z Regt. their leader **Kering Chin**. Informed his captors He had wanted to surrender long before , until his commander **Ah Soo Chye** had gone across the border to Thailand 2 others were named as **Senagit & Regek** ---]
Sun.	28th	Combined Operations continued throughout Malaya---]
Mon.	29th	RAN HMAS *QUEENBOROUGH*. Began her fourth tour of duty in Malayan coastal waters. Combined Operations continued throughout Malaya---]

MARCH

Tue.	1st	}
Wed.	2nd	} Combined Operations continued throughout Malaya---]
Thur.	3rd	}
Fri.	4th	RAN HMAS 'QUICKMATCH'.. Began her fourth tour of duty in Malayan coastal waters---]
Sat.	5th	Combined Operations continued throughout Malaya---]
Sun.	6th	**6 WOII. A. N. H. Mowett MacOnochie.** R.A.E.C.. Died***[Ashes REP]---]
	+	6 HMT OXFORDSHIRE arrived Southampton with returning Service personnel ---]
Mon.	7th	Combined Operations continued throughout Malaya---]
Tue.	8th	Flt/.Lt. R.F. WYATT. R.A.A.F.awarded the G.M. attempting to save lives in an Aircraft crash Butterworth airfield Perak. (LG 07/10/60.)
Wed.	9th	} Combined Operations continued throughout Malaya---]
Thur.	10th	}

Fri.	11th	**11 Cfn. J. Morley.** R.E.M.E Died ** *Kranji Singapore # 11 / D – 18* ---]
Sat.	12th	}
Sun.	13th	}
Mon.	14th	}Combined Operations continued throughout Malaya---]
Tue.	15th	}
Wed.	16th	}
Thur.	17th	**Sgt. Mohd. Shah S/O Nabi Bakhah.** F. M. Police Killed on Ops. 6th m/s Kampong Java Rd. Pahang---]
Fri.	18th	} Combined Operations continued throughout Malaya---]
Sat.	19th	}
Sun.	20th	**20 Rfn./ Ck . Manbahadur Gurung.** 6th Queen Elizabeth's Own Gurkha Rifles Died *** *Kluang # 1 / A – 1* Johore --]
	+	**20 HMT OXFORDSHIRE** sailed Southampton bound for Singapore / Hong Kong with replacement Service personnel---]
Mon.	21st	**21 Cpl. L. Ellis.** 1st. Battn. Cheshire Regt. Died***[No known Grave]Terandak Wall Memorial Malacca---]
Tue.	22nd	Combined Operations continued throughout Malaya---]
Wed.	23rd	**23 Signm. J.D. Brass.** Royal Signals Died of disease *Kranji Singapore # 11/ D – 19* ---]
Thur.	24th	}Combined Operations continued throughout Malaya---]
Fri.	25th	}
Sat.	26th	**26 PC. Mured B. Abdullah.** F. M. Police Died by Accident on Ops. Gurun Kedah.---]
Sun.	27th	} Combined Operations continued throughout Malaya---]
Mon.	28th	}
Tue.	29th	}
Wed.	30th	} Combined Operations continued throughout Malaya---]
Thur.	31st	**31 Pte. G. W. Amas.** 2nd. Battn. Royal New Zealand. Regt. Killed in Action Engaging CT's at Hutan Lasah *Taiping # K / 29* Perak---]

APRIL

Fri.	1st	Kuala Lumpur His Majesty Tuanku Sir. Abdul Rahman The first King & Ruler of the Independent Federation of Malaya (Yang di-Pertuan Agong) & concurrent Ruler of Negri Sembilan died peacefully in his sleep in Instana Negara Kuala Lumpur ---]
	+	RNZM HMNZS *'PUKAKI'* Completed her third support role of duty & left Malayan coastal waters, whilst
	+	HMNZS *'ROTOIT'l* Began her second support role if duty in Malayan coastal waters.---]
	+	R.A.F. 93 Sqdn Royal Air Force Regt. (Malaya) Returned to Changi & were Disbanded ---]
Sat.	2nd	}Combined Operations continued throughout Malaya---]
Sun.	3rd	}
Mon.	4th	Kuala Lumpur: The Deputy Head of State, Sultan of Selangor H.H. Hisamunddin Alam Shah assumed the function of King & Ruler of the Malayan Federation. Until a new Head of State is elected by the The Conference of Rulers His Majesty. Tuanku Sir. Abdul Rahman, was buried in the Royal Mausoleum Negri Sembilan ---]
Tue.	5th	5 HMT DUNERA sailed Southampton bound for Singapore with replacement Service personnel ---]
Wed.	6th	} Combined Operations continued throughout Malaya---]
Thur.	7th	}
Fri.	8th	}
Sat.	9th	}
Sun.	10th	} Combined Operations continued throughout Malaya---]
Mon.	11th	}
Tue.	12th	}
Wed.	13th	} Combined Operations continued throughout Malaya---]
Thur.	14th	Kuala Lumpur :The Conference of Rulers, elected His Majesty .Hisamunddin Alam Shah & was sworn in as King & Ruler of the Federation of Malaya (Yang di-Pertuan Agong) His Deputy Head of State His Highness.Syed Putra ibni Al- Marhum. Raja of Perlis, was elected for a five year term of office ---]
Fri.	15th	**15 Sgt. Ithnin Bin Haji Tahir** R. A. O. C (MOR) Died *** *Claimed by next of Kin* ---]
	+	**15 L/Cpl. McGregor** Royal Engineers Died*** *Western Road # 2172* George Town Penang ---]
	+	**15 Pte. Ithnin Bin. Hadji.Tahir** . R. A.O. C. (MOR) Died***-*Claimed by next of Kin*---]
	+	RAN HMAS *'MELBOURNE"* Began her fifth tour & HMAS *'VOYAGER"* Began her fourth tour of duty in Malayan coastal waters.---]
Sat.	16th	Combined Operations continued throughout Malaya---]

Sun. 17th	Kuala Lumpur: The decision of the Government of Malaya to end on July 31st. The 12-year long Emergency was announced by the new King in Kuala Lumpur. In his speech to Parliament the Yang di-Pertuan Agong. Stated: 'Although victory over the Communist Terrorist had not been easy, Malaya could claim the distinction of being the only country to have fought & conquered "these forces of evil" & the past years would "remain a glittering period in our history". Adding that the dept owed. to the Security Forces both Malayan & Commonwealth, could not be over-emphasized. The need to retain permanent powers of detention, "need no cause for fear". The Government was following the example of many other countries 'Whose Governments have shouldered squarely their responsibilities for securing internal "peace & order." In the public interest, & no loyal law –abiding citizen has cause to feel alarmed at the proposed constitutional amendment. ---]
Mon. 18th	} Combined Operations continued throughout Malaya---]
Tue. 19th	}
Wed. 20th	20 HMT DILWARA sailed Southampton bound for Singapore with replacement Service personnel ---]
Thur. 21st	21 HMT OXFORDSHIRE arrived Singapore with replacement Service personnel enroute Hong Kong 21st.---]
Fri. 22nd	Kuala Lumpur: After a three day reading of the Amendment to the Bill of Constitution. The Malayan Government was given a majority of 75 votes to 13. The amendment did not refer specifically to preventive detention (as previous) but extended a previous Article of the Constitution to give Parliamnet special powers to deal with Action Engaging CT's prejudicial to its definition of security ---]
Sat. 23rd	} Combined Operations continued throughout Malaya---]
Sun. 24th	}
Mon..25th	}
Tue. 26th	}
Wed. 27th	}
Thur. 28th	} Combined Operations continued throughout Malaya---]
Fri. 29th	29 Dvr. Tapah Bin. Abdullah Hanon. R.A.S.C.. (MOR) Died*** Claimed by next of Kin ---]
Sat. 30th	Combined Operations continued throughout Malaya---]

MAY

Sun. 1st	Kuala Lumpur: A Bill was passed by the Federation of Malaya's Legislative Council. Nominating the successor to the Malayan Auxiliary Air Force to become The Malayan Air Force ---]
Mon. 2nd	}
Tue. 3rd	} Combined Operations continued throughout Malaya---]
Wed. 4th	}
Thur. 5th	5 EM1 R.S. Cotton. Royal Navy. HMS 'TERROR' Died*** [Ashes REP] ---]
+	5 HMT DUNERA arrived Singapore with replacement Service personnel enroute to Hong Kong 5th.---]
Fri. 6th	6 HMT OXFORDSHIRE arrived/ sailed Singapore bound for Southampton with returning Service personnel']
Sat. 7th	Combined Operations continued throughout Malaya---]
Sun. 8th	8 Cpl. L. Burtenshaw. 1st. Battn. Cheshire Regt. Died***Kranji Singapore # 11 / D - 21---]
Mon. 9th	9 Cpl. A. E. Cotton. R.A.S.C.. Killed struck by lightning. Kranji Singapore # 11 / D - 20 ---]
Tue. 10th	}
Wed. 11th	}
Thur. 12th	} Combined Operations continued throughout Malaya---]
Fri. 13th	}
Sat. 14th	14 Pte. K. Merry. A.C.C.. Died*** Kranji Singapore # 11 / D - 22---]
+	14 A/POM. D. L Green Royal Navy HMS 'ALBION' Died *** [Ashes REP]---]
Sun. 15th	Combined Operations continued throughout Malaya---]
Mon. 16th	16 Pte L.R. Smedley. 1st. Bttn R.A.R. Died *** Taiping # K / 30 Perak---]
Tue. 17th	Combined Operations continued throughout Malaya---]
Wed. 18th	18 Pte. J.W.N. Hall. R.A.M.C.. Died***Kranji Singapore # 11 / E - 18---]
Thur. 19th	19 HMT DILWARA arrived Singapore with replacement Service personnel ---]
Fri. 20th	} Combined Operations continued throughout Malaya---]
Sat. 21st	}
Sun. 22nd	}
Mon. 23rd	}
Tue. 24th	} Combined Operations continued throughout Malaya---]
Wed. 25th	25 HMT DUNERA arrived Singapore sailed bound for Southampton with returning Service personnel ---]

Thur. 26th	} Combined Operations continued throughout Malaya---]
Fri. 27th	}
Sat. 28th	**28 Sgt. L. Nelson.** R.A.S.C..Died Transport incident.*Kuala Lumpur # 33 / 1278* ---]
+	**28 Pte. H.M. McGill.** R.A.M.C, Died*** *Kuala Lumpur # 33 / 1280* ---]
+	28 HMT OXFORDSHIRE arrived Southampton with returning Service personnel---]
Sun. 29th	}Combined Operations continued throughout Malaya---]
Mon. 30th	}
Tue. 31st	**31 Cpl. J. R. Harrison.** 1st. Battn. R.A.R. Died from Wounds recv'd in ambush
	Kranji Singapore # 11 / D – 23 -]

JUNE

Wed. 1st	R.A.F. 81 Sqdn. Meteor. PR10 Completed Operations R.A.F. Seletar---]
Thur. 2nd	Combined Operations continued throughout Malaya---]
Fri. 3rd	3/06/1960 LG # 42057 p. 4031 The following awarded the Distinguished Flying Cross
	SQD/LDR. S.R. DIXON, DFC ROYAL AIR FORCE
	The following awarded the Distinguished Flying Medal
	SGT. J.E. PAYNE. DFM ROYAL AIR FORCE
Sat. 4th	}
Sun. 5th	}Combined Operations continued throughout Malaya---]
Mon. 6th	}
Tue. 7th	7/06/1960 LG # 42058 p. 4037 The following awarded the British Empire Medal
	SGT. A. J. MCHUGH . BEM ROYAL AIR FORCE
Wed. 8th	Combined Operations continued throughout Malaya---]
Thur. 9th	**9 Fg./Off. K.C. Carter.** R.A.F. Died*** *[Ashes REP]*---]
Fri. 10th	10/061960 LG # 42061 p. 4145 The following awarded the British Empire Medal (Military)
	SGT. F.G. KEABLE. BEM ROYAL ELECTRICAL MECHANICAL ENGINEERS
	SGT. J. J. O'REARDON. BEM LOYAL REGIMENT.
	SGT D.H. STEVENSON. BEM ROYAL ORDNACE CORPS
	SGT. F.L. NICHOLLS. BEM ROYAL AUSTRALIAN ENGINEERS
	p. 4146
	S/SGT. T.T. BABBINGTON. BEM ROYAL NEW ZEALAND INF.
	The following awarded the Distinguished Flying Cross
	CAPT. H.G. STENSON. DFC ROYAL REGIMENT. ARTILLERY
	The following awarded the Distinguished Flying Medal
	SGT. W.A. PATRICK. DFM ARMY AIR CORPS
Sat. 11th	Combined Operations continued throughout Malaya----]
Sun. 12th	**12 Sgt. J. H. Wilkle.** R.A.M.C. Died*** *Kranji Singapore # 11 / D – 24* ---]
Mon. 13th	}
Tue. 14th	} Combined Operations continued throughout Malaya
Wed. 15th	}
Thur. 16th	Kuala Lumpur: A British Army spokesman gave details of the concentration of British troops within certain areas of the Federation, agreed upon under the UK-Malayan Treaty of Defence & mutual assistance concluded, when Malaya became Independent. Explained that:-
	'The Bukit Terandak Wall Memorial Cantonment (Fort George) would be the main base for all overseas forces in the Federation. Housing British, Australian & New Zealand troops
	All overseas land forces not within this cantonment, would be Stationed elsewhere in Malacca & Johore States, in which connection building project's. in progress at Kota Tinggi, Kluang & Johore Bahru, where British & Gurkha troops were already Stationed. Bases in Northern Malaya, Kuala Lumpur, Sungei Betsi, Sungei Batani, Ipoh, & Taiping, would be vacated & taken over by the Federation Army.
	Only one base in Northern Malaya would be retained indefinitely for the use of Commonwealth Forces- the Military Hospital & Rest camp in the Cameron Highlands. Adding that the Bukit Terandak Wall Memorial Cantonment would be biggest Army base in South East Asia The British Battalion Manning Fort GEORGE base is the 1st/3rd. East Anglian Regt. Moved there from Ipoh. To be joined by the 26th. Field Regt. Royal Artillery (from Britain) & by a Field Battery of the Royal Australian Artillery'. ---]
Fri. 17th	}
Sat. 18th	} Combined Operations continued throughout Malaya---]

Sun. 19th	}	
Mon. 20th	RAN HMAS *'MELBOURNE"* Completed her fifth & final tour of duty in Malayan coastal waters.---]	
Tue. 21st	21 HMT OXFORDSHIRE sailed Southampton bound for Singapore with replacement Service personnel---]	
Wed.22nd	22 HMT DUNERA arrived Southampton with returning Service personnel ---]	
Thur. 23rd	Kuala Lumpur. The Federation House of Representatives passed a Bill effective to come into force from the ending of the Emergency. Its three point aim was to :-	
	'Empower the responsible Minister to detain persons for up to two years if, there was reason to believe they were carrying out subversive activities.	
	Provided the Head of State (on the advice of the Cabinet) considered detention to be justified.	
	Gave detainees the right of appeal to an advisory board & Authorised periodic reviews of individual cases'--]	
+	23 HMT DILWARA arrived Southampton with returning Service personnel ---]	
Fri. 24th	}	
Sat. 25th	} Combined Operations continued throughout Malaya---]	
Sun. 26th	R.A.F. 90 Sqdn. Vulcan B1 Completed Operations at R.A.F. Butterworth.---]	
	} Combined Operations continued throughout Malaya---]	
Mon. 27th	RAN HMAS *'QUIBERON'*. Began her second tour of duty, whilst HMAS *'VAMPIRE'*. Began its first tour of duties in Malayan coastal waters---]	
Tue. 28th	}	
Wed. 29th	} Combined Operations continued throughout Malaya---]	
Thur. 30th	}	

JULY

Fri. 1st	R.A.F. 45 Sqdn. Canberra B2 Completed Operations R.A.F. Tengah---]	
+	R.A.F. 48 Sqdn. Beverley C1 Completed Operations R.A.F. Kuala Lumpur---]	
+	R.A.F. 52 Sqdn. Valetta C1 Completed Operations R.A.F. Kuala Lumpur---]	
+	R.A.F. 81 Sqdn. Canberra PR7- Meteor PR10 Completed Operations R.A.F. Tengah---]	
+	R.A.F. 110 Sqdn. Sycamore H/C HR14 Completed Operations R.A.F. Butterworth.---]	
+	R.A.F. 209 Sqdn. TE Pioneer CC1 Cmpleted Operations R.A.F. Seletar ---]	
+	R.A.F. FEC Sqdn. Valetta C1/2 - Hastings C1/4 Completed Operation R.A.F. Changi---]	
+	R.A.F. 205 Sqdn. Shackleton MR1 Completed Operations R.A.F. Changi---]	
+	R.A.F. 205 Sqdn. Sunderland MR1 Completed Operations R.A.F. Changi---]	
+	R.A.F. 656 Sqdn. Auster 5/6/7/9 Completed Operations R.A.F. Kuala Lumpur---]	
+	R.A.A.F. 2 Sqdn. Canberra B1 Completed Operations at R.A.F. Butterwoth ---]	
+	R.A.A.F. 3 Sqdn. Sabre 32 Completed Operations At R.A.F. Butterworth.---]-	
+	R.N.Z.A.F. 41 Sqdn. Bristol Freighter Completed Operations R.A.F. Kuala Lumpur---]	
+	R.N.Z.A.F. 75 Sqdn Canberra B2 Completed Operations R.A.F. Butterworth.---]	
+	R.N.Z.A.F. 77 Sqdn. Sabre 32 Compleded Operations R.A.F. Butterworth.---]	
+	M.A.A.F. Kranji Singapore Sqdn. Chipmonk Completed Operations R.A.F. Seletar ---]	
Sat. 2nd	RAN HMAS *QUEENBOROUGH*. Completed her fourth & final tour of duty in Malayan coastal waters—]	
Sun. 3rd	RAN HMAS *VENDETTA* Completed her first & final tour of duty in Malayan coastal waters---]	
Mon. 4th	}	
Tue. 5th	} Combined Operations continued throughout Malaya---]	
Wed. 6th	}	
Thur. 7th	}	
Fri. 8th	**8 Pte.'s D. W. Logue. Pte D. W Low** 1st. Batt. Sherwood Foresters. Killed in action	
	Kranji Singapore # 11 / D – 25 - 15---]	
+	**8 Cpl. P. C. Crouch**. R.A.F. Police FEAF. Died from injuries received in an accident on July.6th.	
	Kranji Singapore # 14 / A - 11---]	
Sat. 9th	}	
Sun. 10th	} Combined Operations continued throughout Malaya ---]	
Mon. 11th	}	
Tue. 12th	}	
Wed. 13th	**13 Sgmn. Harkabahadur Limbu.** Gurkha Signals Drowned on Ops. Perak *Seremban # 83* Negri Sembilan-]	
+	**Pte. S. B. Mohamed.** ACC. (MOR) Died*** *Claimed by next of Kin ---]*	
+	**Spr. A.C. Williams.** Royal Engineers Died*** *Kuala Lumpur # 33 / 1279---]*	

Thur. 14th	**14 Lt./Col. G.F. Blyth.** Royal Engineers Deid***_Kranji Singapore # 11 / C – 23_ ---]
+	14 HMT **DUNERA** sailed Southampton bound for Singapore with replacement Service personnel ---]
+	14 HMT **OXFORDSHIRE** arrived Singapore with replacement Service personnel---]
Fri. 15th	15 HMT **OXFORDSHIRE** sailed Singapore bound for Southampton with returning Service personnel
Sat. 16th	HMT **DILWARA** renamed **KUALA LUMPUR** ---]
Sun. 17th	**17 Drv. Humbahadur Thapa.** Gurkha Army Service Corps. Died by Accident. _Kluang # 1 / A - 3_ Johore---]
Mon. 18th	}
Tue. 19th	}Combined Operations continued throughout Malaya ---]
Wed. 20th	}
Thur. 21s	}
Fri. 22nd	22 HMT **OXFORDSHIRE** arrived / sailed Singapore bound for Southampton with returning Service personnel]
Sat. 23rd	} Combined Operations continued throughout Malaya---]
Sun. 24th	}
Mon. 25th	}
Tue. 26th	**26 Cpl. B. C. Brown.** Elect/Fit. R.A.F. Tengah Died resulting from accident._[Ashes REP]_---]
+	Operation _"Hammer"_ by the 3rd. RAR began against the 12th. District Asal Organisation in the Lasah area.of Kedah---]
Wed. 27th	}
Thur. 28th	} Combined Operations continued throughout Malaya ---]
Fri. 29th	RNZN HMNZS _ROTOITI_ completed her second support role of duty & left Malayan coastal waters.---]
Sat. 30th	**30 S/Sgt. J.H. Bews.** Royal Singals Died *** _Kuala Lumpur # 33 / 12 81_
	The last Serviceman to die in the 12 year Emergency (War). Yet others would die in the following months. ---]
Sun. 31st	_Kuala Lumpur_ In a broadcast at Midnight the **Yang Pertuan Agong (King) Hisamuddin Alam Shah of Malaya** announced :

The 12 year "Emergency" ?? WAR was Declared Over.

Declaring that the ending of the Emergency was "Not only a victory for our nation but also a victory for democracy. The first occasion on which the democratic countries have defeated Communism." Adding; The kind of war we have fought usually produces one of three results :

Victory for the Communist. –

The division of the country into two parts or, --

A state of endless struggle.

At the same time he gave a warning that the Communist, though defeated militarily might still try to achieve their aims by such methods as infiltration into the trade unions & into student & youth organisations

In a Separate Broadcast The Prime Minister Tengku Abdul Rahman referred to the same point.

AUGUST.

1st. The Day was celebrated as public holiday. In Kuala Lumpur. Large crowds watched a parade of 6,000 ~ Malayan, British, Australian, New Zealand & Gurkha troops, including a Fly-past of Planes of the British, Australian, New Zealand & Malayan Air Force. The Yang Pertuan Agong. H.M. King Hisamuddin Alam Shah of Malaya. Awarded to Field Marshall Sir. Gerald Templer for his part in the defeat of Communism in the Federation:

The Grand Knight of the Most Distinguished Order of Merit.

Which carries the title of "Tun" equivalent of Earl.

The State of Emergency ended with all Malaya cleared of the Communist Terrorist, Except for **Chin Peng** and approx. 400 of his army, then settled or making their way across the Malaya Border into Thailand:-

A truly Beaten MALAYAN RACES LIBERATION ARMY .

Nevertheless the stragglers were stil being hunted by the Security Forces---]

4th. Fort GEORGE The New Commonwealth Army & HQ of the 28th. Commonwealth Brigade base.12 miles North of Malacca was officially inaugurated---]

10th. 20 HMT **DUNERA** sailed Singapore with returning Service personnel ---]

12th. **SAC. B. Milner.** M/T Drv. R.A.F. Died Road Traffic Accident. _[Ashes REP]_---]

+ Operartion _"Hammer"_ Ended ---]

15th. **Cpl. Mohamed Noor B. Hamid.** F. M. Police Killed on Ops. Sado South Thailand---]

20th. **Pte. B. D. Cooke.** R. A. M. C. Died***_[Ashes REP]_---]

22nd. **L/Cpl. R.J. Guest** 13/18th Hussars Died Transport accident *** _Kranji Singapore # 11 / E – 4_---]

+ HMT **OXFORDSHIRE** arrived Southampton with returning Service personnel ---]

24th **Pte. B. H. Ferrell.** 1st. Battn. R.A.R. became the last Serviceman to be Killed on Active Service _Taiping # K / 31_

Perak ---]

SEPTEMBER

5th. **Sgt. J. Kerr Cook** R. A. F. Kuala Lumpur Died ***_Kuala Lumpur # 38/ M -1_---]

12th. **Mre. R.Wright** (42Commando) Royal Marines Died*** [Ashes REP] Ipoh Perak---]

OCTOBER

1st. R. A. F. Kuala Lumpur was officially handed over to the Royal Malayan Air Force---]

5th. **Cpl. B.S Powell** Royal Engineers Died*** _Kuala Lumpur_---]

+ **5 Sgt. J. Kerr.** Cook at R.A.F Kuala Lumpur Died*** _Kuala Lumpur_ ---]

+ **5 HMT FLAMINIA** sailed from GeorgeTown Penang bound for Brisbane Austraila on board was the 3rd. Battn.Royal Australian Regt. having completed their two years operation in Malaya---]

7th. 7/10/1960 LG # 42164 p. 6861   The following awarded the George Medal
FLT/LT. R.F. WYATT. GM.   ROYAL AUSTRALIAN AIR FORCE
His award of the George Medal was for his bravery on the the 5th. March. 1060. He was the Navigator on board a Canberra. During take off power was lost and the Canberra run off the runway at Butterworth & caught fire. The Pilots foot was trapped in the cockpit & Wyatt struggled to free the Pilot whilst the plane still burnt. He freed the trapped Pilot and they were dragged out.
The following awarded the British Empire Medal (Military)
SGT.V. ANDERSON. BEM   ROYAL AUSTRALIA AIR FORCE
Sgt. Anderson was able to coordinate the Fire fighting unit & control the blaze therefore preventing the plane to explode.--]

17th. **Sgt. T.J. Day.** The Queen's Royal Regt. Died***_[Ashes REP]_---]

30th. 30 HMT DUNERA arrived Southampton with returning Service personnel ---]

NOVEMBER

14th. 14 Jnr. / Tech I.W. Law Eng/ Fit R. A. F. Changi Died from injuries Motor Veh acc.
Kranji Singapore # 1 / A – 12]

DECEMBER

2/12/1960 LG # 42211 p. 8319   The following awarded the Air Force Medal
SQDN/LDR. F. BARNES AFC   ROYAL AIR FORCE
27/12/1960. LG # 42237 p. 8941   The following awarded the British Empire Medal (Military)
C/SGT. R.H.J. HEWITT BEM   THE ANGLIAN REGIMENT.
SGT. R. LANDY. BEM   ARMY CATERING CORPS
SGT. W.H. MCAVOY. BEM   ROYAL ARMY MEDICAL CORPS
SGT. D.I. MACKINTOSH. BEM   NEW ZEALAND IN REGIMENT.
Awards for act's. of gallantry from 1st Jan 1960 to 31st July 1960

R. A. F. OPERATION _"FIREDOG"_ END OF YEAR STATISTICS 1960

No of Sorties	No. of Strikes	1,000 Lb.Bombs	500 Lb. Bombs	350 LbCluster	20 LbBombs	R/P's	20mm	.5 mm	.303mm
/	/	/	/	/	/	/	/	/	/

[Authors Note No figures available for 1960. However there were- As detailed in Table below]

R. A. F. SUPPORT 1960

	Soties	Troops/Lift/	Casac	Pass/Lift	Supply Wt. Lbs	Leaflets drop (1,000)	B Flying Times No / hrs	Broadcsting No / hrs	Crashed
Air SupportA/C*	1250	/		/	5,018,733	/	/	/	
Auster**	/	/	/	/	/	/	/	/	Canberra RAAF No. ??
Pioneer	N/A	830	13	110	96,807	/	/	/	
H/C Light	N/A	/	/	/	/	/	/	/	
848 Sqdn	/	/	/	/	/	/	/	/	
155 Sqdn	N/A	4,003	173	378	76,186	/	9,184	/	
Target/MK**	/	/	/	/	/	/	/	/	
Vis/Air OBs**	/	/	/	/	/	/	/	/	
Communication**	/	/	/	/	/	/	/	/	
Leaf. Sorties*	N/A	/	/	/	/	/	/	/	
Leaflets Drop*	/	/	/	/	/	9.899	/	/	
Leaf Sorties **	/	/	/	/	/	/	/	/	
Leaflets Drop**	/	/	/	/	/	/	/	/	
Broad Sorties*	N/A	/	/	/	/	/	/	/	

Broad Hrs *	/	/	/	/	/	/	64	/	
Broad Sorties**	/	/	/	/	/	/	/	/	
Broad Hrs **	/	/	/	/	/	/		/	
Photo RECCE***	/		/	/	/	/	/	/	

*   Air Support A/C Dakota -Valetta- Hastings Bristol

** Auster

*** Photo Rec Anson,,Spitfire, Mosquito, Meteor, Pembroke

CHAPTER 19
Solving The Mystery of the 'Marie Celeste' Liberator KH326

[The Author Joe] When I arrived in Singapore in September 1955. Within 10 hours I was on guard on a train in Malaya. Totally unaware that a war that began in 1948, was ongoing, Was soon to find out when I reached my posting in Ipoh. Through the daily radio news bullitins of reports of:- "Contacts being made. A follow up is in progress." - " RAF aircraft dropped bombs on a known Terrorist Camp." – " A number of security forces were Killed in the area of Kinta. A follow up is in progress."

My posting was at 3 Coy REME LAD attached to the Royal Australian Army Service Corps. Part of the newly formed 28th. Commonwealth Independent Infantry Brigade engaged in a war. The camp next to ours, was the Base camp of the 15th. /19th. Royal Hussars, and Heli Pad. ½ a mile down the road, was the base camp of the 1st. Battalion. Royal Scots Fusiliers, further out was the base camp of the 2nd. /6th. Gurkhas also the 4th. Battalion Malay Infantry. At Ipoh airport there was a landing strip with a Detachment of the RAF, not forgetting the Federation of Malay Police. All within the close vicinity of IPOH. All engaged in seeking out and destroying members of the Malayan Races Liberation Army (MRLA) The Military section of the Malayan Communist Party. Under the Command of **Chin Peng**.

In 1957. After spending 18 Months on active Service in IPOH North Malaya. I returned home to England, then very much aware of the fact that there was absolutely no coverage of the war in Malaya (called an Emergency by some idiotic Political Statement) so called for Insurance purposes??? During the following years I had purchased and read a few books written by former National Servicemen, all interesting but none relating to anyone's period on Active Service. I also found a book, with lists of named Service Personnel by Regiment and date Killed in Malaya. However, it was many years later alter I had retired from Commercial Life, I took to writing. Specifically, about my own experience as a Conscripted National Serviceman in Malaya. I had a lot of photos and a good memory, and during my period of time out there came into contact with several Regiments. That was when I referred back to the. "Book with the list of casualties." which had me thinking of creating a separate book, with more if possible, pertinent details of any of the various incidents, and was determined to do something about it. In 2012. I published my 2nd, Book My own memoirs of a National Servicemen called:
"UP TO THEIR NECKS" THE STORY OF A NATIONAL SERVICEMEN "

Nevertheless, during my own research of Malaya. Not too certain as to the date, when I actually began researching this book possible 25 years ago?. Like many of the other Regiments contacted during the period 1993/4 to present day 2019. Gradually collated scraps of information in books, including contacting various Regiments about their involvement on Active Service in Malaya. My first contact with the Royal Highland Fusiliers was in September 1999, asking if they could or would provide pertinent information to the incidents relating to the deaths of 8 Fusiliers of 1st. Battn Royal Scots Fusiliers. A reply from Maj.(Retd.) Willie. Shaw, provided me with some information about the role the 1st Royal Scots Fusiliers as detailed in their Army Journal (He sent a copy of their appropriate journal, received and read). Willie Shaw also informed me that a fire (not stated where) in 1985, had destroyed a lot of their history. However, the time passed and eventually in September 2006. I made further contact with Alex Burdon of the Royal Scots Fusiliers Association for more information. He put me in touch with Anthony Gordon residing in South Africa. Then from October 2006, we began communicating, initially by telephone then E/Mal. Anthony's circular E/Mail dated 23 Dec. 2006, as a "Gordon Newsletter." Stated the following:

23rd. Dec 2006 Anthony Gordon to a host of ex listed (I assumed RSF's). The last mentioned was
Joe Plant   joaann@btinternet.com
Dear everybody.
    With very best wishes to you all for Christmas and New Year from Pat and Anthony.
    From a very warm and dry Cape Town with no fog! Over 20o C this week. Sorry to rub it in! We had a very good winter with good rains, well separated so that most could sink in and help the dams. Our dams are now 88% full, the best for years, last summer and the two before we had very severe water restriction- garden watering only for 30 minutes per week! Our back lawn looks by Weetabix and now lots of the Kikuyu grass has given way to Queak and Buffalo (both indigenous whilst the Kikuyu is from Kenya and need lots of water!) Since last summer we now have very few moles, snails and ants!
    Antony's newsletter gives a lot of their doings but I must say, this email was going to mainly Regimental and Military Friends in desperate hopes to get you something by Christmas! We would far rather send it with a card but, as usual, we are so late that there is no hope of a letter to you soon.
    Most of you will not recognise Joe Plant at the end of the list. He was a REME Craftsman mechanic at 3 Company LAD RASC   and so knows some things about events there. He is writing his own memoirs and has collected a number of other events with difficulty. From the Internet he saw our 1st. RSF Malaya 1954- 57 gathering at Kilmarnock on 7th. September and wrote to our HQ. Asking for help, his letter was passed around the gathering and some of us have made contact with information

for which. He is very grateful. I sent copies of the maps and some photos. I have just found copy of the Police Operation Order for the arrest and movement of about 15 families from KATHAN BAHRU new village (just North of Chemor between the main road and railway) on? Feb 1956? As MTO I was much involved and we had a whole Company fully committed. I cannot remember which Company! I remember that only 2 or 3 of the families were away when the camp was put down. Each family got three trucks, to load all their possessions, including the house, and over 24 hours before they were taken to 3 different places well off the West Coast. I remember that 6 or 8 of houses had secret underground rooms down below the floor which it hid the illegals!

3 Company RASC were much involved. I have also found a feint copy of my "handing over notes" about the MT for, I presume, Bill Kerr who took over. This is interesting and mentions the many vehicle problems and spares shortages.

With very best wishes for Christmas and the New Year Anthony and Pat.

[Author note] Fast forward to 2007] The following is a recap of how I became deeply involved in trying to solve the mystery and later discovery of a 'Marie Celeste' RAF B24 Liberator Bomber referred too in Chapters 1 & 11

Following on from Anthony Gordon's E/M.:- In January 2007. I was contacted by the RSF's (RHF) Association in Glasgow, and conversed with their Secretary Mr. Andrew Blackley . Requesting information on the 8 named RSF Soldiers who had been Killed during engagements with the Communist Terrorist. The 'conversation led to information of an incident when an RSF Platoon, whilst on an Operational Patrol, near the top of a range of mountains close to the Malay / Thailand Border, discovered in deep bamboo. The wreckage of a crashed B24 Liberator Bomber, with all its supplies intact. It was assumed ready for a supply drop to the SOE Force 136. Notice of the wreckage had been given to the RAF and as far as he Andrew, was aware it was still there? Andrew also made mention of a second Liberator bomber had been found by another Regiment down near Seremban but no further details?

THIS SNIPPET OF INFORMATION INTRIGUED Joe
Subsequently led to the following trail of correspondence

What was to follow was.The co-operation of many person's inputs of their thoughts, suggestions, detective work, with the passing of countless documentation in order to fathom out possibilities of, **"What, When and How."** Trying to solve too many questions, relating to a crashed Aircraft including the fate of its crew. Furthermore, the physical determination of the Malayan search parties of. **Capt. Zuraiman Malayan Army** and **Shaharom Ahmad of the Malaya Historical Group.** Who undertook arduous forays into the jungles and hills of North Malaya, to the eventual successful finding of Liberator KH326. Also, the endeavours of one-person, part of the team, **Matt Poole an American Researcher,** who doggedly sought out the families of the missing Liberators Crews, to advise them of the fate of their beloved ones, to at least give them peace of mind.

The 2 RSF Officers who were physically involved at the Crash site in 1955. **Antony Gordon the Motor Transport Officer,** who took control of all the weapons found. And **Blair Agnew a National Service Officer** who arrived at the crash scene, 2 days later after its discovery. Blair was instrumental in obtaining the vital RSF War Diary of "Operation Unity" from Glasgow, found by **Maj. (Rtd.) Willy Shaw.** Which opened the key to Pandora's box, to reveal the true GR (grid reference) of the fatal crash site. To all the other RSF Fusiliers involved in finding the Liberator.

Many Thanks to all those who became involved through the following corresopondence. There are too many names to record, in this fascinating story of its find. Nevertheless, their names are recorded as and when they entered into the story. Chronologically day by day in the following 156.

1.	**7 February 2007** Joe sent a letter to the Armed Forces Personnel Administration Agency. Requesting for any information on the crews of the 2 lost Liberators in Malaya during WWII. (Copy mislaid?)

2.	**21 February 2007** dated. The RAF return letter. Requested as follows: -

Thank you for your letter dated 7 February 2007 and your enquiry regarding the fate of the crews of 2 Liberators lost in the jungles of Johore (Joe's] letter referred to 2 separate finds: The RSF's in North Malaya, and another unknown Regt. Find, operating in the Seremban area South Malaya.)

Before we can carry out further research we do, however, require some more details. We shall be grateful if you could provide either the serial numbers of the aircraft, the names of at least one of the crew members from each aircraft and /or the date of the accidents.

Their statement in this letter, reversed the onus. They wanting information from Joe who had requested same from them???

Not perturbed by this request, Joe, knew due to his brother Jack's period of time in Burma 1944 /45 knew the Army Navy and RAF Squadrons operating in India and Burma were under the heading SEAC (South East Asia Command). Possibly a clue to finding something on the Internet as:- Internet ref: www. rquirk.com/lib99.html.
SEAC Liberators. 99 Squadron

This was created by of a Canadian Researcher by the name of **Robert Quirk:**

27/02/ 2007 Reading through it, Joe downloaded each list of the 9 RAF Sqdn. With comments of the fate of each Numbered Liberator. The number of Liberators missing in each Squadron were namely: -

Sqdn: 99 = 41 - Sqdn 160 = 87 - Sqdn 292 = 8 - Sqdn 215 = 34 - Sqdn 354 = 42 – Sqdn 355 = 95 - Sqdn 356 = 61 - Sqdn 357 = 38 - Sqdn 358 = 47.

Total Liberators listed missing with comments = 453 All tabulated as illustrated below:

Serial	Squadrons	Mark	Notes	Ref.
EW236	159/99	VI	Missing in Bad weather 6.10.45	AB
Most Important				
EV940	355	VI	Lost 8. 10. 1944 NFD	AB
KL654	356	VI	Missing on SD flight over Thailand 23 04 1945	AB
KH326	357	VI	Missing 6.6.1945 NFD	AB

AB stands for Air Britain   NFD ?...

This took time to identify any "likely" missing Liberators from the 453 listed, before sending an E/Mail to Robert Quirk for any information he could provide.

3.   1 Mar. 2007   Joe Plant to Robert Quirk As follows

Subject: Missing Liberators

I have perused with interest, details of your web site. The above subject. My interest is researching the Malaya Emergency 1948 - 1960 another forgotten war. Trying to piece together the combined military involvement against the MPABA (Malaya Peoples Anti British Army) the predecessors of the MPAJA (Malaya Peoples Anti Japanese Army)1942-1945 both under the Leadership of **Chin Peng**. I served in the REME in Ipoh 1955-1957 became hooked on the events that took place.

Located next to ours was the 1st. Battn. Royal Scots Fusiliers who in Nov. 55 **[Author Note this was my error should read May 55]**: during 'Operation Unity', one of their Patrols found in deep jungle close to Kroh on the Malay / Thailand border a Liberator. It was intact with all suppliers in pristine condition? The RAF were contacted and it took 10 Helicopter trips to remove all supplies. Information the RSF's provided, it was one of two Liberators which went missing on supply drops. to 136 Force. Possibly before Operation Zipper the intended British invasion against the Japanese. The second was found by another Infantry Battn.? 3 years later in the jungles of Johore S. Malaya, Still being researched by others.

I have contacted the RAF Air Historical Group for information and the National Archives without results. The find is most intriguing, as many questions still remain unanswered to the find by the RSF's.

There was no evidence of any member of the crew. Did they bale out? Who were they and What was their fate. The Liberators I.D. Number Squadron and Base.

The Japs never found it? Were the arms to be dropped for 136 Force?

The irony of this find was that the RSF's were searching for a CT camp, disturbed a hornets nest, they scattered and found the Liberator, then found a CT jungle track 10 yards away from the hidden Liberator, which led them to the abandoned camp approx. 100 yds further on, suitable for 100 persons. Who the CT's would have dearly loved to have found the arms cache on their doorstep. The RSF's cleared the site for the Helicopters to land.

Your web site has revealed Numbers of possible missing Liberators as Follows

Sqdn 190. BR 939: Sqdn. 355 BZ938 - EV940: Sqdn 358 - EW124 – EW174 - EW188 - KGB 877: Sqdn 356 KL 654: Sqdn. 358 EW 124 -EW 174 EW 188 KGB 877 .   More possible Sqdn. 355?

Please can you assist wuth this puzzle to identify all missing details.

Most grateful.

Joe. P. Plant.

4.   1.Mar 2007 :   Robert Quirk to Joe Plant with copy of another E/M.

3/1/2007 you wrote:??

Roberts comment.

Back in 2000 I had made a list of RAF Libs lost in '45 in the area.

EW 124 355/356 VI Missing 19.6. 45 Code name "H" Location unknown AB

EW 174 358 VI Damaged by Ki 43s and crash-landed in jungle 29.5.45 AB

Code was "P" this was Smith's a/c - claims shot down over Thailand, but Roe's account in Merrick's book claims they were over Alor Star.

EW 180 FE VI Missing 19.3. 45 AB

Squadron unknown –no details

EW 188 358 V1 Missng 26.3.45

Code "H" on sortie to French Indo China believed lost over Northern Burma

EW 263 156/99 VI Missing in bad weather 6. 10. 45   AB -

Code "K" on flight from Cocos? To Singapore

KG 877   355/358 VI Flew into hill in cloud near Rathedsung on SD mission 11. 6. 45 AB
Code letter "O"

KH 326   357 VI Missing 6. 6. 45. NFD AB
F/O Timmerman

KH 654   356 VI I Missing on SD flight over Thailand 23 .8. 45 AB
Code "R"

[Author note: Comparing my list to Roberts, noted that 4 were the same number, and 4 , numbers were different:- EW180. – EW 236 – KH 326 & KH 654.]

5.   1ˢᵗ March 2007   Robert Quirk to Joe Plant.   <u>With attached copy of e-mails</u>

I have forwarded your e-mail to a few of my contacts who may be in touch with you.

1)   One of the Liberators is probably KL654 / R 356 Squadron - I have been involved in the investigation of this for a number of years - finally, the British government sent a representative to the site (with the Malaysian armed forces) they now have the date plate from the engine which confirm the aircraft as an RAF aircraft - something they had been denying for years. "Google" And you will find some articles in British papers on this

2)   the second maybe the one referred to in the following e/mail ---

Copy E-mail attached.   **Shaharom to Robert Quirk 18 /02 /2004** you wrote :

Dear Sir.

Today I received an E mail from **Gerald Howse** which his uncle was in **Liberator KH326 X** which lost near Kroh Isthmus / Malay border The Information given to me was detail with report from RAF Air Historical Group which stated the findings in 1955 which near to Malaya / Thailand border. Can you get any more info about this aircraft?

We would like to visit this wreck

Thank you very much

Shaharom Ahmad.

MHG –Researcher

<u>**Copy e-mail 18 /02 / 2004**</u>   **Robert Quirk to Shaharom Ahmad**

Gerald has been in contact with me – he said he had some documentation which may describe the crash site – and would try to find it – that was about a week, and I have not heard from him since - note that the one survivor was a prisoner on the South Andermans Is. After baling out (died in captivity)

The record in the Canadian casualty book says "shot down in the Bay of Bengal between Bunting and Anderman Island

[Authors note:] Noted the date <u>18 /2/ 2004</u> 3 years earlier. SOMEONE else? Was searching for maybe the same Liberator? It appeared one Liberator KL654 was the one in South Malaya. The other was KH326 near Bunting? And if I remembered at that time, having read through the e-mail, noted they wanted more Information on the Lib. Maybe Andrew Blackley RSF's Secretary could have that info? Will make a call. Also thought there was somewhat confusion about their two E/Ms, recollecting my 'conversation with Andrew Blackley. The RSFs were operating on the Fringes of the Malaya / Thailand Border, nowhere near Bunting (Langkawi) Also, who was this Gerald Howse? And Robert Quirk's <u>other contacts</u>??]   Did not have long to wait 2 E/Ms arrived: date: -

6.   1. Mar 2007   (E-mail 1) Shaharom Ahmad to Joe Plant.

"Glad to hear some news from you.

About the location of the crash. It is a blur since it was only reported last saw near Pulau Dayang Bunting which now is Langkawi Island. I assumed that the aircraft must be damaged and all the crews were baled out (over sea) and the aircraft using auto pilot travelled much further inland where it was maybe run out of fuel or heavily damaged and crashed in a mountain range. The Coordinates which given by RAF Air Historical Group was their DZ. I hope we can get a positive info into the exact location so that we can start our search for the wreck. If in Malaysia we can do any time, but if the wreck was in Thailand or Burma there will be a problem

Gerald was confident that **KH326** was crashed near Bunting Kedah area which approx. 30 miles from Thailand border and and a very very remote place which the nearby village was 40 km. But I'll check with other source. Maybe here were some Police or army post nearby built after the war to monitor CT activities. The only way to visit the site was using helicopters.

Shaharom Ahmad Hope to get more info from you.

7.   2 March 2007   E/Mail Shaharom Ahmad to Robert Quirk cc <u>Joe Plant</u>

Sub: SEAC COMMAND LIBERATORS

Dear all.

Thank you, Mr. Robert Quirk, for forward the email to me. **[Joe Plants]** Yes, I've just finishing collecting several info from my records together some documents which given by Gerald Howse who searching for his uncle missing in B- 24 Liberator KH 326 / X US Serial 44-44197 in June 6, 1945.

The records which give details of the expeditions in 1955 which found the wreckage together with some details on grid location which similar to what you give to Mr. Robert Quirk near the Kroh (Malay/Thailand Border)

Right now, I would like to know if you have any records or information which might lead to the exact spot where the Lib was? Kroh were large and it was near to the border where I need get clarification from Malaysian Military who still controlled the area to comb the jungle

From the RAF records in 1955 they mention the plane was in Auto Pilot and crashed on a straight flight pattern. Broke in 3 pieces where the supplies were intact All crew members were not found and from the evidence on board where emergency pack was opened and all parachutes were missing it assumed that the crews were bailed out and might be lost or found by Japanese and were executed.

One of KH326/X crew members was Wop/Ag William Peter McLeod

The location was put on QY300814 grid where I hope you can decode it into Lat and Long using 1950 map

About RAF or MOD who did not have the records, yes, I agree on that especially when they responded to our call about KL 654/ R Regarding another B24 wreck at South Johore or Johore? (which one). Could it be KL 654/R Found near Seremban Town? Any reports were given by the Patrols who found the wreck I need to know if they found any remains on the wreckage

Hope you can contact me as soon as possible

Shaharom Ahmad.

[Author Note] From this e-mail Joe gathered that the sender was a Malaysian Researcher and the mysterious Mr. Howse was the nephew of a crew member of the Liberator, who he Mr. Howse was seeking information about his uncle. Peter McLeod? At least they had a Map ref.

In regards to the Liberator in South Malaya, that accordingly had already been found, although of interest. Was not the one found by the RSF's.

8.   2 March 2007   (E/mail No. 2)   From Matt Poole to Joe Plant

Hi Joe

My RAF Liberator research pal, Robert Quirk, sent me a copy of the enquiry he received from you regarding the identities of two crashed Liberator found in the 1950's in the Malay Peninsula area. I just wanted to let you know I'll delve into my records of crashed RAF Liberators to see what serial numbers might best match up, I can tell you now that of the serials you listed in your e-mail to Robert, the following can be disqualified

Here Matt gives detailed information on the following which are basically not relevant to the missing two briefly mentioned.

Sqdn. 190: BR939 : Rangoon. –
Sqdn. 355: BZ938 : Rangoon.- EV940 Siam -
Sqdn. 358: EW124: Bay of Bengal. - EW174 Bankok - EW188 French Indo China - KGB 877Akyab
Sqdn. 356: KL654: The Seremban Liberator.
Contd.:

I have one other great candidate for you **KH326 of 357 Squadron** Lost 6 June 1945 in the Kroh area! Gerald Howse has researched this one – family history matter. I think. He did create maps and images which were put on the website, but the main link no longer works, However, going in" through the back door" I have at least rediscovered a roundabout way of access to some of the site

Fortunately, I saved the two most pertinent images a couple of years ago. I am sending these to you as e-mail attachments one per e-mail in 2 successive e-mails

Robert Quirk was the one who had corresponded with Gerald and had pointed out the website and e/mail address to me Possibly Robert had made more recent contact with Gerald

Anyway, when you see the maps, I'm Attaching you'll be very excited. And if Gerald has not heard your interesting news, I can guarantee you that he too, will be amazed. I think we're on to something her!

Furthermore, there is a possibility that your information will tie in with the story of KL 654 and can add to what is known of the mystery.

"Who knows if, KH326 is the Liberator found by the 1st. Battalion Royal Scots Fusiliers in November 1955 **(Authors Note my mistake, actually May 1955)** Then possibly through the "old boy" network it may be possible to locate someone who visited the crash site. There MUST be photos around somewhere. And the fact that RAF helicopters were involved means there are records.

Ah you've have opened a can of worms on this. I love the thrill of the hunt!"----

So, I still have more searching to do and will get back to you as time permits, I may be slower than I want, but I won't forget.

Cheers

Matt Poole

Wheaton Maryland USA

(son of a Liverpool woman whose husband, Sgt. George Plank, was shot down and Killed over Rangoon on Liberator BZ962 RAF 159 Squadron 29 Feb 1944)

[Author Joe's comment: This second email, solved two bits of information:

a) Only one Liberator KH326 appeared to be the one the 1st. RSF's had discovered.

b) Matt Poole another Researcher in America, who had a different personal interest in finding Liberators.

It suddenly dawned on [Joe], just by chance, asking a relevant question, to what [Joe] wanted from the RSF's for his Malayan Emergency research. Had then become the leading force, in trying to unravel to him, a mystery, that according to the date of the crash of Liberator KH326 6th. June 1945 was 62 years old. [Joe] Knew at that time. More exiting discoveries lay ahead, more so, with Matt Poole. A developing and truly interesting friendship in trying to solve this mystery, including Shaharom Ahmad the Malaysian Researcher.

8.   3 March 2007:   Joe Plant to Matt Poole.

Many thanks for your e-mail, which I read with great interest. "A can of worms"? More of a HORNETS NEST, as the RSFs found out, which led to the discovery. One of their Patrol disturbed a hornet's nest, and being very angry, they buzzed around, causing the Platoon to disperse very quickly in a military-controlled fashion as taught, into undergrowth. The Sergeant heard one of them call out, "*Sergeant, there's an airiyplane!*" It was 10 yards into the jungle from the CT's path, which later led to their camp 100 yards further on. From my experience those hornets are bloody big buggers and pack a sting.

My contact in the RSF is one of 2 Officers in charge of the Patrol at the time of the find:

1.   Lt. Staheli has since passed away and gone to higher grounds;

2:    2nd./Lt. Blair Agnew. I spoke with him yesterday, informing him of Robert Quirk's information. He is now in contact with the RSF's Regimental Archives.

Yet another RSF officer, Anthony Gordon, was the Transport Officer in charge of transporting the armaments and supplies from Baling to Kuala Lumpur. His twin brother Ian took over from him when he left the Regimental Headquarters at IPOH, where I was stationed at the same time and was a NS in the REME attached to the RAASC (Aussies but that is another story?). I have been in touch with him during the latter part of 2006. He is also aware of the latest information.

Blair Agnew told me that the CT camp was near the top of a hill obviously on a level spot. The top of the hill was about 2-3000 feet high? and they found the Liberator 200 feet from the summit, which indicates that the Liberator in auto pilot was on a controlled gentle downward glide upon impact?? Assumed just a guess!

I know that the RAF took 10 lifts in helicopters to bring out the supplies. Their Landing Zone was the CT camp, which the RSFs cleared for the landing, and their records are where???

However, I have thought of an alternative. The Fleet Air Arm (FAA) were flying S55 Sykorski helicopters during 1954-57. It might have been 858 Squadron which did the lift. I have another mate who was out in Malaya with me, and I contacted him today, as he knows a Rear Admiral (Retired) who is the curator of their (FAA) museum and will contact them on Monday. They must know the actual Landing Zone (LZ) position Grid Reference, (GR) if it is in their archives and if it was them? However, I will go back to the RAF and try them again.

Do you have any information of the names of the crew on board so I can find out where they are buried??? Assumed?

The Seremban Liberator: I will try and find out what Regiment was located in that area at the time. It could have been one of many English, Gurkha or, Malay units. As I have said, I am researching the Malaya Forgotten War 1948-60, hence my quest to find the Liberators' history, which has now become more of a purpose. To resolve the mystery behind it. A jigsaw puzzles. I will still keep buzzing about.

9.   3 March 2007:   Matt Poole to Joe Plant,

After I sent the info to you yesterday I went back and actually read the material Gerald Howse had completed on the loss of KH326 'X' of 357 Squadron. His comments were incorporated into his map artwork. Now I understand that he was perfectly aware that the Lib was found in 1955 From the detail he wrote.

An attempt to drop supplies to Force 136 Note: the flight path of this map is inaccurate as the crash location has been decoded KH326 'X' recorded to be located at least 21 km NE of Alor Setar. This will be confirmed when a party attempts to go to the crash site in 2004 An attempt to drop supplies to Force 136; KH326X arrives Bunting Island just West of Yama small island about 1 mile long West coast Malaya at 00: 40 local Malaysia time June 7 1945 the attitude of the B24 would have been 50-500 feet above sea level to avoid enemy radar and it is night-time. Possible flight paths of the B24 are shown in red square, they are in route to drop supplies to Force 136 who are waiting at the drop point marked as a red square. These men would have been within 15 -20 miles of the wreck site. **KH326X does not reach the drop point and is found in 1955 with supplies in the wreck but no trace of human remains.** *The crew has abandoned KH326X somewhere between Bunting Island and the Kroh area. Kroh is where the 3 roads meet. The B24 is within 50 miles of the sea. About 20 min flying time at 150-165 mph.* **KH326 X has crashed on autopilot with possibly one engine feathered, mid-section burns but rest of craft is intact. Sten Guns and ammo are found in the wreck, no one has touched the site. The men waiting at the drop point may know the fate of the crew Most likely executed by the Japanese, no record of them has been found.**

Gerald obviously had a source for this specific information on the wreck Very likely he wrote to the UK Ministry of Defence Air- Historical Group and received a report or two which summed up the 1955 findings. From what little I can understand from what I can see on Gerald's defunct website. it seems he was related to William Peter McLeod RCAF serial J47871 who must have disappeared with the remainder of the crew of KH326'X'. Also, I can read a photo caption (photo links don't work) to a 1945 document called a circumstantial Report, which was a standard form written right after the disappearance of an aircraft and crew. The report would have listed time of take-off, basic details on the nature of the operation, and a listing of crew name, rand serial number and maybe crew position. Alas I can't see this information for myself and never saved a copy of this document when it was accessible.

I still have some more liberator serial data base searching to do for you

Cheers for now Matt

10.   3 March 2007   Joe Plant to Matt Poole:

Having read the lastest message, I believe I was wrong in my assumption that the Lib was flying high to avoid detection. It appears it is the opposite. It was on a climbing path. The area on the border **[Malaya-Siam border]** is very mountainous, aprox 3,000 feet plus. The distance the Lib had to travel to those ranges from sea shore, flying at an altitude of 50-250 ft., was less than maybe 20 miles, with a time of 15-20 minutes to Kroh. Anything up to 7 minutes into the overland flight, they would have started to climb to avoid flying into the mountains. They set the autopilot. Hence, the altitude when the Lib crashed. However, for whatever reason, a real big question is why in that short distance did all crew members bale out? They must have landed in dense jungle which appears on my map of Malaya 1950 as mostly uninhabitable jungle area.

11.   3 March 2007:   Matt Poole to Joe Plant,

Robert Quirk just sent me a few original documents he had received from Gerald Howse back in '04 or so. These are fantastic and are just what you are looking for. I must send them one at a time to you. I've resized some of them for speed in

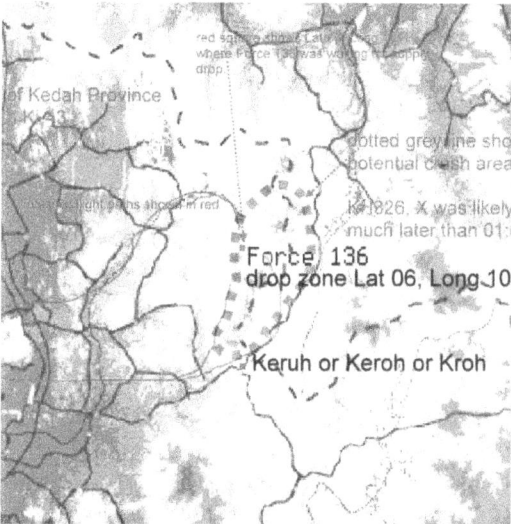

sending via dial-up internet...hopefully you can read these well enough and they won't take too long to download.

I have not yet analyzed your theory on the path taken by aircraft X. I suppose it's all just speculation, anyway. When I get a moment I'll mull over your analysis.

The documents Robert sent me prove that Gerald did, indeed, correspond with the MOD people to acquire what was known at the time. I just wonder if the wreck is still there, in large part. But if they did not find human remains in 1955, I must lean toward the theory that all crewmen baled out after suffering engine trouble. The documents I'm sending really do paint an interesting picture -- possible engine problems due to water in the petrol tanks. The fates of the crew? Either death from the bale-outs (too low an altitude, or Killed in the landing, or hung up in a tree, etc), from wounds, from the evils of the jungle (predators, illness), or at the hands of adversaries. Not pretty.

Above This is a copy of Gerald Howse map. Showing his annotation of the flight path of KH326 and his analysis of the probable crash site. It is apparent that Gerald Howse area of search was North East of Alor Star.That is quite a distance away from the DZ of KH326. Based on information from the RAF Air Historical Branch   Source By Matt Poole

Copy Letter from Ministry Defence London. **Dated 25 February 1988** Copied from Matt 4/03

Dear Mr. Howse

Thank you for your letter of 29 November 1987 in which you enquire upon the flight on which our uncle. the late Flying Office W.P. McLeod lost his life.

Our records show that on the 6. June 1945 Liberator KH326 of No 357 Squadron took off from its base at 0858 hours on 6 June 1945. It was last seen by another aircraft at about 1640 hours over Bunting island. The aircraft did not return and nothing was ever heard of it or its crew; it was eventually declared missing and the names of its crew were recorded on the Air Force Memorial at Singapore.

his memorial is dedicated to those airmen who lost their lives in SouthEast Asia and have No known Graves. The full Crew are:

Can	J 12779	F/O Timmerman. A.F.	- Captain.
Can	R217478	Sgt. Dellis. D. 1	- 2nd Pilot.
Can	J 47344	P/O Peron. J.J.	- Navigator.
Can	J 47321	P/O Reeve. W. W.	- Air Bomber.
Can	J 47871	P/O McLeod. W. P.	- Wop/Ag.
Can	J 47869	P/O Faulkner. G.	- Wop/Ag.
Can	R279733	Sgt. Andrews. H. H.	- A/Gunner.
Can	R278843	Sgt. Giesbrect. R.	- A/Gunner.

The ranks shown above are those held at the time the aircraft was lost; all the crew were advanced one grade after being declared missing. As you will see all the crew are Canadian

I will attempt to answer your remaining question in the order posed.

1, In 1955 the wreckage was found in deep jungle; there do not appear to have been any "local people" nerayby that could be questioned.

2. Because of the thick jungle and poor access to the wreck site, there appears to have been no attempt tpmove the wreckage exceot for one or two small parts for idenficatio purposes .

3 Any question of 'permmision to remove the wreckage', ould be a matter for the Burmese Government, I view of the difficulties involved by the jungle this would not , in all probability be a very practical proposition. The wreck is some 50 miles from the sea .

4 We have no maps to show the area.

5 There is no evidence of allied troops being in the vicinity at the time of the crash

6 The area was nominally under occupation by the Japanese. However, in view of the dense jungle it seems unlikely that there were any Japanese troops in the area

7 We have no record of POW camps in the vicinity

8 Although of 357 Squadron, the Liberator was a on detachment to No 8 Squadron Royal Indian Air Force. The base of RIAF is not shown in our records; the base of No 357 Squadron at the time of the loss of KH326 was Jessore.

9 The operation was to drop supplies to Force 136 at a location given in Lat/ Lon terms 06.00 North 101.00 East

I note that you have a copy of the RAF Far East Air Force letter of 16 June 1955. This letter gives the only clues which are to hand on the loss of the Liberator; as you will see no trace of the crew was found on board the aircraft when its wreckage was found. It was considered that the crew had abandoned the aircraft before it crashed. In view of the apparent deep Jungle it is unlikely that the crew could have survived in such conditions.

I am sorry I cannot be if greater assistance than this.

R. A. Muncay.

Air Historical Group S (RAF)

12. 3 March 2007 Joe Plant to Matt Poole

Recv'd all docs very good print out's many thanks

Reading through the MOD & RAF letters. I made a mistake thinking it "KH326" Waa discovered in Nov 55.

[Author Note this was an error I made, sending an E/M to Robert Quirk 1 Mar 2007 it was May 1955 not Nov.]:

RAF Singapore letter dated 16th. June 55. which reports its discovery. The RSF's took over from the Manchester Regiment in April 55 the Operation they were engaged in was 'UNITY' Flushing out CT's along the Thailand Border. Therefore, the Patrol must have found it between the 1st. to 16th June 55. I will check that detail my error.

The other RAF letter June 45, probably give a better rendition of the incident. I took time to plot a straight-line course from Trincomalee Ceylon their base? **[Author Note: No It was Minneriya Corrected by Matt Poole]** to Kroh Malaya.

It passes South of Alor Star over Bunting Is. In a map of Malaya, just North of Kroh there is a mountain on the Malaya side (G. Lang Ht. 2,987 FT. on the Thailand side slightly NE is another one (Bt. Prenggan Ht. 3276 FT. which is right on the Border line, which appears and could be in the same vicinity as the RSF's report maybe that's the one.??? I'm guessing.

The straight-line flight path goes South of SIK there appears to be nothing but uninhabitable dense jungle from there until the road running North from BALING. If the crew did bale out in that area, I don't hold up much hope?? Who knows. Good point about List of Missing Airmen Thanks Good Hunting Joe.

13. 4 March 2007: Matt Poole to Joe Plant,

You were incorrect on one thing -- 357 Squadron on 6 June 1945 was flying from Minneriya, Ceylon, not from Trincomalee, Ceylon. I will soon send an excerpt of a book, *"Flights of the Forgotten"* by K.A. Merrick, which spells out the history and gives you a few interesting tidbits to read about Special Duties Liberator flights to the Malaya area in 1945. Your theory of flight path from Ceylon to the Kroh, Malaya area is sound. With the long flight times, no doubt aircrew wanted to take as little fuel as possible, or they sure didn't want to fly any more dogleg courses than necessary. I'll have to check back with you, in time, to learn more of your findings. Is your research going to make it into book from this ultimately?

14. 5 March 2007 Matt Poole to Joe Plant

Glad to hear all the documents successfully ended up in your computer. I have one more- attaché for you – an alternative map graphic that Gerald Howse had sent to Robert Quirk. I haven't compared it to the other similar graphic I already sent, so I didn't know yet which ones more accurate.

You were incorrect on one thing – 357 Squadron on 6 June 45 was flying from Minneriya Ceylon, not from Trincomalee Ceylon.

I'd also love to be able to acquire further evidence on either or both of the downed Libs. Photos would be amazing to added to my collection. There are amazing gems to be rediscovered in places such as Kew the RAF museum and the fleet Air Army Museum I hope the records of the chopper involvement regarding the Lib can be ferreted out!

Attached Source Matt Poole

Arau Kodiang Kampong Padang Sanai

Kedah and Perak are Provinces of Malaysia

Pengkalan Tok Puteh   Ban Nang Sata   Rangae

Jitra Kedah

KI-43 fighters were based at Alor Setar

Japanese Airbase Kampong Masjid
Alor Setar, est 1941-42

Red Star is Supply Drop Point
410 Lat 06 Long 101
Force 136 awaiting supplies.

Tanah Merah   Kampong Tobiar

Kampong Watt Dalam   Kampong To   Sungai Ko-lok

Circle is 50 Miles diameter,
20 minutes at 150 mph

Simpang Tiga Pendang Kampong Relong   Waeng

Loss of B24 KH326 X
at approximately

Sungai Limau Yan Kechil Kampong Jeneri   Kampong Jedok
01:00 Local Malaysian Tim, June 7 1945

Bunting Island
Red Dot   Kampong Sadu   Betong   Kampong Kalai
Singkir Darat   Bongor   Kroh Area

Last sighting by "M" 16:40 hrs at red dot   Merbok   Baling   Kampong Lawa   Jeli

Sungai Petani   Tanah Hitam

Pinang Tunggal   Tawar

67   Perak Kampong Kerunai   Malaysia

Labu Besar   Batu Dua   Kampong Bersia   Jerimbong   4

Tanjong Bunga

Likely location of wreck shaded red but may be on the Thai side awaiting further details

B24 KH326,"X" and B24 "M" departed China Bay, Trincomali, Celyion at 08:58 GMT
June 6, 1945 to drop supplies to Force 136 in Malaysia, the round trip estimated at
about 20 hours. B24 "M" returned to base B24 "X" did not. B24 "X" was found in 1955 at
the Kroh area near the Malay/Siam border, no human remains or traces were found.
Crash site is in high mountainous jungle.
Force 136 was waiting at the drop point Lat 06, Long 101 shown as a red star.
The departure time of the mission would have been roughly 17:00 hrs
local time in Malaysia (GMT+8) or 5:00pm, sighting at Bunting Island by Simms in aircraft
"M" was at 16:40 hrs GMT, 7 hours 40 minutes later. GMT+8 hours would have made the
local Malaysian time 00:40, twenty minutes to 1:00 am, the time of the last sighting over
Bunting Island. A B24 flew between 150 and 165 mph, given the distance from the sea to
the crash site of 50 miles, the aircraft perished within 20 minutes or so as it only traveled 50
miles before crashing in the Kroh area, possibly within 15-20 miles from Force 136 waiting at
the drop point. At the time of the parachute of the crew it was dark.
The crew could have baled out anywhere between Bunting Island and Kroh.
It remains a mystery why they abandoned the aircraft, as the crash investigation
indicated 3 engines were running with possibly one engine feathered, and they had not
yet reached the drop point. Speculation suggests they determined they would be unable
to make it back to Ceylon, however this does not explain why they abandoned the mission
to drop the supplies when they were so close. It is unknown whether aircraft "M" last
sighting of KH326,X was when "M" was proceeding to the drop point or if "M" was
heading back to Ceylon. "M" reported that there was no enemy encountered on the

15.   5 March 2007:   Joe Plant to Matt Poole,

The second map made by Gerald Howse refers too Two Bunting Islands. The large island at the top is in the Langkwi
group of islands. The lower Island is called P. Daysag Bunting (1950 Malay map), not Bunting.

However my initial gut feeling after reading the excerpts from the narrative is the Canadians were well aware of the dangers likely to be encounted by bumping into Jap fighters located in the Alor Setar aerodrome. If their flight headed for the Langkawi Island top path, which is to the North of Alor Setar, it would be more prone to attack than the lower. Turning up behind Alor Setar would appear unsuitable for their intended Drop Zone. Looking at the map, the reference stated appears more in line with an interception by Jap fighters.

Fleet Air Arm archives: my mate is visiting them possibly 'Thursday? RAF Historical wants it in writing one more time. The National Archives have 155 Squadron Helicopter records for viewing only. Will have to visit Kew one more time.

Sorry.My writing a book? Ultimately yes, but have to research at least 110 Army Regt.s. British, Gurkahs, Aussie, NZ, Fiji, Malay, Rhodesian, Sarawak Rangers including RAF, Royal Navy, Malay Federation Police records. A daunting task, but well on the way. The discovery of the Liberator will be included, hence my search for a solution, as will be the Seremban Liberator. This was a forgotten war and only pieces were written about it. Never mind, I lived through it.

16. March 6 2007 Matt Poole to Joe Plant

My take on Bunting Island: Gerald Howse said there were two Buntings one a large feature, the other a tiny speck in the ocean, really Given the night-time landfall, one would initially wonder how a navigator could have pinpointed the smaller bunting as a reference point. But if the moon phase was one of brightness it may have been easier than one would thing for example the navigator could have used larger identifiable landmarks to determine where the smaller Bunting was and then Bunting may have been seen even low.

ON Gerald Howse's Topographic colour graphics that I sent you, note the topography near the smaller Bunting. Immediately inland there is a large hilly feature which rises for an otherwise flat coastal plain. Between the Larger Bunting island and the Penang area to the South this terrain ONLY such features on the coastal plain. Thus, it may have been a key aid in navigating to the Drop Zone. From the low known altitude flight across water given the correct moon and weather conditions, this feature may have been THE essential visual reference point in crossing the coast at the correct point, South of Alor Star, North of Penang Georgetown and more or less over the smaller Bunting Island. Also, there is a large inlet just North of the terrain feature- potentially a total landmark on the coast?

The thought of flying over/very near the large Pataya Daysag Bunting doesn't make too much sense either. It would have been populated maybe with Japanese. Why announces one's arrival to the area? Logically making landfall (and a noisy one at that in a 4 Engine Lib) at a point where human habitation was limited makes sense to me. And keeping away from Alor Star also makes sense not wanting to attack a swarm of Japanese hornets. You know what those Asian hornets were! So, I'm leaning toward the approach over the smaller Bunting Island

Here is a wonderful site for finding out moon phases/Sunrise/Sunset data. This could be very useful to you in other Aspects of your research, too:

http://aa.usno.navy.mil/data/docs/RS_OneDay.html

One must know the time zone situation in 1945 versus Greenwich Mean Time, or a war standard time, to get the accurate data. That can be tricky, and I am not certain of the wartime time keeping situation, but still, you should be in the vicinity, within an hour perhaps. And anyway, even without the precise time zone info, you'll have the dates and lat/long, which will allow you to get the overall surise/Sunset/moon data for that day or night.

Here is a great source for place names anywhere in the world (includes maps):

http://www.fallingrain.com/world/index.html

That's the home page. For some of your specific work, here are the links:

Sri Lanka page:

http://www.fallingrain.com/world/CE/

Minneriya (clearly separate from Trincomalee):

http://www.fallingrain.com/world/CE/30/Minneriya.html

Thailand page:

http://www.fallingrain.com/world/TH/

Malaysia page:

http://www.fallingrain.com/world/MY/

I searched on "Bunting" in Malaysia: nothing obvious.
I searched on "Dayang Bunting" (name on 1980s map I have): nothing obvious.
I searched on "Daysag Bunting" (name on 1950 map you have): nothing obvious.

Regarding maps, are you familiar with Google Earth? It is absolutely fantastic, because you can view modern imagery of anywhere. Some areas are covered by extremely detailed high resolution images, but places like the interior jungles of Malaysia are just covered by poor-resolution images.

The thing about Google Earth: it included digital terrain elevation data. You can check this feature "on" and then use the tilt bar scale at upper right to angle your view of anywhere on the earth. Then you can see features in 3-D. And then you can spin and rotate your view of anywhere. It is absolutely amazing.

If you have high-speed internet, downloading Google Earth is easy and quick. Then you use it when you are connected to the internet by simply clicking on the Google Earth icon. I keep mine on my desktop. In "Tools" in the menu at the top of the page you would be able to navigate to an "Options" page. Here you can look at terrain exaggerated vertically up to 3 times its true vertical value. This helps in areas where the mountains are not really that distinct. Then the "lay of the land" really pops. out -- incredible to any researcher!

You can also search on a place name, OR on a latitude/longitude. It will relocate on that spot. Zooming in and out gives one the close-in and faraway views. You can also save images to your hard drive. Wonderful!

In lieu of downloading Google Earth (which is free), you can see the same images simply by going to google.com. On the resulting home page, just hit the MAPS option at top. This will bring you to a new Google maps home page. By holding the left mouse button down and moving it, you can reposition where you are anywhere in the world. Then zoom in using a double click of the left mouse button, or by using the scroll bar on the left.

There will be three options for viewing on the right: Map, Satellite, and Hybrid. In Malaysia, the Map option is just the basic coastline and international border. In places like the UK, however, you'll get a very detailed map with this option. The Satellite option will be the imagery. Great in some areas, basic in others. The Hybrid combines an overlay of some map info atop the Satellite image, for orienting the viewer. This is great for areas like London, for example.

I'm not sure if you can save these images to your hard drive. My computer is slow today, and my attempt to save a sample didn't get me anywhere. But I know you can save Google Earth images, even the oblique (tilted) views. At upper left on Google Earth there will be a save function. Then you choose to save it to whatever location you decide on your computer.

I'll let you figure this Google stuff out. It is an eye-opener if you've never used it.

More ideas...Shaharom Ahmad is an aviation researcher who was instrumental in visiting KL654's crash site and positively identifying the airframe. He is part of the Malaya Historical Group (or runs it?).

[Authors Note: Dec 2018: There are 2 Islands named "Bunting" Ref 1950 Map of Malaya.
   a) **5 miles to the North of Alor Star In the Lankawi group of Islands. Is another large Island named Pukai. Daysag Bunting.**
   b) **Approx 19 miles South of Alor Star, lies Pukai Bunting. Approx 31 miles South is Georgetown Penang**

17.   6 March 2007   Joe Plant to Matt Poole,:

I spoke with my cousin Ray who was a Navgator in the Fleet Air Arm in 42-47 and served in Ceylon. He informed me he flew from Minneriya which is North East of KANDY in central Ceylon. I plotted a flightpath from there to KROH, which within reason offers a direct flight path flying South of Bunting, over Merbok.**[Approx midway between Bunting and in Japanese controlled Georgetown.]** At low altitude they would have spotted the white sandy shores of Malaya in an almost black sea, and if in moonlight, which I am sure would have been the case. It was not Monsoon time, which is in Sept. Having experienced the view of the seashore on those moonlight nights, I can honestly say they would not have had any doubts as to where they were heading?

I have sent an e-mail to Shaharom as you suggested, so I will keep him informed. A good contact for my book.

17   6. March 2007   Joe Plant to Shaharom Ahmad

I have been in contact with Matt Poole who has provided me with a lot of info on the history of the hunt for KH326, which has further triggered my imagination.

As I explained to Robert Quirk I am researching the Malayan emergency 48 – 60 having started my own autobiography of my time in Malaya IPOH 55 – 57. Decided to expand it to before and after my time. Found a roll of honour and am now establishing cause of all fatalities, which occurred during that period of time. And I might add FORGOTTEN, I intend to do something about it?? To remember all those fellow comrades who did not return home. I came to know about the Liberator through my contacts with the RSF's, there is only one of the two officers alive who found the wreckage, he is not on email. I speak to him on the phone. He is currently looking in their archives, for anything to do with that find. I will report back later

My quest was therefore to identify the members of the crew I knew that they were on a mission to Force 136 and seeing Chin Peng was a former member it was a coincidence which drove me forward stop possibly you might understand my reason however, I discovered they were all Canadian with No known Graves.

18. 7 March 2007   Matt Poole to Joe Plant,

Glad Minneriya's location is well understood now. To see a crystal clear image of it today, go towww.maps.google.com. Type "minneriya, sri lanka" in the search window, and return, and it will center right on a modern view of the airport. If necessary, make sure to hit the "Satellite" button on the upper right so that you get the image, not the map.

I hope Shaharom and you can learn from one another. I will be making contact with him myself pretty soon, I think. He works with a Royal Malaysian Air Force officer, Goh Keng Loon, who also visited KL654's site with him recently. I'm sure they will be pleased to hear of your research, and if they are like me, they come alive when given the opportunity to be involved with further research into this forgotten part of the world.

It must have been amazing flying on a moonlit night toward the Malaya coast...never mind the war part...just the beauty of that unique perspective on the earth. Those white beaches, as you say, must have looked brilliant at night. Some of us forget just how bright things can be when the moon is out, mainly because we live in cultures where streetlights, etc., confuse us as to the real nature of the night sky.

You wrote . *"I will keep him informed a good contact for my Book, but don't let me take your story away "* No it is not my story at all. I've gathered things here and there from others who have done all the work on the KH326 and KL645 investigations. I am going to join in to the KL645 team in the hope that my participation can help them find more next-of -kin. So far, I'm told , only two families are in touch with them – in both cases children of crewmen. I've had tremendous success finding kin so far and wide, so maybe I can add something positive to reach more.

I do understand that the Liberators wreck stories will only get a small mention in your book . I am like you though, I like to find answers to mysteries, even if they are not associated with the main focus at the time .One day I will buy your book and enjoy every word of it. Keep you focus and drive and you will succeed.

19.   8 March 2007   Shaharom Ahmad to Joe Plant

Thank you for the info. The mystery of those KH 326 crews still surrounding me and relatives. Why they all bailed out when the plane was not damage?

What happened to them which they took their decision to leave the plane?

And no one did not know what happened since there were no survivors to tell the tale. the crews might be captured and executed. The last sightings of KH 326 was near Bunting Island which another B – 24 flew along but after that they were separated

I've talked to Tony Tamblyn who mention to ask 848 RN Squadron if they knew which he found out their diaries match to the date "3rd. June 1955 send inspection party to Siamese border to check aircraft wreck."

I hope that we can find the coordinates QY 300814 into Lat and Long

20.   9 March 2007   Joe Plant to Shaharom Ahmad

Good news. The RSF's have found the records of the find of the Liberator it is detailed and I am awaiting a hard copy of same. It provides map references and indicates the crew members were on board at the time of the crash. There remains possibly disposed of by animals. Tigers or???

However the map ref QY300814 appears to be wrong???

Please provide details of your address so I can send a hard copy of the records upon receipt.

21.   9. March 2007   Shaharom Ahmad to Joe Plant

Thank you for your email my address number Shaharom Ahmad (deleted)

The grid was wrong? OOps. The grid was taken from their letter dated 1955 (Authors note *The RAF Letter*) which I attach it to you before. The crew remained on board? Hmmmm.

Will check the records first thank you very much.

22.   9 March 2007   Joe Plant to Matt Poole

I still think that the mystery lies in why they baled out. You will see the possible area of jumping. I feel that if they baled out either over the sea or inland there would have been some chance, and evidence, of maybe not ALL, BUT AT LEAST 1, being captured by the Japs.

[Authors Note: If any of the crew had baled out over the sea. The other B24 crew would have see them. All was said. Last seen flying into clouds] .

Nevertheless they were posted as missing and again one can assume that they might have been strung up underneath the jungle canopy never to be found???

My theory is of it being nightime once over the land. I worked out 47 miles as the crow flies to Kroh where the mountain range rises to 3,000+ feet. They possibly misjudged their height (possibly not true), but when they realised they were not going to make it over the mountains, they set the autopilot, so the plane would crash, and they destroyed everything before baling out. A nightime landing in the Jungle is not very inviting. Only a theory. Don't really know anyway.

23.   9 March 2007   Joe Plant to Matt Poole:

Christmas has arrived early this year...The hornets are nested?? Excellent news: the RSFs have located the documents and a full report of the find. Blair called me today and advised me, he is awaiting a hard copy, so I will advise soon.

However within the report it strongly indicated that the crew were still in the plane when it crashed, althought no remains were found. Another point: the Map Reference everyone has been searching at appears to be wrong? Nevertheless I will report asap.

24. **9 March 2007:** **Matt Poole to Joe Plant,**

Wow...Merry Christmas-in-March to you, too. That's great news -- the finding of the RSF report. I would be most grateful for a copy after you get yours from the RSF and after you find the time. I am just plain intrigued by possibilities here...such as the fact that if there is any chance of human remains being found, then the Canadian government may want to get involved. I think I mentioned that I have been working with Major James McKillip of the Directorate of History & Heritage in Ottawa on two RAF Lib crashes/burials in Burma, each containing 6 Canadian crewmen. In each case remains were found in 1945 and buried, but then just plain forgotten. Major McKillip is fighting for funding for the initial site visits, but I have friends who will accomplish this on their own if the money is not forthcoming AND Burma allows the investigations.

Anyway, because the entire KH326 crew is Canadian, I know Major McKillip will be all ears. Seeing a copy of the report from 1955 will be a revelation. I am a bit skeptical, however. If numerous helicopter trips were required to remove supplies, then it is clear at this point that the Liberator wreck was pretty well investigated...yet no human remains? Maybe it was not nearly as intact as I thought. In the jungle, of course, it doesn't take much to hide evidence. After all, this huge wreck wasn't even discovered by the rebels whose camp the RSF were approaching!

I don't have old maps of the area, but I would assume that Shaharom can get them. The original vintage map of the area would have the correct grid coordinate system where the crash reference location was derived. Later editions of a map can have an updated military grid coordinate system, with slight geodetic shifting due to a different datum employed. Thus, a six-digit grid coordinate reference on a 1955-era edition of the map could be a different position on the earth than the same six-digit reference on a later edition of the same-scale map.

Gerald Howse apparently knew someone with topo maps of the area, but since he has disappeared, I guess he's a tough one to track down again...

I wonder if, other than Gerald Howse, any other KH326 kin are at all "in the know" about the fact that the wreck was found. I also wonder if any photos exist of the wreck...I may have said that previously...If any come your way via Blair, then ya gotta lemme see 'em!! (There, I'm proving how greedy I am...No, not really, just incredibly curious.)

25. **11. March 2007** **Joe Plant to Robert Quirk**

Robert

I sent a EM last 'Friday but found out that it was never received?

But good news. Blair Agnew the officer who found the wreck visited their museum in Glasgow, found the detailed report and it has co-ordinates. I am waiting for a hard copy and will revert soonest. From our Tel/con it appears that the crew were still on board at the time of the crash. Another thing the map ref's appear to be far from correct

I have informed that Matt Poole I and Shaharom of the news

26. **11 March 2007** **Robert Quirk to Joe Plant**

Interesting news John? **(Joe)**-- it is amazing what you have managed to dig up, and I look forward to seeing it Robert.

27. **11 March 2007** **Matt Poole to Joe Plant,**

I was just reviewing documents and I realized what I think is a fundamental error in Gerald Howse's understanding of the timing of the KH326 operation. Records indicate that KH326 "X" took off at 08.58 and was seen by aircraft "M" in the "target area" between 16.33 and 16.45 hours. (It is possible that "target area" was a very broad description of Malaya, not the actual Drop Zone; I've seen such gross generalisation regarding target area in other records.)

Obviously "X" did not drop its supplies, so one must presume it was still destined for the Drop Zone at the time of its demise. "M" may have already reached the DZ and Thus was on the return leg to Minneriya when "X" was spotted

Based on my understanding of other records in this theatre of war, the times would have been reported in RAF documents as LOCAL TIME. However, Gerald Howse's map graphics assume that the times given were actually Greenwich Mean Time, not local time. Thus, he thinks KH326 was over Malaya during darkness, crashing in the first hour after midnight, local time

I am betting that KH326 took off in daylight, crossed the Malayan coast in daylight, reached the general Drop Zone vicinity in daylight and then was lost -- in what must have been daylight **[ditto last comment]** If I had access to the 357 Squadron Operations Record Book, there might be something else written which clarified matters. But I feel strongly, at this point, that it was a daylight affair.

I am going to write to my Japanese air combat Friend, Hiroshi Ichimura. He might know something about activity out of

Alor Setar in June 1945, if there was any. I just don't know how late the Japanese flew from here. Regardless, I do know that Japanese aerial activities were very, very slight by this time. Thus, the British did much more flying in daylight late in the war.

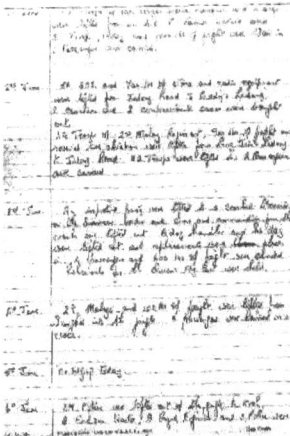

28.   **12 Mar 2007**   Jacko to Joe Plant with attatched: This s a copy of the 848 Sqdn. Sykorski Pilots note book when engaged on the lift dated 2nd to 6th June, re the KH326 Liberator For clarity it reads :

2nd. June 56 SAS 700 lbs of stores, and radio equioment were lift from Jalong Road to Paddy's Ladang 2 casvacs and 2 compassionates were lifted out.

43 troops of the Malay Regiment. 900 lbs of freight and several live chickens were lifted from Long Jim's Ladang to Jalong Road. 32 troops were lifted in and 2 passengers were carried.

3rd.   *An inspection party were lifted to a crashed Liberator on the Siamese border and arms and ammunition from the crash were lifted out. A dog handler and his dog were lifted out and replacements were flown in. A passenger and 600 lbs of freight were carried.*

Rehearsals for the Queen's fly past were held

4th,   *28 Malays and 150lbs of freight were lifted from Sungkei into the jungle 8 passengers werecarried on a rrecce*

5th.   *No Flying.*

29.   **12 March 2007:**   Joe Plant to Matt Poole,

I spoke to the Royal Observatory Edinburgh this afternoon. They confirmed that time in Penang 6th June would be GMT + 8. If they took off from Minneriya @ 8.58, that would mean it was about 17.00 hrs Penang /Singapore time. Twilight in Malaya is roughly 18.45 local time, so within 2 hours of their GMT take off time it would be dark in Malaya? I might be wrong but it needs clarification. Records should prove that.

I had a call from Tony Gordon in S. Africa yesterday, the RSF's transport Lt. who did the transfer*[of armaments*] from Gerald Howse's take on time being GMT was incorrect. Robert Quirk has the 357 Squadron records on microfilm, and he will be taking a look, hopefully this week, to see what turns up. He says sometimes GMT is used, sometimes local time, Beling to Kuala Lumpur. He has maps of the actual area and is sending them across.

30.   **13 March 2007**   Matt Poole to Joe Plant,

I just wanted to get off a quick acknowledgement of your latest news and surmising re the times. I certainly might be wrong in thinking that but the GMT should have a Z (Z is always GMT in records). I'll be intrigued with those maps from S. 'Africa, that's for sure.

31.   **14 March 2007**   **Matt Poole to Joe Plant,**

I just received a reply from Japanese military aviation historian/author Hiroshi Ichimura. I asked him if there was Japanese fighter activity at Alor Setar airfield, near to where KH326 came down. Here's the reply (I have tidied up his English slightly):

The JAAF [Japanese Army Air Force] 12th Kyoiku Hikotai (educational squadron) was Stationed at Alor Setar [Alor Star]airfield at that time. It was the fighter pilot training unit. They came to there on 20th February 1945. 12th Kyoiku Hikotai was ordered onto air defence around the area. Their fighter should be Ki27 (or Ki43).

The JAAF 3rd Air Force was ordered to stop the pilots' education programme in the beginning of April 1945. All flying units should be trained for "Kamikaze". My father, Cpl. Kikusaburo Ichimura, was one of these pilots. He was assigned to the 1st Rensyu Hikotai (Practice Squadron) in Java.

I am very sorry, but I have no evidence of any JAAF or JNAF [Japanese Navy Air Force] fighters claiming to have destroyed the Liberator KH326 on that day. The combat activity of the 12th Kyoiku Hikotai seemed to be dull. But they might have shot KH326 down. I will try to find further information for this unit.

So, at this point, we still don't know for certainty whether Japanese fighter activity was associated with the loss of George's Liberator. But there were flyable aircraft at Alor Setar. *[Alor Star]*

I keep mulling over the time situation, and it gets more and more complicated

31.   **19. March.2007**   **Joe Plant to Matt Poole**

Blair Agnew: No news as of yet. I believe he is waiting the receipt of a map of Malaya in colour from Antony Gordon in South Africa, who is also sending me a couple of A4 sheets of a map of the area.

Antony did speak with me on 'Thursday night about the maps, and I had already given him the Force 136 Drop Zone point. Having worked it out, he feels that the crash at Kroh in relationship to the DZ was approximately 12 miles slightly Northwest. We shall see.

However, my mate Jacko told me he remembers a newspaper article about the find and believes there was a photo printed. I am in the process of searching the British Museum Library for evidence, but I feel that will not come to anything.

Blair spoke to me about their find, as did Antony. (They are conversing verbally on the subject.) They both were on the scene at the same time and both have reiterated that the RAF Inspection Party could not wait to get out of the jungle. They did not like it? Their assumption was pig's bones???

The RSF's Patrol had already spent five weeks in there when they found it.

Jacko did locate the records of the Royal Navy Fleet Air Arm choppers. They took the Inspection Party in and came out the same day. Date: 3rd June 1955. I am researching the RAF (helicopter) Sqdn from the National Archives for their records. Wiil wait to see.

Antony says there were 12-14 air lifts to remove all the cargo, which in my opinion definitely rules out any Japs locating the site. Beside guns and ammo, there was medical, KD clothing and other materials stored, and only one container was damaged. The Japs would certainly have wanted the medicines and also guns. Your first theory might be right.

Burnt clothing was found and bones. Any crew members escaping the fire on board would very quickly lose their way. They were not equipped for jungle survival. The RSF's account *[7 Platoon]* was it took them 10 hours of cutting through dense bamboo to advance 1,000 yards and that was not far from the elephant track which eventually led to the crash site.

The RSF report and other map details will provide far more evidence to draw a sensible conclusion to all theories. Nevertheless, an inquisitive mind still remains.

I have had no contact with Shaharom since he acknowledged my early Christmas greetings His statement about doing a site visit was in his e-mail date 2 March, 2nd paragraph. He needs the correct Lat/Lon. which we are all waiting for, and I believe the original to be the wrong Lat/Lon. where everyone was searching??

My address: Firleigh Cottage Maryfield Torpoint, Cornwall PL11 2PE. Tel:

PS. Have just this minute received a phone call from the British Library. *[referring to found Straits Times issue 2nd. June 1955]* No photograph found in newspapers. Tough. And I know that the RSF did not have cameras with them. They carried out dead bodies for I.D. – a normal practice.

32.   20 March 2007   Joe Plant to Shaharom Ahmad

Shaharom

Blair Agnew the RSF Officer who was at the crash site in May/June 1955 called me this afternoon with news that he had received a copy of the RSF REPORT from Glasgow complete with a map. He has reviewed a copy with a map he has reviewed same and we spoke about the crash site and LZ of the helicopters. Both were identified with a map reference. I'm sorry to say the crash site ref was not QY300814 as stated in the LETTER DATED THE 16TH. JUNE 1955 BUT!! 818300. Everyone has been looking searching in the wrong place

The LZ Heli. is 818301 very close to it. there is a 'Y 'Mentioned on the map but no 'Q' but there again the RSF's were not reading from the same grid reference??? He also stated that the crash site is approx. 400yds due WEST of the border on the Malaysian side AND approx. 15,000 yds further WEST to the nearest road running NORTH from BALING to Kg. BAREMBANG. We have agreed to meet soon, to discuss the situation and hand over hard copies, which no doubt will be forwarded on to be seen.

I trust this news will be of significant importance to all concerned. All for now.

[Authors Note: This is the point in the search. Which defined the error in Grid References]

33.   20 March 2007   Shaharom Ahmad to Joe Plant.

Dear Joe

THANK YOU FOR YOUR Email

It seems that grid ref. QY300814 was INCORRECT GIVEN BY RAF Inspection party who wrote the 1955 letter. I'll check the new grid to my Friend who knew how to read the grid.

Will check the place again with the map or if you have another map with u that u can pinpoint the grid and scan it to me much appreciated

Yes, this news will be more valuable since right now we are searching for the wrong grid

Hope will get some more news from you

Thank you very much

34. **20 March 2007** **Matt Poole to Joe Plant:**

Was the newspaper story from back in 1955? If there was any press coverage at all, can you obtain a copy? I know Shaharom's other Lib project in Malaysia recently got coverage in a London newspaper, so I was wondering if your mate Jacko had seen that story, and that there was no 1955 story A link to the recent story:

http://www.thisislocallondon.co.uk/mostpopular.var.1200285. most viewed.lost_war_hero_plane_discovery.php

Another point of confusion: You wrote, *"I have had no contact with Shaharom since he acknowledged my early Christmas greetings."* This was back in December? Or by "early Christmas" do you mean the "Christmas comes in March" feeling we had when the RSF report's discovery in the archive reached you? You had even put it in those terms when you first wrote to me about the report. *[Author note: Correct Christmas is a time of giving gifts]*

I have not written to Shaharom yet...I just want to say to him. I'm sure that sooner or later he will hunt for the wreckage of KH654...too good an opportunity. I think he has known about this wreck for several years. Gerald Howse, whose uncle William McLeod died in the KH654 loss, added text to one of his maps, once found on his now-defunct website. The text said the following:

> *"Note: the flight path of this map is incorrect, as the crash location has been decoded, KH326,X recorded to be located at about 21 km NE of Alor Setar. This will be confirmed when a party attempts to go to the crash site in 2004."*

I assume that Gerald was referring to his contact with Shaharom or maybe to Shaharom's associate and fellow researcher Goh Keng Loon. I know from the remnant of Gerald's website (text only is viewable) that Goh Keng Loon had been in contact with Gerald. Goh, recently trekked with Shaharom to the wreck of RAF Liberator KL654,. So maybe Shaharom and Goh KL (as he signs his name on the internet sometimes) have planned to some day visit the KH326 wreck. Of course, the new positioning info/maps that are going to reach you will be a huge boost to that attempt to reach the wreck.

[Author Note re Matt's comment : [Shaharom's team did not attempt to rediscover the crash site until 2007, soon after the correct grid reference had been revealed in the 1955 RSF report. Gerald's plot of the crash location had been based on the erroneous QY300814 grid ref recorded in the RAF HQ, FEAF report of 1955.]

35. **20 March 2007** **Joe Plant to Matt Poole:**

I don't know about the story in a newspaper. Its Jacko's memory. I don't know? Try to find something??

Yes, you were right. Christmas Greetings in March but I wonder at the new revelation???

Flight path of KH326: I think I was right with my assumptions, but we shall see?

36. **20 March 2007** **Joe Plant to Matt Poole, Robert Quirk,**

Blair Agnew, the RSF officer who was at the crash site in May/June 1955, called me this afternoon with news that he had received a copy of the RSF REPORT from Glasgow, complete with a map. He has reviewed same, and we spoke about the crash site and LZ of the helicopters. Both were identified with a map reference.

I'm sorry to say the crash site reference was not QY300814, as stated in THE RAF LETTER DATED THE 16TH JUNE 1955, BUT as 818300. Everyone *[Authors note: Cannot be everyone.]* has been looking/searching in the wrong place?? The heli LZ is 818301, very close to it. There is a 'Y' mentioned on the map, but no 'Q' stated, but there again the RSF were not reading from the same grid references??? He also stated that the crash site is approx 400 yds due WEST of the Malay /Siam border, on the MALAYSIAN side, and it is approx 15,000 yds further WEST to the nearest road, which we assume is the road running NORTH from BALING to Kg. BAREMBANG. We have agreed to meet soon, to discuss the situation and hand over hard copies. Which no doubt will be forwarded on to be seen.

37. **21 March 2007:** **Joe Plant to Matt Poole**

Shaharom e-mail received. Thinks basically they are presently searching wrong place whether that's physically or map reading???

Further info about DON a very leading question. Where did he get the info from, and what initials are reported? Need more info to establish Identification?

I've checked 8/200 Sqdr. records. 8 was disbanded and became 200. *[Authors Note : error 200 Squadron became 8 Squadron in May 1945.]* They were in Minneriya same time *[as the 357 detachment of 4 Liberators, including KH326]*, but I doubt if their records would reveal any other person in another Sqdr. or Flight?

Sims: Was he the pilot of the other Liberator which spotted KH326 over Bunting?

IF the secret agent baled out and was captured, where was he captured? The plane would have had to change course from Bunting and fly Southbefore turning North for the flight to the DZ at Force 136?? IFhe flew North, he would have flown very close to ALOR SETAR. I think improbable??

38.   <u>23 March 2007</u>:   **Joe Plant to Matt Poole,**

Your reference to Don **[Timmermans]** and the statement about a ninth member on board came as a surprise, which just adds intrigue to the outstanding mystery. I discussed it with Blair Agnew, and we thought if he baled out and was captured and interned by the Japs, dying 4-6 weeks later, the cause of death: brutal torture for information.

The Liberator, after reaching the Malay coast, would have banked Southinland, allowing him to bale out, before banking North to reach his scheduled DZ. Unfortunately it crashed close to the top of a mountain. It would be difficult to ascertain if this was correct even if the crashed Liberator pointed to the North, as that would have been its pre-intended flight path. Only assumed; conclusion still remains a mystery.

However it got me thinking: where could I obtain information about Force 136 and its members? I contacted the Imperial War Museum, CWGC, National Army Museum, SEAC POW Assn. None had any records relating to Force 136. I spoke with the National Archives, who do hold records for viewing purposes only. I will have to make a trip to London to see myself. Is there any further info you could obtain re the initials of this bloke which would assist when I do go? Date yet to be planned.

Blair Agnew believes that it was the RNFAA *[Royal Navy Fleet Air Arm]* Heli that did the pick up, although his memory is a little bit shaky after 50 odd years, but we still have the RAF records to view. You were correct about 8/200; I was wrong. I should have inscribed 200/8 I only read the squadron movements, not records.

39.   **23 March 2007**   **Joe Plant to Matt Poole, again**

Looking through old e-mails, I came across the first one I received from Robert Quirk – 2nd. March, which attached a message dated 18 Feb 2004 to Shaharom. Script mentions, *"Note that the one survivor was a prisoner on the South Andamans Island after baling out (died in captivity)."* Comments believed were from Gerald Howse??

Is this one and the same? I doubt it if he baled out over the Andamans. He must have been in a Liberator taking off from a base in Madras. He would have been too far North if he was in KH326. Are we looking for someone else????

40.   <u>24 March 2007</u>   **Anthony Gordon to Blair Agnew & Joe Plant**

At long last I posted you both a big envelope of "Liberator" map copies and one sheet of the actual crash site map for Blair. IT IS REALLY FASCINATING WHAT JOE HAS FOUND! AND PROBABLY MORE TO COME!

I have sent you a lot of black and white and colour copies of the maps more than one copy of each in most cases.

I have sent Blair a black-and-white copy of the large "Melaya 1950" map 1: 760 320 (12 miles to the inch. Joe has already got a copy. You will see that I marked, off the East coast, not far N of Singapore where the late Prince of Wales and Repulse were Sunk!

I have also sent Blair the original copy of the Betong sheet 2J/1 which the crash site is (near the W edge) grid reference 818 300. This map belongs to David Christie (Blair will know him) he was a Cameroonian operating in the N. Melaya in the late 50s and early 60s with the Malayan Rangers. He later took only orders (so now "The Rev") and retired to a village about 50 miles inland. As he has another copy of this sheet (joint with three others covering most of the "Betong Slient") he said you could have it. I have a big sheet at present.

You will see that the maps were all made at the terribly difficult scale 1: 63 360 (1 inch to the mile) with the **grid squares each of 1000 YARDS**. I have made a copy of the scale line with the diagram of the maps sheets. It is only as we have used METRIC maps of 1: 50 000 or multiples of that MANY years (NATO Sandard!) does one realise how terrible the old scaling was!

You will see that the four sheets around the intended dropping zone of 101 E 06 N are:

No.2E 16	No. 2F 13 (Betong)
(which we do not have)	(original copy to Blair)
DZ	
No. 2 I 4	No. 2J1

You will see that the map sheets are exactly sized by Degrees of Longitudinal and Latitude and the intended target dropping site is exactly on the NW corner of the Betong sheet (101 E. and 06 N.) only about 6 miles slightly W of North of the crash site. These lines are on the big Melaya map.

Unfortunately we do not have the sheet to the end N W of the dropping site.

I have also made other copies of the critical areas, including Kroh and area (which is also at the junction of 4sheets but you can see our, rifle range and airstrip just S of the village.).

I have also made a number of ENLARGEMENTS mostly at 190% of the crash site in b and w and, for Blair to see if he can pick up the CT camp site and actual crash site. I do not know if the grid reference of 818 300 is the CT camp or the crash. Blair may be able to work it out. But remember that the maps were not very accurate!! This map is dated 1958 AFTER WE WERE THERE, so could be more accurate than ours were.

Some of my copies are duplicated (vertical and horizontal) in some cases and vary by colour, b and w and strengths of print ("Fast" in the fastest i.e., the worst uses less ink!! And BEST is just that)

you will just have to fit copies together!

The crash site, close to the border water- shed, is easy to find as it has the distinct U shaped bend. It is noticeably high ground around their with a number of hills over 3500 or even 4000 feet, I wonder what they were briefed about the area? Maps were very bad in the 1940s and as, I understand they were flying on automatic pilot it is not surprising that they crashed!

Joe's latest E/mail continues the incredible story! I find it fascinating and quite possible, that there was a 9th. person trying. Quite possibly a Force 136 person or a Chinese/Malay going to join Chin Pengs people. The book (The Jungle Is Neutral I think describes them receiving people, including signallers with the airdrops.). I wonder if Chin Peng mentions this in his big book My Side Of History I have it but have not read much of it!

Anthony Gordon.

41. <u>23 March 2007</u>   **Matt Poole to Joe Plant,**

Thanks for your latest. First of all, I have solved the mystery about the Andamans. There is a Canadian book called *"They Shall Grow Not Old"*, which is a compilation of information about Canada's war dead...I think WW II only. I knew the book had some details in it that were not in the Commonwealth War Graves Commission "Debt of Honour Database", so I asked Robert Quirk to peek at his copy for any biographical evidence on the KH326 all-Canadian crew. At the time I did not even know all the home towns, since the CWGC often does not have this info.

Robert found this additional information for the navigator J.J.P. Perron:

> *Perron, Joseph Jean Paul F/O (N) from Three Rivers, Quebec (or Trois Rivieres)*

In Perron's writeup is:

> *"One other member of the crew, Sgt. Wynne, bailed out, was captured and imprisoned at SouthAndaman Island and died on August 17, 1945."*

This is clearly in error. I have found that Sgt. Wynne was 23 year old F/Sgt Harold Wynne, a 355 Squadron air gunner whose Liberator, KH 250 "H", crashed near Port Blair, Andamans on 17 May 1945. Per the Commonwealth War Graves Commission:

Name:	*WYNNE, HAROLD*
Nationality:	*United Kingdom*
Rank:	*Flight Sergeant*
Regiment/Servic	*Royal Air Force Volunteer Reserve*
Unit Text:	*355 Sqdn.*
Age:	*23*
Date of Death:	*17/08/1945*
Service No:	*1516012*
Additional information	*Son of Edwin and Florence Wynne.*
Casualty Type:	*Commonwealth War Dead*
Grave/Memorial Reference:	*3. F. 5.*
Cemetery:	*KIRKEE WAR CEMETERY*

I then found Harold Wynne and crew in the book *"Burma Liberators, RCAF in SEAC, Vol. II"* by John R.W. Gwynne-Timothy. The narrative, from the 355 Squadron chapter, with typo's corrected in *[brackets]*:

> *Aircraft "H" bombed Chatham Island. The weather forced aircraft down and bombing had to be carried out from 2,000 feet. Flak was heavy and accurate. Most aircraft were hit. Aircraft "H" was hit on its dummy run over the target area at Port Blair. Smoke came out of the no. 2 engine. The aircraft was seen to turn around, bomb its target and then gradually lose height until it crashed into the ground and burst into flames on impact. The aircraft was captained by F/O R. Totham. It was his first trip with a new crew and they were being screened by F/S Duckworth, R.J.*

> *The missing crew of aircraft "H" were F/O Totham, captain; F/S McDowall, J.H., second pilot; P/O I.B.* **[I.A.]** *Morgan, bomb aimer; F/S Emerson, H.W., navigator; W/O Johnson, H, wireless operator; W/O Campbell, H, wireless operator; Sgt Bennel, L. ball gunner; P/O F.E. Rumsey-Williams, front gunner; F/S Wynne, H., mid-upper gunner; and F/S McPherson, R., rear gunner.* **[F/S R.J. Duckworth was left out of the above list.]**

> *The results of the bombing in the target area of Port Blair were generally good but the Squadron was much saddened by the loss of Duckworth, Totham, and their crew.*

The book's Appendices list the crew again:

> *Crew 54*
>
> *F/O   Totham, R.*   *F/S   Duckworth, R.J.*

F/S	McDowell, J.H		P/O	Rumsey-Williams, F.E.
F/S	Emerson, H.W.		F/S	Wynne, H.
P/O	Morgan, I.A.		F/S	McPherson, R.
W/O	Johnson, H.		Sgt	Benfell, L.
W/O	Campbell, H.			

Sortie: 183, missing

A recent privately-published book, *"Signed With Their Honour"*, edited by Mike Jones, is the history of 355 and 356 Squadrons. The narrative for May 1945 did not list names, but it corroborates the above details from the book *"Burma Liberators."* One important addition, however, to *"Signed With Their Honour"*:

KH250 made a second run, bombed the target and then gradually lost height before crashing in to the ground. One person was seen to bale out.

Using the names of Harold Wynne's 10 crewmates, I searched the CWGC database for their casualty details. I found that all 10 are officially missing and Thus are commemorated on the Singapore Memorial only. Only Wynne has a known grave in a war cemetery.

So Harold Wynne was the only one to be seen to bail out. He was captured, incarcerated, and probably murdered by the Japanese. Of the eleven-man crew of KH250, only Wynne's body was recovered for reburial post-war.

This incident is completely independent from the ordeal of the KH326 crew on 6 June 1945. J.J.P. Perron may have been creWed. with Wynne at some point, perhaps in training, but they dled In separate circumstances and were on different Liberator squadrons in India.

I highly suspect that the information about the alleged ninth KH326 crewman, attributed by Don Timmermans to his father Dick (pilot Arie Timmermans' brother), directly relates to Wynne. Don told me that his dad had a copy of the 1945 Circumstantial Report, which listed the names, ranks, Service numbers, and crew positions of the full KH326 crew. It is very possible that when Dick was searching for details about his brother's fate, someone -- perhaps at the local Canadian Legion post where Dick was a member -- showed him a copy of *"They Shall Grow Not Old"*.

They then matched each name on the 1945 report to its corresponding entry in the book. This would have led them to the slight error in the J.J.P. Perron details, with the reference to crewmate "H. Wynne" dying in Japanese hands on SouthAndaman Island a few weeks after KH326 went down. It would have seemed to make sense; Dick could not have known the book's error. Harold Wynne was just another RAF Liberator airman flying from India who died in SouthEast Asia, but whose downing and death were unrelated to the Timmermans crew. (There are many errors in the book, though it is a superb and valuable book.)

Dick said that only the initials of the ninth man aboard KH326 were known. Here's my take on that. Only Harold Wynne's first initial, H, was given in *"They Shall Grow Not Old"*, not his full name. It is easy to understand how Don was led to his conclusion of "initials only" when, in fact, it was "first initial only, and surname". I will query Don again to see what he thinks of my theory.

I think I've just solved this part of the mystery...though there is always a chance that I was wrong. But, reviewing the circumstantial evidence, I'd say that there was NO AGENT aboard KH326 who parachuted from the aircraft, was captured, and who died weeks later.

The personnel file of J.J.P. Perron at the National Archives of Canada could reveal something here. Maybe I can call on a connection to peruse this file and those for the other seven KH326 crewmen.

By the way, I have a great connection at the Imperial War Museum: Dr. Rod Bailey, who is writing a book about -- of all things -- some of the unSun.g heroes of Special Duties flying in WW II. I have helped Rod considerably with one such hero, who Among many other incredible accomplishments in the war, commanded 159 Squadron Liberators for 6 Months in 1944 and revolutionised the distance/bomb load/supply load capabilities in this theatre of war where distances were so vast. Rod came to Washington DC in late '05, and we had a great evening together at a Malaysian restaurant called Penang in downtown DC.

He's busy with his many duties, but I could run this past him at some point and see what he thinks. First, however, I'll run it past Don Timmermans for his point of view. I am hoping that Don can yet find some written notes that his father left in a folder or somewhere, which might give more evidence. Because I know that Dick (Don's dad) was a member of the local Canadian Legion, I suspect that one of the old timers in the Blind River, Ontario Group will remember some details. Hope so.

Thanks for the news that Blair Agnew believes that it was Fleet Air Arm choppers that did the pick up. Certainly it is understandable that Blair's memory is vague on this. Unfortunately, the only way to verify it is to slog through the RAF heli squadron records at Kew and hope it's not a waste of time.

42. __23 March 2007__   **Matt Poole to Joe Plant,**

I had rushed off my earlier analysis this morning, and now that I reread what I wrote this morning, I see a small hole in my logic. My explanation about initials is not quite valid. Don Timmermans' father Dick said he found out that a ninth man was aboard KH326, known only by initials. I'd surmised that Dick's source of this info might very well have been the J.J.P. Perron entry in the book "They Shall Grow Not Old", but I somehow missed the fact that the entry was not "H. Wynne" (first initial only), but simply "Sgt. Wynne". The complete book quote:

"One other member of the crew, Sgt. Wynne, bailed out, was captured and imprisoned at South Andaman Island and died on August 17, 1945."

I'd suggested that perhaps what Dick Timmermans may have been told is that the first name of the ninth man aboard KH326 was unknown, rather than both his first and last names.

OOps...Nevertheless, it may still turn out to be true that the source of the information relayed to Dick Timmermans was the book. Maybe not...so much for solving a mystery with confidence. Perhaps Don Timmermans can still solve this one for sure.

And certainly F/Sgt Harold Wynne was NOT aboard KH326. No doubt about it! Just thought I'd correct my error.

43.   24 March 2007:   Joe Plant to Matt Poole,

Antony Gordon called me from Cape Town yesterday and said he had sent the maps which I believe pinpoint not only the crash site but also the DZ for the Force 136. I shall have to be patient. He also said it was very interesting and an incredible story with the new twist to the ninth member. He suggested it could also have been a Chinese / Malay person going to join Chin Peng (the very person we were in arms against 48-60).

44.   24 March 2007   Gordon to Blair Agnew Joe Plant

Dear Blair and Joe

1. Joe gave me the D Z as to be 101 E., 06 N. this is on the big Melaya 1950 map and is the NW corner of the Betong sheet 2J1 which I sent Blair and I made copies of. I also made copies of the SW corner of the sheet N of Betong 2 F/13 as this is also the DZ. This Z is in the middle of deep jungle and in big hills **so is totally unsuitable for parachuting supplies!**

However about a mile N and NE of the given DZ there is the big River S BAHO which has a wide valley and our 1953 maps also has a track along it. This is also shown on the Betong cheat sheet disappearing in a NW direction.

2. Joe tells me they could have been an extra, unarmed, passenger in the Liberator. Quite possible an officer or signaller going to Force 136??? This valley would be an excellent DZ for supplies and a "passenger" it would probably have been visible if the aircraft had been anywhere near his route to the given DZ. The track would help the rapid dispersal and carry on the way of the supplies into the hills well known to Force 136. Various books on Force 136 mention men being dropped.

3.   When looking at the match carefully, with a magnifying glass, I see a slight difference in the given heights. The big 1950 map gives a height of the highest hill about 2 miles NE of the crash site, Bukit Lata Papalang as 4155 feet but the 1958 1 inch betong sheet gives it as 4152 feet. This shows that there was a change noted so obviously the heights were being rechecked.

4.   I understand, and I remember being told this at the time of the crash discovery, that the Liberator was flying on "Auto Pilot"I wonder if any heights were recovered from the altimeter. I suspect that they just did not know----had not been told-- the very high hills in the area. We certainly, even in the early 1950s, found the maps inaccurate at times so often regarded them as a useful bit of paper! I wonder if we will **ever** be able to discover what heights they were briefed for. I know from four years personal experience with the fleet air arm, that this is one of the most important items to be included in any sortie brief. One would get "stick" it one was wrong at the post strike debrief!! And our chaps were in highly sophisticated aircraft, (Buccaneers) with radar etc., And good maps! It is easy, now, to be boys after the event but one must remember that in 1944 things and procedures were much simpler than now with things like GPS etc

5 . Joe's latest another letters : I think the earlier choppers into the site were RAF but I think I remember refuelling the 13 or 15 later flights which were RN (848 and 845 squadrons). The RN flew the US Sikorsky 51S had a much better payload than the R AF who had the British copy.

6.   I was the MTO (Transport Qfficer) for 1RHF at Kroh at the time and when John Staheli's first signal came in everything stopped, with the efforts put in to help first JS and then Blair Agnew with him. I think Ken Todd was the intelligence (Operations) officer with the wonderful Lt/Col Tim Hope Thompson as CO I would have thought there should be a Battalion Ops. Report in the War Diary which went, I am pretty certain, to Brigade Division and HQ Melaya every week. Ken died some years ago but was succeeded by David Balfor Scott who lives at Brampton (PH. (01899) 830430). I think his memory, like a lot of us, is not too good. But he has is letters to his parents for all his Service (in India with the BW, 1 RSF in Germany, Korea at Brigade HQ, Depot RSF Ayr, 1 RSF Melaya etc,. I just wonder if he has anything by chance on the Liberator??

I hope these thoughts may be of interest

Anthony Gordon

45.   24 Mar 2007   Blair Agnew to Antony Gordon cc Joe Plant

Thank you for your two emails. I will try to answer all the points which you raised and whilst the answers may not be in the same order as the questions, I hope everything will covered.

The first and most important thing is that I now have the operational diary kept by D Coy and specifically by Gordon. This diary covers all their Ops. and I have a full report of the whole of Op. Unity. Even more helpful, the diary has all the maps and these are marked up! Until I got this, I had not realised that D Coy were lifted in at start of the Op. I now believe that they started well North and East of where we were operating.

Now to specifics; the crash site is clearly stated in the report to be at 818300.on the map, bearing the legend in Red Cross is "LZ FOR EVAC OF ARMS BEING CRASHED AIRCRAFT" and the GR here is 818301 or 818302; it is hard to differentiate but this confirms to my memory of the proximity of the LZ to the crash. The LZ was cut on high ground and was in fact on the site of that CT. Camp. Again this is confirmed as it was from the LZ/CTcamp that we could see a light at night which gave us cause to go and search for it, thereby nearly losing John down the cliff! 12 Platoon made their camp round the edge of the LZ and in due course we joined them there.

When 12 Platoon were brought out they had to move to a LZ GR 881346 and when we were lifted out we also had to go there for the lift. I think this is significant as 881346 is lower in altitude than 818302 and therefore was more suitable for lifting troops than the higher one. My memory is that we were lifted out by the RAF and not the Navy but obviously I could be mistaken.

What is clear from the report is that it was the Navy who did the evacuation of the weapons from the crash.

The entry in the diary for 'Friday 3rd. reads;

Helicopter with RAF pers arrived in approximate 09:30 hrs Took them down to examine the wreckage also Staff Sergeant from War Graves Commission. RAF removed portions of a/cfor identification. War Graves Cmmission Sergeant looked for remains But could not find none. Party finally left with "spoils" at approximately 16:00 hours. I. O. Came in with helicopter and briefed us on further task. This was to Patrol an ambush along Gore border track to our N andE within our area. All weapons and all visitors left the same night. Sergeant Fulcher and War dog evac Dog handler and dog arrived.

I cannot imagine that the Navy would have let their chopper stay for the whole day doing nothing and so I think it is clear that they made the various flights that you were aware of.you may well say that the report says nothing about the chopper being from the Navy, but Joe's friend Jacko found the record at Yeovilton showing that 855 Squadron flew in and removed kit on that day.

[Author Note Refer to 12 Mar. Jacko to Joe E/M Jacko's verbal comment was They were not the best kept records very brief to say the least]

{ An inspection party were lifted to a crashed Liberator on the Siamese border and arms and ammunition from the crash were lifted out. A dog handler and his dog were lifted out and replacements were flown in. A passenger and 600 lbs of freight were carried.

Rehearsals for the Queen's fly past were held ....}

Cont. My memory is very clear that when I met up with John, he told me that the so-called R AF experts were very uncomfortable in the jungle and their top priority seemed to be to get out again. In today's language their examination of the bones which were found could be described as "cursory"at best or perhaps" cavalier ". The Jocks were not vastly impressed!

When I arrived I was also told that the examination of the aircraft and shown that the auto pilot was set and the radio frequency was clear. I would have thought that these details would have been checked and recorded by the RAF "experts" but may be that would have delayed the departure! If they did record it, then the RAF crash report should show that but Joe's research has shown that details are sparse.

With regard to the possibility that there was a ninth person on board, I think this might be a bit of a red herring. We believe that the crew did not escape and were Killed in the crash but no one can state with certainty that they were eight or nine men on board just as no one can say that two or three bailed out. For the same reason it would seem to me that the fate of one member of those on board was the fate of them all. I would also imagine that it would have made sense for the agent, if there was one, to have been dropped on the same DZ as the supplies.

Finally: I confirm that Ken Dodd was the I. O. And although I have spoken to David B-S I am not sure that he had even arrived. I did ask him if he had any info, but he had none.

The strange thing is that I can see in my minds eye the ground as though it were under my feet. If you imagine the LZ as a rectangle with the long side running left to right, then the ground fell away from the top side down to a straight where the washing areas were, and from the bottom right corner a track rundown a ridge following an reversed "S"shape and came to a stream. Approximately 10 to 15 yards before you cross that stream there was a slit trench with another a little further up the hill towards the LZ. I hope this may be useful.

46.   25 March 2007:   Matt Poole to Joe Plant,

It most certainly is possible that there was a 9th person aboard KH326, although we know for certainty that it was not Harold Wynne of 355 Squadron. But a Chinese or Malay agent, or even a British agent? Surely a possibility. Don Timmermans is asking around, but chances are we shall never get to the bottom of this mystery. Yesterday I phoned all of the "Andrews" listings in the Sudbury, Ontario phone book. No luck, BUT...

One gentleman writes occasionally for the Sudbury newspaper and knows the editors. He is a bit of a historian, too, and he has offered to personally pester the editors regarding the printing of an appeal for the kin or friends of KH326 crewman Harry Andrews. I'd written to the two Sudbury newspapers last weekend, but most newspapers never reply, even if they print the appeal. So having an ally who can directly bring this to the attention of the editors is a great bit of luck on my part.

Another Andrews gentleman I phoned comes from 'NEWFOUNDLAND'. When I related the story of the hornets forcing the RSF men to scatter, leading to the discovery of the Liberator, this man gasped. Said he had goosebumps, because he remembers hearing this very story back in 'NEWFOUNDLAND'. Huh??? Not only that, but he swears that there was a local family in 'NEWFOUNDLAND' named Andrews. And he believes there was a Harry Andrews married to Isabella, or Henry married to Isabella. Our Harry Henry Andrews was the son of Henry and Isabella Andrews, but three different sources say they were from Sudbury, Ontario.

I don't think the gentleman on the phone was pulling my leg. He sounded like a kind hearted man. Well, now I need to dig a little deeper and acquire the wartime address of the Andrews family.

Was there a 1955 newspaper story on this crash, after all, that the gentleman actually did read in 'NEWFOUNDLAND' back then???

ARGHHHHH!!! These mysteries keep intensifying.

[Authors note: Yes on the 19ᵗʰ Novemeber 2018. I did find a newspaer article in the Straits Times issue 2 June 1955 under the heading: -

Warime arms spotted at wreck

A Royal Air Force team will leave here tomorrow to inspect the wreckage of a wartime Liberator bomber discovered by a security force Patrol 2,800 feet above sea level near Kroh on the Malay Siam border.
<u>*One of their tasks*</u> *will be to recover a large stock of guns and ammunition found in the wreckage.*
An R AF spokesman said today that the plane is believed to have crashed sometime in 1945 it is possible that it was ferrying arms to Malayan guerrillas in the jungle at the time the aircraft carried the normal armaments of a war time Liberator plus a number of sten guns and other small arms. The plane crashed on a heavily forested ridge it carried a crew of from 10 or 12 men. A Patrol the Royal Scots Fusiliers discovered the wreck last month but could not report the find until they came out of the jungle on monday. The Patrol was taking part in the joint Siamese Malayan operations on the border. End.

[Authors Note] The report was confusing They the RAF. Did not remove the small arms. Number of persons in the Liberator 10 or 12 ? The RSF's reported the Find on the same day. Not after coming out of the jungle.

You asked about the Dellis connection to the Dominican Republic. I had a long chat with Don Dellis' niece, who lives maybe 30 miles from me. Lovely woman. She explained the family's link to Canada.

Her great-grandfather was a Greek sponge/conch fisherman who married a British woman and lived in the Turks and Caicos Islands (UK, North of Haiti/Dominican Republic, and at the southEast end of the Burmudas). Their son, Don Dellis' father George, took over the business eventually. George's brother-in-law set up a shipping business in the Dominican Republic, so George and his wife (I don't have her name) relocated there.

In fact, they had their own island. Sound like they prospered economically. It was a wonderful, enriChin life for the family. There were four boys and one girl. All were sent off to boarding schools in Canada or the US -- what culture shock, what climate shock!! Don actually went to a military preparatory school in the US and disliked it. I'm not sure if he switched to go to Upper Canada College, where I know his brother John went. Must learn more facts still.

All the brothers were smart and athletic. Alexander became a pilot in the RCAF and served in the UK. I don't know squadron details. David became a US citizen and served in the Pacific. John served in the Canadian military.

Marilyn Dellis Higgs, with whom I spoke, is the daughter of their sister Effie. Alexander met some S. African bloke on the boat returning him from the UK to Canada and told the guy to phone his sister, Effie. Bingo! They married. Lived mostly in the Cape Town area. Effie now has severe dementia and lives with Marilyn and her family. Don was the youngest. The family did not want him to join up, but you know these young lads. The war was exciting, AND many felt compelled to actively get involved in the fight to beat tyrrany.

47. <u>26 March 2007:</u>   Joe Plant to Matt Poole,

Your latest info re Don Dellis' brother John, to be honest, disturbs me. This guy has been waiting 60 years + for some news about his brother, and somehow, I have linked the past with the present, with the results still to be defined. Possibly at the end of the day, it will only be an assumption as to the cause of his death along with others. But I admire you for finding John, and his rendition of how it happened, which brings a new twist: A STORM...but a very close possiblity to the real fate of KH326?

Sims' letter to Don's parents suggests he ditched into the sea but HE REPORTED THAT KH326 WAS FLYING NORMALLY, SOUTH OF BUNTING. SO THAT NEVER HAPPENED. Was this a point where Sim's could not relate the possibility that they had crashed inland and been captured by the Japs, which was a worse fate than drowning?? I don't know, but I would assume that his letter gave some compassion to Don's parents. Everyone knew what treatment was given to POWs. Just another theory of mine.

Back to the crash. It was found basically intact. The centre section had been on fire and burnt clothing was found. Was this caused by a strike by lightning? The rain was blinding and they could not see where they were heading. Auto pilot set on, and if it was too late to pull up, why did neither Timmermans nor Dellis knock out auto pilot and take hold of the controls, bearing in mind they were gaining altitude and steaming full power at about 250 mph??

I have spoken to both Blair and Antony; the latter, the Transport Officer, was on the scene when the chopper arrived, so he was aware of the situation. They informed me that they firmly believe the crew perished in the crash. Another thing which Antony reminded me about was insects. Termites, to be precise, apart from other wild animals looking for prey. These buggers eat everything, and as he said, it was almost 10 years to the day when they found the Liberator. Things rot bleedin' quickly in the jungle, and they - excuse my phrasoligy - "would have made a bean's feast of any remains." Hence, no bodies were found apart from burnt articles of clothing and a few bones???

I pondered long and hard over the times. It has bugged me about the 01.00 drop time and the 16.45 sight time. What did they do with the 7 hours, make a trip to Singapore and back? JOKE. I believe one thing was missed. Everything points to their takeoff time as 8.58, sighting 16.45. I believe their T/O time was Ceylon local time, not GMT, and whilst flying @250 mph, they were catching up on time as normal flights always do. So the flying time at sighting would be about 8 hours flying time. Another assumption. I'm not a navigator.   As you say, speculations, speculations.

48.   26 March 2007   Matt Poole to Joe Plant,

Oh, brother, have I had luck finding things out over the weekend. In short, I found Gordon Hercus, the rear gunner on the Lib of S/Ldr Sims, and he gave me TREMENDOUS detail. In short, he said the cumulonimbus storm they flew through near the coast of Malaya was mild compared to some he'd experienced. He said that storm on 6 June was NOT SCARY! Tame is one of the words he used to describe it. He believes it was probably not a major factor in the demise of KH326. Of course, all it takes is one lightning strike, as you suggested. But if struck by lightning near Bunting, a fire would have brought them down in pieces eventually...they were loaded with petrol. Given the relatively intact nature of the wreck, except for the fire, I can't imagine that a lightning strike 50 or so miles away could bring the Lib down in a controlled glide. The usual gets inserted here: Who the hell knows??

49.   29 March 2007:   Joe Plant to Matt Poole,

One thing for sure is that as it disappeared into the storm clouds it was gone, AND it still had 50 miles to go. The ravages of a storm, as they flew through it, cannot be revealed. Nobody knows, but you can bet your bottom dollar it was not a joy ride.

Your constant communication with other members or families slowly brings out the information that will reveal a ton when all is submitted and collated. On my part I was expecting to receive the maps from South'Africa today, but I think the Forked Stick Carrier was gorged by lions Still waiting. However, I have arranged to meet with Blair Agnew. Wednesday for a brief meeting in Exeter, half way between our residents. Hopefully, by then, I will have received maps and, together with the report, will send out hard copies. Later I will visit the National Archives in London to see what goodies they reveal. At present I am in limbo just waiting.

50.   29 March 2007   Joe Plant to Matt Poole, again,

I have pondered over your recent e-mails and have found discrepancies in some of the evidence you have received from other sources. Not your problem, but I believe some of the evidence contributed to the final fate of the KH326. The following are my observations and theories associated with the new evidence gained, but we have to start off from Ceylon.

a) I suspected, and I agree with your point: the local Ceylon time was the basis for times stated in the Circumstantial Report of 25/7/45. Enough said.

b) Both planes on the mission were bowsered up the night before takeoff.

c) Sims was allocated a pristine Liberator for the mission [**Author note: Matt found out, since proven not to be true; KH326 had been with the squadron since at least 12 March 1945**], and his old plane was to be flown by Timmermans. Timmermans obviously knew of the problem, regarding what the old plane had been through, and was not happy at the thought of flying it, whereas Sims knew his old plane and was happy to fly it. Subsequently, at the last minute at the end of the tarmac both crews swopped planes and took off.

d) I now understand that both planes went on the inward flight. I had thought previously that Sims was on his outward flight when he spotted Timmermans near Bunting.

e) Somewhere close to Malaya Simms picked up Tokyo Rose, who informed them that they had water in the petrol and they were destined to die on that mission. The crew took this to heart, as they had been purposely singled out. The Japs knew of the incoming mission (which is another factor in the equation). They were worried and frantically checked the petrol for water. Radio silence between the planes was paramount, so no contact was made to Timmermans.
How did Rosie know??? Possibly there was a spy watchign the fuel load or who was part of the team which contacted Rosie, also possibly informing her (the Japs) that Sims was in a new plane?

[Authors note: Ref Matt:Joe later told me that "Tokyo Rose" was his generic term for the Japanese radio broadcaster, although he knows this was not THE Tokyo Rose, a female broadcaster situated in Japan.]

Timmermans was contacted by Minneriya Base at 12.18 hrs about the water in the petrol. How did Base know? Possibly picked up Rosie's chat. Anyway, they said it would not effect them?

Circumstantial Report: how far towards landfall was KH326 when this message was received? Also, why did they not contact Sims' plane? (Sims had already been informed by Rosie, the Japs thinking he was flying the pristine aircraft.) So Timmermans and his crew and passenger? were destined to meet their fate.

f) The last sighting of KH326 was near Bunting. Hercus was a rear gunner and at Action Stations, being in the target area. Their plane was either flying alongside or in front of Timmermans. He possibly was the last, or Sims and the Co-Pilot were the last, to sight KH326 before it disappeard into the storm cloud. They, too, would have entered the clouds and got enveloped in blackish grey. The bulk of the Liberator would have caused some cloud disturbance at its rear and Hercus, as he stated, was not in a SCARY situation. However up front might have been a different matter. Now, seeing that Hercus stated the effect of water in the tanks had them jumping about, the same would have happened to the Timmermans crew. Lightning hitting Timmermans' plane anywhere near Bunting: you can rule that out; otherwise, it would have been spotted by Sims' crew. And seeing they were flying at 50-200 feet(per one statement) or 500-700 feet (another statement) below Japanese radar, the possiblity of them coming down near the sea or inland was nil. They were still airbourne, and it is now a known fact that they were climbing and crashed into a mountain at an altitude of 3000+ feet.

g) Sgt. Wynne, mentioned in the J.P.P.Perron biography: is this a red herring? Wynne died about 2 Months after J. P. P. Perron went missing on the 6th of June. (How strange: 1 year after D-Day 1944)

h) I do not doubt Gordon Hercus. He was there. But there is still a lot of speculation going on and becoming more positive up to the last sighting. Will study further and figure out some more queries.

50. **30 March 2007   Blair Agnew to Antony Gordon cc Joe Plant**

Thank you for all the maps which arrived today. Strange to say the maps that were in Gordon's diary are rather better as they seem to have a little more detail with regard to streams. At the LZ from where the weapons were extracted there are an extra couple of streams shown which conforms to my memory. I have tried to draw a sketch plan in this email, but my IT skills are not up to it and I have just deleted my effort as it would have been incomprehensible. I am meeting up with Joe on Wednesday next and we will then be able to go through the info which we have.

51. **1. April 2007   Shaharom Ahmad to Joe Plant**

Any news regarding the map and the coordinates? My friend managed to decode QY 300814 into QT 300814 found it was close to Lake Muda jungles. Right now QY was at sea... So he changed it to QT where it was under Kedah state. Keep in touch.

52. **1.April 2007   Matt Poole to Joe Plant**

The June page from Gordon Hercas' logbook is attached.

you will see that Gordon flew as a passenger with Arie on third June Gordon said with a laugh, that this must have been a booze run.

On 6 June, Gordon take off time is listed as 0 8.00, in "Lib 162"this was serial number KH 162. He flew as a G, A,, on

Squadron Leader O. A. H. (Haig) Sims crew. The 'OPS.' referred to an op or mission with the hours being added to his total needed to complete a tour of Ops. The aircraft flew from Minneriya to Melaya and back to Minneriya. Total time aloft 9hr 10 min of daylight flying an eight-hour 45 minutes of night flying 17 hours 55 minutes total.

Gordon also noted F/O Timmermans -- missing. The reference to FIGHTER is not in reference to the loss of Arie Timmerman's; there was no knowledge of fighter activity that day. Instead fighter was the drop zone code. Other drop zones listed in June were FUNNEL, SERGENT and CARPENTER . I note in the surviving July 45 357 Squadron records that FIGHTER was a drop zone destination then, as well. So it's not to be confused with Japanese fighter aircraft attacking: Source Matt Poole.

The times in the logbook are usually not exact to the minute. Often within a few minutes, but rounded to the nearest five minute interval, or sometimes to the nearest 15 minute interval. Now if only the time mystery can be resolved soon! **Attached is copy of The Log Book.**

[Authors Note] Ref. is made to the Map on page 17 indicates the code names for Guerrilla Forces under Force 136 - FIGHTER & SERGEANT were code names for. AJUF 8 operstng in Kedah - FUNNEL was code name for AJUF 5

323

operating in Perak – CARPENTER was code name for AJUF 4 operating in Johore. Others were as per shown on map. Indevidual Drop Zones of dates, times and Grid reference, were agreed between Force 136 and HQ in Ceylon.

53.   2. April 2007   Blair Agnew to Shaharom Ahmad cc Joe Plant

My name is A.J. B. Agnew. In 1955 was serving in Malaya with 1 Battalion the Royal Scots Fusiliers. We took part in Operation Unity in the area of the Thailand border. 12 Platoon of D Company 1 RSF fou nd the remains of KH 326. I was ordered to move North to join up with 12 Platoon and moved with my men of 7 Platoon and did so. I visited the crash site and saw the wreckage of the aircraft. I have in my possession the map of the area and on the map the exact location of the crash site is clearly marked as to is the site of the LZ from which the weapons, which were the cargo on the aircraft, were evacuated. The grid ref of the crash site is 818300 NOT repeat NOT 300814. The grid ref of the elder said from which the weapons were evacuated is 818302. The LZ is approx 2500 yds West South West of -BUKIT LATA PAPALANG. There is, or was, a track winding down from the LZ, which passes approx 10 yards from the crash site. This winding track has been used by the Terrorist and had two slit trenches dug at points where the track curved. These trenches would have been dug for protection of the Terrorist camp which was sited at the location which became the LZ. The crash site is approx 250 yards from the LZ.

For the avoidance of doubt grid references are looked at in the following manner the NORTHING grid line directly to the left of the site is 81. Dividing that's where to the right NORTHING 81 into units of 10 gives the information that the site lies on the NORTHING 818. Similarly, moving up the map, the grid line running West to East and just below the crash site is 300. From this the site can be identified as 818 300.

Although the experts who were sent in by the RAF said there were no remains of the crew, we who were there, were always convinced that the crew had been on board at the time of the crash and that they had died on the aircraft. The presence of remains a Mae West, a flying jacket together with personal weapons and flying gloves point in that direction. I hope this information assist you in your search. The incident remained very vivid in my memory.

54.   2 April 2007   Shaharom Ahmad to Joe Plant

Any new rules regarding the match and the coordinates? My friend managed to decode the QY 300814 into QT 300814 found it was close to Lake Muda jungles. Right now QY was at sea . So that he changed it to QT where it was under Kedah state.

55.   2 April 2007   Matt Poole to Joe Plant

From Gordon Hercus (on the other Lib) I received four photos of Aire Timmerman's yesterday, plus a copy of Gordon's logbook page covering the 6 June operation. You guessed it.... It adds to the confusion regarding time! Gordon's book says his Liberator took off at 0800 which is 58 minutes before the circumstantial report says Timmerman's and crew took off.

Gordon said that he can't remember if the aircraft took off one after the other. He said it is possible that the Timmerman's Lib was late due to the switch in aircraft, because they were going to a new Lib, maybe the model and a few new whistles and bells that Timmerman's and crew to get familiar with before they took off. I know that S/Ldr Sims (Gordon's)Lib was KH 162, which was built in Fort Worth, Texas in construction block be 20 4J – 80 – CF. The Timmerman's Lib, KH 3 to 6, was the – 20 4J – 90 – CF, later construction block built in Fort Worth. I don't know if the Libs were identical, or if the latter block at some changes.

Gordon said it was possible that if KH 326 took off late, it eventually caught up with his Lib, since the distances were so great.

I just don't think this is logical.... Wasting so much petrol to catch up, when running short of petrol could spell disaster. And then after water in petrol bowser message reached KH 326, Timmerman's would have wanted to be extra conservative.

Soooooooo..... I have a new hunch... Gordon's logbook could be a clue that the takeoff time of KH 326 was around 0800, not over 0900. If so, local time in India was 4/5 hours ahead of GMT. This is a thought.

Gordon is sending me all pages of his logbook. In July 357 Squadron records are extremely detailed on individual aircraft/takeoff times... Always recorded in GMT here! Maybe I can compare Gordon's logbook with the official records in July and once and for all figure out this time mess.

But until I get to the bottom of this, it is not worth you wasting your time speculating on this Aspect of the mystery. Nothing more now except attached photos sent they show Aire Timmerman is the blonde one he looks like he could have been an the of the American football player if he wanted! Strong! In the photo of the men in the back of the truck, whoever is to the viewers right of Timmerman's is definitely an athlete was either been very active around the farm say or has lifted weights. Attached.photo. by kind permission of Matt Poole.

56.   3 April 2007   Shaharom Ahmad to Blair Agnew cc Joe Plant

Thank you for your email. I believe on your story regarding the grid ref. Which now 818300 and not 300814 which stated by RAF. I hope that you could scan the map show the exact location of the wreckage and send it to me via email as attachment stop right now, we don't have any details map of the area mentioned so far. I have to send a request to Malaysian Army which it will take a few weeks for them to reply.

From your story, there is no doubt that the crews still there. Based from the findings like flying glass, shoes and personal weapons clealy show the proof. Our RAF must thinking to cut short trip and the investigation and mention that the crew were not on board. I don't think that the crews were crazy to bail out from Japanese held territory, which the plane was not damaged at all. The plane might damaged and crashed landed which Killed entire crew on impact . If the CT found the remains and buried it near the wreck site. There must be someone survive from the crashed but later died of injuries.

Based from your story, we will start to reopen back our research and hope we will find the wreckage and trace the graves and hope to rebury them in Taiping

57. 3 April 2007   Blair Agnew to Shaharom Ahamd cc Joe Plant

I believe that the aircraft either was struck by lightning,and caught fire or else it caught fire when it crashed. The fuselage had clear signs of fire and the Mae West and flying jacket had been damaged by fire. There is no possibility of the body's been found by the CTs. If they had found them, they would have found all the weapons any ammunition. It will be better if I sent you a photocopy in colour of the map. The map as all the original markings on it which were made by the Patrol which found the. It is in colour and therefore will be much easier to use to identify the site. Please let me have your address and I will send you the map. Research and hope we will find the wreckage and trace the graves and hope to rebury them in Tiaping for now I wait your email together with the attached map and thanks for your kindness.

58. 7 April 2007   Joe Plant to Matt Poole,

Good meeting. Blair Agnew was a National Serviceman like myself but an Officer. Copy of map and excerpts from report in snail mail post to you. Should receive Tuesday.

59. 9 April 2007   Blair Agnew to Joe Plant

I have been giving some thought to the cargo in the plane and I think that there are certain questions which if answered, might prove interesting. I do not know anything about the weapons which were the defensive arms for the. Aircraft, more importantly, how ammo was carried for them. According to the Patrol report approx. 2000 rounds of unspecified ammo were recovered. To the best of my memory, a Sten gun mag holds 20 rounds and as 22 were found I think it would be reasonable to surmise that there would have been sufficient ammo to say 2 mag's per gun. That would mean approx. 850 to 1,000 rounds of .9mm. A Bren mag.holds 28 rounds and I would have thought that at least 50 to 100 rounds would have been sent with the gun. There is no mention of .38 ammo although there was 18 revolvers of that calibre and 1 Police special revolver. There is no mention of .303 ammo and my thoughts here is the reception party from Force 136 may well have been armed with US carbines, which are .300 calibre, In fact that was the weapon I myself carried. The really interesting question surrounds the 2 x .5 Browning. The report says that . 5 ammo was found but does not say how much. I believe that the .5 Browning is belt fed rather than drum or magazine fed. I find it hard to believe that each gun would have no more than 500 rounds. It is also a well known fact that air gunners always tested their guns shortly after take off and so they would probable have fired a burst of say 20 rounds to test each gun. I think your contact in the US wo has been doing all his research on Liberators may well know all about the armaments of the plane and also how much ammo they carried for each gun. The point I am making is that there may well be belts or drums of ammo somewhere near the crash unless they went off on impact .If that was the case . then it begs the question as to why the rounds that were found did not go off. The pointis that the guns themselves were not damaged by fire . It is a real Puzzle!

60. 10 April 2007   Joe Plant to Shaharom Ahmad

Ref. Blair Agnew's message to Shaharom . Please understand regarding the point of the 2nd. Liberator found. Was NOT repeat NOT found by the 1st. RSF's. This was only a verbal statement made at the time. It the 2nd. Liberator was found later after the RSF's had left Malaya . Another Inf. Battalion found it. I am in the process of trying to etablish which Inf Battalion that was??? But it does point to the fact. It was the SEREMBAN Liberator which you have already found Many Congratulations.

By now you should have received the package I sent you.

Another point I wish to make. Blair asked about the ammunition for the Liberators Browning M/guns these would definitely be belt fed for contiuous firing during attack, all aircraft were fitted with this type of weapon. Matt Poole sent me a photo of McLeod Wop/Airgunner with belts of ammo dangling over his shoulders. There was no way that a magazine was used to feed those M/guns. I trust this clarifies the situation.

61.   Sent by Joe Plant to Matt Poole by snail mail, received 12 April 2007: .

Excerpts from the 1955 "Malay Emergency" Action diary of the Royal Scots Fusiliers, reporting the discovery and investigation of the wreck of

RAF 357 Squadron Liberator KH326 (lost 6 June 1945)

Blair Agnew on behalf of the 1st. Royal Scots Fusiliers gave me permission to use the report, in the story I was researching and compiling information on the Malayan Emergency. The full report can be read in Chapter 13 1955

FRI. 27 MAY

Force 1

Started today on the task of searching the four map squares. Two Patrols went out to Grid Ref. 8031, 8131. Nothing found except game tracks along tops. of ridges. Going in this area quite difficult. Steep hills, thick undergrowth and a large amount of bamboo near to the streams. No sign of CT activity.

Force 2

Found natural clearing of fern at 881390 and one of bamboo at GR 873393. Both these had been reported as being suspected hill paddi.

SAT. 28 MAY

Force 1

Two Patrols out today to search map squares 8030, 8130. Patrol into area 8030 found nothing but animal trap at 815309 on the way out along ridge. Also elephant tracks along streams in the area. Patrol in 8130 on the way S, whilst following the stream, cut up through bamboo thicket and found the remains of crashed wartime Liberator bomber with British markings on tail and wings. Bomber was found at GR. 818300. Wreckage was scattered about over a considerable area and part of the fuselage had burned out. Clothing, arms, ammunition, grenades, medical eqpt and personal clothing (kit) had been packed in CLE (*Central Landing Establishment*)containers which remained in the bomb bays or were scattered near it. The aircraft was presumed to have been on a supply run for Force 136. Also what we thought to be the charred remains of human bones were unearthed. This was later stated by experts not to be the case. I (*Lt. Stahell*) still feel very sceptical and from personal clothing found later feel quite convinced that crew did not bale out. This find, made by Fus. McGill, the leading scout of Sgt Dummelow's Patrol, was reported to Bn HQ and we started to salvage equp. whilst waiting instructions.

Force 2

Patrolled boundary from 907360 to B.P. 49. No tracks other than intermittent game trail along border. Patrolled GR 9240.

SUN. 29 MAY

Force 1

Salvaging of eqpt continued today. We were told to get out all we could without disturbing wreckage unduly. We asked for tools to dismantle 2 brownings from the rear turret We asked for tools to dismantle 2 brownings from the rear turret which were dropped to us by Auster. By the end of the day we had recovered approx 2000 rounds of .5, .303, .300, .45, .9 mm ammunition, two .5 browning guns, 22 sten-guns, 1 bren gun, 18 .38 revolvers, 1 .38 Police special revolver, 1 .45 US pistol. Two medical kits, an assortment of army clothing. Also 3 survival knives, a charred remains of BD with whistle attached charred flying boots and goggles, a lighter, 1 pr of civilian shoes, charred flying jackets, remains of one Mae Westand navigators protractors. All these latter articles together with the position of the wreck convinced us that some at least of the crew members must have crashed with the aircraft. The amn, with the exception of the .300, was in excellent condition. Of the stens 18 were assembled and undoubtedly would have worked, also about 40 sten mags were Serviceable. The bren was in poor shape externally though the inside of the barrel and working parts were as new. The revolvers if cleaned by an armourer I am certain would almost have worked. The .5 brownings seemed to be in good condition. They had however been adapted for electrical firing and would have needed some modification for use by ground troops With the exception of about 2 pairs of gym shoes all articles of clothing were US. In the medical packs, such items as plaster, bandages, etc, were US. However bottles of iodine, insect repellant, etc, also jars of Whitfields ointment were in perfect condition and were used by Pl Medical Ord. We also salvaged in Serviceable condition two artery forceps, a pair of surgical scissors, three thermometers and a scalpel. All these were immediately appropriated by Pl Med Ord who was hovering around seizing all useful items to make up his kit. All arms and stores were evacuated to base camp. We then started to clean and assemble weapons whilst awaiting instructions as to their disposal.

Force 2

Patrolled to GR 8939 via GR 8739. NTR Continued crop destruction in ladangs.

MON. 30 MAY

Force 1

Received instructions today to cut L.Z. So that experts could be flown in to view wreckage. Requested drop of explosives, saws, axes, etc. Took airdrop of rations & eqpt. Started cutting L.Z. Continued to search a/c but could find nothing more of interest. Searched surrounding area but found nothing but scattered wreckage. Large piece of broken wing was discovered further down the valley next to large tree which had its top broken off. From this we assumed that a/c must have hit tree and thought this might be reason for crash. Searched wreckage for a/c identification number. Which we were unable to find. We were instructed that we were not to move out of M.S. we were in and the Police were Patrolling to our S. Our task was to finish the cutting of the L.Z. as quickly as possible.

Force 2

Made ready to move to L.Z. (2)

TUE. 31 MAY

Force 1

Continued with preparing L.Z. also blasting trees with plastic explosives dropped. Progress was regretably much slower than expected.

Force 2

Moved to L.Z. (2).

WED. 1 JUNE

Force 1

Still cutting L.Z. Work was going rather slowly owing to axes and saws breaking. At the end of the day L.Z. virtually complete. Target day for completion was P.M. 2nd.

Force 2

Received airdrop. Patrolled area around base.

THUR. 2 JUNE

Force 1

L.Z. completed. During the course approx 1430 hrs shooting was heard to the S. of our location. This was 2 single shots followed by burst of automatic fire, 5 – 6 rounds. Took out Patrol immediately and searched around our location but discovered nothing. No further sounds heard. It was discovered subsequently that this shooting was due to the Police who had had a contact. Took our air drop today.

Force 2

Patrolled spur N. of base to GR 863333, also area GR 8835. NTR.

FRI. 3 JUNE *[Matt Poole: This heading was also cut off from my photocopy.]*

Force 1

Helicopter with RAF pers arrived in approx 0930 hrs. Took them down to examine wreckage also S/Sgt from War Graves Commission RAF removed portions of a/c for identification. War Graves Commission Sgt looked for remains but could find none. Party finally left with "spoils" at approx 1600 hrs. I.O. came in with helicopter and briefed us on further task. This was to Patrol and ambush along border track to our N & E within our area. All weapons were evacuated by Heli and all visitors left the same night. Sgt Fulcher & War Dog evac. Dog handler & dog arr.

Force 2

Patrolled to 870368. Also area 8934. NTR.

SAT. 4 JUNE

Force 1

This was observed as a rest day.

Force 2

Ambushed track at GR 864333. Patrolled area of food dump at GR 868338. NTR

62.   **13 April 2007   Matt Poole to Joe Plant**

Yippeee!! Got your materials, and it is so good to now understand where KH 326 came down.

The green maps are printed later than the brown map on the left (which is in the style of the mid-1940s British 1:63. 360 maps of Burma and Siam that I have seen). I am going to try to track down the full originals of these maps, via my employers map library, although this may be difficult. Some of the maps are held in storage in Arizona. So it may be a long process to order copies... And they may not have the maps which cover the general border area in the vicinity of KH 326's crash.

Thanks so much for sending the copies. To be able to see maps and to read the report is a huge. Step forward

Shaharon is making good progress in setting up the team to visit the area. Great news. I have taken the liberty of writing to him, but I should CC you on anything from here onward. I don't want to leave you out of any other thought process/discussion Shaharon and I have from here onward.

63.   **13 April 2007   Sharharom Ahmad Blair Agnew cc Joe Plant**

I received the map and RSF report yesterday (12th Apl) in good order . Thank you very much . I would say that the map will give us extra help to located the wreckage and hope that someone was not found it yet and disturbedthe wreckage and bring her parts out for scrap. The area were still declared as black area under military supervision and it protect the wreckage too from outsider.

I would like to know about her cargo, Did the ammos and weapons were scattered or still wrapped inside drop container? Right now I'll assembled a few people who have experience in jungle trekking (hacking our way into thick jungle) We have to make our way and hope there will e some small tracks leading into mention area. If not we will nedd to make it by ourself.

Thank you very much for your valuable support and wish us giood luck on the expedition. We will give you some udatrs later.

64. <u>13 April 2007</u>   **Matt Poole to Shaharom Ahmad cc Joe Plant**

I have typed up the RSF report and added a few notes of explanation, just in case you need to send this to anyone via email. Also, I have scanned Blair's maps and have enclosed a cropped portion of this at the end of the RSF report. See the enclosed documents. It is a bit large due to the size the scan map. Joe, if this is too large for you let me know and I will simply send you the document without the map added. Then it will be quite small and easy to download.

Shaharom, your Lat/Long is very accurate. I came up with 5° 54' 06" E. 101° 01' 18" (rounded up the seconds) of course it is a bit of guesswork, and each time I look for it I get a slightly different number. The important thing is that we clearly understand the geographical location, within a small fraction. That is exceptionally fortunate.

I have also saved snapshots Google Earth imagery showing the crash site. Joe, I have your address but Shaharom I need your address to send you a CD containing all the images I have so far.

I know how some families might not want to disturb any human remains found. However of the four families I have found so far, nobody has expressed concern over this yet stop

The Canadian government policy is very clear if human remains are found, Canada considers it their duty to recover them, even if the families do not agree. But that is looking far ahead. If remains are found. I feel 100% certain that Canada will immediately start the diplomatic work with Malaysia to be given permission to send a full excavation team. This will be a Canadian project, I believe, and it will not involve the RAF unless one of their representatives wants to come along anyway. I would insist that you Shaharom be a part of the team, if you would want this. Canada has been involved in aircraft wrecks- such as a Canadian creWed. Dakota lost in the Burmese jungle and discovered in the mid-1990's, the Canadians were then allowed in to excavate in deep jungle and this was followed by a reburial ceremony in Taukkan war cemetery outside of Rangoon. A Very moving documentary of this story was produced by the National film board of Canada I cannot help but shed a few tears when I watch it, the love ones of the airmen are interviewed., including the wartime girlFriend of one airman. Very, very touching. And extremely well done. It is available as a videotape from the National film board of Canada but, I don't know if the format is the same as what you would view Shaharom. I think it is only produced in the American/Canadian format and not on DVD hope I'm wrong though.

As I think I mentioned in an earlier email, the problem with Canada concerning my two other RAF Liberator wrecks investigation is two fold.
1.   they involve Burma and politics with Burma a very challenging.
2.   The Canadian government authorities do not want to spend Canadian taxpayers money UNLESS they can be certain that human remains will be recovered Canada does not want to go all the way to the Far East and find nothing but shattered machinery.

However, because KH 326 came down in Melaya could be a different story that's why am hoping that major Jim McKillip will be able to convince his bosses to spend a little money, even though human remains have not yet been found.. I will phone him next week, that said my guess is still that Canada wants others to find the bones first. And then they will spend money too bad that Malaysia/Thailand politics will make your trip to the site more difficult (having to go the more difficult route through Malaysia not through Thailand) and I do imagine that there are scattered villages so that you can reach the site. The road may be poor for travel and this could increase but I sense that you enjoy the thrill of the hunt. I have a great friend Clayton Kuhles from Arizona USA who has found something like 6 aircraft in the Hump area so far. We work together well. He trekked far into jungle and mountain country in China India and Burma when no other westerner hss visited in decades and he loves it. Been an out of doors man/adventure who has climbed mountains it is difficult work sometimes very dangerous but that is what brings him great pleasure and a sense of Satisfaction when aircraft are found.

If remains are eventually found, I would think that they would be buried a Kranji not typing as long as there is room in Kranji

Shaharom you have done brilliant work on KL 654 I can just imagine huffing and puffing through the jungle and all that digging and grunting. I wish I could somehow be there with you in May or June or whenever get your trip to KH's 3 to 6 on the road

Joe it appears that one or more lines of Lt. Staheli's personal comments were cut off of the bottom of my copy of the RSF report covering Saturday 28 May perhaps copy received from Blair also missing this? Or if your copy has this further titbit of information could you type it up and email it to me? Many thanks old Chap!

65. <u>13 April 2007</u>   **Shaharom Ahmad to Matt Poole cc Joe Plant**

Thank you again for your email I receive the same map as yours. I've to check with my Google Earth and pinpoint the location might be closer to N.5 degrees 54'06 78" E.101° 01'1527" it seems that we have to start our journey from Malaysia not Thailand

100% will be greater for political issues and troublesome if we entered the border I agree that coming from Thailand is quite easy but better from Malaysia

I don't mind if the wreckage were scattered we can slowly trace down any human remains it will take a few days or weeks but if the wrecks area were disturbed it will be hard for us to trace Like what happened to KL4 case. The area was too deeply disturbed by visitors who visited it enroute to nearby mountain trail. Most of the her parts were missing and luckily some personal effects not rings knife and harness were found untouched very near the wreckage. Most of the equipments, oxygen bottles, emergency axes were removed by local I hope that KH 326 wreckage was untouched

Quite interestingly we found one Type D canister nearby. A large and heavy container if dropping onto cars the car will be smashed beyond recognition but the container was empty. You can send the zip files to me I can opened it here.

I will orgnise my scattered team again an hope May June , will make our way to the site . For Me . we have to use our own expenses and were not being sponsored . Like my friend says to me "Labour of Love" When we gather reasonable funds and manpower we will go there.

I would like to know if we found human remains. That will to the remains? Do the next of kin families want it to be sent home or buried it in a CWGC graves in Taiping or Kranji ? Do they fully agreed on this ? It is quite troublesome for us to take KL654 case where one family want it home but others not agreed.

66.   14 April 2007   Blair Agnew to Shaharom Ahmad cc Joe Plant.

Thank you for your email. it is 50 years since I went into the jungle and so I may be a bit out of date in my knowledge, but I hope you will not be upset if I make some suggestions which I think may help you.

The first thing is that the jungle in that area is very thick the going is very hard. The main reason for that is that there is a lot of bamboo and it has fallen so lies parallel to the ground so that you have to do a lot of crawling through and underneath this bamboo. This makes progress very slow as I told you, on one occasion whilst going to the site of the crash, my Platoon and I only managed to cover 1000 yards in 10 hours! Ground is very rugged with many steep and high ridges. Unless there has been logging in the area, I would doubt whether there is any sign of a track into the area. You should remember that it took us approximately three weeks to get to the area although we were Patrolling which was obviously a factor in slowing us down, I would think that if you were to try to go in from the nearest point on the nearest road, you might take 5 to 7 days to get there.

My preferred solution would be to get onto the border track and make your way along it until you are directly due East of the crash site. Would then have to drop from the border ridge and then climb back up to the next ridge to locate the site of the Landing Zone, the border track was one which was used by animals and is wide enough for one person. It tends to run along ridges and so is reasonably going. The best way in will be by helicopter, but you would have to have an LZ reasonably near the site and that of course would mean that someone would have to go in and cut it.

I look forward to hearing how you get on.

From your last email I see that the Liberator carried 10 Brownings only two were recovered from the wreck and special tools are to be sent in to let the soldiers demount from the aircraft, no report was made of the other 8 guns which should have been there, but I am absolutely sure that they could not have been removed by aborigines and we know that the CT's never found the site. if you look at the report you will see that the weapons were in CLE containers I suspect that any ammo for the Brownings which was not found probably exploded on impact. Good luck and regards wish I was going with you.

67.   14 April 2007   Joe Plant to Matt Poole,

My deepest apology for copies sent [*with some missing lines of text*]. I too was in a rush to catch post so must have handled them wrongly. However Shaharom was sent the full copy. The size of paper was larger than A4. I just took copies of the relevant pages as sent to you.

However, the following are noted [*missing notes in bold*]

SAT. 28 MAY

. . .I (Lt Staheli) stil feel very sceptical and from personal clothng found later feel quite convinced **that crew did not bale out. This find, made by Fus. McGill the leading scout of Sgt Dummelow's Patrol was reported to Bn HQ and we started to salvage equp. whilst waiting instructions.**

THUR. 2 JUNE
Force 2

Patrolled spur N. of base to GR863333 also area GR8835. NTR.

FRI. 3 JUNE [From here forward, already in your possession]

I trust this clarfies the situation. Once again apologies.

I do not think Blair made the marks on the map. This was the original as documented at time.

68.   15 April 2007   Joe Plant to Matt Poole,

As you say, it is amazing how this project reaches out. I pondered awhile over this point with still 4 families for you to search for. You have done an amazing piece of tracking down in the past and no doubt you will suceed. Lady Luck must be on your side.

However, my thoughts went back to six weeks ago when I started on this mystery, never knowing that it would come this far. Upon reflection after you sent me the details of the RAF letters, and unknown at the time and in the past, the fact that the GR was typed wrong. IF it had been CORRECT at the time in 1955, Gerald Howse or Don Dellis' brother and the rest of the crew's relatives would not have suffered the pain of not knowing the fate of that last mission. It would have been cut and dried years ago, and our recent extemely interesting communication would never had happened.

However, the last six weeks have revealed that a **"stupid mistake"**, until corrected last week, was the cause a lot of undue agro/cost to many families and researchers alike.

[Authors note : 'Stupid mistake' That was a bit harsh but at the time in question that was my thoughts Matt commented on this on my above statement. I stand corrected.]

Matts Comment: Yes Gerald Howes nephew of KH326 crewman William McLeod did waste time analysing the QY300814 reference (and plotting it on his website now defunct), but this was not an issue that caused other families great problems. A Grid reference whether correct or incorrect is not plattable Latitude/Longdtitude : one would have to refer to aifficult to access 1950's British/ Military map of the area to translate any grid reference number inti Lat /Long. Only Gerald Howse did this] However, Later 3 years later on approx. 8 Oct 2010 Anthony Gordon raised a query covering the Grid Reference read forward 8 Oct 2010.

69.   14. April 2007   Matt Poole to Joe Plant.

Thanks for setting me straight on the missing lines of the report. It's good to know the names of McGill and Dummelow... Wonder where they are?

I also wrote to a first Battalion RSF veteran Peter O'Reilly, whose email found on the National Malaya & Boneo Assoction site. His granddaughter is his web link, and she wrote back to say that Peter remembers but was not there.

Also found another first Battalion veteran George Masson. He gave his dates in the RSF as 1/10/ 53 to 1/10/55 Presume this is the English date format Not the Bloody American. Flip Flop (Month Day Year)

Good news I finally got through to Gerald Howse in Edmonton Son of KH326 casualty Bill McLeod. Gerald is an intelligent and Friendly bloke. He has some good information which might help me to find next-of-kin of one or more of the 4 remaining airmen whos kin I have not discovered yet. He has letters received by his grandmother (Bill McLeod's mother) from 2 or 3 of the other families and will scan them in due time.

Just for completeness, I am attaching the updated written version of the RSF report which now includes the missing lines you provided, This version for speed in open it does not include the map and image it has a unique file name, so that you will not overwrite the one with the photos. I forgot if I asked you.... Do Blair or Anthony keep in touch with anyone else who was part of the Lib discovery? I know that Lt Staheli has passed away. And how many total 1st Battalion men would have been part of the Patrol which found the Lib? Force 1 not force 2.

One of he photos sent to me by Gordon Hercus aboard S./Ldr Sims' Lib on 6 June 1945 shows crewmen from both the Timmerman's and Sims crew in a truck as they prepare for some hunting fun. Gordon pointed out Timmerman the tall blonde but no one else however I have a photo of George Faulkner of the Timmerman's crew and I compared his face to the athletic big bicep bloke standing to Timmerman's left (viewers right) see the attached photo.

Are, it is amazing how this project reaches out and touches someone, positively, in a way we could not have imagined six weeks ago. You put a query out to Robert Quirk, who contacts me, which starts my involvement in the mystery of KH 326. Then, through Robert, I get an address this of the Burma Bombers Association Members (the final address this, as it has disbanded formally), and one of the names I phoned, of the 357 Squadron veterans listed was Gordon Hercus lots of tell me, and he sends me photos of Harry Timmerman's.crew. I thought it was a good match. In the meantime,I found Kathy Blanchard niece of George Faulkner. I sent her photo and bingo! [Authors Note: Received 4th Apr.]

Sure enough, after I sent the hunting photo to Kathy Blanchard, neice of George Faulkner, she wrote back that it was him. Absolutely thrilled with this photo of her uncle , never seen it before.

Would you be willing to give me the addresses and phone numbers Gordon Blair? I may call them eventually, just to say hi and hear them describe things. Nothing like hearing it from the horses mouth!

70.   15 April 2007   Alan Robertson to Matt Poole

[The 1955 RSF report revealed that Fusiliers McGill had been responsible for the discovery of the KH 326 Liberator wreckage. On 14th of April. I posted a query, regarded McGill and his Patrol leader, Sgt. Dummelow, to the guestbook on the National Malaya & Borneo Veterans Association UK. This is the response]

I received the address of George McGill, [**his addrees deleted**] This is the last known address I have so I hope it is helpful. I was in the RSF George Masson & I now live in Canada Brandon Manitoba. George send me a copy of this letter. I was at the reunion with the twin Gordon from South 'Africa couple of years ago. He was motor transport officer, when I was transferred to the MT after having had my share of the jungle. Later I was invalided out to Blighty after a spell at BMH (British Medical Hospital) in Singapore after contracting tropical sprue. I hope this is of some help.

71. 16 April 2007   George Masson to Matt Poole

Got your email regarding the crash Liberator. Yes, I was on the operation when it was found but my Platoon had nothing to do with the discovery. I've been in touch with one or two lads that may help. One of them has very good memory of the time. This made is George Cahoon who isn't on the Internet so its either post or telephone he lives at 4 Seaford Road Peterhead Aberdeenshire AB 42 XF

I spoke to him last night and he said that McGill found the propeller first, and it was when they were following a compass reading through a bamboo clump before hitting the Hornets nest, and they had to scatter when you rightly said in your email McGill was in D Company 10 Platoon.

[Authors note: This dosen't seem correct previous comments refer to McGill finding the B24's Tail Fin.?? And MaGill was in 12 Platoon.]

My Platoon was 11, and we went another way to the bandit camp , so we were involved with the crash site. I don't know where Sgt Jimmy Dummelow came into it, because he was in C Company unless C Company was ordered to secure the site for the R AF to investigate later.

[Authors note. Sgt. Dummelow was the Sgt. In charge of the Patrol that found the Liberator.]

I know there were revolvers, bren guns and thousands of rounds of ammunition, which was about hundred yards from the bandit camp we were after, but it was so long ago that your memory fades a bit.

Lt. Staheli was in 10 Platoon. My Platoon had 2/Lt Robertson I was Cpl. acting Sergeant at the time I think?

[Authors note Lt. Steheli was the Commander of 12 Platoon]

I remember when we entered the camp. it was huge. it had a parade ground, perhaps, even prison. I think it was a Japanese camp in the war, and bandits were using it The bandits had fled by the time we got there.

We also found bandit bashes on the border or what you could call Ladangs. Our Company was a very deep penetration unit, and workd on that operation nine weeks in the jungle at that time, so we had to carry on with the operation. We destroyed all of them. In one of them we found about 6 cwt of rice, 10 boxes of Quaker porridge oats, a few tins of Dutch condensed milk, and potatoes. The Platoon had a feast at night when we bedded down. We destroyed the rice we could not carry.

Getting back to report Force one was 12 Platoon and Forced two was 11 Platoon. In a report Force 2 did go to the LZ to help to cut down the trees, finishing up by blowing some down.

Then we carried on Patrolling the area and receiving the airdrops. We then went on further Patrol and finished on the wrong side of the border, and the reason I can tell you that was when we came up through the jungle we came to a track offended trig point in concrete. 1 side said Siam the other said Malay.

As for the spoils getting loaded onto helicopters, we weren't there but what we were told, there was human remains at the site. But that's all I know. I've spoken by email to another mate George Donaldson, who keeps in touch with Tony Gordon and Andrew Blackley I sent him your email and he said he will get back to me. Another person who is not on email is Jim McSorely I keep in touch with him he was in 12 Platoon. Yes just moved house from Irving to Largs I myself is living in Wakefield Yorkshire so I only see Jim when I am in Irving

George Cahoon said last night that Chad Stuart, who was a bren gunner with 10 Plt attempted to get a daily diary of his time in the army so he may well have recorded the incident. But we don't know where he is but will start making enquiries and maybe find something for stop will give you an email address to Alan Robertson lives in Canada he may be able to help as well yes heard of the crash is email is cludgie@mts.net

72. 16 April 2007   Joe Plant to Matt Poole,

George McGill...Made a cursory phone to E. McGill this a.m. George passed away two years ago, Elizabeth his wife informed me. But she knew nothing about the Liberator. I did not dwell on the subject but said I would keep her informed

Sgt. Dummelow passed away several years ago, as did John Staheli.

73. 16 April 2007   Matt Poole to Joe Plant,

Sorry to hear that George passed away, as have Sgt. Dummelow and of course John Staheli. It is always a gamble picking up the phone and calling "out of the blue". I did this a few weeks ago when trying to speak to one of the 357 Squadron pilots. He passed away a year ago, and I spoke with his daughter, who happened to be visiting her mother.

You wrote: *"As a point of interest I cannot see how Shaharom would have found it later. Even the RCAF did not know where it crashed ????"*

What I meant is this. If the RAF report from 1955 had included the accurate grid reference, it would have been known to Gerald Howse he wrote to the UK Ministry of Defence Air Historical Group. (I know he wrote to the AHB back in 1988, and I presume he received the RAF document soon thereafter, and not from a Canadian source.) When Gerald built his website in

2004 One way or another he and Shaharom got in touch, and Shaharom then wanted to find the wrecksite. So my point is that if the grid ref had been correct in the 1955 report, Shaharom would have learned this correct number two or three years ago. He would have then, not now, mounted an initial expedition to that location.

I am assuming that Shaharom would have had access to 1950s-era maps showing the military grid. However, for all I know Shaharom needed the map Blair provided in order to key him to the exact spot.

74.   16 April 2007   Joe Plant to Matt Poole,

The RAF report. That is exactly my point. Yes, Gerald would have found it through Shaharom the real crash site, but what I have read from your valuable information was that everyone was on a wild goose chase. Nobody, but nobody, knew where they crashed even in 1945. Last seen South of Bunting Island. If the 1st Battalion RSF had not stumbled upon it, the crash site MIGHT never had been found. Whoever typed the report up got the Grid Reference back to front. The RAF Officer Commanding Singapore read it and signed. That was the evidence which Gerald was finally given by the RAF Historical Group in 1988, and we are talking about a big area to search as highlighted in those Google Links maps (in dense thick jungle, as has now been pointed out by Shaharom, & at least he has now got a pinpoint to locate). Our correspondence has mainly been based on our assumptions & speculations. Where did they crash, where did they bale out, etc., etc. Even the time was stated wrongly: after midnight Malaya time. Don't get me wrong. My point is that the RAF bungled it??

And the mystery continues?

75.   16 April 2007   Allan Robertson to Matt Poole

Thanks for your letter. Sorry you came up empty. And sorry to McGill passed on. But now I have more light.the McGill I gave you was the CEO why, and McGill you are looking for was in see CEO why, because Sgt Dummelow was in C:

When we first arrived in the Malaya we were Stationed at Butterworth, and on our first operation in the Bong Su area I was on the fan Patrol with three others we got lost. Cpl. could not read a map anyway, we spent the night rough at daylight we continued our wanderings. and we came across a basher with four bandits, we Killed two, but we did not get them registered until two days later, meanwhile Sgt Dummelow was on Patrol with C: somewhere in the Cameron Highlands area when he ran into some bandits, and they got their kill registered before us, they had the first kill, when in actual fact it was ours.

George Masson sent me a copy of your letter, and George now lives in or near York in England, where he has resided since he got out of the mob. But he originally was full serving Scott. I've been looking for his address but have missed it sorry but I will email him to contact you. There are a lot of empty spaces in our albums now, and they grow thinner every day now. I am a member the MBVA they are a Group here in Canada on Vancouver Island. A Canadian Group registered to the one in Blighty. Sorry can't help you any more, and I was not on the op. that found the plane, but remember guys talking when they came in. George was on the op I have some pics of them but they were taken on it, but none of the actual plane or arms cache et cetera so can't assist any more.

76.   17 April 2007   Antony Gordon to Blair Agnew cc Joe Plant

Many thanks for your information my file regimental/Malay/ Liberator gets thicker and thicker I can imagine now thick Joe's is?? (Blair. Many thanks your copy of the excellent article drafted for the R HF journal and Joe for the large selection of copies of maps et cetera.)

It is really TERRIBLE to put it mildly, that the R AF, both Far East (Melaya) and especially UK Ministry, did not report the basic fact that it was Canadian lost aircraft to the Canadian authorities!! These facts are quite clear even from the original Far East Air Force letter is of 16 June 1955? And then, to complicate matters they get the Grid Reference reversed. This has Thus led many people on the wrong trail!

I must say that AT THE TIME from my (comfortable) position as MTO (Motor Transport Officer of 1 RSF Kroh working on the radio and verbal reports that we got. I was fully convinced that there were human remains at the wreck also that the RAF " experts" who came to examine the wreck were very casual and wanted out of the jungle as soon as possible. I remember they said the bones that were found were of "Pig" I cannot think any wild pig would choose such places to die. I believe they did not even stay a night on site. You may be able to confirm this from D Company War Diary which you have now see. But my impression, and memory, tells me that these "experts" really did not know the job and were not really interested! We certainly gained the impression, when the crash was reported, that the R AF (obviously the senior ones) really were interested, but I do remember that the experts did not give that impression!

From the copies of the fascinating report that Joe has sent a number of queries arising my mind:-

1 What was the target purpose of the other Liberator which did return? Were they also doing a supply drop at the same time and to the same DZ?? The fact that they had seen KH 326 as they cross the coast of Melaya (before the storm) indicates that they must have been on almost the same track (heading) to still be so close after such a long flight as a "Pongo" and aircraft controller in HMS Eagle 21 years after the sortie to supply drop I would have suggested that they cross the Malayan coast well to the South of the anAlor Star Japanese air base and also clear of Penang they could Thus fairly easily fix their position visually and then make any alterations for the approach to the DZ. Must remember that the maps, at the time, were very poor! Did the

other Liberator achieve its target? I read that the two crews swopped aircraft very shortly before takeoff to do this indicates that both were similarly loaded and must have had the same target!

2 The initial report to the air Ministry from Far East Air Force states that the automatic pilot panel indicated that the aircraft of flying----- through straight and level possibly one engine "feathered" I wonder if there is any detail of the height at which the automatic pilot was set to is mentioned anywhere? This question ties in with my next.

3 It is a pity that there seems to be no records of the briefing details for the sortie for either aircraft. One of the basic bits of information are crew needs for sorties is minimum altitude (to avoid the ground!) This was always pounced upon for details of "fluffy clouds with a hard centre" that might be met! I feel pretty certain that the automatic pilot KH 326 was set at the height far lower than the hills in the target area. In some cases just NE of the crash site there is a height of 4152 ft much closer (just of the South of the given DZ) Lat 006 Long 101 there are heights over 3000 ft.

4 All indications point to the other Liberator making for the same target but I wonder if this can be confirmed? It will be wonderful if any details of their flight and successes, or otherwise can be found!

5 Back to the "human remains" I would have thought that if humans were in the crash then the skull at least would remain possibly the backbone but no doubt there are jungle wild animals which would remove even these and everything rots very quickly!

77.   23 April 2007   Joe Plant to Matt Poole,

Returned from London Archives where I researched the Force 136 Roll of Honour, hoping to identify the extra sercret agent on board KH236 Unfortunately the RoH only contained a list of medals, commendations and awards, quite a few to Malays of different races, but no fatalities. However I DID GAIN SOMETHING out of it . I took a look at the 357 Sqdn Records , unfortunately being on microfilm with my eyesight as it is? Was not able to read much if anything of that mission m so drew a blank But at least Robert Quirk has them in Canada .

Your last E//M refers to Andrew Blackley. Andrew was one of the first persons to contact me in October 2006, Who informed me of the second liberator down South (Seremban) but knew nothing about the find.

78.   23 April 2007   Matt Poole to Joe Plant

Records researchs are always intriguing, though the tedium can be wearying . In the past at Kew I'd set out to find one thing and be distracted by other things ....with "bonus" points that were sometimes more useful than the material I'd been specifically searching for.My guess is. That of force 136 facts are so secretive that the truth will not come out, conserning KH 326

Gordon Hercus   said that they never carried only supplies for dropping and sometimes carry multiple agents/passengers. Ah well, that maybe in his Liberator, but some July 45' 357 Squadron records showed that some of the Lliberators just carried supplies. So the possibility does exist that KH 326 only had eight men onboard,the crew.

Here are the 1st. Battn. Guy's I know about associated with the Crash find

12 Platoon

Tony Gordon   (you interviewed.)
Blair Agnew   (you interviewed.)
Jim McSorley   (not yet interviewed.)
George McGill (deceased)
Jimmy Dummelow (deceased)
John Staheli (deceased)
11 Platoon

George Masson (we have correspondence by E/M)
Allan Robertson (George M. Said Allan was with Him) Platoon unknown
George Donaldson.(George M. said George D. will get back to him)
Peter O'Reilly   (has been contacted was not involved , but he remembers the Lib find)
George Cahoon (was not on the wreck . but has a good memory)
Chad Stewart   (George M. said Stewart was in 10 Platoon but he misidentified others in 12 Platoon as being in 10 Platoon So I will have to ask George M. to verify . Stewart kept a diary , but his whereabouts may be unknown)

If Stewart was in 12 Platoon D can be found...... That would be nice, seing he kept a diary

[Authors Note: also Willie Shaw, Alex \Burden, put me in touch with Antony Gordon and Blair Agnew. Andrew Blackley, who was instrumental with his info to Joe Plant in Oct 2006]

79.   24 April 2007   Joe Plant to Matt Poole,

Have I stumbled onto some information which could be relevant to the project of KH326?

Last night I took to reading an old book published in 49 by Spencer Chapman about Force 136. Within the pages references to 357, 160 & 8 Squadrons glared out of the text. We all know about their activities, but something caught my eye: that they were put at the disposal of Force 136 by the RAF for the build up for Operation "ZIPPER", the intended invasion of Malaya, as Submarines could not cope with the demands of supplies being transported into that region.

This was introduced on the 1st June 1945. 357, 160 & 8 Squadrons were designated to fly from CEYLON, from China Bay & Minneriya. Between the months of June and July they made 249 sorties, carrying equipment and personnel. 69% of the missions were successfully carried out over DZs where supplies were dropped. No mention was made of the total number of agents carried, but including 356 & 99 Squadrons from the COCOS Islands in August and September, 510 bodies were delivered behind enemy lines

There were only 2 incidents where Jap fighters attacked the Libs. However, none were lost due to enemy Action AND only two casualties were incurred throughout the whole missions:
1. an officer (unamed)
2. an N.C.O. who DROWNED in a pool upon landing (certainly not our man).
Would this officer be the person we are seeking who flew on that fatal flight??? I have checked with the Commonwealth War Graves Commission. They only have three likely persons who died on the 6th June (No known Grave for any of them):
1. an R.A. Gunner;
2. an Indian Pioneer Corp member;
3. a Sapper (Engineer) from the Johore Volunteer Corps. A possibility, but I suspect he was with the Johore group. I tried the M.O.D. No luck, and the Imperial War Museum retains only books, so are we chasing a wild goose, but the single officer is, I feel, very likely???

80.   25 April 2007   Joe Plant to Matt Poole,
The names of the three persons are: L/Bd. Charles Carson, - Rank?, Indian Pioneer Corp and Spr. S.A. Hjerrild, Johore Volunteer Engineers. There is no records of the OFFICER without a name. As I said, it's most intriguing.

The e-mail from George Masson was also very interesting The real info comes from the Fusilliers who were there, although the officers make up the report, as you have read. The 'conversations which take place between soldiers is quite something else. They see things that the officers don't, and it would be most interesting to collate their stories

81.   25 April 2007   Matt Poole to Joe Plant,
Thanks for the names of the three men with No known Graves who died on 6 June 1945. The complete info on these men, via the CWGC database follows. Too bad there isn't a name for the officer!

Name: **CARSON, CHARLES**
Initials: C
Nationality: United Kingdom
Rank: Lance Bombardier
Regiment/Service: Royal Artillery
Unit Text: 95 Bty., 48 Lt. A.A. Regt.
Age: 28

Date of Death: 06/06/1945
Service No: 1543769
Casualty Type: Commonwealth War Dead
Grave/Memorial Reference: Column 9.
Memorial: SINGAPORE MEMORIAL

Name: **HJERRILD**
Initials: S A
Nationality: United Kingdom
Rank: Sapper
Regiment/Service: Johore Volunteer Engineers

Date of Death: 06/06/1945
Casualty Type: Commonwealth War Dead
Grave/Memorial Reference: Column 463.
Memorial: SINGAPORE MEMORIAL

Name: **HANIF**
Nationality: Indian
Rank: Pioneer
Regiment/Service: Indian Pioneer Corps
Unit Text: 13th Bn.
Date of Death: 06/06/1945

Service No: 163137
Additional information: Son of Abdulla, of Navapura, Nasik, India.
Casualty Type: Commonwealth War Dead
Grave/Memorial Reference: Column 363.
Memorial: SINGAPORE MEMORIAL

82.   25 April 2007   Joe Plant to Matt Poole
I do agree that to find this officer is going to be most difficult. We do not know his regiment. Even the three mentioned on 6/6/45, as they have No known Graves, therefore it means going through their activities on their last engagements via regimental achives. Furthermore, records out of India?? and Johore??? They also might have been POWs??? Who knows? But I always look for the needle???

83.   25 April 2007   Matt Poole to Joe Plant

This is mushrooming.... More of the 12 Platoon lads are being tracked down, this is what George Masson just sent me fantastic!

And by the way I think congratulate you on your detective work coming up with a list of three others, one of more of whom may have been aboard KH 326. I think I asked you in my last e-mail for the name of the officer , but if you can get the CWGC to give you the names of all three , then I can do some more snooping.

OK. Here's some good news on this incredible project. Gerge M. sent some photos… will have to send them to you later….
[Authors note : never recv'd. Matt forgot].
84.   25 April 2007   Joe Plant to Matt Poole
Had a talk with George Cahoon on Saturday he said he had a nice chat with you Matt . but he didn't know whether you understood him well because of his accent and he said something happened and got cut off.

I've got good news for you after's spreading the news around I got an email from Jim Stewart he was in 12 Platoon who lives in Fenwick he was there and I spoke today with Dougie Thom he was a Cpl in 12 Platoon, who was also on the site helping to organise the removal of all the ammunition and weapons and it was McGill who found it. There were two McGill's one in 10 Platoon and one in 12 Platoon, my mate Jim McSorely who was a lance corporal in 10 Platoon. McGill was his Basha mate on the operation and the 12 Platoon McGill is the one who has died and Joe Plant spoke to his wife. When I spoke to Dougie Thom today I asked if it would be okay to give you his phone number, he is not on email he said it would be all right, he also said that he visits Jim McIntyre he was taken out by the helicopter because he cut his tendons on his Thumb when cutting the bamboo when a machete, he lives in Troon and Dougie is going to get in touch and will phone me with the information Dougie's phone number Kilmarnock*********. He is a mine of information because he was there and will tell you a lot where as myself and George Cahoon were on the same operation, but not involved with the site, we are only telling you what was told to us and George has a better memory than I have. I'm sending you the email I received from Jim Stewart and you will get his email address from that and by them way George Cahoon says don't take too much notice of what Alan Roberts from Canada says, because he said he was a transport driver he knows him better than I do. I just met him through E Mails. If you go to www.rhf.org.uk site again click the OCA and the photographs come up the coloured ones from last years reunion , double click the ones I tell and you will get the faces of the lads I'm talking about. , go right to the bottom row of all the coloured photos with the dates, on the left hand side is Dougei Thom and my mate Archie McMillan with the moustache, 2nd, row up LHS is George Cahoon on his own, 2nd row up middle is Andrew Blackley with the blazer badge. 3rd. row up LHS is Dougie Thom ??? with Major Wilmott who led the operation. 4th. row up on RHS with dark glasses is Geoge Donaldson on LHS is Jim McSorley my mate. I'm not in photo I took these all the best George.   Attched ??
85.   22 April 2007   Fenwick Stewart@ aol .com to George Masson
Had a visit from the D Thom on 'Friday let me read the email you sent to Archie Mac. I was in 12 Platoon I remember a boot from the cockpit also a pistol which seem to be in good nick for the time it had been there don't remember much more except it was there that Ben McIntyre badly injured his hand and that to be airlifted out by one of the helicopters don't know if you remember me George Sat. next to you in the reunion Jim Stewart.
86.   26 April 2007   Matt Poole to Joe Plant,
If I'm reading your info correctly, only the three men whose names we know have a 6 June '45 date of death. The officer's name AND date of death are not known, right???

One thing I must emphasize is that we do not know, for certain, that KH326 was carrying an extra passenger or two or three or more. Gordon Hercus said that they NEVER carried only supplies, but I've found that he was wrong. The July records of 357 Squadron do show that some flights were supply dropping-only, and other times they carried up to several agents!
87.   26 April 2007   Matt Poole to Joe Plant, again,
Did the Spencer Chapman book mention the DATES when there were two Japanese fighter attacks upon Liberators involved with the agent/supply drops.?
88.   26 April 2007   Joe Plant to Matt Poole,
According to the CWGC, the chap I discussed this with identified 11 on the Singapore Memorial in Kranji War Cemetery
8 were the Canadians of KH326, the other three as you have.
As for Carson, I intend to ask question of the Royal Artillery Museum in Woolwich, London. *[See Item 98 for the result.]*
Yes it is not going to be easy, but we can but try.
Spencer Chapman answer: No.
89.   27 April 2007   Matt Poole to Joe Plant,
"The Moonlight War" by ex-357 Dakota flight C.O. Terrence O'Brien, has some interesting stuff. Haven't had a chance to go through it fully for things pertaining to our cases, but here's an interesting passage:
*The statistics are interesting. We aircrew at Jessore suffered forty times greater loss of life than did the men whom we landed safely down there in the jungle; only five parachutists were subsequently Killed in Action in Burma and **none at all in Siam and Malaya**, but we lost over two hundred aircrew - the French soldiers who parachuted and landed to join their army in Indi-*

China are not included in these figures. Parachuted agents were in greatest peril not down in the jungle on their operation but while they were sharing our danger in the air; eight of them were Killed with aircrew in planes which were shot down or crashed.

What is equally surprising is that **there are only three recorded fatalities in the actual drops.** One had a faulty parachute, and a Karen whom I dropped into one of the trees scattered about a "Character" site was probably a victim of fouled static lines *[in Burma].* **The third fatality was a sergeant on the "Funnel" operation in Malaya; the despatcher reported on return that all the team had landed in the DZ but we heard from the field next day that the sergeant had actually fallen into an old tin-mining pit and drowned. The surface was carpeted with water lillies and he probably thought it was a patch of luscious grass, for he did not release himself just before impact as trained to do when entering water; the outcome was that he became entangled under the water with the shroud lines of the collapsed chute and so drowned under the canopy.**

Another casualty, according to some people, was a Shan who was never heard of again after being dropped blind - at a map-chosen site with no one waiting on the ground. He was thought to have landed fatally in a tall tree, for his parachute was seen floating down perfectly all right into a valley along the Chinese Border. But it seems to me more likely that once he was safely back in his own country he may have simply decided to go home to his village and have nothing more to do with our dangerous wars. Several of the Chinese dropped early into Siam took that very sensible course.

I don't know if O'Brien's statistics cover the entire war. I assume so, as his book seems very detailed

[Authors note: The Sergeant dropped into Malaya and drowned could well have been dropped by either of 357 or 355 Squaron Liberators dropping supplies / passengers to "FUNNEL" Guerillas operating in PERAK.]

90.   28 April 2007   Letter George Cahoon to Joe Plant

[Authors Note: Altho' this letter was received early in June. It has been relocated to this date, prior to Matt Poole's interview with Dougie Thom, on 28 April. It reveals the passage of 11 Platoon's real time before, during and after the find of the Liberator.]

June 2007 letter received from George Cahoon.

To begin Mr Joe Plant contacted me early April 2007. Mr Plant asked me if I had been involved in Operation Unity during 1955 on the Siamese border.

When I told him that I was, he asked me if I could inform him if I had been involved with the finding of a Liberator bomber that had been shot down by Japanese fighters in WW2 - I informed Joe Plant I had not been involved with the discovery of the Liberator but had just been part of the same. Operation Unity.

[Authors note: Correction during my 'conversation with George, there was no mention of any Japanese fighters shooting down the Liberator]

Mr Plant asked me about certain things I can only answer truthfully to the best of my memory.

A few days later a Mr. Matt Poole telephoned me and asked me the same questions and informed me, that one of his relations had been on the said Liberator. Again I told him what I had already written and hoped that I could help him.

[Authors note: I doubt if Matt mentioned that ONE of his relations, was on the plane, He possibly referred to Gerald Howse's relationship].

Mr Poole I believe comes from Wheaton Maryland USA. His contact has been Mr George Masson ex NCO i.e. Cpl number 11 Platoon 1st.RSF having recently met George Masson at two Fusiliers Reunions, I have been in contact with George and Jim McSorley, who were both on the same operation and have decided to help Mr Plant and Mr Poole if it is possible with my memory is of Operation Unity as Mr Plant requested.

April 1955 LENGGONG PERAK MALAYA "D COY" 1st. RSF.

The Company was ordered to parade in front of Company officers and Major Wilmot advised us to be prepared to move out as a Major operation will begin sometime in May 1955.

1955 APRIL BALING PERAK

At this time the Malayan peace talks were taking place at a village called Bailing between the Malayan Communist Party MCP and the British Army.

In the event of the peace talks breaking down. The agreement was to give the MCP i.e. **CHIN PENG** OC a week's grace. After this the Company would be deployed on a military term, which was the search and destroy. in support of this would be "A" Company 1st. R SF.

April 30, 1955 KROH

Left Lintang in convoy to Kroh, spent night in tents. Next day Major Wilmot said we had been given the okay to proceed with the operation.

1 MAY 1955 OPERATION UNTY

The Company gathered on the Padang. Boarded helicopters and flew into LZ Major Wilmot marshalled us in the jungle beside LZ, an old Tin Mine. Gave the order to move out. Myself and Fusiliers Hendry were first and second Scout, behind us were Sgt Fulcher Dog handler and Major Wilmot with the Company behind!

First week on Patrol nothing out of the ordinary, virgin jungle. This Patrol continued with the dull Company until about the 24th or 25th of May 1955 until a most unfortunate accident occurred in which one of our comrades was severely injured. This incident triggered the discovery of the Liberator.

The person injured was medical orderly L/Cpl McFadden RAMC. Attached 1/RSF. Whilst making our way down a steep incline, McFadden slipped and landed on a wooden tree stump. As myself and Hendry were well up on the other side of the incline we heard this terrible scream and everyone froze, Major Wilmot ordered me to find out what had happened. I in going back down the ravine, I could see Sgt Dummelow, Sgt Gilmore and some others, around the injured McFadden pulling pieces of wood out of his rectum.

I duly reported to Major Wilmot who then ordered us to make a camp, then ordered the radio operator David English to contact HQ and inform them of what had happened. The radio operator did this. He was asked by HQ what?' Starlight'? Code for medical orderly and how serious it was? The radio operator replied 'Starlight' was the injured man, HQ informed Major Wilmot not to give the injured man anything to eat, only sweet tea to drink and to make a suitable landing zone for the evacuation of McFadden.

At this time we were about 3000 feet up according to the map, which I had been supplied with from Joe Plant. Anyway, at that time we were in the most accessible terrain and had to make for the lower ground. Major Wilmot ordered a makeshift stretcher for McFadden also a cutting party to clear undergrowth.

26th of May 1955

Following animal tracks along a mountain path, suddenly the War dog went mad and started pulling Sgt Fulcher! Major Wilmot notice this, called a meeting and decided this was CT activity and ordered Lt Staheli 12 Platoon, to take a party and pursue this trail.

Lt. Staheli took Sgt Fulcher, Sgt Shanley, Sgt Dummelow, Cpl Thom and 12 Platoon including Fusilier McGill. This left 10 and 11 Platoon to make our own way down to get McFadden evacuated.

About two days later Lt Staheli had discovered the Liberator and also a large bandit camp nearby, which had been deserted. This we heard over the radio operator set and also that Fus. McGill had found the propeller and other debris.

MR. STAHELI'S REPORT YOU ALREADY HAVE.

10 Platoon and 11 Platoon 1955

Meanwhile 10 Platoon and 11 Platoon and McFadden were still labouring to get through the jungle: the cutting party was led by Lance Cpl J Poole. After two days is and his party's hands were red raw and bleeding! The stretcher party took turns and were Trojans carrying medic McFadden! McFadden was in constant pain and to cap it all, we ran out of water and there only recourse was to tap the bamboo. This entailed making a hole, then filtering track water through our field dressings, then boiling it-this is not to be recommended, it was discussing, but needs must!

The next morning myself and Major Wilmot started down the track with the rest of the Company following us. About midday, we could hear and AUSTER PLANE circling over our position, Major Wilmot ordered me to let off a smoke bomb, which I did. The pilot of the Auster then dropped a SITREP flag, red, yellow and blue. Attached to the flag was a report for Major Wilmot, who upon reading the report and consulted his map ordered me to stay and inform Lt. Robertson of 11 Platoon OC, that Major Wilmot would return shortly! As we were well ahead of the Company he would try for water.

About two hours later I noticed the movement further down the track and saw Major Wilmot struggling up towards me with a large army water bag full of water. To this day, I can still see Major Wilmot. When I went to his aid he said 'CAHOON take this up to the men!' I was amazed how Major Wilmot managed to carry this amount of water. Taking this water back to the Company whose progress was a lot slower than us, was greatfully accepted. Major Wilmot ordered us to bash up, then told us we were not far from a likely Landing Zone.

The next day we reached the LZ and cut down surrounding trees and undergrowth. The helicopter came and evacuated McFadden also Major Wilmot and a few others, mainly from the cutting party.

Command of the Company passed to Lt Robertson whose orders were to proceed to the original landing site and destroy LADANGS (cultivations) ; this Patrol consisted of 10 and 11 Platoons. On reaching our original LZ, Lt Robertson split us into two groups ie. About eight of us and Radio Operator to remain behind beside the LZ as a holding group, as he and the rest of the Patrol searched for LADANGS. This was on the Thailand's border and I must say as holding Company, we had it made.

Lt. Robertson and the rest of our Patrol set about destroying LADANGS whilst as I have said we the eight or nine bodies, had nothing to do except watch the perimeter of the Landing Zone. One day a Cpl. Sharkey arrived from up river and approached Fusilier Hendry. He told Fusilier Hendry that he had to join him on his Patrol as Scout. At first Fusilier Hendry in military parlance told Cpl. Sharkey to Fuck Off! Cpl Sharkey said. 'OK, go up and asked Lt. Robertson!' As a soldier Fusilier Hendry had no other option but to comply! Changing into wet clothes and arming himself, Fusilier Henry said ' Right lets go.' Whereupon corporal Sharkey said.' I'm only kidding.' Fusilier Hendry then said. 'Fuck you I am coming now.' This Patrol consisted of Cpl. Sharkey Fusilier Hendry Fusiliers Feeney and several others.

As I have already written, this LZ was magic, with a tributary stream running through about 4 foot wide and side about 3 foot deep with water running about 6 inches deep. To this day I cannot remember who suggested making a dam on this steam, but the idea of having a swim definitely appealed to us.

The eight of us set about like the proverbial beavers and made a dam of sorts. This strem began to risead made a first class swimming pool, which we of the Holding Party really enjoyed. About 5.30 pm we all had to stand to and I happened to mention to Fusilier Lynass about the Patrol that had left with Cpl. Sharkey and Fusilier Hendry and the rest of the Patrol. Fuilier Lynass was not noted for his wit said to me. 'Fuck Knows. You know Sharkey he could get lost opening a door.'

The next morning after Stand to and still no sign of Sharkey and the Patrol. The eight of us were wondering, if we should contact (Robertson went out of the surrounding jungle Cpl. Sharkey, Hendry and Feeney and other members of the Patrol appeared. Corporal Sharkey's first words were. 'What the fuck have you done to the fucking river?' Needless to say we were very twitchy as going by the words and expressions we could only give very larne excuses. Sharkey and the Patrol were a wee bit upset; Lt Robertson was a very thoughtful and dour man could see the funny side of this thankfully, and decided to let sleeping dogs lie. Corporal Sharkey and his Patrol later on, laughed about this event Cpl. Sharkey had made this his map reference and guide!

The next day an AUSTER PLANE flew over us and as we stood at the edge of the LZ the pilot dropped a SITREP, which we recovered and gave to Lt Robertson it was orders for us to move to a new location

While he was reading these orders the Auster circled us and started to waggle his wings, we were waving back when the Auster suddenly dived into the swamp area of the LZ. We were stunned then Lt. Robertson ordered us to get over and see if the pilot was all right.

Luckily the plane had not caught fire or exploded, we successfully got the pilot out and his first words were 'At least my watch is still working!' Lt. Robertson ordered David English our Radio Operator to inform HQ about this and they send a helicopter to collect the Auster pilot. We salvaged everything that could have been any use to anyone from that plane. The Auster is still there to this day!

Two days later Patrol was ordered to a new location. Lt. Robertson led us to the LZ that had been used for McFadden and ordered Cpl Wilson 'POP' to take 10 Platoon to a new map ref on the SUNGEI BAHO and SUNGEI TEBUS rivers to Patrol surrounding areas. Corporal Wilson acting Sgt, was in command of this Patrol including Cpl. Sharkey and L/Cpl. McSorley, we set up base camp at the junction of the two said rivers. We then started to Patrol the area on given map references. To whom of you read this, we were in an alien environment and had been for about six weeks and as young men we developed a sense of "black humour" le **CPL.** SHARKEY'S PATROL.

Anyway Cpl. WILSON ordered L/Cpl MCSORLEY to take a Patrol down the right bank the SUNGEI BAHO, in search of any CT activity. This Patrol consisted of Fusiliers McGugan Scout. L/Cpl McSorley, Fusiliers Feeney Fusilier LYNASS and I. About two hours into this Patrol the only sound was a river rushing by when suddenly McGugan held up his hand, we all went into defensive positions. McGugan signalled us to come forward, which we did, then he pointed to the ground and we saw these enormous pug marks McGugan whispered "Tiger' 'On this Patrol! We were all from Kilmarnock and Glasgow!

Hunting CT's is one thing, but a Tiger, this was definitely not on our remit. After a few moments Lance Cpl McSorley signalled let's go and we went forward, but with a wee bit of extra care. McGugan to give his due, did his job as Scout now with a bit more vigilance. McGugan came to a fallen tree, right in his path and as he approached put his left hand on the tree and made to jump over onto the track. At this point L/Cpl McSorley held up his hand waved us to stop. He then waited as McGugan came to the fallen tree and prepared to climb over it, when L/Cpl McSorley then let out a Roar or a Growl. To this day I can still see McGugan's hat in mid air, as McGugan flew past us at about 100 miles an hour, the rest of us fell about in hysterics, to us it was hilarious..

McGugan when he realised what was happening, came back and was not a happy soldier, he had a very hard time to keep himself from shooting someone, but eventually calmed down. L/Cpl McSorley apologised, but like the rest of us couldn't stop laughing. Somehow if McGugan reads this he will swear he will never forget that Tiger.

When I meet L/Cpl's McSorley this is one of the many memories and I have many memories, too many to write about that we, the whole Company experience during this operation. We continued to Patrol the surrounding area for about a week, then we received orders to return to the LZ to rejoin Lt. Robertson and 11 Platoon as we would be join soon with 12 Platoon.

At this time, as we now know, 12 Platoon had almost completed the evacuation of most of the arms and ammunition is, the Graves Commission had also given up as there was no bodies or, any remains and were preparing to rejoin the rest of us at BASH LZ. LT. Robertson ordered 10 Platoon to search various areas , also 11 Platoon. This continued for 2 weeks when we got a surprise visitation from our new Battlion Commander Lt/Col.Delano Osbourne .

Lt. Staheli and 12 Platoon re-joined us and swopped stories as well as different tales to tell for example Fus. Magill did say he discovered the Liberator by accident. All of 12 Platoon confirmed that. Lt. Staheli took command and we headed North to the border and on the crest of hill we found deserted CT Camp of huge preportions, there was even a smsll Parade Ground and several machine gun nest around the hill. Some days later we were airlifted to Kroh then to a new HQ Back to normal.

AT LINTANG CAMP

About 6 weeks later a 3 ton truck pulled up and out stepped L/Cpl. McFadden RAMC.   He had volunteered to rejoin "D" Coy. He had made a full recovery but would not show us his arse. .... END.

91. 27 April 2007   Matt Poole to Joe Plant.

I phoned Dougie Thom on Saturday. He was there in the initial stage of the Liberators discovery. I'm transcribing my interview with him, but it is a slow process he talks fast and of course with a Scottish accent, it will take time for me to finish the transcription.

But I thought I'd get things going by sending this much of the interview. Pretty interesting stuff! As always, each man sees things slightly different. According to Dougie. Blair and Tony were not involved in the early part of the mission. I don't think Dougie is being "us versus them." in his choice of words.

Since there's more to this interview, might I suggest not sending it on to others yet?

Recollections of Dougie Thom ex12 Platoon First Battalion Royal Scots Fusiliers, who was there in late May 1955 when Liberator KH 326 was rediscovered in the Malayan jungle:

I was there after the discovery. What happened was we were on Patrol up in one of the camps on a nine week Patrol. So we were in one of the camps there. One of the Patrols went out and came upon the Liberator. McGill would be the Scout. He is dead now by the way. Sgt Dummelow was the Sgt on it.

And what happened is, they came down the track which we used from our camp to get to one of the streams to get our water. What they did, they went down so far and then they cut in to the right into the jungle a bit. They hadn't travelled far any distance in their. 150 yards, 200 yards, when they came upon the Liberator. What Dummelow did

And what Dummelow did with the rest of his Platoon it could have been about 7, 8 or 9, they left a big boy by the name Ben McIntyre. He stood by the plane while he (Dummelow) came back up to the camp to get the rest of us. We were in the camp, because I'd been in a Patrol at a previous day. And they brought us down to take the stuff off the plane, because there were canisters and various things all over. Even the Browning guns were mounted on the front of the Liberator. And Dummelow went away to get us, somehow or other, he could manage to get back up to the camp very quickly {mild laughter}.

What happened is Ben McIntyre who was standing at the Liberator waiting, naturally for the rest of us to come down to dismantle all the things that were round about the Liberator, couldn't wait any longer, so he came up off the Liberator himself. Just walked out onto the track, straight up to the camp, and he got us in the camp.

Then we came down to where the Liberator was, and we started to dismantle it. About a couple of hours later Dummelow came upon us again. So he had got lost for a couple of hours. We started to dismantle the actual Liberator. Naturally we got Sten guns, a lot of clothing. I tried a pair of boots on, but they just disintegrated. But the Sten guns were all greased and in greaseproof paper. We cleaned one up and put ammunition in it and find it was perfectly okay all right.

So that was after about 10 years. There were various things their pistols that we found and all that. But we certainly searched around about quite an area,. But we never found any signs of life

[Matt mentioned Blair Agnew]

Blair Agnew, he was not there, I can assure you. He may have come upon it later, but the Platoon that was on that was 12 Platoon. That was not Blair Agnew's Platoon. His Platoon was either 10 or 11, which was not there at the time. We were there at the camp. It was Staheli, he was the one officer in command

[Matt then mentioned another officer Anthony Gordon of South'Africa]

These people were not at that particular point. They were not there. What happened is you kept moving about on these operations. They may have, upon that and then had something else to do with it later on. But at the immediate time it was found, it was certainly our Platoon. That got there and it was us that certainly took all the stuff out that we could get, and took it back up to the camp After that I think they. Blair Agnew and or Anthony Gordon, came upon it and I think it was them that dug the DZ for the helicopters to come in.

You see we only had five or six days in that camp. Then we moved along to another camp.

So that could have happened. But the immediate finding of the Liberator was by one of our Patrols that went out then it was our Patrol who did all the rest of it on that mission. We were the ones that went down and got the actual Liberator, found it at first, and then took all the stuff off of it. We certainly did not dismantle the Brownings or anything like that. They were still on the plane when we left.

[Matt mentions Regarding the removal of the Browning machine guns on the Liberator]

I would take it that was whoever came after us, we would move on to another camp, and somebody else will come in and the next proceedings on the plane will be handled over to them. But it was certainly as they found it.

[Matt Regarding finding the Liberator]

It was absolutely out of the blue. He *[John Staheli 12 Platoon officer]* was down in the plane with us. He was there to when we were all collecting..... Because he was encamped at the time with us. Naturally, when you're in a Platoon you may be have anything up to maybe 60 or 70 men out. You're always doing Patrols from that point in the jungle, and you get rid references to go to and do your various Patrols around the area, then come back to. Camp. That was procedure right throughout and I think that was about a nine week course, right up nearly to the North Siamese. border.............

Intervwiew transcript to be continued.

92.   **29 April 2007**   **Matt Poole to Joe Plant.**

I think Timmerman's and Sims were just skippers who qualified on Liberators and were sent, where needed to the Far East to join a bombing Squadron. It turned out that they went to 357 Squadron, flying the special duties Ops.

Then they were both sent on detachment to Minneriya. (Ceylon) Nothing special! Somebody had to go, and they needed S/Ldr. Sims to oversee the detachment.

Because the 357 records are so poor, there is, so far, no evidence as to whether Sims and Timmerman's were both headed to the same DZ. Good have been, or maybe they were near to one another. No idea whether there were agents aboard either Liberator. Gordon Hercus, rear gunner on the Sims crew, couldn't recall this either, though he said. "We never took only supplies." But I found evidence in the July 357 Sqn. Records that their Libs sometimes only carried supplies. So I just don't know about the agent situation on 6th.of June 1945.

Because he said a photocopy of his logbook, I know that his crew's (Sims) DZ was in support of "FGHTER." According to a list of SOE (Force 136 being the Far East Arm of SOE) acronyms Robert Quirk recently sent me (from a document he found at Kew), "FIGHTER" was described in this way.

"FIGHTER": Malaya - to establish reception committees for " MULTIPLE" in the Kedah— Perlis region, 1945

Then I looked up " MULTIPLE" in the same source

"MULTIPLE" Malaya – to organise resistance in Pahang area 1944 – 45 similar operations in Kedah "FIGHTER" and Kuala Lipis "BEACON"

Gordon inked "D. N.C.O." in the logbook for the 6th. June 1945 Operation. D.N.C.O. stands for "Duties Not Carried Out." This means that S/Ldr. Sims and crew did not successfully drop their supplies (and possibly agents) on the drop zone. The reason for this is not found in the surviving 357 Squadron records, but Gordon told me that if the recognition signal on the ground was not exactly as briefed, the airmen did not drop on the primary DZ for fear that something terribly wrong at happened on the ground. For example, had the Japanese learned of the DZ through their own methods, a drop of supplies and agents (if any were carried on 6th. June) would have been a mistake.

Possibly Gordon's crew drop supplies at a secondary DZ, but this is not noted in the logbook. Possibly all materials were returned to Minneriya for use on a future special duties assignment, or dumped over the ocean (not any agent, though!!)

Gordon does not know the whereabouts of any of his crew except the one who, he said, is pretty much a basket case from alcoholism. Gordon suggested that I'd be wasting my time trying to interview the guy, and I have not tried.

So in summary, it's the usual "WE JUST DON'T KNOW ANY MORE"about the 6th. June Op.

That's the best answer I can give you Joe.

I've made more progress on the Dougie Thom transcript. Also, I received an email from Jim Stewart, who was there with 12 Platoon and Dougie Thom. I said I would like to interview him by phone, but he did not send his phone number. He hardly remembers anything, he said so I'll leave him in peace his email to George Masson said this much.:-

I was in 12 Platoon. I remember a boot from the cockpit, also a pistol which seemed to be in good nick for the time it lay there. Don't remember much more except it was there that Ben McIntyre badly injured his hand and had to be airlifted out by one of the helicopters.

Now his Jim Stewart's response to my direct email said this.

I am sorry I cannot add much more to what I have said before, regarding the crashed Liberator, as my memory is not great at the best of times. I will try to help. First of all, I do not remember the main body of the plane. Only the cockpit area, where we found the boot (black leather army issue). Also the pistol, which, if my memory serves me right, was a Lugar type. I cannot be 100% sure.

I do not recall seeing any bones!

Shortly after that we were involved in cutting down trees and clearing the area for the helicopters to land, what with that and guarding the site in case of bandit activity. I did not get back to the plane. Hope this helps in some small way.

Yes, it does help

Dougie Thom will search for Ben McIntyre, who is alive. If Dougie finds him, then we'll really luck out. Ben was in the original Patrol with Lt. Jim Steheli. George McGill, and maybe five or six others. If any other names can crop up to interview, after Ben is intervieWed., will be in even better shape..... Keeping fingers crossed!

Dougie was a wonderful interview. Sharp and very pleasant. A happy person sounds like a Sort o' the Earth bloke. He sure treated me nicely.

Will send more of his interview to you. Perhaps later today.

93.   29 April 2007   Matt Poole to Joe Plant   Joe. Picking up from Part one.
Part two of two Dougie Thom recollections of finding the Liberator 28th of May 1955

Re-George Masson. George was in 11 Platoon. He wasn't in the actual finding of the plane George was another Platoon you see? But I think, as I say, it may have been then that it. [*continuation of the recovery*] how it was handed over from us. He may have moved on and they may have come in and did something. George was in 11 Platoon He was a corporal the same as me. Corporal.

[Authors note See the previous corresponding letter from George Cahoon.]

[*Dougie continued talking about walking along the wide elephant track on the ridgeline, which served as the border between Malaya and Siam. He says they were told not to cross into Siam was the rebels were lying in ambush there he further talks about Dummelow and Shanley, being the world's worst map readers ever. {Authors note this is the same opinion as George Cahoon} Dougie goes on to describe the wreckage*]

I'm trying to recollect. As I say, you're doing these things and you're probably not taking in much detail, but as I remember, right, everything in the front of the plane was [*sounds like stengley??*] with the exception of the Brownings. The Brownings were sticking out. The glass was broken all over the gun turret, and part of the plane was all open and away, there were tiny pieces scattered around the wings and everything, as far as I could see were away. They were shattered to bits when they came down into this trees 10 years ago [*or possibly earlier*] they must have got torn to bits.

[*Matt says it's that Stehelis report said that the wing was found downhill, and that a tree had been shorn off, so they figured it went into the trees and broke the tree, Thus contributing to the wreckage scatter*]. Dougie simply agrees.

There was very little left of the actual plane. There was bits and pieces of the fuselage and things like that on the plane, but it was a wreck. A lot of the actual canisters was just sitting outside where they had fallen out and come out the plane and some of them were still inside part of the plane. One of the canisters that was lying at the side of the plane, was the one with the Sten guns. Two of which with Sten guns. There must have been, what, I reckon 20 to 30 Sten guns

[*in total there were 22 Sten guns*]

There were two canisters and they were just circular canisters; and they were packed at each end [*unclear what ws really said]* and so were all the others with various things .Along with ammunition, and there were pistols, or something like that. It was separate from the rest of them.

[*Matt says there was one US. .45 calibre pistol*]

I remember one of the pistols, we reckoned it may have been a pilots pistol, or something like that it was separate from the rest of them

That's right, I remember that getting picked up I couldn't give you the details on who picked it up, but I remember that has been found. And the rest, some of the other pistols were in the actual plane, which were being dropped.

[*Matt tells Dougie that there were 18 .38 calibre revolvers and 1.45 calibre revolver*]

That will be may be where maybe George Masson became involved. They would take all of the inventory up, all the material it was found, which we didn't do. We took up as much as we could, as far as I can gather, but then I'm quite sure that we, at that time, moved on. Then somebody else would take over on that camp

I'm quite sure that's what happened .

But what I'm going to do, I going to get in touch with Ben McIntyre, who is still living .And Ben is the boy who was left in charge when Dummelow found the thing, when their Patrol found it, and he Dummelow went to come back up to the camp to get us and then got lost. And Ben left the plane and walked up to us in five minutes to call us in the camp. We all came down near into the plane and started to dismantle it, and still Dummelow was lost

[*Matt asked if Ben is the one who sliced his Thumb tendons on sharp bamboo there. But Dougie corrects the story*]

It was not there, though, Not there no. What he did, he lost a couple of tendons in his finger. What happened was in one of the camps at night, he sharpened up his machete, and then he went to stick it in the ground, and he actually hit a root and his hand slid right down the machete. I was there when that happened and he slid it right down and cut his finger inside his hand. He lost the feeling in his fingers I guess that was in May.

[Dougie was guessing that all of this took place maybe May of 1955, The plane , actually was discovered on the 28th. May. So his recollection was excellent.]

I've also been in touch with Jim Stewart who was in my Platoon as well. *[Matt and Jim can communicate by e-mail]* Jim will maybe recollect bits and pieces that I can't do for you. Because we were all wandering all over the plane, getting things and Jim and I were pals. We went into the army together, from the same place and did our training the in the Cameroonian's. Before we transferred to Royal Scots Fusiliers. Jim and I entered the army together came together and we were pals during the whole thing, so Jim will probably be able to maybe say something, other parts of it and I'll get Ben. Who is actually one on the Patrol that found it see what he can recollect as well.

Most of the people who were on that, quite a few of them are dead there are also two or three of them away, one Bob Kirkpatrick he is in Australia as far as I know. I don't know where. He was one of the ones that came and found it. I don't know where he is and I don't know if I'll ever be able to find out where he is. [Re Jim McSorley] Jim McSorley was not there that I know he was not in 12 Platoon McSorely was in 11 Platoon with George Masson he was one of the ones that maybe came and carried on with the thing. Maybe he'll have some insight as well

[Re Human remains] We looked about for human remains because that was when one of the first things that we tried to see if there were any form of life, even bones or anything round about we certainly didn't see any

[Matt reads from the words of Lt Staheli report: Also what we thought to be the charred remains of human bones were unearthed this was later stated by experts not to be the case. That summarises further, that's Staheli author of the Action diary. believes that the crew did not bail out]

If they didn't bail out, then they could only have been in close proximity of that. As much as I can recollect again I would say that the plane was in a condition that had they still been in that plane there must have been one or two of them still in it. I don't think they would all have been thrown out because the plane wouldn't have travelled terribly far when it hit that jungle. No matter what speed it was going because some of the trees were massive. I wouldn't have thought that that plane coming down there, that's why one of the wings was torn off, and the other one must have been wee bit *[unclear]* but I don't remember a wing still being actually attached too the plane

[Matt asked how much of the fuselage was intact]

Oh. There was quite a bit. The fuselage the guns in the front, turret of the Liberator, the actual front of it was still as far as I is the framework went still there

[Matt askes about the unofficial RAF report which said that the autopilot control in the cockpit was abled to be inspected and that Jim Stewart sent an email saying that he remembers a boot been found in the cockpit. Stewart did not say bones just about, so the assumption for now is that Jim did not see bones and there was something left in the cockpit].

As the years go by, I don't know if they would be eaten by something. There is a possibility that could have happened you have a good reference on it *[the position of the cockpit I think he means]* You'll know the exact point where it was

[Re: The remoteness of the crash area]

We went there, we were dropped off and we made our way to that area so you get there once you get in. What they can do is actually all they need to do, what used to do is blow the trees with the plastic. Blow them down with plastic for LZ's [Matt explains that the Royal Scots Fusiliers report describes using Satchel charges to blow down trees to make the LZ for the choppers which flew out the contents of the Liberator

We used to use plastic, and a big boy who was a woodcutter, that was all what he did. Felled trees and he used to lay the trees down where we wanted them to fall. Rammed the plastic behind it and bang, the biggest trees we could possibly get, so that they knocked down every other tree in the vicinity we used to do that .

[Matt says per the Fusiliers report: A charred flying jacket and a Mae West life preserver vest were found in the wreckage, which is partly why Lt. Steheli believed that there were human remains around]

As I say, I don't recollect finding any bones .I don't recollect that all, but don't get me wrong I mean, although we were doing that I was maybe down there doing it a couple of hours , 3 hours and then up and then maybe the next day I was out Patrol and somebody else went down . That situation when like that you still had to do your Patrols it's possible that there were still a lot of activities going on, when I wasn't there I can only give you the information, I had when I was there

[Matt mentions a Chad Stewart not in 12 Platoon who supposedly kept a daily diary a Bren Gunner maybe in 10 Platoon. Dougie can't specifically recall this man explaining that there were many faces and names 30 or so men in each Platoon. He talked generally about his two years in Service and his philosophy, to do the best he could in his National Service commitment. He tells the story of coming up upon fresh warm elephant dung and sprinting down the trail to try to find

the elephant. Not once did they ever see an elephant. Story of finding opium stash that was flown out by helicopter regarding helicopters , Dougie had interesting comments]

The Navy will come down to the DZ in a spiral. If we got the RAF coming, they wanted a 35° take off for their helicopters They would not come in unless they could get the clearance made to come into the DZ and then go off at 35° maximum 40. Whereas the Navy boys, with a big beards and that, they used to come in and say. 'Oh it'll do us, and then they come stalling roundabout and drop into us. We didn't need to clear a bigger space .

[Dougie tells a further story} Of a Navy helicopter he was aboard, that damage the rotor and it was brought down on a main road, where they waited for a replacement rotor, which was changed. Tells a story of his Patrol shooting a Malayan Home Guard. That was in the area where anything that moves was considered fair game. The injured man, erroneously shot as a bandit, was manhandled out of the area. Very tiring and made a full recovery]

[Re: His Friend Jim Stewart.]

Jimmy and I were there at the same time Jim and I were part of the ones that came down from the camp Jim and I slept in the same basher .We were pals all through it .We were chums.

[Brief talk of McGill dying and Dummelow two of the men on the Patrol which found the Liberator]

Bill will be able to tell us who was on that Patrol. Ben McIntyre. He will be able to tell is who was out on that Patrol with them probably. If he can do that and name them, then we can probably get in touch. But the point is, they left the plane once they found it and came to get us and got lost for a couple of hours. We were actually down on the plane when they still were lost.

[Matt tells a story that Dummelow's team was lost and then they ran into a hornets nest, scattered, and then McGill discovered the wreck]

I can never recollect that, but what happened is they went down the path leaving our camp. Naturally, you always left on a path and then you made your way to wherever your grid reference was where you were supposed to be. You made your way there with compass bearings and such and started find your way to it. But what he did is, he went down there, then they cut their way in to the right as far as I can..... I'm trying to think they cut into the right, off the track there was a hornets nest on the way down, but I don't think they .....unless they disturbed the hornets nest on the way down. But anyway they went down through there. They must have, well you think he would have gone up a short away or something like that Not off the track. I reckon they were only 150 to 200 yards, probably somewhere in that area where the plane was found. That's when Dummelow said, 'Will leave you here Ben and go up and get the rest of the men down here then will see about getting this stuff out. He didn't come back on the track. He went up. You would think he would have gone up a short away or, something like that. However we found out that he didn't get out? He got lost and Ben was sitting there waiting five minutes or whatever 10 minutes, as he said I can't understand this, on going my way up there and Ben just walked up from there, he was no Sgt just an ordinary bloke in a Patrol. Ben just walked, retracing steps back on the track back up into the camp, got us. Ben took us straight back down straight to the plane. It was a simple way was the matter of they had to go away into the jungle and get lost, they did know their way the jungle, because I can assure you we were down there in shorts, just wee shorts on and sandals I think I pulled on my boots I remember rightly. We were down there in anything no time at all, it was that close to our We were 1 million miles away by any chance. The jungle is very difficult to read.

[Matt asked Dougie to describe the kind of jungle around the wreck]

To me it was trees. There may have been bamboo about to. Taking details like that, I can't really go back there but I thought there would trees mainly trees, some of that had sprung up in 10 years after that, all new growth. I didn't think at the time I saw it that there were massive trees because we were able to get right close to the plane get around about it and that site was of that massive trees about, whether it [the crash and fire] destroyed anything at tatl there, and that, and over 10 years ago hadn't really got itself started *[regrowth]* properly it was accessible

[Matt asked Dougie if he was aware of a newspaper story 1955 about the liberators discovery]

He could not remember any such story. I think if I remember rightly someone had taken a number of the aeroplanes or something.

[Authors Note: There was one. I found the article dated June 1955 .researching in 2018.]

[Matt explains that the official R AF report states that the data plate removed from the interior of the wreck. It contained the serial number. Identifying the aircraft also and engine data plate was removed, it was later match to the record of engines attached to KH 326]

We had officers there. The man you are talking about, Blair Agnew was only 21 years old, when he was over there couldn't be much more. And he was an officer. I can assure you, he had no idea, he was not the man you would have wanted to really going to battle with, because he didn't have the experience. But I think it was only in for the two years as well. He wasn't regular, or anything like that. I remember he stayed at his father's house in Broadmeadows in Ayrshire , is a big house down between Kilmarnock and Ayr .That was where his father stayed and where Blair was brought up *[I left this comment in because Dougie was not being mean only matter-of-fact, any man would have preferred a leader with that the experience of course]*

As I said Blair may have come into the picture after we left, to guard to do something else, I wouldn't know but he certainly wasn't in one of the ones that found it

[Re George Cahoon] Dougie remembers the name probably would recognise a face he certainly was not in 12 Platoon which found the Liberator and Dougie says George Cahoon was probably in George Masson Platoon]

[Matt talks about the RAF flying in a team of investigators with the, Commonwealth War Graves Commission rep]

They only spent a few hours on site.

[Matt explained that these men were scared of the jungle and just wanted to get the hell out, According to Blair Agnew and Anthony Gordon one theory is that they glossed over the possibility of remains been in the aircraft]....

I would have thought, they would have needed to search a little bit more than *that* I certainly don't remember them coming

[Matt explains that the RAF and CWGC investigators arrived at the site 09 30 on 'Friday third of June, which was six days after 12 Platoon discovered the Liberator wreckage. This explains why Dougie did not have direct experience with the investigators]

[Matt gives his explanation that the R AF could not do a proper investigation at that time, due to the fact that there was a war going on. Matt says he just wishes the families had been notified]

Dougie, again, said he will seek out Ben McIntyre and get me some more information or, at least the phone number

[Matt explains that the Liberator crew were all Canadians and that the Canadian Government wants to go after human remains]   End of tape 'conversation with a 56 or so minutes recorded.

Authors Note: I feel that it is necessary to insert an Officers report on the discovery of the Libertor. This extraxt is by Col Blair Agnew who in 2005 submitted his recollection of the discovery. To be entered into the Royal Highland Fusiliers Journal. Due to changes in the British Army In 1979 The Royal Scots Fusiliers became part of the RHF Regiment.:-

94.   Blair Agnew's Recollection from The RSF Journal.

In mid-1955 the director of operations in Malaya launched Operation Unity, designed to flush out terrorist activity along the Siamese now Thailand border.

It is now 49 years since these events occurred, and consequently relying on my memory without the benefit Patrol reports carries with it the risk of falling down on exact detail. Not only that, but the author did not participate in the event until approximately 48 hours after it had happened. Thus to some extent, is say is involved, any errors in the take stand to be corrected if any members of the Patrol involved can do so.

Obviously a considerate number of troops were deployed on Op Unity, but this story concerns primarily 12 Platoon the Company 1 RSF commanded by Lt John Staheli and 7 Platoon see Company commanded by 2nd./Lt. Blair Agnew.

The Siamese border drops. to the Southto form a V with Kroh, the Battalion headquarters situated near the bottom. 12 Platoon were deployed to the Westof the border and well North of Kroh. 7 Platoon travelled from Kroh to Bailing and then North on the Westerly Road, to debus and enter into the jungle following a two-hour march across paddy field. After entering the jungle normal Patrolling took place. As we gradually move North

After approximately four weeks Fusilier Eddie Kerr, the 7 Platoon Radio Operator, reported to me that he had been listening to 12 Platoon's radio traffic and had heard them using the word 'Liberator.' He asked me if that was a codeword, but I could not find no trace of it in my list. Within 24 hours 7 Platoon were ordered to move North to join 12 Platoon at the grid reference which indicated a distance achievable in a day.

This turned out to be a total fallacy and when the Platoon set out the next morning, they embarked on the worst journey they could imagine. The going was through bamboo over a series of steep ridges, travelling 1000 yards. Exhausted we bashed up on the top of a hill and the following morning found. That in fact we had spent the night in. Siam. We moved off just after first light and regained what we believe to be. The border track running along the ridge

In mid-morning we came across an abandoned small terrorist camp just off the track and subsequently we came to the conclusion that this was a small outpost acting as a guard camp for the main CT camp. A little later we started to drop down with the track winding in front of us until we reached,a stream at the bottom. The track crossed the stream and started to ascend a ridge again winding upwards, and in approximately 25 yards we came round the corner to find ourselves facing three slit trenches sited to give a perfect killing ground at the corner. It was clear that we had virtually .arrived at 12 Platoon's located and after proceeding for a further 250 yards joined up with 12 Platoon.

What follows is John Stahel's account of what his Patrol that found: As stated earlier, 12 Platoon had been operating North of 7 Platoon and after four weeks they had discovered this recently abandoned CT camp. It was large, being capable of holding approximately 100 terrorist. It jad a small playground, armourer's shop, ablutions for both men and women,. and a cookhouse area. Potentially it was an important case and the defences around it gave credence to that. It has to be remembered that the

CT 's were known to operate near the borders so that they could, if necessary, cross into the sanctuary of Siam, where technically they could not be followed

Having found the camp 12 Platoon made it their base and Patrolled from it in the hope of following up and Engaging any of its former occupants. One Patrol was dispatched back down the approach track with a view to Patrolling the valley. Which carried the stream The Patrol was led by Sgt Dummelow, as it passed the slit trenches, one of the Patrol brushed against what turned out to be a hornets nest. And these hornets exited their nest at high speed and were potentially very angry. The Patrol reacted in the correct manner and scattered before regrouping and proceeding. The leading scout asked Sgt Dummelow where he should go and was told go round the next and 10 yards to the right. This he did and within about 10 yards.he stopped, and according to Sgt Dummelow said "Sargeant- there's an aity plane."

Lying hidden in the jungle, no more than 10 yards from a main terrorist track was the remains of a Liberator bomber. A Jock was invited to call under the wing to get its number and the investigation began. It was virtually intact, auto pilot was set, the radio frequency setting could be seen, there appeared to be the fuel tanks. The Browning machine guns were in place and on the ground were flying gloves and some personal armaments.

The plane was thoroughly searched, for the fuselage was virtually intact, and here the finds became more incredible. It appeared that there were three categories of cargo waiting to be dropped. The first was medical supplies, and not surprisingly it was quite clear that these were well past their sell-by -date and quite unusable. The second was clothing which included KF shirts and other items of clothing, but damp and time had done their worst and none of this kit was Serviceable. The third category was the most important and consisted of weapons and communications. The weapons, including Sren gun parts, were well wrapped in greaseproof paper and proved to be in good condition, so much so that 12 Platoon swore that they had switched their working parts of their Sten guns for those in the plane, as a latter were in better condition. They further swore the REME armourers had said that the parts sent out by helicopter {removed from the jungle crash site by helicopter} were in poor condition. This may well have been apocryphal, but it made for a good story.

Obviously it was vital that all this hardware should be evacuated and RAF experts should be called in to examine the wreck and some bones which had been found nearby. 12 Platoon set to work to cut down the trees around the camp, thereby creating an LZ for helicopters. The R AF flew in but according to 12 Platoon, were not enamoured with the jungle environment and flew out rapidly, having pronounced the bones to be those of pigs.

What must the terrorist have thought when news reached them of this find? Therer they were with one of the major camps, well - sited and well - defended, and there, no more than 10 yards from their main approach track, was a supply of arms and ammunition which they could never have imagined themselves capable of acquiring. Perhaps it illustrates how dense the jungle is and proves what those who spent weeks Patrolling no, namely that visibility in thick jungle varies between 5 and 10 yards. Interestinly ad lmost as a postscrip , the other missing Liberator was found about 3 years later.

[Authors note: The Seremban Liberator]

Patrols of 7 Platoon and 12 Platoon did not end with this discovery, for we discovered that at night we could see what appeared to be a flashing light coming from the West. We took bearings of this light, and although the maps of the area were extremely bad we believe that the light must be coming from a cliff, on a long high ridge to the West.

It was decided that a Patrol consisting of John Staheli, myself, Sgt.Jackman, Sgt. Dummelow and Fusilier Greenside would investigate. We set out found ourselves on a knife edge ridge with a track with a maximum width of 3 feet. There appeared to be no way spot the cliff face, but eventually a relatively clear but very steep slope on the North side of the ridge apparently ended in a precipice over a sheer drop. It was decided to investigate, and Greenside went down first, followed by Sgt Dummelow. Sgt Jackman then went down, indicating that a fine hanging down was not securely anchored. I then went down, followed by John Staheli who stumbled, grabbed the vine which gave way, and he hurtled down the slope, as he passed me I grabbed his Carbine, hoping to stop him, but this had no effect. At the cliff edge he hit a tree with the crook of his right arm and spun right round the tree before falling into overhanging vines. Which by the grace of God held him. We dragged him out and retreated to the ridge path where all of us set and dragged at cigarettes. Deeply shocked.

John had lossed his jungle hat that and by chance a week later we found it at the bottom of what was a 300 foot cliff. When we returned to the camp still shocked, Johns remarked to me perhaps summed him up well:

"Blair for God's sake don't tell Patricia."

12 Platoon moved North two weeks later and were lifted out, having spent six weeks on Patrol 7 Platoon went North a week later carrying as many of our resupply parachutes as we could manage, and we were also lifted out, having spent exactly 7 weeks on Patrol our longest ever sojourm in the jungle but one that has remained extra on the memory as probably the most unusual Patrol carried out by 1 RSF.

95. **2 May 2007** **Joe Plant to Matt Poole,**

From my other 'conversations with Blair Agnew he did not find the Lib. He was instructed to connect up with Lt. Staheli but was at the scene of the crash maybe a day or so later when they took over. As for Tony Gordon, the MT Officer, he was at Base HQ in Kroh and was called out to the scene. Again, I understand that the heli airlift took the supplies back to Kroh. There they were put on the MT lorries and taken down to REME Base workshops. in KL . I am waiting for an answer back from the RA about Charles Carson and trying to establish contact with other sources for the other two who are listed as missing. That, I believe, will take a long time, as will details of the officer. Need patience, that's all.

96.   8 May 2007   Matt Poole to Joe Plant

This is the email that Don Timmerman's sent me. Interesting !!

I believe that I have evidence support fact that the R AF did indeed notify the RC AF of the discovery of Liberator KH 326 in 1997, my father (Dick) wrote to her member of Parliament seeking what information the government had regarding the disappearance of. Arie and his crew His letter was forwarded to the National Archives of Canada and in 1998, Dad received the document which I have attached The circumstantial and discovery report you already have. However, you will notice that the cover letter to the discovery report clearly states that it was sent by the British Air Ministry to the Canadian Chief of the Air Staff on or about ninth of September 1955. This (the 1998 document) was the first time a family and heard of this discovery of KH 326 43 years later. We know that Gerald's family was not informed, nor lightly the others. More than just an oversight I think. This should not have happened. Anyway, I hope this helps to answer one question.

97.   16 May 2007   Joe Plant to Matt Poole

Found Ben McIntyre in Troon and spoke with him. He seemed a very quiet fellow. He was a bit shaky at first. His memory is not all that good, but I did explain the circumstances. He was one of the Platoon which found the Liberator. He does not remember McGill or Dummelow or any officers, just a couple of the guys. Cannot remember how they found it, but he said it was in terrible undergrowth and thick bamboo. He does remember the hornets and being chased. Did not want to get stung by those besties!! He is reluctant to go to any reunions and prefers to forget about the army. I suspect he was a National Service conscript like me.

He was shocked to find even today that the Lib had not been found I explained about the wrong GRs. He remembers clearing the trees for the LZ, a terrible job. They had to use explosives that were dropped in. He mentioned the RAF and CWGC arriving, but that they left quickly. Anyway, he said if he speaks with anyone else, he will give them my contact number, but I don't hold out much hope.

98.   22 May 2007   Joe Plant to Matt Poole,

I received a message about the (RA)Royal Artillery about L/Bdr. Charles Carson. We can eliminate him, as he was a POW in Sandakan, where he died in Borneo. His unit was captured when the Japs invaded Java. I still think a possible agent carried as a passenger aboard KH326 was an officer??? Could be wrong

99.   22 May 2007   Matt Poole to Joe Plant.

Thanks for the Charles Carson details good detective work !

You may recall that rear gunner, Gordon Hercus aboard S/Ldr Sims Lib on 6th. June 45, told me that as far as he knew, only crewmate John 'Pop' . Flannigan was still alive today was in his 90s was not well . Don't waste your time contacting him said Gordon. I decided at long last, not to take Gordon's advice . And I Phoned on Saturday 'Pop' is 94 and a happy-go-lucky sounding man his memory is very spotty and really can't help with specifics of 6th. June, but he put me in touch with his daughter Nancy.

Nancy, with whom I'm in touch by computer, is thrilled with the story, and she will be sending me some photos and copies of her dad's logbook. Already she scanned the page covering 6th. June, and it has the same takeoff time is shown in Gordon's logbook : 0800 . Local time this is 58 minutes the takeoff time of KH 326, as found in the RAF circumstantial report. I believe both Libs took off within minutes of one another because:

1 The Sims crew spotted Timmerman's crew over Bunting Island and

2 The rate of petrol consumption was critical. On such a long flight it would have been illogical for Timmermans crew to have burned excessive petrol in order to catch up with a Lib that had taken off nearly. An hour earlier. NO way!!

Also, per the Hercus and Flannigan logbooks, the Sims crew was airbourne for 17 hours 55 minutes. Call it 18 hours, given an 0800 take-off time, the halfway point would have been in the vicinity1700. Time of Sunset on 6 June was 1658, with Twilight lasted until 1721 (with no moon) .The drop needed just a little light for being able to see the DZ and to drop without hitting terarain .So the 1700 time, give or take, makes perfect sense as Hercus Sims crew is approximately .Halfway point (I know the logbook shows the "D.N.C.O", or Did Not Complete Operation", and we don't know why they couldn't complete the drop,)

The 1945 Circumstantial Report says the Sims crew spotted Timmerman's between 1633 and 1645 over bunting, which was only 20 or so minutes from the Drop Zone .That ties in with the DZ been reached by Sims circa 1700. Then it was approx nine hours of flying back to Minneriya for Sims

My point is this .An 0858 takeoff time for Timmerman's makes no sense, given the known round-trip time of about 18 hours for Sims .That would have put Timmerman's the halfway point -long after dark making for an impossible drop situation .

It is my opinion that the 1945 Circumstantial Report takeoff time is off by about an hour .Given this error one can't trust the accuracy of the other time references in the same report, including the 1633 1645 "Last sightings of Timmerman's, by the Sims crew, even if these numbers are wrong, it still makes sense Sims took off at about 0800, reached the halfway DZ Mark around 1700 with enough light to a drop (though they didn't drop), and then turned for home for the second half of the flight .Logic dictates that Timmerman's flying behind Sims (and independently) would have been on a similar schedule, planning a nine-hour outward passage and a 9 hour return flight.

So I'm finally Satisfied with the time in question!

100.   22 May 2007   Matt Poole to Joe Plant

Some pleasant tidbits of evidence showed up in my mailbox today photos of Harry Andrews and two wartime newspaper stories from the Sudbury Star Sudbury Ontario Canada

FLYER REPORTED MISSING AFTER BURMA MISSION

Stationed in India since March of this year, as a member of the crew of a Liberator bomber with an R AF Squadron, Sgt. Air Gunner , Harry Andrews is reported missing in Action. This news received by the airmen's parents, Mr and Mrs H. Andrews of 208 Pine Street.

Since going into Action as a wireless airgunner Sgt Andrews has completed a number of operational flights over such targetsas the jungles of Burma, the islands of Penang and other points near China, where the Allied fliers meet with the Jap Zeros.

During an interview with the Sudbury Daily Star earlier this year that the young airman expressed the wish that he would like to receive a posting to the Burma Theatre. The 19-year-old flyer got his wish, and was posted as a tail gunner in the Liberator bomber in the Far East.

OUT IN SPACE

"You seemed to be perched out in space on the tail of a bomber." He wrote in the letter home. "Of course there is the intercom, but you don't get the throb of the engines out on the tail. You look up down sideways all there is sky. That's how I like it a bare sky.

Keen on getting into aircrew Harry enlisted for gunnery and took to his pre-aircrew training at Edmonton later been posted to Mattmen. The youthful flyer graduated with his Gumley wing and three books in July 1944 was then posted the West Coast for operational training completing this training.

Born in South Shields England Harry came to Canada with his parents in 1929. He was a student at Elm Street public-school and later took his commercial course at the Sudbury mining and technical school, joining the staff of the Canadian National Railway in the ticket office at the conclusion of his schooling he remained in that job the two years

So we have two very useful clues

1   He was born in South Shields UK
2   He and his parents emigrated from England to Canada in 1929. This also implies that his sister Margaret was much younger and was born in Canada.

101.   30. May 2007   Joe Plant to Matt Poole

I sent an E/M to the Local Studies Library South Sheilds dated 27th May Outlining the Story of the Missing Lib and Harry's part and emigration the following is their prompt reply.

Hello Joe

Check of the St Catherine's index (Gen register office) on microfiche has found the following:

Biirth registered April/ May /June 1925- Harry Andrews (mother's maiden name Milburn) SouthShields 10 a 1608

Marriage-registered October/November/December 1924-Harry Andrews and Isabella B Milburn SouthShields 10 a 1507

I have not traced a birth for Margaret between 1925 and 1929'

There is only one Andrews in South Shields, listed in the phone book J.J. Andrews 80 Trinity walk SouthShields

Good luck with your research.

102.   14 June 2007   Matt Poole to Joe Plant

Huge news from the daughter of KH326 pilot Arie Timmermans ...Read on its proof that KH 326 was NOT carrying any agents , just supplies

++

Thanks for the Peter O'Reilly news the other day sorry I forgot to reply at the time to thank you! Did you know that I'd heard from Peter's daughter a while ago, so I did not knowing already that Peter was at Kroh and remembered hearing about the Lib find? But you talked directly with Peter, so that's good to hear.

Read on my friend. This is a wonderful gift that Aire's daughter has to share with me.

Mary Constance Timmerman's (widow of Aire Timmerman's) to Frank Joseph and Maud Gladys Timmerman's (Arie's parents). 22 January 1946:

[Susan Zurakowski daughter of Aire and Mary Constance Timmerman's, sent Matt Poole the 1946 letter along with a preface and a note at the end]

When I returned to Canada at the end of May. I went through my father's and mother's papers unfortunately the pilot log entries from my father were prior to his deployment overseas. I'm surprised that I don't have his logbook or, the letters my mother wrote to him. While he was overseas I also don't have any of his personal effects except the picture of my mother. In an RCAF frame I don't know if he had it only in Canada or, if he took it overseas with him?

There was one letter that my mother wrote to my father's parents that has the account of the events of the mission when my father was lost, as recounted to my mother by Haig Sims when he returned to Canada. The following is copied from his letter (Squadron Leader Haig Sims piloted the second Liberator sent out to Northern Malaya with KH 326 on 6 June 1945)

Haig and Barbara (presumably Haig's wife) both came for dinner and stayed till midnight. Haig was simply grand. He brought the maps, the very ones that Tim has with him (waterproof silk guaranteed to last 50 years even underwater).. They are extremely detailed Haig told me every detail he could think of, and I will try to report as much of it as I can.

In the first place, the job of 357 Squadron was the dropping of supplies and men (Dad guessed that last summer) behind the enemy lines, particularly in the Malay Peninsular. This particular mission was to drop supplies only. It seems there were about 20 men naked in the jungle in Malaya and the object was to fly up a certain valley. And drop supplies to these men. Haig said it was an honour for him and Tim to be chosen out of the Squadron to do that particular mission and they both felt very keen about finding these men. They planned the trip very carefully.. They flew out of Ceylon.

Haig last saw Tim's plane just as they crossed the coast just above Penang Island . The target was in the Northern most part of Malaya. The weather was perfect. Haig dropped his supplies on what he hoped. Was the target. He said it was almost impossible to be sure. because rains had swollen the rivers so much that it was difficult to follow the map accordingly to rivers And the target was vague.

At the risk of their own lives, these geurrillas responded to a signal from Ceylon, as soon as they thought Tim was missing, to say that only one Liberator had flown up the valley. Haig says this may have been himself or it may have been Tim. If it actually was Tim we haven't much of a clue as to where Tim's plane went down - it could even be in Sumatra or anywhere. But it seems more likely that he came down between the time that Haig saw his plane last and the arrival at the target because Pete (must be Joseph Jean Paul Perron Airey Timmerman's navigator.) Is a very keen navigator and I'm sure he would have been dead on target. He always is. In that case the plane must have come down in an area of less than 400 square miles , more likely in an area of less than 100 square miles.

As soon as Tim did not return everyone started a very thorough search, Planes, cruisers, Submarines . And the geurrillas themselves. Haig says the whole district had been gone over. With a fine tooth comb. During this search they found 4 Liberators [?] None of which was Tim's, one of them as far away as the North Andaman's.

This is the way it seems to me .If Tim's plane had crashed .Haphazardly it would have been found.In this search and identified since it had not been found, then Tim and the crew must have got out of the plane safely. It is my idea that they may have either destroyed or hidden the plane so thoroughly that it could never be found I'm sure that is what Tim would do since he would want to make sure theJaps found absolutely. No trace

I asked Haig particularly. About their equipment absolutely everything is on their person -when they jump weapons, indestructible maps, compass, medicine, concentrate food supply, and heavens no what else? Haig says there were men who lived alone in the jungle ever since the fall of Singapore in 1939 and still survive. I know Tim would know how to get along in such a situation .

Well mom and dad, it is very much as it? And yet I found it encouragingly .I believe that Tim will eventually get home safely . Haig told me about the dream one of the the chaps in the Squadron, in which Tim walked into the mess one night and said. He was quite all right.

The only other information I have from the letters my father wrote to his mother just before his last mission is that Monsoon season had begun, hence the swollen rivers .This mission seems to have been delayed because of weather conditions .But other missions were being flown my father was tired in getting to bed about 2:00 a.m. He had lost about 10 pounds but attributed it to the extreme heat at the time of the year. I am still going through my mother's papers but doubt if I will find more. Of course if I do I will forward information that might be relevant to you all. I am anxious to hear about the jungle expedition and hope all is going well. for them. I can't remember for sure but I think you said that Haig Sims isn't still alive. Certainly have been wonderful to talk to him.

{This is the end of Susan's email.}

103. 14 June 2007:   Joe Plant to Matt Poole,

I wonder if Haig Sims was being cautious and kind to Arie's Mum & Dad about the conditions prevailing and the survival kit, etc., etc. It does not make any sense to me. From the facts which have been previously revealed, I understood that Sims did not complete his mission, i.e., did not drop supplies, but returned back to base with his cargo? He even commented on the rain swollen rivers and the target was vague??

Also if it was good weather, there were only 2 planes in the sky but they did not see him go down, and if he was flying second in the queue why did the rear gunner not spot him? He was the last to see him over the Malayan coast before they entered thick cloud. This sure is a mystery.

And the comment about Sumatra, strange I assume, would be on their homeward flight path. But we know they did not drop the supplies.

Sorry to be a bit negative, but it still seems strange and contradictory at this moment in time.

However another snippet. I contacted a friend of mine Tony Hamilton a Royal Hampshire soldier who served in Malaya 1954-56. Who knows quite a lot about their involvement. He told me he had a photo of Brigadier Erskine DSO, Commander of the Guards Division – the last-known photo of him standing in front of an Auster plane with its pilot Capt J.F. Churcher Royal Artillery stood beside him. The plane crashed into the jungle. Both were listed as missing. That was on the 11 Nov.1949. A few years later, 16th June 1955 (not 10 years), another Hampshire army Patrol found the plane near the Bentong Gap. No survivors, only a set of Medal Ribbons which were identified as Erskine's, a shirt tab with the name of a London Army Offiercs supply shop. . And of course the plane number. TJ664.

The moral of this is similar to Timmermans, where hardly anything was found: wild animals, etc., etc. Not a conclusion however.

104. 14 June 2007   Matt Poole to Joe Plant

Oh damn you immediately caught something which I temporarily forgot: the fact that according to Gordon Hercus logbook, the Sims crew did not complete their drop successfully (D.N.C.O). The logbook of Gordon's crewmate John Flanagan is a teaser though it has D.C.O. written for their next flight but for 6/7 June there is neither a DNC or nor a D.N.C.O!!

And if you look at Hercus logbook entry, that the. D.N.C.O.Is actually written level with Gordon's notes of the Timmerman's crew been missing. It makes no sense that Gordon would note Timmerman's Op as a D.N.C.O. and then not know the success/failure of his own aircraft mission. So is safe to assume that, indeed, the Sims crew did not complete their drop. successfully 6 of June.

These are conflicting tidbits of evidence can drive one mad! On the other hand, they make the study of history a fascinating puzzle too.

As to why anyone on the Sims Liberator did not see the Timmerman's Lib off the Bunting island, I can understand this

1 Timmerman's was probably not RIGHT behind Sims.

2 Although the comulonimbus clouds may have been confined to the coast, or right off the coasts (according to Gordon Hercus), perhaps overland there were still clouds, which at times obscured the view back towards the Timmerman's Lib.

3 The atmospheric haze must always be significant in that climate, just from the amount of water vapour around. A huge Liberator is really just a spect in the sky, anyway. These Libs were natural metal (unpainted), so in a grey haze they can all but disappear from sight, even from close range.

4 The Sun. was about to set, adding to the difficulty in spotting the Timmerman's aircraft.

5 The Sims crew were totally focused upon their task : finding the needle in a haystack DZ, communicating with the ground and spotting the correct ID signal, lining up for the drop, and then getting the hell out of that dangerous environment.

6 They were flying at low altitude-with hills around. And they were climbing after crossing the coast, in order to stay above the terrain all of this jostling etc, would have added to the sensory overload each crewman experienced.

7 And they were keyed up and probably scared to some extent .At least I would have been!!

These same conditions could have added to explain how a fire from a crashed Liberator, and the noise of the crash, could have been missed by Japanese and anti-Japanese alike. Plus the incredible sound absorbing qualities of jungle vegetation and hilly terrain. The fire probably went out quickly and given nightfall, the smoke must not have been easily pinpointed. Again a large Liberator is really just a spect when compared to its larger environment air or ground .

I'll certainly let you know as soon as I hear from the trekkers. Fingers crossed!!

That Auster crash stories a great one! Wild animals got them, unless the CT's or others did not remove the bodies first.

105. 28 June 2007   Matt Poole to Joe Plant

A 357 Squadron airmen George McGregor in Canada date with this take on things

George McGregor (Art Coy crew 357 Squadron) to Matt Poole 25 June 2007

It will be quite easy to determine extra bods (agents been dropped by Parachute) were aboard when the wreck is reached. The special ramp would have been installed for them to sit upon before being dropped. The ramp, or remains of one, would still be there.

The Timmerman's crew would have used the great Nicobar Island as its last fix before heading to the coast of Malaya.

Maybe I should run through the procedure in making a drop. The drop area would be a clearing in the jungle. It would have a group of fires in the form of T. There would also be an Aldus lamp flashing a letter. If the letter was not one we had been briefed for, we did not drop, as the Jackson probably taken over. We mostly at the second drop site to then go to.

At any rate, when getting close to the DZ we would select the point from which to make a timed run. At this point the pilot was given a course to fly, and the bomb aimer when DZ appeared would guide the pilot over the DZ using the bomb site. When lined up, the bomb aimer would say steady the bomb aimer would open the bomb doors and with about a minute to go would put on a red light to prepare the dispatcher for the drop. Would put on a green light when time to drop. If he decided it unsafe, but the red light back on in some cases it meant making second run.

If agents were involved, they would sit on a ramp above the bomb they when the green light was put on, the dispatcher will give each one a little shove to get them to slide out, you had to be very careful to do things right and not get them all up in trees. The dispatcher would be one of the air gunners trained for the drops. They men on the ground in the jungle were able to get word back to base on the success of the drop out crew never had a bad report comeback I would take with a grain of salt Tokyo Rose, Bent aircraft, water in petrol and switching planes.

[Authors Note. Dec 2018 : George's point about the last navigation fix at the Great Nicobar Island would be on Timmermans PORT side inbound to Malaya. STARBOARD return homeward route.]

Of .course, we do have the official 1945 R AF report stating that water had been found in the petrol bouncer and this had been radioed Timmerman's crew, although Gordon's account has a few errors in it (after all, it was 62 years ago that these events happened)

I have to believe they were switched aircraft, and that the weather front they hit right off the coast was not a factor he was absolutely sure about ending up in the bent aircraft after switching from KH 326, but he was in error when he said that KH 326 was brand-new. NOT true at all had been on the Squadron since at least January. So it was well used Gordon was wrong in stating that they NEVER only carried supplies, meaning that they must have dropped agents on 6 June.

My biggest question is whether the Japanese really taunted them and named the skipper that day, but Gordon insisted it was true the fact that he told me that they named Squadron Leader Sims is just not the kind of thing that an intelligent man like Gordon would have made up I could be wrong of course, but I will believe Gordon on this it sure makes a story interesting! And it's not exactly far-fetched the 357 attachment and just moved to Minneriya, and it is reasonable to expect that the Japanese had their own agents on so long who had tried to sabotage the petrol someone could have learned that Squadron Leader Sims was the C.O. of the detachment, and are taken off on 6 June bound for Malaya. Thus, a simple radio broadcast directed at the Sims crew could have happened.

106.   26 July 2007   Joe Plant to Matt Poole,

No News is good news, so they say?

Been busy on my memoirs and Malayan history 1948-60. I have found out the origins of the AJUF (Anti Japanese Union & Forces) and MPAJA (Malayan Peoples Anti Japanese Army), both originating from the MCP (Malayan Communist Party).

The AJUF, it appears, was originally formed in 1941 or thereabouts. My theory is that the name was chosen by the MCP. However, in 1942 after the British surrendered to the Japanese, the term MPAJA appears possibly to have been named by the British, to join forces with Force 136 – a group which you know about. It did extend their capacity into Burma, Indo China, etc. The missions to drop supplies by Liberators is testiment to their extent.

However I also found out that the dropping of supplies, arms, medical, etc. to separate MPAJA units (consisting of approx 10,000 members) by the end of July 45 was 1,904 small arms (rifles, sten guns, etc.) 4,608 grenades, and 0.85 tons of explosives. By mid-July 187 British staff and 32 wireless Stations were operating in Malaya.

I have a copy of the programme for the Victory Parade held in London in 1946, listing all the forces taking part. Under the Malayan Contingent the above two names do not appear, but a strong contingent was present under the name of Guerrilla force and Police. Possibly this was because they were recognised as the military section of the MCP, which had never been accepted by the British Government. The origins of the 1948-60 MPABA (Malayan Peoples Anti British Army) seems to trace right back to the AJUF, if you understand my reasoning?

107.   21 August 2007   Joe Plant to Matt Poole,

In a book written "My Side of History" by *Chin Peng*, the leader of the CT revolt in Malaya. Within his script he refers to Liberators. He mentions being invited to the first supply drop on the 26th Feb 1945, which dropped supplies and two Force 136 officers, into a DZ at a Tin Mine off the Tapah-Bidor Road. (Tapah is the town where we used to join the armoured convoy up into the Cameron Highlands.)

[Authors Note. Dec 2018. Ref is made to Brian Moynahans book "JUNGLE SOLDIER" that states this specific drop of suppliers and 2 Officers. Named as Major's. Hannah & Harrison.

In fact there were 3 Drops. on the same day 26th. Feb. 1945:   2 of Personnel : 1 of just supplies :

Drop 1. Major Hannan or Hislop landed in thick jungle in Kedah, together with 5 Chinese Members.

Drop 2. 150 miles? South. Major Harrison along with 2 Radio operators named as : Cpl. Hempleman & Chuen a Chinese Member. Were dropped near Bukit Bidor. This I believe is the one *Chin Peng* was at the DZ

Drop 3. Another B24 Liberator flew in shortly after to drop further supplies. It needed 100 men to collect and carry into the jungle the weighty content of suppliers dropped. Chapman was at this drop as was *Chin Peng*.

Dates of other Drops. with named personnel are as those listed on pages 9-10]

He also mentions that Davis (another Force 136 officer) was in radio contact with Ceylon. *Chin Peng* advised him on specific areas in the Kedah, Perak region, where his forces were operating in. (Kedah and Upper Perak are border states of the Malaya/Siam (now Thailand) Border.) This information was radioed back to Ceylon.

He also wrote:

> *"The safe arrival of Broome and Chapman [Spencer Chapman, British agent] in Ceylon in late May coincided with the dramatic call by military planners for Operation Zipper's readiness date, to be advanced from late November to mid August. All the old calculations had to be dumped and replaced by the new arrangements, a massive acceleration to the programme. Supply operations in earnest from Ceylon began on June 6th, where three newly arrived RAF Liberators flying from airstrips in Minneriya and China Bay were required to fly round trips of 2,500 to 3,000 miles, under all-weather condition. Very few sorties were cancelled because of weather. Pilots frequently encountered heavy rain and mist over the Malayan drop zones."*

He also went on to say that the RAF drops. were very accurate, although some DZ's were like handkerchiefs on the side of hills, and the dropping of SOE officers and wireless operators began in July???

[Authors note Dec 2018: Freddy Spencer Chapmn was a "stay behind" with Force 136, had been in the jungle since early 1942. when he was cut off and went into the jungle with Force 136. He was captured by the Japanese and escaped. Chapman together with Broome. Finally left Malaya at Pankor Island onboard a Submarine on the 13th. May 1945 & arrived in Trincamallee 6 days later 19th/ 20th. May. 1945. Both men were required to assist in the final preparations of Operation Zipper.

RAF 357 Squadron began operations from Minarriya Ceylon, in Late May 1945. He refers to 6th June would that be reference to the ill fated KH326 ???]If we could get hold of *Chin Peng* (apart from wringing his neck), he might be able to cast a thought on KH326?? What do you reckon?

108. 23 August 2007   Matt Poole to Joe Plant

The *Chin Peng*. Stuff is fascinating. I'll have to dig through some of my books and records to see if I can match up the first. Malaya drop with the Liberator Squadron base.

Hmm.... I wonder what *Chin Peng*. Does know about KH 326 probably nothing much, since they didn't discover it, on the other hand, once it was found by the RSF, could there be some records of their visits in CT archives somewhere? Probably there are no such archives, maybe I'm wrong.

As for the wreck being rediscovered, I'm waiting, waiting, waiting for any news from Shaharom Ahmed and/or Capt. Zuraiman. They should have been back from the trip by now.... If they ever got away?

109. 12 Septmber 2007   Sharharom Ahmad to Matt Poole

Just got back to my office after one day recovery from most hardcore tracking in the world we had to encounter.

It is a shame for me to say I'm so sorry that we did not reach the wreck site. The trail were so great and we only achieve 5 km tracking for three days and three nights. The terrain was so inhabitable and we had to use local guide to guide us into the thick jungle, wading across several rivers, walking down and up into 60° slope where one error can make you down into the ravine. Plus lots and lots of bamboo jungles similar to RSF reports, which stated they encountered bamboo jungles. And rains! Once rains, we do some drifting in the jungle which so dangerous since we carried heavy backpack with several day rations.

Our journey started at 7 September where we drive using logging road to our starting point where the road ends there. We trekked using old logging road cutting some hills and rivers to make and journey faster. At night, it's raining heavily. The next day, we walked again and climbing up to 900 m of slopes until reaching the end of logging trail. It is near to Gunong Bayu. From there, we go down and reaching the river at 5:30 PM. We stop there and proceed to the next day. At this point, there were no trails or anything to lead us to the wreck site. From our GPS, it shows we were only 4.5 km from the wreck site. We start climbing, descending and reaching the highest reach where we were stuck into the thick bamboo jungles.

It is 4:30 PM and rains start pouring down. We have to go down into the valley where we stop for our third night in the jungles. Malaysian Army which control the area give us 4+1 days to go in, but we spend three days right now. A decision need to make which some of us including me. Were heartbroken and ration were only last for another day and we could not proceed which from our research, it will took us another four days to going out. We have to aborted our mission and the next day (fourth day). We walked out we only bought out from the jungle at 11 PM exhausted, bruised and broken hearts. From our GPS, it only shows 2.1 km from the wreck site.

But we determined to visit it soon. Our plan is to use helicopter to insert at one operational LZ 2 km North of Bukit Papalang where we can achieved one or two days. Reaching the wreck site

I'm so sorry which we felt to achieved our mission. But I promised you that we will visit soon very soon later I have attached some photos of the jungles to you.

Right now, I'm making a slow recovery of the most hazardous trip we ever encountered. And we glad that we did not encountered any dangerous snakes or anything and post danger to us.

110. <u>13 September 2007</u>   **Matt Poole to Joe Plant**

First my apologies for not getting back to you with follow-up info in answer to some of your ongoing queries.

The expedition to KH 326 crash site was finally granted a small window to proceed on foot.

Unfortunately, despite a valiant effort, the first attempt was foiled by that same dense, trackless jungle, steep slopes and incessant rains that have been described to me by the RSF Lads Shaharom Ahmed, in his two messages to me yesterday, was clearly depressed that his team had not succeeded, but he's more determined that ever to make it to the site... Eventually.... Using (he hopes) helicopter trips into the jungle to save time.

From the description of the jungle, however, it sounds like any attempt will be challenging. And the other factor is getting permission from the Government again... For not just a trip, but helicopter support. Apparently Captain Zuraiman of the Malaysian Army Museum thinks he can use his influence to get the team the desired helicopter transportation to a landing zone used to resupply the Malaysian border Patrols in the area. But even if they do get choppered in, it's still a strenuous hike through thick jungle.

So read on below I think you'll agree that Shaharom gave it his all, despite turning back with a couple of kilometres of the site. So near, so far.... And he is recovering from his arduous trek if you want to write to Ahmed to thank him or give him support, I'm sure it would boost his spirits

I suppose it will be a few Months before the next attempt I'm not sure about whether there. I believe it rains all the time there, with no clear dry season/Monsoon season like. In parts of Burma but there are rainier Months on average, and maybe they need to shoot for the statistical dry season. But the HEAT and HUMIDITY.

Cheers Joe and I'm sorry to the news is not what we had hoped, but it's an ongoing project that may still have. The outcome we hope.

The RSF, just had their reunion and Blair Agnew spoke about the wreck to the 200 or so who were gathered. Perhaps you heard from Blair or one of the others in attendance.

111. **19 September 2007**   **Joe Plant to Shaharom Ahmad.**

Hi Shaharom

I have just returned back from my vacation yesterday when I checked my email to find your sitrep from Matt on the trek into the Ulu. Disappointing but do not flag as we say in England 'If you don't succeed the first time try try again. ' And my friend you will succeed that I and many others are with you all the way in spirit to guide you to the ultimate find. And when you do you will call out EUREKA (I have found it)

Having read with your report we sympathise with your thoughts and arduous trek. Yes leeches, rain pouring down and the hacking through the terrain in those mountainous regions not very pleasant, but unfortunately necessary to reach your goal. I spoke with Blair Agnew today who suggested that there was an animal track running along the top fringe of the border about 2500/3000 elevation which might provide a better route and be easy sure that the track will not have overgrown as animals use the same track years but it is by luck. And judgement you will win

one thing is positive that is Gerald Howse as been possibly searching for 70 years to find somewhere where KH 326 crashed and searched in the wrong place. Now there is a correct identification of the crash grid reference and I'm sure within a short space of time with perseverance your goal will be reached.

GOOD LUCK and GOOD HUNTING we are all behind you. Best regards and salutations. Joe

112. <u>20 September 2007</u>   **Shahaom Ahmad to Joe Plant.**

Thank you very much for your email and your supportive morale Thank you very much

Regarding animal track, yes, due to our 'conversation with 2nd. Ranger Officers who accompanied us confirmed there were a trail along the top fringe of the border about 2500/3000 elevation close to the border which wide and not overgrown used by border control. We opted to use this trail, but our guide insists that we need to trek near water point (stream or river) to make sure that we have continuous water supply. Another thing that using this trail will be take more time since we need to climbing up to the peak ridge and down back again and climbed again which is not suitable for us who carry heavy backpacks. So our routes used by hunters and shortcuts have to be made cross in this ridges.

He (the guide) quite seems to be true a lot when we entered the jungle. When we at the peak of elevation of 1500 m, there were no source of water. We have to walk down to the valley, which took us another half day to reach the water point, which valuable for us. For cooking and replenish water supply

So our trail was close to water point and some point that we have to climbed the peak and walked down in a day to make sure that we arrive at the water source not more than 5 pm. At 6 pm, it was dark in the jungle.

So our future plan was to insert using helicopters which save us sometimes and prepared to walk out from the jungles using straight-line from the wreckage towards. Nearest village possibly that will start as second expedition firmly in October or November. Where weather permits right now at Kedah was a peak of monsoon time with some of the low areas were flooded. So keep in touch and see you soon for more report.

113.   **30. September 2007**   <u>**Blair Agnew (ex-Royal Scots Fusiliers officer) to Joe Plant (in e-mail sent by Joe to Matt Poole**</u>

Obviously a long time has elapsed since I was in that part of the jungle, but if I might be permitted to offer some advice, I would suggest that rather more planning might be undertaken before the next attempt is made to find the wreck.

The first thing to understand is that the border track does allow any party to make reasonable progress without having to hack a path through thick jungle. The border track may well go up and down but it does allow for relatively easy movement, and therefore the sooner the search party can get on to it, the better.

Using GPS it should not be too difficult to select a position on the track which would be due EAST of the crash site and of course very close to the site of the CT camp from which the original Patrol set out and found the wreck. The grid reference of the CT camp was given in the RSF Patrol report.

The significance of the CT camp is that it had a stream running to the East of the camp and just below it. The camp itself Sat on a ridge and the stream was just below it. That stream provided plenty of water for the approximately 100 CTs in the compound for our soldiers when we occupied it.

My next suggestion would be that there is no need to find a place beside water to make camp. Of course it would be nice if such a place could be found, but if not, then we very often based up on any reasonable level ground near the top of a ridge and sent two soldiers down to fill water bottles at the stream below. The advantage of doing that is that you do not need to start the next day's march by climbing up to the top of the hill which you decended from the night before. Nothing is worse for morale than feeling the previous day's work had been wasted.

Unfortunately I no longer have the map of the area and therefore I am not sure where Bukit Palabang lies in relation to the crash site, but I presume it lies to the North. I wonder whether it would be possible to plan for and to get the necessary permissions for an extended search window to allow for insertion by helicopter and extrAction on the next chopper resupply flight two weeks later. This would allow a longer time at the site, and if an LZ is not too far from the site, the search party could leave extra days' rations at the LZ and resupply themselves as and when necessary.

From veiwing the photographs I feel that perhaps too much time might have been taken in establishing camp each night. We slept on the ground and did not make beds as a general rule. In fact, the only time that I slept on a raised platform was when we were in that CT camp, and that was only because 12 Platoon had been there for about 10 days before we arrived, and they had quite a number of parachutes which provided something to lie on.

I realise that this may sound a little critical but that is the last thing which I wish to be, as I am well aware that those who are going in should not be expected to "rough it" as we did, and in all probability they may well be rather older than we were. I sincerely hope that what I have written may be of assistance, and above all I hope for and wish them to achieve a successful outcome. It is very worthwhile thing that.

Good luck to them all and I do wish that I could be with them.

114. **30 September 2007**   **Joe Plant. Matt Poole.** Joe sent a copy of above message to Matt .

115. **1 October 2007**   **Matt Poole to Joe Plant.**

Thanks for Blair's constructive criticism I am not quite sure if you forwarded this to Shaharome , so I'll go ahead and send it anyway. Blair has some good advice. I imagine that access to the border trail may have been restricted on their first trip, given that the border is a very sensitive area these days. But Captain Zuraiman, using his army connections, is working on getting greater access the LZ, says Shaharon, is 2 km North of Bulit Papalang, the highest point on the rich the LZ is still roughly 7 km from the crash site... Based upon the old map and just eyeballed (not measured carefully) that is a formidable height, unless the border trail is still quite possible.

Shaharom sent me a modern road map of the area, and the streams look quite different when compared to the old map. It is my guess that the original map has much error in its topography and drainage, the art of Geodesy has advanced tremendously since the time of the survey flights to make this particular topographic map. I found that the old British maps of the scale in hilly terrain surrounding two of my other crash sites in Burma, are very inaccurate, invaluable nonetheless.

I just hope that the 1955 map really is good enough to get these guys to the wreck without too much trouble.

Enclosed is Shaharom's map , showing the path of their recent expedition. I guess the path is based on GPS and then plotted on the map. I don't quite agree on where he has the wreck located, when compared to the RSF map, but Shaharom's map site.may have been a rough guess only.

Shaharom's map below courtesy of Shaharom Ahmad

I can't remember…does Blair have a e-mail? I know he has a S. African Friend who wrote to me by e-mail, but I have not aquired Blair's e-mail address yet is there any problem with sharing that with me. Its your call mate!

116. 3 October 2007 Joe Plant to Matt Poole

Blair's email apologies I thought I had sent it to you no problem drumbarr@yahoo.com

Many thanks for the attached map received well. As you say everything has advanced so quickly since those long days years ago. However I'm sure they will succeed in the long run , my only comment is they seemed to be a long way away from the crash site . I thought they would have tried a different route to make it easy for themselves , but with the area being Black they know better.

117. 3 October 2007   Matt Poole to Joe Plant.

Thanks for Blair's email address. I will send him the map, plus see what else he wants.

The map route… I do believe Shaharom and gang had to take the route shown because there just are not any closer roads and villages on the Malaysians site. The village of KG ULU LEGONG does seem closer to the border ridge line, however, and the map from Sharharom seem to have a dashed line adjacent to a stream leading uphill toward that ridge line. If they had tried this route, perhaps they would have reached a maintained or less impassable border trail which they could have used to move Northward towards the wreck the overall length of the track would have been longer but perhaps it would have been much easier than the path travelled

Really, though, we don't know the full story regarding permission. And they only had four days total to get in and get out. Which was an impossible short time to really accomplish anything.

The early part of the track was a long and old logging road, but even that was overgrown and difficult, I think. It's all a matter of geography and politics on the Thailand side of the border, very close to the wreck site, people have cleared land I have on the slope to ridgeline. Shaharom told me earlier on and it was impossible for them to use Thailand as a point of entry, all due to politics…

118. 8 October 2007   Blair Agnew to Shaharom Ahmad cc Joe Plant.

In my last email, I tried to make some suggestions that might help you in your search and since then I have been trying to think whether I could help you in any other way. It is of course a long time since I was the crash site but I do have a fairly clear recollection of the ground and I think I might be able to give you some pointers which may help

You do have the grid reference of the crash site and I suggest that you should draw a line due EAST from there and then work out the exact reference spot where the line meets the border track. You should then be able to reach that exact spot using GPS and when you reach the spot this is what I think you will find:

if you stand on the border track facing NORTH, the ground on your left (i.e. due West) will fall away from the border ridge and at the bottom of that fall away there should be a stream. I think that this will be the stream that the CT's used as is ablution point for the camp that we found and which we occupied. If I am correct, the site of the CT camp will be approximately 50 feet above the steam. The site the CT camp was on the top of ridge rather lower than the border ridge and it was a level site that level ground did not extend very far but as I remember it was roughly in the shape of a rectangle which ran NORTH to SOUTH with the short sides at the SOUTH and the NORTH. The track which led down to the crash site left the CT camp from the BOTTOM LEFT corner of that rectangle and when down a mini ridge the CT's had dug 2 sets of slit trenches on the way down and if you could find the remains of these or, the indentations in the ground where they had been dug, you will be very close to achieving your aim, it was just below the lower of these slit trenches that the leading Scout brushed against the Hornets nest and it is at that spot you should leave the track and head NORTH WEST to find the site. The site should be no more than 20 to 30 yards from that point. I hope this may help if you feel that I can give you any further assistance please let me know

119. 9 October 2007   Blair Agnew to Matt Poole.

Shaharom has made a good try finding the site but I am afraid that he started from the wrong spot through no fault of his own. To go in from the West meant that they had a long and arduous trek through thick jungle and with the further disadvantage that they were climbing across the grain of the country it was for that reason that we were lifted out of the area at the end of our Patrol as it was considered too far for us to walk out after a long Patrol, when we were needed for other operations indeed when we were lifted out, we had two days rest and then were back in the jungle in a different area.

From your email, I realise that I did not make myself clear on the full details of the topography . When 12 Platoon moved up to the CT camp before the wreck was found, they occupied the CT camp which was on a fairly level ridge top and I suppose the actual camp covered an area roughly 30 x 15 yards. The description which I was given when I arrived there with 7 Platoon, was that there was a parade around and bashes in which the CT's lived were grouped around the site of this space on the East side there was a track leading down the washing points which showed a clear division into male and female washing points the washing points late approximately 50 feet below the camp you will note that in my email to Shaharom , I suggested that they

354

should approach the site from the East and that the stream which provided the washing points would help them to identify the site.

When the wreckage was found, the LZ for the incoming choppers was made by clearing the area of the CT camp as this involved the minimum clearance effort and want on a level ground Thus the LZ and the CT camp were one and the same location.

You are quite correct in saying that 50 years is a long time and there will have been a great deal of growth but there may still be differences in the growth that might help in the identification interestingly enough, when I was serving in Malaya, and our base was at Kroh and on the road between Kroh and Baling the remains of WW2 slit trenches which had been dug by the Argyll's during the retreat to the South before the advancing Japs were quite clearly visible. You are right in saying that materials deteriorate rapidly in the wet tropical climate, but the materials which they will be looking for are in fact metal and therefore I think they have survived very well. Certainly when I saw the wreck, the markings on the wings were clearly visible and I see no reason why there should have been any material change it occurs to me that carrting the metal detector might help in the search although I do not know at what rains these devices can operate.

With regards to human remains, I am convinced that the crew were on board when the plane went into the hillside, though I think that the formation of the wreckage indicates that the aircraft "pancaked" into the jungle rather than flying directly into the hillside. The list of the kit recovered points to the crew being on board as a would not have bailed out without taking personal weapons and items of clothing that would blatantly personnal to the crew. I was not present when the R AF "experts" came into view the wreck and to look at some bone that been found when I talked to John Staheli , he was very scathing in its view that they were primarily interested in getting back to civilisation and therefore pronounce the bones to be pig bones. Perhaps we were being harsh as we had to spend long periods in the jungle and therefore were not put off by the conditions, in fact I truly believe that we really enjoyed been in the Ulu as we were well away from the confines and constraints of life in camp and we all felt that we were doing a useful job.

You ask about their photos of the area but I am afraid that these do not exist. The Patrol report from 12 Platoon is the best record of the whole incident and of course, it contained the marked up maps of the area and the actual crash site the problem with the maps that we use was that they had been come by from air photographs and will really not very accurate as a mapmaker you might be amused when I tell you that there were quite a few white patches on the map sheets and these generally bore the legend "cloud no air cover" not exactly helpful when you were trying to navigate we used to say: "you're never lost, you just don't know where you are." If the jungle taught me one thing it was that you must trust a compass and once that lesson was learnt then the jungle held no fears

120.   9 October 2007   Matt Poole to Blair Agnew

Thanks for your long email which gives me even more than detail to add to my running research diary, a copy of which I have attached to this email for your files.

Please note that this document records many things which have proven to be irrelevant, and various things that were avoided by later findings. It is not a final report just to run in chronological diary of the project started in March when I was put in touch with Joe Plant until the last few entries I have added comments in brackets to explain some of the writing or to link it to an earlier entry

I will send a second email, which will have as an attachment the list of only the headings to each of the hundred and 52 separate entries in research diary I have highlighted the more important/more relevant entries in this headings list so that you can perhaps bypass the lesson material and concentrate on the more pertinent entries I quickly reviewed the whole document to make sure they was no comments that might offend you the only thing I found the might ruffle your feathers of Dougie Thom's recollections but I absolutely feel that the words were not meant to insult, but only to emphasise that he would not on site at the time of the Liberators discovery .Yes just making sure I had the facts straight transcript does not include any questions, so Dougie's emphasis that you were not there at the start of Liberator excitement seems like he's beating a dead horse .... But he was just making sure I understood the basics,No insult intended I am quite sure.I like Dougie -no line shooter.

121.   9 October 2007   Blair Agnew to Shaharom Ahmad

I have just been re-reading your emails and in particular your idea that following insertion by chopper you will carry out your search and then walk out to the nearest road. It once again I might be permitted to offer advice, it is that you should try to arrange for your party to be lifted out as well as chopper in. The reason for this is that you will only have a fun finite supply of rations, perhaps five days and if we assume you take one day to reach the area of the crash and then perhaps two days to search the area and presuming that you find the remains you will have to spend time really thoroughly investigating what you find, then at the most optimistic predictions you would have only two days rations left. You will not be able to reach any road in two days! It was for that reason that seven Platoon were told to march North to an LZ to be lifted out, as the best estimate of the time it would have taken us to march out was five days. Knowing the type of jungle which covered the area, I think that to do the distance in five days would have been very difficult and you have to remember that we were used to the jungle and were very young and fit. I think therefore that you should do your best to try arrange that you should be given a full two weeks, including rations and the ride in a chopper at each end.

122. **9 October 2007**   **Matt Poole to Blair Agnew**

Shaharom forwarded me a copy of your latest email to him and his reply, your memory is sharp, and I hope it serves Shaharom well and his team is faced with a daunting task -rediscovering that "needle in the haystack" in a difficult environment over 60 years after KH 326 crashed .The jungle swallows everything in no time, so I can't imagine that he will find the CT camp easily maybe it will be a case of comparing vegetation helicopter LZ hacked out of the jungle to allow the chopper to land (to remove the Liberator's cache of guns et cetera) might stand out as an area of less mature tree growth. Something like that somewhere in the UK archives there are aerial photos of that area, dating back to 1950s I imagine it is still all classified I am a professional mapmaker, and I know that the air photos reveal details and landmarks (such as the CT camp and the LZ you made) that are not on the maps I also know that the maps were often very poor in their geodesy. Trying to represent mountainous three-dimensional is on a flat piece of paper was not easy (things are improving with technology nowadays), and I bet that the maps you used were generally okay but not nearly as accurate as you would have liked to the compare them with 1955 vintage aerial coverage of the area will be a godsend with the R SF archives old any such imagery???

I'm keeping my fingers crossed in the hope that Shaharom and his crew will succeed not just in finding the site, but in discovering human remains. Only they find this evidence will the Canadian government the send a team out to do a proper excavation, of course it may be that all the crew bailed out before the crash I have a hunch at least that some were aboard such as men in the cockpit, but then why were no bones found in 1955??? Mysteries, mysteries. Perhaps animals scavenge and scattered the remains nearby, bodies were rejected during the violent crash I don't trust the R AF and War Graves Commission effort at the crash site, that's for sure and from what Joe said to me, you thought the investigation were team the scared the jungle (not that I wouldn't be quaking in my boots either!) And just wanted to get the hell out of there .

Perhaps a bit more snooping around soon will uncover something is. Abstention

this fascinates me so even if the remains are not found, I am pleased that I have been able to find the Kin of 7 of the 8 airmen KH 326 to share information they never knew

Yes the cloud voids in the maps must have been exASP.erated for you and your men on the maps of the crash vicinity there are couple of huge cloud voids-but only on the Thailand side of the border where the CT is were taking refuge (knowing that you were ordered not to make incursions across the border) maybe they were hiding under the clouds!

No doubt if you were on site which Shaharom and his team, the sensory recollections will kick in and it would be as if 52 years with just the blink of an eye to bad they can't transmit real-time videos to so that you can provide guidance from a nice comfy chair in front of a warm fire thousands of miles away that wouldn't be the same as being there, as the cameras point of view so confining, while an on-site visit would allow one to take in the whole atmosphere thanks for emphasising that the CT camp and the LZ were one and the same I can understand without having been in such situation wide been in the do with genuinely enjoyable on some levels. At least for many young men I have a friend who combined his love of adventure with his passion finding wrecked aircraft in Burma, India and China. He treks where no wihteman has been in many decades, or ever, and he reaches some very remote areas stop he says he loves being in the middle of nowhere, such as the 12,000 foot crash site is discovered in the Himalayas, he faces the shares of danger especially in Burma where easing during somebody attainment and running out of food and living off the land but he just loves being out there and I can appreciate why so many of your young National Service lads of defining moments in their lives some hated it, some were thrilled by adventure, but the parent experience could not have been read in books or learnt from watching movies ....

123. **10 October 2007**   **Blair Agnew to Matt Poole..**

Thanks for your email. No feathers have been ruffled as I always make clear that I was not the commander of the Platoon which found the plane, and was in fact Patrolling with my Platoon some distance to the South. My first knowledge of the discovery was when we heard the radio transmissions of 12 Platoon referring to "liberator", my signaller and I searched through our code books but could find no mention of "liberator" and it was only when I received a signal. Which ordered me to move up to join 12 Platoon, that I found out that they had found a Liberator bomber, one thing however, is that John Staheli and I were close Friends and in fact were on the same course at the Jungle Warfare School as he arrived in Malaya a week after myself, it was natural therefore that when I brought my Platoon up to join his, he would give me a very thorough briefing on all that happened regard to the finding of the plane. I went down to see the remains with John and thereafter the two Platoons work closely together with regard to the pattern of Patrolling, and a few days later John and I and our respective Platoon sergeants went out on a special Patrol with one other Jock to try and find from where a light appeared to be coming. That special Patrol nearly ended in disaster when John almost fell over a cliff but that is another story. It does however raise one point and that is that the CT camp sat on top of a ridge and overlooking the jungle, at night you could see over the tOps. of the trees and into the distance, that indicates that the ground fell away quite dramatically to the West of the CT camp. As far as the terrain is concerned, I would agree with Dougie Tom that the plane was amongst trees rather than in bamboo. We did however go through the thickest bamboo that I ever encountered when making our approach march to join up with 12 Platoon .This was to the South of the crash site and it was so thick that we only managed to cover 1000 yards in 10 hours of marching with five-minute haults every hour!......

124. <u>10 October 2007</u>   **Joe Plant to Blair Agnew and Matt Poole,**

My apologies to Blair. I was under the impression that I had sent your e-mail address to Matt, as I did with Gordon's and a few other RSFs. However, the contact has been made, and may I say with very interesting reading, more ideas evolving from the hornets' nest, positive thoughts about metal detectors, and the thought that KH326 "pancaked" into the hillside. One thinks that when a plane "pancakes", it is on flat ground. However, in this case a very strong possibility, seeing that it was found with the controls set at a "climbing altitude". This, if you remember Matt, I suggested that the 2 planes flew low over the Malayan coast before climbing to fly over the inboard mountain range, at what height over the coast they were maybe can be established through your contacts?

And so the mystery continues, and I'm sure that Shaharom will take this latest information & advice on board and be very sucessful in their next excussion

125. <u>18 October 2007</u>   **Sharharom   To Blair Agnew cc Joe Plant.**

Thank you for your advice. Yes, we already check with local guide that there were several option which we will consider.

1. Insert by Heli and lifted out by Heli. (During crash find it took 12 days to lifted out personnel and supplies)

2 And walked out using old logging track 2 km West of the wreckage and walked close to Sungei Lasau (2 days to reach road)

3. Insert by Heli and walked out another 2 km and reached our third camp (1st. trip) and from there we can straight walked one day out into our RV point (Tango 2 bar).

From my point of view, we will might choose option number three and will consult with Captain and Rangers Platoon.

Regarding their thick bamboo, yes, we have all we have already reached one site where bamboo were so thick that we stuck there, wondering how the world we will get out all walked inside the bamboo. Luckily our guide had his sharp parang which easily cut the bamboo and we walk slowly out from there.

Our guide also told us he found CT tunnel South of Tango 3 bar near to border. Large enough to accommodate hospital Hall et cetera. Thank you for your support

126. <u>3 December 2007</u>   **Joe Plant to Matt Poole**

I spoke to the Royal Observatory Edinburgh this afternoon. They confirmed that the times in Penang 6 June 1945 would be GMT +8 if they took off from Minneriya at 8.58. that would mean it was about 17:00 hours Penang /Singapore time. Twilight in Malaya is roughly 1845 local. Time so with Intel two hours of their GMT takeoff time. It would be dark in Malaya? Might be wrong but it needs clarification, records should prove that.

127. <u>3 December 2007</u>   **Matt Poole to Joe Plant**

Re-times I certainly might be wrong in thinking that Gerald Howe's take, on time being GMT was incorrect. Robert Quirk has a 357 Squadron records on microfilm. And he will be taking a look, hopefully this week. To see what turns up, he says sometimes GMT issues, sometimes local time, but the GMT should have a Z (Z is always GMT in records)

127. <u>23 June 2008</u>   **Joe Plant to Matt Poole,**

In previous correspondence apparently Sims & Timmermans swopped planes on the tarmac, just before taking off. If that was the case, can we define which pilot was in charge of which Lib on previous Ops.? If they were one and the same, would that eliminate the theory or suggestion of swopping planes on that crucial flight?

128. <u>23 June 2008:</u>   **Matt Poole to Joe Plant,**

The main problem in answering your questions is that I don't have the complete 357 Squadron Operations Record Book, only a few portions sent to me by Robert Quirk in Canada. He has the ORB on microfilm, but he has not found the time to scan it all for me. He also has a painful nerve problem in his neck, which has slowed. him down from fulfilling my request for things like the ORB scans. Maybe if I get a chance I'll pester him with a request to review the ORB and compile a list of all recorded dates KH326 and KH162 were flown on Ops. through 6 June '45. But with his neck problem, and work, and family, etc., he may not be able to review the microfilm for a while.

What he has sent me shows that the ORB was very incomplete. There were the Lib operations and the Dakota Ops. at that time, and it seems the records were haphazardly compiled. Then the four-Lib detachment to Minneriya (including Sims and Timmermans) were essentially forgotten in the records for a while.

So I don't have a complete record of Lib flights and who was in which aircraft. Gordon Hercus was definitely wrong in his recollection that KH326 was a brand new Liberator. NOT AT ALL TRUE!!!

That said, look through my research write up and you'll find a few clues. Review the following entries: 50, 111, 119, 120, 122, 124, 125, 128, 131, and 136.

A relative of Wop/Ag Bill McLeod (from the KH326 crew) sent me one photocopied page from Bill's surviving logbook. This page only covers May 1945, and Timmermans was his skipper for all 10 flights. Regarding KH326 and KH162, here are the flights:

2.5.45 Lib 326 Local drops. 1:10 day flying.
19.5.45 Lib 162 Air test 30 minutes, day flying
19.5.45 Lib 162 Air test 45 minutes, day flying
20.5.45 Lib 162 NONE. OP. JESSORE - CEYLON 8:15 day flying.

Another clue: The logbook of AG Gordon Hercus from the Sims crew proves that Timmermans piloted KH162 at least once at Minneriya:

June 3 Lib 162 Pilot: F/O Timmermans Duty: Passenger. Sigeriya & Minneryia Ceylon (Transit) 20 minutes, day flying.

That's all...but it's significant, because it shows that Timmermans piloted the allegedly bent-out-of-alignment KH162 at least four times -- two simple air tests, one short hop between airfields in Ceylon, and one long flight to Ceylon. I don't know the date when allegedly the Sims crew flew KH162 through a thunderstorm and got all hell beat out of them, and when the airframe was twisted. Could it have occurred between the date Timmermans flew it to Ceylon on 20.5 and when it was flown on 6 June??? Because of the lack of detachment records in the 357 ORB, I am not certain, except that the 357 Squadron portion of Gordon Hercus' logbook (which I have in its entirety) shows only ONE pre-6 June flight in KH162 with S/Ldr Sims as skipper:

15 May OP cancelled, gas leakage. Duty Not Carried Out. 2:30 day flying.

The ONLY other flight in KH162 before 6 June was the one I mentioned above, when Timmermans flew on 3 June from Sigeriya to Minneriya, Ceylon for 20 minutes.

Could the gas leakage on 15 May have been caused by flying into a Thur.nderstorm and having to cancel the op???? I just don't know. Gordon did not seem to be a line-shooter in any way. So the thing about the Japanese coming on the radio seems improbable, but I'll have to believe him. And the bent-up airframe story has to have some link to truth...but maybe it was one of the other Libs he flew, not KH162 (or KH326). His tale of switChin aircraft is so firm in his mind. How could it be a tall tale? It must be true, but maybe the reasoning for the switch had nothing to do with a bent-up airframe.
Oh, human memory, it is so hit-and-miss!

I'm glad you wrote me, as I'd never realized that the evidence in logbooks makes for an iffy match with the Hercus story. Yet it could be perfectly true. Wish I had more details on the 15 May cancelled op in KH162. It WAS cancelled -- they had to turn around -- and a petrol leak is certainly a possible result of a bad encounter with cumulonimbus clouds. Maybe at some point I'll run this past Gordon again, but I have to do so delicately, so as not to insult him.

Lastly, here are Gordon's flights in KH326, each with S/Ldr Sims as skipper::

25 April KH326 2:00 day flying
2 May KH326 Night Circuits [practice night flying] 2:20 night flying
3 May KH326 X/C Jessore-Burma-Jessore 6:00 day flying, 2:20 night flying
12 May KH326 OPS. Jessore-Malaya-Jessore. Duty Carried Out. 10:30 day flying, 9:50 night flying.

129. 23 June 2008   Joe Plant to Matt Poole, also

Many thanks for your reply. Your a mind of information, which is real great. As you explained about Robert, I'm sorry he has a problem. But his microfilm records would, no doubt, provide a clearer picture of the squadron's plane changes, if any. But we will have to wait and see. Still very intriguing. Will we ever get to know the full story? That is doubtful? But hopefully sucess is just the other side of June

130. 24 July 2008:   Joe Plant to Matt Poole,

Stumped!!! The jungle is a cruel, relentless, vicious place not willing to give up its secrets. We are now talking about a lapse of 50 + years of jungle growth, which from what I can remember, grows overnight. And it grows stronger. Nevertheless they have tried, and congratulations for their efforts (not in vain).

I read your comments as to how certain persons might assist in releasing photos, etc. I will bear that in mind. I have only just two weeks ago made contact with The British Army Intelligence Museum in relation to the deaths of some of their members during the 48-60 war. I did receive a welcome response and details of their involvement as well (information I had already collated). However I do believe if I make the right roads inwards something might just happen to spring from their files, etc.

At the moment we have come to a fork in the road. One will lead in the right direction, so to speak. Nothing is lost. On the other hand, I do not think that the RAF Air Historical Group would come up with anything of value, but it is worth a go from this side of the pond. I started this wild trail off by finding an error in the Grid Ref. which I believe is correct. What they need out there is a giant Metal Detector. Some Hopes?

131.   26 July 2008   Joe Plant to Matt Poole

Contacted the Imperial War Museum in London. They might be able to help with further details.

The Air Historical Group has recently moved from their previous HQ and have sent all their recon photos to a place in Edinburgh, which I contacted yeterday. They informed me that they have got the stuff but it's uncatalogued, and it would be difficult to search through the mass. However, it is in some semblance of order. If I could give them further info, which I have to obtain from the Air Historical Group, they might be able to narrow down the search and help that way. However, it's a long shot in trying to solve the problem from this side of the pond.

132.   28 July 2008   Joe Plant to Matt Poole,

Spoke with the Air Historical Group this p.m. to find out which squadron did air reconnaissance up in that area. Most likely out of Butterworth, it could have been either an RAF, Aussie, or Malay squadron who operated from there to cover the Northern Territory. Also squadrons at Kuala Lumpur could have been involved, and any type of plane could have been used, specifically fighter type. However he said all the squadron paper records are at the National Archives in Kew, that will take a month of Sundays to search through. But he is willing to look into his papers at Northolt first. If I can pinpoint the squadron, I can go back to TARA [The Aerial Reconnaissance Archive in Edinburgh] and ask them to search their recce photos.

I have also thought that there might be a possibility of the Army Air Corps– who flew Austers for communication with ground forces – also spotting CT camps. They might have some material available. Worth a try.

A Fleet Air Arm 848 Squadron S55 Heli did the pick up. Jacko did get the pilot's notes. They contained nothing, and as we know there were no photos taken by anyone at the scene, so that would be a dead end, I'm afraid.

I take your point about writing AHB a letter If I remember rightly, one of the crew members originated from South Sheilds. Good starting point, eh?

133.   28 July 2008   Joe Plant to Matt Poole,

Ghost!! I know the Chinese Malays and other Easterns believe in the other world. Perhaps his friend does have something. It is not far-fetched, but something puzzles me.

During our previous discussions we touched on the subject of a ninth member on board, and could find no proof. If he was on board, he did not descend by parachute. It would have been too early for his drop.

The second thing is that a search was carried out, by Force 136 immediately after the loss of KH326. but no chutes caught in the upper group of trees were ever spotted, which points to the fact that all died in the crash including the Chinese agent?

I still think that the intended drop was to a party which included *Chin Peng* – something I have been trying to find out, if that is true. He is still alive and resides over the border in Thailand, where he escaped from the Brits in 53 'ish, and where the peace talks were held in Bailing in '55. The RSFs were engaged in an operation to protect him, as far as I know. Don't know why, but that's politics.

I will contact Jacko to see if he can locate the chopper pilots of 848 Squadron – a long shot but worth a try.

134.   29 July 2008   Joe Plant to Matt Poole,

I did read somewhere, either in "The Jungle is Neutral" or in *Chin Peng's* book, that he was engaged in supply drops. when he was with Davis in the same vicinity or, thereabouts, about the same time as KH326 was doing drops. I cannot confirm if this is correct; it is only my assumption.

Chin Peng disappeared over the frontier into Thailand when things were getting too hot for him. He and his followers made camp on the Thailand side of the border near to Kroh, as I understand. At the time the RSFs were engaged on Operation UNITY when they found KH326, they were not allowed to stray over the border (as Blair's party did before he discovered he was out of bounds).

However, later the RSFs, amongst others, were engaged in security protection to *Chin Peng* in that area, which was basically sealed off from November '55 til December '55 due to the peace talks between Tunku Abdul Rahman, Davis and *Chin Peng* and his other nominated representative. Davis was then a liason officer and had known *Chin Peng* from Force 136 days. When Davis died in 2006 his obituary in the Times explained his days in the SOE. *Chin Peng* wrote a reply praising his old Friend yet later, as he explained, his adversary. I have tried to get in touch with Chin Peng but without success. He is still in and about the same area just over the border of Thailand. The Malaysian governement has refused his entry back into Malaysia, even to see his aged parents (must be ghosts by now).

I am only summising about the connection with KH326, but it was possible. It still requires investigation.

I think the reference to parachutes hanging in trees was more directed to the search which apparently did take place after KH326 crashed [by Force 136 in the area], and I'm sure in our earlier e-mails we discussed this at length, including tigers and other wild beast which just might have eaten human flesh. I cannot say how true it is, and I don't think anyone can tell exaclty what did happen on that fatal climb into oblivion. Speculation, speculation? That never will be answered and will remain a mystery. But the main objective now is finding the wreckage.

I have a copy of the FAA lifts as sent to me by Jacko. As he explained, the pilots did not make out much of any reports. The following is as entered into the pilots' log book (as available)

> **2nd Jun.** *56 SAS. 700 lbs of stores and radio equipment lifted from Jurong to Paddy's Ladang. 2 Casualties and two compassionate cases brought out. 42 troops of 2nd Malay Regiment, 900 lbs of freight, and several live chickens were lifted from Long Jims Ladang to Jalong Road. 32 troops were lifted in. 2 passengers were carried.*

> **3rd Jun.** *An inspection party were lifted to a crashed Liberator on the Siamese Border and arms and ammunition from the crash were lifted out. A dog handler and his dog were lifted out and replacements brought in. 4 passengers and 600 lbs of freight were carried.*

> **4th Jun.** *29 Malays and 150 lbs of freight were lifted from Slighs into the jungle. 3 passengers were carried on a recce.*

> **5th Jun.** *No flying today.*

That is all that Jacko was able to discover, when he went to the Fleet Air Arm Museum, as he said, was confirmed by a Senior Archivist. Pilots in 848 Squadron did not bother too much about writing up notes, as the RAF used to. I'm sorry to disappoint you, but you have what I have.

[Authors note: When John Davies died on October 27th. 2006. Chin Peng wrote his obituary on John Davies]

Quote :   Many people tend to believe that friendships cannot bridge the divisions of international conflict particularly in situations where those with close bonds of trust and understanding find themselves in bitterly opposing camps.

I would differ: and would even suggest that perhaps there might be a lesson for our troubled world today in the decade's long relationships the next listed between myself and my friend John Davies obituary October 31 2006.

I first met John in September 1943 in Japanese occupied Malaya. He was there to establish links to the outlawed. Communist Party Malaya (CPM) the only active anti-Japanese resistance group then in existence in the country.

[Author note Not strictly true there was another Guerrilla force before the CPM. The Chinese Kuomintang were the first to be accepted by the British to fight a sabotage war against the Japanese. The Communist Party of Malaya came in later after being finally accepted by the British to fight against the Japanese].

John's credentials were signed by Admiral Louis Mountbatten head of the British Ceylon based South-East Asia Command (SEAC) I (Chin Peng) was representing the Perak State Committee of the CPM.

That meeting forged an association that was expedient: We wanted to rid Malaya of a common enemy [The occupying Imperial Japanese Army]. But we both realised ultimately that the period of been allies in a common cause would eventually end. It did but I can never have forget my time with John in the Malayan jungle. He was an impeccable leader in the most harrowing of circumstances.   Unquote.

135.   12 September 2008   Matt Poole to George Mansson

I'm sending this to Blair Agnew and Joe Plant to

Glad you made the reunion – – the grand gathering of your band of brothers you're a born reporter. It's a fine summary of the RSF reunion! Can't thank you enough for the info from Robert Walter and John Reid – intriguing to say the least. Yet it seems confusing (without my knowing more) that they would have blown up the wreck after removing so many guns, et cetera and flying them out by Sikorsky helicopter. Why would they have blown up the wreck that prop possibly would have yielded human remains (or more human remains)?

Dog tags taken from the bodies also makes little sense as me, since the official report says no human remains were found Dougie Thom's clear recollection counters Roberts and John's account.

Now, if the aircraft was blown up at a later date, then shouldn't this be in the official Action diary – just like the one describing the late May/early June initial discovery and LZ clearing? We should be able to get record of A Company diary from the RSF archivist. I'll talk more about this with Blair.

Meanwhile I will, indeed be in touch with Robert and John after I buy some more cassette tapes, so that I can record my 'conversation with them. Maybe when I hear what they say, I'll have a better idea whether I think they were on the wreck stop my Malaysians wreck hunter buddy Shaharom will probably be up to tell me whether what other R AF aircraft were lost during the Malayan emergency. And perhaps we can roll out one by one, all other aircraft. I know there was at least one Valletta lost, plus the Auster you mentioned, and others no doubt.

Interesting to, that Alex Hamilton ties in to the story, as typist of an official report on the aircraft. How I'd like to find that people if it isn't one I've already have. I'll be getting in touch with Alex to share what I have, and maybe the wording will ring a bell, or, maybe he will know that he typed something completely different.

I reckon Blair will give me a report soon and probably he talked with a few other lads or with Alex, Robert and John.

This is so fascinating... And time-consuming! And worthwhile! I'm going to be slow-acting to follow up on it.

136.   13 September 2008   Joe Plant to Matt Poole,

Although George M. has dug out another bit of information, I'm mystified as to the validity of this latest info. Over the past eighteen months, when I started on this trail. no one who had any knowledge of the discovery has ever referred to another plane being found on Operation Unity.

In The RSF report Lt. Staheli only mentions the discovery of KH326. On the same day the RAF flew in, a Sgt in the CWG Commision also found no evidence of human remains except bones, possibly pig bones. Even Blair never mentioned another plane.

[Authors note: This came to light when George Cahoon wrote in his letter in June 2007 referring to The Platoon being deployed to rescue The Auster Pilot who had crashed after dropping a Sitrep to the Crash party.]

So where are the dog tags which were removed from the dead bodies mentioned? And the identity as those being Canadians? If anything, any remains would be skeletal with some remains of clothing, boots, belts, etc. I certainly have my doubts as to its authenticity. The sound of a plane being blown up about an hour after they left the scene could well have been the LZ party blowing up trees.

The only other mention of a similar plane made to me was by the RSF Secretary, **[Andrew Blackley]** who mentioned the discovery of another plane down south. This, we have discovered, was the Seramban plane, which when discovered by Shahrome, was in bits. I still have not found out which battalion found the plane, but as the story goes it was a Malay Regt. . who found it. Another mystery.

I do not want to sound negative, but where would the instructions come from to blow up a plane the size of the Lib after it had been cleared of its contents? Was it the RAF in Singapore? I doubt it. If that was the case, the letter sent to the Canadian RAF would have mentioned the disposal of same.

There appear to be too many if's in this latest story, or is it someone trying to confuse the issue as it stands? I might be wrong. However, to me, it does not ring true.

Now I will search through my files and try to identify a plane which crashed during the Emergency in the same vicinity of Kroh, but I would like to add that very few planes were found. And the RAF, RAAF crew and passengers, many from 55 Company RASC on supply drops., have No known Grave. And all 151, including Infantry, are listed on Terandak War Memorial in Malacca. Again, I have a full list.

I'll make up a list of lost planes and e-mail asap, OK?

[Authors note: this has now been completed as listed in the preceeding Chapters]

137. 23 Aug 2009:   Joe Plant to Joe Bamford (KL654 historian), cc to Matt Poole,

It was most pleasant and interesting speaking with you yesterday evening regarding your discovery of KL654. How you came to get involved with its disappearance must be very intriguing, but I assume it was the memorial stone in the church that began the search.

As for KH326 that is an entirely different story, that originally revolves about my writing my own memoirs of National Service, still to be completed. Having been sent out to Malaya in 1955, I spent 18 months in the REME LAD attached to the Australian RAASC in and around Ipoh. Like many NS guys, we were unaware that we were going into a war zone and were soon greeted with news of guys getting Killed. Writing my memoirs made me think of how it began and that there must have been many Killed after I left.

Thus, I began researching Malaya 1948-1960, which transpired to be the "Second Forgotten War". I contacted many Regimental Associations for information on those Battalions. Some were forthcoming with information, but they were more inclined to refer to books published by an officer or Regimental Historian. There was nothing of great interest in the National Archives – more about foreign policies regarding Malaya.

The Royal Scots Fusiliers were located in Columbo Camp about a quarter of a mile away from us; we were adjacent to the 15/19th Hussars. Bill Speakman VC who was attached to the RSFs, was a regular visitor to our NAAFI. Anyway in Nov 2006 I contacted Andrew Blackley, Secretery of the RSF Association, who informed me that their 12 Platoon had discovered the remains of a Liberator. It was almost intact and had all the supplies, medicines, guns, ammo, and clothing still in their canisters. Apart from the clothing, in mint condition. The guns were wrapped in greaseproof wadding. It took the RN helicopters 10 or 12 trips to bring out the supplies.

An RAF team did visit the site along with a War Graves Commission WO. There were a couple of bones discovered, but they were declared PIG bones, not human. The party beat a hasty retreat, as they did not like the confines of the jungle.

Andrew's story interested me, as it would add intrigue into the 'my' manuscript. I contacted the RAF Air Historical Group who knew nothing of it. After receiving their information, I pursued my interest on the Internet and found Robert Quirk's site with all the list of missing Liberators lost in the Far East. Concentrating on Libs lost in Malaya, I came up with two possibles, details of which I enquired from Robert, explaining why I was researching the planes. This was on the 1st March 2007.

Imagine my surprise when I received a reply from Robert and also an e-mail from the Malayan Historical Group's Shaharom Ahmad. The following day Matt Poole e-mail contacted me and provided information that it was a Canadian crew. He sent a copy of a letter with the names of the lost crew, issued by the RAF in Singapore June 1955. The letter inferred that the Lib had been found by the RSFs on the 28th May 1955. The plane and crew went missing on the 6th June 1945, almost 10 years to the day. It went missing on a secret supply drop to Force 136.

Matt also informed me that some relatives had been searching for its location for some time. So began a co-ordinated effort to establish its whereabouts. I contacted the RSFs again and explained its discovery and asked if they could provide me with any records of their discovery. This they were able to do, Nevertheless, the known grid reference provided by the RAF was totally different from that recorded in the RSF records. and I sent these to Shaharom Ahmad and Matt Poole. Hence, the Canadian relatives had been searching in the wrong area.

Nevertheless through my inquisitive nature and interest. I had been able to relocate KH326.

[Authors note: With tongue in cheek. Should have identified that the grid reference provided by the RAF in 1955 and used by Gerald Howes as QY 300814 in his efforts to locate KH326. That information was provided to me when I received an e-mail from Sharome Ahmad on the 2nd. Mar. 2007. stating the GR as QY 300814. I was totally unaware of where that was in North Malaya. It was only, when I received a copy of Gerald Howse Map from Matt Poole on te 5th, March I noticed that he Gerald, indicated he was searching near to Alor Star, that did not appear right to me. As the 1st. RSF's were operating on the Malay / Siam border near Kroh. I contacted Blair Agnew and he contacted, Willie Shaw in Glasgow who found the War Diary of Operation Unity, sent it to Blair who Identified their operational area and crash site. Blair Agnew advised me by telephone on the 20th. March of the (GR) Grid Reference of the crash site of KH326 as QY 808300. Which obviously revealed the true GR of the crashed Liberator KH326. Definitely relocating the crash site of KH326. This information was sent by e- mail to Shaharom Ahmad on the 20 March 2007. That was the pivot point of the beginning of a team effort to find the missing Liberator.]

Since then, I believe two expeditions [Authors Note: By Shaharom Ahmad and Jim Zuriaman in Sept 2007 did not succeed and a further attempt in July 2008 did not succeed] have been carried out in an attempt to find the plane that crashed about 2-300 feet from the top of a mountain. It still remains a total mystery that both Matt and I are trying to resolve. Matt has located all but one of the Canadian crew's relatives and must be congratulated on his efforts. I do have two full files relating to our search that will have to wait until a search does reveal its true resting place, hopefully sooner that later. We all live in hope.

[Authors note: At the time the above e-mail was sent, The author was unaware that the wreck of KH326 had been accidently found by two separate Malay Army Patrols. The following e-mails reveal the incidents.]

138. 16.June 2010   Capt. Zuraiman to Matt Poole
I think the 4 WD guy. [Authors note: No knowledge] back in the summer of 2009 was referring to another wreck site not the KH 326 site

The KH 326 find was actually by Army troops of A Company last year but not reported. Later B Company went wrong on their Patrol routing and found this wreck in February this year. They kept silent about this for almost 4 months because they took the wrong route. A company of the Malaysian Army found the wreck in 2009 but did not report it then in February 2010 the company found the wreck by accident when they got lost on their Patrol, they kept silent for four months before reporting it so as not to get in trouble or be made fun of.

139. 16 June 2010   Capt. Zuraiman to Matt Poole again
I will recover more photographs and speak with the army people involved in finding the wreck, it was mentioned that they usde more than one camera, so far all the photos have been from one camera only.

140. 17 June 2010   Matt Poole to Laurie Clegg Canadian Director of History and Heritage
I've been trying to understand WHO rediscovery of wreck KH 326. language has been the problem Shaharom and Jim Zuraiman thankfully can communicate in English, but it is not perfect and I was confused. Here is the account chronologically Jim's agreement and Shaharon Ahmed learnt last summer that a four-wheel-drive group discovered some wreckage. Because of their commitments on other projects (like theRAF Liberator KL654 site excavation) Jim and Shaharom did not track down the four WD guy for some months

When I asked him early in 2010. If he had found the guy, he replied that the four WD adventurer had found some other stuff but not KH 326 I don't think the adventurers were very close to the KH 326 area really

The Malaysian Army controls the board region in dense jungle. A Company of the army found the KH 326 wreckage in 2009 while on Patrol but they did not report it

B Company of the army found the wreck by accident when they got lost on the Patrol in February 2010 (this explains why the photos were dated ninth Feb 10) they were embarrassed by getting lost and afraid maybe of getting reprimanded by Seniors before reporting it. Nobody else has been in the site yet I've asked the only Patrol to the GPS fix, but I've not been given an answer yet.

141. 17. June 2010   Shaharon Ahmed to Matt Poole

Jim's reports were correct both parties (4x4 and army Patrols) found wreckage but the 4x4 guys later told Jim they had found other wreckage and not KH 326 since the location of the wreckage site that they found was far from the border.

We could only rely on the two army reports. Jim submitted to us. One Patrol A Company of the Royal Malay Regiment found the wreckage KH 326 in 2009, did not report it to their officer in command, because they were put Patrolling a wrong section of the jungle, when they discovered the wreck it had reported the finding their CO would have known that they were made walking far from their Patrol area and they would have been punished.

Also B Company Royal Rangers Regiment RRR found the wreckage in 2010 and also had a similar story of entering the wrong Patrol area and finding the wreckage. But the Officer of the Regiment who joined us on two previous occasions heard of the findings and asked the soldiers about the findings.

Seems like a coincidence right? With the wrong Patrol areas losing their way and similar stories to the RSF's and their encounter with hornets seems quite a coincidence to me.

As it is right now our info and photos have been obtained from the RRR officer and he will ask the soldiers again for the location of the wreckage and the grid reference report which was taken by their squad leaders. Then we will meet them, and we hope that the soldiers who found the wreckage can lead us to the site. The RRR officer told Jim that the location described by the soldiers was not far from our last camp during our second mission in 2008 The soldiers noted that they found our abandoned campsite and walked 500 m down to the ravine and found the wreckage.

I still remember the terrain and will plotted it back. Without jungle guides who know every part of the jungle and I hope that we we will be inserted using the shortest routes. I will remember that the guides also lead us back to civilisation by using the shortest route, took us three days to march then reach the campsite area and when we were going back we took one day to reach our last checkpoint at the chalet.

Regarding the informer [4WD Guy] these years we are getting more info regarding wrecks in the same area but when we checked it thoroughly was not the KH 326 that we were searching for sorry for the trouble.

142. 21 June 2010   Shaharom Ahmad to Blair Agnew

Yes, we might now think what those boys in our RSF and later Patrol found the wreckage both of them found this wreckage accidentally and later could be punished if they reported it to top brass but it still leaks thanks for the leaks which we could determine the wreckage and location for I exhibition next week hope clear they will be on our side

Regarding the panel, we will look for it. From the photos, it shows that someone were visited the wreckage and pulled out some parts the front section (bombardier and navigator office) still intact with front turret the damage look obvious do the damage from the recovery in 1955 or current one.

I would like to say that some of the crew's plight survived based from the photograph and the wreckage itself that what we called a textbook crash where pilot used to belly downloads up crashed and hope that the belly of the plane which hit the trees and absorb the impact it would be a control crash which pilots still control the plane and try to crash landed in the jungle but something happen when the plane hit the trees the plane might break in pieces and caught fire , probably most of the crews were bailed out or positions himself in an aft of the pilot copy crash landing procedures where the plane structures have the most strong section to withatand crash .But it is just my opinion we will check when we visit the site

143. 23 July 2010   Sharharom Ahmad to Matt Poole

Just coming out from the jungle and finding the wreckage after getting into the most challenging tracking. It took us three days and two nights to reach the site.

On sorry to say that we only had three hours at the site, since we needed to track back to base camp which was located 2.7 km from the crash site. What we saw at the site was not satisfying.

The wreckage was scattered due to previous activities. I do not know who did it, but it was touch and broken up by scrap hunters who came from Thailand.

The even made a campsite near the wreck.

We could see the remains of the no section without the cockpit, two wings with burnt landing gear, the separated tail stabiliser, for engines (two of them burnt), and a tail turret detach completely.

A large amount of aircraft remains were scattered down to the valley below, which we assumed to be. A 45° slope section of wing spar was located/50 m from the wreck. I will attach the wreck plan. When arrived in my office on Monday

from the wreck, I assume that KH 326 flew straight and its wing hit a tree, and the plane spun several times and hit the hill on a less site. We did not know where the . Fuse a large always section have gone could they have been broken up and are missing a scrap

The RSF report from 1955 shows that the fuselage was still intact,. But we did not find it only the nose section. All instruments were gone, metres pages. Were pulled out and some fittings were gone. Could be from scrap hunters

I believe my report should help you and the 8H to finalise your future action. We did not have time to excavate the area, but we are sure that the HH, with full manpower, could visit the site by air. And escalated properly- the crash site was big-- approximately 80 m wide,, and most of the wreckage was in bamboo which would be difficult to clean up only with proper manpower and equipment can be cleaned to get the excavation. Properly

I believe some of the remains could be on site. And some crew bailed out I should. Reconsider water in the fuel tanks the plane may have had trouble, flew back towards base, and the pilot opted to bail out near the border to make sure they would reconnect Force 136 easily. The plane flew straight, and I wonder why the pilot flew it straight. There were no high hills. Until the plane hit the peak at the border but it's just my opinion. We need to sit down again to check the truth beyond the crash. I'm happy that we finally found KH 326 on our third attempt

I need to rest first, and we will communicate once again back to KL.

By the way the plane was found 500 m from the border. And not 500 yards he he he but the map sent by Blair Agnew was correct. It showed the location of the crash. Very near to the actual site

144. 25 July 2010   Matt Poole to Joe Plant cc Blair Agnew

Hi Joe and Blair

I received an email from Shaharon Armad in the Malaysians jungle, returning from the arduous trek to reach crash site of KH 326. They made it, but the difficulties in reaching the site meant they had only three hours on-site. The condition of the debris shows that someone, probably scrap metal merchants, crossed over from Thailand at some point(asked for clarification, if they know), and had torn apart much of the intact part the wreckage. Including the cockpit see the note below.

It is widely scattered site, too. That's not surprising to me, but given the realities the steep terrain and dense bamboo, together with the fact that the physical wreckage, has apparently been torn apart, I am guessing that a full excavation. Just will not become a reality now I hope. I turn out to be wrong

Photos in a sketch map will reach us. This upcoming week I hope we can get a GPS fix, plotted accurately in Google Earth in 3-D, and then. Look at it from different angles the map of the debris field will help us to make. Sense of the circumstances of the wreck

Is not over yet, but it's a disappointment that the wreckage was not more intact that, of course, is no indication as to whether or not. Human remains can be found on site the dense, difficult bamboo would make any excavation. Especially difficult

In my opinion, just finding it and visiting the wreck is a great victory. It's just not an ideal victory

145. 25 July 2010   Joe Plant to Matt Poole,

That is disapointing news. Whoever took the sections of the plane must have used the elephant track that the RSF report referred to. Bloody marvellous it lay undiscovered for 10 years. Even the CTs who were camped close by did not discover the arms cache plus other items. Nevertheless, its exact whereabouts remained undiscovered (said with tongue in cheek) until 2007 when the correct grid ref was unearthed in the1st. RSF Operational Report on "Operation Unity". However, in those 50 years someone did find it, possibly Sakis (Malayan aborigines) who passed on the word to Thailand scrap merchants who ravaged the site??

I can't get my head around the comment made by Shaharom that *'the plane flew straight and its wing hit a tree and spun several times"*. The B-24 is a big beasty, and most likely it did hit the top of a tree on an upward climb and slewed. into a crash position. The tree in question was most likely very tall and would have snapped off at the top. By now it is dead and has succumbed to the jungle floor.

Shaharom's other comment re the possibility of crew members bailing out (I already passed along my theory on that issue) and water in the fuel tank (something Matt discovered in some reports at Minnereya). Why did the pilot fly it straight? There were two B-24s on that mission. KH 326 was last sighted by the other crew flying into heavy cloud in-between Bunting Island and Penang Isand. Both I assume were on the same mission to drop supplies to Force 136 waiting at the DZ at Lat 06°N.Lat, Long. 101° E. Long.

I attach a section of a map I made out in July 2007 showing the possible flight path to the DZ. It is flat across that section of Malaya, but it soon starts to rise rapidly into mountanous country as Blair will confirm. I believe the pilot, as discovered, for some reason had it on autopilot and, flying through thick cloud and a rainstorm, did not realise how close they were to the mountains. He tried to lift her over the top, but the wing hit a tree, they lost the wing, and it slewed. before impact. If two engines were discoverd burnt (starboard or port) and the fire was quickly extinguished by the rain, the crew on board may all have been concussed or bleeding from wounds received.

Who survived is a mystery. It is a theory, but without either Flight Report Books *[??]* it will remain a mystery.

Hey, let's not be despondent. Shaharom and Jim have actually found KH 326 after 3 attempts during the past 3 years. Congratulations to them and their crew. And that alone must bring peace of mind to the aircrew's families that Matt has discovered. It's up to us to try and somehow sumise and piece together the crew's ending.

146. 21 July 2010   Joe Plant to Shaharom Ahmad

Long time no speak as they say. Congratulations on your success I have been out of the loop due to complete in my book that has been successfully launched last 'Friday 17th.July.

But wish to make comment re-possible survivors. That I doubt ever got out alive from the crash. Many moons ago Matt and I discuss what could have happened IF anyone did jump over that terrain they can appear will get caught up in the high canopy of the trees and would have been spotted by any Japanese fighter plane operating out of their base in Alor Star

if any did get out the crash site the chances of survival were not great. Any who were injured were possible make the Malayan tigers and bears that roam in the jungles who just might drag the body's away into deep jungle. It is all supposed with it out the discovery of any bones.

There was another incident where an army step plane that Brig. Erskine was a passenger crashed into the jungle in 1949 the crash site was not discovered until 1956 by a Patrol f the Royal Hampshire Regiment at the Gap. The only identifying more items was his medal ribbons and officers broke shoe and a shirt nametag, there were no bones of either him or is army pilot what happened to the bodies???.

I too am eager to see the closing stages of this saga due to my involvement right from the start by chance finding of either RSF the correct grid references as they had identified it and I am still waiting to see if they both match, furthermore I wish to conclude the scenario of KH 326 within my manuscript about the history of Malayan War 1948- 1960. I will read back through my old emails to see what assumptions for Matt and I came up with during the initial stages.

147.   21 July 2010   Blair Agnew to Matt Poole cc. Joe Plant. Shaharom Ahmad George Masson.

Well done on the late this batch of photos annual comments with regard to this photo, what is the tubular frame appears to be covering the rudder? It appears to be dome-shaped and could it have been covered by plexiglass?

The details of the discovery of fascinating they give an interesting insight into the mindset Patrol I would have thought that reporting the fine would have outweighed any disc disciplinary problems resulting from been in the wrong area and the Patrol must all have been very tightlipped to keep the secret!

It might be worth making the point to a Malaysian friends that when the 1st. RSF found the wreck, the control panels were there and they were able to ascertain that the aircraft was flying on auto and the heading on which they were flying. These remains must still be there and perhaps there may be more photos to come which will show them.

Anyway may be obsessive but you are doing a great job and eventually the families will be very grateful to you.

148.   26 July 2010   Shaharom Ahmad to Joe Plant and Matt Poole,

Regarding the expedition, we just came out from the jungle on 'Friday last week. The terrain and trekking into the thick jungle tested our morale and strength in reaching our target goal of finding the wreckage and ending our long search for the plane. On the map, it seemed to be easy, but on the ground walking a few hundred meters was pushing our limits. Both ways from the South and trekking along the same river, we needed to cross it 20-30 times in a day. It makes me wonder how the crew could ever have walked out safely if they managed to bail out successfully.

In the jungle, we do have wild animals and I'm agree with you that anything that smells, will attract animals. Most probably, wild pigs will eat flesh if they manage to find one. Like what you have said to me about Major Erskine tragedy. His remains could be eaten by wild boars and other animals. Unlike B– 24 KL 654, most of the remains were burnt buried in the ground which we could find stop if the remains were lying on top of the ground inside mangled wreckage, probably these animal will get into them stop do you have any info regarding Major Erskine missing Auster? I mean the location? The gap was located in Fraser's Hill.

The correct location of the KH326 wreckage is **05 degree 53' 59.1" N., 101degree 01' 20.1" E.** Very close to the Thailand border. My suggestion is clear: Get into the wreck site again with plenty of manpower and equipment, clear out all vegetation and debris, and only then we can see how the remains could be located. We only had 3 hours time after we found the wreck, and I'm frustrated because I know that we could have done better if we had more time.

Next year, the site will be opened for loggers, and most probably a logging road will be created. This will enable us to bring our vehicles closer to the wreck site and bring more supplies to the site for excavation purposes. I already gave my word to the loggers, and they promised to inform me and my team when they reach the site next year.

My close examination of the wreckage shows that the plane was flying straight until one of her wing edges hit some tree on the highest peak, slicing the wing in two, and the plane tumbled down in a flat spin into a valley. In that spin, the plane hit more trees and broke into several sections and scattered. I don't know how to explain, but some might have bailed out before the crash, and some might have been Killed in the impact. I do believe that since the wreckage was scattered, no one survived the impact.

The only way to get this clear is to visit the site and follow my suggestion. I believe DHH Canada has lots of expertise on this...

149.   26 July 2010   Matt Poole to Shaharom Ahmad cc Zuraiman Joe Plant Blair Agnew

Thanks for the very detailed explanations, the excellent map, and the great photos.

First off, the photo showing where instruments were fitted is definitely the panel found DIRECTLY in front of the pilot seat (on the left side of the cockpit). Immediately to the right of this piece, and slightly lower, is where the autopilot control panel would have been found.

This piece of control panel, minus the gauges, is a great find. Also, the framing to the pilot/co-pilot windows is a unique find that in only found on a Liberator.

Do you have photos of the rear turret I think the photo looking into the turret is the front turret. I would like to send rear turret photos to the sister of Harry Andrews, the rear gunner

I agree with you that a thorough search of the area cleared vegetation would succeed in finding many more items, and possibly human remains I have left a telephone message when laurel Clegg of the DHH, but she may be out of the office this week I will push, push push them to commit to a recovery project-or financial offering to you to help pay for one! I do not expect any fast Action on their part, so I do not wait by the computer for the decision!!

Wow-when I think of your intense efforts I am really grateful for your dedication I just hope Canada reward you for your devotion to THEIR war dead the wreck site: it sure is a twisted debris field am I correct in thinking that the bomber was flying EASTWARD when it clipped the tree with its port wing near the trail you marked on the map? (This is where the port wing edge is marked on the map) If so then it did hit the HIGHEST point in the immediate area .

Please correct me if you think the bomber was flying from another direction .

The NO STEP (that's what it must say) sure makes sense for recovering on the circular opening where the Liberator originally had a ball turret . Of course, this 357 Squadron special duties Liberator had no ball turret and no appetite so this perfectly explains why there is a round fairing or covering, over the whole and painting NO STEP is logical.

I don't know what the canister is-- being held in one photo I don't think it is for you and consumption of a liquid looks like a reservoir of some sort for a mechanical part

many thanks for the GPS Lat/Long. I have a map at work, one: 50,000 scale, that I am not allowed to show to you but it has much more accurate relief on it than the RSF map, and the lat/long you gave me is almost exactly where I suspected the wreck to be!

I will look at Google both very soon. You do know that you can view the area in 3-D in Google Earth, right? They've recently updated the imagery with some better resolution imagery, but the old low revs imagery made it easier to view the terrain because of its shadowing now it is not easy.

150. 26 July 2010   Shaharom to Matt Poole

Thank you for your reply all the photos which I sent to you will come from my camera so it would be better to put MHG as a contributor of the photos. Sorry for the quality since I only managed to bring my El cheapo camera with 3.2 megapixel rather than bring my DS LR. He he save space and weight just enough to bring some foods and equipment

The instrument was taken away from the site and was dumped at the lower part of the hill near the engine. Could be someone interested in bringing it out but changed his mind the water container was a water bottle used by army could be used by the crews? Or later troops who do the excavation and discarded at the bottom.

About your theory. Yes the plane came from the direction where the wingtip was found the plane hit the trees first before hit the slope the L Z's(highest point) was further up in Captain Zuraiman got the coordinates and the measurement in height. I'm too busy checking the wreckage and did not have time to visit the LZ. We can see clearly that there were no other obstacle from this direction where the plane coming, it just flew straight from Pulai Bunting and hit this tree

I hope that DHH have solution to co-ordinate another expedition and a hope this time they have proper manpower and equipment to clean off the wreckage site only then, we could see the hidden parts which cannot be seen clearly inside the bamboo and bushes.

I don't mind if you want to use the photos and sending it to the relatives for me, it will be a relieving matters for them to see the plane that their loved ones flew and died together, we hope that they would get another trip back home when they were found. We hope that you and Laurel could discuss back the situation and hope they would come here

151. 14 August 2010   Joe Plant to Sue Raftree, MoD Joint Casualty and Compassionate Office,

Many thanks for your e-mail and pleasant 'conversation regarding the recent discovery of the missing Liberator bomber KH326 of SEAC RAF Sqdn 357.

As a matter of courtesy I contacted the CWGC to inform them of its discovery in the Malaysian jungle close to the Malaysia/Thailand border. They in turn suggested that I should contact you to inform you of the find. The following is a brief summary of the fate of Liberator KH326.

On June 6th 1945 at approx 08.58 Ceylon Local Time two Liberators, one of them KH326, took off from their air base at Minneriya in central Ceylon. Their Special Duties Ops. mission was to drop supplies to members of Force 136 engaged in acts of sabotage against the Japanese in Malaya. The ground crew's last sighting was high in the blue sky as the two planes disappeared out of sight. KH326 never returned from that mission.

A search was organised but nothing was ever found. The circumstantial report regarding the missing Liberator was issued by the W/Cdr commanding 357 Sqdn. on the 1st July 1945. In turn, that was sent on to the Canadian authorities in

Ottawa. However in the 1980s Gerald Howse, a nephew of F/O McLeod, a crew member of the fated KH326, tried to seek out the whereabouts of the unknown crash site somewhere near Alor Star in North Malaya. He was unsuccessful in his search.

Almost 10 years to the day since KH326 disappeared, during the Malayan Emergency (war) against the Malayan Peoples Anti British Army, 12 Platoon of the 1st Battalion, Royal Scots Fusiliers, engaged in Operation "UNITY", were on Patrol in the area close to the Malay/Thailand border approx due East of Kroh. One of the leading scouts disturbed a hornets nest, causing the hornets to attack anyone. To escape their venom members of 12 Platoon sought refuge in the undergrowth of the jungle.

One stumbled upon the remains of a plane, which became the subject of further investigation. For all intents and purposes it was found almost intact and the inside of its fuselage contained its cargo of unopened canisters. Upon investigation these revealed Sten guns, ammunition, small arms, medical kits, and clothing. There was very little evidence of any human remains, but some articles of possible crew members' clothing were found.

The discovery was radio'd to base, who informed the RAF, who despatched a team of investigators to the site. The plane was identified as B-24 Liberator KH326, certainly on a supply drop during the war. Some bones were found but dismissed by the investigators as pig bones.

After this, the removal of the arms cache was carried out by a number of helicopter sorties.

The RSF's resumed their intended operations, having discovered a Communist Terrorist camp (including a parade ground), capable of holding at least 100 of their troops, approx 100 yards away from the crashed bomber that, due to the surrounding dense tangle of jungle and bamboo, the CTs had never discovered.

In Oct 2006, whilst I (Joe Plant, ex-veteran of Malaya 1955-1957) was researching the history of the Malayan Emergency (war), I had been contacting various Associations of Regiments, museums, the National Archives, RAF, etc., regarding those who had been engaged during that period of conflict, in an attempt to piece together the involvement and history of all the fatalities that had occurred during the period of 1948-1960. I made contact with Andrew Blackley, the Secretary of the Royal Scots Fusiliers Association.

During our 'conversation Andrew mentioned their find of a Liberator bomber with its cargo intact way back in May 1955. He also stated that another bomber had also been found by another Regiment down in SouthMalaya. (This has since been established as the Seremban Liberator *[KL654 of 356 Sqn]* discovered by the Gurkhas.) Andrew's statement intrigued me so much that I felt I must try and find out more about its being located in the Malayan jungle.

February 2007. After contacting the RAF Air Historical Group also the establishment at Innsworth House and getting no feedback, I located the Internet site of Robert Quirk that revealed a host of information about SEAC Liberator squadrons, including those that were shot down or notified as missing. Studying the possible Liberators missing in the region of Malaya and Siam, I established 5 possibles.**[Authors note: this was wrong. The number I sent to Robert was 11]**

These I e-mailed to Robert for his comments; that date was March 1st 2007. The same day I received his answer

[After comparing. My List of 11 Liberators sent to Robert and with Robert Quirks reply list of 8 missing Liberators in the region. I establish 4 already on my list EW124 – EW 174 EW188 & KG877 , EW180 DID NOT HAVE A SQDR.ref ? Plus 4 possibles EW180 – EW234 - KH326- & KH 654. Only 4 possibles.] advising me that his colleagues would make direct contact with me.

The following day I received two e-mails, one from Shaharom Ahmad, head of the Malaya Historical Group, and the second from Matt Poole, a researcher in America with details of possible crashed Liberators in that area. Matt speculated that it could well be KH326, its crash site being something of a unsolved mystery. Both were eager to know what I could tell them about the RSF's discovery of the crashed Liberator and its location. I had indeed disturbed a "hornets nest."

Subsequently, the three persons mentioned – Matt, Shaharom, and myself – via e-mails, became an integrated team in the quest to find the missing Liberator KH326.

I immediately contacted Andrew Blackley (who was in Malaya at the time of the find) for further information. He informed me that Lt. John Staheli, the Lt. in charge of the Platoon which found the Liberator, had passed away but suggested I contact other members who were present at the find. This I did, making contact with a few names before I contacted Blair Agnew, who was another Lt. in charge of a second Platoon that arrived two days after the find and were responsible for clearing the helicopter LZ (Landing Zone) and the removal of the arms cache, etc., found in and around the wreck.

Over the following days Matt Poole was able to provide me with plenty of information, including the list of crew members and a copy of a letter dated 16th June 1955 from RAF Singapore informing the Air Ministry at Stanmore, Middlesex of the RSF's discovery. Within the text it stated a map reference QY300814. Subsequently that map reference did not match with the Grid Reference provided by the RSF's.

In April Blair Agnew obtained the Operation UNITY war report from the regimental archives, and then it was discovered that the Grid Reference did not match that stated by the RAF. This explains the unfortunate wild goose chase encountered by Gerald Howse in his search for the crash site. This vital piece of information was sent to Matt and Shaharom, and the correspondence on a daily basis stretched into weeks and months as we tried to put together theories of what really did happen, all being speculative. Nevertheless, many other people did become involved throughout its passage of discovery, far too many for me to account for. But there was a hell of a lot of paperwork.

What has happened over the following three years has been quite intense, exciting, and puzzling, involving many ex-RSF's who also wanted to know all about their discovery in 1955. Sadly quite a few members of the two Platoons which reached the crash site have since gone to higher grounds. Three joint attempts have been carried out by the Malaysian Army Museum headed by Capt. Jim Zuriaman, and Shaharom Aharam heading the Malaya Historical Group, whilst Matt Poolebhas been in contact with the families of the missing crew. As you stated, Matt was someone who you had previously been in contact with over other matters. Nevertheless, the wreckage of KH326, when discovered in February this year, had been previously found and scavenged by scrap metal dealers, possibly Thailands, who randomly scattered large parts of the Liberator over the surrounding area while taking cockpit instruments and such – like pieces of evidence that possibly could provide some idea of WHY it crashed on June 6th 1945.

One thing for certain is that the disappearance of KH326 and its Canadian crew as listed below will possibly remain an unsolved mystery of World War II.

I trust the above brief history of the search for KH326 provides you with sufficient information as requested for your further Action.

152. 5 September 2010   Anthony Gordon To all
This is another Officers report on the find This was written by Anthony Gordon (S. 'Africa) dated 5. Sept. 2010

DISCOVERY OF A CRASHED LIBERATOR BOMBER IN NORTH MALAYA IN 1955.

I am sending this to a few Friends and other interested in this event.

A lot has recently been written about the discovery of this crashed Liberator number KH 326 which crashed in North Malaya 6 of June 1945. An article about the crash appeared in the new Straits Times (Singapore) on second of August 2010. There are obviously some errors and omissions in the article which have caused problems.

As I was slightly involved at the time of the discovery of this aircraft. I would like to include a few notes.

I also have a few questions which some of you may be able to help with.

We are holding our Royal Scots Fusiliers Malaya gathering on 9th. of September in Irvine in our Ayrshire regimental area. Andrew Blakley (who was serving in the Battalion at the time of the crash (when he was one of my Scout car drivers) is one of the main organisers. This is an annual gathering of anybody who served in the Battalion in Malaya in 1953 to 57 we usually get about 200 men turning up! It is a wonderful meeting though a few die off each year.

At the time of the Liberator crash I was a Lieutenant in the Royal Scots Fusiliers and was motor transport officer (MTO) in Headquarter Company 1st. Battalion the Royal Scots Fusiliers. Maj Dennis Halstead MBE was our Company Commander with Lieutenant-Colonel M.R.J. HopeThompson DSO as our Commanding Officer. We were based at camp just South of Kroh village north Malaya (about 6 miles from the border with Siam (now Thailand). The Battalion was very scattered with HQ and A and C Companies in Kroh but D Company (under Maj Gordon Wilmot MC) in Grik, about 30 miles to the South (but with no road from us). B Company (Maj. Duncan MC and Maj. Williamson MC) at Lenggong, another 20 miles further South and Support Company at Sungei Siput further South on the main road to South Malaya. We also had a training camp at Minden Barracks on Penang Island. Because we were very scattered and as we had an airstrip at Kroh, we usually had an Army Air Corps Auster aircraft of 1706 flight based with us. The CO use this aircraft to visit our Companies as it was 200 miles to do this by road and, of course, much quicker by air as they were strips at each place.

By 1955 the anti-terrorist operations were much less intense than before, **Chin Peng** and his headquarters were known to be in camps in South East Siam (Thailand). The place was known but we were not allowed over the border at all! Thus we could not bomb his camps,

The actual border ran along the water-shed ridge with very occasionally border posts but sometimes an animal track along the ridge.

In about May 1955 a joint Malayan and Siamese operation was planned "Operation Unity". The head Malayan Police Officer was John Penley based in Kroh. He usually lived in our Officer's Mess. Our living quarters were tents. Kroh was over 1000 feet above sea level, so much cooler than lower down and at night a thin blanket was needed! There were joint meetings between the Malayan Police and Siamese in the nearby Siam town of Betong. Our Intelligence Officer Capt. K.L. (Ken) Todd usually went with John Penley.

Part of the "Operational Unity" plans was for the Royal Scots Fusiliers to search for CT (communist terrorist) camps on our side (Western) of the border which ran roughly north – south from the Kroh. Part of this was given to number 11 Platoon D Company Commanded by Lt John Staheli from Grik. I cannot remember how they got up to the border but I think it was by an lift of three Royal Navy S 51 helicopters from a good site some miles up to the North on a good road from Baling (down the pass from Kroh). I had to refuel the choppers and have a photograph of the R N "Choppers" and of the pile of "Flimsies"(4 gallon tins of AVGAS. The RN S51s had the normal American piston engines running on petrol) Andrew Blakley is in a photograph of the pile of Tin the RN "Choppers"could only lift about four loaded soldiers each, so it was a slow operation to get about 30 men into the new site. If the take-off point was higher the loads became smaller because of the thin air! The Royal Naval Squadron (845 and 848) were very helpful and efficient in every way. They were trained to land in very limited spaces and they obviously enjoyed our type of tasks!

Our Patrols reported to Battalion Headquarters (and to their own company) each evening when the radio work was easiest, though at Battalion HQ radio was open for the full 24 hours each day. Generally this was done using Morse code.

At Battalion HQ at Kroh we knew where each Patrol was and an outline of their tasks – – – even though I was not directly involved. Any unusual news spread fairly quickly!

On the evening of 25 May 1955 **[Authors note: This according to the Operational report was 28 May]** we heard from Lt John Staheli's 11 Platoon that they had discovered the remains of a crashed R AF bomber which was still loaded with the containers of weapons, that it was to drop to the wartime British Force 136. John had found three of the four huge engines and got their numbers which he radioed to us. I think he already identified it as a Liberator. His detailed report and the subsequent reports are in that the company war diary which Major Gordon Wilmot kept in great detail.

How it was discovered as a story by itself! Apart of 11 Platoon under Sgt Dummelow was searching for signs of "CT" camp's etc. at some stage they disturbed a "Hornets Nest" they are like a very dangerous type of Bee but much worse! There is a recognised "Drill" of what to do when you meet Hornets as they are most dangerous! Normally everything on Patrol is SILENCE but if Hornets are struck and the nest disturbed they will attack anybody in reach with a very sore bite! So the drill is just split up and separate as quickly as possible (no "encouragement" is required!!) After about 10 minutes the Hornets will return to the nest and the Patrol can begin to gather again a bit further away!

When Sgt Dummelow was getting the Patrol together again one of the Jocks (Scottish soldiers) told Dummelow to come and look as he had stumbled upon an aircraft. Dummelow told him not to be stupid but was then persuaded to have a look. Sure enough! There, only about 15 to 20 yards from them was the huge remains of this aircraft. John Staheli was called and quickly realised what it was and did a quick check of the remains.

The full report is in D Company's "War Diary" kept by the Company Commander Major Gordon Wilmot (a pre-war soldier who had been in Dunkirk!), This is held in the library the Regimental Headquarters of the (now) Royal Highland Fusiliers (second Battalion of the Royal Regiment of Scotland) in Glasgow.

When the importance and size of the task of clearing out all the weapons loaded in the crashed aircraft was reliesed, it was necessary to have help of another Platoon. At the time the Platoon of C Company under (then) Lieftenant J.B. Agnew (Blair) Blair was operating some distance of the South of 11 Platoon so he was told to join John Staheli. This was easier ordered than done, as a country is very steep and very thick. On one day Blair travelled only 1100 yards through very thick bamboo but this was usual for that type of vegetation.

I know Blair Agnew very well and after leaving the Army as a Colonel he finally retired from his very good position in a Financial Company. He is the only senior member of the 2 Platoons is still alive (and very active!) He told me recently that the Hornets Nest was only about 15 or 20 yards from the crashed aircraft! Also that it was almost at some small defensive positions dug by the Terrorist on a main path going down the hill which had been found before the Hornets found them!

I think, but am not absolutely certain, that a short report about the crash find was published in the Malayan newspaper. About six months later. It struck me how very angry *Chin Peng* would have been, when he heard about the find of all the weapons in the crash! The CT's were very short of arms and ammunition and yet here only 20 yards from the positions was enough for many years!! I always give this an explanation of how thick the jungle is! *Chin Peng* does not mention this in his autobiography: "My Side of History" which is a good description of their activities. Though he does not mention all their activities.

When we received John Staheli's first report it was reported to our army HQ's and, I believe to the Royal Air Force Headquarters. Very soon 2 RAF men were flown up to inspect the site. I think they were both Sgt's. We, even then, were interested to find out as much from the aircraft's instruments as possible and particularly if they were any human remains.

The 2 RAF did not impress our men as it was quite obviously they just wanted to get "out" of the jungle as quickly as possible! They said the aircraft was on "Automatic Pilot" when it crashed. They also said the bones that were there were from wild pigs and not human bones, (I find this difficult to believe as wild pigs do not move in those areas).

After a few days Royal Navy helicopters came to Kroh to get out the weapons and ammunition that had been got out of the wreck. The latest reports say there were about 11 helicopter loads. I did not count in detail but I thought it was 12 or 13. Anyway we (of the MT Section) had to supply the petrol and were running rather low by the time we had finished and the choppers returned South. I think there were six or seven unspoiled weapons containers (from the bomb bay) and 1 that was broken open. There were also the .5 Browning machine guns taken from the wreck which were very rusted

All weapons and containers were put out on the MT square on tarpaulin and covered. One day some of us took a Sten gun from the "Finds" and after cleaning most of grease off it, fired it on the range behind our camp.it worked perfectly. I cannot remember if we used our ammunition or that from the aircraft.

<u>Anthony Gordon's questions</u>

Do not know the exact grid reference of the crash site that certainly is recorded in some of the earlier correspondence I think it was about 708105! If perhaps somebody can give me the exact figure?? I believe the load was to be dropped at 62° North and 101° East, is this correct? it is certainly about 40 miles North of the crash site and North of the heights I have given. It looks a good site, at it is in a very wide valley running down the Northwest from the border ridge with a small river and a track.

Matt Poole's answer: Your latitude is not close! There is only one source for the lat/long of the Drop Zone, a1988 letter from the RAF Air Historical Branch to Gerald Howse nephew of KH 326 crew man William McLeod.

The operation was to drop supplies to Force 136 at a location given in lat/long terms as 06 deg North   101 deg 00 East

I measured this site as 7 miles NNW of the crash site, as measured using Google Earth (a wonderful true Internet download). My guess is that the lat/long of DZ is really more precise than the nice round numbers given. The 357 Squadron records, to which I have access, never provide DZ lat/long. As this info was considered ultra secret at the time.**Anthony's question.** I understand there was some misunderstanding about the site, as we (in the Army) read Easting FIRST and Northing SECOND this is opposite to the Air Force and Royal Navy!!!! But, I believe it led to a lot of difficulty in finding the site?

Matt Poole answer:

Anthony, that is an excellent point. The 1955 1st. Royal Scots Fusiliers report with reference – 818 300 – is indeed a near reversal of the Northing and Easting values found in the HQ FEAF reference QY 300 814 so, the two seemingly different grid reference may be very close after all.

My copy of a piece of the RSF 1: 63, 360 map from 1955 does not include the legend, where presumably the QY when zone designation is identified (as it would be on modern military maps) would your copy of the old 1: 63, 360 map include the legend? If so, can you confirm that the grid so is QY? This will be helpful to know.

Comparing the two grid reference's of course the '300' is the same in both, and we now know this is the Northing 814 versus 818 difference, is the Easting is only 4, which actually represents 4 x 100 yards.The 1: 63, 360 scale of the British map of this area – though the most detailed contemporary topographical map of its day, is not really sufficient for a true accurate pinpoint determination. In light of this, and the recognised geodetic impression of maps of that era (I'm a professional cartographer and can vouch for this, especially in rugged terrain), the 400 yard difference between the two reported grid reference is not great

[Authors note: Ref: My comment ' Srupid mistake' made in an e-mail 15 April 2007. Matts above statement, vindicates the RAF's original stated Grid Reference.]

Anthony's question: Does anybody know the details of the readings on the crashed aircraft instrument??? The RAF men told us as it was on "Automatic Pilot" if the readings included the height of even 2500 feet, the aircraft was asking for a crash in that country, as there are many heights more than that! Especially along the International border!

Matt Poole's answer

Have an excerpt of the 1955 R AF report (the only known to exist) which analyses the wreckage of KH 326. As you can see for yourself there is not much of an explanation, just this brief statement.

The automatic pilot panel indicated that the aircraft was flying through straight and level with possibly one engine feathered.

This implies that the Autopilot was engaged, but it doesn't give definite proof of anything. The fact that the Autopilot was on or off does not prove anything either.

Sadly the scrap merchants have removed all four propellers. I do not know if there will be surviving evidence to prove which, if any, engine had been feathered. Maybe the next time Shaharom and Jim Zuraiman reach the site, they can take detailed photographs of each of the four engines, in search of the gear teeth/prop hub evidence, which could determine the answer

Feathering is the mechanical rotating (by motor) of the three blades of any particular engine to create a "knife edge" and the least wind resistance possible in flight. A feathered prop Thus indicates a cockpit control engine shutdown or else an outright engine failure. Were a propeller not feathered, the drag of the flat blades would have a major effect upon the flight characteristics of the bomber.

Furthermore, a non feathered prop could windmill – turning faster and faster as the air hits the blades. A windmilling prop, eventually, could break free of the shaft and slice through the fuselage or wing with dire consequences.

There was no equivalent of a Fight Data Recorder on a Liberator, though the positions of flaps, cockpit control levers, engine throttles and switches (left in the on/off position) could have been frozen in position at the moment of impact. Even then, some switches could have been altered by the impact, so an Investigator would have to keep an open mind.

Lastly the subject of the Thailand scrap metal merchants. My guess is that the wreck has been pilfered by the CT is various fairly soon after the Fusiliers were out of the area. It would have been obvious to them after all the RSF activity, and the wreck would have yielded many potential useful tidbits. Then, over the years, the Thailand side of the border has been successfully cleared of jungle. Look on Google maps and you will see how much of the land has been cleared, almost up to the border, near the border. The border is porous, to, I suspect that the wreck has been found other times over the years, and that some point it became a target for the opportunities looking to haul away some aluminium for its scrap metal value. The border is only 400 or so metres away, pretty close to the scavengers. I do recall that Shaharom found out that the wreck hah been found in the 1980s by the Malaysians Police quoting from Shaharom in July 2007

I heard the Royal Malaysian Police patrol found the wreck in the early 1980s, but no one from the Malasian Police Museum remembers the event. Will dig further you should know that the Malaysian people were not good at keeping records. Regarding the Police Museum yes, the Police also have a museum, and past data and records were beautifully by them, but in most cases they were not, it depends on luck, and their staff were not aware of anything about finding KH 326, since the museum was established in the late 1990s some of the records of staff were still new.(Shaharom has found Nothing)

153.   5 October 2010   Joe Plant to Matt Poole,

No, I have not had any feedback from the RSF reunion but intend to make contact with Andrew in the near future.

I have been trying to trace a copy of the 6th. June RAF Operational Report for Minneriya Sqdn. Not mentioned? that I have recieved from the Nat Archives, there is no mention of KH326. Plenty about Spitfies, etc. Do not understand why no mention.

I think I have found one of the chopper pilots of 848 Sqdn Royal Navy who did the lifts. I am waiting for info back. He is in his 80's. Hopefully something will come of that.

Also trying to find some info about the report that was submitted by the two RAF guys who surveyed the crash site. That is going to be difficult, according to a researcher at the Nat Arch, but will continue to review.

154.   5 October 2010   Matt Poole to Joe Plant,

First, WOW!! I hope you did find one of the chopper pilots. I'd love to hear how you found him. I had left a plea for info on who these men were via the Fleet Air Arm message board...or something like that...must rediscover the reference, which I have in my records somewhere. I have never received even one response, though I have not checked the site lately.

Only four Libs from 357 was on detachment at Minneriya at the time, and the individual records of these flights are missing from the 357 Sqn Operations Record Book. I already had the Station records from Minneriya -- from you? or my Friend Robert Quirk?? Attached -- the two appropriate pages.

Now I'm fuzzy on 8 Sqn records. I have two pages, announcing the move to Minneriya, but nothing else. Oh, my record keeping is lacking, as I don't know who sent these pages. See attached. Maybe Robert Quirk has further 8 Sqn records from Minneriya...I must check with him, but I must assume that I've previously done this and the records revealed NOTHING.

In short, any records of the 357 detachment's flights from Minneriya were lost in the shuffle, it seems.

The RAF guys at the wrecksite -- I was wondering where a further record of their activities could be found...with their names. How marvellous would that be to find this info??? Your sleuth at Kew might come up with something in, say, records of the Commander-in-Chief of the Far East Air Force, but it could be a tough slog. Perhaps the name of G/Capt O.A. Morris, whose name is at the bottom of the 16 June 1955 letter with details of the wreck visit, will prove useful. Hope so!

I don't know if Gerald Howse has submitted the letter yet. Via Skype maybe I can catch him home later this week...though it is a busy week for me

155.   24 November 2010   Joe Plant to Matt Poole,

I did send an e-mail to Gerald Prince of the 848 Heli Sqdn but did not get a reply. You prompted me to get back in touch and find out what has happened. I found his telephone number and spoke with him this morning. Nothing is the reAction. He said that he had lost the details of my original e-mail. However, he is going to re-open the case and see if anyone can recollect the discovery. He did mention PHOTOS. Again a mystery, but if they have some, it would be greatHe does remember the incident, but he was a ground crew maintenance member in Singapore, not in Kuala Lumpur where the squadron was based. Most of his Association members are groundcrew, but he will try to find out what he can and get back to me verbally. I'll have to wait and see what transpires in the next couple of weeks. I have informed him that the "NAVY IS THE MISSING LINK." Bit of bullshit really. Nevertheless I am eager to see what he comes up with.

156.   19 July 2011   Joe Plant to Matt Poole,

Just received e-mail from Gerald Prince, 848 Sqdn Helis. He sends his apologies as he is not available during the winter months. Possibly he goes abroad? Anyway, he has little or no news to offer, as he says they are all depleting in numbers. Last year it was 27, now its down to a handful, but he will still keep trying for information. The two heli pilots are amongst those depleted. So I do not hold out much hope for photos, but you never know. I have asked him to chase up any still available, so I await his next e-mail. No response was ever received.

[Author note]: Thus ended my involvement with the disappearance and finding of Liberator KH326 A truly amazing mystery adventure —

I am extremely pleased, that I had the pleasure. To be just one of a team, to take part in an epic passage of time in trying to solve a mystery that began in 1945. But truly still partly unsolved, regarding the fate of the 8 Canadian Members of the Crew of KH326. My thanks go to all those mentioned in the foregoing write up, especially to Matt Poole who became a good friend. His great knowledge of finding airplane wrecks and his part in finding all the relatives of the deceased Crew not only of of KH326. But many others. Shaharom Ahamad of the Malaysian Historical Group - Jim

Zuraiman of the Malaysian Army, who along with their teams, made 3 Arduous trips into the Ulu. in an attempt to find the missing Liberator. Twice being unsuccessful, due to arduous jungle terrain. The 3rd, was 'Eureka.' Antony Gordon and Blair Agnew. Officers of the 1st. Battalion Royal Scots Fusiliers who were there at the crash site in 1955 along with many other Old RSF Sweats. Who provided so much very useful information, and assistance to the search team. My Salutations to all.

Joe P. Plant

oooOooo

CHAPTER 20
MILITARY CEMETERIES - MALAYA PENINSULAR

~~Memorial~~ Stone: 4 Km. Jalan Langor Road Alor Star. [1]

SARAWAK RANGERS
Ungkok.　A.J.　L/Cpl.

Buried at the Old Gurkha Cemetry Sungei Patani. [22]
Roll of Honour.

2ND. KING EDWARD VII'S OWN GURKHA RIFLES

Gharti.	B.	Rfn.	Gurung.	B.	Lt.			

7th.DUKE OF EDINBURGH'S OWN GURKHA RIFLES

Rai.	B.	Rfn.	Limbu	B.	Rfn.	Rai.		P.M.C Capt.
Limbu.	B.	Rfn.	Rai.	J.	Rfn.			

10th.PRINCESS MARY'S OWN GURKHA RIFLES

Limbu.	D.	Rfn.	Rai.	J.	L/Cpl.	Sunwar.	M	Recruit
Rai.	G.	Rfn.	Limbu.	J.	Rfn.	Limbu	P.	Rfn.
Tamang.	G.	Rfn.	Rai.	M.	Recruit	Rai.	S.	Rfn.

GURKHA SIGNALS
Chhetri　R. Sgmn

GURKHA ENGINEERS

Bura.	K.	Spr.	Tamang.	L.	Spr.

DEPOT THE BRIGADE OF GURKHAS

Rai.	P.	Boy.	Pun.	P.	Boy.

Buried at the New Gurkha Cemetry Sungei Patani. [23]
ROLL OF HONOUR

2ND. KING EDWARD VII'S OWN GURKHA RIFLES

Thapa.	B.	Rfn.	Pradham.	P.	Cpl

6TH. QUEEN ELIZABETH'S OWN GURKHA RIFLES

Thapa.	A.	Rfn.	Gurung.	G.	L/Cpl.	Pun.	R.	Rfn.
Thapa.	A.	Rfn.	Pun.	G.	L/Cpl.	Thapa.	P,	Cpl.
Rana	B.	Rfn.	Chhetri	G.	Rfn.	Thapa.	T.	Rfn.
Gurung.	B.	Rfn.	Gurung.	K.	Rfn.	Pun.	T.	Capt.(KGO)
Gurung.	B.	Rfn.	Gurung.	K	Recruit	Thapa.	T.	Recruit
Thapa.	C.	Rfn.	Pun.	L.	Rfn.			
Thapa.	D.	Rfn.	Rana.	N.	Rfn.			
Pun.	D.	Rfn.	Gurung.	R.	Lt.(KGO)			

Kuala Terengganu Cemetery [1]
Roll of Honour

ROYAL NAVY
Breen.　J.J. TO/Mech.

Buried at Western Road Cemetery Penang. [54]
Roll of Honour.

1ST. BATTALION MANCHESTER REGIMENT.

Broadbent.	J.	Cpl.	Cooper.	A.	Pte.	Hiscox.	K.	Pte.
Buckley.	E.F.	Pte.	Fitzpatrick.	L.E.	L/Cpl.	McGibbons.	E.	Pte.

1ST.& 2ND. BATTALION THE KINGS OWN YORKSHIRE LIGHT INFANTRY.

Carter.	A.	Pte.	James.	R.A.	Pte.	Walker.	C.	Pte.
Fee.	A.G.	Pte.	Kelly.	H.	Pte.	Ward.	K.W.	Pte.
Guy.	R.	Pte.	Mills.	J.	Pte.	Whitehead.	J.D.	L/Cpl

1ST. BATTALION. ROYAL SCOTS FUSILIERS

Lyon.	J.	Fus.	Vine.	W.J.	Cpl.

KINGS OWN REGIMENT
Hornby.　B.　WOII

22 SPECIAL AIR SERVICE
Eakin.　P.G.R. Cpl.

ROYAL CORPS. OF SIGNALS

Byde.	W.C.	Cpl.	Meiklejohn.MBE	G.D.	Maj.	

ROYAL ARMY SERVICE CORPS.

Breese.	M.	Sgt.	King.	P.O.	Dvr.

ROYAL ARMY ORDNANCE CORPS.
James.　G.T. Pte.

CORPS. OF ROYAL ELECTRICAL & MECHANICAL ENGINEERS

Wright. T. Cfn.

INTELLIGENCE CORPS.

Golder. W. WOII

ARMY CATERING CORPS.

Godfrey. J.J.H. Pte.

ROYAL AIR FORCE

Berry.	M.F.J.	Plt./II	Harris.	A.I.J.	Nav.II	Parsons.	R.	Flt./Lt.
Blackmore.	L.B.	SAC.	Hobson.	F.W.T.	Fg./Off.	Rathbone.	P.M.	Plt./Off.
Bowler.	J.E.	Fg./Off.	Hollands.	R.E.	ACI.	Russell.	R.J.	Fg./Off.
Carus.	R.	Cpl.	Jones.	J.B.	Flt./Lt.	Swindells.	G.J.	Fg./Off.
Cain.	F.	W/O.	Lacy.	B.P.H.	Fg./Off.	Woods.	A.J.	Sgt.
Cooper.	R.C.F.	LAC.	Leppard.	W.H.	SAC.			
Fifeild.	L.W.	Ch.Tech.	Murphy.	M.	Cpl.			

ROYAL AUSTRALIAN AIR FORCE

Duffy.	W.P.	LAC.	Lawson.	J.G.	AC	O'Donnell	J.M.	Cpl.
Hall.	D.J.	LAC.	Rowe.	C.J.	LAC.			

ROYAL NAVY

Berkely.	P.D.	A/B	Frost.	N.H.	TO2.
McTaggart.	T.J.	Sto/Mech.			

Buried at the Christian Cemetery Taiping. [124]
Roll of Honour.

40 COMMANDO

Alexander.	C.	Mne.	Coop.	J.R.	Lt.	Mathieson.	K.	Mne.
Chadwick	J.	Mne.	Dayes.	G.A.	Mne.	Ryder.	R.T.	Cpl.
Cherry.	R.J.	Mne.	Dowling.	M.G.	Lt.	Taylor.	M.J.	Sgt.
Clarke.	R.A.	Mne.	Ireland.	L.C.	Cpl.			

9TH./12TH. ROYAL LANCERS (PRINCE OF WALES)

Britnell.	J.F.	Trp.	Bryant.	E.H.S.	Sgt.

13TH./18TH. ROYAL HUSSARS (QUEEN MARY'S OWN)

Richardson.	R.	Trp.	Warner.	M.J.	Trp

15TH/19TH. KING'S ROYAL HUSSARS

Bruce.	D.C	Trp.	Fitchett.	P.J.	Trp.	Thompson.	C. E.	Sgt.
Campbell.	G.	Trp.	Jones.	R.F.D.	Trp.	Walker.	A. G.	Trp.
Davies.	J.A.	2/Lt	Summers.	G.	Trp.	Wells.	S.W.J.	Cpl.

3RD. ROYAL TANK REGIMENT

Hibbs.	J.A.	Lt.	Whipp.	R.	L/Clp

ROYAL REGIMENT OF ARTILLERY (RA)

Cuniff.	F. D.	Gnr.	Little.	D.S.	Gnr.
Golldin.	G.J. L.	Lt.	Moffat.	G.R.	Capt.

1ST. BATTALION MANCHESTER REGIMENT

Arands.	T.	Pte.	Grady.	J.	Pte.	Smith.	R.H.	Pte.
Baillie.	W.M.	Pte.	Harrison.	M.	Pte.	Traynor.	T.	Pte.

1ST. BATTALION LINCOLNSHIRE REGIMENT

Barson.	A.D.	Pte.	Duckett.	F.R.	Sgt.
Dodd.	W.	Cpl.	Jack.	D.	Pte.

1ST. & 2ND. BATTALION THE KINGS OWN YORKSHIRE LIGHT INFANTRY

Baddeley.	W.C.	Sgt.	Gilpin.	J.	Sgt.	Maritt.	J.R.	Pte.
Gee,	R.	Pte.	Foley.	J.	Pte.	Price.	D.A.	CQMS.

1ST. BATTALION WEST YORKSHIRE REGIMENT

Brown	P.S.	Pte	Silverwood.	A.	Pte.

1ST. BATTALION. ROYAL SCOTS FUSILIERS

Fleming. A.W. L/Cpl.

1ST. BATTALION WORCESTERSHIRE REGIMENT

Dunn.	R.E.	Pte.	Sellwood.	A.	Sgt.

GLOUCESTER REGIMENT

Mercer. P.C.D. Capt.

1ST. BATTALION LOYAL REGIMENT (NORTH LANCASHIRE)

Gardner.	K.	Pte.	Nelson.	R.	Pte.
Morley.	R.H.	Lt.	Turner.	E.	Sgt.

1ST. BATTALION SEAFORTH HIGHLANDERS ROSS-SHIRE BUFFS (THE DUKE OF ALBANY'S)

Eglington. J.B. Pte.

1ST. BATTALION GORDON HIGHLANDERS

Fairgreive.	J.H.	Pte.	Rose.	K.S.	2/Lt.
MacKenzie.	J.S.	Pte.	Wright.	K.W.	Pte.

ARGYLL & SUTHERLAND HIGHLANDERS

Docherty. E. Pte.

ROYAL ULSTER RIFLES

Salter. MBE.MC. E.M. Maj.

22 SECIAL AIR SERVICE

Bond	C.W.	L/Cpl.	Goulding.	G.L.	Lt.	Moffatt.	J.R.	Capt.

ARMY AIR CORPS.

Dalley.	P.J.L.	Capt.						

ROYAL ARMY SERVICE CORPS.

Birnie.	L.	Dvr.	Jeffries.	B.	L/Cpl.	Smith.	A.T.	Capt.
Edland.	N.	L/Cpl.	Lewis.	A.	Sgt.	Staples.	P.J.	Pte.
Hoye.	T.G.	Dvr.	Naylor.	D.	L/Cpl.			
Hoye.	F.L.	Capt.QM	Quinn.	T.M.	Cpl.			

ROYAL ARMY MEDICAL CORPS.

Brown.	R.M.	Capt.

CORPS. OF ROYAL ELECTRICAL & MECHANICAL ENGINEERS

Bligh.	L.J.	Cpl.	Giles.	D.V.	Cpl.
Brown.	R.	Cfn.	Richards.	H.W.	Sgt.

ROYAL MILITARY POLICE

Trotter.	J.T.	Cpl.

INTELLIGENCE CORPS.

Turrall.	G.W.R	Capt.	Hunt.	P.W.	Lt.

QUEEN ALEXANDER'S ROYAL ARMY NURSING CORPS.

Fenelon.	P.M.	Pte.

SARAWAK RANGER

Kumpang.	A.T.	Pte.	Nyambik.	A.P.	Pte.
Leton.	A.K.	Pte.	Ugap.	A.U.	Pte.

ROYAL AUSTRALIAN ARTILLERY

Blanch.	S.J.	Gnr.	Ducat.	R.M.	Gnr.	Sutton.	D.K.	Bdr,

1st. BATTALION ROYAL AUSTRALIAN REGIMENT

Ferrell.	B.H.	Pte.	Smedley.	L.R.	Pte.

2nd. BATTALION ROYAL AUSTRALIAN REGIMENT

Allan.	J.N.	Cpl.	Holland.	T.B.	Pte.	MacVicar.	D.	Pte.
Anderson.	C.C.	Sgt.	Ingra.	C.C.	Pte.	Metcalf.	J.N.	Pte.
Decent	J.	Pte.	Jay.	C.A.	Pte.	Potts.	J.P.	Pte.
Ewald.	H.H.	Sgt.	Jephson.	H.M.	Pte.	Wilson.	J.	Pte
Fritz.	G.C.	Pte.	Keen.	A.W.	Pte.			

3rd. BATTALION ROYAL AUSTRALIAN REGIMENT

Haynes.	P.L.	Pte.	Seesink.	D.A.	Cpl.
Ryan.	M.	Sgt.	Tulloch.	A.J.	Pte.

ROYAL AUSTRALIAN SIGNALS

James.	K.V.	Sgmn.	Norris.	E.R.	Sgmn

ROYAL AUSTRALIAN ARMY SERVICE CORPS.

Thompson.	E.F.	Pte.

ROYAL AUSTRALIAN ELECTRICAL & MECHANICAL ENGINEERS.

Henderson.	B.A.D.	Cfn.

1st. BATTALION. NEW ZEALAND REGIMENT

Breitmeyer.	R.M.	Pte.	Kawha.	T.	Pte.
Brown.	P.	L/Cpl.	Tuxworth.	B.J.	Pte.

2nd. BATTALION. NEW ZEALAND REGIMENT

Amas.	G.W.	Pte.	Solia.	T.F.	Pte.

ROYAL AIR FORCE

Hurn. BEM.	H.E.A.	Plt./I.	Orr.	J.	Cpl.

Buried at Batu Gajah Ipoh Perak. [52]
Roll of Honour

42 COMMANDO

Eatough.	B.	Mne.	Rowe.	W.R.N.	Sgt.
Mackay. MC.	P.L.	Capt	Storey.	J.	Mne.

45 COMMANDO.

Barnett.	T.W.	Mne.	Miller.	L.O.	Mne.	Westwood.	G.	Sgt.
Budgen.	P. K.	Lt.	Nevard.	E.J.	Mne			
Fordham.	P. D.	Mne	Parr.	D.	Mne			

4th. QUEEN'S OWN HUSSARS

Finch.	J.E.	Cpl.	Johns	T.	Trp.	Questler.	M.	Lt.
Grayson.	B.	Trp.	Lynch	B.G.	Trp.	Read.	R.J.	RS
Hunter.	S.G.	Trp	Mitchell.	D.J.	Trp.			

ROYAL REGIMENT OF ARTILLERY (RA)

Villar.	J.H.	Capt.

2ND. BATTALION COLDSTREAM GUARDS

Brown.	J.D.	Gdsmn.	Lawson. BEM	I.D.	Sgt.	Parkin.	J.F.	Gdsmn.
Dowson.	J.R.	Sgt.	Medley.	H.J.	Gdsmn.	Rowe.	P.S.	Gdsmn.

ESSEX REGIMENT

Barnes.	R.G.	Maj.

1ST.& 2ND. BATTALION THE KINGS OWN YORKSHIRE LIGHT INFANTRY.

Boden.	W.J.	Pte.	Cough.	J.E.	Pte.	Hutchinson.	K.	L/Cpl.
Brown.	V.	L/Cpl.	Hall.	R.L.	Pte.	Jones.	D.	Pte.
Dobson.	A.	Pte.	Harrison.	C.M.	Pte.	Woodhouse.	H.	Pte.
Elliott.	J.	Pte.	Hudson.	J.K.	Pte.			

1ST. BATTALION SOMERSET LIGHT INFANTRY

Lock.	D.G.	Capt.	Pyemount.	D.S.	2/Lt.

THE GREEN HOWARDS

Fisher. G.A. Pte.

1ST. BATTALION WORCESTERSHIRE REGIMENT

Thompson. J. Pte.

ROYAL ARMY SERVICE CORPS.

Baldwin.	R.	Dvr.	Hopper.	T.F.J.	Dvr.	Whitwell.	C.E.	Dvr
Hand.	F.	Cpl.	Jessop.	P.B.	Capt.			
Hoggett.	N.	L/Cpl.	Ritter.	C.R.	Sgt.			

CORPS. OF ROYAL ELECTRICAL & MECHANICAL ENGINEERS

Stedeford. B.W. Capt.

ROYAL ARMY MEDICAL CORPS.

Dunn. A. Pte.

ROYAL AIR FORCE.

Blakey.	P.	Sig.III	Marshall.	D,C,	Flt.Lt.	Wigglesworth.	R.S.	Flt.Lt.

Buried at the Gurkha Cemetery Sulva Lines Ipoh. [52]
Roll of Honour.

2ND. KING EDWARD VII'S OWN GURKHA RIFLES

Gurung.	B.	Lt.(KGO)	Gurung.	I.	Rfn.	Pun.	L.	Rfn.
Pun.	D.	Rfn.	Gurung.	K.	L/Cpl.			

6TH. QUEEN ELIZABETH'S OWN GURKHA RIFLES

Ale.	A.	Rfn.	Gurung.	L.	Rfn.	Ale.	P.	Rfn.
Gurung.	B.	Sgt.	Bura.	M.	Rfn.	Thapa.	P.	Rfn.
Thapa.	B.	Cpl.	Gurung.	M.	Rfn.	Gurung.	R.	
Rana.	D.	Sgt.	Mall.	M.	Rfn.	Capt.(QGO)		
Newar.	I.	L/Cpl.	Gurung.	P.	Rfn.	Thapa.	Y.	Sgt.

7th.DUKE OF EDINBURGH'S OWN GURKHA RIFLES

Pickin. A.R. Capt.

10th.PRINCESS MARY'S OWN GURKHA RIFLES

Gurung. K. Rfn.

GURKHA SIGNALS

Gurung. R. Cpl.

Buried at Cheras Road Kuala Lumpur.[417]
Roll of Honour

ROYAL REGIMENT OF ARTILLERY (RA)

Bailey.	C. M.	Gnr.	Griffiths.	L.P.	Capt.	Mather.	M. R.	Cpt.
Brooks.	A.R.	Gnr.	Harper.	J. G.	Gnr.	Rawlings.	A.	Gnr.
Chick.	P.	Gnr.	Hillman.	G. B.	Gnr.	Stansbei.	M.H.	Gnr.
Daunt.	N. R.	BQMS.	Hipwell.	J.	Gnr	Taylor.	E.	BQMS.
Fitzgerald.	T.	Gnr.	Houghton.	F. R.	Gnr.	Vickers.	G.A	Gnr
Wallett.	F.	Gnr.	Whitear.	W. J.	Gnr.			

4TH. QUEEN'S OWN HUSSARS

Archibold.	N.	Trp.	Mills.	H.G.G.Maj.		Stares.	R.D.	Trp.
Guy.	K.	Trp.	Platts.	E.	Trp.	Totman.	P.J.	Trp.
Hartley.	W.J. H Cpl.		Roberts.	A.J.	Trp.	Ward.	P.T.	Trp.
Lane.	W.	Trp.	Skiba.	F.	Trp.			

11th. HUSSARS (PRINCE ALBERT'S OWN)

Hornigold.	N.	Trp.	Houlsley.	C.	Cpl.	Slack.	C.E.	Sgt.

13TH/18TH. ROYAL HUSSARS (QUEEN MARY'S OWN)

Hall. R. Trp.

1ST. KINGS DRAGOON GUARDS

Godrich.	J.A.	Trp.	McInnes.	J.	L/Cpl.
Mawdsley.	T. R.	Trp.	Ross-Wilson.	J.	L/Cpl.

3RD. BATTALION GRENADIER GUARDS

Chriscoll. MM.	J.P.	L/Cpl.	Herrett.	V.T.	Gdsmn.	Ryan.	T.	Gdsmn
Hall.	J.R.	Gdsmn.	Martin.	A.E.	Gdsmn.			

2ND. BATTALION COLDSTREAM GUARDS

Tate. M. L/Sgt.

2ND. BATTALION SCOTS GUARDS

Clucus.	W.	Gdsmn	Forbes-Leith	J.A.	2/Lt.	Ferguson.	A.	L/Sgt.
Duffell.	E.J.	Gdsmn	Graham- Watson.	P.W.B.	2/Lt.	Holland.	K.	Gdsmn

Lea.	H.L.	L/Sgt.	McKenzie	R.A.C.	Lt.	Morrice.	M.J.	2/Lt.
MacMillan	D.	Sgt.	Moore.	D.	2/Lt.			
Raich.	W.A.P.	Sgt.						

1ST. BATTALION THE QUEEN'S REGIMENT (WEST SURREY)

Braybrooks.	D.A.J.	Pte.	Mack.	J.V.	2/Lt.
Duff.	H.M.C.A.	Pte.	Townsend.	R.M.	2/L

EAST SURREY REGIMENT

Shaw.   D.   Sgt.

1ST. QUEEN'S OWN ROYAL WEST KENTS

Bardell.	J.	Pte.	Hand.	L.J.	Pte.	Lowday.	W.J.	Pte.
Brown.	D.P.	Pte.	Heath.	G.H.	Pte.	Manning.	D.W.	2/Lt.
Chambers.	R.J.	L/Cpl.	Henderson.	T.H.	Cpl.	Molland.	D.P.	L/Cpl.
Cheeseman.	J.	Pte.	Hollebon.	L.G.	Pte.	Newell.	E.C.	L/Cpl.
Coleman.	D.C.	Pte.	Holman.	L.W.	Pte.	Pelling.	M.	Pte.
Deed.	E.A.	Capt.	Knight.	J.A.C.	Pte.	Stevenson.	H.C.	Pte.
Denton.	C.	Pte.	Latter.	D.W.	Pte.	Sulley.	H.	Cpl.
Elsley.	D.R.I.	Pte.	Lepper.	A.G.	Pte.	Whitmore.	P.A.	Pte.

ROYAL FUSILIERS

Argyle.	A.F.	Sgt.	Villiers.	R.E.	Fus.

ROYAL WARWICKSHIRE REGIMENT

HENSLEY.   K.A.   2/LT.

1ST. BATTALION SUFFOLK REGIMENT

Ansell.	B.V.	Pte.	Mallows.	F.T.C	L/Cpl.	Sommonds .	H. R.	L/Cpl.
Ashdown.	J.A.	Sgt.	Mills.	R.A.	Pte.	Swann.	M.S.	Bdsmn.
Bailly.	S.J.	Cpl.	Moore.	R.	Pte.	Thompson.	S.E.	L/Cpl.
Edwards.	J.O.	Pte.	Nobbs.	D.	Pte.	Walker.	H.C.	Pte
Killick.	L.G.	Pte.	Payne.	L.R.	Pte.	Westin.	D.B.	Sgt.
Larman.	B.	Pte.	Pearce.	W.G.	Pte.	Wilson.	D.	Pte.
Lewis.	F.L.	Pte.	Riches.	E.A.	Pte.			

1ST. BATTALION LINCOLNSHIRE REGIMENT

Marshall.	J.A.	Pte.	Ogden.	R.D.	2/Lt.

1ST. BATTALION DEVONSHIRE REGIMENT

Bone.	A.B.	Pte.	Hall.	G.C.	Pte.	Rayner.	J.W.	Cpl.
Browne.	J.M.	Pte.	Kimmel.	M.O.F.	2/Lt.	Vizor.	R.M.	L/Cpl.
Glass.	F.M.	Cpl.	Lawery.	W.G.	Pte.	Wareham.	N.J.	Cpl.
Greene.	M.J.	Pte.	Price.	R.W.	L/Cpl.	Wright.	M. A.	Capt.

1ST.& 2ND. BATTALION THE KINGS OWN YORKSHIRE LIGHT INFANTRY

Mc. Gee.   J.   L/Cpl.

1ST. BATTALION SOMERSET LIGHT INFANTRY

Beaumont.	R.	Sgt.	Hanlon.	M.J.	Sgt.	Mathews.	W.B.	Pte.
Bennett.	A.B.	Pte	Heath.	B.B.	2/Lt.	Pheasant.	E.W.V.	Pte.
Cleveland.	G.F.	Pte.	Johnson.	A.K.	Pte.	Plympton.	B.W.G.	Pte.
Clothier.	D.M.	Cpl.	Leeworthy.	J.A.	Pte.	Shaw.	G.H.	Cpl.
Down.	E.J.	L/Cpl.	Martin.	E.G.	L/Cpl.	Spurr.	P.W.P.	Pte.
Farrance.	A.C.H.	L/Cpl.	Mather.	J.R.S.	Capt.			

THE GREEN HOWARDS

Bamblett.	W.D.	Pte.	Mayle.	A.G.	Cpl.	Smith.	H..	Pte.
Higgins.	D.G.	Pte.	Owen.	J.	Pte.			
Lord.	R.	Pte.	Parrish.	P.	Bdsmn.			

1ST. BATTALION WEST YORKSHIRE REGIMENT

Sayner.   D.C.   Pte.

1ST. BATTALION CHESHIRE REGIMENT

Bancroft.   K.B.   Pte.

1ST. BATTALION. ROYAL SCOTS FUSILIERS

Cartwright.   P.B.S .   Lt.

2ND. BATTALION WELSH FUSILIERS

Catleugh.	D.J.	L/Cpl.	Fieldhouse.	G.C.	Fus.	Sutton.MC	P.G.F.	Maj.
Davies.	J.M.B.	Capt.	George.	A.	Cpl.	Taylor.	C.B.	Fus.
Evans.	J.	Fus.	Rowlands.	D.G.	L/Cpl.			

1ST. BATTALION CAMERONIANS. (SCOTISH RIFLES)

MCammont.   W.J.   Sgt.

BLACK WATCH. R.H.R.

McKee,	R.	L/Cpl.	Tarleton.	R.B.	Cpl.

ROYAL BERKSHIRE REGIMENT

Moore.   J.P.   Pte.

1ST. BATTALION LOYAL REGIMENT (NORTH LANCASHIRE)

Brook.   T.R.   Maj.

1ST. BATTALION ROYAL HAMPSHIRE REGIMENT

Ainsley.	J.R.	Pte.	Archer.	P.J.	Pte.	Hill.	W.	Pte.
Amor.	A.E.	Maj.	Bolam.	D.W.	2/Lt.	Mumford.	C.J.G.	Maj.

Masterman.	P.W.	Pte.	Swain.	B.D.	L/Cpl.			
Smith.	B.D.	Pte.	Watton.	R.C.	L/Cpl.			

1ST. BATTALION SEAFORTH HIGHLANDERS ROSS-SHIRE BUFFS (THE DUKE OF ALBANY'S)

McIntyre.	K.F.	Lt.	Frew.	D.J.	Pte.

1ST. BATTALION GORDON HIGHLANDERS

Campbell.	A.	Pte	Duff.	R.D.	Capt.	Leggat.	J.	Pte.
Caulfield.	G.	Capt.	Duggan.	T.	Lt.	Murray.	G.P.	Pte.
Cronin.	T.E.	Pte.	Gray.	A.	Pte.			

ARGYLL & SUTHERLAND HIGHLANDERS

Roxburgh.	J.	Pte.

22 SPECIAL AIR SERVICE

Bancroft	K.	Cpl.	Duckworth.	E.	Spr.	Pearce.	J.P.	Tpr.
Barker. BEM.	E.C.R.	Maj.	Fotheringham.	J.L.C.	Lt.	Powell.	B.	Tpr.
Boylan.	P.G.	Sgmn	Howell.	A.E.	Tpr.	Watson.	B.	Pte.
Cartwright.	P.B.S.	Lt.	Marselle.	W.R.J.	Tpr.	Wilkins.	F.W.	Tpr.
Dean.	A.G.H.	Lt.	Morgan.	J.A.S.	Tpr.			
Donnelly Wood.	F.M.	2/Lt.	O'Leary.	J.E.	Tpr.			

ROYAL ARMY SERVICE CORPS.

Anderson.	E.P.	Pte.	Hodgson.	G.	Dvr.	Roberts.	E.	Dvr.
Boardman.	H.F.	Dvr.	Kearney.	C.	Dvr.	Smith.	J.	Dvr.
Bolden.	T.E.	Dvr.	Malsom.	R.J.	L/Cpl.	Smith.	P.	Dvr
Brown.	T.E.	Dvr.	Marsh.	H.D.	Cpl.	Studd.	P.	Dvr.
Burke.	M.	Dvr.	Mathews.	B.R.	Sgt.	Thurlby.BEM.	J.A.	Sgt.
Carter.	R.W.	Dvr.	McAlister.	L.F.	Dvr.	Vickers.	R.D.	Pte.
Chew.	C.	Sgt.	McKay.	L.M.	Cpl.	Waite.	H.W.	L/Cpl.
Davidson.	B.F.	Dvr.	McLeary.	J.A.	Dvr.	Wakefield.	M.	Dvr.
Dixon.	J.	Dvr.	McMullin.	J.	Dvr.	Walsh.	C.	Dvr.
Driver.	A.A.	Dvr.	Merrett.	F.J.	Dvr.	Walters.	M.S.	Cpl.
Franklin.	W.R.	Capt.	Moon.	F.J.	Maj. QM.	Waterhouse.	W.B.	Dvr.
Hanslar.	G.A.	L/Cpl.	Nelson.	L.	Sgt.	Wellman.	J.E.	Cpl.
Henderson.	R.W.	Maj.	Pickard.	M.	Capt.			
Hickman.	A.H.G.	Dvr.	Randle.	T.H.	Cpl.			

CORPS. OF ROYAL ENGINEERS (RE'S)

Armstrong	D.	Spr.	Creighton.	L.	Cpl.	O'Connor.	W.	Spr.
Brading.	C.J	Sgt.	Gibson.	J.	Spr.	Powell.	B. S.	Cpl.
Brown.	V. C.	Spr.	Gold.	I.L.	Spr.	Sidebottom.	G.W.	Spr.
Collins.	N.	Spr.	Langstaff.	H.	Spr.	Willians.	A. C.	Spr.

ROYAL CORPS. OF SIGNALS.(RS)

Bews.	J.H.	S/Sgt.	Halliwell.	E.	Dvr.	Robertson.	G.	L/Cpl.
Booth.	D.	Cpl.	MacDonald .	D.	L/Cpl.	Thompson.OBE	F.C.	Col.
Craig.	A.	W/OI	Peach	P.R.	Cpl.	Twigg.	W.J.	Sgm
Curd.	W. A .	SQMS	Plumpton.	D.J.	Sgmn.			
Ford.	J.M.	Dvr.	Roberts.	C. F.	W/OII			

ROYAL ARMY MEDICAL CORPS.

Barratt.	F.V.	Pte.	Shufflebottom. R.		Pte.	Sumner.	F.	Pte.
McGill.	H.M.	Pte.	Summers.	E.T.	Pte.	Williams.	J.D.	Pte.

ROYAL ARMY ORDNANCE CORPS.

Reeves.	A.	Pte.	Thorn.	J.A.	Pte.	Bachan	Singh.	Sgt.

CORPS. OF ROYAL ELECTRICAL & MECHANICAL ENGINEERS

Beck	G.	Cfn.	Harris.	W.E.M.	S/Sgt.	Smart.	C.A.	L/Cpl.
Drummond.	D.A.	L/Cpl.	Hitchen.	B.	Cfn.	Smith.	S.A.	L/Cpl.
Gallacher.	L.M.	Cfn.	Marles.	F.J.	Cfn.	Turner.	J.J.	Cfn.
Greenwood.	W.	Cfn.	Pipe.	D.F.	Cfn.			
Young.	C.B.	Sgt.						

ROYAL MILITARY POLICE.

Brandon.	J.	L/Cpl	Edgar.	G.W.J.	L/Cpl.

ROYAL ARMY EDUCATION CORPS.

Taylor.	C.	Capt.

ROYAL ARMY PAY CORPS.

Durham.	D.J.	Pte.

INTELLIGENCE CORPS.

Goldsmith.	R.J.	Cpl.

ARMY CATERING CORPS.

Jackson	J.	Pte.

QUEEN ALEXANDERS ROYAL ARMY NURSING CORPS.

Brown.	D.E.	Pte.

GENERAL LIST.

Ford. MBE.	C.	Lt/Col.	Skone.CBE.DSO	H.E.	Brig.

2ND. KING EDWARD VII'S OWN GURKHA RIFLES

Gurung.	B.	Rfn.	Rana.	B.	Rfn.	Newar.	I.	Rfn.

Thapa.	J.	Rfn.	Thapa.	P.	Rfn.	Gurung.	P.	Rfn.
Gurung.MBE. DSM.	P.	Maj.	Pun.	P.	Rfn.	Truss.	D.A.	Maj.

6TH. QUEEN ELIZABETH'S OWN GURKHA RIFLES

Pun.	C.	Sgt.	Ranan.	I.	Rfn.			

7th.DUKE OF EDINBURGH'S OWN GURKHA RIFLES

Limbu.	B.	Rfn.	Rai.	I.	Rfn.	Rai.	M.	Rfn.
Gurung.	B.	Rfn,	Rai.	J.	Rfn.	Rai.	M.	Capt.(KGO)
Rai.	B.	Rfn.	Gurung.	K.	Rfn.	Thapa.	P.	Rfn.
Rai.	C.	Rfn.	Rai.	K.	Rfn.	Thapa.	S.	Rfn.
Limbu	H.	Rfn.	Ale.	K.	Rfn.	Rai. MBE.	T.	Maj(KGO).
Limbu.	H.	Rfn.	Rawar.	M.	L/Cpl			

10th.PRINCESS MARY'S OWN GURKHA RIFLES

Rai.	B.	Rfn.	Rai,	G.	Rfn.	Limbu.	R.	Rfn.
Rai.	C.	Rfn.	Rai.	J.	Rfn.	Sunwar.	S.	Rfn.
Rai.	D.	Rfn.	Rai	K.	Sgt.			
Rai.	G.	Rfn.	Rai.	N.	Rfn.			

GURKHA SIGNALS

Gurung.	T.	Sgmn.

GURKHA SIGNALS

Gurung.	H.	Spr.

GURKHA MILITARY POLICE

Rai.	R.	Lt. (KGO)

RHODESIAN SPECIAL AIR SERVICE

Davies.	J.B.	Cpl.	Ernst.	O.H.	Sgt.	Visagle.	V.E.	Cpl.

1ST. KINGS AFRICAN RIFLES

Ajetumbaya.	M.	Cpl.

3rd. KINGS AFRICAN RIFLES

Alfred	S.	Cpl.	Lesukukwa.	S.	Pte.	Salmon.	U.	Pte.
Barnet.	M.	Pte.	Malia.	B.	Pte.	Saulos.	M.	Pte.
Javenalisi	D.	Pte.	Mambana.	K.	Sgt.	Willard.	S.	Pte.
Kipkorir.	S.	Pte.	Moso.	K.	L/Cpl.	Willie.	M.	Pte.
Kiptebelio.	K.	L/Cpl.	Moulana.	M.	Pte.	Winecon.	L.	Cpl.
Ziyalure.	C,	Pte.						

NORTHERN RHODESIAN REGIMENT

Esekia.	S.	Pte.	Peterson.	M.	WOPC.	Simushi.	M.	Pte.
Msope.	B.	Pte.	Salweko	F.	Pte.			

SARAWAK RANGERS

Bulan.	A.K.	Pte.	Rejup.	A.B.	Pte.
Kelambu.	A.G.	Pte.	Untang.	A.E.	Pte.

ROYAL AUSTRALIAN ARTILLERY

Tucker.	L.A.	Sgt.

ROYAL NEW ZEALAND SAS REGIMENT

Buchanan.	A.G.	Sgt.	Thomas.	A.R.	Trp.

ROYAL AIR FORCE

Albutt.	H.T.	Flt./Lt.	Foster.	S.	Sqd.Ldr.	Pickrell.	J.D.	Sgt.
Armstrong.	J.B.	Sgt.	Hall.	R.H.	Plt./lll	Pound.	R.	F./Sgt.
Brothwick.	R.	LAC.	Hayter.	S.V.	Sgt.	Ross.	J.	ACII
Boyatt.	B.T.	Sgt.	Hillman.	T.	Flt./Lt.	Scutt.	J.E.	Sqd.Ldr.
Brougginton.	J.T.	Sgt.	Hodge.	T.W.	Cpl.	Sherlock.	P.J.	Sgt.
Brodie.	D.	Sgt.	Janicki.	J.	Plt./lll	Simpson.	R.	Cpl.
Brown.	L.	Plt.lll.	Johnson	A.E.	Flt./Lt.	Slater.	C.D.	AC.
Clisby.	C.R	Fg./Off.	Kerry.	J.	Sgt,	Smith.	L.S.R	Fg./Off.
Cochrane.	B.A.	Fg./Off.	Loxton.	E.H.	Plt./lll	Stubbins.	D.B.	Flt./Lt.
Cosens.	P.A.S.	Cpl.	Manners.	G.B.	Sgt.	Thorpe.	B.L.	Cpl.
Cox.	J.C.A.	Jnr.Tech.	Maulden.	J.R.	Flt./Lt.	Towner.	D.A.	Sgt.
Daly.	P.	Flt./Lt.	McColl.	T.J.	Plt./Lt.	Tucker.	J.A.M.	Nav.
DeBoer.	P.C.M.	Nav.	McGibbon.	J.	Cpl.	Walters.	B.F.	Fg./Off.
Draper.	E.W.	Flt./Off.	Mitchell.	A.G.A.	Flt./Lt.	Woods.	W.C.	Sgt.
Dray.	L.W,D.	Flt./Lt.	Motton.	D.J.W.	AC.			
Ford.	G.C.	F/Sgt.	O'Sullivan.	J.	Cpl.			

ROYAL AUSTRALIAN AIR FORCE

Tait.	G.R.	W/O

ROYAL NEW ZEALAND AIR FORCE

Devicovi.	W.A.	F/O	Nelson.	D.F.	F.O.	Tie.	A.S.	Sqd.Ldr

ROYAL NAVY.

Breen.	J.J.	Sto/Mech

Buried at the Loke Yew Road Buddist Burial Ground Kuala Lumpur. [1]
Roll of Honour

ROYAL PIONEER CORPS. (CEYLON)

Somadasa.	T. B.	Pte.	Karunaraine.	H.M.	Pte.	

Buried at Seremban Christian Cemetery Negri Sembilan. [31]
Roll of Honour.

13TH/ 18TH. ROYAL HUSSARS (QUEEN'S OWN)

Carpenter.	G.E.	2/Lt.	Cook.	D.R.	Trp.	Harden.	J.B.	2/Lt.

ROYAL REGIMENT OF ARTILLERY (RA)

Chapman.	G.E.	Bdr.	Heyburn.	D.	Sgt.	Prett.	R.S.C.	Gnr.
Gibson.	J.H.	Gnr.	Higgs.	N.	Gnr.	Thompson.	J.	Gnr.
Hayes.	J.P.	Gnr.	Hughes.	G.O.	Gnr.			

1ST. BATTALION THE QUEEN'S REGIMENT (WEST SURREY)

Fisher.	R.W.	Pte.						
Jones.	R.E.	Sgt.	King.	S.P.	Pte.	Palmer.	A.V.	2/Lt.

BORDER REGIMENT.

Pyrnne.	R.	Capt.

THE GREEN HOWARDS

Alcock.	G.	Pte.	Daynes.	W.J.	Pte.	Porter.	R.W.	Pte.
Baldam.	N.	Pte.	Hartley.	W.	Pte.	Wray.	A.	Sgt.
Crosthwaite.	F.L.	Pte.	James.	G.S.	Pte.			

HIGHLAND LIGHT INFANTRY

Whitney.	W.G.	Capt.

22 SPECIAL AIR SERVICE

Garrett.	W.F.	WOII.

CORPS. OF ROYAL ENGINEERS (RE'S)

Webb.	A.A.M.	L/Cpl.

CORPS. OF ROYAL ELECTRICAL & MECHANICAL ENGINEERS

James.	D.H.	Cfn.

ROYAL MILITARY POLICE

Morris Jones.	A.E.	L/Cpl

ROYAL AIR FORCE

Ellis.	B.A.	Sgt.	Kent.	W.	Sgt.

Buried at the Gurkha Cemetery Seremban Negri Sembilan. [53]
Roll of Honour.

2ND. KING EDWARD VII'S OWN GURKHA RIFLES

Forester-Walker. MBE.	A.I. Lt/Col.		Thapa.	M.	Cpl.

6TH. QUEEN ELIZABETH'S OWN GURKHA RIFLES

Thapa.	B.	Rfn.	Gurung.	N.	Rfn.	Tshering Lama.	P.	Lt.(QOG)
Tamang.	D.	Rfn.	Gurung.	P.	Rfn.	Thapa.	S.	Rfn.
Gurung.	K.	Rfn.	Pun.	P.	L/Cpl.	Gurung.	S.	L/Cpl.
Rana.	M.	Rfn.	Gurung.	P.	Rfn.	Gurung.DSM.	S.	Capt.(KGO)

7TH.DUKE OF EDINBURGH'S OWN GURKHA RIFLES

Rai.	A.	Rfn.	Limbu.	D.	Rfn.	Sunwar.	K.	Recruit
Rai.	A.	Cpl.	Sunwar.	D.	Cpl.	Rai.	K.	L/Cpl.
Sunwar.	A.	Rfn.	Rai.	D.	Recruit	Sunwar.	L.	L/Cpl.
Rai.	B.	Rfn.	Limbu.	D.	Rfn.	Limbu.	M.	Recruit
Rai.	B.	Rfn.	Rai.	G.	Rfn.	Rai.	P.	Rfn.
Gurung.	B.	Cpl.	Limbu.	G.	Rfn.	Limbu.	P.	Rfn.
Limbu	B.	Rfn.	Rai.	G.	Rfn.	Rai.	R.	Rfn.
Rai.	B.	WOII	Rai.	H.	Rfn.	Gurung.	R.	Rfn.
Rai.	B.	Rfn.	Limbu.	J.	L/Cpl.	Rai.	R.	Lt.(QGO)
Rai.	B. Capt.(KGO)		Tamang.	J.	Rfn.	Gurung.	S.	Rfn.
			Rai.	J.	Rfn.	Limbu.	T.	L/Cpl.
Tamang.	B.	Rfn.	Tamang.	K.	Rfn.			
Limbu.	C.	Rfn.	Tamang.	K.	Rfn.			

10th.PRINCESS MARY'S OWN GURKHA RIFLES

Limbu.	J.	Rfn.	Sunwar.	N.	Rfn.

GURKHA SIGNALS

Limbu.	H.	Sgmn.	Chhetri	N.	Sgt.

Buried at Terendak Military Cemetery Malacca. [4]
Roll of Honour

ROYAL REGIMENT OF ARTILLERY (RA)

Estell.	J.A.	Gnr.	Hills.	P. H.	Capt.

QUEEN'S OWN CAMERON HIGHLANDERS

Fothergill.	J.N.	Pte.

CORPS. OF ROYAL ELECTRICAL & MECHANICAL ENGINEERS

Dixon.   J.   Cfn.

Buried at Christian Cemetery Malacca. [3]
Roll of Honour

QUEEN'S OWN CAMERON HIGHLANDERS
Shaw.   W.   Maj.

ROYAL CORPS OF SIGNALS (MOR'S)

De.Costa.	N.	Sgmn.	Manteiro.	L/Cpl. L/Cpl.

Terandak Wall Memorial Wall Malacca. [134]
NO KNOWN GRAVE.
Roll of Honour

ROYAL REGIMENT OF ARTILLERY (RA)

Bridge.	J.	2/Lt.	Costerton.	P.J.D.	Capt.
Churcher.	J.F.	Capt.	Kemp.	P.M.P.	Gnr.

2ND. GUARDS BRIGADE COMMANDER
Erskine. DSO   M.D.   Brig.

1ST. BATTALION MANCHESTER REGIMENT
Raingill.   M.W.   2/Lt.

KINGS REGIMENT.
Gaitley.   R.Q.   Maj.

1ST. BATTALION CHESHIRE REGIMENT
Ellis.   D.N.   Cpl.

1ST. BATTALION THE LOYAL REGIMENT (NORTH LANCASHIRE)
Proctor   J.H.   Maj.

ROYAL ULSTER RIFLES.
Foley.   P.J.   Rfn.

ROYAL ARMY SERVICE CORPS.

Bryant.	P.	Cpl.	Lammond.	C.T.	WOI	Taylor.	P.E.	Dvr.
Dagg.	B.	Dvr.	Lane.	W.H.	Cpl.	Whitty.	A.	Dvr.
Goldsmith.	O.A.	Dvr.	McShane.	F.	Dvr.	Wilson.	R.T.	Dvr.

2ND. KING EDWARD VII'S OWN GURKHA RIFLES

Gurung.	A.	Rfn.	Gurung.	G.	Rfn.	Thapa.	N.	Cpl.
Pun.	B.	Rfn.	Thapa.	G.	L/Cpl.	Thapa.	P.	Rfn.
Gurung.	B.	Rfn.	Pun.	G.	Rfn.	Gurung.	P.	L/Cpl.
Gurung.	B.	Rfn.	Gurung.	G.	Rfn.	Pun.	R.	Rfn.
Sahi.	B.	Sgt.	Thapa.	H.	Rfn.	Gurung.	R.	Rfn.
Thapa.	B.	Cpl.	Thapa.	H.	Rfn.	Thapa.	R.	Rfn.
Ghale.	B.	Rfn.	Tamang.	J.	Rfn.	Ghale.	S.	Rfn.
Thapa.	C.	Rfn.	Ghale.	J.	Sgt.	Gurung.	S.	Rfn.
Gurung.	C.	Rfn.	Pun.	J.	Cpl.	Thapa.	S.	Lt.
Rana.	D.	Rfn.	Thapa.	K.	Rfn.	Gurung.	T.	Rfn.
Thapa.	D.	Cpl.	Pun.	K.	Rfn.	Gurung.	T.	Rfn.
Mall.	D.	Rfn.	Gurung.	L.	L/Cpl.			

6TH. QUEEN ELIZABETH'S OWN GURKHA RIFLES

Ale.	C.	Sgt.	Damal.	J.	Rfn.	Damal.	R.	Rfn.
Gale.	D.	L/Cpl.	Gurung.	L.	Rfn.	Gurung.	S.	Rfn.
Mukhiya.	G.	Cpl.	Thapa.	L.	Rfn.	Ale.	T.	Sgt.
Gurung.	G.	Rfn.	Limbu.	M.	Sgt.	Thapa.	T.	Rfn.
Rana.	H.	Rfn.	Gurung.	P.	Rfn,			

7th.DUKE OF EDINBURGH'S OWN GURKHA RIFLES

Rai.	B.	L/Cpl.	Pun.	P.	L/Cpl.
Rai.	J.	Rfn.	Limbu.	S.	L/Cpl.

10th.PRINCESS MARY'S OWN GURKHA RIFLES.

Rai.	L.	Rfn.	Rai.	R.	Sgt.
Rai.	M.	Rfn.	Rai.	R.	Sgt.

GURKHA MILITARY POLICE
Roka.   C.   L/Cpl

ROYAL PIONEER CORPS (CEYLON)

Jaladeen.	A.M.	Sgt.	Ramon.	A.	Pte.

SARAWAK RANGERS

Adrian.	A.T.	Pte.	Manit.	A.C.	Pte.	Nysra.	A.T.	Pte.
Empati.	A.D.	Pte.	Mat.	A.A.	Pte.			
Entap.	A.T.	Pte.	Nyantua.	A.J.	Pte.			

ROYAL AIR FORCE

Ashton.	A.H.	Fg./Off.	Baxter.	A.B.J.	Fg./Off.	Bowen.	K.J.	LAC.
Axon.	H.A.	Fg./Off.	Bone.	A.E.	LAC.	Broardbent.	D.	ACI.
Bullard.	P.G.	Flt./Lt.	Bouttell.	W.A.S.	Flt./Lt.	Burden.	L.E.	SAC.
Burnley.	P.C.	Sgt.	Bowater.	S.	Fl./Lt.	Carpenter.	G.C.	Nav.III.

Caton.	A.K.	ACl.	Leetham.	J.B.	Sqd.Ldr.	Sketch.	P.M.	Fg./Off.
Clark.	A.P.	Flt./Lt.	Lloyd.	C.	Sig.III.	Smith.	T.W.	Nav.III.
Cauzens.	G.F.W.	Sgt.	Mann.	D.	Sgt.	Stewart.	J.M.	Sig.
Dean.	V.H.	Sqd.Ldr.	Marshall.	P.	Sgt.	Talbot.	E.R.	Plt./Off.
Dench.	R.J.	Fg./Off.	Moore.	A.C.	Flt./Lt.	Tyson.	W.J.	Sig. II.
Dolittle.	G.P.	Fg./Off.	Morley.	F.J.	Sgt.	Visard.	W.J.	Fg./Off.
Gooding.	M.P.	SAC.	O'Toole.DFM.	T.	Sig.1.	White.	F.	Nav.II.
Hall.	K,	Sgt.	Owen.	E.L.	F./Sgt.	Woods.	T.R.	Fg./Off.
Harben.	N.B.	Fg./Off.	Richardson.	R.W.	Flt./Lt.	Wojelechowski.	T.	F./Sgt
Hayes.	D.K.	Sqd.Ldr.	Robinson.	G.A.	Sgt.			
Jones.	M.A.C.	Fg.Off.	Sixsmith.	J.E.	Sgt.			

ROYAL AUSTRALIAN AIR FORCE

McDonald.	G.J.	Plt. III

ROYAL NAVY.

Chappel.	J.	Ele c/Off.	Rutherford,	R,W,	REM	Bulmer.	J.J.	O/S
Brennan.	P.	ABS.						

Buried at the Gurkha Cemetery Kluang. [30]
Roll of Honour

2ND. KING EDWARD VII'S OWN GURKHA RIFLES

Pun.	K.	Rfn.

6TH. QUEEN ELIZABETH'S OWN GURKHA RIFLES

Ale.	D.	L/Cpl.	Gurung.	M.	Rfn/Cook.	Gurung.	S.	Rfn.
Thapa,	D.	Lt. (QGO)	Khan.	N.	Rfn.	Gurung.	S.	Rfn.
Thapa.	D.	Sgt.	Thapa.	P.	Rfn.	Rai.	T.	Rfn.
Gurung.	H.	L/Cpl.	Thapa.	P.	Rfn.	Rana.	T.	Rfn.
Gurung. MM	I.	Rfn.	Thapa.	P.	Rfn.			
Gurung.	L.	Rfn.	Gurung.	S.	Rfn.			

7th.DUKE OF EDINBURGH'S OWN GURKHA RIFLES.

Limbu.	D.	Rfn.	Limbu.	K.	Rfn.	Rai.	K.	Cpl.
Limbu	D.	L/Cpl.	Lepcha.	K.	Cpl.			

10th.PRINCESS MARY'S OWN GURKHA RIFLES

Rai.	J.	Rfn.	Rai.	K.	Recruit	Limbu.	N.	Recruit

GURKHA SIGNALS

Sunwar.	N.	Sgmn.

GURKHA ENGINEERS

Gurung.	B.	Spr.	Limbu.	N.	Spr.	Gurung.	O.	Spr.

GURKHA ARMY SERVICE CORPS

Thapa.	H.	D

Buried at Kranji Military Cemetery Singapore. [417]
Roll of Honour

45 COMMANDO

Smith.	D.	Mne.

ROYAL REGIMENT OF ARTILLERY (RA)

Anderson.	C.F.F.	Maj.	Dowbiggin	W. H.	L/Bdr.	Maroney.	W.M.	Gnr.
Barrett.	C. J.	2/Lt.	Girling.	R.	Gnr.	Nicholls.	A R.	Gnr.
Brown.	T.A.	Gnr.	Glynn.	O.K.	Gnr.	Williams.	K .H.	Gnr.
Davis.	G.S.	Maj.	Hanson.	L.E.	Grn.			
Daw.	R.D.	Lt.	Kay.	R.	L/Bdr.			

1ST. KINGS DRAGOON GUARDS

Forte.	A.J.	Trp.	Walsh.	T.	Trp.

4TH. QUEEN'S OWN HUSSARS

Hovell.	C.J.	Trp.

13TH./18TH. ROYAL HUSSARS (QUEEN MARY'S OWN)

Burgess.	J.	Trp.	Hammond.	L.W.	Trp.
Guest.	R. J .	L/Cpl.	Skillen.	J.	Trp

3RD. BATTALION GRENADIER GUARDS.

Wedderburn.	D.M.A.	Maj.

1ST. BATTALION THE QUEEN'S REGIMENT (WEST SURREY)

Purves.	J.A.	Pte.	Smith.	L.W.J.	Pt

ROYAL EAST KENT REGIMENT

Huntley	S.J.	Capt.

1ST. QUEEN'S OWN ROYAL WEST KENTS

Gibson.	J.M.T.	Capt.

ROYAL NORTHUMBERLAND FUSILIERS

Marshall.	W.H.	Fus.

1ST. BATTALION LINCOLNSHIRE REGIMENT.

Davies.	J.	Pte.	Stone.	S.	L/Cpl.

1ST. DEVONSHIRE REGIMENT

Coomber.	G.H.	L/Cpl.	Pearson.	D.R.	Pte.	Ward.		L.M.C.Pte.
Gardiner.	J.C.	Pte.	Roe.	D.	Cpl.	Wonnacott.	A.J.	Pte.
Lawrence.	G.N.F.	L/Cpl.	Skelley.	G.C.	Capt.			

1ST.& 2ND. BATTALION THE KINGS OWN YORKSHIRE LIGHT INFANTRY.

McAdam.	A.	Pte.	Agutter.	B.	Cpl

1ST. BATTALION SOMERSET LIGHT INFANTRY

Cox.	G.J.	Pte.

THE GREEN HOWARDS

Clark.	J.C.	Pte.

1ST. BATTALION EAST YORKSHIRE REGIMENT (DUKE OF YORKS OWN)

Annders.	J.G.	Pte.	Garnett.	K.	Drum Maj.	Secrett.	A.J.	L/Cpl.
Bamford.	P.	Sgt.	Green.	W.B.	Pte.	Wilcox.	B.	Pte.

1ST. BATTALION CHESHIRE REGIMENT

Hartenshaw.	L.	Cpl.	Readioff.	F.J.	Cpl.
Finnerty.	J.	Pte.	Walker.	B.	Pte

1ST. BATTALION ROYAL SCOTS FUSILIERS

Scott.	H.	Fus.	Seymour.	G.V	Maj. MC

1ST. BATTALION ROYAL WELSH FUSILIERS

Lee.	T.	W/OI	Cane.	P.F.	Capt QM

1ST. BATTALION KINGS OWN SCOTTISH BORDERERS

Harper.	R.M.	Pte.

1ST. BATTALION INNISKILLING FUSILIERS

Dunne.	P.	Fus.	Newell.	J.S.	Fus.	Whelan.	F.	Fus.
Gordon.	G.P.	CQMS.	O'Brian.	J.J.	Fus.			

1ST. BATTALION CAMERONIANS. (SCOTISH RIFLES)

Barker.	C.	Sgt.	Lisle.	R.A.S.	Maj.	Vallance.	J.W.	Rfn.
D'Arcy.	A.	L/Cpl.	McGlinche.	H.	Rfn	Weir.	A.	Rfn.
Hall.	W.D.	Sgt.	McHalr.	W.S.	Rfn.			
Hoy.	T.	Rfn.	Tennant	R.T.	L/Cpl.			

1ST. BATTALION WORCESTERSHIRE REGIMENT

Banner.	J.C.	Pte.	Harvey.	R.	Pte.	Plant.	G.	Pte.
Davies.	R.J.	Pte.	Marsden.	D.J.	Pte.	Whittaker.	S.D.	Pte.
Dykes.	N.	Pte.	Petherbridge.	S.C.	CQMS	Wilson.	B.	Pte.

1ST.BATTALION SHERWOOD FORESTERS.(NOTTINGHAM & DERBYSHIRE REGIMENT)

Johnson.	E.	Cpl.	Cook.	G.	Pte.
Logue.	D.W.	Pte.	Low.	D.W.	Pte.

1ST BATTALION THE LOYAL REGIMENT (NORTH LANCASHIRE)

Allen.	D.E.	Pte.

SOUTH LANCASHIRE REGIMENT

Herbert.	G.D.	Maj.

1ST. BATTALION SEAFORTH HIGHLANDERS ROSS-SHIRE BUFFS (THE DUKE OF ALBANY's)

Anderson.	M.I.	Lt.	Kurton.	A.C.	Pte.	Swift.	J.H.	Pte.
Barr.	A.	Pte.	MacKay.	G.	L/Cpl.	Verney.	J.	Pte.
Falconer.	G.B.	Pte.	Newall.	T.E.	Pte.	Ward.	A.H.	Pte.
Hambrook.	F.	Capt.	Newman.	H.	Pte.			
Kerr.	T.	Pte.	Street.	J.H.	Pte.			
Ward.	W.E.L.	Pte.						

QUEEN'S OWN CAMERON HIGHLANDERS

Campbell.	W.M.	Maj.

1ST. BATTALION GORDON HIGHLANDERS

Watt.	C.A L.	Maj.	Weed.	I.F.	Sgt.

ARGYLL & SUTHERLAND HIGHLANDERS

Patterson.	D.H.	Cpl.

GLIDER PILOT REGIMENT

Gay.	W.D.	S/Sgt.

22. SPECIAL AIR SERVICE.

Tulk.	F.S.	Lt. QM	Fergus.	A.	T.

2ND. KING EDWARD VII'S OWN GURKHA RIFLES

Rai.	B.	Rfn.	Thapa.	H.	Rfn.	Gurung.	M.	Rfn.
Rana.	B.	L/Cpl.	Pun.	H.	Rfn.	Thapa.	N.	Rfn.
Ale.	B.	Rfn.	Gurung.	J.	Rfn.	Gurung.	P.	Rfn.
Ale.	C.	Rfn.	Rana.	K.	Cpl.	Rana.	N.	Rfn.
Gurung.	C.	Rfn.	Pun.	K.	Jemadar.	Mall.	R.	Rfn.
Thapa.	D.	L/Cpl.	Rana.	K.	Rfn.	Thapa.	R.	Cpl.
Thapa.	D.	Rfn.	Pan.	K.	Rfn.	Rana.	S.	Rfn.
Gurung.	D.	Rfn.	Pun.	L.	Cpl.	Thapa.	T.	Rfn.
Gurung.	G.	L/Cpl.	Pun.	L.	Rfn.	Rana.	T.	Rfn.
Thapa.	H.	Sgt.	Thapa,	L.	L/Cpl.	Gurung.	T.	Rfn.

Wimbush. T.A. Maj.

6TH. QUEEN ELIZABETH'S OWN GURKHA RIFLES

Gurung.	C.	Rfn.	Tering Sherpa.	C.	Sgt.	Thapa.	K.	Rfn.
Thapa.	C.	Rfn.	Gurung.	D.	Rfn.	Thapa.	M.	Sgt.

10th. PRINCESS MARY'S OWN GURKHA RIFLES

Rai.	A.	L/Cpl.	Limbu.	G.	Rfn.	Rai.	M.	
Limbu.	A.	Rfn	Rai.	I.	Rfn.		Capt.(QGO)	
Sunwar.	B.	Rfn.	Rai.	K.	Rfn.	Tamang.MM.	M.	Lt. (QGO)
Rai.	B.	L/Cpl.	Tamang.	K.	Rfn.	Limbu.	N.	Rfn.
Tamang.	B.	Rfn.	Rai.	K.	Rfn.	Ale.	P.	Rfn.
Thapa.	B.	L/Cpl.	Limbu.	K.	Lt.(KGO)	Rai.	P.	Sgt.
Rai.	B.	Cpl.	Limbu.	K.	C/Sgt.	Rai	P.	Sgt.
Magur.	B.	Rfn.	Sunwar.	K.	Rfn.	Rai.	P.	Rfn.
Rai.	B.	Sgt.	Limbu.MM	K.	Lt. (KGO)	Rai.	P.	Rfn.
Rana.	B.	L/Cpl.	Sunwar.	K.	Rfn.	Limbu.	S.	L/Cpl.
Limbu.	B.	Rfn.	Limbu.	K.	Cpl.	Limbu.	T.	Rfn.
Limbu.	B.	Rfn.	Hewar.	K.	Rfn.	Chhetri	T.	Rfn.
Rai.	D.	Rfn.	Limbu.	M.	Rfn.	Lama.	T.	Lt.
Rai.	D.	Rfn.	Limbu	M.	Rfn.	Chhetri.	T.	Rf

10th. PRINCESS MARY'S OWN GURKHA RIFLES TRAINING WING

Tanang	D.	Recruit	Tamang	D.	Recruit	Sunwar.	G.	Recruit

GURKHA ARMY SERVICE CORPS.

Rai. R. Dvr.

SARAWAK RANGERS

Dempi.	A.B.	Pte.	Janggak.	A.I.	Pte.

2nd. KINGS AFRICAN RIFLES

Michaya. D. Pte.

3rd. KINGS AFRICAN RIFLE

Kipkorir. T. Pte.

1st. RHODESIAN AFRICAN RIFLES

Jonah	Pte.	Mjikielwa.	Pte.	Tongogaru.	L/Cpl.
Josephe.	Pte.	Tayengwa.	Cpl.		
Wanyana.	Pte.				

CORPS OF ROYAL ENGINEERS

Black.	J.	Maj.	De Rohan.	H.O.M.J.R.	Cpl.	Rothnei	A.I.	Spr.
Blyth.	G.F.	Lt.Col.	Harper.	G.E.	Maj.	Savarimuta .	J.	Spr.
Brennan.	G.F.	Spr.	Haycock.	J.	Spr.	Sudbury. BEM	E.H.	Capt.
Brigett.	R.	Capt.	Howard.	D. C.	Capt.	White	A. E.	W/OI
Broadley.	R.	Spr.	O'Neil.	J.J.	L/Cpl.	Yates.	G.C,	W/OII
Clark.	M.H.	Spr.	Parker.	J.	L/Cpl.			
Davidson.	J.	Cpl.	Pringle.	E.A. L.	W/O2			

ROYAL CORPS OF SIGNALS

Brass.	J.D.	Sgmn	Hamilton.	H.H.	Sgt.	Marr.	H. W.	Sgmn.
Chambers.	D.F.	Sgmn.	Hardwick.	K.	W/OII	Moore.	E.A.	Sgmn.
Ellery.	H.A.	Sgmn.	Howard.	D.C.	Cpl.			

ROYAL ARMY SERVICE CORPS

Anderson.	D.	Sgt.	Clarke.	R.C.	Dvr.	Jones.	J.C.	Dvr.
Atkinson.	J.	Dvr.	Cooper.	F.G.	Cpl.	Jones.	W.	Dvr.
Barnard.	G.	Cpl.	Cotton.	A.E.	Cpl.	Legge.	G.	Dvr.
Barrie.	A.	Sgt.	Gray.	J.P.	Capt.	Muller.	E.H.	Dvr.
Box.	A.D.J.	Dvr.	Howitt.	A.C.	Cpl.	Saunders.	D.E.	Dvr.
Champion			Humphreys.	S.D.	Lt.	Smith.	H.W.	L/Cpl.
De. Crespigny V.T.	Maj.		Jones.	D.A.	Dvr.	Wroe.	D.	Dvr.

ROYAL ARMY MEDICAL CORPS

Hall.	J.W.N. Pte.	Jessop.	R.V.	Cpl.	Wilkie. J.H. Sg

ROYAL ARMY ORDNANCE CORPS

Darby.	R.	Pte.	Leather.	E.P.	Pte.	Morris.	W.O.	2/Lt.
Fenton.	W.	Maj.	Low.	G.H.	Cpl.	Philip.	J.	Pte.
Hunt.	J.	Sgt.	McDonald.	J.D.R	Lt.	Ward.	B.	Pte.

CORPS OF ROYAL ELECTRICAL & MECHANICAL ENGINEERS

Baker.	C.E.	Cfn.						
Bowden.	G.W.A. Cpl.		Cushway.	W.	Capt.	McAuley.	W.F.	Pte.
Bissell.	E.A.	L/Cpl.	Hancox.	D.	Cfn.	McNicol Moncur W.T	Sgt.	
Boyd.	W.	S/Sgt.	Hanson.	J.T.C.	Cfn.	Morley.	J.	Cfn.
Broughton.	A.F.	WOi	Kirk.	A.W.	WOII	Robinson.	S.E	Cfn.
Charnock.	C.	Pte.	Legge.	C.A.	Cfn.			
Sanderson.	PSJ.	WOII	Thompson.	G.	Cpl.	Row.	A.D.	L/Cpl.
Sinclaire.	J.W.	Cpl.	Greenwood.	G.R.	L/Cpl.	Taylor.	D.J.	L/Cpl
Stobie.	N.	Cpl.	Grindley.	D.W.F.	L/Cpl.	Morrison.	C.	L/CPL

ROYAL ARMY EDUCATION CORPS.
Gibbs. P. Capt.

ROYAL ARMY PAY CORPS.

Spinner.	D.J.O.	Pte.	Keeble.	D.B.	WOII

ARMY CATERING CORPS.

Hurren.	D.	Pte.	Merry.	K.	Pte.

ROYAL PIONEER CORPS.
Broughton. P.R. WOII

WOMENS Royal Army Corps.

Atkinson.	B.	Pte.	Davies.	H.M.	Sub.	Patterson.	E.	Sgt.
Chapman.	C.M.	L/Cpl.	Patten.	L.C.	Sgt.			

ROYAL PIONEER CORPS (CEYLON)

Abraham.	KK.	Pte.	Francis.	L.	Pte.	Plyadasa.	H.R.	Pte.
Appuhamy.	M.R.D.	Pte.	Jamis.	A.G.	Pte.	Simion.	V.K.	Pte
Davith Hamy.	S.M.A.	Pte.	Perera.	M.A.W.	Pte.	Weerasinghe.	W.	Pte.

CORPS OF MILITARY POLICE (CEYLON)
Jayasena. M.G. L/Cpl.

INDIAN ARMY ORDNANCE CORPS.
WynneHannah. G. Capt

1st. BATTALION ROYAL AUSTRALIAN REGIMENT

Harrison.	J.R.	Cpl.	Reynolds.	P.E.	Lt.

ROYAL NEW ZEALAND INFANTRY REGIMENT.
Nepiia. G. Sgt.

ROYAL AIR FORCE

Ainsley.	S.	Fg/Off.	Habergham.	G.	LAC.	Moodie.	J.H.W.	Fg./Off.
Armstrong.	J.H.	Sig.II	Hall.	L.G.	Flt./Lt.	Moore.	D.L.	Fg./Off.
Arundell.	P.	Jnr.Tech.	Harding.	R.B.	ACI.	Morling.	M.V.	SAC.
Baser. DFC.	W.J.	Sqn/Ldr.	Harris.	F.T.	Sgt.	Naish.	A.H.	Plt./IV.
Bate.	J.F.	ACI	Hartley.	H.	Flt./Lt.	Nelson.	H.E.R.	Wg.Cdr.
Binks.	E.R.	Jnr.Tech.	Harvey.	W.	W/O.	Nesbit.	R.E.	SAC.
Baxter.	E.S.	W/O.	Hauxwell.	M.	Jnr.Tech.	Noel.	J.E.B.	Cpl.
Bell.	P.H.	Cpl.	Hayes.	B.W.	Jnr.Tech.	O.Toole.	J.J.	Cpl.
Birrell.	D.N.	Flt/Lt.	Hayes.	G.	Sgt.	Owen.	B.	Plt./Off.
Blackburn.	F.	Flt./Lt.	Hedges.	H.R.	ACI	Patterson.	J.D.	Plt.III
Blewett.	G.L.	Flt./Lt.	Hewett.	W.L.	ACI	Pike.	A.E.	Flt./Lt.
Bocek.	H.	Sgt.	Hickman.	G.E.	Flt./Lt.	Pithey.	N.	Jnr.Tech.
Bowden.	V.	Sgt.	Hill.	J.N.	SAC.	Plumtree.	J.J.	Cpl.
Brie.	G.C.A.	Fg/Off.	Horsman.	G.	LAC.	Poling.	P.C.	Flt./Lt.
Brown.	C.A.M.	Sgt.	Howson.	G.E.	Sgt.	Poole.	M.	LAC.
Brown.	D.H.M.	Nav.	Hylton.	S.	Sgt.	Powell.	E.C.	F/Sgt.
Brown.	W.G.	Sig.AI	Jones.	E.	LAC.	Price.	J.M.	F./Sgt.
Cantwell.	T.E.	Plt.I.	Kay.	D.	LAC.	Price.	J.M.	Fg./Off.
Casling.	B.S.	Fg./Off.	Kearney.	W.H.J.	Flt./Lt.	Reeve.	D.G.	AC.I
Cersell.	R.W.	Flt./Lt.	Keen.	R.C.	ACII.	Ryan.	A.E.	LAC.
Clark.	J.Y.	ACI.	Hilton.	P.C.	Gp.Capt.	Scutt.	E.S.	Cpl.
Craddock.	R.A,	Fg./Off	Kellet.	J.	Cpl.	Sharkey.	C.	F/Sgt.
Crough.	P.C.	Cpl.	Kell.	R.T.	SAC.	Short.	M.	Flt./Lt.
Dancy. D.FC.	D.H.G.	F/Sgt.	Landbeck.	B.R.	Fg./Off.	Smith.	R.T.	LAC.
Danton.	G.H.W.	Nav. II.	Langley. DFM.	L.	Flt./Lt.	Smith.	W.S.J.	Cpl.
DeRosa.	R.F.	Sgt.	Law.	I.W.	Jnr.Tech.	Sprott.	J.	SAC.
Eaton.	J.E.	AC2.	Longstaff.	C.W.	Ch.Tech.	Starling.	P.J.	Flt./Off.
Ellens.	J.G.J.	LAC.	Lyne.	W.E.	Fg./Off.	Stevens.	E.E.	F./Sgt.
Emuss.	R.A.	Plt.I.	Mcguire.	J.	SAC.	Stirk.	A.	F./Sgt.
Fullager.	K.J.	Fg./Off.	Marry.	J.	F./Sgt.	Sykes.	G.E.	Fg./Off.
Gibson. DFM.	J.W.M.	Sig.	Martin.	R.F.	Cpl.	Tarling.	P.G.	Flt./Lt.
Gillett. G.C.	I.J.	ACI.	Mason.	B.	Cpl.	Veale.	D.J.	LAC.
Golding.	A.M.	LAC. W.	Massey.	B.	Flt./Lt.	Walters.	F.S.	Cpl.
Gooch.	J.R.H.	Cpl.	McConnell.	F.G.	Sgt.	Ward.	J.H.	Nav.II
Grant.	J.R.	Cpl.	McConnell.	J.J.	Flt./Sgt.	Watkins.	D.	Cpl.
Gratton.	R.J.	Sgt.	McGuire.	J.	SAC.	Wells.	J.A.	Sgt.
Green.	E.	F/Sgt.	Mathews.	R.E.	F/O.	White. MBE.	C.T.	Sqn.Ldr.
Gregory.	H.L.P.	F/Sgt.	Metcalfe.	P.	Nav.III.			

ROYAL AUSTRALIAN AIR FORCE

Brown.	H.B.	W/O	Murphy.	M.	LAC.

ROYAL NEW ZEALAND AIR FORCE
Finn. D.L. F/O

ROYAL NAVY.

Baker.	R.V.	Ldg	Bradbury-Flint	S.C.	ABS	Caskin.	E.	Ldg/Wtr.
Boukley.	A.F.	Sto/Mech.	Camp.	C.A.	ABS.	Coggin.	J.	Ldg,Av/Mech.

385

Conifrey.	M.S.	ABS.	Lobb.	G.A.	C/PO.	Rhodes.	A.G.	Lt. Comd.
Cowling.	O.P.	4th.Eng.	Lones.	W.L.	Lt.	Richardson.	J.E.	Mech.
Galipeau.	L.M.	ABS.	McAdam.	D.J.	ABS.	Scrivener.	J.C.	P/O
Glen.	R.	ABS.	McKenzie.	R.H.C.	Sub/Lt.	Smith.	J.	Sen.Com/Eng.
Heard.	W.J.	Lt.	Moore.	A.R.	Ord/Telg.	Sugar.	W.G.	BS
Jones.	F.	W.Ship/Wt.	Murphy.	J.	Mech/Elect.	Warburton.	N.	
Larkin.	C.B.	Ldg.Smn.	Noakes.	R.N.	L/AirMech.			

Buried at the Jewish Cemetery Thompson Road Singapore.. [1]
Roll Of Honour

ROYAL AIR FORCE
Gee.   N.J.   Flt./Lt

Buried at the Kuala Belua. Cemetery. Brunei. [4]
Roll of Honour.

ROYAL AIR FORCE

Carpenter.	J.A.	Flt./Lt.	Pointer.	D.A.	Nav. III
Harker.	D.A.	Fg./Off.	Wallace.	G.R.	Nav. II

Remains Cremated or Repatriated. [217]

40 COMMANDO
Eames.	R.H.V.	Mne.	Orr.	S.	Sgt.			
Lamb.	E.	Mne.	Howe.	N.S.	Cpl.			

42 COMMANDO
Rose.	H.H.	Mne.	Wright.	R.	Mne

45 COMMANDO
Genge.	T.J.H.	Sgt.	Henry.	J.	Cpl.	Keyes.	D.C.	Mne.
Turner.	L.J.	Mne.	Pearce.	B.J.	Bdsn.			

1ST. KINGS DRAGOON GUARDS
Readman.	D.	Trp.	Leiper.	J.S.	L/Cpl.

9TH. /12TH. ROYAL LANCERS (PRINCE OF WALES)
Brougham.   J.H.P. 2/Lt.Hon.

11TH. HUSSARS (PRINCE ALBERT'S OWN)
Myres.	J. P.	Trp.	Priddice.	E.E.	Sgt.

15TH/19TH. KING'S ROYAL HUSSARS
Smith.   W. J.   Trp.

3RD. ROYAL TANK REGIMENT
Hudson.   R.   L/Cpl.

ROYAL REGIMENT. OF ARTILLERY (RA)
Bridgewater.	G.W.	Gnr.	Lewis.	T.B.	Gnr.	Shannon.	P.J.	Sgt.
How.	J.E.	Maj.	Randall.	H.	Lt.	Wilson.	F.W.	W/O

3RD. BATTALION GRENADIER GUARDS
Farrar.   J.R.S. L/Sgt.

2ND. BATTALION COLDSTREAM GUARDS
Palfrey.   S.   Gdsmn.

2ND. BATTALION SCOTS GUARDS
Bax.   M.G.   Cpl.

1ST. BATTALION THE QUEEN'S REGIMENT (WEST SURREY)
Palmer.	D.W.L.	Capt.	Day.	T.G.	Sgt.

EAST SURREY REGIMENT
Mitchell.   R.R.   Cpl.

1ST. BATTALION MANCHESTER REGIMENT.
Kelley.   T.   Pte.

1ST BATTALION SUFFOLK REGIMENT
Holland.   H.   Cpl.

1ST. BATTALION LINCOLNSHIRE REGIMENT
Thompson.	D.T.	Pte.	Coupland.	B.	Pte.

1ST. BATTALION DEVONSHIRE REGIMENT
Banton.	E.	L/Cpl.	Hewitt.	C.S.	Cpl.	Sysum.	K.A.	Pte.

1ST.& 2ND. BATTALION THE KINGS OWN YORKSHIRE LIGHT INFANTRY.
Gregory.	J.D.	Pte.	Hicks.	D.C.	Pte.

1ST. BATTALION SOMERSET LIGHT INFANTRY
Clare.   R.J.   Pte.

OXFORD & BUCKS LIGHT INFANTRY
Clifton.   C.   Lt. Col.

THE GREEN HOWARDS.
Bottomley.	B.	Pte.	Gill.	J.	Pte.

1ST. BATTALION WEST YORKSHIRE REGIMENT (P.W.O)
Clarke.   J.B.   Pte.
Hoe.   F.W.   Maj.

1ST. BATTALION WEST YORKSHIRE REGIMENT
Brocklesy.	G.C.	L/Cpl.	Boreham.	G.J.	Cpl.	Ellingworth.	C.	Cpl.

Chadwick.   H.P.   Maj.

1ST. BATTALION. ROYAL SCOTS FUSILIERS

Goodwin.	W.M.	L/Cpl.	Gibson.	J.	Fus.			

1ST. BATTALION CHESHIRE REGIMENT

Hart.	W.	Pte.	Kirby.	J.H.	Pte.			

1ST. BATTALION. ROYAL WELSH FUSILIERS

Owen.	J.	Fus.	Evans.	G.R.	Fus.	Bryde	H.E.	Fus.

1ST. BATTALION KINGS OWN SCOTTISH BORDERERS

Coulter.	P.R.	Cpl.	Seaton.	D.P.	Pte			

1st. BATTALION CAMERONIANS. (SCOTISH RIFLES)

Bald.	R.R.G.	Lt.	Mazzetti.	J.H.	Rfn.	Thompson.	G.	Rfn.
Gray.	W.	2/Lt.	Shaw.	R.	Rfn.	Ure.	W.	Rfn.
Holland.	T	Rfn.	Shennan.	A.G.	Cpl.			
McDonald.	A.J.D.	Maj.	Sims.	A.M.	L/Cpl.			

BLACK WATCH R.H.R

Hoare. MC.   J.N.R.   Lt.

1ST. BATTALION WORCESTERSHIRE REGIMENT

Brooks.	A.H.	C/Sgt.	Rowley.	J.A.	Sgt.	Walker.	D.C.	Pte.
Leadham.	B.J.	Pte.	Stanton.	B.	Cpl.			
Rowberry.	H.	Pte.	Taylor.	B.D.E.	Pte.			

1ST. BATTALION SEAFORTH HIGHLANDERS ROSS-SHIRE BUFFS(THE DUKE OF ALBANY'S

Christie.	W.	Sgt.	McCreary.	D.	Cpl.			
Covell.	C.	Pte.	McMurdock.	J.MacD.	Pte.			

1ST. BATTALION GORDON HIGHLANDERS

Learmonth.	J.	L/Cpl.	Nutt.	J.	Pte.			
Newlands.	A.	Pte.	Wright.	T.	Pte.			

2nd. KING EDWARD VII'S OWN GURKHA RIFLES

Rana,	B.	Rfn.	Gurung.	D.	Capt.(QG)	Gurung.	S.	Capt.(QGO)
Gurung.	C.	Cpl.	Thapa.	K.	L/Cpl.			

6th. QUEEN ELIZABETH'S OWN GURKHA RIFLES

Gurung.   T.   Rfn.

7th. DUKE OF EDIBURGH'S OWN GURKHA RIFLES

Rai.   D.   Rfn.

10th. PRINCESS MARY'S OWN GURKHA RIFLES

Sunwar.	A.	Rfn.	Rai,	D.	Rfn.	Rai.	P.	Rfn.
Rai.	B.	Rfn.	Sunwar.	K.	Rfn	Rai.	R.	Rfn.
Rai.	C.	Rfn.	Limbu.	K.	WOI			
Tamang.	C.	Lt.(QGO)	Rai.	K.	Rfn.			

1st. BATTALION FIGIAN REGIMENT.

Baleilakebu.	A.	Pte.	Marawa.	V.	Pte.	Tanicakau.	T.	Pte.
Bucknell.	A.W.	Sgt.	Nadaka.	N.	L/Cpl	Turaguvakace.	H.	Pte.
Canavanua.	M.	Pte.	Nagata.	S.	Pte.	Yakaruru.	S.	Pte.
Genge.	R.	Maj.	Oasevakaatini.	E.	Pte.	Valu.	M.	Cpl.
Kasiva.	L.	Pte.	Rabonu.	M.	Pte.	Valabua.	S.	WOI.
Komaiwai.	M.	Cpl.	Sinclair.	J.	Pte.	Vukica.	E.A.	Pte.
Luwei.	J.	Pte.	Taloga.	P.	Sgt.	Waqumaitia.	A.	Pte.
Wara.DCM.	N.	SGT.						

ROYAL NEW ZEALAND INFANTRY REGIMENT.

Hargest.	P.M.	2/Lt.						
Peke.	H.R.	Pte.						

ROYAL ARMY SERVICE CORPS.

Brown.	H.	Dvr.						
Denning.	K.M.	Maj.	King.	A.C.	Dvr.	Tennant.	D.M.	Dvr.
Humpherson.	J.	Dvr.	Richards.	W.J.	2/Lt.	Trehearne.	C.C.	Capt.
Jeeves.	A.	Pte.	Smith.	F.E.	Dvr.			
Jones.	R.H.	Dvr.	Smith.	J.A.L.	Capt.			

CORPS. OF ROYAL ENGINEERS

Binmore.	C.M.	Spr.	Searff.	M.S	Spr.	Wealleans.	J.	L/Cpl.

ROYAL CORPS. OF SIGNALS (RS)

Ashworth.	T.H.	Sgt.	Ford.	P.M.	Sgmn.	Lovell.	I. F.	Sgt.
Cook.	F.J.	Maj.	Short.	L.	Sgmn.			

ROYAL ARMY MEDICAL CORPS.

Cooke.	B.D.	Pte.	Green.	G.M.	Lt.QM	Rooney.	J.	Pte.
Cruickshank.	J.D.	Lt/Con.	Hobbs.	C.E.A.	Pte.	Skelton.	H.E.	Capt.
Geddes.	J.	Capt.	Kiddell.	R.G.	Cpl.	Tipler.	J.A.	Pte.

ROYAL ARMY ORDNANCE CORPS.

Allcock.	H.M.	WOII	Blucke.	F.C.	Maj.	Pedley.	N.C.	Pt
Benham.	W.	Cpl.	McQuinllan.	R.F.	Pte.			

CORPS. OF THE ROYAL ELECTRICAL & MECHANICAL ENGINEERS.

Biddle.	R.W.	Cfn.	Biles.	F.E.	Cfn.	Burness.	R.	Sgt.

Caley.	B.	Cfn.	Johnston.	W.H.P.	Cfn.	Parker.	R.	Cfn.
Hodds.	G.E.	Cpl.	Joyce.	J.B.	Sgt.			

ROYAL MILITARY POLICE.

Elliott.	E.	L/Cpl.	May.	A.	L/Cpl.

MILITARY PROVOST STAFF CORPS.

May. A.N. Sgt.

ROYAL ARMY EDUCATION CORPS.

Hargreaves.	E.W.	Sgt.	Mowat-		
Howie.	W.T.F.	S/Sgt.	MacOnochie	A.N.H.	WOII

INTELLIGENCE CORPS.

Stephen-Smith. E.P. Capt

ARMY CATERING CORPS.

Hill. R.J. Pte.

ARMY PHYSICAL TRAINING CORPS.

Gelder. G. Lt/Col

ROYAL AIR FORCE

Bartlement.	M.O.	LAC	Best.	N.E.	ACWI			
Benton.	K.L.	Sgt.	Bradford.	J.W.	Flt/Sgt.			
Braithwaite.CBE. F.J.St.G.			Haslop	G.M,	Flt/Lt	Mulligan.	A.N.	SAC.
Air Vice Marshal			Hatcher.	A.V.L.	Jnr. Rech.	Pickering.	G.A.	LAC
Brown.	B.C.	Cpl.	Hollands.	R.I.	Flt/Lt.	Rolfe	J.I.T.	Flt/Lt.
Calthorpe.	W.	ACI	Isaacs.	V.W.	Cpl	Selth.	J.A.N.	Fg/O.
Carter.	K.C.	F/O	Jackson.	R.	Plt/O.	Shillaker.	J.A.	Fg/O
Crocker.	H.W.	Ft/Lt.	Kilbank.	L.L.	ACI	Thothard.	F.	Snr.Tech.
Davies.	J.W.	W/O	Ledson.	A.	SAC.	Walker.	A.R.	Flt/Lt.
Donaldson.	D.W.	Eng. II	Lincoln.	J.D.	Fg/O.	Waterman.	D.J.	Flt./Sgt.
Douglas.	S.L.i.	Cpl.	Loughlin.	W.A.	SAC.	Witham.	J.H.	Fg/O
Faulkner	R.E.	Cpl.	Lyne.	A.	Flt/Lt.	Woodward.	W.G.	LAC.
Ford.	J.R.	Flt/Lt.	Milner.	B.	SAC.			

ROYAL NEW ZEALAND AIR FORCE.

Bucknell.	A.W.	Cpl.	Gudsell.	J.A.R.	LAC	Fraser.	R.	Flt/Sgt.

ROYAL NAVY.

Nicholls.	F.J.	ABS.	Turner.	P.	ABS	
Pointer.	D.A.	Nav.III	Wallace.	G.R.	Nav.II	

List of MALAYAN ORDINARY RANK'S (MOR's) [92]

The following list of MOR's. Volunteers. Enlisted into the Britiah Army. Mainly Corps/Regt. & therefore should be named as part of the British Army Forces.1948-1960

Bodies claimed by next of KIN.

Roll of Honour

ROYAL REGIMENT OF ARTILLERY

B. Harun.	A.H.	Grn.	B.Md. Moor	I.	Bdr.	B.Yunos.	S.	Grn.
B. Yaacob .	A.	Grn.	B. K.Ahmad.	K.I.	Grn	B.Othman.	Z.	L/Bdr.
B. Othman.	A.	Grn.	B.Buyong.	O.	L/Bdr.			
B.. Saad.	H.	Grn.	B.Manap.	O.	Bdr.			

CORPS OF ROYAL ENGINEERS

B. Marth.	A.H.	Spr.	B.H.Sen.	A.	Spr.	Charles	S.	Spr.
B.Hassan.	A.M.	Spr.	B.M. Idris.	M.	Spr.	B.Dollah.	Y.	Spr.
B.K.Raman.	A.B.R.	L/Cpl.	B. Din.	M.N.	Spr.	B Mahmud.	Y.	Spr.
B.Kassim.	A.	Spr.	B.Saad.	O.	Spr.	B.L. Latif.	Z.	Spr.
B.Taib.	A.	Spr.	B.Ahmad.	S.	Spr.			
B. Abdullah.	A.	Spr.	B.Shaft.	S.	Spr.			

CORPS OF ROYAL SIGNALS

L.B.Swee.	W.	Cpl.	Vanisi.	T.E.	Sgmn.	B.Ibraham.	K.	Pte.
Kennsdy.	A.S.	Cpl.	B.Musa.	A.R.	L/Cpl.	B.A.Samad.	Y.	Pte.

ROYAL ARMY SERVICE CORPS.

B.A.Hamid.	A.G.	Dvr.	B. Osman.	H.	Dvr.	Geok Soon.	S.	Dvr.
B.Saringat.	A.M.	Dvr.	B.Ismail.	I.	L/Cpl.	B.Sujab.	S.	Pte.
B.Ibraham.	A.	Dvr.	B.Ishak.	I.	Dvr.	B.Ali.	S.H.	Dvr.
B.Sir.at.	A.	Dvr.	B.Raok.	K.	Dvr.	B. Roseh.	T.	Cpl.
B.H.A. Zam.	H.A.R.	Dvr.	B. Matzim.	M.	Cpl.	B.A. Hanan.	T.	Pte.
B. Abbas.	H.	Dvr.	B.Abdullah.	O.	Dvr.	B.Othman/	Y.	Dvr.

ROYAL ARMY MEDICAL CORPS.

B.Kassim.	M.	Cpl.	B.Daud.	S.	Pte.			

ROYAL ARMY ORDNANCE CORPS.

B. Mohamed.	A.M.	Cpl.	B.M. Wall.	I.	Pte.	Bok Hol.	T.	Pte.
B.Mohajir.	H.	Pte.	B.H. Tahir.	I.	Sgt.			

CORPS, OF ROYAL ELECTRICAL & MECHANICAL ENGINEERS

B.Ahmad.	A.A.	Cfn.	B.Din.	I.	L/Cpl.	B.Talib.	M.Y.	Cfn.
B.Hassan.	A.	Cfn.	B.Jaapur.	I.	Cfn.	B. Awal.	P.	L/Cpl.
B.Duras.	H.	Cfn.	Ming Kool.	L.	Cfn.			

ARMY CATERING CORPS.

B.Mohmad.	S.	Pte.	B.H. Amari.	A.	Pte.	B.H. Osman.	H.	Pte.
B.NaSir..	O.	Sgt.	B. Senawi.	D.	Pte.			

ROYAL AIR FORCE REGIMENTS

Aziz.	A.	SAC.	B.Ahmad.	A.	LAC.	B.Chik.	O.	AC1.
B.A.Manus.	A.B.	Cpl.	B.Sumad.	M.	AC2.	Mahamud.	M.	J/tech.
B.Dol.	A.S.	LAC.	B. Yusof.	M.	Cpl.	B.Hassan.	S.	P/Off.
B.Chik.	A.	Cpl.	B. Ramli.	M.A.	AC2	B.Jaffr.	S.	AC1
B.M. Noor.	A.	LAC.	B. Awang.	M.N.	SAC.	B.Warjan.	W.	AC1.
B.Massin.	A.	SAC.	B.Hassan.	M.Y.	LAC.	B.Buyong.	Y.	A
B. Shaffle.	H.	Cpl.	B.Ahmad.	M.Y.	AC1.			
B.Mahmood.	I.	SAC.	B. Ahmad.	O.	LAC.			

1-7 Battn's ROYAL MALAY REGIMENTS Killed = 101 (Not included in above list Grave Locations not known)

FEDERATION OF MALAY POLICE

Were engaged in a similar roll as per the Commonwealth Forces : Jungle Patrols
Total number of Officers and Ordinary Ranks. 1948- 1960 = 1,026   Grave Locations not known.
Named British Federation Malaya Police. (Below [125] Incl. in above figure)

Rolls Of Honour

Jalan Hanzah Christian Cemetery Kota Bahru Kelantan

O'Hara-Murray.	CMC.	Cdt/ASP.	Wedgewood.	D.	Pol/Lt.

Jalan Pertana Christian Cemetery Penang

Bernard.	A.	Pol/Lt	Franks.	VH.	Astn/Supt.	Stork.	D.	Aux/Insp.
Buleel	AEB.	Aux Supt.	Godwin	CM.	Asst/Cdr.	Thonger.	FJJ.	Pol/Lt.
Davies	KW.	E/Sgt.	Hathaway.	BK.	Pol/Lt.	Young.	FR.	E/Sgt.
Dawson.	KF.	Cdt/Supt.	Hugo.	JP.	Pol/Lt.	Wilmot.	AR.	Pol/Lt.
Fitzgerald.	LJ.	Aux/Sgt.	McBoyle.	GEM.	E/Sgt.	Weide.	N.	Pol/Lt.

Christian Cemetery Kuala Lipis Pahang

Dixon	R.	Pol/Lt.	Hacket.	EP.	E/Sgt.
Fookes	RH.	Cdt/Supt	O'Keefe.	CH.	Pol/Lt.

Christian Cemetery Tiaping Perak.

Bennet.	T.G.	Pol/Lt.	Livingstne.	MR.	Pol/Lt.	Wernham.	LW.	E/Sgt.
Evans.	PRJ.	CdtAsp	Mundy.	GTG	Pol/Lt.			
Hemsley.	CPM.	HR. Pol/Lt.	Webb.	KI.	E/Sgt.			

Batu Gajah Christian Cemetery Ipoh Perak

Abercrombie.	JDA.	Pol/Lt.	Chapin.	DH.	Pol/Lt.	Humble.	P.	E/Sgt.
Benson	AE.	Pol/Lt.	Cowan.	HF.	E/Sgt.	Lord.	RE.	Pol/Lt.
Bradley.	JS.	Pol/Lt.	Craig.	DA.	Asst/Supt.	Middleditch.AE.		Pol/Lt.
Brown	A.	Aux/Supt.	Garnham	J.L.	Aux/Pol.	Murray	L.A.	Aux/Insp
Brown.	L.V.	Asst/Sup.	Gates	GD.	Aux/Pol.	Park.	C.R.	Aux/Pol.
Bruce	FL.	Pol/Lt.	Grant.	W.	E/Sgt.	Sansom MC.	DJ.	Pol/Lt.
Burns	GM.	Aux/ Insp.	Good.	RL.	Pol/Lt.	Tulson KPM CPM.	GDC.	Asst/Cmdr.

| Wells | V. | E/Sgt. | | White. | D.J. | Aux/Pol. | | Whittingham L. | Pol/Lt. |

Teluk Intan Christian Cemetery Perak

Nightingale. A.F. Aux/Insp.

Kuala Lipis Christian Cemetary Pahang.

| Batchelor. | VA. | Cdt/ASP | | | | |
| Embery. | JA | Cdt/ASP | | Talks. | B | Cdt/ASP |

Christian Cemetery Kuantan Pahang

Bates.	CEA.	Pol/Lt.		Jones.	R.	E/Sgt.		Sutton.	CFD.	Pol/Lt.
Cook	SS.	Aux/Insp.		Mansfield	LR.	Pol/Lt.		Valpy.	LG	Asst/ Cdr.
Harrison	A.	Pol/Lt.		Marcon.	HG.	Pol/Lt.		Yapp.	JG.	Pol/Lt.
Hartley GM. GO. Pol/Lt.				Murphy	PJ.	E/Sgt.				

Christian Cemetery Ruab Pahang

Miller KPM. CPM. EJ Pol/Lt.   Campbell CPM. ILF. Aux/Pol.

Cheras Road Christian Cemetery Kuala Lumpur

Almond.	WA.	Pol/Lt.		Jarvis.	FH.	Pol/Lt		Murrim	NMH. Cadet
Blenkinsop.	G.	E.Sgt.		Jesse.	RH.	Asst/Supt		Nelder.	DR.	Pol/Lt.
Caffrey.	FJ.	E/Sgt.		Magill.	NNR.	Pol/Lt.		Quick.	JG.	Pol/Lt.
Cookham	AS.	Aux/Insp.		Malone.	PFA.	Pol/Lt.		Rainsford. DSOMC. EF.
Doohan.	PA.	Dep/Supt.		Milton.	AW	Supt.		Asst/Supt.
Harrison	RJE . E/Sgt.			Mothersole. AE.	Pol/Lt.		Wilstone.	ICF.	Pol/Lt.

Gutsal Road Christian Cemetery Seremban Negri Sembilan

Aylot.	DJ.	E/Sgt.		Hope.	D.	Cadet.		Ritson.	JB.	Aux/Ispt.
Cooper.	BFS. Asst/Supt.			Hurst.	NHH. Pol/Lt		Watson MM. R.	Pol/Lt.
Gutsell	VA.	Aux/Pol.		Johnson	M.	E/Sgt.				
Harding.	ED.	Aux/Insp.		Maddem	PRB. Aux/Insp.				

Military Cemetery Kranji Singapore

Aldridge	EJ.	E/Sgt.		Charlton.	TA.	Pol/Lt.		Freeborough.EA. Asst/Supt.
Belsham.	FC.	Pol/Lt.		Chown.	JW.	Pol/Lt.		Grant.	D.	Pol/Lt.
Berry.	WJ.	Pol/Insp.		Darling.	T.	Pol/Lt.		Hughes.	EJ.	Pol/Lt.
Cain.	GWB. Pol/Lt.			Ford.	JOl.	Pol/Lt.				
Cawthra.	LC.	Pol/Lt.		Frazer.	AR.	Pol/Lt.				

NO KNOWN GRAVES

Berling.	S.	Aux/Pol.		Kassim.b. B. Awang. Insp.		Tozer.	CS.	Pol/Lt.
Boxall.	EP.	Pol/LT.		Kinven.	AI.	Pol/Lt.		Watkins.	FH.	Ast.Supt.
Cooke.	T.	Asst/Supt.		Marris.	N.	Pol/Lt.		Yahya.b. Abbis. Aux/Pol.
Devon.	CE.	Pol/Lt.		Ollerton.	RI.	Pol/Lt.		Yassin.b. Moharam. Sup
Harris.	N.	Pol/Lt.		Searle.	PLA. A/Supt.				
Hawkins.	AJ.	Civilian		Thompson. JN.	Pol/Lt.				

CHAPTER 21

Under the leadership of *LAI TE* & *CHIN PENG* 1943 -1960
Known Communist Terrorist Leaders. Possibly 90% named below were Killed?

Ah Chai
Ah Chang
Ah Chat
Ah Chee
Ah Cheung
Ah Chin
Ah Choi
Ah Choon
Ah Chung
Ah Dien
Ah Fuk
Ah He
Ah Ho
Ah Khee
Ah Kin
Ah Ko
Ah Kok
Ah Kong
Ah Ku
Ah Kuk
Ah Lan
Ah Lik
Ah Lik
Ah Ming
Ah Ngew
Ah Peng
Ah Piah
Ah Po
Ah Poi
Ah Sang
Ah Sin
Ah Sui
Ah Thye
Ah Tong
Ah Tung
Ah Wah
Ah Wei
Ah Yee
Ah Yeong
Ah Ying
An Rung
Ang Heng
Anjun. b. Pondak
Au Chi
Au Ha Ho
Au Tien Tsin
Awi Hor Por
Bah Kah
Bah Kiah
Bah Petakan
Bah Poyang
Budin Bin Choh
Chai Ah Chow
Chai Fook Seng
Chai Ko Cha
Chan Ah Siew
Chan Ban Sek
Chan Hong
Chan Poon
Chan Sam Lau
Chan Sam Yin
Chan Sau Poi
Chan Tsng Chuen
Chan Wing
Chang Lo

Chau Choi
Chee Ah Kong
Chee Ping
Chen Chee
Chen Lien
Chen Tian
Chen Tien
Chen Tuk Cho
Cheng Chee
Cheng Ping
Cheong Sah Mei
Cheong Tong
Cheow Yin
Chey Song
Chi Yang
Chia Siow Hwa
Chiang Koon
Chin Lee Sang
Chin Nam Fook
Chin Voon
Chin Ah Ming
Chin Kong
Chio Ying
Chng Kah
Cho Soon Knoon
Choi Ah Chow
Chon Chin Nam
Chong Ah Chan
Chong Ha Cheng
Chong Hock Leng
Chong Kah
Chong Piew
Chong Ping
Chong Teng
ChongTok Cho
Choo Ah Kong
Chou Yong Pin
Chow Ah Che
Chow Ah Sang
Chow Lup
Chow Ying Pu
Choy Budin bin
Chu Kee
Dr. Ong Chon Kee
Fan Heung Mui
Fan Yon Oof
Fong Beng
Fong Chow Loy
Foo Bak Hoo
Foo Tee
Foo Wei Khian
Fuk Lung
Go Peng
Goh Peng Tuan
Goh Peng Tuan
Heup Theong
Hg Gim Cheng
Hiek Liew
Hiew Ah Min
Ho Koi Meng
Hoe Lian Chye
Hoi Lung
Hoi Ming
Hon Kwong
Hoong Poh
Hor Lun

Hor Lung
Hrap Thong
Hsin Hsuch Hung
Hwa Soon
Ismail b. Sharriff
Itam b. Pundak
Jamatu B. M. Mataris
Kadir
Kam Yin
Kan Chye Kia
Kan Chye Kiat
Kasim b. Arahad
Keh She
Khe Kim Thion
Khoo Mon.g
Khoon Kool Sang
Kiah Mat
Kim Siong
Kim Tai
Kok Fool Cheong
Kok Loy
Kong Fa
Kong Ha
Kong Kee
Kong Sang
Kong Shui
Kong Sze
Kony Kee
Kum Chin
Kum Fong
Kum Sing
Kwan Yuk
Kwang Chong
Kwong Min
La Yu Hwain
Lai Yoon Choy
Lam Kim
Lam Kwa
Lam Poh
Lam Swee
Lan Yan
Lau Chen
Lau Kow
Lau Lee
Lau Mah
Lau Shui Mai
Lau Yan
Lau Yew
Lee Ah Tong
Lee Cad Chin
Lee Fatt
Lee Khan Kau
Lee Kim Yen
Lee Kwan
Lee Meng
Lee Sie Tong
Lee Sie Tong
Lee Soong
Lee Soong
Lee Swee
Lee Wai
Lee Wei
Lee Yoon Choy
Leiu Yit Fun
Leo Kim Yin
Leon Wei Chong

Leong Chueng
Li Hak Chi
Li Yau
Lia Ting
Lian Chiang
Liew Yao
Liew Kon Kim
Liew Siew Fook
Liew Yoo
Liew You Taw
Lim Ah Ang
Lim Chang
Lim Chiong Siong
Lim Fong Kroh
Lim Mam wan
Lim Mei Sek
Lim Yu Swee
Lion How
Liuw Kon Kim
Lo Ah Sang
Lo Yu Hwain
Loh Min Sien
Loh Hon
Loh Liet
Loh Min Sien
Loi Tak
Lon Yan
Lou Cheng
Lou Mng
Low Kon
Low Ming
Loy Choy
Luan Chu Kiok
Lui Chow
Lui Tong Tai
Magalam
Mah Hoong
Mah YaTinb. Mukasan
Mal Lau
Manap Jepun
Mao Sze chuan
Mat Indra
Mee Chun
Meng Chuan
Meng Soon
Ming Lee
Ming Yuen
Mo Yuen sheng
Moo Yat Mei
Mui Fong
Mui Fong
Musa Ahmad
Ng Gim Cheng
Ng Heng
Ng Ki
Ng.Pak Thong
Ohui Wah
Ong Boon Chiew
Ong Chen Hwa
Ong Cheng
Ong Chin Tong
Ong Ling
Ooi Ah Yen
Ooi Ah Yin
Osman China
Pa Tze Hok
Pah Seng
Pai Tze Moke
Pak Lam
Pan Yoon Yin
Pang Kun Yin

Peck Ha
Pei Fun
Pei Tze Hok
Pen Tuan
Peng Kun Yin
Phien Wee
Phoay Lie
Phong Kee Sang
Phony Liew
Phui Fan
Phui Wok
Pih Yuen
Pitt Yuen
Poh Seng
Pol Tze Moke
Poo Yee
Raja Gopel
Ramasonay Moolhi
Rampah
Rashid Maidin
S. DhorMon.ay
Sam Fatt
San Fat Yee
San Moi Kon Min
Sany b. M. Buscat
Sarlid
Siang Chung
Siao Chang
Siew Chong Kee
Siew Hong
Siew Kool
Siew Lau
Siew Yin Dg
Siew Yit
Sin Yuen
Siow Heng
Soh Eng Loo
Soon Chen Sip
Soon Peng
Soon Yoon Heng
Sue Lin
Sui Chiong
Sui Mah
Sun. Wei Chin
Tab Ah Sang
Tan Ah Kwang
Tan Cheong See
Tan Cho Gee
Tan Fook Leong
Tan Mon.g Kwan
Tan Tak Shin
Tan Yew
Tang Mon.g Kwan
Te Chia Min
Teek Hai
Teh Sigat
Tek Liew
Ten Fook Loong
Ten Geok Lan
The Siew
The Siew Huat
Thep Min
TinBoo
Ting Fook
Ting Fook
Tng Fuk Leong
To Koh Lim
Tomh Paw
Tong Fook Leong
Tong Kwee Wong
Tsang Tong

Tsang Tung
Tsing Lee
TSun.g Hing Luen
Tuan Thiam
Verenansee
Wah Ali
Wahab
Waho Annuar
Wai Ming
Wai Shan
Waiu Chee
Wan Ali
Wan Tai Lui
Wang Chin
Wang Chin
Wang Hing
Who Seong
Willie Kwok
Woh Seong
Won Tai Lei
Wong Ah Tuk
Wong Yeh Lo
Wong Ag Chin
Wong Ah Tuk
Wong Chan
Wong Cheng
Wong Cheng
Wong Chin
Wong Fuk Kwang
Wong Hing
Wong Kim Pat
Wong Koi
Wong Kow
Wong Kwai
Wong Lo Dej
Wong Phool Kee
Wong Quia
Wong Wee Kuan
Wong Wee Kuen
Wu Tien Wang
Wui Tien Wang
Yang Kwo
Yap Jib Hai
Yap Kong Thye
Yap Kow
Yap Lien
Yau Ming
Yau Wei
Yee You
Yeom Kwo
Yeong Cheong
Yeung Kuo
Yeung Kwo
Yi Chou Boo
Yiong Kio
Yip Ah Chew
Yip Ah Chu
Yok Fong
Yoke Chin
Yoke Chin
Yoke Fong
Yoke Kuon
Yong Chor
Yong Hoi
Yong Joi
Yong Kwo
Yoon Heng
You Heng
Yua Fook
Yuk Saki
Zukari b. Be

392

BIBLIOGRAPHY

The following list of Books, Magazines, Newspapers, Museums. Letters. Articles. Web sites, which have been referred too. For extracts of information in the compilation of this book

An Inch Of Bravery: by Colin Bannister
Australian Defence Staff (London)
Australian War Memorials.
British Library.
Brush Fire Wars: by Michael Dewar
Bugles & Kukri: by R.W.L. Mac Alister
Commonwealth War Graves Commission: By their kind permission
                    Photo of the. Terandak Wall Memorial Rear Cover.
4th Royal Hussars.
13/18th. Hussars.
15/19th Hussars.
Cheshire Miltary Museum.
Counter Intelligence Malaya & Borneo : by E. R. Smith
Destiny Malaya: by Peter Stock.
Emergency and Confrontaion: 2nd. Battn. Royal Australian Regt. by Peter Dennis & Jeffrey Grey
FORCE 136: by Tan Chon Tee.
Forgotten War: by Christopher Bayley & Tim Harper.
From Emergency To Confrontation: by Christpher Pugsley.
George Cross Heroes: by Michael Ashcroft.
Green Beret - Red Star: by Antony Crockett.
Hansards
How They Won The DFC. Vol 1 & 2: by Nick & Carol Carter.
Hunting Terrorist In The Jungle: by John Chynoweth.
Paper's by Low Choo Chin:-
        : Immigration Control. During The Malayan Emergency:
        : The Repatriation Of The Chinese As A Counter - Insurgency Policy. During The Malayan Emergency
        : Banishment Of Anti Communist Chinese To Formosa. During The Malayan Emergency:
Imperial War Museum.
Jungle Green: by Authur Campbell.
Jungle Soldier: by Brian Moynahan.
Jungle War In Malaya: by Harry Miller.
London Gazette:
London Guildhall Library. Her Majesties Troopship Logs.
Loyal To The End: by Fredrick. W. Hudson.
Malaya and Borneo: by E.D. Smith.
Malaya Tales Of The Yorkshire Light Infantry: By John Scurr.
Malaya The Undeclared War: by Andrew Bradford Blackley.
Malayan Monument To Force 136 1942- 1945 & Commonwealth Forces 1948-1960 Cover Photo.:
                    By: The Author. Joe. P. Plant
Malayan Railways KTMB.
Malayan Spymaster : by Boris Hembry.
Malayasian High Commission London.
Menace In Malaya: by Harry Miller.
Ministry Of Defence Naval Historic Group.
Ministry Of Defence Air Historical Branch.
Museum Of The Manchester Regt.
My Side Of History: by Chin Peng.
National Archives Kew London.
Netherlands Army
News Of The World Newspapers.
New Zealand SAS .
Operations Most Secret SOE The /Malayan Theatre: by Ian Trenowden.
Orpration 'FIREDOG' by: Malcolm R. Postgate.

Our Man In Malaya by: Margaret Shennan.
Plymouth Central Library: Naval History.
R. A. F. Regiment Museum.
Re-Enter The SAS: by Alan Hoe & Eric Morris.
Royal Electrical Mechanical Engineers Museum of Technology.
Royal Air Force Museum.
Royal Australian Infantry Association 2nd. Battn.
Royal Hampshire Assosiation.
Royal Scots Fusiliers Association.
SAS Operstions: by James D. Ladd,
Shoot To Kill: by Richard Miers
Singapore's Dunkirk: By Geoffrey Brooks.
Singapore Straits Times.
Suffolk Regt. Old Comrades Association.
The Black Watch Museum.
The Camaronians Museum.
The Coldstream In The Cold War Malaya 1948- 1950 By Edwar Crofton.
The Daily Worker : Newspaper Archives.
The Devon and Dorset Regiment HQ.
The Door Marked Malaya: by Oliver Crawford.
The Forgotten Conflict 1948-1960 : by Roy. W.G. Russell.
The Gloucestershire Museum
The Green Howards In Malaya: by Major. J.B. Oldfield.
The Gurkha Museum.
The Gunner : By D.H.T. Reade.
The History of The Suffolk Regt.: by F A Godfrey.
The Military Intelligence Museum.
The Jungle Beat: by Roy Follows.
The Jungle is Neutral: by F.Spencer Chapman.
The Lincoln Museum.
The Malayan Campaign 1948 – 60: by John Scurr & Mike Chappel.
The Malayan Emergency 1948-1960. Roll Of Honour: by Peter Gaston.
The Malayan Emergency & Indonesian Confrontation: by Robert Jackson.
The Malayan Police Force In The Emergency 1948 -1960: by R. Thambipillay.
The Queen's Lancashire Regiment
The New Zealand Embassy London.
The Royal Air Force Museum
The Royal Anglian Regiment.
The Royal Australian Navy.
The Royal Logistics Corps.
The Royal Scots Dragoon Guards.
The Royal New Zealand Navy.
The Suffolk's In Malaya: By Len Spicer.
The History of the Suffolk Regt. 1046 -1959: by F. A. Godfrey.
The History of the Somerset Light Infantry 1946- 1960 : by Kenneth Whitehead.
The Times Atlas.
The War Of The Running Dog: by Noel Barbour.
The Worcestershire Regt.
The Wrexham Museum.
Ulu Itam: by Peter & Kathleen Thomas.
Who Won The Malayan Emergency: by Herbert Andrews.
Zimbabwe Archives. No Response.
www. Britains Small Wars. Com. :
www. Angelfire.Com.:
www. Members.Tripod.com.:

The Malaysian War Monument (Tugu Negara) is located within the Lake Gardens in the capital Kuala Lumpur

Commissioned in 1963, constructed in 1966. The Monument is 15 metres tall, made of bronze. Designed by the Austrian sculptor Felix de Weldon, who was also responsible for the Marine Corps War Memorial in Virginia USA

The sculpture depicts a group of soldiers, with two slumped at the base and one holding the Malaysian National Flag. The bronze figures represent: Leadership, Suffering, Vigilance, Strength, Courage and Sacrifice.

The stones the soldiers are standing on, were imported from the small Swedish town of Karishamn South East Sweden.

The granite base of the sculpture bears the Malayan Coat of Arms, flanked on either side by inscriptions in English (Latin script) also Malay in (Jawi script)

DEDICATED TO THE HEROIC FIGHTERS IN THE CAUSE OF PEACE AND FREEDOM. MAY THE BLESSING OF ALLAH BE UPON THEM

Photo: By The Author Joe P. Plant

The below photograph published by kind permission of the Commonwealth War Grave Committee. Is located in the Terendak War Cemetery Malacca. It is known as the:

Terandak Wall Memorial

Engraved on 7 Plaques are 152 names of the personnel of the three Services of Commonwealth Forces & Federation Police Who have NO KNOWN GRAVES. Lost in the jungles of Malaya? 1948-1960

THEY ARE NOT FORGOTTEN

Printed in November 2021
by Rotomail Italia S.p.A., Vignate (MI) - Italy